Mastercam® 2022

TRAINING
GUIDE
MILL 3D

By Matthew Manton, Duane Weidinger, and Mike Wearne

camInstructor

Mastercam® 2022 Training Guide Mill 3D
Published by
camInstructor Incorporated
285 Fountain Street South
Cambridge, Ontario
N3H 1J2
www.caminstructor.com

Date: June 22, 2021
Author: Matthew Manton, Mike Wearne, Duane Weidinger
ISBN: 978-1-988766-72-0

National Library of Canada Cataloguing in Publication

To order additional copies of the book contact camInstructor Inc. at:

Canadian Office	Phone 1-877-873-6867
285 Fountain Street South	Fax 1-866-741-8421
Cambridge, ON	email sales@caminstructor.com
N3H 1J2	

Notice

camInstructor Inc. reserves the right to make improvements to this book at any time and without notice.

Trademarks

Mastercam is a registered trademark of CNC Software, Inc.

All brands are the trademark of their respective owners.

Printed in Canada

Recommended Software

To get the most out of this book we recommend using Mastercam 2022 Mill Level 3 with Solids Software or Mastercam 2022 HLE Software.
June 22, 2021

Mastercam 2022

TRAINING GUIDE

COURSE SITE OVERVIEW

Before working on the Lessons in this book, you should view the camInstructor Course Site Overview Video.

1. Go to www.caminstructor.com and click on **Log In** using your username and password. NOTE: Your log in instructions are on inside of the front cover of this book.
2. Click on **My Courses** and then click on **Select a Category** and select **Course Site Overview**.
3. Click on the **Course Site Overview** course.

camInstructor

Contents at a Glance Mill 3D

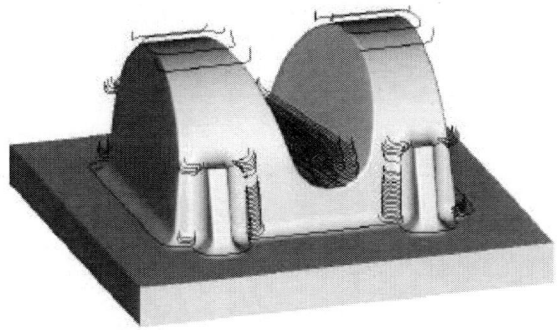

CAD Instruction
- ➲ Wireframe & Solid instruction

CAM Toolpath instruction
- ➲ Surface High Speed - Dynamic OptiRough
- ➲ Surface High Speed - Hybrid

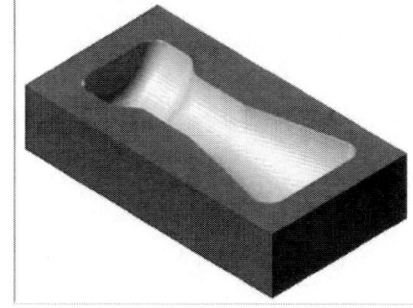

Exercise 9A page 68

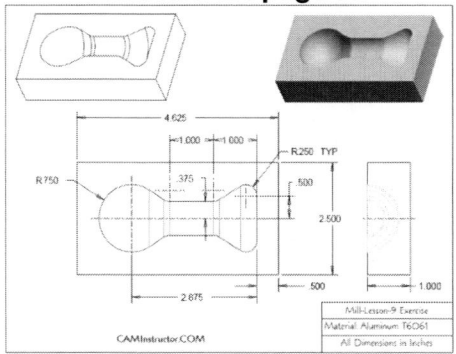

Exercise 9B page 69

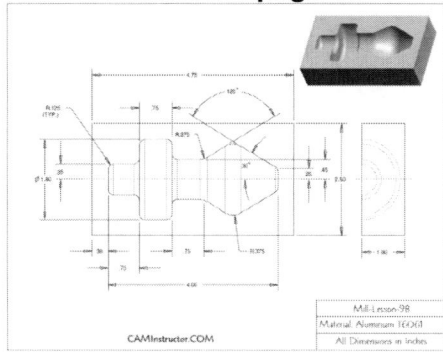

Mill 3D

CAD Instruction
- ➲ 3D Wireframe & Solid instruction

CAM Toolpath instruction
- ➲ Surface Rough Parallel
- ➲ Surface High Speed Raster Rest Pass

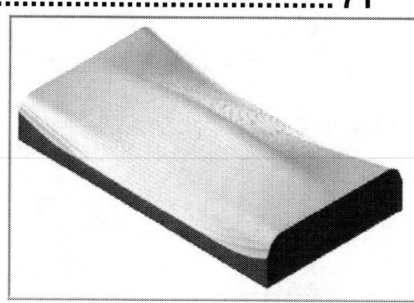

Exercise 10A page 115

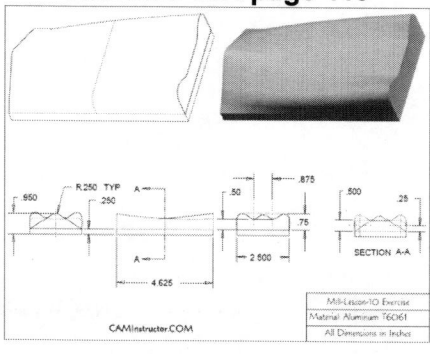

Exercise 10B page 116

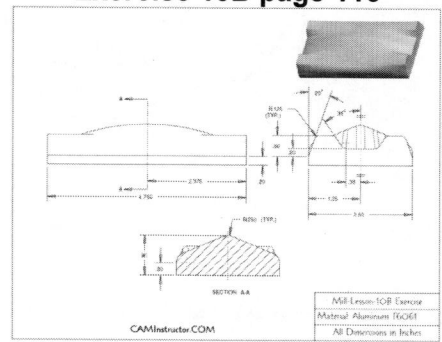

CAD Instruction
- ➲ 3D Wireframe & Surface instruction

CAM Toolpath instruction
- ➲ Surface High Speed - Area Mill
- ➲ Surface – Finish Flowline

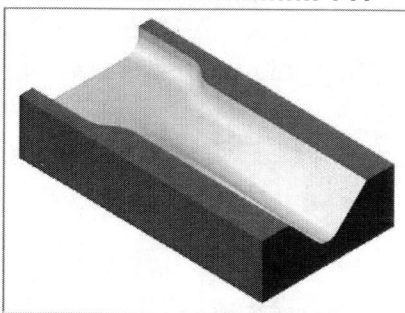

Exercise 11A page 155

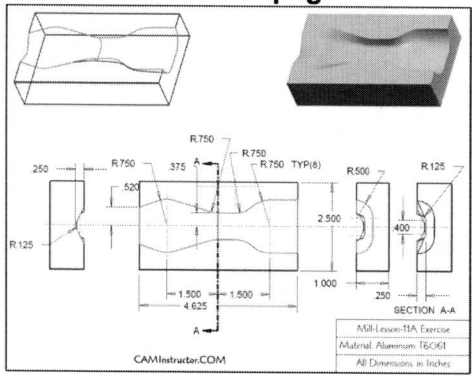

Exercise 11B page 156

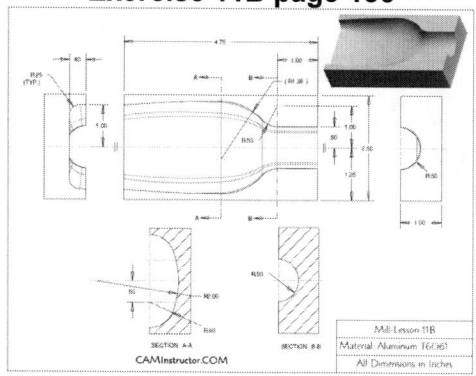

CAD Instruction
➲ Solid Import and Alignment

CAM Toolpath instruction
➲ Surface High Speed - Area Mill
➲ Surface High Speed - Finish
   Flowline

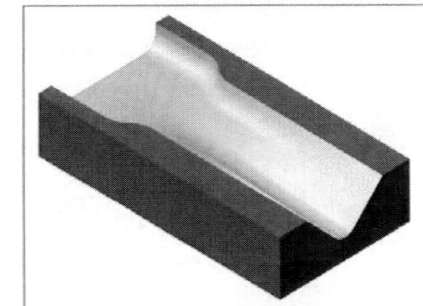

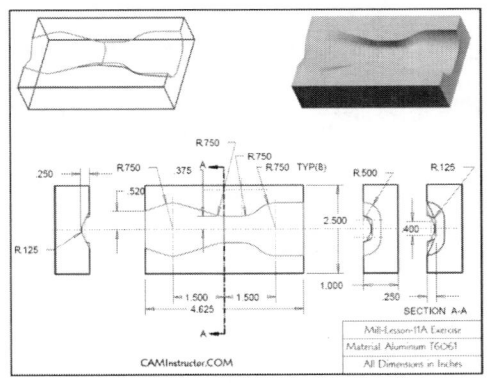

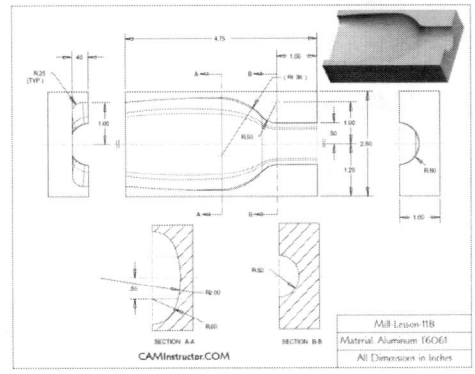

CAD Instruction
➲ 3D Wireframe & Surface instruction

CAM Toolpath instruction
➲ Surface Rough Pocket
➲ Surface High Speed – Waterline
➲ Surface High Speed – Scallop
➲ Surface High Speed – Scallop Rest Passes

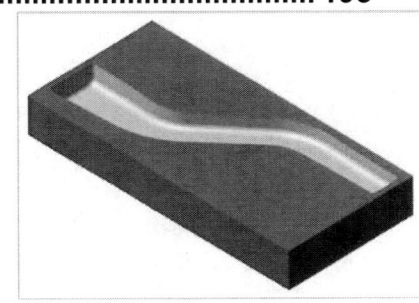

Exercise 12A page 254

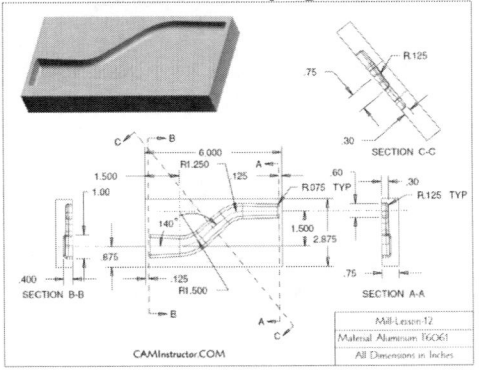

Exercise 12B page 255

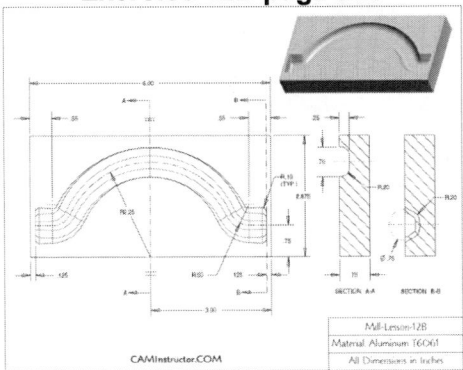

Mill 3D

CAD Instruction
  ➲ 3D Wireframe & Solid instruction

CAM Toolpath instruction
  ➲ Surface Rough Plunge
  ➲ Surface Finish Contour
  ➲ Surface Finish Shallow

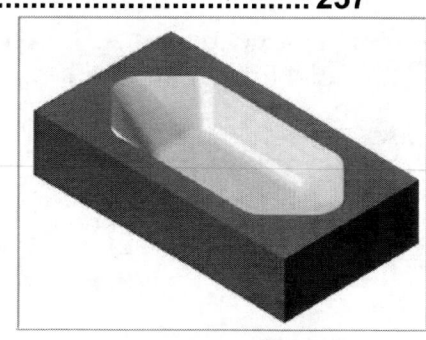

Exercise 13A page 301

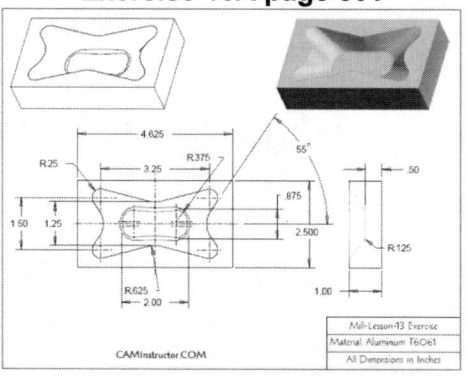

Exercise 13B page 302

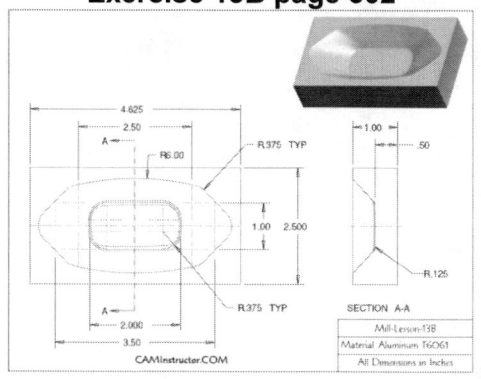

CAD Instruction
  ➲ Wireframe & Solid Model instruction

CAM Toolpath instruction
  ➲ Surface Rough Pocket
  ➲ Surface Finish Contour

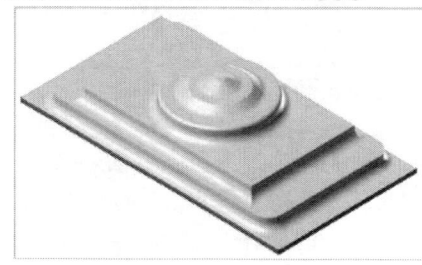

Exercise 14A page 359

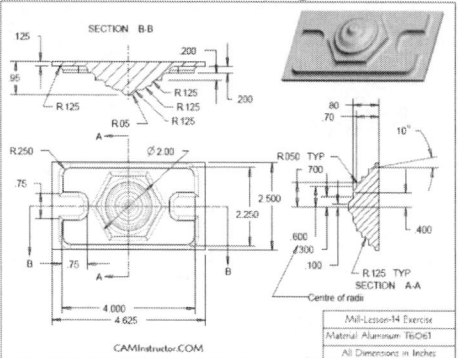

Exercise 14B page 360

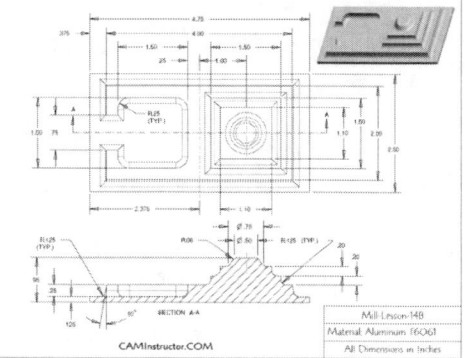

CAM Toolpath instruction
- ➲ Surface High Speed – Dynamic OptiRough
- ➲ Surface High Speed – Waterline
- ➲ Surface Finish Leftover
- ➲ Surface High Speed - Pencil

Exercise 15A page 403

Exercise 15B page 403

CAM Toolpath instruction
- ➲ Surface High Speed – Dynamic OptiRough
- ➲ Stock Model
- ➲ Surface High Speed – Dynamic OptiRest
- ➲ 2D High Speed – 2D Area Mill
- ➲ Surface High Speed – Equal Scallop
- ➲ Surface High Speed – Spiral
- ➲ Surface High Speed - Pencil

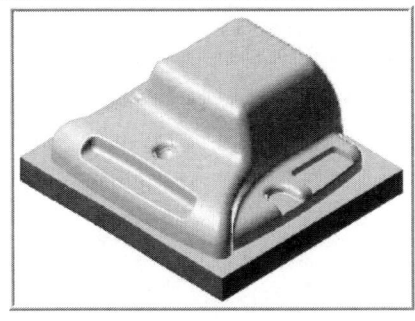

Exercise 16A page 482

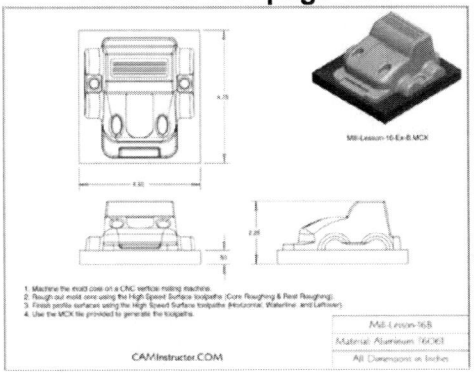

Exercise 16B page 483

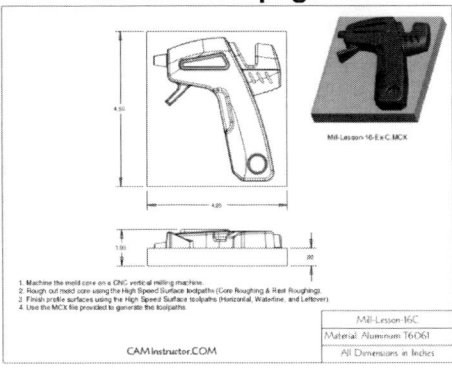

Mastercam 2022

TRAINING
GUIDE

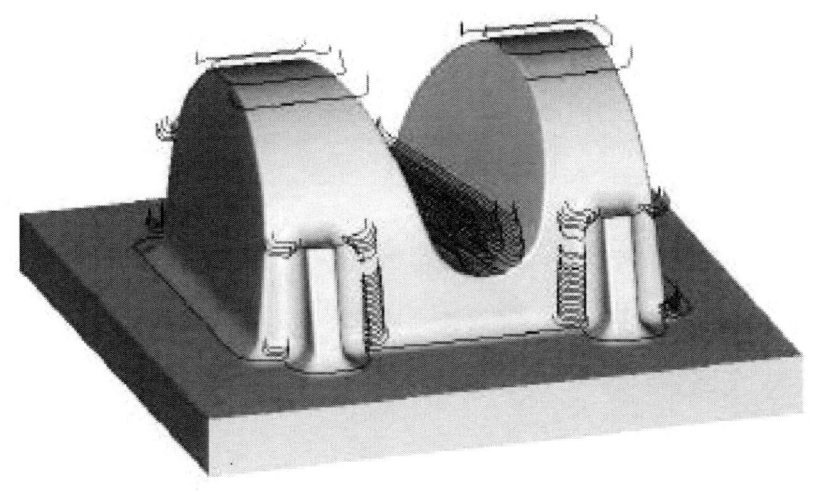

SURFACE TOOLPATH OVERVIEW

camInstructor

3D TOOLPATHS

The following information is a summary of Mastercam Help. This is provided with the Mastercam Software and produced by CNC Software, Inc.

3D roughing

3D roughing toolpaths typically use larger tools, multiple stepovers, and multiple stepdowns to quickly remove larger volumes of stock and leave an even amount of stock for finishing. The roughing toolpaths you choose for your part depend on the shape of the part, shape of the stock, and machining situation. Mastercam provides several roughing strategies

3D finishing

3D finishing toolpaths typically finish a part down to the drive geometry (or to the stock to leave amount if one is specified). Mastercam provides several finishing strategies.

Shown below are the Roughing and Finishing 3D toolpaths in Mastercam 2020 located on the menu bar. These are the most commonly used 3D paths. There are additional 3D toolpaths outside of this menu.

Other 3D toolpaths

Right clicking in the Toolpath manager will allow access to the other 3D paths. You can access 3 menus from this, Surface Rough, Surface Finish, Surface High Speed. Each menu will expose different 3D paths.

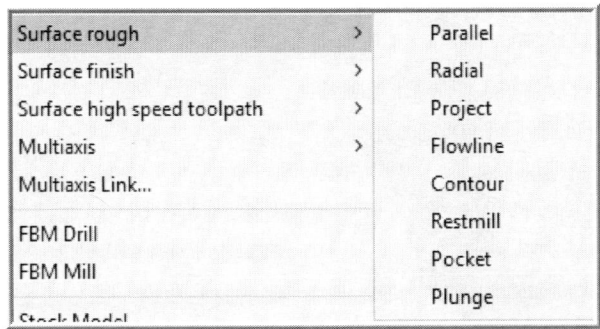

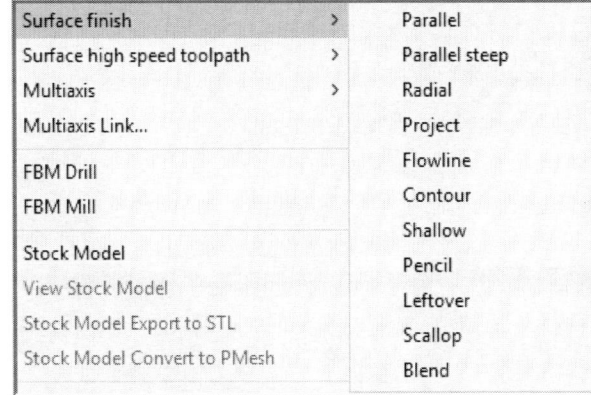

Geometry selection

Both surface rough and finish toolpaths use the same method to select geometry and apply parameters. You can customize how and when Mastercam prompts for surface toolpath geometry by making selections in the Toolpaths page of the System Configuration dialog box. Mastercam prompts for drive geometry, check geometry, and a tool containment boundary for each surface toolpath type.

Depending on the toolpath type, additional geometry may be optionally selected, such as a starting point, a radial center point, or curves. These entities, usually separate from the part, provide Mastercam with additional information about how you want the tool motion created and will improve the final toolpath results.

SURFACE TOOLPATHS

Toolpath Type	Image	Uses
Parallel Toolpath		**Surface Rough Parallel** Remove the bulk of material quickly. **Surface Finish Parallel** Machine over all the surfaces in parallel passes.
Radial Toolpath		**Surface Rough and Finish Radial** Cut from the center point outward, creating cuts like the spoke of a wheel.
Project Toolpath		**Surface Rough and Finish Project** Project either geometry or a toolpath from an earlier operation onto surfaces.

SURFACE TOOLPATHS

Toolpath Type	Image	Uses
Flowline Toolpath	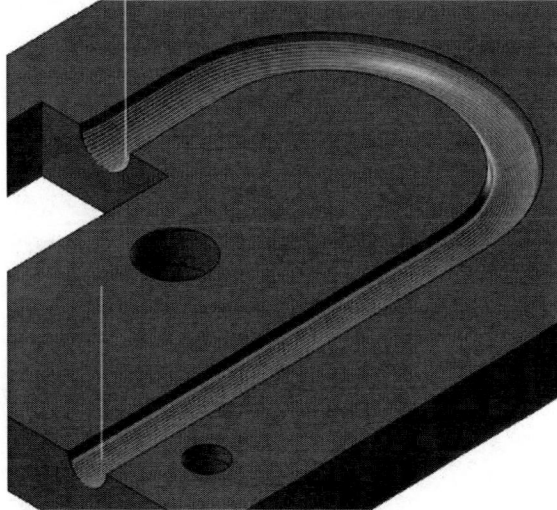	**Surface Rough and Finish Flowline** Follows the shape and direction of the surfaces and creates a smooth and flowing toolpath motion.
Contour Toolpath	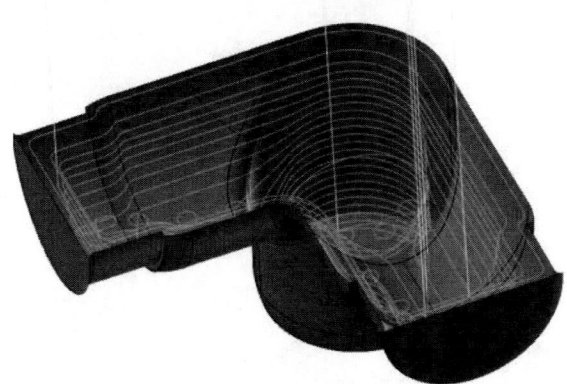	**Surface Rough and Finish Contour** Works well for parts that have steep walls. Allows the tool to step down gradually in the Z axis instead of stepping over in the X and Y axes.
Restmill Toolpath	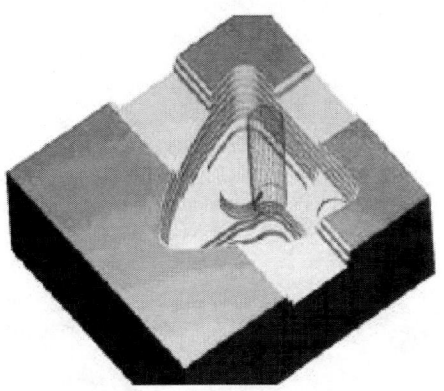	**Surface Rough Restmill** A roughing toolpath that cleans up remaining stock with a constant Z motion.

SURFACE TOOLPATHS

Toolpath Type	Image	Uses
Pocket Toolpath		**Surface Rough Pocket** Removes a lot of stock quickly and creates a series constant Z cuts.
Plunge Toolpath	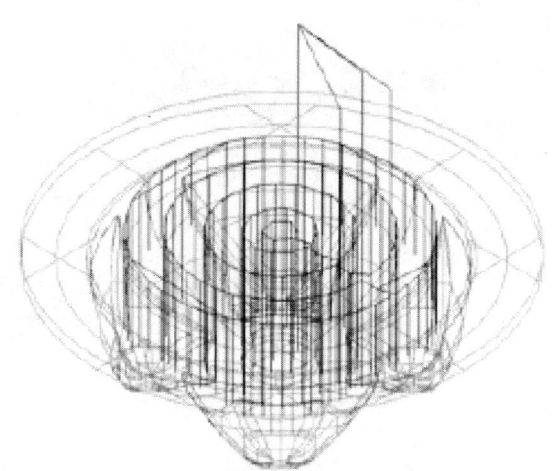	**Surface Rough Plunge** Requires a special Plunge Roughing Tool as it uses a drilling-type motion to remove large quantities of material very quickly.
Finish Parallel Steep Toolpath	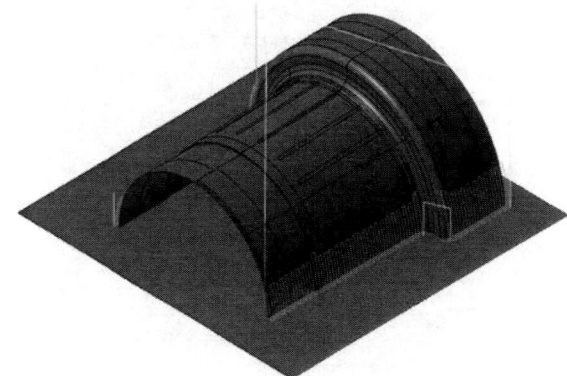	**Surface Finish Parallel Steep** Removes material from surfaces that fall between two slope angles. This toolpath is usually used after a finish parallel toolpath.

SURFACE TOOLPATHS

Toolpath Type	Image	Uses
Finish Shallow Toolpath	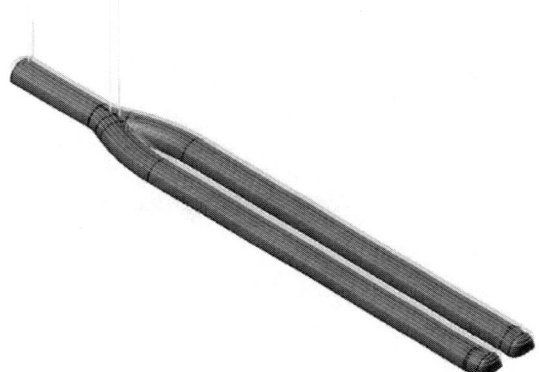	**Surface Finish Shallow** Removes material from surfaces that fall between two slope angles.
Finish Pencil Toolpath	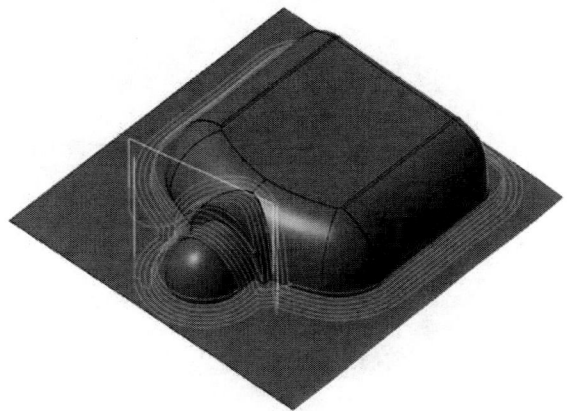	**Surface Finish Pencil** Follows the path where two surfaces meet. It cleans out material by driving the cutter tangent to two surfaces at a time.
Finish Leftover Toolpaths		**Surface Finish Leftover** Removes material left behind by the larger tool from a previous operation. It calculates how much stock is left over and uses the information to create tool motions.

SURFACE TOOLPATHS

Toolpath Type	Image	Uses
Finish Blend Toolpath	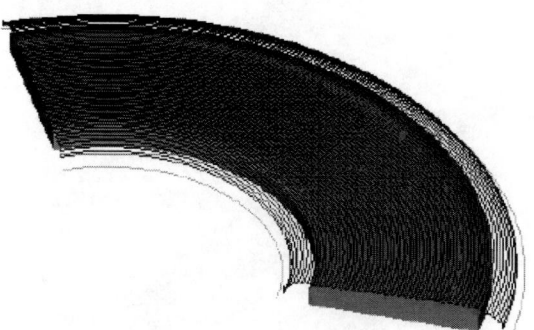	**Surface Finish Blend** Creates motion that is defined by curves that were created along the drive geometry.
Finish Scallop Toolpath	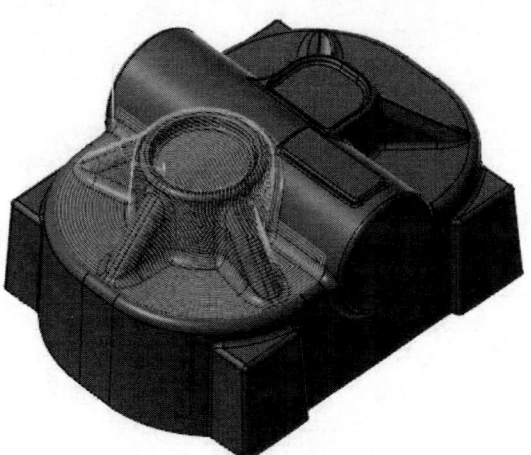	**Surface Finish Scallop** Creates a constant toolpath over the entire surface regardless of whether the surface becomes steep or shallow.

SURFACE 3D HIGH SPEED TOOLPATHS

3D high speed toolpaths (HST) are a set of machining strategies that are specially designed to produce the smoothest, most efficient tool motions when machining surface models (or solid faces). Mastercam uses two main techniques to achieve this:

- Each cutting pass can be configured with advanced corner rounding and toolpath refinement techniques to reduce the impact of corners, sharp angles, and other discontinuities. These parameters help maintain a constant load on the tool, reduce machining time, and improve machined surface quality.
- An advanced suite of linking tools lets you optimize the transitions between cutting passes and the lead in/out to each cutting pass.

In addition, 3D high speed toolpaths extend Mastercam's gouge-checking capabilities to include the tool holder. Use the holder definition page incorporated in the high speed toolpath interface to define custom holder shapes and save them in holder libraries.

Another difference between HST toolpaths and Mastercam's other toolpaths is how they use defaults. Most Mastercam toolpaths read default values from the .mcam-defaults file for each operation type. HST toolpaths dynamically calculate default values based on the selected tool. Whenever you select a new tool for an operation, Mastercam updates the toolpath parameters. Click here to learn more about managing HST defaults.

All of the high speed features are integrated in the Surface High Speed Toolpaths dialog box. This is where you select a machining strategy and configure the cutting passes, linking strategies, and many other toolpath options.

3D HST toolpaths support both roughing and finishing operations. The following HST toolpath types are available:

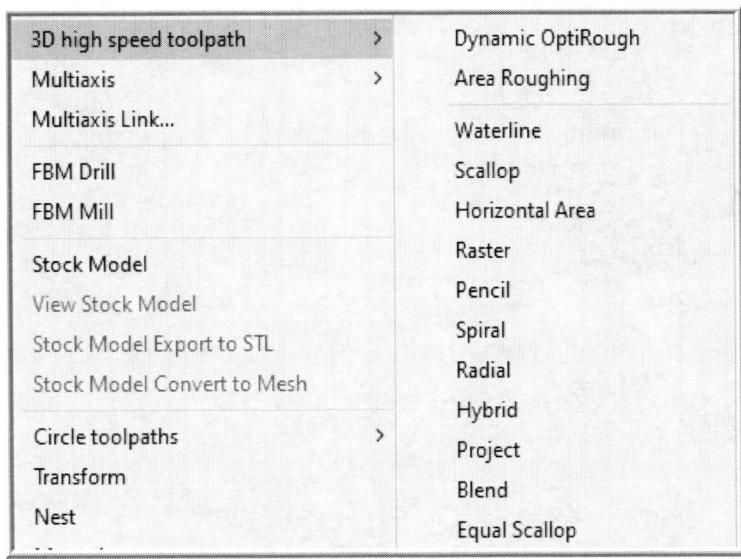

SURFACE HIGH SPEED ROUGHING

Roughing - Area Roughing – Containment boundary – From Outside

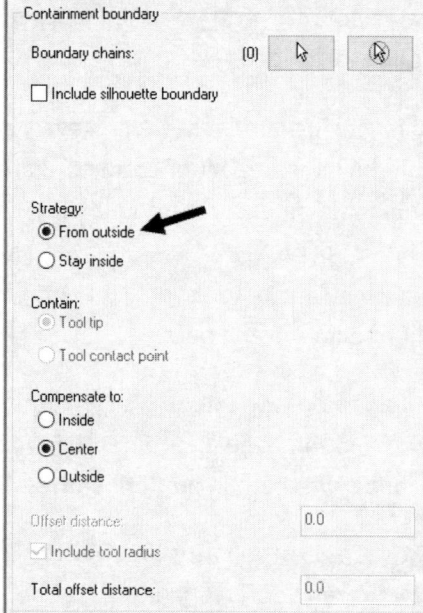

Uses:
Ideal for boss-type parts. On each Z level, the tool approaches the part from the outside with multiple offsets.

Roughing – Area Roughing – Containment boundary – Stay Inside

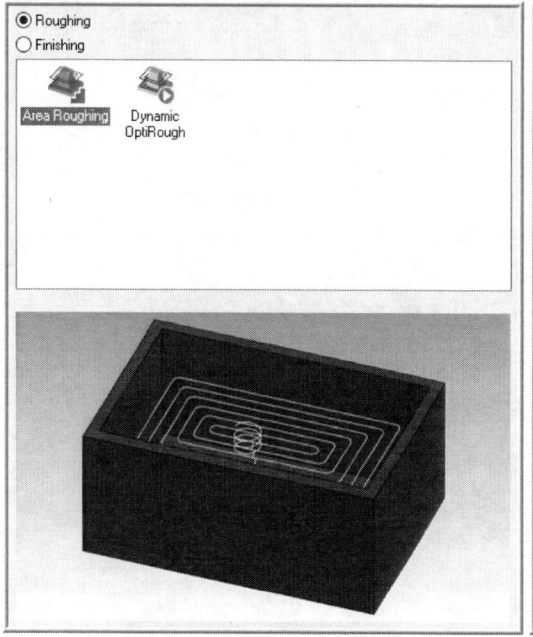

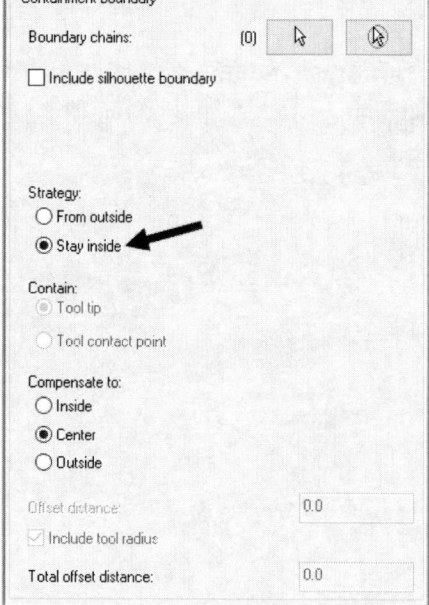

Uses:
Good for parts that need to be machined from the inside out, such as pockets, cavities and molds.

SURFACE HIGH SPEED ROUGHING

Roughing – Dynamic OptiRough – Containment boundary – Stay Inside

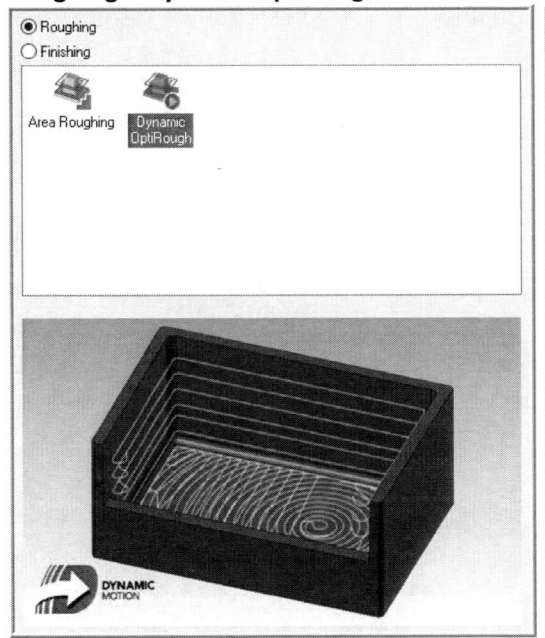 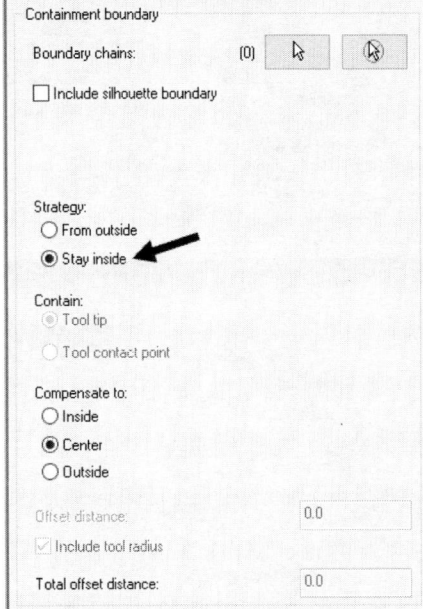

Uses:
An area pocketing approach - used to remove the maximum amount of material with the minimum of step downs, significantly reducing cycle times.

Roughing – Dynamic OptiRough – Containment boundary – From Outside

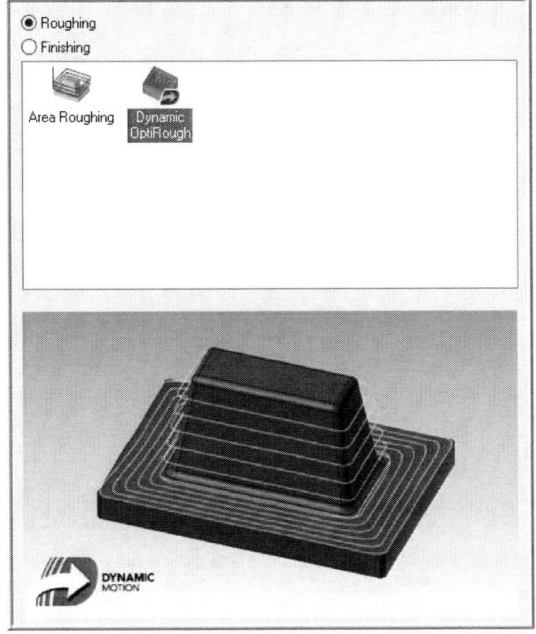 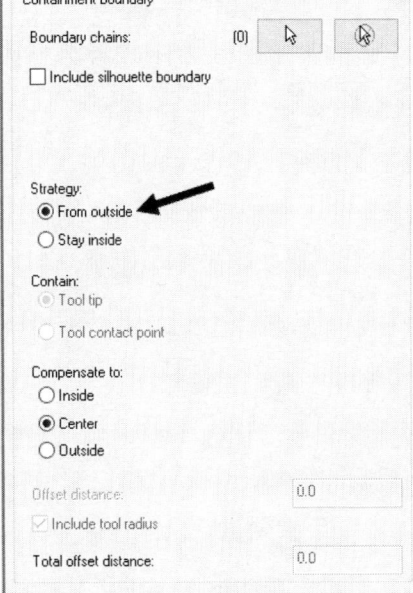

Uses:
A Core from outside approach - used to remove the maximum amount of material with the minimum of step downs, significantly reducing cycle times.

SURFACE HIGH SPEED ROUGHING

Roughing – Area Roughing – Rest Material – Enabled

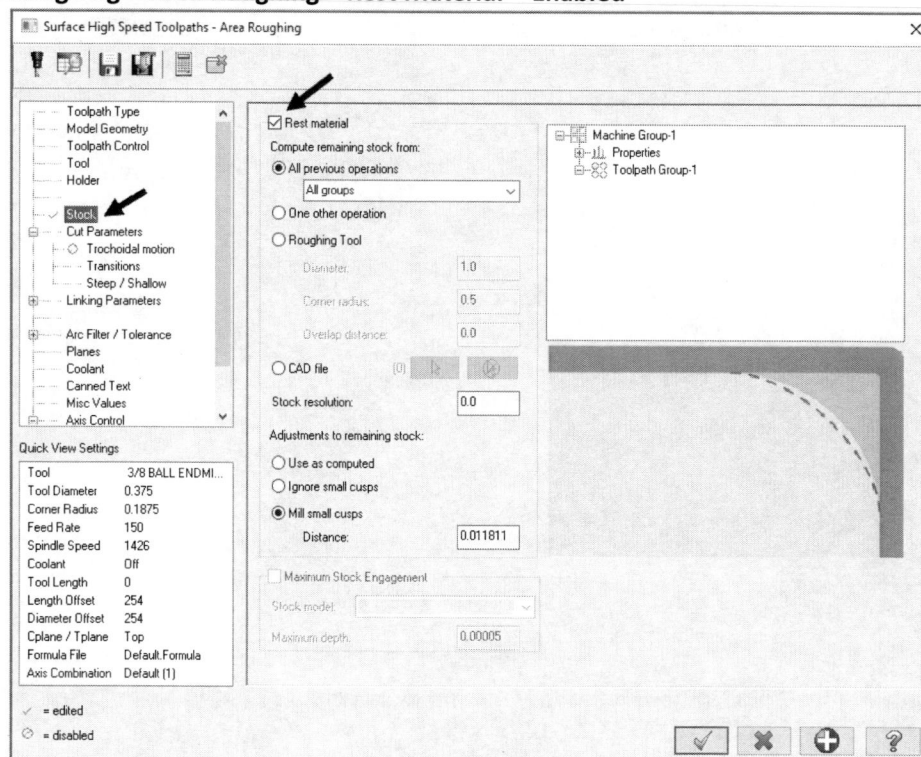

Uses:

Cleans out enough stock in required areas so that a finish tool will NOT encounter and excessive amount of material.

SURFACE HIGH SPEED FINISHING

Toolpath Type	Example	Uses
Waterline	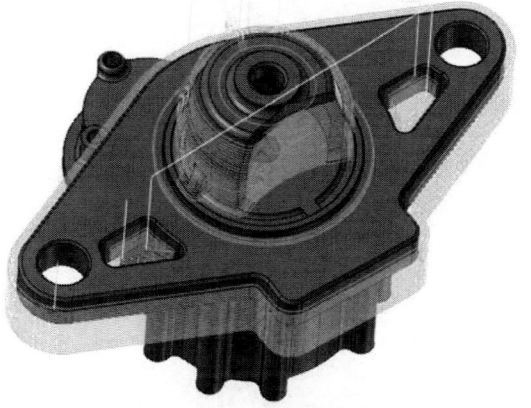	**Waterline** Best for steep areas, like walls of molds or cavities.
Scallop		**Scallop** Also known as constant stepover toolpath. Produces a consistent scallop height across the surface.
Horizontal Area	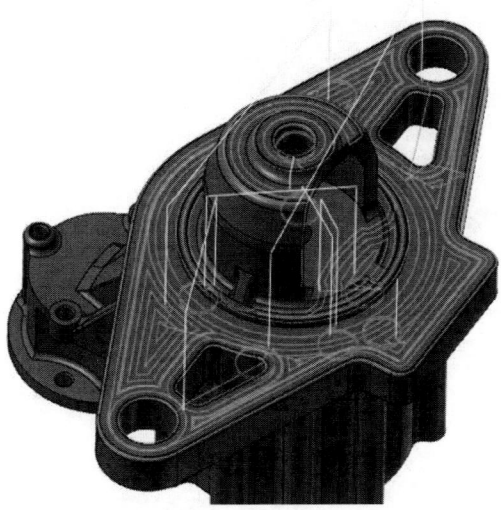	**Horizontal Area** Good to finish flat areas.

SURFACE HIGH SPEED FINISHING

Toolpath Type	Example	Uses
Raster	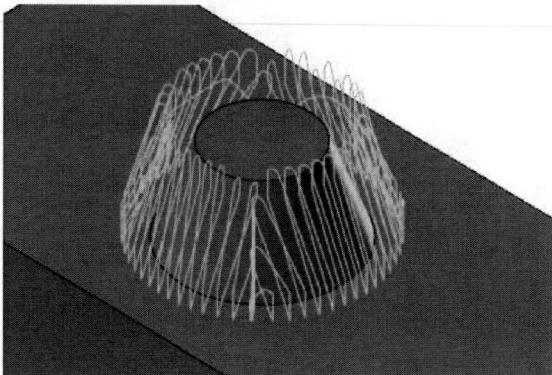	**Raster** Creates parallel cutting passes across the surface. The angle the cutter passes the surface can be adjusted depending on the part features.
Pencil	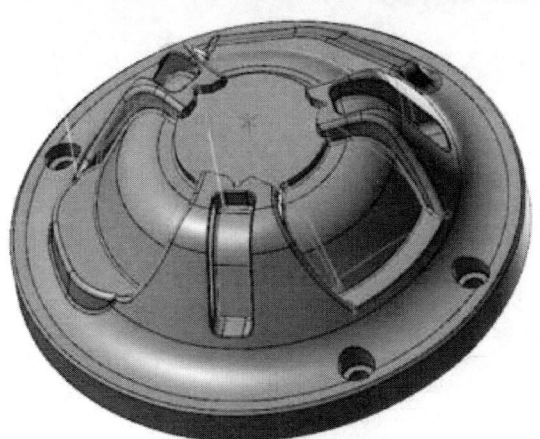	**Pencil** Used to clean out corners and boundaries between surfaces.
Spiral	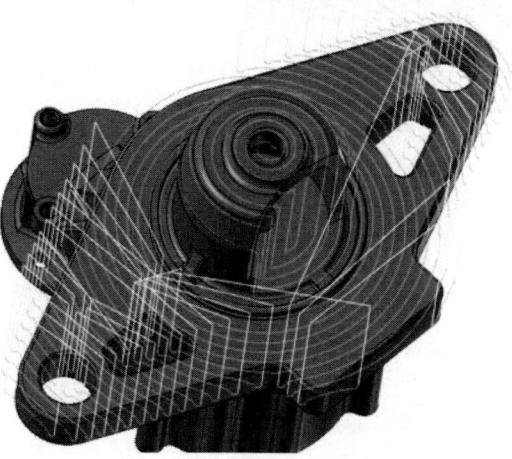	**Spiral** Used to create a toolpath that feeds into the part in a continuous spiral.

SURFACE HIGH SPEED FINISHING

Toolpath Type	Example	Uses
Radial	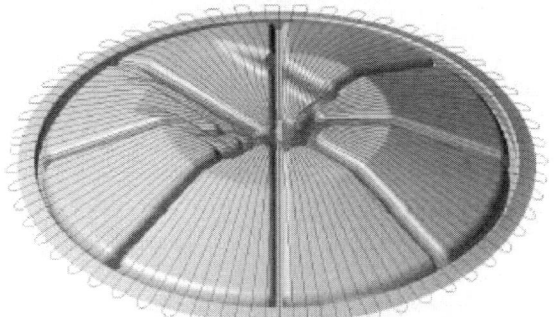	**Radial** Best used when requiring a toolpath that radiates outward from a central point.
Hybrid	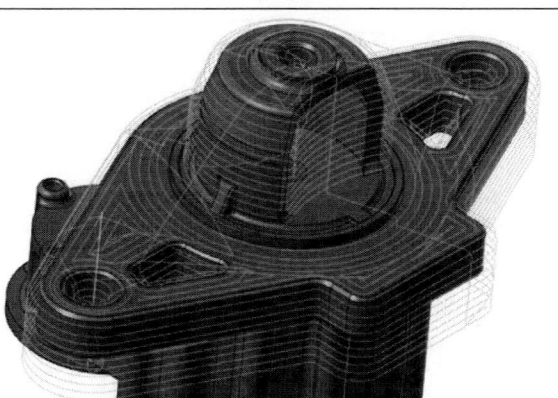	**Hybrid Finish** Used to machine steep and shallow areas utilizing both scallop and constant Z approaches in single toolpath.
3D HST Project		**3D HST Project** A common use of project is engraving created by projecting curves onto a surface as shown to the left.
Equal Scallop	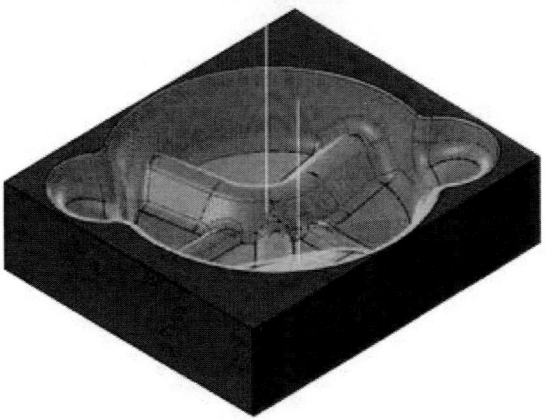	**Equal Scallop Finish** Best used when requiring a toolpath with consistent scallop motion, relative to the stepover distance.

Mastercam. 2022

TRAINING

GUIDE

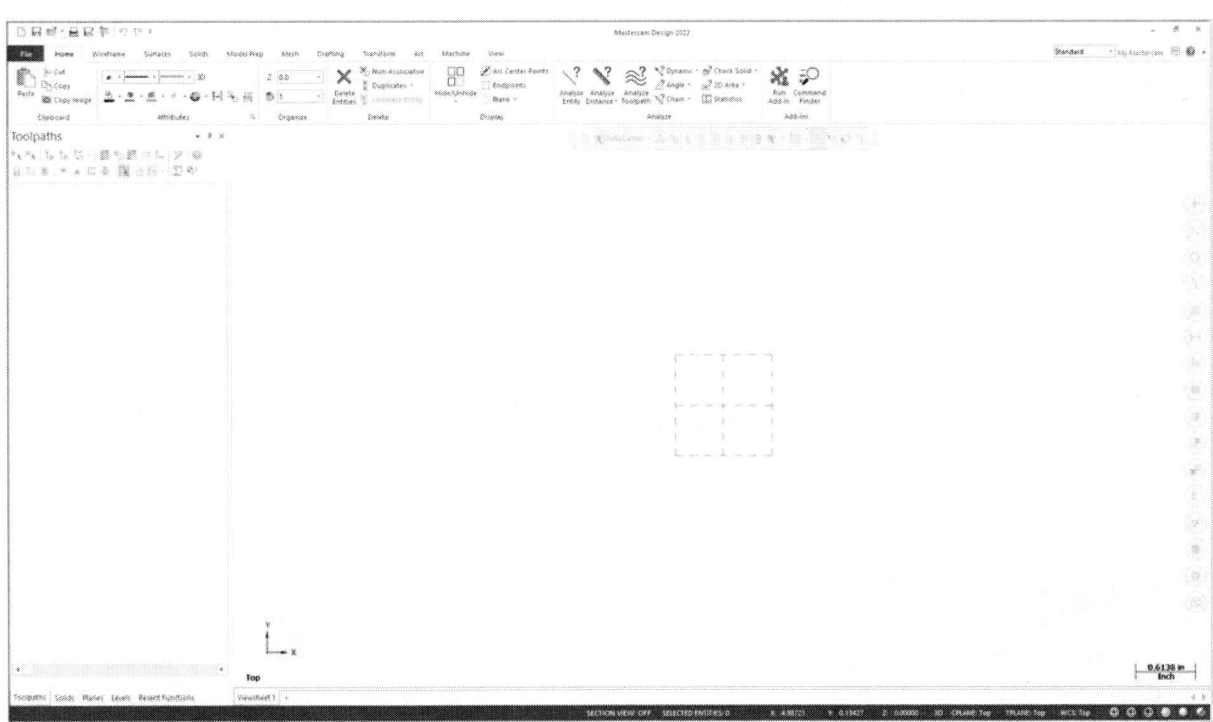

SETTING THE ENVIRONMENT

camInstructor

SETTING THE ENVIRONMENT
COMPLETE THESE STEPS BEFORE STARTING EACH LESSON

Before starting the geometry creation and generating the toolpaths you should:
- ➲ Set up the Grid. This will help identify the location of the origin. There are other methods that can be used each with their own benefits. Refer to the Setting the Environment video for further explanation of these options.
- ➲ Set the machine type to the Default machine based on the lesson topic. The Default machines are capable of all machine motions needed in all the available toolpaths for that machine type.
- ➲ You can install different machine types if needed. Refer to the Adding a Machine video in the Tips and Techniques section for instructions.

SET THE DISPLAY OF THE GRID
1. Launch **Mastercam**.
2. Select the **File** tab in the upper left corner of your screen.

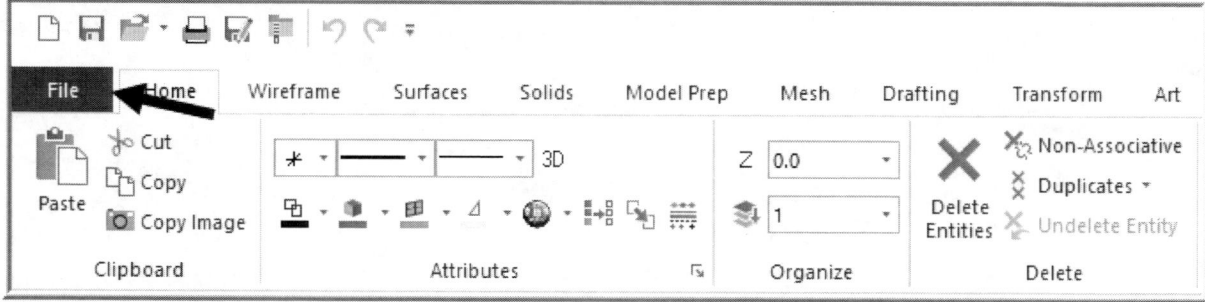

3. From the selections on the left of your screen select **Configuration.**

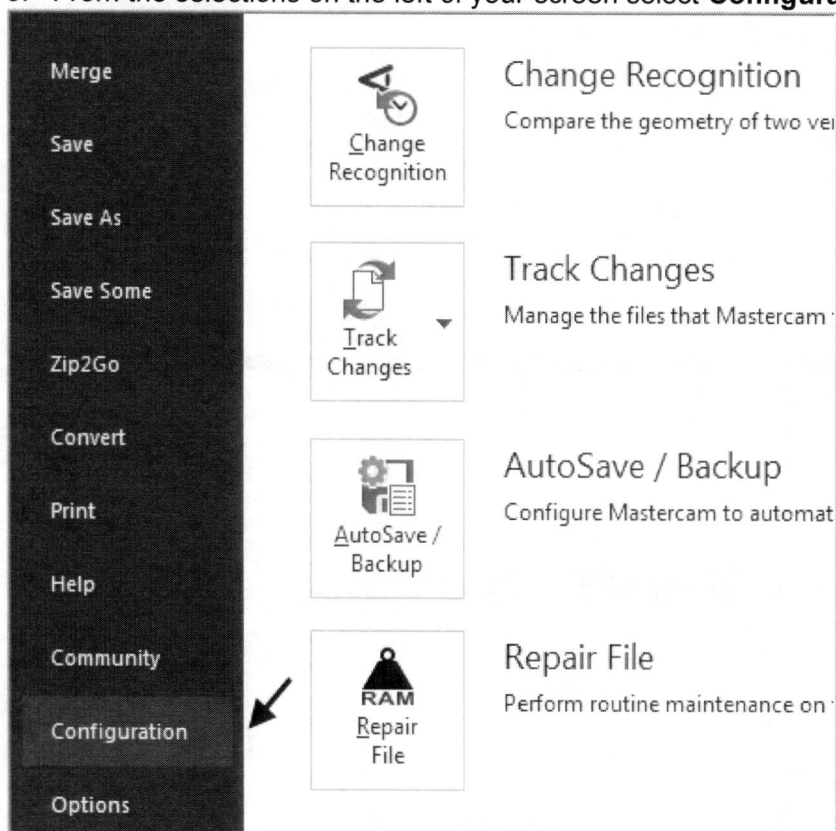

4. From the window on the left side of this window expand the **Screen** topic by selecting the **+ sign** and then select **Grid.**

5. Change the **Size** to 1.

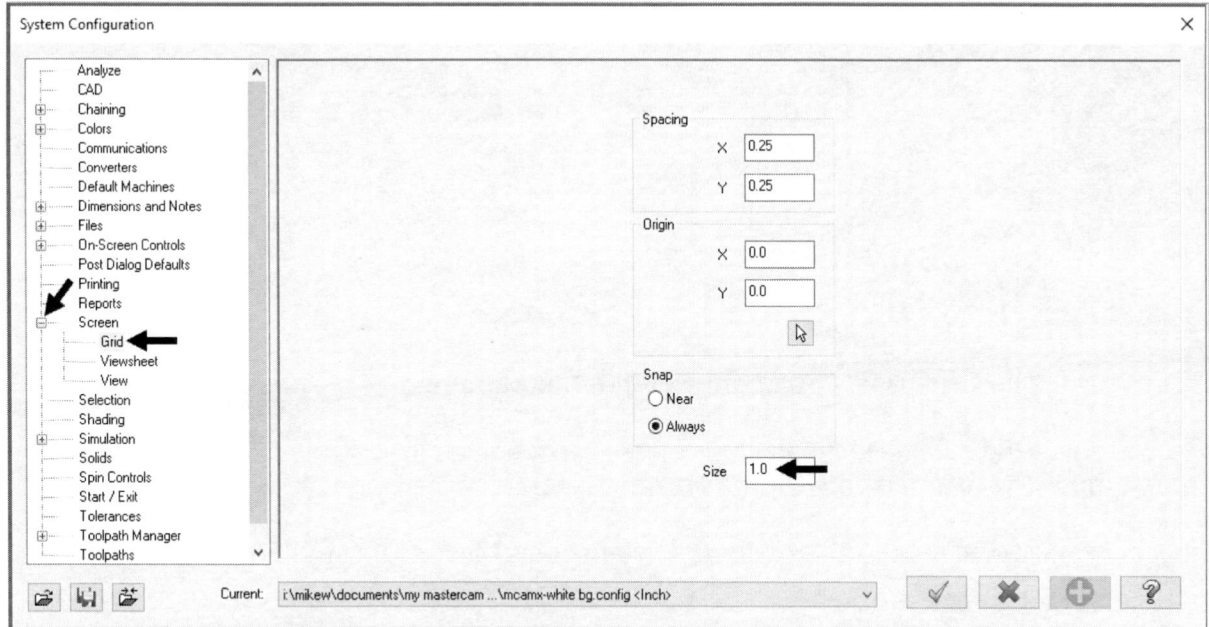

6. Select the **OK** button [✓] to complete this function.

7. When prompted to "**Save all current settings to configuration file**" select **Yes**.

Grid Settings

Use the Grid Settings page to configure the default settings for Mastercam's grid function.

Activate the grid using the **Show Grid** controls on the **View tab**.

Snap to Grid allows the grid to be used as selection points. The selection grid is a matrix of reference points that the cursor snaps to when you sketch a point. Snapping to the selection grid provides a finer level of precision than sketching points freehand. For example, to draw entities whose locations and dimensions are always multiples of a half inch, set your grid X and Y values to 0.5.

We do not recommend turning Snap to Grid on for any of our Lessons.

---

8. Now select the **View** tab and click on **Show Grid** to display the grid on the screen. The button will show with a blue background to show it is active.

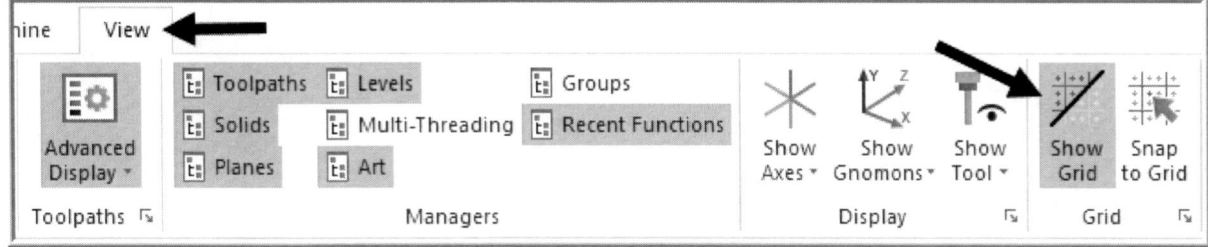

---

9. In the lower right corner of the **Grid** section click on the arrow.

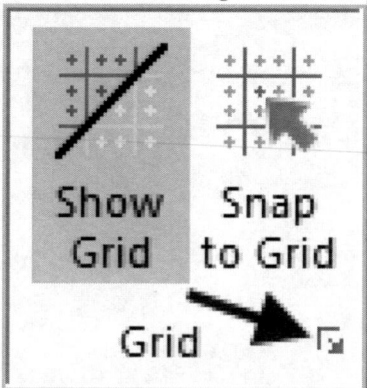

This opens up the **Grid** page – **no changes are required here**.

You can save Grid parameters to the Mastercam configuration file as you did earlier or you can make **temporary changes only for the current session** on this page.

Saved Grid parameters are loaded when you start a new Mastercam session.

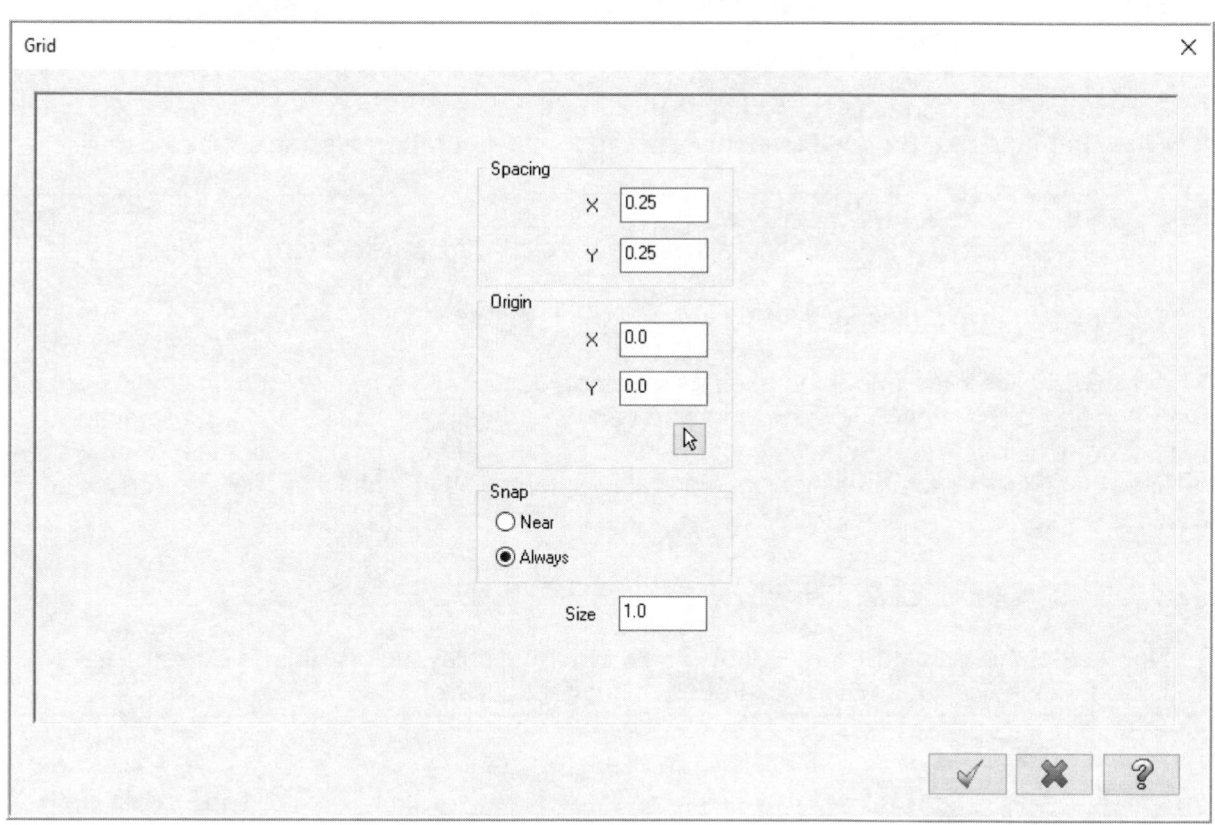

10. Select the **Cancel** button [✖] as no changes are required.

DISPLAYING THE MANAGERS

1. You can close the **Toolpaths/Solids/Planes/Levels Manager** by clicking the **Close** button in the **upper right corner for each manager panel**. To open the Toolpaths Manager again, choose the **View tab**, and select **Toolpaths**.

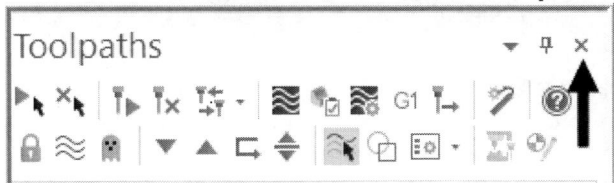
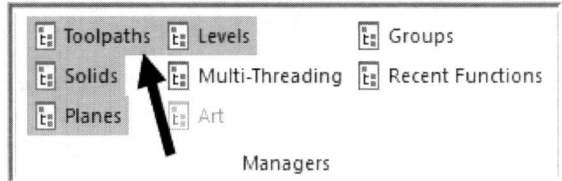

> **Note:**
> Your settings for the Managers are modal between Mastercam sessions. This means that Mastercam "remembers" and maintains the position and size of the Managers, even if you close and re-open Mastercam.

2. When **more than one Manager** is activated, you can display different manager panels by selecting the relevant tab at the lower left of the screen

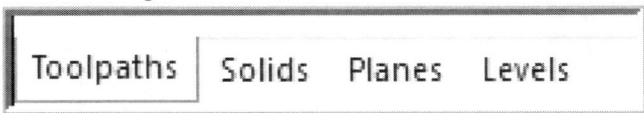

Toolpaths/Solids/Planes Managers Hidden   **Toolpaths Manager Displayed**

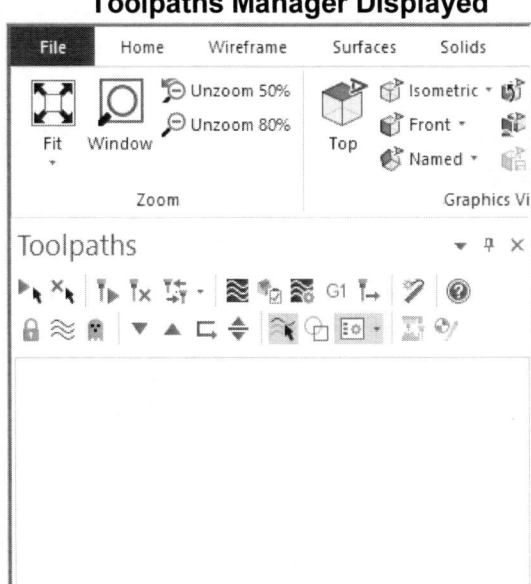

> Mastercam allows you to move the Toolpaths/Solids/Planes Manager to a different location, re-size their window, and close or re-open them whenever you want.
> By default, the Toolpaths/Solids/Planes Managers are docked to the left side of the graphics window. You can undock the Managers and dock them where you like. To do so, drag the Manager pane to a screen position or to one of the docking icons that appear as you drag.
> For more information on the Toolpaths Manager see the **Interface video** in the **Tips and Techniques** section.

SELECT THE TYPE OF MACHINE

*NOTE: Mastercam includes only Default machines for each machine type. Additional **Post Processors** and **Machine Definitions** can be downloaded from the Mastercam website, however this does NOT apply to people using the **Mastercam HLE Software.** It only applies to customers who have purchased full licenses.*

➲ For **all the camInstructor lessons** you will use the **DEFAULT Machine Definition**. If you have access to an alternate machine you wish to use, for example a **Generic Haas 4X Mill**, you can use it if it is capable of the machine motions carried out in the lesson.
➲ Some of the advanced lessons may come with a machine already loaded into the file.
➲ To set the machine type do the following:

1. Select the **Machine** tab at the top of the screen.

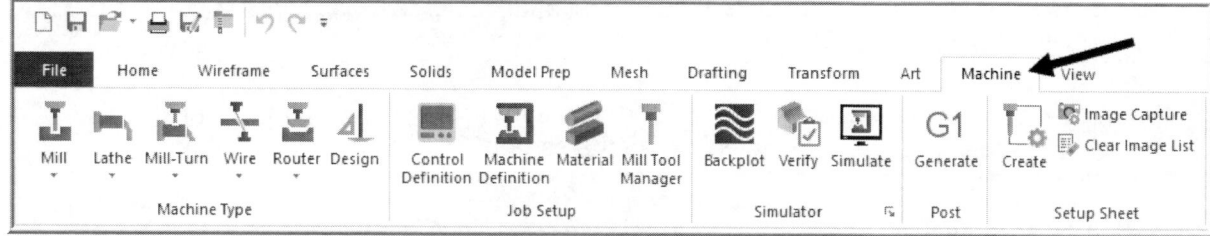

2. Now click on the appropriate **machine type** and from the menu that appears select **Default**. Only select 1 machine based on the lesson you are working on.

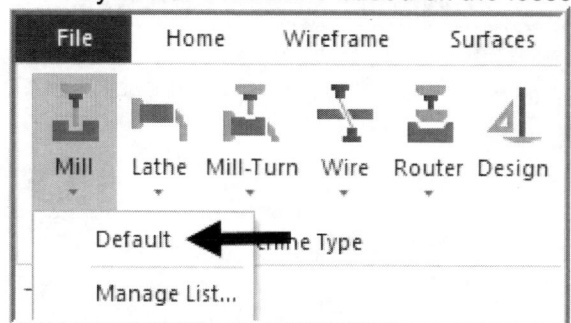 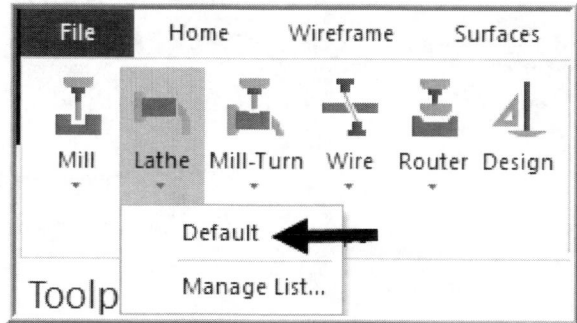

3. You will now see the chosen machine in the **Toolpath Manager**.

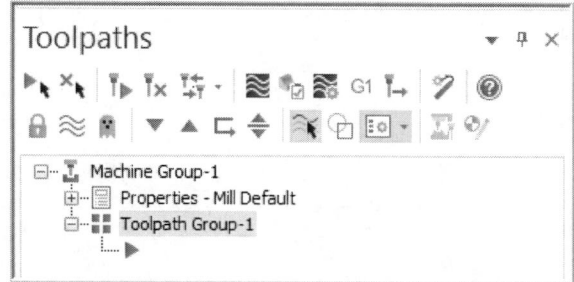 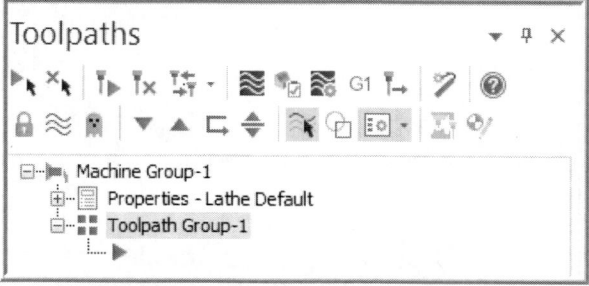

➲ Only 1 machine is needed in the Toolpath Manager. **Left click** on the Machine Group and use the **keyboard Delete key** to remove extra Machine Groups that have been accidentally inserted.

OPTIONAL
CHANGE TO THE DESIGN ENVIRONMENT

➲ If no machining will be done, such as in the Solids course, if desired, Mastercam can be set to a Design mode. This would also free up a machining license if needed.

➲ When Mastercam is launched, it will default to the Design environment.

➲ If you have started Mastercam and have a Machine Group you wish to delete…

1. **Right Click** on the **Machine Group** and select **Groups>Delete all empty**. You may need to perform this twice to completely remove the Machine Group.

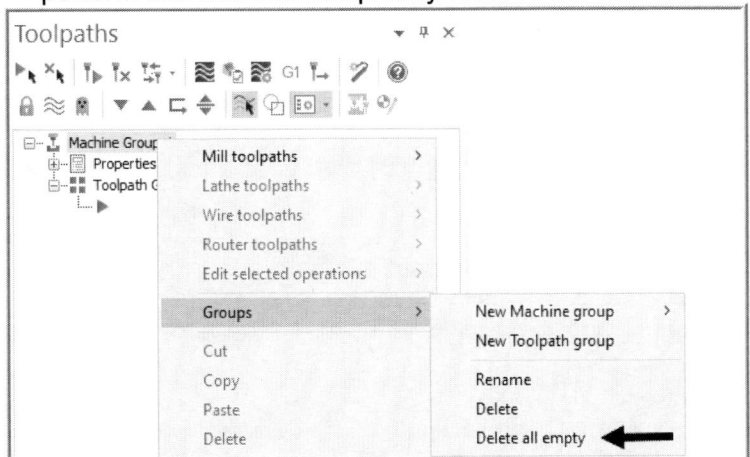

2. Select the **Machine** tab at the top of the screen.

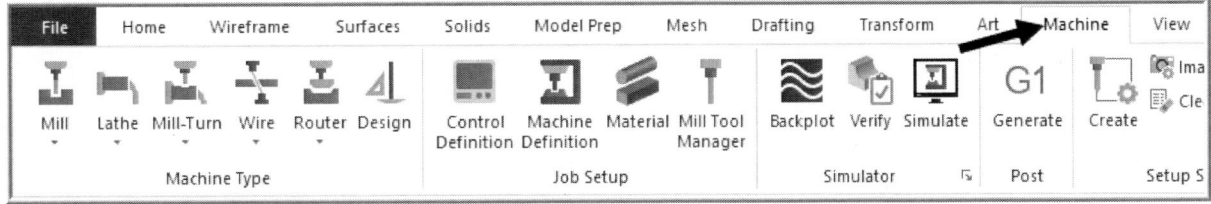

3. Now click on **Design**.

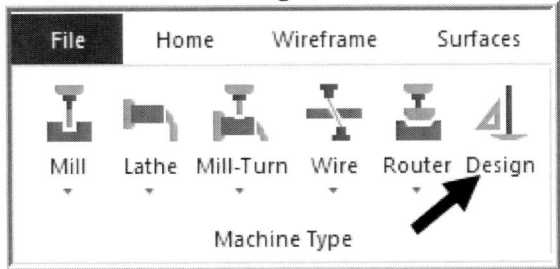

➲ The Toolpath Manager will now be blank and you will be in the Design mode.

OPTIONAL
CHANGING THE MEASUREMENT SYSTEM
FROM ENGLISH TO METRIC

Mastercam can be used in either **Inch (English)** or **Metric**. In order to change from **Inch** to **Metric** follow the instructions listed below:

1. Select **File** in the upper left corner of your screen.
2. From the selections on the left of your screen select **Configuration.**
3. Open up the drop down menu and click on the **mcamxm.config (Metric)** selection as shown below;

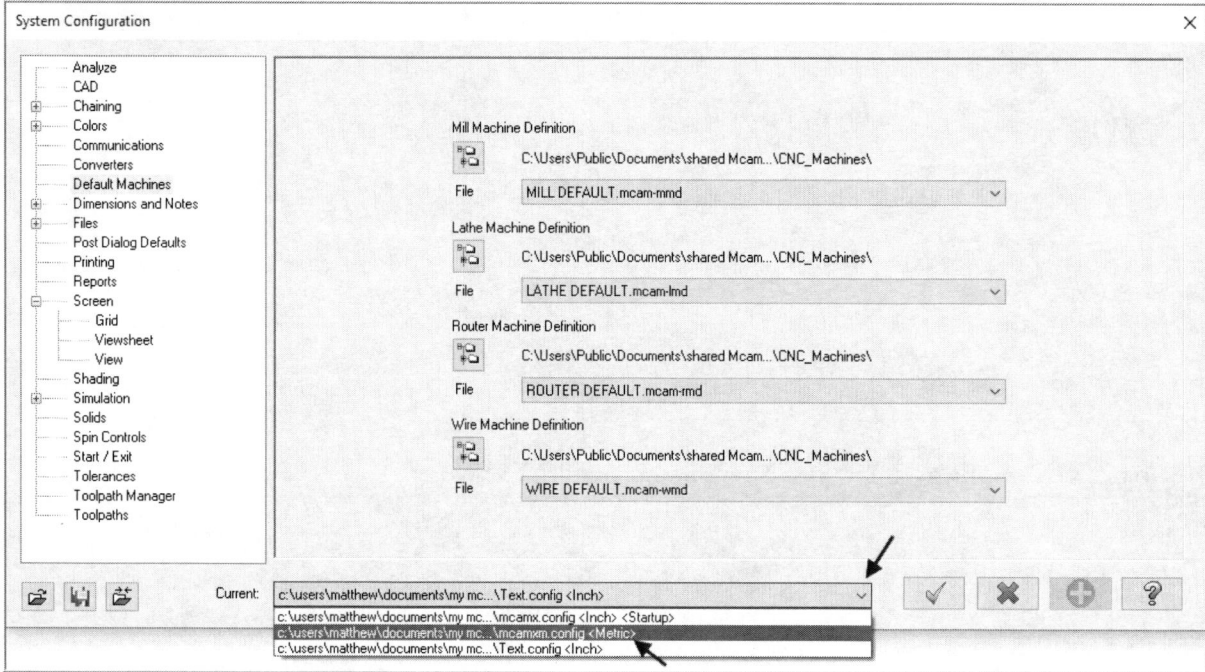

4. Select OK ✓ .

OPTIONAL
CHANGING THE MEASUREMENT SYSTEM
FROM METRIC TO ENGLISH

Mastercam can be used in either **Inch (English)** or **Metric**. In order to change from **Metric** to **Inch** follow the instructions listed below:

1. From the top Mastercam menu, select **Settings>Configuration…**
2. Click on the **mcamx.config (English)** selection as shown below;

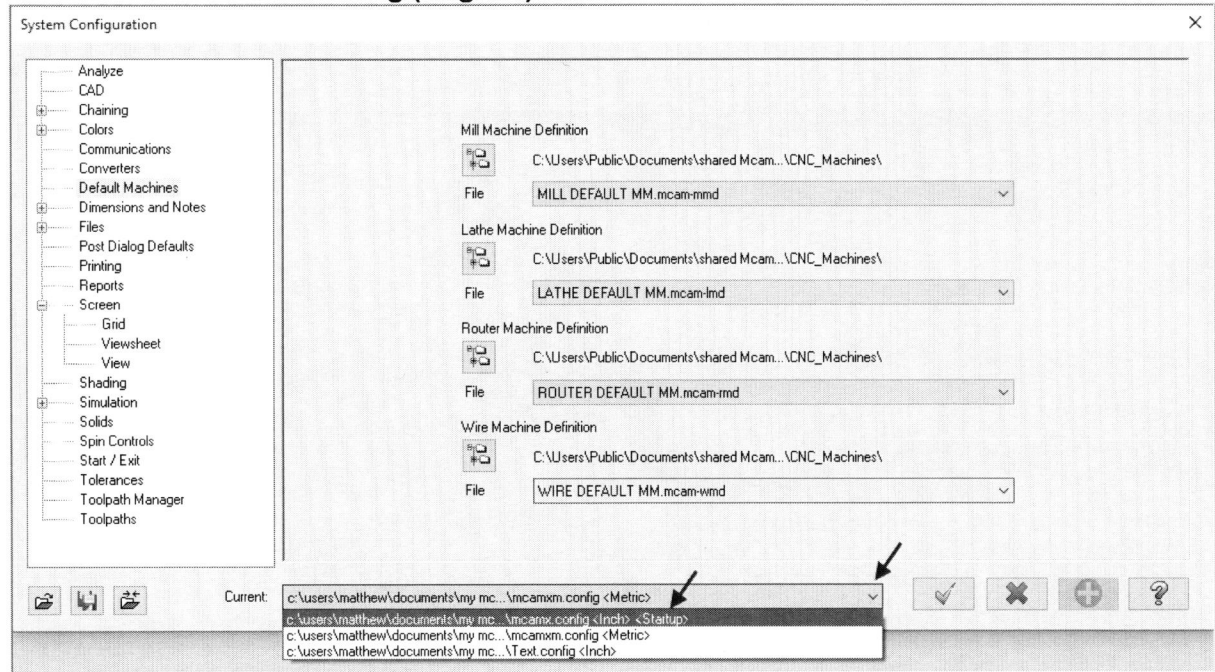

3. Select OK [✓].

Mastercam 2022

TRAINING
GUIDE

MILL-LESSON-9

DYNAMIC OPTIROUGH AND
SURFACE HIGH SPEED HYBRID

camInstructor

Objectives

You will create the geometry for Mill-Lesson-9, and then generate the toolpaths to machine the part on a CNC vertical milling machine. This Lesson covers the following topics:

➲ **Create a 3-dimensional part by:**
Creating lines.
Creating arcs.
Trimming geometry using Divide / Delete.
Creating a revolved solid and an extruded body.

➲ **Establish Stock Setup settings:**
Material for the part.
Feed calculation.

➲ **Generate a 3-dimensional milling toolpath consisting of:**
Surface High Speed - Dynamic OptiRough
Surface High Speed - Hybrid

➲ **Inspect the toolpath using Mastercam's Verify and Backplot by:**
Launching the Verify function to machine the part on the screen.
Generating the NC- code.

High Speed Toolpaths - HST

3D HST Hybrid toolpaths include a new Optimize cut order checkbox which defines the cut order Mastercam applies to different cutting passes in the toolpath. When selected, Mastercam works in tiers, ordering the toolpath's cutting passes based on proximity and safety. Mastercam machines features by area until it reaches a common Z-level, then repeats the process until it reaches the next common ground. The tool stays in a common ground, which reduces unnecessary motion and shortens the length of the toolpath.

Hybrid toolpaths now offer additional options for handling open and closed contours. Closed contours contain continuous motion without a need for a retract or reversal of direction. You can select climb or conventional machining for these contours. Open contours offer One Way or Zigzag cutting options. Open contours set to One Way will use the cutting method selected for closed contours.

The new Automatic Offset method controls how Mastercam handles the boundaries between steep and shallow areas. If the toolpath engages part surfaces that include core and cavity properties, Mastercam applies upper to lower offset methods to core features and lower to upper offset methods to cavity shapes.

The 3D HST toolpaths now calculate more efficient high-speed motion at your part's boundaries. To improve regeneration speed, they now only recalculate the necessary sections of the toolpath instead of processing the entire toolpath when changes are made.

The 3D HST Project toolpath projects either geometry or a toolpath from an earlier operation onto surfaces. Previously, the Project toolpath was only available as a surface roughing toolpath. In Mastercam the full suite of high speed toolpath parameters are available to refine the tool motion.

MILL-LESSON-9 DRAWING

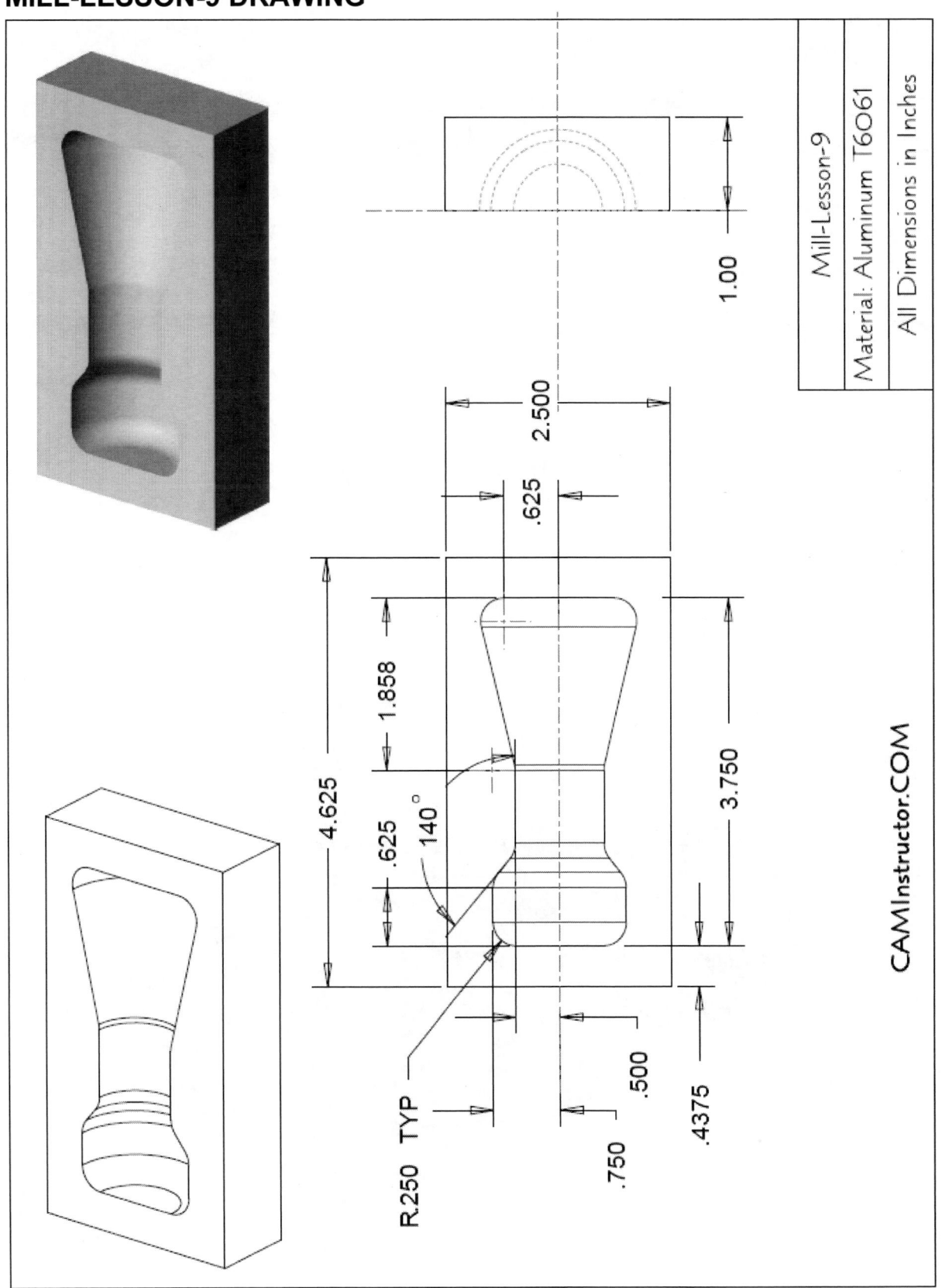

Mill-Lesson-9

Material: Aluminum T6061

All Dimensions in Inches

1.00

2.500

.625

4.625

1.858

.625

140°

3.750

R.250 TYP

.750

.500

.4375

CAMInstructor.COM

TOOL LIST

➲ 0.375 diameter bull end mill with a 0.0625 corner radius to rough machine the pocket.
➲ 0.375 diameter ball end mill to finish machine the pocket.

MILL-LESSON-9 - THE PROCESS

Geometry Creation

TASK 1:   Setting environment
TASK 2:   Create geometry - Profile
TASK 3:   Create geometry - Block
TASK 4:   Create the solid block
TASK 5:   Create the revolved solid
TASK 6:   Save the File

Toolpath Creation

TASK 7:   Define the stock
TASK 8:   Rough using OptiRough
TASK 9:   Finish using Hybrid
TASK 10: Verify the toolpath
TASK 11: Post and create the CNC code file

NOTE: Before starting this Lesson make sure to watch the Course Site Overview Video. Instructions for accessing the video are on Page 1 of this book.

TASK 1:
SETTING THE ENVIRONMENT
Before starting the geometry creation, you should set up the grid and machine type as outlined in the **Setting the environment** section at the beginning of this text:
1. Set up the Grid. This will help identify the location of the origin.
2. Set the machine type to the Default Mill.

TASK 2:
CREATE GEOMETRY - PROFILE
➲ In this task you will create the geometry that will be used to create the revolved surface. First you will create the circles, C1 through C4 and then create the lines 1 through 7. The arc C5 will be created using Fillet.

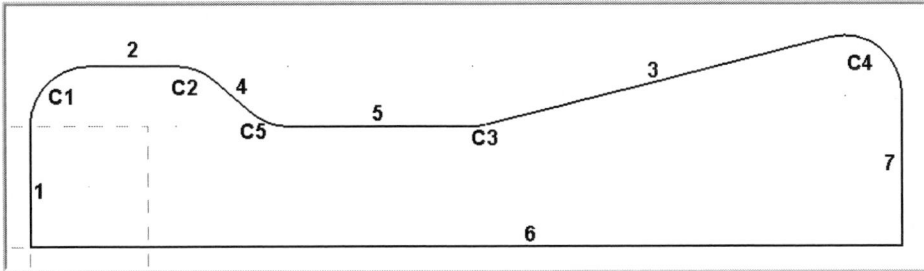

➲ **Create Circle #1**
1. Select the **Wireframe** tab and in the **Arcs** section select **Circle Center Point**.

2. Enter a value of **0.25** for **Radius** and hit the Enter key. Click on the **Lock** icon to "freeze" this value.

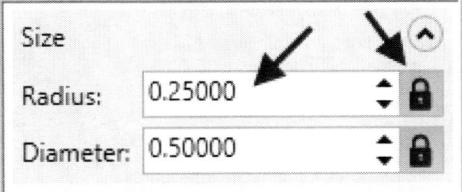

3. To satisfy this first prompt **Enter the center point** click the middle mouse button and then hit the spacebar on your keyboard.
4. The **Fastpoint** box now opens. Input **0.25,0.5** and hit the **Enter** key.

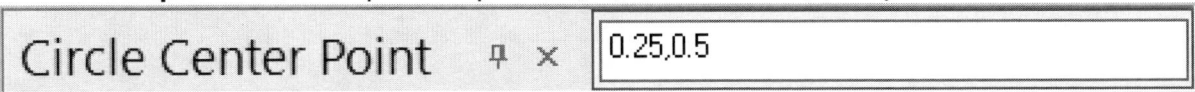

➲ **Create Circle #2**
5. To satisfy the prompt **Enter the center point** just type the coordinate, **type in 0.625,0.5** for the center of the circle. Now hit **Enter**.

⊃ **Create Circle #3**

6. To satisfy the prompt **Enter the center point** just type the coordinate, **type in 3.750-1.858, 0.5+0.25** for the center of the circle. Now hit **Enter.**

⊃ **Create Circle #4**

7. To satisfy the prompt **Enter the center point** just type the coordinate, **type in 3.750-0.25, 0.625** for the center of the circle. Now hit **Enter.**
8. Right mouse click in the graphics area and click on **Fit**.

9. Click on the **OK** icon ☑ to complete this feature.

⊃ **Create Line #1**

10. Select the **Wireframe** tab if required and in the **Lines** section click on **Line Endpoints**
11. On the graphics screen you are prompted: **Specify the first endpoint** and the Line panel appears. **Ensure** the **Tangent** function is activated.
12. To satisfy the prompt **Specify the first endpoint** move the cursor over to the **center of the grid** and as you get close to the **Origin** (X0Y0) a visual cue appears. ⬚ This is the cue that will allow you to snap to the origin, with this visual cue highlighted **pick the origin**.
13. To satisfy the prompt **Specify the second endpoint** move the cursor over the area of the circle shown below. Ensure there is **no visual snap cue** being displayed and click on this point. As **Tangent** is activated on the Line panel the line will snap to the closest tangency point on the circle as shown below right:

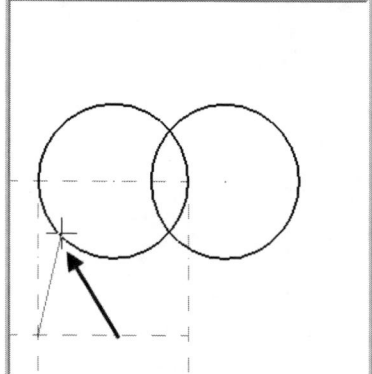 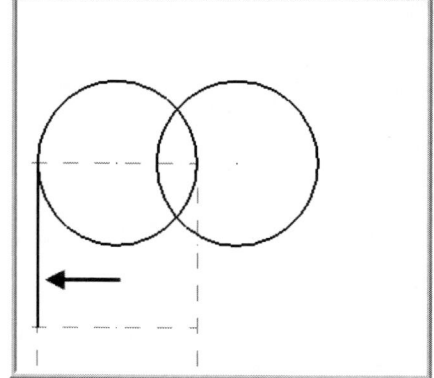

⊃ **Create Line #2**

14. To satisfy the prompt **Specify the first endpoint** move the cursor over the area of the circle shown below. Ensure there is **no visual cue** being displayed and click on this point. As **Tangent** is activated on the Line panel the line will snap to the closest tangency point on the circle.

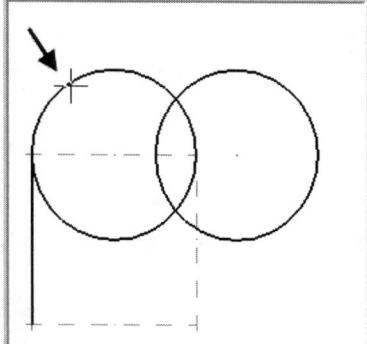

15. To satisfy the prompt **Specify the second endpoint** move the cursor over the area of the circle shown below. Ensure there is **no visual cue** being displayed and click on this point. As **Tangent** is activated on the Line panel the line will snap to the closest tangency point on the circle as shown below right.

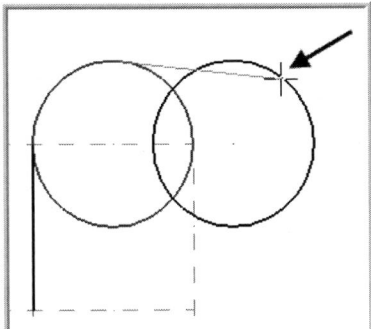 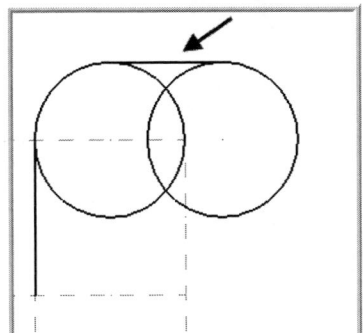

➲ **Create Line #3**

16. To satisfy the prompt **Specify the first endpoint** move the cursor over the area of the circle shown below. Ensure there is **no visual cue** being displayed and click on this point.

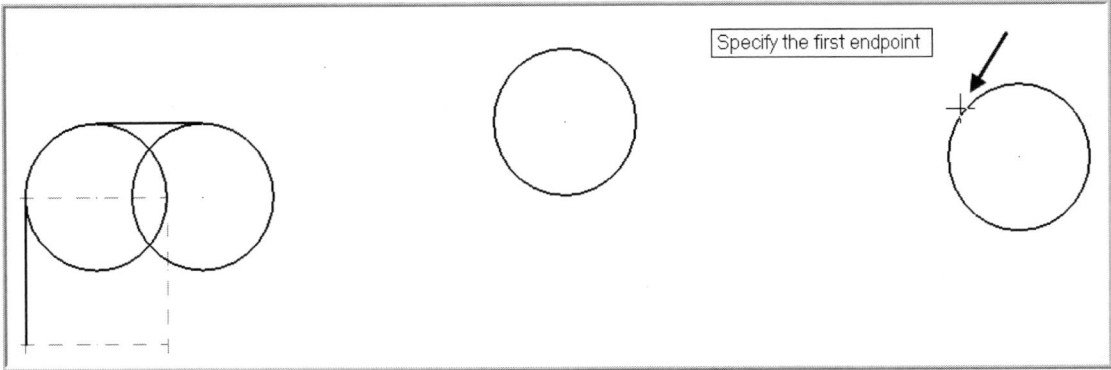

17. To satisfy the prompt **Specify the second endpoint** move the cursor over the area of the circle shown below. Ensure there is **no visual cue** being displayed and click on this point. As **Tangent** is activated on the Line panel the line will snap to the closest tangency point on the circle.

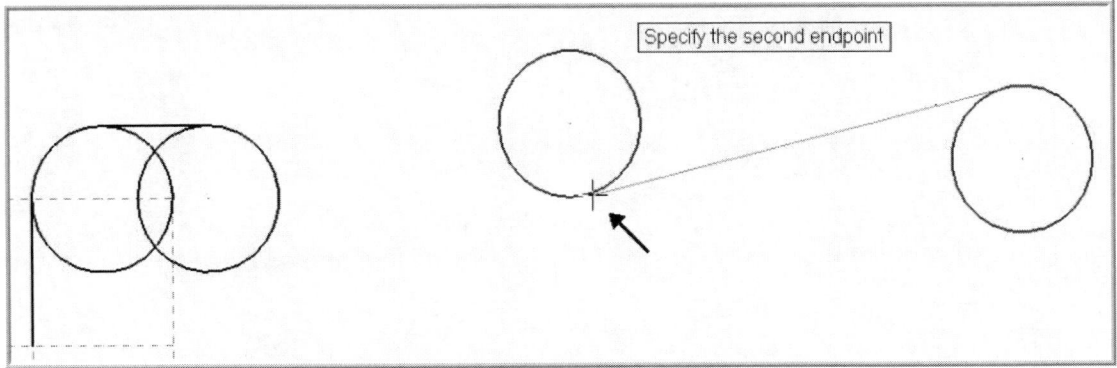

18. Click on the **OK and Create New Operation** icon .

⮑ Create Line #4

19. Click in the space for **Length** and enter a value of **0.5** and then hit the tab key. In the space for **Angle** and enter a value of **-40.0** and hit enter.

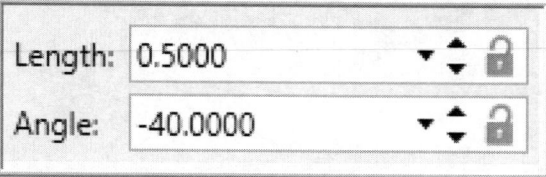

20. To satisfy the prompt **Specify the first endpoint** move the cursor over the area of the circle shown below. Ensure there is **no visual cue** being displayed and click on this point.

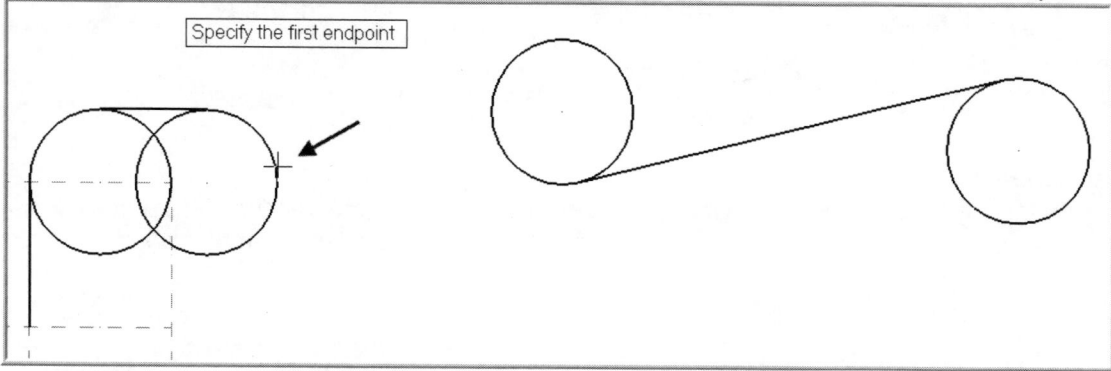

21. To satisfy the prompt **Select a line** pick the lower line as shown below:

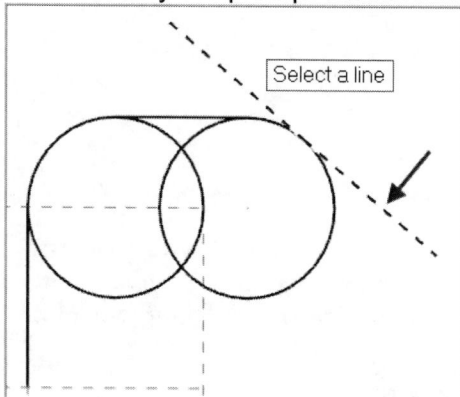

⊃ **Create Line #5**

22. To satisfy the prompt **Specify the first endpoint** use the **AutoCursor Override drop down list**. Open the drop down for **Auto cursor** on the **Selection Bar** menu and select **Quadrant**. Move the cursor over the area of the circle shown below right and click on the circle:

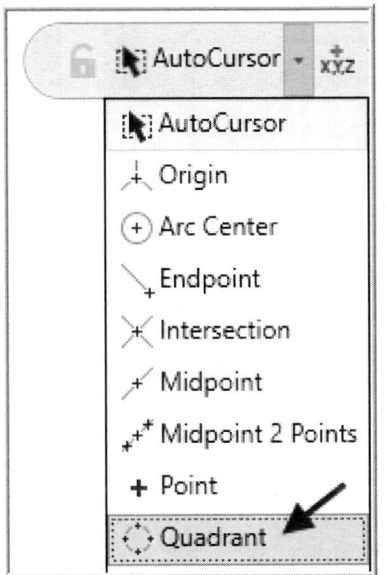 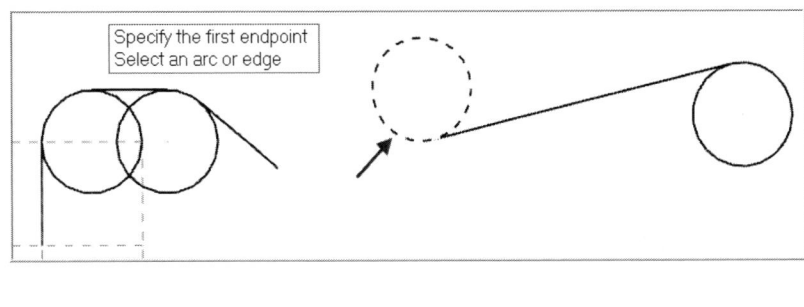

23. To satisfy the prompt **Specify the second endpoint** move the cursor over to the left of the circle shown below. Ensure the visual cue for **Horizontal/Vertical** 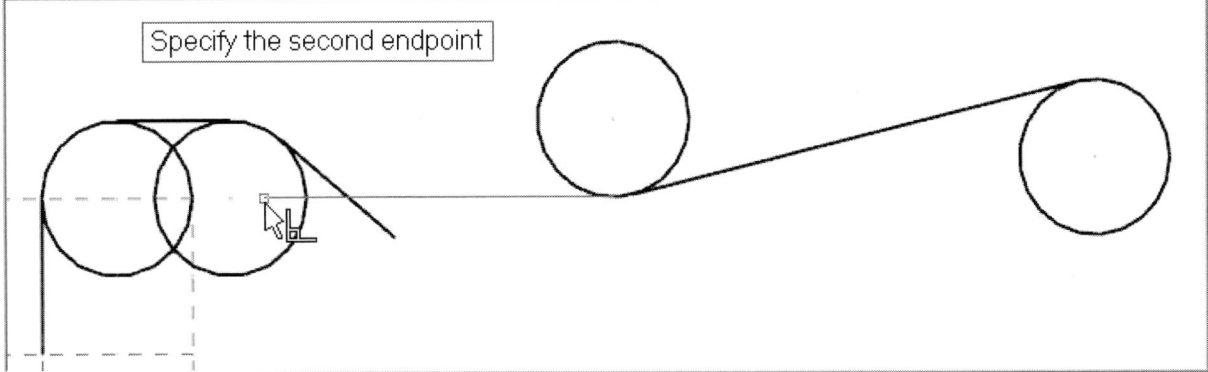 is displayed and click on this point.

⊃ **Create Line #6**

24. Activate **Multi-line** in the Line Endpoints panel.

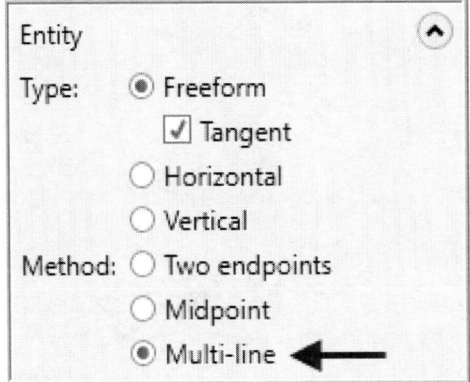

25. To satisfy the prompt **Specify the first endpoint** move the cursor over to the **center of the grid** a visual cue appears. 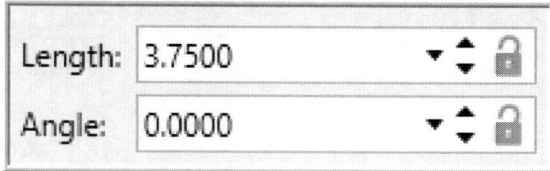 With this visual cue highlighted **pick the origin**.
26. Click in the space for **Length** and enter a value of **3.75** and then hit the tab key. In the space for **Angle** enter a value of **0** and hit enter.

Length:	3.7500	▾ ⬍ 🔒
Angle:	0.0000	▾ ⬍ 🔓

⮕ **Create Line #7**

27. To satisfy the prompt **Specify the second endpoint** move the cursor over to the right of the circle shown below. When the visual cue for Endpoint is displayed click on this point.

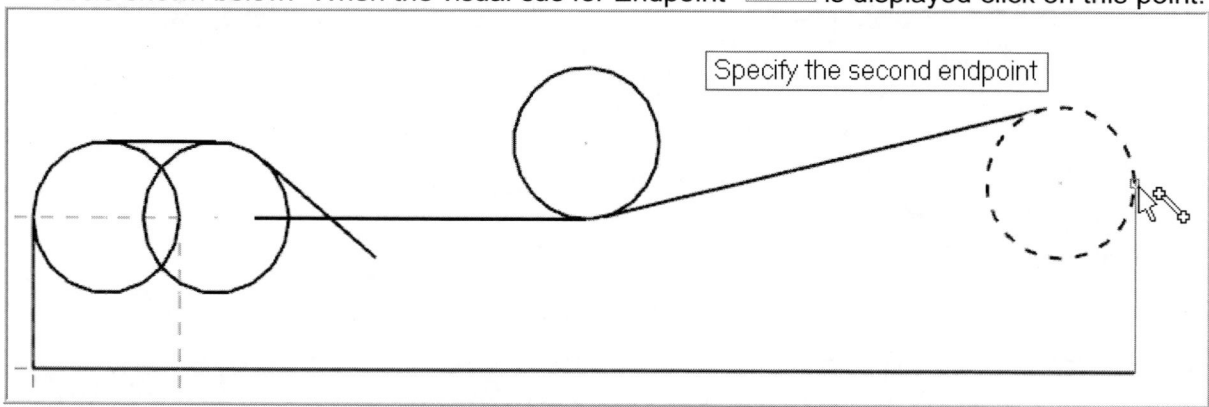

28. Click on the **OK** icon to complete this feature.

⮕ **Create Fillet #5**

29. Select the **Wireframe** tab at the top of the screen and in the **Modify** section click on **Fillet Entities**.
30. The **Fillet Entities** panel appears. If required activate the **Method** to **Normal** and enter a value of **0.25** for **Radius**.
31. Ensure the **Trim** entities box at the bottom of the panel is check marked to turn the trim on. When prompted to **Fillet: Select an entity,** select the two lines shown below:

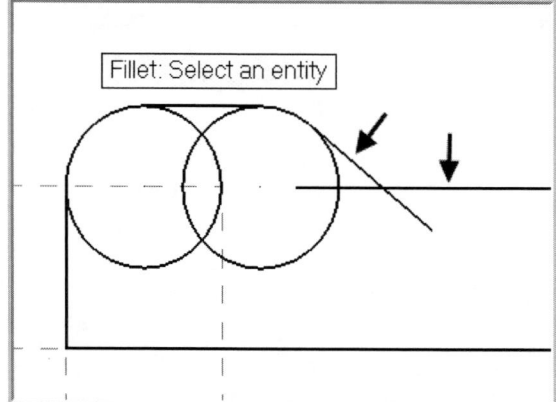

32. Click on the **OK** icon to complete this feature.

⊃ Next, you will trim the geometry using **Divide / Delete**. There are many different ways to accomplish this trimming operation, this is just one method. If you make a mistake using **Divide / Delete** use the **Undo** button to start over.

⊃ **Trim the circles**
33. In the Wireframe
34. Click on **Divide** in the **Modify** section.
35. The **Divide** panel appears. Activate **Trim** if required.

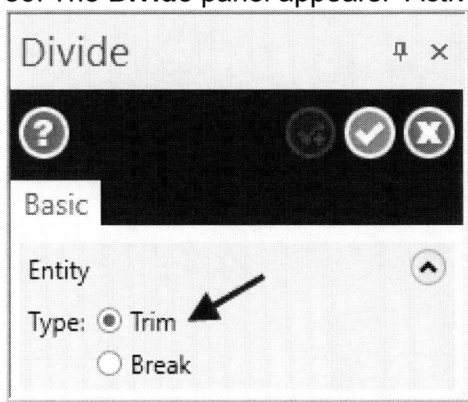

36. To satisfy the prompt **Select the curve to divide / delete.** Move the cursor over the various circles and select in order and position as shown below. The arc is trimmed back to the two closest intersections/end points as shown below. Placing the cursor over the entity to divide / delete shows a preview as shown below left.

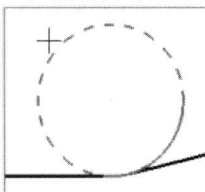
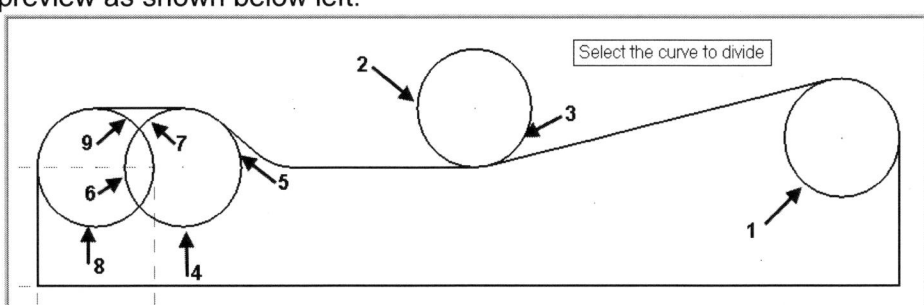

Note: On some of the circles you will need to select them more than once to completely trim them.

37. Click on the **OK** icon to complete this feature.

⊃ The completed geometry is shown below:

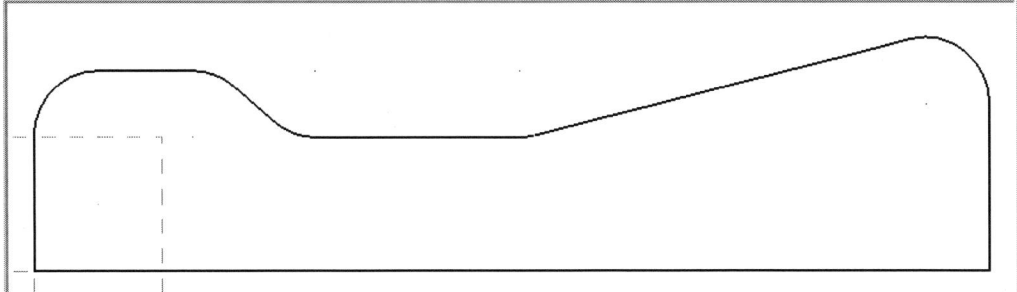

TASK 3:
CREATE GEOMETRY - BLOCK

⮕ In this task you will create the geometry that will be used to create the solid block.

1. On the **Wireframe** tab at the top of the screen and in the **Shapes** section click on **Rectangle.**
2. When the Rectangle menu appears input a **Width of 4.625** and a **Height of 2.50**.

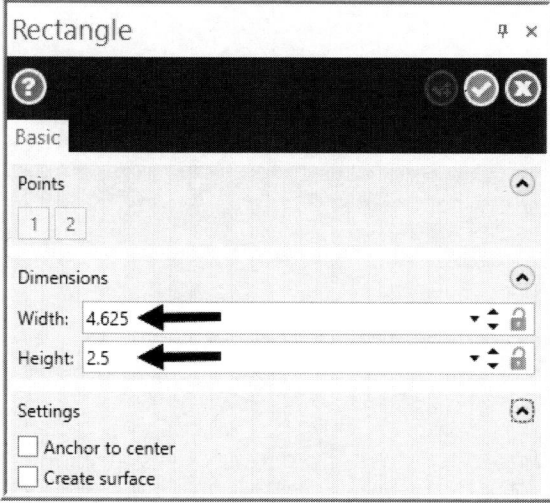

⮕ Since we specified positive values for the Width and Height of the rectangle, when selecting the position for the first corner of the rectangle it will be relative to the lower left corner.

3. To satisfy the onscreen prompt to Select a new position for the first corner, click the **spacebar to use Fastpoint** and **input -0.4375, -1.25**. (you may need to click the middle mouse wheel on the graphics screen to shift focus so the spacebar will trigger Fastpoint)

-0.4375, -1.25

4. Click **Ok** to complete the rectangle creation. You screen should match below.

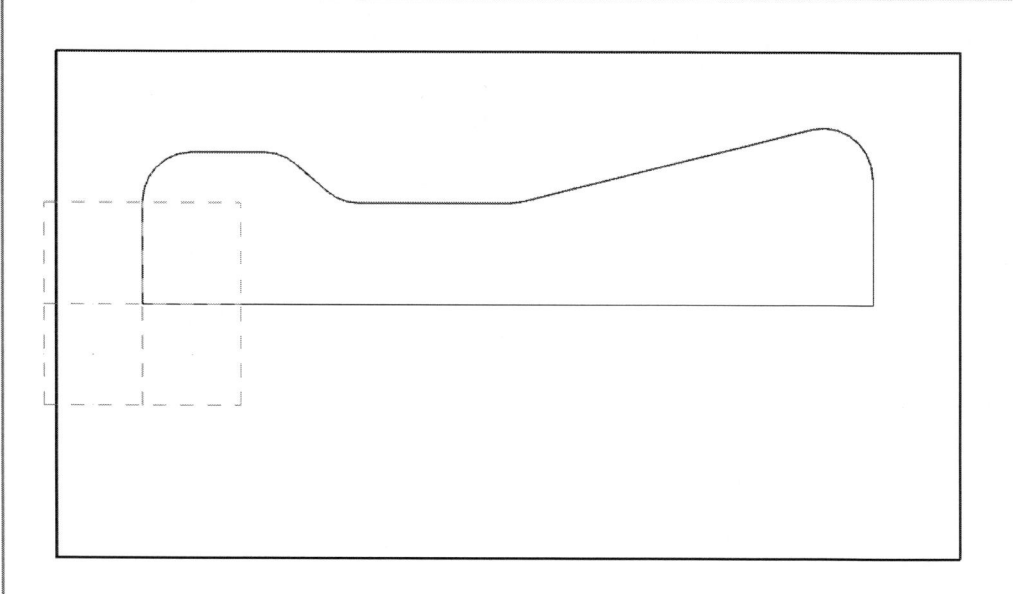

TASK 4:
CREATE THE BLOCK SOLID BODY

1. Activate a **wireframe** image if required by selecting the **Alt and S** keys or by clicking on the **Wireframe** icon at the lower right of the screen:

2. Right mouse click in the graphics area and click on **Top**.

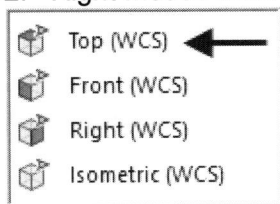

3. On the **Solids** tab and in the **Create** section select **Extrude**.

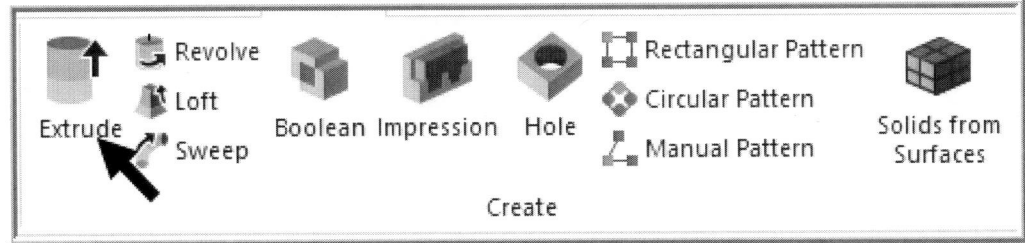

⊃   On the screen you will now see the **Chaining** dialog box, with the **Chain Button** selected as shown by the arrow. In the graphics screen a prompt to **"Select chain(s) to extrude"** is displayed.

4. Select the chain as shown in the **Graphics Screen** diagram:

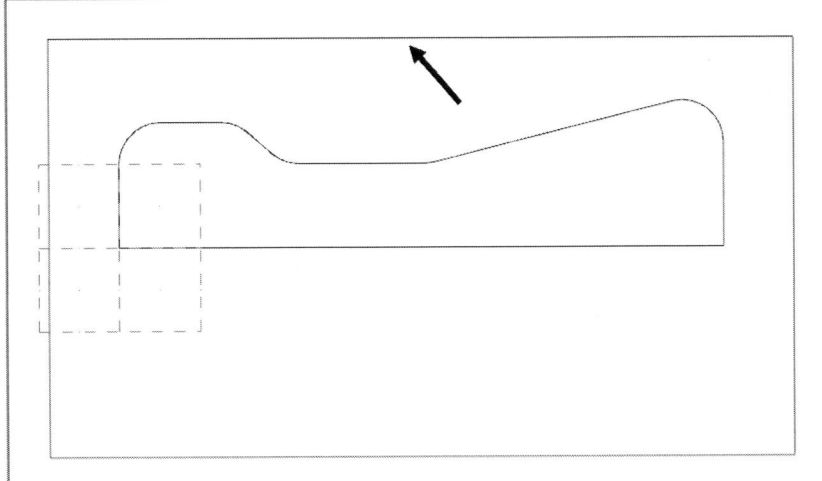

5. Click on the **OK** icon.

6. Right mouse click in the graphics area and click on **Isometric**.
7. An arrow will appear on one of the corners as shown below, make sure the arrow is pointing

   down. If it is pointing up click on the **Reverse All** icon 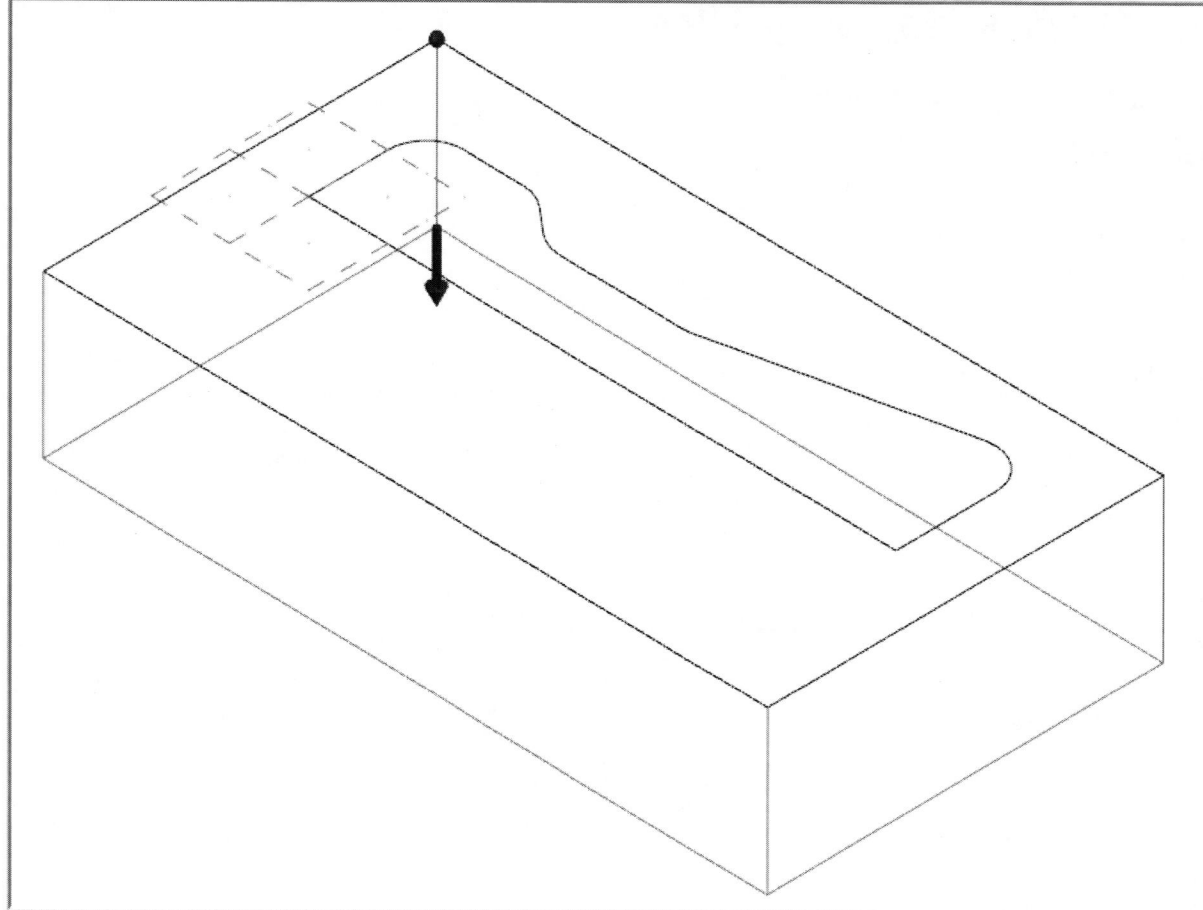 in the Solid
   Extrude panel. **Note:** you may have to unzoom the image to see the direction the arrow is
   pointing.

8. Make the necessary changes as shown below in the Solid Extrude panel. Activate **Create Body** and set the **Distance to 1.0**.

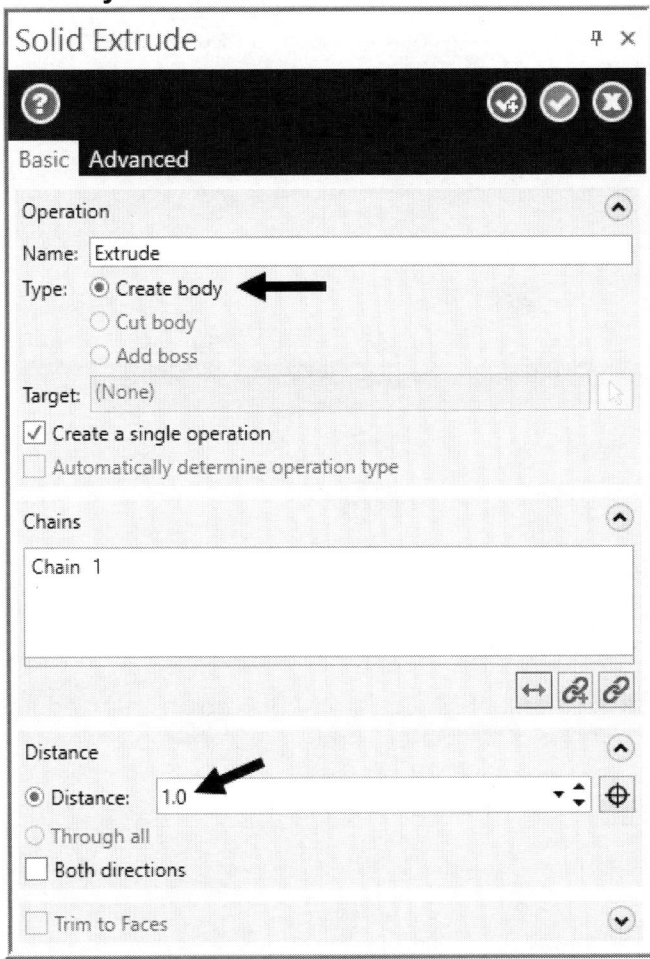

9. Click on the **OK** icon 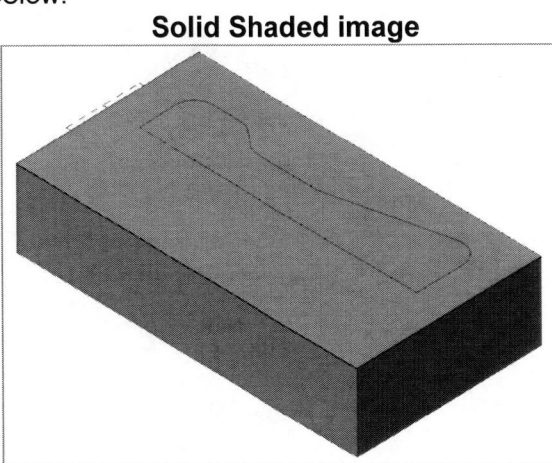 in the Solid Extrude panel.
10. Right mouse click in the graphics area and click on **Fit**.
➲ Your screen should look like the screenshot below:

Wireframe image

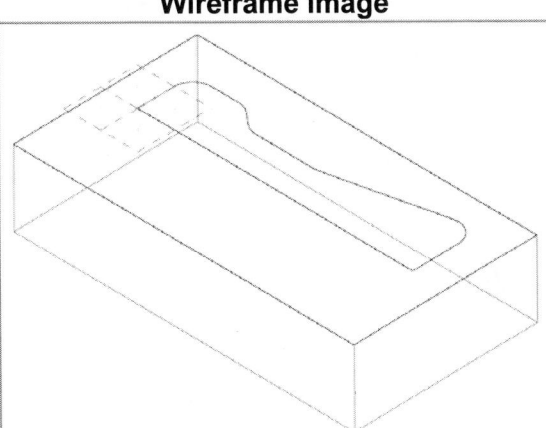

Solid Shaded image

TASK 5:
CREATE THE REVOLVED SOLID
➲ In this task you will create the solid cavity of the part by revolving the geometry created.
1. Right mouse click in the graphics area and click on **Top**.

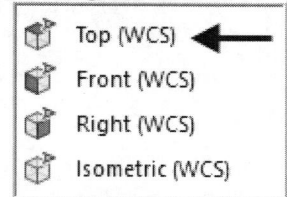

2. Right mouse click in the graphics area and click on **Unzoom 80%** to shrink the display.
3. Click on the **Solids** tab and in the **Create** section select **Revolve**.

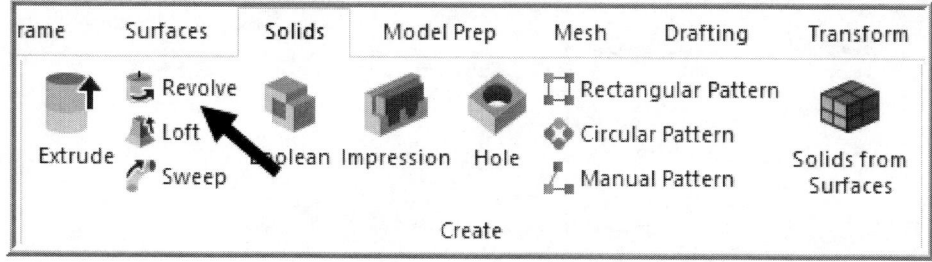

➲ On the screen you will now see the **Chaining** dialog box, with the **Chain Button** selected as shown by the arrow. In the graphics screen a prompt to **"Select chain(s) to revolve"** is displayed.
4. Select the chain as shown in the **Graphics Screen** diagram:

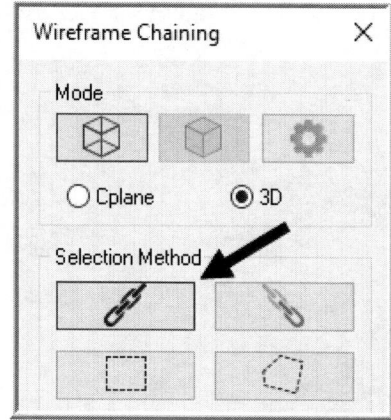 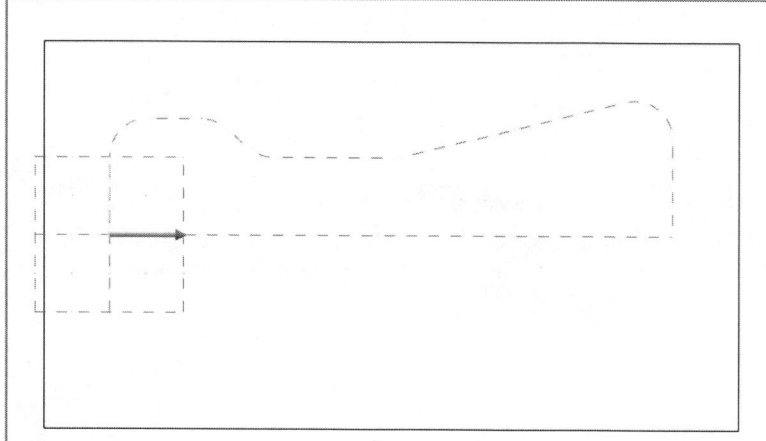

5. Click on the **OK** icon. ✓

6. The **"Select a line to be used as axis of rotation"** prompt appears. Select the centerline of the cavity as shown below:

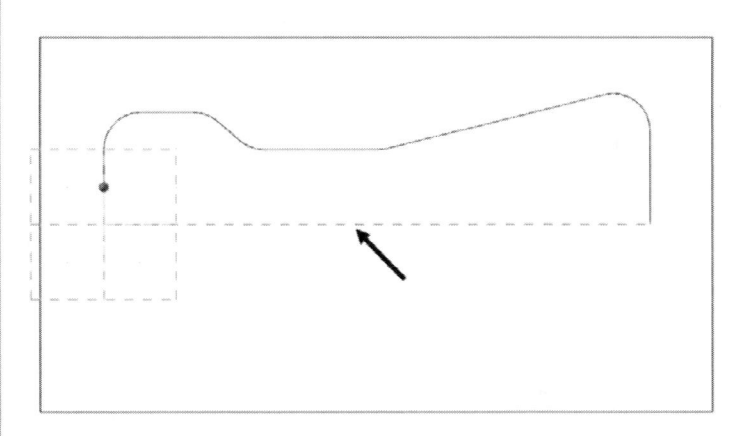

7. Right mouse click in the graphics area and click on **Isometric**.
8. In the lower right corner of the screen click on the **Wireframe** icon to change the display to wireframe.

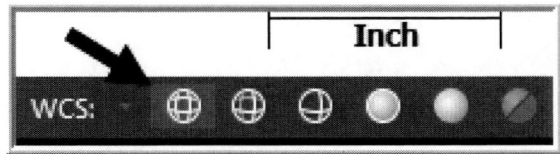

9. The current settings will be creating a revolved body. We do not want this new shape, we want this to cut into the existing model.

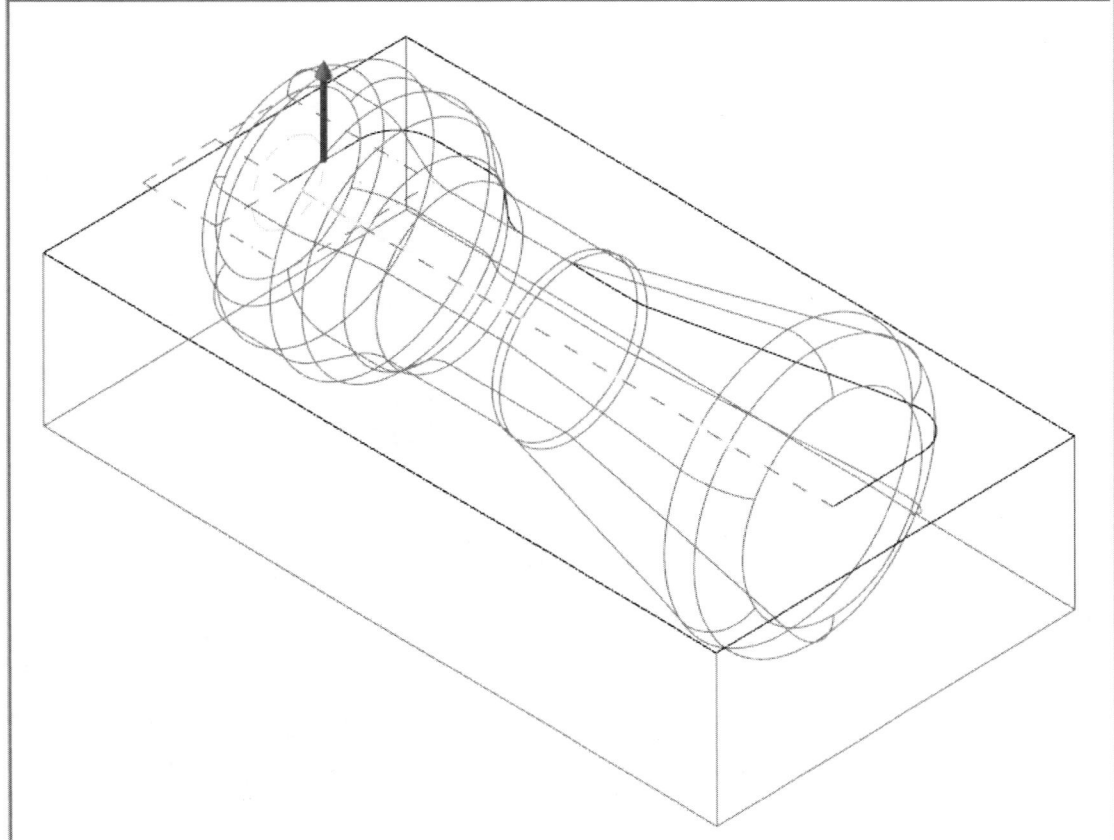

10. Change the Revolve Type to Cut Body. If there is not an existing solid model before creating this operation, Cut Body will not be an option. Therefore, it is important to create the base first.

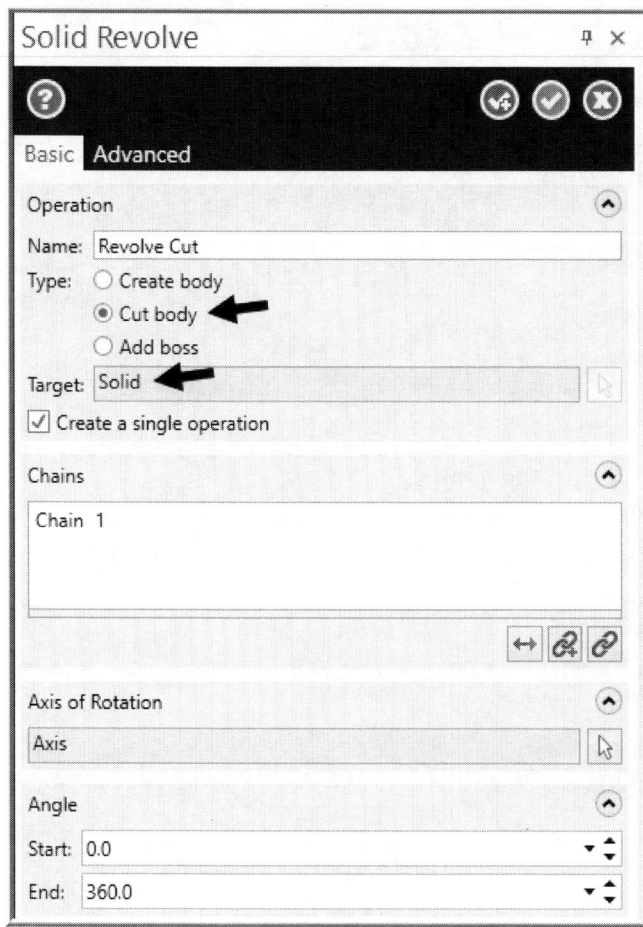

11. Click on the **OK** icon in the Solid Revolve dialog window.

➮ Your screen should look like the screenshot below left:

12. Select **Alt and S** to **shade** the solid extrusion or click on the **Outlined Shaded icon** at the lower right corner of the screen.

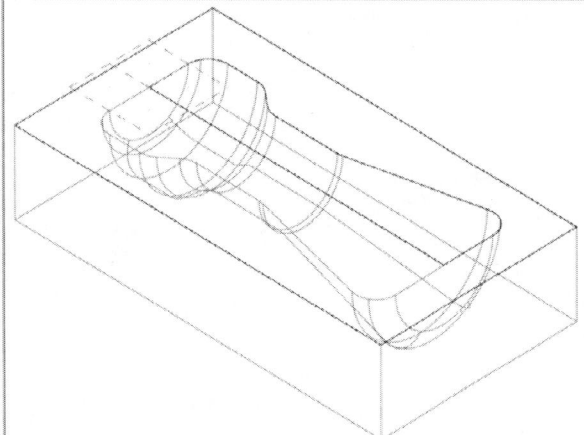
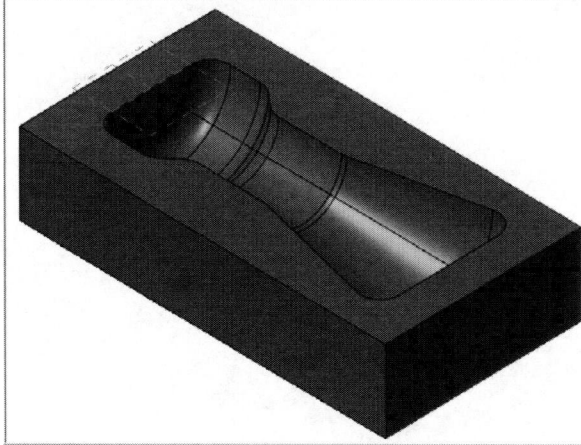

TASK 6:
SAVE THE FILE

1. Select **File**.
2. Select **Save As.**
3. Click on the **Browse** icon.
4. In the File name box, type **Mill-Lesson-9**.
5. Browse to an appropriate location.
6. Select the **Save** button to save the file and complete this function.

Toolpath Creation

TASK 7:
DEFINE THE STOCK

1. Right mouse click in the graphics area and click on the **Fit** icon ⊞.
2. Select the **View tab** and click on **Toolpaths** in the **Managers** section to display the Toolpaths Manager.
3. Select the **plus** in front of **Properties** to expand the Toolpaths Group Properties.

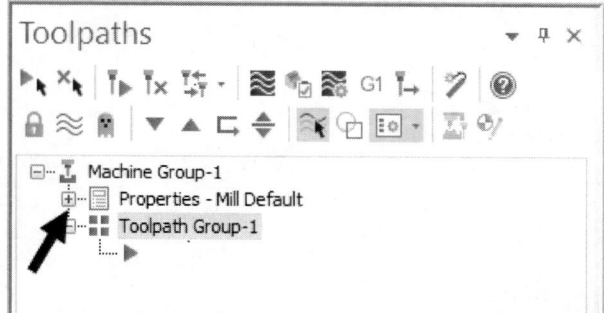
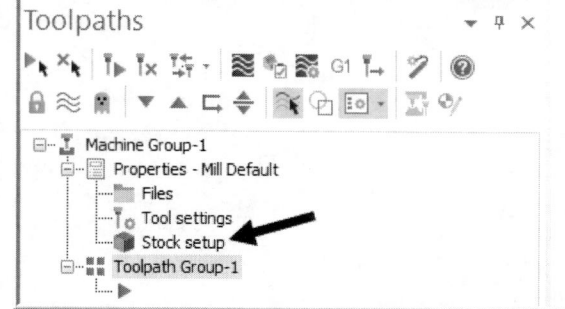

4. Select **Stock setup** in the Toolpaths Manager window as shown above on the right:
5. Change the parameters to match the **Stock Setup** screenshot below:
➲ **Z zero** is at the **top of the part**.

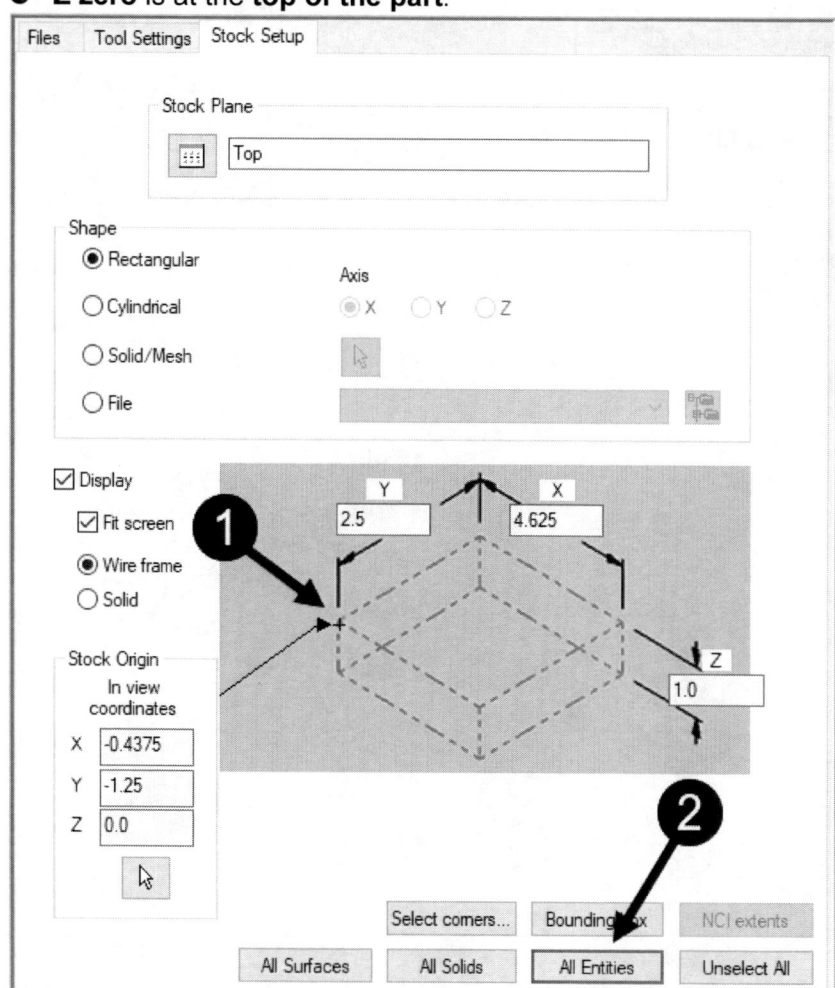

6. Select the **Tool Settings** tab and change the parameters to match the Tool Settings screenshot below. To change the Material type follow the instructions below:

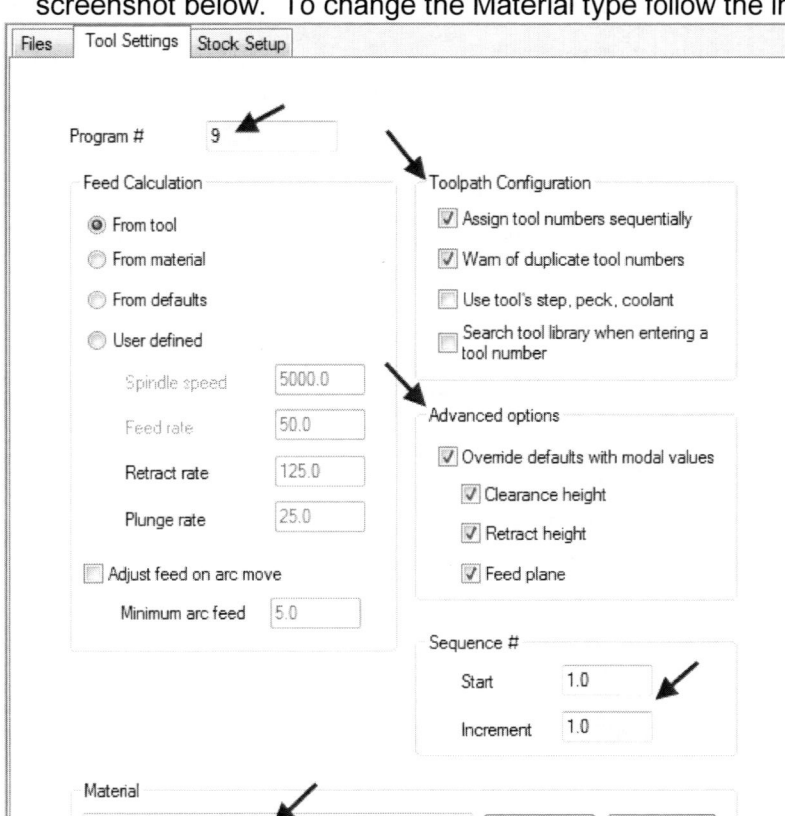

7. To change the Material type to Aluminum 6061 pick the Select button at the bottom of the Tool Settings page.

8. At the **Material List** dialog box open the **Source** drop down list and select **Mill – library**.

9. From the Default Materials list select **ALUMINUM inch -6061** and then select ✓.

10. Select the OK button ✓ again to complete this Stock Setup function.

➲ Your part should look like the screen shot below. With X0 Y0 at the middle left side and Z zero at the top of the part.

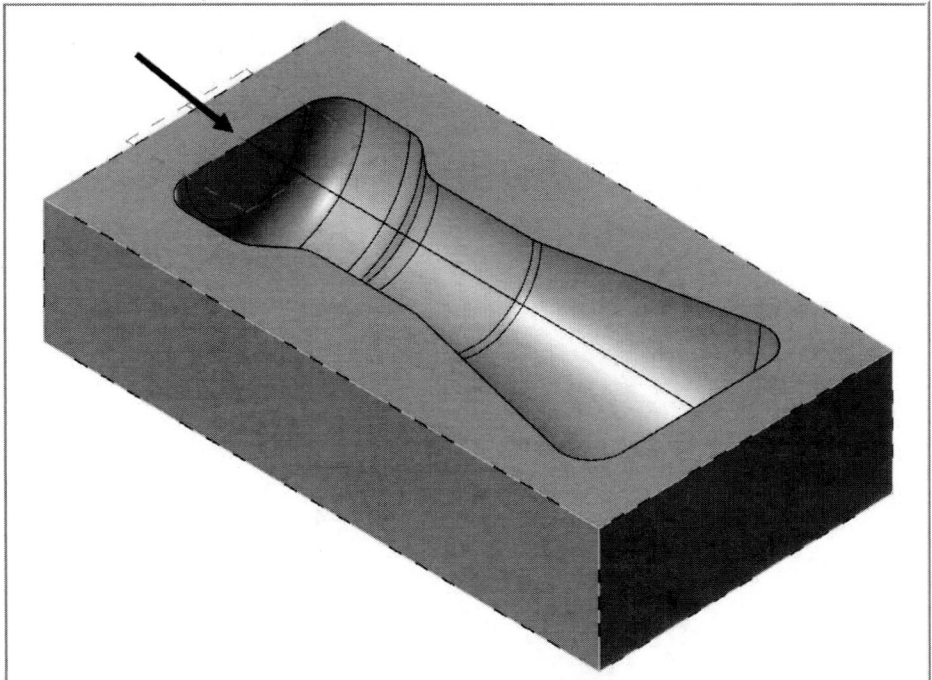

TASK 8:
ROUGH USING OPTIROUGH

⮑ In this task you will use a 0.375 diameter bull end mill with a 0.0625 corner radius to rough out the pocket using **Surface High Speed>Dynamic OptiRough.**

Dynamic OptiRough Toolpaths

The 3D surface high speed Dynamic OptiRough toolpath supports cutters capable of machining very large depths of cut. It uses an aggressive, fast, intelligent roughing algorithm based on Mastercam's 2D high speed dynamic milling motion..

A single Optimized toolpath can cut material in two directions, on stepdowns (-Z) and step ups (+Z). This highly efficient bi-directional cutting strategy removes the maximum amount of material with the minimum of stepdowns, significantly reducing cycle times.

---

1. Right mouse click in the graphics area and click on the **Fit** icon 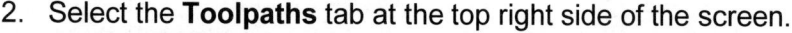.
2. Select the **Toolpaths** tab at the top right side of the screen.
3. Select **OptiRough** in the **3D** toolpath section.

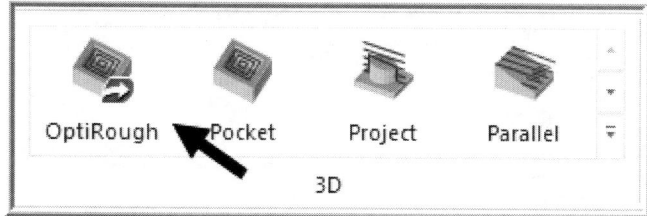

4. On the screen select the **Model Geometry** page, if required.
5. Set both the **Wall Stock** and **Floor stock** to **0.020.**

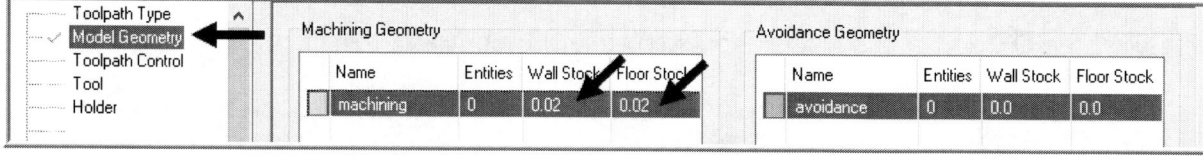

6. At the bottom of the **Model Geometry** page click on the **Select entities** button.

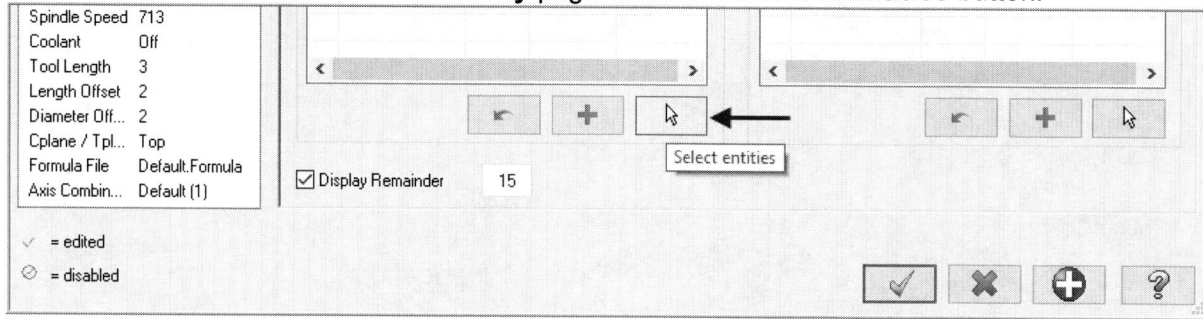

7. Now you will be returned to the graphics screen, select the **Select all advanced** button on the right of your screen.

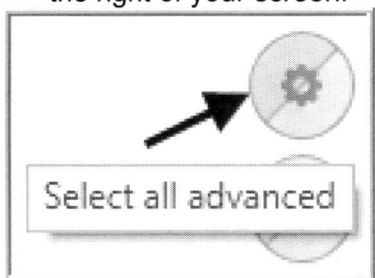

8. The **Select All** dialog box appears on the screen. Click on the OK icon [✓] to complete and exit this feature.

9. To move onto the next step, you now need to pick the **End Selection** icon [⊘].
10. Select the **Toolpath Control** page.
11. Select the **Containment Boundaries** button at the top of this page.

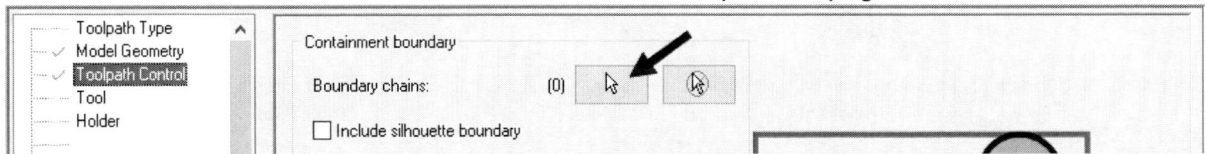

12. On the screen you will now see the **Chaining dialog box.** Switch to the **Solid Chaining** mode and **enable Loop**. Select the line as shown below on the right, click **Ok** on the Pick Reference Face menu when the boundary of the cutout is highlighted. This will select this as the machining boundary for this operation.

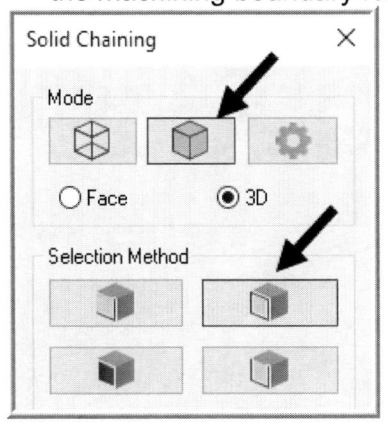

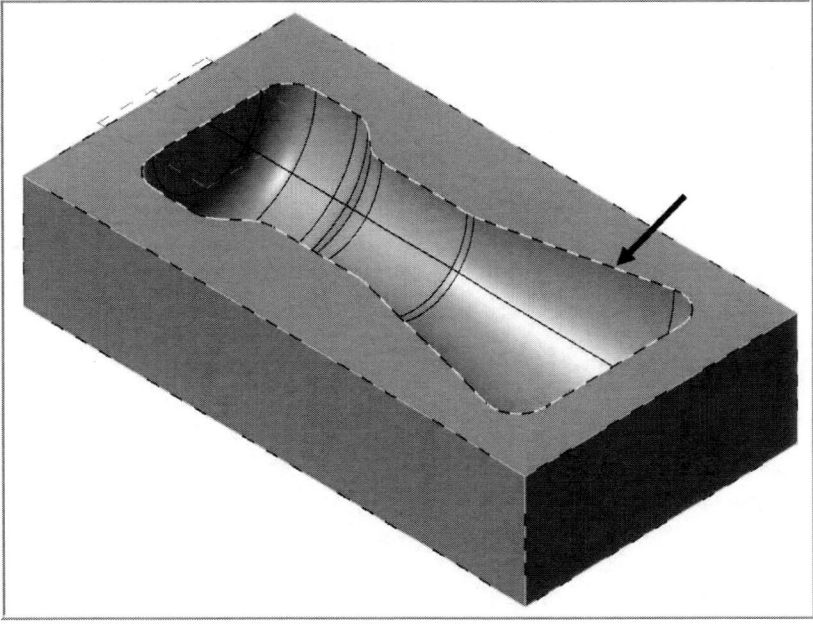

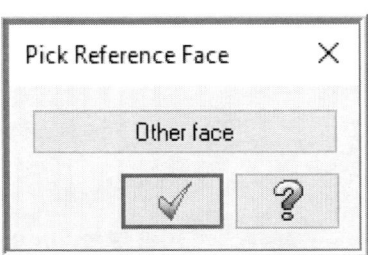

13. After the boundary has been successfully chained select the OK button [✓].

14. Still on the **Toolpath Control** page make changes to this page as shown below.

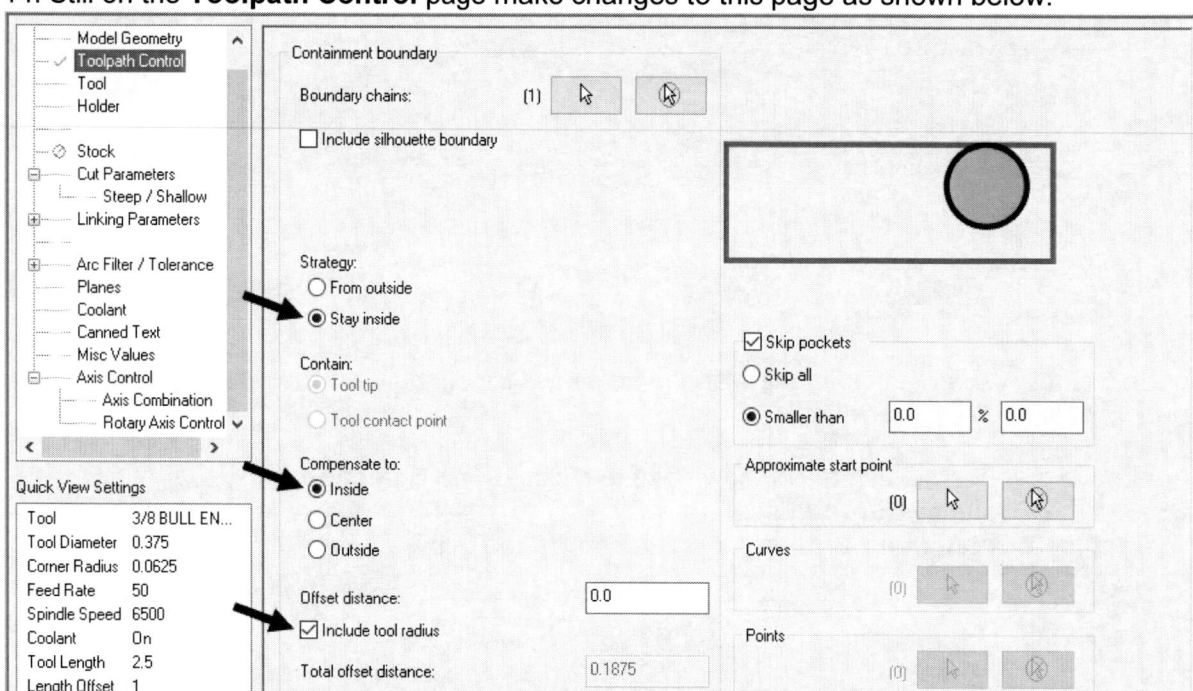

Toolpath Control
Use this page to set tool containment parameters for your surface high speed toolpath. Tool containment boundaries are used to control the tool's position around the boundary of your part.

The boundary is a closed set of wireframe curves which enclose the area to be machined. Mastercam will not create tool motions that violate the boundary, regardless of the selected cut surfaces. They can be any wireframe curves, not necessarily associated with the surfaces that are machined.
For example, you can create custom guide geometry to precisely limit the tool movements. The curves do not have to lie on the part; they can be at any Z-height.

For Area Roughing toolpaths with the Stock page enabled, if a boundary was not specified Mastercam will generate a min/max boundary around the selected drive surfaces. This boundary can be adjusted.

Use Mastercam's Silhouette Boundary function to quickly create a boundary curve that you can use for a containment boundary.

Compensate to Inside
Keep the tool inside this boundary.

Compensate to Center
Keep the tool centerline inside the boundary (allow up to half of the tool to exit the boundary).

Compensate to Outside
Allow the entire tool to exit the boundary but keep the tool edge in contact with the boundary.

15. Now click on **Tool** and in the lower left corner of the **Toolpath parameters** page select the **Select library tool...** button.

16. Use the slider bar on the right of this dialog box to scroll down and locate a **0.375 diameter bull end mill with a 0.0625 corner radius**. Select the end mill by picking anywhere along its row.

17. Select the OK button 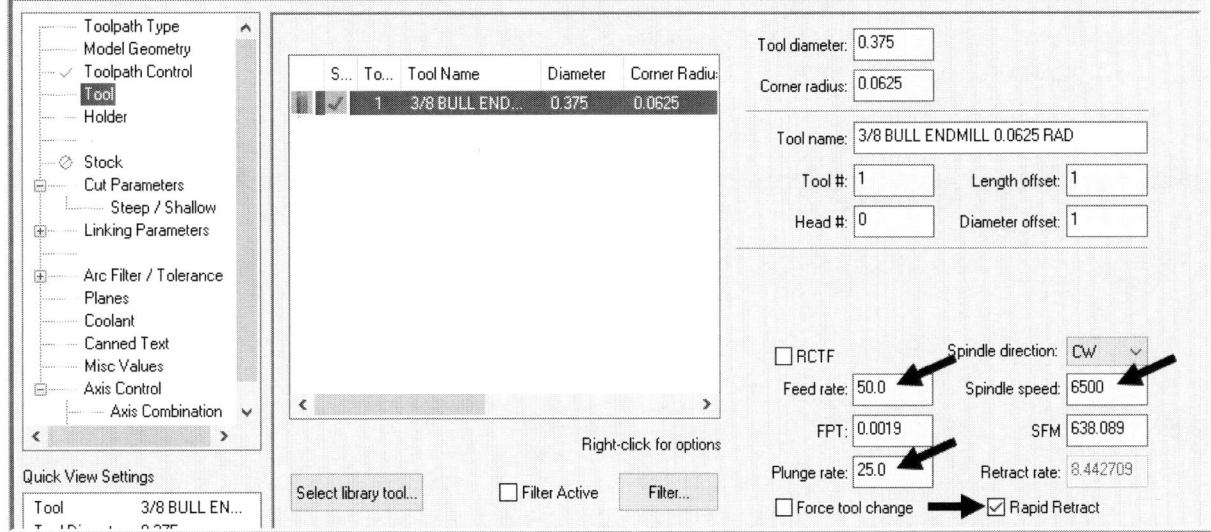 to complete the selection of this tool.

18. Make changes to the **Tool parameters** page as shown below.

19. Select the **Cut parameters** page and make changes to this page as shown below:

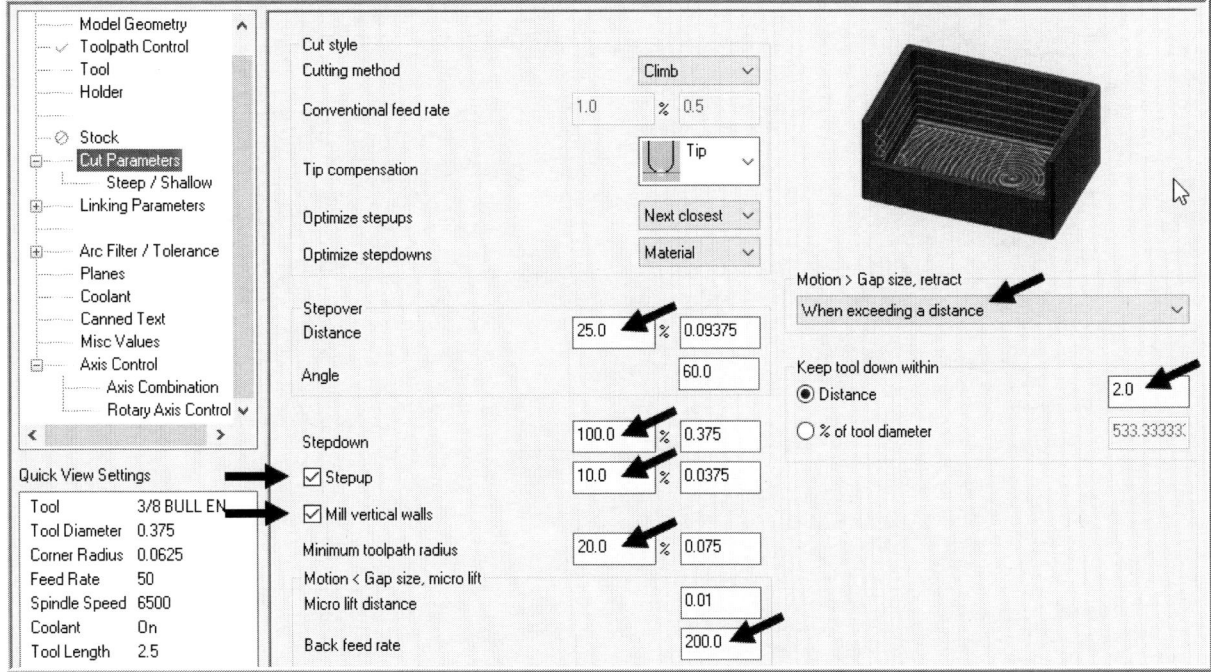

Cut Parameters - Optimized Toolpaths
As stepdowns are calculated, the dynamic roughing motion clears the material in the -Z direction, avoiding any islands.

If you activate Stepup cuts in the toolpath's Cut Parameters, Mastercam calculates additional slices in the +Z direction to remove any material left behind between the step downs—for example, islands or large scallops on angled walls.

The step up cuts use a 2D high speed dynamic rest motion to clear leftover material. Step up cuts are ordered between stepdowns.

Motion > Gap size, micro lift
Controls retracts in the toolpath when making a non-cutting move within an area where the tool can be kept down or microlifted.

Never: Eliminates retracts from the toolpath for these types of tool moves.

20. Select the **Steep / Shallow** page and ensure nothing is activated here.

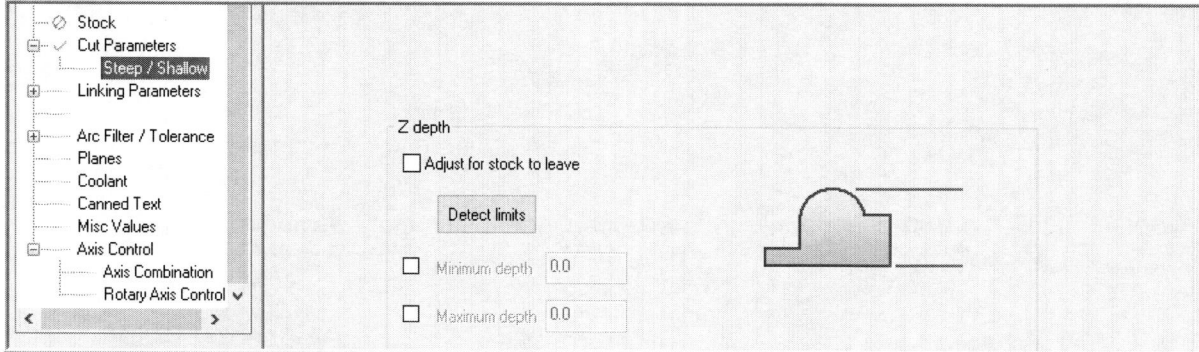

21. Select the **Linking Parameters** page and make changes to this page as shown below.

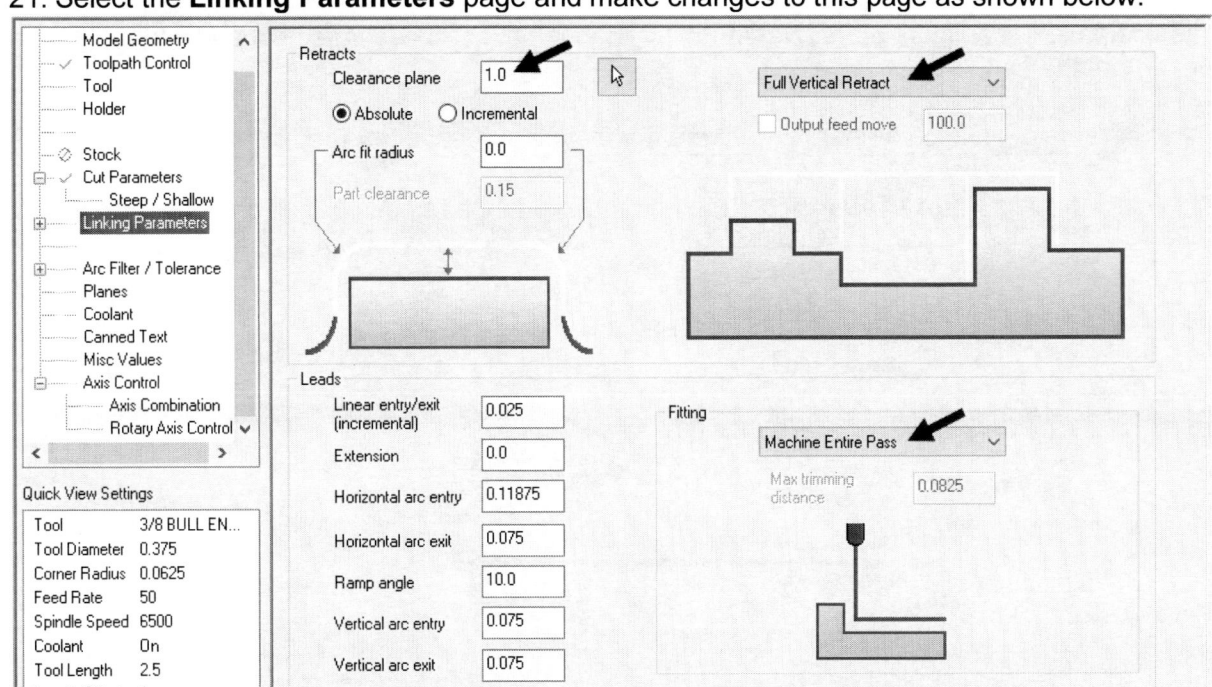

Linking Parameters
Use this page to create the **links between the cutting passes**. In general, you can think of linking moves as air moves when the tool is not in contact with the part, compared to cutting moves which are configured on the toolpath's Cut parameters page.

First, select a retract method. This determines how the tool will move between the end of one pass and the beginning of another. Then, use the **Leads fields** to control how the tool moves onto and off of the part at the start and end of each cutting pass. These moves are applied to each pass no matter which cutting pass is selected.
Finally, select a **Fitting option** to control how the entry and exit arcs will be fit into each pass.

22. **Expand** the Linking Parameters and select the **Transitions** page and make changes to this page as shown below.

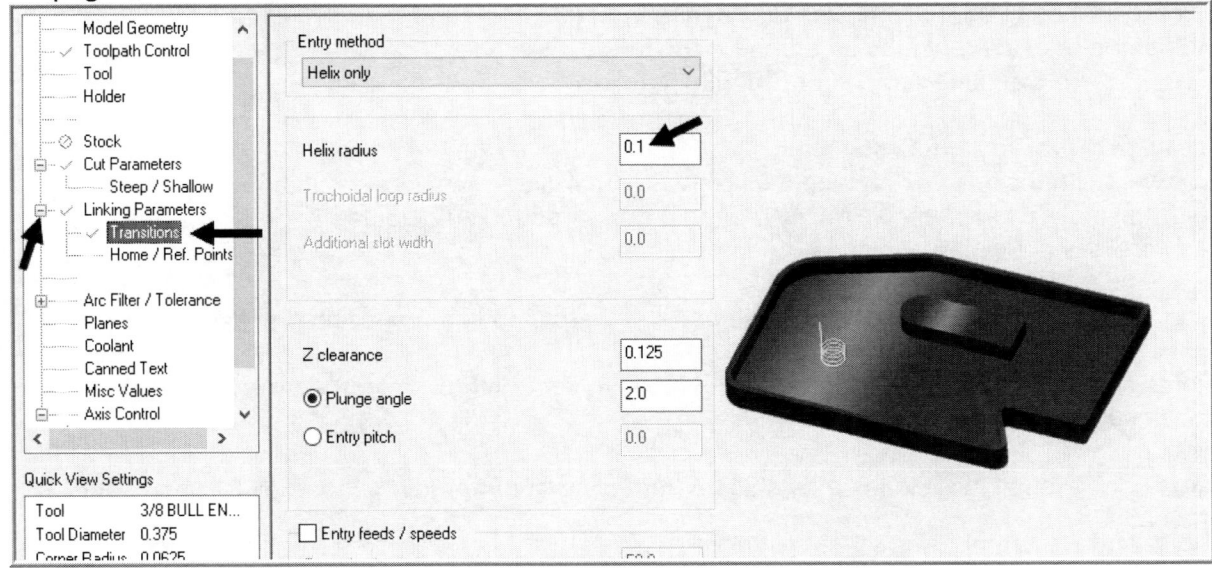

> **Transitions**
> Use this page to configure an entry method for the toolpath. This defines how and where the tool enters the part.
>
> Other parameters let you further refine the entry moves and set entry feeds and speeds.

23. Select the **Arc Filter / Tolerance** page and make changes to this page as shown below.

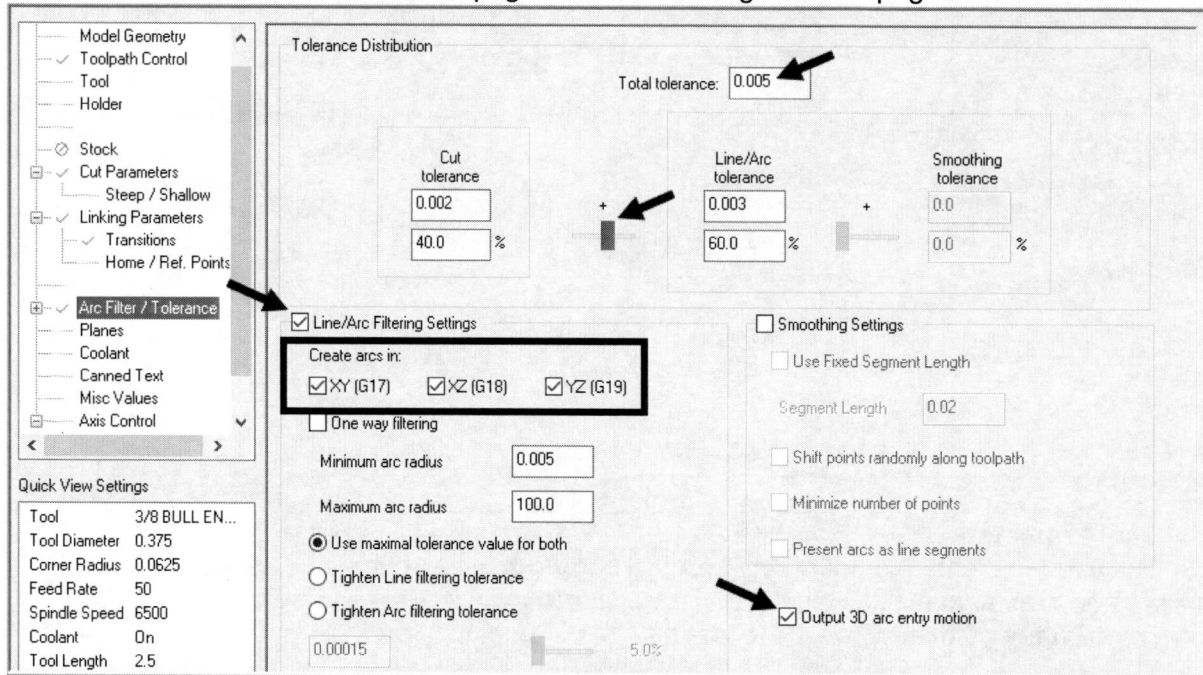

> **Arc Filter/Tolerance**
> Use this page to control toolpath tolerances. Typically, this involves several sets of variables. Mastercam uses the values you enter here to convert the toolpath—originally created using G1, G2, G3 motions—to a refined set of "smoothed" G1 motions wherever possible, and within the tolerances you specify.
>
> **Tolerances Distribution**
> The Tolerances Distribution fields display the total tolerance and the formula used to derive it. Adjust the total tolerance by entering a value in the Total tolerance field or by changing the values of the Cut, Line/Arc and/or Smoothing tolerances.
>
> **Line/Arc Filtering and Smoothing**
> Toolpath filtering lets you replace multiple very small linear moves — within the filter tolerance — with single arc moves to simplify the toolpath. Smoothing distributes a toolpath's node points, avoiding the clustering and grouping of points that can cause marks and other imperfections.
>
> Use the different checkboxes to enable or restrict arc creation in specific planes.
>
> Enter minimum and maximum arc radius values to control the size of the arcs Mastercam creates in the filtered toolpath.
>
> Define the smoothing tolerance by shifting, removing and/or adding node points along your toolpath.

24. Turn the **Coolant** Flood on.
25. Select the OK button ✓ to complete this toolpath.
26. It may take a while for Mastercam to create the toolpath. Mastercam's multi-threading functionality will calculate the toolpath while you continue to work. The green spool of thread indicates threading is active.

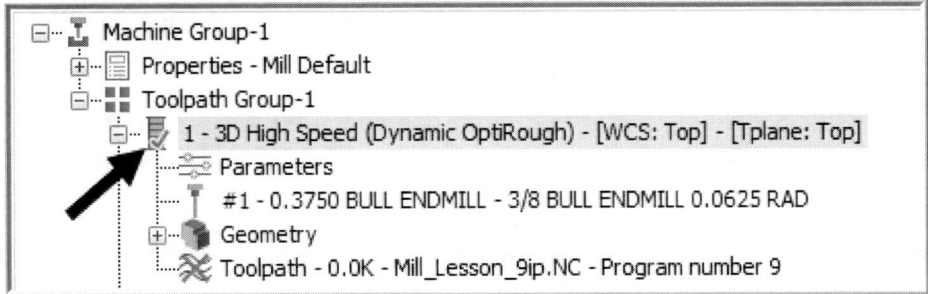

27. If threading is not active, you can turn it on by selecting **File>Configuration...** then making the selection indicated below on the **Toolpaths** tab.

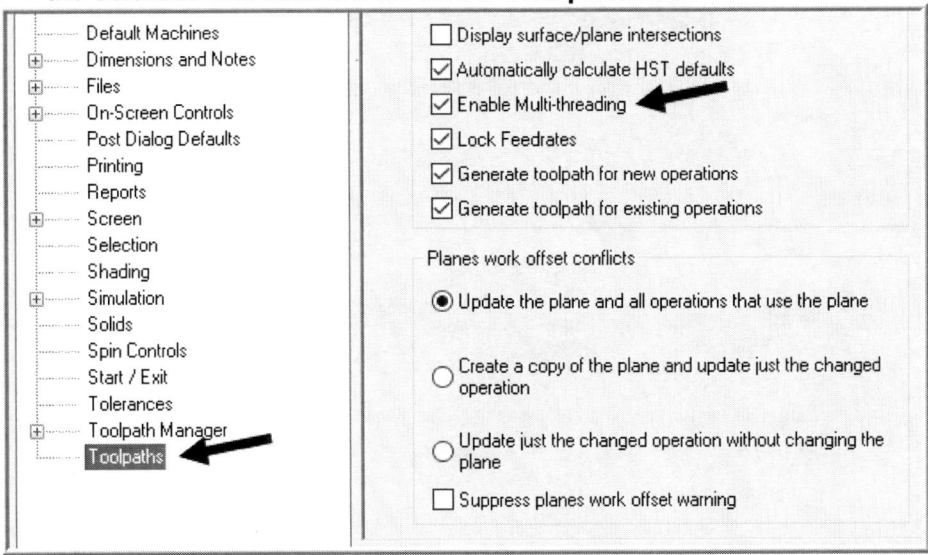

➲ The screen should look like the image below:

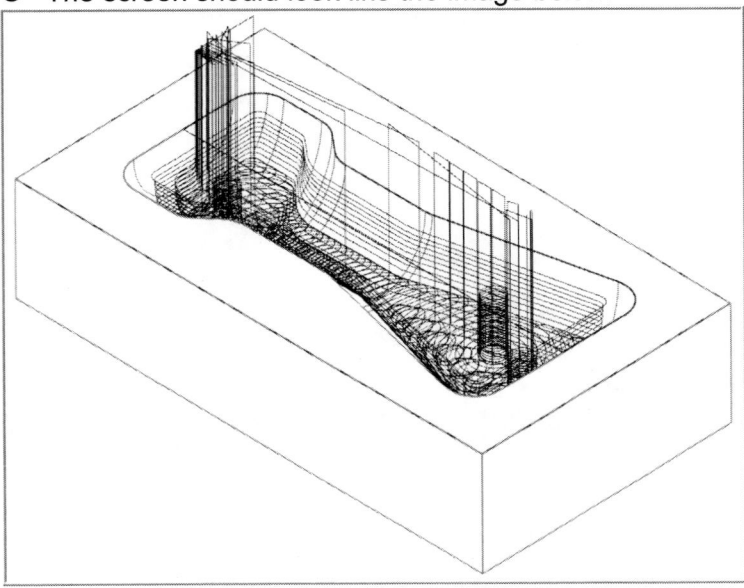

TASK 9:
FINISH USING HYBRID

➲ In this task you will use a 0.375 diameter Ball end mill to finish the pocket.
➲ Mastercam's Hybrid finishing toolpath addresses steep and shallow areas utilizing both scallop and constant Z approaches in a single toolpath.
➲ The toolpath switches seamlessly between both methods and cuts in a logical optimized order.
➲ Most of the parameters you define for the toolpath are similar or the same as other surface high speed finishing toolpaths. However, the Step group of settings on the Cut Parameters page are unique. Use them to control how Mastercam defines steep and shallow areas.

1. Select the **Toolpaths** tab at the top right side of the screen if required.
2. Click on the **Expand gallery** down arrow in the **3D** section and select **Hybrid** from the **Finishing** selections.

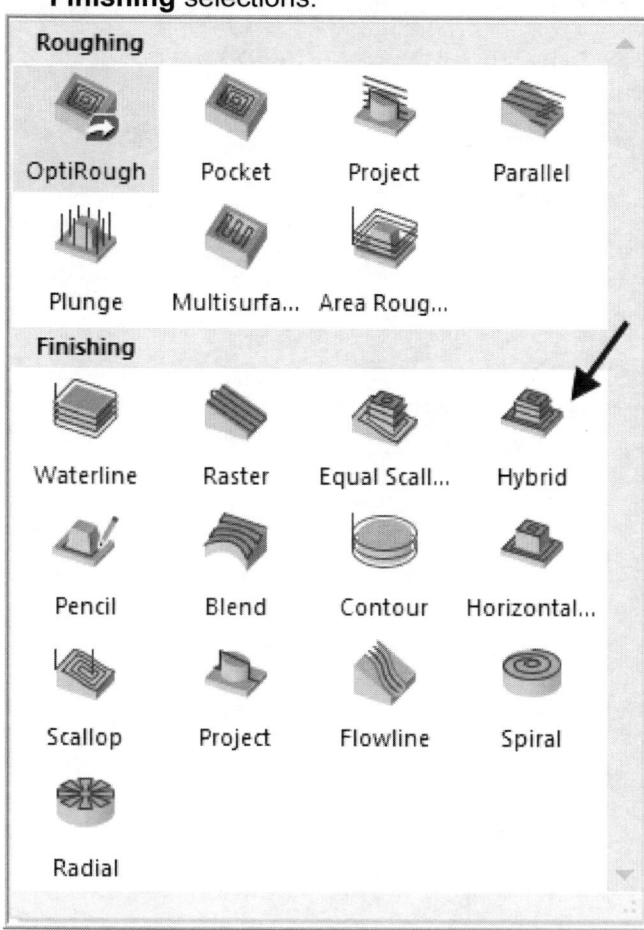

3. On the screen select the **Model Geometry** page, if required.
4. Ensure both the **Wall Stock** and **Floor stock** are set to **Zero.**

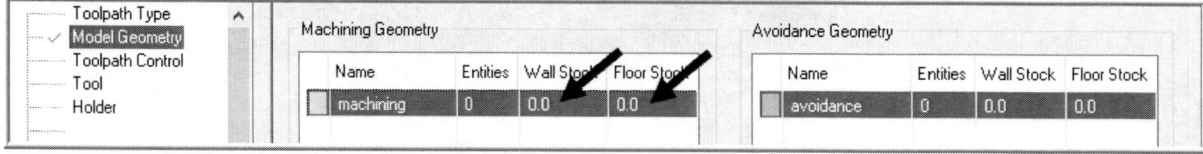

5. At the bottom of the **Model Geometry** page click on the **Select entities** button.

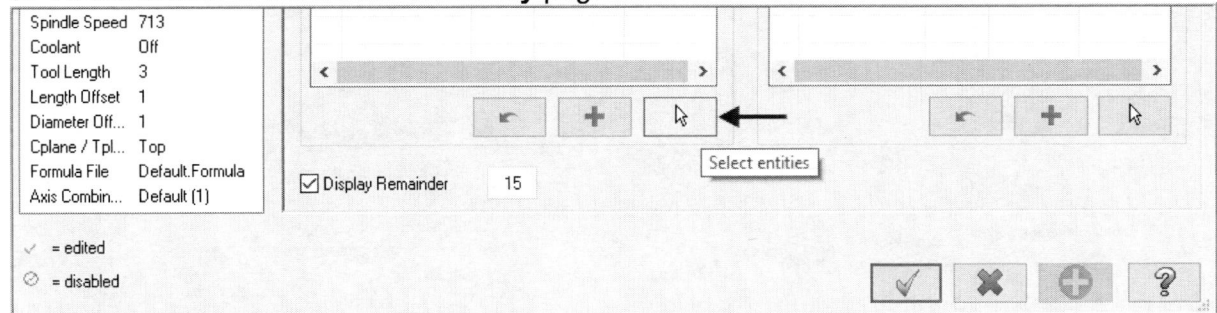

6. Now you will be returned to the graphics screen. Follow the instructions in the on-screen prompt to Double-click on a solid feature, **double click on any face of the revolved feature**. The entire feature should be selected.

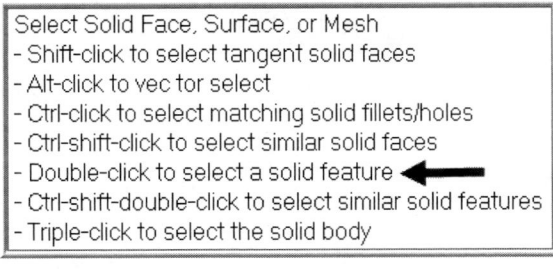

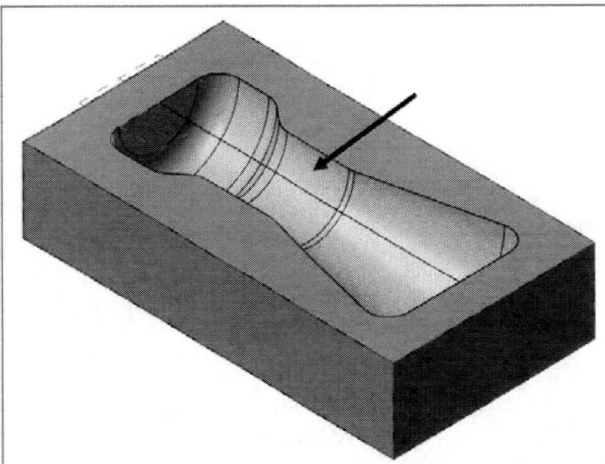

7. To move onto the next step, you now need to pick the **End Selection** icon ⊘.
8. Select the **Toolpath Control** page.
9. Check the **Include silhouette boundary** box at the top of this page.

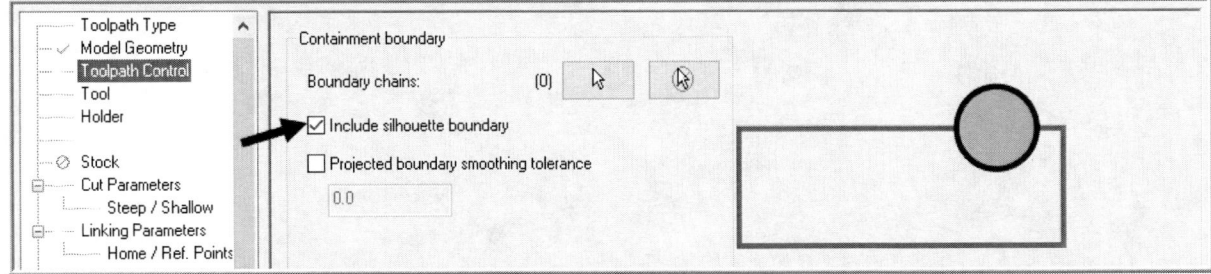

When Include Silhouette Boundary is selected, Mastercam will create a boundary around the selected Machining geometry and use it as a containment boundary in addition to any selected Boundary chains.

10. Still on the **Toolpath Control** page make changes to this page as shown below.

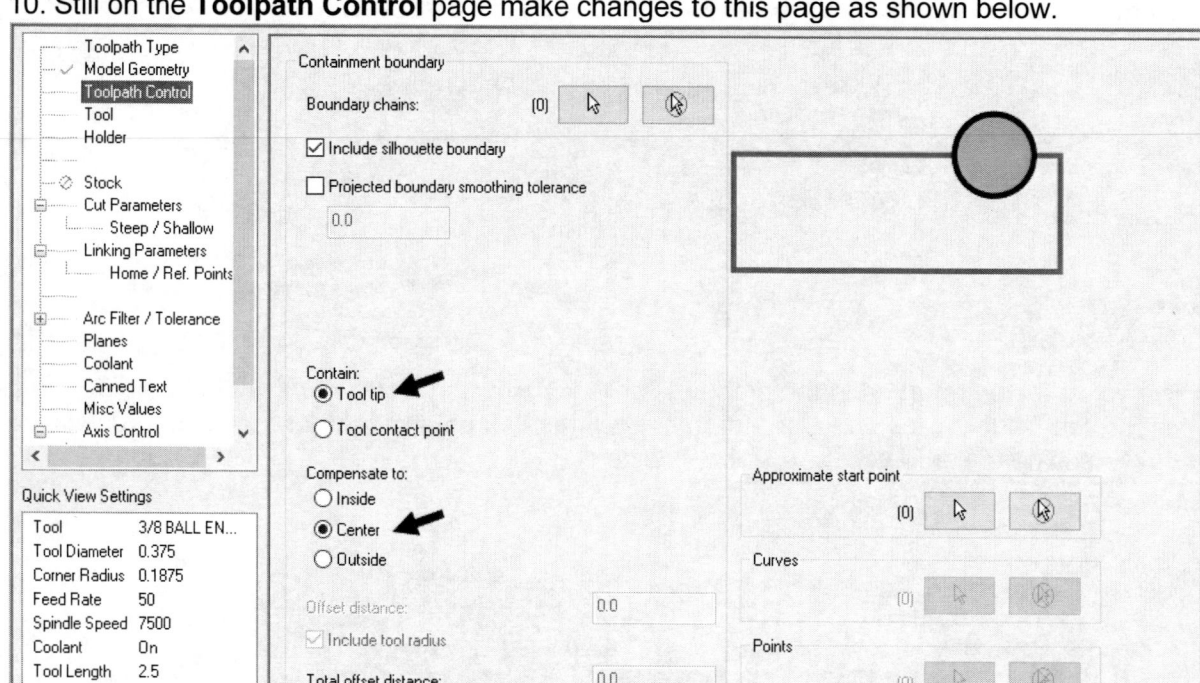

11. Select the **Tool** selection page, then the **Select library tool…** button.
12. Select the **Filter** button on the right side of the **Tool selection** dialog box.
13. Select the **None** (1) button in the Tool Types section.
14. Click on the **Endmill2 Sphere** type icon as shown in the picture (2) below:
15. Select the drop-down arrow in the **Tool diameter** (3) field and set it to **Equal**.
16. Input the tool diameter (4) as **0.375**.

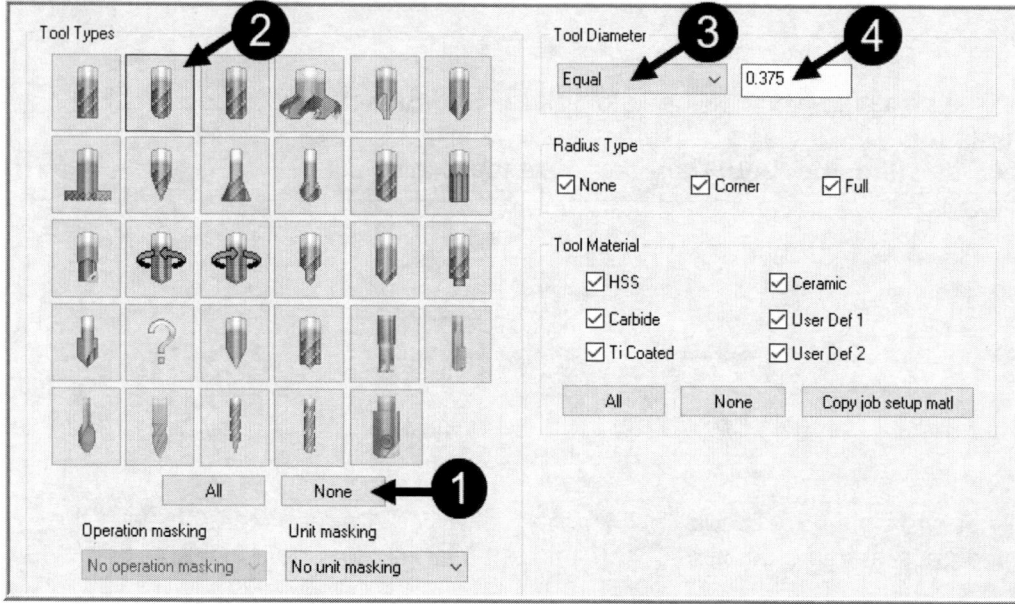

17. Select the OK button ✓ to exit.
18. Select the 0.375 ball end mill.

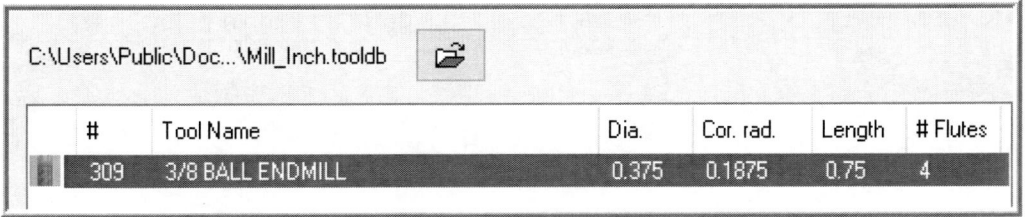

19. Select the OK button ☑ to complete the selection of this tool.
20. Make changes to the **Tool** page as shown below:

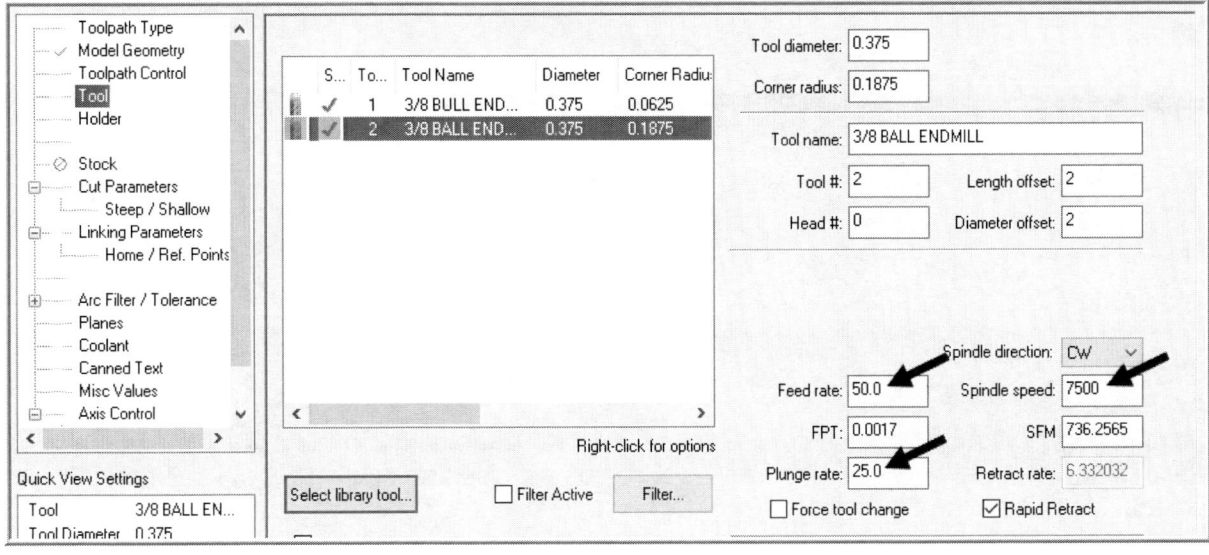

21. Select the **Cut Parameters** page and make changes to this page as shown below.

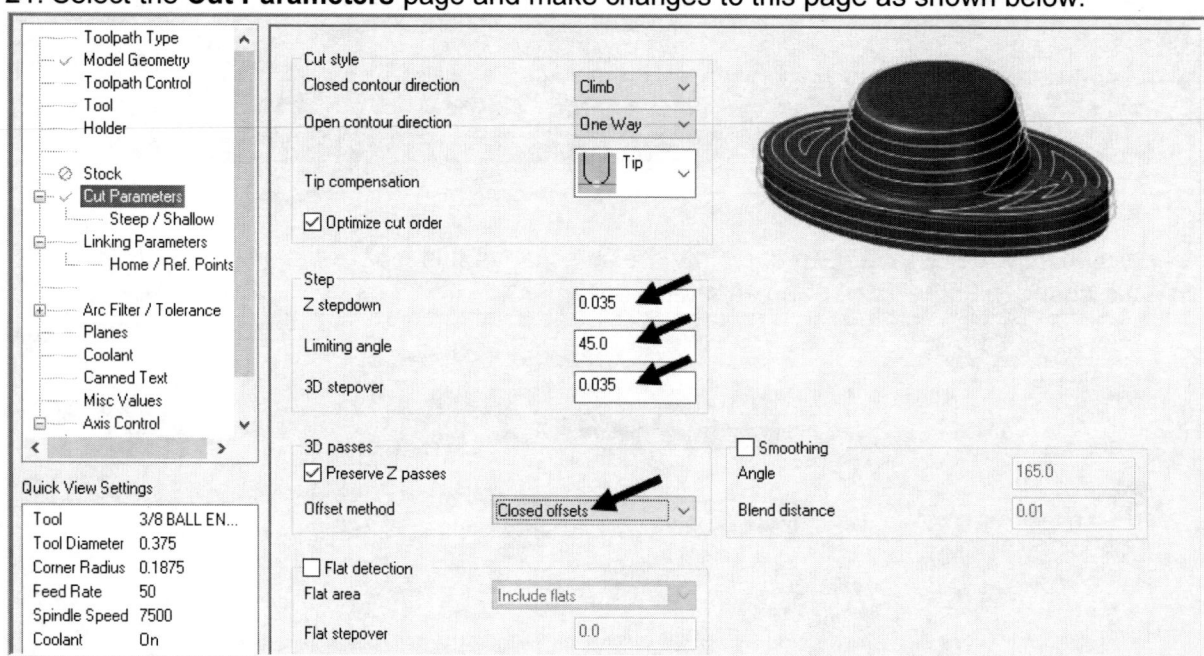

Cut Parameters

Use this page to configure the cutting passes for a hybrid toolpath. This is a finishing toolpath which generates waterline-style cut passes for steep regions and scallop cut passes for shallow regions. Mastercam switches smoothly between both styles to cut in a logical optimized order.

Z stepdown

Defines the constant Z distance between adjacent stepdowns. Mastercam uses these stepdowns in combination with the Limiting Angle and 3D stepover to calculate cut passes for the hybrid toolpath.

Mastercam first slices the entire model into sections defined by the Z Stepdown distance. It then analyzes the drive surface's slope transition between each stepdown along the specified

Limiting Angle.

If the drive surface's slope transition within the stepdown distance is less than the applied limiting angle, the hybrid toolpath considers it steep and a single 2D waterline cutting pass is generated. Otherwise, the stepdown is defined as shallow. Mastercam uses the 3D stepover value to create 3D scallop cut passes along the shallow slope.

3D stepover

Defines the spacing between 3D scallop-style cutting passes in shallow stepdowns.

Preserve Z passes

Select to maintain Z passes in steep areas. Passes in shallow areas are calculated based on the Offset method. Deselect to calculate collapse motion across the entire part when a shallow region is encountered.

Offset method

Select a method for handling the boundaries between steep and shallow areas from the drop-down.

Closed offsets: The boundaries are treated as closed chains when calculating the 3D collapse motion.

22. Select the **Steep / Shallow** page enable Minimum Depth and set it to **-0.05**.

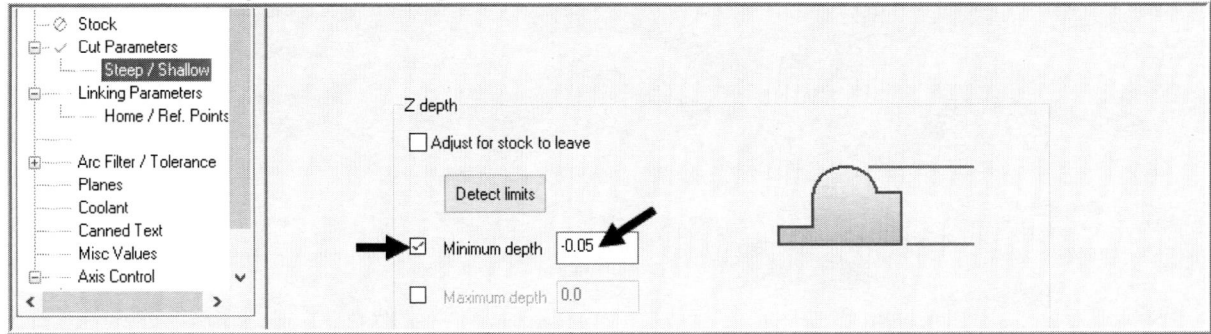

23. Select the **Linking Parameters** page and make changes to this page as shown below.

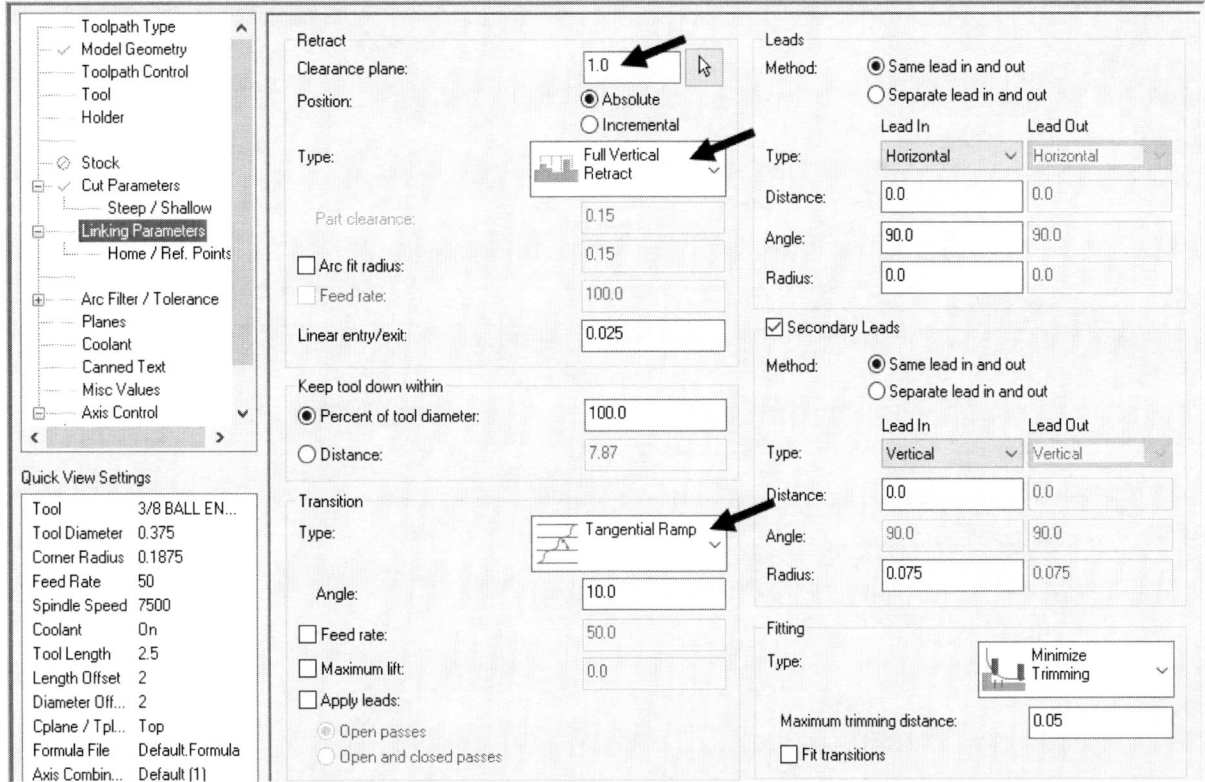

Linking Parameters
Use this page to create the **links between the cutting passes**.

In general, you can think of linking moves as air moves when the tool is not in contact with the part, compared to cutting moves which are configured on the toolpath's Cut parameters page.

Transition
Use these settings to configure the entry moves that the tool will make as it transitions to new Z levels. These moves control the transition to a new set of cuts on a different Z level.

Select **Tangential ramp** to create a true high speed transition between the cutting passes. Mastercam inserts arcs at the beginning and end of the ramp for the smoothest tool motion into and out of the move.

---

24. Select the **Arc Filter / Tolerance** page and make changes to this page as shown below.

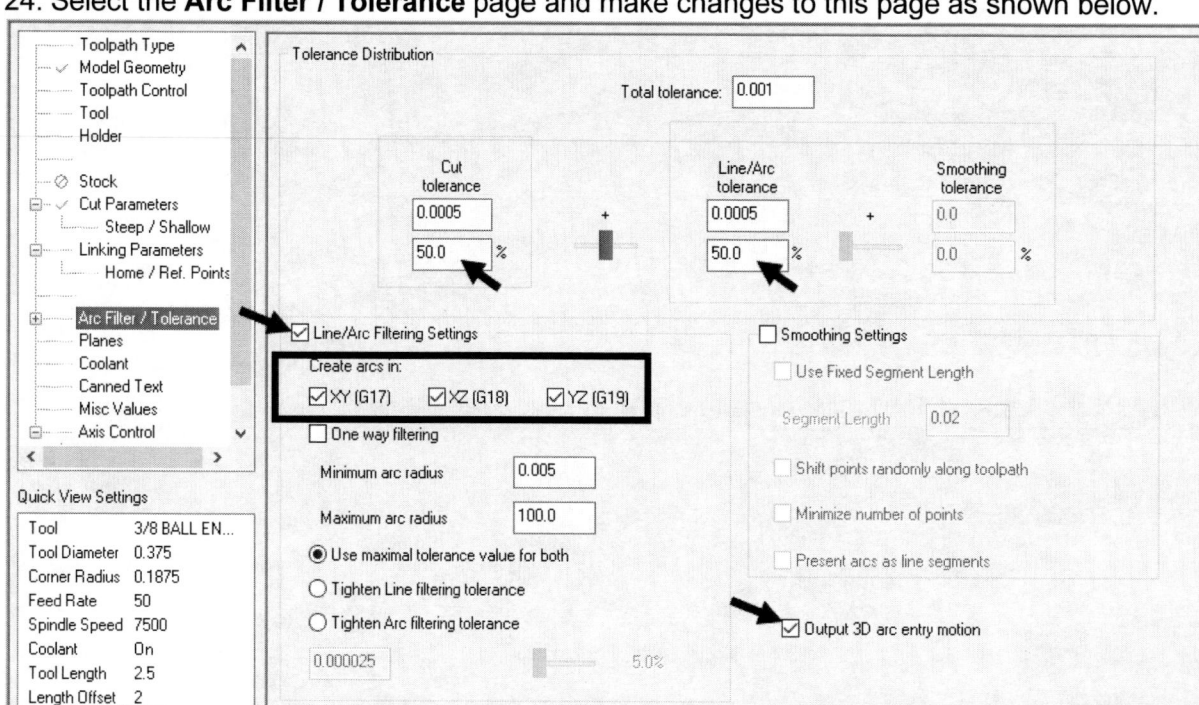

Arc Filter/Tolerance

Use this page to control toolpath tolerances. Typically, this involves several sets of variables. Mastercam uses the values you enter here to convert the toolpath into a more optimized path wherever possible, and within the tolerances you specify.

25. Turn the **Coolant** Flood on.

26. Select the OK button ☑ to complete this toolpath.

27. It may take a while for Mastercam to create the toolpath. Mastercam's multi-threading functionality will calculate the toolpath while you continue to work. The green spool of thread indicates threading is active.

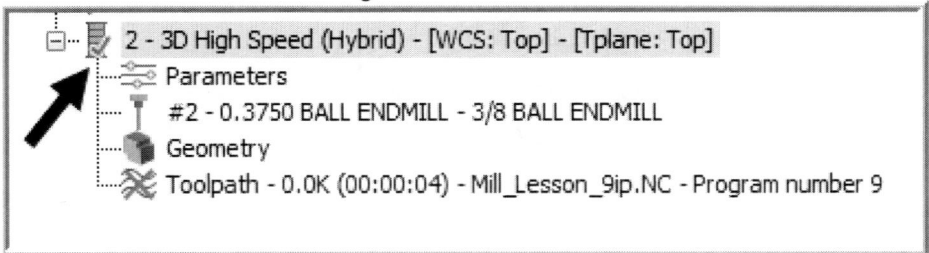

⊃ The screen should look like the image below with just the Hybrid the toolpath displayed:

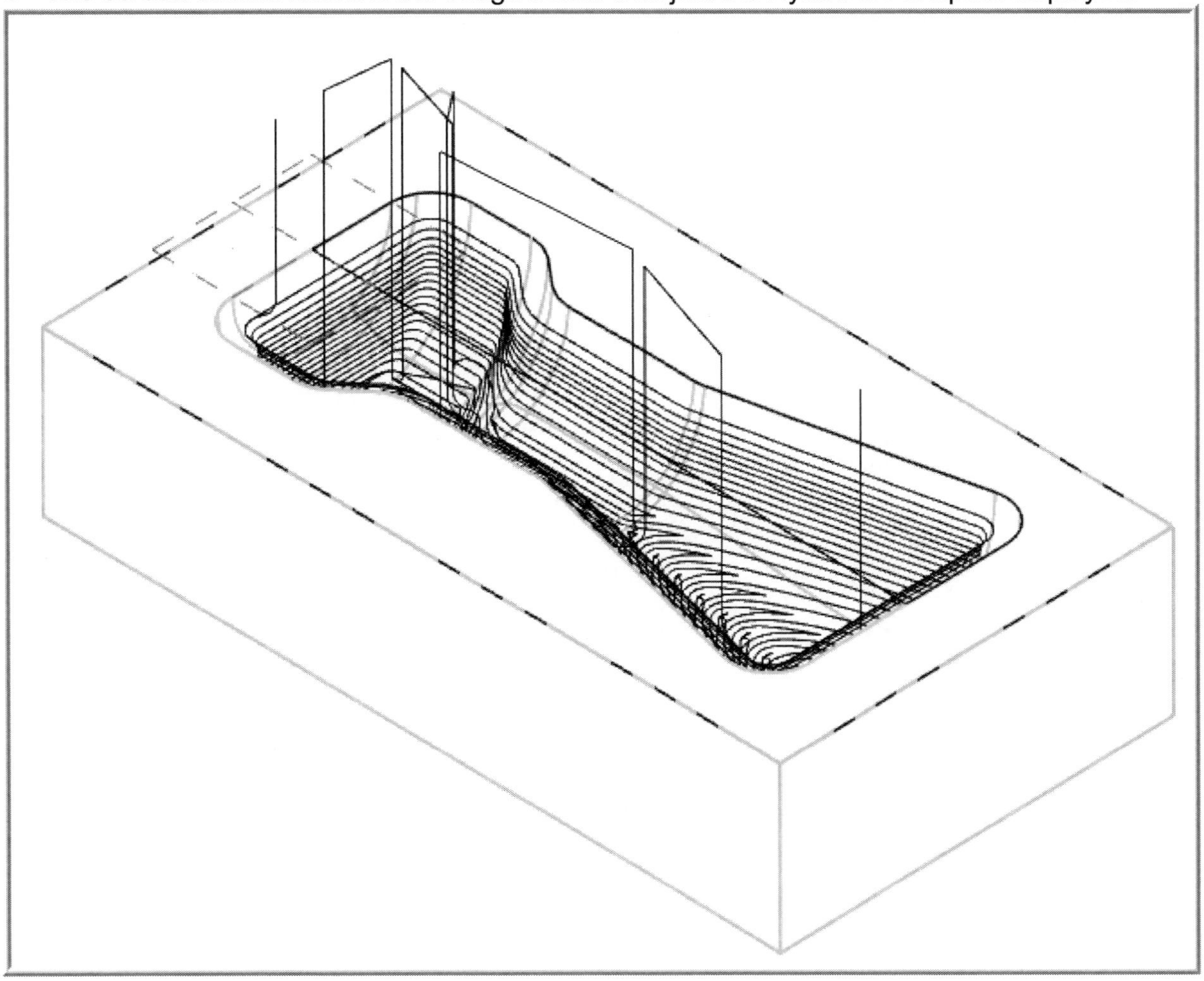

TASK 10:
VERIFY THE TOOLPATH

1. Right mouse click in the graphics area and click on **Isometric**.

2. Right mouse click in the graphics area and click on the **Fit** icon .
3. In the **Toolpaths Manager** pick all the operations to verify by picking the **Select all operations** icon .
4. Select the **Verify selected operations** icon shown below:

5. **Maximize** the Backplot/Verify window if required.
6. Activate the options shown below in the **Visibility** section of the **Home** tab. **Initial Stock** not activated.

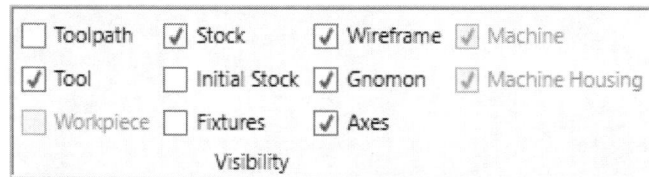

7. At the top of the screen select the **Verify** tab and activate the **Color Loop**.

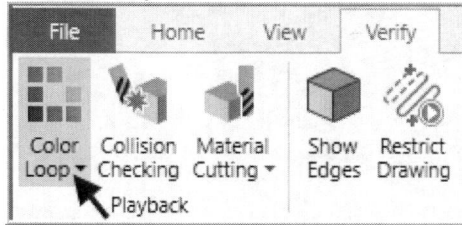

Color Loop
Changes the color of the toolpath or cut stock by operation or by tool change.

Choose **File Options** to set the colors.

8. In the lower part of the screen now set the run Speed to slow by moving the slider bar pointer over to the left as shown below.

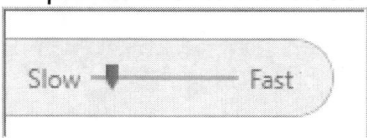

9. Now select the **Play Simulation** button to review the toolpaths.

⊃ The verified toolpaths are shown below:

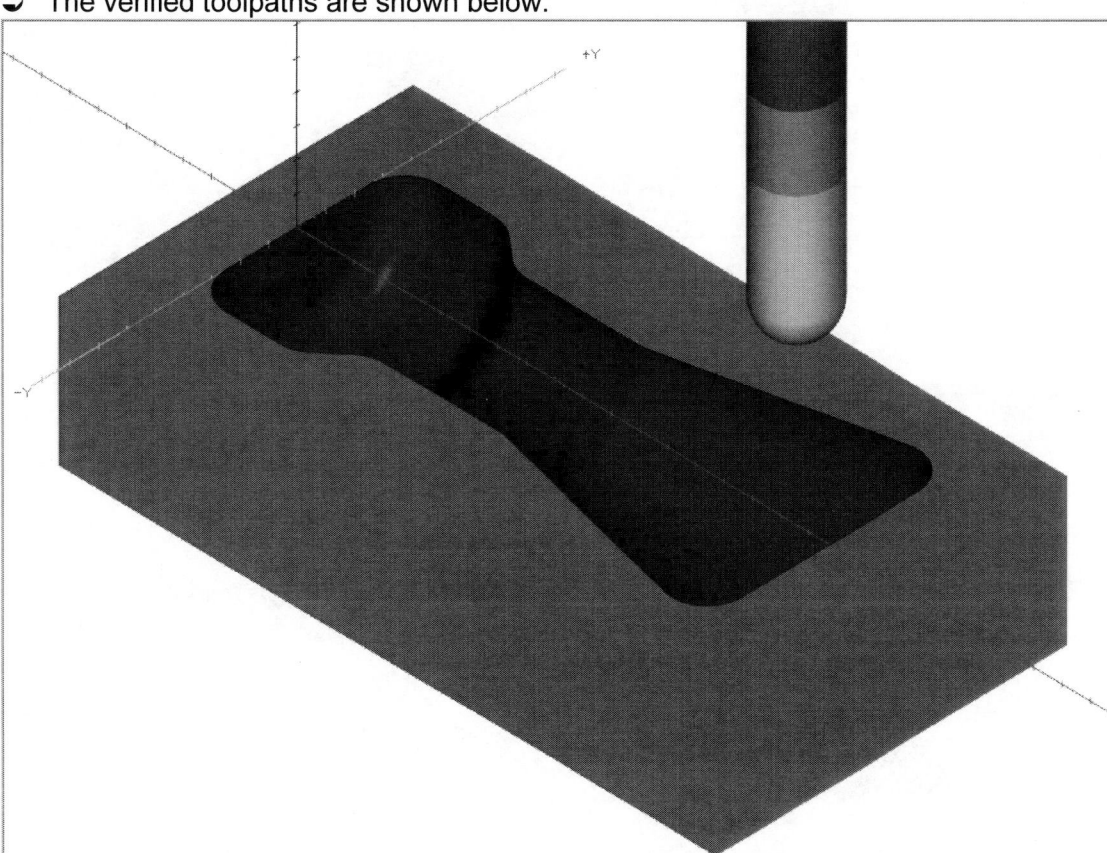

10. Select the **Close** button ☒ in the top right hand corner to exit Verify.

SAVE THE UPDATED MASTERCAM FILE

1. Select the **Save** icon from the **Quick Access** toolbar at the top left of the screen.

TASK 11:
POST AND CREATE THE CNC CODE FILE

Please Note:
Users of the Mastercam **Home Learning Edition** (HLE) will not be able to Post and Create the CNC code file.

1. Ensure all the operations are selected by picking the **Select all operations** icon  from the Toolpaths manager.
2. Select the **Post selected operations** icon **G1** from the **Toolpaths manager.**

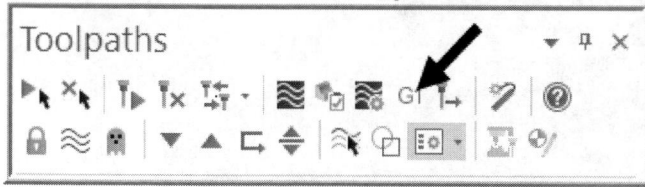

3. In the **Post processing** window, make the necessary changes as shown below:

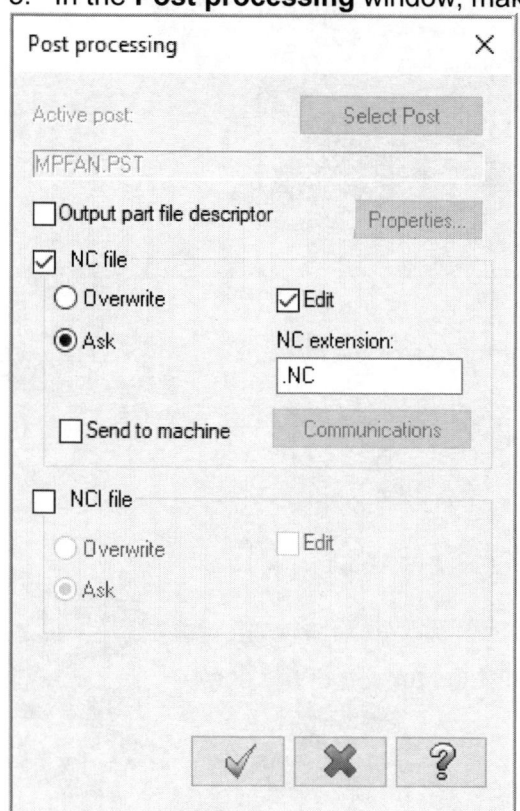

4. Select the **OK** button 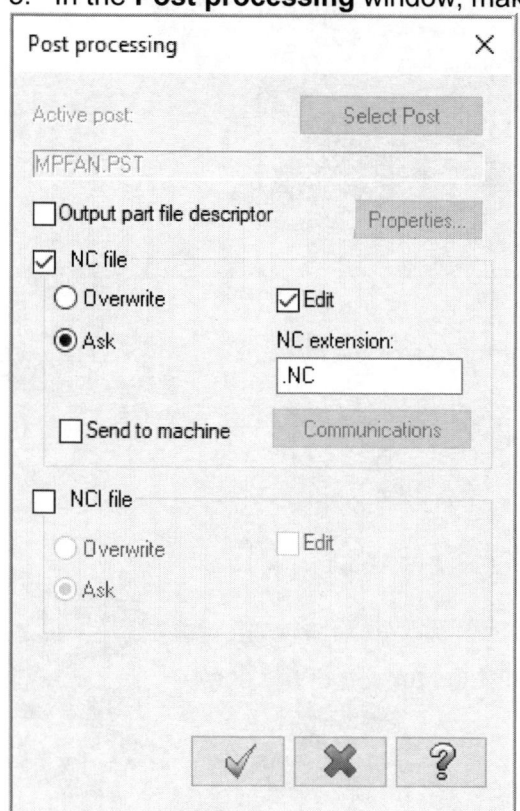 to continue.

5. Ensure the same name as your Mastercam part file name is displayed in the File name window as shown below:

File name: MILL-LESSON-9

Save as type: NC Files (*.NC)

6. Select the **Save** button.
7. The CNC code file opens up in the default editor:

```
Mill_Lesson_9.NC  ×
    7    ( T1 | 3/8 BULL ENDMILL 0.0625 RAD | H1 )
    8    ( T2 | 3/8 BALL ENDMILL | H2 )
    9    N1 G20
   10    N2 G0 G17 G40 G49 G80 G90
   11    N3 T1 M6
   12    N4 G0 G90 G54 X3.1263 Y-.0536 A0. S6500 M3
   13    N5 G43 H1 Z1. M8
   14    N6 Z.2666
   15    N7 G1 Z.2416 F25.
   16    N8 X3.1289 Y-.0425 Z.2019
   17    N9 X3.1362 Y-.0126 Z.1742
   18    N10 X3.1409 Y.0066 Z.1678
   19    N11 G3 X3.143 Y.0244 Z.1646 I-.0729 J.0178 F50.
   20    N12 X3.0858 Y.0973 Z.147 I-.075 J0.
   21    N13 X3.0621 Y.1001 Z.1462 I-.0237 J-.0972
   22    N14 X2.9621 Y.0001 Z.1407 I0. J-.1
   23    N15 X3.0621 Y-.0999 Z.1352 I.1 J0.
   24    N16 X3.1621 Y.0001 Z.1297 I0. J.1
   25    N17 X3.0621 Y.1001 Z.1242 I-.1 J0.
   26    N18 X2.9621 Y.0001 Z.1187 I0. J-.1
   27    N19 X3.0621 Y-.0999 Z.1133 I.1 J0.
   28    N20 X3.1621 Y.0001 Z.1078 I0. J.1
```

8. Select the ⊠ in the top right corner to exit the CNC editor.

➲ **This completes Mill-Lesson-9.**

MILL-LESSON-9-EXERCISE-A

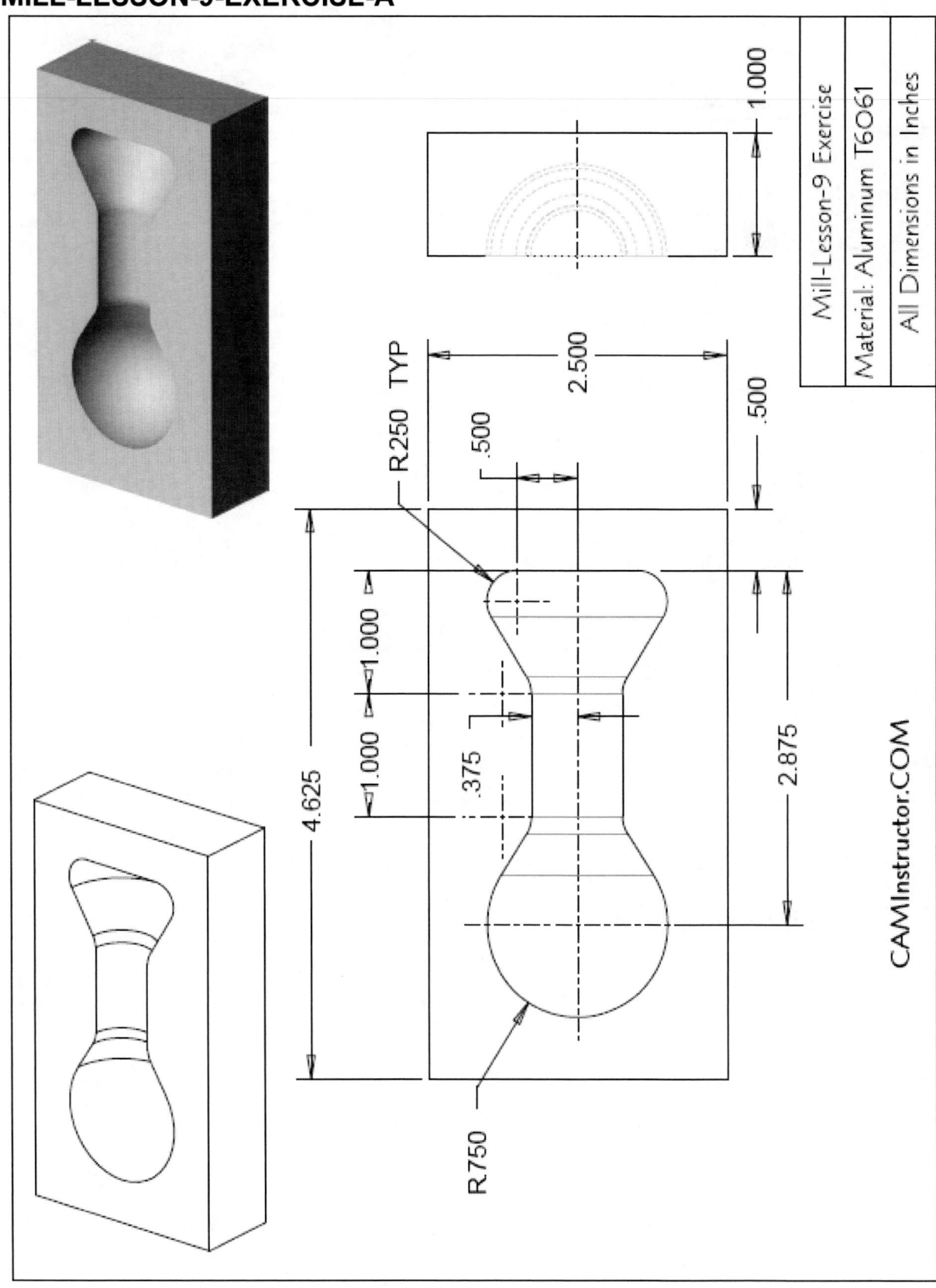

Mill-Lesson-9 Exercise

Material: Aluminum T6O61

All Dimensions in Inches

1.000

2.500

.500

R250 TYP

.500

4.625

1.000

1.000

.375

2.875

R750

CAMInstructor.COM

MILL-LESSON-9-EXERCISE-B

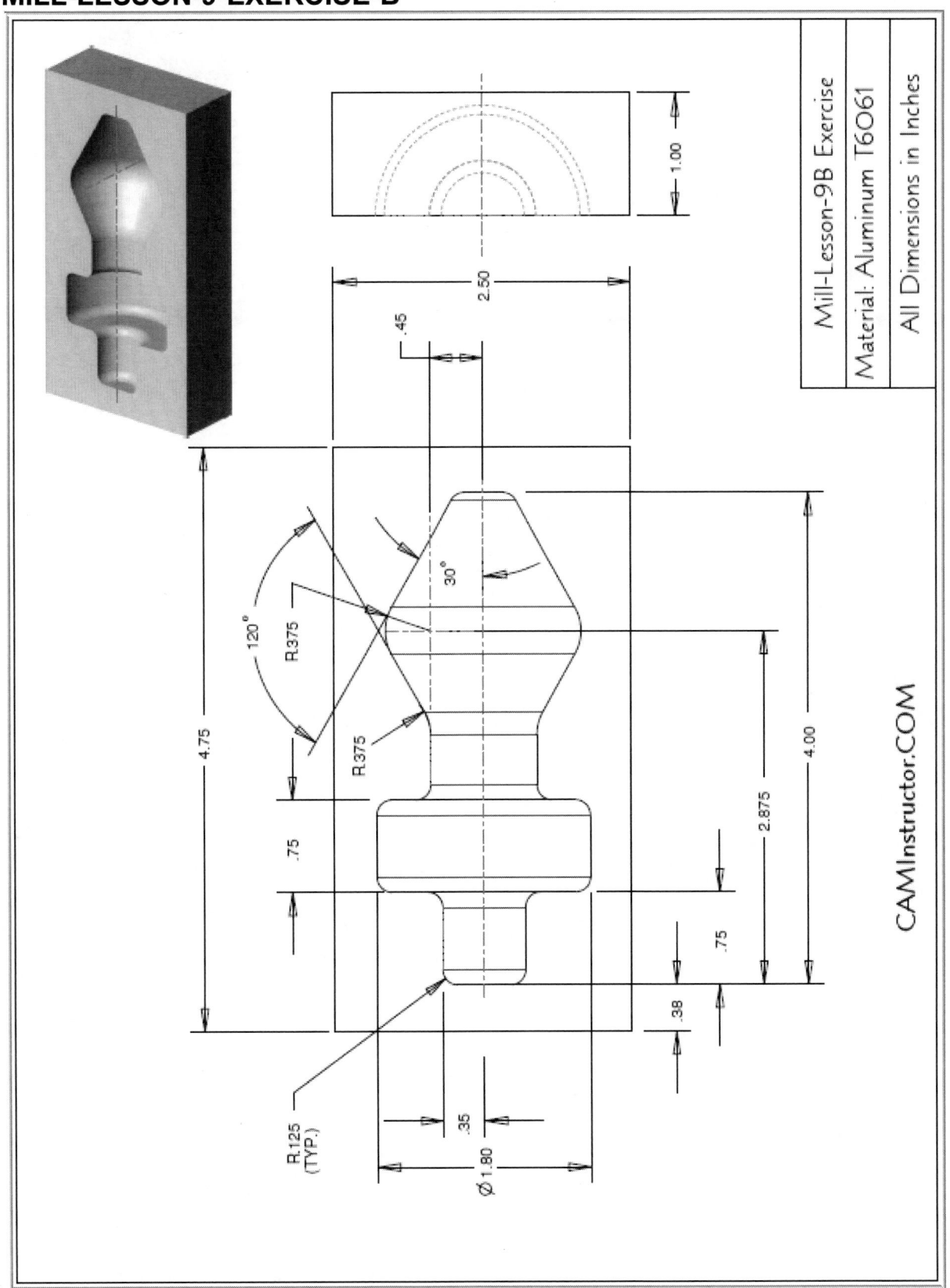

Mill-Lesson-9B Exercise

Material: Aluminum T6O61

All Dimensions in Inches

CAMInstructor.COM

2.50

.45

1.00

120°

30°

R.375

R.375

4.75

.75

4.00

2.875

.75

.38

R.125
(TYP.)

.35

Ø1.80

Mastercam 2022

TRAINING
GUIDE

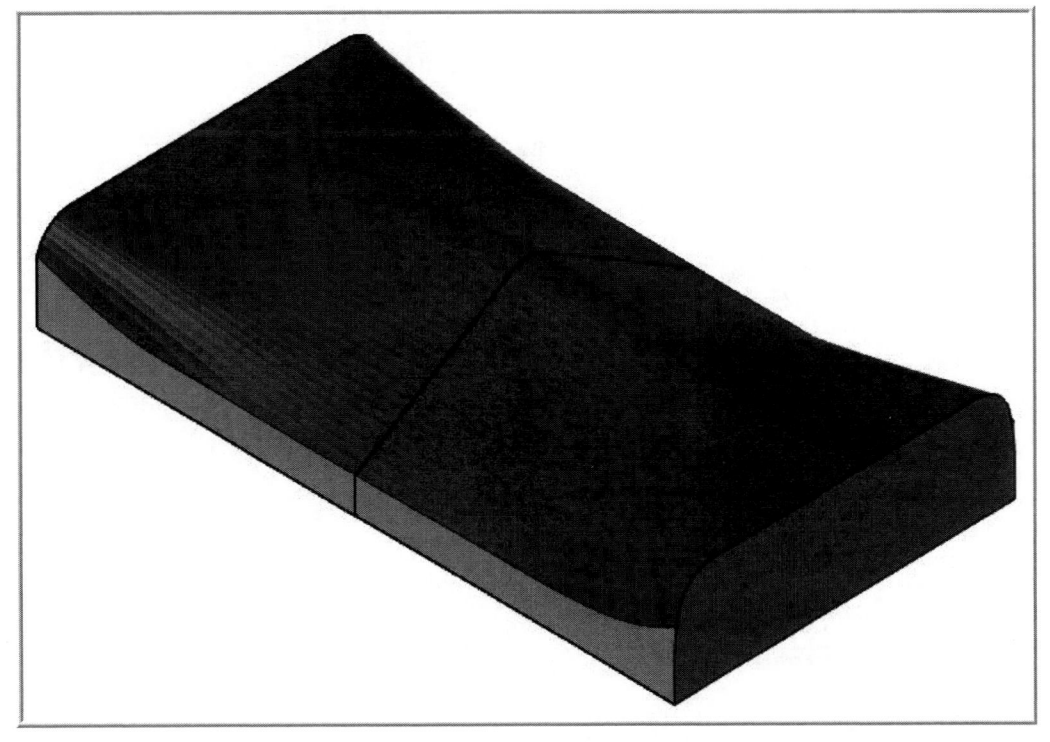

MILL-LESSON-10

SURFACE ROUGH PARALLEL AND
SURFACE HIGH SPEED RASTER

camInstructor

Objectives

You will create the geometry for Mill-Lesson-10, and then generate the toolpaths to machine the part on a CNC vertical milling machine. This Lesson covers the following topics:

➲ **Create a 3-dimensional drawing by:**
Creating lines.
Creating arcs.
Trimming geometry.
Creating a lofted solid.

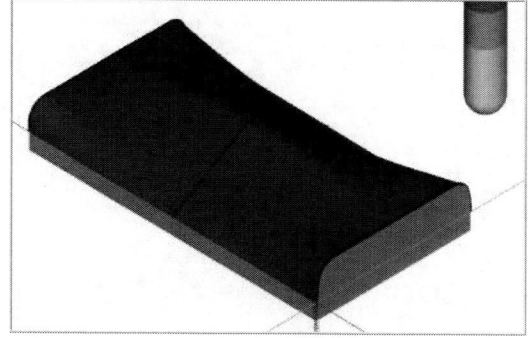

➲ **Establish Stock Setup settings:**
Material for the part.
Feed calculation.

➲ **Generate a 3-dimensional milling toolpath consisting of:**
Rough Parallel Toolpath and Surface High Speed Raster.

➲ **Inspect the toolpath using Mastercam's Verify and Backplot by:**
Launching the Verify function to machine the part on the screen.
Generating the NC- code.

Surface Roughing
Surface roughing toolpaths typically use larger tools, multiple stepovers, and multiple stepdowns to quickly remove larger volumes of stock and leave an even amount of stock for finishing.

The roughing toolpaths you choose for your part depend on the shape of the part, shape of the stock, and machining situation. Mastercam provides several roughing strategies.

Listed below is each of the **Surface Roughing Toolpaths:**

Parallel	**Radial**
Project	**Flowline**
Contour	**Restmill**
Pocket	**Plunge**

Surface Finishing
Surface finishing toolpaths typically finish a part down to the drive geometry (or to the stock to leave amount if one is specified). Mastercam provides several finishing strategies.

Listed below is each of the **Surface Finishing Toolpaths:**

Parallel	**Parallel steep**
Radial	**Project**
Flowline	**Contour**
Shallow	**Pencil**
Leftover	**Scallop**
Blend	

MILL-LESSON-10 DRAWING

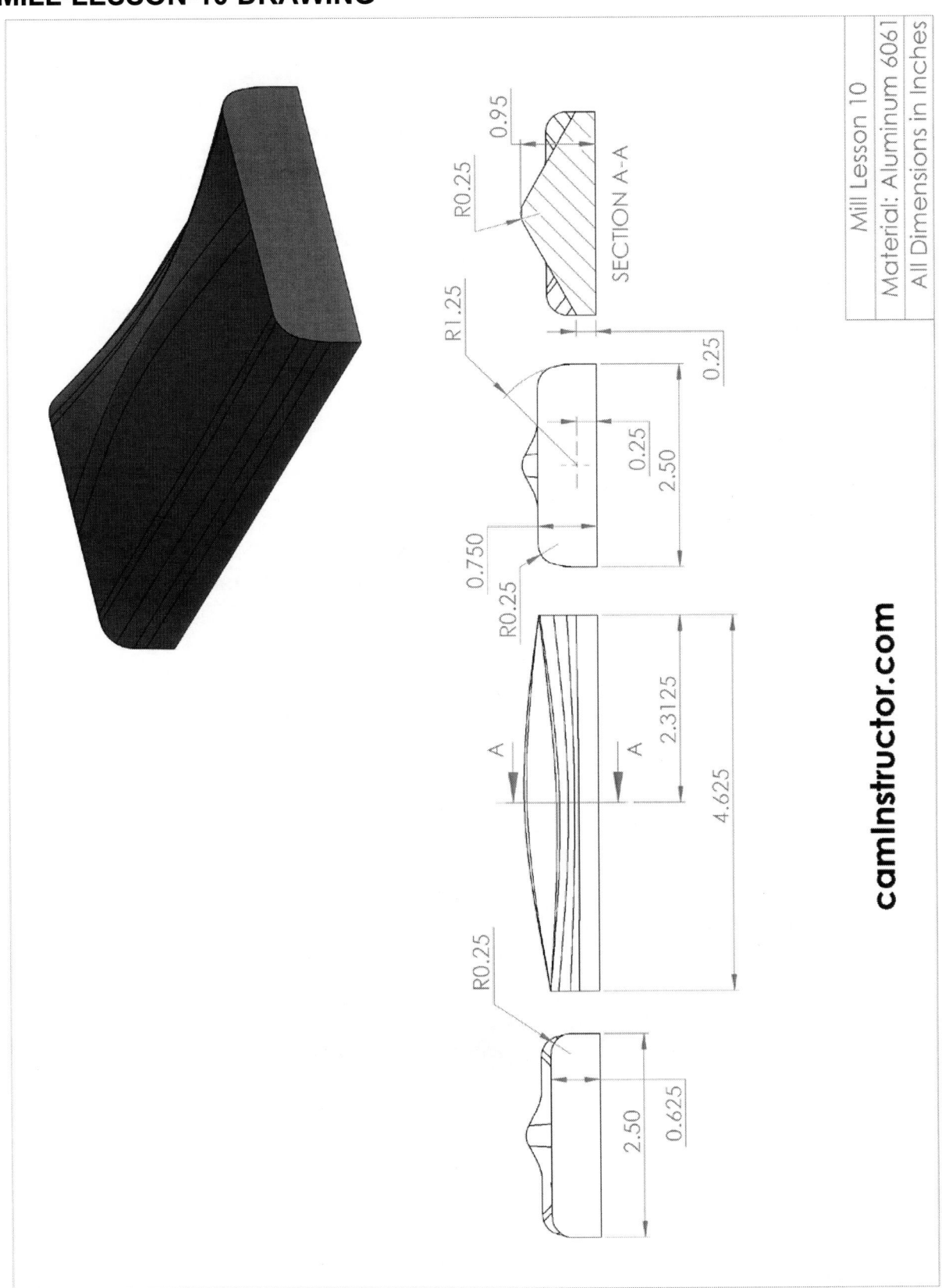

Mill Lesson 10
Material: Aluminum 6061
All Dimensions in Inches

0.95

R0.25

SECTION A-A

R1.25

0.25

0.25

2.50

0.750

R0.25

2.3125

4.625

A

A

R0.25

2.50

0.625

caminstructor.com

TOOL LIST

➲ 0.500 diameter bull end mill with a 0.125 corner radius to rough machine.
➲ 0.500 diameter ball end mill to finish machine.

MILL-LESSON-10 - THE PROCESS

Geometry Creation

TASK 1: Setting the environment
TASK 2: Create geometry – right hand section
TASK 3: Create geometry – center section
TASK 4: Create geometry – left hand section
TASK 5: Create the lofted solid body

Toolpath Creation

TASK 6: Define the rough stock using stock setup
TASK 7: Rough machine using Surface Rough Parallel
TASK 8: Finish machine using Surface High Speed Raster
TASK 9: Optimize the Surface High Speed Raster Toolpath
TASK 10: Verify the toolpath
TASK 11: Post and create the CNC code file

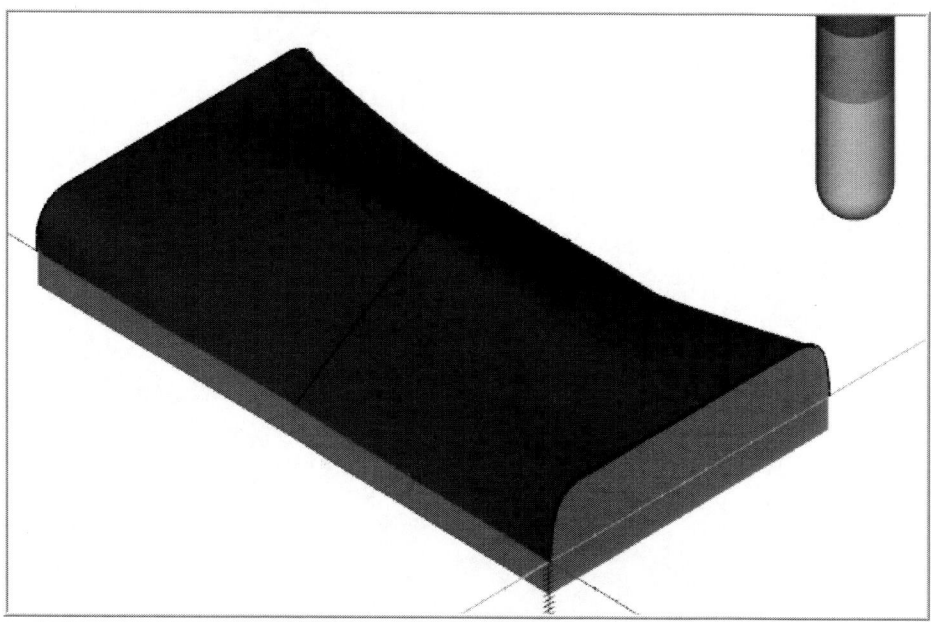

TASK 1:
SETTING THE ENVIRONMENT
⊃ Before starting the geometry creation, you should set up the grid and machine type as outlined in the **Setting the environment** section at the beginning of this text:
1. Set up the Grid. This will help identify the location of the origin.
2. Set the machine type to the Default Mill.

TASK 2:
CREATE GEOMETRY – RIGHT HAND SECTION
⊃ The base of the material is at **Z0.** The bottom face of the material and the 4.625 x 2.5 dimensions has been previously machined to size.
⊃ In this task you will create the right-hand section that will be used to create the lofted body. First will be the creation of the rectangle. Next will be the 1.25 radius arcs (1) using Arc Polar, which will be trimmed. Finally, the 0.25 radius arcs (2) will be created using Fillet.

⊃ **Setup Plane and create right hand side section**
1. Select the **View tab** and ensure the **Planes Manager** is enabled. **ALT + L** is the keyboard shortcut to toggle the Planes Manager.

2. Right mouse click in the graphics area and toggle to **2D construction**. The **Z value** should be at **0**.

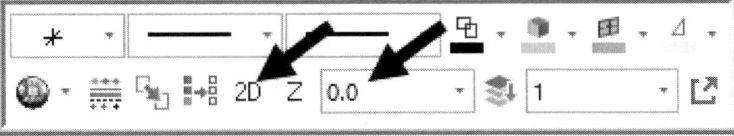

2D/3D Construction Modes
This button switches from 2D construction mode to 3D construction mode. The default setting for this button is 3D construction mode.
In **2D mode**, all the geometry is created parallel to the current construction plane and at the current Z depth setting. However, you can override the Z depth setting by typing coordinate values that include a Z depth value different from the current Z depth setting.

⊃ The **Planes Manager** is shown below

Use the **Plane Manager** as a central point for selecting, editing, creating and managing planes. Some of the tasks that you can accomplish here include:
- Selecting which planes to use for the Cplane, Tplane, Gview, or the work coordinate system (WCS).
- Editing the origin of a plane.
- Assigning a work offset to a plane, so that whenever you select the plane for a toolpath, the work offset code is automatically generated.
- Create new planes relative to an existing plane or by copying existing planes.
- Delete unused or created planes. You cannot delete any of the main system planes.
- Dynamically create a new plane from an existing plane using the Dynamic Plane dialog box.

The large window lists all of the planes that have been defined in the current file. Click on a plane to select it and then set current plane and apply it to the WCS, Cplane, or Tplane.

Tool plane (Tplane)
For most typical toolpaths, this is the plane in which cutting moves (G1/G2/G3) take place. The tool typically approaches and retracts from the part normal to the tool plane in the Z axis. You can align the Tplane with any of the standard planes or a custom orientation. Changing the Tplane typically produces a rotary motion code when you post your toolpath. The exact effect depends on your machine tool and post processor; for example, rotating the tool plane 30 degrees about the X-axis might tilt the tool axis on a 5-axis machining center, or could rotate a fixture on a table, depending on how your post is written.

Construction plane (Cplane)
Cplane is the plane in which geometry is created. Typically this is used in connection with drafting—when you draw entities, select a Cplane to orient the geometry in space. When you create a toolpath, the construction plane is the plane in which the tool is compensated. For almost all toolpaths, the construction plane should be the same as the tool plane (which is the plane normal to Z, or to the vertical tool axis).

Work Coordinate Systems (WCS)
Mastercam also lets you shift and move the coordinate axes themselves. This lets you create a work coordinate system (WCS), which lets you move the coordinate system to your part geometry instead of moving or transforming the part geometry. Think of the WCS view as defining the "Top plane" relative to your part.

3. Right mouse click in the graphics area and click on **Isometric**. Note that the Plane Manager has changed slightly to indicate an Isometric view in the **Gview** column.

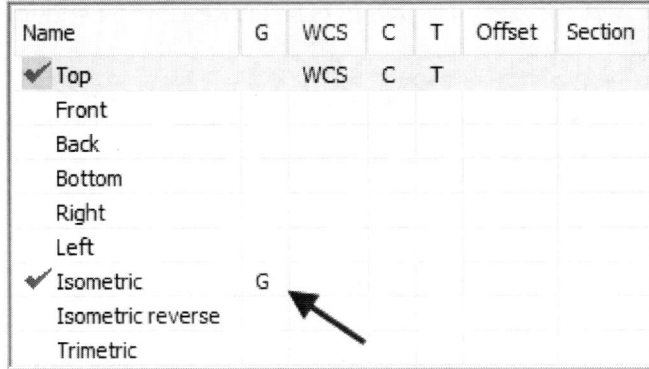

4. Now open up the drop down menu for **Follow rules** ⟲ and **remove all the check marks** to cancel all the rules.

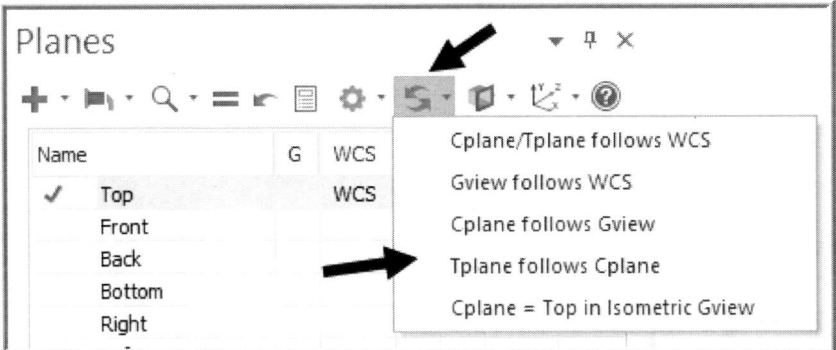

Please Note:
The reason for cancelling all the rules is so that when working through this lesson you will have to make a **specific action** in the **Planes Manager** to change the **Cplane -** the Construction Plane.

Follow Rules ⟲
The state of follow rules are preserved between sessions.

Cplane/Tplane follows WCS: Always aligns the construction plane and tool plane to match the WCS.

Gview follows WCS: Always aligns the graphics view to match the WCS.

Cplane follows Gview: Always aligns the construction plane to match the graphics view. If the Tplane and the Cplane are set to the same plane, the Tplane will also follow the Gview.

Tplane follows Cplane: Aligns the Tplane with the Cplane when the construction plane has been changed by the user, or as the result of another follow rule. The Tplane can still be changed independent of Cplane.

Cplane = Top in Isometric Gview: Aligns the construction plane to the Top plane when the graphics view has been set to isometric.

5. Now click in the **C column (Construction Plane)** for the **Right** plane. The view is still set to Isometric but construction of the geometry will now take place on the Right Side plane. Take note at the bottom of the screen **CPLANE: RIGHT TPLANE:TOP WCS:TOP** as shown below right.

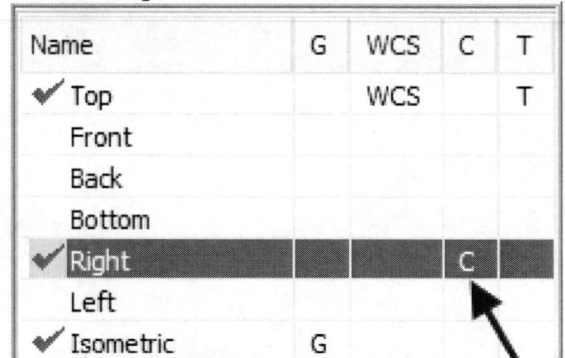 

⊃ **Create the Rectangle**

6. Select the **Wireframe** tab and in the **Shapes** section click on **Rectangle.** On the graphics screen you are prompted: **Select a new position for the first corner.**

7. To satisfy the prompt, move the cursor over to the **Origin** (X0Y0) a visual cue appears. , **pick the origin**.

8. Click in the space for **Width** and enter a value of **2.5** and then hit the tab key or Enter key. In the space for **Height** enter a value of **0.75** and hit enter. (Ensure Anchor to Center is **NOT** enabled).

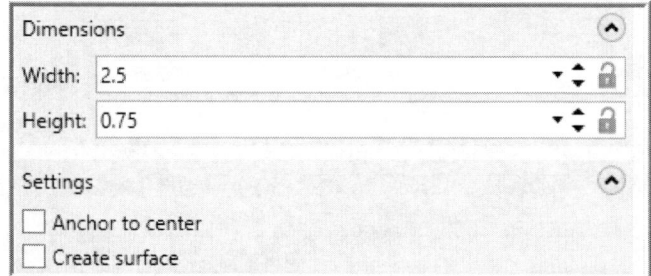

9. Click on the **OK** icon to complete this feature.

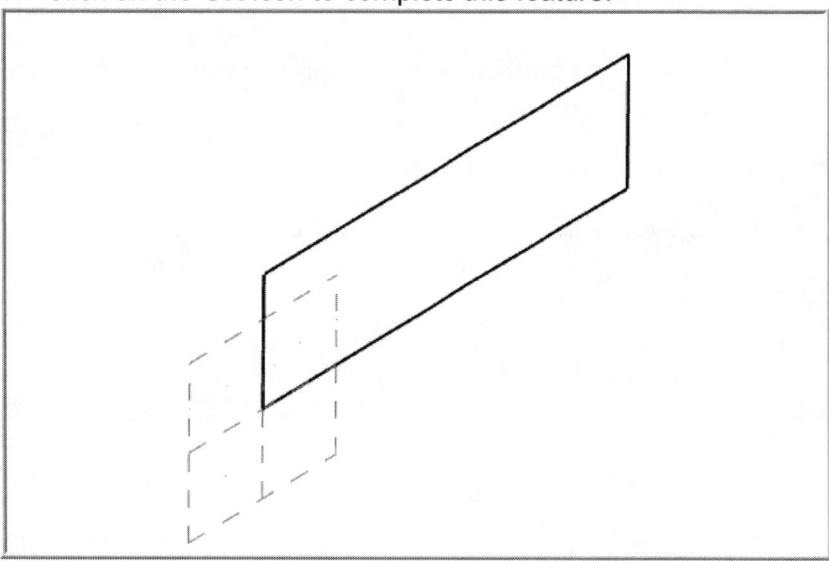

⊃ Create Arc #1

10. On the **Wireframe** tab in the **Arcs** section, click the down arrow and select **Arc Polar.** In the Arc Polar menu, input **1.25 for the Radius** and **180.0 for the End Angle**.

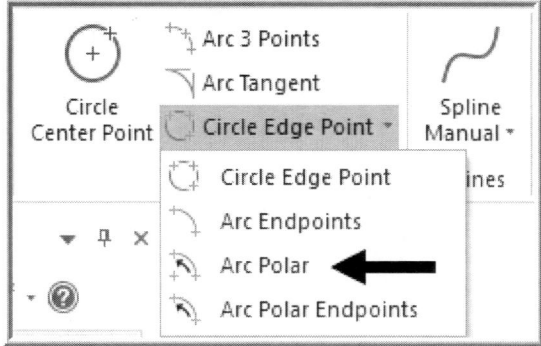

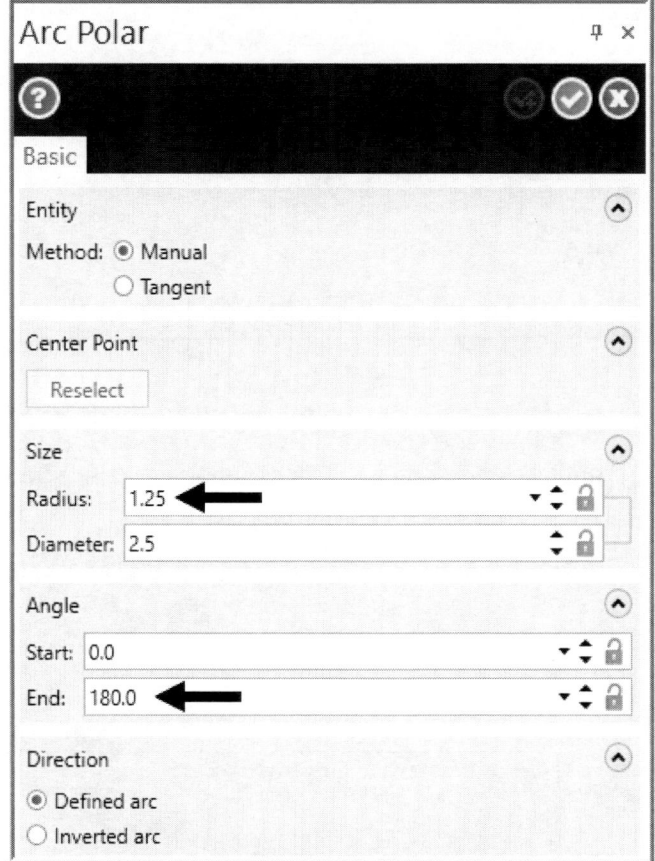

11. To satisfy the onscreen prompt for 'Enter the center point', use **Fastpoint** and input **1.25, 0.25.** (you may need to click the middle mouse wheel in the graphics screen to shift focus). Click **Enter** to complete the arc placement. Click **Ok** to complete the function.

1.25,0.25

⊃ The completed arc…

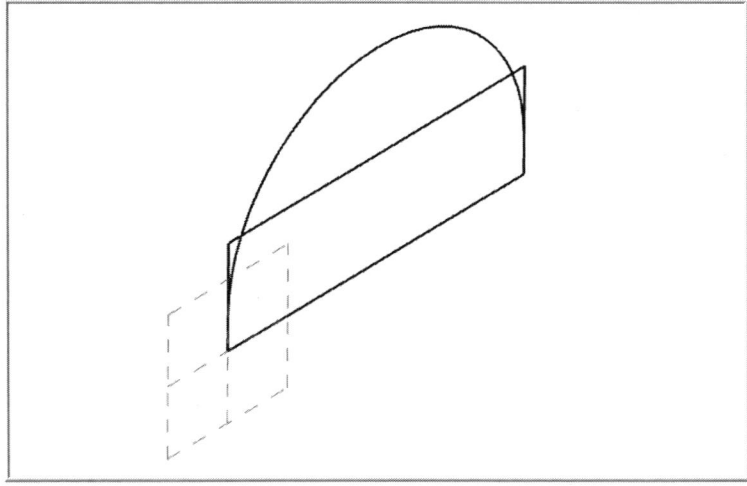

12. Right mouse click in the graphics area and click on **Right**.
13. In the **Wireframe** tab click on **Divide** in the **Modify** section.
14. The **Divide** panel appears. Activate **Trim** if required.

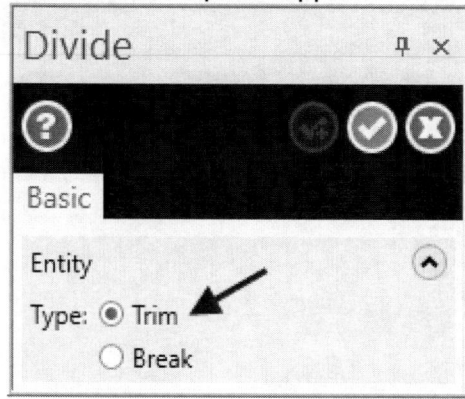

15. To satisfy the prompt **Select the curve to divide / delete**. Move the cursor over the various entities and select in order and position as shown below left:

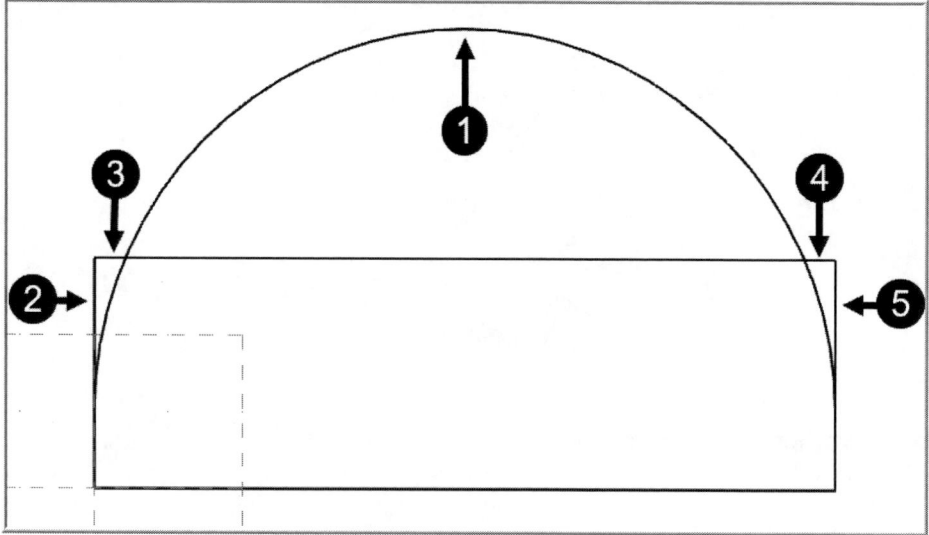

16. Click on the **OK** icon to complete this feature.

➲ The completed geometry is shown below:

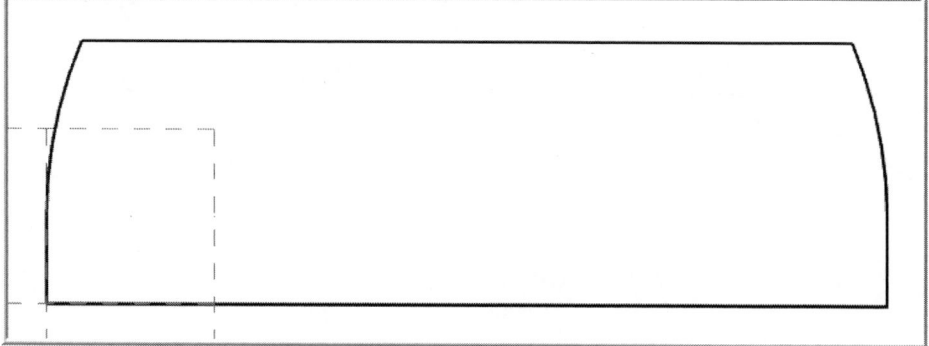

17. Select the **Wireframe** tab and in the **Modify** section click on **Fillet Entities**.
18. The **Fillet Entities** panel appears. If required activate the **Method** to **Normal** and enter a value of **0.25** for **Radius**.
19. Ensure the **Trim entities** box at the bottom of the panel is check marked to turn the trim on.

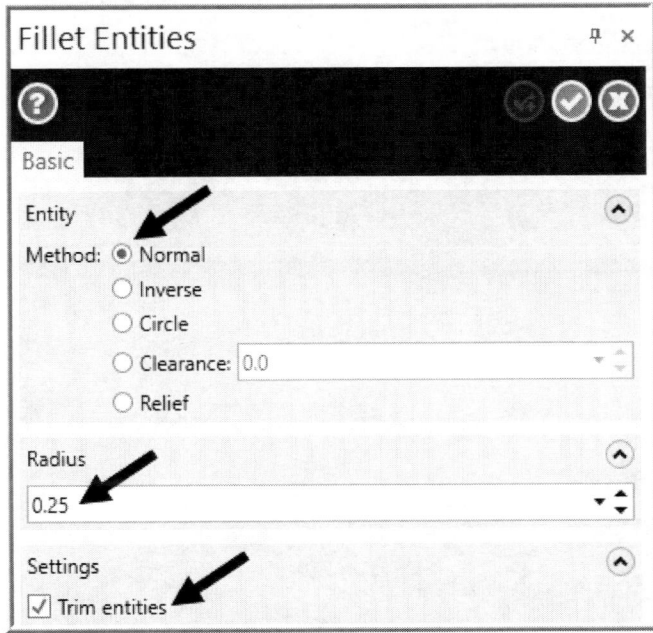

20. When prompted to **Fillet: Select an entity**, select entity 1 and 2 as shown below. The fillet radius appears at the corner of entities 1 and 2. To complete the remaining fillet radii, select: **entities 3 and 4**.

21. Click on the **OK** icon ⊘ to complete this feature.
   ➲ The completed geometry...

TASK 3:
CREATE GEOMETRY – CENTER SECTION

➲ In this task you will create the center section that will be used to create the lofted body. First will be the creation of the rectangle. Next will be the arc at the top, and then the lines connecting the arc to the rectangle. Finally, trimming will be done to leave the shape below.

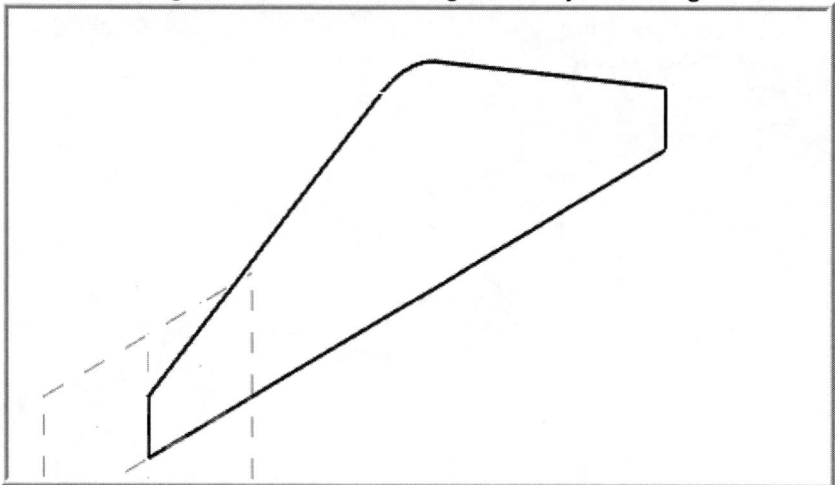

➲ **Create center section**

1. Right mouse click in the graphics area and click on **Isometric**.

➲ The view is still set to Isometric but construction of the geometry will take place on the **Right** plane. Take note at the bottom of the screen **CPLANE: RIGHT TPLANE:TOP WCS:TOP** as shown below right.

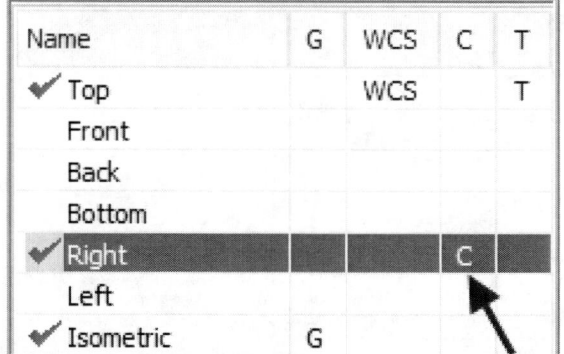

2. Right mouse click in the graphics area. Next click in the space for the **Z value** and enter a value of **-4.625/2** and hit enter. This will then be calculated to **-2.3125**.

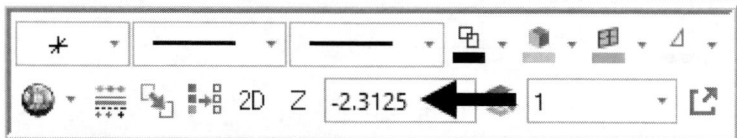

➲ Take note at the lower part of the screen on the status bar **Z: -2.31250**.

⊃ **Create the Rectangle**

3. Select the **Wireframe** tab and in the **Shapes** section click on **Rectangle.** On the graphics screen you are prompted: **Select a new position for the first corner.**

4. To satisfy the prompt, click the middle mouse button in the graphics area and then hit the **spacebar** on your keyboard to activate **Fastpoint**. Input **0,0** and hit the **Enter** key.

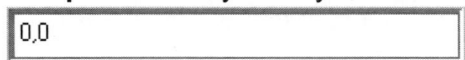

5. Click in the space for **Width** and enter a value of **2.5** and then hit the tab key or Enter key. In the space for **Height** enter a value of **0.25** and hit enter. (Ensure Anchor to Center is **NOT** enabled).

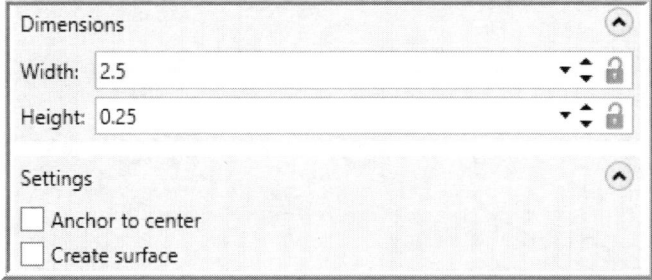

6. Click on the **OK** icon to complete this feature.

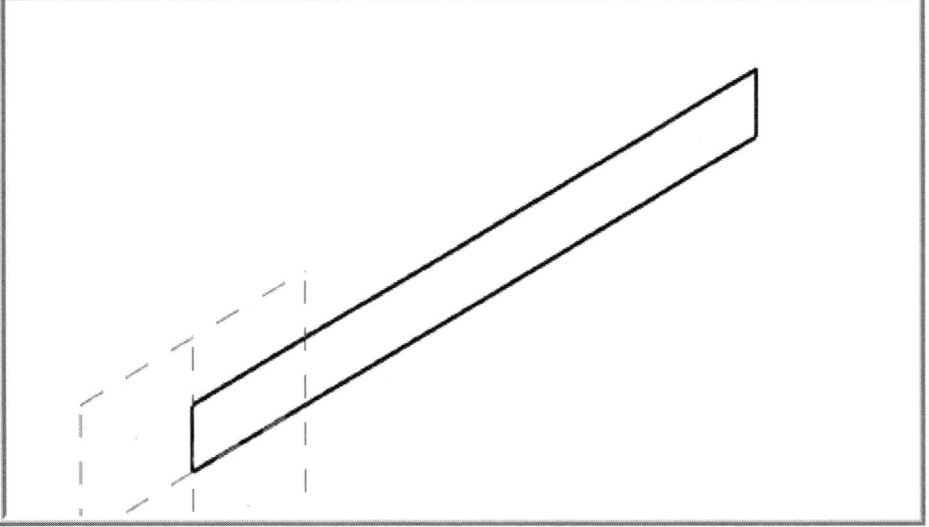

⊃ **Create the Arc**
⊃ The arc is located in the middle of the of the part in Y and at the very top of the part in Z. The top of the part is located at 0.95 (0.7+0.25 from the print)

7. Select the **Wireframe** tab if required and in the **Arcs** section select **Circle Center Point**.
8. The **Circle Center Point** panel appears and you are prompted to **Enter the center point** enter **.25** for the **Radius** and hit enter.
9. To satisfy the prompt **Enter the center point** click the middle mouse button and then hit the spacebar on your keyboard.
10. The **Fastpoint** box now opens. Input **2.5/2,0.95-0.25** and hit the Enter key.
11. Click on the **OK** icon to complete this feature.

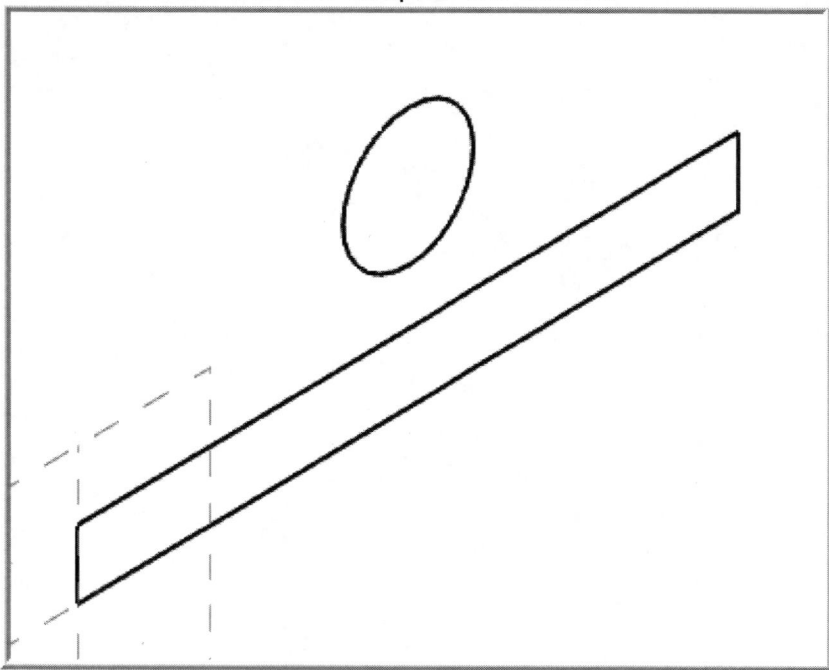

➲ **Create the Connecting Lines**

12. Select the **Wireframe** tab if required and in the **Lines** section click on **Line Endpoints**.
13. On the graphics screen you are prompted: **Specify the first endpoint** and the Line Endpoints panel appears. **Ensure** that the **Tangent** function is activated.
14. To satisfy the prompt **Specify the first endpoint** move the cursor over to the end point of the line shown below and snap to this point.

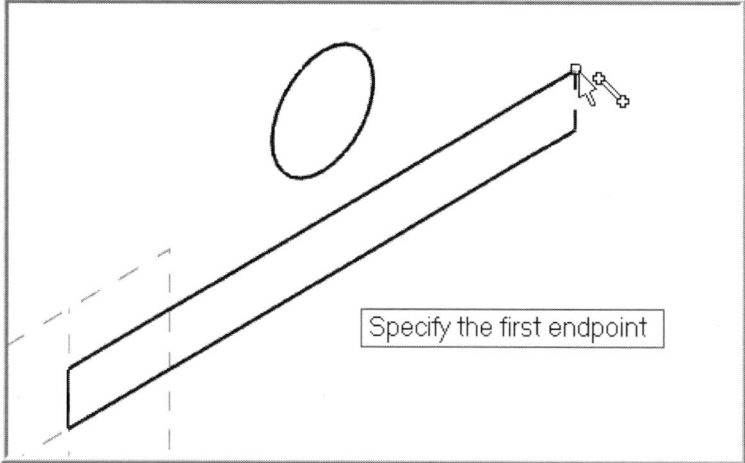

15. To satisfy the prompt **Specify the second endpoint** move the cursor over the area of the circle shown below. Ensure there is **no visual cue** being displayed and click on this point. As **Tangent** is activated on the Line Endpoints panel the line will snap to the closest tangency point on the circle as shown below right:

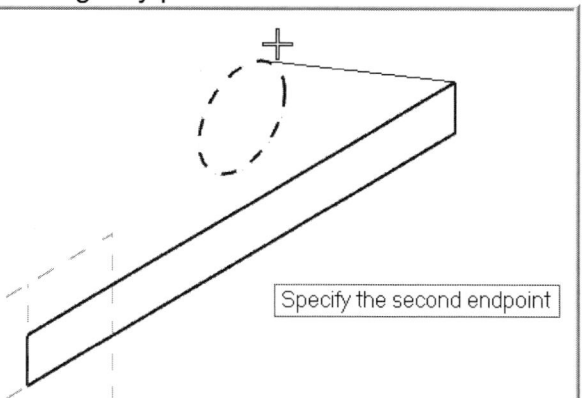 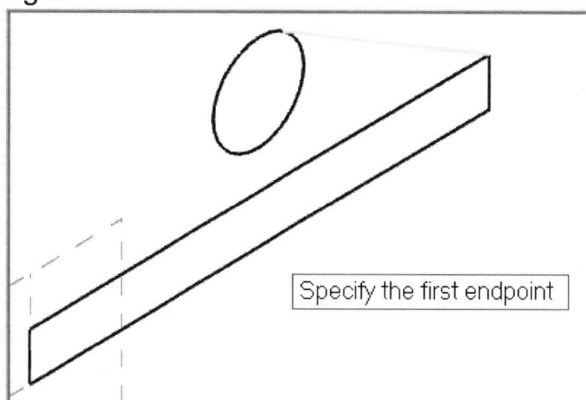

16. To satisfy the prompt **Specify the first endpoint** move the cursor over to the end point of the line shown below and snap to this point.

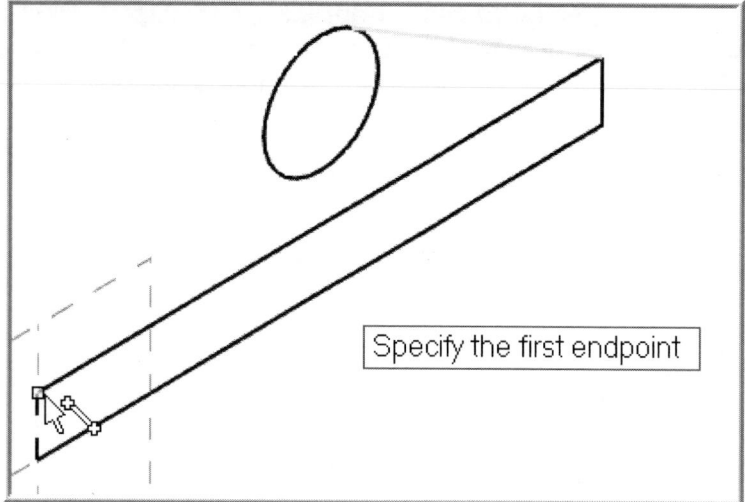

Specify the first endpoint

17. To satisfy the prompt **Specify the second endpoint** move the cursor over the area of the circle shown below. Ensure there is **no visual cue** being displayed and click on this point. As **Tangent** is activated on the Line Endpoints panel the line will snap to the closest tangency point on the circle as shown below right:

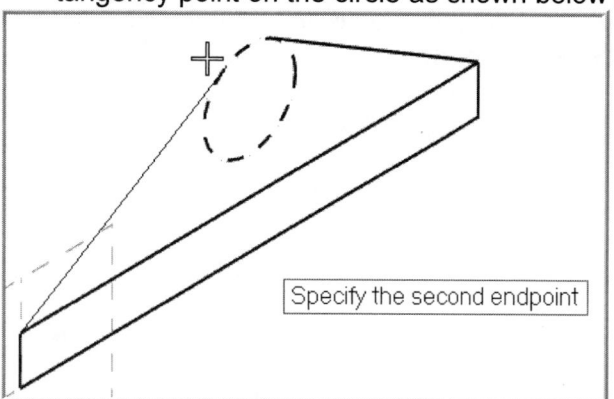

Specify the second endpoint

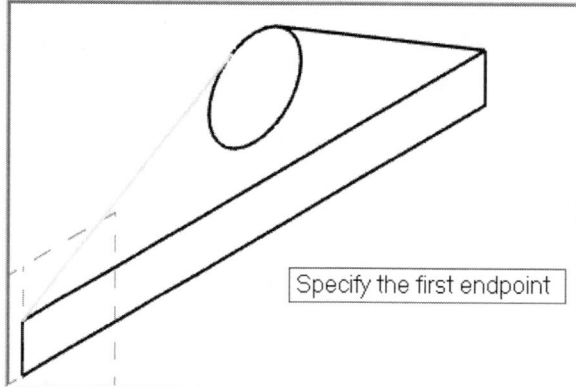

Specify the first endpoint

18. Click on the **OK** icon to complete this feature.

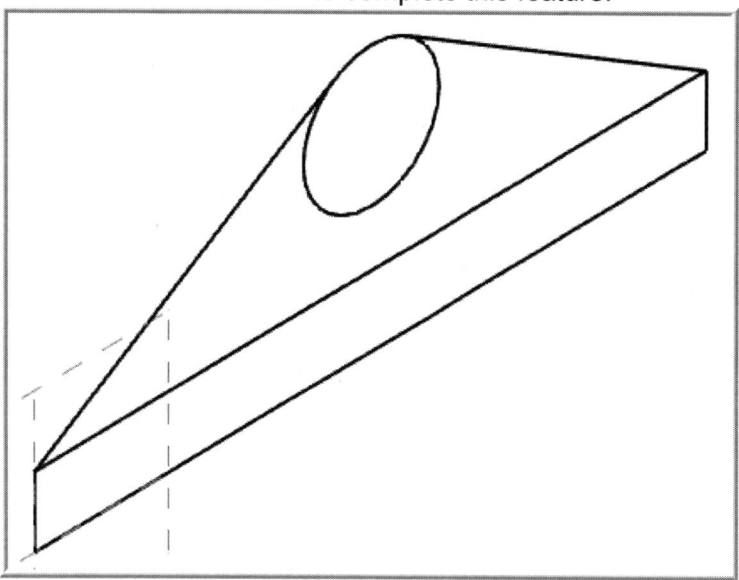

➲ Trimming

19. In the **Wireframe** tab click on **Trim to Entities** in the **Modify** section.
20. The **Trim to Entities** panel appears. Activate **Trim 3 entities.**

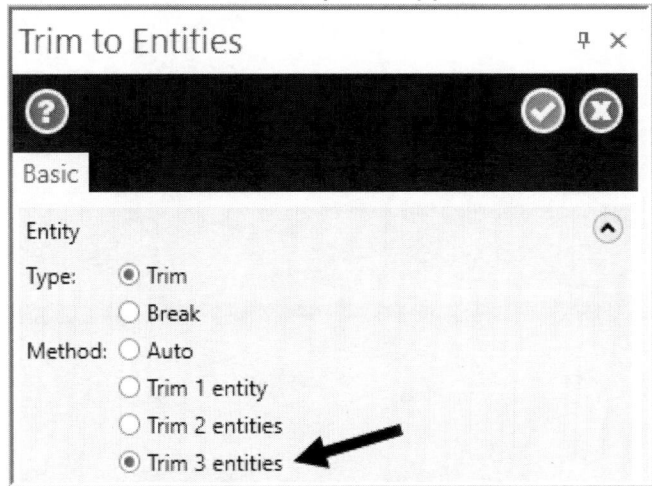

21. Move the cursor over the various entities and select in order and position as shown below left: **The top of the arc is selected last**.

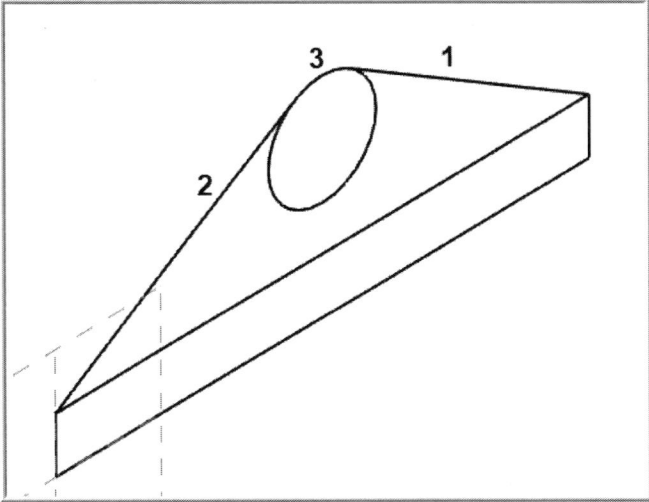

22. Click on the **OK** icon to complete this feature.

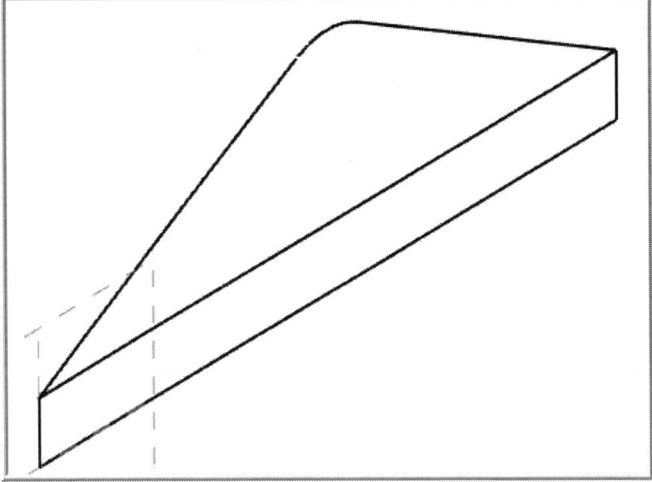

23. Remove the middle line by simply selecting it (left click on the line) and then hitting the Delete key on your keyboard.

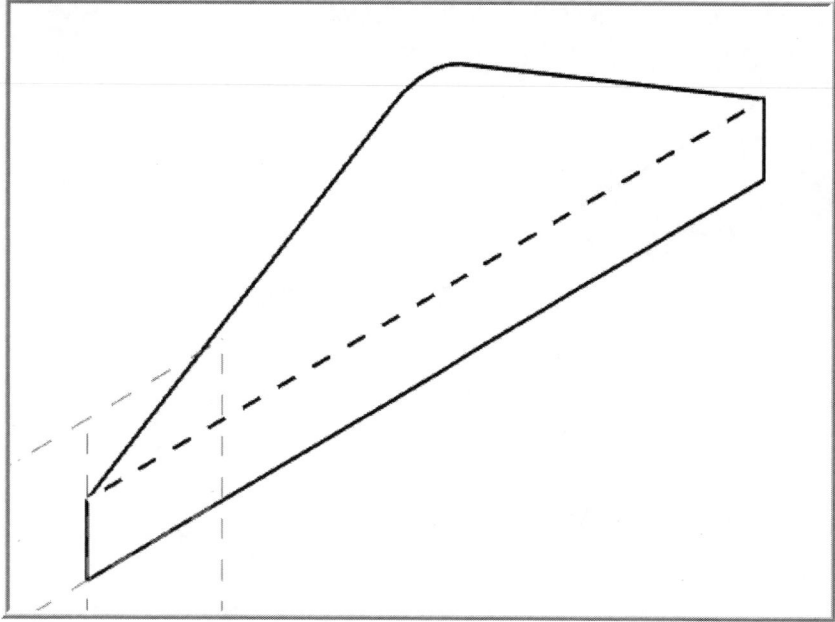

‣ The completed middle section...

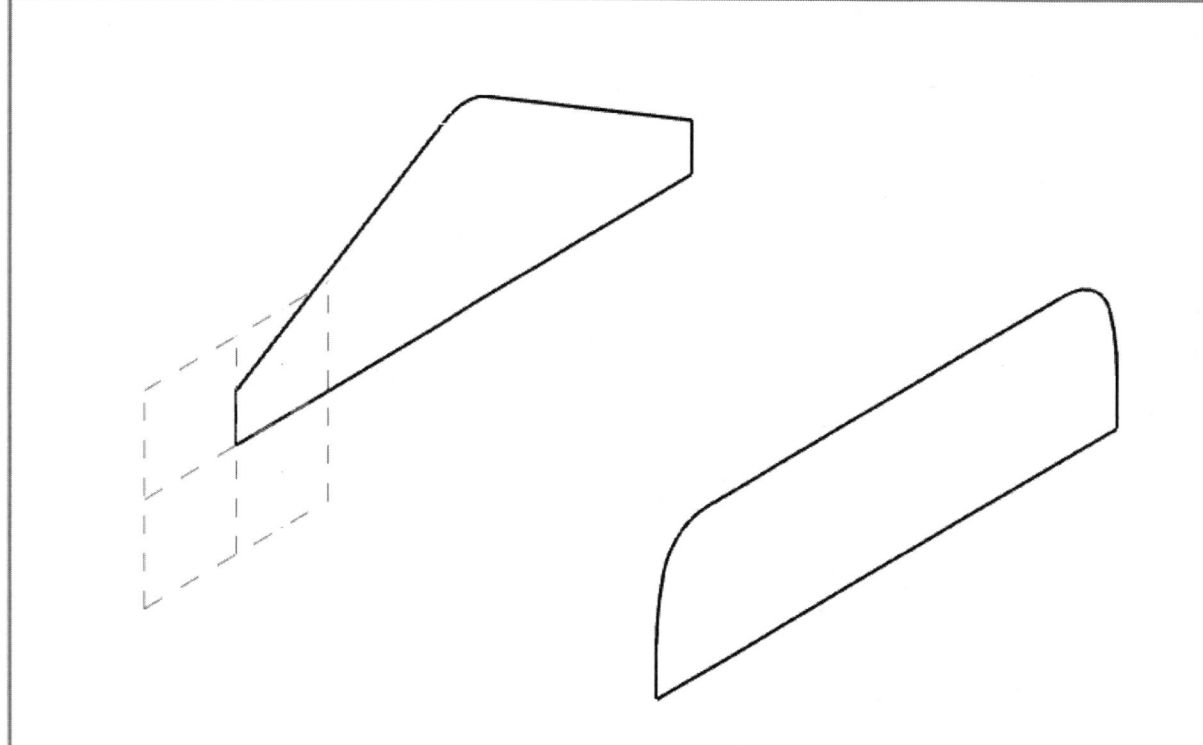

TASK 4:
CREATE GEOMETRY – LEFT HAND SECTION

➲ In this task you will create the left-hand section that will be used to create the lofted body. First a rectangle will be created and then finally the two arcs will be created using fillet.

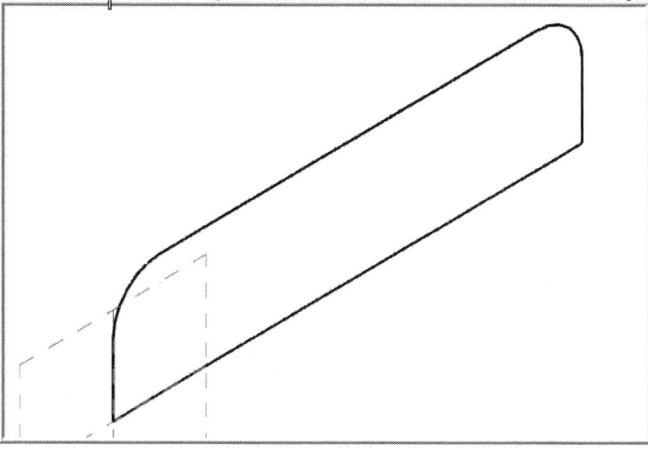

➲ **Create the rectangle**

1. Right mouse click in the graphics area. Next click in the space for the **Z value** and enter a value of **-4.625** and hit enter.

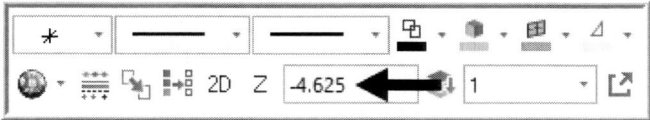

➲ Take note at the lower part of the screen on the status bar **Z: -4.625**.

2. Select the **Wireframe** tab at the top of the screen and in the **Shapes** section click on **Rectangle**. Click in the space for **Width** and enter a value of **2.500** and then hit the Enter key. In the space for **Height** enter a value of **0.625** and hit enter. The **Anchor to center** option – **should not be activated.**
3. To satisfy the prompt click the middle mouse button and then hit the spacebar on your keyboard. The **Fastpoint** box now opens. Input **0,0** and hit the Enter key. Click on the **OK** icon to complete this feature.

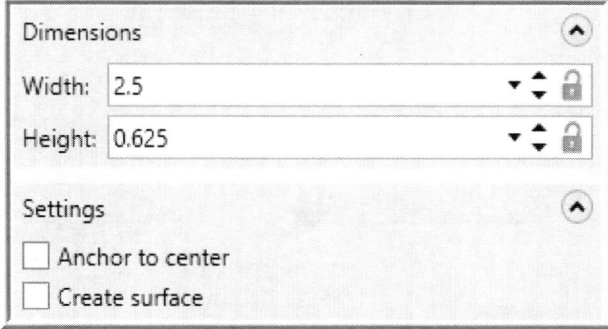

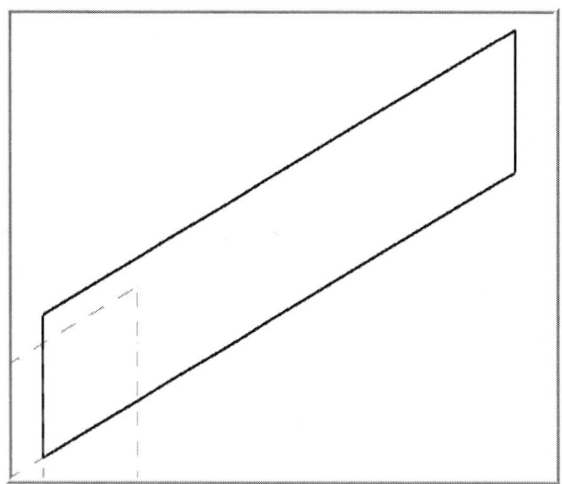

⊃ **Create the Arcs**

4. Select the **Wireframe** tab if required and in the **Modify** section click on **Fillet Entities**.
5. The **Fillet Entities** panel appears. If required activate the **Method** to **Normal** and enter a value of **0.25** for **Radius**.
6. Ensure the **Trim** entities box at the bottom of the panel is check marked to turn the trim on.

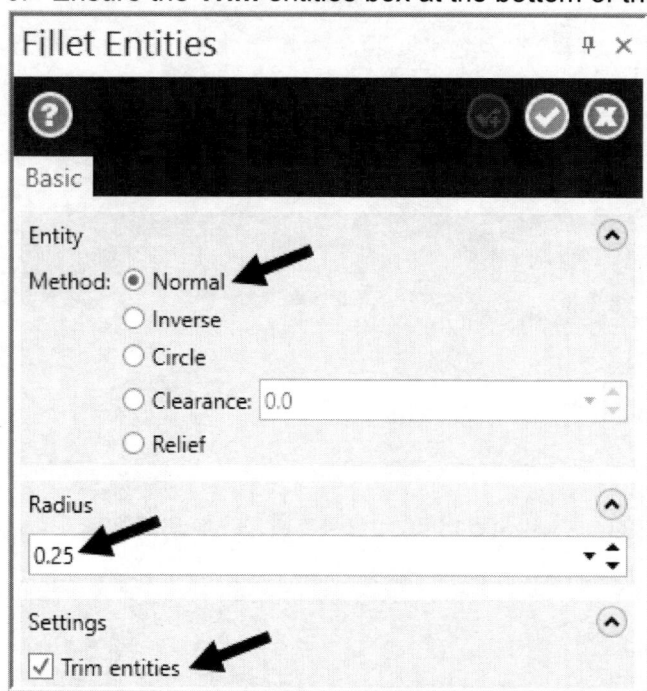

7. When prompted to **Fillet: Select an entity,** select entity 1 and 2 as shown below. The fillet radius appears at the corner of entities 1 and 2. To complete the remaining fillet select: entities 2 and 3. The completed geometry is shown below right:

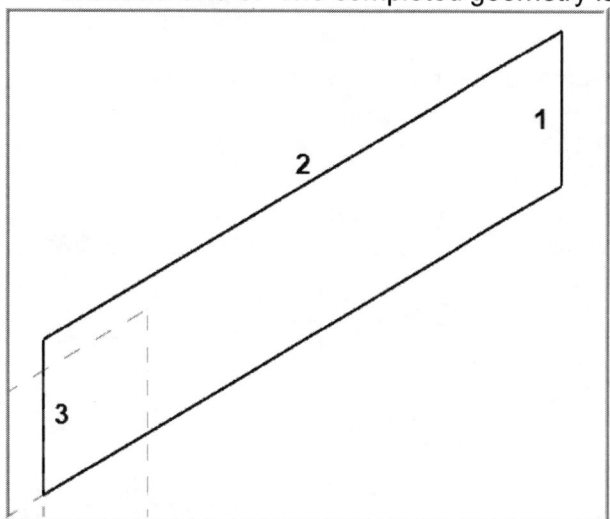
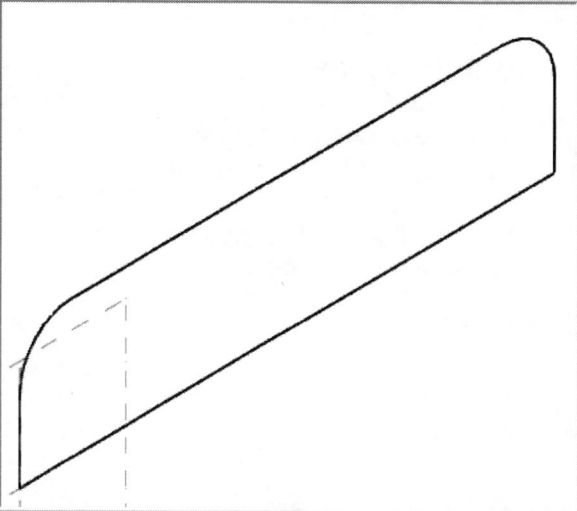

8. Click on the **OK** icon to complete this feature.

⮌ **The Completed Wireframe Geometry**

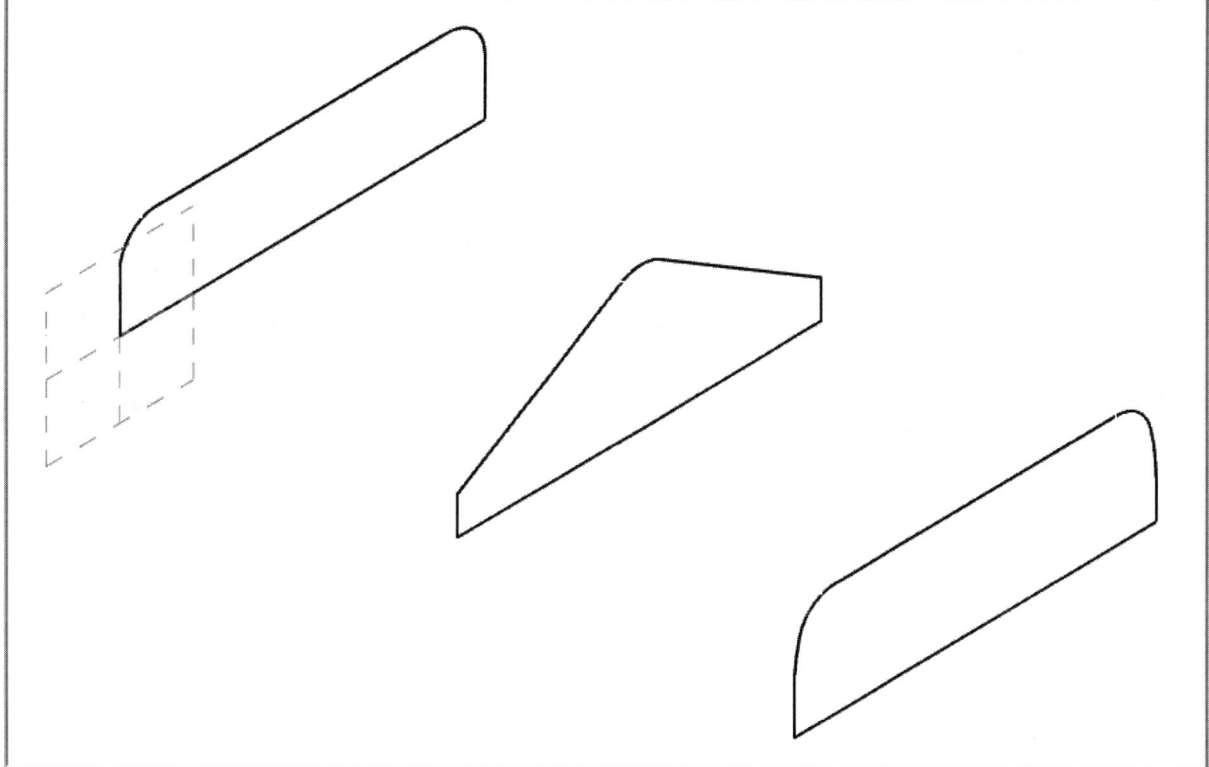

9. Remember to **Save** your file.

TASK 5:
CREATE THE LOFTED SOLID

➲ In this task you will create a lofted solid using the geometry you have just created.
➲ Before creating the solid, since loft is being used to blend between the 3 sections, Mastercam will need to know how to line this blend up. This is done through Syncing.

Sync modes are methods Mastercam uses to align chains. You can select the following methods...

None - Synchronizes the chains by dividing them each into an even number of points. Certain surfaces and toolpaths require more precision than this option provides.

By entity - Matches the chains by the endpoints of each entity. Requires both chains to have the same number of entities.

By branch - Matches the chains at branch points. Can be used for most chain synchronization.

By node - Matches two or more splines by the node points of each spline. Each spline must have the same number of node points. Applies only to parametric splines.

By point - Matches the chains by point entities on the endpoints of each entity. You need to have created the points where you want the chains to sync.

Manual - Matches the chains of user-defined areas.

Manual/density - Matches the chains that you specify and allows you to assign a density for each chain. If an area has small radii, use a higher density (such as 2) for a better finish.

➲ Currently, one of the chains has 8 entities while the other 2 have 6 so By Entity cannot be used (unless we break some lines in two or consolidate some arcs into splines).

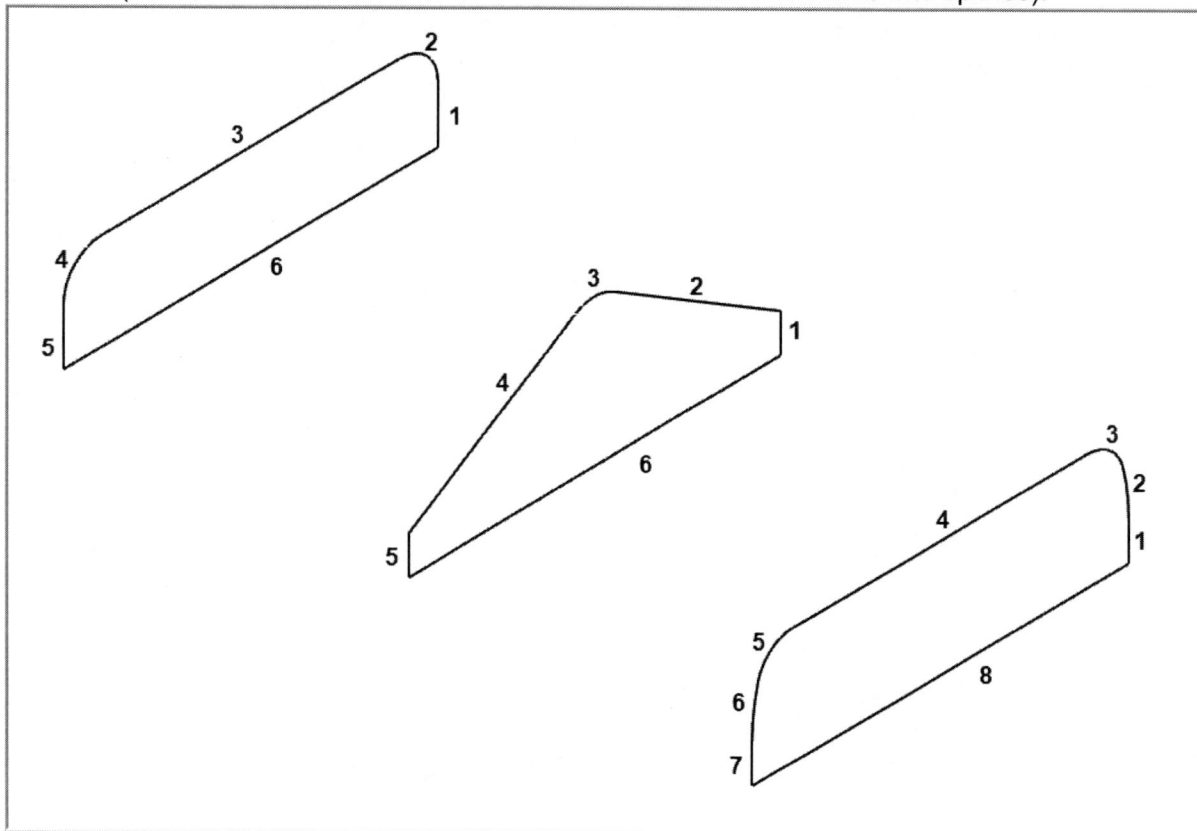

➲ For this part we can use either the By Branch or By Point. Both methods would require additional geometry creation. Next, lines will be created to set the syncing points on what will be the bottom face of the part. It's not necessary to create a line at every sync point, some of the syncing can be left to the software's' digression. You could create points at the endpoint of the lines that are about to be created and then use the By Point sync method.

1. Create lines, using **Line Endpoint**, to represent the sync positions needed for the bottom face. Draw **4 lines** from points **1-2, 2-3, 4-5, and 5-6**. Do NOT draw only 2 lines from 1-3 or 4-6.

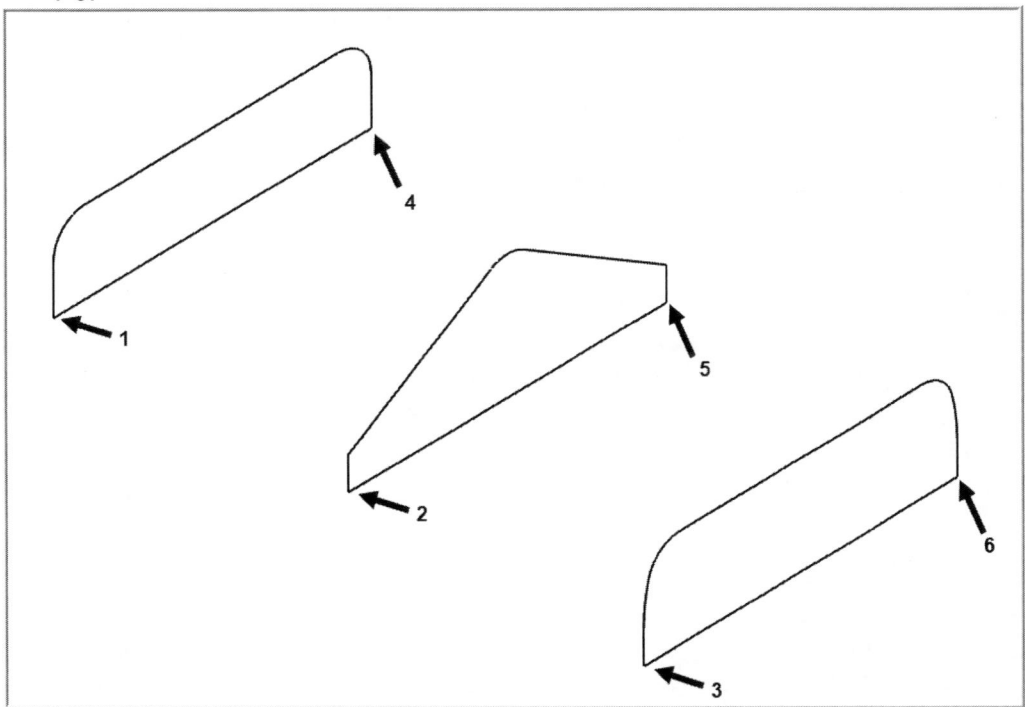

➲ The 4 completed lines…

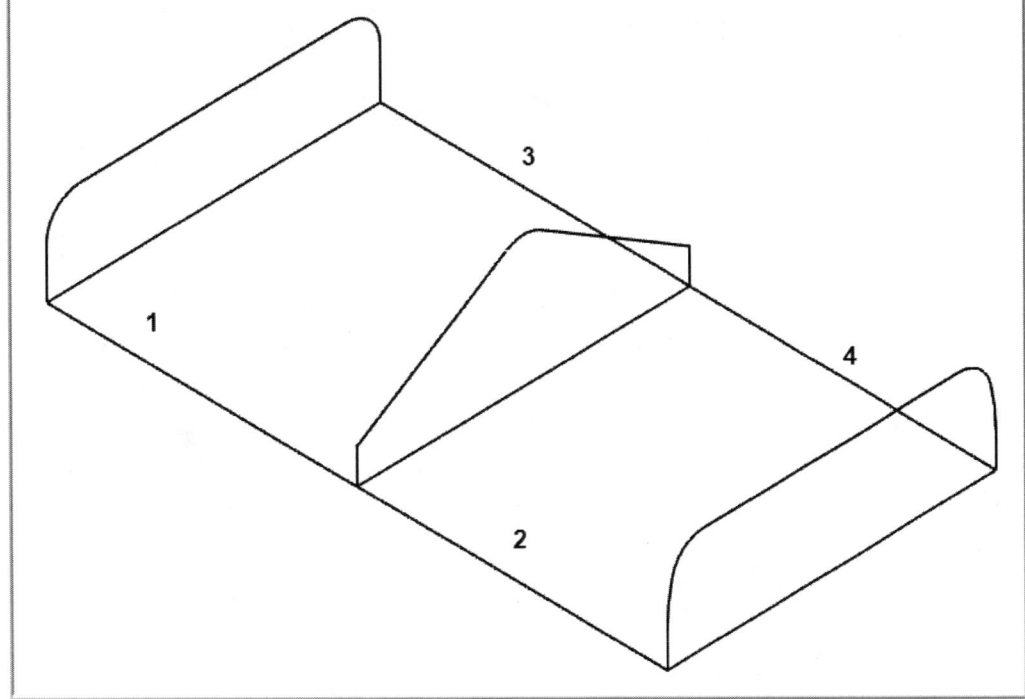

2. Click on the **Solids** tab and in the **Create** section select **Loft**.

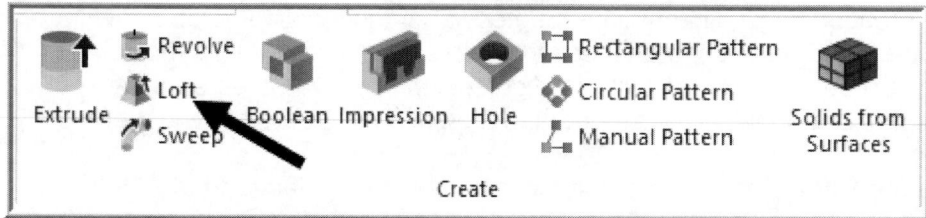

Solid Loft uses a set of closed chains to create one or more new solid bodies, cuts in an existing body, or bosses on an existing body.

Mastercam transitions between two or more chains of curves in the order that you select them by capping the first and last chains with solid faces.

3. On the graphics screen you are prompted **"Lofted surface: define contour 1"** with the **Chain Button** selected.

4. Before selecting geometry, a Syncing mode must be selected. On the **Chaining menu** click the **Options** button. On the **Options menu** set the **Sync mode** to **by Branch**. Click Ok.

   Back on the Chaining menu switch the **mode to Cplane**. This will make chaining easier since it will not see the branch geometry as possible paths for the chain selection.

   The Right plane should still be the active Construction plane. If it is not change this now.

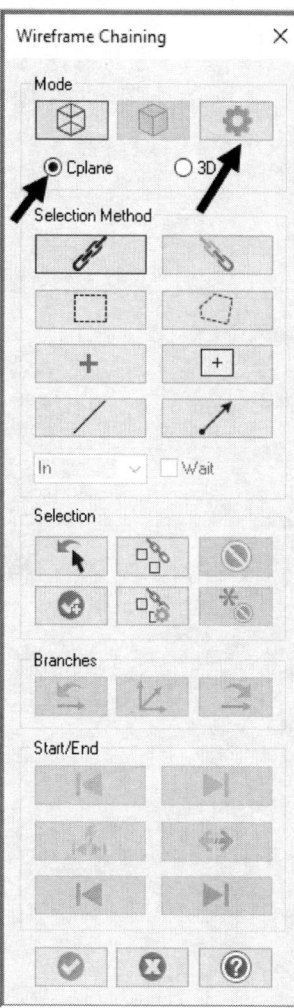

5. The start point and direction of the chains must match. Click each chain as shown...

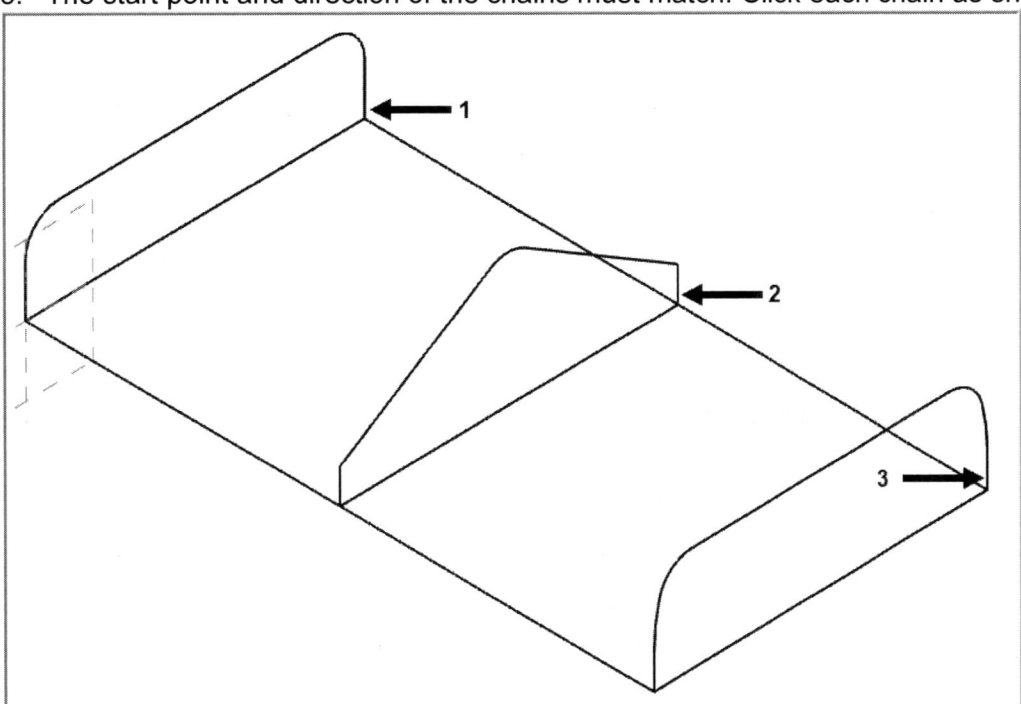

6. Click the **Ok** icon.
7. Make the necessary changes as shown below in the **Loft** panel. Activate **Create Body** if required.

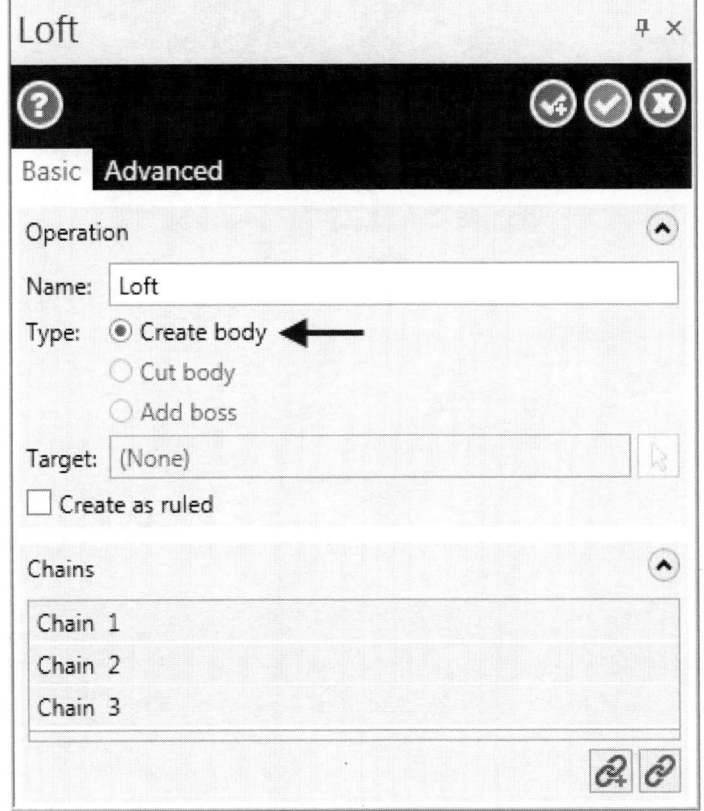

What are the criteria for the selected chains for a Loft operation?

There must be a minimum of two closed, parallel chains.

Each individual chain of curves must be planar.

All of the selected chains must follow the same chaining direction.

You cannot select a chain of curves more than once for a given loft operation.

A selected chain of curves cannot self-intersect

Create as ruled

Select to create the lofted solid, cut, or boss using ruled blending. In a ruled blend, Mastercam transitions from one chain of curves to another, which results in linear sections. Clear to use smooth blending. In a smooth blend, Mastercam considers all of the chains of curves when transitioning between them, which results in smooth sections.

8. Click on the **OK** icon 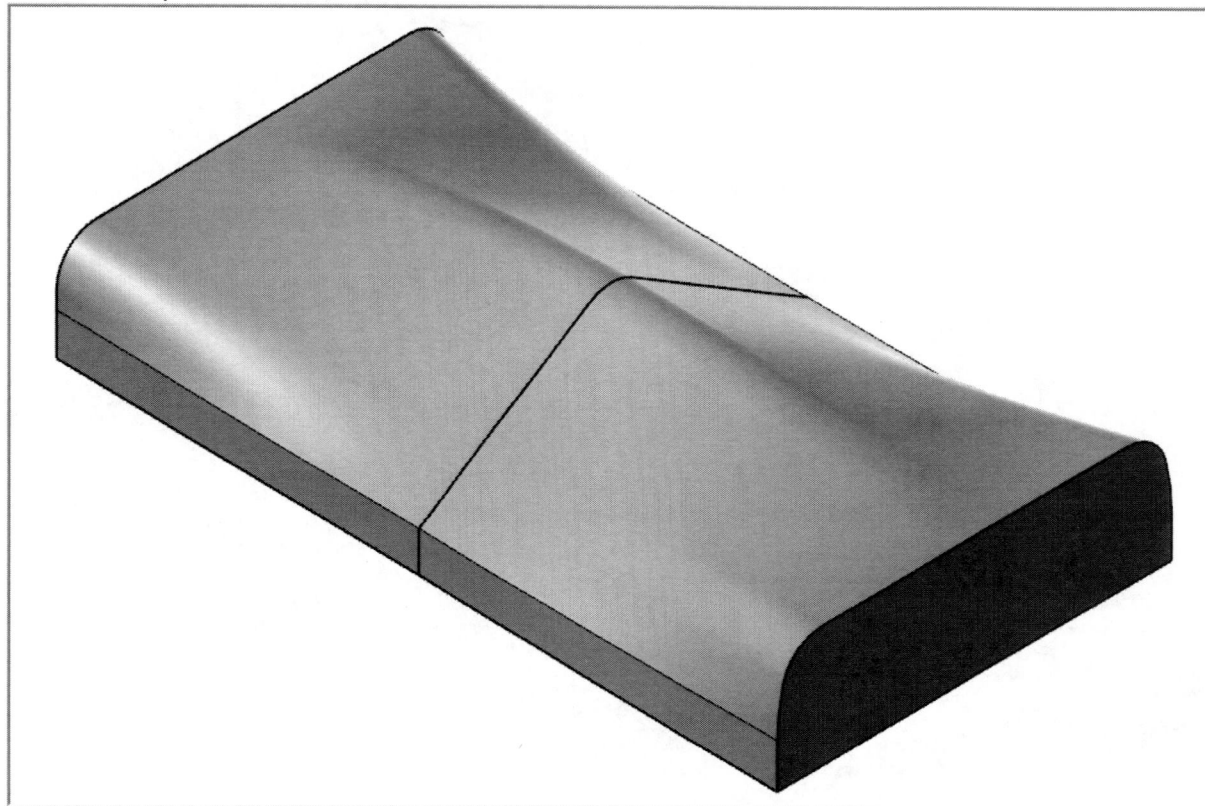 in the **Loft** panel.

➲ The completed lofted solid…

9. Remember to **Save** your file.

Toolpath Creation

TASK 6:
DEFINE THE ROUGH STOCK USING STOCK SETUP

1. If required right mouse click in the graphics area and click on **Isometric**.
2. If required toggle the **Planes Manager to display**.
3. In the Plane Manager click in the **C column (Construction Plane)** for **Top**. Take note at the bottom of the screen **CPLANE:TOP TPLANE:TOP WCS:TOP** as shown below right.

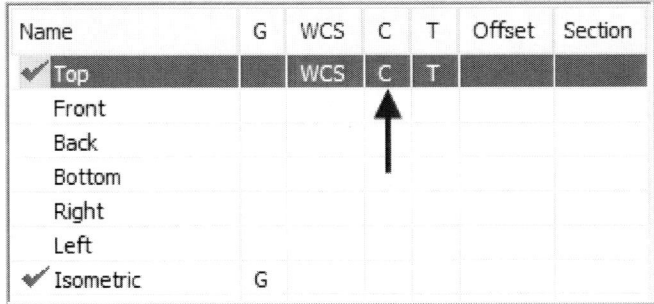

4. Set the Planes Z position back to 0. **Right click** in the graphics screen and input **0.00** for the Z planes position.

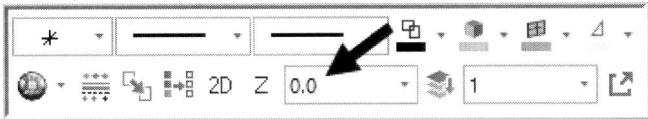

5. On the **Toolpaths Managers,** select the **plus** in front of **Properties** to expand the Toolpaths Group Properties.

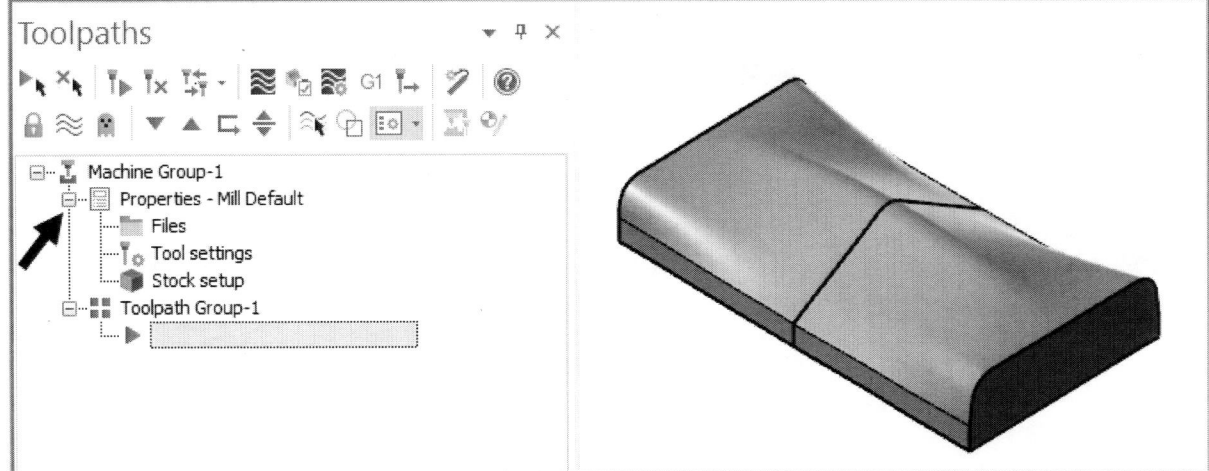

6. Select **Stock setup** in the Toolpaths Manager window.
7. Change the parameters to match the **Stock Setup** screenshot below: The base of the material is at **Z0** and is 1.00 inches thick. The base of the material and the 4.625 x 2.5 dimensions has been previously machined to size.

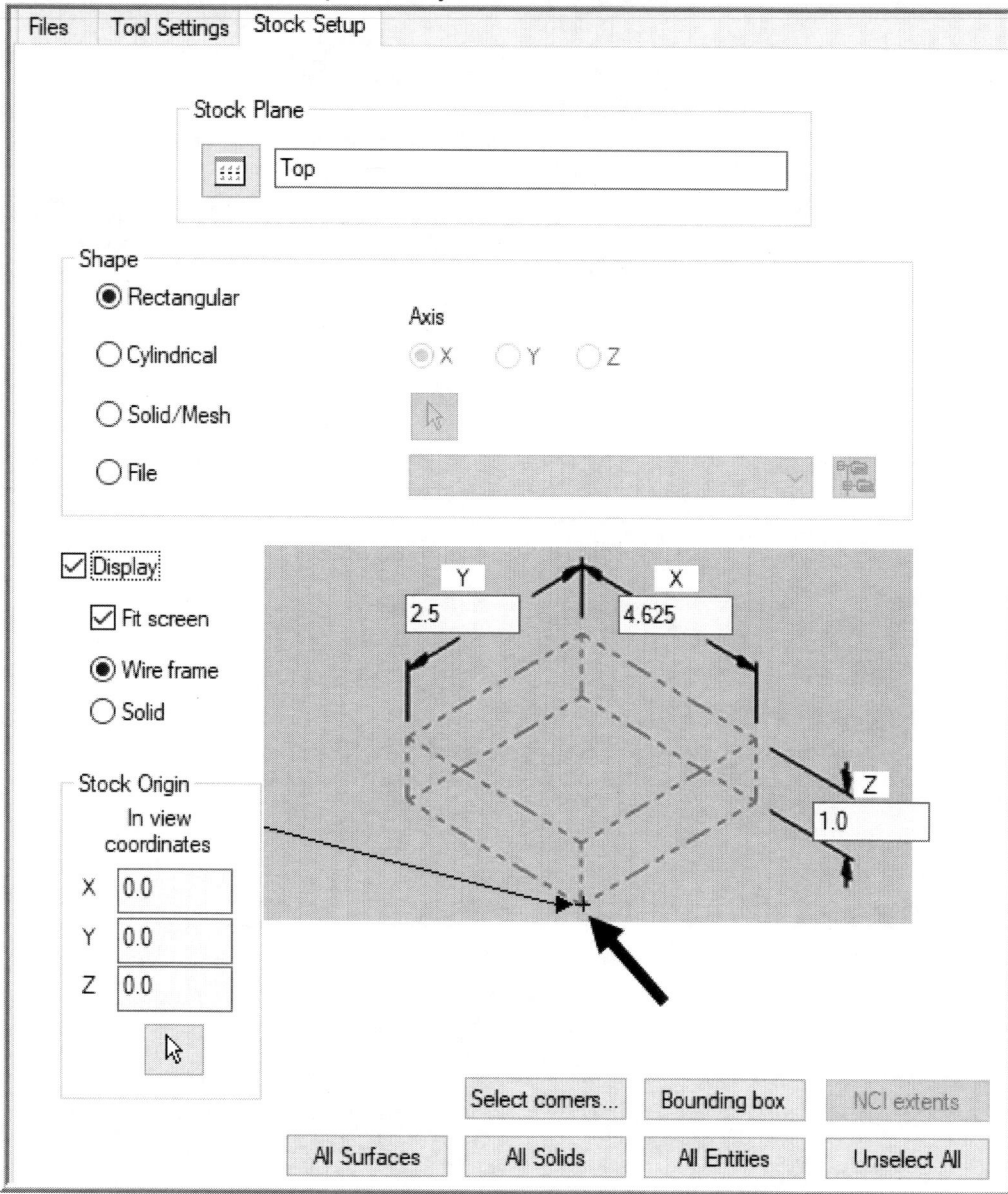

8. Select the **Tool Settings** tab and change the parameters to match the Tool Settings screenshot below. To change the Material type follow the instructions below:

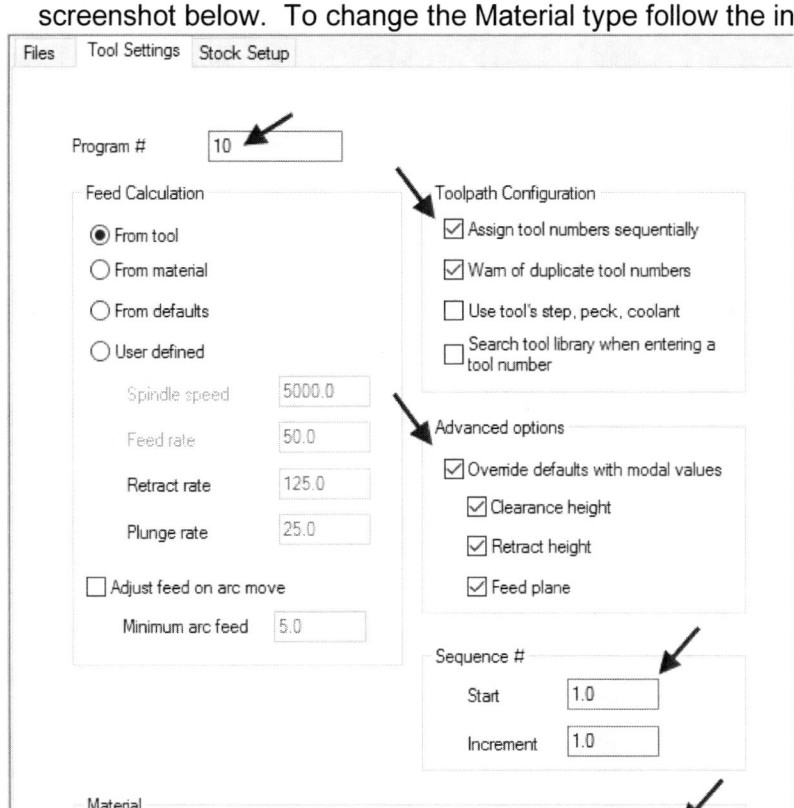

9. To change the Material type to Aluminum 6061 pick the Select button at the bottom of the Tool Settings page.

10. At the **Material List** dialog box open the **Source** drop down list and select **Mill – library**.

11. From the Default Materials list select **ALUMINUM inch -6061** and then select ✓.

12. Select the OK button ✓ again to complete this Stock Setup function.

➲ Your part should look like the screen shot below. With **X0 Y0** at the lower right side and **Z zero** at the base of the stock.

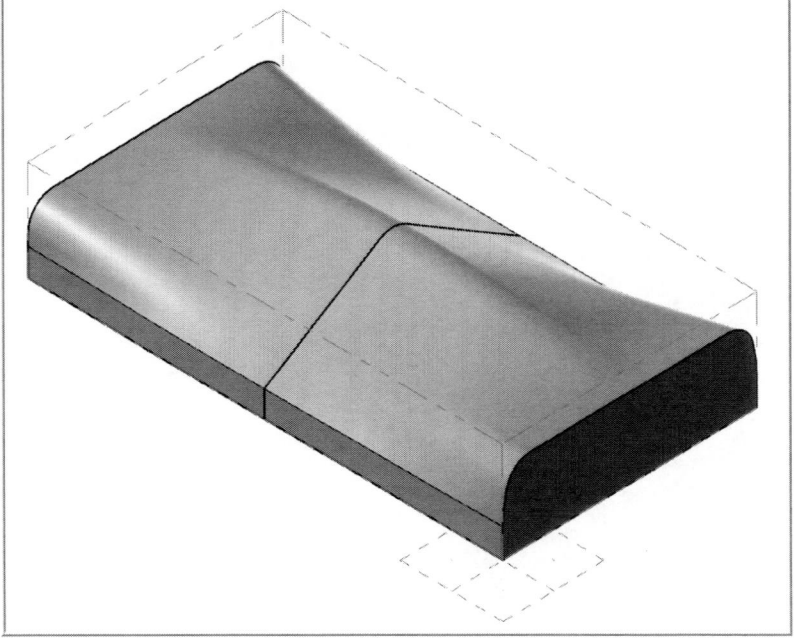

TASK 7:
ROUGH MACHINE USING ROUGH PARALLEL

➲ In this task you will use a 0.5 diameter bull end mill with a 0.125 corner radius to rough the lofted solid.

1. Select the **Toolpaths** tab at the top right side of the screen.
2. Select **Parallel** in the **3D** toolpath section.

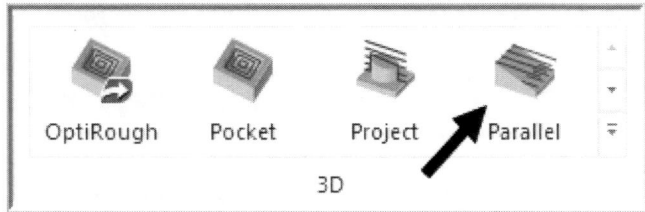

3. Activate **Boss** from the **Select Boss/Cavity** dialog box and then select the **OK** button. Notice the on-screen prompt…

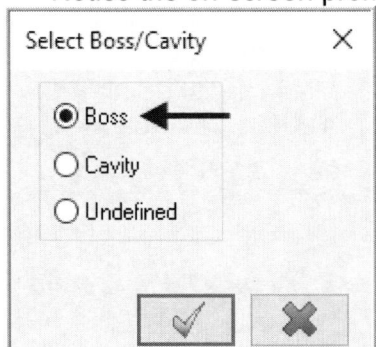

Select Solid Face, Surface, or Mesh
- Shift-click to select tangent solid faces
- Alt-click to vec tor select
- Ctrl-click to select matching solid fillets/holes
- Ctrl-shift-click to select similar solid faces
- Double-click to select a solid feature
- Ctrl-shift-double-click to select similar solid features
- Triple-click to select the solid body ◀━━━━

4. To satisfy the prompt on the screen, **triple click on the solid** so the entire solid is selected.

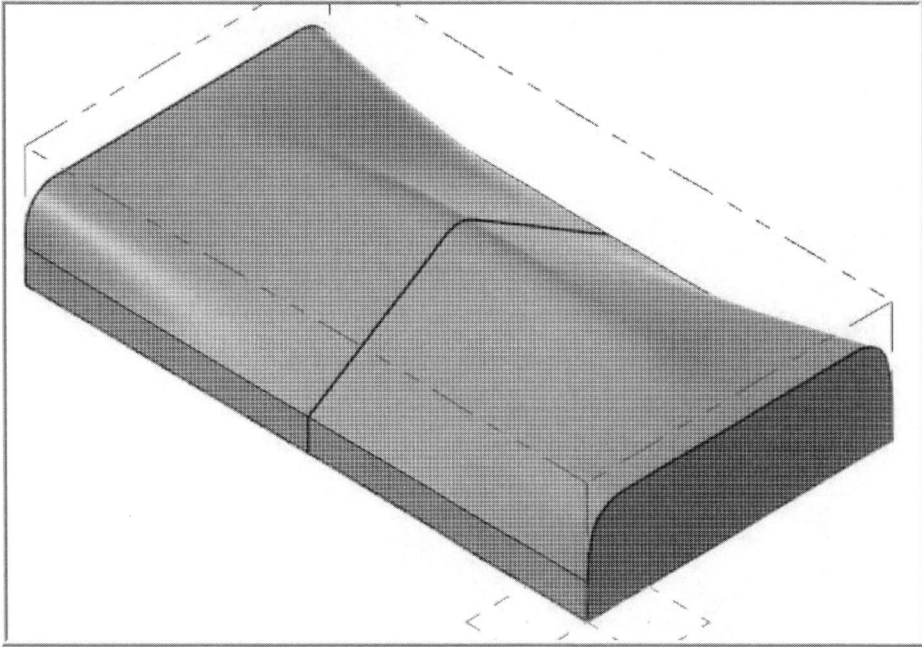

5. To move onto the next step, you now need to pick the **End Selection** icon .

6. Select the OK button [✓] to exit the **Toolpath/surface selection** dialog box.
7. In the lower left corner of the **Toolpath parameters** page select the **Select library tool...** button.
8. Use the slider bar on the right of this dialog box to scroll down and locate a **0.5 diameter bull end mill with a 0.125 corner radius**. Select the end mill by picking anywhere along its row.

	Tool Number	Tool Name	Diameter	Corner Radius	Length	Type	Radius Type
	344	1/2 BULL ENDMILL ...	0.5	0.03125	1.0	Bull endmill	Corner
	345	1/2 BULL ENDMILL ...	0.5	0.0625	1.0	Bull endmill	Corner
	346	1/2 BULL ENDMILL ...	0.5	0.125	1.0	Bull endmill	Corner
	347	5/8 BULL ENDMILL ...	0.625	0.0625	1.5	Bull endmill	Corner
	348	5/8 BULL ENDMILL ...	0.625	0.25	1.5	Bull endmill	Corner

9. Select the OK button [✓] to complete the selection of this tool.
10. Make changes to the **Toolpath parameters** page as shown below. Set coolant **on**.

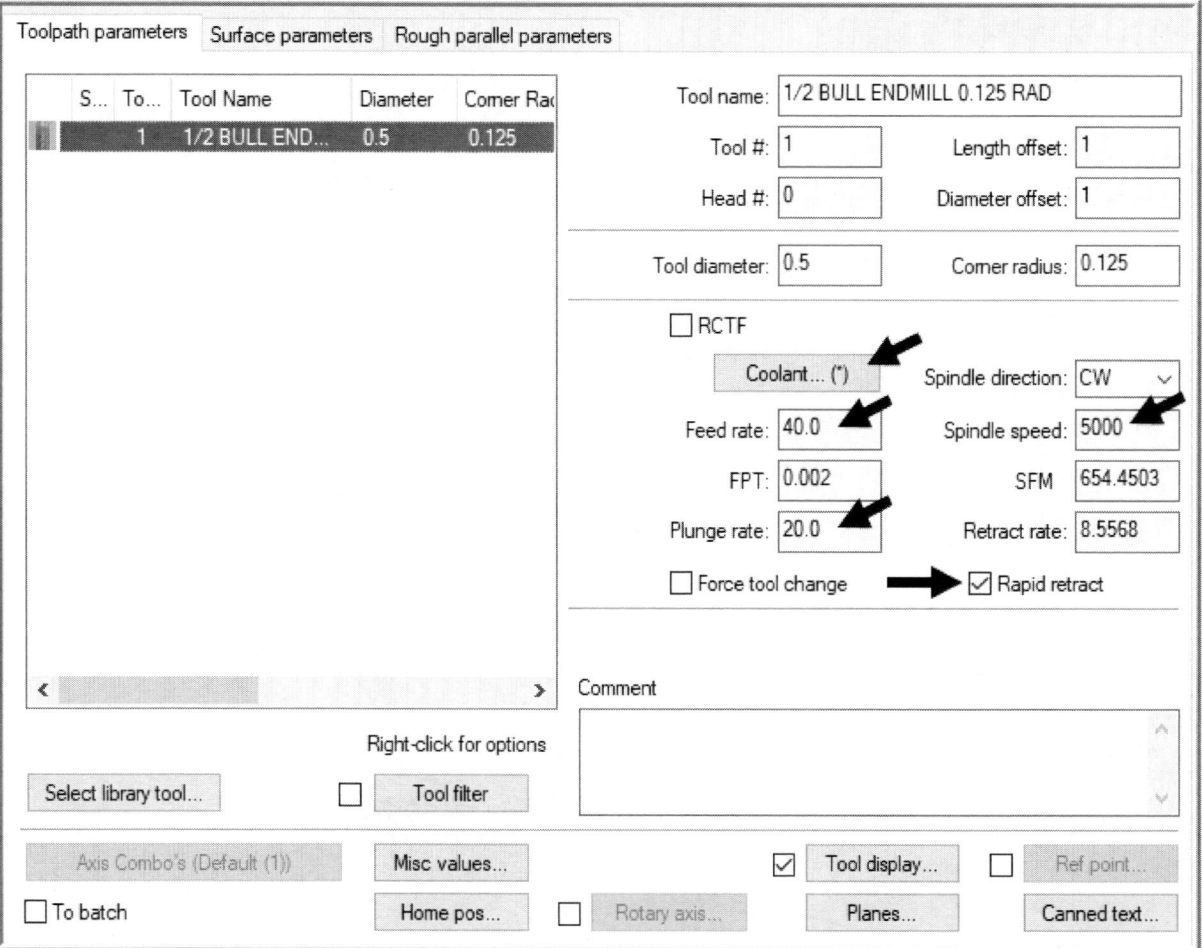

11. Select the **Surface parameters** page and make changes to this page as shown below.
Stock to leave on drive is set to 0.020.

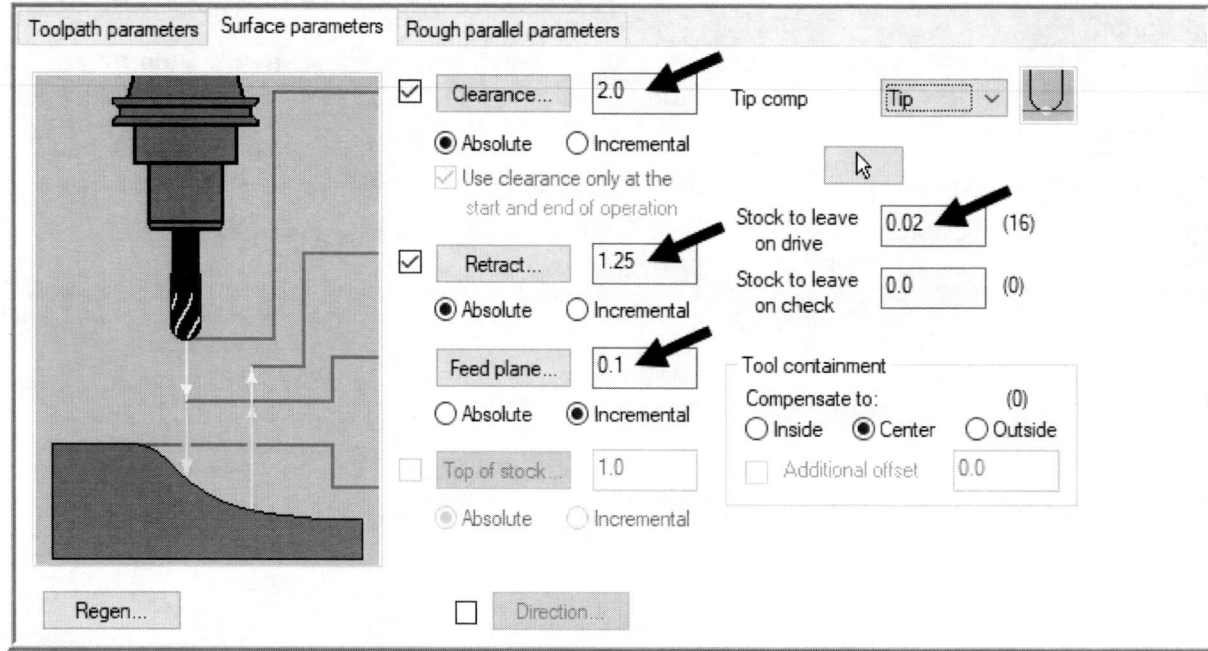

12. Select the **Rough Parallel** page and make changes to this page as shown below.

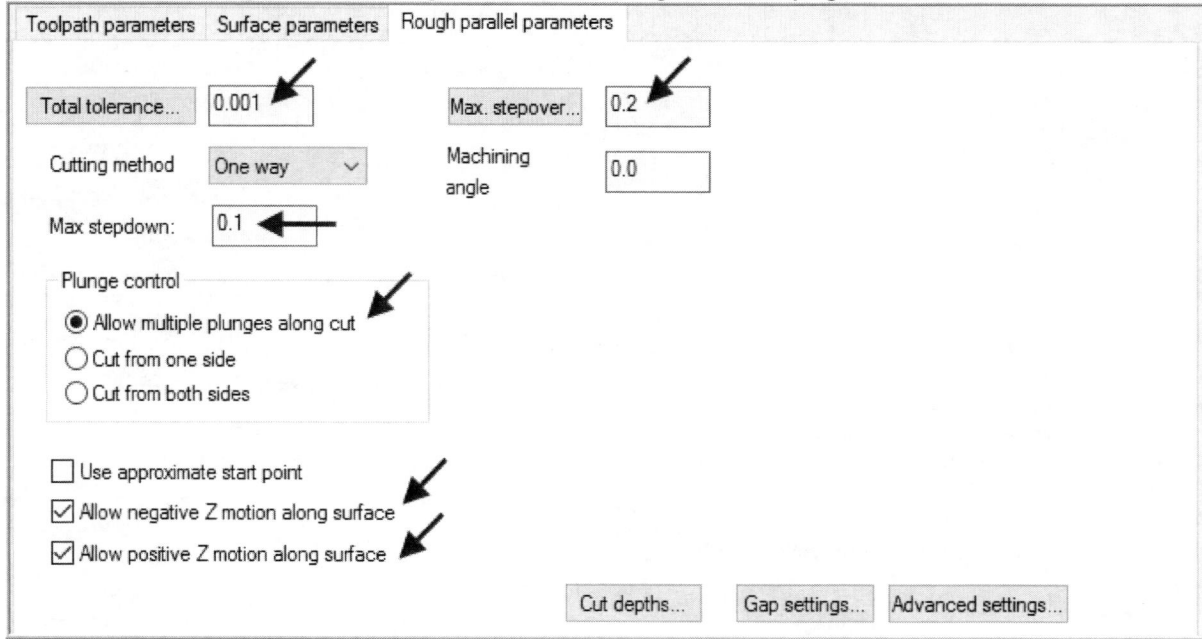

13. Select the **Gap settings** button make the necessary changes.

Gap settings   ✕

Reset

Gap size
○ Distance   0.01
◉ % of stepover   300.0 ◄━

Motion < Gap size, keep tool down

Broken   ⌄
☐ Use plunge, retract rate in gap
☑ Check gap motion for gouge

Motion > Gap size, retract
☑ Check retract motion for gouge

☐ Optimize cut order
☐ Plunge into previously cut area
☐ Follow containment boundary at gap

Tangential arc radius: 0.0

Tangential arc angle: 0.0

Tangential line length: 0.3 ◄━

✓   ✗   ?

By setting a **Tangential line length** that is slightly larger than the radius of the tool **(0.3)** we can ensure that the lead-in after a gap will smoothly engage the tool into the material without a direct plunge.

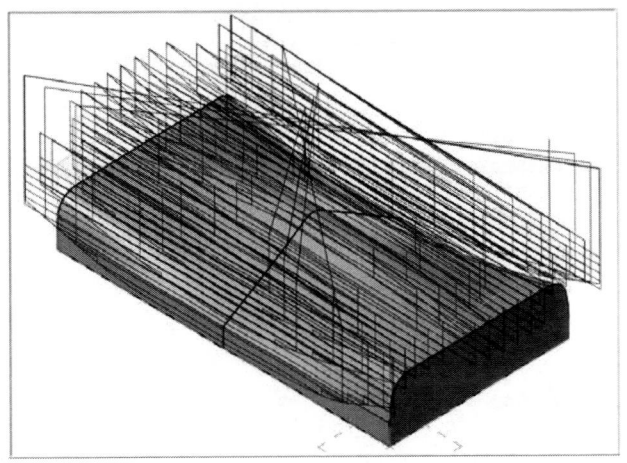

14. Select the OK button [✓] to complete this feature.
15. Select the OK button [✓] to exit **Surface Rough Parallel**.

➲ Your screen should look like the image above on the right:

TASK 8:
FINISH MACHINE USING SURFACE HIGH SPEED RASTER
⊃ In this task you will use a 0.5 diameter Ball end mill to finish the lofted surface.

1. Right mouse click in the white space of the Toolpaths Manager and select:

   Mill toolpaths>Surface high speed toolpath>Raster

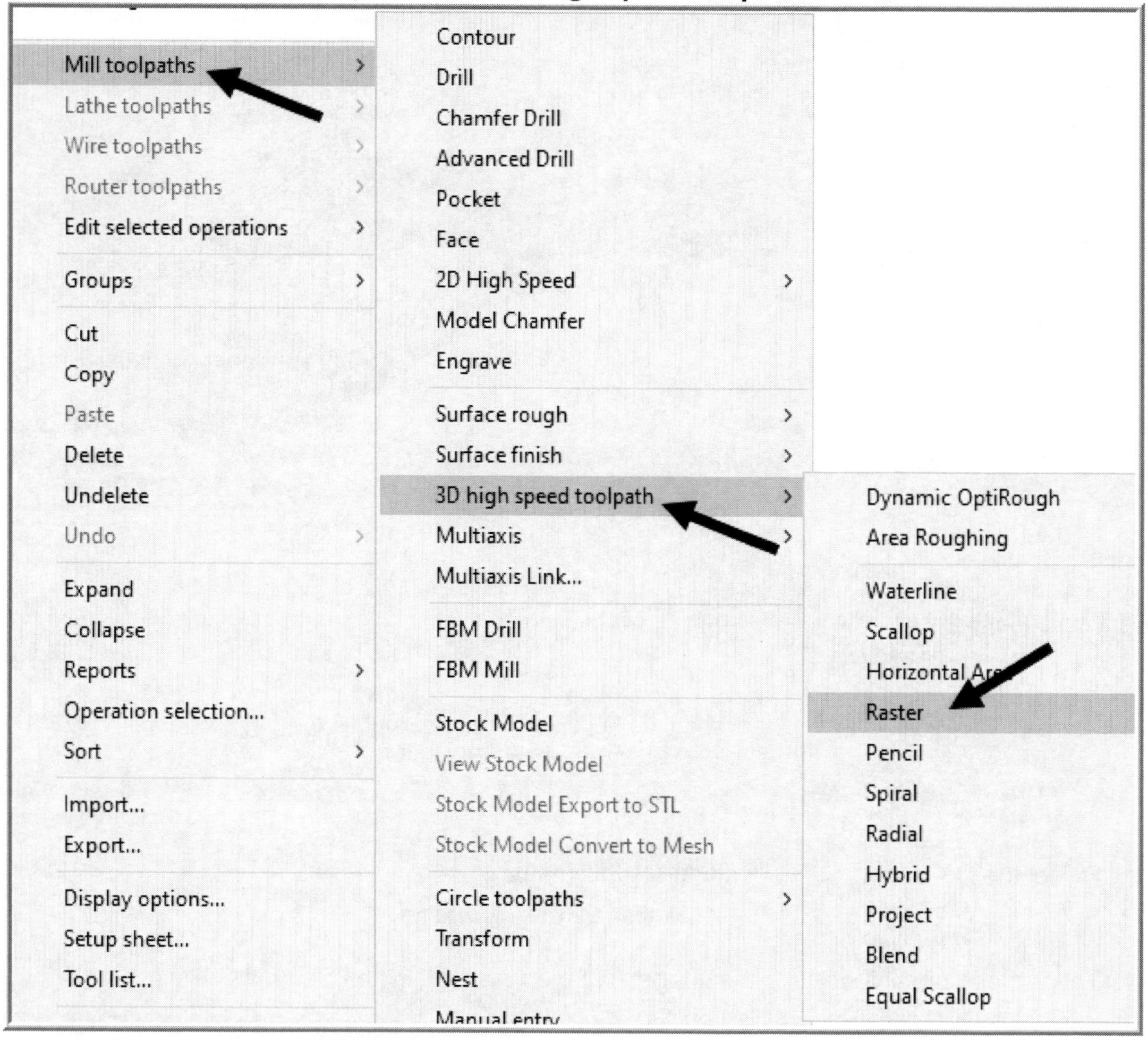

Mill toolpaths >	Contour		
Lathe toolpaths >	Drill		
Wire toolpaths >	Chamfer Drill		
Router toolpaths >	Advanced Drill		
Edit selected operations >	Pocket		
Groups >	Face		
	2D High Speed >		
Cut	Model Chamfer		
Copy	Engrave		
Paste			
Delete	Surface rough >		
Undelete	Surface finish >		
Undo >	3D high speed toolpath >	Dynamic OptiRough
	Multiaxis >	Area Roughing
Expand	Multiaxis Link...	Waterline
Collapse	FBM Drill	Scallop
Reports >	FBM Mill	Horizontal Are
Operation selection...	Stock Model	Raster
Sort >	View Stock Model	Pencil
Import...	Stock Model Export to STL	Spiral
Export...	Stock Model Convert to Mesh	Radial
		Hybrid
Display options...	Circle toolpaths >	Project
Setup sheet...	Transform	Blend
Tool list...	Nest	Equal Scallop
	Manual entry	

2. On the screen select the **Model Geometry** page, if required.
3. Ensure both the **Wall Stock** and **Floor stock** are set to **Zero.**

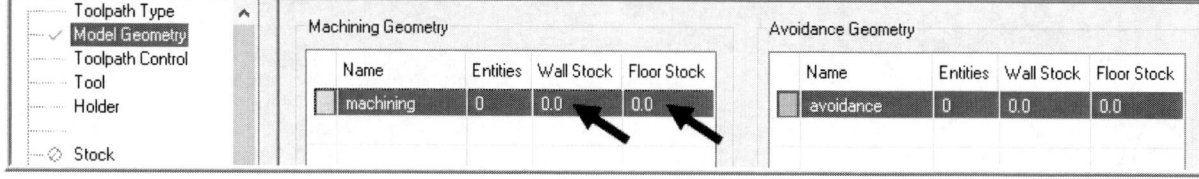

4. At the bottom of the **Model Geometry** page click on the **Select entities** button.

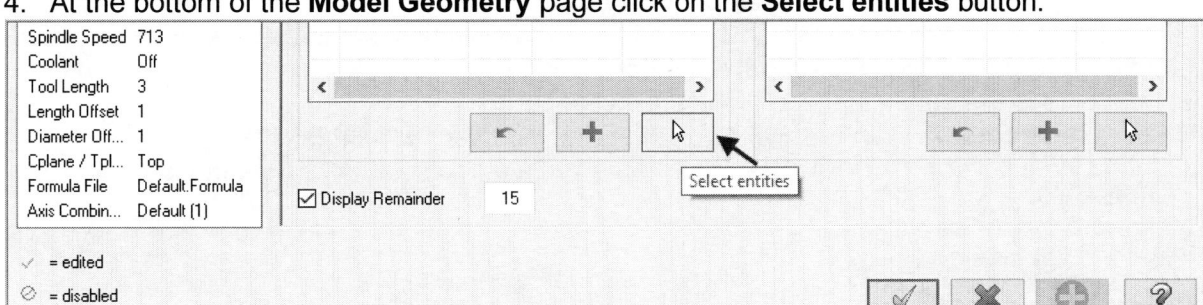

5. Now you will be returned to the graphics screen, select the **entire solid** again.

6. To move onto the next step, you now need to pick the **End Selection** icon.

7. Select the **Toolpath Control** page, no changes needed at this point.

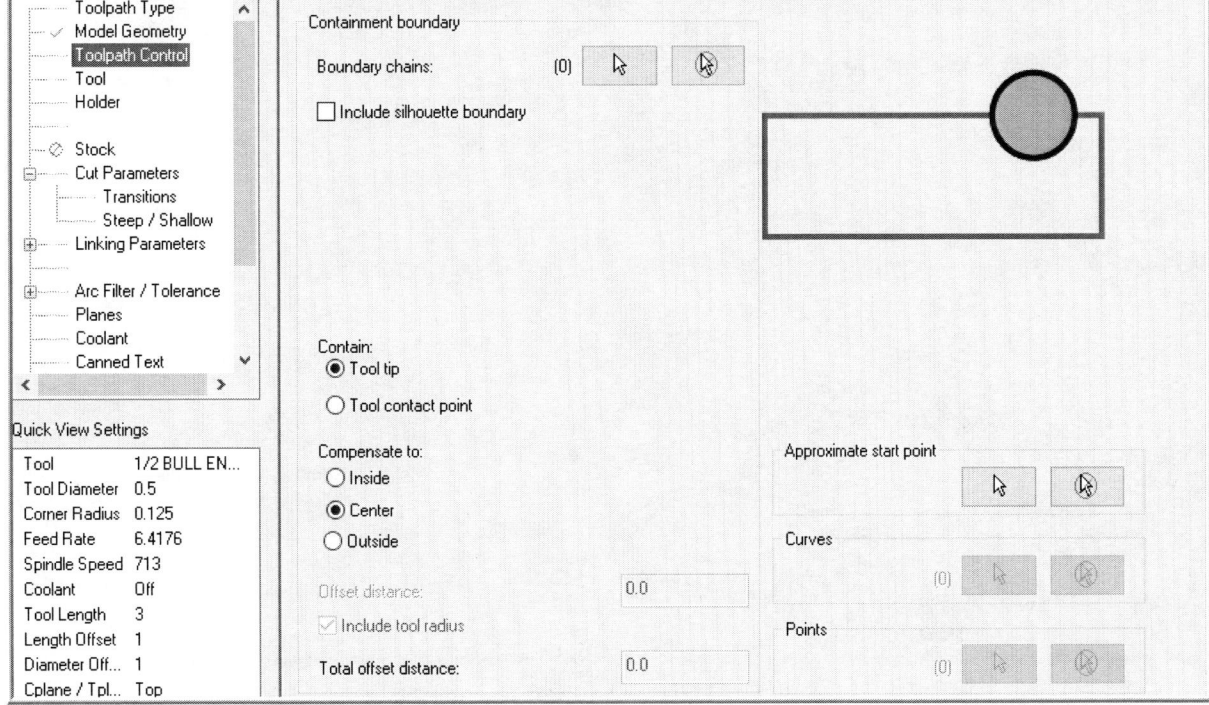

8. Select the **Tool** page, then the **Select library tool…** button.
9. This time we will use the **Filter** function to filter out a selection of cutters. Select the **Filter** button on the right side of the **Tool selection** dialog box.
10. Select the **None** button in the Tool Types section.
11. Click on the **Endmill2 Sphere** type icon, first row, and second icon from the left.
12. Select the drop down arrow in the **Tool diameter** field and set it to **Equal.** Input the tool diameter as **0.5**.

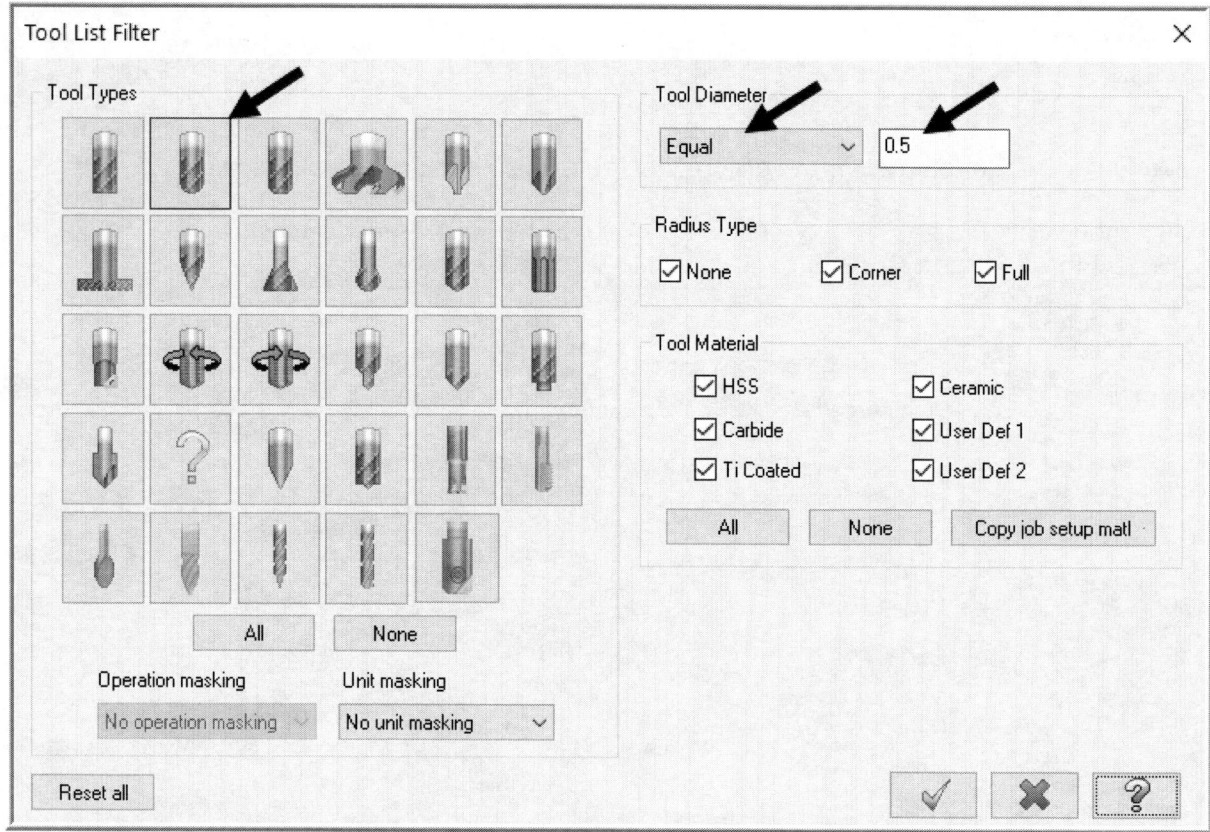

13. Select the OK button [✓] to exit.
14. Select the **0.5 ball end mill**.

	Tool Number	Tool Name	Diameter	Corner Radius	Length	Type	Radius Type
	311	1/2 BALL ENDMILL	0.5	0.25	1.0	Ball endmill	Full

15. Select the OK button [✓] to complete the selection of this tool.

16. Make changes to the **Tool parameters** page as shown below:

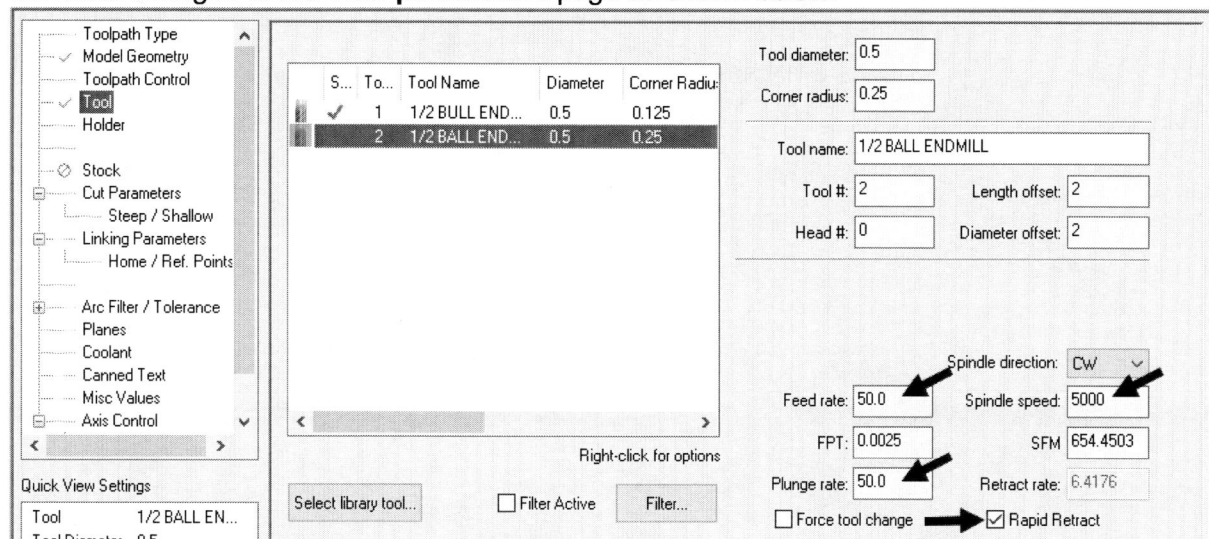

17. Select the **Cut parameters** page and set the Stepover to 0.05. This value could be set smaller but that will add to the toolpath's calculation time.

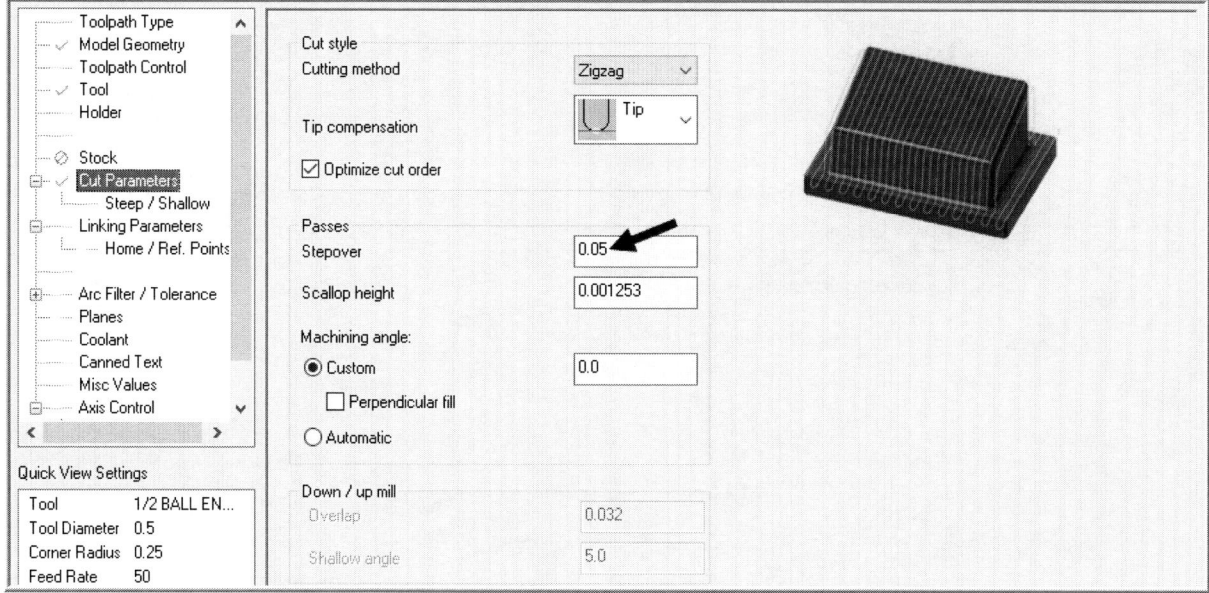

18. Select the **Linking Parameters** page and make changes to this page as shown below:

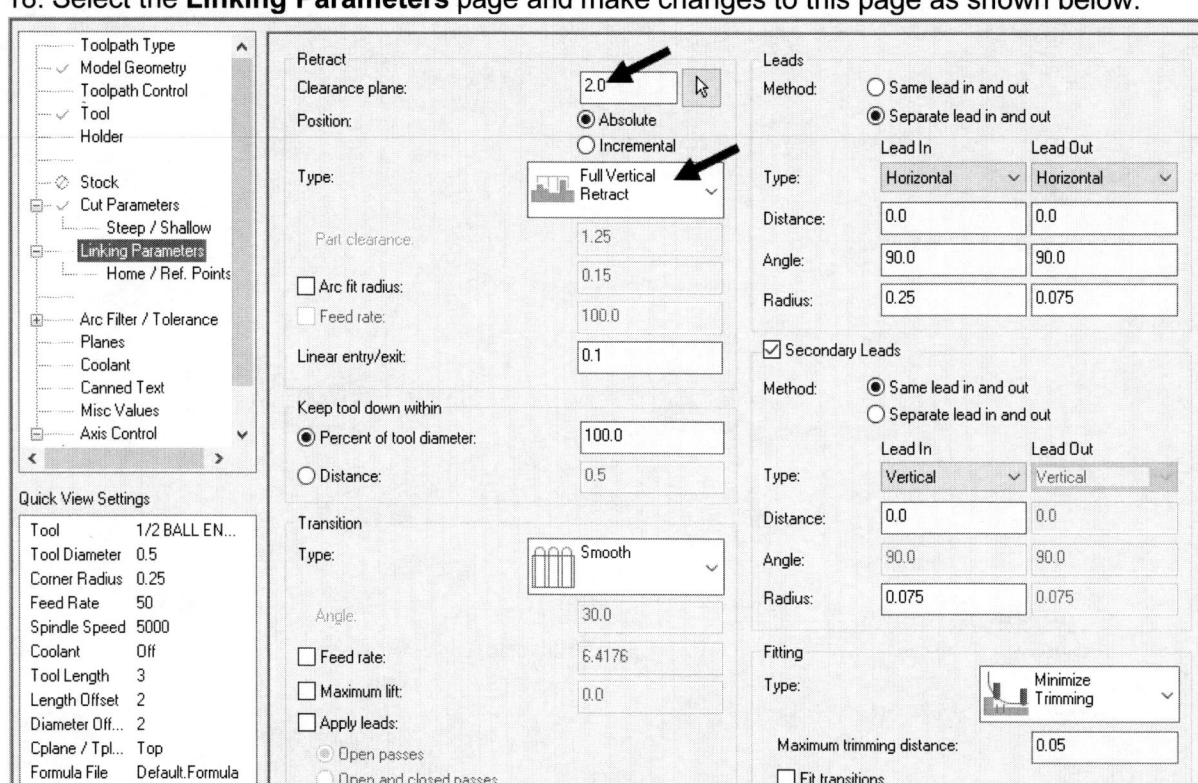

19. Select the **Arc Filter / Tolerance** page, set the **Total tolerance** to .001 and make changes to this page as shown below. Make note of the percentage values used in each tolerance.

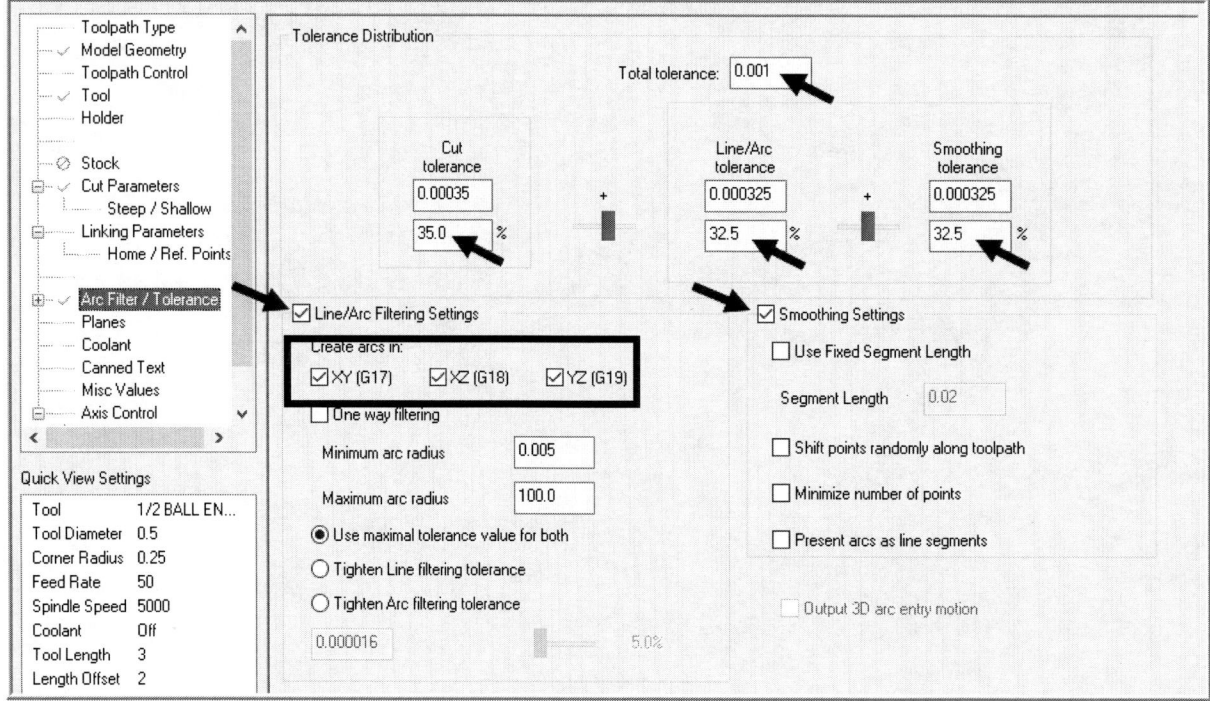

For finishing toolpaths, a tighter tolerance, and an increased **Surface quality** setting will produce the most desirable results.

One way filtering forces the filtering function to filter only from one side of the surface to the other (apply the filtering routine in one direction only). This is effective to avoid a wavy effect between passes of the filtering algorithm.

Smoothing Settings
CNC controllers have a preference for the way they receive coordinate data during high speed machining. Some prefer even spaced points, some prefer a minimal number of points, some prefer no arcs, etc. Make selections here accordingly and use high speed machining modes if your machine/control has support for them.

20. Select **Coolant** from the list on the left and turn the coolant on.

21. Select the OK button  to exit **Surface High Speed Toolpaths - Raster**.

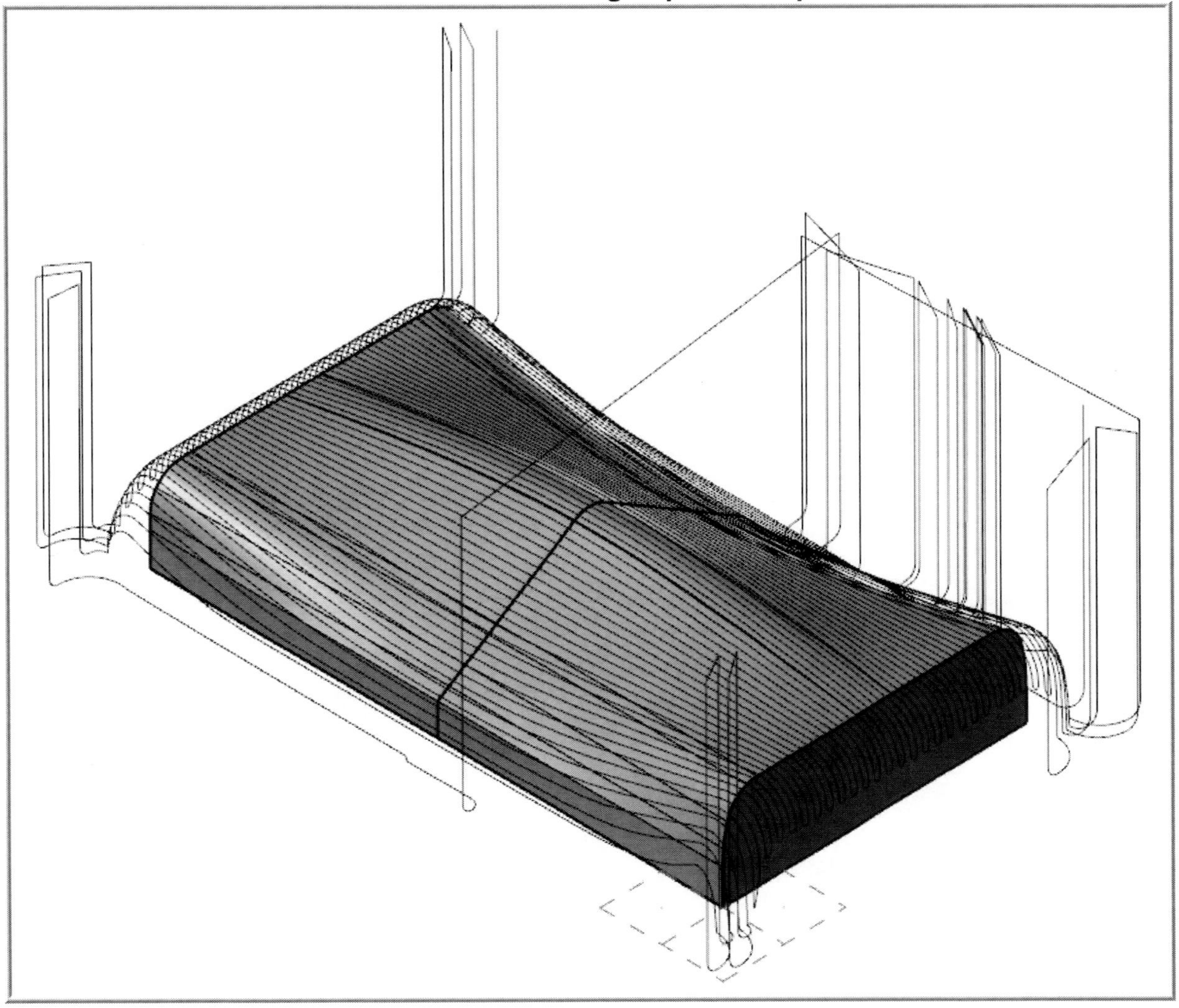

TASK 9:
OPTIMIZE THE RASTER TOOLPATH

➲ The toolpath could be optimized to limit some of the areas being cut. The corners of the part, the toolpath is moving excessively deep in Z. The toolpath is also arcing over the ends of the part in X. Finally, the very front and very back of the part do not need tool motion applied since those faces have already been cut.

➲ To clean up this toolpath, a Containment Boundary will be created, and an Angle Limit will be applied.

1. Create a **new level** for the Containment Boundary and make it the active level.

2. On the **Wireframe** tab, in the **Shapes** section, select **Rectangle**.

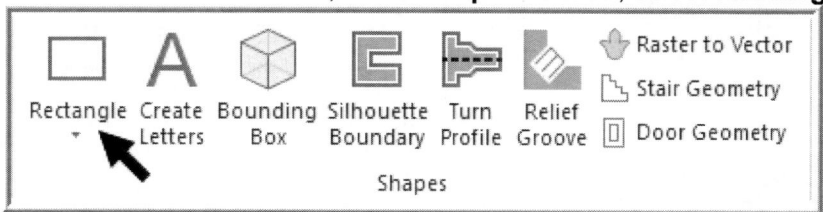

3. Use **Fastpoint** to define the first corner by pressing the spacebar. Input **0,-0.5** and press **Enter**.

```
0,-0.5
```

4. Set the Width at **-4.625** and the Height to **3.50.** Click **Ok** to complete the rectangle.

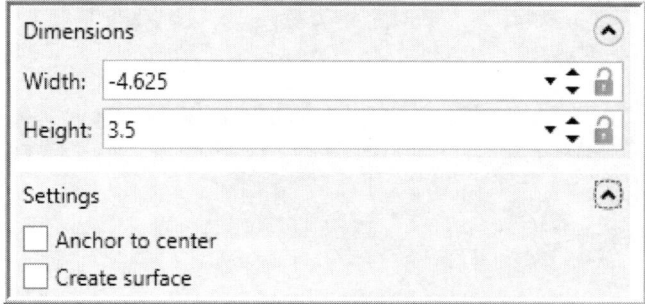

5. Level 1 can now be turned back on. The completed boundary and original part shown below. This boundary will contain the toolpath to the end of the part in X but allow it to machine completely across the part in Y.

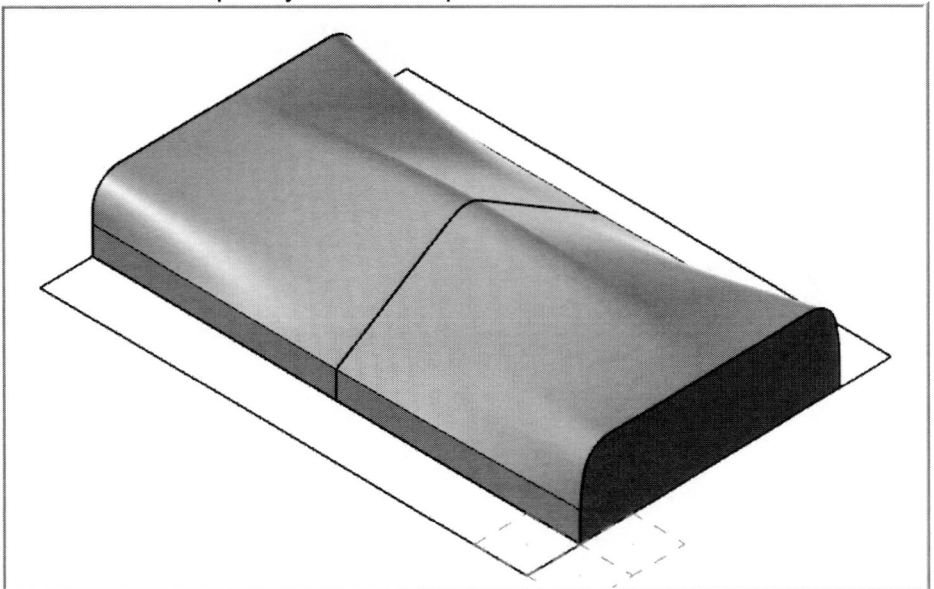

6. Click on **Parameters** for the Raster Toolpath and then select **Toolpath Control**.
7. Click the Boundary chain selection button.

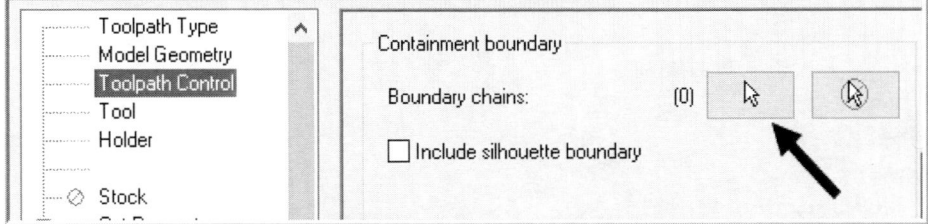

8. Select the rectangle that was just created. Click **Ok**.

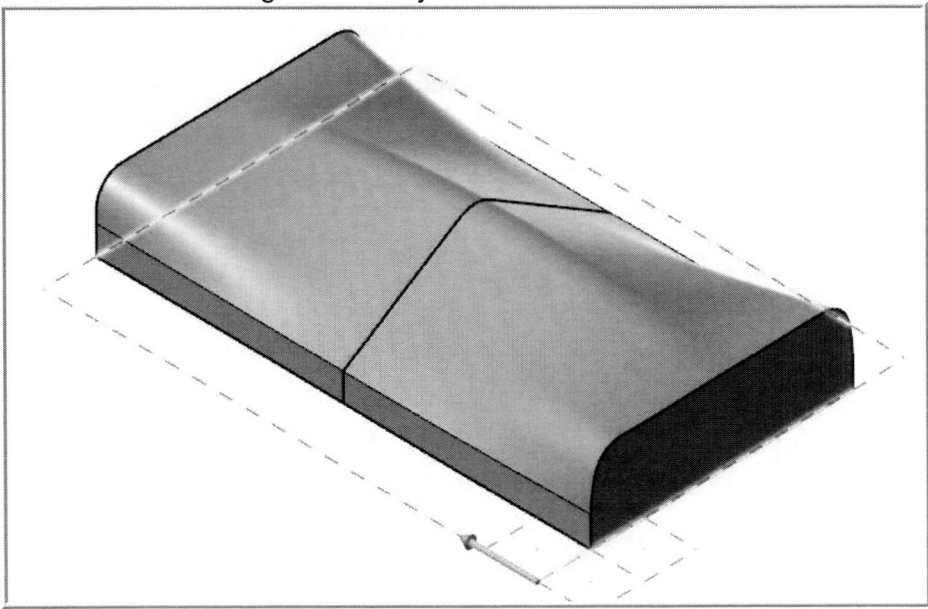

9. From the left menu, select **Steep/Shallow**. Set the To angle at **89** degrees.

10. Click **Ok** to compete the toolpath edits.
11. **Rebuild** the dirty operation is necessary.

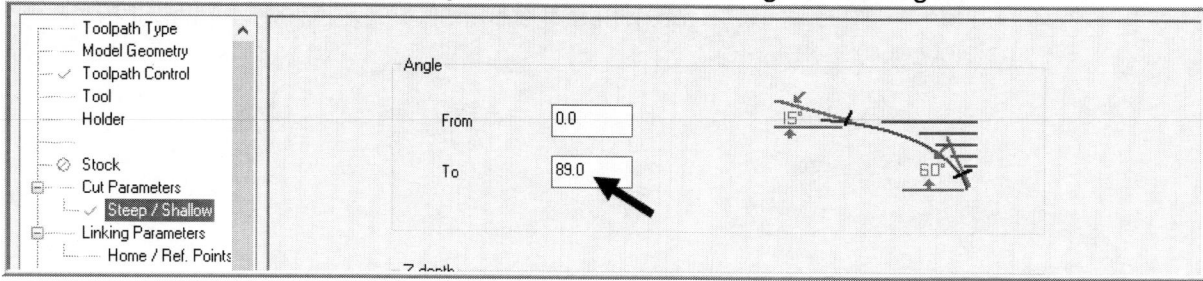

➲ The optimized toolpath no longer machines the front or back face, does not arc over the ends in X, and does not extend excessively deep in Z at the corners.

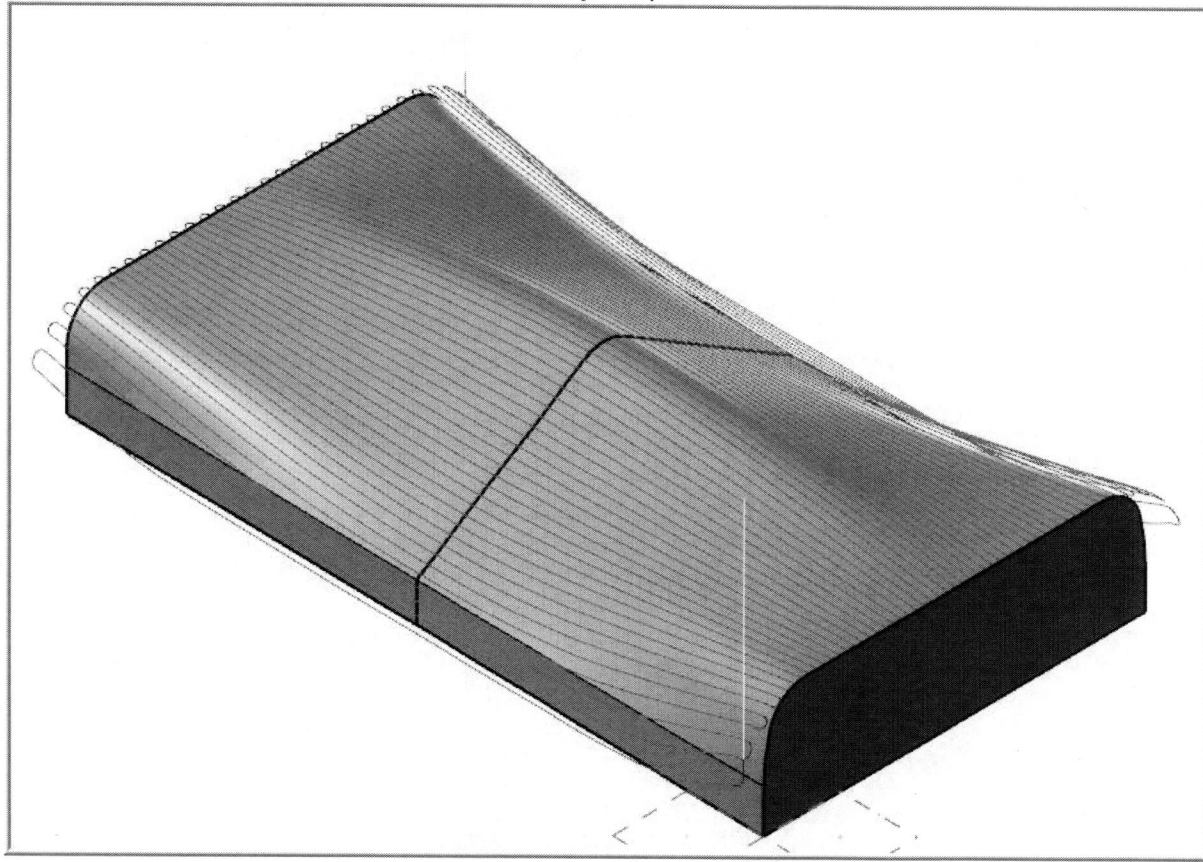

TASK 10:
VERIFY THE TOOLPATH

1. Right mouse click in the graphics area and click on **Isometric**.
2. In the **Toolpaths Manager** pick all the operations to verify by picking the **Select all operations** icon.
3. Select the **Verify selected operations** icon.
4. **Maximize** the Backplot/Verify window if required.
5. Activate the **Follow** option in the **Toolpath** section of the **Home** tab.
6. Activate the options shown below in the **Visibility** section of the **Home** tab. **Initial Stock not** activated.

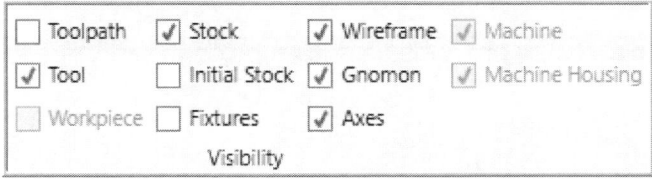

7. At the top of the screen select the **Verify** tab and activate the **Color Loop**.
8. In the lower part of the screen now set the run Speed to slow by moving the slider bar pointer over to the left as shown below.

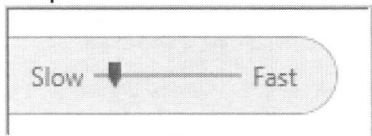

9. Now select the **Play** Simulation button to review the toolpaths.

➲ The verified toolpaths are shown below:

10. Select the **Close** button [×] in the top right hand corner to exit Verify.

TASK 11:
POST AND CREATE THE CNC CODE FILE

1. Ensure all the operations are selected by picking the **Select alloperations** icon  from the Toolpaths Manager.
2. Select the **Post selected operations** button from the Toolpaths Manager.

Toolpaths

3. In the Post processing window, make the necessary changes as shown below:

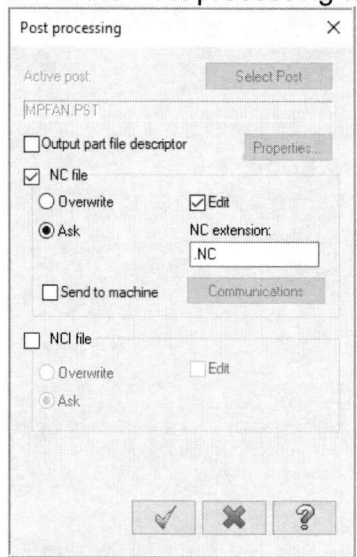

Post processing

Active post: Select Post
MPFAN.PST

☐ Output part file descriptor   Properties...
☑ NC file
   ○ Overwrite   ☑ Edit
   ◉ Ask   NC extension:
                         .NC
   ☐ Send to machine   Communications

☐ NCI file
   ○ Overwrite   ☐ Edit
   ◉ Ask

4. Select the **OK** button to continue.
5. Ensure same name as your Mastercam part file name is in the NC File name field.
6. Select the Save button.
7. The CNC code file opens up in the default editor:

```
MILL-LESSON-10.NC ×
    7    ( T1 | 1/2 BULL ENDMILL 0.125 RAD | H1 | XY STOCK TO LEAVE - .02 | Z STOCK TO LEAVE - 0. )
    8    ( T2 | 1/2 BALL ENDMILL | H2 )
    9    N1 G20
   10    N2 G0 G17 G40 G49 G80 G90
   11    N3 T1 M6
   12    N4 G0 G90 G54 X-4.8805 Y-.1923 A0. S2500 M3
   13    N5 G43 H1 Z1.25 M8
   14    N6 Z.9114
   15    N7 G1 Z.7114 F12.
   16    N8 X-4.5805
   17    N9 X-.0505
   18    N10 X.2495
   19    N11 G0 Z.8114
   20    N12 Z1.1
```

8. Select the ☒ in the top right corner to exit the CNC editor.

➲ This completes Mill-Lesson-10.

MILL-LESSON-10-EXERCISE-A

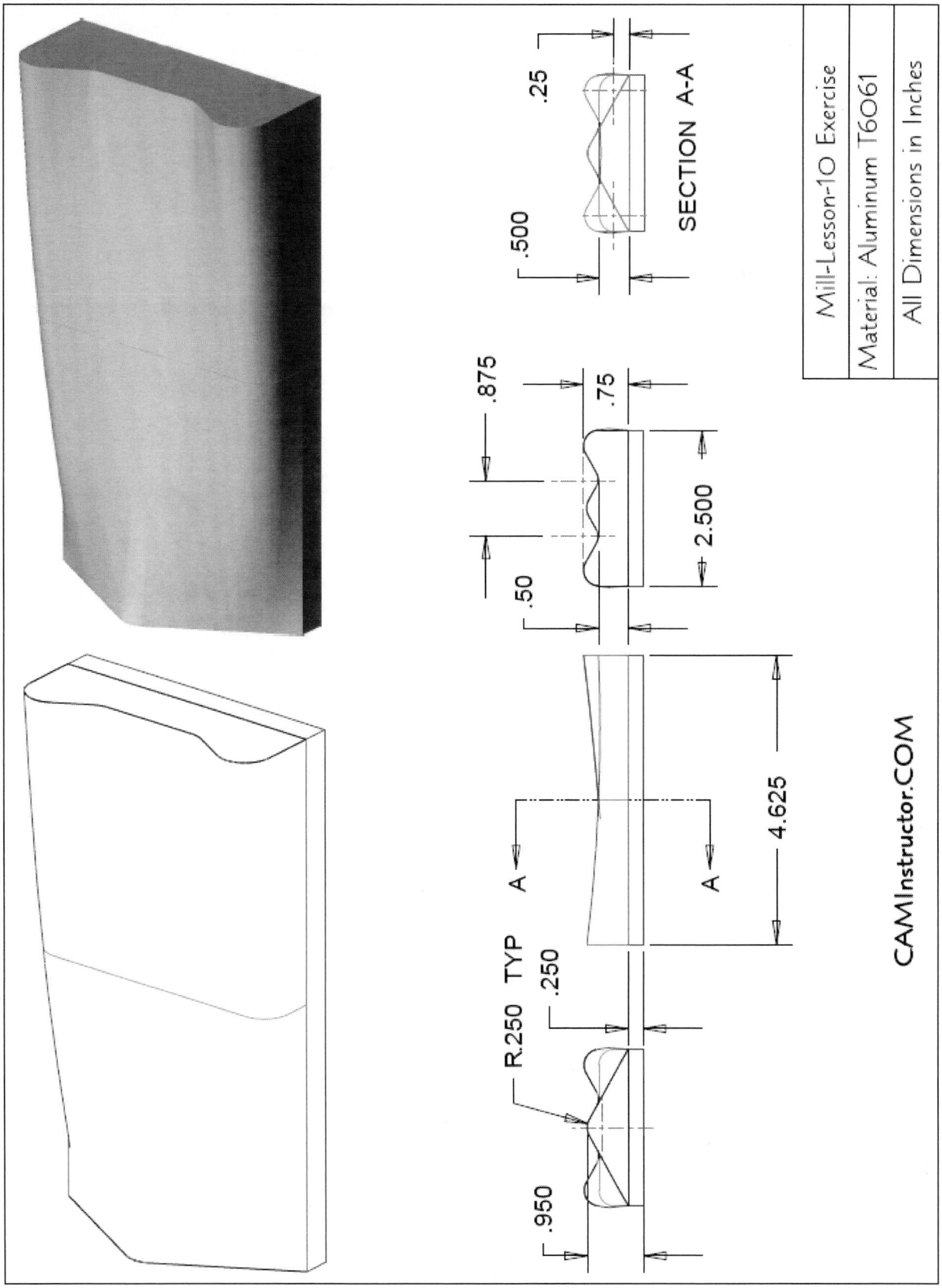

SECTION A-A

.25

.500

.875

.75

2.500

.50

4.625

A

A

R.250 TYP

.250

.950

Mill-Lesson-10 Exercise

Material: Aluminum T6O61

All Dimensions in Inches

CAMInstructor.COM

MILL-LESSON-10-EXERCISE-B

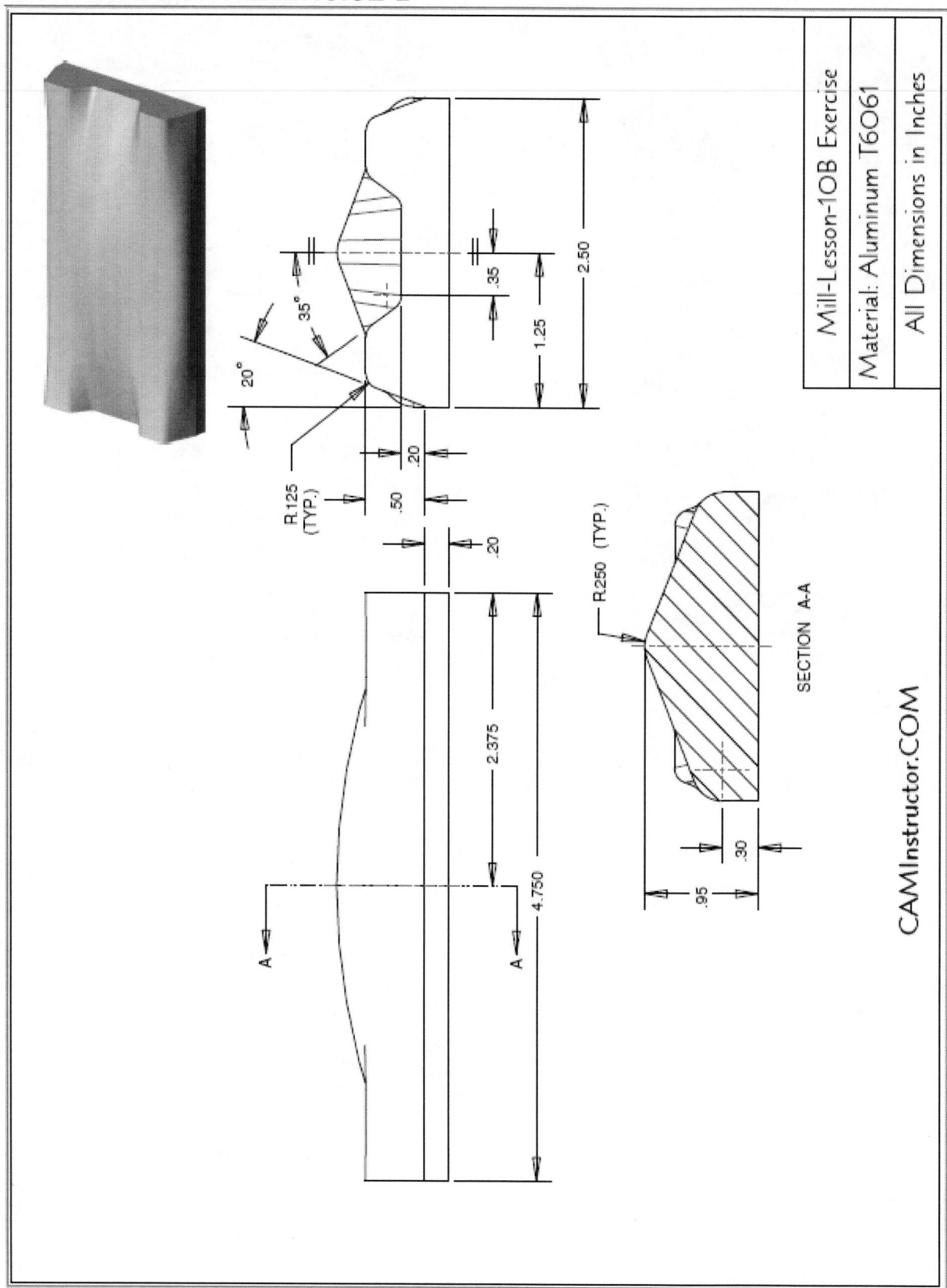

Mill-Lesson-10B Exercise

Material: Aluminum T6061

All Dimensions in Inches

SECTION A-A

CAMInstructor.COM

Mastercam 2022

TRAINING
GUIDE

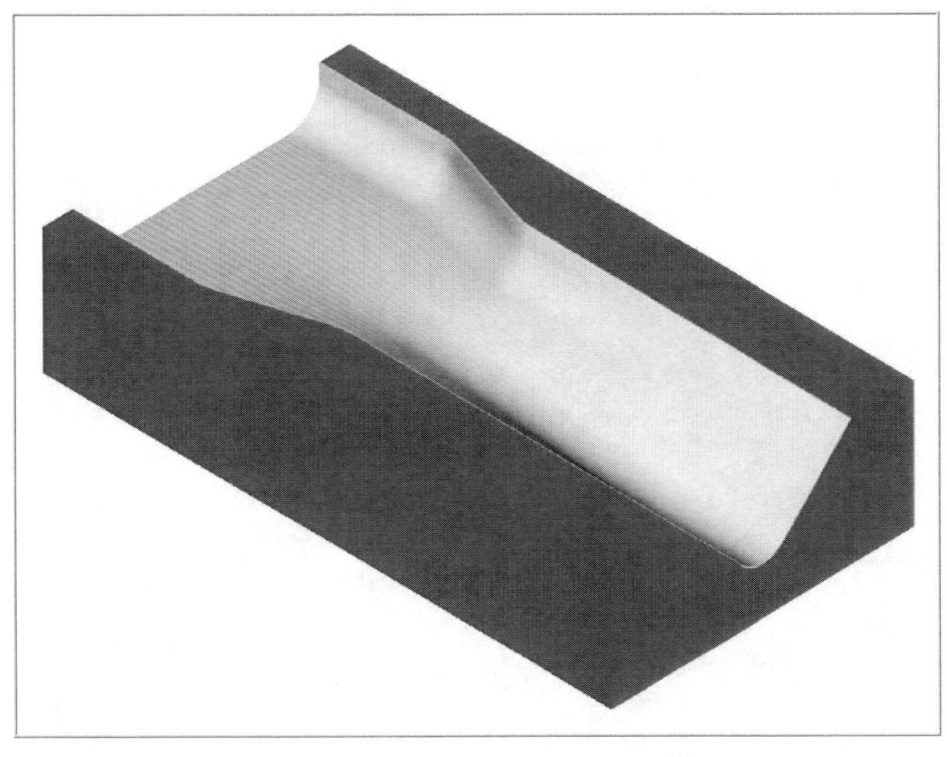

MILL-LESSON-11

SURFACE HIGH SPEED AREA ROUGHING
& FINISH FLOWLINE TOOLPATHS

camInstructor

Objectives

You will create the geometry for Mill-Lesson-11, and then generate the toolpaths to machine the part on a CNC vertical milling machine. This Lesson covers the following topics:

➲ **Create a 3-dimensional drawing by:**
Creating lines.
Creating arcs.
Trimming geometry.
Creating a net surface.

➲ **Establish Stock Setup settings:**
Material for the part.
Feed calculation.

➲ **Generate a 3-dimensional milling toolpath consisting of:**
Surface High Speed Area Roughing.
Finish Flowline.

➲ **Inspect the toolpath using Mastercam's Verify and Backplot by:**
Launching the Verify function to machine the part on the screen.
Generating the NC- code.

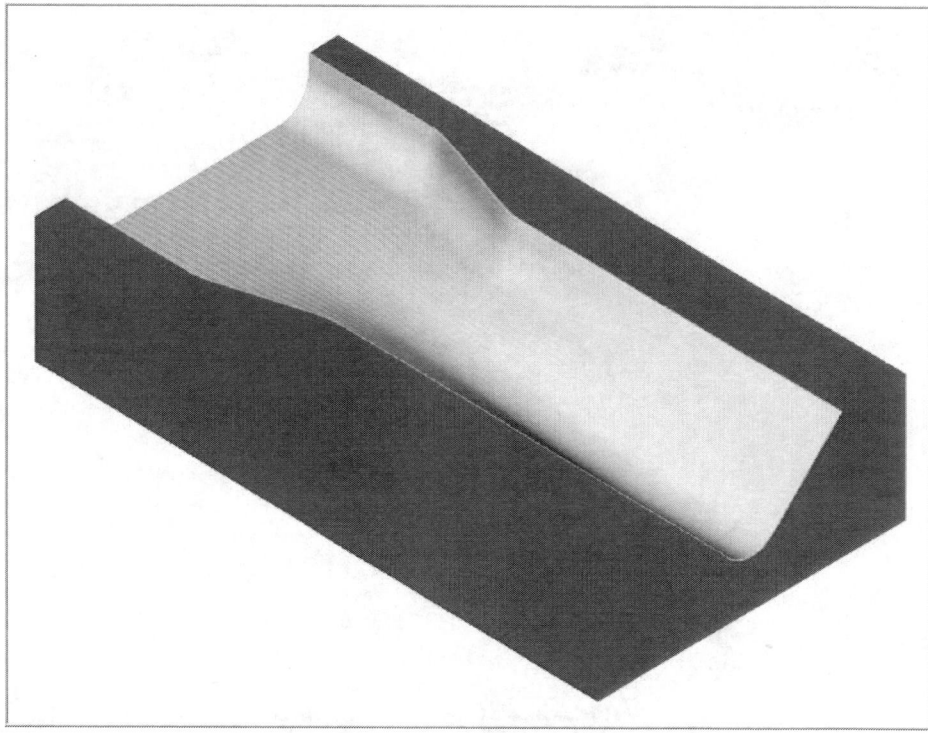

MILL-LESSON-11 DRAWING

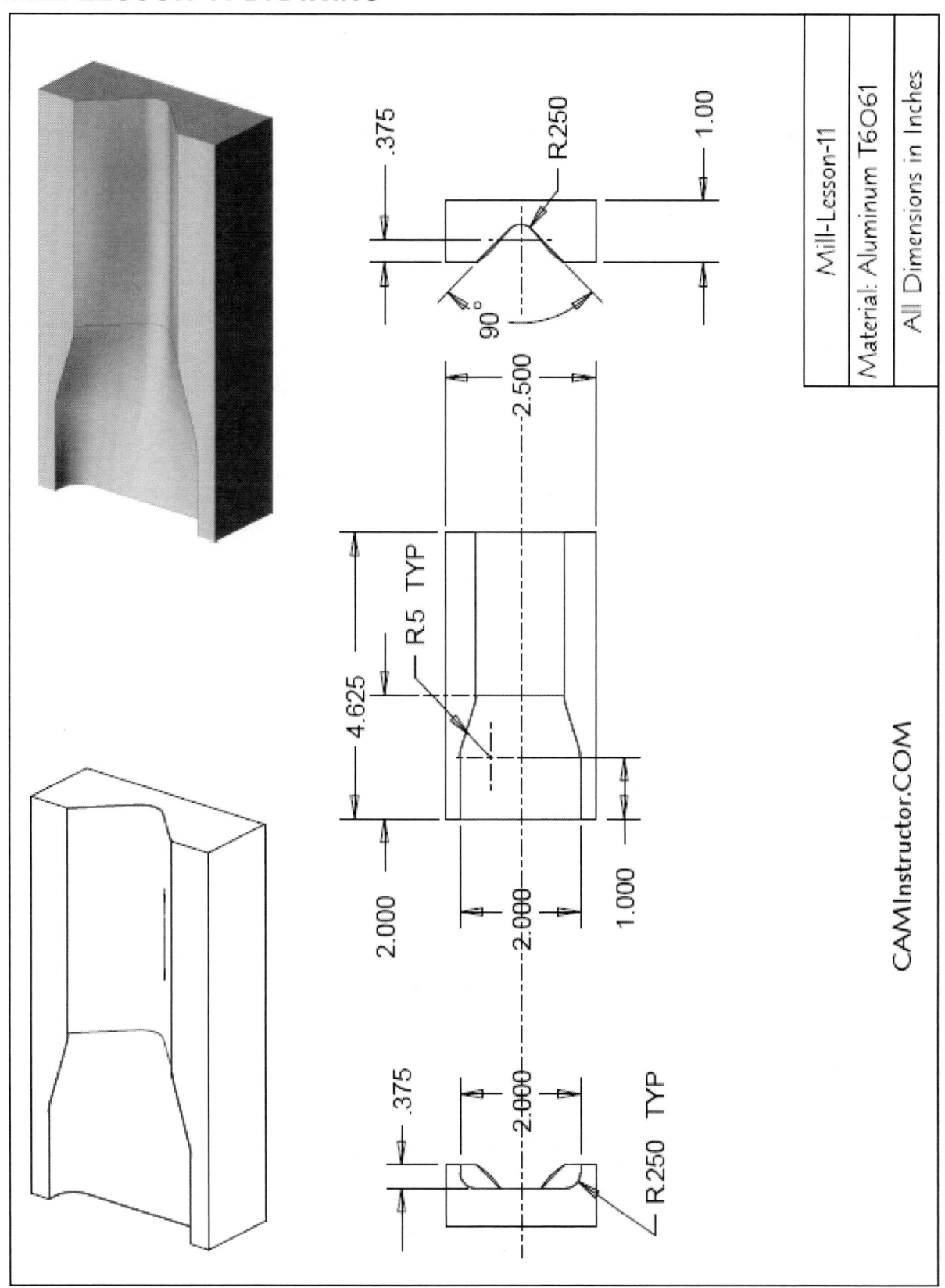

.375

R250

1.00

90°

2.500

R5 TYP

4.625

2.000

2.000

1.000

.375

2.000

R250 TYP

Mill-Lesson-11

Material: Aluminum T6O61

All Dimensions in Inches

CAMInstructor.COM

TOOL LIST

0.500 diameter bull end mill with a 0.125 corner radius to rough machine.
0.500 diameter ball end mill to finish machine.

MILL-LESSON-11 - THE PROCESS

Geometry Creation

TASK 1: Setting the environment
TASK 2: Create geometry – right hand section
TASK 3: Trim right hand section geometry
TASK 4: Create geometry – left hand section
TASK 5: Create the profile
TASK 6: Trim profile geometry
TASK 7: Mirror profile geometry
TASK 8: Create the net surface
TASK 9: Save the drawing

Toolpath Creation

TASK 10: Define the rough stock using stock setup
TASK 11: Rough machine using surface high speed Area Roughing
TASK 12: Finish machine using finish flowline
TASK 13: Verify the toolpath
TASK 14: Save the updated Mastercam file
TASK 15: Post and create the CNC code file

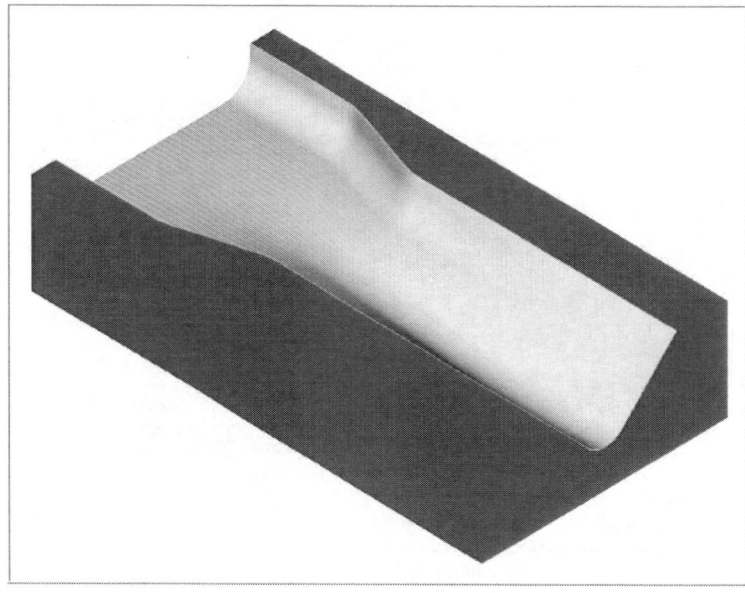

TASK 1:
SETTING THE ENVIRONMENT
⮑ Before starting the geometry creation, you should set up the grid and machine type as outlined in the **Setting the environment** section at the beginning of this text:
1. Set up the Grid. This will help identify the location of the origin.
2. Set the machine type to the Default Mill.

TASK 2:
CREATE GEOMETRY – RIGHT HAND SECTION
X0 Y0 Z0 UPPER LEFT CORNER
⮑ The top of the material is at Z 0. The base of the material and the 4.625 x 2.500 dimensions have been previously machined to size.
⮑ In this task you will create the right hand section that will be used to create the net surface. First will be the creation of line 1 next will be Arc 1 followed by line 2 and 3.

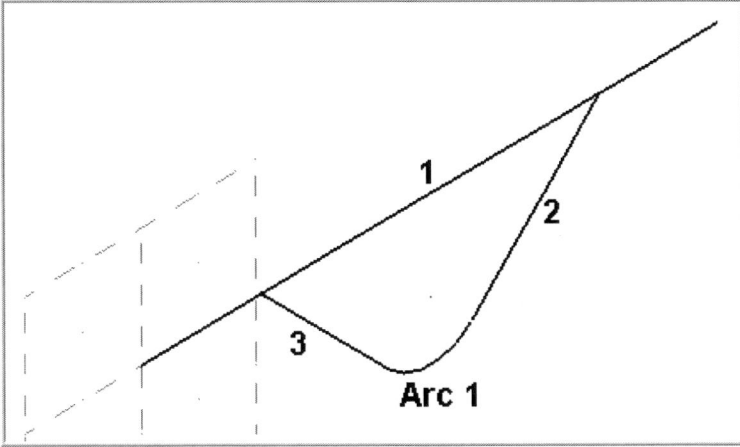

⮑ **Create right hand side section**
1. Select the **View tab** and ensure the **Planes Manager is set to display**.

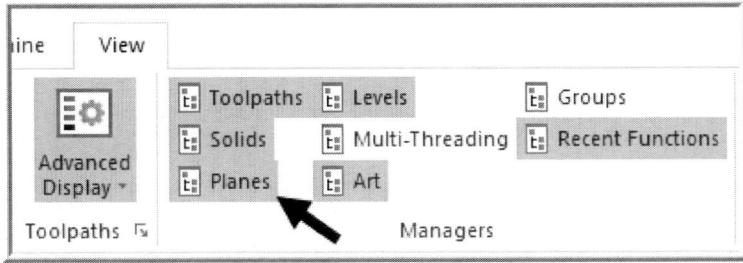

2. Right mouse click in the graphics area and toggle to **2D construction**. The **Z value** should be at **0**.

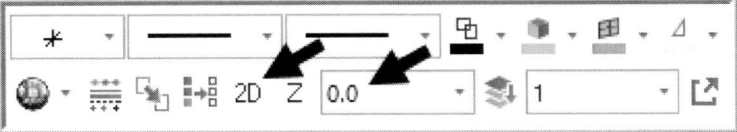

3. Right mouse click in the graphics area and click on **Isometric**. Note that the Plane Manager has changed slightly to indicate an Isometric view in the **Gview** column.

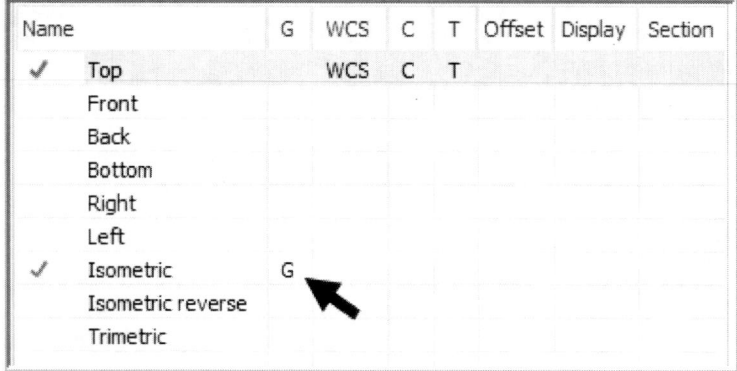

4. Now open up the drop down menu for **Follow rules** 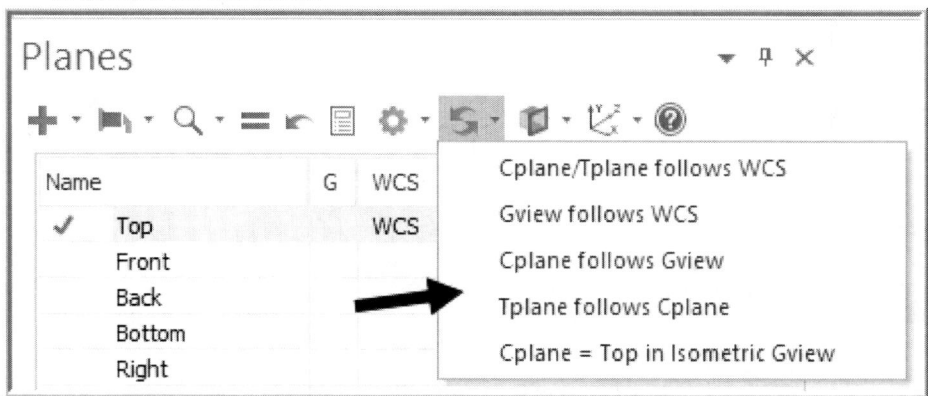 and **remove all the check marks** to cancel all the rules.

Please Note:
The reason for cancelling all the rules is so that when working through this lesson you will have to make a **specific action** in the **Planes Manager** to change the **Cplane -** the Construction Plane.

5. Now click in the **C column (Construction Plane)** for the **Right** plane. The view is still set to Isometric but construction of the geometry will now take place on the Right Side plane.
Take note at the bottom of the screen **CPLANE: Right TPLANE:Top WCS:Top** as shown below right.

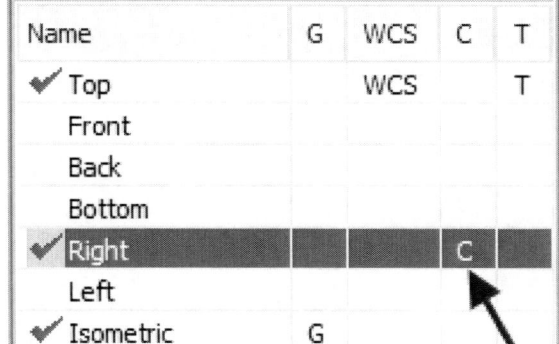

CPLANE: Right   TPLANE: Top   WCS: Top

⊃ **Create Line #1**

6. Select the **Wireframe** tab and in the **Lines** section click on **Line Endpoints.** On the graphics screen you are prompted: **Specify the first endpoint** and the Line Endpoints panel appears

7. To satisfy the prompt **Specify the first endpoint** move the cursor over to the **Origin** (X0Y0) a visual cue appears. 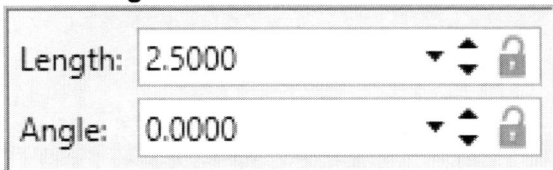, **pick the origin**.

8. Click in the space for **Length** and enter a value of **2.5** and then hit the tab key. In the space for **Angle** enter a value of **0** and hit enter.

Length:	2.5000	▾ ♦ 🔒
Angle:	0.0000	▾ ♦ 🔒

9. Click on the **OK** icon to complete this feature.

⊃ **Create Arc #1**

10. Select the **Wireframe** tab if required and in the **Arcs** section select **Circle Center Point**.

11. The **Circle Center Point** panel appears and you are prompted to **Enter the center point** enter **.25** for the radius and hit enter.

12. To satisfy the prompt **Enter the center point** click the middle mouse button and then hit the spacebar on your keyboard.

13. The **Fastpoint** box now opens. Input **2.5/2,-0.375** and hit the Enter key.

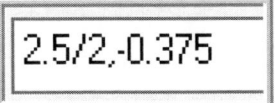

14. Click on the **OK** icon to complete this feature.

⊃ **Create Line #2**

15. Select the **Wireframe** tab if required and in the **Lines** section click on **Line Endpoints**.
16. First click in the space for **Length** and enter a value of **1.0** and then hit the Tab key. In the space for **Angle** enter a value of **45** and hit enter.

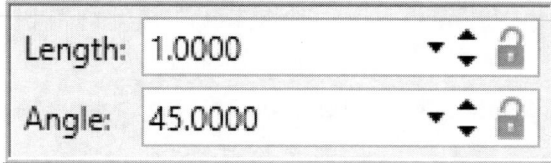

17. On the graphics screen you are prompted: **Specify the first endpoint**. Ensure that the **Tangent** function is activated.
18. To satisfy the prompt **Specify the first endpoint** move the cursor over the area of the circle shown below left. Ensure there is **no visual cue** being displayed and click on this point. After selecting the circle you will be prompted to **Select the line** pick the line shown below:

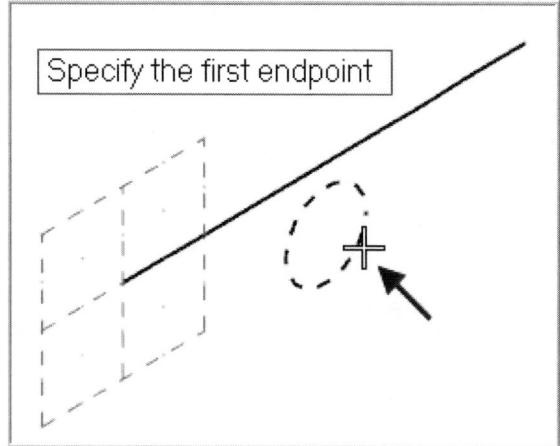
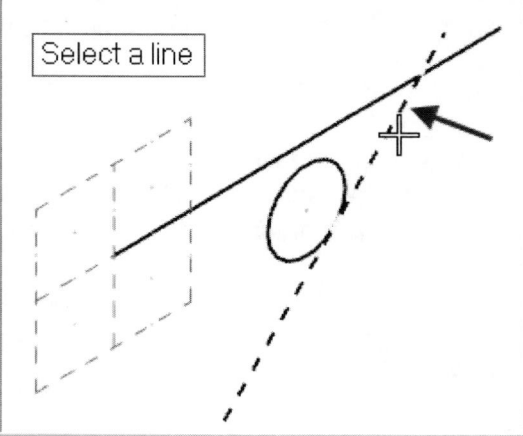

19. Click on the **OK and Create New Operation** icon .

⊃ **Create Line #3**

20. Click in the space for **Length** and enter a value of **1.0** (if required) and then hit the tab key. In the space for **Angle** enter a value of **90+45** and hit enter.

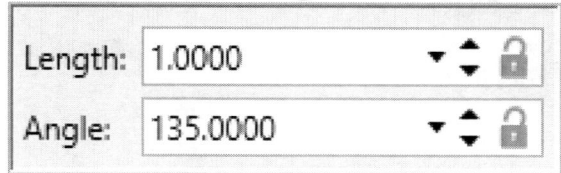

| Length: | 1.0000 |
| Angle: | 135.0000 |

21. On the graphics screen you are prompted: **Specify the first endpoint**. **Ensure** that the **Tangent** function is activated.

22. To satisfy the prompt **Specify the first endpoint** move the cursor over the area of the circle shown below left. Ensure there is **no visual cue** being displayed and click on this point. After selecting the circle you will be prompted to **Select the line** pick the line shown below:

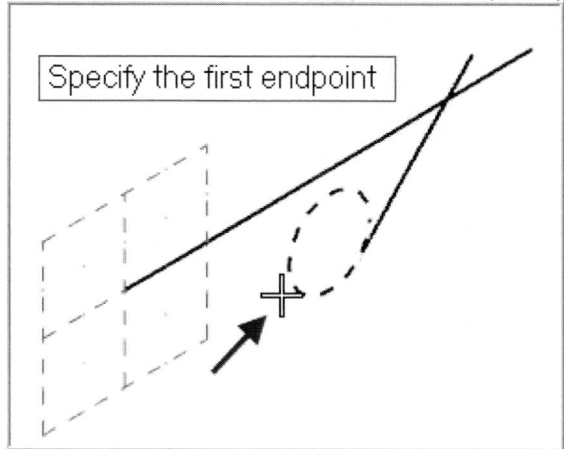
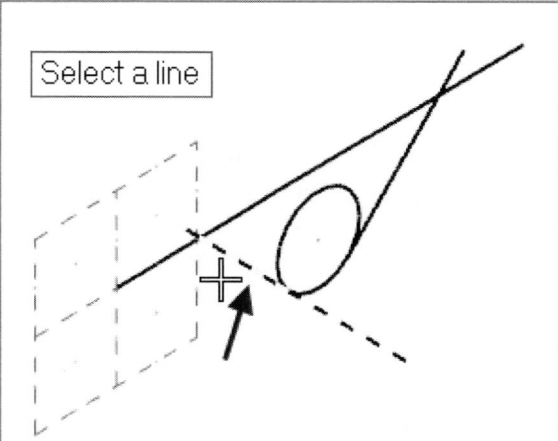

23. Click on the **OK** icon 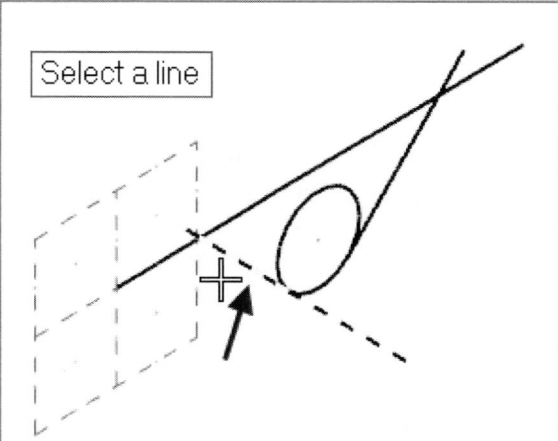 to complete this feature.

TASK 3:
TRIM RIGHT HAND SECTION GEOMETRY

➲ In this task you will trim the geometry using Divide / Delete.

1. In the **Wireframe** tab click on **Divide** in the **Modify** section.
2. The **Divide** panel appears. Activate **Trim** if required.

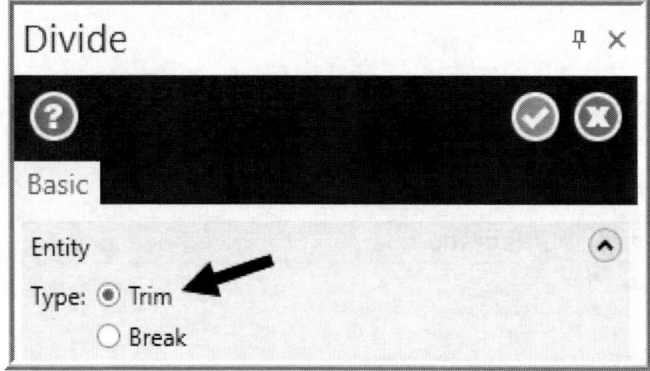

3. You are prompted to **Select the curve to divide / delete**. Move the cursor over the various entities and select in order and position as shown below left:

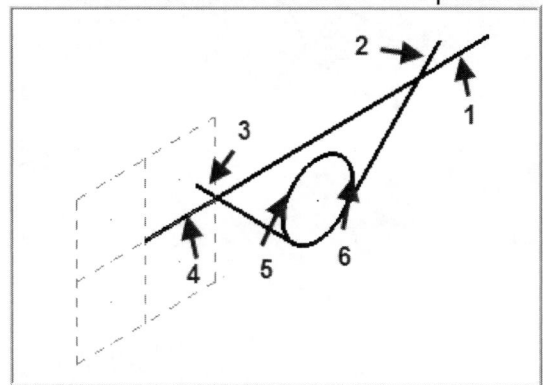
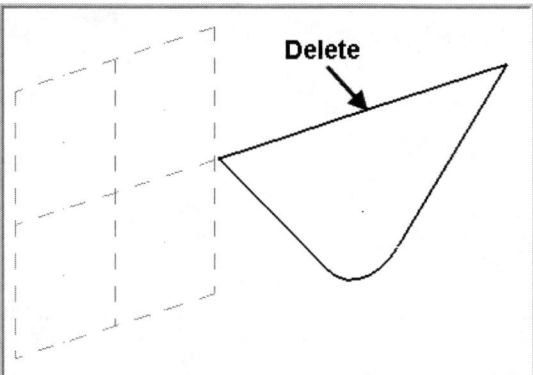

4. Click on the **OK** icon 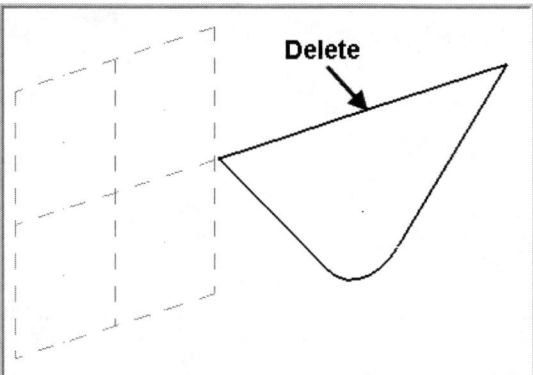 to complete this feature.
5. **Delete** the line shown above right by clicking on the line with the mouse and hitting the **Delete key** on keyboard.

TASK 4:
CREATE GEOMETRY – LEFT HAND SECTION

➲ In this task you will create the left hand section that will be used to create the net surface. First a rectangle will be created and then finally the two arcs will be created using fillet.

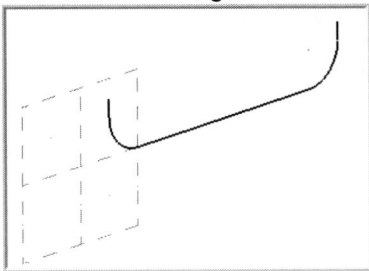

➲ **Create the rectangle.**

1. Right mouse click in the graphics area. Next click in the space for the **Z value** and enter a value of **-4.625** and hit enter.

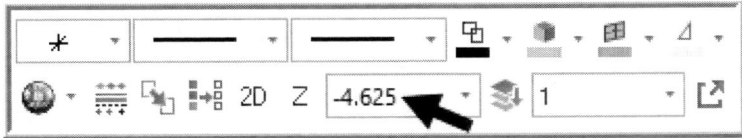

➲ Take note at the bottom of the screen **Z: -4.62500**.

2. **Unzoom** to enable the grid to be seen.
3. Select the **Wireframe** tab at the top of the screen and in the **Shapes** section click on **Rectangle**.
4. Click in the space for **Width** and enter a value of **2.0** and then hit the tab key. In the space for **Height** enter a value of **0.375** and hit enter. The **Anchor to center** option – **should not be activated**

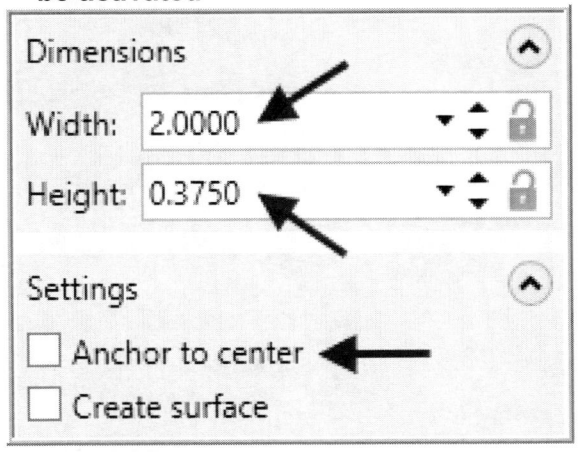

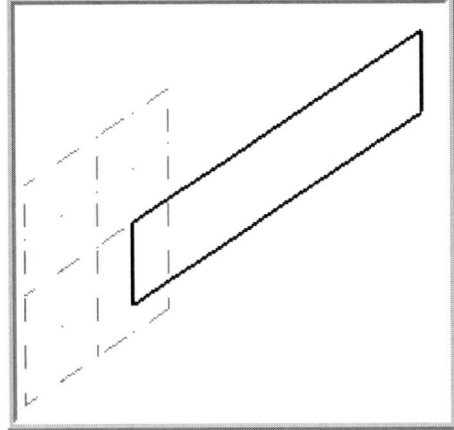

5. To satisfy the prompt click the middle mouse button and then hit the spacebar on your keyboard.
6. The **Fastpoint** box now opens. Input **0.25,-0.375** and hit the Enter key.
7. Click on the **OK** icon to complete this feature.

⮥ The completed rectangle is shown above right.

⮥ **Create Arc #2 and #3**

8. Right mouse click in the graphics area and click on the **Fit** icon 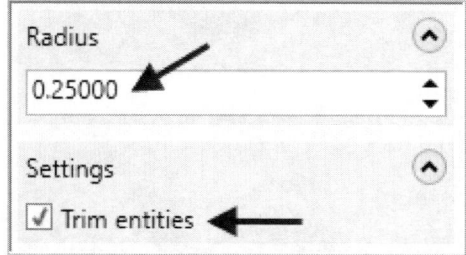.

9. Select the **Wireframe** tab and in the **Modify** section click on **Fillet Entities**.

10. The **Fillet Entities** panel appears. If required activate the **Style** to **Normal** and enter a value of **0.25** for **Radius**.

11. Ensure the **Trim** entities box at the bottom of the panel is check marked to turn the trim on.

12. When prompted to **Fillet: Select an entity,** select entity 1 and 2 as shown below. The fillet radius appears at the corner of entities 1 and 2. To complete the remaining fillet select: entities 2 and 3. The completed geometry is shown below right:

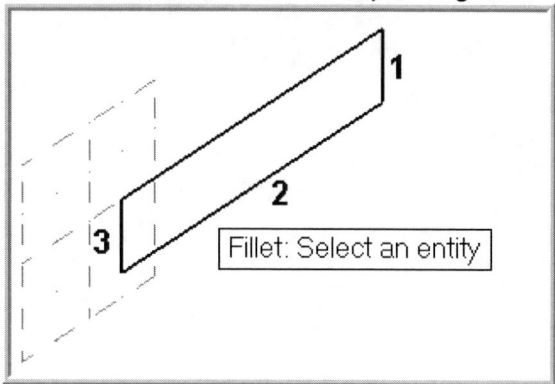
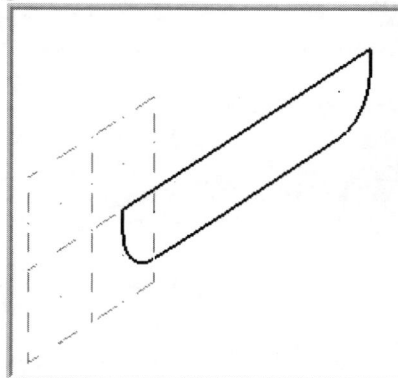

13. Click on the **OK** icon to complete this feature.

⮥ **Delete Construction line**

14. **Delete** the line shown below by clicking on the line with the mouse and hitting the **Delete key** on keyboard.

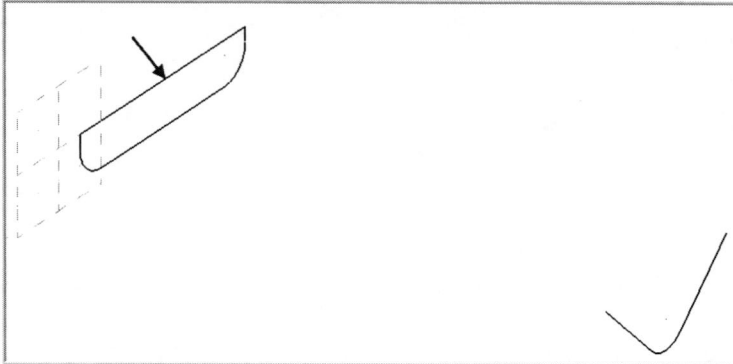

TASK 5:
CREATE THE PROFILE
➲ **Create Line #1, #2, #3, Arc #1 and Arc #2**
➲ It is **recommended** that you watch the **Mill-Lesson-11 Task 5 video** before completing this task.

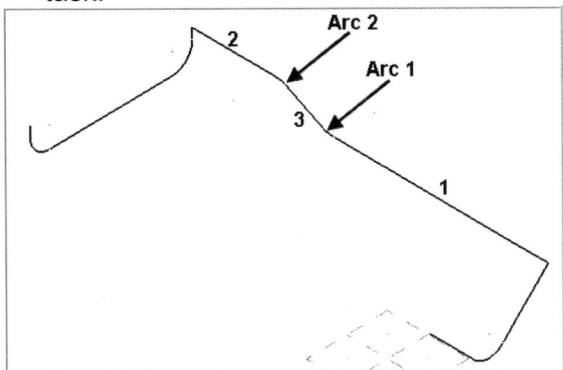

1. Right mouse click in the graphics area. Next click in the space for the **Z value** and enter a value of **0** and hit enter.

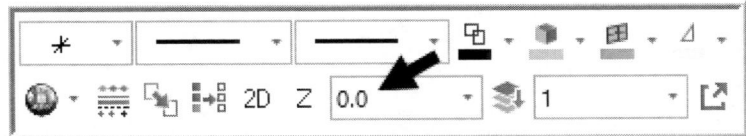

2. Right mouse click in the graphics area and click on **Isometric**.
3. If required toggle the **Planes Manager to display**.
4. In the Plane Manager click in the **C column (Construction Plane)** for **Top**. Take note at the bottom of the screen **CPLANE:TOP TPLANE:TOP WCS:TOP** as shown below right.

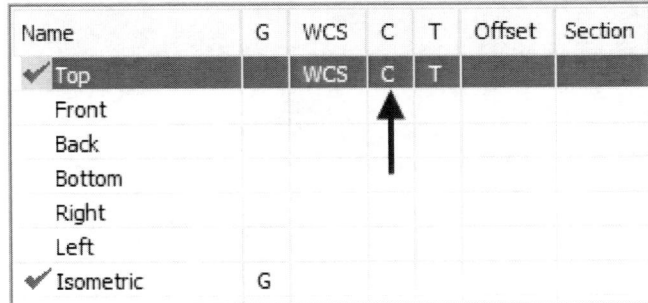

5. Close the Plane Manager.

➲ **Create Line #1**

6. Select the **Wireframe** tab if required and in the **Lines** section click on **Line Endpoints.**

7. To satisfy the prompt **Specify the first endpoint** move the cursor over the endpoint of the line shown below. When the visual cue for endpoint appears pick this point.

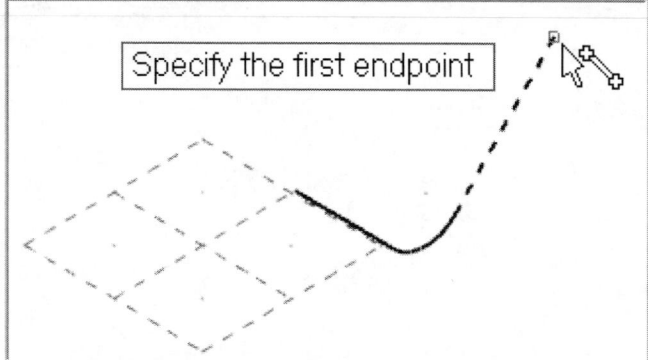

8. Click in the space for **Length** and enter a value of **4.625-2.0** and then hit the tab key. In the space for **Angle** enter a value of **180** and hit enter.

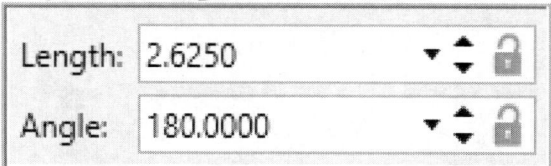

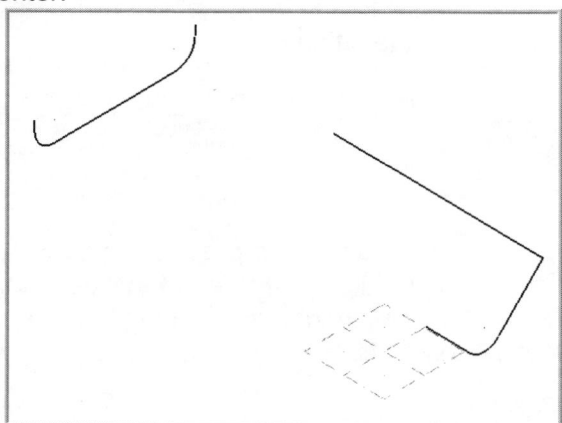

9. Click on the **OK** icon to complete this feature.

➲ The line is shown above right:

⊃ **Create Arc #1**
⊃ **Construction line for Arc #1**

10. Select the **Wireframe** tab if required and in the **Lines** section click on **Line Parallel**.
11. On the graphics screen you are prompted: **Select a line** and the Line Parallel panel appears.
12. First click in the space for **Offset Distance** and input **0.5** then hit **Enter**
13. To satisfy the prompt **Select a line**, move the cursor over the line shown below and select it.

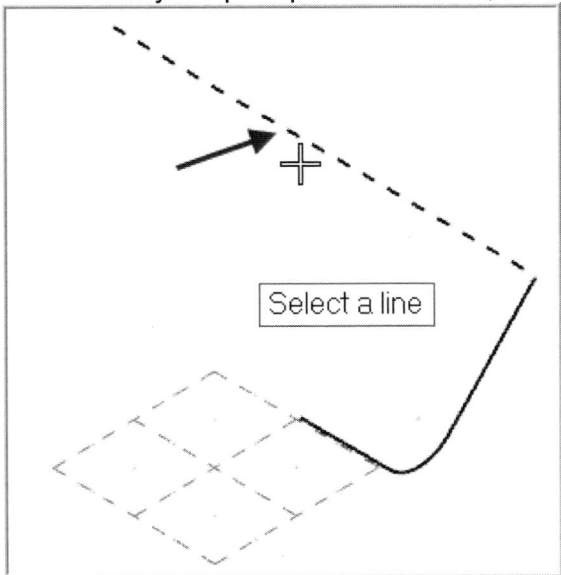

14. To satisfy the next prompt **Indicate the offset direction** move the cursor above the line and pick a point as shown below. The line appears as below right:

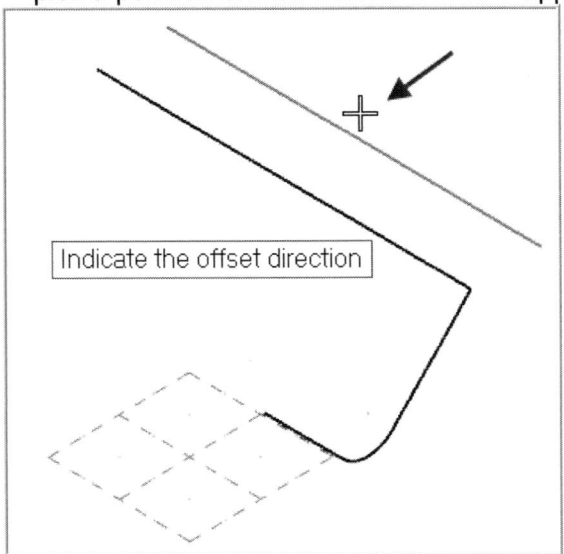 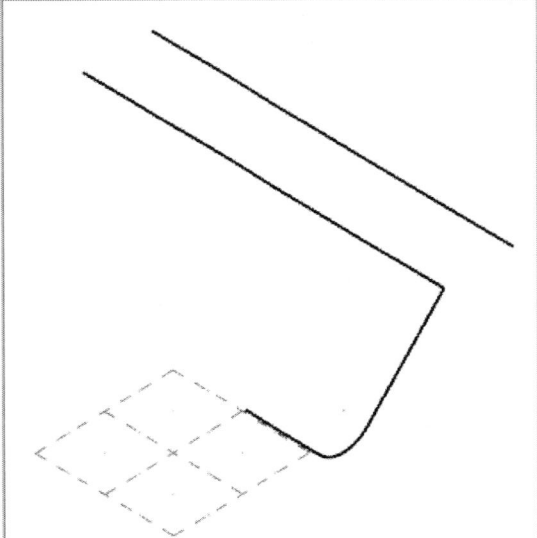

15. Click on the **OK** icon to complete this feature.

16. Select the **Wireframe** tab and in the **Arcs** section open up the drop down menu and select **Arc Polar**.
17. In the **Arc Polar** panel enter a value of **0.5** for **Radius**.
18. Click in the space for the **Start Angle** and enter **180** and hit the tab key. Enter a value of **0** for the **End angle** and hit enter.
19. To satisfy the prompt **Enter the center point** move the cursor over the endpoint of the line shown below left. When the visual cue for endpoint appears pick this point. Activate **Inverted Arc** to place the arc in the correct position **if required**.

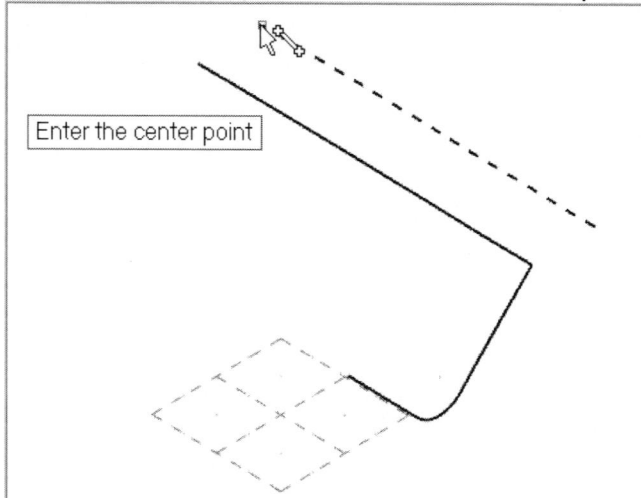
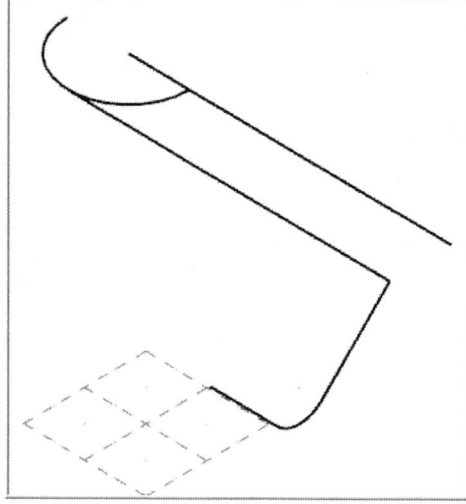

20. Click on the **OK** icon to complete this feature.

➲ The completed arc is shown above right:

➲ **Create Arc #2**
21. Select the **Wireframe** tab if required and in the **Arcs** section select **Circle Center Point**.
22. The **Circle Center Point** panel appears and you are prompted to **Enter the center point** enter **.5** for the radius and hit enter.
23. To satisfy the prompt **Enter the center point** click the middle mouse button and then hit the spacebar on your keyboard.
24. The **Fastpoint** box now opens. Input **-4.625+1.0,1.75** and hit the Enter key.

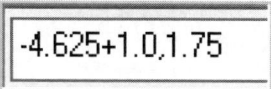

25. Click on the **OK** icon to complete this feature.
➲ The completed geometry is shown below:

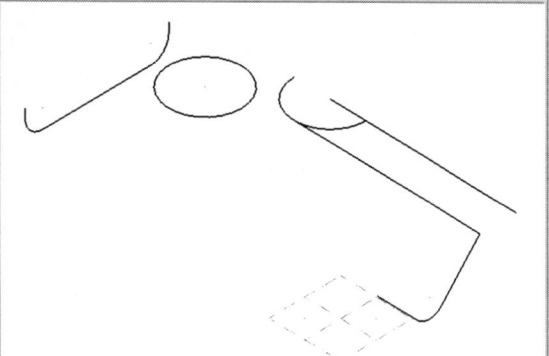

➲ Create Line #2

26. Select the **Wireframe** tab if required and in the **Lines** section click on **Line Endpoints**.
27. On the graphics screen you are prompted: **Specify the first endpoint** and the Line panel appears. **Ensure** that the **Tangent** function is activated.
28. On the graphics screen you are prompted: **Specify the first endpoint** and the Line panel appears. **Note** that the **Tangent** function is activated.
29. To satisfy the prompt **Specify the first endpoint** move the cursor over the area of the circle shown below. Ensure there is **no visual cue** being displayed and click on this point.

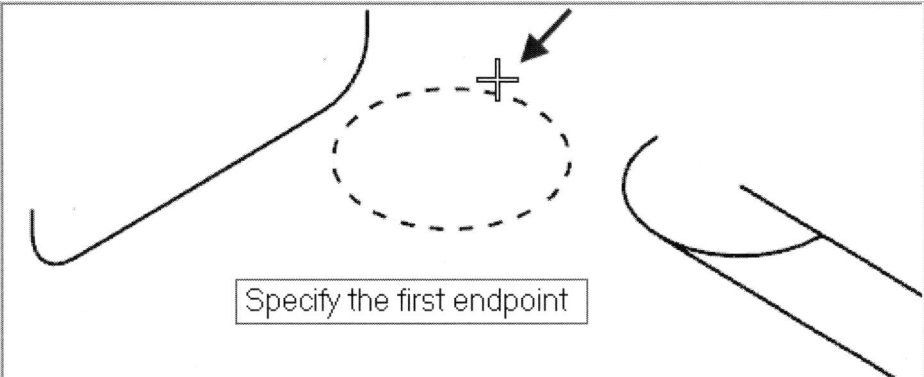

30. To satisfy the prompt **Specify the second endpoint** move the cursor over the endpoint of the line shown below. When the visual cue for endpoint appears pick this point.

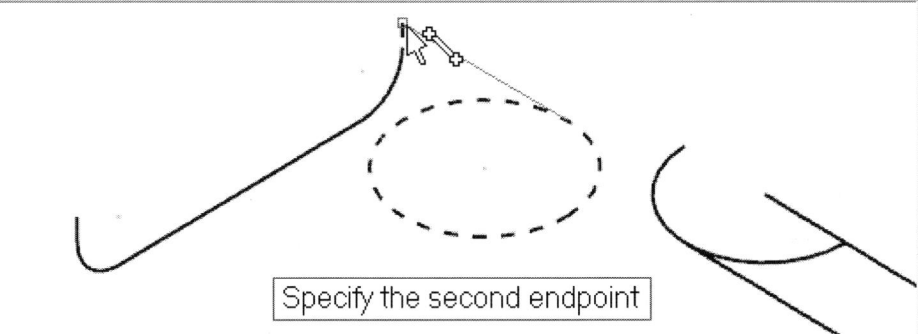

● **Create Line #3**

31. To satisfy the prompt **Specify the first endpoint** move the cursor over the area of the circle shown below. Ensure there is **no visual cue** being displayed and click on this point.

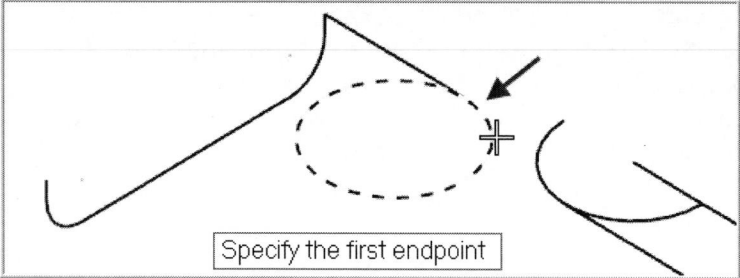

32. To satisfy the prompt **Specify the second endpoint** move the cursor over the area of the circle shown below. Ensure there is **no visual cue** being displayed and click on this point.

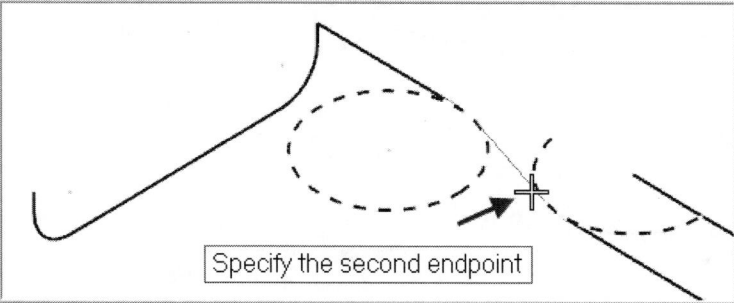

33. Click on the **OK** icon to complete this feature.

● The completed geometry is below:

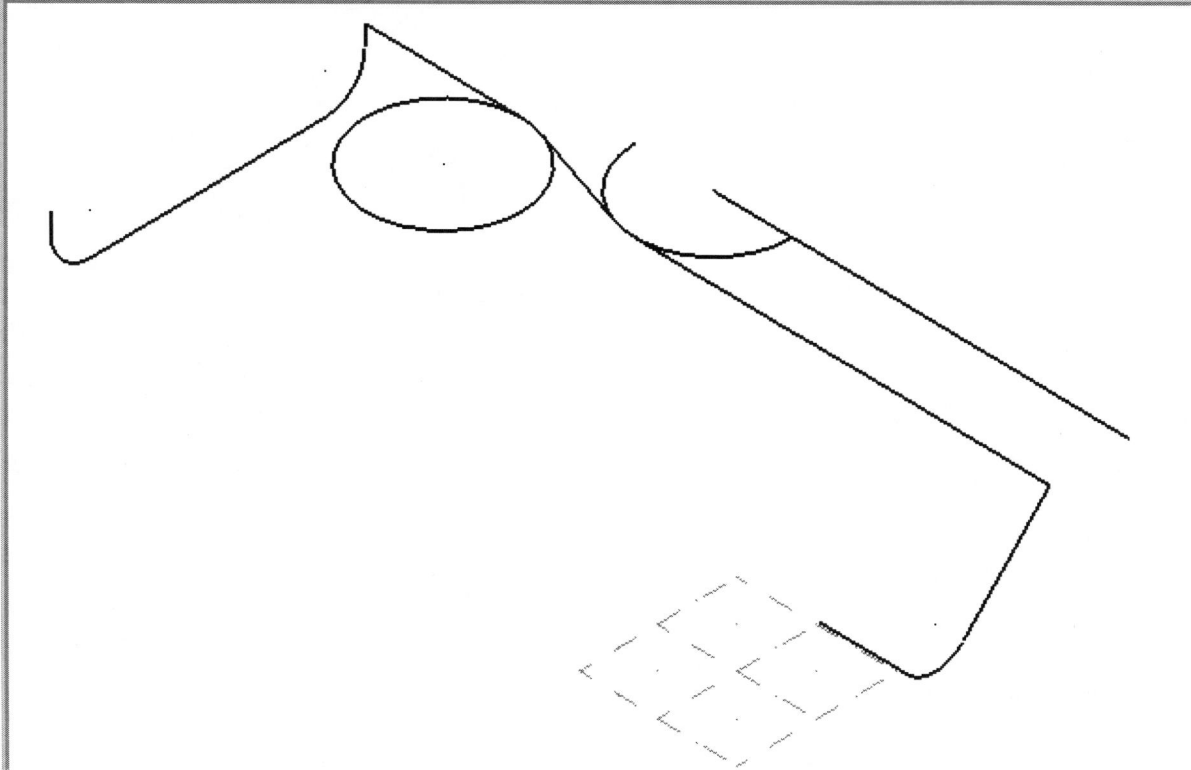

TASK 6:
TRIM PROFILE GEOMETRY

➲ In this task you will trim the geometry using Divide / Delete.

1. In the **Wireframe** tab click on **Divide** in the **Modify** section.
2. The **Divide** panel appears. Activate **Trim** if required.
3. You are prompted to **Select the curve to Divide / Delete**. Move the cursor over the various entities and select in order and position as shown below left:

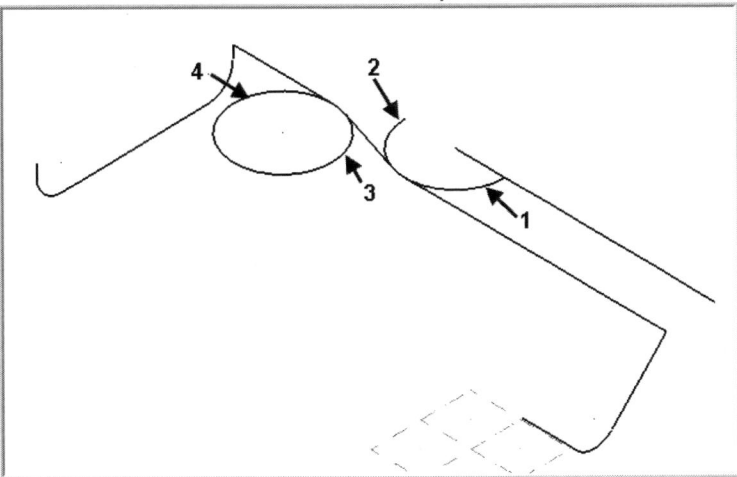

4. Click on the **OK** icon ⊙ to complete this feature.
5. **Delete** the line shown above right by clicking on the line and hitting the delete key on the keyboard.

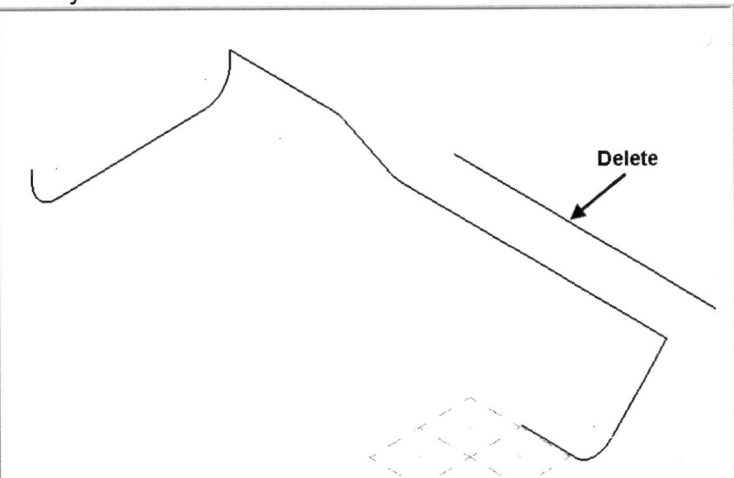

TASK 7:
MIRROR PROFILE GEOMETRY
➲ In this task you will mirror the geometry.
1. Select the **Transform** tab and in the **Position** section select **Mirror**.
2. You are first prompted to **Select entities**. Click on **line 1**, then click on **arc 2**, then click on **line 3**, then click on **arc 4**, then click on **line 5** as shown below: Note, the lines and arcs will become dashed as you select them.

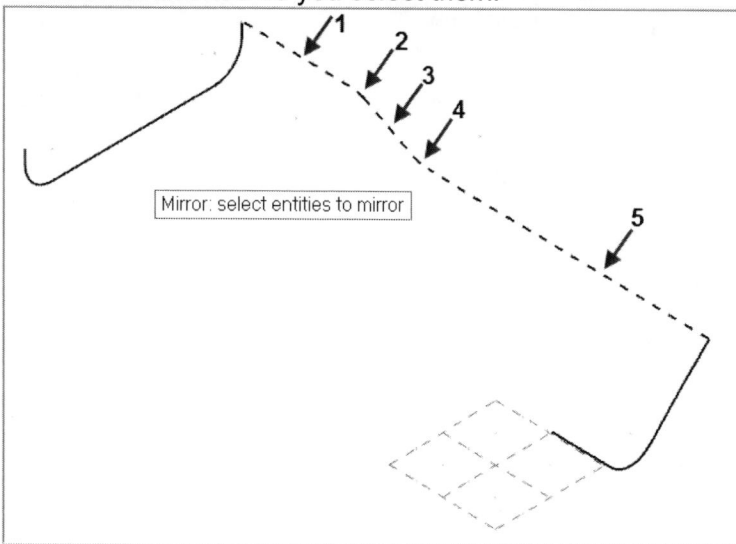

Mirror: select entities to mirror

3. To move onto the next step you now need to pick the **End Selection** icon.
4. After selecting End Selection the **Mirror** panel appears. Set the following values:

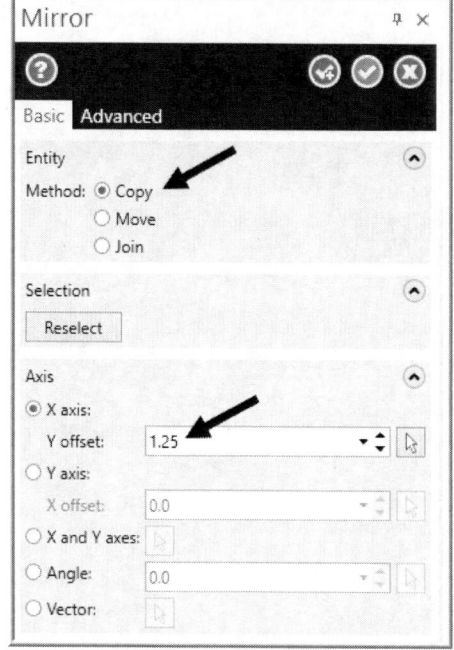
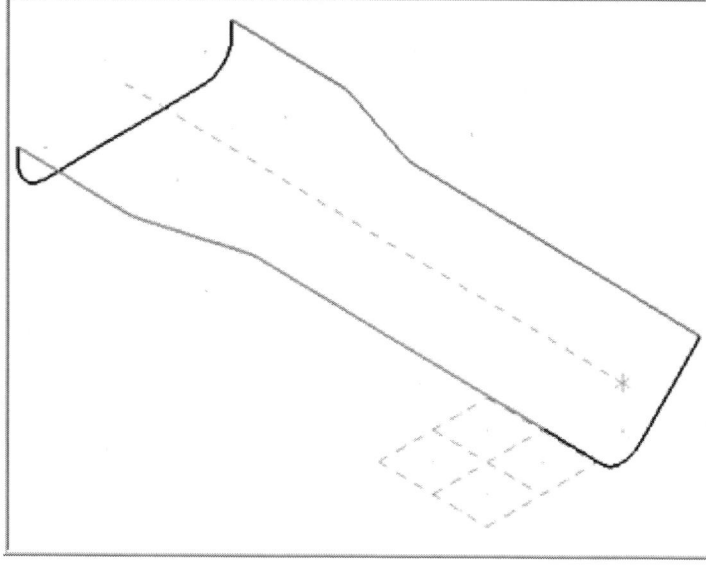

5. Click on the OK icon to complete this feature.

6. Right mouse click in the graphics area and click on the **Clear Colors** icon.

TASK 8:
CREATE THE NET SURFACE
➲ In this task you will create a net surface using the geometry you have just created. The net surface will be created using four chains.

Net Surfaces are surfaces constructed from a network of intersecting curves.

Generally, you chain a minimum of two across curves intersecting with two along curves. The exception is when all of the across contours meet at one or both ends,

When you click OK in the Chaining dialog box, the net surface is created within the intersections of the chained curves.

Each along contour will be intersected with each across contour to determine the net surface boundaries.

➲ **Create Net Surface**
1. Click on **Surfaces** tab and in the **Create** section select **Net**.
2. In the Chaining dialog box set to **Partial** chain.
3. On the graphics screen you are prompted: **Select the first entity. Activate 3D and Partial Chain.** Select the **partial chain** by first selecting line 1, **ensure the arrow is pointing downwards** and then select line 2.

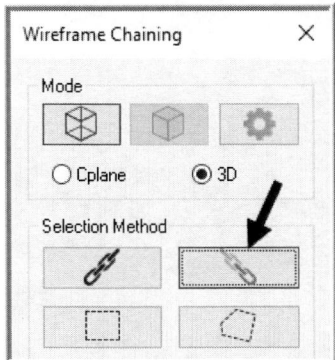
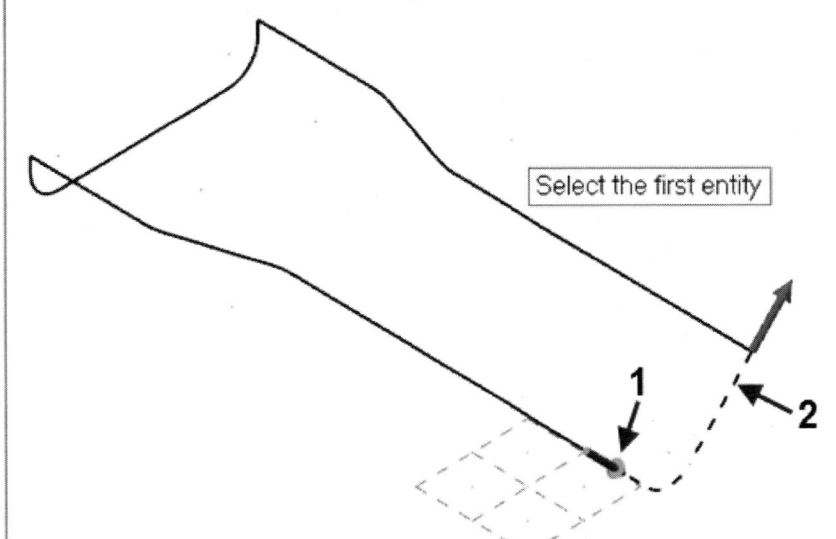

4. On the graphics screen you are again prompted: **Select the first entity.** Select the partial chain by first selecting line 1, ensure the arrow is pointing downwards and then select line 2.

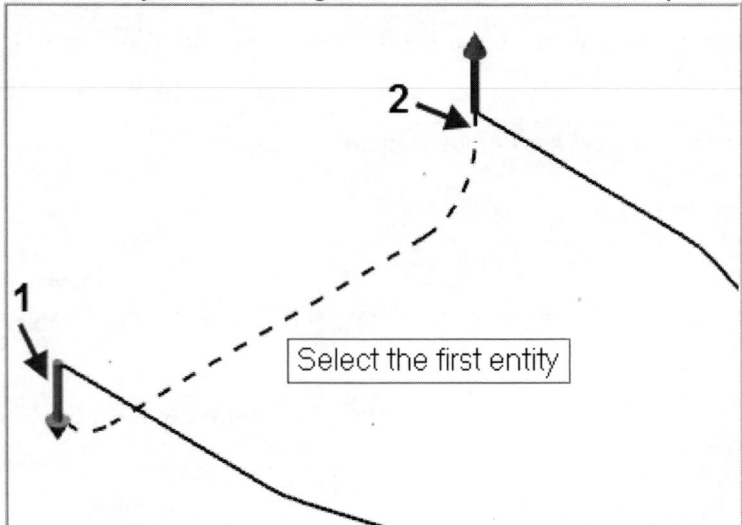

5. On the graphics screen you are prompted: **Select the first entity.** Select the partial chain by first selecting line 1, ensure the arrow is pointing to the left and then select line 2.

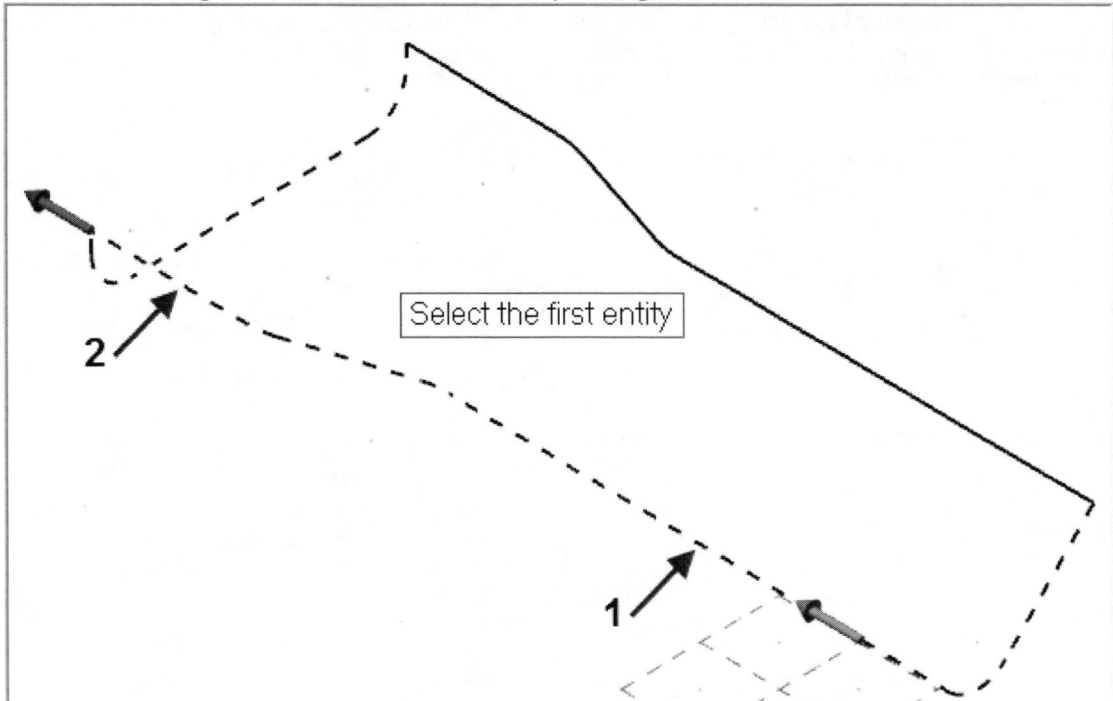

6. On the graphics screen you are again prompted: **Select the first entity.** Select the partial chain by first selecting line 1, ensure the arrow is pointing to the left and then select line 2.

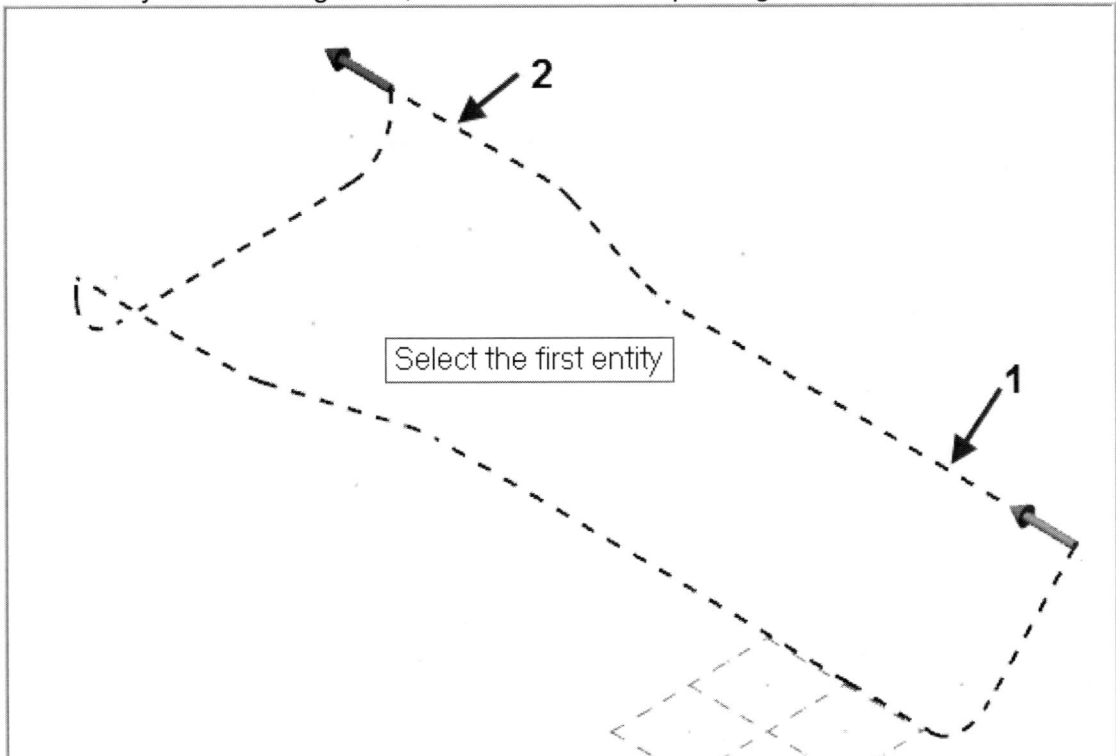

7. Click on the OK icon [✓] in the Chaining dialog window.

8. Click on the **OK** icon [✓] to complete this feature.

➲   The completed net surface is shown below:

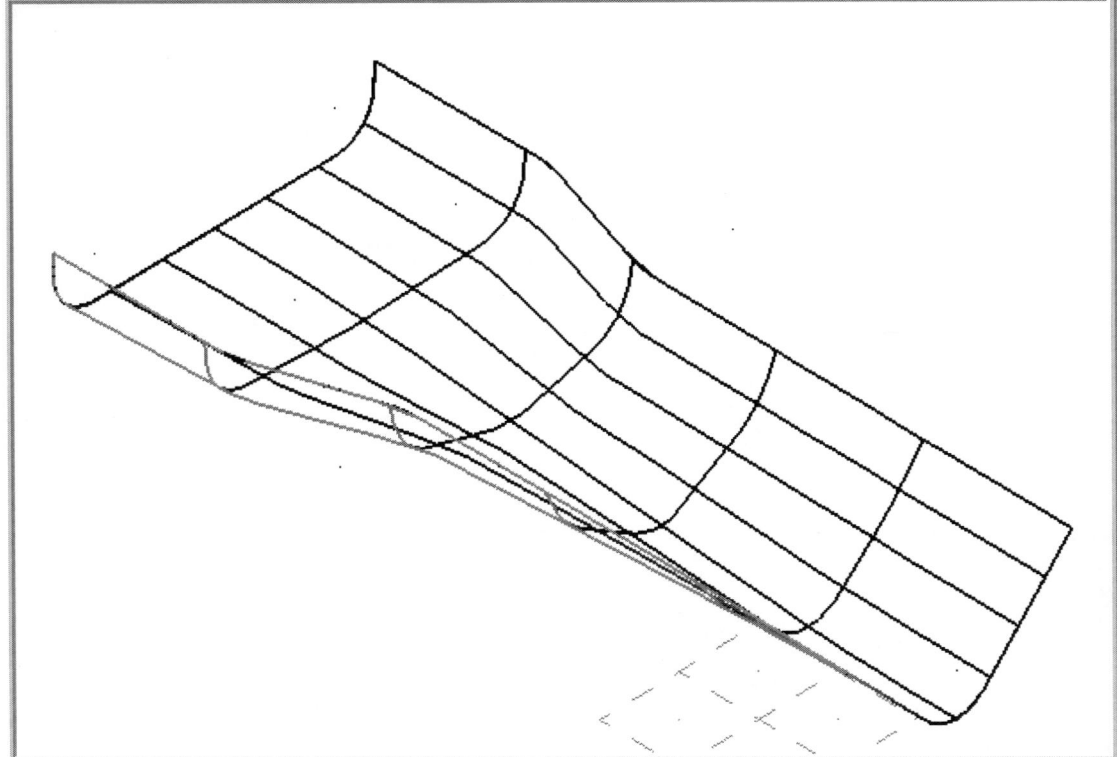

TASK 9:
SAVE THE DRAWING

1. Select File.
2. Select **Save as**.
3. Click on the **Browse** icon.
4. In the File name box, ensure **Mill-Lesson-11** is visible as shown below:
5. Save to an appropriate location.
6. Select the **Save** button to save the file and complete this function.

Toolpath Creation

TASK 10:
DEFINE THE ROUGH STOCK USING STOCK SETUP

1. Select the **View tab** and click on **Toolpaths** in the **Managers** section to display the Toolpaths Manager.
2. Select the **plus** in front of **Properties** to expand the Toolpaths Group Properties.
3. Select **Stock setup** in the Toolpaths Manager window.
4. Change the parameters to match the **Stock Setup** screenshot below: The top of the material is at **Z 0**. The base of the material and the 4.625 x 2.500 dimensions has been previously machined to size.

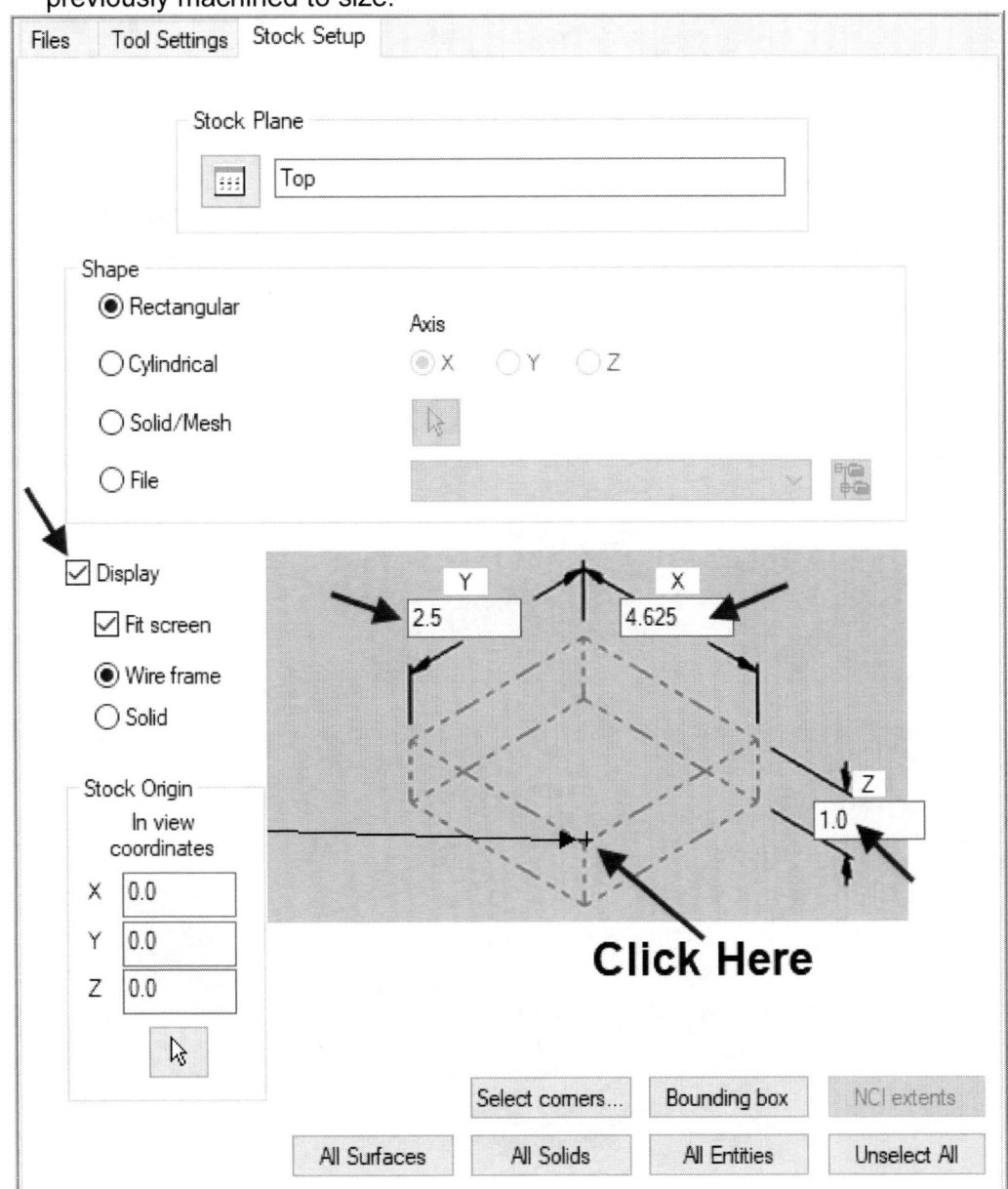

5. Select the **Tool Settings** tab and change the parameters to match the Tool Settings screenshot below. To change the Material type follow the instructions below:

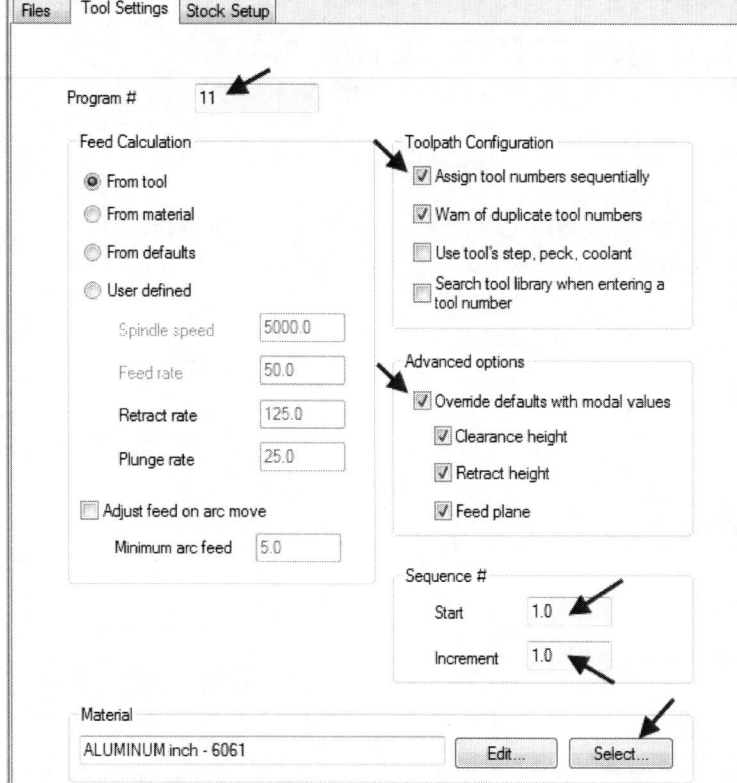

6. To change the Material type to Aluminum 6061 pick the Select button at the bottom of the Tool Settings page.

7. At the **Material List** dialog box open the **Source** drop down list and select **Mill – library**.

8. From the Default Materials list select **ALUMINUM inch -6061** and then select ☑ .

9. Select the OK button ☑ again to complete this Stock Setup function.

10. Right mouse click in the graphics area and click on the **Fit** icon ⊞ .

➲ Your part should look similar to the screen shot below. With X0 Y0 at the lower right side and Z zero on top of the stock.

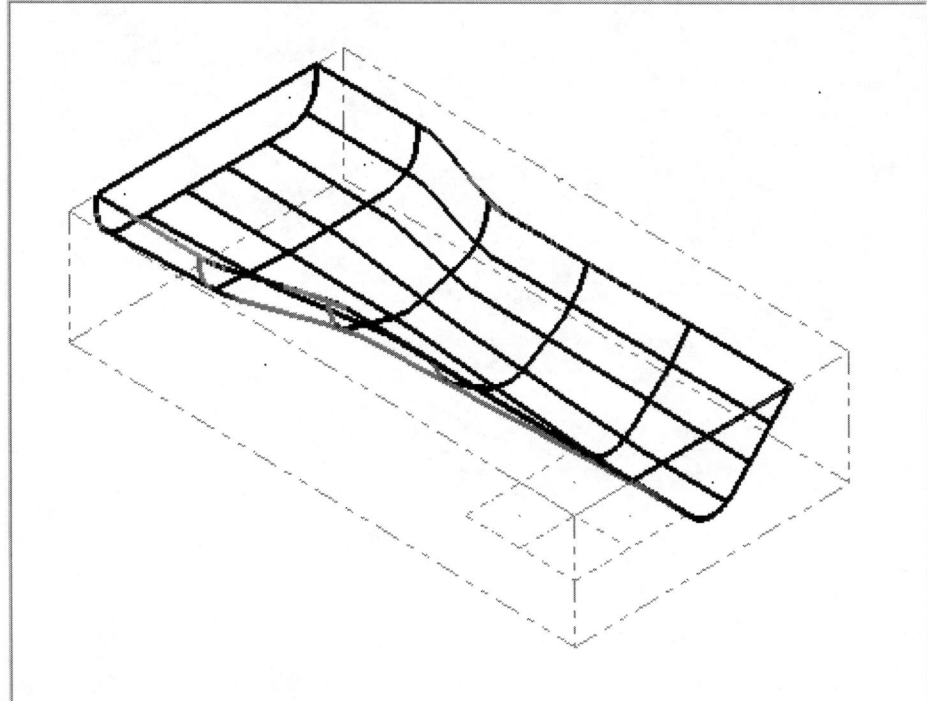

TASK 11:
ROUGH MACHINE USING SURFACE HIGH SPEED AREA ROUGHING
➲ In this task you will use a 0.5 diameter end mill with a 0.125 corner radius to rough the net surface.

1. Select the **Toolpaths** tab at the top right side of the screen.
2. Select **OptiRough** in the **3D** toolpath section.
3. Select the **Toolpath Type** page, select **Area Roughing**.

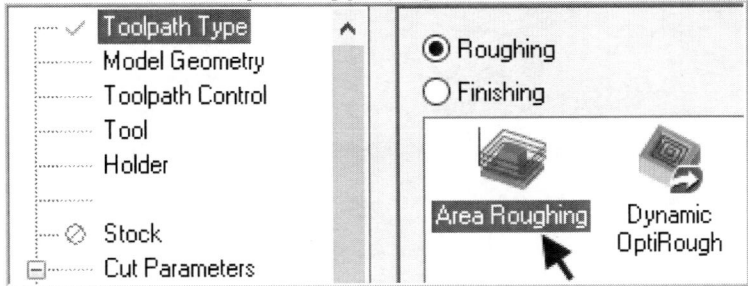

4. Select the Model Geometry page and set both the **Wall Stock** and **Floor stock** to **0.020.**

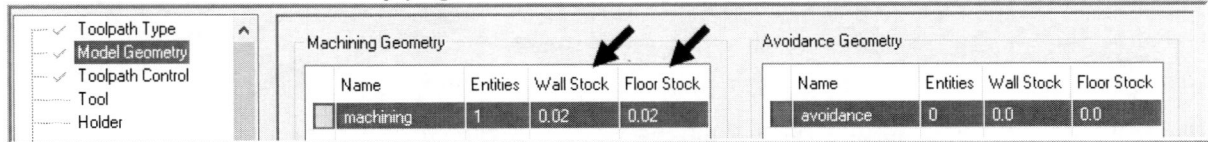

5. At the bottom of the **Model Geometry** page click on the **Select entities** button.

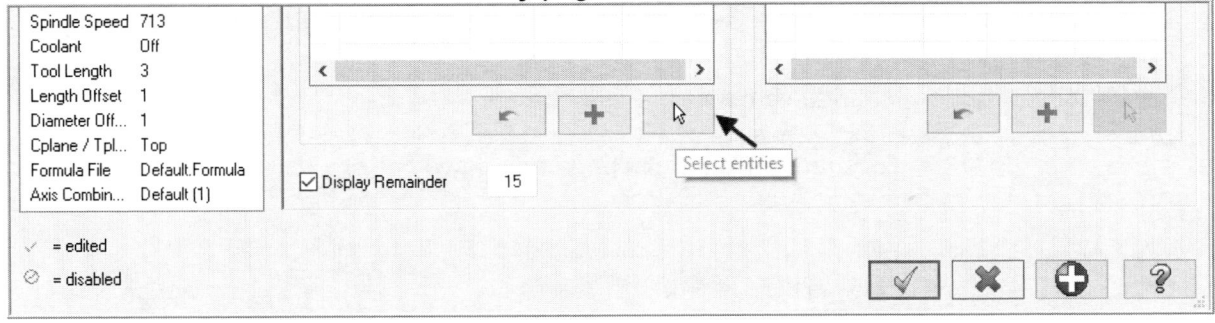

6. Now you will be returned to the graphics screen, select the **Select all advanced** button on the right of your screen.

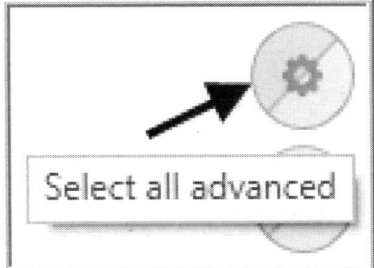

7. The **Select All** dialog box appears on the screen. Click on the OK icon ✓ to complete and exit this feature.

8. To move onto the next step, you now need to pick the **End Selection** icon ◎.

9. Select the **Toolpath Control** page, make changes as shown below.

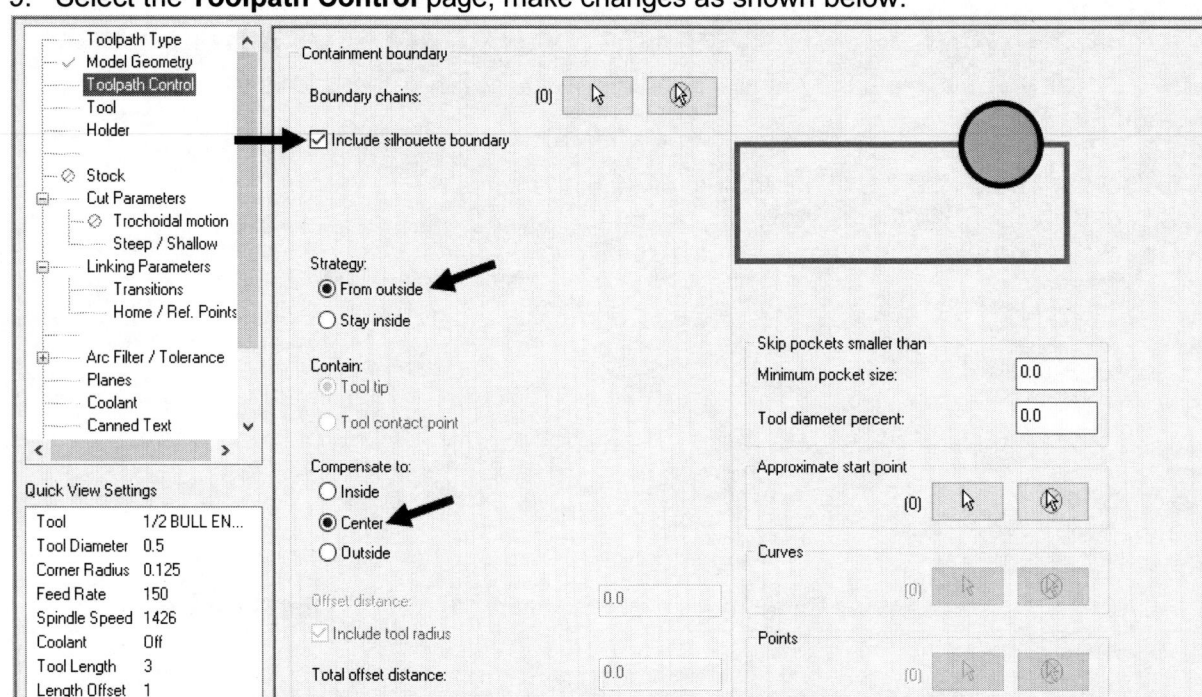

10. Select the **Tool parameters** page, then the **Select library tool…** button.
11. De-activate **Filet Active**.
12. Use the slider bar on the right of this dialog box to scroll down and locate a **0.5 diameter bull end mill with a 0.125 corner radius**. Select the end mill by picking anywhere along its row. **Deactivate Filter Active** if required.
13. Select the OK button [✓] to complete the selection of this tool.

14. Make changes to the **Toolpath parameters** page as shown below

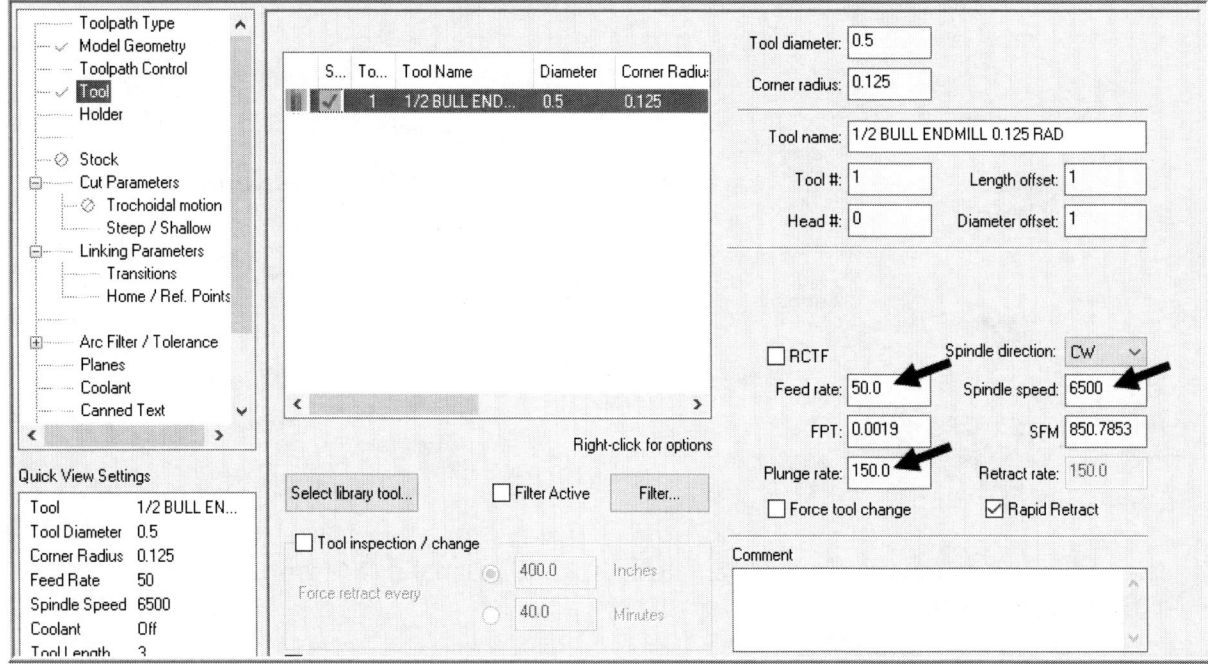

15. Select the **Cut parameters** page and make changes to this page as shown below.

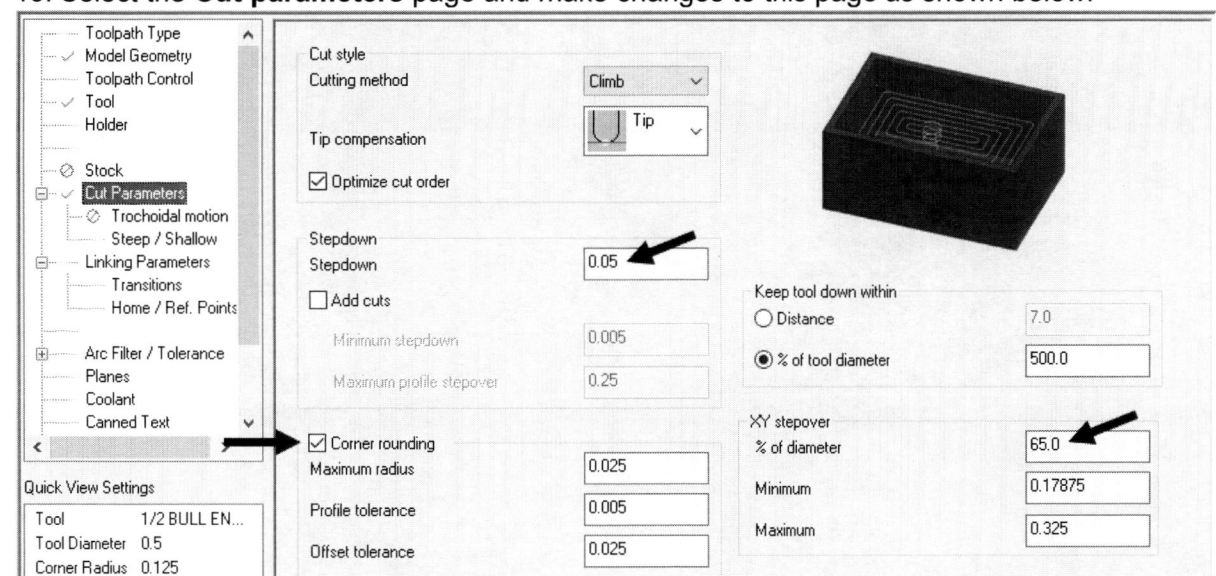

Profile tolerance
This sets the maximum deviation from the calculated toolpath that the smoothing will adjust the 'smoothed' toolpath to.
Offset tolerance
Works the same way as the smoothing tolerance. This affects offset passes (toolpath steps that are away from the drive geometry).
Loosening the tolerances here will result in smoother motion on the machine. The tradeoff is accuracy. The **profile tolerance** for finishing toolpaths should be the same or tighter than the total tolerance

---

16. **Trochoidal motion is not activated**.
17. No settings are needed on the **Steep / Shallow** page.

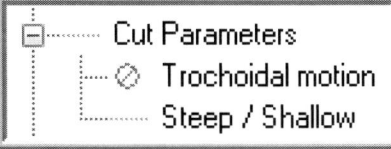

---

18. Select the **Linking Parameters** page and make changes to this page as shown below.

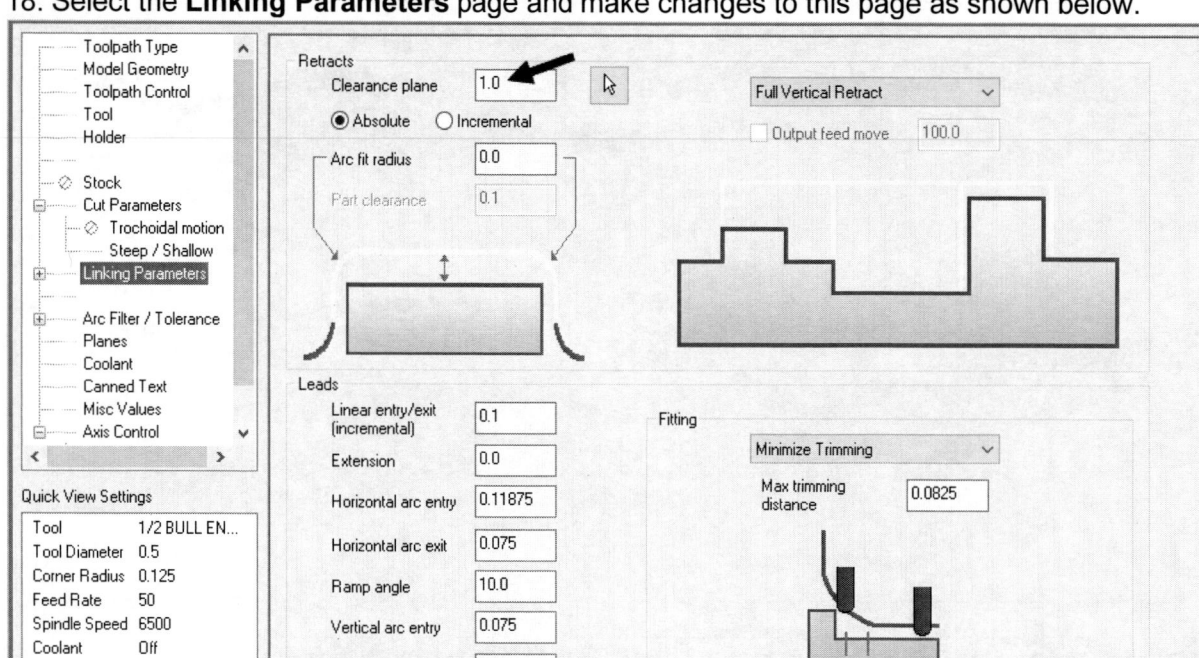

19. No settings are needed on the **Transitions page**.

20. Make the following settings on the **Arc Filter / Tolerance**.

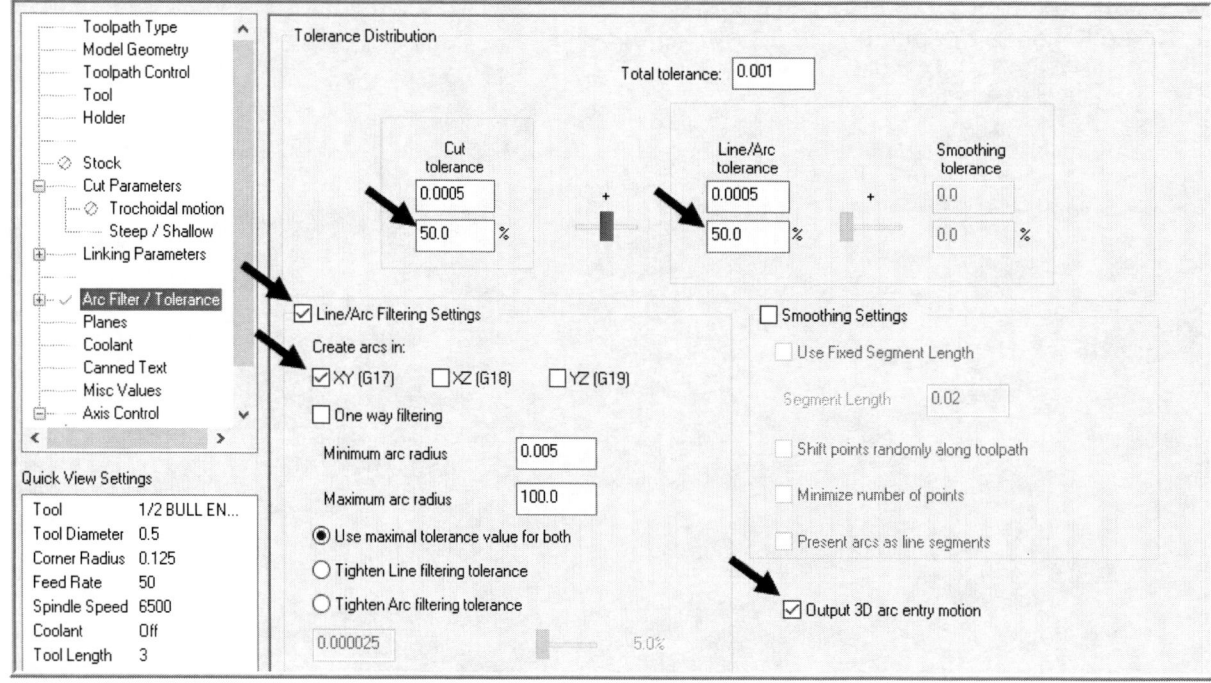

21. Turn on coolant on the **Coolant** page.

22. Select the OK button ✓ to exit and generate the toolpath.

23. Verify the new toolpath.

➲ The verified image should look like the image below:

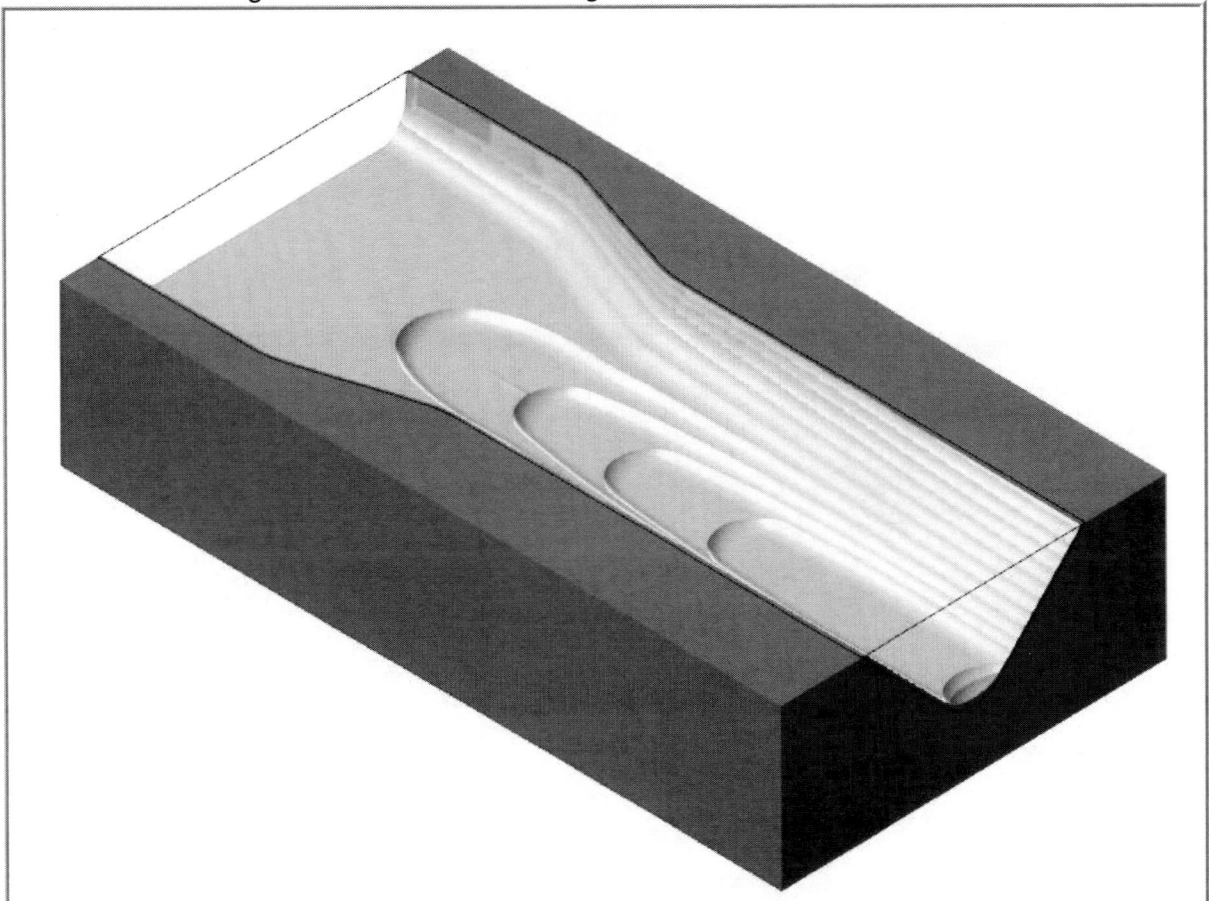

TASK 12:
FINISH MACHINE USING SURFACE FINISH FLOWLINE

 ⮩ In this task you will use a 0.5 diameter Ball end mill to finish the net surface.

1. Select the **Toolpaths** tab at the top right side of the screen.
2. Click on the **Expand gallery** down arrow in the **3D** section and select **Flowline** from the **Finishing** selections.
3. To satisfy the prompt first select the **Surface**.

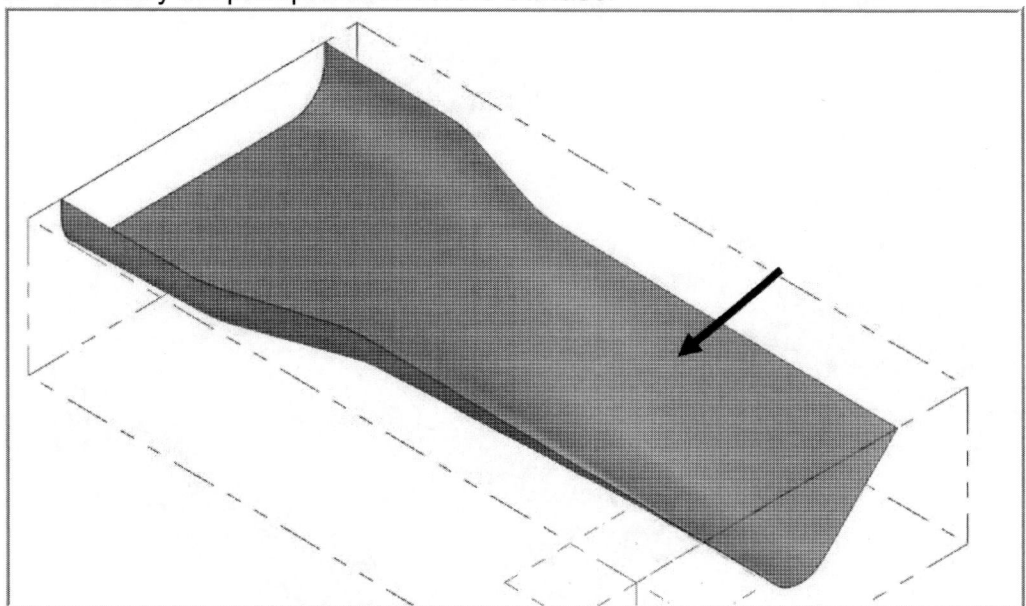

4. To move onto the next step, you now need to pick the **End Selection** icon .
5. Click on the **Flowline** button on the **Toolpath/surface selection** dialog box.

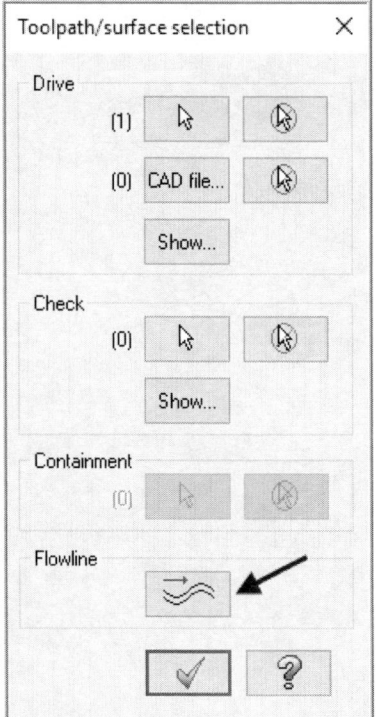

6. Click on the **Cut direction** button to toggle the toolpath direction as shown below: Note, the lines should be inside the cavity as shown below: if they are on the outside click on the Offset button. If the toolpath display for the roughing path is in the way press the shortcut **Alt+T** to remove it.

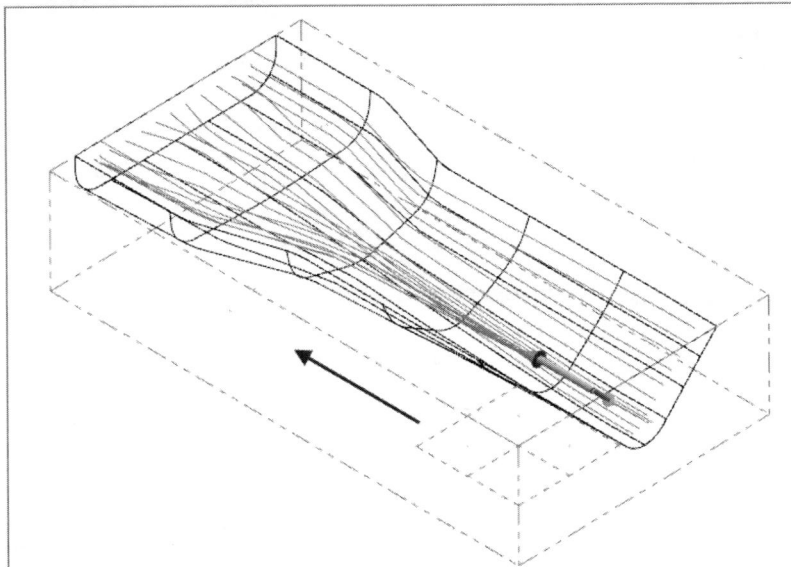 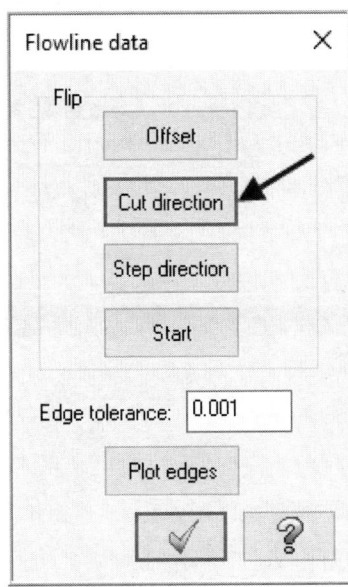

7. Select the OK button to exit the **Flowline data** dialog box.
8. Select the OK button to exit the **Toolpath/surface selection** dialog box.
9. In the lower left corner of the **Toolpath parameters** page select the **Select library tool...** button.
10. Use the **Filter** function to filter out a selection of cutters. Select the **Filter** button on the right side of the **Tool selection** dialog box.
11. Select the **None** button in the Tool Types section.
12. Click on the **Endmill2 Sphere** type icon, first row, and second icon from the left.
13. Select the drop down arrow in the **Tool diameter** field and set it to **Equal.** Input the tool diameter as **0.5**.

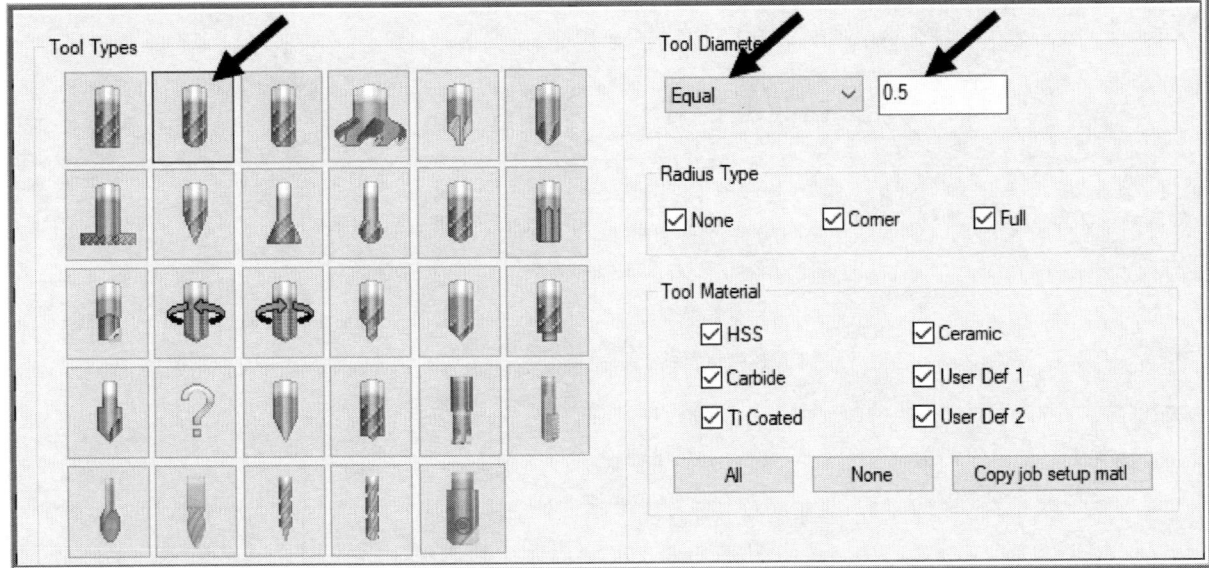

14. Select the OK button to exit.

15. Select the **0.5 ball end mill**.

	Tool Number	Tool Name	Diameter	Corner Radius	Length	Type	Radius Type
	311	1/2 BALL ENDMILL	0.5	0.25	1.0	Ball endmill	Full

16. Select the OK button [✓] to complete the selection of this tool.
17. Make changes to the **Toolpath parameters** page as shown below. Coolant flood is on.

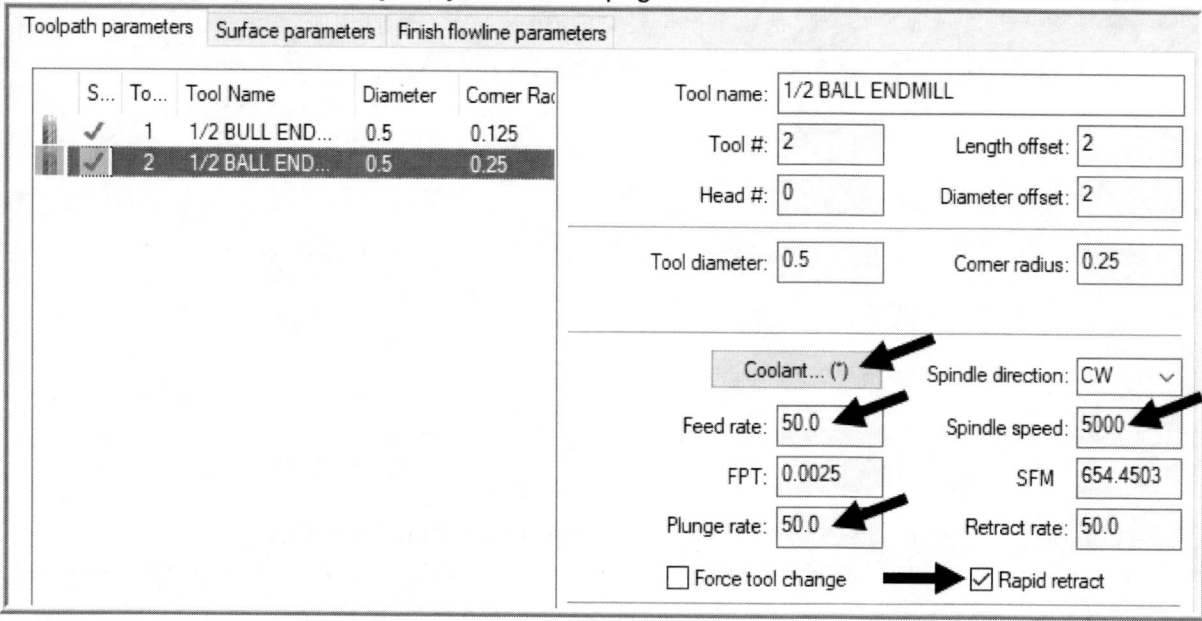

18. Select the **Surface parameters** page and make changes to this page as shown below:

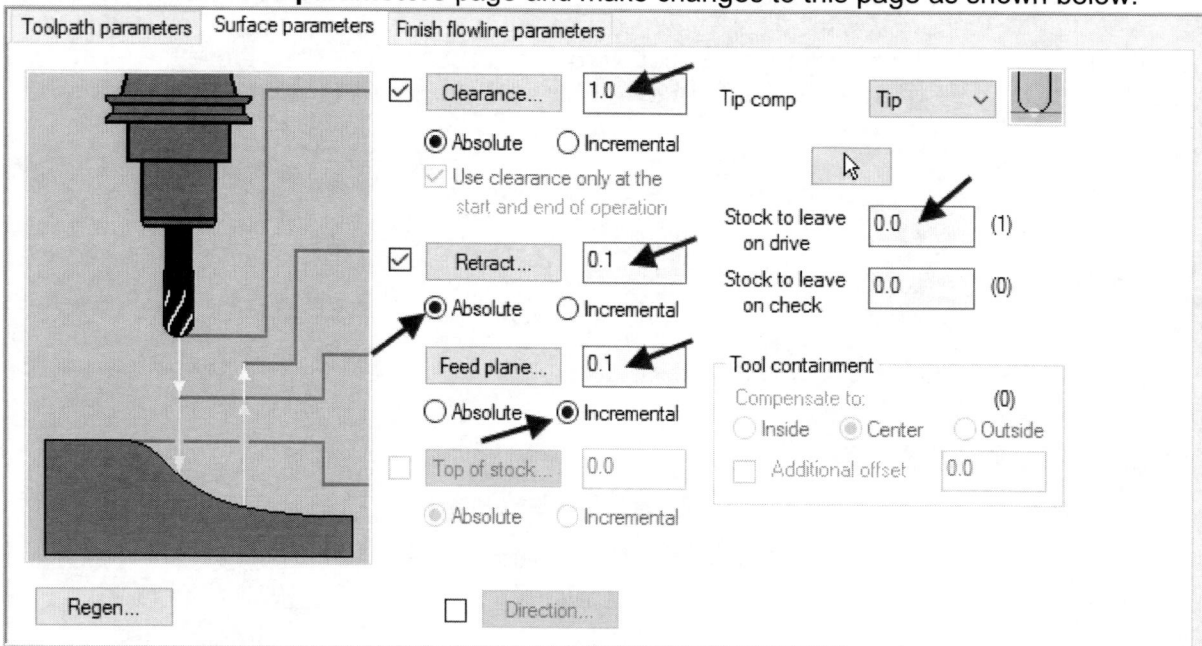

19. Next, on the **Finish flowline parameters** page make changes to this page as shown below:

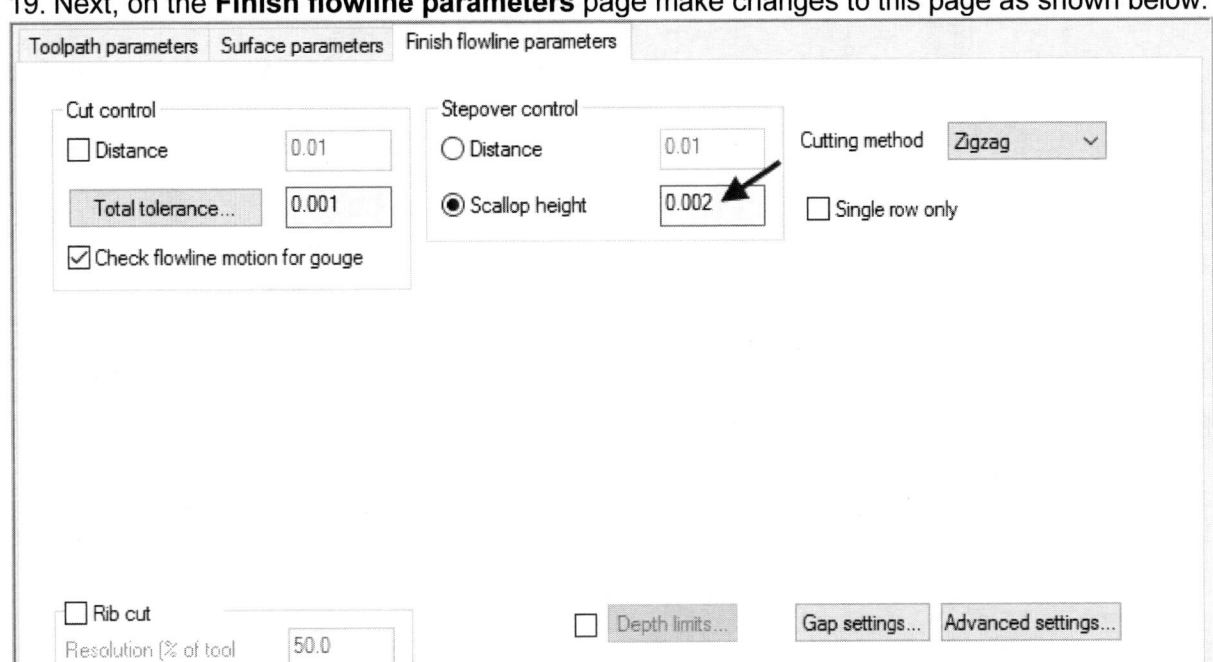

Scallop height

This adjusts the stepover between cuts to create leftover material at a specific height.

Surface rough and finish flowline toolpaths give you precise control of scallops left on the part.

Scallop height can be set either as a stepover distance or as an actual height.

When using the scallop height option, Mastercam automatically adjusts the stepover between cuts, although this amount is not shown in the stepover entry field.

20. Select the **Gap settings** button and make changes to this page as shown below:

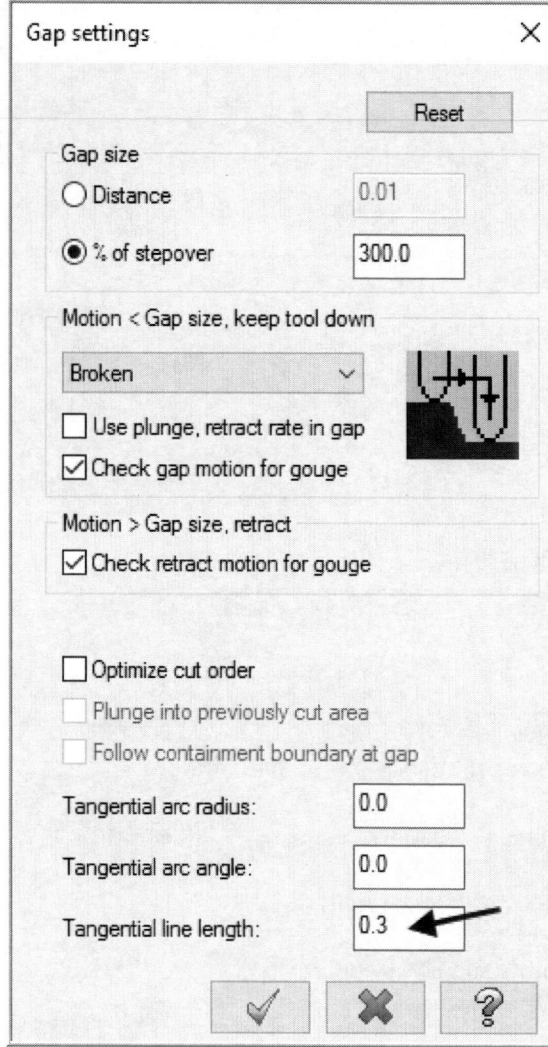

Tangential line length
Sets the line length at the entry and exit points of a gap. Not available for multiaxis toolpaths.

Motion
Determines the tool motion in areas smaller than the gap size.

Direct moves the tool directly from position to position.
Broken moves the tool up and over or over and down.
Smooth moves the tool in a fluid motion.
Follow surface(s) matches the Z motion of the surface.

21. Select the OK button ✓ to exit Gap settings.
22. Select the OK button ✓ to exit Finish Flowline parameters.
➲ The screen should look like the image below:

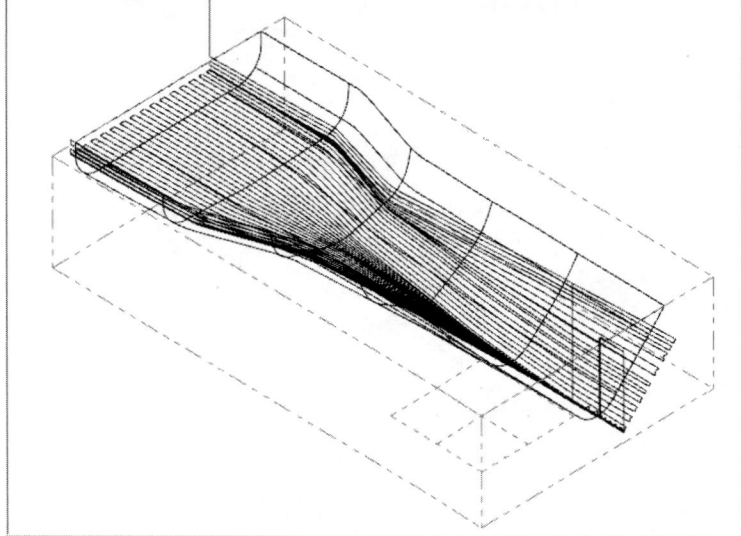

TASK 13:
VERIFY THE TOOLPATH

1. Right mouse click in the graphics area and click on **Isometric**.
2. In the **Toolpaths Manager** pick all the operations to verify by picking the **Select all operations** icon.
3. Select the **Verify selected operations** icon.
4. **Maximize** the Backplot/Verify window if required.
5. Activate the options shown below in the **Visibility** section of the **Home** tab. **Initial Stock not** activated.

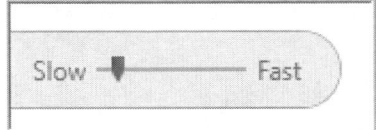

☐ Toolpath	✓ Stock	✓ Wireframe	✓ Machine
✓ Tool	☐ Initial Stock	✓ Gnomon	✓ Machine Housing
☐ Workpiece	☐ Fixtures	✓ Axes	
	Visibility		

6. At the top of the screen select the **Verify** tab and activate the **Color Loop**.
7. At the top of the screen select the **View** tab, the **Isometric** icon and then select **Fit**.
8. In the lower part of the screen now set the run Speed to slow by moving the slider bar pointer over to the left as shown below.

Slow ——▼———— Fast

9. Now select the **Play** Simulation button to review the toolpaths.
⮕ The verified toolpaths are shown below:

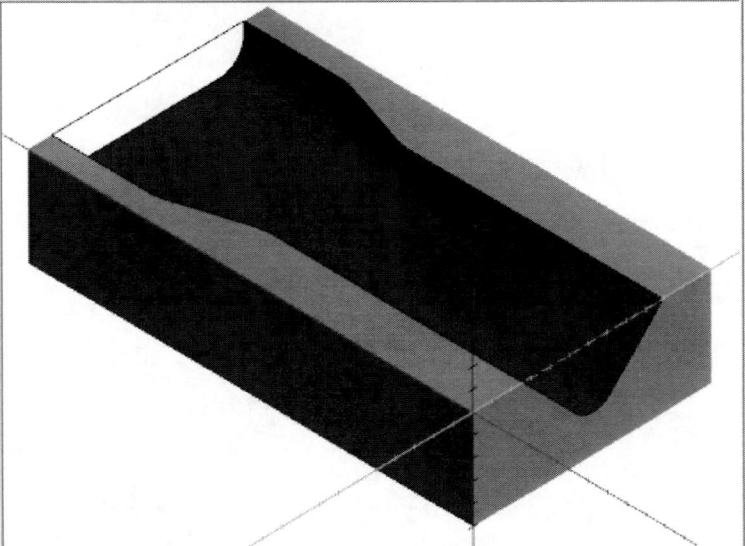

10. Select the **Close** button [×] in the top right hand corner to exit Verify.

TASK 14:
SAVE THE UPDATED MASTERCAM FILE

1. Select the **Save** icon from the **Quick Access** toolbar at the top left of the screen.

TASK 15:
POST AND CREATE THE CNC CODE FILE

1. Ensure all the operations are selected by picking the **Select all operations** icon  from the Toolpaths Manager.
2. Select the **Post selected operations** button from the Toolpaths Manager.

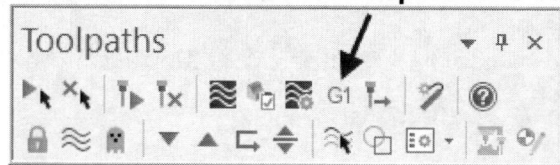

3. In the Post processing window, make the necessary changes as shown below:

4. Select the OK button to continue.
5. Ensure the same name as your Mastercam part file name is in the NC File name field.
6. Select the Save button.
7. The CNC code file opens up in the default editor:

```
MILL-LESSON-11.NC  ×

   7   ( T1 | 1/2 BULL ENDMILL 0.125 RAD | H1 )
   8   ( T2 | 1/2 BALL ENDMILL | H2 )
   9   N1 G20
  10   N2 G0 G17 G40 G49 G80 G90
  11   N3 T1 M6
  12   N4 G0 G90 G54 X-3.6123 Y1.2593 A0. S2500 M3
  13   N5 G43 H1 Z1. M8
  14   N6 Z.2461
  15   N7 G1 Z.2211 F12.
  16   N8 X-3.6127 Y1.2595 Z.2133
  17   N9 X-3.6139 Y1.2598 Z.2055
  18   N10 X-3.6158 Y1.2604 Z.1979
```

8. Select the ☒ in the top right corner to exit the CNC editor
➲ This completes Mill-Lesson-11.

MILL-LESSON-11-EXERCISE-A

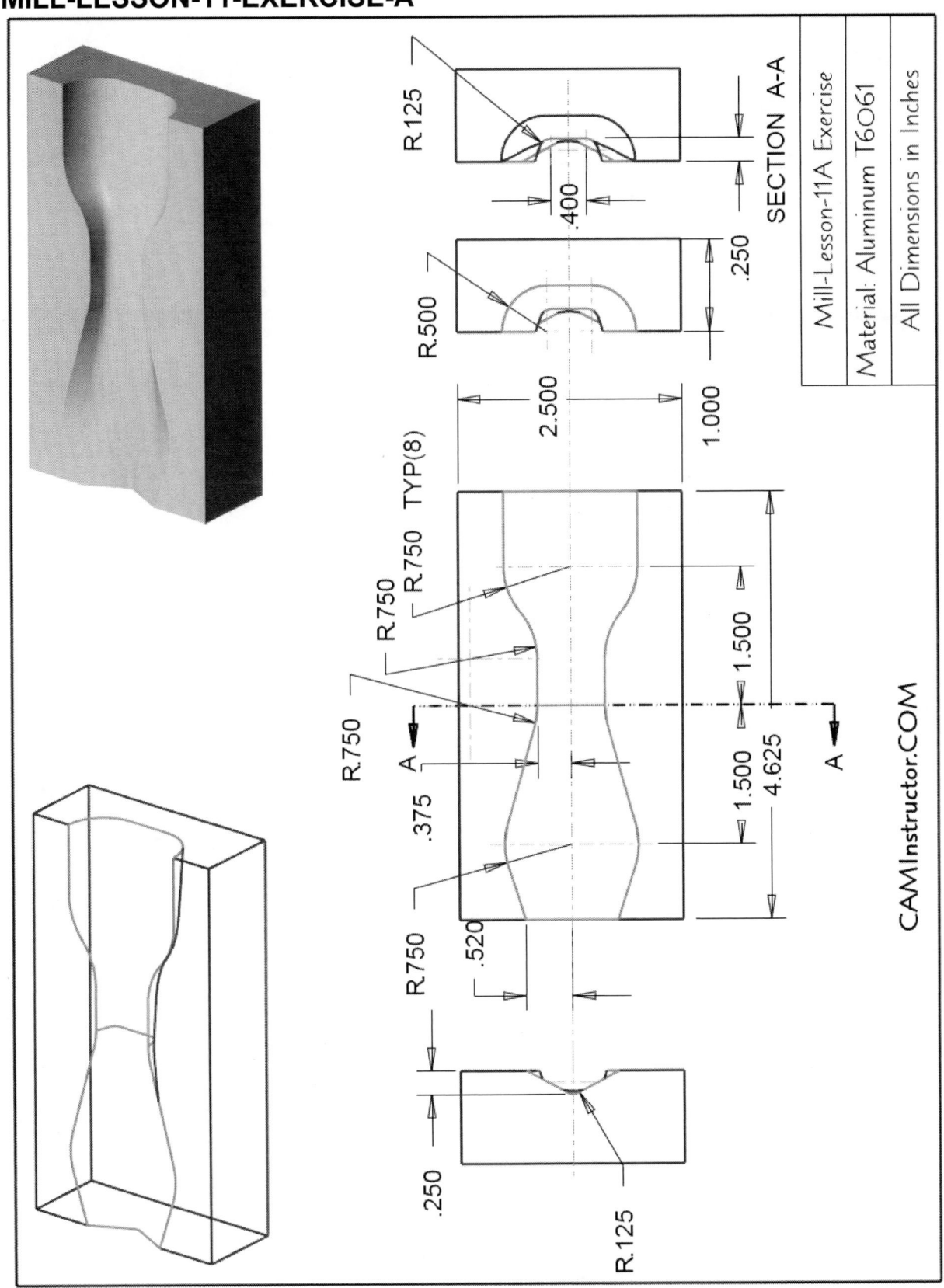

R.125

SECTION A-A

.400

R.500

.250

Mill-Lesson-11A Exercise

Material: Aluminum T6061

All Dimensions in Inches

2.500

1.000

R.750

R.750 TYP(8)

R.750

A

.375

1.500

1.500

4.625

R.750

.520

.250

R.125

CAMInstructor.COM

A

MILL-LESSON-11-EXERCISE-B

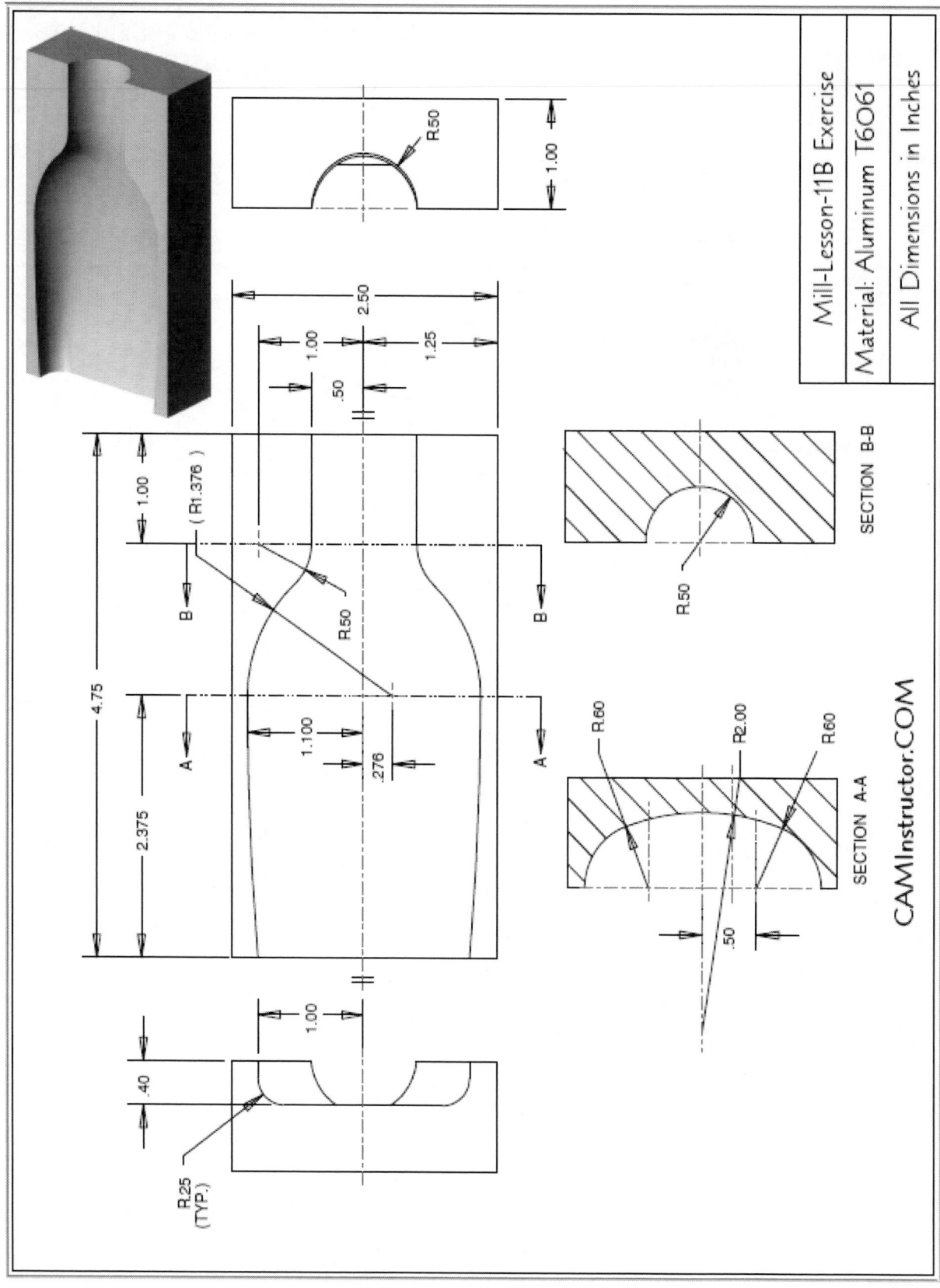

Mill-Lesson-11B Exercise

Material: Aluminum T6O61

All Dimensions in Inches

SECTION B-B

SECTION A-A

CAMInstructor.COM

Mastercam 2022

TRAINING
GUIDE

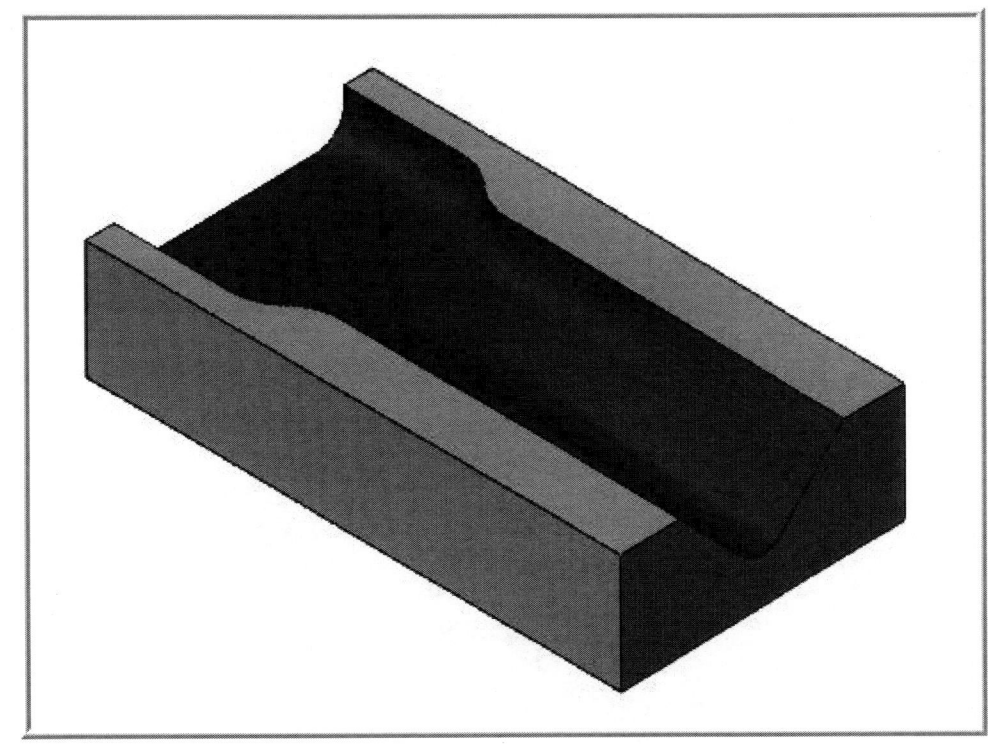

MILL-LESSON-11B

IMPORT A SOLID MODEL

SURFACE HIGH SPEED AREA ROUGHING
& FINISH FLOWLINE TOOLPATHS

camInstructor

Objectives

You will import the CAD file for Mill-Lesson-11B, and then generate the toolpaths to machine the part on a CNC vertical milling machine. This lesson covers the following topics:

➲ **Import and Position the Part in Mastercam**

➲ **Establish Stock Setup settings:**
Stock size using Bounding Box.
Material for the part.
Feed calculation.

➲ **Generate a 3-dimensional milling toolpath consisting of:**
Surface High Speed Area Roughing.
Finish Flowline.

➲ **Inspect the toolpath using Mastercam's Verify and Backplot by:**
Launching the Verify function to machine the part on the screen.
Generating the NC- code.

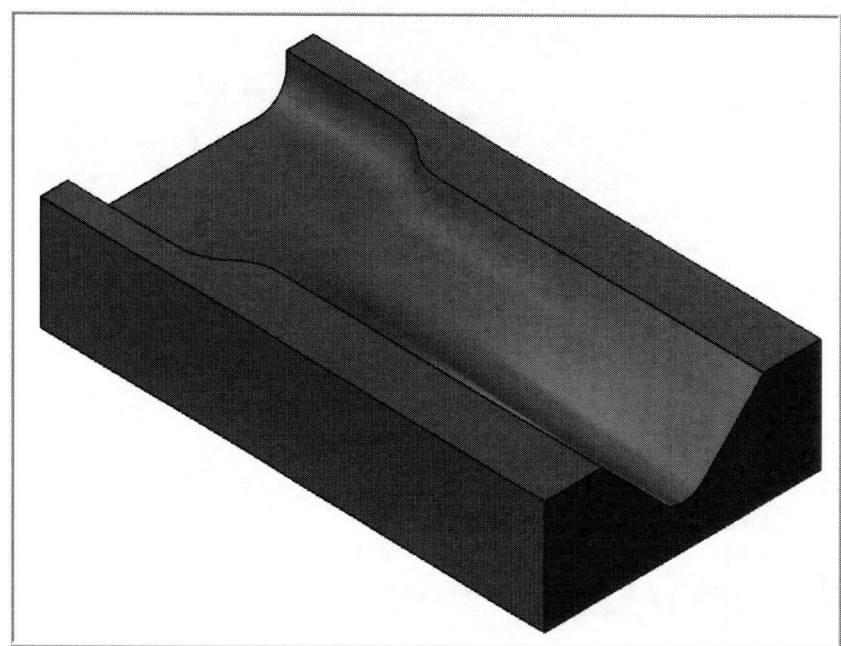

MILL-LESSON-11 DRAWING

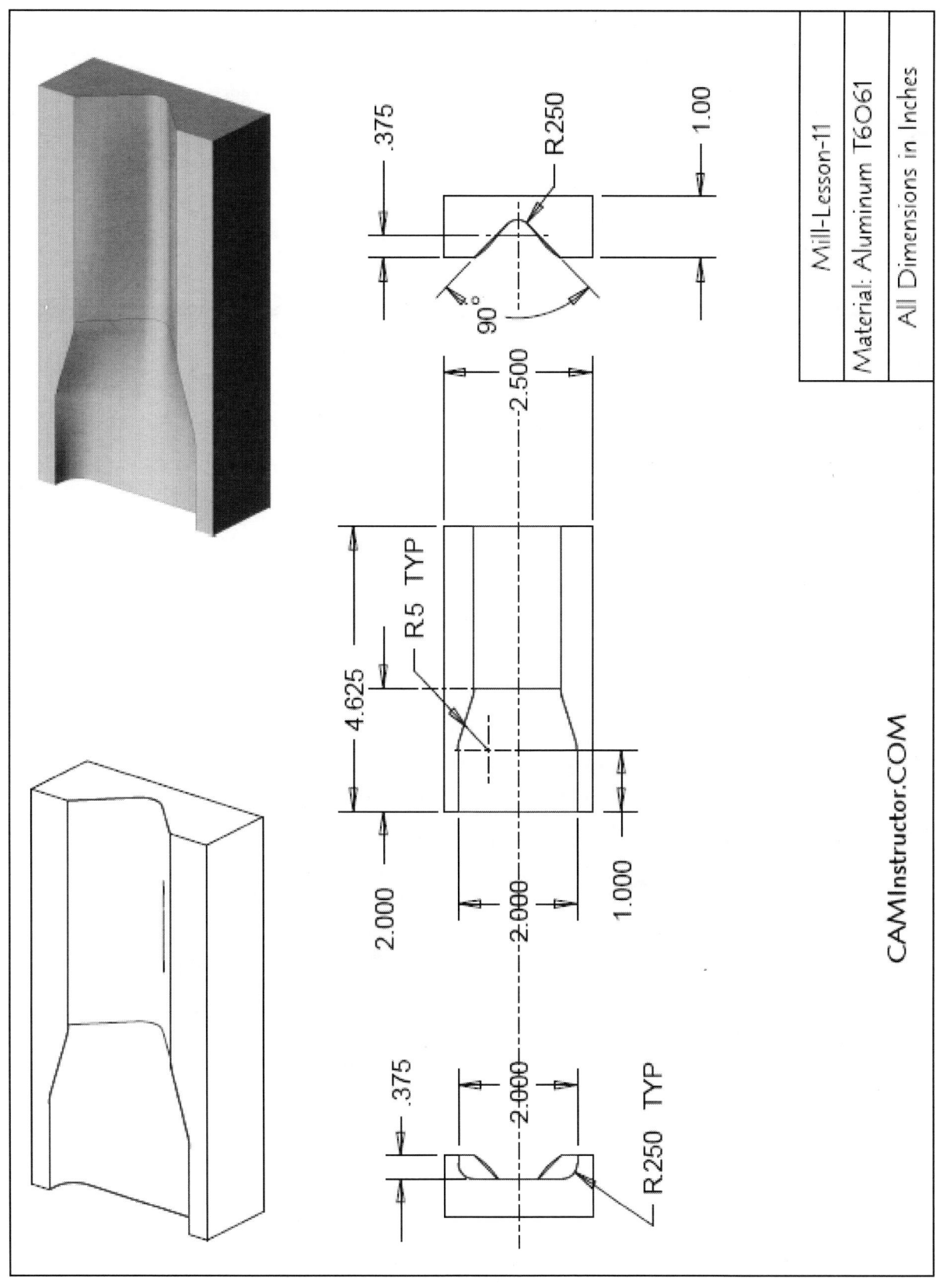

Mill-Lesson-11

Material: Aluminum T6O61

All Dimensions in Inches

CAMInstructor.COM

.375

R250

1.00

90°

2.500

R5 TYP

4.625

2.000

2.000

1.000

.375

2.000

R250 TYP

TOOL LIST

➲ 0.500 diameter bull end mill with a 0.125 corner radius to rough machine.
➲ 0.250 diameter ball end mill to finish machine.

MILL-LESSON-11B - THE CAM PROCESS

Toolpath Creation

TASK 1: Import the CAD file into Mastercam
TASK 2A: Align the part to a default plane
TASK 2B: Create a new plane at the part
TASK 3: Define the rough stock using stock setup
TASK 4: Rough machine using surface Area Rough
TASK 5: Finish machine using surface Hybrid
TASK 6: Verify the toolpath
TASK 7: Post and create the CNC code file

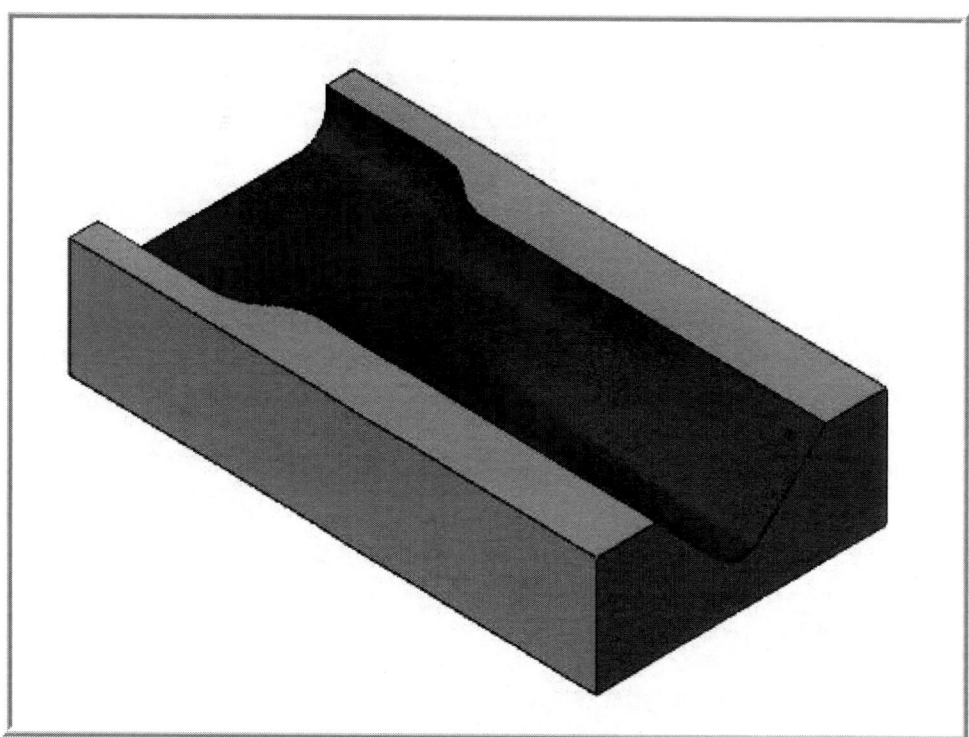

TASK 1:
IMPORT THE CAD MODEL

➲ Before importing the model, you should set up the grid and as outlined in the **Setting the environment** section at the beginning of this text:

1. Set up the Grid. This will help identify the location of the origin.
2. The machine will be selected after opening the model.
3. On the **View** tab enable the Managers for **Toolpaths, Levels, Solids, and Planes**.

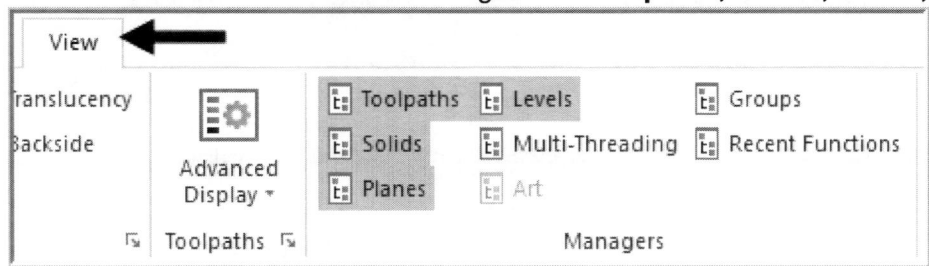

4. Select the **Open** icon from the **Quick Access** toolbar at the top left of the screen.
5. Click the **File Type** button (currently says **All Mastercam Files**) as shown below.

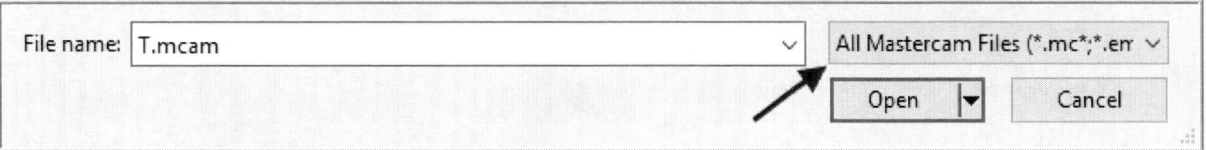

6. Scroll through the menu and select the **STEP Files** as shown below.

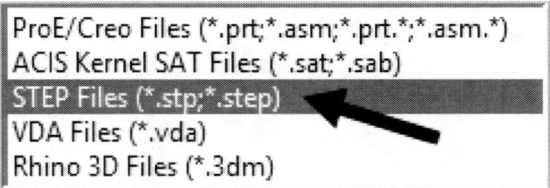

7. Find the location of the **Mill-Lesson-11B.stp** file and click on the file.

Note: If you are using the CamInstructor Online Course, the file can be downloaded in one of the steps in the Lesson.

8. Now click on **Options**.

9. Uncheck the **Edge Curves** box. This will disable the creation of wireframe geometry on the solids edges when it is imported into Mastercam. We will not be needing any wireframe geometry for this lesson.

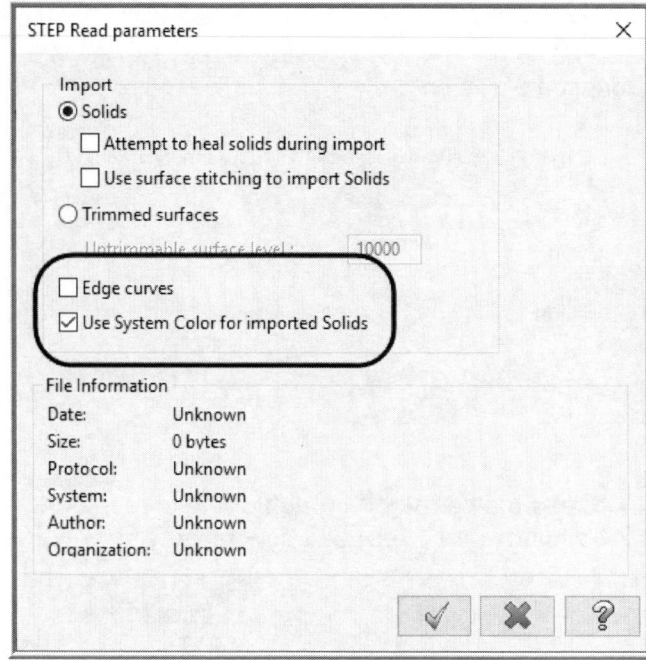

Edge Curves
Turning on Edge Curves tells Mastercam to add Lines and Arcs to all the Edges on the Solid.

Use System Colors
Enable to import the solid in the color set in Mastercam.
Disable to import the solid as the color it was created with.

10. Click on **OK** ✓.

11. Click on **Open**.

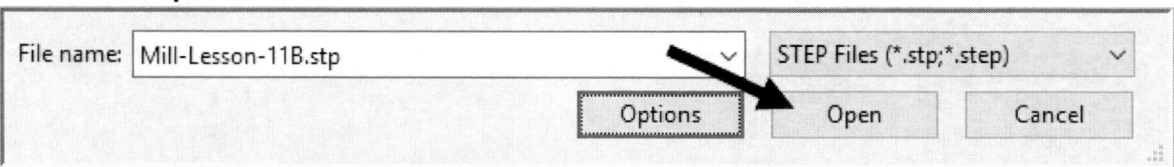

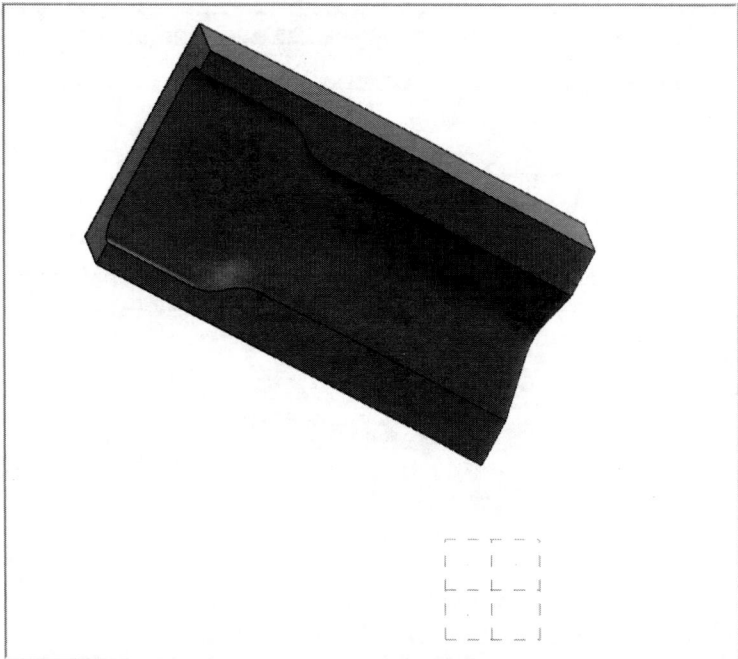

The part will import in the position and orientation that it was in when created in the CAD software.
In the next few steps, we will explore two options for dealing with this models imported location.

12. Set the machine type to the **Default Mill**.

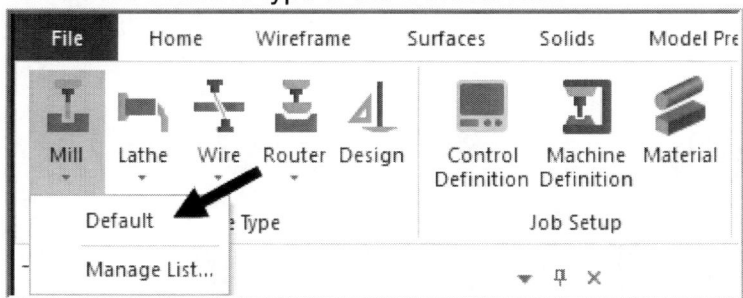

13. **Save** the file as **Mill-Lesson-11B** in an appropriate directory.

TASK 2:

➲ The model needs to have its datum located at the lower right corner and at the top face.

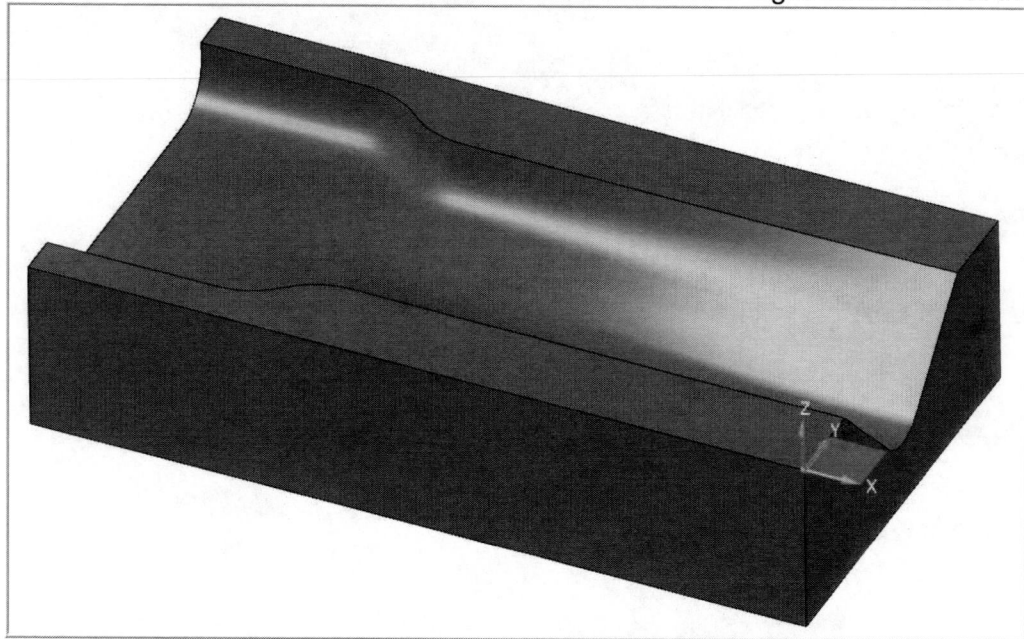

➲ The model has imported in the orientation and position that it was created with in the CAD software. Currently it is not aligned to the desired datum location.
➲ The model has been skewed in the picture below to show the difference in orientation and position of the default Top plane and the desired datum location on the model.

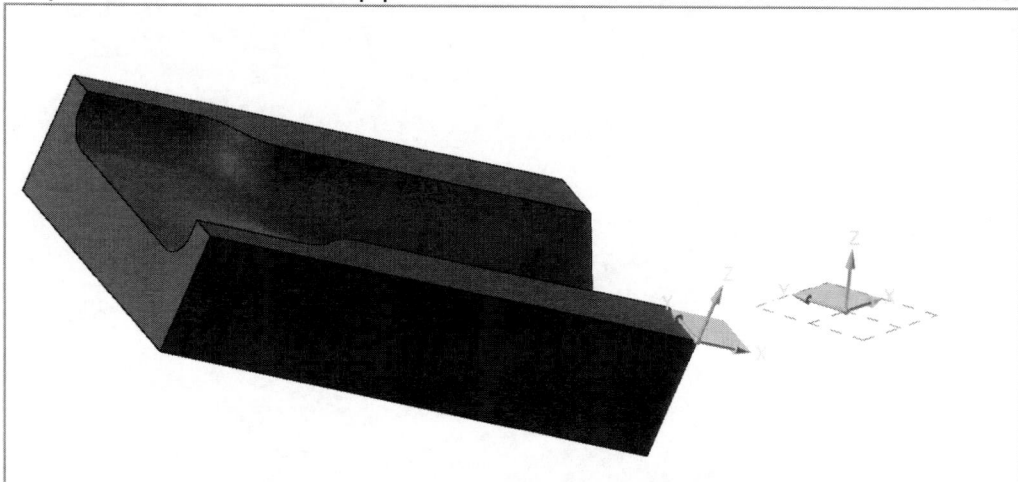

➲ There are a couple of options to change the Work Offset (datum) location.
   a. **Option A** is to move the part to the required Plane.
   b. **Option B** is to create a new Plane at the parts location.

TASK 2A:
MOVE THE PART TO THE DEFAULT TOP PLANE

➲ We want the Work Offset (datum) to be set to the lower right corner and top of the part. In this task we will align and position the part to the default Top plane relative to the required datum location

1. Make sure **Top** is selected in the list of planes.

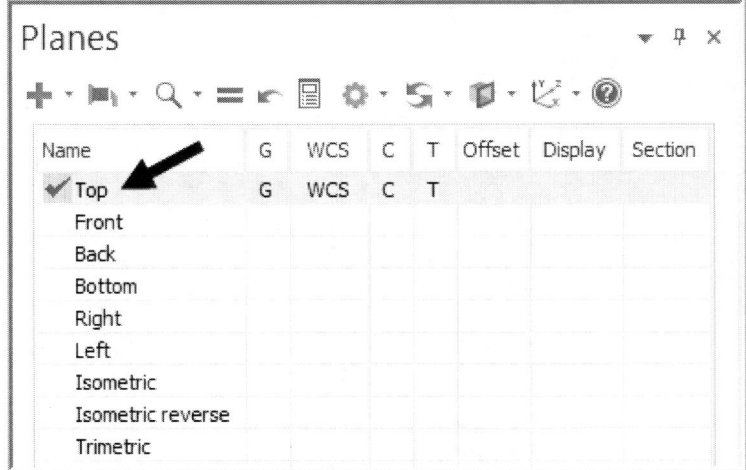

2. On the **Transform** tab in the Position section, click on **Dynamic**.

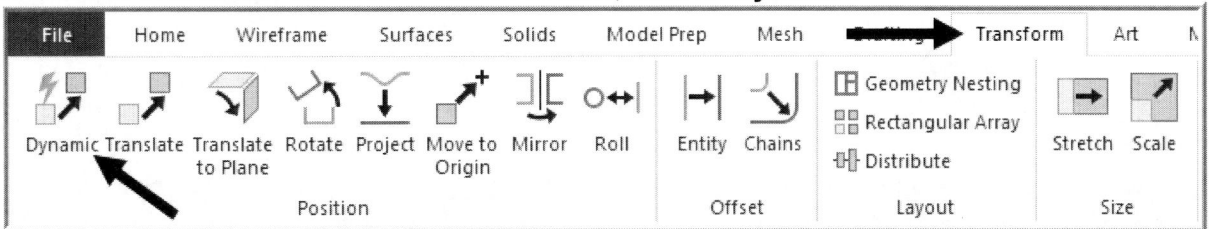

Use the **Dynamic function** to manipulate geometry orientation and location with an interactive gnomon. Dynamic provides a visual representation of Mastercam's transform/translate movements as you make changes. You also have access to Translate, Translate to Plane, and Rotate all within one powerful function.

3. You will be prompted to **Select entities to move/copy**. **Click anywhere** on the solid to select it. Click **End Selection**.

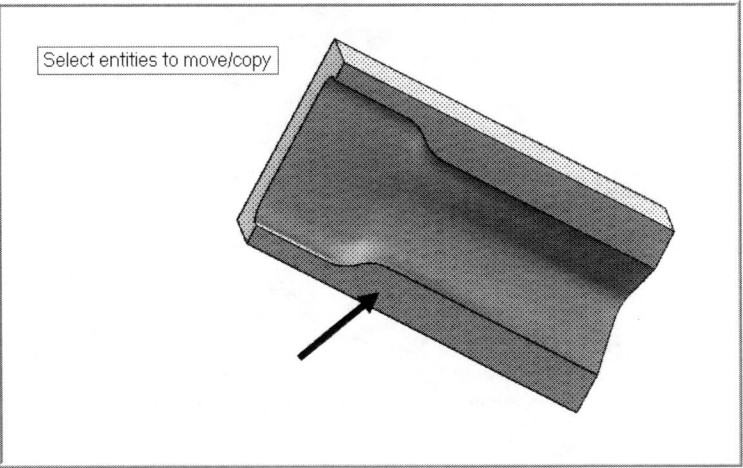

4. You are now prompted to **Pick gnomon origin position**. Place the gnomon on the lower left corner of the part by left clicking when the end point visual cue appears.

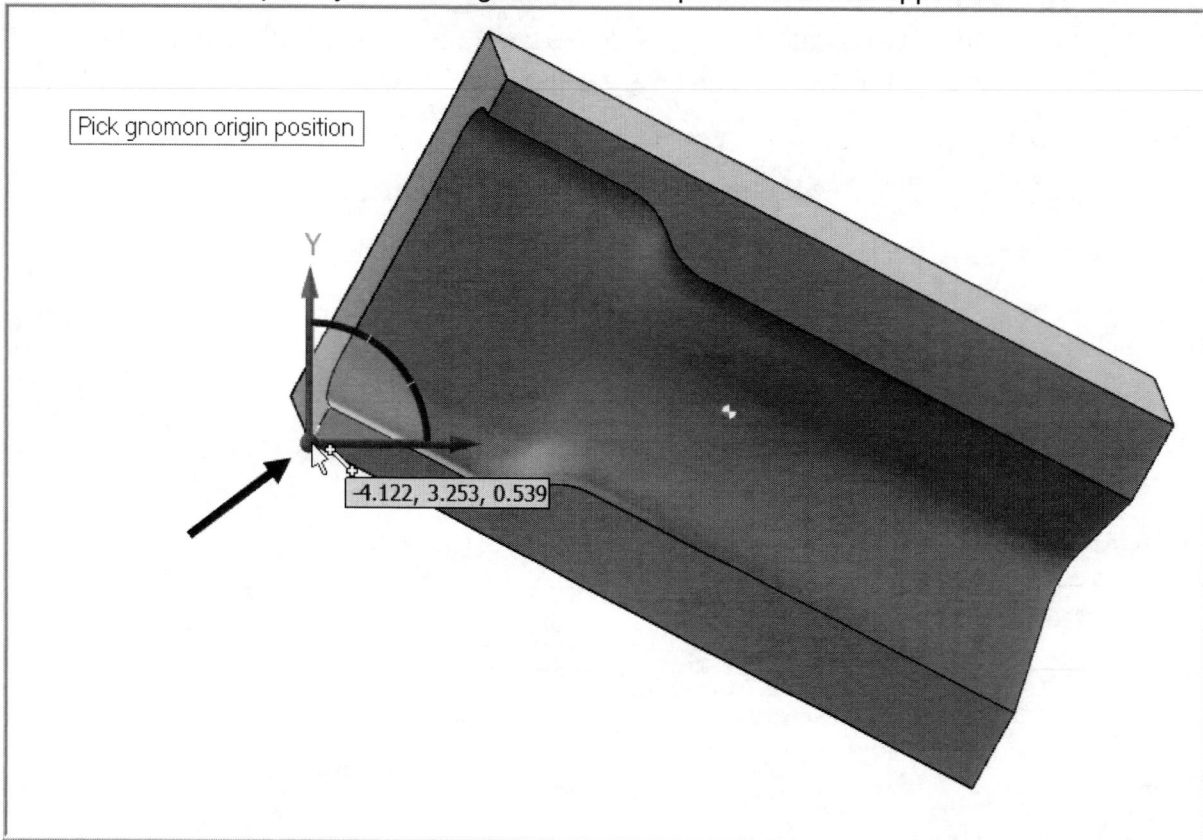

Pick gnomon origin position

-4.122, 3.253, 0.539

➲ Once the gnomon is placed, the manipulation type that is active will be shown just below and to the left of the gnomon with an icon. This mode can be toggled by clicking on the icon.

Manipulate axes - allows movement of the gnomon.

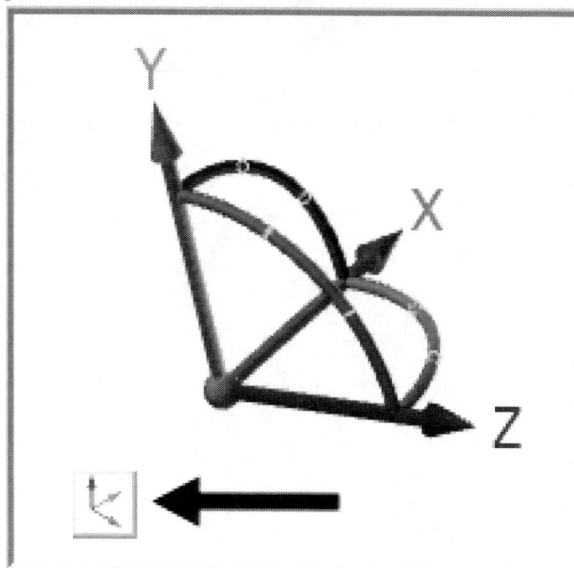

Manipulate geometry - allows movement of the selected geometry.

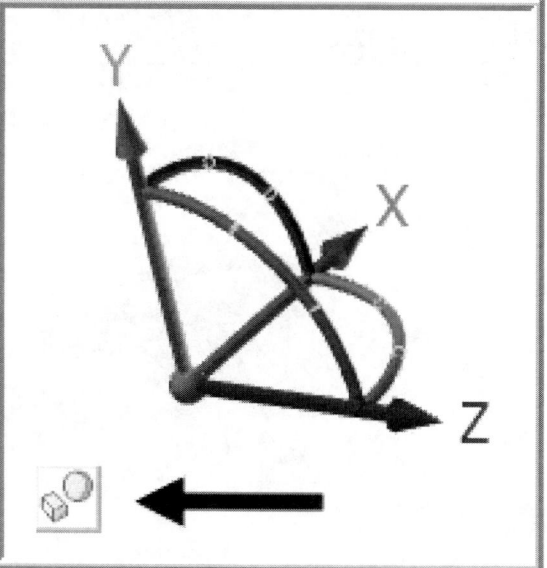

⮕ The gnomon can be manually moved. The type of movement will depend on the section of the gnomon that is clicked on.

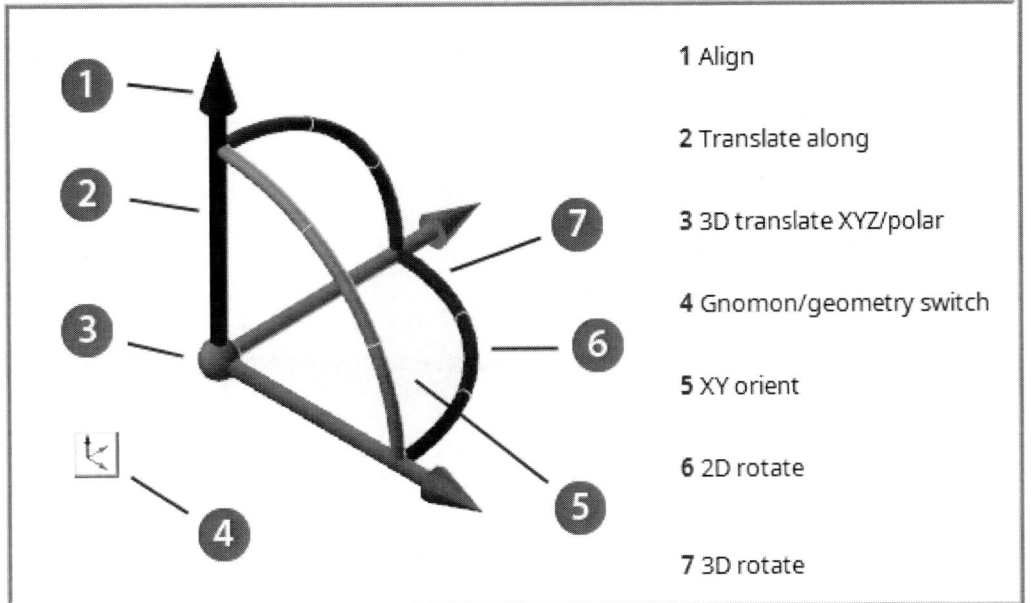

1 Align

2 Translate along

3 3D translate XYZ/polar

4 Gnomon/geometry switch

5 XY orient

6 2D rotate

7 3D rotate

⮕ For this translation we will be using automatic axes and origin placement found in the Dynamic dialog menu.

Origin	**Axes**

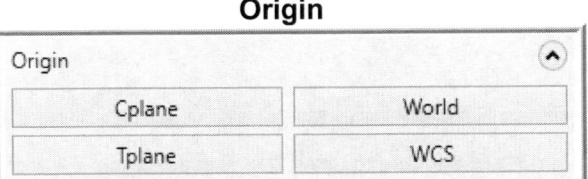
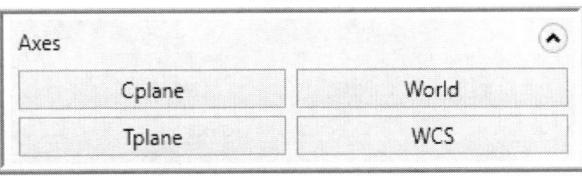

Moves the selected geometry **from the current gnomon center point** to the origin of the current **Cplane, Tplane, World,** or **WCS.**

Orientates the selected geometry based on the **current gnomons Z axis** to the orientation of the current **Cplane, Tplane, World,** or **WCS** Z axis.

⮕ Before using the automatic alignment, the gnomon will have to be aligned with the geometry so the Z axis of the gnomon is pointing in what will be the Z axis of the machining setup.

5. Switch to **gnomon manipulation** by clicking the gnomon switch.

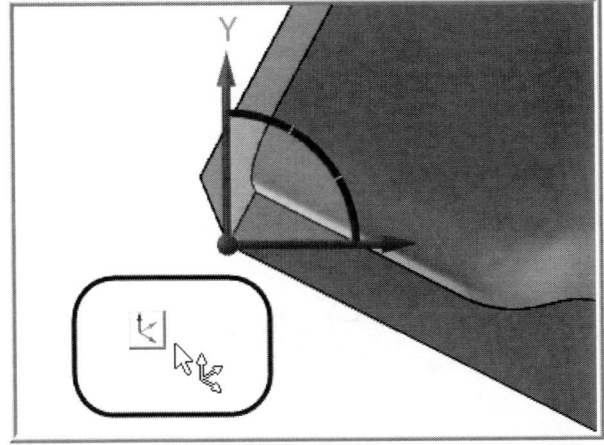

6. Click on the **blue arc** segment closest to the X axis.

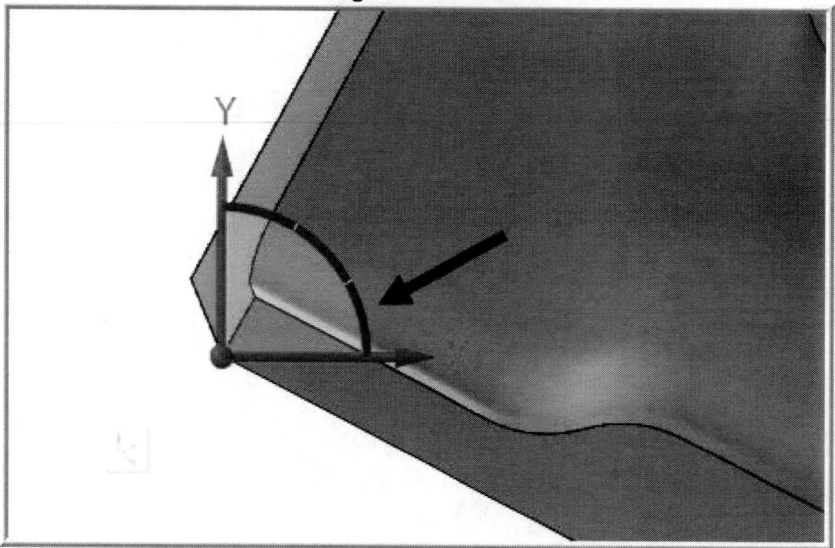

7. Click on the **lower right corner** of the solid. This will properly align the X axis of the gnomon to the part.

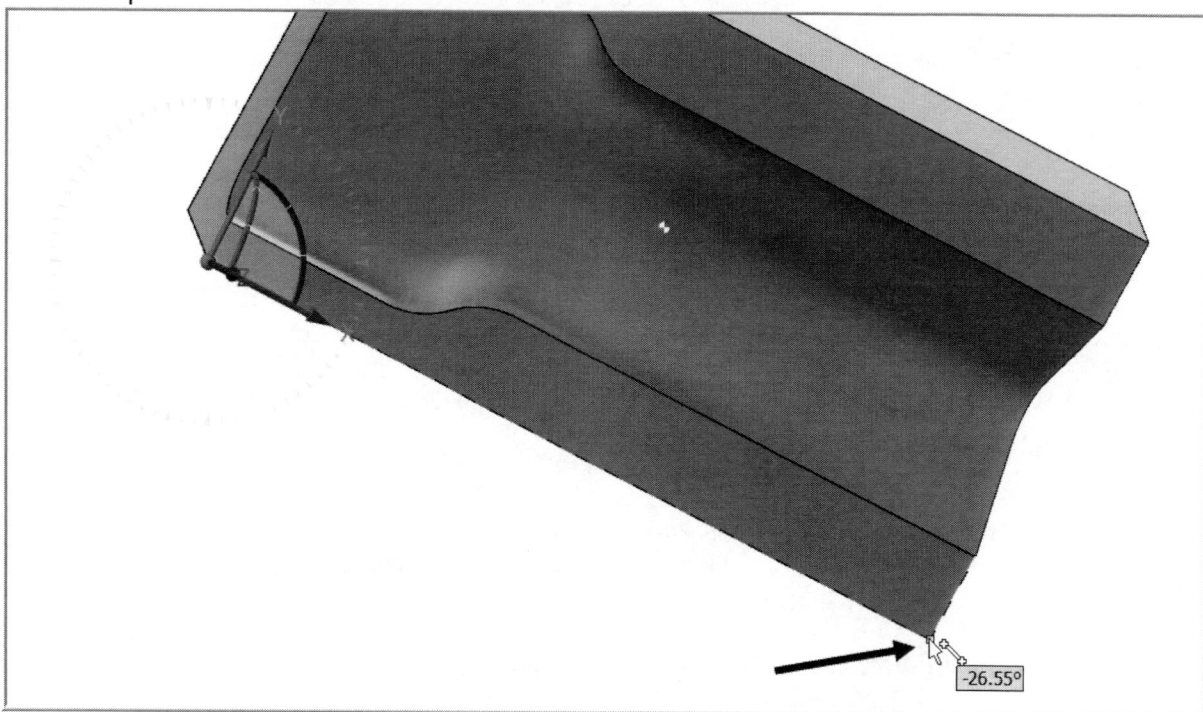

➲ The X axis of the gnomon is now aligned with the part. Y and Z still need to be adjusted. Skew your part so you can get a better view of the Y axis if the gnomon.

8. Click on the **red arc** closest to the Y axis.

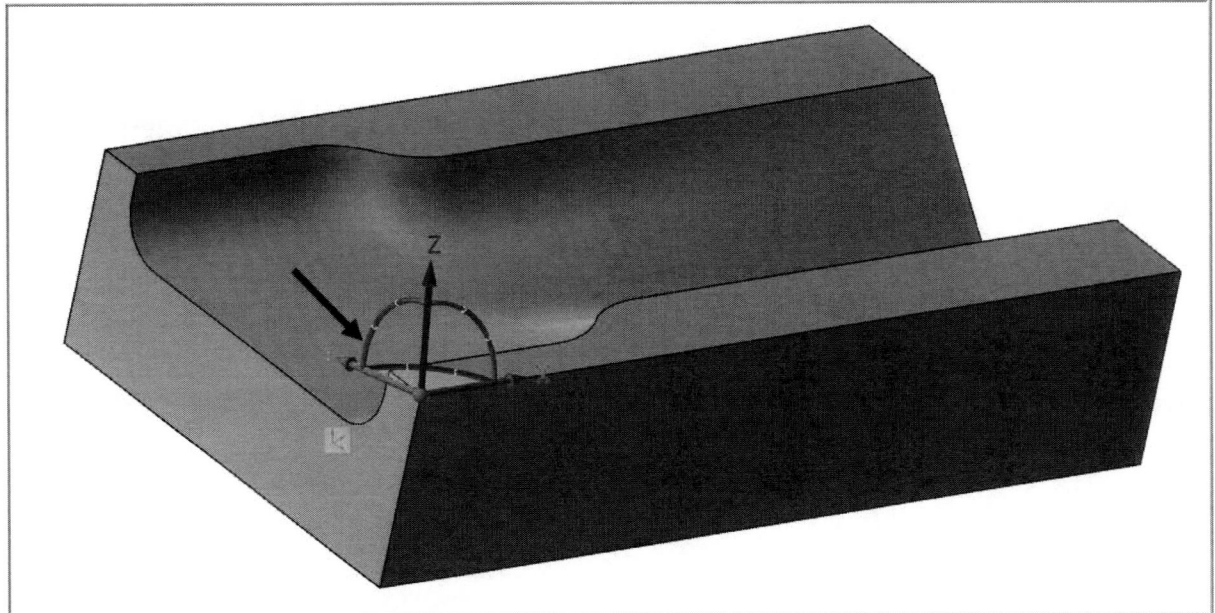

9. Click on the top left corner of the part. If you are not seeing the visual que, ensure you have zoomed out enough so the selection point is outside of the graduated dial.

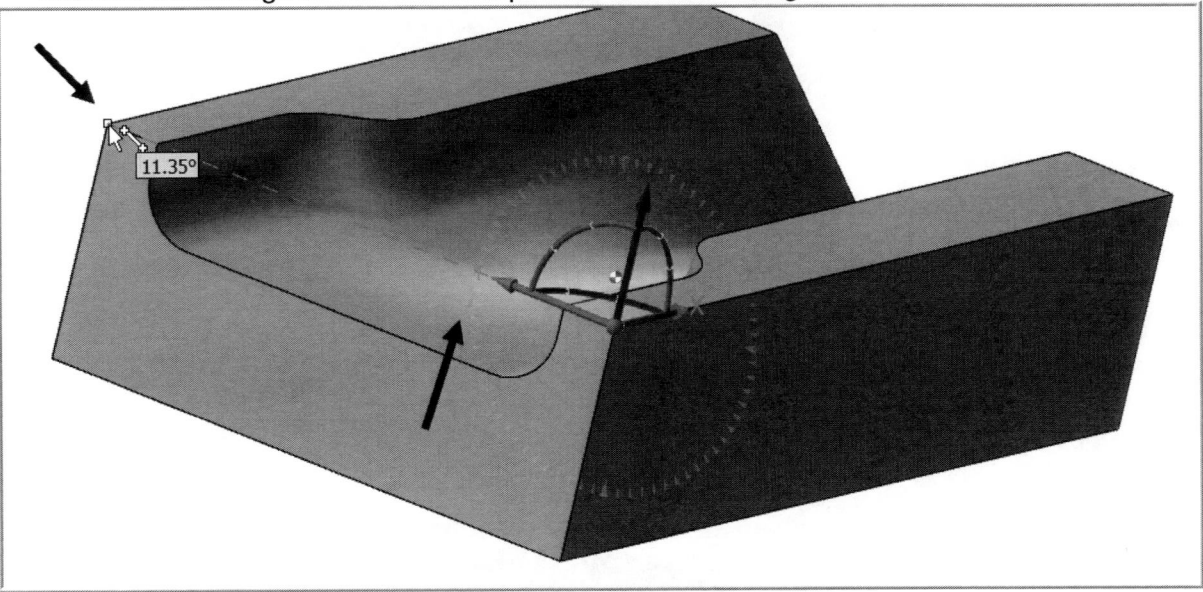

When rotating the part or the gnomon, if your cursor is inside of the graduated dial it will snap to angles that increment by 5 degrees. If your cursor is outside of the graduated dial you can click on snap points, such as visual cues, or click on any point in space. The angle will be set to the exact degree based on your click point.

Cursor inside dial	Cursor outside dial
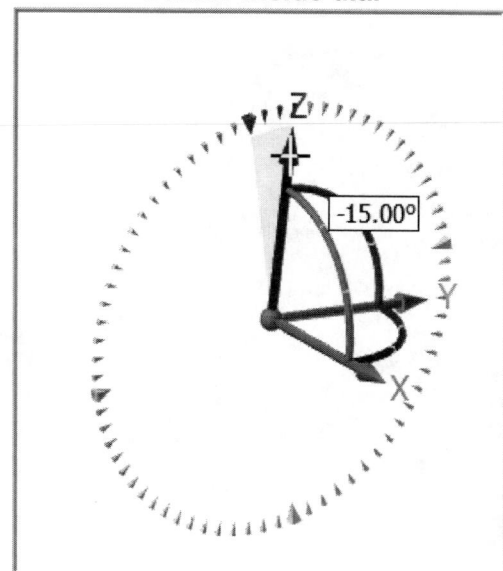	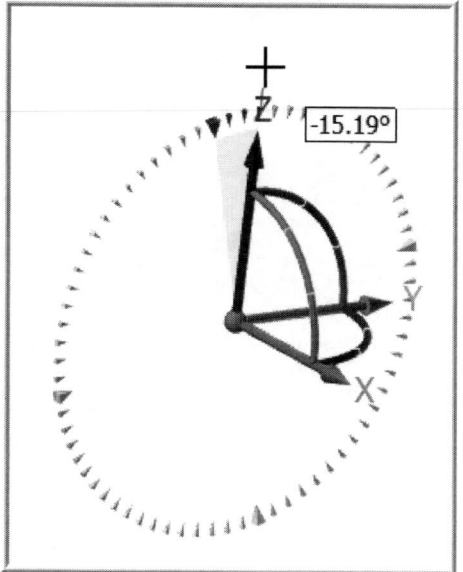

10. With the orientation now complete, we need to move to gnomon to the datum location in the lower right corner. Click on the ball of the gnomon.

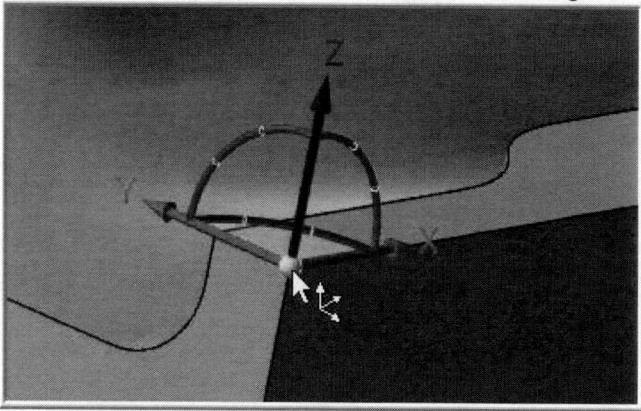

11. Place the gnomon at the lower right corner of the part, at the top face.

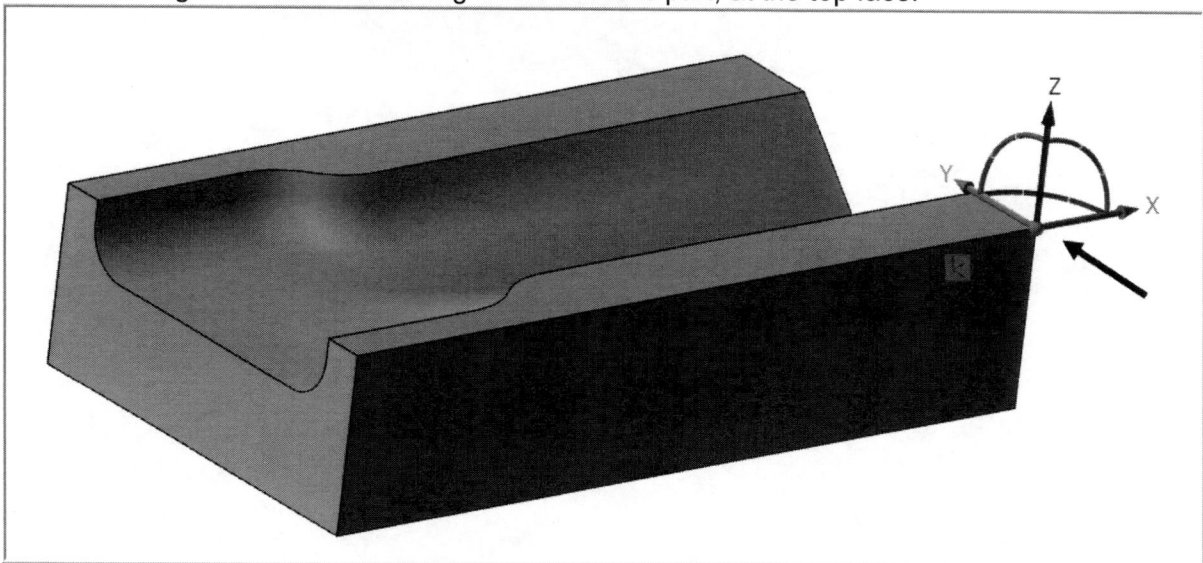

12. With gnomon placement complete, switch back to part manipulation mode.

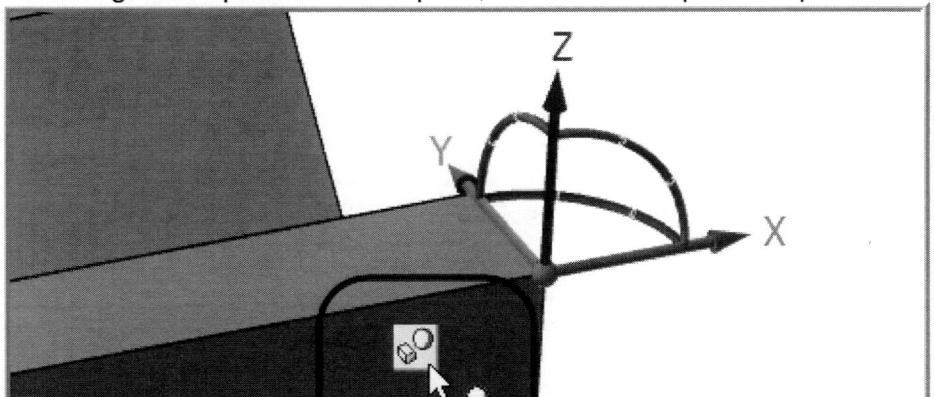

13. On the Dynamic dialog menu click **WCS for Origin**.

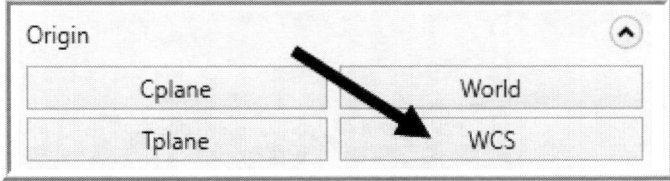

14. On the Dynamic dialog menu click **WCS for Axes**.

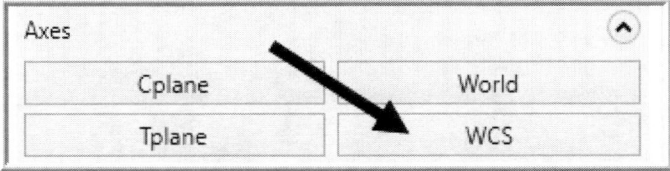

15. Click the **green check** to complete the Dynamic Transform.
16. On the **View** tab click **Fit** and switch to an **Isometric** view. On the **Home** tab click **Clear Colors**.

➲ The part is now perfectly aligned with the Top plane.

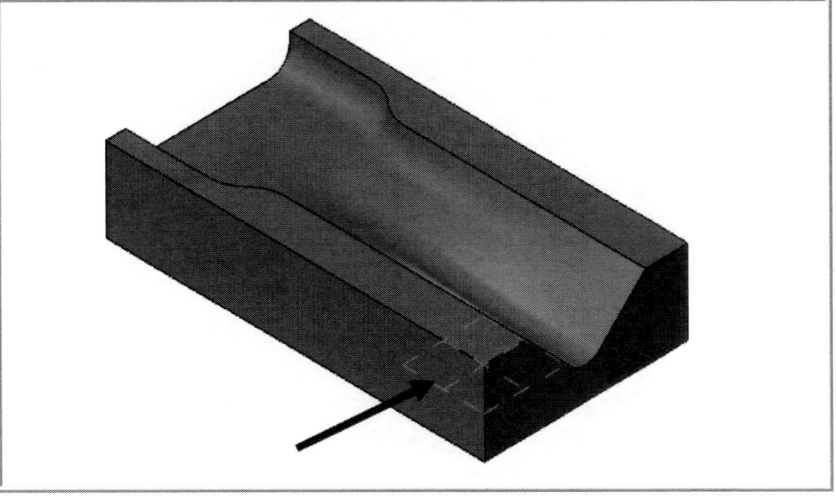

TASK 2B:
CREATE A NEW PLANE AT THE PART

➲ If you completed the previous task (2A), you would need to undo the transform before attempting this task. This would place the part back at its original imported location.

1. On the **Planes** menu, from the **Add Plane** pulldown, select **Dynamic**. Alternatively, you can click on the **gnomon in the lower left corner** of the graphics screen. This will launch into the same Dynamic Plane creation function.

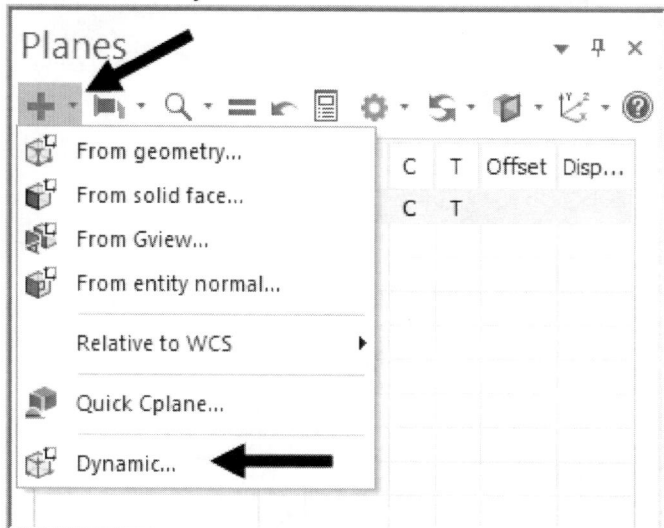
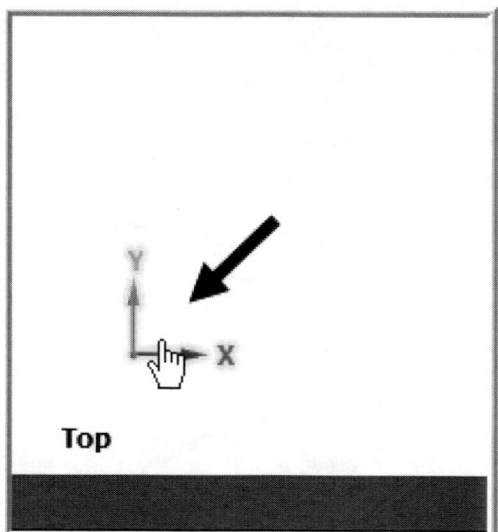

2. On the **View** tab, click **Fit**.
3. Place the gnomon on the **lower left bottom corner** of the part. Look for the line **endpoint** visual cue.

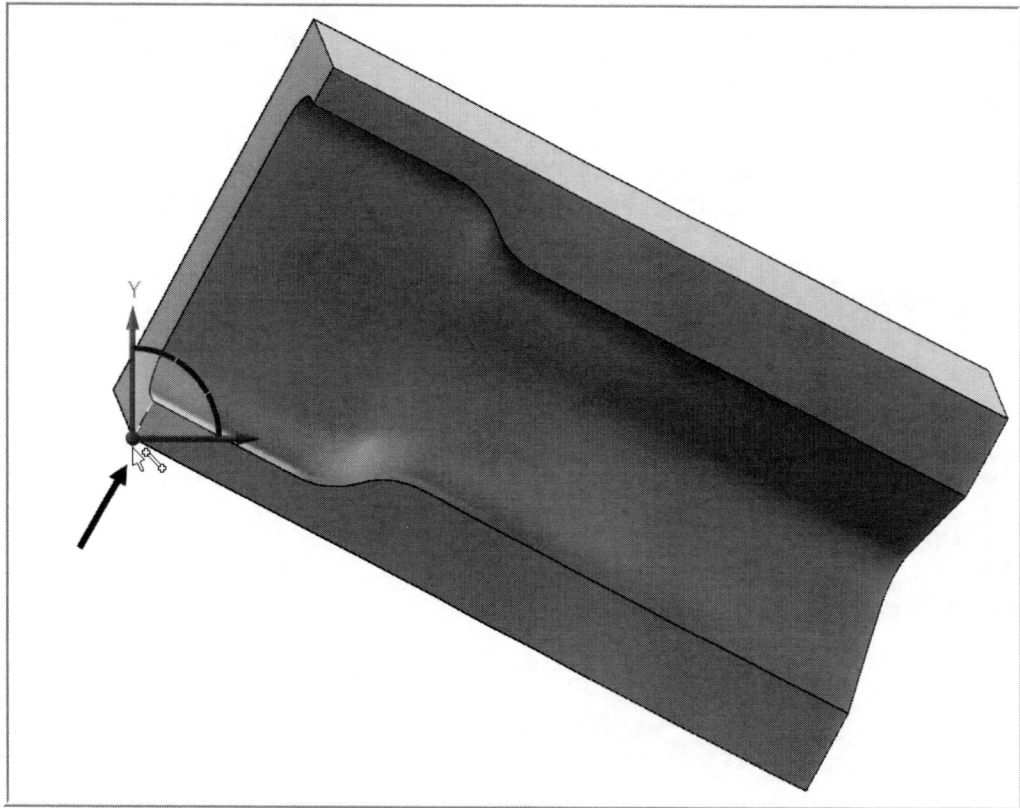

⤳ The Dynamic Planes gnomon is similar to the Dynamic Transform gnomon. The only difference is there is no switch for geometry/gnomon with the Dynamic Planes gnomon. For more information on the clickable parts of this gnomon, refer to the previous section.

4. Click on the **blue arc** closest to the X axis.

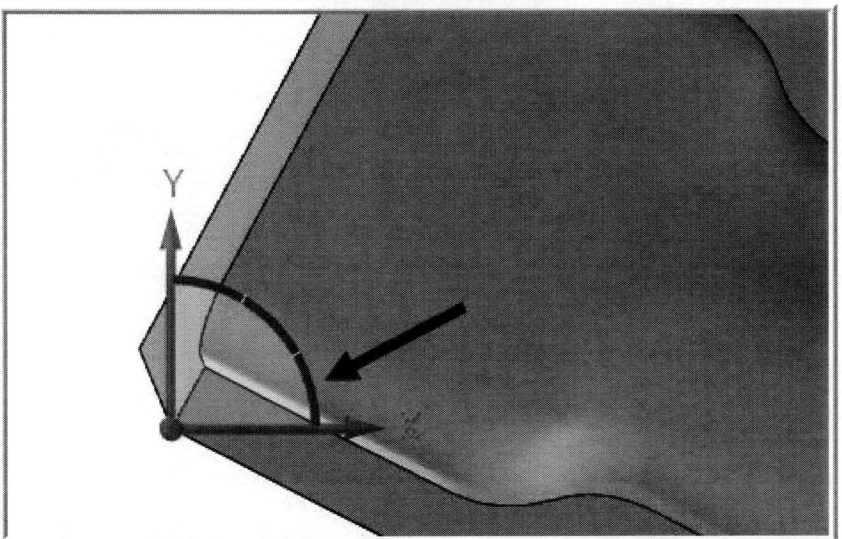

5. Click on the lower right corner of the part. Watch for the endpoint visual cue. This completes the X axis alignment.

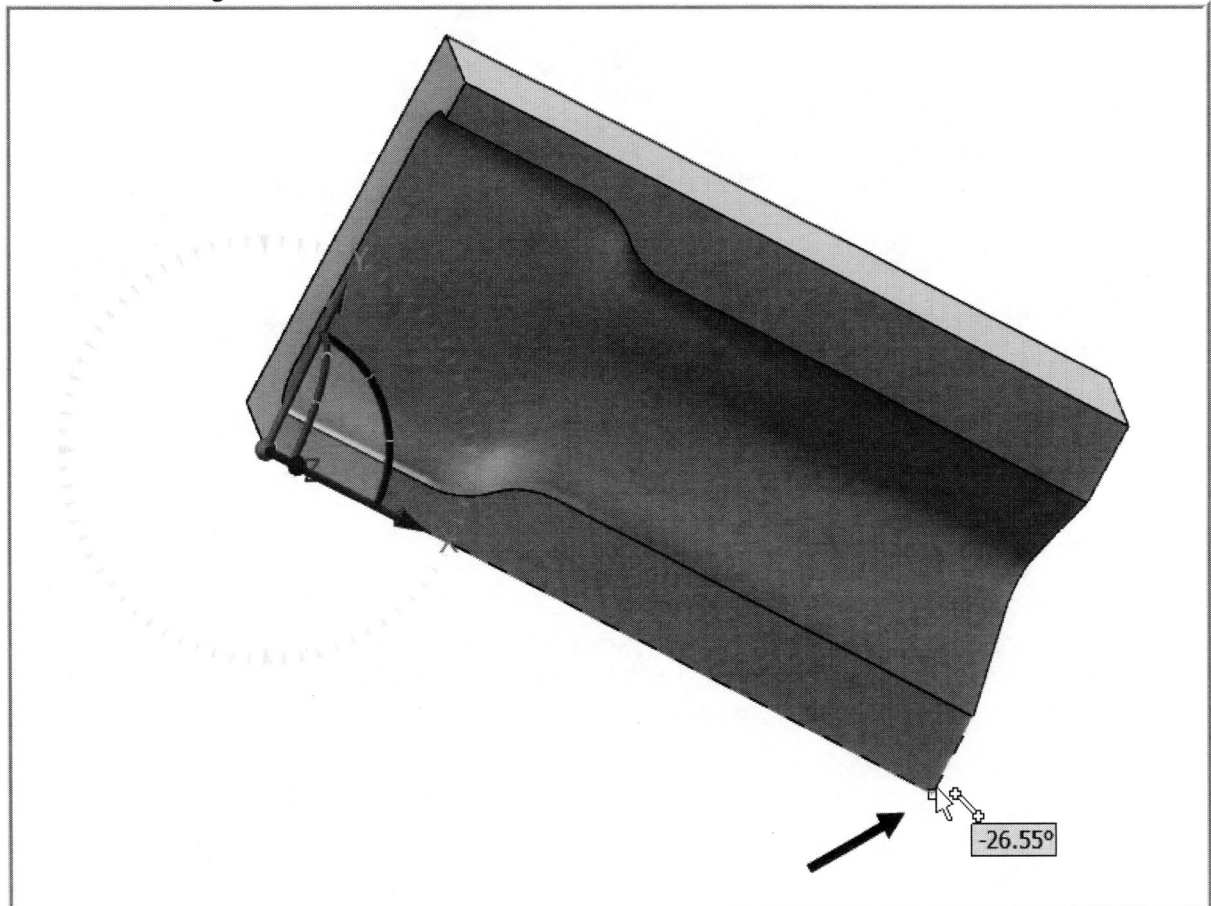

6. Skew the part to get a better view of the left side. Click on the red arc closest to the Y axis.

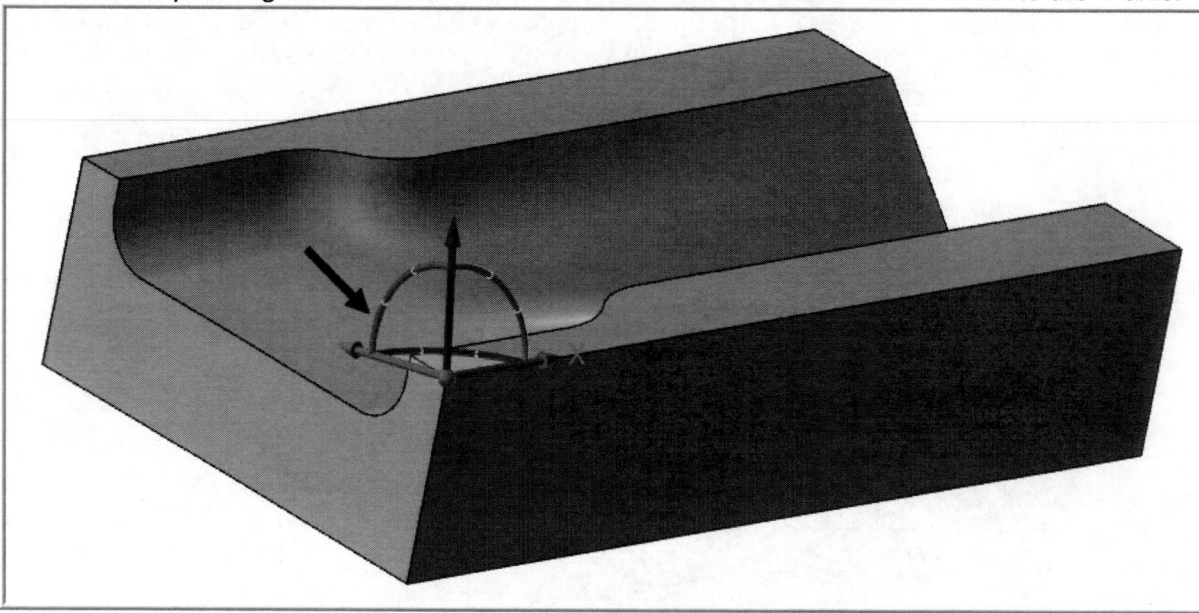

7. Click on the **upper left corner** to complete the Y axis alignment. If you do not see the visual cue appear, ensure you are zoomed in enough so your cursor is outside of the graduated dial.

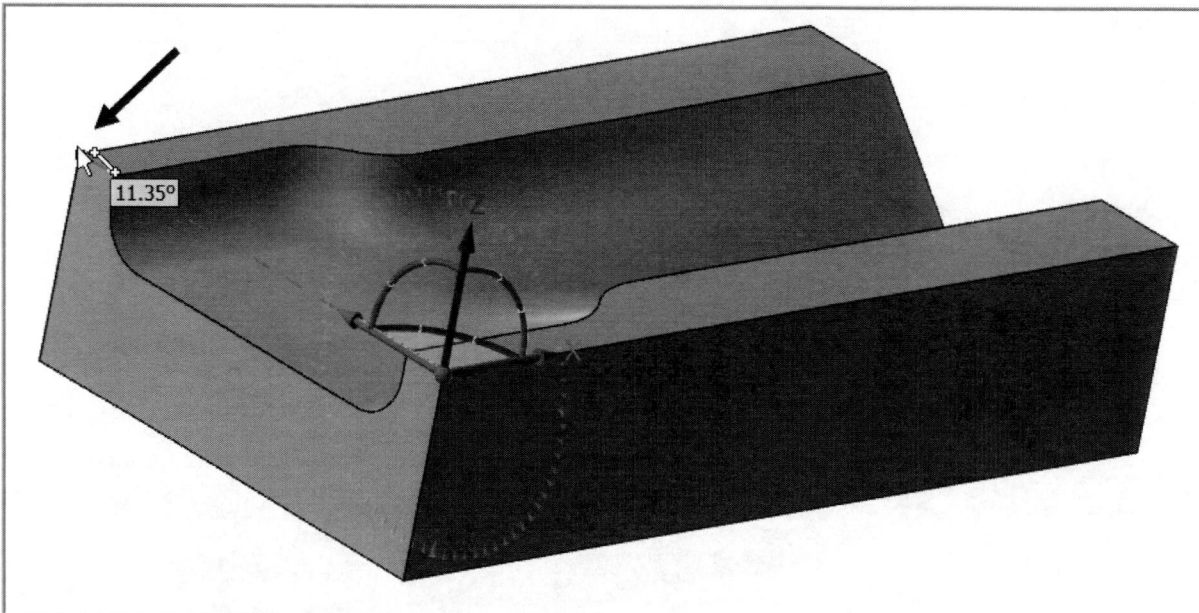

When rotating the part or the gnomon, if your cursor is inside of the graduated dial it will snap to angles that increment by 5 degrees. If your cursor is outside of the graduated dial you can click on snap points, such as visual cues, or click on any point in space. The angle will be set to the exact degree based on your click point.

8. Click on the **ball** of the gnomon and move it to the **lower right corner** of the part, at the top face. This completes the plane orientation and positioning creation.

 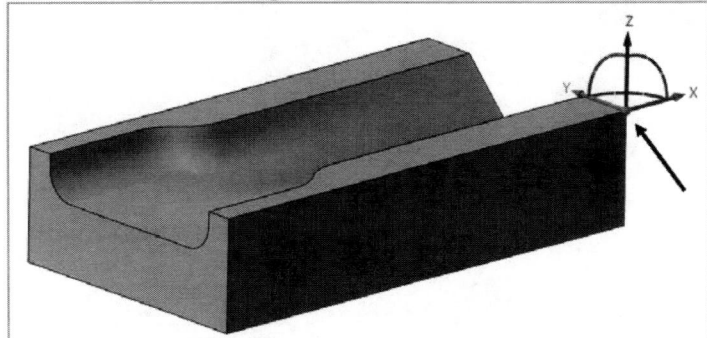

9. On the New Plane dialog menu make the following changes…

   Name - 11B Imported Top

   In the **Set As** section, enable **WCS**, **Tplane**, and **Cplane**.

   Set As will set the selected planes to this newly created plane once plane creation is complete.

   Click **Ok** to complete the plane creation.

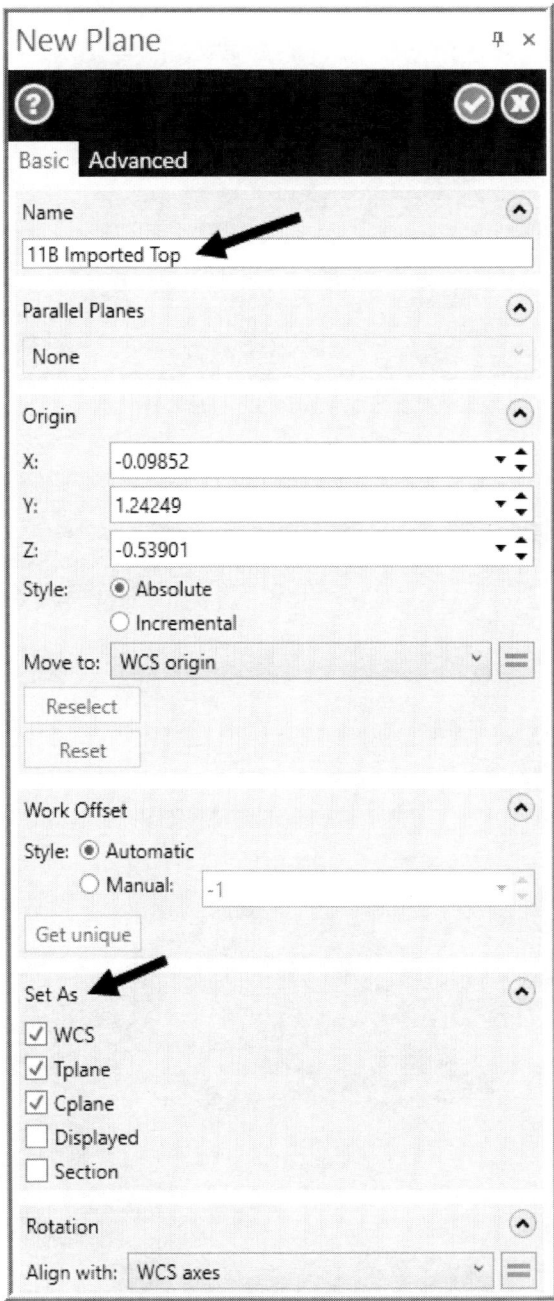

10. Switch to a **Top** View, **Fit** the screen, and then **Unzoom 50%.**

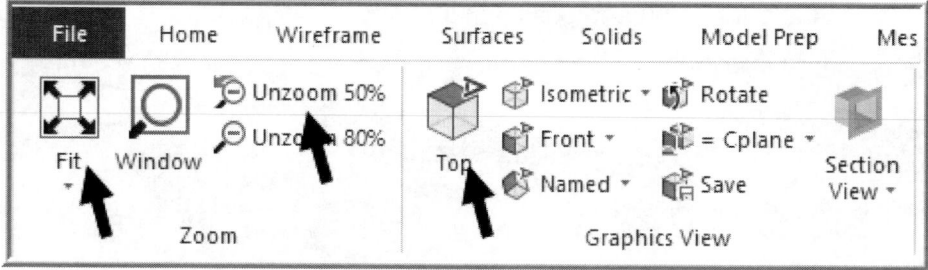

➲ Your **Planes Manager** and **Graphics screen** should match below.

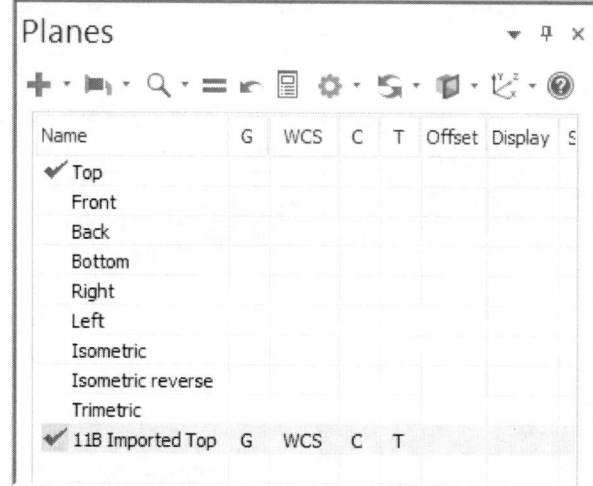

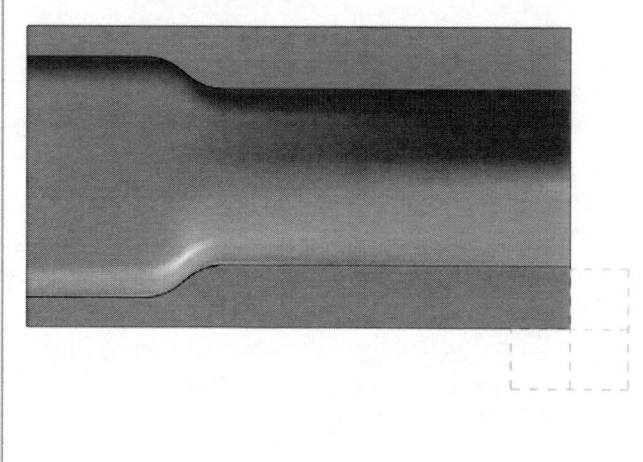

11. On the **View** tab set the view to **Isometric**, **Fit** the screen, and **Unzoom 80%.**

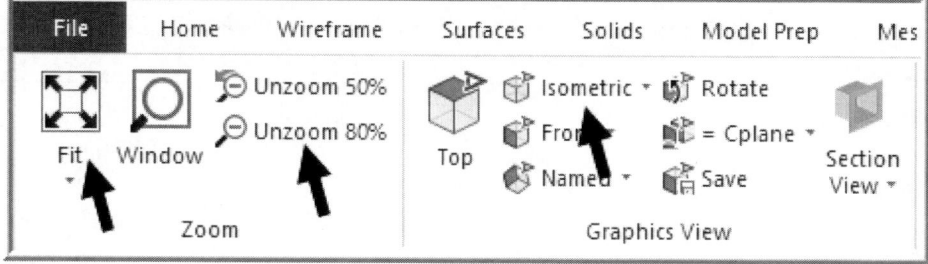

➲ Your graphics screen should match below.

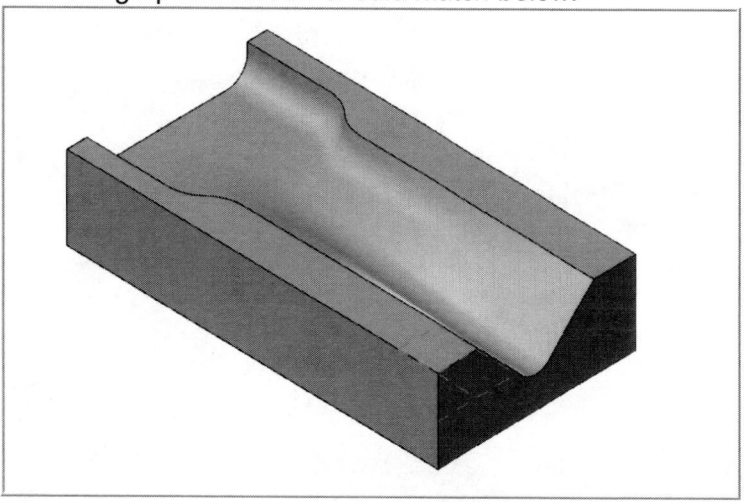

TASK 3:
DEFINE THE ROUGH STOCK USING STOCK SETUP

1. Set the machine type to **Mill Default**, if required.
2. Select the **View tab** and click on **Toolpaths** to display the Toolpaths Manager.
3. Select the **plus** in front of **Properties** to expand the Toolpaths Group Properties.

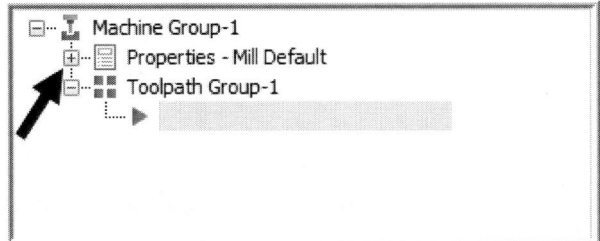 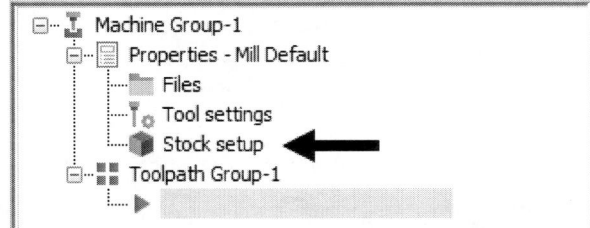

4. Select **Stock setup** in the Toolpaths manager window. If you followed **Task 2A,** you should see **Top** set as the Stock Plane. No additional steps are needed. If you followed **Task 2B**, the Stock Plane needs to be changed **to the created plane**. Click the plane selection button.

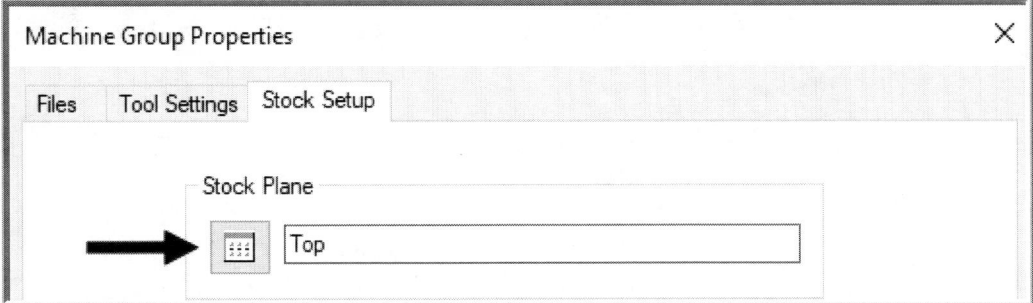

5. Select the created plane from the list and then click **OK**.

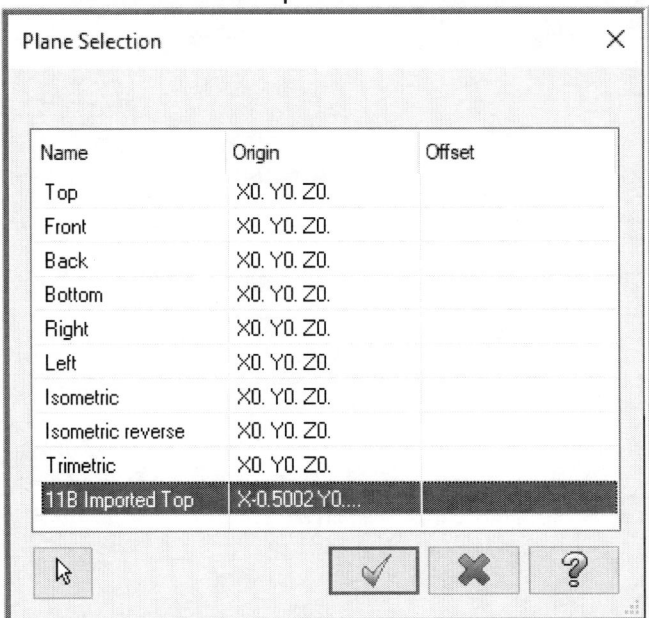

‹ The Stock plane will now be set to the created plane.

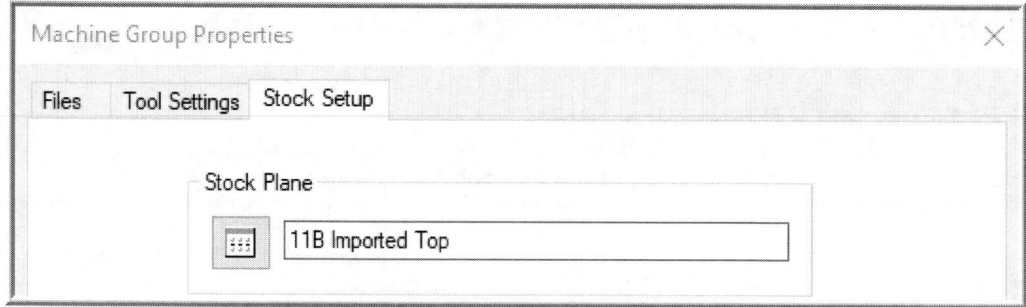

‹ The following steps will be the same regardless of method used previous.

6. Change the parameters to match the **Stock Setup** screenshot below:

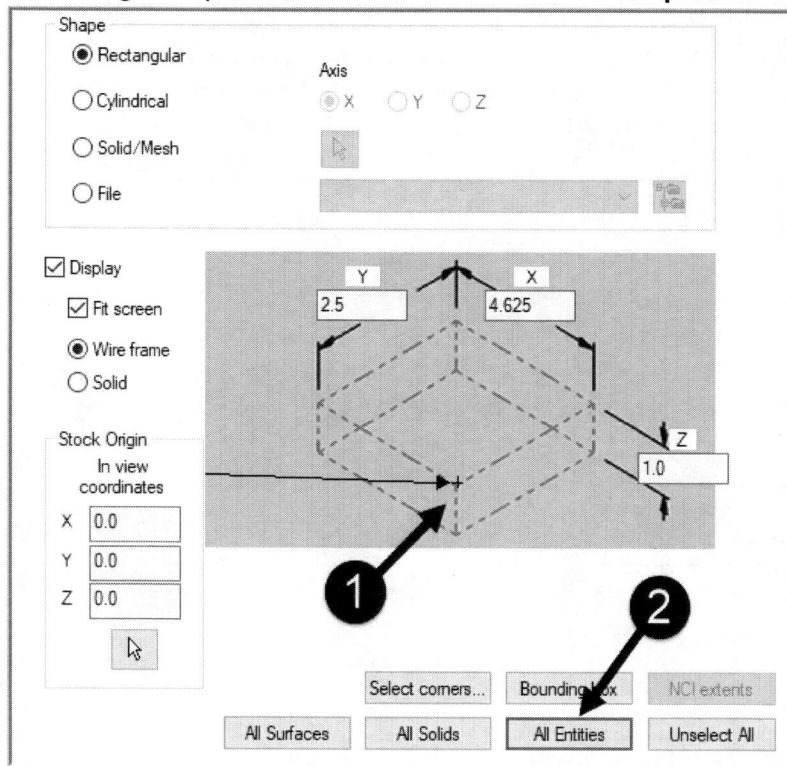

Please Note:

The Stock Plane will be automatically set to the active WCS plane when the machine is selected. If you used method **2A, this should be set to Top**. If you used method **2B, this will be set to 11B Imported Top**.

Follow numbers in the picture for setting the stock.

1 - Set the stock origin to the lower right corner, at the top face.

2 - Click All Entities. Mastercam will make a stock size that encases all visible entities in the graphics screen.

7. Select the **Tool Settings** tab and change the parameters to match the Tool Settings screenshot below. To change the Material type follow the instructions below:

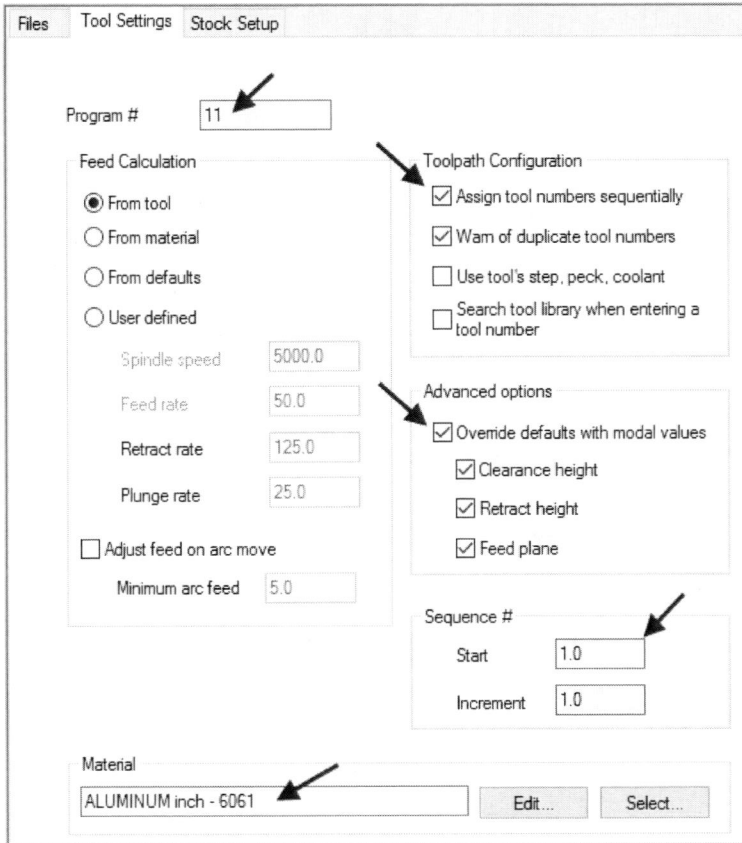

8. To change the Material type to Aluminum 6061 pick the Select button at the bottom of the Tool Settings page.

9. At the **Material List** dialog box open the **Source** drop down list and select **Mill – library**.

10. From the Default Materials list select **ALUMINUM inch -6061** and then select [✓]

8. Select the **OK** button [✓] again to complete this Stock Setup function.

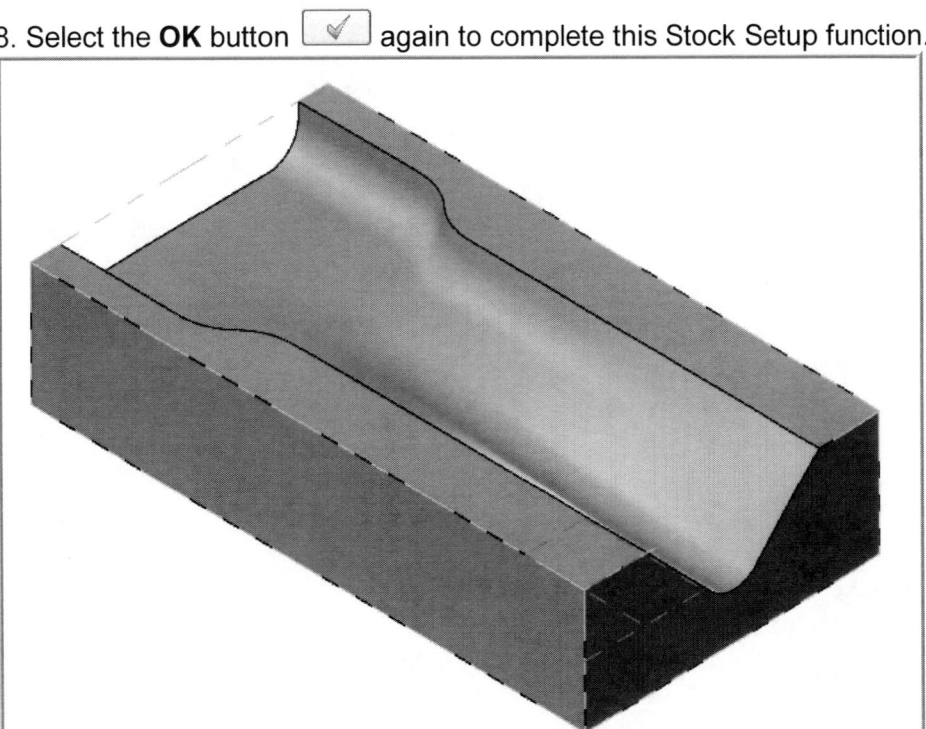

TASK 4:
ROUGH MACHINE USING SURFACE HIGH SPEED
AREA ROUGH

➲ In this task you will use a 0.5 diameter end mill with a 0.125 corner radius to rough machine the part.

1. Select the **Toolpaths** tab at the top right side of the screen.
2. Select **OptiRough** in the **3D** toolpath section.
3. Select the **Toolpath Type** page, select **Area Roughing**.

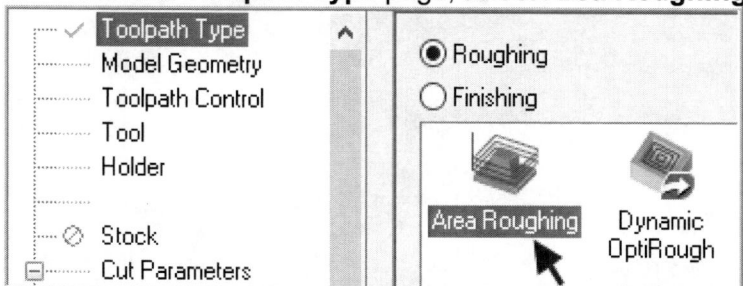

4. On the **Model Geometry** page set both the **Wall Stock** and **Floor Stock to 0.02.**

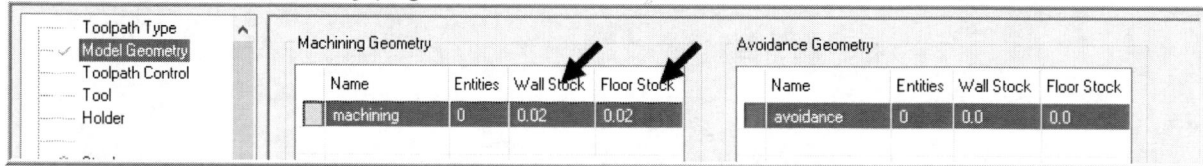

5. At the bottom of the **Model Geometry** page click on the **Select entities** button.

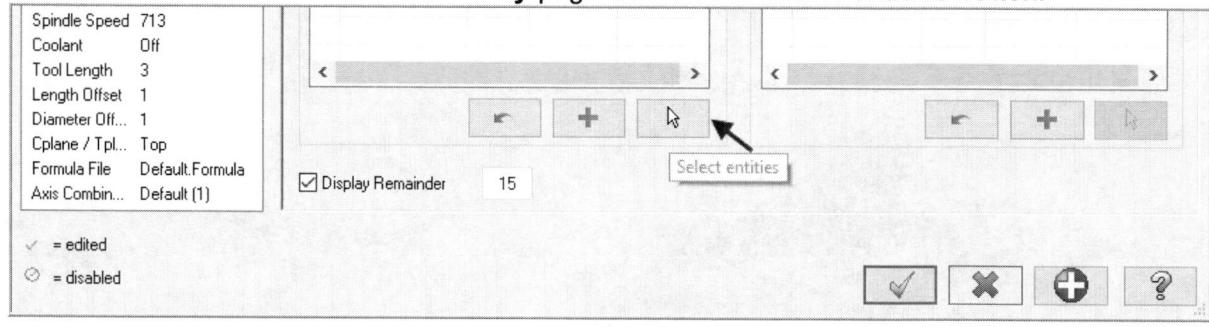

6. To satisfy the prompt **triple left click on any solid face**. This will select the entire solid.

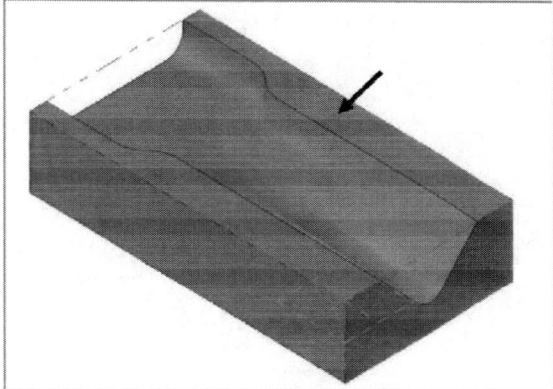

7. To move onto the next step you now need to pick the **End Selection** icon .

8. Select the **Toolpath Control** page, make changes as shown below.

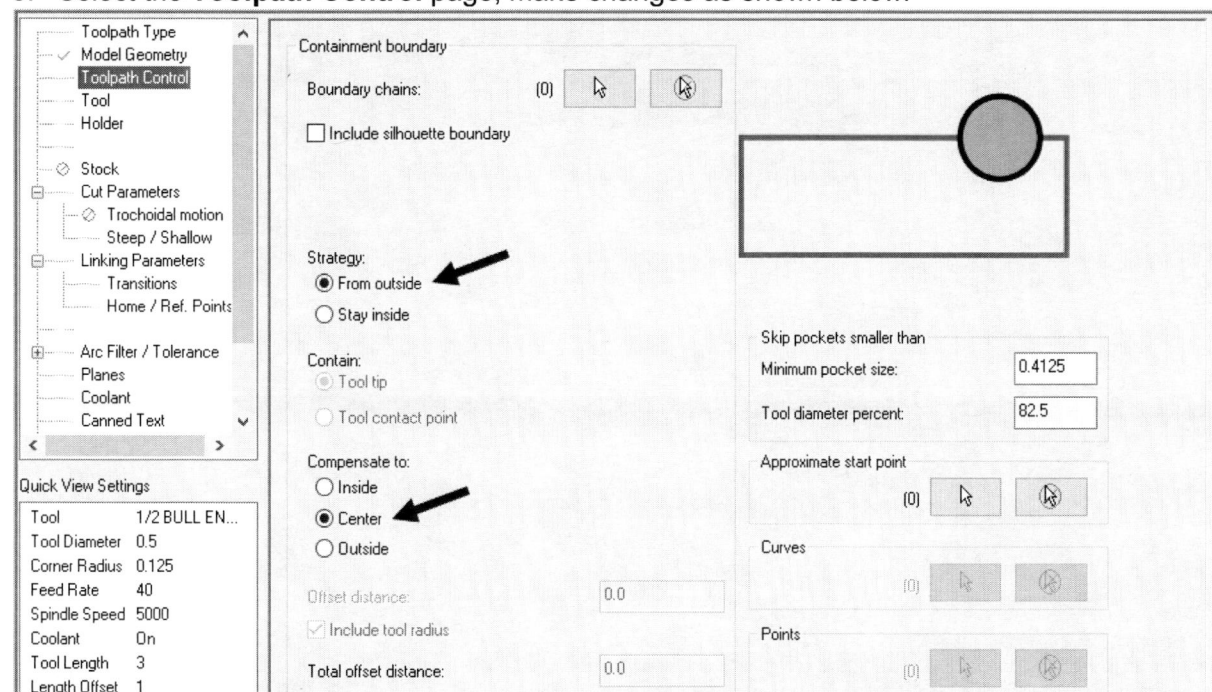

9. Select the **Tool** page
10. In the lower left corner of the **Tool** page select the **Select library tool...** button. **Disable Filter active** if required.
11. Use the slider bar on the right of this dialog box to scroll down and locate a **0.5 diameter bull end mill with a 0.125 corner radius**. Select the end mill by picking anywhere along its row.

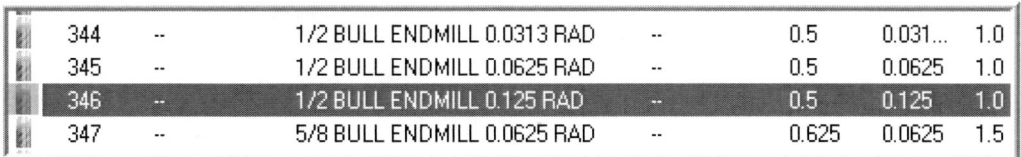

	344	--	1/2 BULL ENDMILL 0.0313 RAD	--	0.5	0.031...	1.0
	345	--	1/2 BULL ENDMILL 0.0625 RAD	--	0.5	0.0625	1.0
	346	--	1/2 BULL ENDMILL 0.125 RAD	--	0.5	0.125	1.0
	347	--	5/8 BULL ENDMILL 0.0625 RAD	--	0.625	0.0625	1.5

12. Select the OK button [✓] to complete the selection of this tool.

13. Make changes to the **Tool** page as shown below.

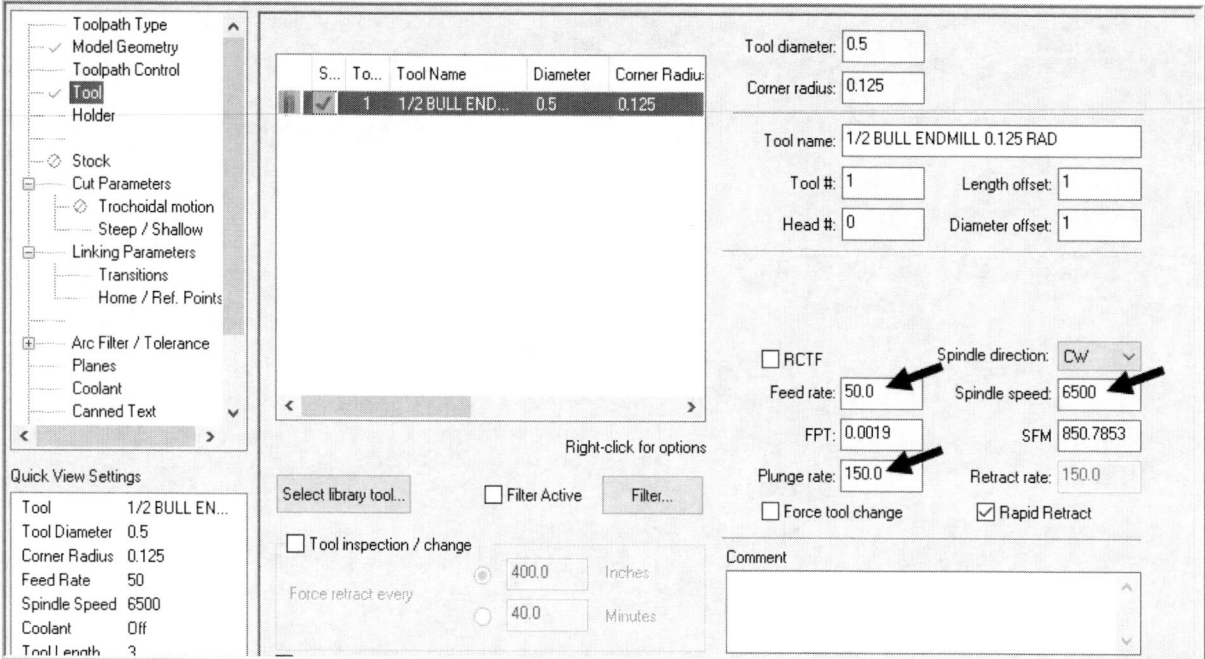

14. Select the **Cut parameters** page and make changes to this page as shown below.

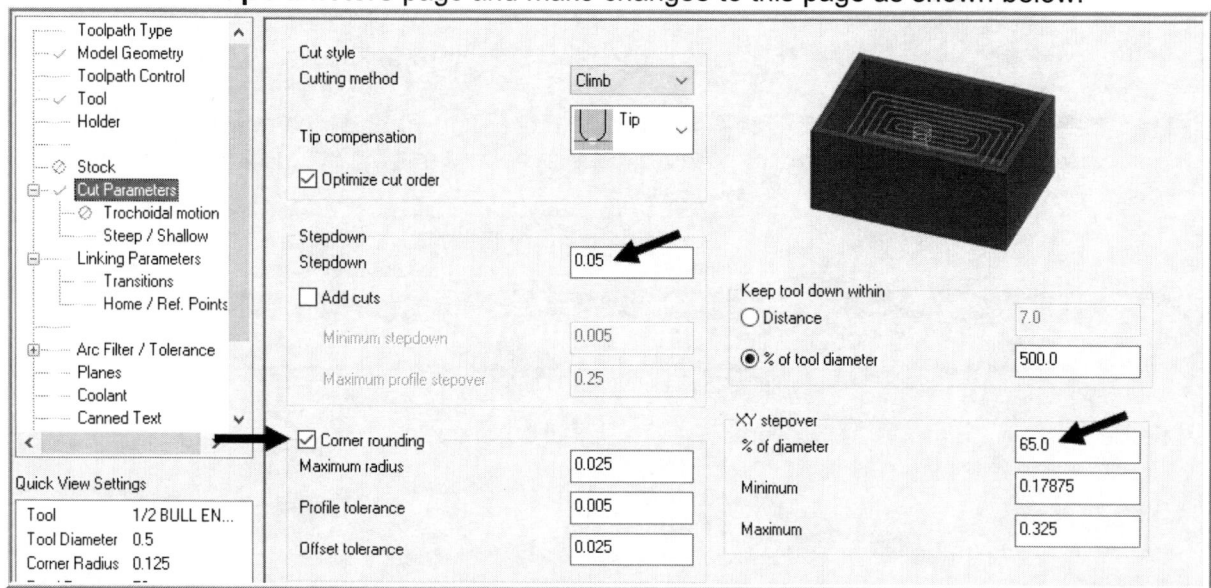

Profile tolerance
This sets the maximum deviation from the calculated toolpath that the smoothing will adjust the 'smoothed' toolpath to.

Offset tolerance
Works the same way as the smoothing tolerance. This affects offset passes (toolpath steps that are away from the drive geometry).

Loosening the tolerances here will result in smoother motion on the machine. The tradeoff is accuracy. The **profile tolerance** for finishing toolpaths should be the same or tighter than the total tolerance

15. No changes on the Trochoidal Motion or Steep/Shallow pages.

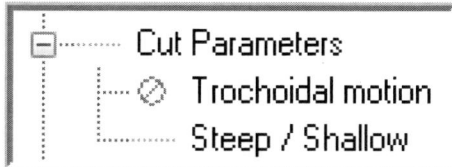

16. Select the **Linking Parameters** page and make changes to this page as shown below, if required:

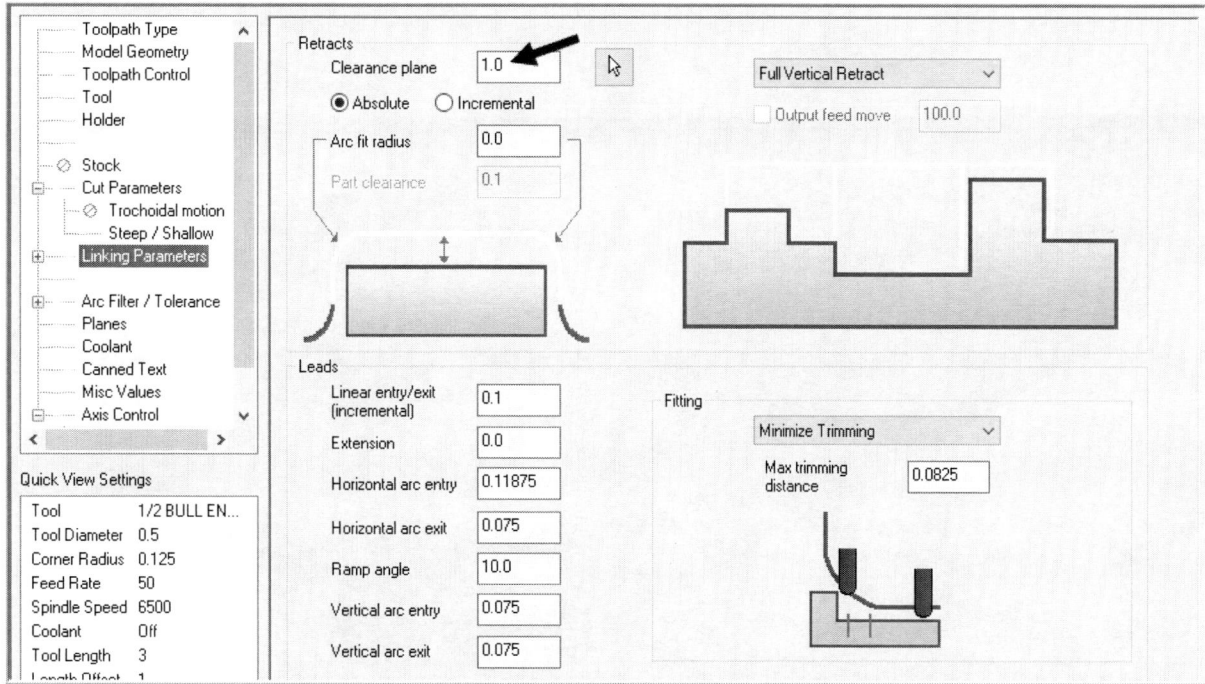

17. Make the follow changes on the **Arc Filter / Tolerance** page.

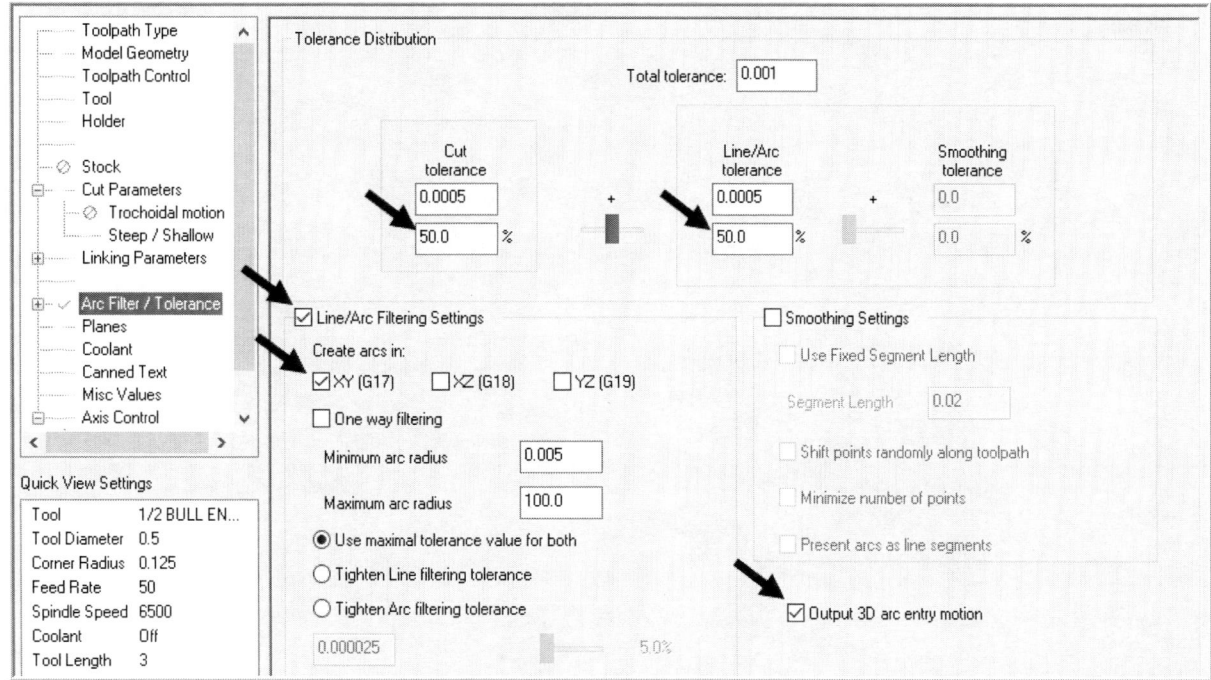

18. Turn on Flood coolant on the **Coolant** page.
19. Select the OK button ☑ to exit and generate the toolpath.
20. **Verify** the new toolpath.

➲ The verified image should look like the image below:

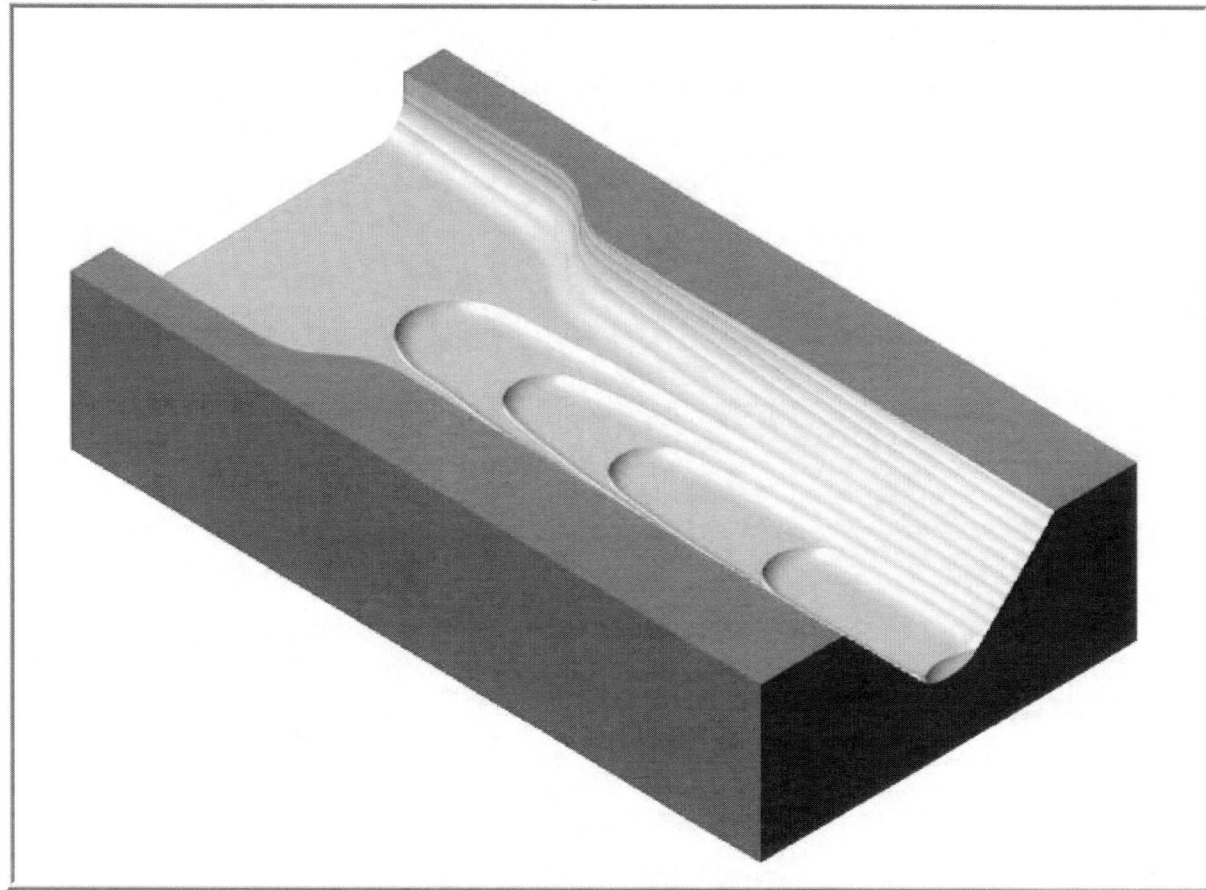

TASK 5:
FINISH MACHINE USING SURFACE FINISH FLOWLINE

➲ In this task you will use a 0.250 diameter Ball end mill to finish the surface.

1. Select the **Toolpaths** tab at the top right side of the screen.
2. Click on the **Expand gallery** down arrow in the **3D** section and select **Flowline** from the **Finishing** selections

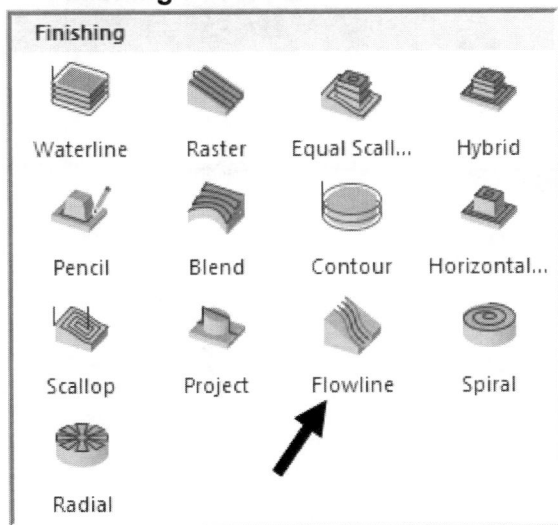

Mastercam's Surface flowline toolpaths follow the shape and direction of the surfaces and create a smooth and flowing toolpath motion.

Both rough and finish flowline toolpaths require an orderly row or grid of surfaces. You can change the start point and direction of the cuts in the Flowline data dialog box.

3. Select the surface shown below for the finishing operation. Click End Selection. The Toolpath/Surface selection menu will then appear, click on the **Flowline** button.

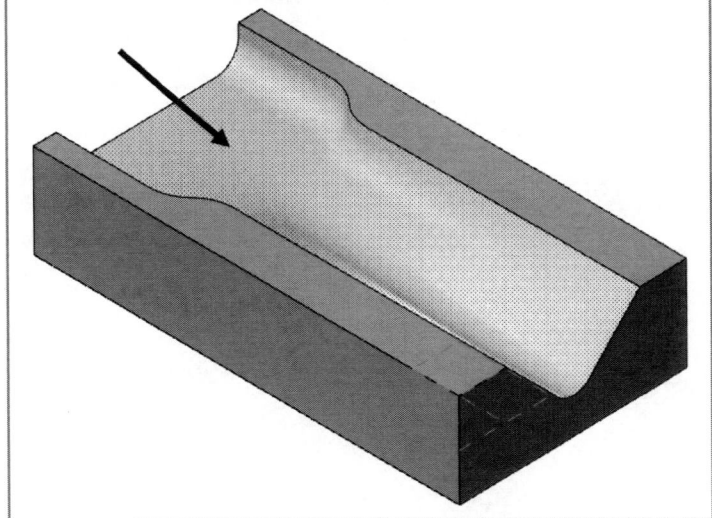

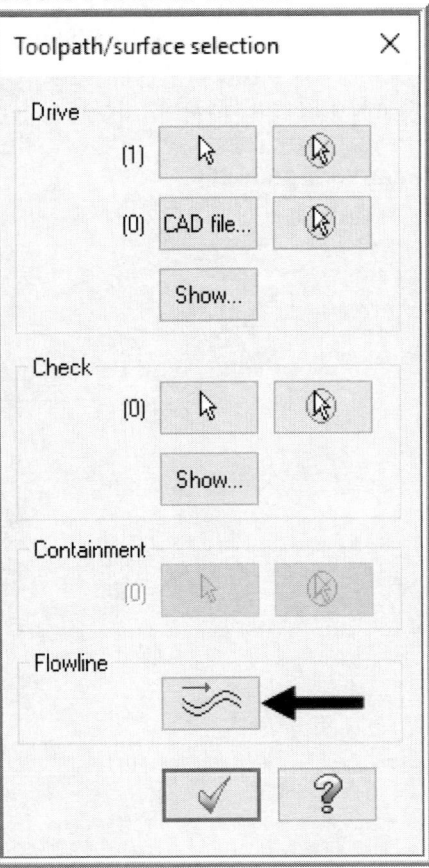

4. Click on the **Cut direction** button to toggle the toolpath direction as shown below: Note, the lines should be inside the cavity as shown below: if they are on the outside click on the Offset button.

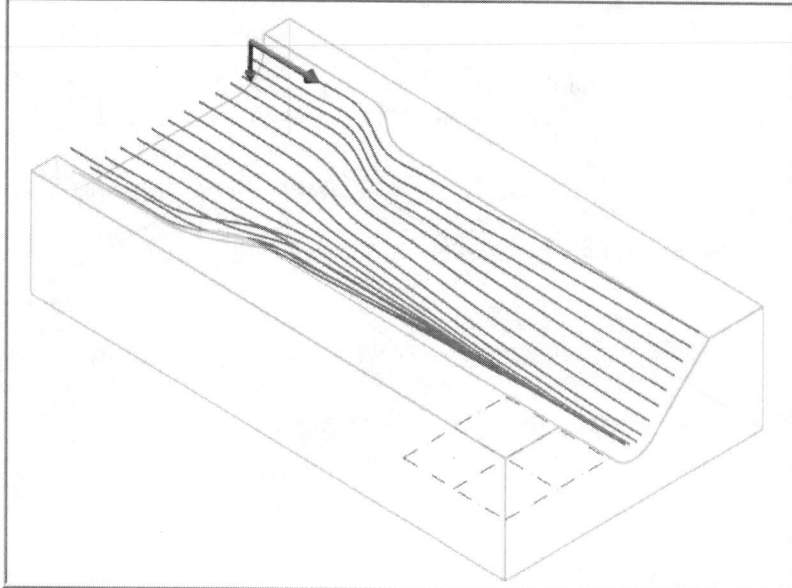 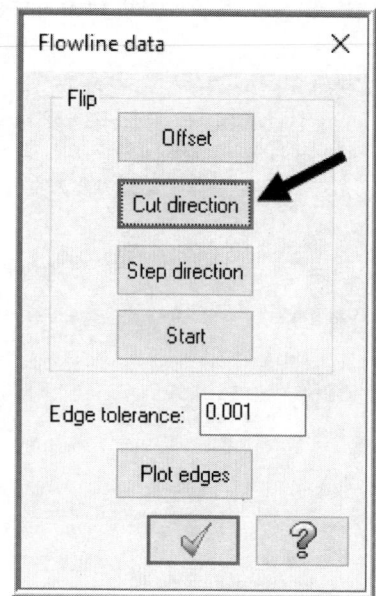

5. Select the OK button to exit the **Flowline data** dialog box.
6. Select the OK button to exit the **Toolpath/surface selection** dialog box.
7. In the lower left corner of the **Toolpath parameters** page select the **Select library tool...** button.
8. Use the **Filter** function to filter out a selection of cutters. Select the **Filter** button on the right side of the **Tool selection** dialog box.
9. Select the **None** button in the Tool Types section.
10. Click on the **Endmill2 Sphere** type icon, first row, and second icon from the left.
11. Select the drop-down arrow in the **Tool diameter** field and set it to **Equal.** Input the tool diameter as **0.250**.

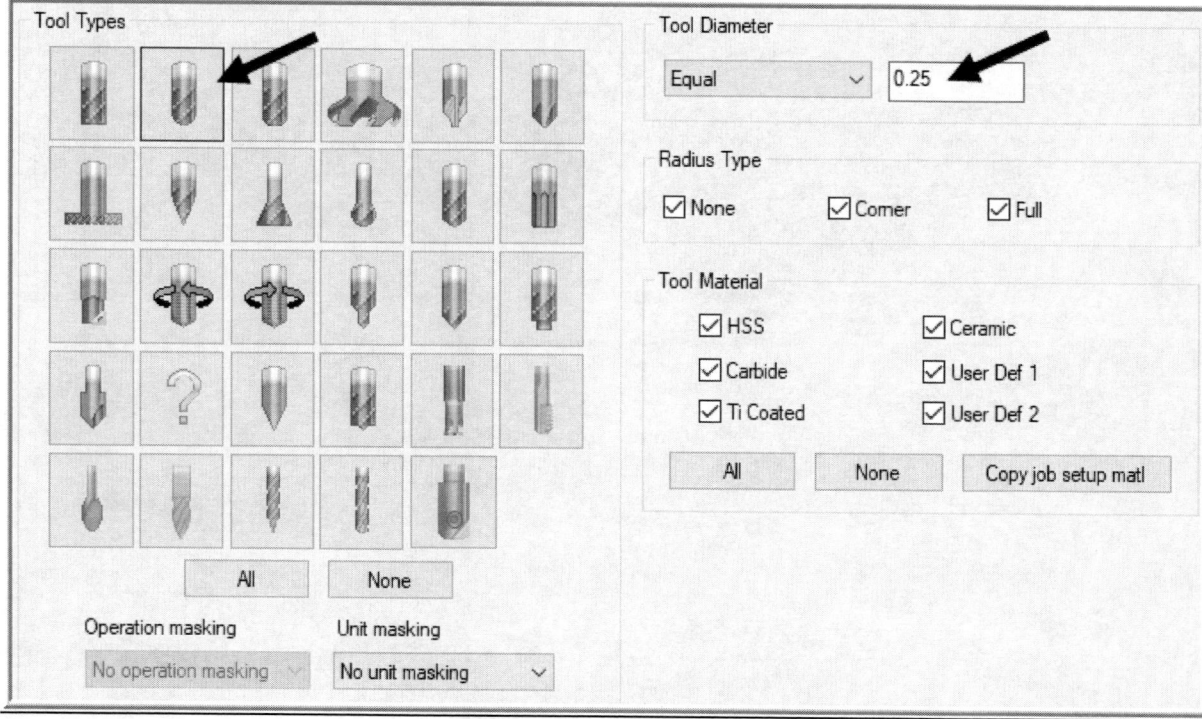

12. Select the OK button [✓] to exit.
13. Select the **0.25 ball end mill**.

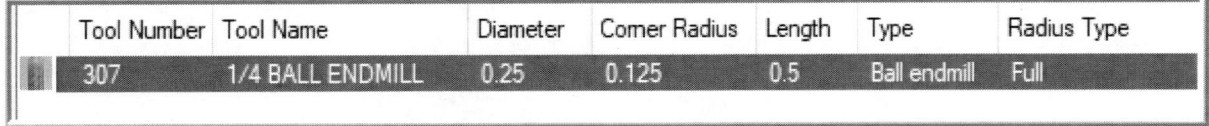

Tool Number	Tool Name	Diameter	Corner Radius	Length	Type	Radius Type
307	1/4 BALL ENDMILL	0.25	0.125	0.5	Ball endmill	Full

14. Select the OK button [✓] to complete the selection of this tool.
15. Make changes to the **Toolpath parameters** page as shown below. Coolant flood is on.

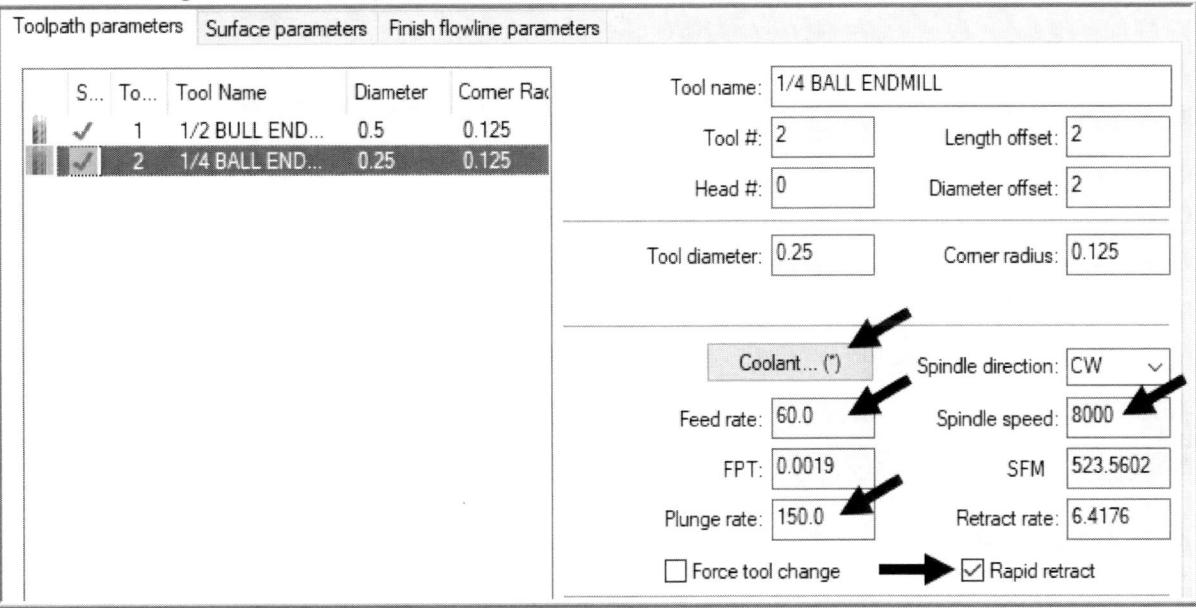

16. Select the **Surface parameters** page and make changes to this page as shown below:

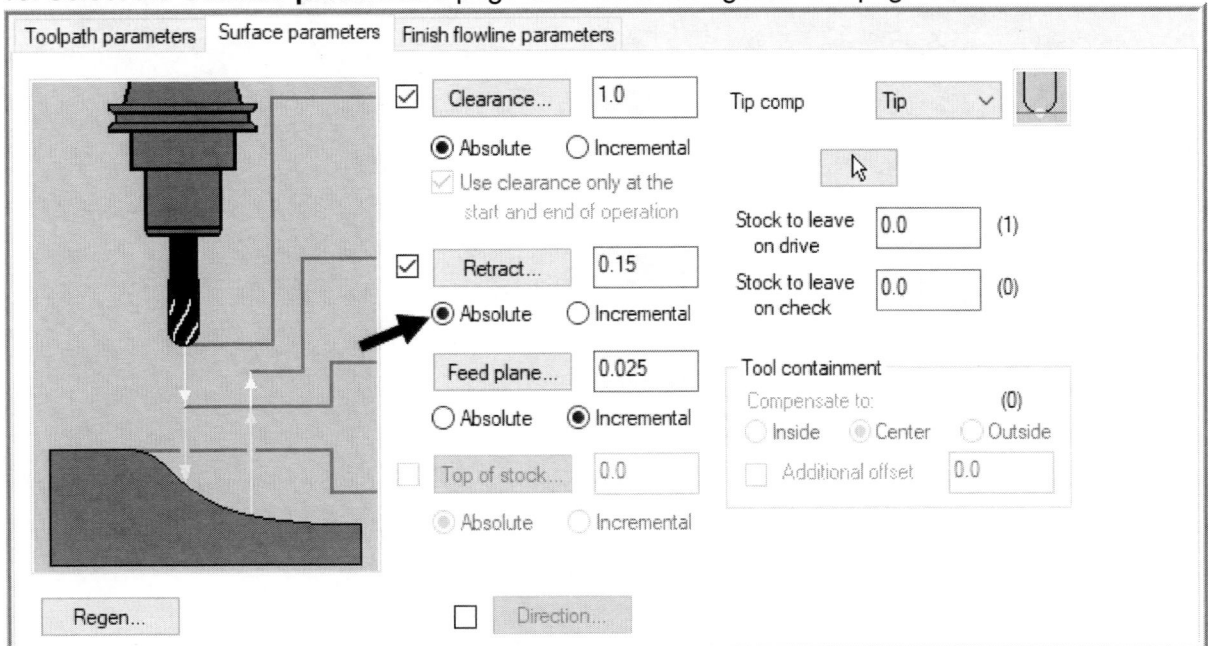

17. Next, on the **Finish flowline parameters** page make changes to this page as shown below:

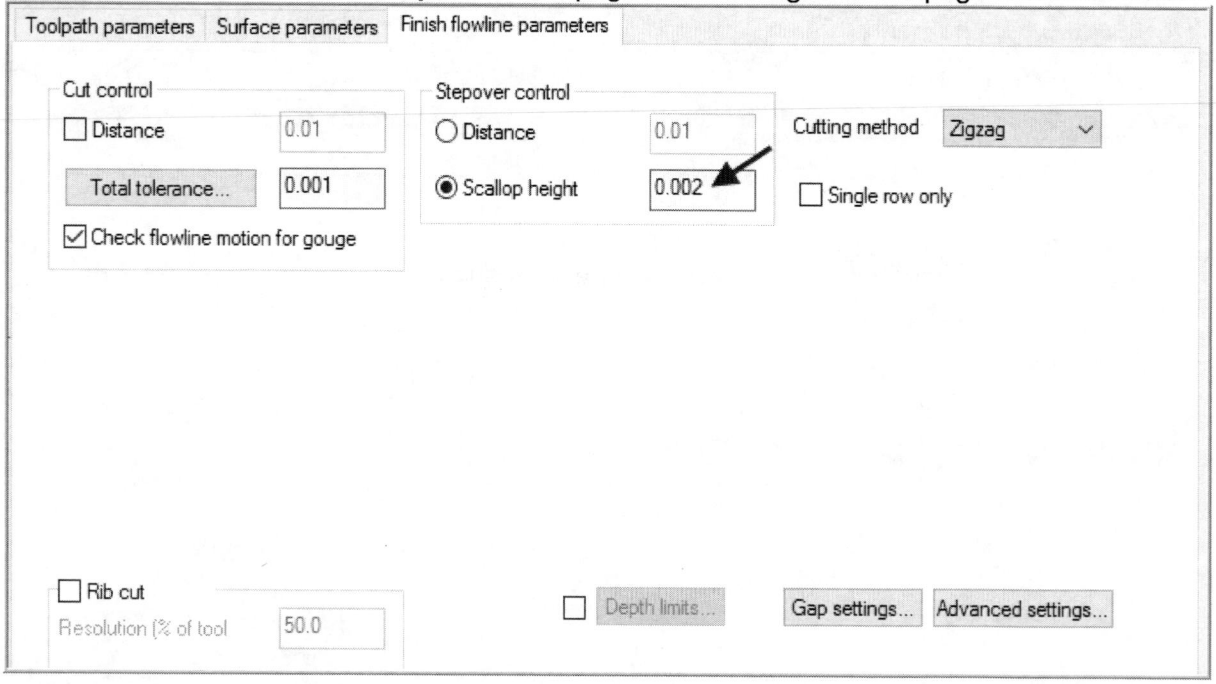

| Toolpath parameters | Surface parameters | Finish flowline parameters |

Cut control
- ☐ Distance   0.01
- [Total tolerance...]   0.001
- ☑ Check flowline motion for gouge

Stepover control
- ○ Distance   0.01
- ⦿ Scallop height   0.002

Cutting method   Zigzag ∨

☐ Single row only

- ☐ Rib cut
- Resolution (% of tool   50.0

☐ Depth limits...   [Gap settings...]   [Advanced settings...]

Scallop height

This adjusts the stepover between cuts to create leftover material at a specific height.

Surface rough and finish flowline toolpaths give you precise control of scallops left on the part.

Scallop height can be set either as a stepover distance or as an actual height.

When using the scallop height option, Mastercam automatically adjusts the stepover between cuts, although this amount is not shown in the stepover entry field.

---

18. Select the **Gap settings** button and make changes to this page as shown below:

Gap settings ⨯	**Tangential line length** Sets the line length at the entry and exit points of a gap. Not available for multiaxis toolpaths. **Motion** Determines the tool motion in areas smaller than the gap size. **Direct** moves the tool directly from position to position. **Broken** moves the tool up and over or over and down. **Smooth** moves the tool in a fluid motion. **Follow surface(s)** matches the Z motion of the surface.

Gap settings dialog contents:

Reset

Gap size
- ○ Distance — 0.01
- ◉ % of stepover — 300.0

Motion < Gap size, keep tool down
- Broken
- ☐ Use plunge, retract rate in gap
- ☑ Check gap motion for gouge

Motion > Gap size, retract
- ☑ Check retract motion for gouge

- ☐ Optimize cut order
- ☐ Plunge into previously cut area
- ☐ Follow containment boundary at gap

Tangential arc radius: 0.0

Tangential arc angle: 0.0

Tangential line length: 0.2 ⬅

19. Select the OK button ✓ to exit Gap settings.

20. Select the OK button ✓ to exit Finish Flowline parameters.
The screen should look like the image below:

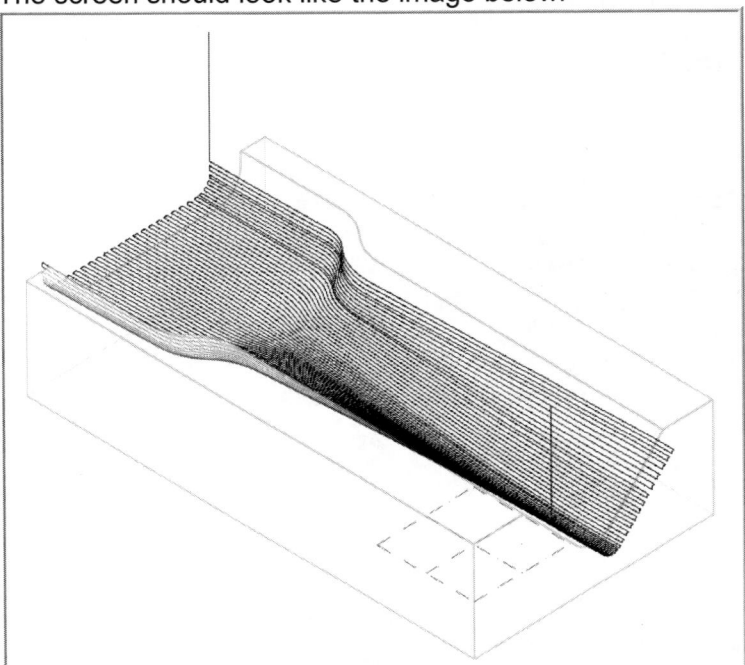

TASK 6:
VERIFY THE TOOLPATH

1. Right mouse click in the graphics area and click on **Isometric**.
2. In the **Toolpaths Manager** pick all the operations to verify by picking the **Select all operations** icon.
3. Select the **Verify selected operations** icon.
4. **Maximize** the Backplot/Verify window if required.
5. In the **Home** tab, select the following **Visibility** options.

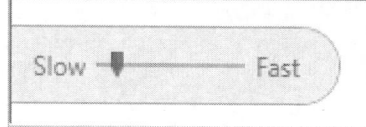

6. At the top of the screen select the **Verify** tab and activate the **Color Loop**.
7. In the lower part of the screen now set the run Speed to slow by moving the slider bar pointer over to the left as shown below.

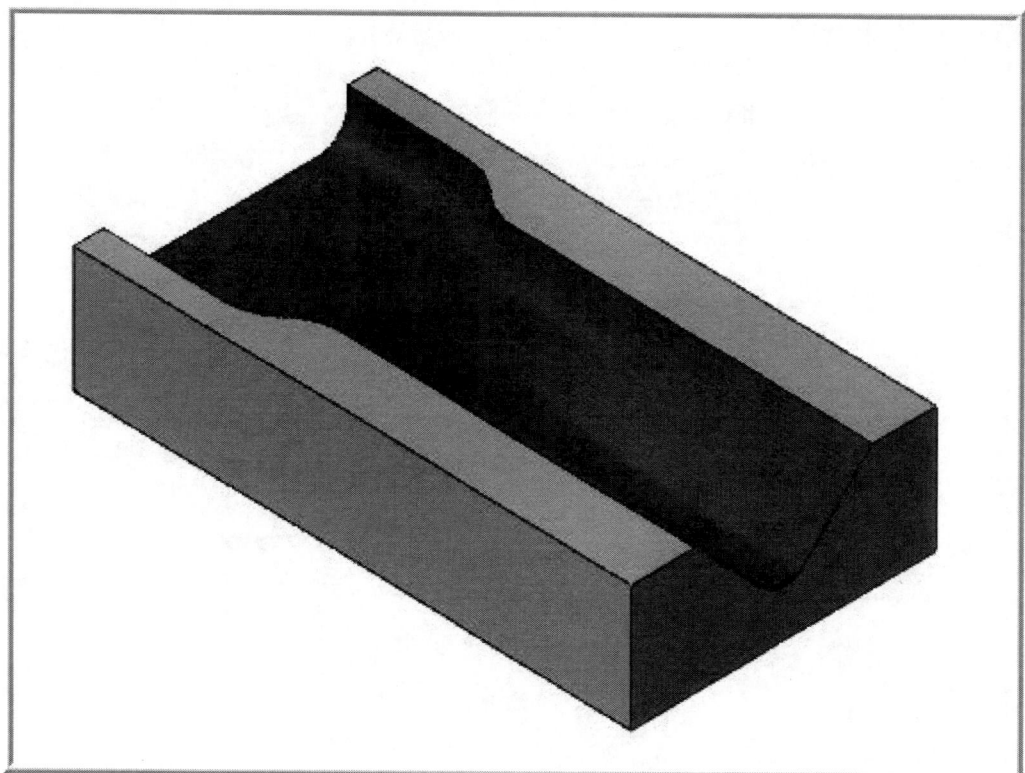

8. Select the **Close** button [×] in the top right hand corner to exit Verify.

TOOLPATH TASK 7:
POST AND CREATE THE CNC CODE FILE

1. Ensure all the operations are selected by picking the **Select all operations** icon  from the Toolpaths Manager.
2. Select the **Post selected operations** button from the Toolpaths Manager.

3. In the Post processing window, make the necessary changes as shown below:

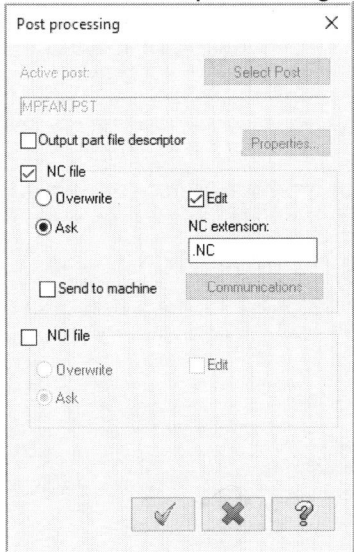

4. Select the OK button [✓] to continue.
5. Ensure the same name as your Mastercam part file name is in the NC File name field.
6. Select the Save button.
7. The CNC code file opens up in the default editor:

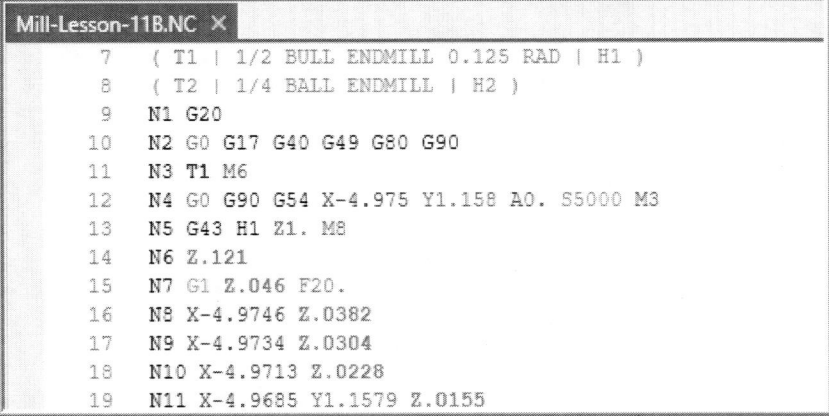

```
 7    ( T1 | 1/2 BULL ENDMILL 0.125 RAD | H1 )
 8    ( T2 | 1/4 BALL ENDMILL | H2 )
 9    N1 G20
10    N2 G0 G17 G40 G49 G80 G90
11    N3 T1 M6
12    N4 G0 G90 G54 X-4.975 Y1.158 A0. S5000 M3
13    N5 G43 H1 Z1. M8
14    N6 Z.121
15    N7 G1 Z.046 F20.
16    N8 X-4.9746 Z.0382
17    N9 X-4.9734 Z.0304
18    N10 X-4.9713 Z.0228
19    N11 X-4.9685 Y1.1579 Z.0155
```

8. Select the [×] in the top right corner to exit the CNC editor
➲ This completes Mill-Lesson-11B.

MILL-LESSON-11 EXERCISES

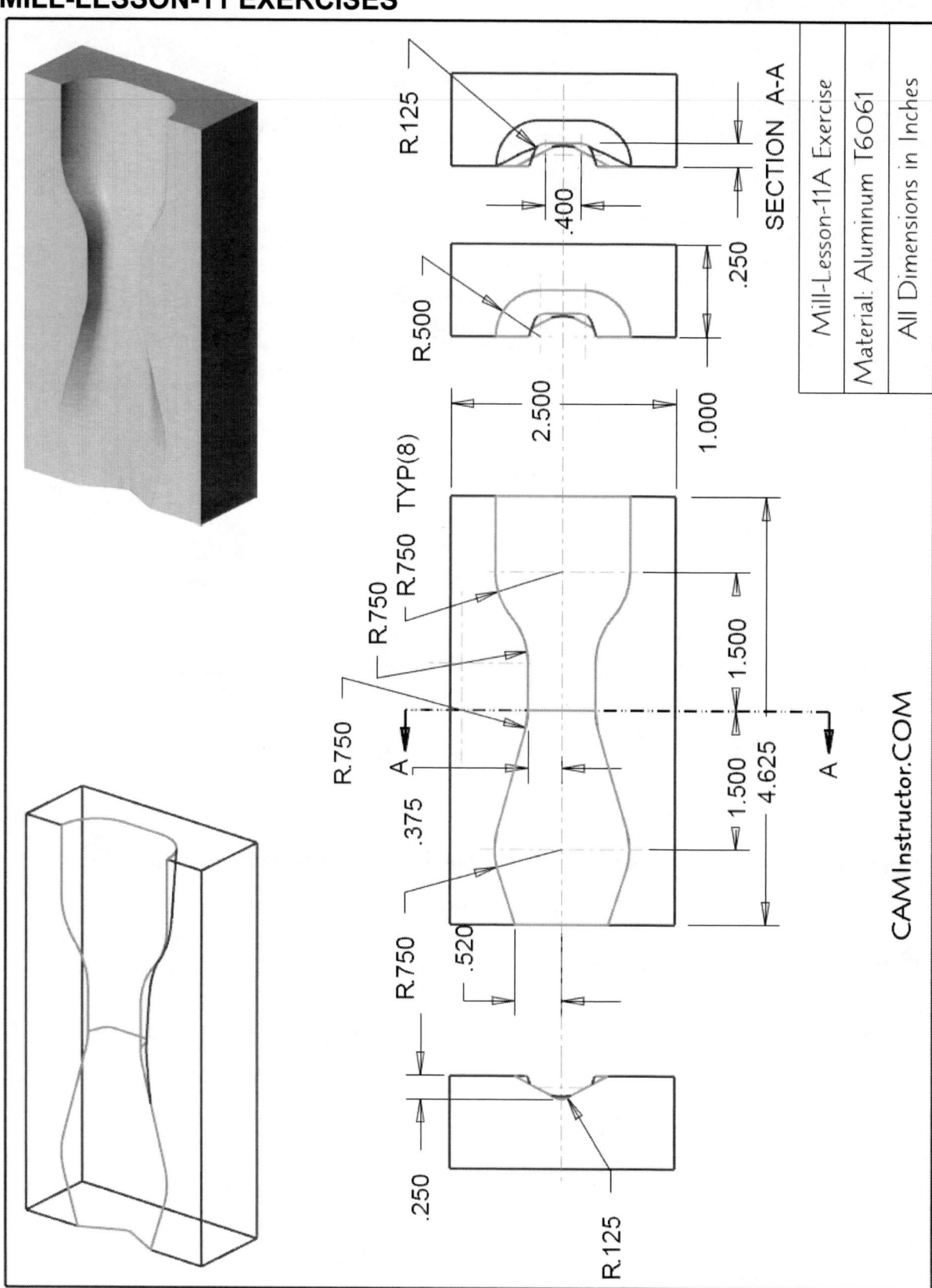

SECTION A-A

Mill-Lesson-11A Exercise

Material: Aluminum T6O61

All Dimensions in Inches

R.125

.400

R.500

.250

2.500

1.000

R.750 TYP(8)

R.750

R.750

1.500

1.500

4.625

A

A

.375

.520

R.750

.250

R.125

CAMInstructor.COM

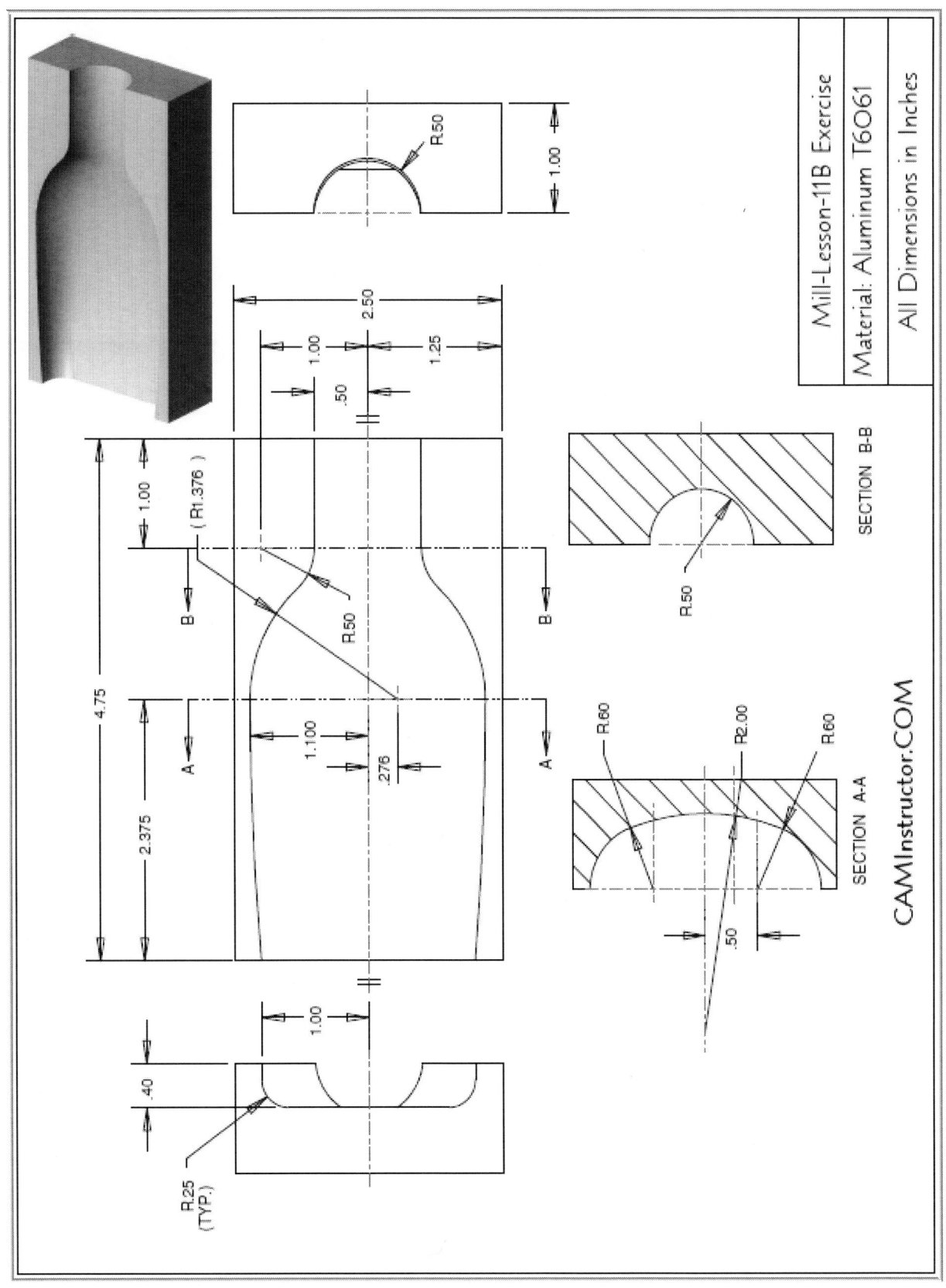

SECTION B-B

R.50

SECTION A-A

R.60

R2.00

R.60

.50

R.50

2.50

1.00

.50

1.25

1.00

(R1.376)

R.50

B

B

4.75

2.375

A

A

1.100

.276

1.00

.40

R.25
(TYP.)

R.50

1.00

Mill-Lesson-11B Exercise

Material: Aluminum T6O61

All Dimensions in Inches

CAMInstructor.COM

Mastercam. 2022

TRAINING
GUIDE

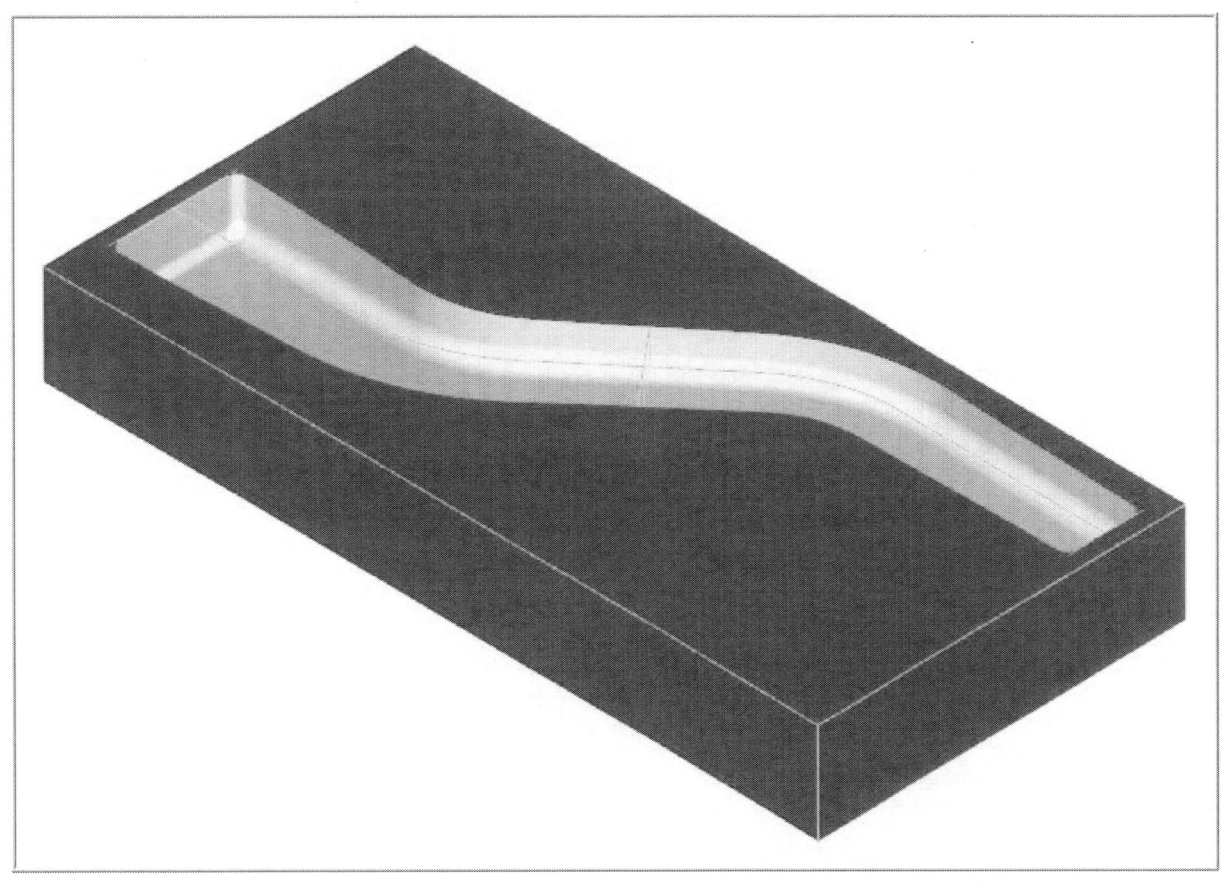

MILL-LESSON-12

SURFACE ROUGH POCKET, FINISH
SCALLOP & FINISH WATERLINE

camInstructor

Objectives

You will create the geometry for Mill-Lesson-12, and then generate the toolpaths to machine the part on a CNC vertical milling machine. This Lesson covers the following topics:

➲ **Create a 3-dimensional drawing by:**
Creating lines.
Creating arcs.
Trimming geometry.
Creating a swept surface.
Creating a flat boundary surface.
Creating a filleted surface.

➲ **Establish Stock Setup settings:**
Stock size using Bounding Box.
Material for the part.
Feed calculation.

➲ **Generate a 3-dimensional milling toolpath consisting of:**
Surface Rough Pocket Toolpath.
Finish Surface High Speed (Waterline) Toolpath.
Finish Surface High Speed (Scallop) Toolpath.
Finish Surface High Speed (Scallop) Rest Passes Toolpath.

➲ **Inspect the toolpath using Mastercam's Verify and Backplot by:**
Launching the Verify function to machine the part on the screen.
Generating the NC- code.

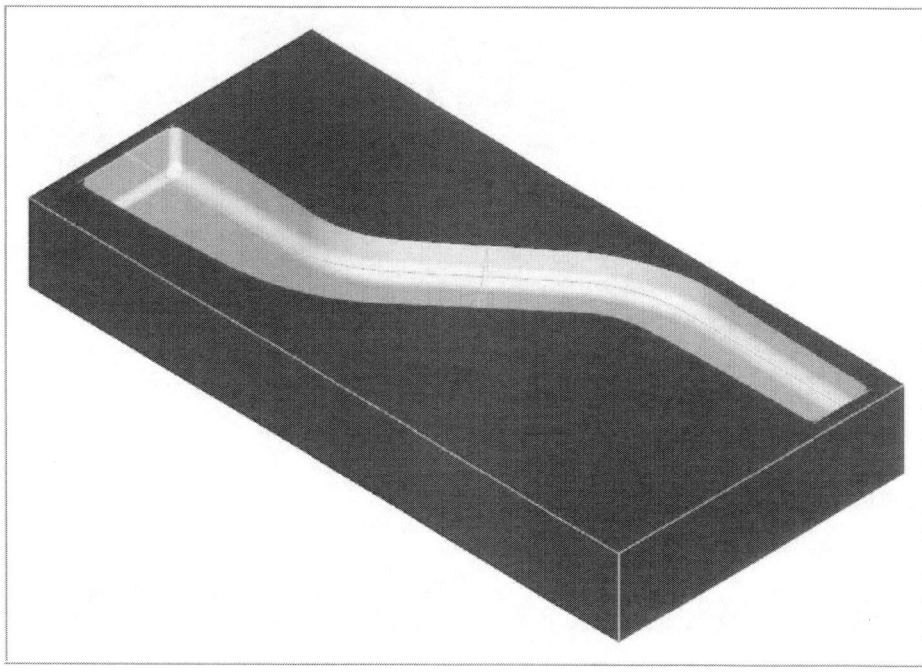

MILL-LESSON-12 DRAWING

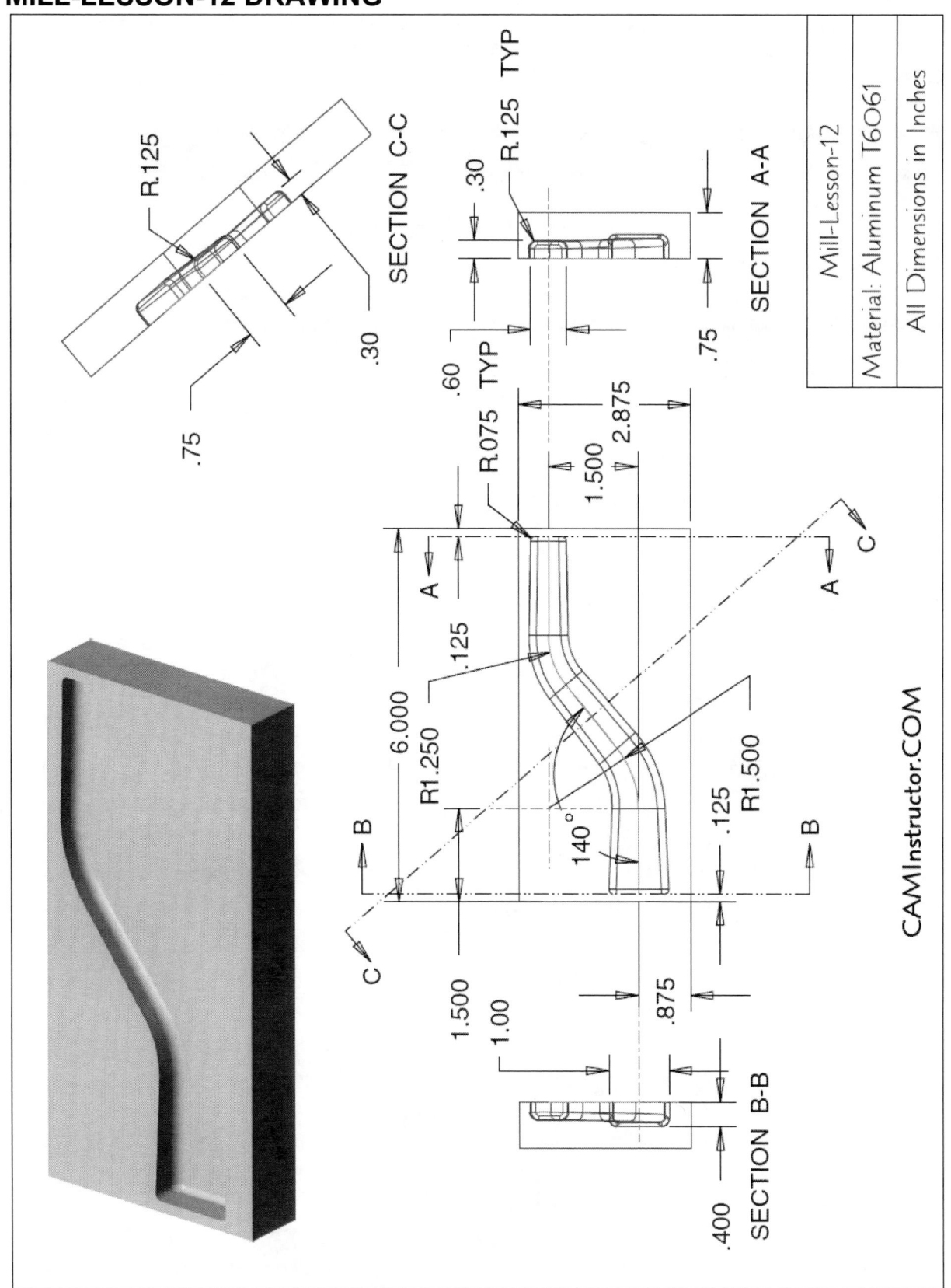

SECTION C-C

R.125

.30

.75

SECTION A-A

R.125 TYP

.30

.60

R.075 TYP

.75

2.875

1.500

A

A

C

C

6.000

.125

R1.250

140°

R1.500

.125

B

B

1.500

1.00

.875

.400

SECTION B-B

Mill-Lesson-12

Material: Aluminum T6O61

All Dimensions in Inches

CAMInstructor.COM

TOOL LIST

➲ 0.500 diameter bull end mill with a 0.125 corner radius to rough machine.
➲ 0.250 diameter ball end mill to finish machine.
➲ 0.1875 diameter ball end mill to finish machine the corners of the pocket.

MILL-LESSON-12 - THE PROCESS

Geometry Creation

TASK 1: Setting the environment
TASK 2: Create geometry – material blank 6.0 x 2.875 x .75
TASK 3: Create the profile for the sweep on top of material
TASK 4: Trim geometry for the sweep
TASK 5: Create right hand section geometry for sweep
TASK 6: Create left hand section geometry for sweep
TASK 7: Create center section geometry for sweep
TASK 8: Create the swept surface
TASK 9: Create flat boundary surface at ends of sweep
TASK 10: Create fillet surfaces
TASK 11: Save the drawing

Toolpath Creation

TASK 12: Define the rough stock using stock setup
TASK 13: Rough the pocket using Surface Rough Pocket
TASK 14: Finish walls using Surface High Speed (Waterline)
TASK 15: Finish floor and fillets using Surface High Speed (Scallop)
TASK 16: Finish using Surface High Speed (Scallop rest passes)
TASK 17: Verify the toolpath
TASK 18: Save the updated Mastercam file
TASK 19: Post and create the CNC code file

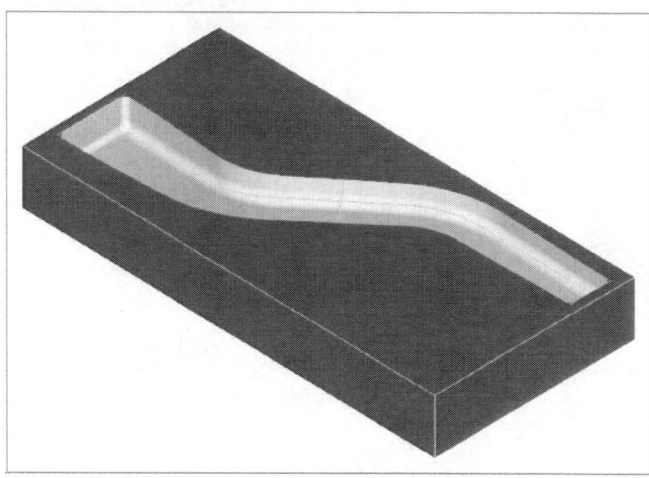

TASK 1:
SETTING THE ENVIRONMENT
➲ Before starting the geometry creation, you should set up the grid and machine type as outlined in the Setting the environment section at the beginning of this text:
1. Set up the Grid. This will help identify the location of the origin.
2. Set the machine type the Default Mill.

TASK 2:
CREATE GEOMETRY – MATERIAL BLANK 6.0 X 2.875 X .75
X0 Y0 Z0 LOWER LEFT CORNER
➲ The top of the material is at **Z0**. The material has been previously machined to size, 6.0 x 2.875 x .75.
➲ In this task you will create the geometry that make up the material blank, a box 6.0 x 2.875 x .75.

1. On the **Wireframe** tab in the **Shapes** section click on the drop-down menu arrow under **Rectangle** and select **Rectangular Shapes**.
2. The **Rectangular Shapes** panel appears and you are prompted to **Select a base point**.
3. Set the following values shown below left:

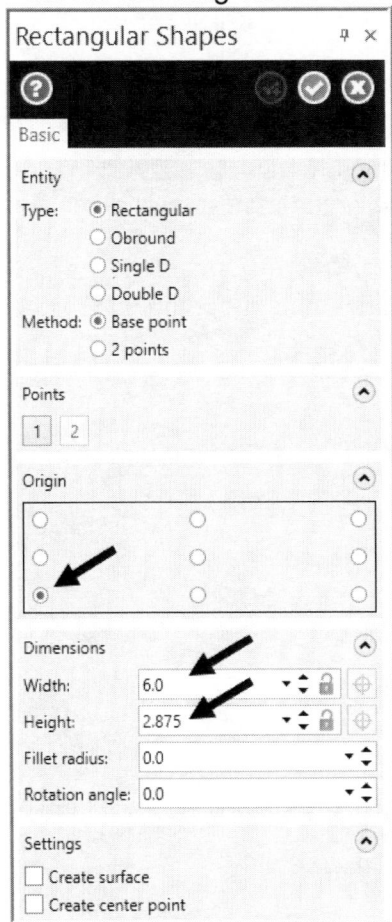

4. Now you need to **Select the position of the base point**. Move the cursor over to the graphics screen and position the cursor at the **center of the grid** and **pick the origin**.
5. Click on the OK icon to complete this feature.
6. Right mouse click in the graphics area and click on **Isometric**.
7. Right mouse click in the graphics area and click on the **Fit** icon.

➲ The completed geometry is shown below:

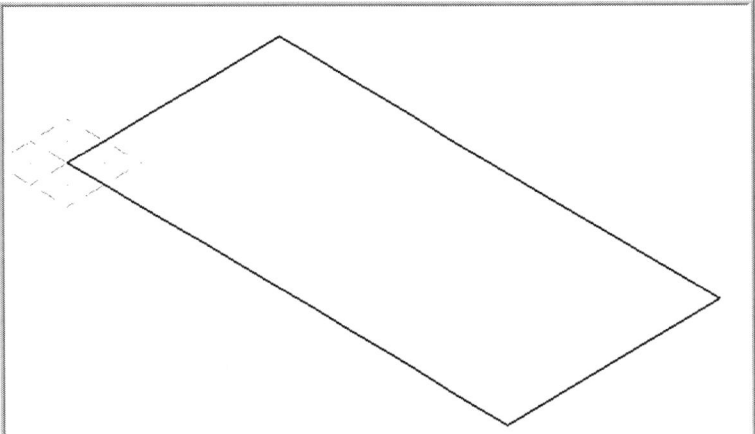

⊃ **Create the 3D box to represent the material blank.**

8. Select the **Transform** tab and in the **Position** section select **Translate**.
9. You are now prompted to **Translate: select entities to translate.** Hold the **shift** key down and select one of the lines. This process then selects all four lines.

10. Now you need to pick the End Selection icon 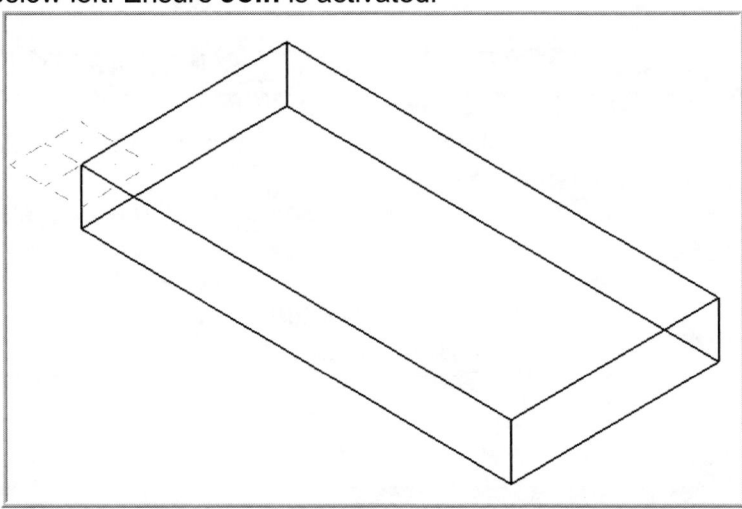.
11. Set the following values shown below left. Ensure **Join** is activated:

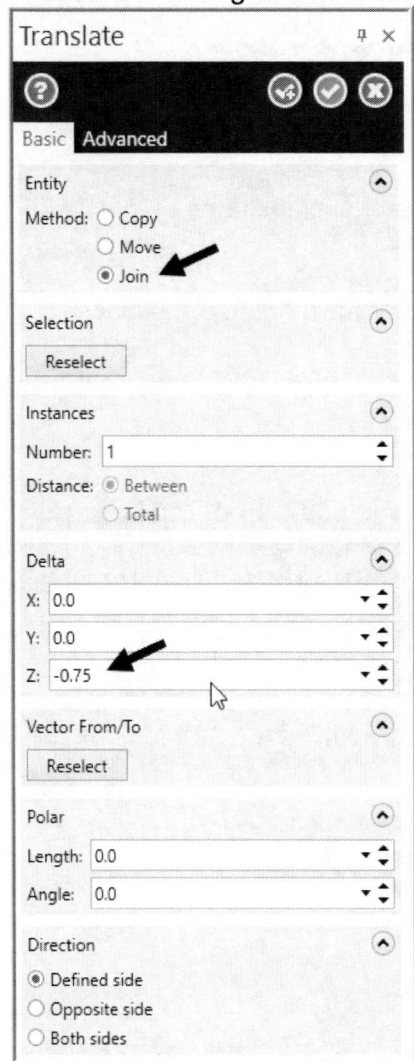

Join:
Transforms a copy of the selected entities to a new position in the graphics window and maintains the position of the original entities.

Mastercam creates lines or arcs to connect the endpoints of the original entities to the endpoints of the transformed entities.

Mastercam cannot join surfaces or solids.

12. Click on the OK icon ![icon] to complete this feature. The completed geometry is shown above.

13. Right mouse click in the graphics area and click on the **Clear Colors** icon ![icon].

14. Right mouse click in the graphics area and click on the **Fit** icon ![icon].

TASK 3:
CREATE THE PROFILE FOR THE SWEEP ON TOP OF MATERIAL
➲ Create Line #1, #2, #3, Arc #1 and Arc #2

➲ **Create Line #1**
1. Select the **Wireframe** tab if required and in the **Lines** section click on **Line Parallel**.
2. On the graphics screen you are prompted: **Select a line** and the Line Parallel panel appears.
3. To satisfy the prompt **Select a line**, move the cursor over the line shown below and select it.

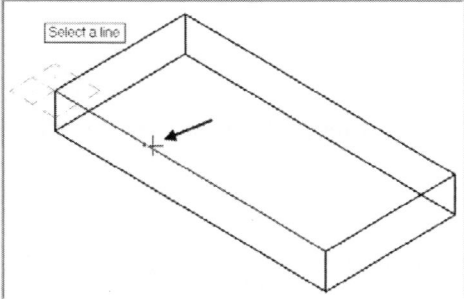

4. To satisfy the next prompt **Select the point to place a parallel line through** move the cursor above the line and pick a point.

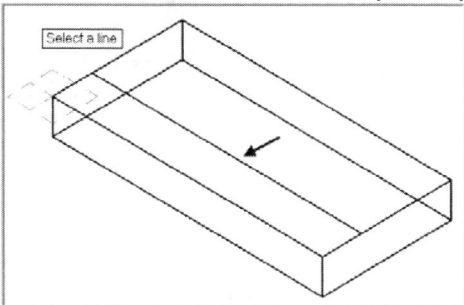

5. For the **Offset Distance** input **0.875** then hit **enter** as shown below:

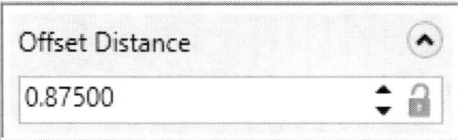

6. Click on the **OK and Create New Operation** icon .

➲ **Create Line #2**
7. To satisfy the prompt **Select a line**, move the cursor over the line shown below and select it.

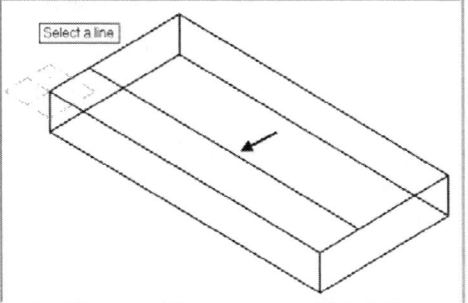

8. To satisfy the next prompt **Select the point to place a parallel line through** move the cursor above the line and pick a point.
9. For the **Offset Distance** input **1.5** then hit **enter**. The line appears as shown below:

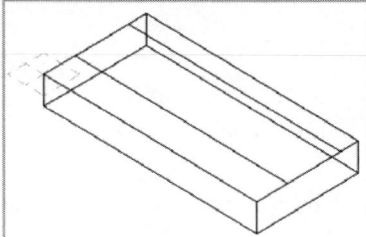

10. Click on the **OK** icon to complete this feature.

➲ **Create Arc #1**

11. Select the **Wireframe** tab if required and in the **Arcs** section open up the drop down menu and select **Arc Polar.**
12. To satisfy the prompt **Enter the center point** click the middle mouse button and then hit the spacebar on your keyboard.
13. The **Fastpoint** box now opens. Input **1.5,0.875+1.5** and hit the Enter key.

1.5,0.875+1.5

14. In the **Arc Polar** panel enter **1.5** for the radius and hit enter. Click in the space for the **Start Angle** and enter **-90** and hit the Tab key. Enter a value of **0** for the **End angle** and hit enter as shown below.

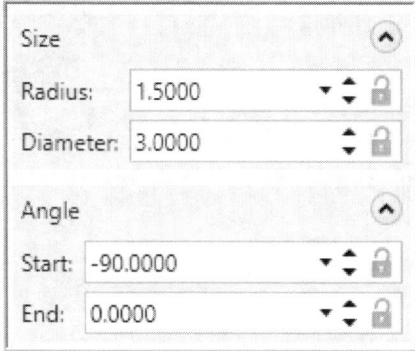

15. Click on the **OK** icon to complete this feature.

➲ The arc is shown below:

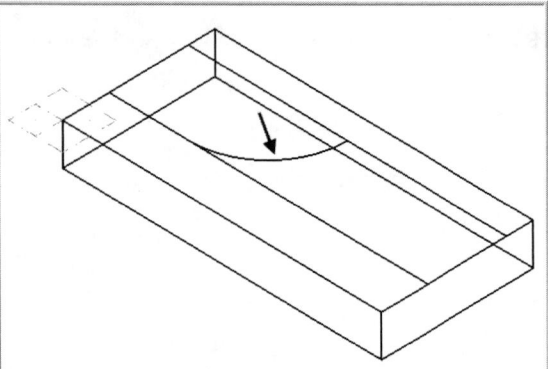

⊃ Create Line #3
16. Select the **Wireframe** tab if required and in the **Lines** section click on **Line Endpoints**.
17. First click in the space for **Length** and enter a value of **1.0** and then hit the Enter key. In the space for **Angle** enter a value of **180-140** and hit Enter.

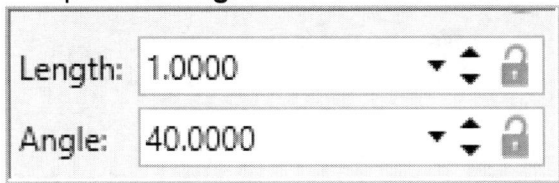

18. On the graphics screen you are prompted: **Specify the first endpoint**. **Ensure** that the **Tangent** function is activated.
19. To satisfy the prompt **Specify the first endpoint** move the cursor over the area of the arc shown below left. Ensure there is **no visual cue** being displayed and click on this point. After selecting the arc you will be prompted to **Select a line** pick the line shown below:

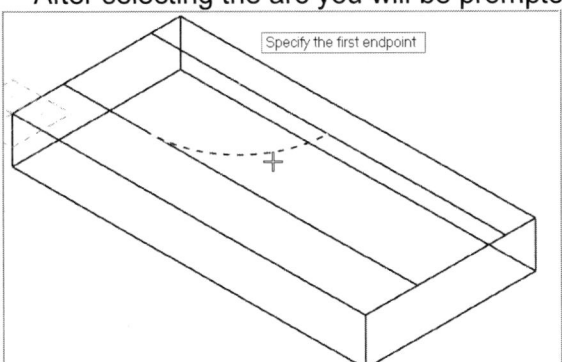 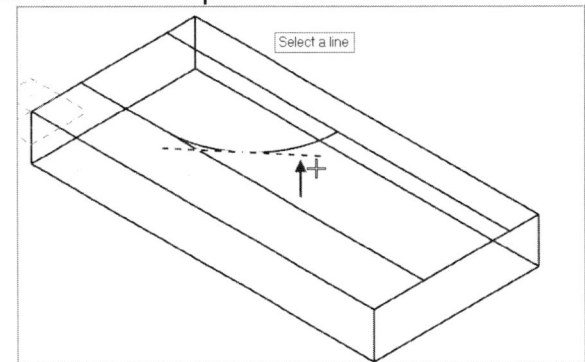

⊃ **Please note** if the line appears on the other side of the arc hit the **undo** key and try again, picking the arc in the position prescribed above.

20. Click on the **OK** icon to complete this feature.

⊃ Create Arc #2
21. On the **Wireframe** tab and in the **Modify** section click on **Fillet Entities**.
22. Enter **1.25 for the radius** and hit enter. Ensure the **Method** is set to **normal** and **trim on**.
23. When prompted to **Fillet: Select an entity,** select the two lines shown below and the fillet radius appears. The completed geometry is shown below right:

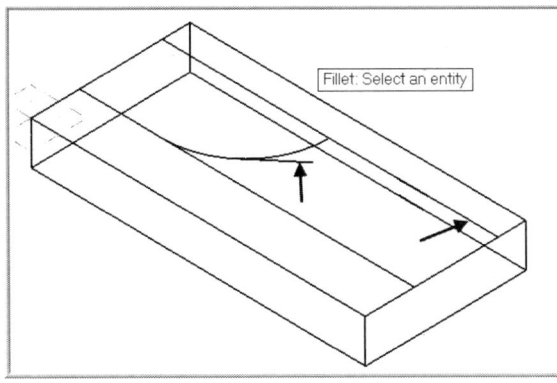 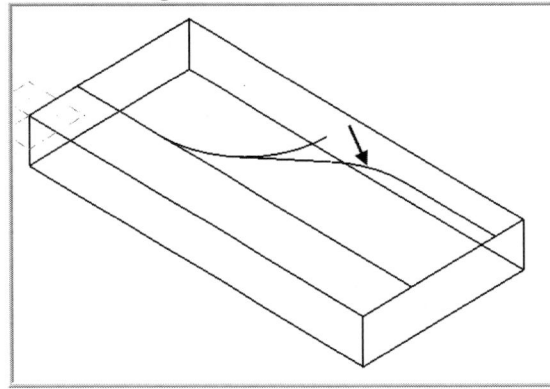

24. Click on the **OK** icon to complete this feature.

TASK 4:
TRIM GEOMETRY FOR THE SWEEP
➲ In this task you will trim the geometry using **Trim 1 Entity** and **Analyze Entity Properties**.

1. In the **Wireframe** tab click on **Trim/Break/Extend** in the **Modify** section.
2. The **Trim Break Extend** panel appears. Activate **Trim 1 entity** in the **Method** section.
3. For the first prompt move the cursor over **line 1** shown below and select it.
4. For the next prompt **Select the entity to trim/extend to** select **entity 2** the arc at the position shown below:

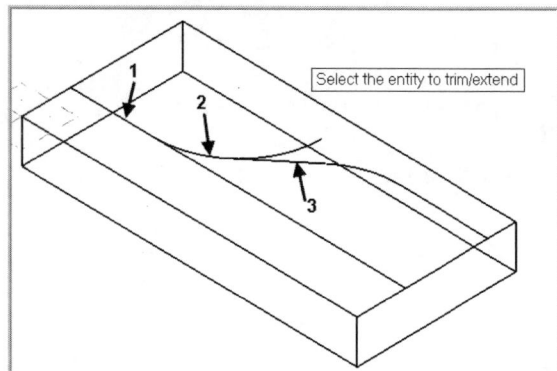
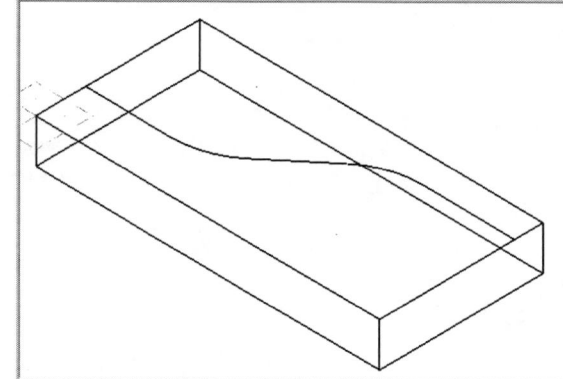

5. For the next prompt **Select the entity to trim/extend** select **entity 2** the arc again, same position as before.
6. For the next prompt **Select the entity to trim/extend to** select **line 3**.
7. Click on the **OK** icon ⊙ to complete this feature.
➲ The trimmed entities are shown above right.

➲ Now you will use **Analyze Entity** to change the endpoints of a couple of lines.
8. Click on the **Home** tab and select **Analyze Entity**.

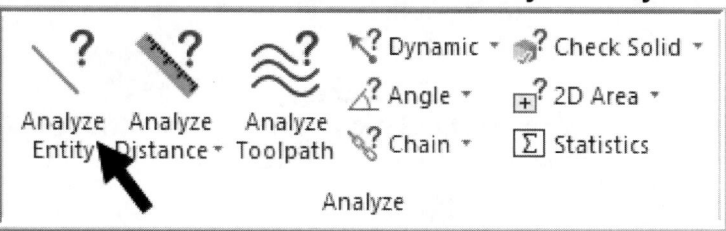

9. Select **line 1** as shown below and the **Line Properties** dialog box appears. Change the **X value of 0** to **0.125** as shown below:

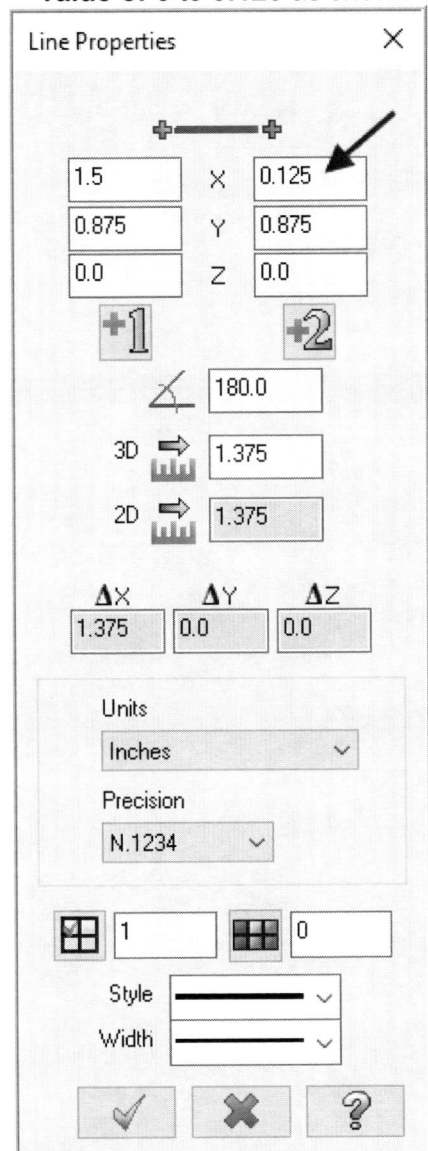

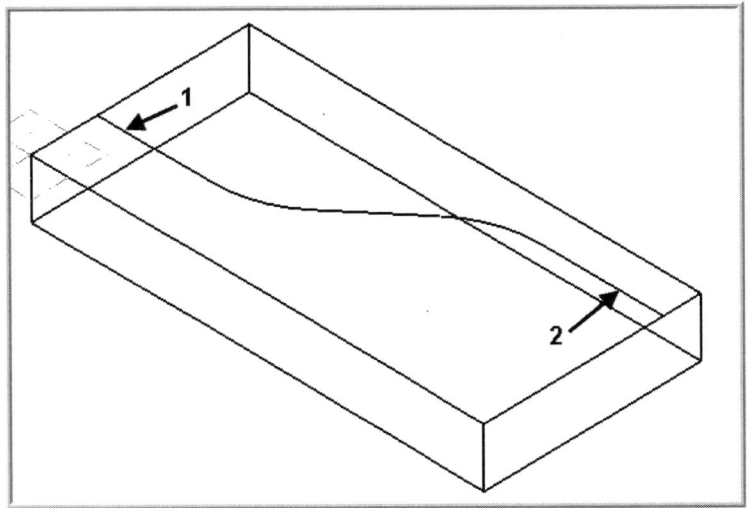

Use this dialog box to view and edit line entity properties, including the length, angle between endpoints, and endpoint positions (XYZ coordinates).

You can also edit the level, color, and point style entity attributes.

10. Click on the OK icon ✓ to complete this feature.

11. In the **Home** tab click on **Analyze Entity** again.
12. Select **line 2** as shown below and the **Line Properties** dialog box appears. Change the **X value of 6.0** to **5.875** as shown below:

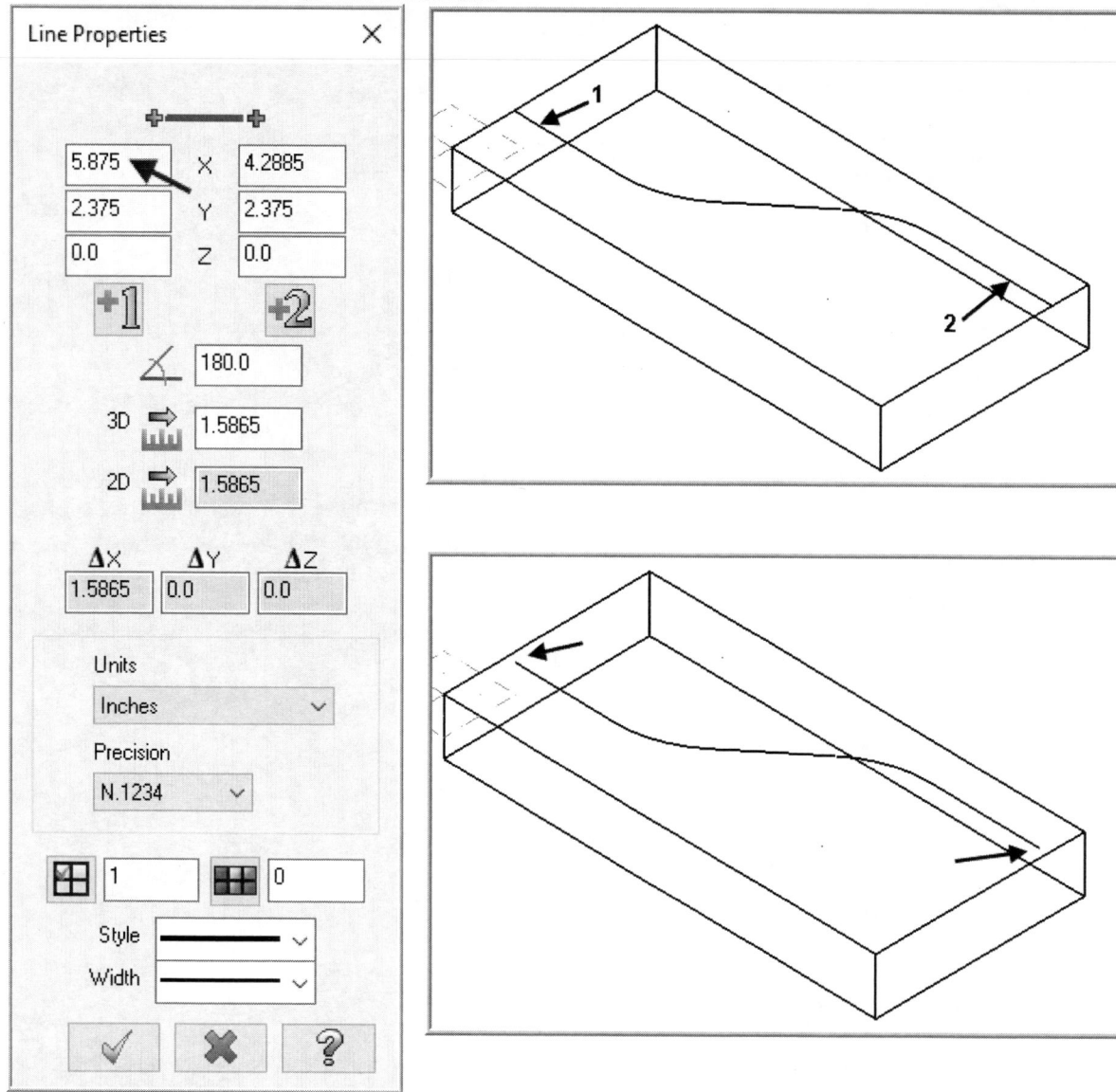

13. Click on the OK icon ✓ to complete this feature. The completed geometry is shown above right.

TASK 5:
CREATE RIGHT HAND SECTION GEOMETRY FOR SWEEP
➲ Create right hand side section using **Rectangular shapes** and **Fillet**.

1. Select the **View tab** and ensure the **Planes Manager is visible**.

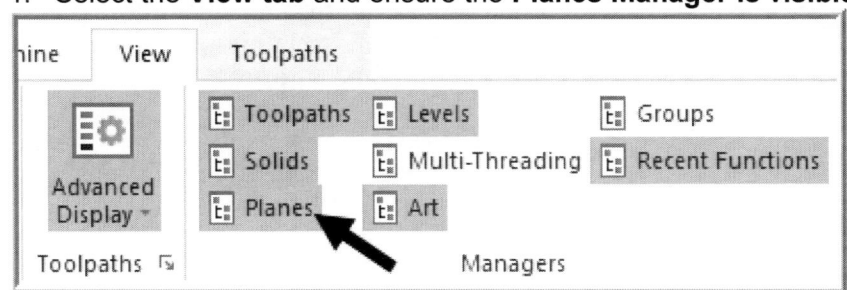

2. Now open up the drop down menu in the Planes Manager for **Follow rules**  and **remove all the check marks** to cancel all the rules.
3. Now click in the **C column (Construction Plane)** for the **Right** plane. The view is still set to Isometric but construction of the geometry will now take place on the Right plane. Take note at the bottom of the screen **CPLANE: Right TPLANE:Top WCS:Top** as shown below right.

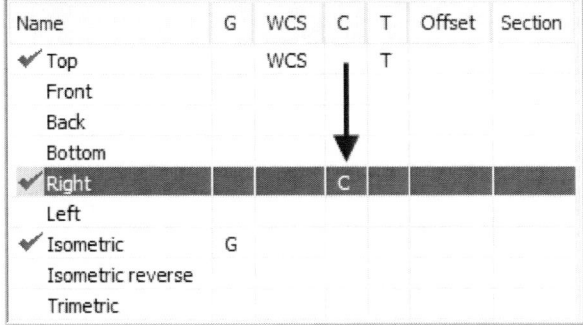

4. Right mouse click in the graphics area and toggle to **2D construction**. Change the **Z value** to **5.875**.

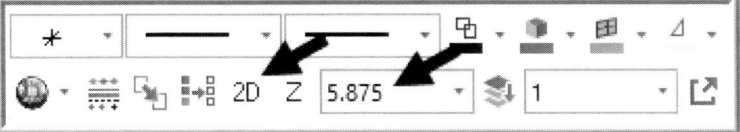

5. On the **Wireframe** tab in the **Shapes** section click on the drop down menu arrow under **Rectangle** and select **Rectangular Shapes**.
6. The **Rectangular Shapes** panel appears and you are prompted to **Select a base point**.
7. Set the following values shown below left:

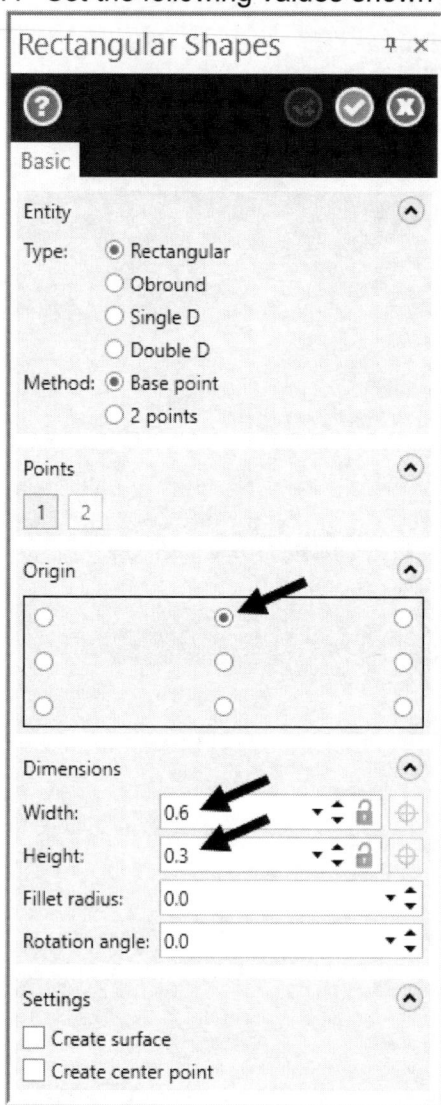

8. Now you need to **Select the position of the base point**. Move the cursor over to the graphics screen and position the cursor at the **endpoint of the line** shown below and pick this point.

9. Click on the OK icon to complete this feature.

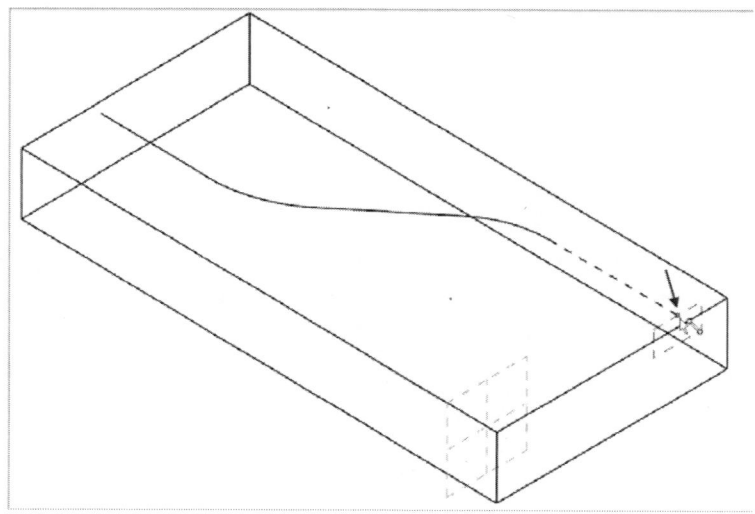

⮑ The completed rectangle is shown below:

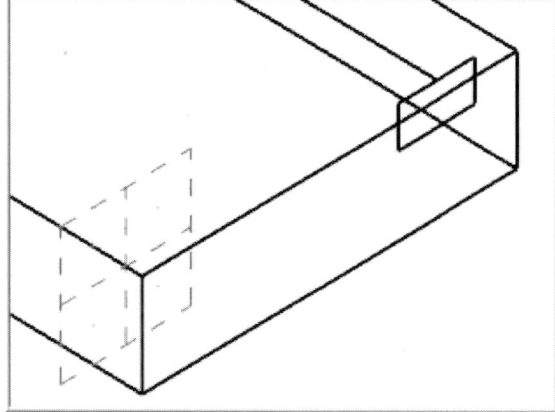

⊃ **Create Fillets**

10. Select the **Wireframe** tab and in the **Modify** section click on **Fillet Entities**.
11. The **Fillet Entities** panel appears. If required activate the **Style** to **Normal** and enter a value of **0.125** for **Radius**.
12. Ensure the **Trim** entities box at the bottom of the panel is check marked to turn the trim on.
13. When prompted to **Fillet: Select an entity,** select entity 1 and 2 as shown below. **Note, you may have to zoom in.** The fillet radius appears at the corner of entities 1 and 2. To complete the remaining fillet select: entities 2 and 3. The completed geometry is shown below right:

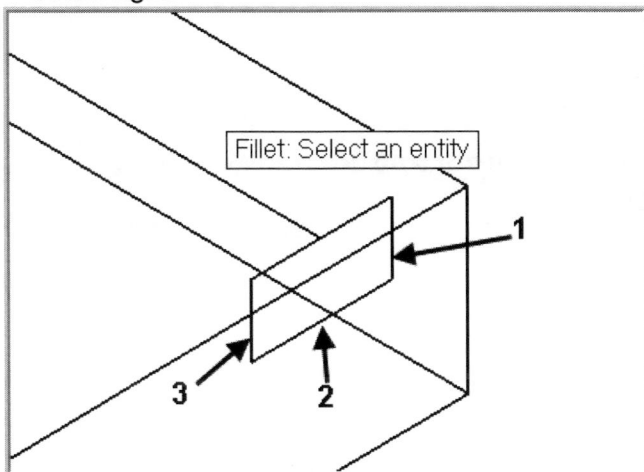 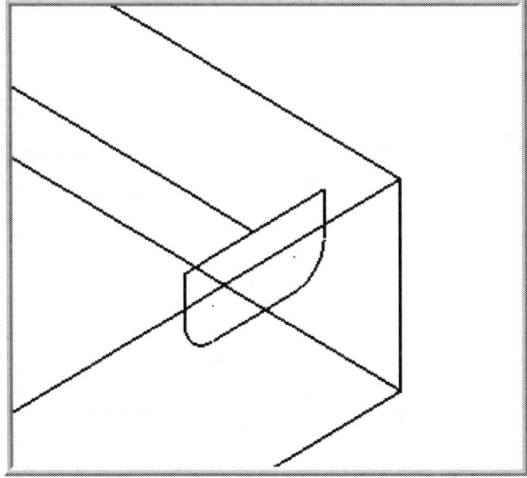

14. Click on the OK icon to complete this feature.

TASK 6:
CREATE LEFT HAND SECTION GEOMETRY FOR SWEEP

➲ Create left hand side section using **Rectangular shapes** and **Fillet**.

1. Right mouse click in the graphics area and click on the **Fit** icon .
2. Right mouse click in the graphics area and change the **Z value** to **0.125**. Notice the **Grid** change location.

3. On the **Wireframe** tab in the **Shapes** section click on the drop down menu arrow under **Rectangle** and select **Rectangular Shapes**.
4. The **Rectangular Shapes** panel appears and you are prompted to **Select a base point**.
5. Set the following values shown below:

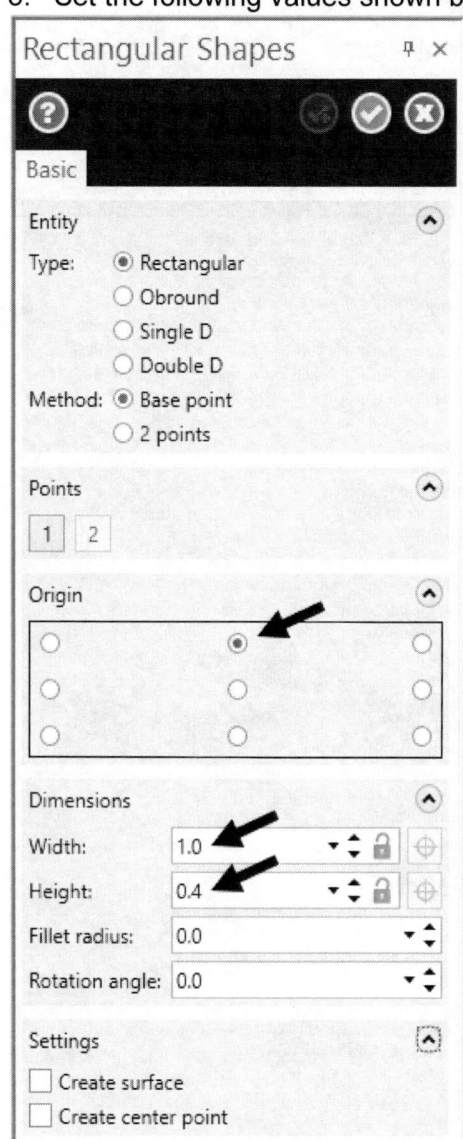

6. Now you need to **Select the position of the base point**. Move the cursor over to the graphics screen and position the cursor at the **endpoint of the line** shown below and pick this point.

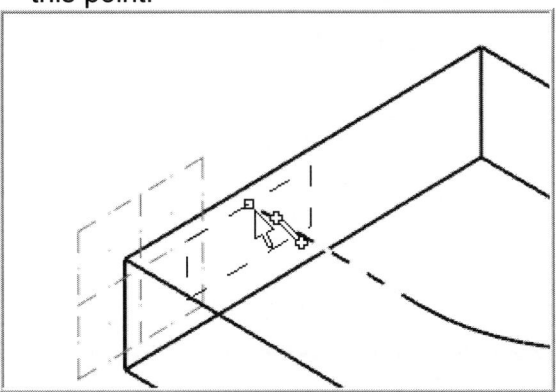 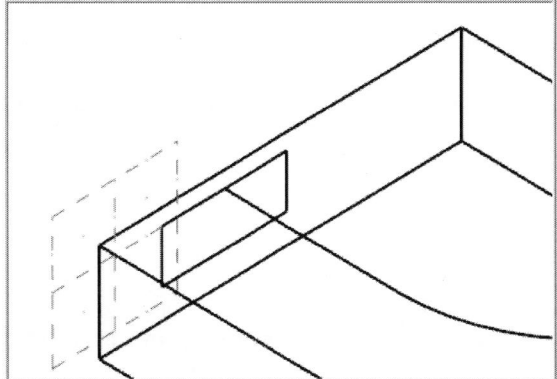

7. Click on the OK icon 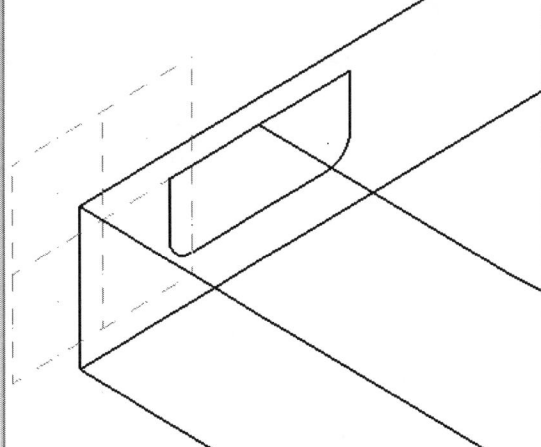 to complete this feature. The completed rectangle is shown above right.

⊃ **Create Fillets**

8. Select the **Wireframe** tab and in the **Modify** section click on **Fillet Entities**.
9. The **Fillet Entities** panel appears. If required activate the **Style** to **Normal** and enter a value of **0.125** for **Radius**.
10. Ensure the **Trim** entities box at the bottom of the panel is check marked to turn the trim on.
11. When prompted to **Fillet: Select an entity,** select entity 1 and 2 as shown below. The fillet radius appears at the corner of entities 1 and 2. To complete the remaining fillet select: entities 2 and 3. The completed geometry is shown below right:

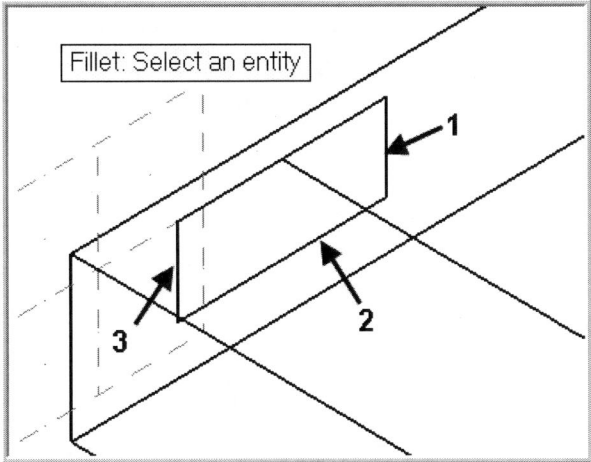 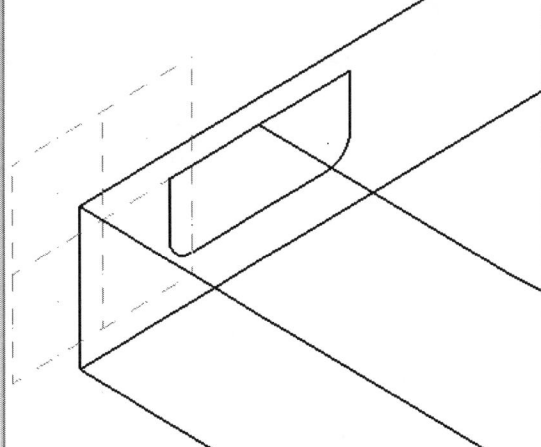

12. Click on the OK icon to complete this feature.

13. Right mouse click in the graphics area and click on the **Fit** icon.

TASK 7:
CREATE CENTER SECTION GEOMETRY FOR SWEEP
➲ Create the user defined construction plane.
➲ Create the center section using **Rectangular shapes** and **Fillet**.

1. Right mouse click in the graphics area and change the **Z value** to **0.**

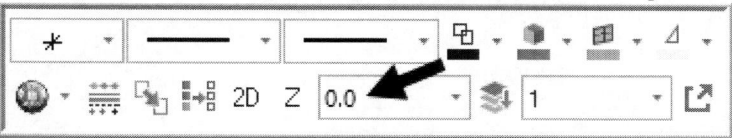

2. If required toggle the **Planes Manager to display**.
3. In the Planes Manager click in the **C column (Construction Plane)** for **Top**. Take note at the bottom of the screen **CPLANE:Top TPLANE:Top WCS:Top** as shown below right.

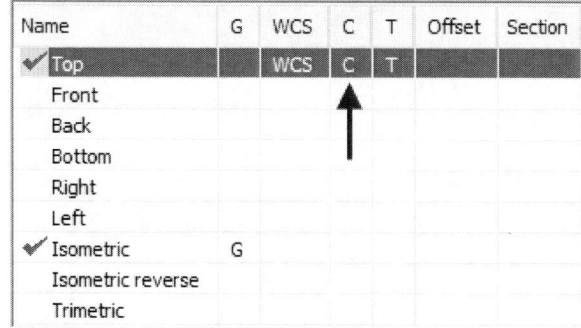

4. **Close** the **Planes Manager**.

➲ **Create Line #1.**
5. Select the **Wireframe** tab and in the **Lines** section click on **Line Endpoints.**
6. First click in the space for **Length** and enter a value of **1.0** and then hit the Enter key. In the space for **Angle** enter a value of **90+40** and hit enter.
7. To satisfy the prompt **Specify the first endpoint** move the cursor over the **midpoint** of the line shown below left. Ensure the **visual cue** for midpoint is being displayed and click on this point.

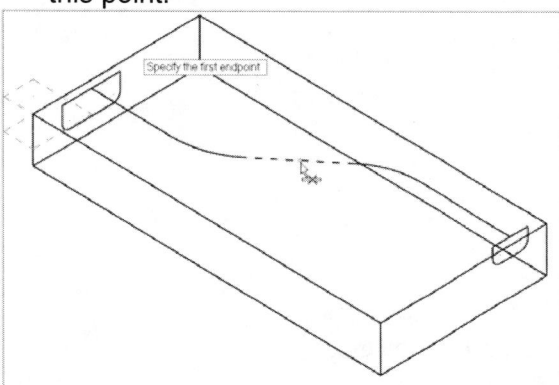

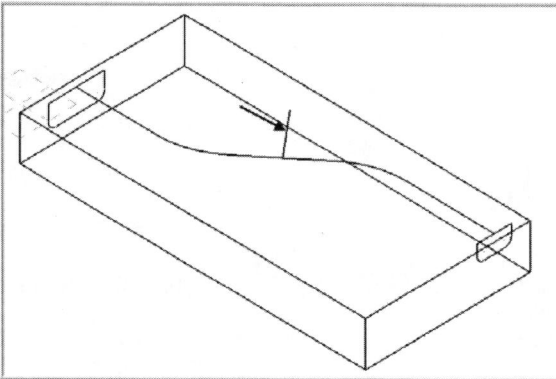

8. Click on the **OK and Create New Operation** icon ![icon].

⊃ Create Construction lines for construction plane.

9. Open the **Planes Manager**. The keyboard short cut is **ALT+L**.
10. Now click in the **C column (Construction Plane)** for the **Right** plane. The view is still set to Isometric but construction of the geometry will now take place on the Right plane. Take note at the bottom of the screen **CPLANE: Right TPLANE:Top WCS:Top** as shown below right.

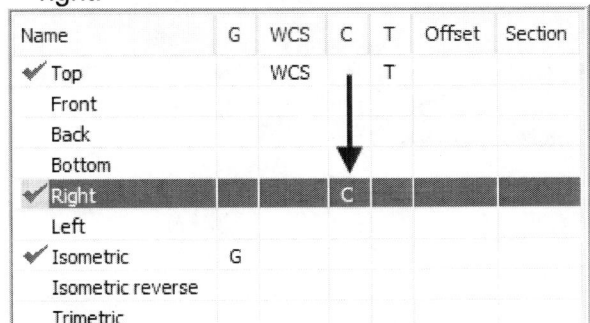

11. Right mouse click in the graphics area and toggle to **3D construction**. The **Z value** should be at **0**

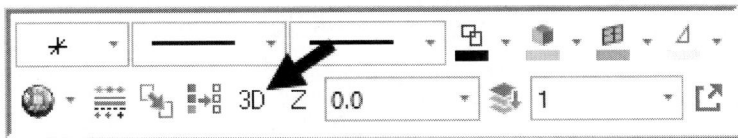

12. Select the **Line Endpoints tab** at the lower left of the screen.
13. To satisfy the prompt **Specify the first endpoint** move the cursor over the **endpoint** of the line shown below left. Ensure the **visual cue** for end point is being displayed and click on this point.

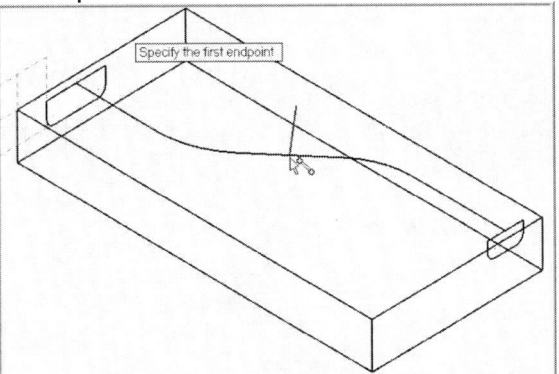
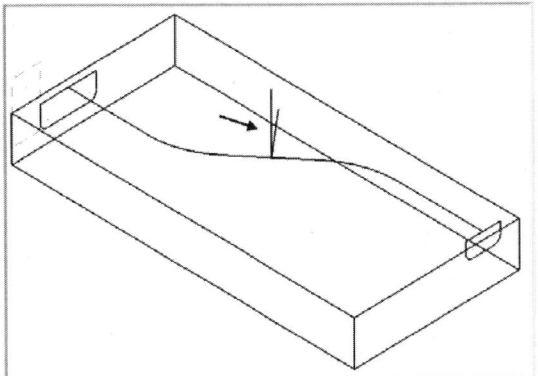

14. Next click in the space for **Length** and enter a value of **1.0** and then hit the Enter key. In the space for **Angle** enter a value of **90** and hit enter.

15. Click on the **OK** icon to complete this feature.

⊃ **Change to Planes using Dynamic Planes**

16. **Some tricky moves coming up: Watch the video on this section.** The video can be found online in **Lesson 12 Task 7**.

---

17. In the **Planes Manager** click on the down arrow and select **Dynamic...**

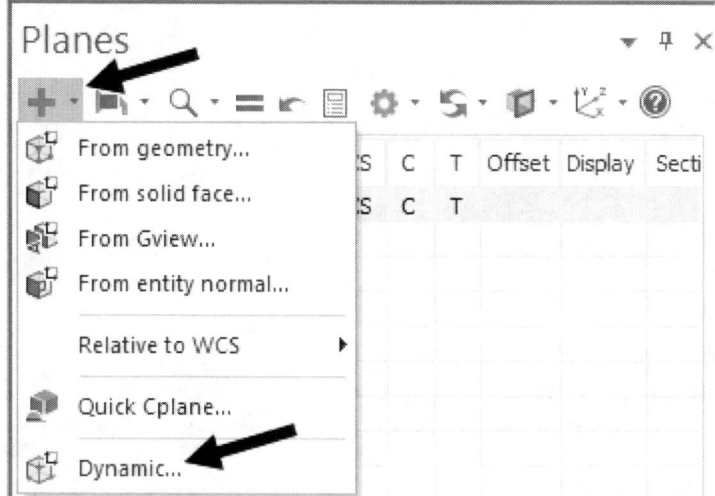

⬚	From geometry...
⬚	From solid face...
⬚	From Gview...
⬚	From entity normal...
	Relative to WCS ▶
⬚	Quick Cplane...
⬚	Dynamic...

Dynamic Planes extremely useful function that allows easy visual manipulation of planes.

Origins can be created by snapping to entity features.

Coordinate system orientation can easily be changed by grabbing an axes and rotating it with the mouse.

When using Dynamic Plane use an interactive gnomon to create a plane in the graphics window. The gnomon comprises three axes connected at the origin, with selection points on the gnomon's segments.

To create a plane or update the origin of an existing plane, start by locating the origin of the gnomon, which creates the origin for the plane.

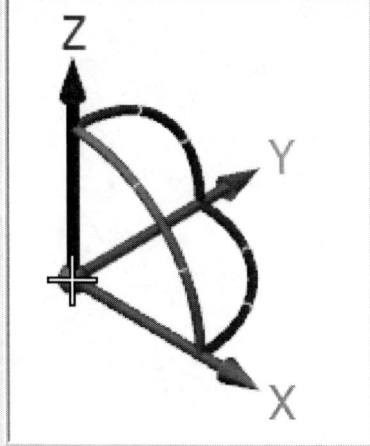

---

18. The New Plane panel appears and on the graphics screen you are prompted: **Pick entity to align to**, snap to the **endpoint of the line** you just created (shown below):

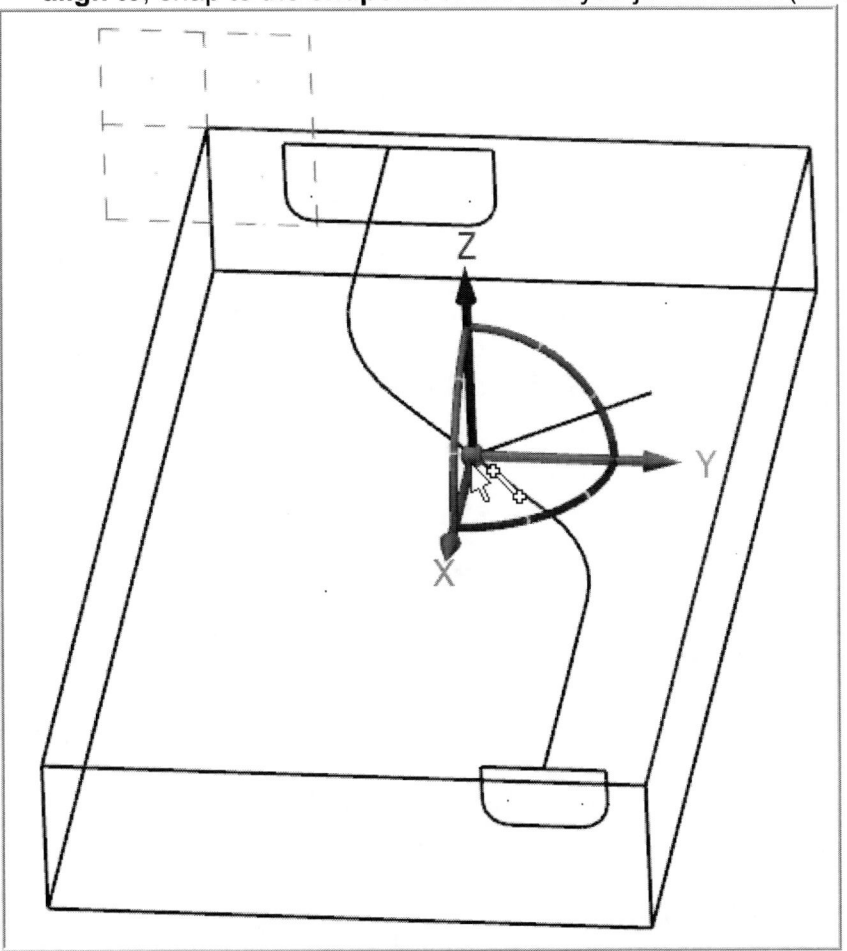

19. The next prompt is as shown:

Select gnomon axes to edit or hit OK/Double-click the mouse to accept the results

20. Select the arrow at the tip of the Z axis, **the blue arrow** (this is to align the current axis), then move your cursor down to the line shown below right to align the Z axis in this direction.

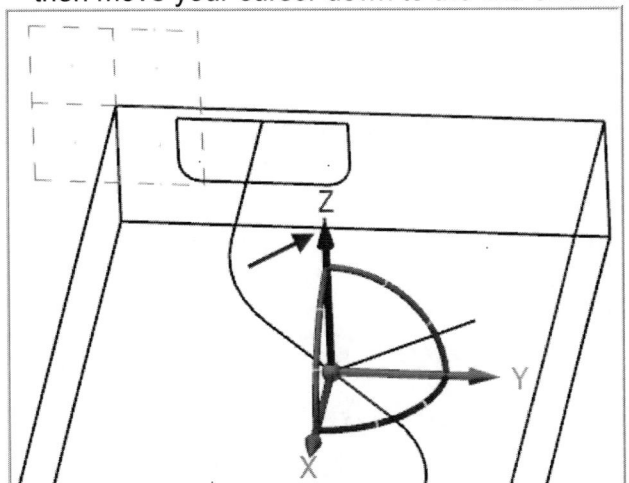 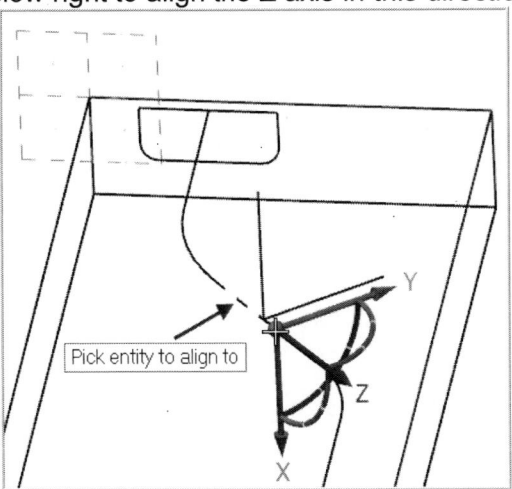

Pick entity to align to

21. Next, click on the **origin** of the **Dynamic Planes Arrows** (shown below left), and drag it back to the end point of the newly created line.

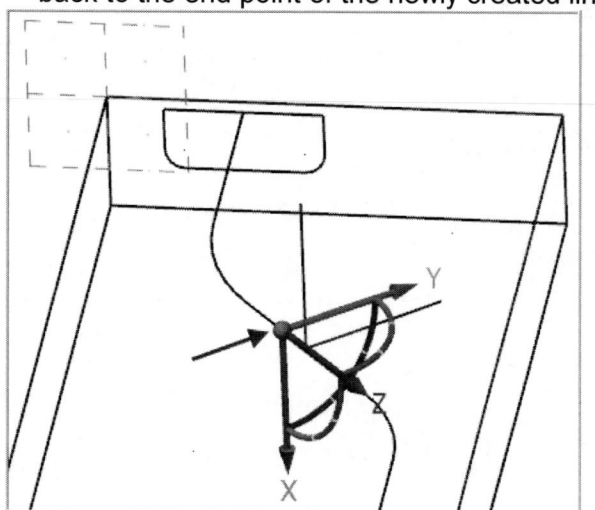
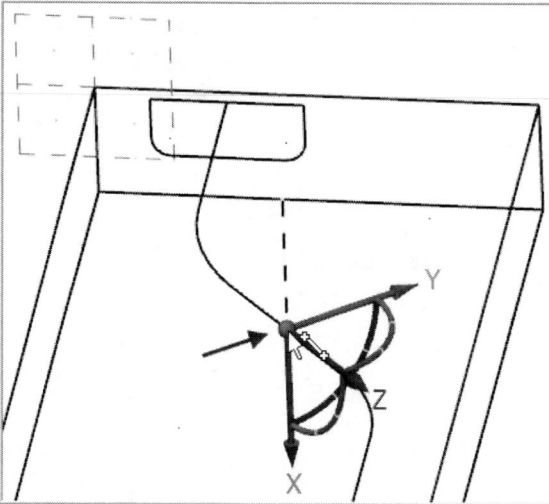

22. The Z axis **the blue arrow** is in the **correct position** but the X axis **the red arrow is not**. To correct this, click on the portion of the arrow just before the tip of the X arrow - **Red** as shown below left. This will rotate about the Z axis. Note the **Rotation** selection can be used as a visual cue while dragging the X arrow **or you can type in the value**. Enter a value of **90** and press enter as shown below in the **Dynamic Plane** dialog box.

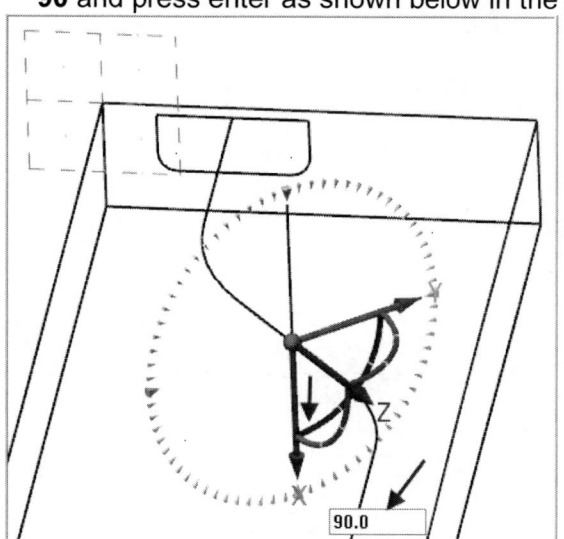
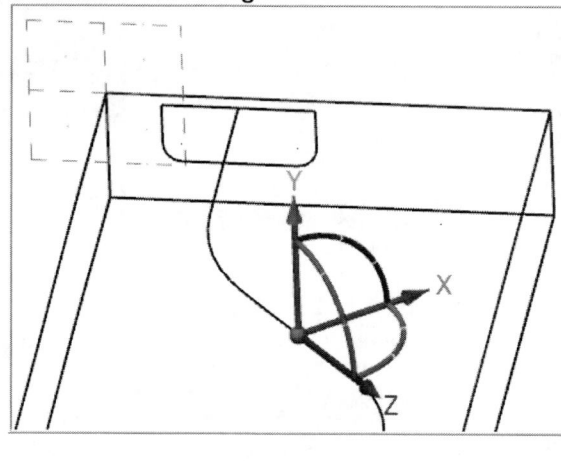

➲ After pressing the enter key the axis tripod should be as the image above right.

23. Review the **New Plane** panel. Name this new plane **Angled Mid**.
24. Activate **Set As Cplane** at the bottom of this panel.

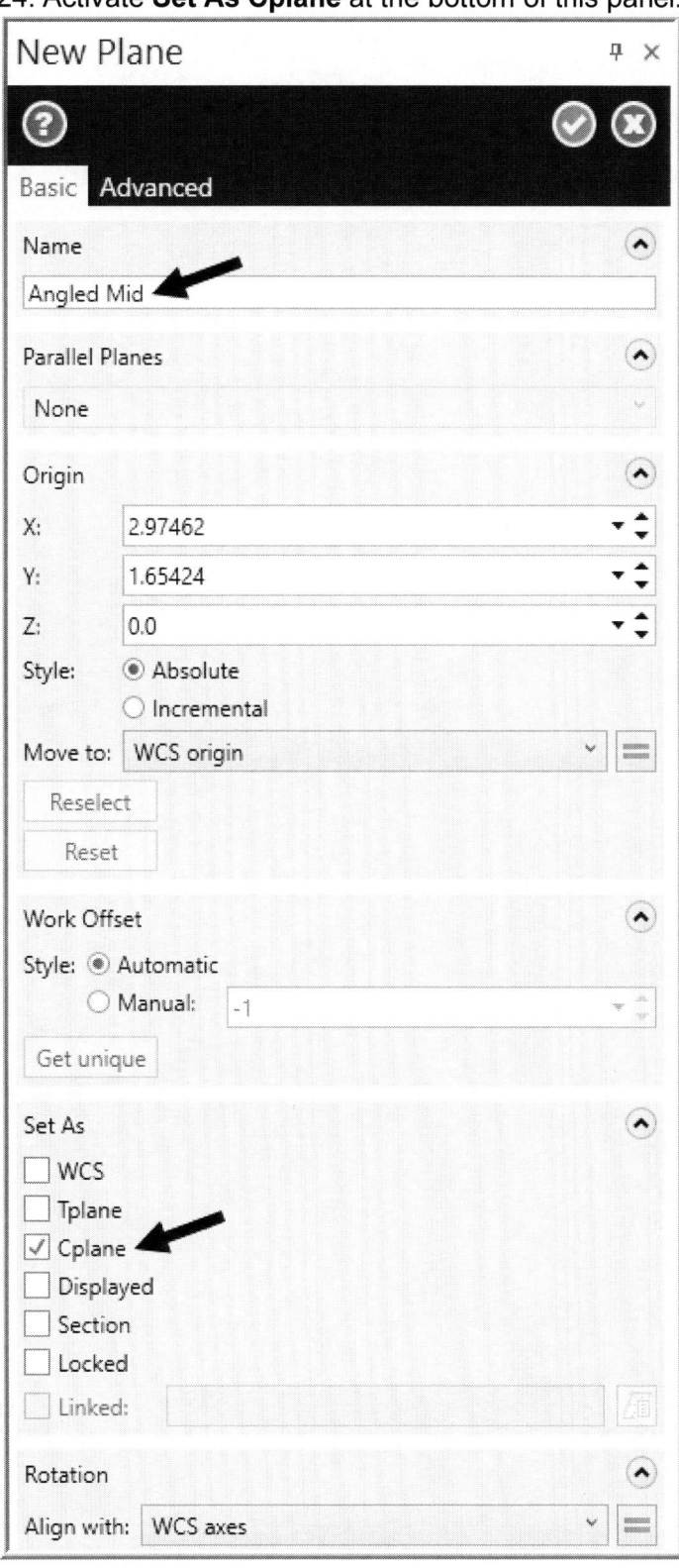

Use the **New Plane** function panels to create or edit user-defined planes. Once you define and name a plane, you can select that plane by its name and use it for other functions in your part file.

Select Dynamic from the Planes Manager to create a new plane menu, or click the View Axes in the lower left corner of the graphics window to activate the Dynamic Gnomon.

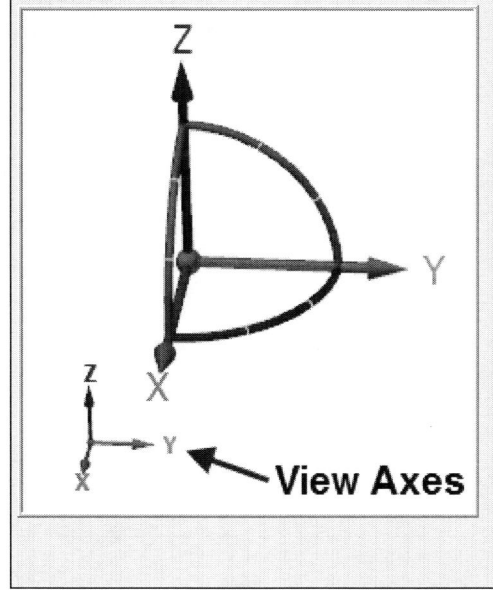

25. Click on the OK icon ⊘ to complete this feature.

26. Click in the **T column (Tool Plane)** for **Top** to make this the Tool Plane, if required.

➲ Note that the **C column** (Construction Plane) is set for the new plane **Right-side-1**. Construction of the geometry will now take place on this new plane. Take note at the bottom of the screen **CPLANE:Angled Mid   TPLANE:Top   WCS:Top** as shown below right.

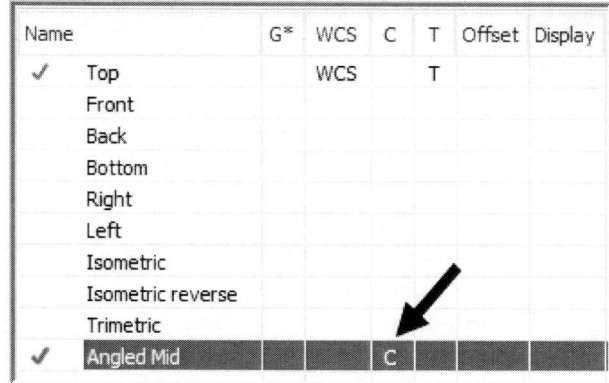
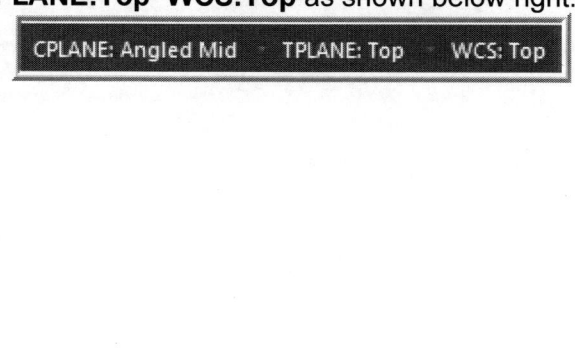

27. Holding down the **Middle Button or Scroll Wheel** on your mouse rotate the view similar to below:

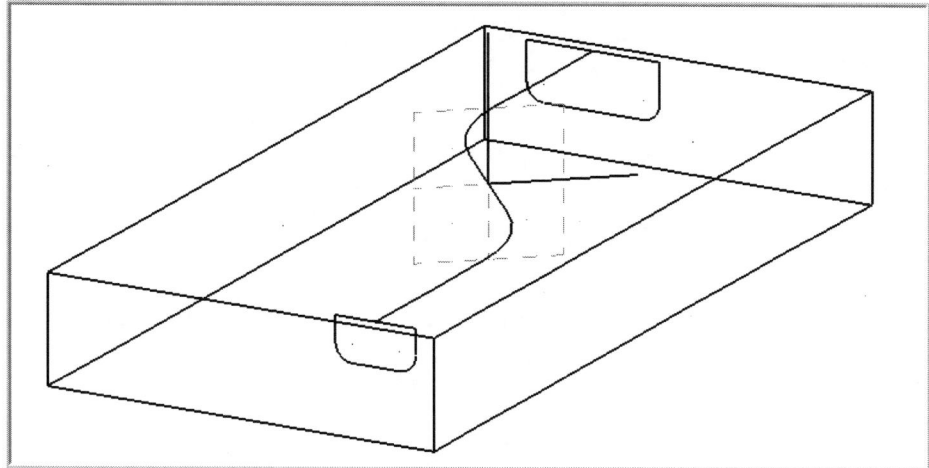

28. On the **Wireframe** tab in the **Shapes** section click on the drop down menu arrow under **Rectangle** and select **Rectangular Shapes**.
29. The **Rectangular Shapes** panel appears and you are prompted to **Select a base point**.
30. Set the following values shown below left:

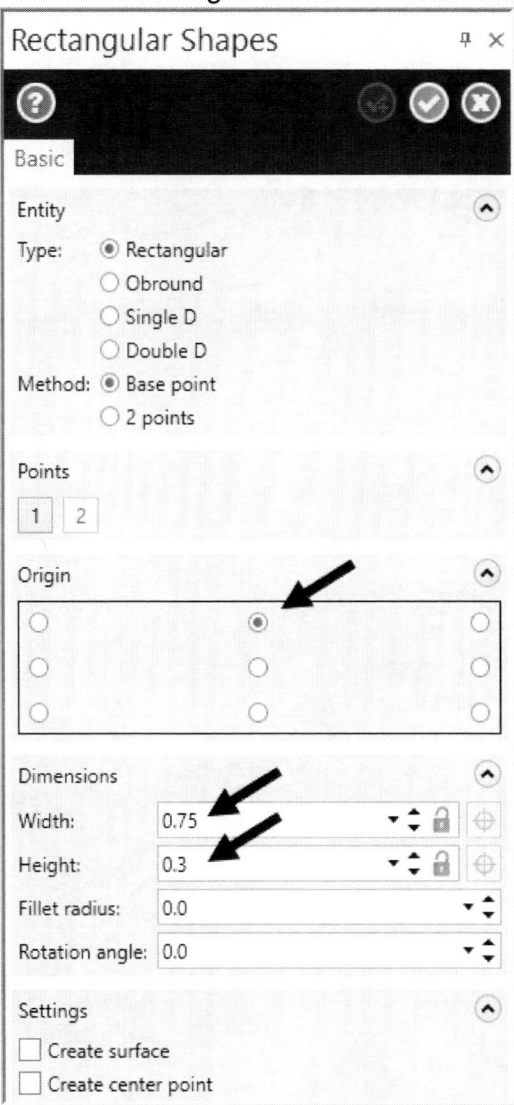

31. Now you need to **Select the position of the base point**. Move the cursor over to the graphics screen and position the cursor at the **Origin** shown below and pick this point.

32. Click on the OK icon ![OK] to complete this feature.

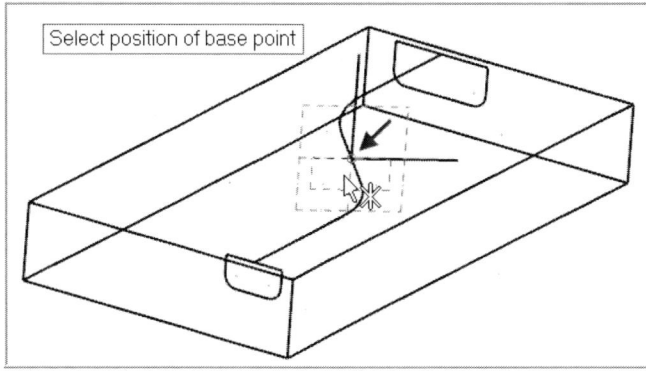

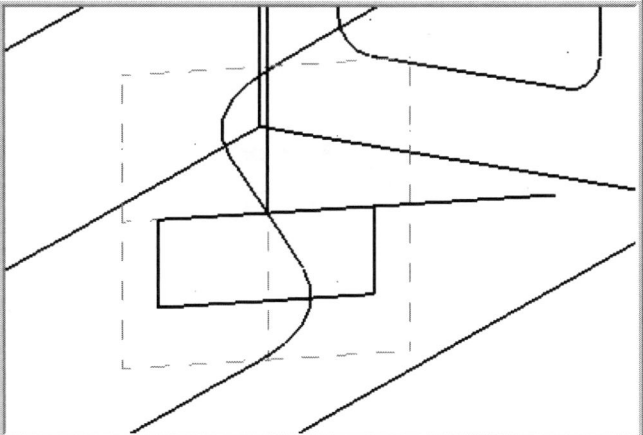

➲ The completed rectangle is shown above.

⟳ **Create Fillets**

33. Select the **Wireframe** tab and in the **Modify** section click on **Fillet Entities**.
34. The **Fillet Entities** panel appears. If required activate the **Style** to **Normal** and enter a value of **0.125** for **Radius**.
35. Ensure the **Trim** entities box at the bottom of the panel is check marked to turn the trim on.
36. When prompted to **Fillet: Select an entity,** select entity 1 and 2 as shown below. The fillet radius appears at the corner of entities 1 and 2. To complete the remaining fillet select: entities 2 and 3. The completed geometry is shown below right:

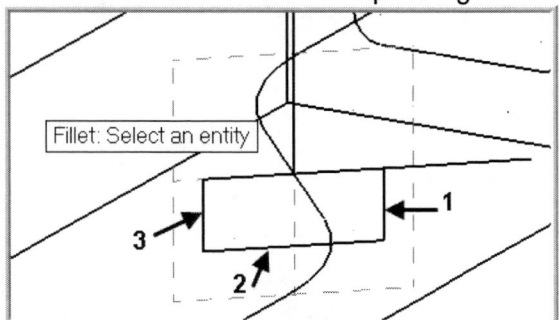
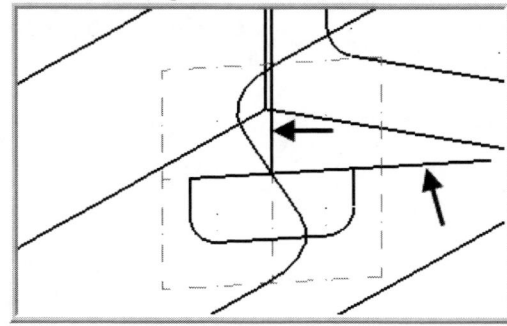

37. Click on the OK icon to complete this feature.
38. **Delete** the two construction lines created earlier for the construction plane as shown above right by clicking on the lines with the mouse and hitting the **delete key** on keyboard.
39. Right mouse click in the graphics area and click on **Isometric**.
40. In the Planes Manager click in the **C column (Construction Plane)** for **Top**. Take note at the bottom of the screen **CPLANE:Top TPLANE:Top WCS:Top** as shown below right.

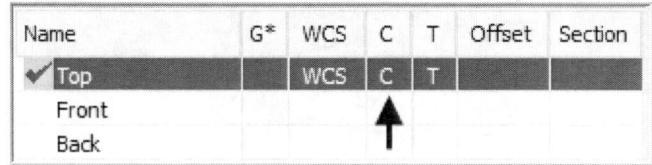

41. Right mouse click in the graphics area and click on the **Fit** icon 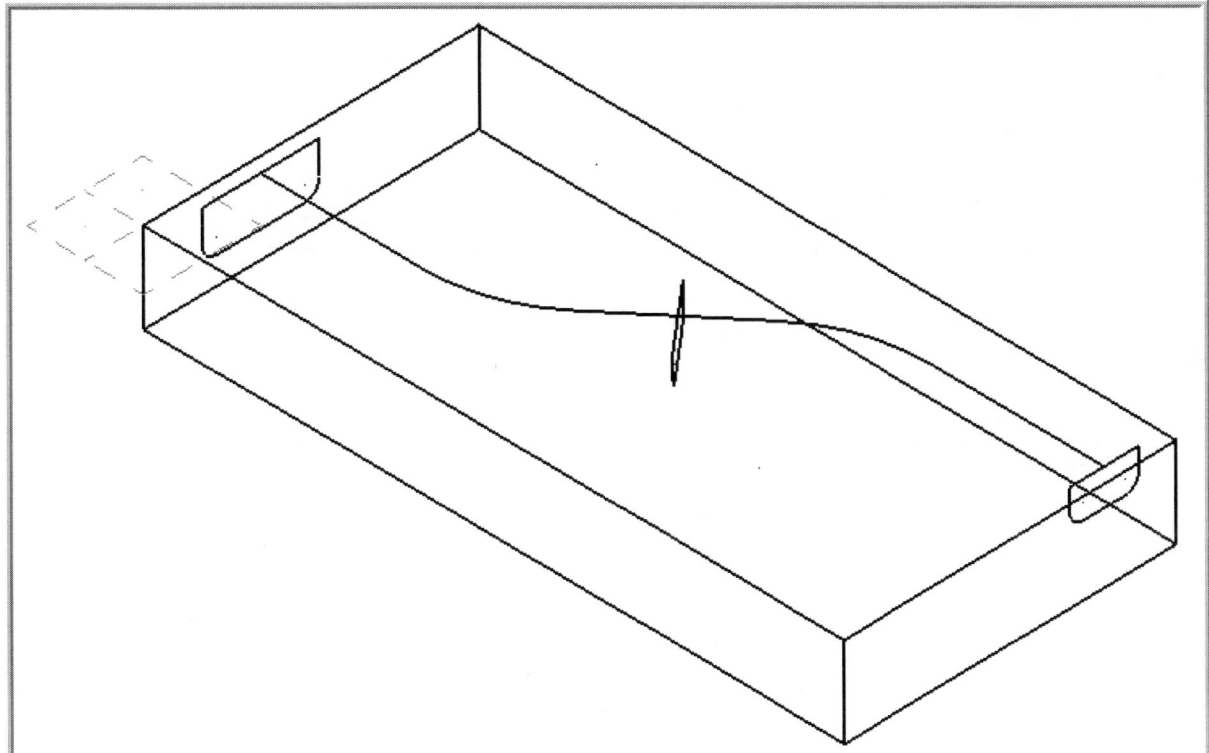.

➲ The completed geometry is shown below.

TASK 8:
CREATE THE SWEPT SURFACE
➲ In this task you will create a swept surface using the geometry you have just created. The swept surface will be created using four chains.

➲ **Create Swept Surface.**
1. Click on the **Surfaces** tab and in the **Create** section select **Sweep**.
2. In the Chaining dialog box set to **Partial** chain.
3. On the graphics screen you are prompted: **Swept surface: define the across contours.** On the right hand section select the partial chain by first selecting line 1, ensure the arrow is pointing downwards and then select line 2. You may need to **zoom in** to select the entities.

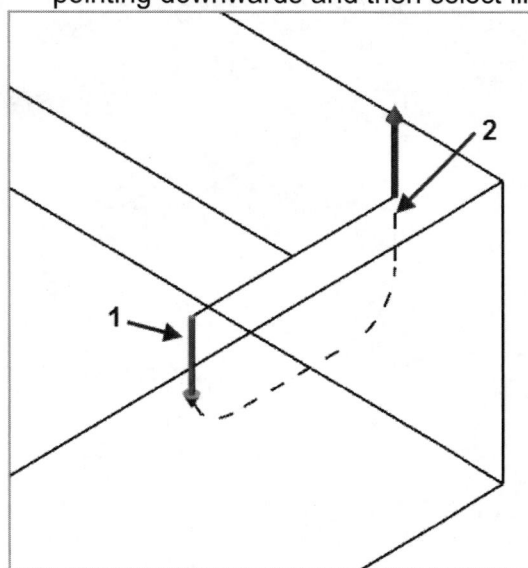

4. Position the view so it is similar to the image below by using the **Middle Button** or **Scroll Button** on the mouse.
5. On the graphics screen you are again prompted: **Swept surface: define the across contour (2).** On the center section select the partial chain by first selecting line 1, ensure the arrow is pointing downwards and then select line 2.

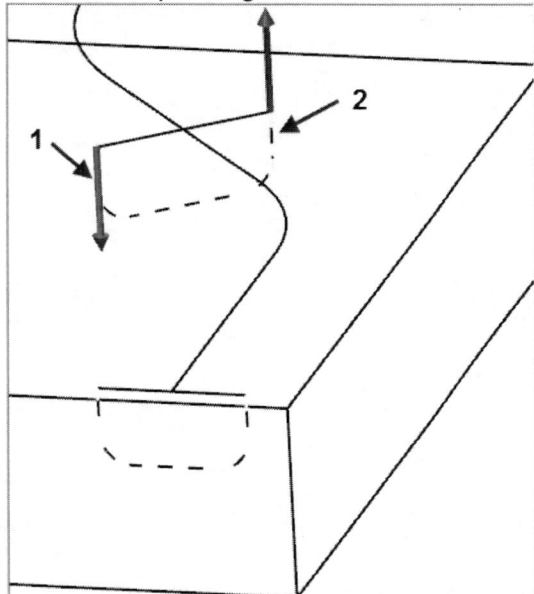

6. Position the view so it is similar to the image below by using the **Middle Button** or **Scroll Button** on the mouse.

7. On the graphics screen you are prompted: **Swept surface: define the across contour (3).** Select the partial chain by first selecting line 1, ensure the arrow is pointing down and then select line 2.

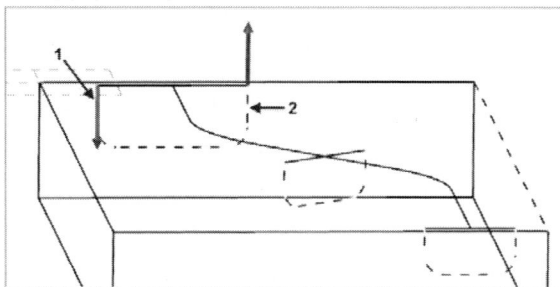

8. Click on the OK icon ☑ in the Chaining dialog window.

9. Right mouse click in the graphics area and click on **Isometric** and then **Fit**.

10. On the graphics screen you are prompted: **Swept surface: define the along contours.** Select the chain by selecting line as shown below:

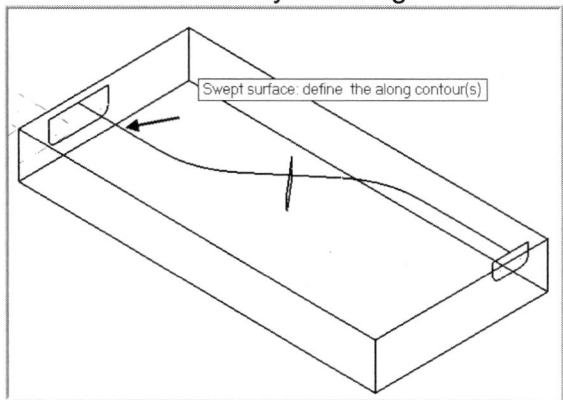

11. Click on the OK icon ☑ in the Chaining dialog window.

12. Click on the **OK** icon 🗹 in the Surface Swept panel to complete this feature.

➲ The completed swept surface is shown below:

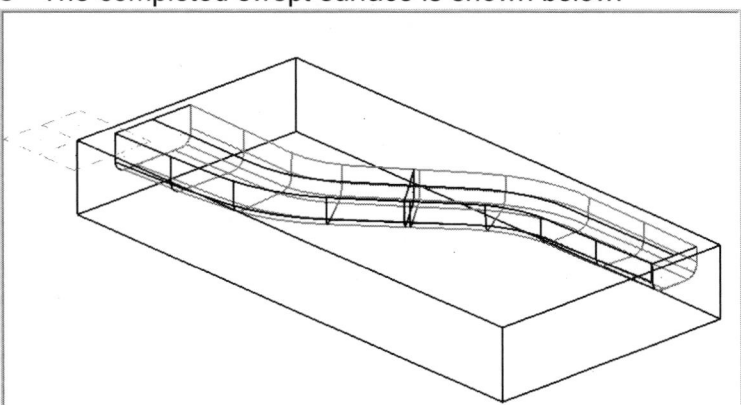

13. In the **View** tab click on **Outline Shaded** in the **Appearance** section to display the part in shaded mode. Now click on **Wireframe** to un-shade the surface.

TASK 9:
CREATE FLAT BOUNDARY SURFACE AT ENDS OF SWEEP
➲ In this task you will create two Flat Boundary surfaces at both ends of the sweep.

➲ **Create Flat Boundary Surface - right hand section.**
1. Click on **Surfaces** tab and in the **Create** section select **Flat Boundary**.
2. In the Chaining dialog box ensure the **Chain** button is activated.
3. On the graphics screen you are prompted: **Select chains to define flat boundary.** On the right hand section select the chain by selecting the line shown below. You may need to **zoom in** to select the entities.

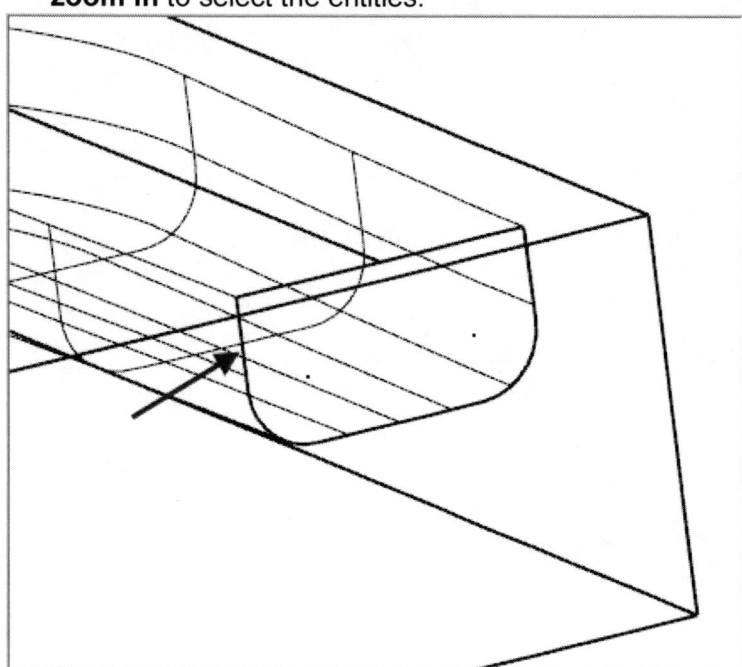

4. Click on the OK icon [✓] in the Chaining dialog window.
5. Click on the **OK and Create New Operation** icon [icon].
6. Right mouse click in the graphics area and click on the **Fit** icon [icon].
7. Zoom in on the **left end** of the sweep.
8. On the graphics screen you are prompted: **Select chains to define flat boundary.** On the left hand section select the chain by selecting the line shown below:

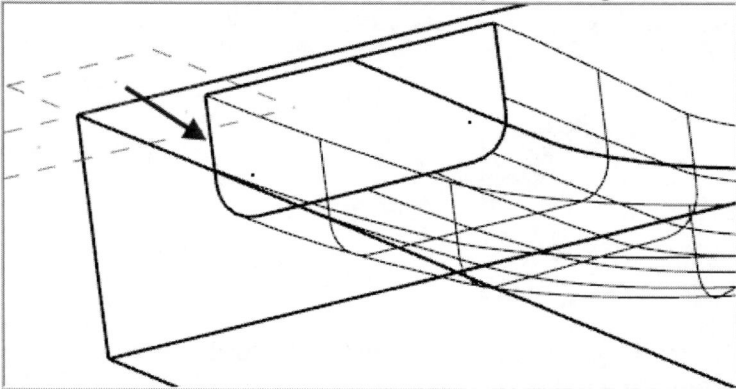

9. Click on the OK icon in the **Chaining** dialog box.
10. Click on the **OK** icon in the **Flat Boundary Surface panel** to complete this feature.

⮕ The completed boundary surfaces are shown below:

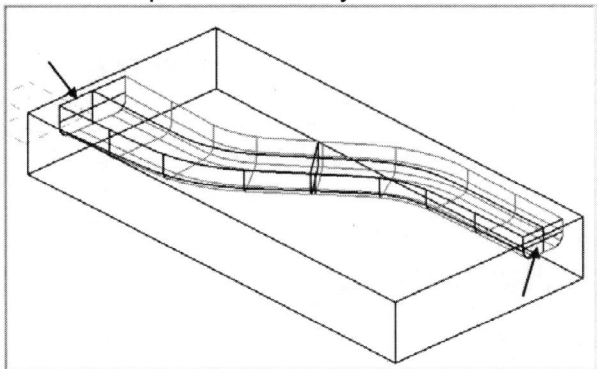

TASK 10:
CREATE FILLET SURFACES
⮕ Create surface to surface fillet .1 radius left and right hand end.

1. Watch **the Mill Lesson 12 Task 10 video** in the online course.
2. In the **View** tab click on **Outline Shaded** in the **Appearance** section to display the part in shaded mode, this will make it easier to select the surfaces. **Wireframe shown below for clarity**.
3. Click on **Surfaces** tab and in the **Modify** section select **Fillet To Surfaces**.
4. Zoom in on the left hand end of the **sweep surface** as shown below:

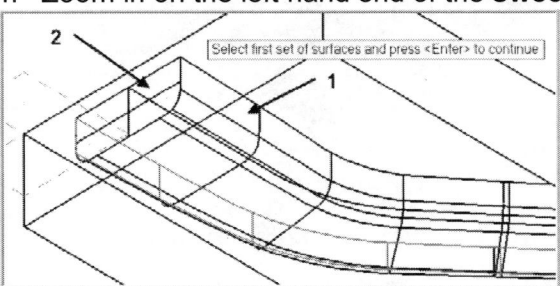

5. On the graphics screen you are prompted: **Select first set of surfaces and press <Enter> to continue.** Select the **sweep surface (1)** as shown above and then **hit Enter**. Note: The surface will highlight when the cursor is over it.
6. For the next prompt **Select second set of surfaces and press <Enter> to continue.** Select the **flat boundary blend (2)** as shown above and then **hit Enter**.
7. In the **View** tab click on **Wireframe** in the **Appearance** section.

8. The Surface Fillet to Surfaces panel appears, **set the radius to 0.075** and other values as shown below:

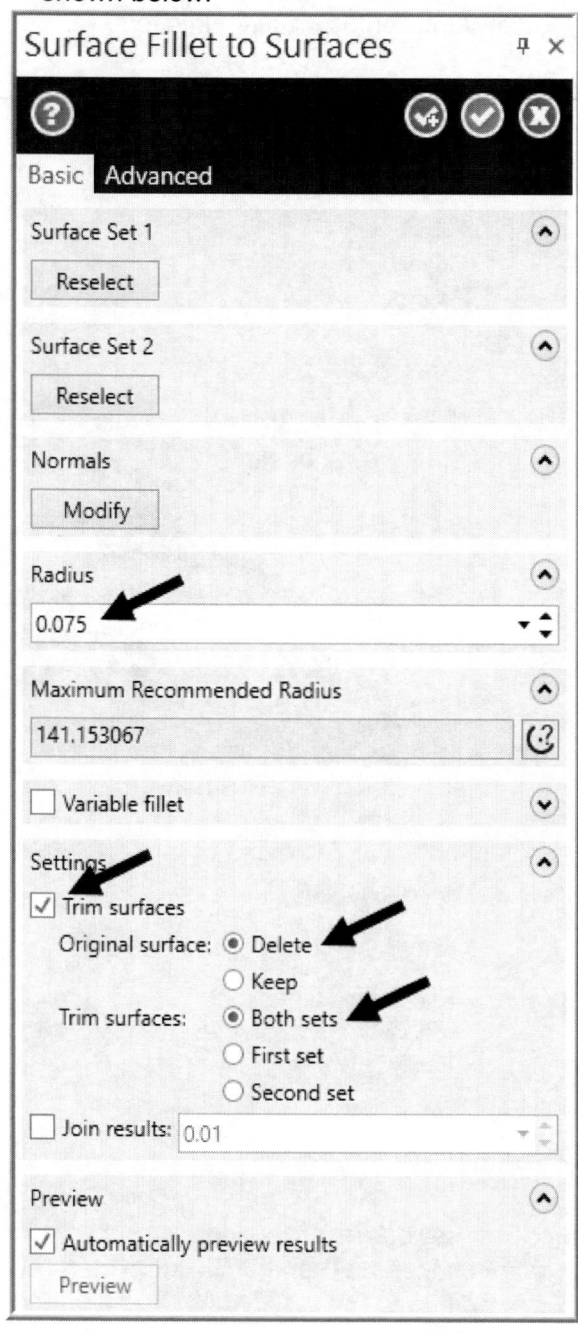

Use this function to create one or more fillet surfaces, each of which is tangent to two surfaces.

You are prompted to select two sets of surfaces. The system attempts to create fillet surfaces by pairing each surface in the first set with each surface in the second set.

You can select one set, but it must contain at least two surfaces. With one set, the system attempts to create fillet surfaces by pairing each surface in the set with every other surface in the set.

If the fillets appear to be backward, as shown below, it is typically the result of surface normal facing the wrong direction.

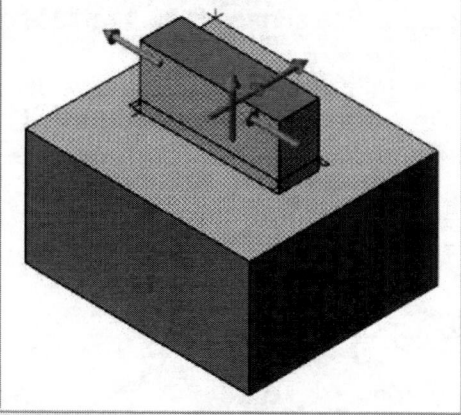

Click Modify and then click the surface to switch the normal to the opposite direction.

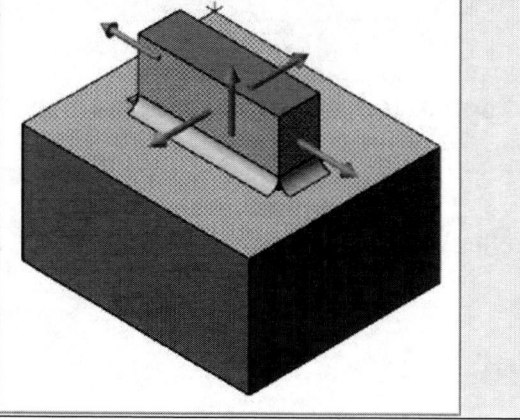

9. Click on the **OK and Create New Operation** icon .

➲ The completed fillet is shown below:

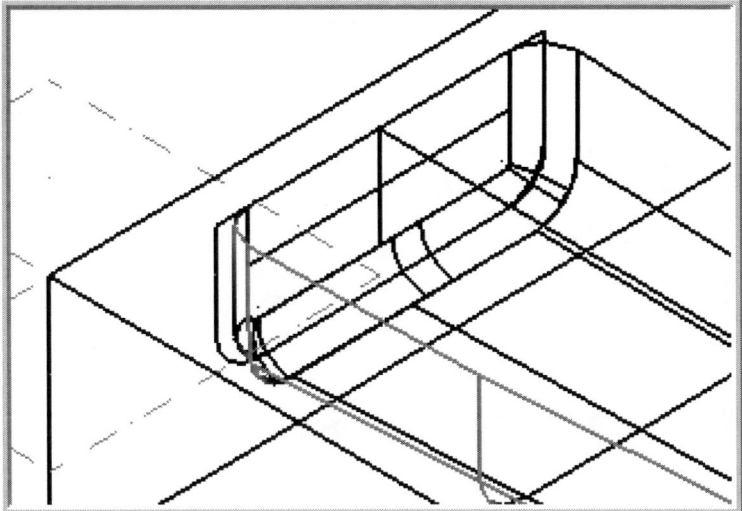

10. Right mouse click in the graphics area and click on the **Fit** icon ▦.
11. Zoom in on the right hand end of the sweep as shown below:

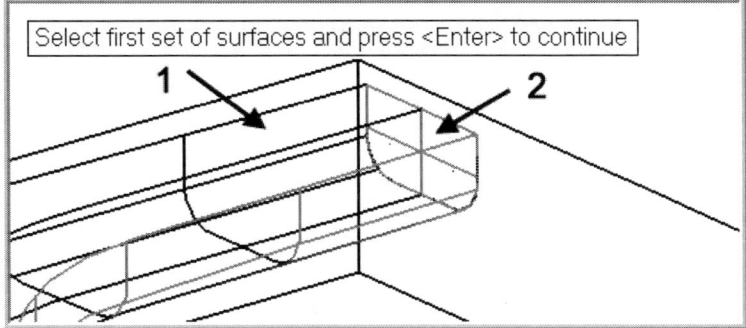

12. On the graphics screen you are prompted: **Select first set of surfaces and press <enter> to continue.** Select the **sweep surface (1)** as shown above and then hit enter.
13. For the next prompt **Select second set of surfaces and press <Enter> to continue.** Select the **flat boundary blend (2)** as shown above and then **hit enter**.

14. The Surface Fillet to Surfaces panel appears, **set the radius to 0.075** and other values as shown below:

15. Click on the **OK** icon  in the **Fillet Surfaces to Surfaces panel** to complete this feature.

➲ The completed fillet is shown below:

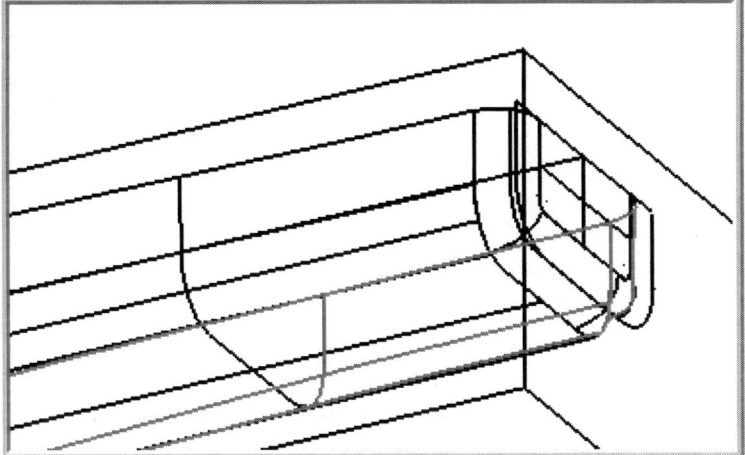

16. Change the graphics view to **Isometric**.
17. Now select the **Fit to screen** icon.

TASK 11:
SAVE THE DRAWING

1. Select File.
2. Select **Save as**.
3. Click on the **Browse** icon.
4. In the File name box, ensure **Mill-Lesson-12** is visible as shown below:
5. Save to an appropriate location.
6. Select the **Save** button to save the file and complete this function.

Toolpath Creation

TASK 12:
DEFINE THE ROUGH STOCK USING STOCK SETUP

1. Select the **View tab** and click on **Toolpaths** in the **Managers** section to display the Toolpaths Manager.
2. Select the **plus** in front of **Properties** to expand the Toolpaths Group Properties.
3. Select **Stock setup** in the toolpath manager window.
4. On the **Stock Setup** page select **Bounding box**.

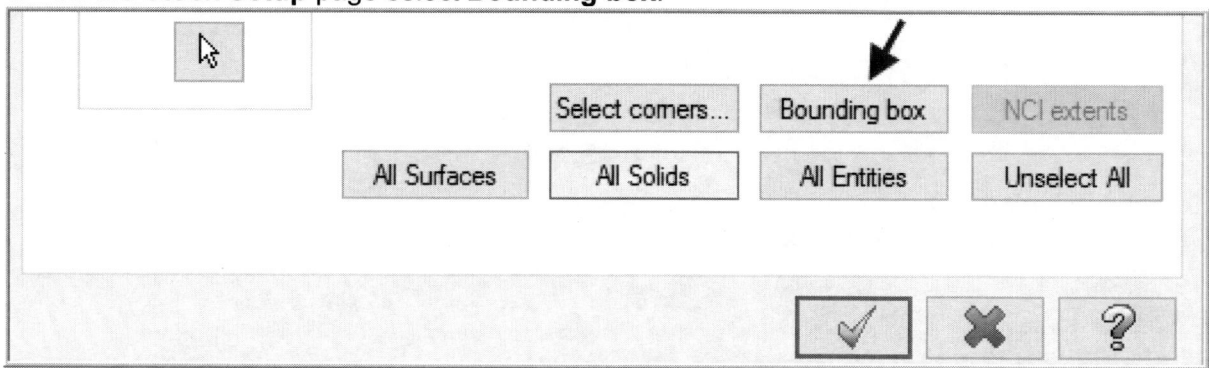

Bounding box
Returns you to the graphics window to select geometry that defines the limits of the bounding box.
Use **Bounding box** to create a rectangular or cylindrical boundary around selected entities in the graphics window. Bounding box creates wireframe geometry, a solid model, or a stock model.
You can also use Bounding box to check the overall dimensions of a part.

5. You are now prompted to **"Select one or more entities. Use Ctrl-A to select all"**. Click CTRL-A. This will select all visible geometry.

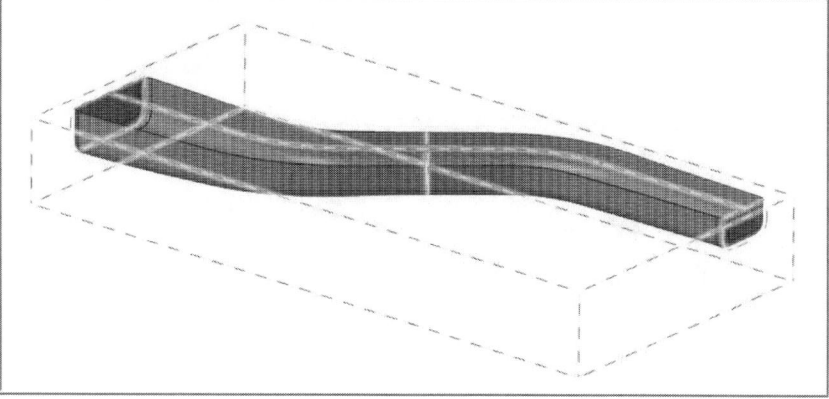

6. Click on **End Selection** to move onto the next step. The Bounding box panel appears.

⊃ Take note of the X, Y and Z values Mastercam has calculated for the stock size and the
preview on the graphics screen.

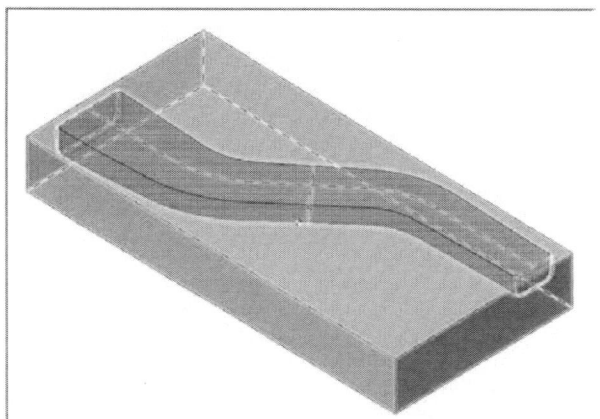

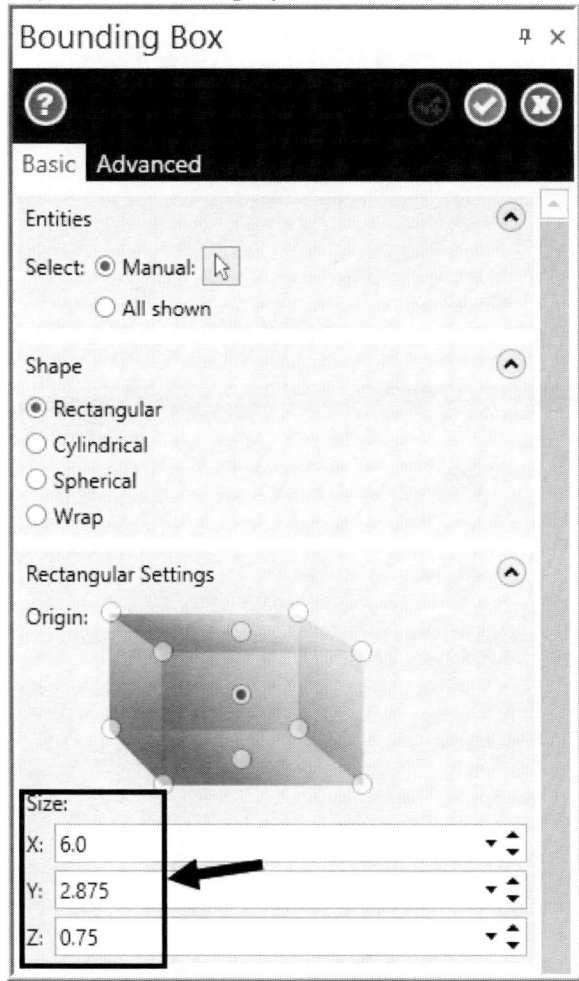

7. Now click on the **OK** icon 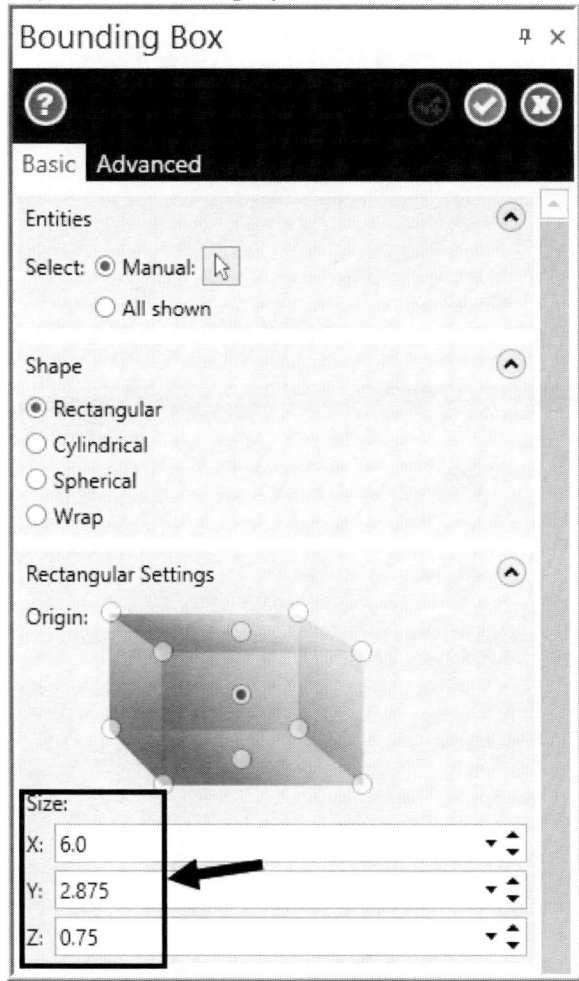 in the Bounding box panel.

⊃ **Bounding box** calculates the sizes and is then input into the X, Y and Z values.
⊃ The top of the material is at Z 0. The material has been pre-machined to size.

8. Mastercam returns the appropriate values to the Stock Setup page:

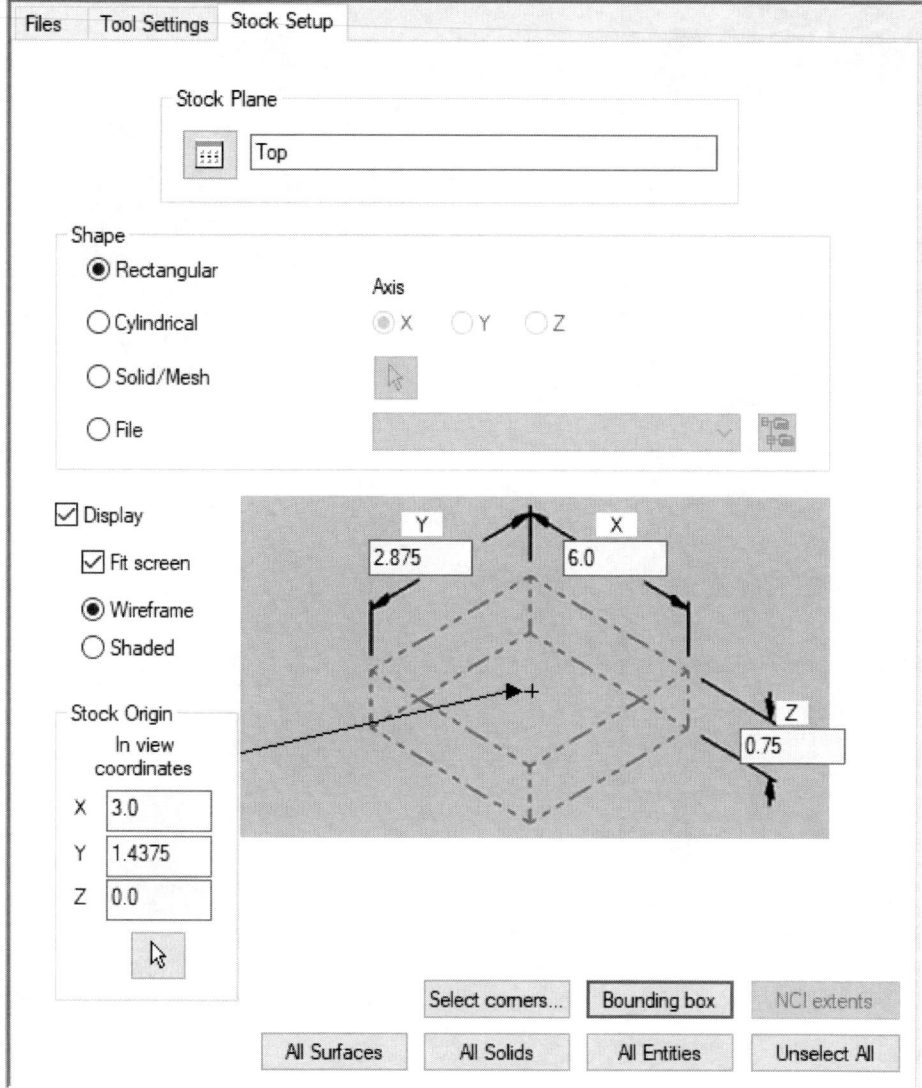

9. Select the **Tool Settings** tab and change the parameters to match the Tool Settings screenshot below. To change the Material type follow the instructions below:

10. To change the Material type to Aluminum 6061 pick the **Select** button at the bottom of the Tool Settings page.

11. At the **Material List** dialog box open the **Source** drop down list and select **Mill – library**.

12. From the Default Materials list select **ALUMINUM inch -6061** and then select 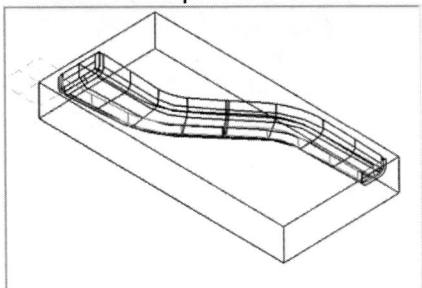.

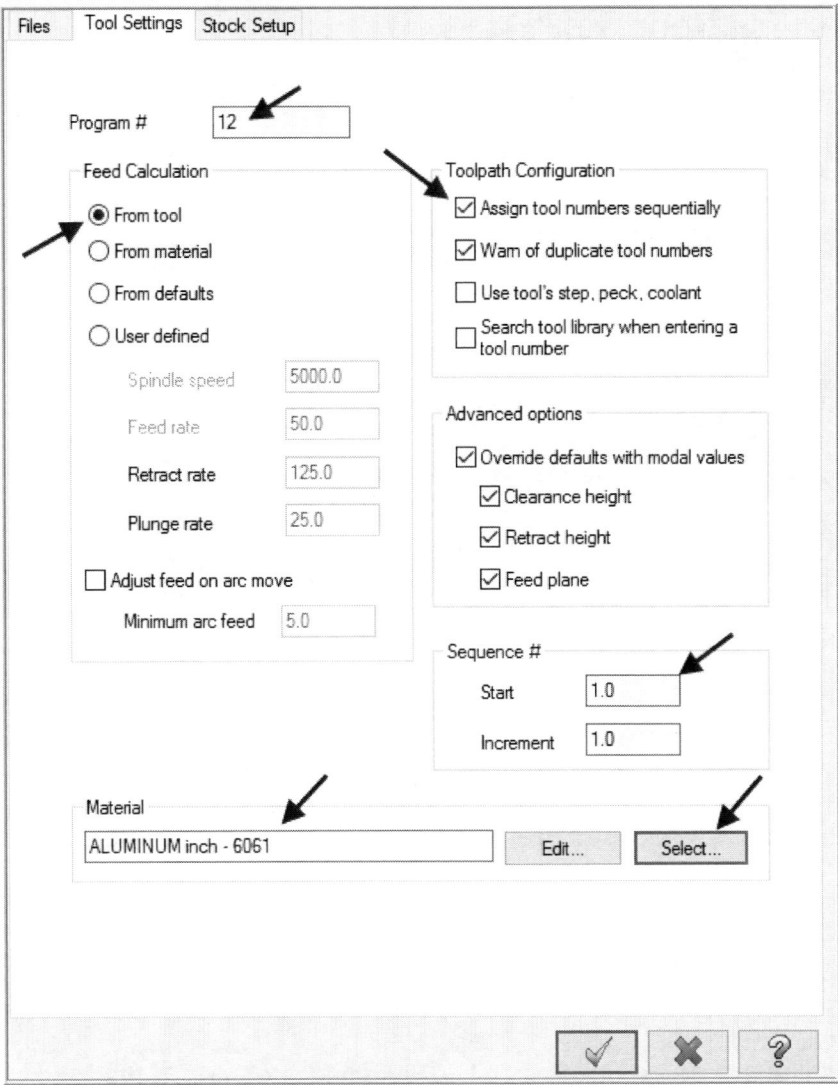

13. Select the OK button ☑ again to complete this Stock Setup function.

14. Right mouse click in the graphics area and click on the **Fit** icon.

➲ Your part should look similar to the screen shot below. With **X0 Y0** at the left side and **Z zero on** top of the stock.

TASK 13:
ROUGH THE POCKET USING SURFACE ROUGH POCKET

⋑ In this task you will use a 0.375 diameter end mill with a 0.031 corner radius to rough out the pocket. Rough pocket toolpaths remove a lot of stock quickly by creating a series of planar cuts (or constant Z), which is the preferred cutting method for many roughing tools.

1. Select the **Toolpaths** tab at the top right side of the screen.
2. Select **Pocket** in the **3D** toolpath section.
3. To satisfy the prompt, you can select each surface individually or **use CTRL-A** again to quickly select all.

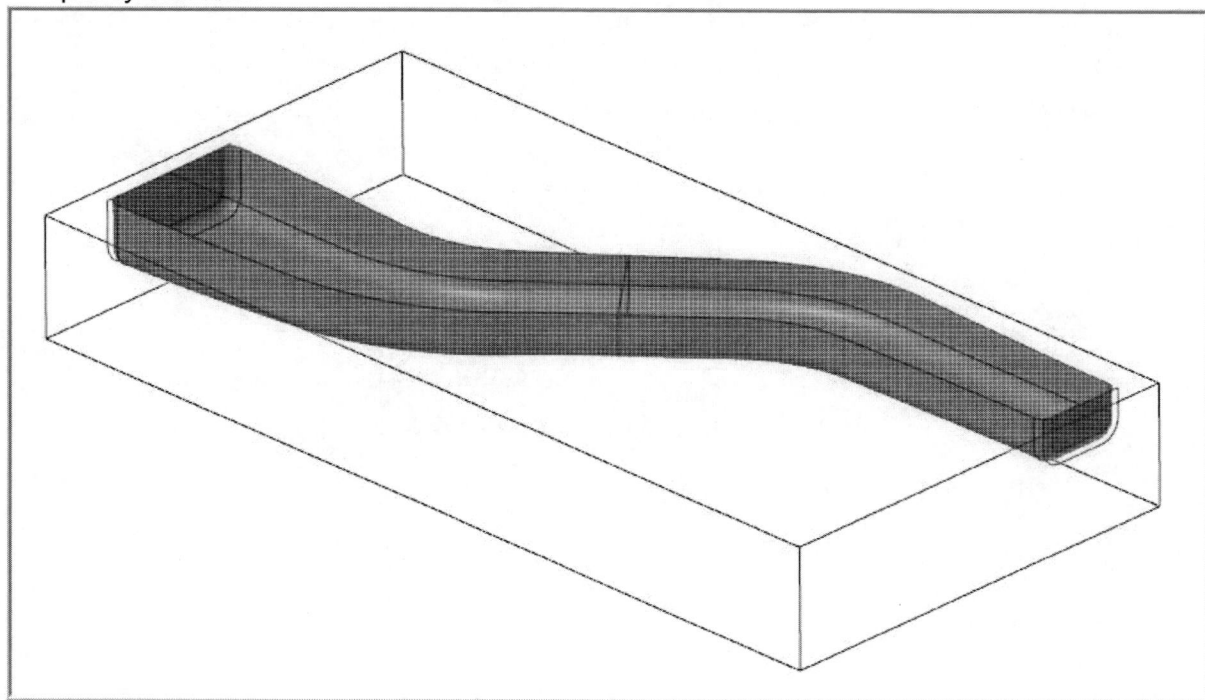

4. To move onto the next step you now need to pick the **End Selection** icon [◎].
5. Select the OK button [✔] to exit the **Toolpath/surface selection** dialog box.
6. In the lower left corner of the **Toolpath parameters** page select the **Select library tool…** button.
7. Use the slider bar on the right of this dialog box to scroll down and locate a **0.375 diameter bull end mill with a 0.03125 corner radius**. Select the end mill by picking anywhere along its row.

Tool Number	Tool Name	Diameter	Corner Radius	Length	Type	Radius Type
338	3/8 BULL ENDMILL ...	0.375	0.0625	0.75	Bull endmill	Corner
339	3/8 BULL ENDMILL ...	0.375	0.03125	0.75	Bull endmill	Corner
340	3/8 BULL ENDMILL ...	0.375	0.125	0.75	Bull endmill	Corner

8. Select the OK button [✔] to complete the selection of this tool.

9. Make changes to the **Toolpath parameters** page as shown below. Set coolant on.

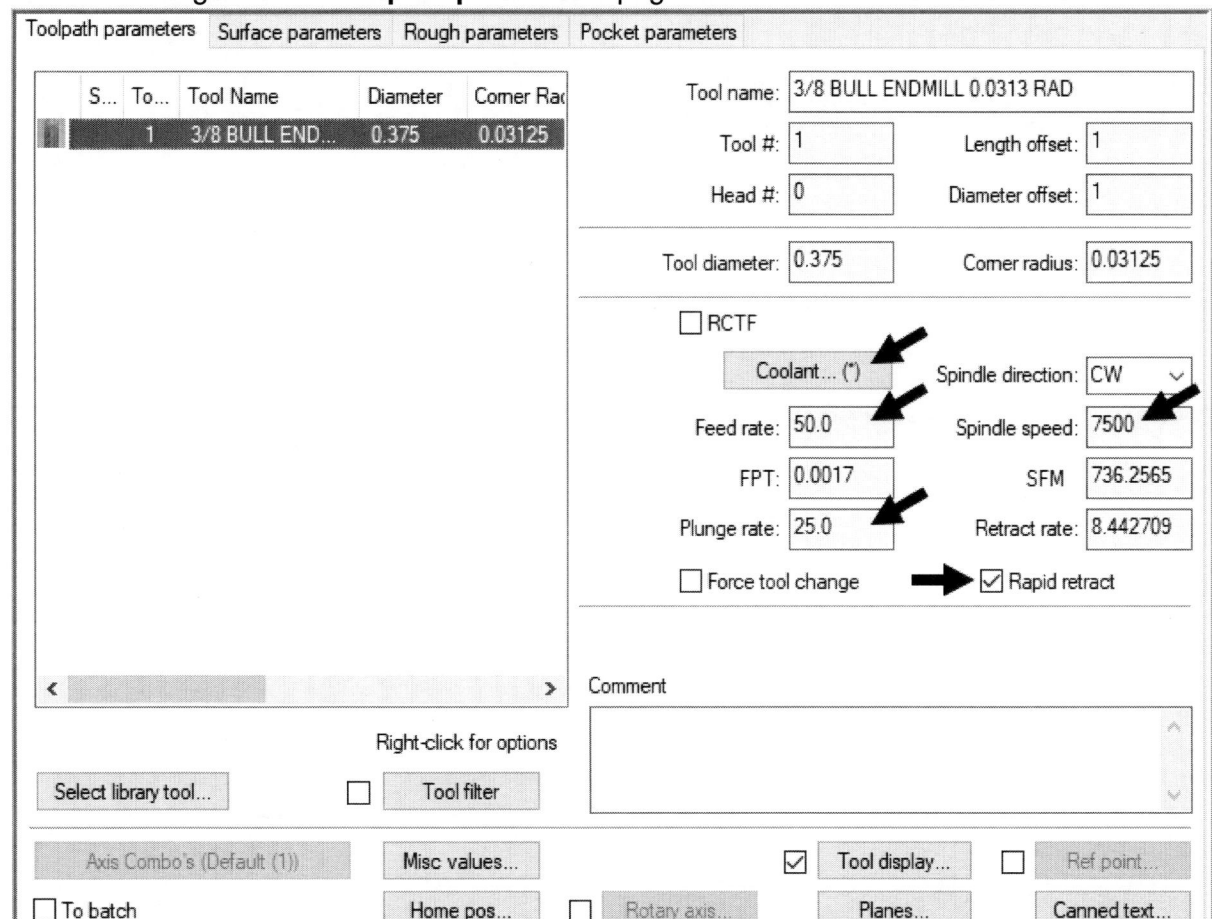

10. Select the **Surface parameters** page and make changes to this page as shown below.
Stock to leave on drive is set to **0.015**.

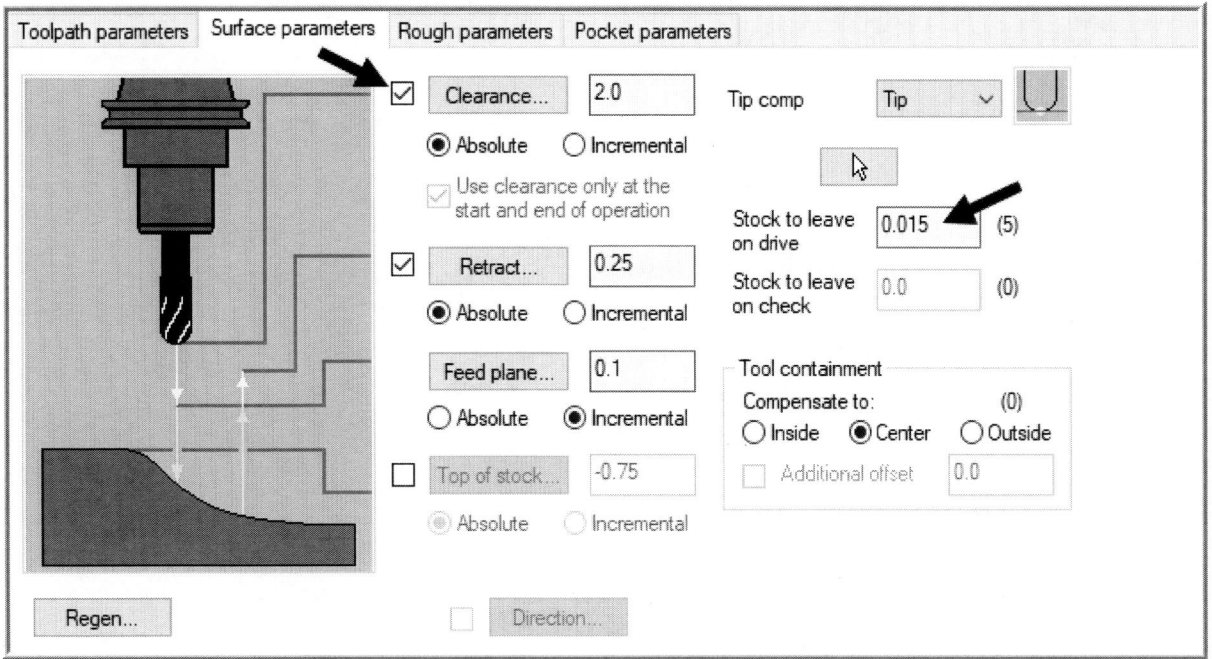

11. Select the **Rough parameters** page and make the following selections:

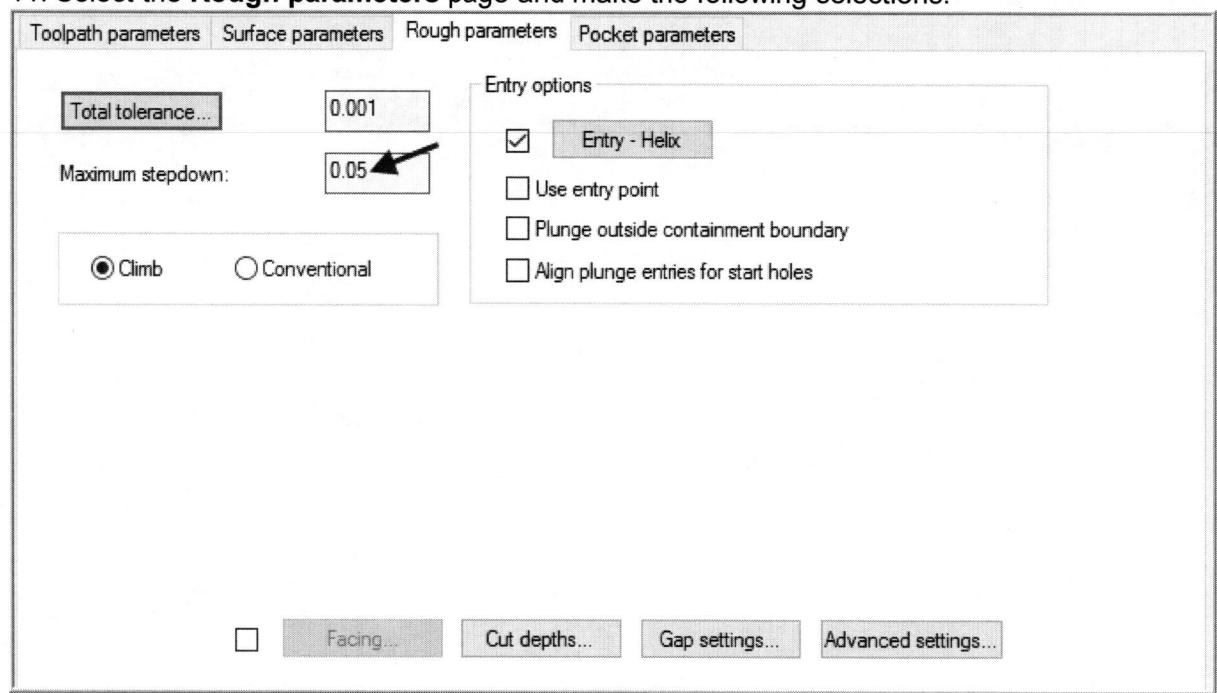

12. Select the **Total Tolerances** button then make the following selections.

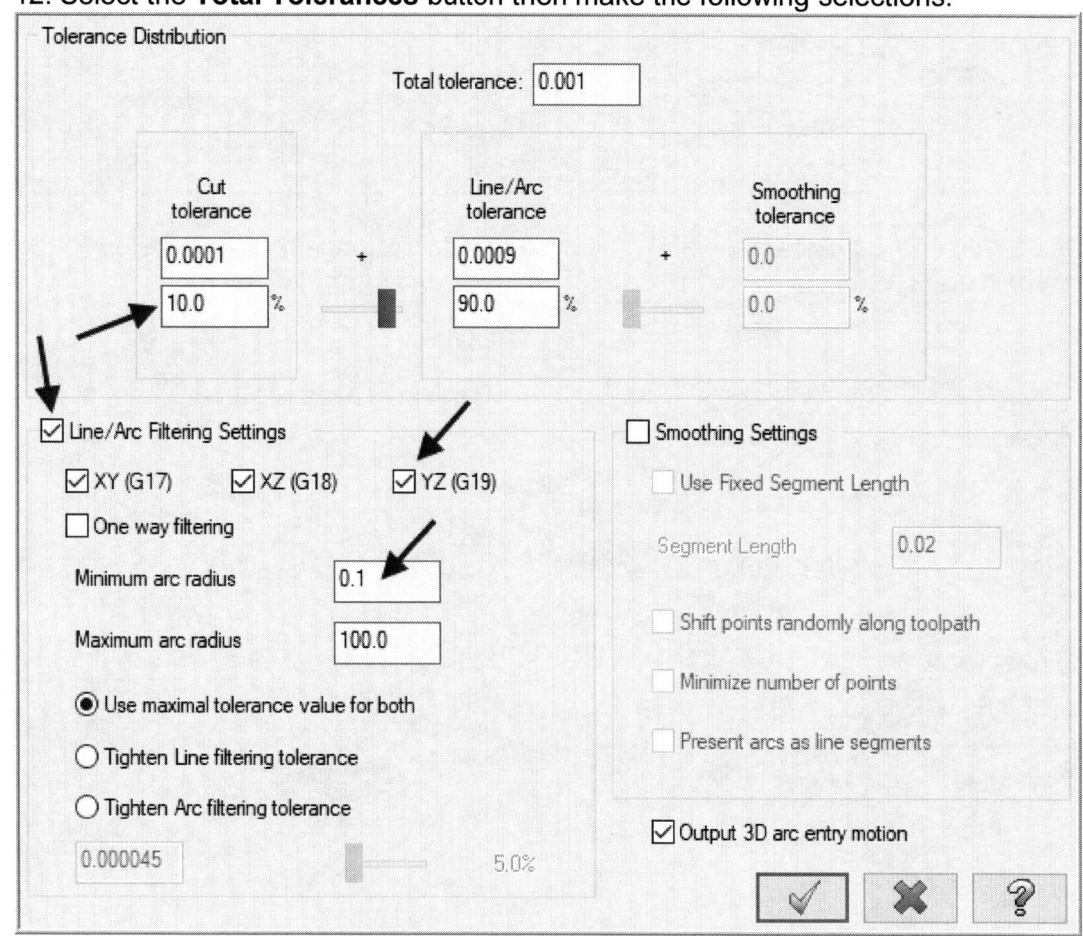

13. Select the **OK** button ✔ to complete this feature.

14. Select the Entry Helix button and **reduce the Max and Min radius** values. Click **OK** to complete this setting.

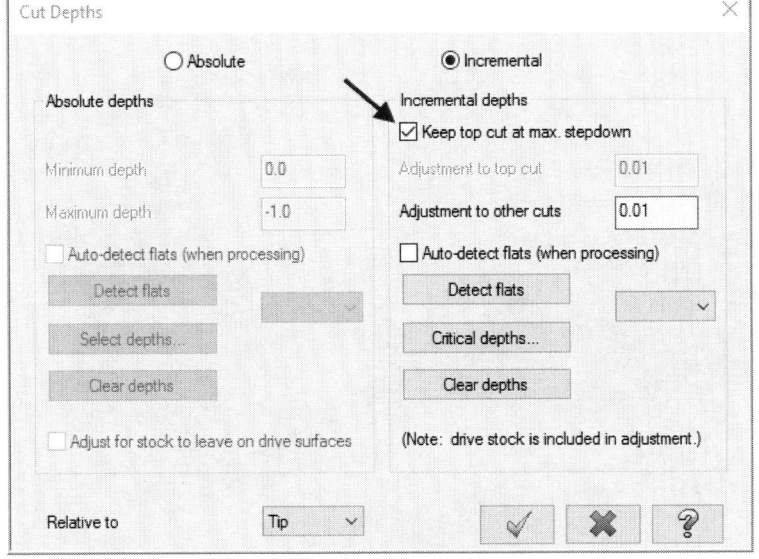

15. Select the **Cuts depths** button make the necessary changes.

	Cut depths specify the placement of Z-axis cuts for all rough surface toolpaths and for finish contour toolpaths. **Incremental cut depths** Incremental cut depths are measured from the top and bottom of the part for most rough surface toolpaths and for finish contour toolpaths. **Keep top cut at max stepdown** Available only for rough pocket toolpaths. Forces the tool to make the first cutting pass at the max cut depth instead of the top of the part.

16. Select the **OK** button ☑ to complete this feature.

17. Select the **Pocket parameters** page and make changes to this page as shown below:

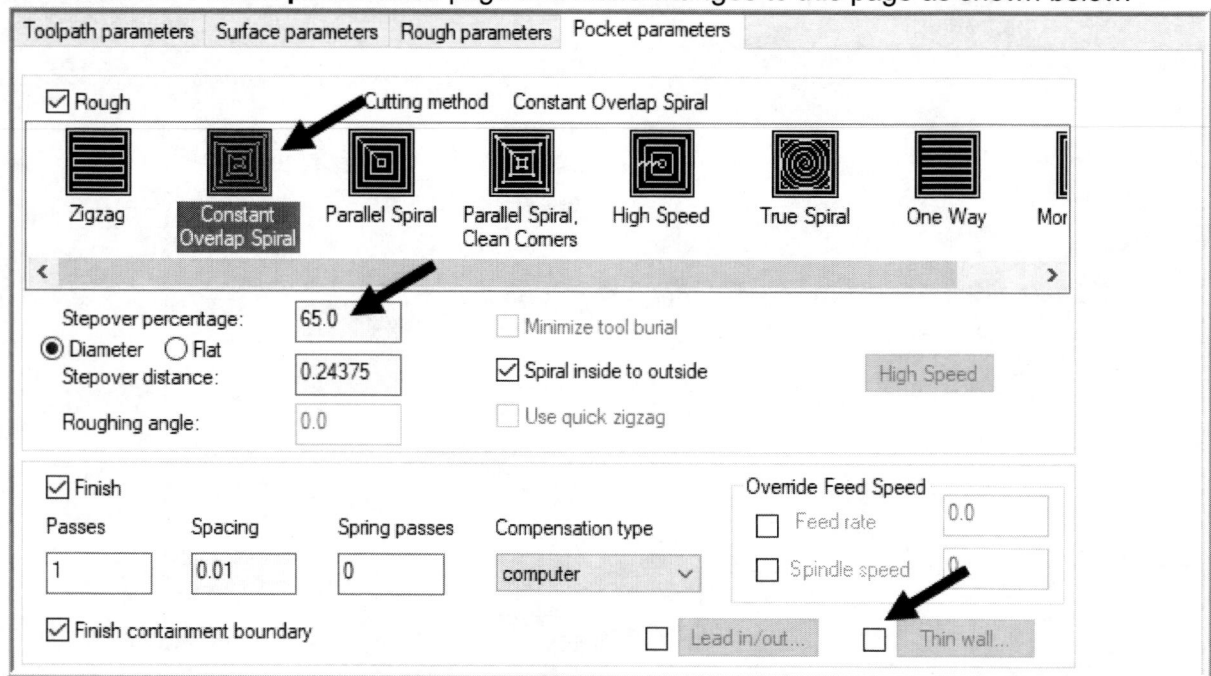

18. Select the **OK** button 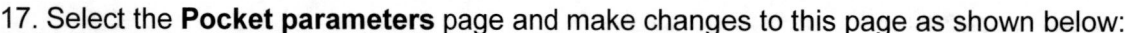 to exit **Rough pocket** parameters.
19. **Verify** the new toolpath.

➲ Your screen should look similar to the image below.

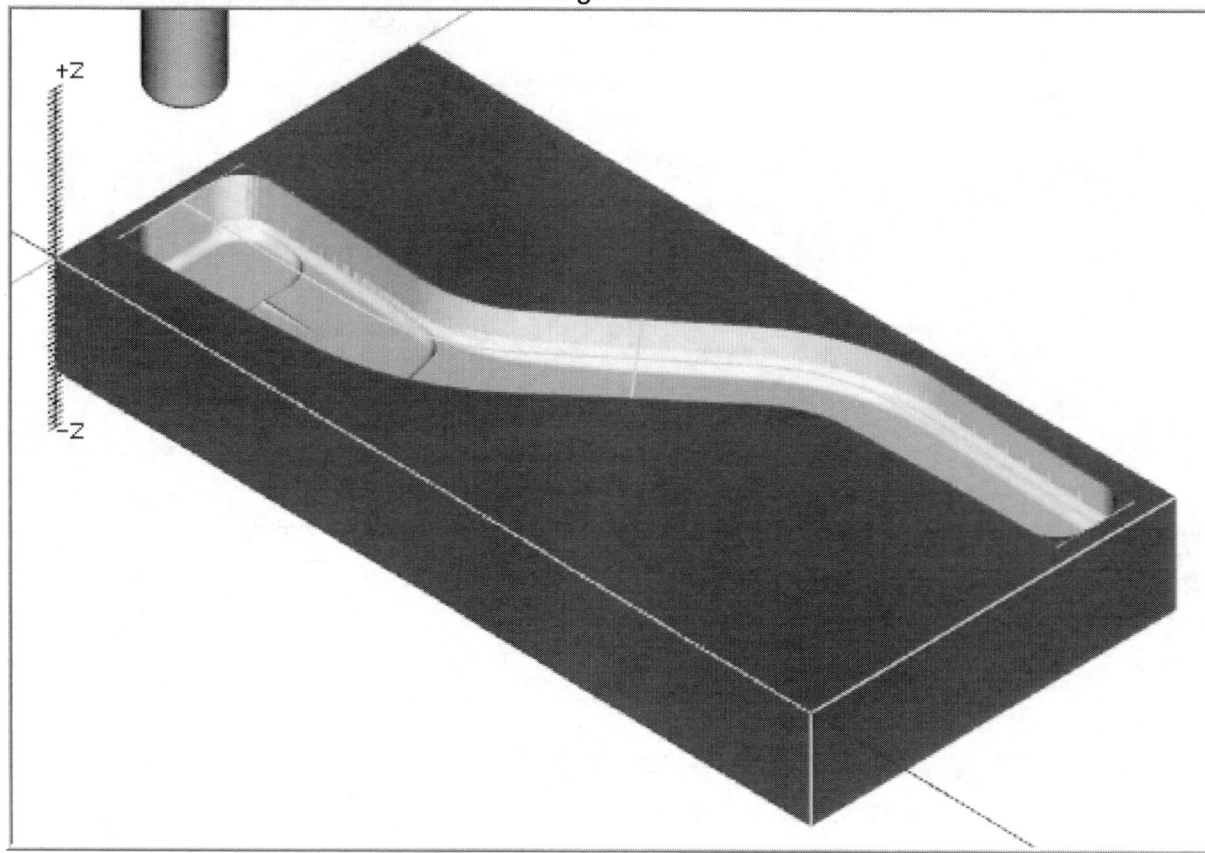

TASK 14:
FINISH USING SURFACE HIGH SPEED WATERLINE TOOLPATH
➲ In this task you will use a 3/16" diameter Ball end mill to finish the walls of the pocket.

> Surface high speed toolpaths are a set of machining strategies that are specially designed to produce the smoothest, most efficient tool motions when machining surface models (or solid faces).

1. Right mouse click in the white space of the Toolpaths Manager and select:
   Mill toolpaths>Surface high speed toolpath> Waterline.

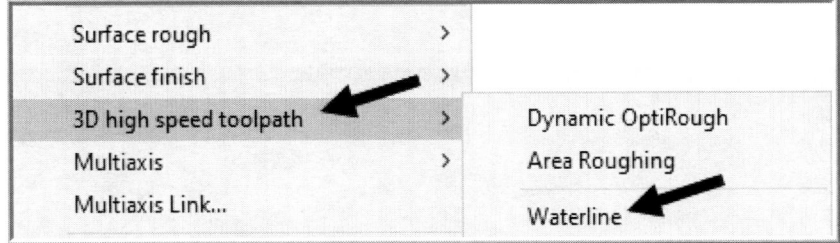

2. On the screen select the **Model Geometry** page, if required.
3. Ensure both the **Wall Stock** and **Floor stock** are set to **Zero.**

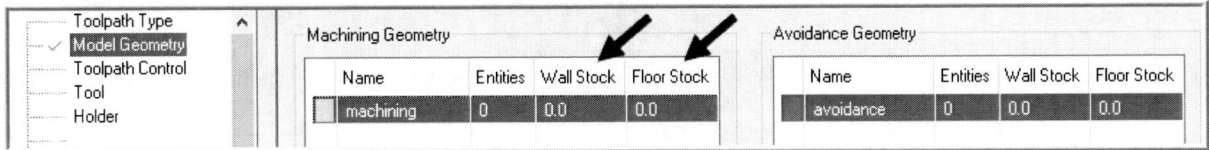

4. At the bottom of the **Model Geometry** page click on the **Select entities** button.

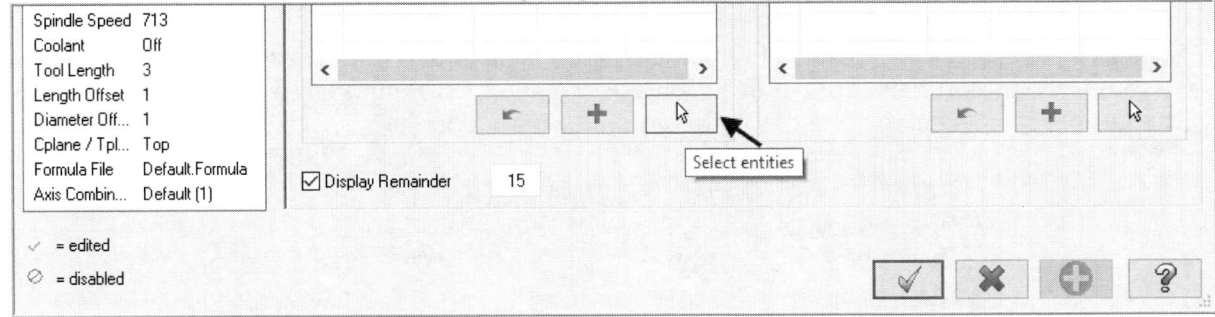

5. Now you will be returned to the graphics screen, click **CTRL-A** to select all visible surfaces.

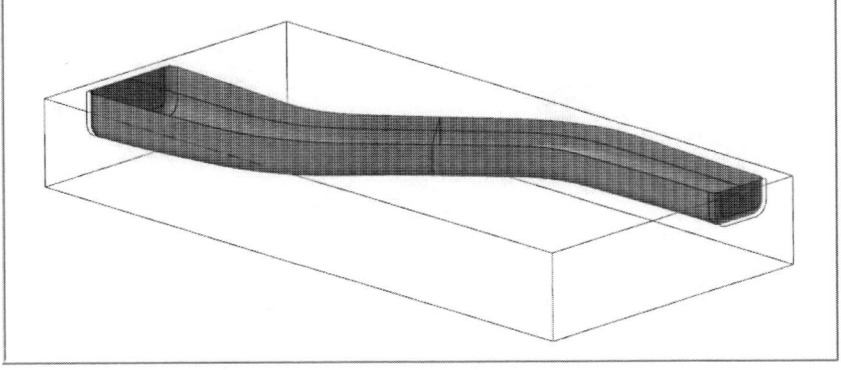

6. To move onto the next step you now need to pick the **End Selection** icon .

7. Select the **Toolpath Control** page, make changes as shown below.

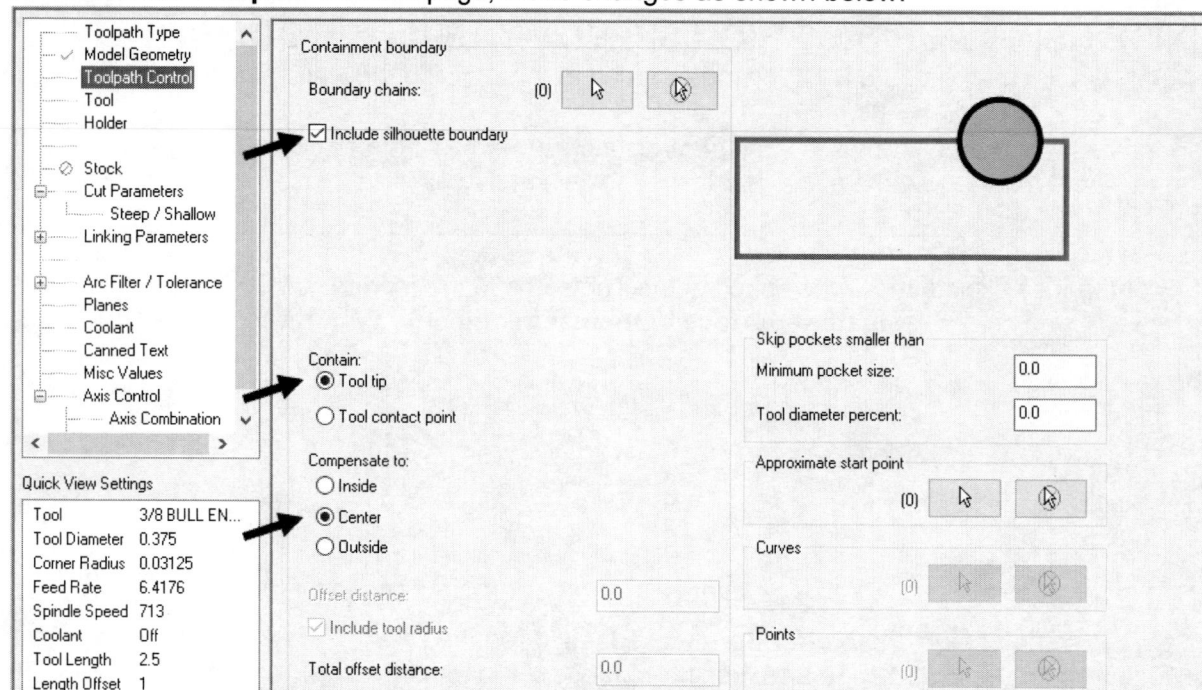

When **Include Silhouette Boundary** is checked, Mastercam will create a silhouette boundary around the selected **Machining geometry** and use it as a containment boundary in addition to any selected **Boundary chains**. A silhouette boundary is a boundary curve around a set of surfaces, solids, or solid faces.

8. Select the **Tool** page from the list on the left hand side.
9. Select the **Select library tool...** button. **Disable Filter active** if required.
10. Use the slider bar on the right of this dialog box to scroll down and locate a **0.1875 diameter ball end mill**. Select the end mill by picking anywhere along its row.

Tool Number	Tool Name	Diameter	Corner Radius	Length	Type	Radius Type
301	1/32 BALL ENDMILL	0.03125	0.01563	0.375	Ball endmill	Full
302	1/16 BALL ENDMILL	0.0625	0.03125	0.375	Ball endmill	Full
303	3/32 BALL ENDMILL	0.09375	0.04688	0.375	Ball endmill	Full
304	1/8 BALL ENDMILL	0.125	0.0625	0.375	Ball endmill	Full
305	5/32 BALL ENDMILL	0.15625	0.07813	0.375	Ball endmill	Full
306	3/16 BALL ENDMILL	0.1875	0.09375	0.4375	Ball endmill	Full
307	1/4 BALL ENDMILL	0.25	0.125	0.5	Ball endmill	Full
308	5/16 BALL ENDMILL	0.3125	0.15625	0.75	Ball endmill	Full
309	3/8 BALL ENDMILL	0.375	0.1875	0.75	Ball endmill	Full

11. Select the OK button ✓ to complete the selection of this tool.

12. Make changes to the **Tool** values page as shown below:

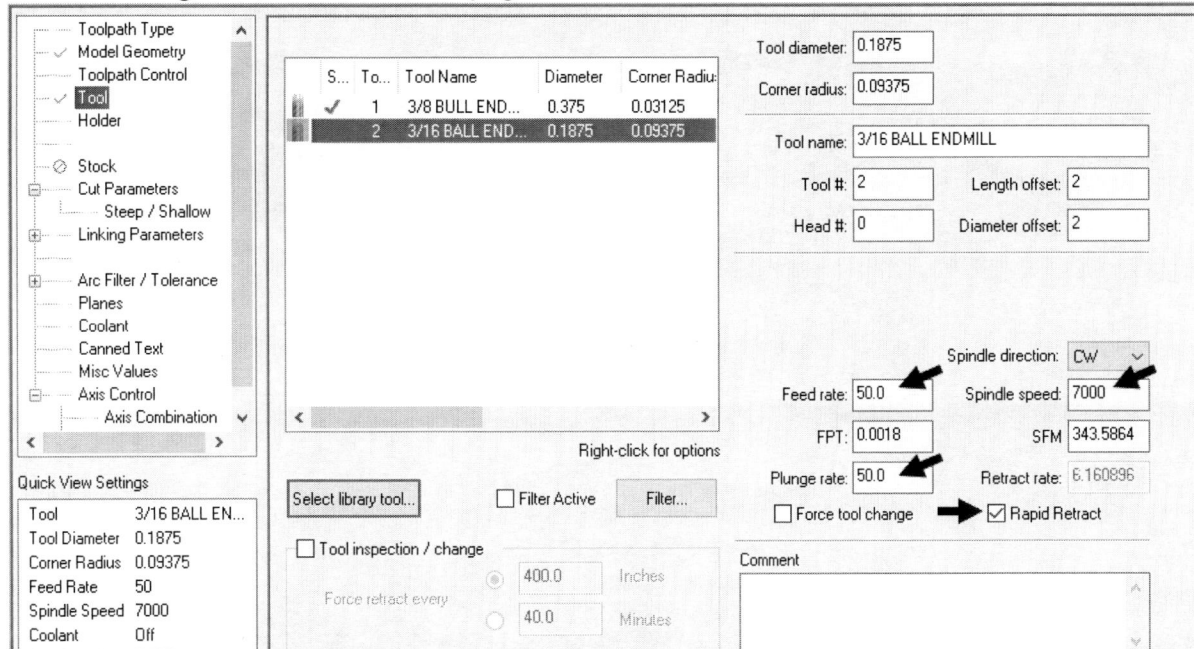

Using the largest ballnose endmill possible will keep wall and floor scallops to a minimum.

However, by selecting one with a corner radius that that is slightly smaller than the fillets running the length of the part will finish the fillets more effectively.

13. Select **Cut Parameters** from the list on the left and make changes as shown below:

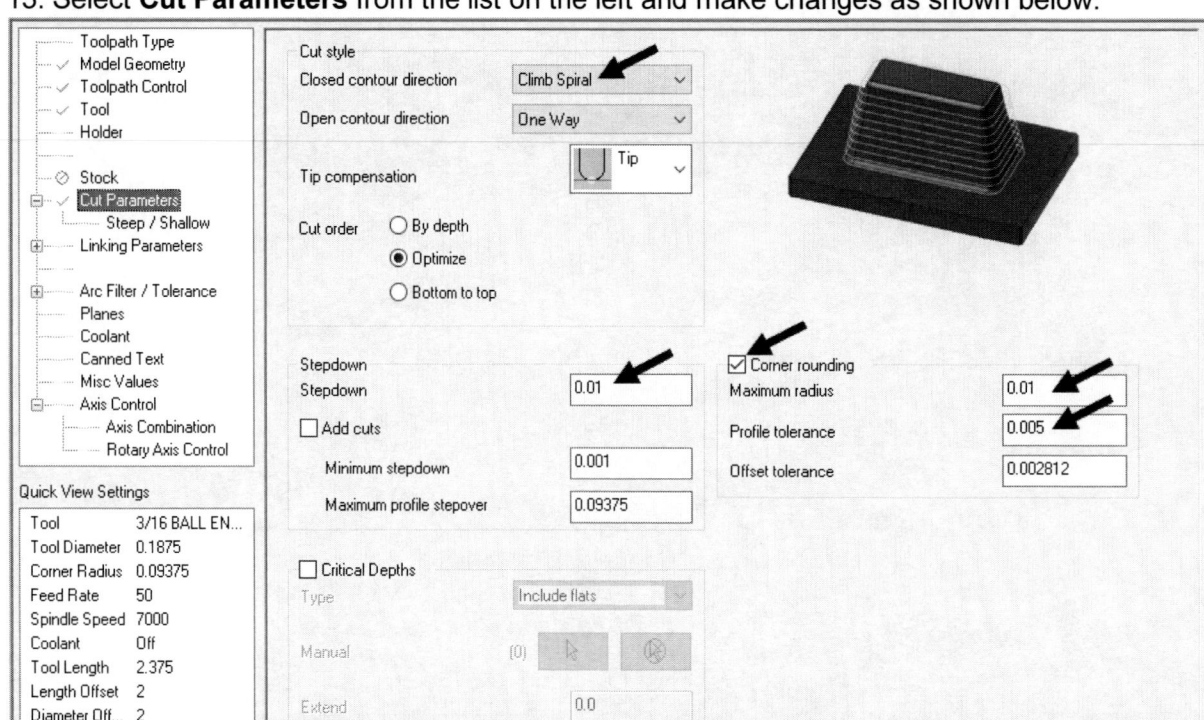

Closed Contour Direction sets the motion type for closed loops around the part. Options are Climb, Conventional, Climb Spiral, and Conventional Spiral.

Open Contour Direction sets the motion type for open loops on the part. Options are One way, which will take its direction from the above selection, and Zig Zag.

Corner rounding

Activates toolpath corner rounding, which replaces sharp corners with arcs for faster and smoother transitions in tool direction.

Maximum radius: Enter the radius of the largest arc that you will allow Mastercam to insert to replace a corner. Larger arcs result in a smoother toolpath, but with greater deviation from the originally programmed toolpath.

Profile tolerance: Represents the maximum distance that the **outermost profile** of a toolpath created with corner rounding can deviate from the original toolpath.

Offset tolerance: Represents the maximum distance that a profile of a toolpath created with corner rounding can deviate from the original toolpath. This is the same measurement as the profile tolerance but is applied to **all the profiles except the outermost one**. This lets you maintain different tolerances for the first profile and subsequent profiles.

14. Select **Steep / Shallow** from the list on the left. **Activate Use Z depths**. Click on the **Detect Limits** button. This will show the top and bottom of the surfaces to machine. Complete the other settings as shown below left and explained below right:

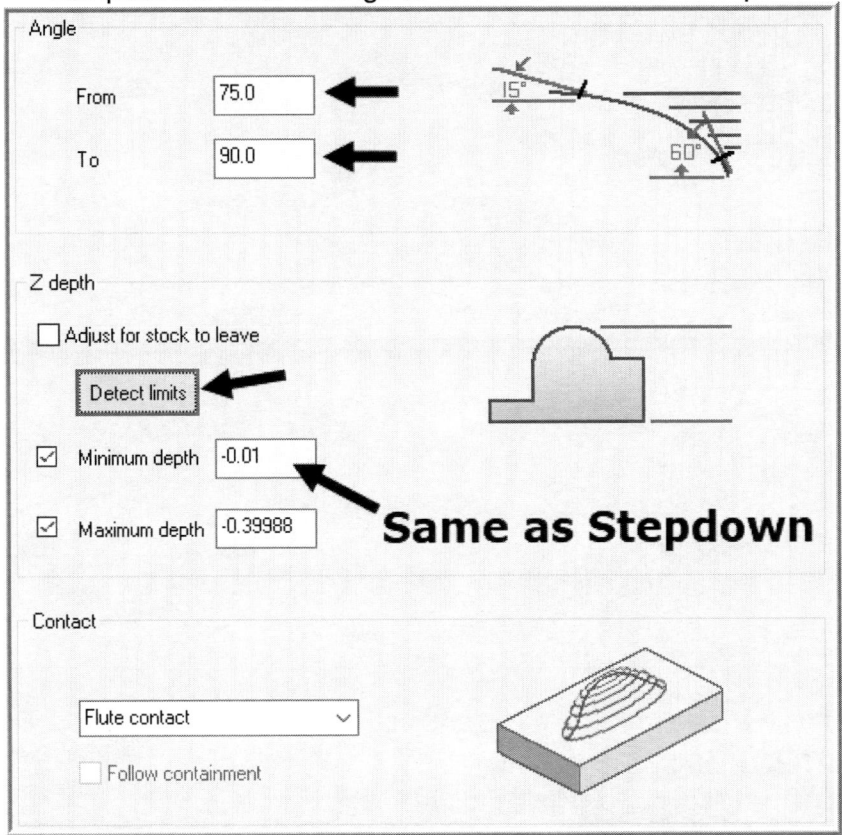

It is possible to use both the **Angle** and **Z depth** selections to setup the machining area. These selections work in combination with the **Containment Boundary**.

Here, we want to limit cuts to the walls. The bottom of the walls varies in Z depth so **Angle** will work well here.

Also use Z depth to keep the first cut one **Stepdown** below the top of the surface.

15. Make the following settings on the **Linking Parameters** page.

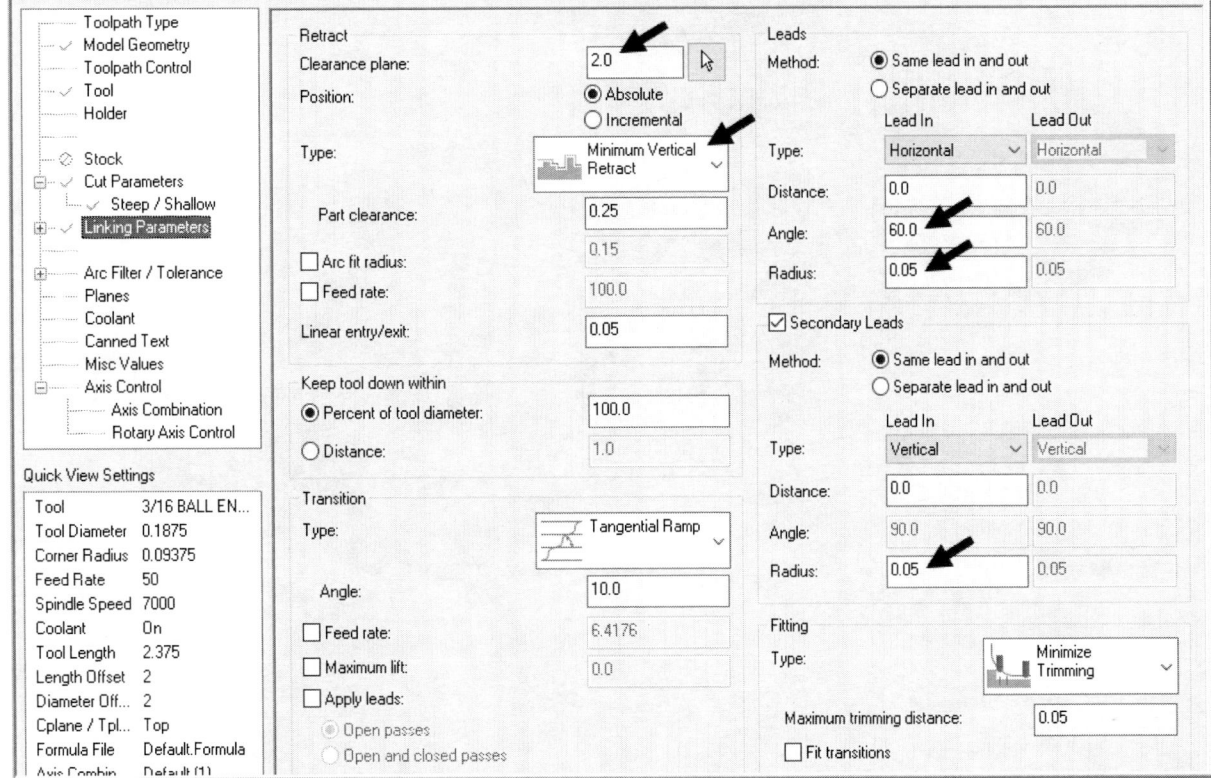

16. Make the following settings on the **Arc Filter / Tolerance** page if required.

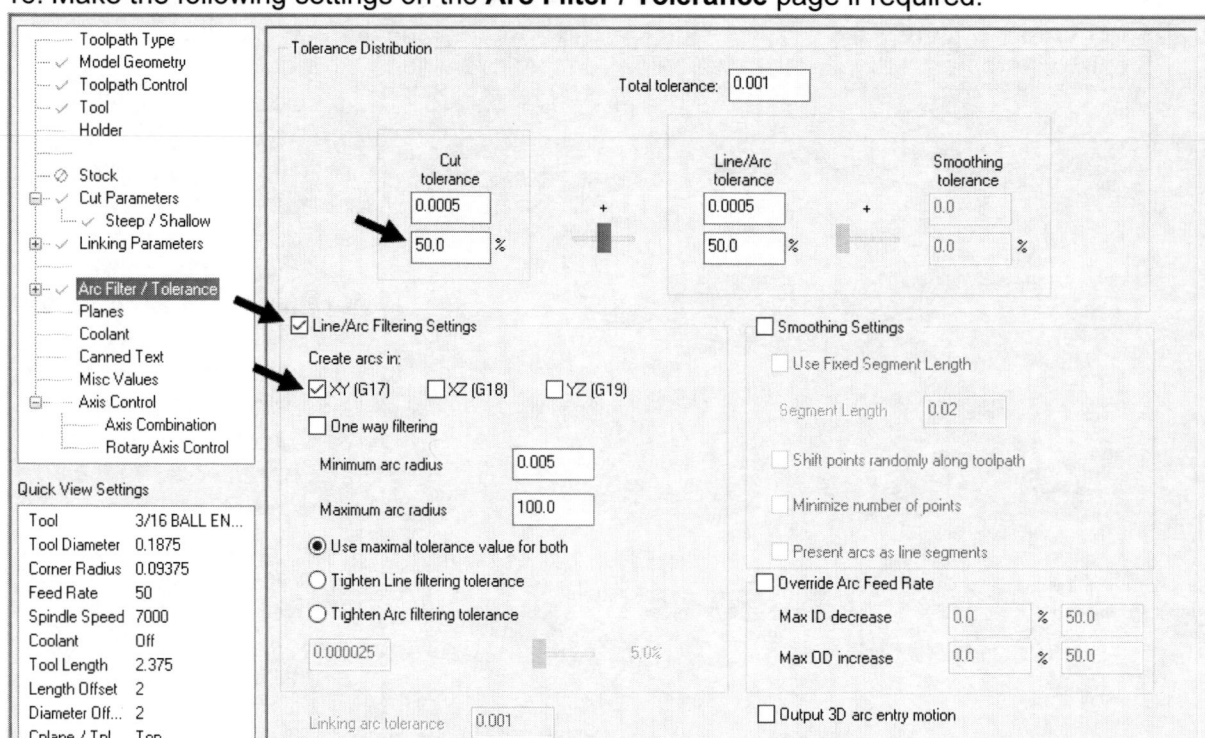

17. Select **Coolant** from the list on the left and turn the coolant on.

18. Select **OK** to exit **Surface High Speed** toolpath.

19. Verify the 2 toolpaths. Your screen should look similar to the image below.

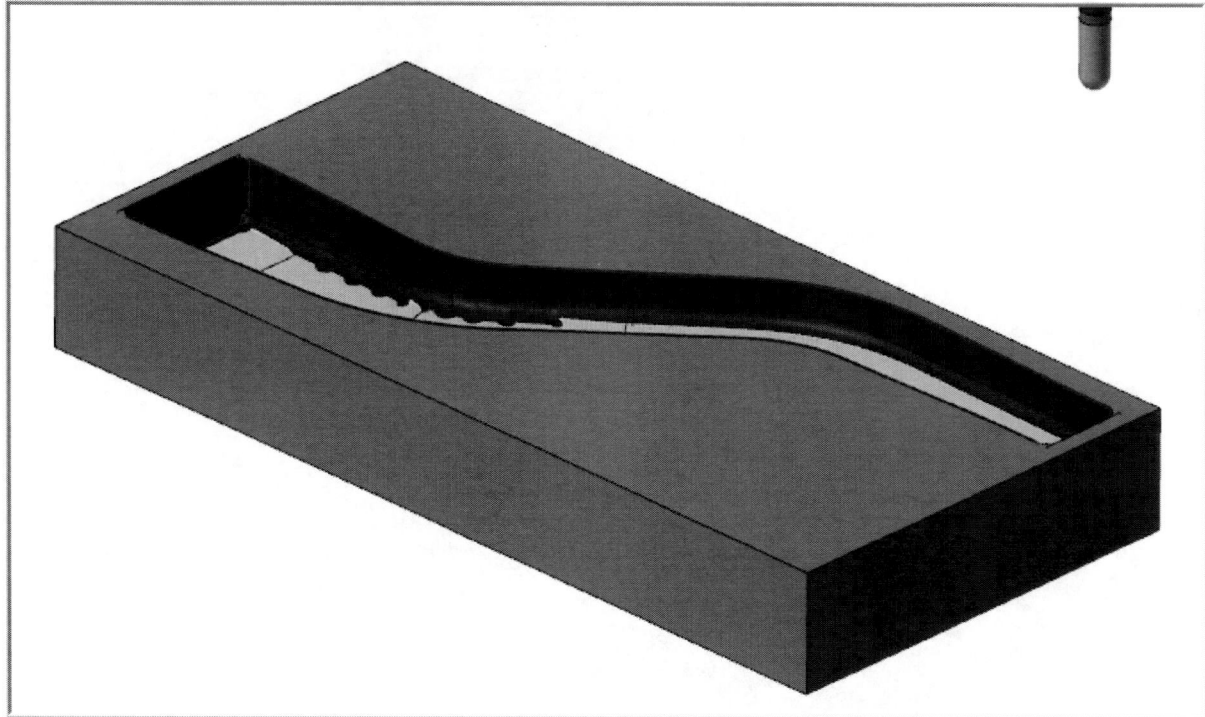

TASK 15:
FINISH USING SURFACE HIGH SPEED SCALLOP TOOLPATH
➲ In this task you will use the same 3/16" diameter Ball end mill to finish the floor and fillets of the pocket.

Climb or **Down Milling** will produce the best surface finish on the machine. The walls have been finished by climb cutting in one direction. Finishing the walls first by stepping downwards ensures that stock will not interfere with the tool shank during cutting. If that cutting direction were to continue onto the floors the tool would no longer be climb cutting. Next, the floor and fillets will be finished to continue climb cutting.

1. Left click on **Operation 2**. This will place a green check on Operation 2.
2. In the Toolpaths Manager, right click on the newly created operation 2 and drag the operation down. You will be prompted as shown below. Select **Copy after**.

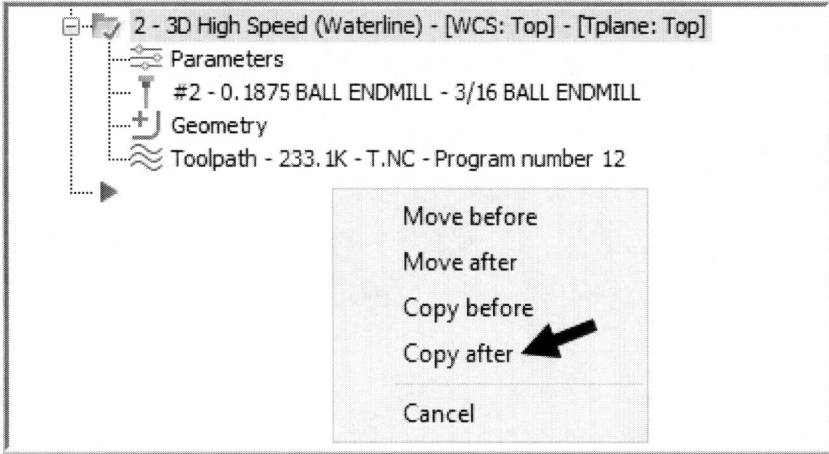

3. Move the Insert arrow ▶ to the bottom of the list of operations by clicking the ▼ icon on the Toolpath manager toolbar.
4. Click on the **Parameters Folder** of the newly copied operation as shown below.

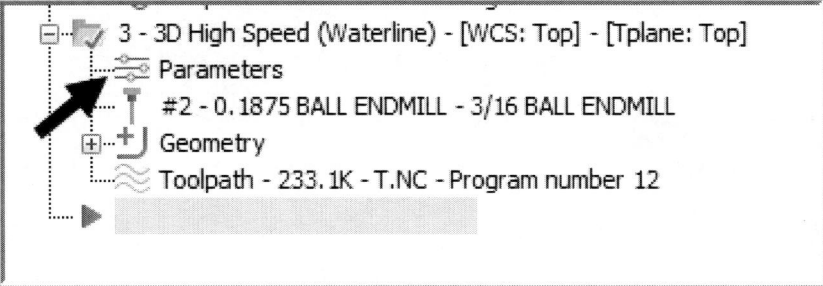

5. Select **Toolpath Type** and make the appropriate selections as shown below. Select **Scallop** and ensure **Finishing** is activated.

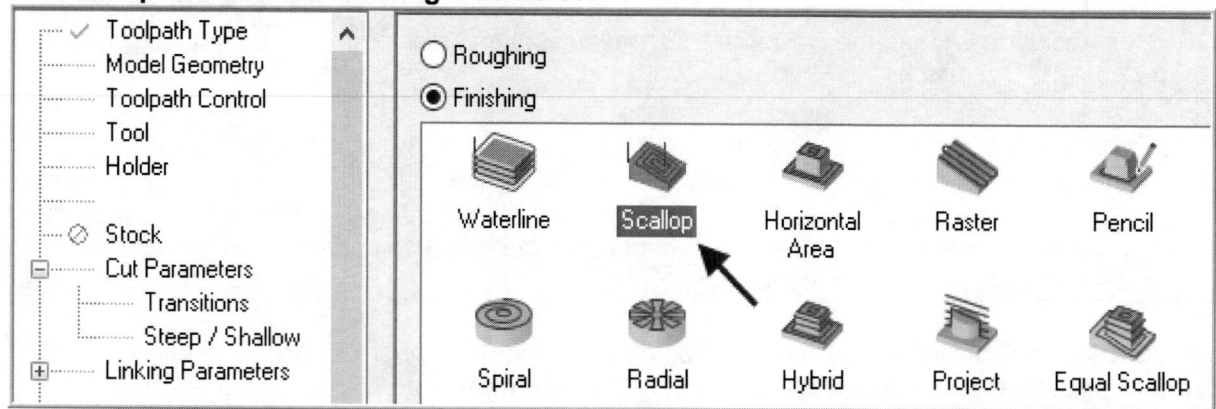

> Because the operation was copied, all settings have carried over from the other operation. You will not need to redo selections for **Tool**, **Arc Filter / Tolerance**, **Coolant**, etc.

6. Select **Cut Parameters** and make the appropriate selections as shown below.

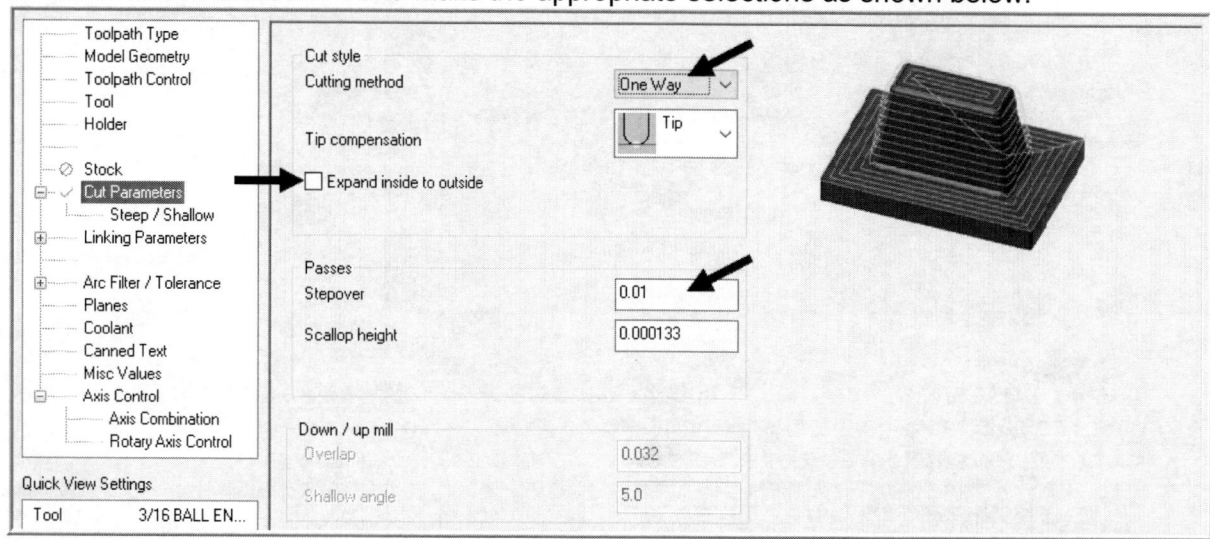

> If you find the cut is not climb milling, changing the Cutting Method to Other Way can solve this problem.

7. Select **Steep/Shallow** and make the appropriate changes as shown below.

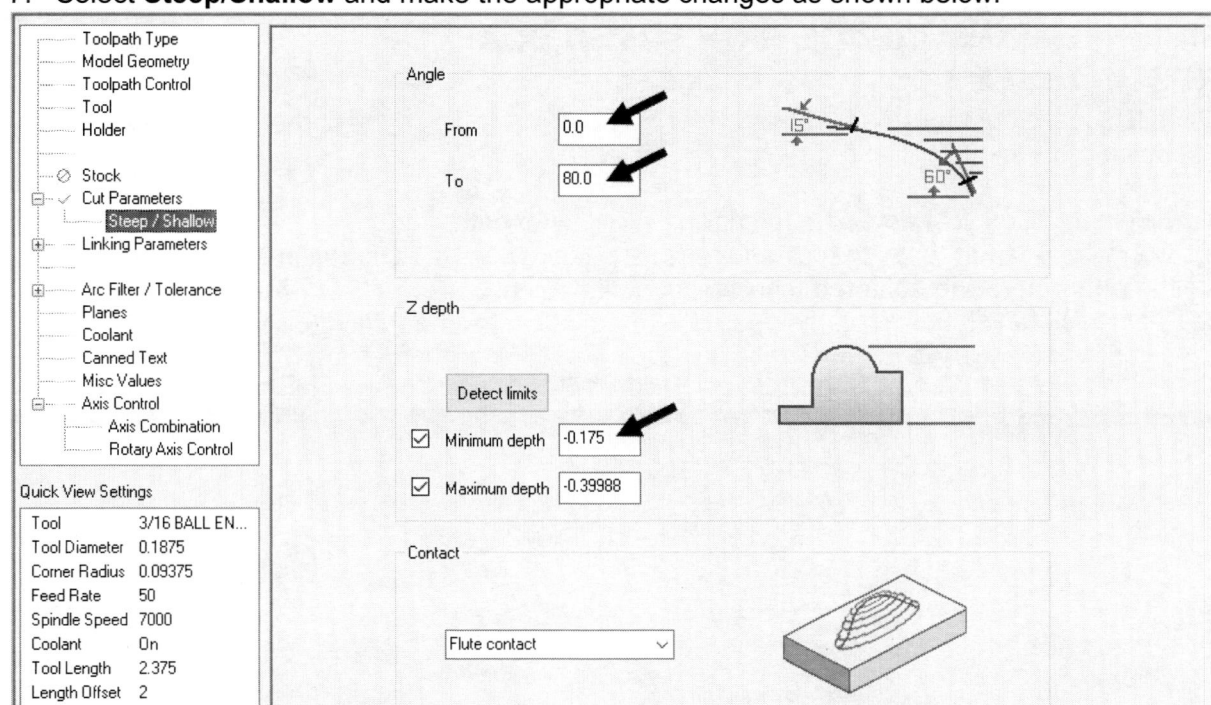

Enter the **Minimum depth** as a point that is somewhere just above the top of the fillets. This is so the calculation does not include cuts at the top of the walls.
Angle will keep machining area restricted to the floors and fillets. It is important to note that this is not the angle of the surface itself. It is the offsetting or tangency angle of the tool from that surface

8. Select the OK button ✓ to exit Surface High Speed Toolpaths.
9. Click on **Regen all dirty operations** to have the toolpath updated.
10. Verify the 3 toolpaths. Your screen should look similar to the image below.

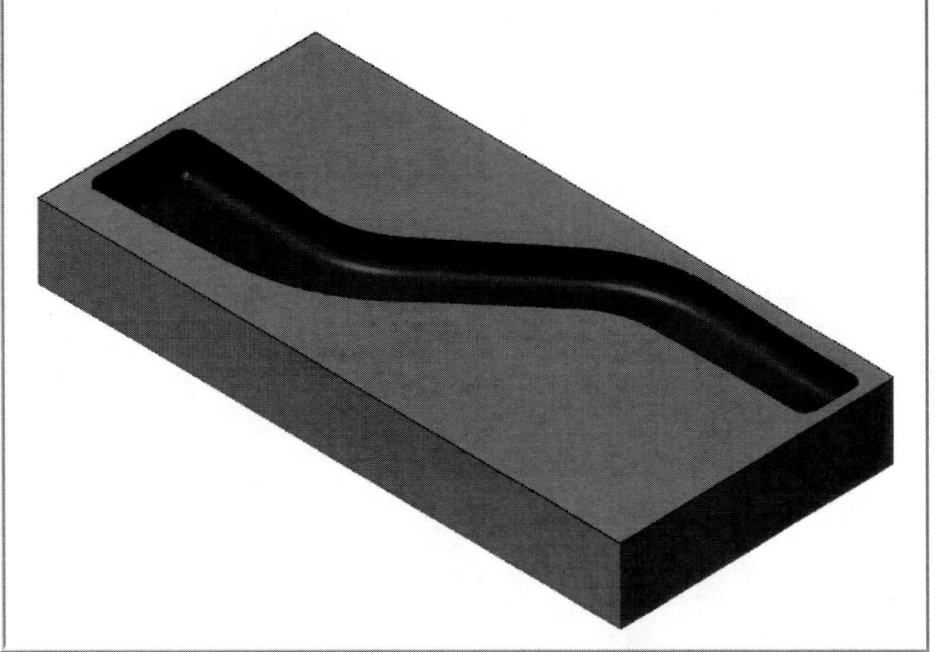

TASK 16:
FINISH USING SURFACE HIGH SPEED SCALLOP
REST PASSES

➲ In this task you will use a 0.125 diameter Ball end mill to finish the corners of the pocket which have the .075 fillet radii.

1. Select **Alt-T** on your keyboard to show the display of path.
2. Copy the **Scallop** toolpath created previously. Make sure the Operation you want to copy is the **only operation selected** (checkmark on the folder).
3. Right click (and holding) on the operation, drag below this operation (operation 3), then selecting **Copy after**.

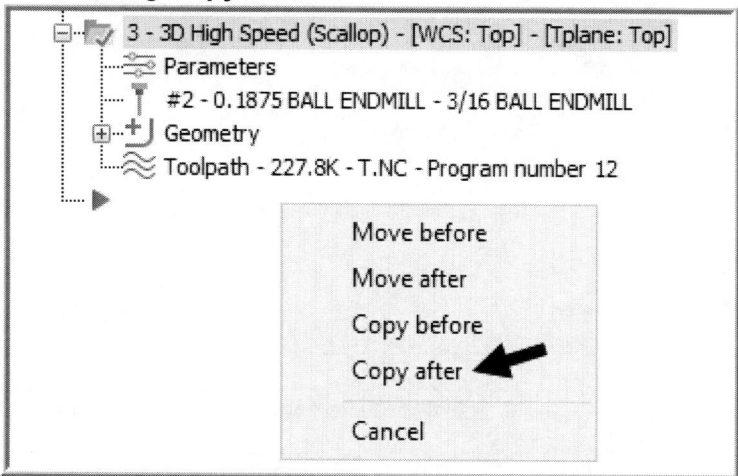

4. Move the Insert arrow 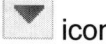 to the bottom of the list of operations by clicking the ▼ icon on the Toolpath manager toolbar.
5. Click on the **Parameters** folder of the newly copied **Operation (4)** as shown below.

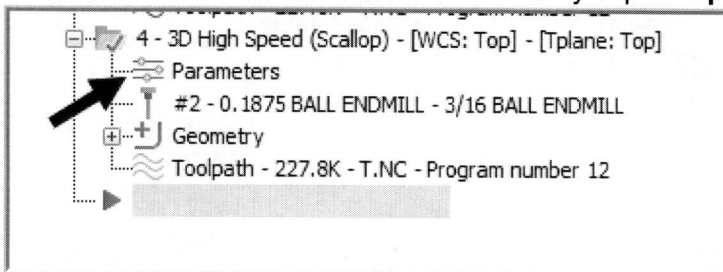

6. Click on **Tool** from the list on the left.
7. On the **Tool** page click **Select Library Tool**. Turn off the **Filter** and use the slider bar on the right of this dialog box to scroll down and locate a **1/8" (0.125) diameter ball end mill**. Select the end mill by picking anywhere along its row.
8. Select the OK button to complete the selection of this tool.
9. Make changes to the **Toolpath parameters** page as shown below:

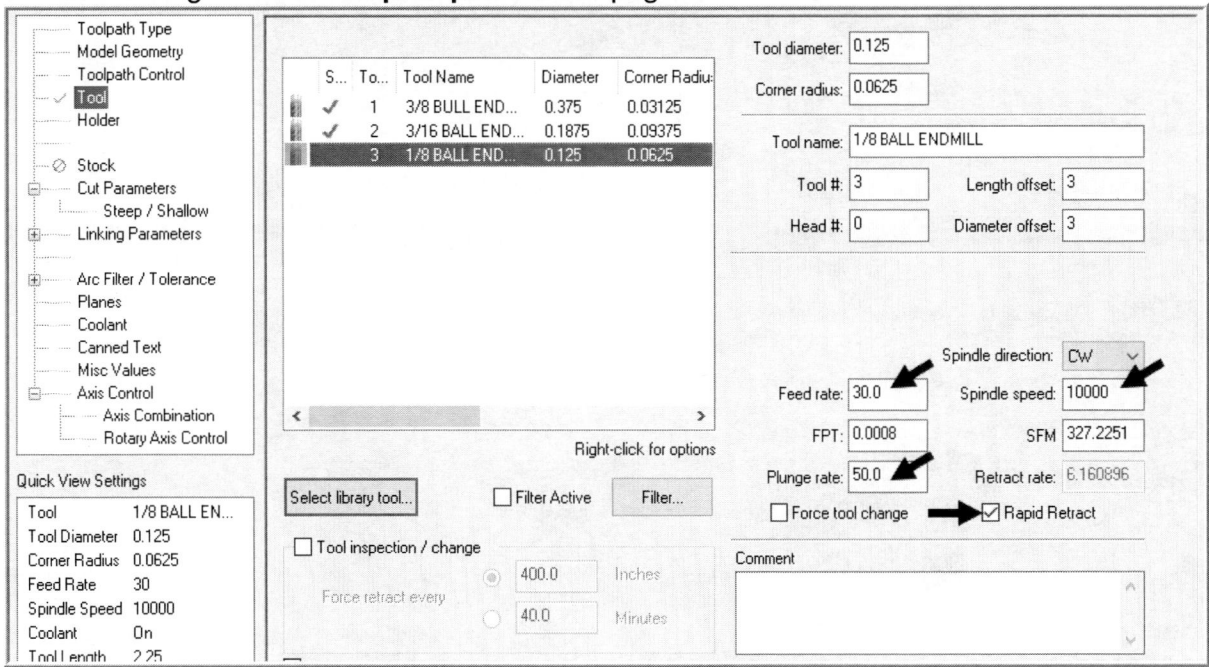

10. Select the **Stock** page and make changes to this page as shown below.

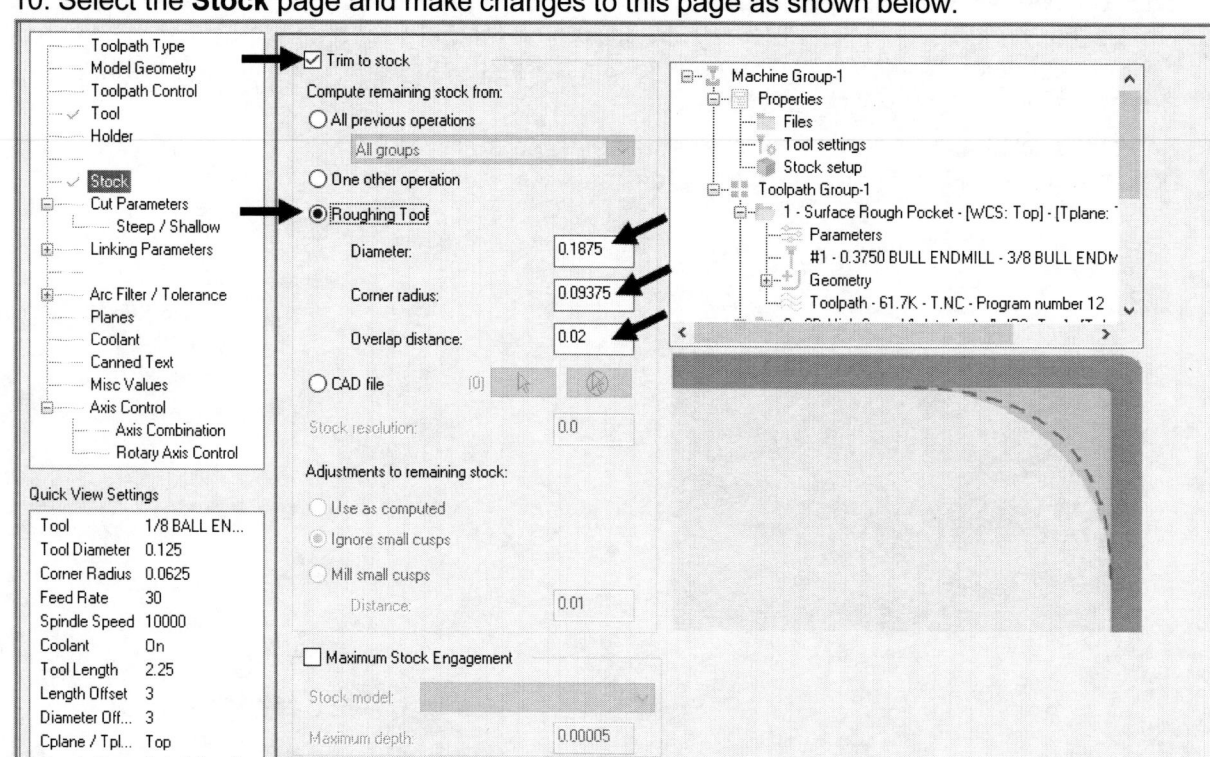

Trim to stock
Use this page to define how Mastercam calculates the stock model for a surface high speed toolpath. The stock model defines the amount of stock to be machined by the toolpath.

Choose one of the following approaches:
- Calculate the stock remaining from one or more source operations in the current part file. Choose groups from the drop-down menu or select one or more other operations from the list in the window. If the part file includes a Mastercam stock model operation, you can select it for use as the stock model. The source operation does not have to be another high speed toolpath.

- Enter the dimensions of the roughing tool. Mastercam calculates a stock model based on the areas of your part that could not be cut or accessed by such a tool.

- Select an external CAD file, such as an STL file. Use this option when your stock model is an irregular shape, like a casting.

11. Set the **Stepover** so the Scallop Height is like the previous finishing toolpaths. A 0.008 stepover with this tool nets close to 0.0001 scallop.

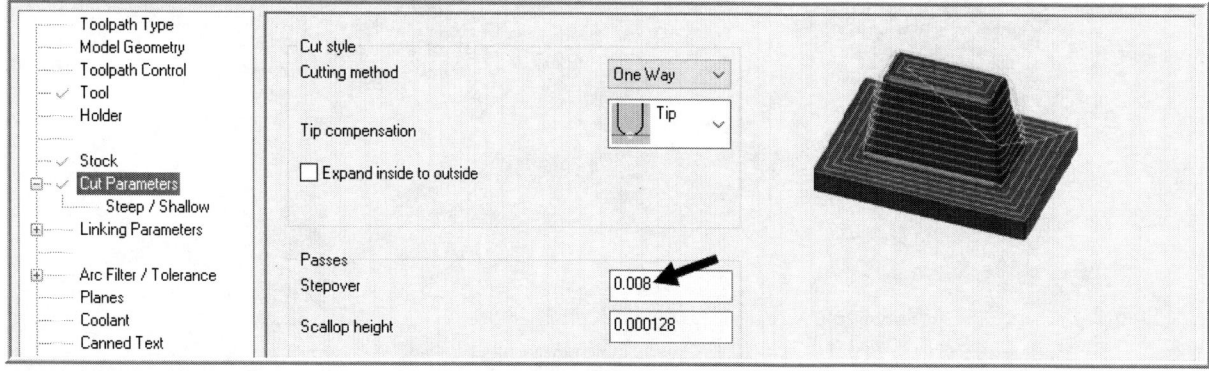

12. The **Steep / Shallow** parameters from the previous toolpath will limit cutting. Select
    Steep/Shallow and make changes as shown below.

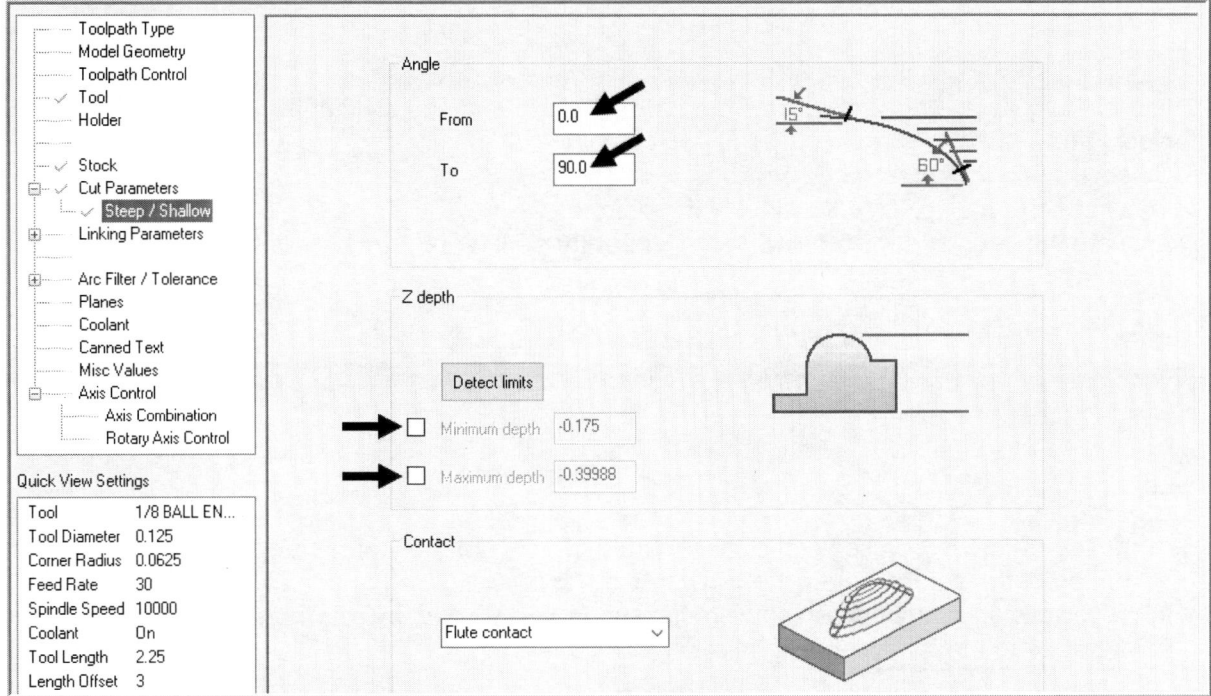

13. No changes are needed on the **Linking Parameters** page.

14. Select the OK button 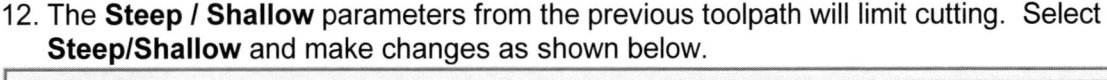 to complete the toolpath.
15. Click on **Regenerate all dirty operations** if needed. The toolpath will take a bit of time to
    calculate.

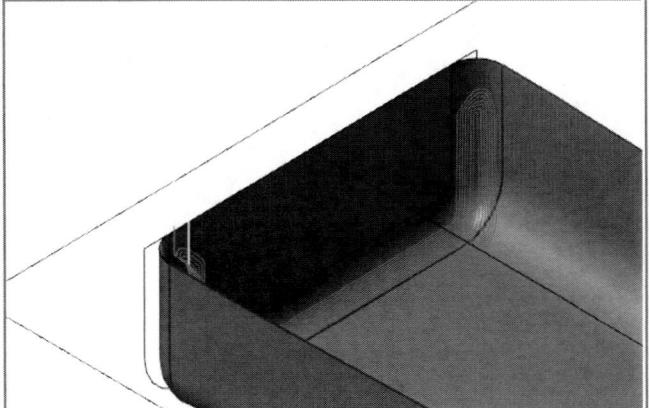
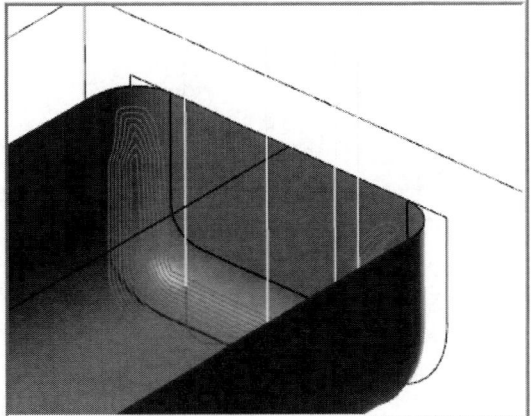

TASK 17:
VERIFY THE TOOLPATH

1. Right mouse click in the graphics area and click on **Isometric**.
2. In the **Toolpaths Manager** pick all the operations to verify by picking the **Select all operations** icon.
3. Select the **Verify selected operations** icon.
4. Maximize the Backplot/Verify window if required.
5. Activate the options shown below in the **Visibility** section of the Home tab. **Initial Stock not** activated.

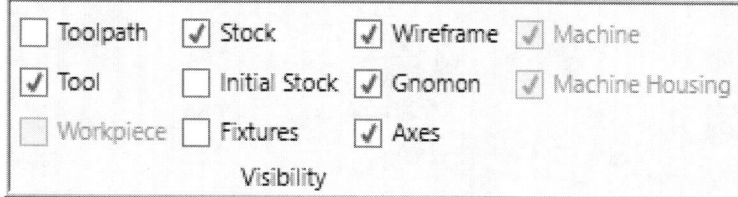

6. At the top of the screen select the **Verify** tab and activate the **Color Loop**.
7. At the top of the screen select the **View** tab, the **Isometric** icon and then select **Fit**.
8. In the lower part of the screen now set the run Speed to slow by moving the slider bar pointer over to the left as shown below.

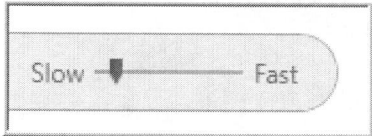

9. Now select the **Play** Simulation button to review the toolpaths.
➲ The verified toolpaths are shown below:

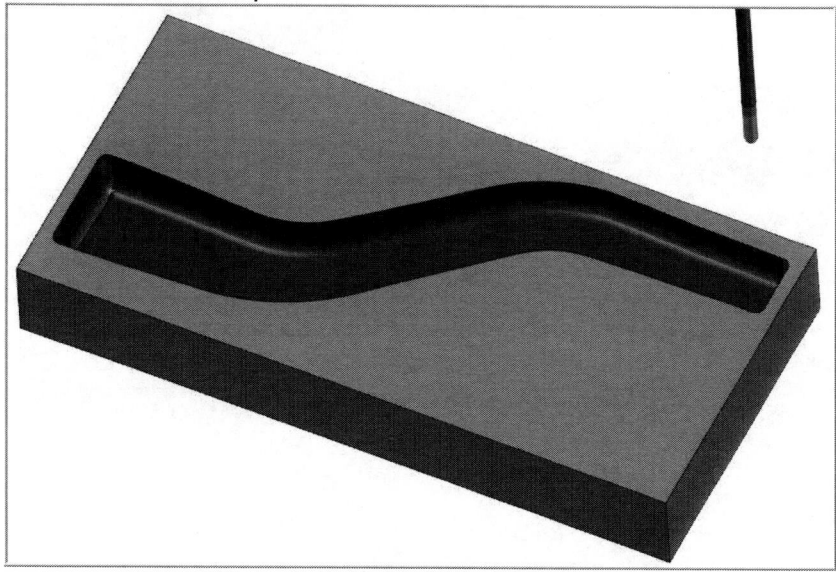

10. Select the **Close** button ⊠ in the top right hand corner to exit Verify.

TASK 18:
SAVE THE UPDATED MASTERCAM FILE

1. Select the **Save** icon from the **Quick Access** toolbar at the top left of the screen.

TASK 19:
POST AND CREATE THE CNC CODE FILE

1. Ensure all the operations are selected by picking the **Select all operations** icon 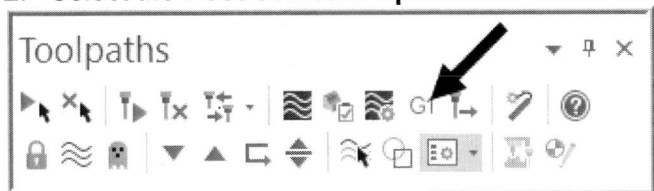 from the Toolpath manager.
2. Select the **Post selected operations** button from the Toolpath manager.

3. In the Post processing window, make the necessary changes as shown below:

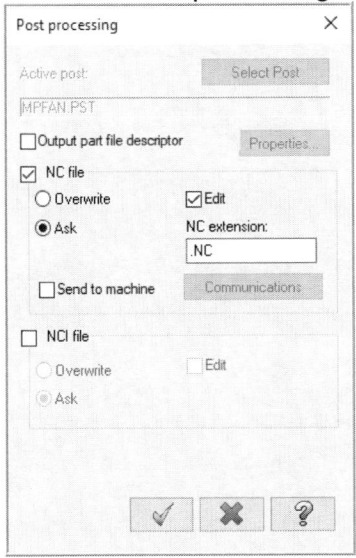

4. Select the OK button ✓ to continue.
5. Enter the same name as your Mastercam part file name in the NC File name field **Mill-Lesson-12**.
6. Select the Save button.
7. The CNC code file opens up in the default editor:

```
6    (MATERIAL - ALUMINUM INCH - 6061)
7    ( T1 | 3/8 BULL ENDMILL 0.0313 RAD | H1 | XY STOCK TO LEAVE - .015 | Z STOCK TO LEAVE - 0. )
8    ( T2 | 3/16 BALL ENDMILL | H2 )
9    ( T3 | 1/8 BALL ENDMILL | H3 )
10   N1 G20
11   N11 G0 G17 G40 G49 G80 G90
12   N21 T1 M6
13   N31 G0 G90 G54 X.5409 Y1.0203 A0. S7500 M3
14   N41 G43 H1 Z2. M8
15   N51 Z.215
16   N61 G1 Z.115 F25.
17   N71 G2 X.6062 Y1.0334 Z.1115 I.0653 J-.1556
18   N81 X.7749 Y.8647 Z.0976 I0. J-.1687
```

8. Select the ✕ in the top right corner to exit the CNC editor.

➲ This completes Mill-Lesson-12.

MILL-LESSON-12-EXERCISE-A

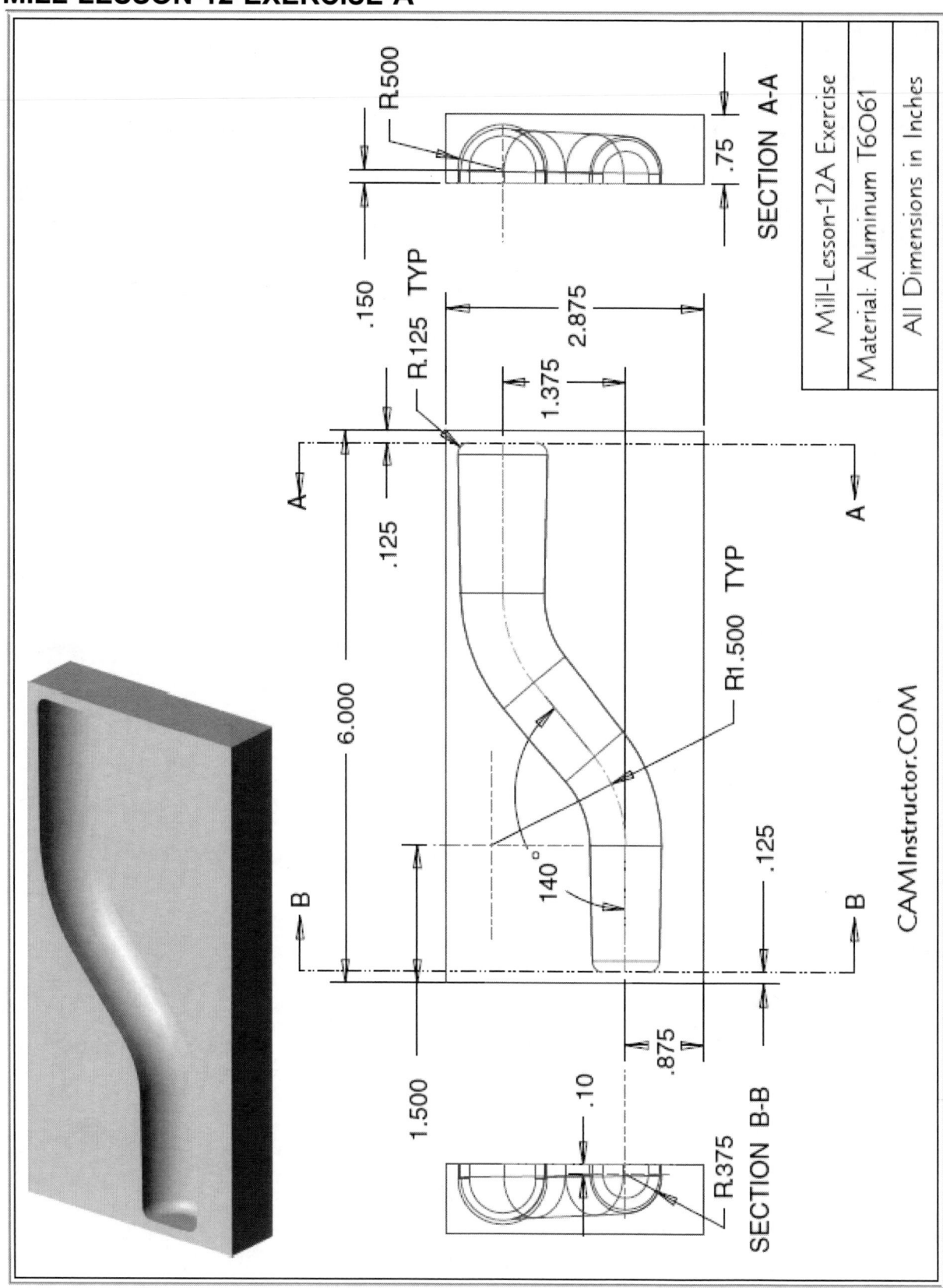

SECTION A-A

R.500

.75

Mill-Lesson-12A Exercise

Material: Aluminum T6O61

All Dimensions in Inches

.150

R.125 TYP

2.875

1.375

A

R1.500 TYP

.125

6.000

CAMInstructor.COM

140°

B

.125

B

1.500

.875

.10

SECTION B-B

R.375

MILL-LESSON-12-EXERCISE-B

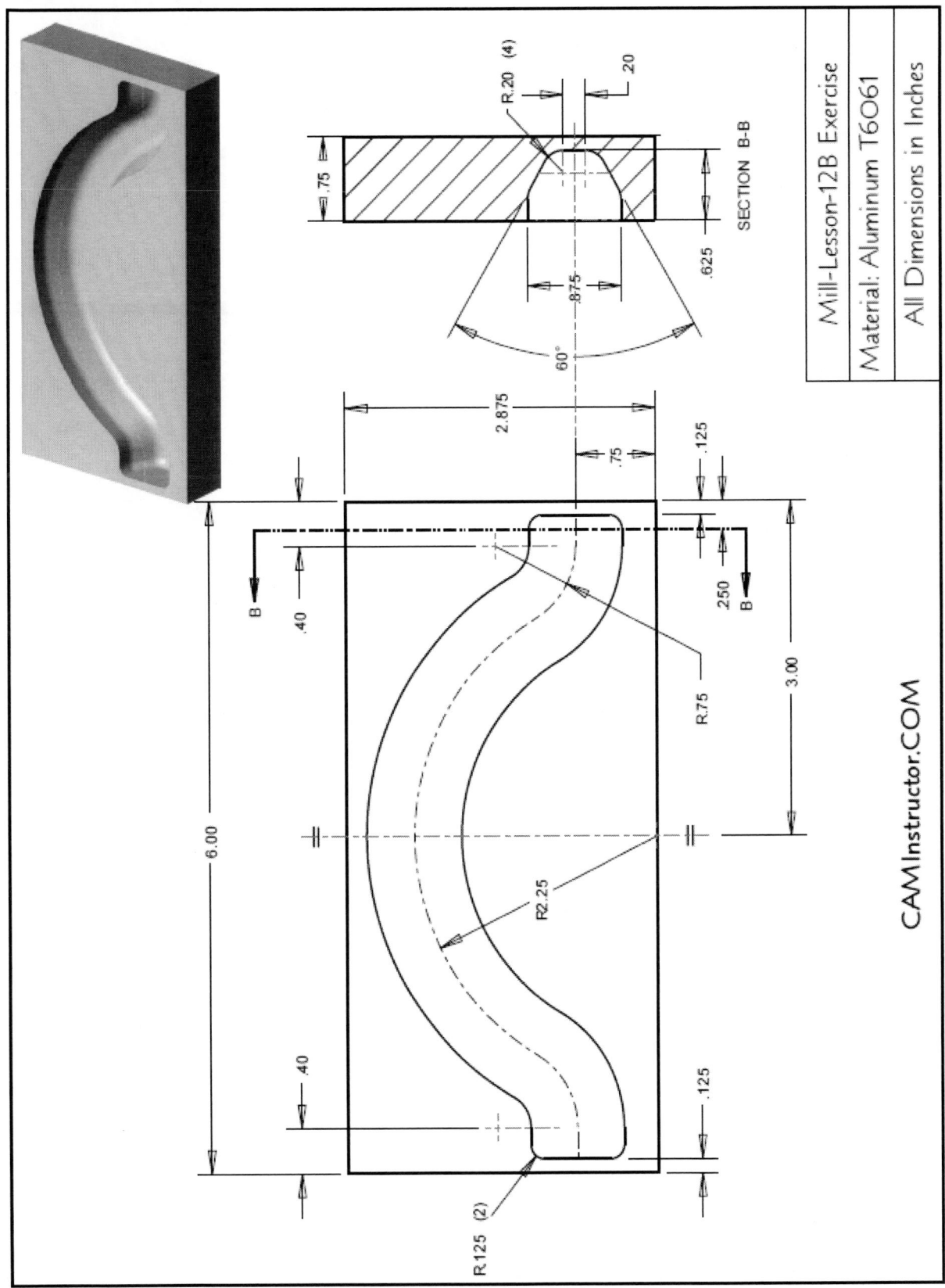

Mill-Lesson-12B Exercise

Material: Aluminum T6O61

All Dimensions in Inches

SECTION B-B

R.20 (4)

.20

.75

.625

.875

60°

2.875

.75

.125

.250

3.00

6.00

.40

.40

R.75

R2.25

.125

R.125 (2)

B

B

CAMInstructor.COM

Mastercam 2022

TRAINING GUIDE

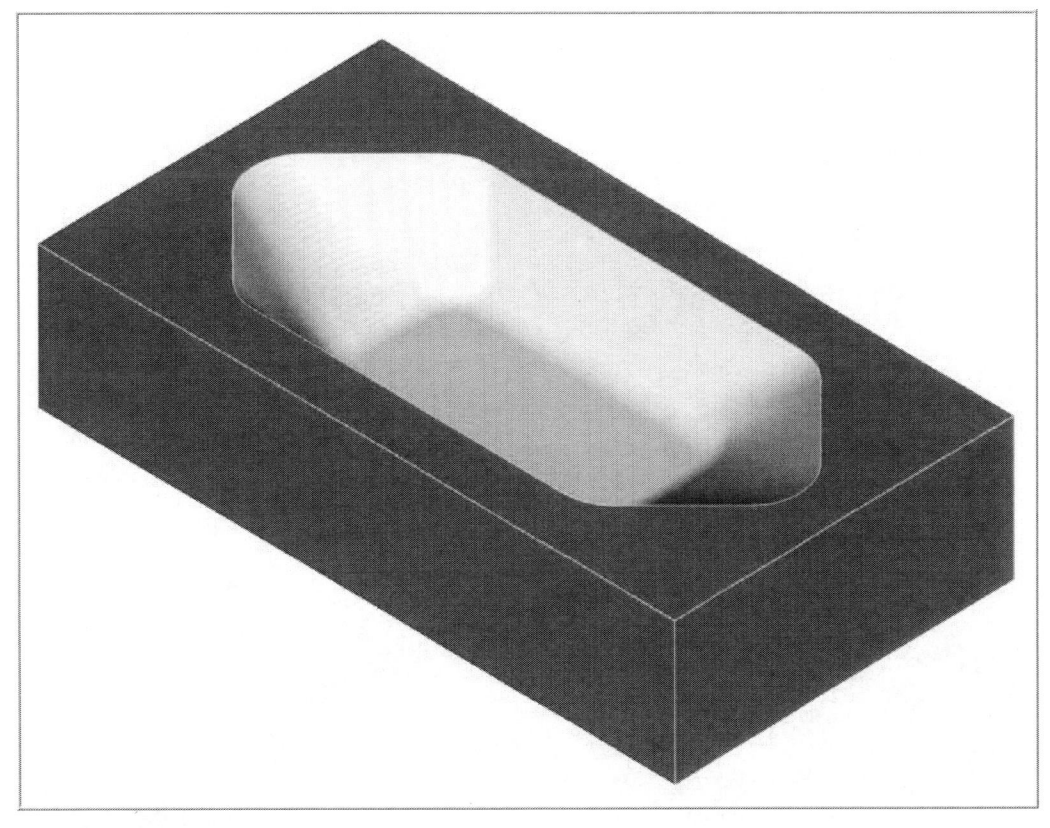

MILL-LESSON-13

ROUGH PLUNGE, FINISH CONTOUR & FINISH SHALLOW TOOLPATHS

camInstructor

Objectives

You will create the geometry for Mill-Lesson-13, and then generate the toolpaths to machine the part on a CNC vertical milling machine. This Lesson covers the following topics:

➲ **Create a 3-dimensional drawing by:**
Creating lines.
Creating arcs.
Trimming geometry.
Creating a ruled surface.

➲ **Establish Stock Setup settings:**
Stock size using Bounding Box.
Material for the part.
Feed calculation.

➲ **Generate a 3-dimensional milling toolpath consisting of:**
Surface rough plunge Toolpath.
Surface finish contour Toolpath.
Surface finish shallow Toolpath.

➲ **Inspect the toolpath using Mastercam's Verify and Backplot by:**
Launching the Verify function to machine the part on the screen.
Generating the NC- code.

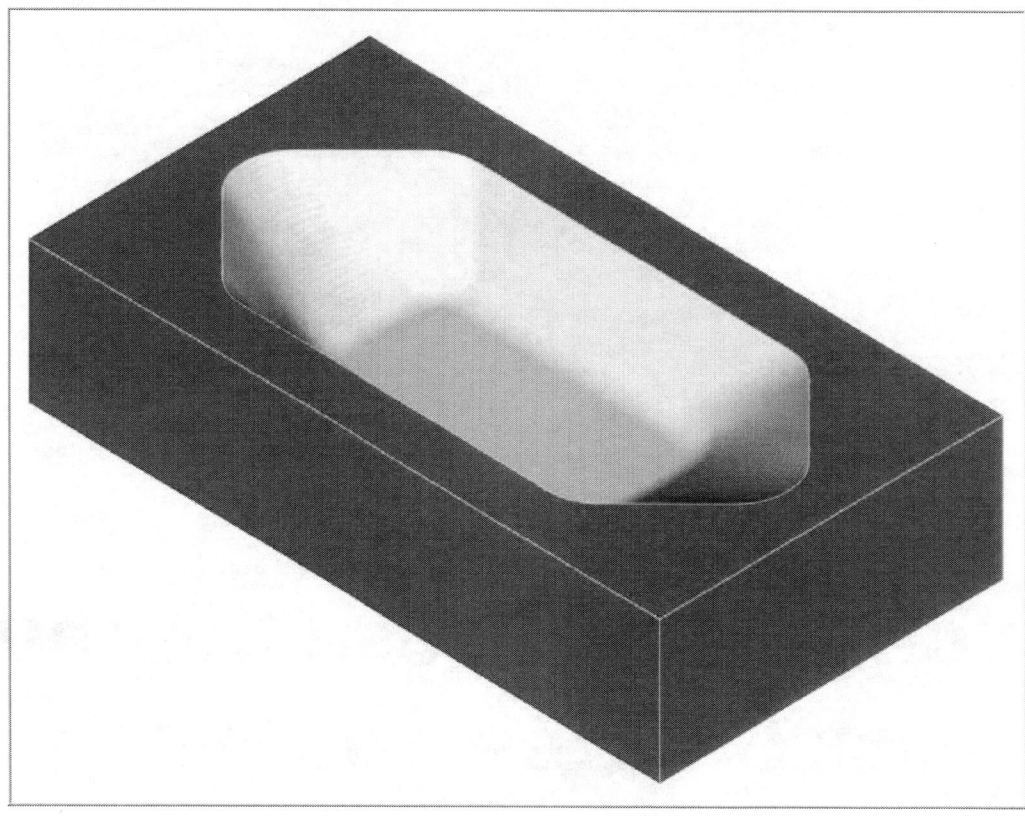

MILL-LESSON-13 DRAWING

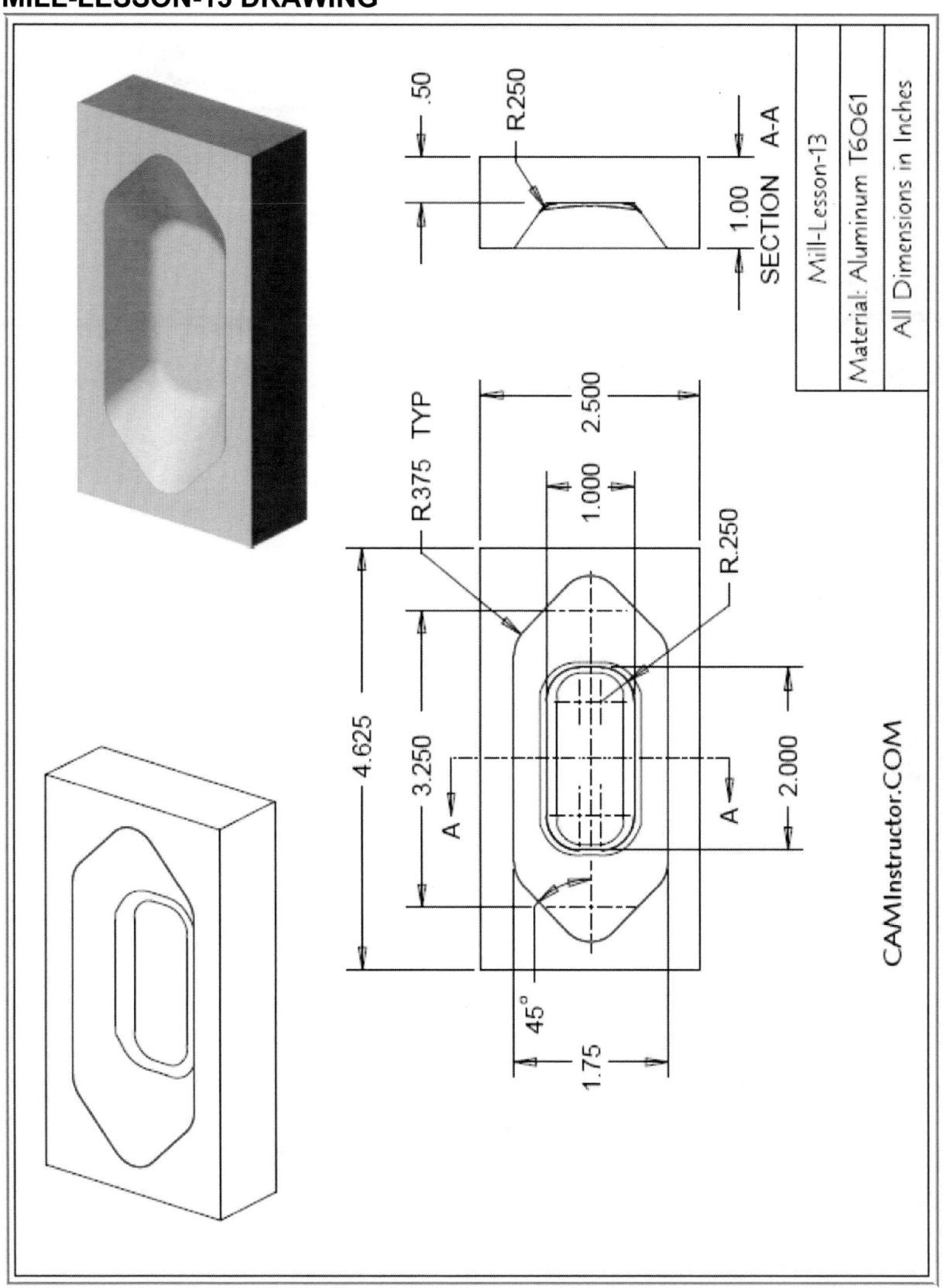

SECTION A-A

.50

R.250

1.00

Mill-Lesson-13

Material: Aluminum T6O61

All Dimensions in Inches

R.375 TYP

2.500

1.000

R.250

4.625

3.250

2.000

A

A

45°

1.75

CAMInstructor.COM

TOOL LIST
➲ 0.500 diameter flat end mill to rough machine.
➲ 0.375 diameter ball end mill to finish machine.

MILL-LESSON-13 - THE PROCESS

Geometry Creation

TASK 1: Setting the environment
TASK 2: Create geometry for bottom of pocket
TASK 3: Create geometry for top of pocket
TASK 4: Trim geometry – top of pocket
TASK 5: Create geometry – material blank 4.625 x 2.5 x 1.0
TASK 6: Translate geometry to bottom of pocket
TASK 7: Edit geometry for loft syncing
TASK 8: Create a lofted solid
TASK 9: Create the base solid body
TASK 10: Boolean subtraction of a solid
TASK 11: Create 0.25 fillets at bottom of pocket

Toolpath Creation

TASK 12: Define the rough stock using stock setup
TASK 13: Rough out surface using surface rough plunge
TASK 14: Finish using surface finish contour
TASK 15: Finish bottom surface using finish shallow toolpath
TASK 16: Verify the toolpath
TASK 17: Post and create the CNC code file

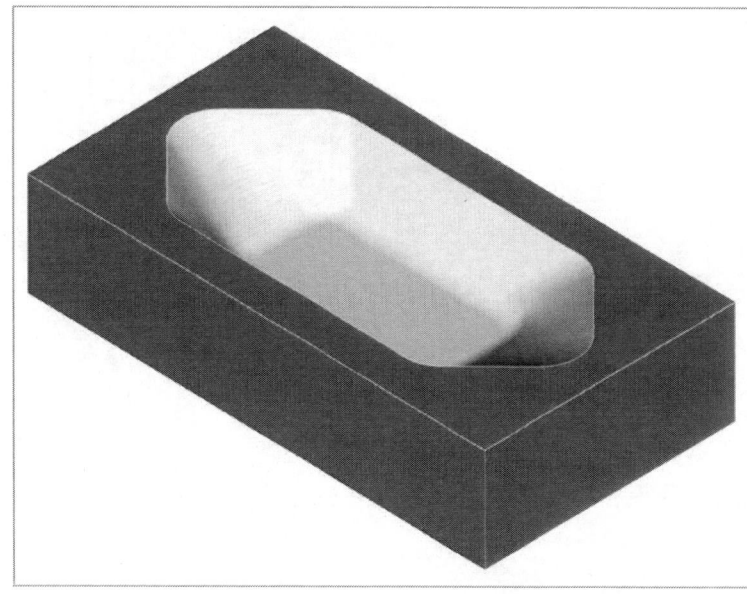

TASK 1:
SETTING THE ENVIRONMENT
➲ Before starting the geometry creation, you should set up the grid and machine type as outlined in the Setting the environment section at the beginning of this text:
1. Set up the Grid. This will help identify the location of the origin.
2. Set the machine type the Default Mill.

TASK 2:
CREATE GEOMETRY FOR BOTTOM OF POCKET
X0 Y0 CENTER OF PART Z0 TOP OF PART
➲ The top of the material is at **Z 0.** The material has been previously machined to size: 4.625 x 2.5 x 1.0.
➲ Later in this lesson you will use Transform Translate to translate the bottom of the pocket geometry down to a Z level of -0.5.

➲ **Create bottom of pocket section**
1. Hide the Toolpaths Manager, Solids and Planes pane.
2. On the **Wireframe** tab in the **Shapes** section click on the drop-down menu arrow under **Rectangle** and select **Rectangular Shapes**.
3. The **Rectangular Shapes** panel appears and you are prompted to **Select a base point**.
4. Set the following values shown below left:

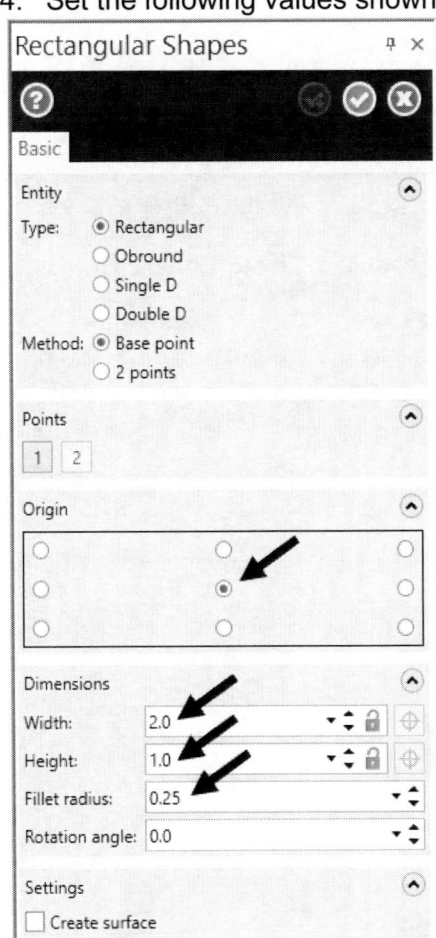

5. Now you need to **select the position of the base point**. Move the cursor over to the graphics screen and position the cursor at the **center of the grid** and **pick the origin**.
6. Click on the OK icon to complete this feature.
7. Right mouse click in the graphics area and click on **Isometric**.
8. Right mouse click in the graphics area and click on the **Fit** icon.

➲ The completed geometry is shown below:

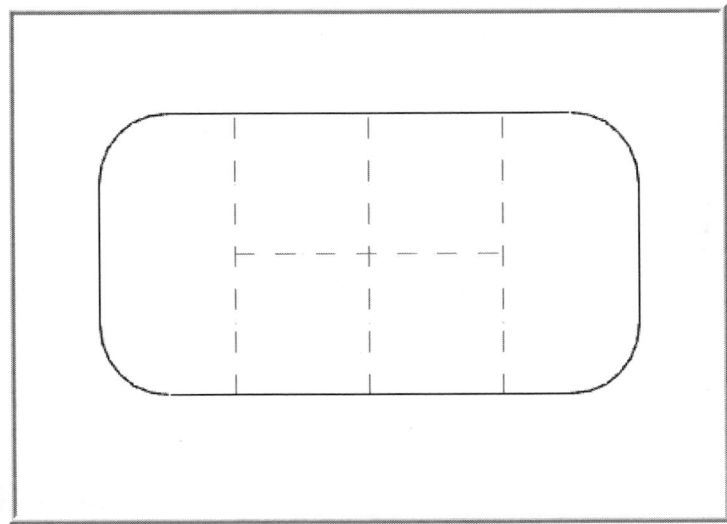

TASK 3:
CREATE GEOMETRY FOR TOP OF POCKET

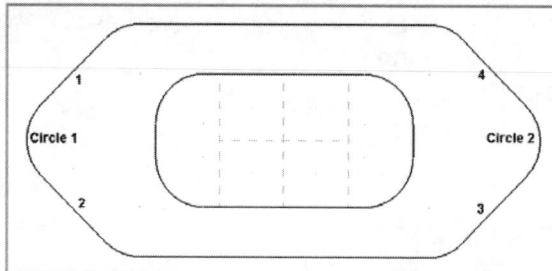

1. On the **Wireframe** tab in the **Shapes** section click on **Rectangle**.
2. Click in the space for **Width** and enter a value of **3.25** and then hit the Enter key. In the space for **Height** enter a value of **1.75** and hit enter. Activate **Anchor to center**.
3. Now you need to **Select a base point**. Move the cursor over to the graphics screen and position the cursor at the **center of the grid** and **pick the origin**.
4. Click on the **OK** icon 🔘 to complete this feature.

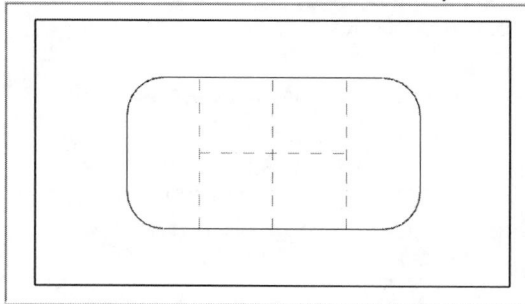 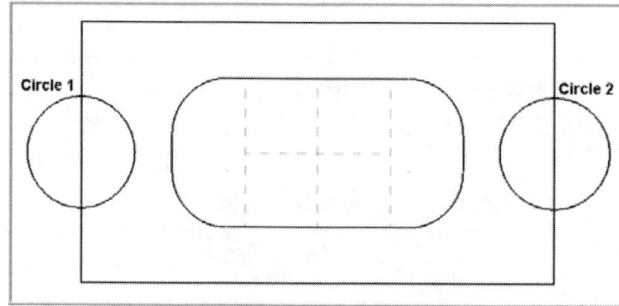

➲ **Create Circle #1 & #2**

5. Select the tab at the top of the screen and in the **Arcs** section select **Circle Center Point**.
6. Enter **.375** for the radius. Click on the **Lock** icon 🔓 to **"freeze"** 🔒 this radius value.
7. To satisfy the prompt **Enter the center point** move the cursor over the **midpoint** of the line shown below left. Ensure the **visual cue** for midpoint is being displayed and click on this point.

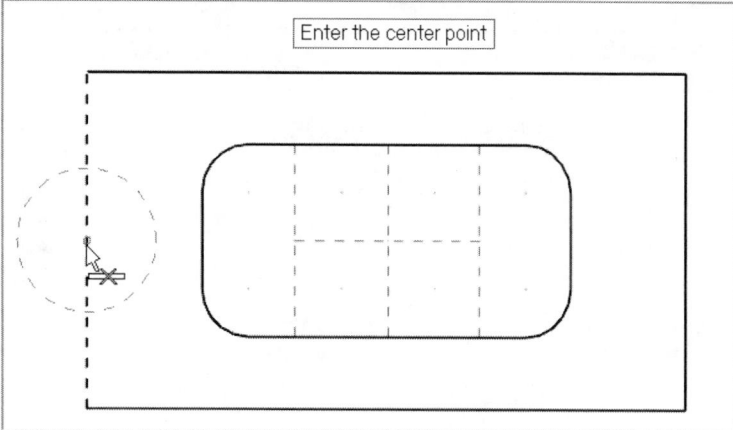

8. To satisfy the prompt **Enter the center point** move the cursor over the **midpoint** of the line shown below left. Ensure the **visual cue** for midpoint is being displayed and click on this point.

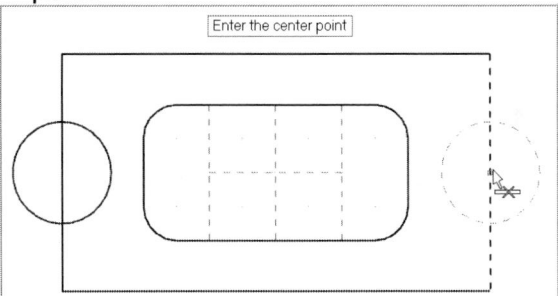 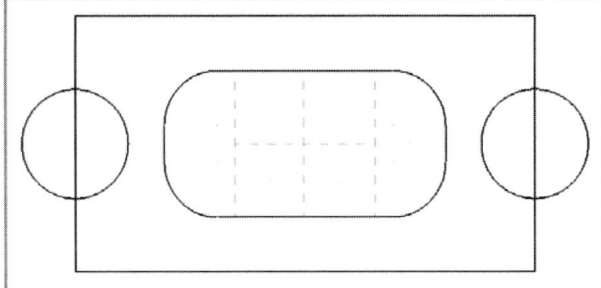

9. Click on the **OK** icon to complete this feature.

➲ **Create Lines #1,2,3 & 4**
➲ **Create Line #1**

10. Select the **Wireframe** tab if required and in the **Lines** section click on **Line Endpoints**.
11. First click in the space for **Length** and enter a value of **1.0** and then hit the Enter key. Click on the **Lock** icon 🔓 for **Length** to "freeze" 🔒 this **1.0**. In the space for **Angle** enter a value of **45** and hit enter. **Note** that the **Tangent** function is activated.
12. To satisfy the prompt **Specify the first endpoint** move the cursor over the area of the circle shown below left. Ensure there is **no visual cue** being displayed and click on this point.
13. After selecting the circle you will be prompted to **Select a line** pick the line shown below:

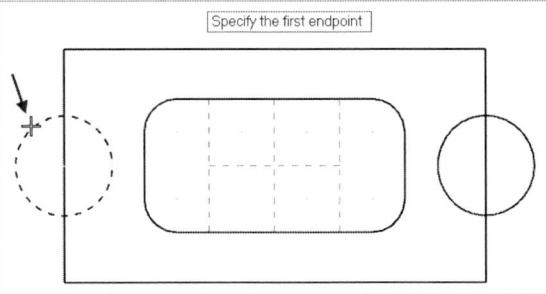 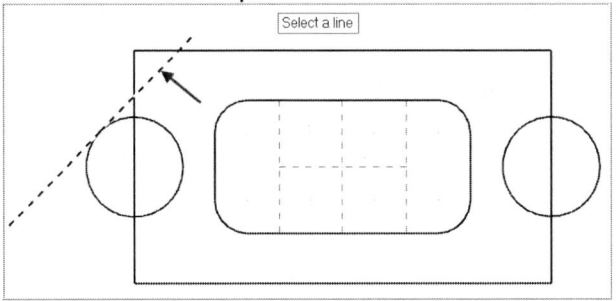

14. Click on the **OK** and **Create New Operation** icon 🔵.

➲ **Create Line #2**

15. In the space for **Angle** enter a value of **-45** and hit enter.
16. To satisfy the prompt **Specify the first endpoint** move the cursor over the area of the circle shown below left. Ensure there is **no visual cue** being displayed and click on this point. After selecting the circle you will be prompted to **Select a line** pick the line shown below:

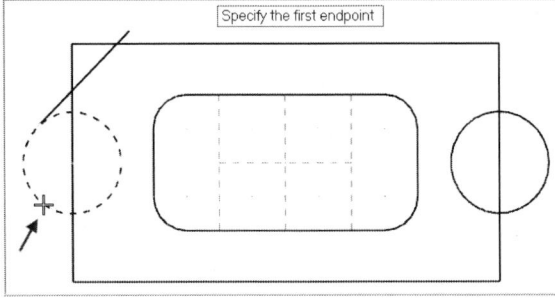 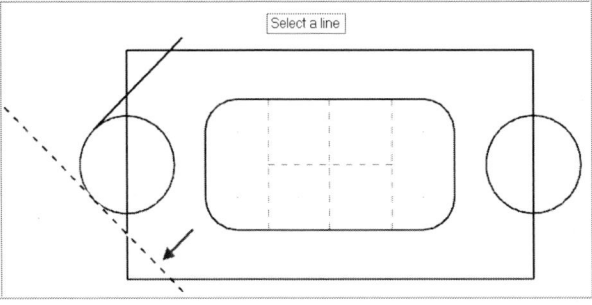

17. Click on the **OK** icon ✅ to complete this feature.

➲ **Create Line #3**
➲ **For Line #3 and Line #4 we will explore a different method in the construction of these two lines.**

18. In the Wireframe tab click on **Line Endpoints**.

19. Click on the **Lock** icon ![lock] for **Length** to **"Un-freeze"** ![unlock] this **1.0.**

20. To satisfy the prompt **Specify the first endpoint** move the cursor over the area of the circle shown below **left**. Ensure there is **no visual cue** being displayed and click on the circle.

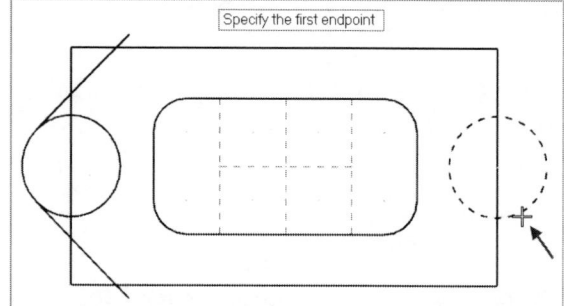 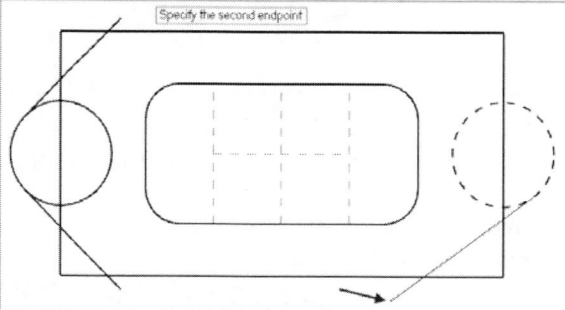

21. To satisfy the prompt **Specify the second endpoint** move the cursor to the point shown **above right** and click on this point. This is just an approximate point as we will be trimming the lines in a later task.

22. In the space for **Angle** enter a value of **180+45** and hit enter.

23. Click on the OK and Create New Operation icon ![icon].

➲ **Create Line #4**

24. To satisfy the prompt **Specify the first endpoint** move the cursor over the area of the circle shown **below left**. Ensure there is **no visual cue** being displayed and click on the circle.

25. To satisfy the prompt **Specify the second endpoint** move the cursor to the point shown **below right** and click on this point. This is just an approximate point as we will be trimming the lines in a later task.

26. In the space for **Angle** enter a value of **90+45** and hit enter.

27. To satisfy the prompt **Specify the first endpoint** move the cursor over the area of the circle shown below left. Ensure there is **no visual cue** being displayed and click on this point.

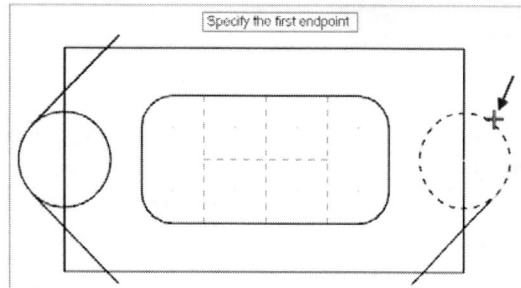 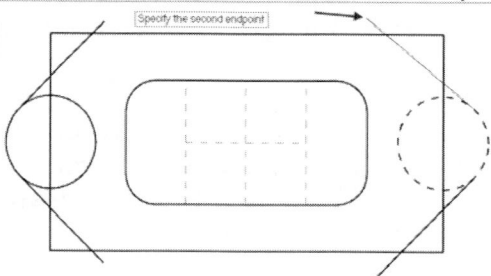

28. Click on the **OK** icon ![icon] to complete this feature.

➲ **Create Fillets**

29. Select the **Wireframe** tab and in the **Modify** section click on **Fillet Entities**.
30. Enter **.375 for the radius**. Ensure the **Method** is set to normal and the **Trim** is **activated**.
31. When prompted to **Fillet: Select an entity,** select entity 1 and 2 as shown below. To complete the remaining fillet select: entities **3 and 4**, entities **4 and 5**, entities **6 and 1.** The completed geometry is shown below right:

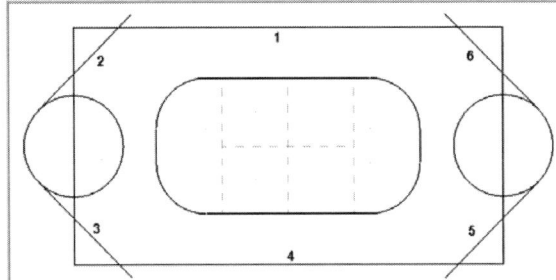 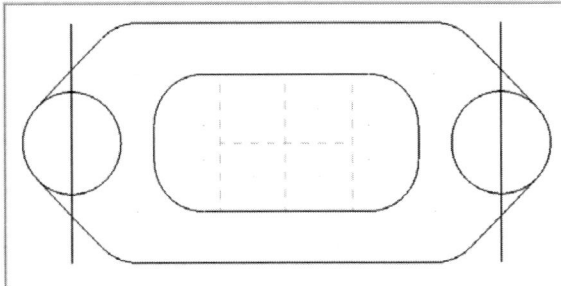

32. Click on the **OK** icon 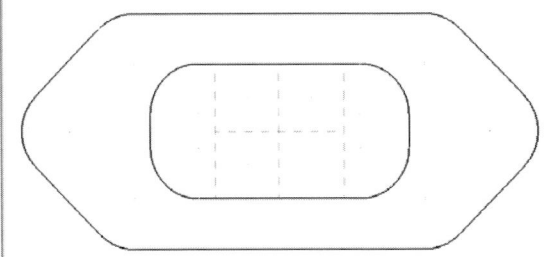 to complete this feature.

TASK 4:
TRIM GEOMETRY – TOP OF POCKET

➲ In this task you will first delete two lines and then trim the geometry using Divide / Delete.
1. **Delete** the two lines shown below by clicking on the lines and hitting the **delete key** on the keyboard.

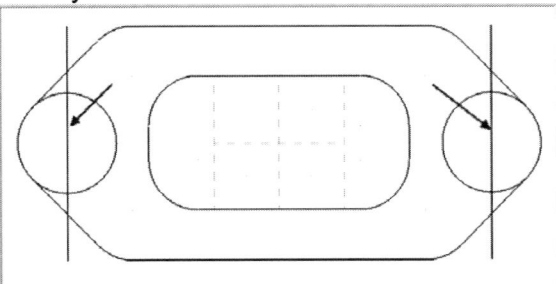

2. In the **Wireframe** tab click on **Divide** in the **Modify** section.
3. To satisfy the prompt **Select the curve to divide / delete**. Move the cursor over the various entities and select in order and position as shown below left:

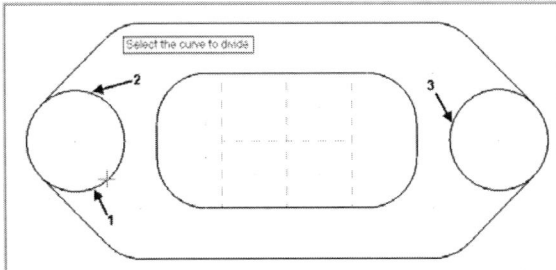 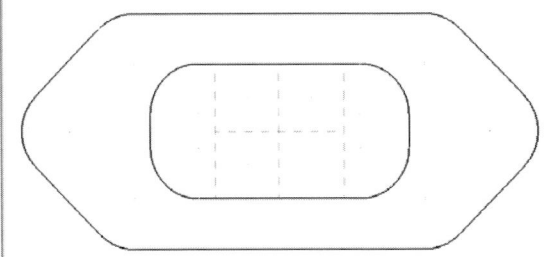

4. Click on the **OK** icon to complete this feature.

TASK 5:
CREATE GEOMETRY – MATERIAL BLANK 4.625 X 2.5 X 1.0

1. Select the **Wireframe** tab and in the **Shapes** section click on **Rectangle**.
2. Ensure **Anchor to center** is activated.
3. Click in the space for **Width** and enter a value of **4.625** and then hit the Enter key. In the space for **Height** enter a value of **2.5** and hit enter.

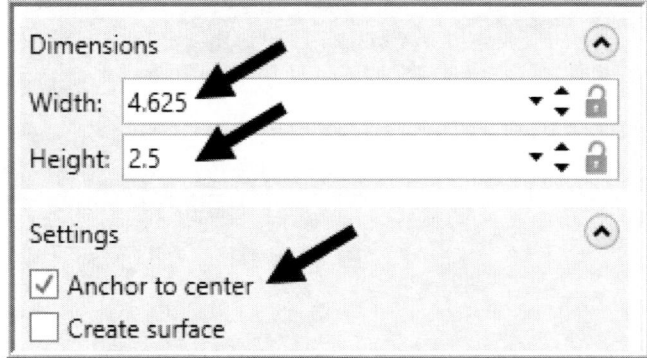

4. Now you need to **Select a base point**. Move the cursor over to the graphics screen and position the cursor at the **center of the grid** and **pick the origin**.
5. Click on the **OK** icon ⊘ to complete this feature.
6. Right mouse click in the graphics area and click on **Isometric**.
7. Right mouse click in the graphics area and click on the **Fit** icon ⊞.

➲ The completed rectangle is shown below:

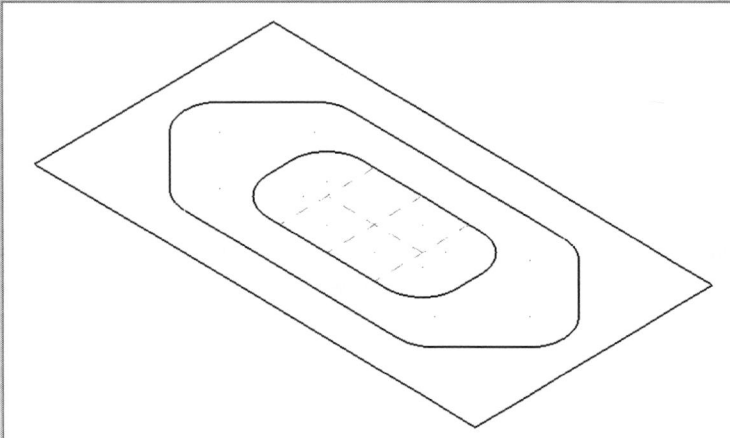

TASK 6:
TRANSLATE GEOMETRY TO BOTTOM OF POCKET
➲ Translate the geometry at Z0 down to Z-0.5

1. In the **Transform** tab select **Translate** in the **Position** section.
2. You are now prompted to **Translate: select entities to translate.** Hold the **shift** key down and select the line shown below. This process then selects the complete chain.

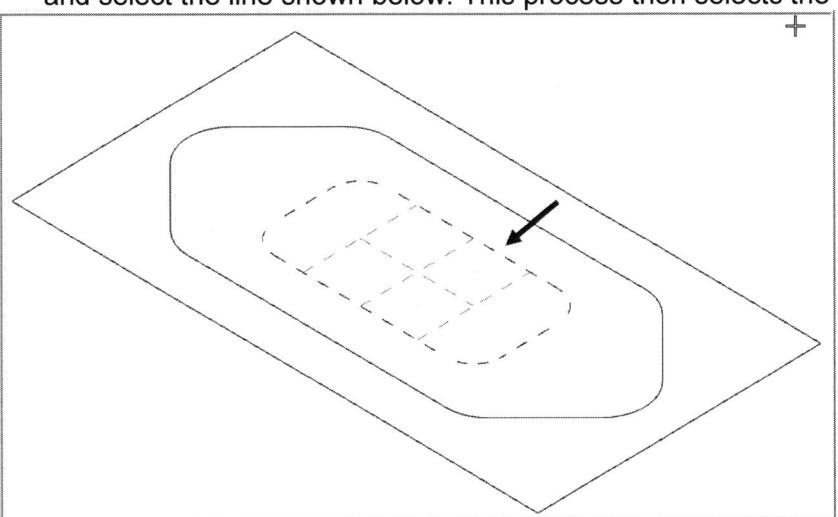

3. Pick the **End Selection** icon.
4. Set the following values shown below left. Ensure **Move** is activated, **Z is set to -0.5**.

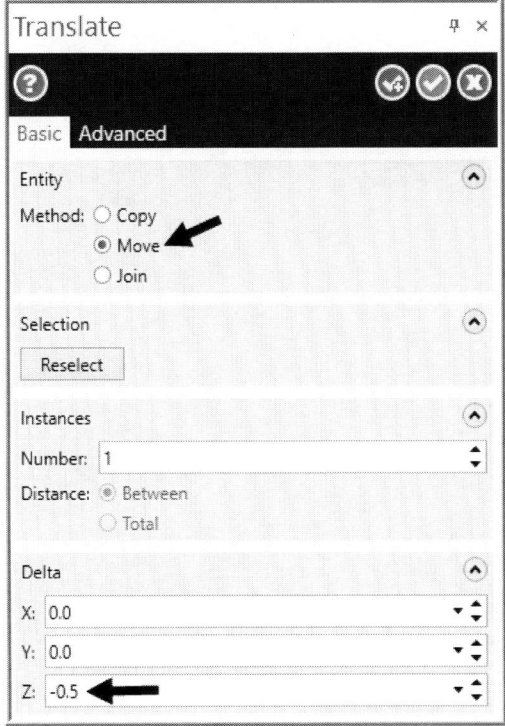

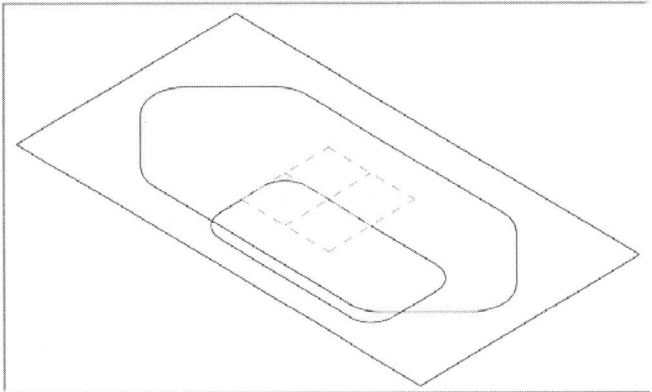

5. Click on the **OK** icon to complete this feature. The completed geometry is shown above.
6. Right mouse click in the graphics area and click on the **Clear Colors** icon.
7. Right mouse click in the graphics area and click on the **Fit** icon.

TASK 7:
EDIT GEOMETRY FOR LOFT SYNCING

➲ Later, when the lofted solid is created, Mastercam will need to know how to align or blend the two pieces of geometry together. This is done though Syncing options. There are many options, the most common is 'by Entity'. With this setting each chain must contain the same number of entities. Mastercam then uses these entities to create the edges for the blends.

➲ The top chain currently has 12 entities and the bottom has 8. For best results, the 4 rads of the bottom chain can be broken in half. This will provide the needed 12 entities and provide even blend points.

1. On the **Wireframe** tab in the Modify section, select **Break Two Pieces**.

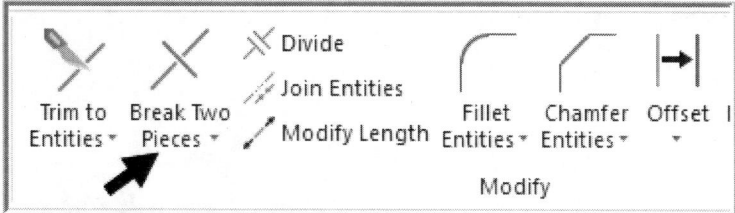

2. You are then prompted to '**Select an entity to break**'. Click on one of the bottom radii.

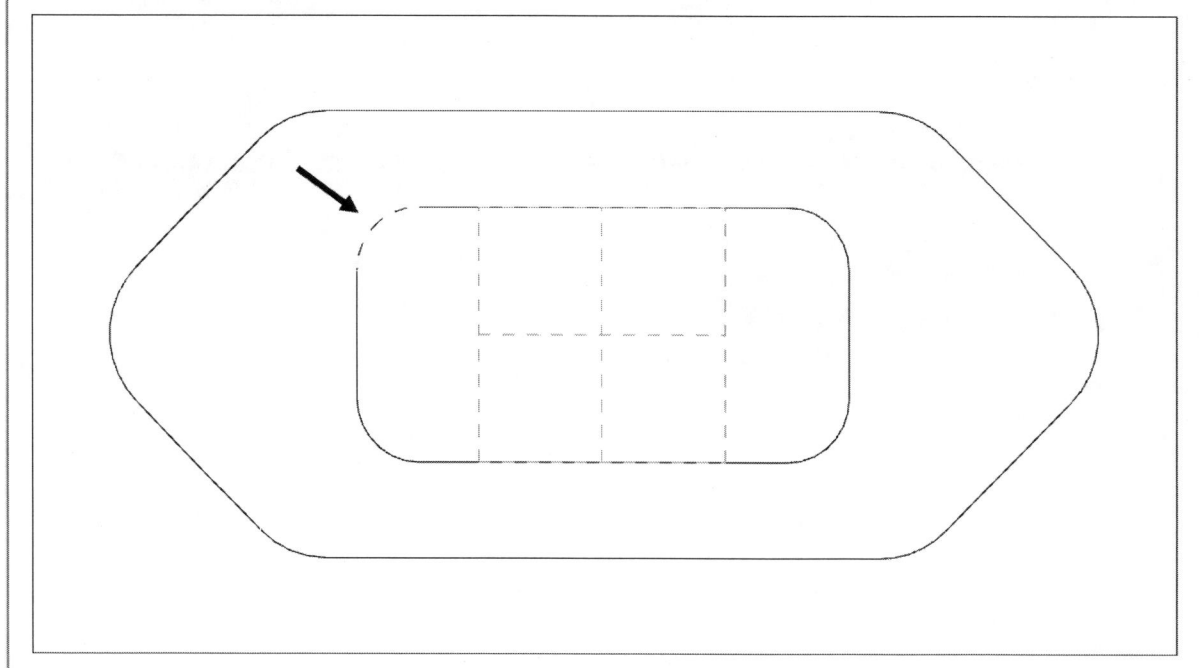

3. You are then prompted to '**Indicate the break position**'. Near the middle of the selected rad you will see the **visual cue appear for midpoint**, click when it appears.

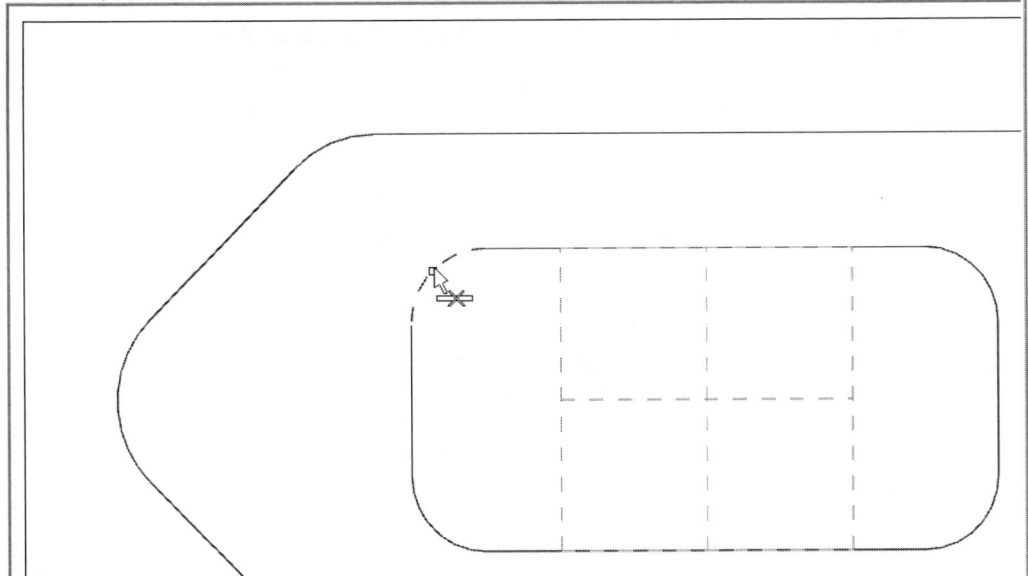

➲ The rad will now be broken into two pieces at the middle of the original radius.

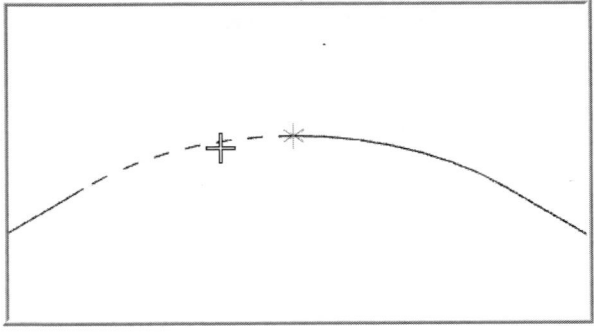 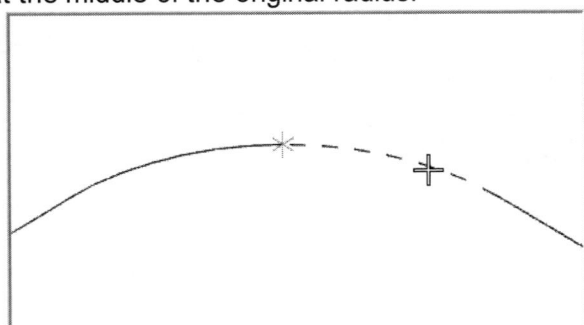

4. **Repeat** for the remaining 3 rads.
5. To exit the Break Two Pieces function, click **the Esc key**.

➲ The bottom chain should now have 12 entities, 4 lines and 8 arcs

SAVE THE DRAWING

1. Select **File.**
2. Select **Save As...**
3. Click on the **Browse** icon.
4. In the **"File name"** box, type **"Solids_Lesson_4"**, if required.
5. Browse to an appropriate location.
6. Select the **Save** button to save the file and complete this function**.**

TASK 8:
CREATE THE LOFTED SOLID BODY
➲ In this task you will create the solid cavity of the part by creating a ruled solid.

1. Click on the **Solids** tab and in the **Create** section select **Loft**.

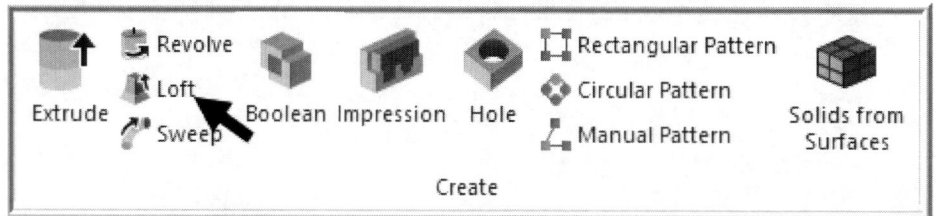

Solid Loft uses a set of closed chains to create one or more new solid bodies, cuts in an existing body, or bosses on an existing body.
Mastercam transitions between two or more chains of curves in the order that you select them by capping the first and last chains with solid faces.

---

2. On the graphics screen you are prompted **"Lofted surface: define contour 1"** with the **Chain Button** selected.

3. Before selecting geometry, a Syncing mode must be selected. On the **Chaining menu** click the **Options** button. On the **Options menu** set the **Sync mode** to **by Entity**.

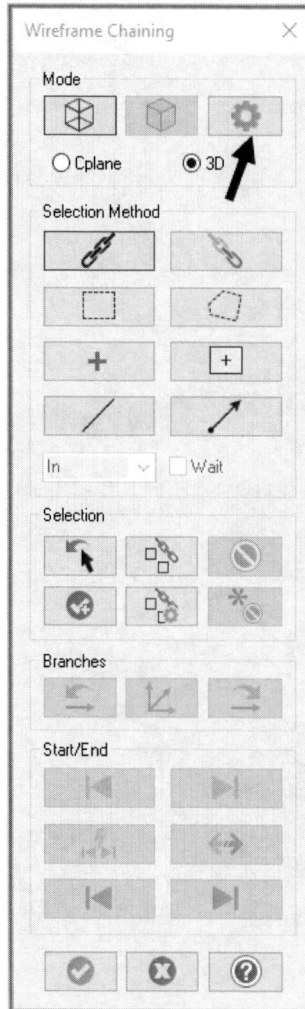

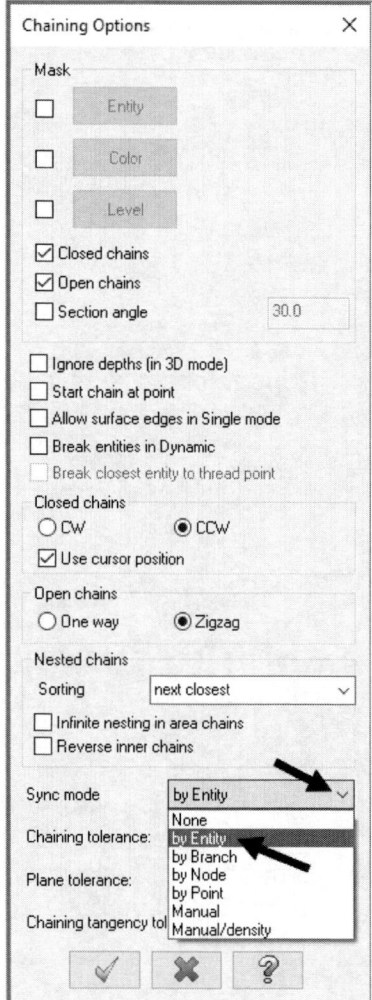

4. Select the **2 chains** as shown in the **Graphics Screen** diagram:

> The **position and direction of each of the arrows is crucial** when creating a loft or ruled solid.
> Ensure that the arrows are pointing in the same direction and at a similar point in both chains.
> Try to select the point on each chain as close as possible to the arrows in the image above.

 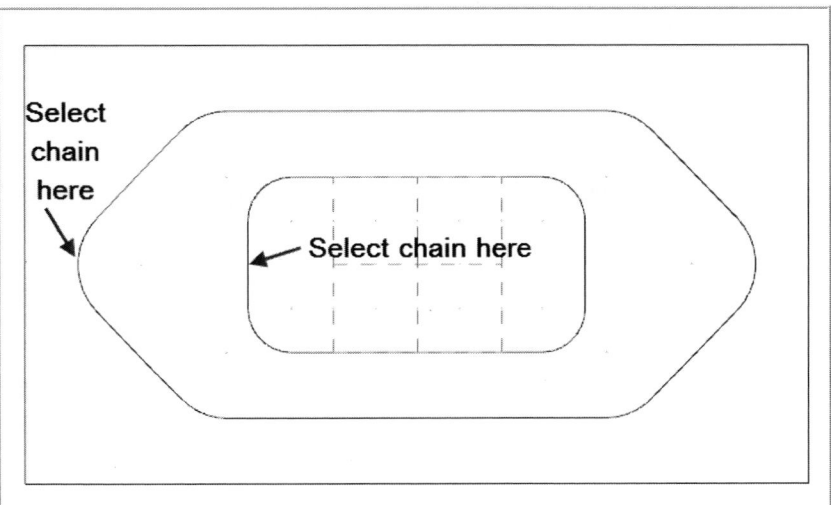

5. Right mouse click in the graphics area and click on **Isometric**.

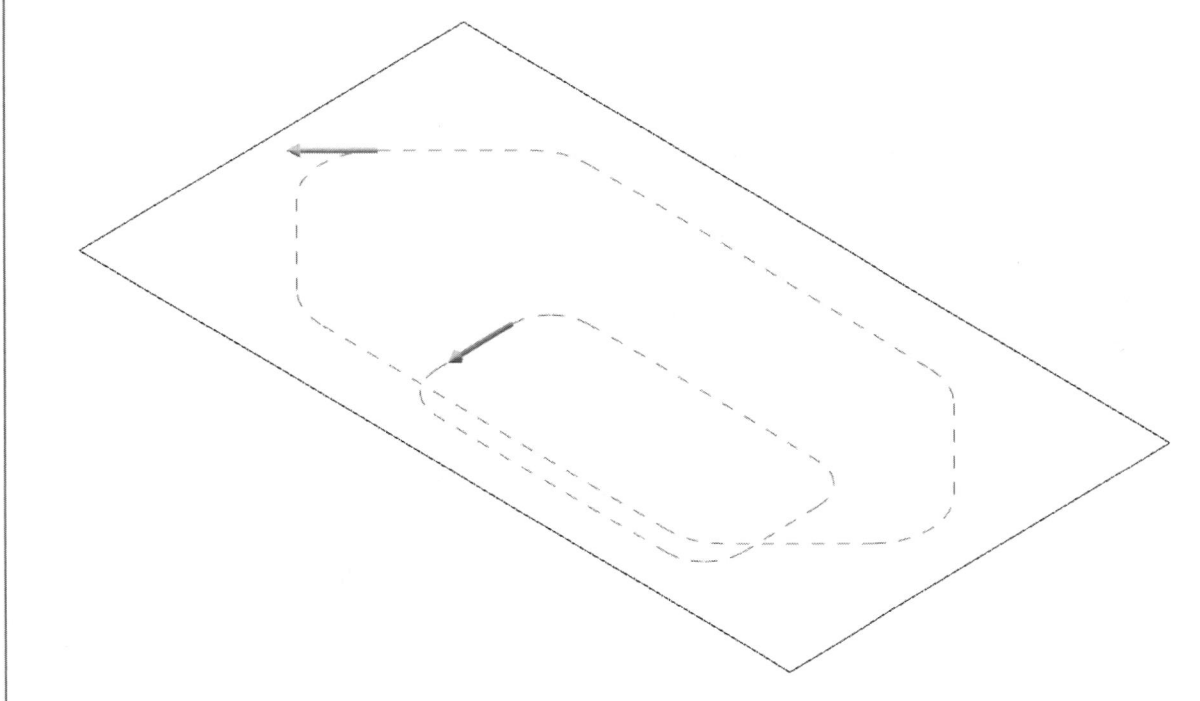

6. Click on the **OK** icon.

7. The **Loft** dialog window should appear as shown below.

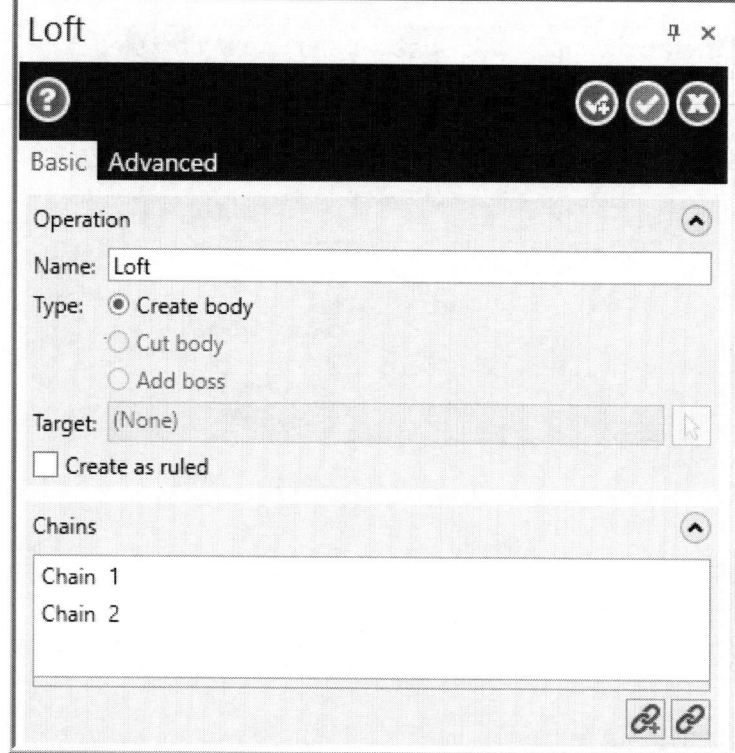

What are the criteria for the selected chains for a Loft operation?

There must be a minimum of two closed, parallel chains.

Each individual chain of curves must be planar.

All of the selected chains must follow the same chaining direction.

You cannot select a chain of curves more than once for a given loft operation.

A selected chain of curves cannot self-intersect

Create as ruled
Select to create the lofted solid, cut, or boss using ruled blending. In a ruled blend, Mastercam transitions from one chain of curves to another, which results in linear sections. Clear to use smooth blending. In a smooth blend, Mastercam considers all of the chains of curves when transitioning between them, which results in smooth sections.

8. Click on the **OK** icon ✅ in the **Loft** dialog window.

➲ Your screen should look like the screenshot below:

Wireframe image	Solid image

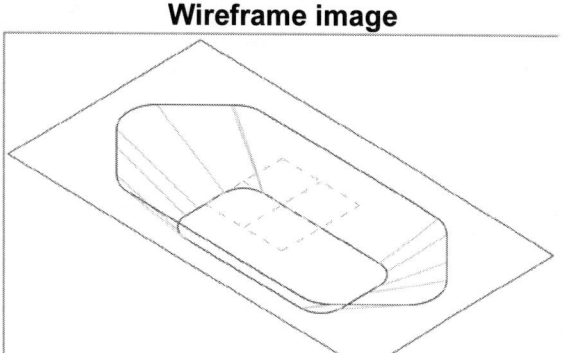 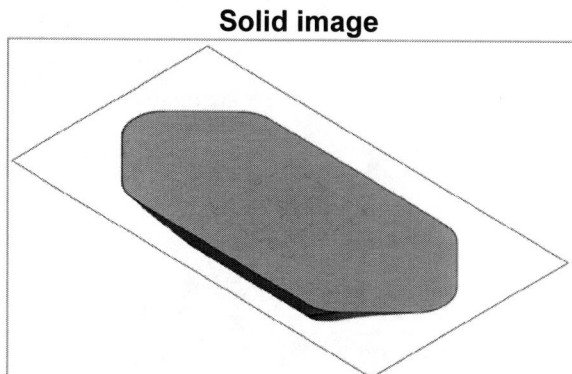

TASK 9:
CREATE THE BASE SOLID BODY

1. Activate a **wireframe** image if required by selecting the **Alt and S** keys or by clicking on the **Wireframe** icon at the lower right of the screen.
2. Right mouse click in the graphics area and click on **Isometric**.
3. On the **Solids** tab and in the **Create** section select **Extrude**.

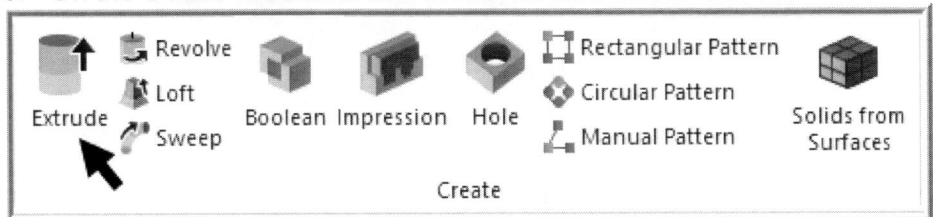

⮕ On the screen you will now see the **Chaining** dialog box, with the **Chain Button** selected. In the graphics screen a prompt to **"Select chain(s) to extrude"** is displayed.
4. Select the rectangular chain as shown below.

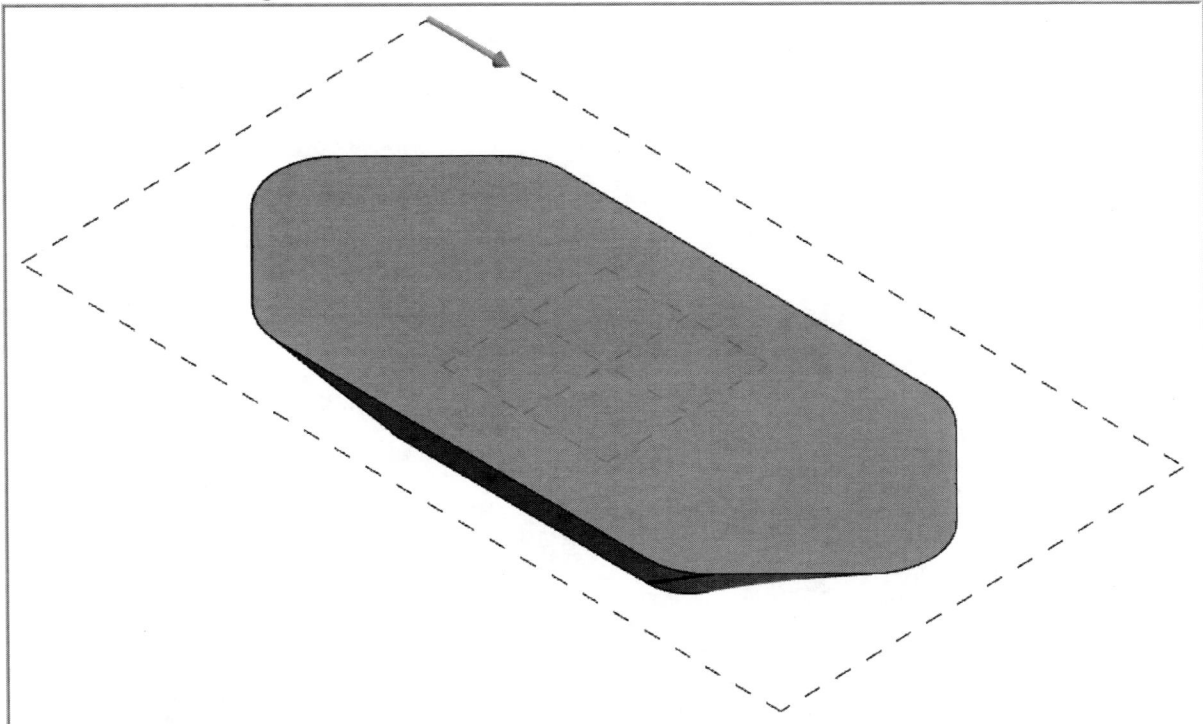

Chaining Box
Cplane: Allows the user to select entities only within a Construction (2D) plane rather than having to select from all entities available.

5. Click on the **OK** icon.

6. An arrow will appear on one of the corners as shown below, make sure the arrow is pointing

   down. If it is pointing up, click on the **Reverse All** icon 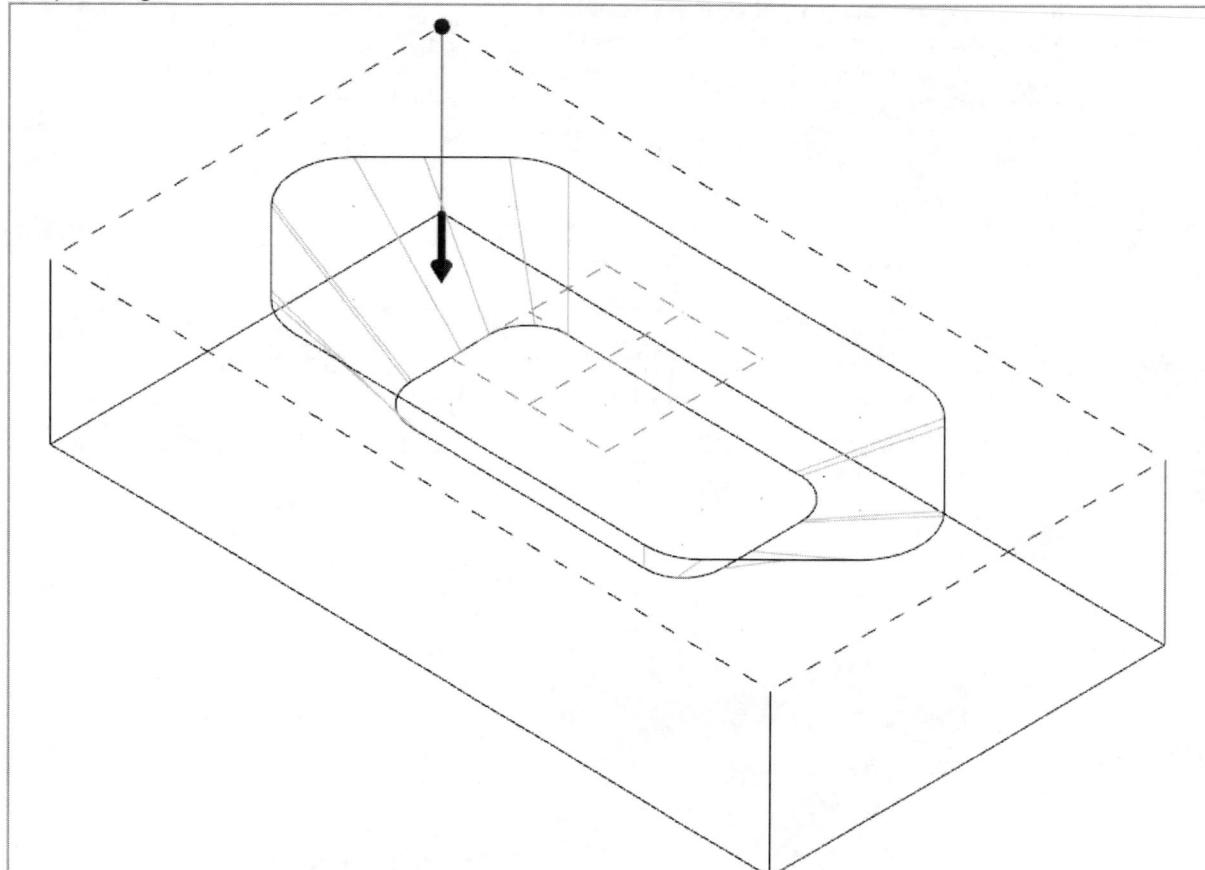 in the Solid
   Extrude panel. **Note:** you may have to unzoom the image to see the direction the arrow is
   pointing.

7. Make the necessary changes as shown below in the Solid Extrude dialog window. Activate **Create Body** and set the **Distance to 1.0**.

Solid Extrude

Basic Advanced

Operation

Name: Extrude

Type: ⦿ Create body ◀━━━
    ○ Cut body
    ○ Add boss

Target Solid body

☑ Create a single operation
☐ Automatically determine operation type

Chains

Chain 1

Distance

⦿ Distance 1.0000 ◀━━━
○ Through all
☐ Both directions

☐ Trim to Faces

8. Click on the **OK** icon in the Solid Extrude dialog window
➲ Your screen should look like the screenshot below:

Wireframe image	Solid image
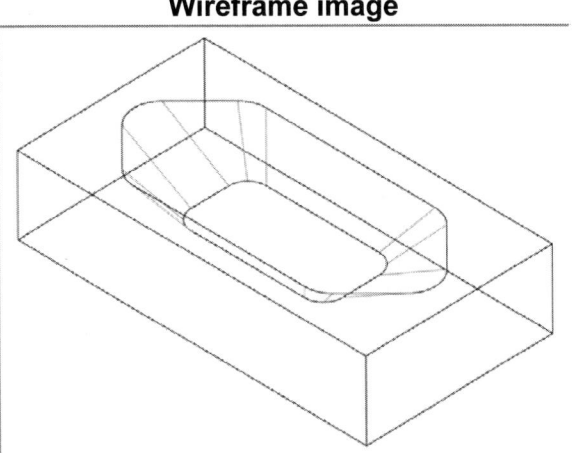	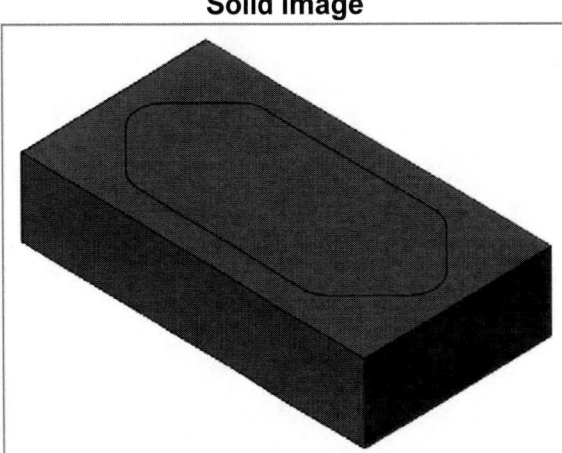

TASK 10:
BOOLEAN SUBTRACTION OF A SOLID

⊃ In this task, the two separate solid bodies that have been created will be combined. In the solids tree, both bodies are present as shown in the image below. Using **Boolean remove** the solid body representing the cavity can be removed from the solid representing the stock material.

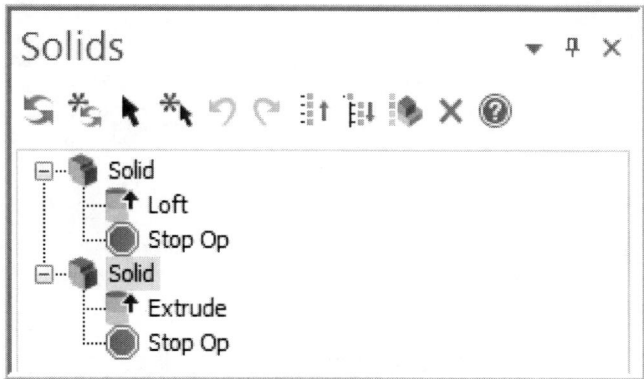

1. Activate a **wireframe** image by selecting the **Alt and S** keys or by clicking on the **Wireframe** icon at the lower right of the screen:
2. Click on the **Solids** tab and in the **Create** section select **Boolean**.

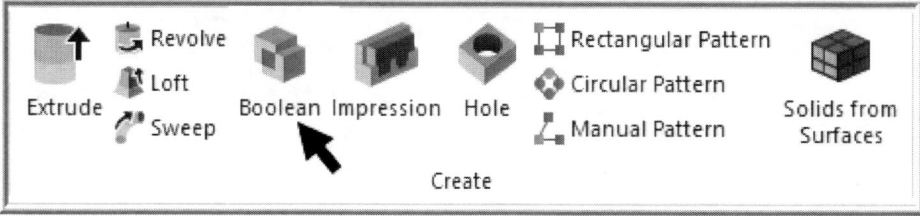

Boolean
Boolean functions construct a solid from combinations of two or more existing solids. You can merge solids, remove solids from one another, and find the common region of overlapping solids.

3. When prompted to "**Select a target body**", select the stock solid body shown below.

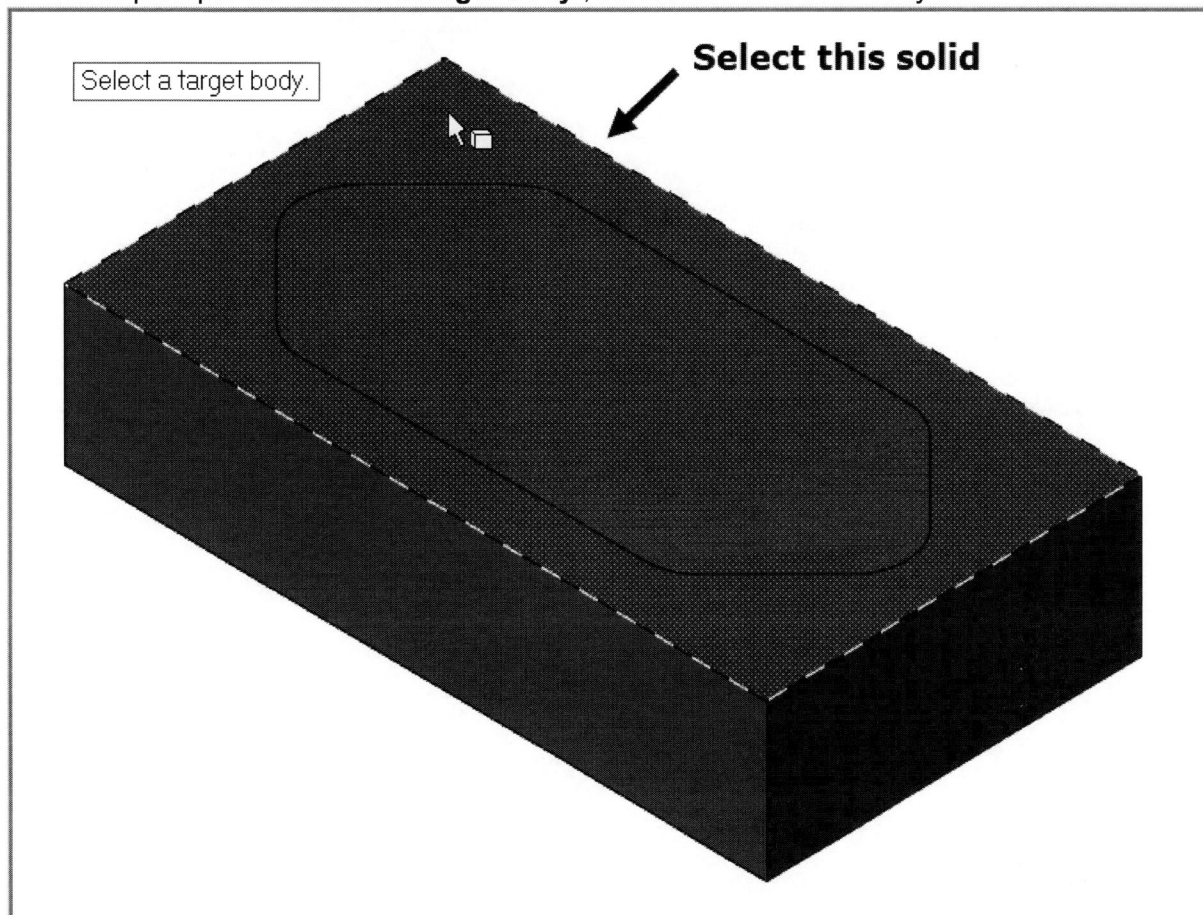

4. The Boolean panel will now activate and the Target Solid will be set with the body that was just selected.
5. On the Boolean panel, activate **Remove.**

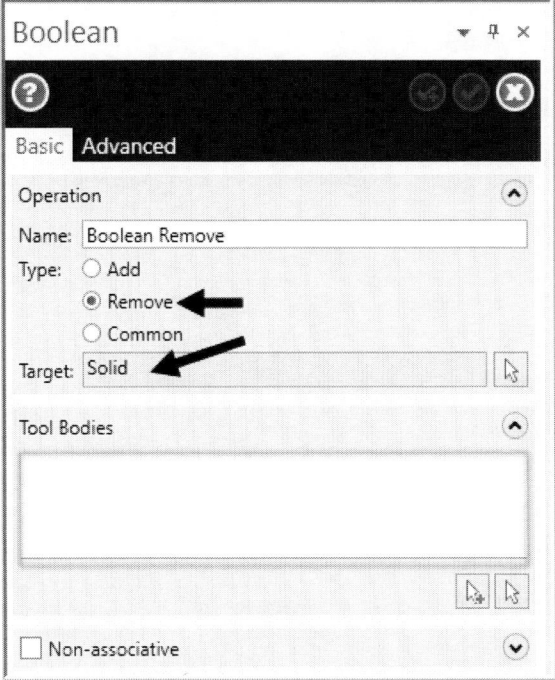

6. Click on the selection arrow shown below left to **"Add Selection"** to the Tool Bodies.

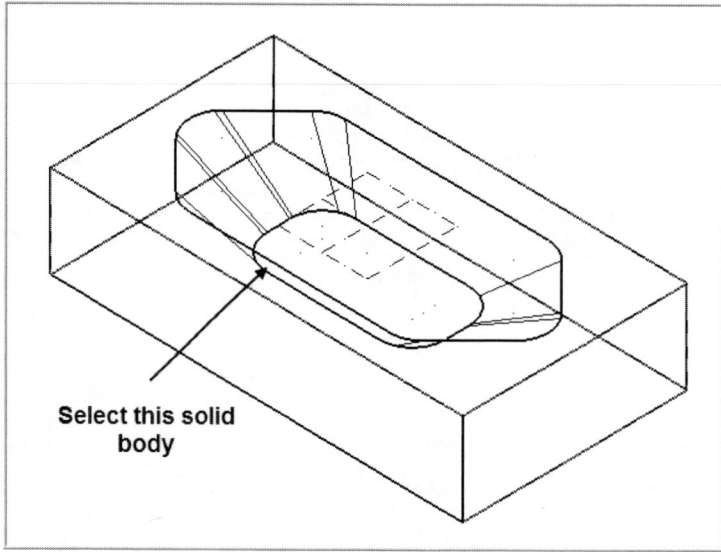

Select this solid body

7. The prompt **"Select one or more tool bodies"** will now be displayed and the **Solid Selection** dialog box appears. In the Solid Selection dialog box **only activate Body** selection. Select the **cavity solid body** as shown above right, the Loft solid.

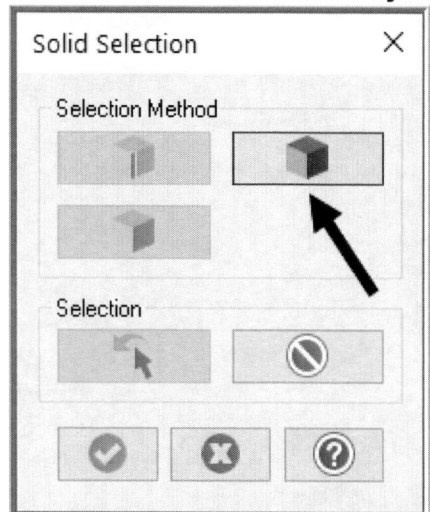

8. Click on the **OK** icon in the Solid Selection panel.

9. Make the necessary changes as shown below in the Boolean dialog window. Ensure **Remove is activated**.

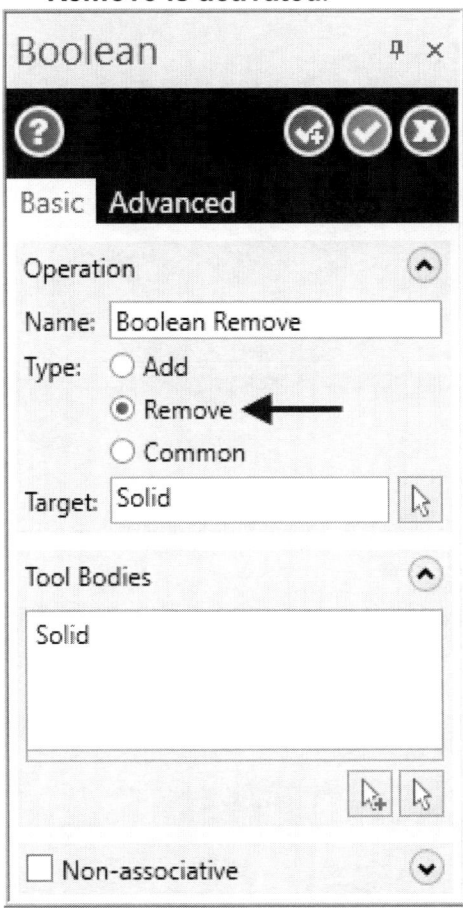

10. Click on the OK icon  in the **Boolean** panel.
11. In the solids tree there is now only one solid entity which contains the **Boolean Remove** feature, as seen below:

12. To change from a **wireframe image** to a **solid image** select the **Alt and S** keys or the **Shading** icon. Your screen should look like the screenshots below:

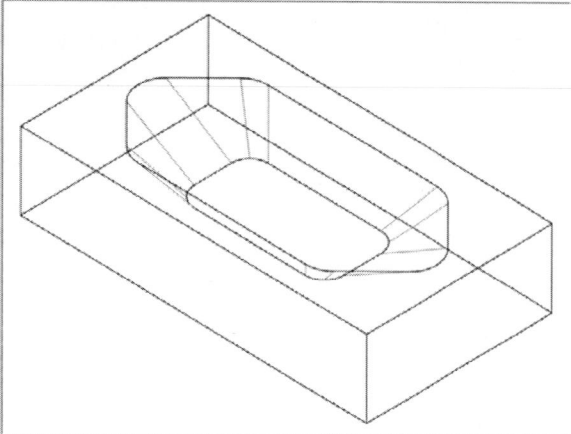
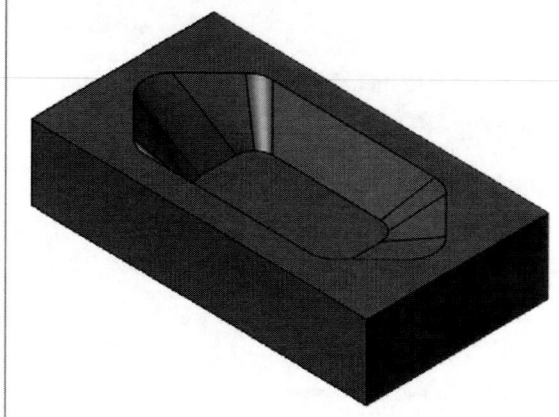

TASK 11:
CREATE 0.25 FILLETS AT BOTTOM OF POCKET

➲ In this task you will create 0.25" fillets on the bottom of the pocket.

1. Activate a **wireframe** image if required by selecting the **Alt and S** keys or by clicking on the **Wireframe** icon at the bottom right of the screen.

2. On the **Solids** tab and in the **Modify** section select **Constant Fillet**.

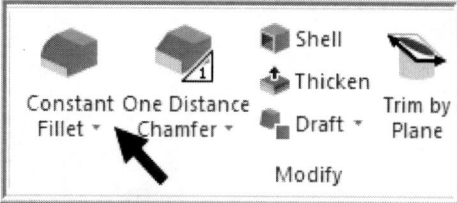

Constant Fillet uses edge blending to produce a rounded edge, introducing new faces that are tangent to the edges' adjacent faces.
You determine the extent of the fillet by inputting a constant radius value.

Variable Radius Fillet
Variable Radius Fillet uses edge blending to produce a rounded edge, introducing new faces that are tangent to the edges' adjacent faces. You determine the extent of the fillet by inputting various radius values along the edge. You can also specify radius positions
Face-Face Fillet
Face-Face Fillet uses two faces or two sets of faces that are blended together to create a fillet. Mastercam will use various ways of creating the fillets depending on the operation type that is selected

3. On the screen you will now be prompted to **"Select one or more entities to fillet"** and the **Solid Selection** dialog box appears. In the Solid Selection dialog box **only activate Face** selection. Now select the **face at the bottom of the pocket** as shown below.

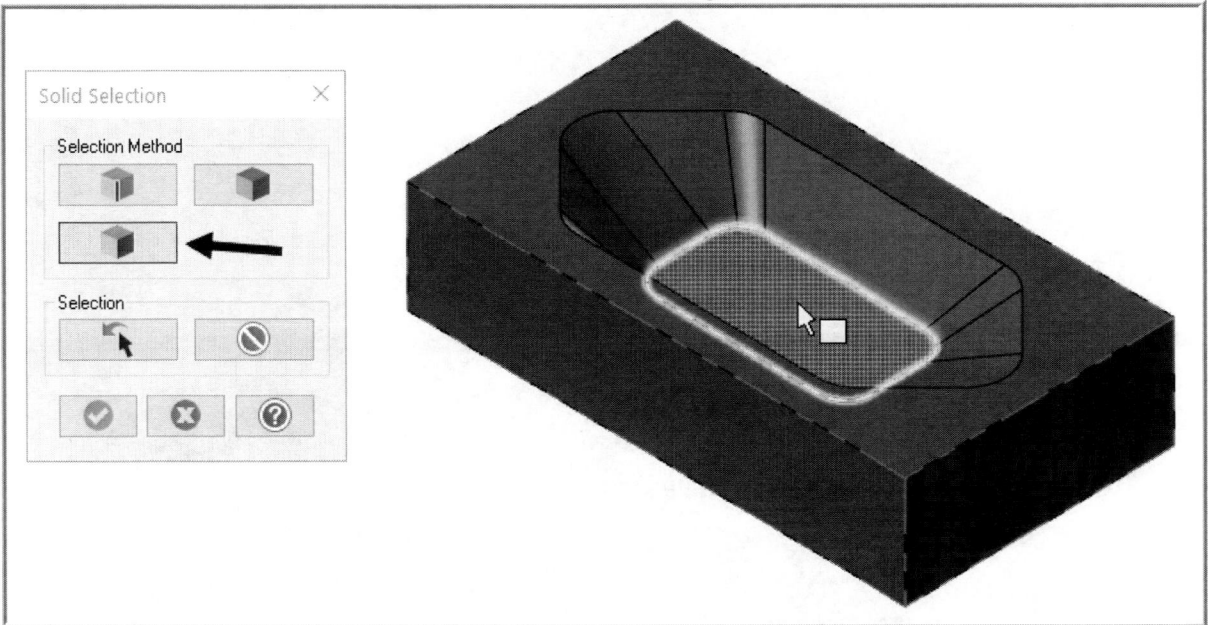

4. Click on the **OK** icon after completing the selection of the face.
5. Make the necessary changes as shown below in the **Constant Radius Fillet** dialog window. Set **Radius to 0.25**.

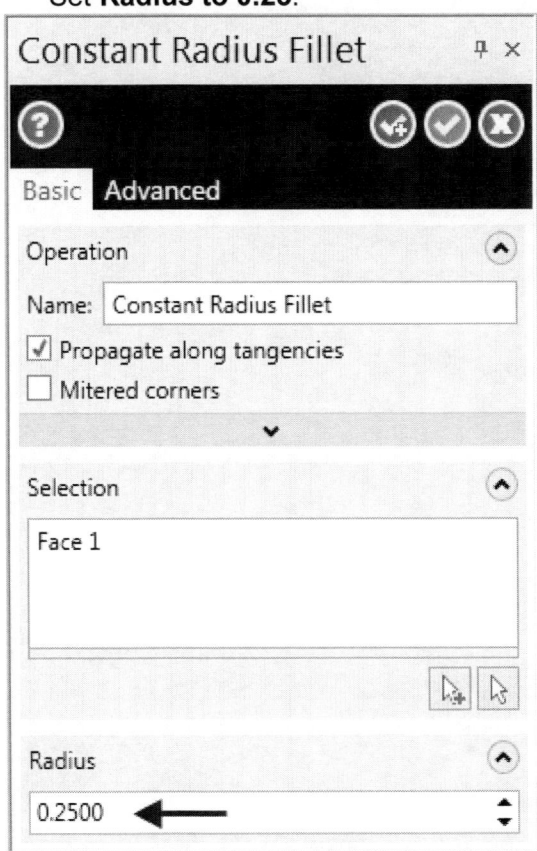

6. Click on the **OK** icon in the **Constant Radius Fillet** panel.

7. Select **Alt and S** to **shade** the solid extrusion or click on the **Outlined Shaded** icon at the top of the screen.
➲ Your screen should look like the screenshot below:

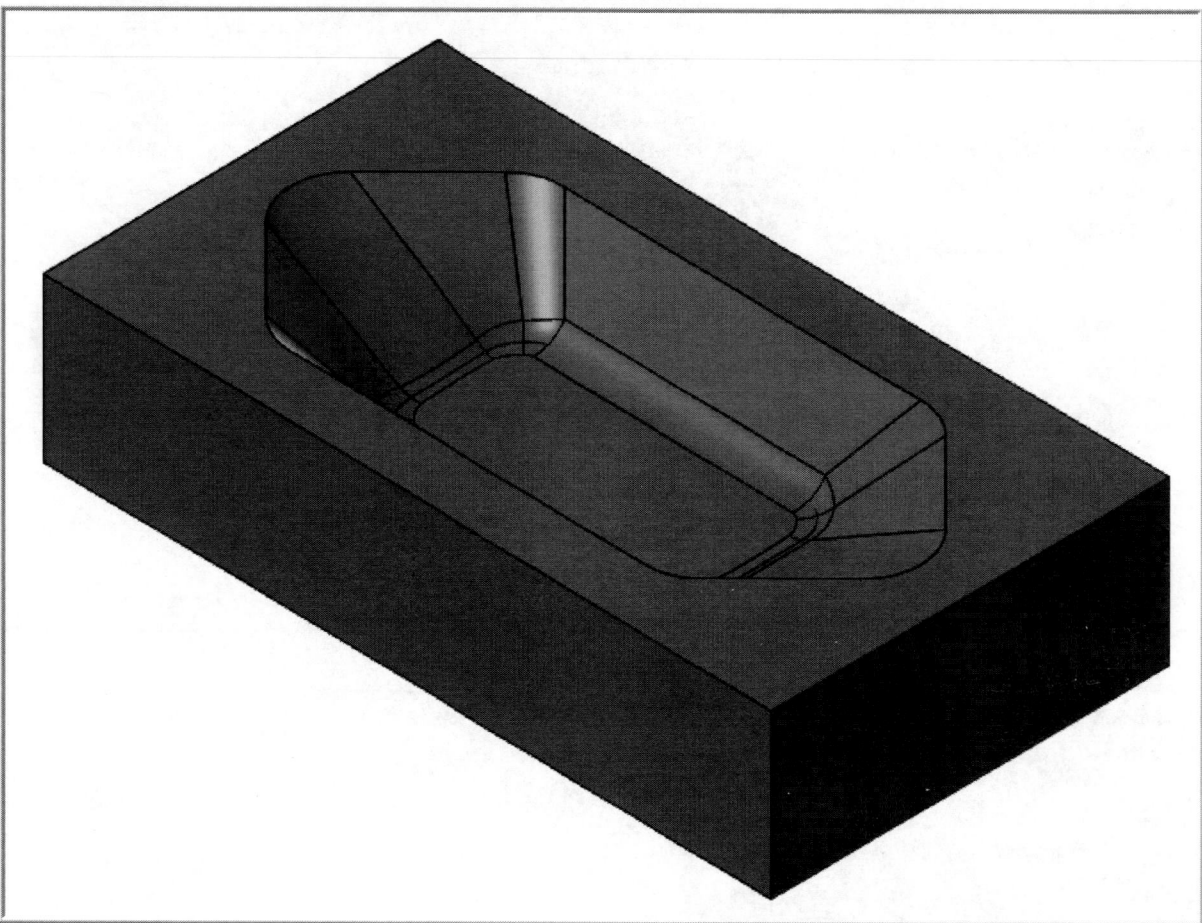

SAVE THE DRAWING

8. Select the **Save** icon from the **Quick Access** toolbar at the top left of the screen.

Toolpath Creation

TASK 12:
DEFINE THE ROUGH STOCK USING STOCK SETUP

1. Select the **View tab** and click on **Toolpaths** in the **Managers** section to display the Toolpaths Manager. **Alt-O** will **Show/Hide** Toolpaths Manager pane.
2. Select the **plus** in front of **Properties** to expand the Toolpaths Group Properties. Select **Stock setup** in the Toolpaths Manager window.
3. On the **Stock Setup** page select **All Entities**.

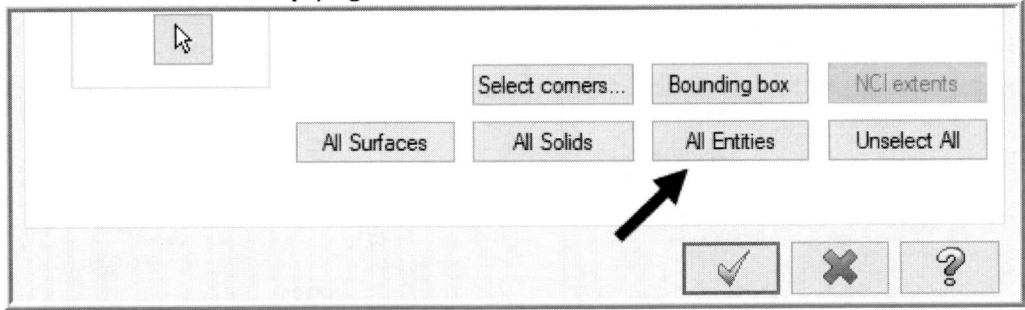

⮕ The Stock setup should now have the values shown below. If required, enable the stock Display.

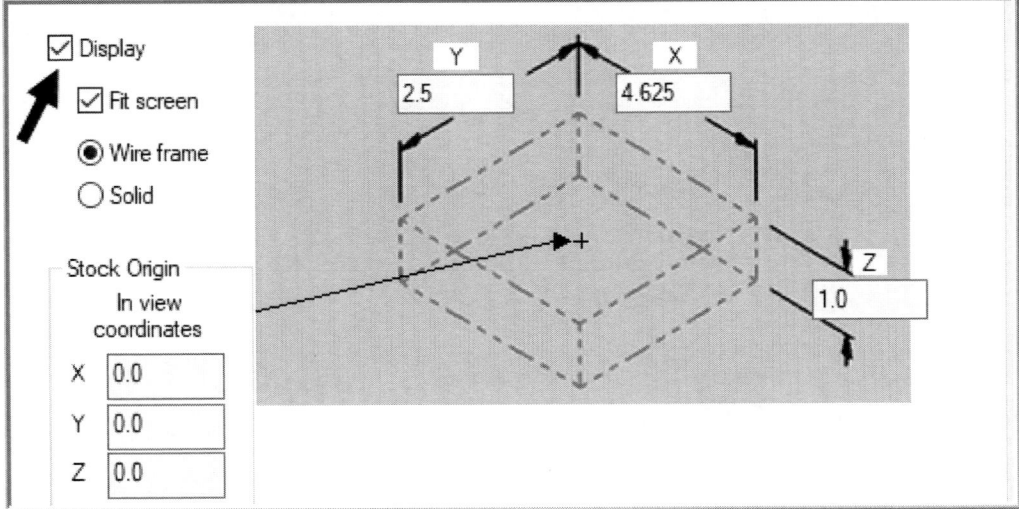

4. Select the **Tool Settings** tab and change the parameters to match the Tool Settings screenshot below. To change the Material type, follow the instructions below:
5. Pick the **Select** button at the bottom of the Tool Settings page.
6. At the **Material List** dialog box open the **Source** drop down list and select **Mill – library**.
7. From the Default Materials list select **ALUMINUM inch -6061** and then select 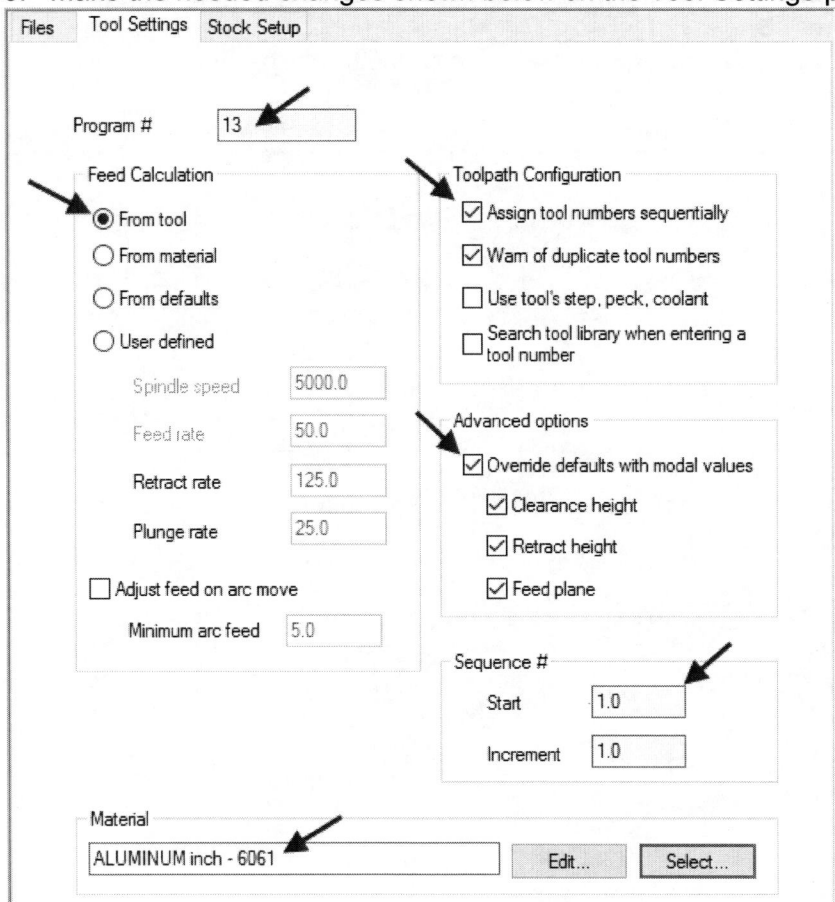.
8. Make the needed changes shown below on the Tool Settings page.

9. Select the OK button again to complete this function.

TASK 13:
ROUGH OUT SURFACE USING SURFACE ROUGH PLUNGE
➲ In this task you will use a 0.5 diameter center cutting flat end mill to rough the pocket.

> **Rough Plunge Toolpaths** machine surfaces quickly with a drilling-type motion. One application for rough plunge is to clean out a deep cavity using special plunge milling tools often with through-tool coolant to help evacuate chips.
> Rough plunge can project a toolpath onto the drive geometry and create plunge points in that pattern. Selecting **NCI** requires that you have the pattern operation already present in the file.
>
> **Note:** In this task you will first create a 2D pocket **to provide the pattern for the rough plunge toolpath**.
>
> **This 2D toolpath will only be used as a pattern it will not be used to machine the part.**

1. Select the **Toolpaths** tab.
2. Click on the **Expand gallery down arrow** to view additional options in the **2D** toolpath section. In the **Milling** section select **Pocket**.

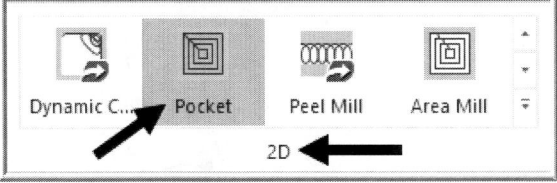

3. On the screen you will now see the **Chaining dialog box** with **Chain set**. Activate the radio button for **C-Plane**.

> **Cplane:** Chains only entities that are parallel to the current construction plane and at the same Z depth as the first entity you chain.

4. For the prompt to **Select Pocket chain 1**. Select the line as shown below:

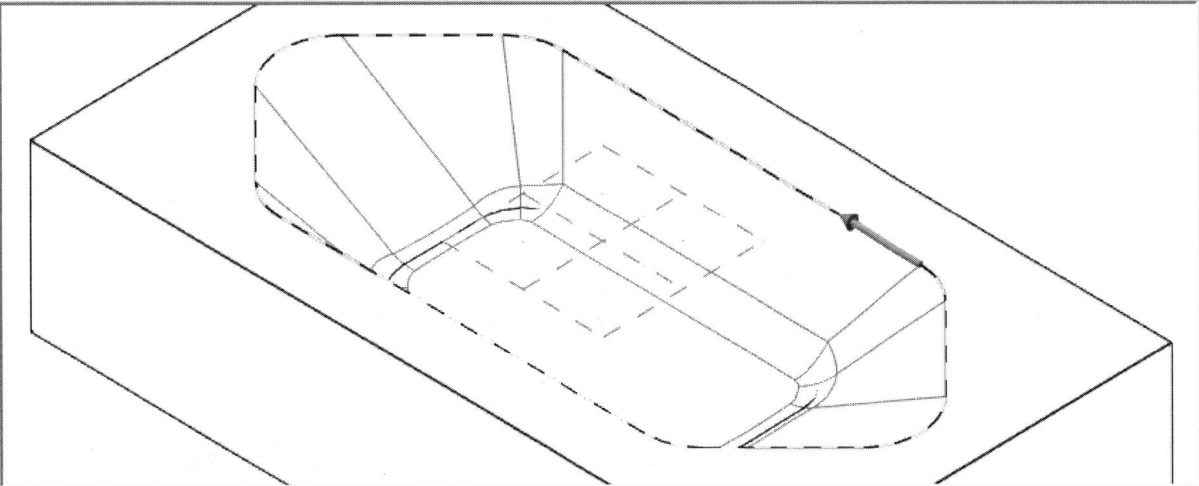

5. After selecting the line your graphics screen should look like the screenshot above, with the green arrow pointing to the right.
6. After the pocket has been successfully chained select the **OK** button ☑ at the bottom of the Chaining dialog box.

7. Select Tool from the list on the left. In the lower left corner of the **Tool** parameters page select the **Select library tool...** button.
8. Use the slider bar on the right of this dialog box to scroll down and locate a **0.5 diameter flat end mill**. Select the 0.5 diameter flat endmill.

Tool Number	Tool Name	Diameter	Corner Radius	Length	Type	Rad
289	7/16 FLAT ENDMILL	0.4375	0.0	0.8	Flat endmill	Nor
290	1/2 FLAT ENDMILL	0.5	0.0	1.0	Flat endmill	Nor
291	17/32 FLAT ENDMILL	0.5312	0.0	1.0	Flat endmill	Nor

9. Select the **OK** button to complete the selection of this tool.
10. Changes to the **Toolpath parameters** are not needed. This toolpath is simply providing a path for the plunge operation, it's speeds and feeds will not effect the final toolpath.

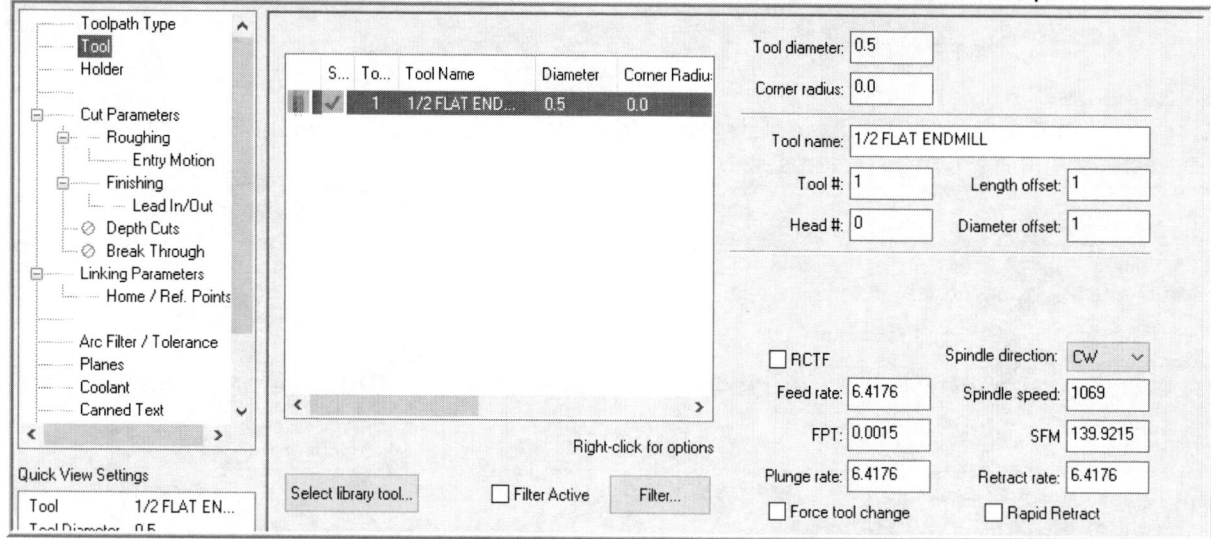

11. On the **Cut Parameters** page, set the stock to leave on **walls to 0.05** and the stock to leave on **floors to 0.0**

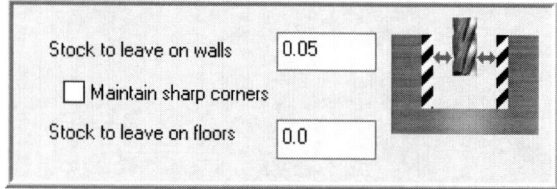

12. Select the **Cut Parameters>Roughing** parameters page and make changes to this page as shown. **Cutting method** is set to **Parallel Spiral** and a **Stepover percentage** of **40**.

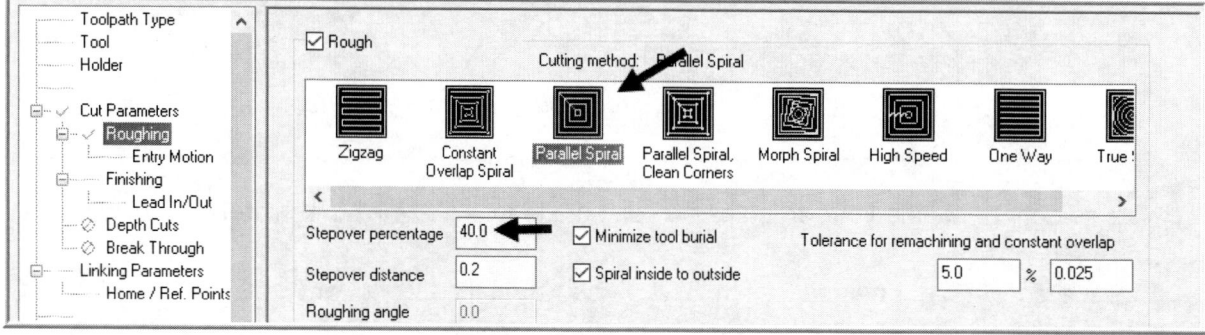

13. Select the plus sign to the left of **Roughing** (if required) from the list on the left and then select **Entry Motion**. On the **Entry Motion** parameters page turn the **Entry Motion Off**.

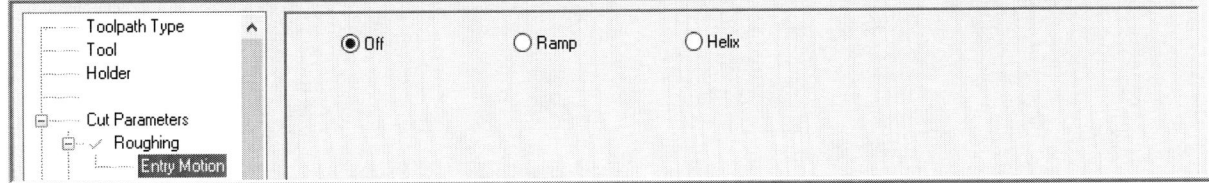

14. Select **Finishing** parameters page and **uncheck** Finish.

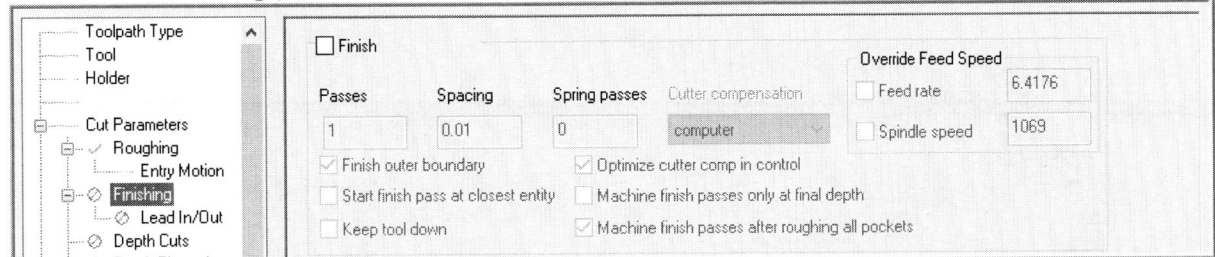

15. On the **Linking Parameters** page, **disable Clearance and Retract**. Set Feed plane, Top of Stock, and Depth to **Absolute 0**.

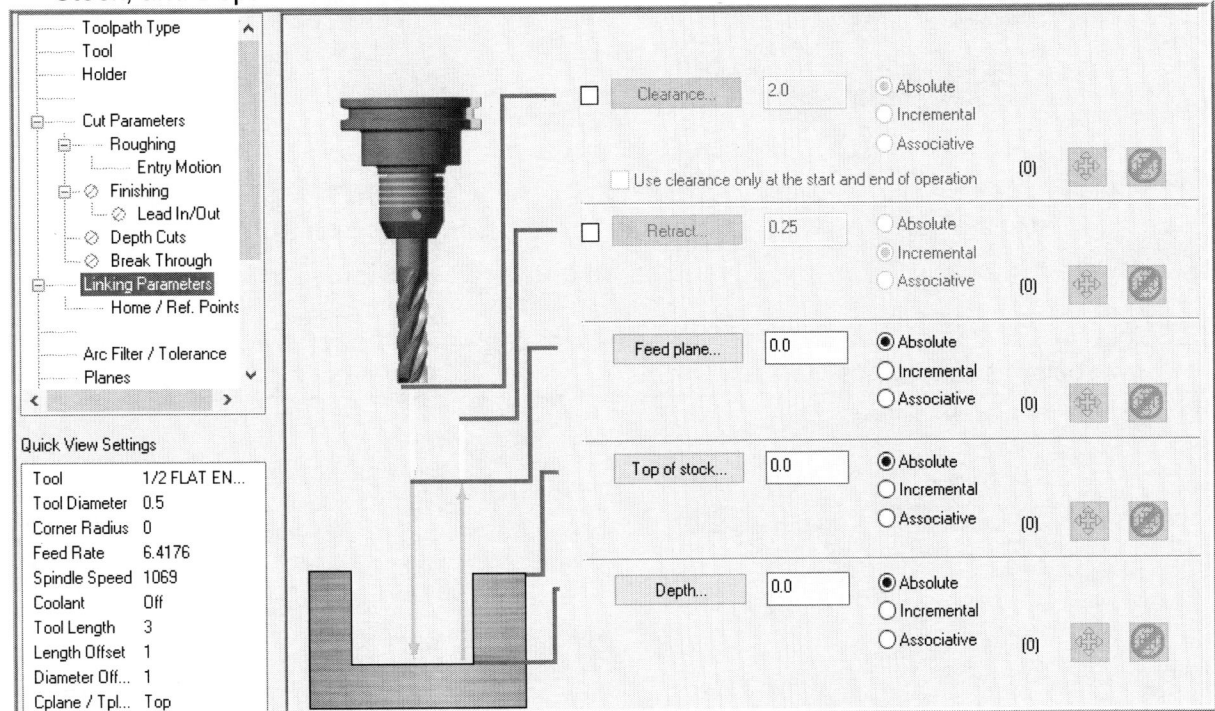

16. Select the **OK** button to complete the toolpath.

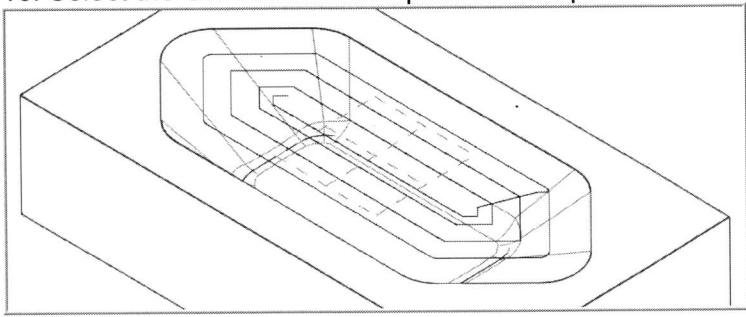

⇒ Rough Plunge Toolpath

17. On the **Toolpaths** tab click on the **Expand gallery** down arrow in the **3D** toolpath section and select **Plunge**.

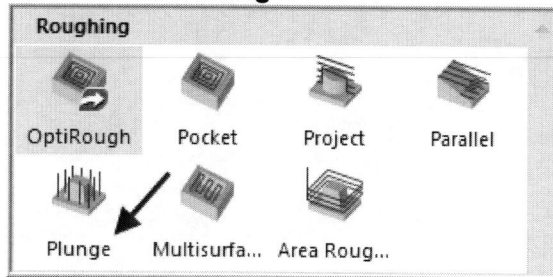

18. To satisfy the prompt, **triple left click** on a solid face. This will select the entire solid body.

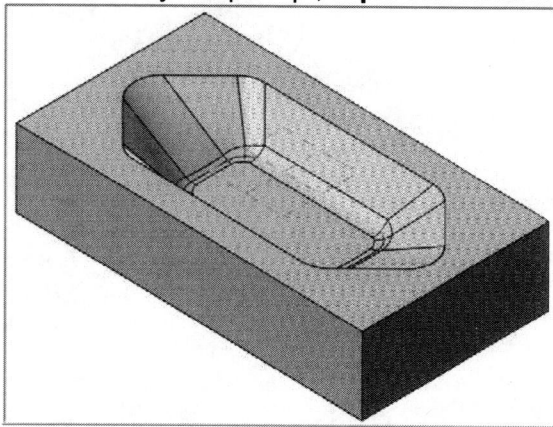

19. To move onto the next step, you now need to pick the **End Selection** icon.

20. Select the OK button to exit the **Toolpath/surface selection** dialog box.

21. Select the 0.5 diameter end mill and make changes to the **Toolpath parameters** page as shown below. Set **Coolant** on.

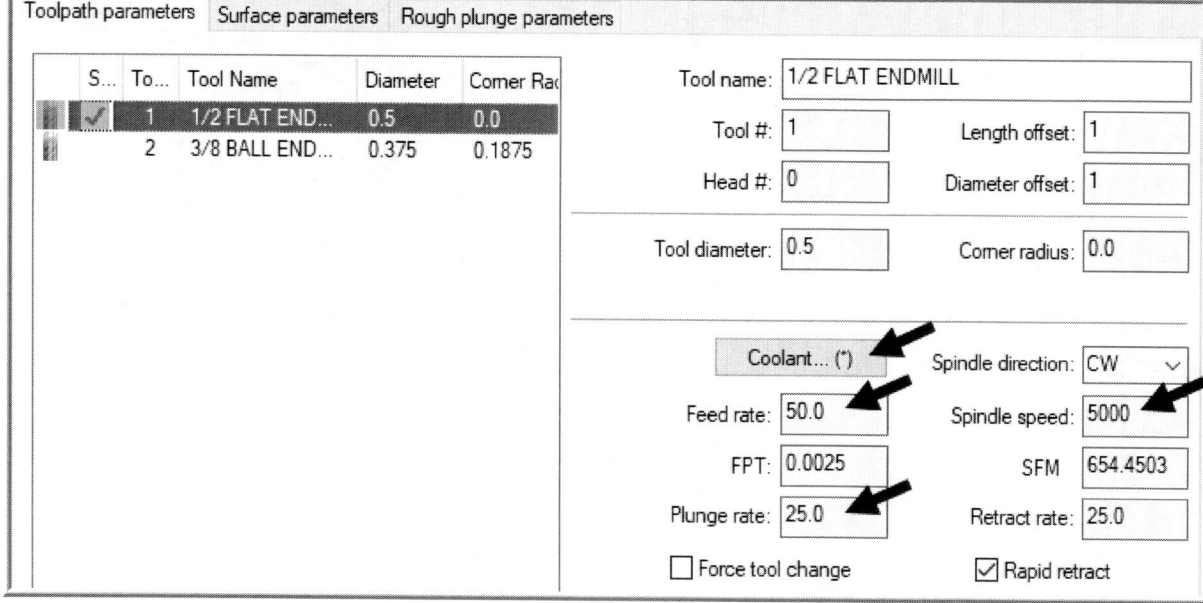

22. Select the **Surface parameters** page and make changes to this page as shown below: **Stock to leave on drive** is set to **0.02**.

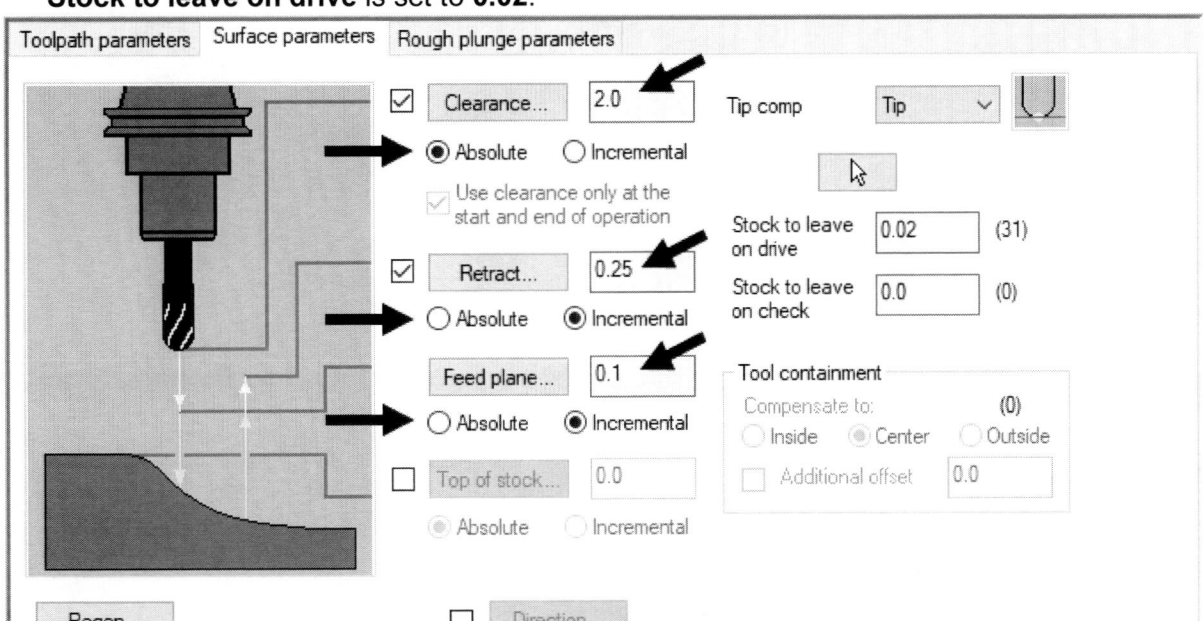

23. Select the **Rough plunge parameters** page and make changes to this page as shown below. Ensure **NCI** is activated and the **Pocket** is selected in the **Source operations**.

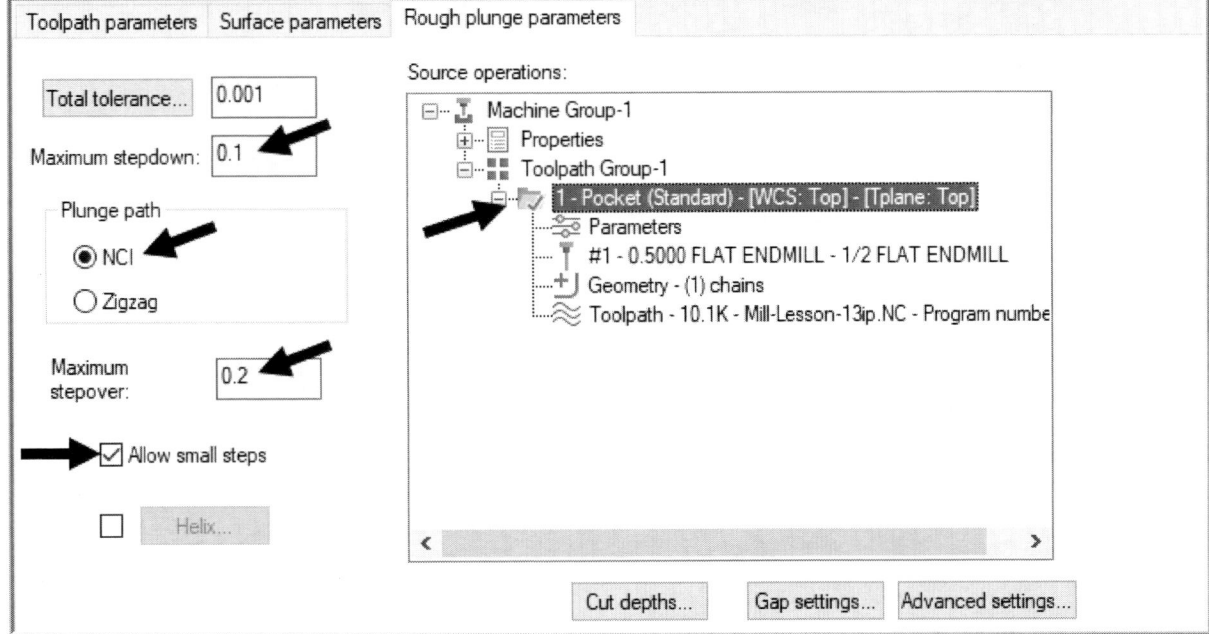

24. Select the **Cut depths** button make the necessary changes. **Note**: both depths are **negative** values.

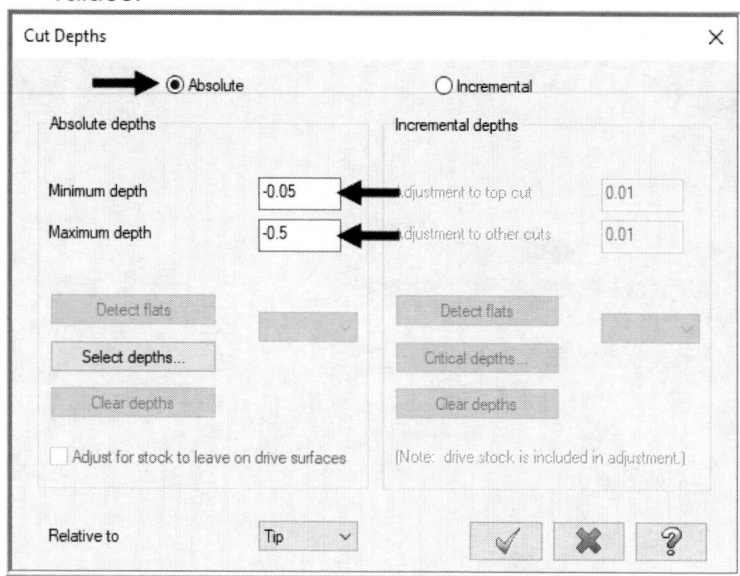

25. Select the OK button to complete this feature.
26. Select the OK button to exit Rough plunge parameters.

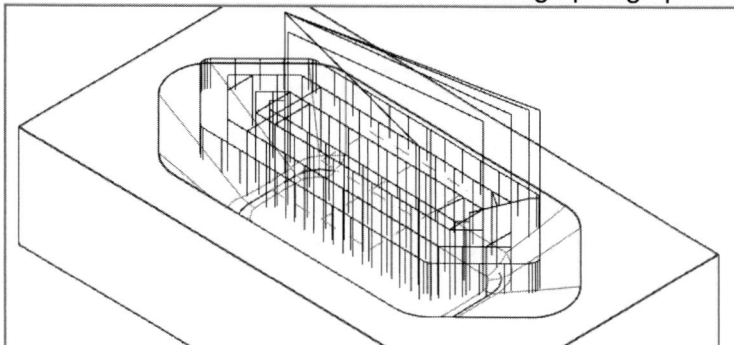

27 Toggle the posting ability of the Pocket toolpath.

With **only the pocketing** operation selected, click the **ghost icon** in the toolpath manager. The ghost icon should now show on the selected operation and a note will show 'POSTING OFF'.

This will keep this operation from being posted in the final g-code program as well as omit it from any Backplotting or Verification.

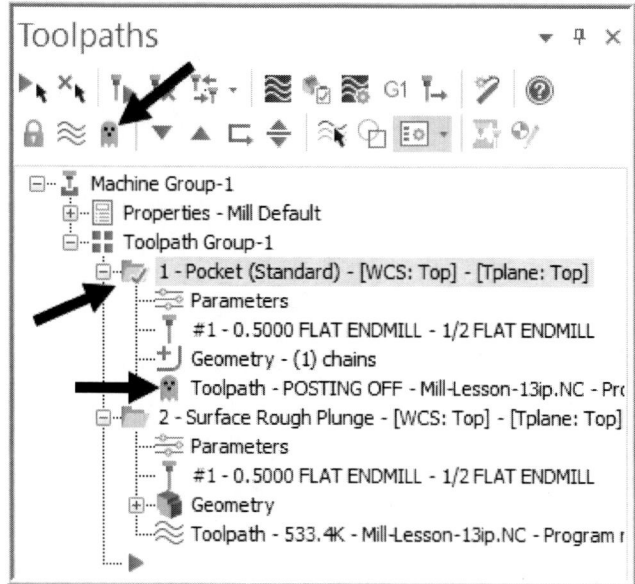

28. Select both operations and click **verify**. (NOTE: the pocket toolpath will not be simulated)
➲ Your screen should look like the image below.

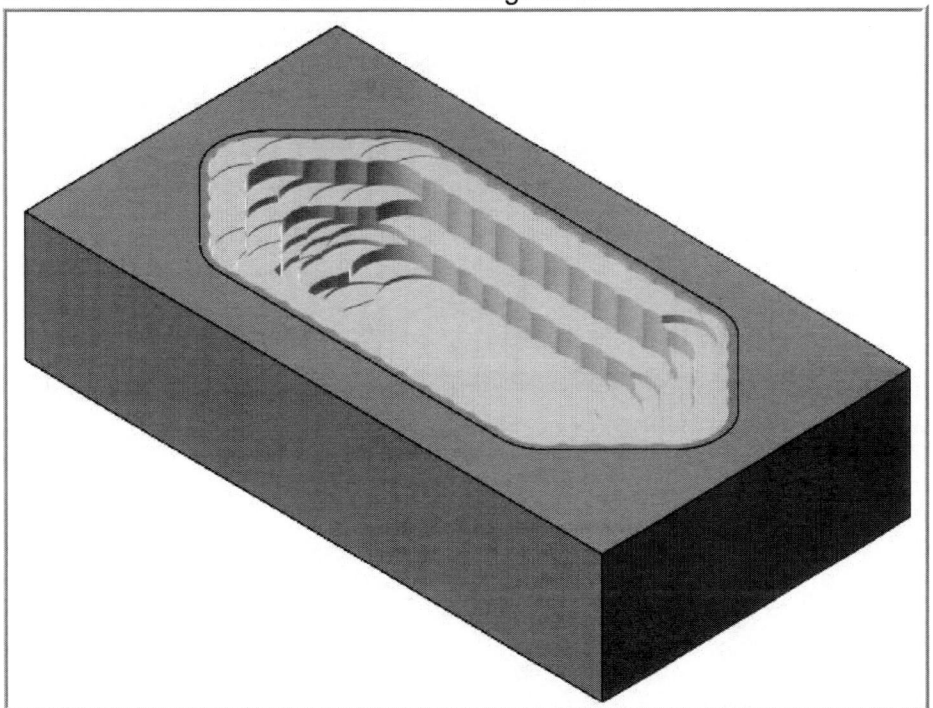

TASK 14:
FINISH USING SURFACE FINISH CONTOUR
⊃ In this task you will use a 0.375 diameter ball end mill to finish the pocket.

1. In the Toolpaths Manager pick all the operations by picking the **Select all operations** icon
    and then select the **Toggle toolpath display on selected operations** to **hide** the toolpaths.

2. On the **Toolpaths** tab click on the **Expand gallery** down arrow menu in the **3D** toolpath
    section and select **Contour** in the **Finishing** section.

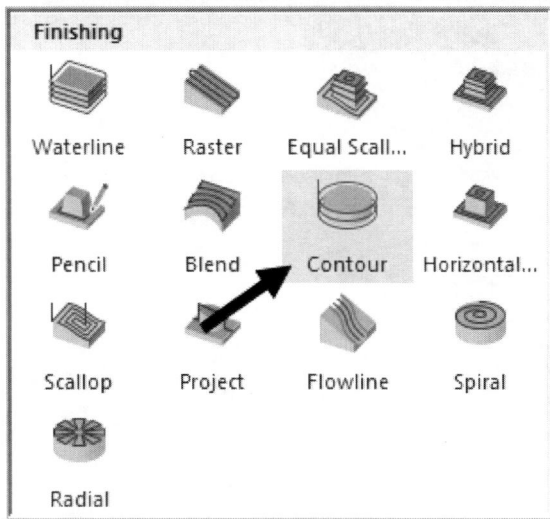

3. To satisfy the prompt, **triple left click** on a solid face. This will select the entire solid body.
4. To move onto the next step, you now need to pick the **End Selection** icon.
5. Click on the **Containment** button on the **Toolpath/surface selection** dialog box.
6. Select the line shown below to chain the top of the pocket.

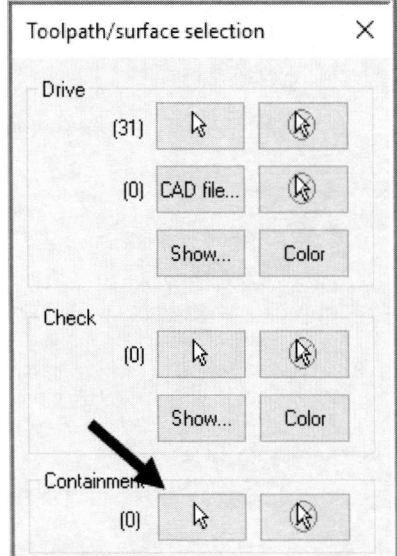

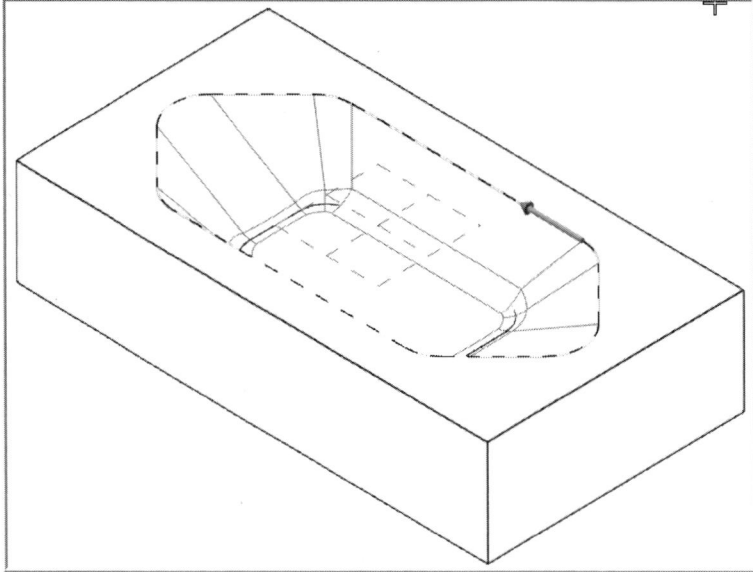

7. Select the OK button 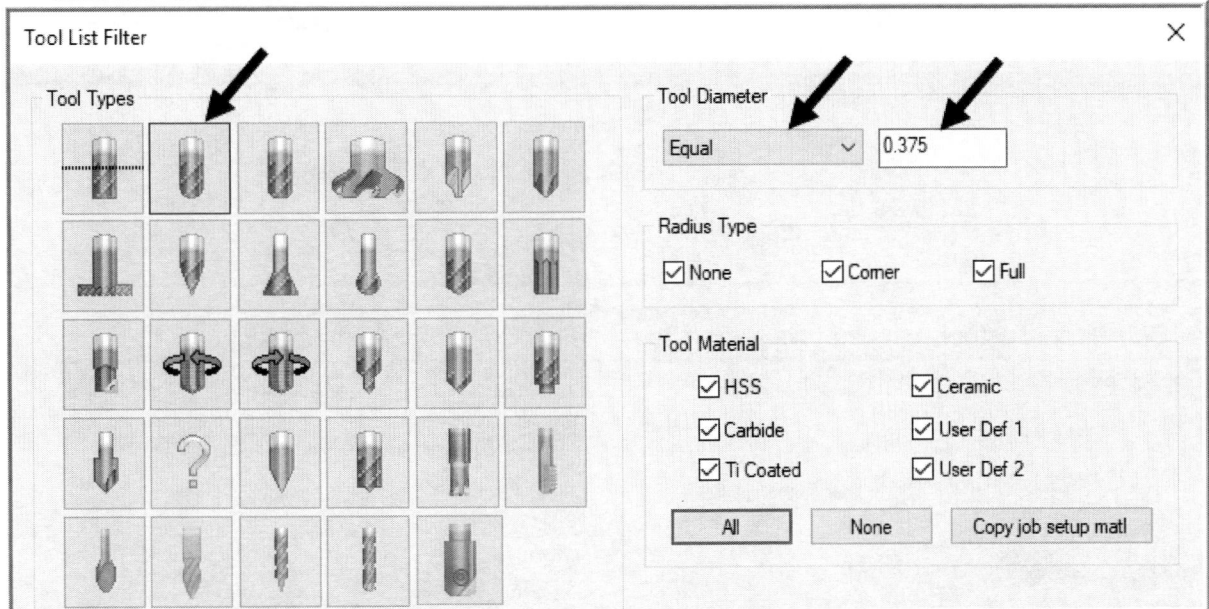 to exit the chaining dialog box.
8. Select the OK icon in the **Toolpath/surface selection** dialog box.
9. In the lower left corner of the **Toolpath parameters** page select the **Select library tool...** button.
10. Use the **Filter** function to filter out a selection of cutters. Select the **Filter** button on the right side of the **Tool selection** dialog box.
11. Select the **None** button in the Tool Types section.
12. Click on the **Endmill2 Sphere** type icon, first row, and second icon from the left.
13. Select the drop-down arrow in the **Tool diameter** field and set it to **Equal.** Input the tool diameter as **0.375**.

14. Select the OK button to exit.
15. Select the **0.375 Ball Endmill**.

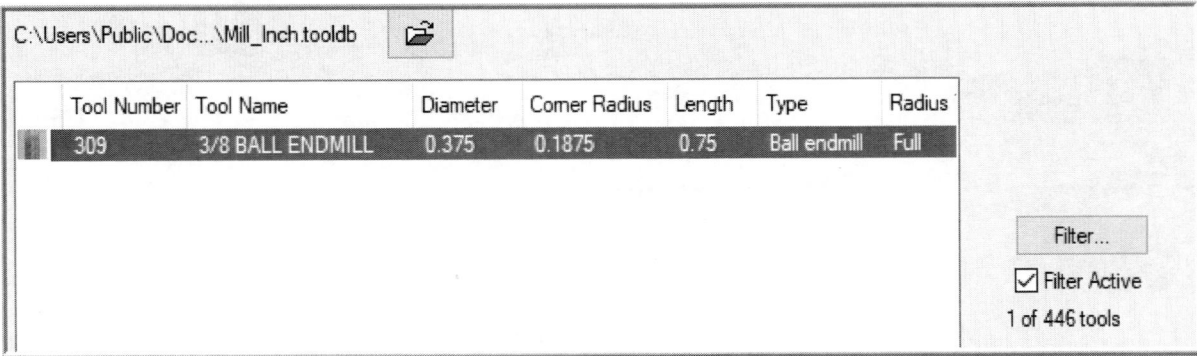

16. Select the OK button to complete the selection of this tool.

17. Make changes to the **Toolpath parameters** page as shown below. Turn **Coolant** on.

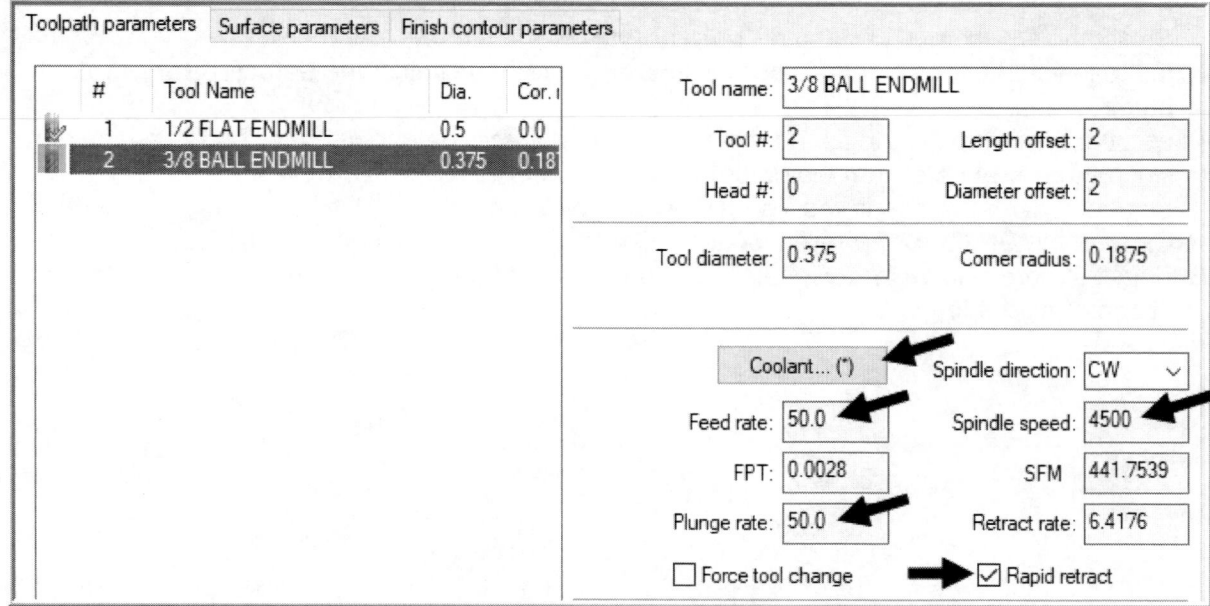

18. Select the **Surface parameters** page and make changes to this page as shown below:

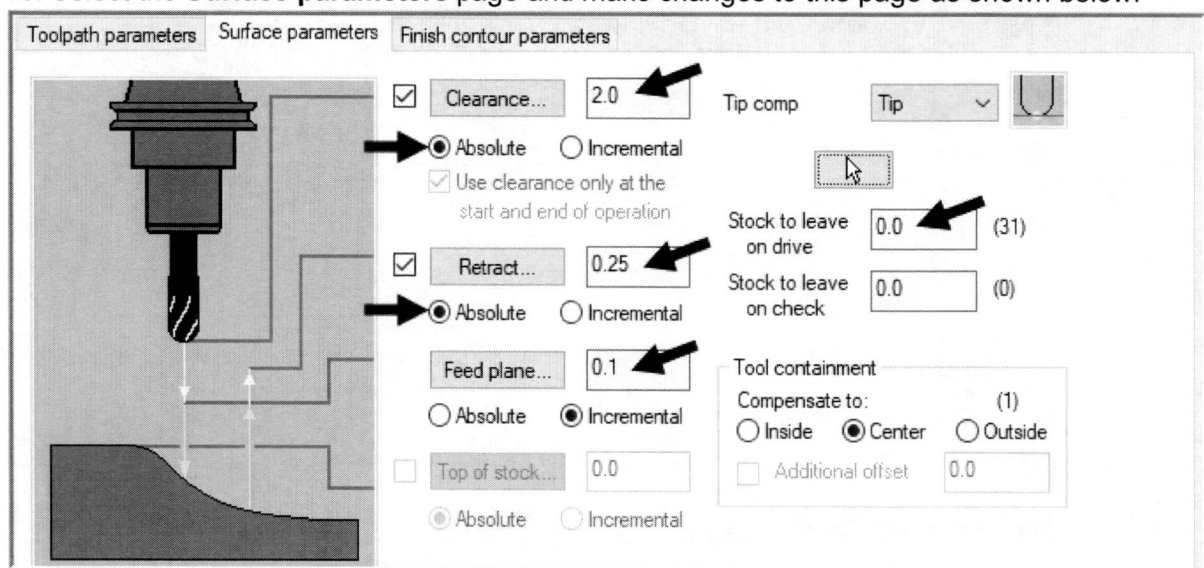

19. Next on the **Finish contour parameters** page make changes to this page as shown below:

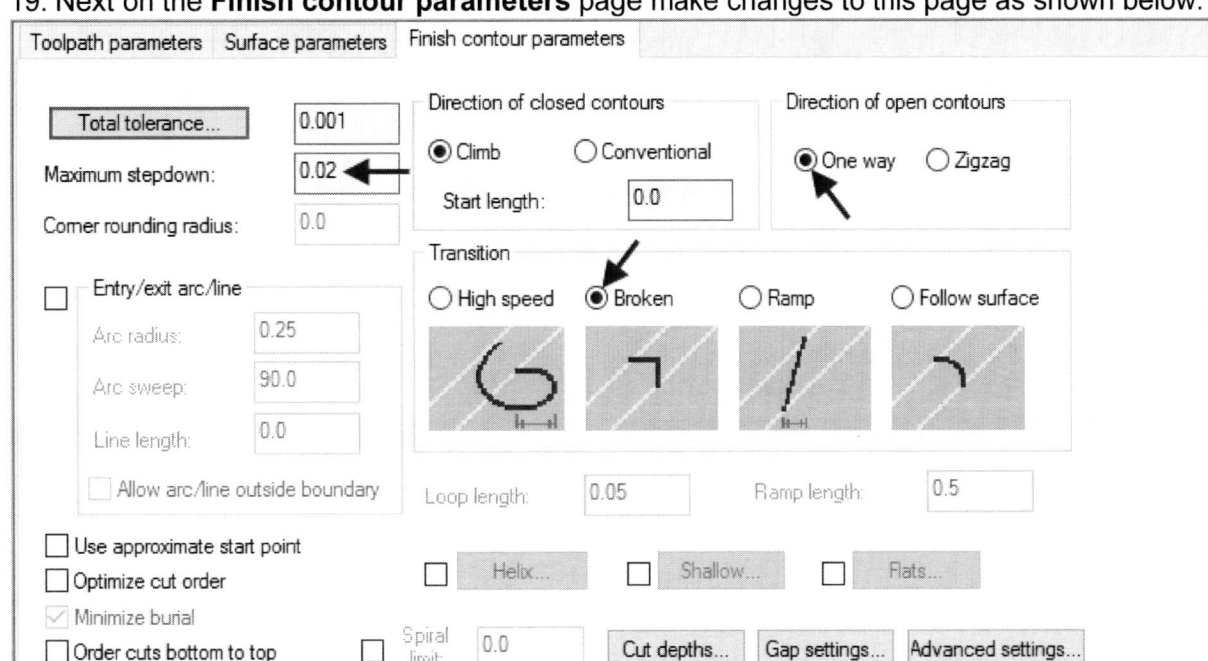

20. Select the **OK** button 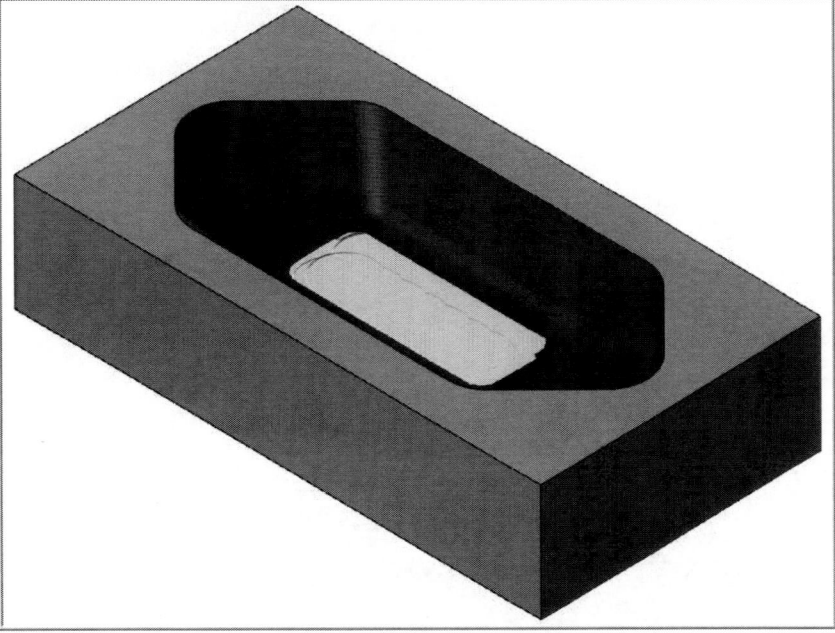 to exit Surface Finish Contour parameters.
21. **Verify** all toolpaths.
⊃ Your screen should look like the image below.

This last toolpath did not machine the bottom surface of the pocket.

Rough and Finish contour toolpaths make multiple cuts using constant Z steps. Rough and finish contour can be used for parts with steep bosses.

To finish machine the bottom surface you will use **Surface finish shallow toolpath**.

TASK 15:
FINISH BOTTOM SURFACE USING FINISH SHALLOW TOOLPATH
⊃ A finish shallow toolpath removes material from surfaces that fall between two slope angles.
⊃ In this task you will use a 0.375 diameter ball end mill to finish the bottom of the pocket.

1. In the Toolpaths Manager pick all the operations by picking the **Select all operations** icon and then select the Toggle toolpath display on selected operations **twice** to hide the toolpaths.

2. Right mouse click in the white space of the Toolpaths Manager and select:
Mill toolpaths>Surface finish>Shallow.

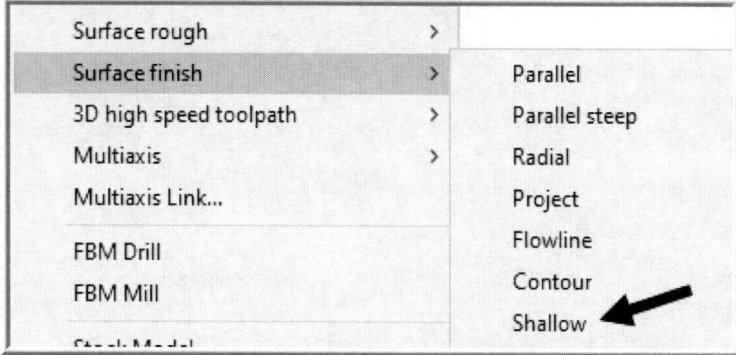

3. To satisfy the prompt, triple left click on a solid face. This will select the entire solid body.

4. To move onto the next step, you now need to pick the **End Selection** icon ⊘.
5. Click on the **Containment** button on the **Toolpath/surface selection** dialog box.
6. Select the line shown below to chain the top of the pocket.

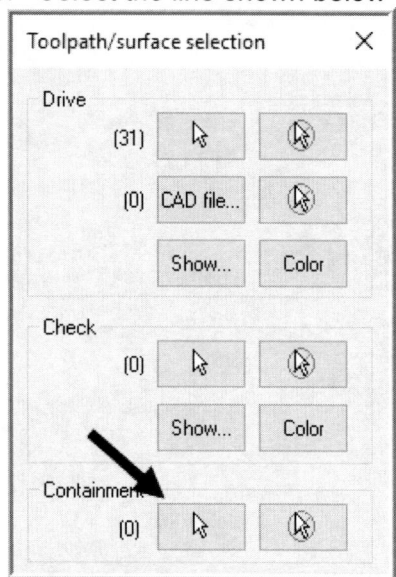

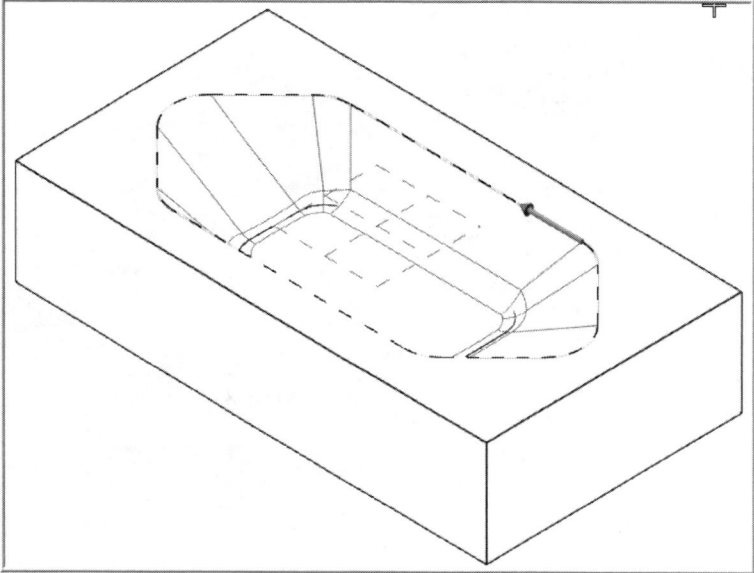

7. Select the OK button ☑ to exit the chaining dialog box.
8. Select the OK icon ☑ in the **Toolpath/surface selection** dialog box.

9. Select the **0.375 ball end mill** on the **Toolpath parameters** page.
10. Make changes to the **Toolpath parameters** page as shown below. **Coolant** flood is On.

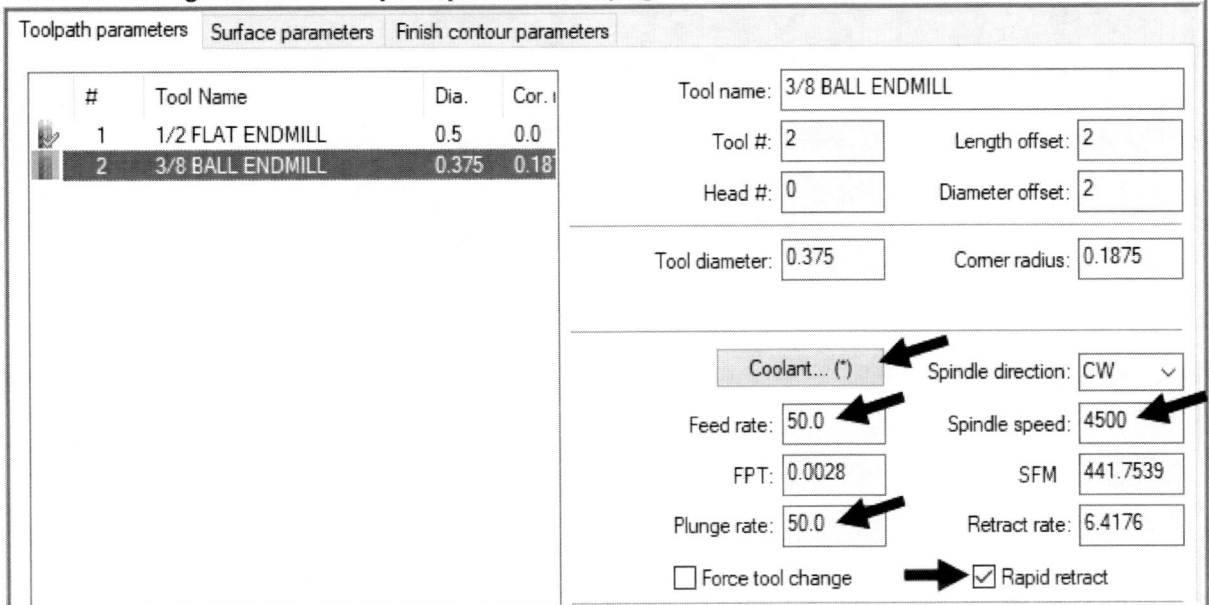

11. Select the **Surface parameters** page and make changes to this page as shown below:
Change the **Tool Containment** to Inside.

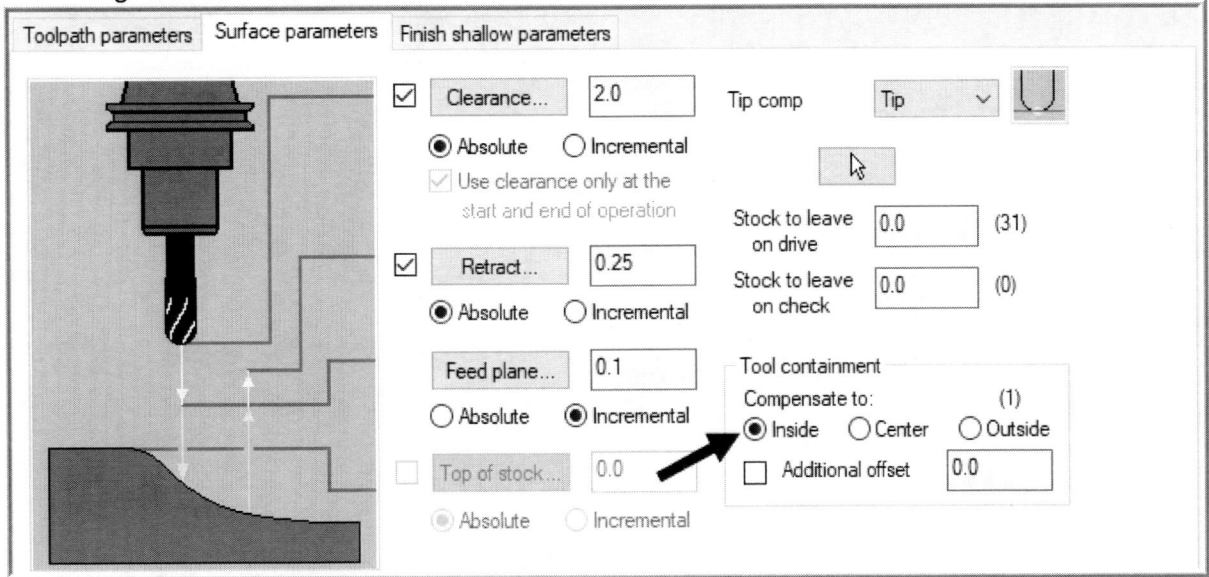

12. Next on the **Finish shallow parameters** page make changes to this page as shown below:

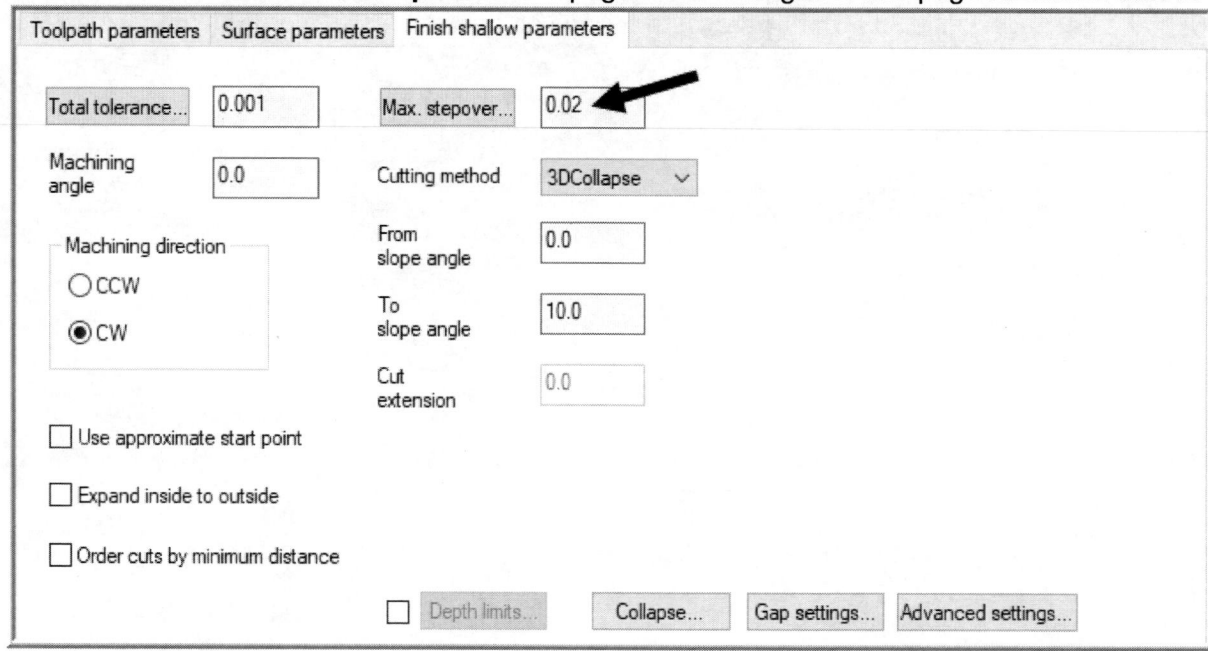

13. Select the OK button ☑ to exit Finish shallow parameters.

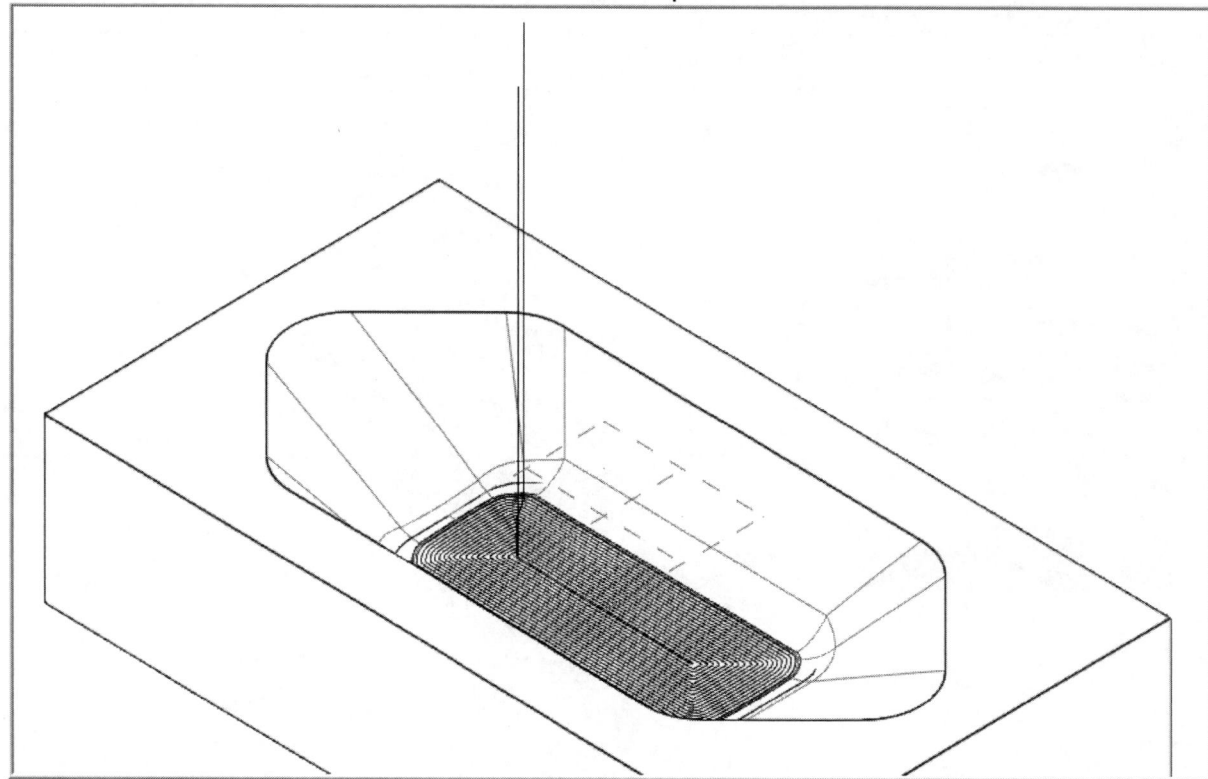

TASK 16:
VERIFY THE TOOLPATH

1. Right mouse click in the graphics area and click on **Isometric**.
2. In the **Toolpaths Manager** pick all the operations to verify by picking the **Select all operations** icon.
3. Select the **Verify selected operations** icon.
4. **Maximize** the Backplot/Verify window if required.
5. Activate the options shown below in the **Visibility** section of the **Home** tab. **Initial Stock not** activated.

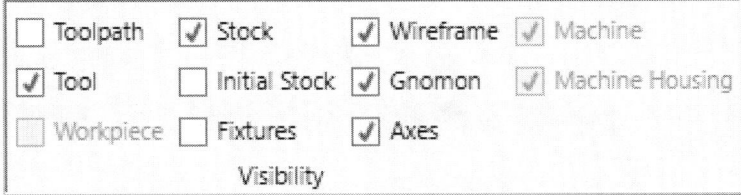

6. At the top of the screen select the **Verify** tab and activate the **Color Loop**.
7. At the top of the screen select the **View** tab, the **Isometric** icon and then select **Fit**.
8. In the lower part of the screen now set the run Speed to slow by moving the slider bar pointer over to the left as shown below.

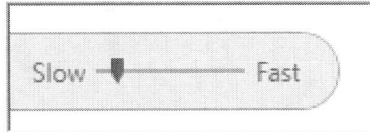

9. Now select the **Play** Simulation button to review the toolpaths.
➲ The verified toolpaths are shown below:

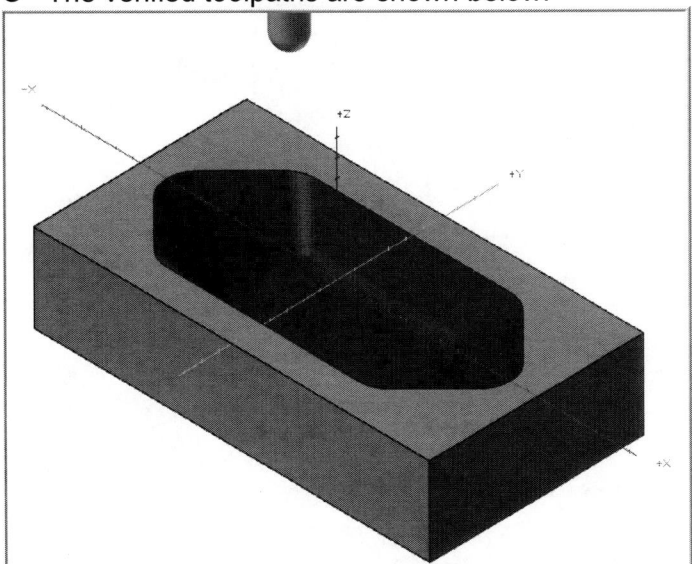

10. Select the **Close** button ☒ in the top right-hand corner to exit Verify.

SAVE THE UPDATED MASTERCAM FILE

1. Select the **Save** icon from the **Quick Access** toolbar at the top left of the screen.

TASK 17:
POST AND CREATE THE CNC CODE FILE

1. Select all the operations and then click **Post selected operations** button 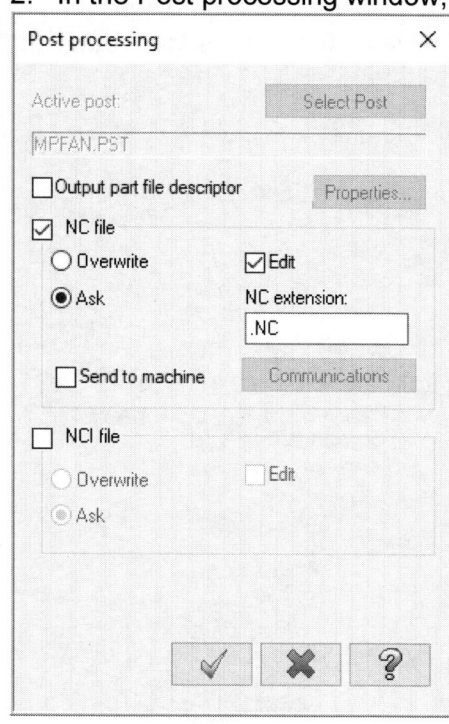 from the Toolpaths Manager.
2. In the Post processing window, make the necessary changes as shown below:

3. Select the OK button [✓] to continue.
➲ If you did not use the ghost to disable posting of op1 you will have to manually select ops 2-4. With this method when you post to gcode you are warned that **Not all operations have been selected for posting, Post all?** **Select No** so only operations 2 through 4 are posted.
4. Ensure the same name as your Mastercam part file name is in the NC File name field **Mill-Lesson-13**.
5. Select the Save button.
6. The CNC code file opens in the default editor.

```
 7   ( T1 | 1/2 FLAT ENDMILL | H1 | XY STOCK TO LEAVE - .02 | Z STOCK TO LEAVE - 0. )
 8   ( T2 | 3/8 BALL ENDMILL | H2 )
 9   N1 G20
10   N2 G0 G17 G40 G49 G80 G90
11   N3 T1 M6
12   N4 G0 G90 G54 X-.949 Y.075 A0. S45000 M3
13   N5 G43 H1 Z1. M8
14   N6 Z.14
15   N7 G1 Z-.05 F10.
16   N8 G0 Z.25
17   N9 X-1.024 Y0.
18   N10 Z.14
19   N11 G1 Z-.05 F10.
```

➲ This completes Mill-Lesson-13.

MILL-LESSON-13-EXERCISE-A

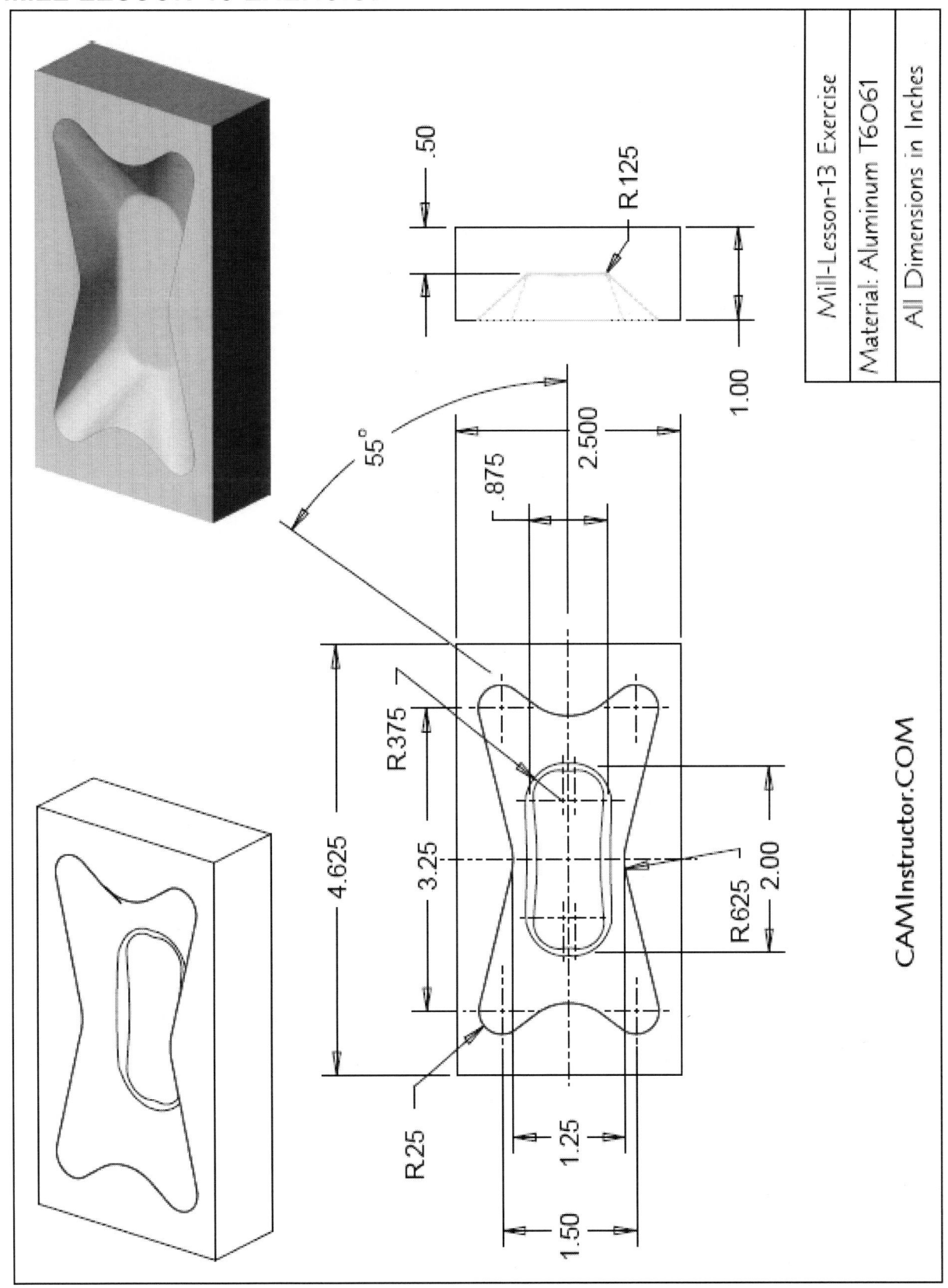

Mill-Lesson-13 Exercise

Material: Aluminum T6O61

All Dimensions in Inches

.50

R.125

1.00

55°

.875

2.500

R.375

4.625

3.25

R.625

2.00

R.25

1.25

1.50

CAMInstructor.COM

MILL-LESSON-13-EXERCISE-B

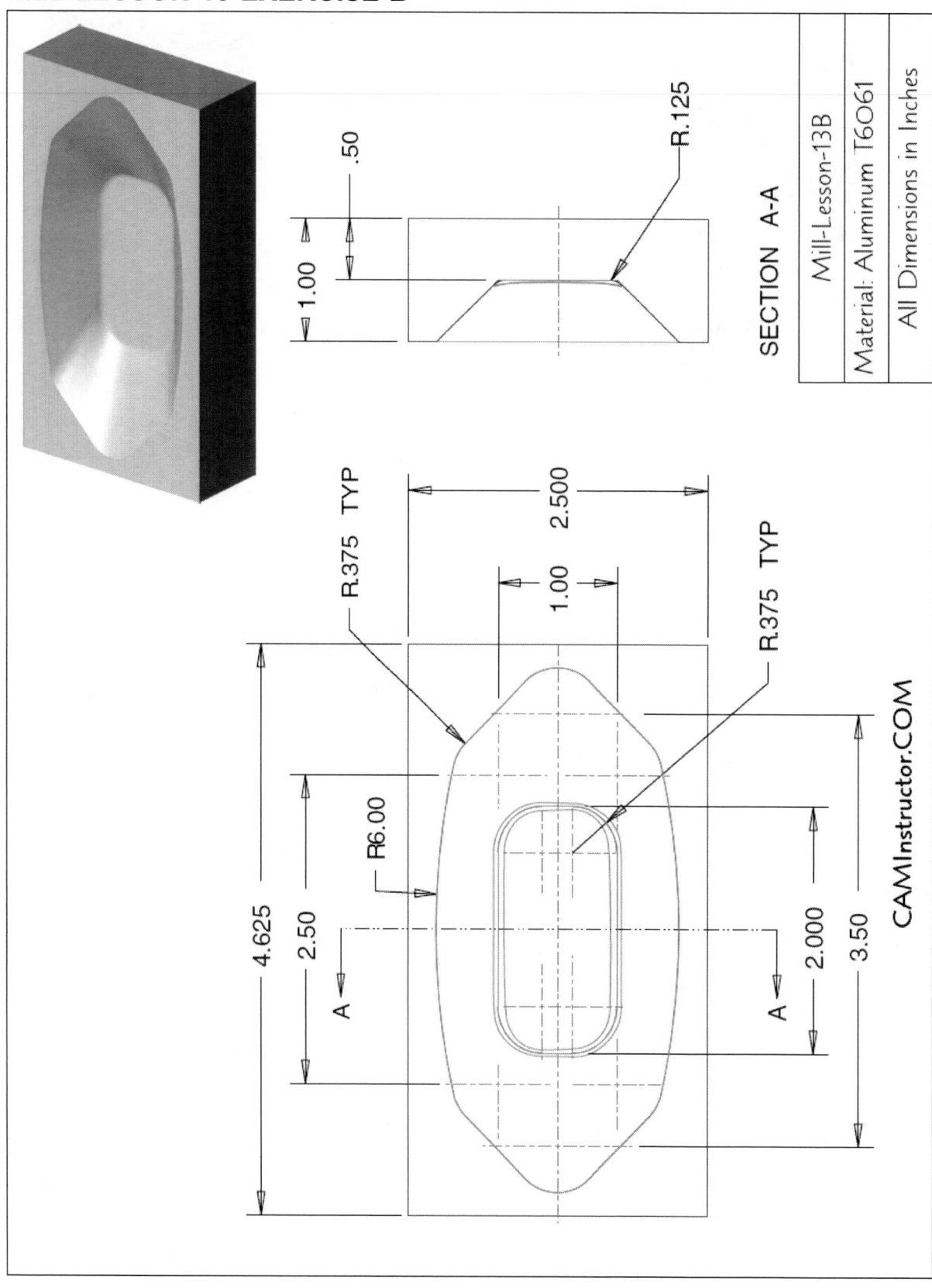

SECTION A-A

R.125

.50

1.00

Mill-Lesson-13B

Material: Aluminum T6061

All Dimensions in Inches

R.375 TYP

2.500

1.00

R.375 TYP

4.625

R6.00

2.50

A

2.000

3.50

A

CAMInstructor.COM

Mastercam 2022

TRAINING
GUIDE

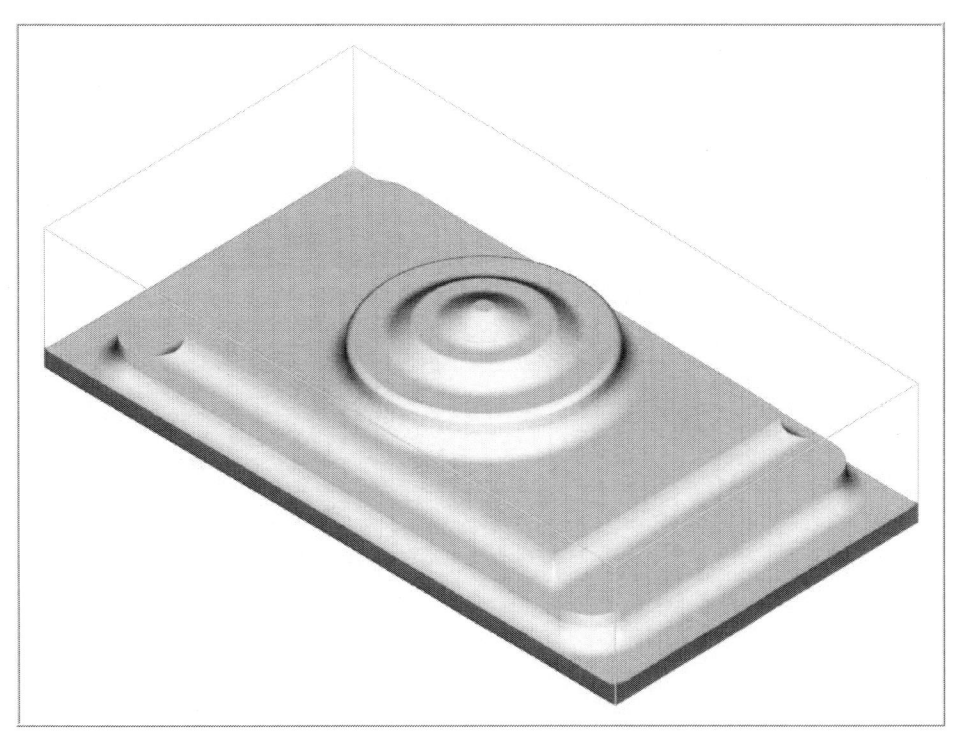

MILL-LESSON-14
ROUGH POCKET &
FINISH CONTOUR TOOLPATHS

camInstructor

Objectives

You will create the geometry for Mill-Lesson-14, and then generate the toolpaths to machine the part on a CNC vertical milling machine. This Lesson covers the following topics:

⊃ **Create a 3-dimensional drawing by:**
Creating lines.
Creating arcs.
Trimming geometry.
Analyze geometry.
Creating solid bodies.
Creating an extruded solid.
Creating a revolved solid.
Creating filleted solids.
Creating Levels.

⊃ **Establish Stock Setup settings:**
Stock size using Bounding Box.
Material for the part.
Feed calculation.

⊃ **Generate a 3-dimensional milling toolpath consisting of:**
Surface rough pocket toolpaths.
Surface finish contour toolpath.

⊃ **Inspect the toolpath using Mastercam's Verify and Backplot by:**
Launching the Verify function to machine the part on the screen.
Creating a STL file.
Generating the NC- code.

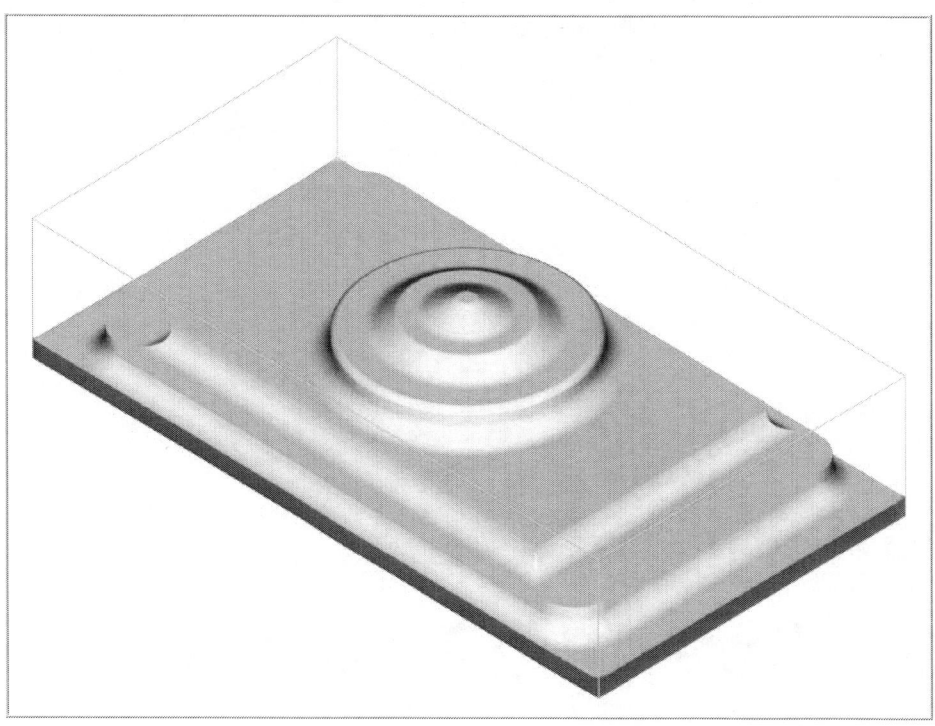

MILL-LESSON-14 DRAWING

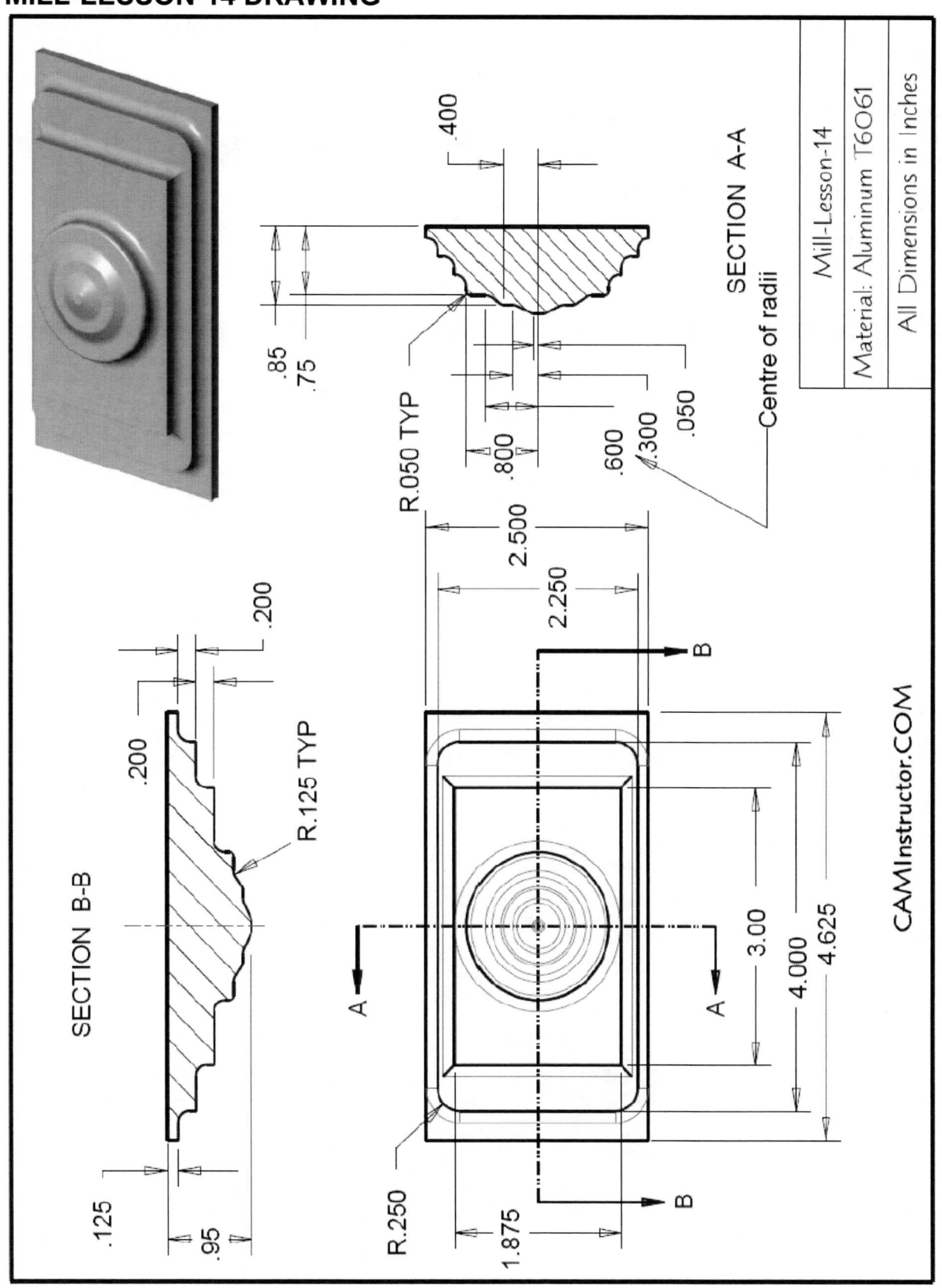

SECTION A-A

Centre of radii

R.050 TYP

.400

.85

.75

.800

.600

.300

.050

2.500

2.250

B

CAMInstructor.COM

Mill-Lesson-14

Material: Aluminum T6O61

All Dimensions in Inches

SECTION B-B

.200

.200

R.125 TYP

.125

.95

R.250

1.875

A

A

B

3.00

4.000

4.625

TOOL LIST

➲ 0.500 diameter bull end mill 0.125 corner radius to rough and finish machine.

MILL-LESSON-14 - THE PROCESS

Geometry Creation

TASK 1: Setting the environment
TASK 2: Create geometry for the solid body
TASK 3: Create geometry for the revolved solid
TASK 4: Trim geometry
TASK 5: Create the solid body
TASK 6: Create the revolved solid
TASK 7: Create fillets on the solid body
TASK 8: Hide the 2D construction entities
TASK 9: Create a box to represent the boundary of the part
TASK 10: Save the drawing

Toolpath Creation

TASK 11: Define the rough stock using stock setup
TASK 12: Rough out surface using surface Rough Pocket Toolpath
TASK 13: Verify the rough toolpath and save as an STL file
TASK 14: Finish using surface finish contour
TASK 15: Verify the toolpath
TASK 16: Save the updated Mastercam file
TASK 17: Post and create the CNC code file

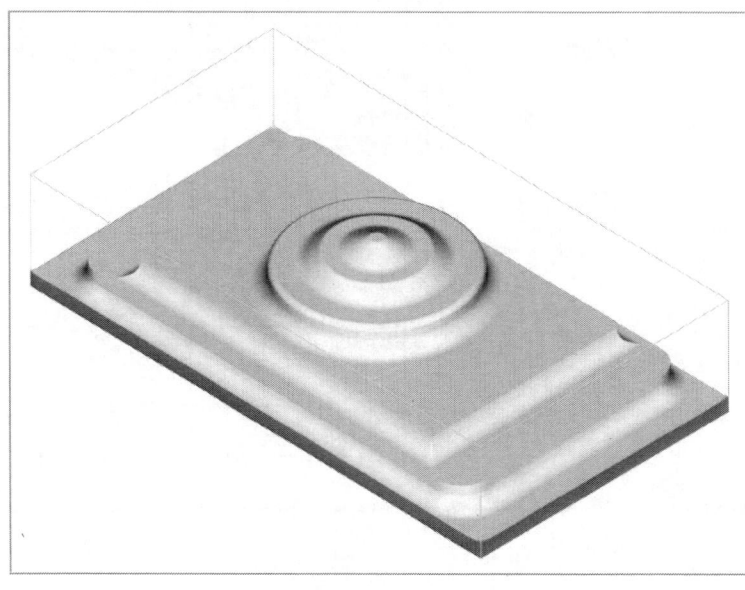

TASK 1:
SETTING THE ENVIRONMENT

Before starting the geometry creation, you should set up the grid and machine type as outlined in the **Setting the environment** section at the beginning of this text:

1. Set up the Grid. This will help identify the location of the origin.

TASK 2:
CREATE GEOMETRY FOR THE SOLID BODY
X0 Y0 CENTER OF PART Z0 BOTTOM OF PART

➲ The material has been previously machined to size: 4.625 x 2.5 x 1.0.

➲ Create bottom of part using Create Rectangle

1. Right mouse click in the graphics area and set the **Wireframe color** to **Green,** color 10, found in the Default Colors.

 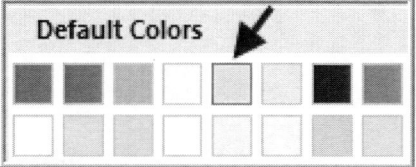

2. Select the **Wireframe** tab and in the **Shapes** section click on **Rectangle**.
3. Ensure **Anchor to center** is activated.
4. Click in the space for **Width** and enter **4.625,** hit the Enter key. In the space for **Height** type in **2.5** and hit enter.

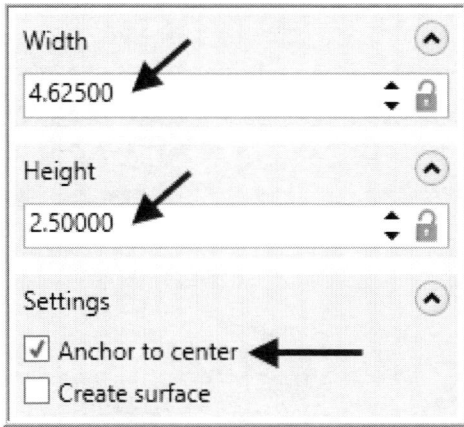

5. Move the cursor over to the graphics screen and position the cursor at the **center of the grid** and **pick the origin**.

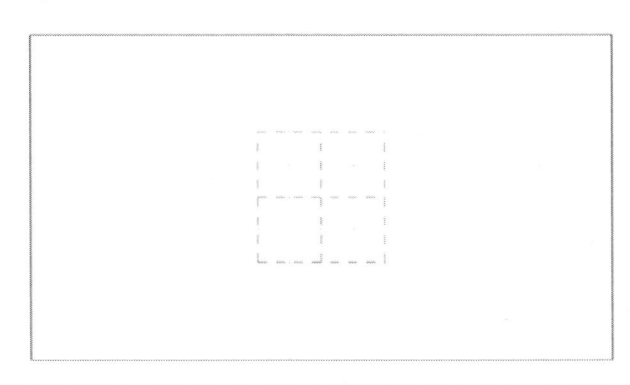

6. Click on the **OK** and **Create New Operation** icon 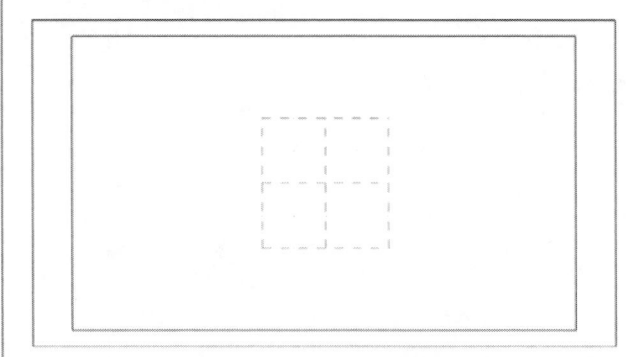.
7. Right mouse click in the graphics area and click on the **Fit** icon.
8. Click in the space for **Width** and enter **4.0**, hit the Enter key. In the space for **Height** type in **2.25** and hit enter.
9. Move the cursor over to the graphics screen and position the cursor at the **center of the grid** and **pick the origin**.

10. Click on the **OK** and **Create New Operation** icon.
11. Click in the space for **Width** and enter **3.0**, hit the Enter key. In the space for **Height** type in **1.875** and hit enter.
12. Move the cursor over to the graphics screen and position the cursor at the **center of the grid** and **pick the origin**.

13. Click on the **OK** icon to complete this feature.
➲ Your screen should look like the image below:

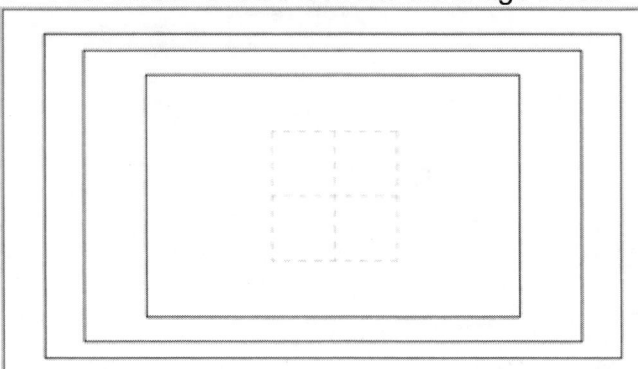

TASK 3:
CREATE GEOMETRY FOR THE REVOLVED SOLID

➲ In this task you will create the geometry that will be used to create the revolved solid.

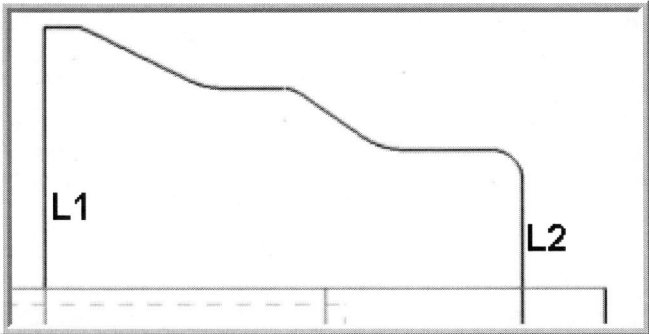

➲ **Create Line #1**

14. Select the **View tab** and click on **Toolpaths** and **Solids** in the **Managers** section to **hide** them and toggle the **Planes Manager to display**. The keyboard short cut is **ALT+L**.

15. Now open up the drop down menu in the Planes Manager for **Follow rules** 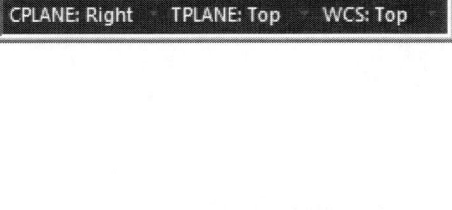 and **remove all the check marks** to cancel all the rules.

16. Right mouse click in the graphics area and click on **Isometric**.

17. Now click in the **C column (Construction Plane)** for the **Right side** plane. The view is still set to Isometric but construction of the geometry will now take place on the Right Side plane. Take note at the bottom of the screen **CPLANE: Right, TPLANE: Top, WCS: Top,** as shown below right.

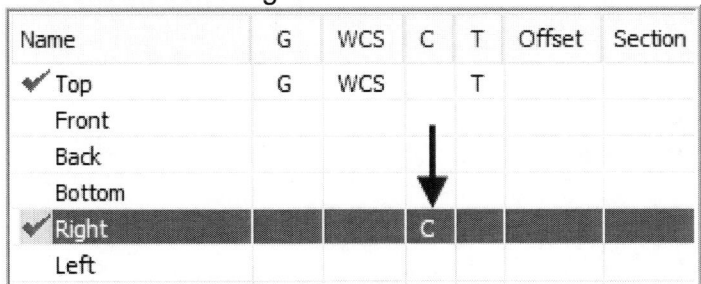

18. Select the **Wireframe** tab and in the **Lines** section click on **Line Endpoints**.

19. On the graphics screen you are prompted: **Specify the first endpoint** and the Line Endpoints panel appears. Move the cursor over to the graphics screen and position the cursor at the **center of the grid** and **pick the origin**.

20. Click in the space for **Length** and enter a value of **0.95** and then hit the Enter key. In the space for **Angle** and enter a value of **90.0** and hit enter.

21. Click on the **OK** icon to complete this feature.

⊃ **Create Line #2**

22. Select the **Wireframe** tab if required and in the **Lines** section click on **Line Parallel**.
23. On the graphics screen you are prompted: **Select a line** and the Line Parallel ribbon bar appears.
24. To satisfy the prompt **Select a line**, move the cursor over the line(1) just completed as shown below and select it.

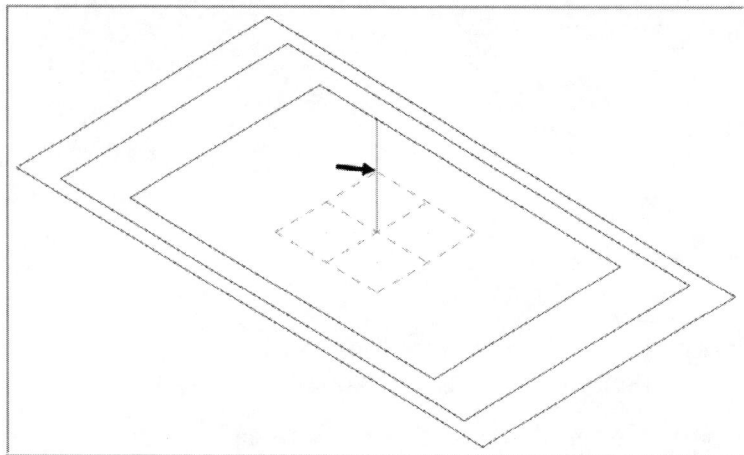

25. To satisfy the next prompt **Select the point to place a parallel line through** move the cursor to the right of the line and pick a point.
26. For the Offset **Distance** input **0.8** then hit **enter** as shown below:

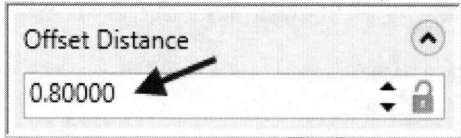

27. Click on the **OK** icon 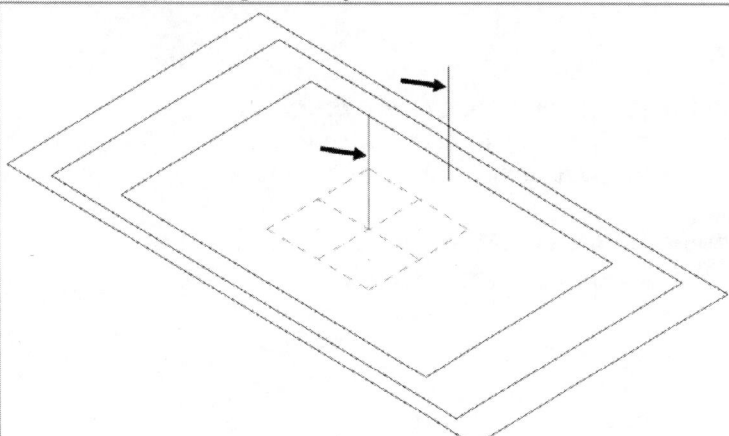 to complete this feature.

⊃ The completed geometry is shown below:

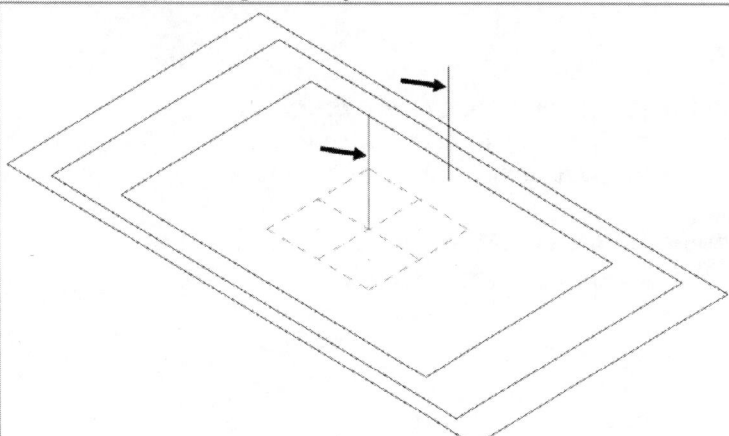

➲ **Create Circle #1 - 0.050 radius**

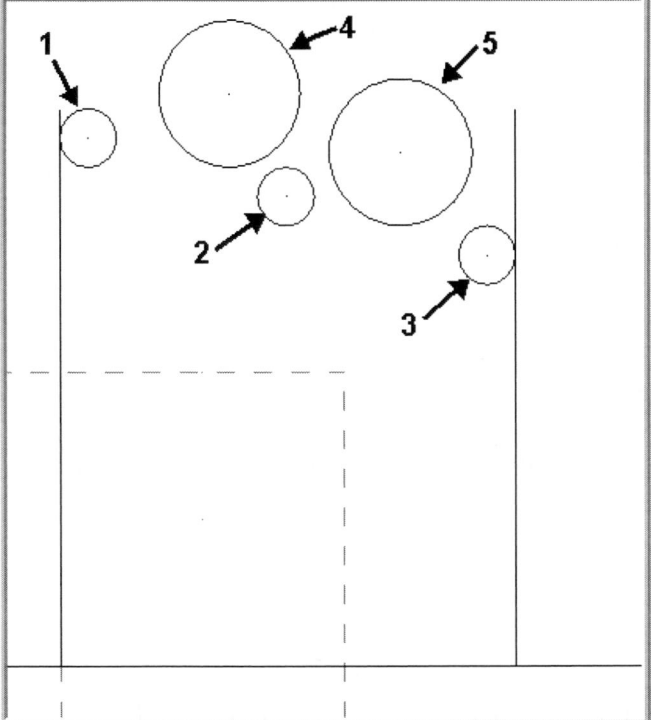

28. Right mouse click in the graphics area and click on **Right (WCS)**.

29. Right mouse click in the graphics area and click on the **Fit** icon ⊞.

30. Select the **Wireframe** tab if required and in the **Arcs** section select **Circle Center Point**.

31. Enter a value of **0.05** for the **radius**. Click on the **Lock** icon 🔓 to **"freeze"** 🔒 this radius value

32. To satisfy the prompt **Enter the center point** click the middle mouse button and then hit the spacebar on your keyboard.

33. The **Fastpoint** box now opens. Input **0.050,0.950-0.050** and hit the Enter key.

0.05,0.95-0.05

34. Click on the **OK** and **Create New Operation** icon 🔘.

➲ **Create Circle #2 - 0.050 radius**

35. To satisfy the prompt **Enter the center point** click the middle mouse button and then hit the spacebar on your keyboard, **type in 0.4,0.850-0.050** for the center of the circle. Now hit **Enter**.

36. Click on the **OK** and **Create New Operation** icon 🔘.

➲ **Create Circle #3 - 0.050 radius**

37. To satisfy the prompt **Enter the center point** click the middle mouse button and then hit the spacebar on your keyboard, **type in 0.8-0.050, 0.750-0.050** for the center of the circle. Now hit **Enter**.

38. Click on the **OK** and **Create New Operation** icon 🔘.

⊃ **Create Circle #4- 0.125 radius**

39. Click on the **Lock** icon 🔓 to **"un-freeze"** 🔒 this radius value

40. Now click in the space for **radius** and enter a value of **0.125**. Click on the **Lock** icon 🔓 to **"freeze"** 🔒 this radius value.

41. To satisfy the prompt **Enter the center point** click the middle mouse button and then hit the spacebar on your keyboard.

42. The **Fastpoint** box now opens. Input **0.3,0.85+0.125** for the center of the circle. Now hit **Enter**.

43. Click on the **OK** and **Create New Operation** icon 🔘.

⊃ **Create Circle #5- 0.125 radius**

44. To satisfy the prompt Enter the center point click the middle mouse button and then hit the spacebar on your keyboard, **type in 0.6,0.75+0.125** for the center of the circle. Now hit **Enter.**

45. Click on the **OK** icon ✅ to complete this feature.

⊃ **Create Line #3**

46. Select the **Wireframe** tab if required and in the **Lines** section click on **Line Endpoints**.

47. **Ensure** that the **Tangent** function is **activated**.

48. To satisfy the prompt **Specify the first endpoint** move the cursor over the endpoint of the line shown below: When the visual cue for Endpoint 🔖 is displayed click on this point. **Zoom** as required.

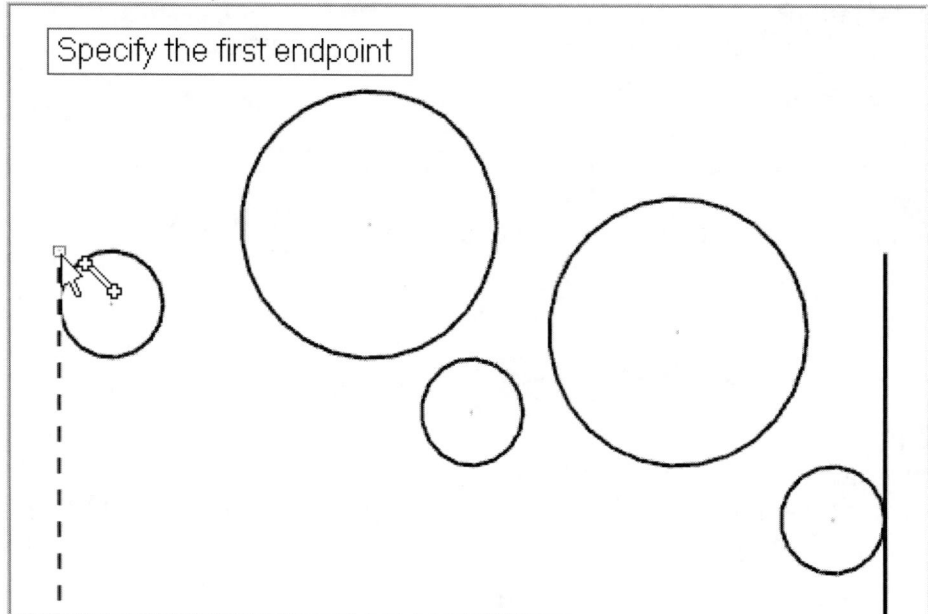

Specify the first endpoint

49. To satisfy the prompt **Specify the second endpoint** move the cursor over the area of the circle shown below: When no visual que appears but the circle is highlighted, click on this point as shown below, this will create the line **tangent to the circle.**

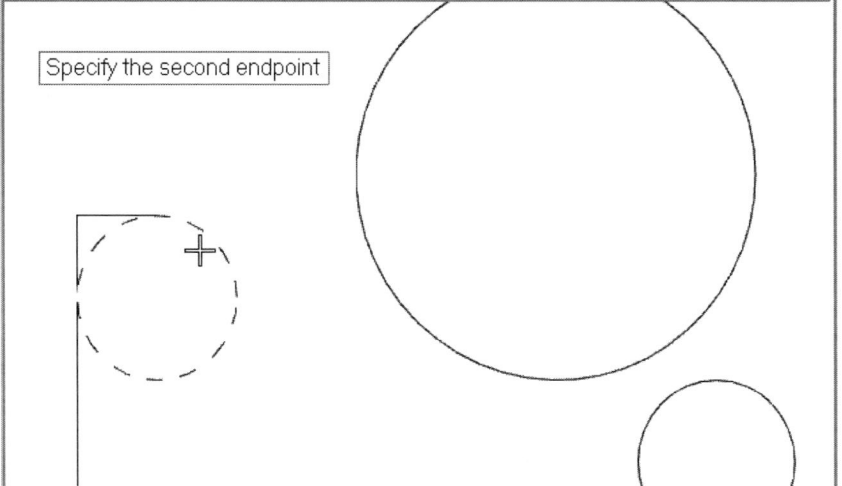

Specify the second endpoint

⊃ **Create Line #4**

50. To satisfy the prompt **Specify the first endpoint** move the cursor over the area of the circle shown below **1**. Ensure there is **no visual cue** being displayed and click on this point. As **Tangent** is activated on the line ribbon bar the line will snap to the closest tangency point on the circle as shown below.

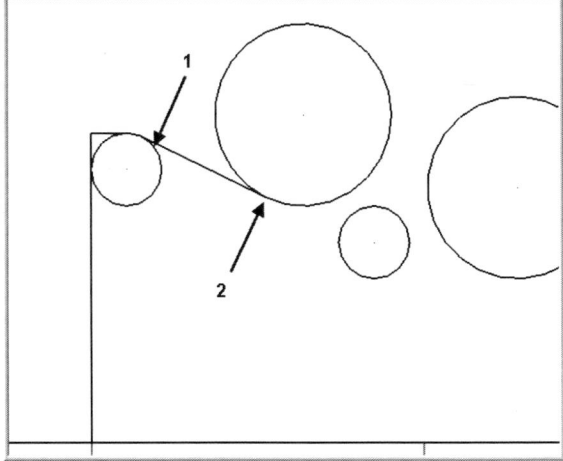

51. To satisfy the prompt **Specify the second endpoint** move the cursor over the area of the circle shown above **2**. Ensure there is **no visual cue** being displayed and click on this point. As **Tangent** is activated on the line ribbon bar the line will snap to the closest tangency point on the circle.

⊃ **Create Line #5**

52. To satisfy the prompt **Specify the first endpoint** move the cursor over the area of the circle shown below **1**. No visual cue should appear, this allows selection of the entire circle to create the line tangent from it.

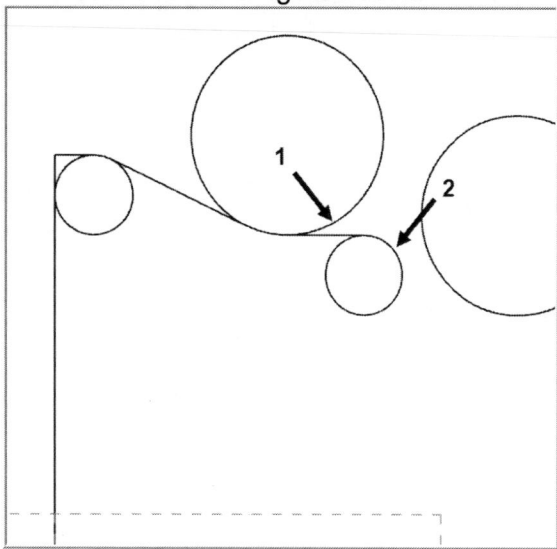

53. To satisfy the prompt **Specify the second endpoint** move the cursor over the area of the circle shown above **2**. Again, no visual cue should appear. This connects the previous tangent line to this arc tangent. The result is a horizontal line in this case.

54. To satisfy the prompt **Specify the first endpoint** move the cursor over the area of the circle shown below **1**: Ensure there is **no visual cue** being displayed and click on this point. As **Tangent** is activated on the line ribbon bar the line will snap to the closes tangency point on the circle.

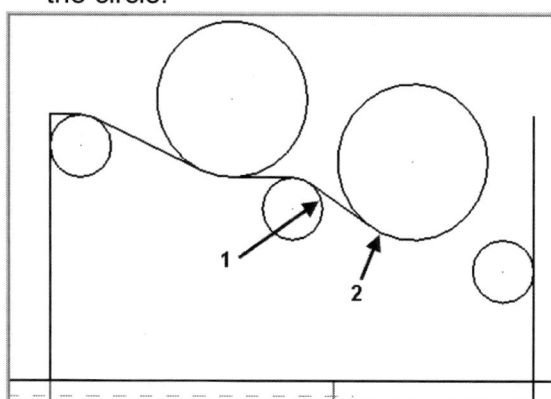

55. To satisfy the prompt **Specify the second endpoint** move the cursor over the area of the circle shown above 2. Ensure there is **no visual cue** being displayed and click on this point. As **Tangent** is activated on the line ribbon bar the line will snap to the closest tangency point on the circle as shown below above:

⮑ **Create Line #6**

56. To satisfy the prompt **Specify the first endpoint** move the cursor over the area of the circle shown below **1**: No visual cue should appear. If the line does not extend correctly when moving to the next selection point, you may need to try moving your mouse around to get the correct tangent extension.

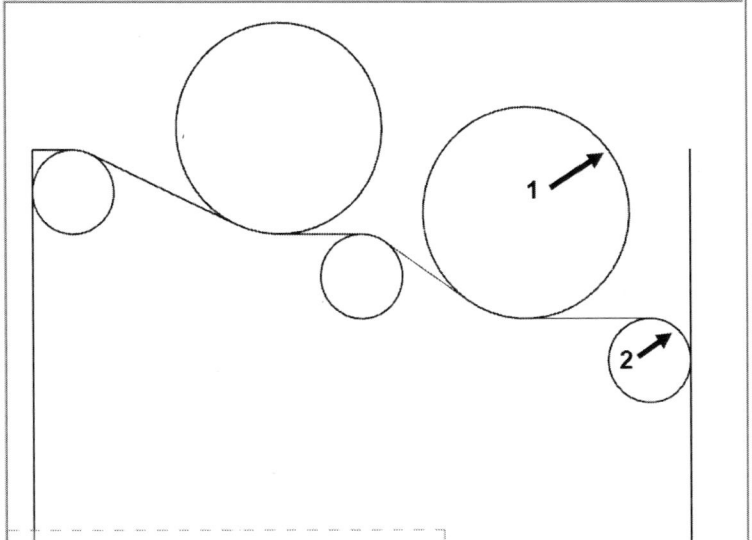

57. To satisfy the prompt **Specify the second endpoint** move the cursor over the area of the circle shown above **2**: Again, no visual cue should show.

58. Click on the **OK** icon to complete this feature.

TASK 4:
TRIM GEOMETRY

➲ In this task you will trim the geometry used to create the revolved surface using **Divide / Delete**. There are many ways to accomplish this trimming operation, this is just one method. If you do make a mistake using **Divide / Delete** don't forget the **Undo** button is just one click away.

➲ **Trim the circles.**
1. In the **Wireframe** tab click on **Divide** in the **Modify** section.
2. The prompt changes to **Select the curve to divide / delete.** Move the cursor over the various entities and select in order and position as shown below: The arc is trimmed back to the two closest intersections. **Note:** On some of the circles you will need to select them more than once to completely trim them.

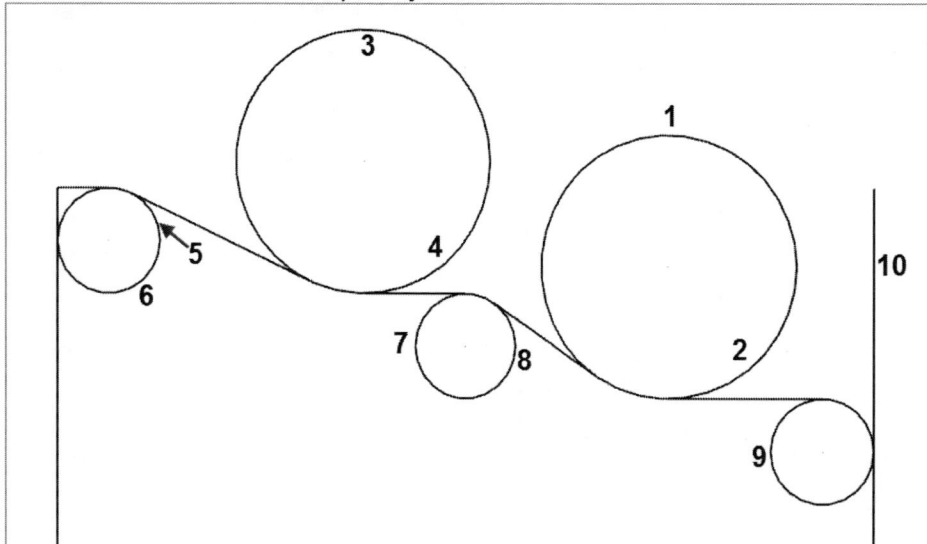

3. Click on the **OK** icon ![icon] to complete this feature.

➲ The completed geometry is shown below:

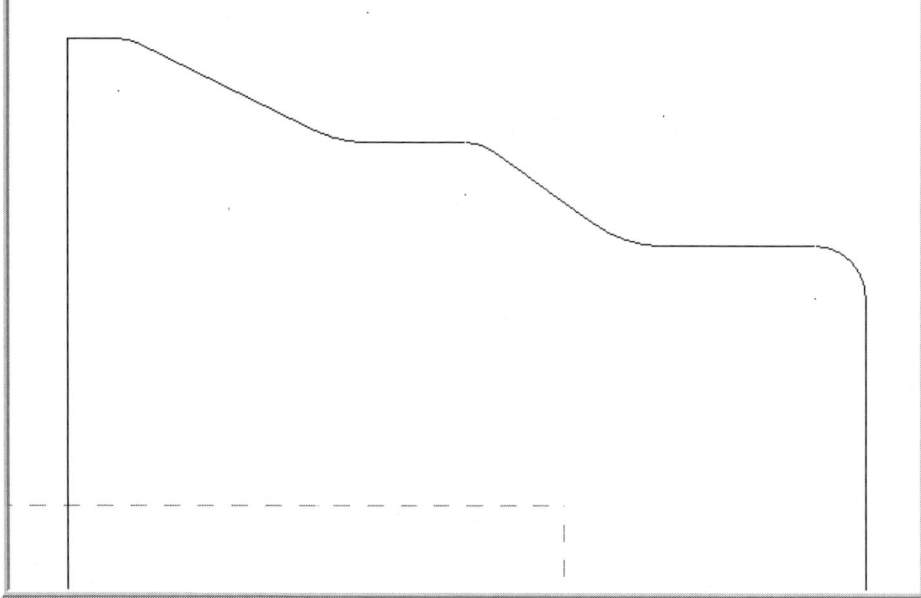

➲ Now you will use **Analyze Entity Properties** to change the endpoints of the right-hand line.

4. Click on the **Home** tab and select **Analyze Entity**.
5. Select the right hand line as shown below and the **Line Properties** dialog box appears. Change the **Y value of 0** to **0.525** as shown below:

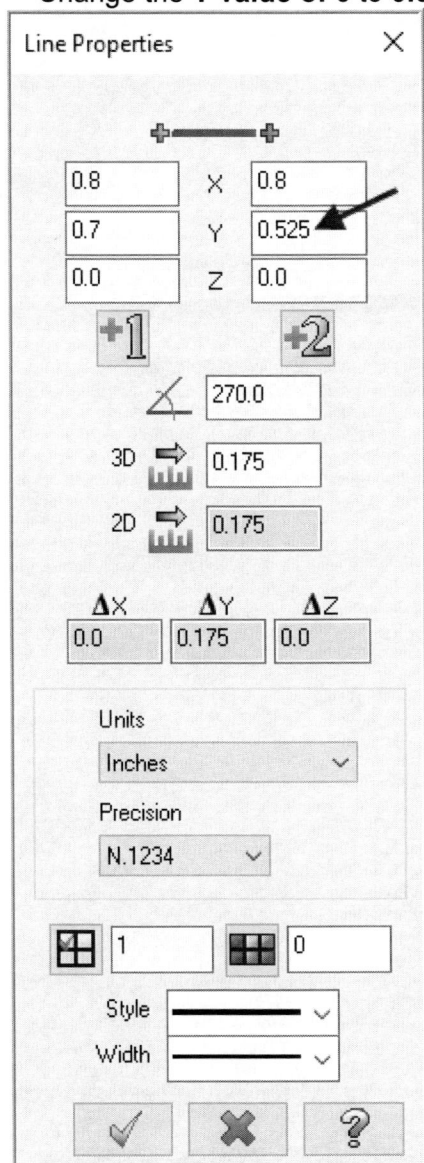

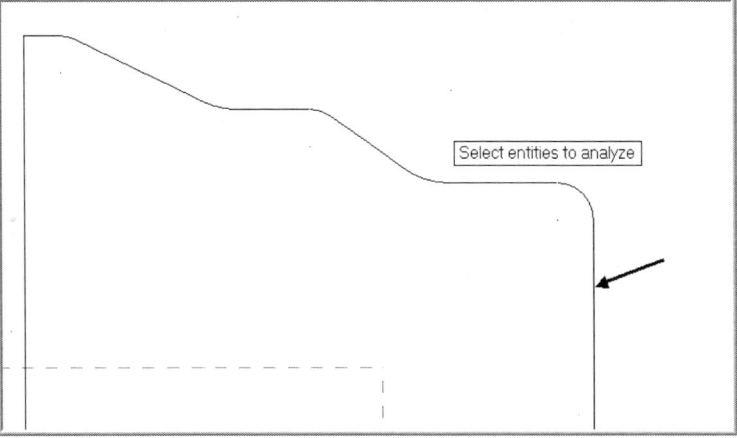

Use this dialog box to view and edit line entity properties, including the length, angle between endpoints, and endpoint positions (XYZ coordinates).

You can also edit the level, color, and point style entity attributes.

6. Click on the OK icon to complete this feature.

7. On the **Home** tab select **Analyze Entity**.
8. Select the left hand line as shown below and the **Line Properties** dialog box appears. Change the **Y value of 0** to **0.525** as shown below:

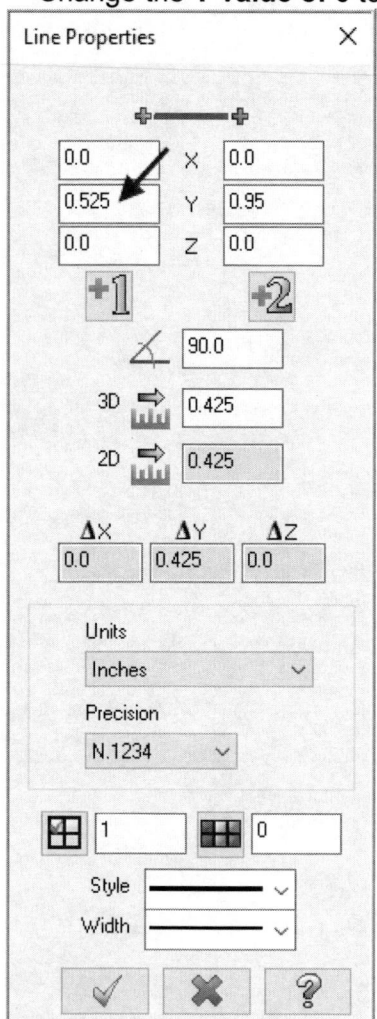

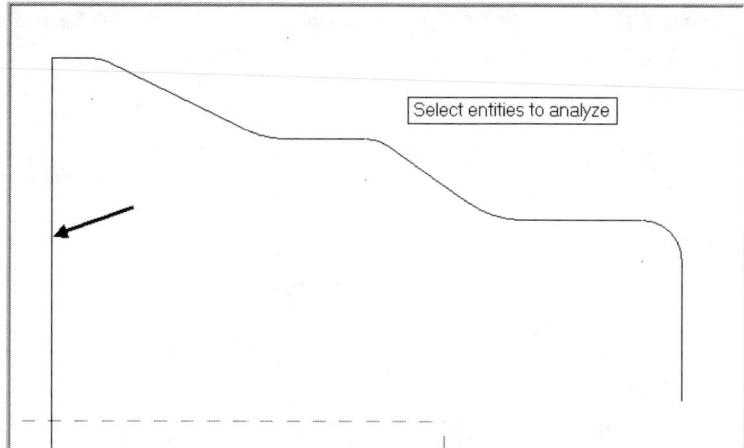

9. Click on the OK icon 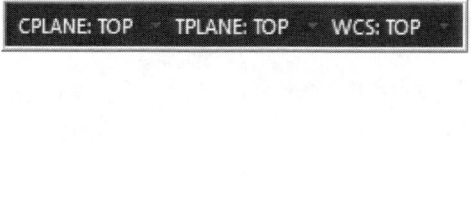 to complete this feature.
10. Right mouse click in the graphics area and click on **Isometric**.
11. In the **Planes Manager** click in the **C column (Construction Plane)** for **Top**. Take note at the bottom of the screen **CPLANE:TOP TPLANE:TOP WCS:TOP** as shown below right.

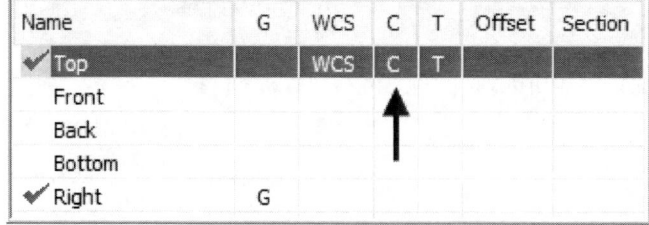

12. **Close** the **Planes Manager**.

13. Right mouse click in the graphics area and click on the **Fit** icon ⊞.

⊃ **Create Line to close Geometry**

14. Select the **Wireframe** tab and in the **Lines** section click on **Line Endpoints**.
15. On the graphics screen you are prompted: **Specify the first endpoint** and the Line ribbon bar appears.
16. To satisfy the prompt **Specify the first endpoint** move the cursor over the endpoint of line **1** shown below: When the visual cue for Endpoint [icon] is displayed click on point **1** as shown below:

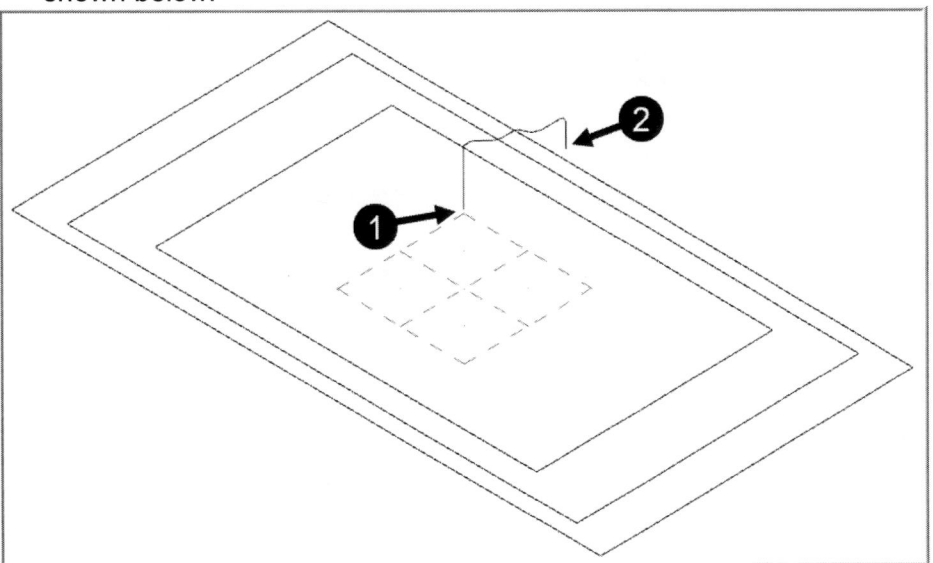

17. To satisfy the prompt **Specify the second endpoint** move the cursor over the endpoint of line 2 shown above: When the visual cue for Endpoint [icon] is displayed click on point 2 as shown above:

18. Click on the **OK** icon [icon] to complete this feature.

⊃ The completed geometry is shown below:

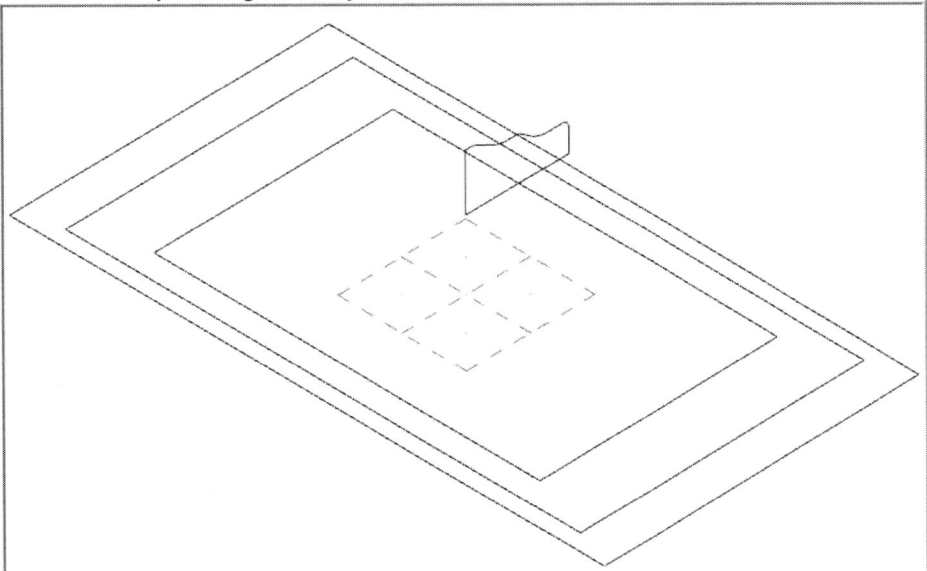

TASK 5:
CREATE THE SOLID BODY
⊃ **Create the .125 Solid Body**

1. Right mouse click in the graphics area and set the **Solids Color** to **Grey, color 7**.

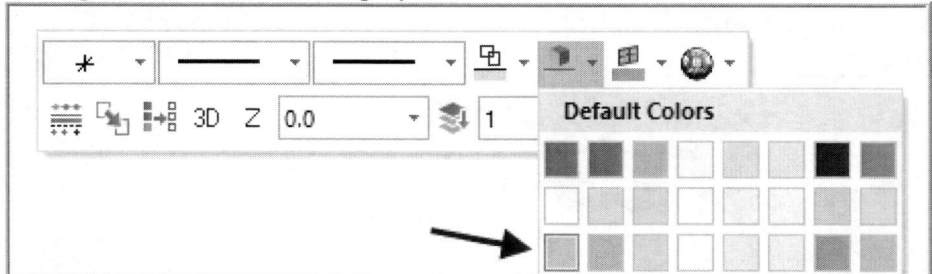

2. Select the **View tab** and click on **Levels** to **show** the **Levels Manager**. The keyboard short cut is **ALT+L**.

3. Add a **new Level** by clicking on **the plus sign** at the top of the **Levels Manager**.

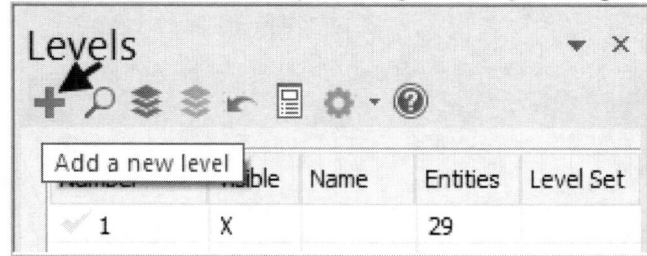

4. The **Level** is now set to **Level number 2** as shown below.

If you cannot see the Level properties click on the **level properties** icon to toggle the display.

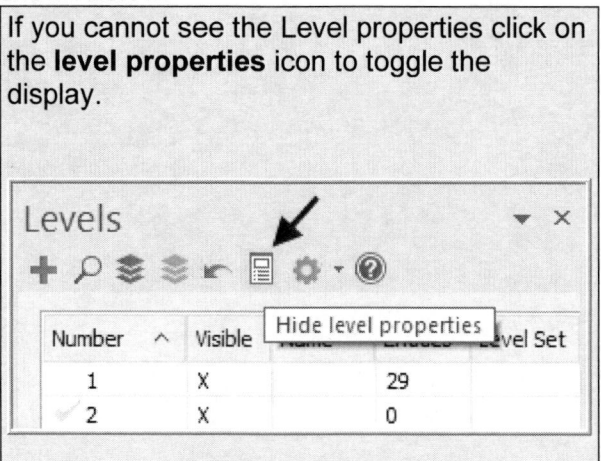

5. Click on the **Solids** tab and in the **Create** section select **Extrude**.
6. On the graphics screen you are prompted: **Select chain(s) to extrude 1.** Select the line as shown below:

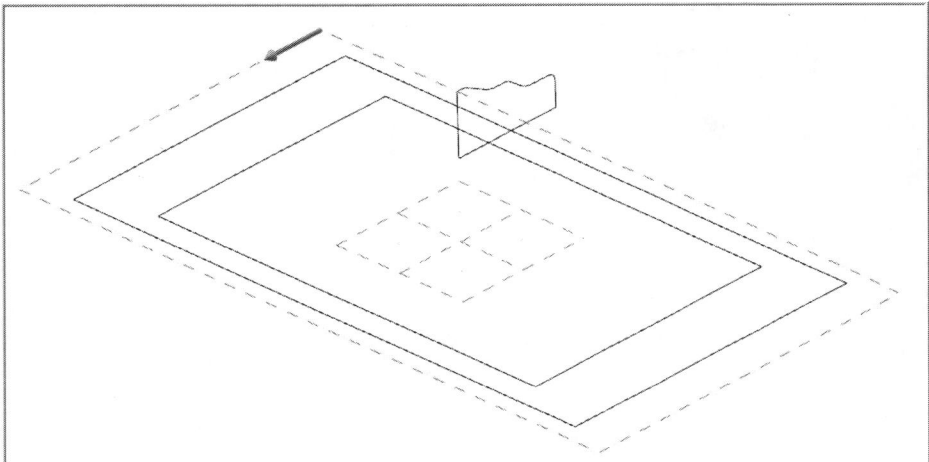

7. Click on the OK icon 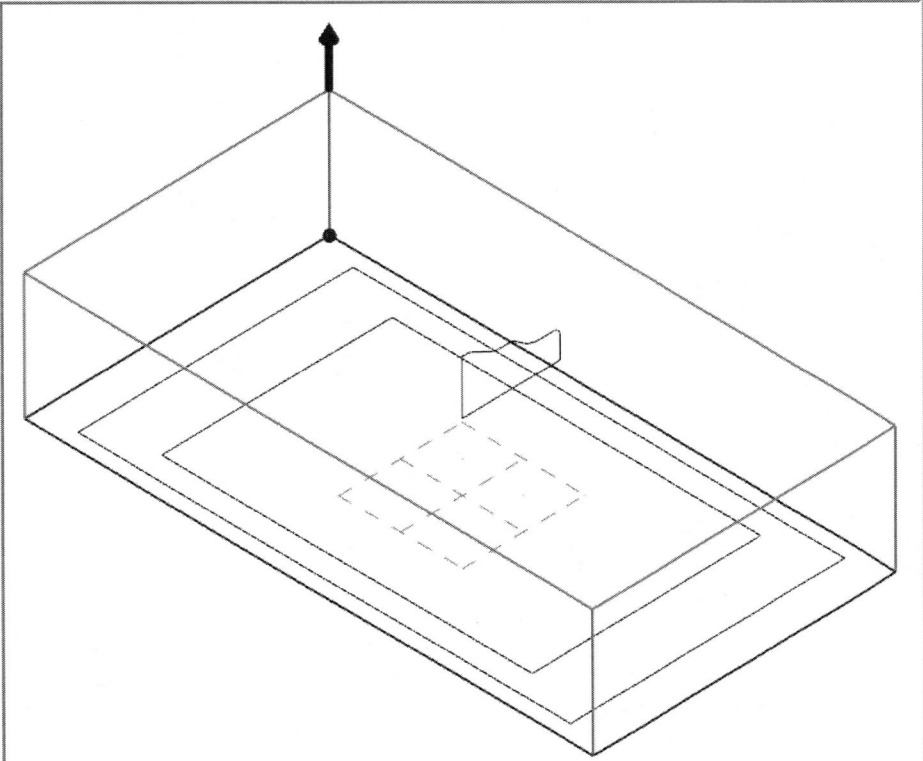 in the Chaining dialog window.
8. An arrow will appear on one of the corners of the rectangle as shown below, make sure the arrow is pointing up. If it is pointing down click on the **Reverse All** icon ↔ in the **Chains** section to change the direction so it is pointing up: **Note:** you may have to unzoom the image to see the direction the arrow is pointing.

9. Make the necessary changes as shown below in the Solid Extrude dialog window. **Distance is set to 0.125. Both directions option is deactivated**.

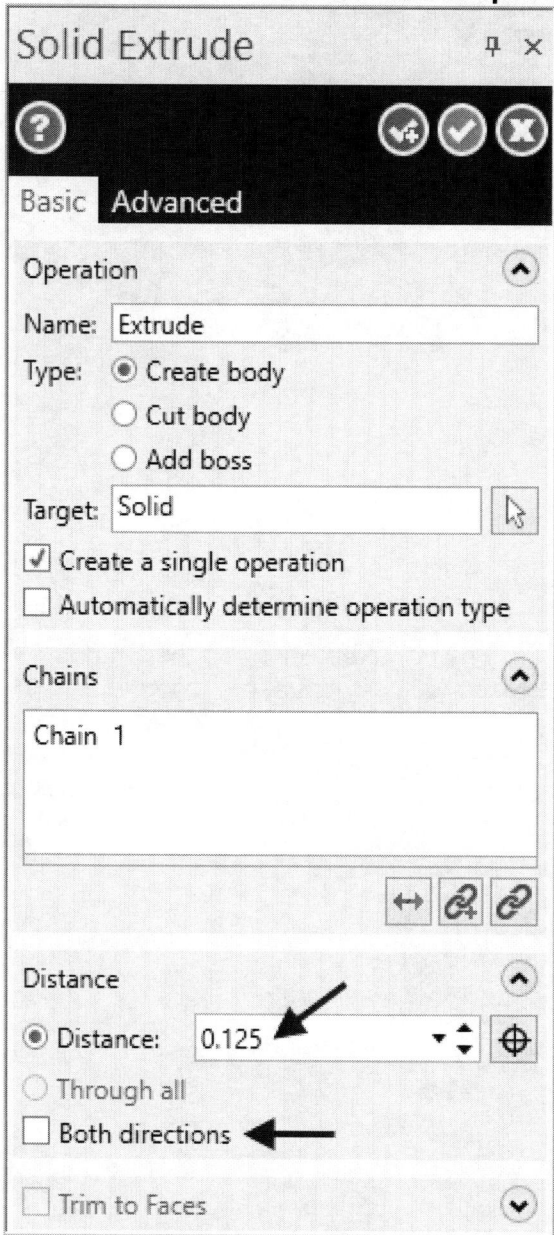

10. Click on the **OK and Create New** icon to complete this feature but remain in the Extrude function.
11. In the **View** tab click on **Outline Shaded** in the **Appearance** section to display the part in shaded mode.
12. In the **View** tab click on **Wireframe** to un-shade the solid. This will make it easier to create the remaining solids.

Create the .200 Solid body

13. Click on the **Solids** tab and in the **Create** section select **Extrude**.
14. On the graphics screen you are prompted: **Select chain(s) to extrude 1.** Select the line as shown below:

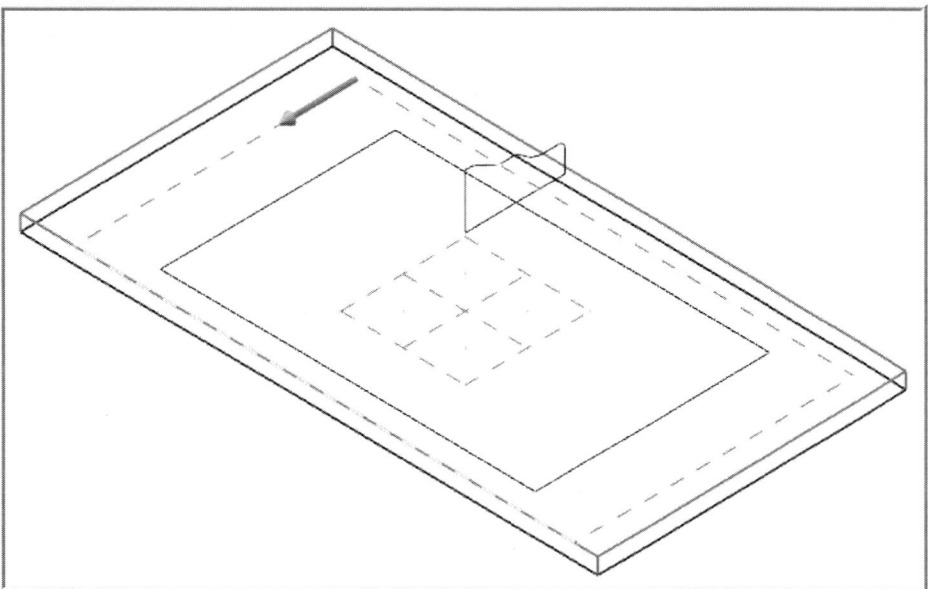

15. Click on the OK icon in the Chaining dialog window.
16. An arrow will appear on one of the corners of the rectangle as shown below.

➲ **Tip:** Click and drag the arrow on the solid to change the extrusion distance or type a distance while the arrow is highlighted and press **[Enter].**

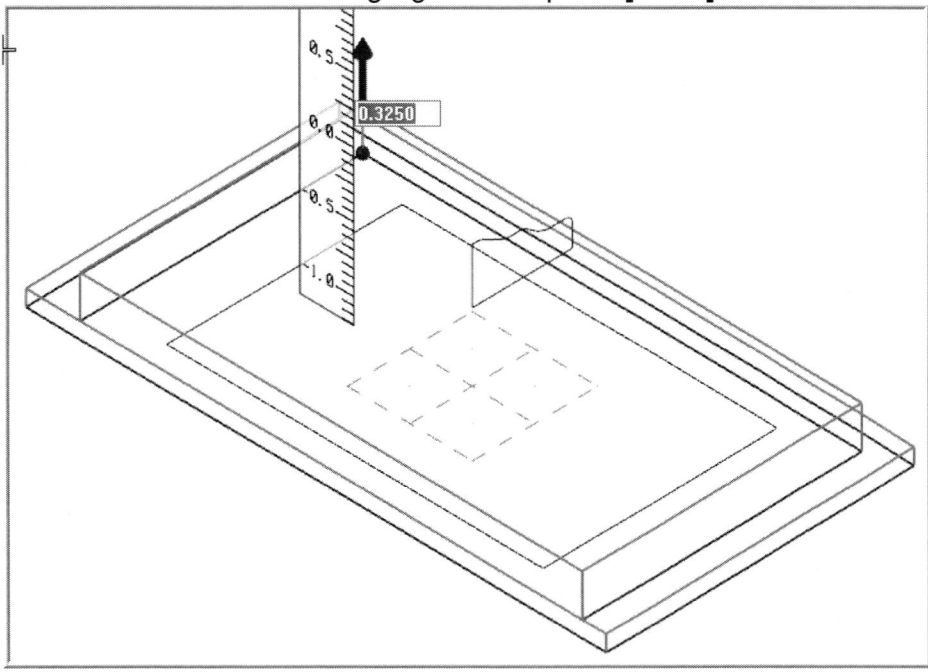

17. Make the necessary changes as shown below in the **Solid Extrude** dialog window: Note: You will enter **.125+.2** in the **Distance** window. **Both directions option is deactivated**.

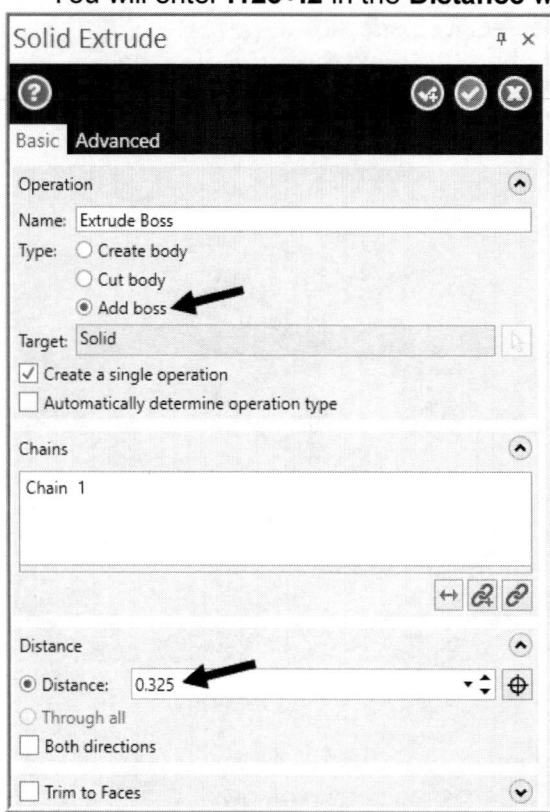

➲ Add Boss will merge this solid function into the previously created solid. This saves the need to Boolean Add two separate solids.

18. Click on the **OK and Create New** icon ![icon] to complete this feature but remain in the Extrude function.
19. In the **View** tab click on **Outline Shaded** in the **Appearance** section to display the part in shaded mode.
20. In the **View** tab click on **Wireframe** to un-shade the solid. This will make it easier to create the remaining solids.

➲ Create the second .200 Solid body

21. Click on the **Solids** tab and in the **Create** section select **Extrude**.
22. On the graphics screen you are prompted: **Select chain(s) to extrude 1.** Select the line as shown below:

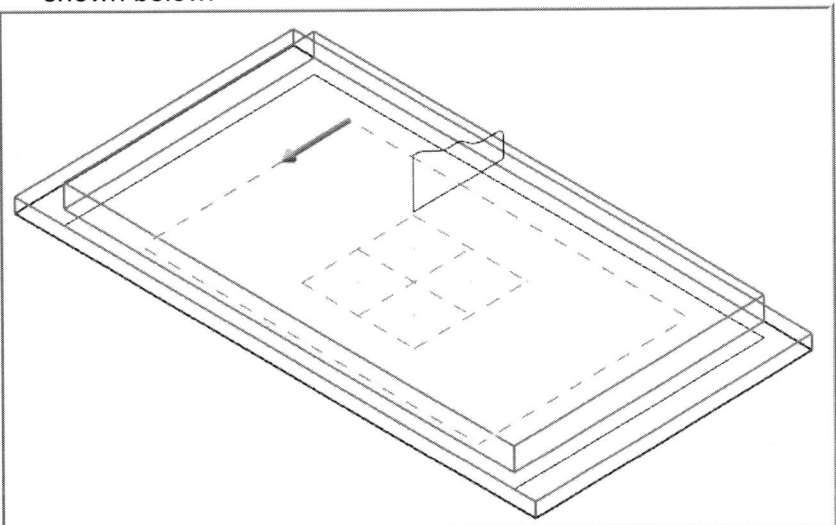

23. Click on the OK icon [✓] in the **Chaining dialog window**.
24. An arrow will appear on one of the corners of the rectangle. Make the necessary changes as shown below in the Solid **Extrude** Note: You will enter **.325+.200** in the **Distance** window.

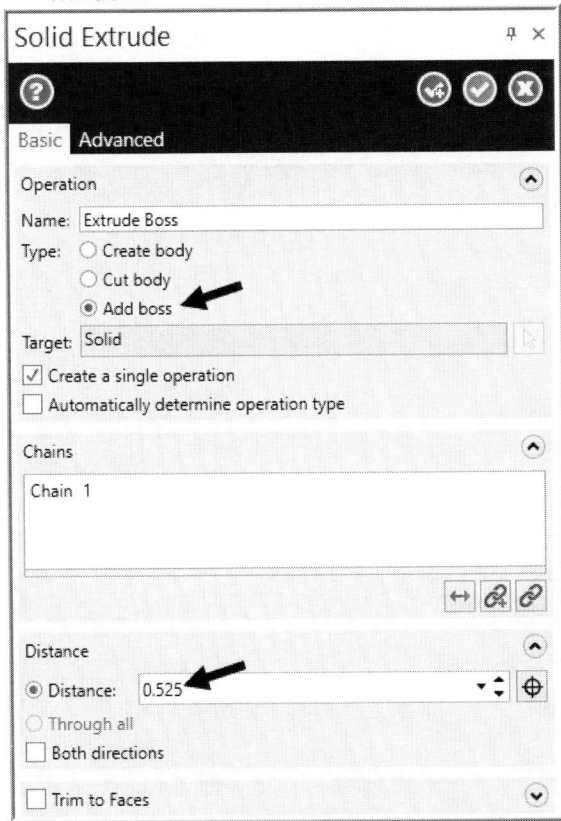

25. Click on the **OK** icon [✓] in the Solid Extrude dialog window.

26. In the **View** tab click on **Shaded** in the **Appearance** section to display the part in shaded mode.

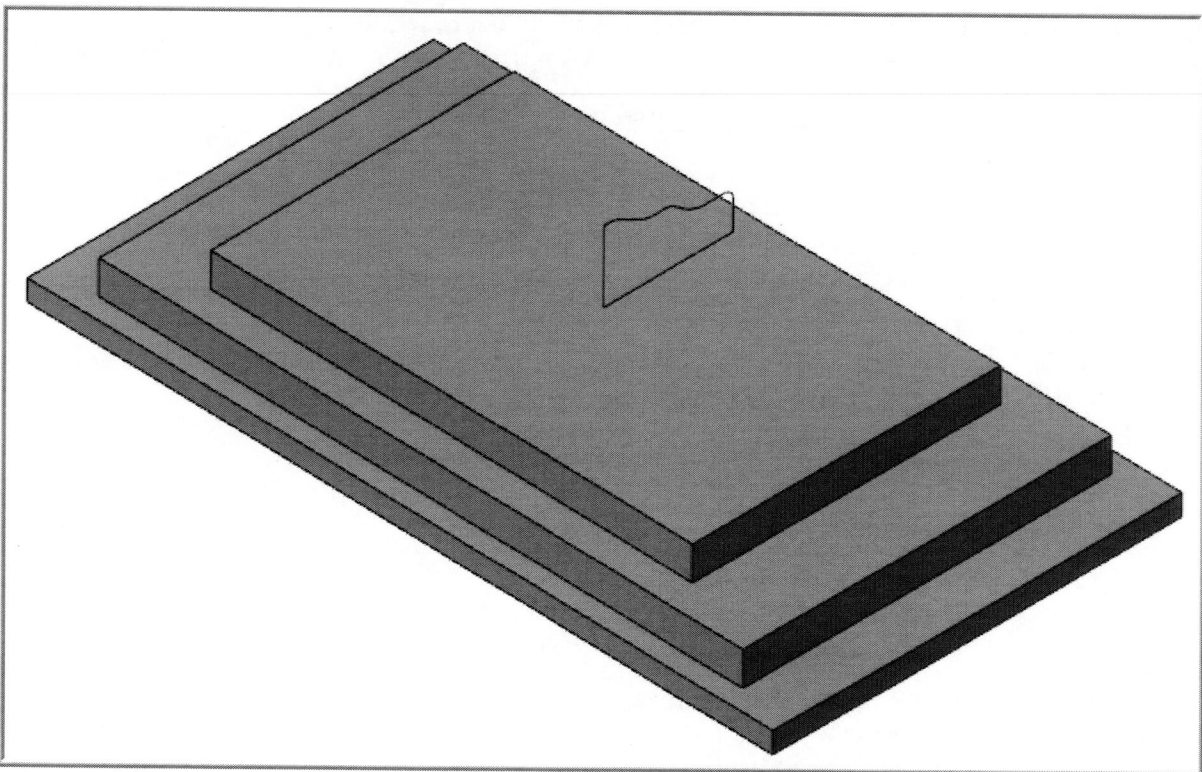

➲ The Solids tree up to this point.

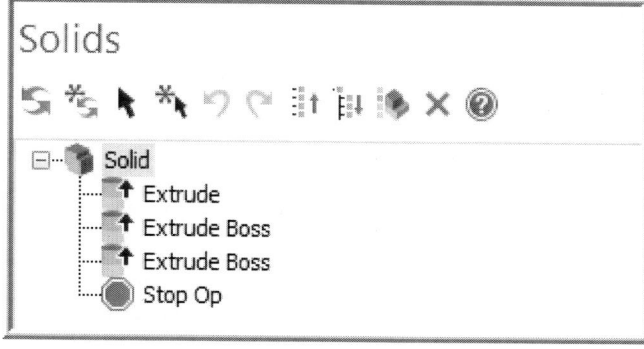

➲ The Levels manager.

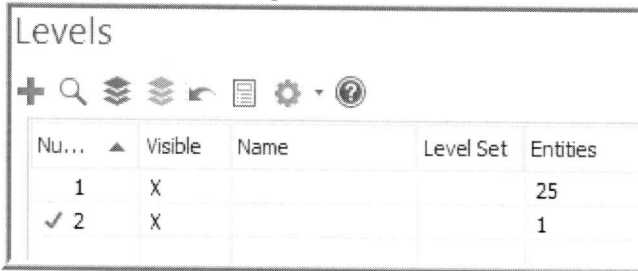

TASK 6:
CREATE THE REVOLVED SOLID BOSS
➾ In this task you will create a revolved solid using the geometry you have just created and revolve the geometry 360 degrees about the Z axis.

> The **Solid Revolve** function lets you revolve planar chains of curves to create one or more new solid bodies, cuts on an existing body, or bosses on an existing body. Mastercam revolves chains of curves by driving the shape of the curves about an axis using given start and end angles and other parameters that further define the results. The number of resulting solids, cuts, or bosses depends on the number of chains that you select, whether the chains are nested, whether you combine operations, and what construction method you use.

➾ **Create Revolved Solid**

1. Click on the **Solids** tab and in the **Create** section select **Revolve**.

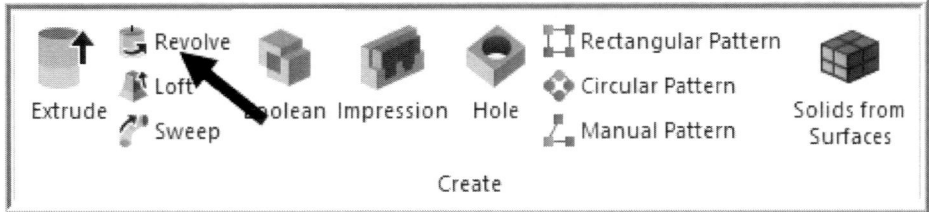

2. Switching to a Wireframe view may make geometry selection easier.
3. Zoom in on the geometry for the revolved solid as shown below:

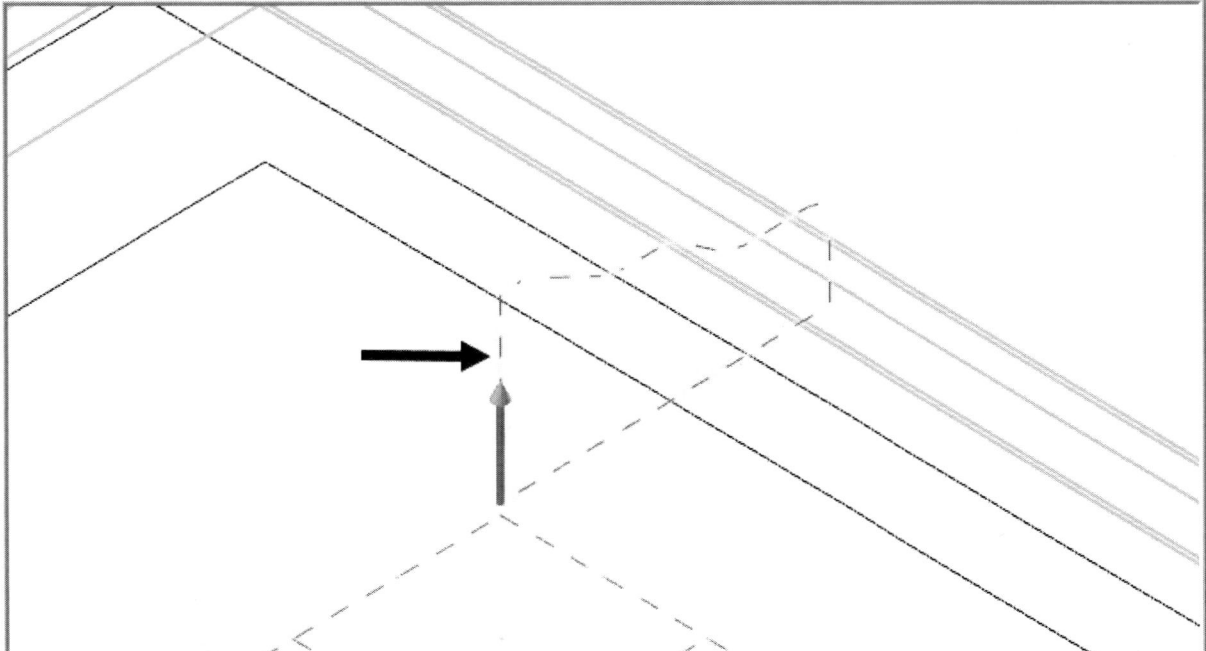

4. On the graphics screen you are prompted: **Select chain(s) to revolved 1** and in the **Chaining** dialog window ensure **Chain** is selected.
5. Select the line on the left as shown above.
6. Click on the OK icon ✓ in the Chaining dialog window.
7. The prompt now changes to **Select line to be used as axis of rotation**, select the axis line shown above.

8. Ensure Add Boss is checked in the **Solid Revolve** window, click on the **OK** icon 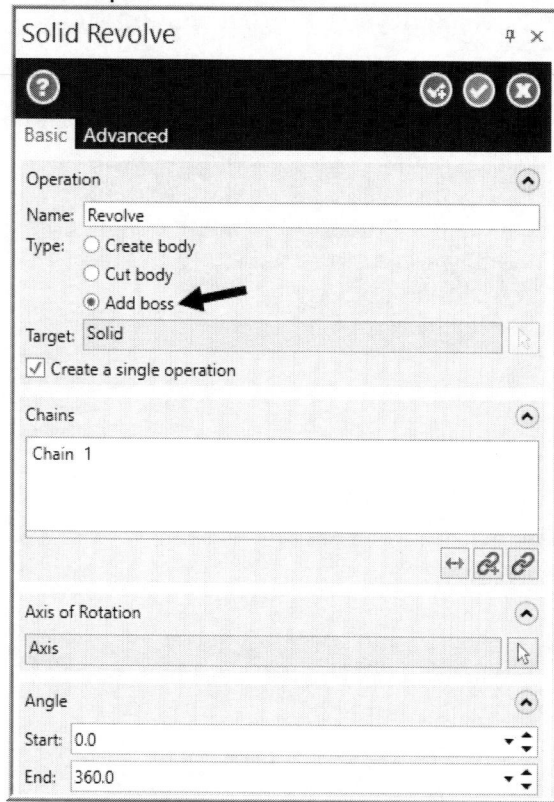 to complete this feature.

9. Right mouse click in the graphics area and click on the **Fit** icon .
10. In the **View** tab click on **Outline Shaded** in the **Appearance** section to display the part in shaded mode.

➲ Your screen should look like the image below:

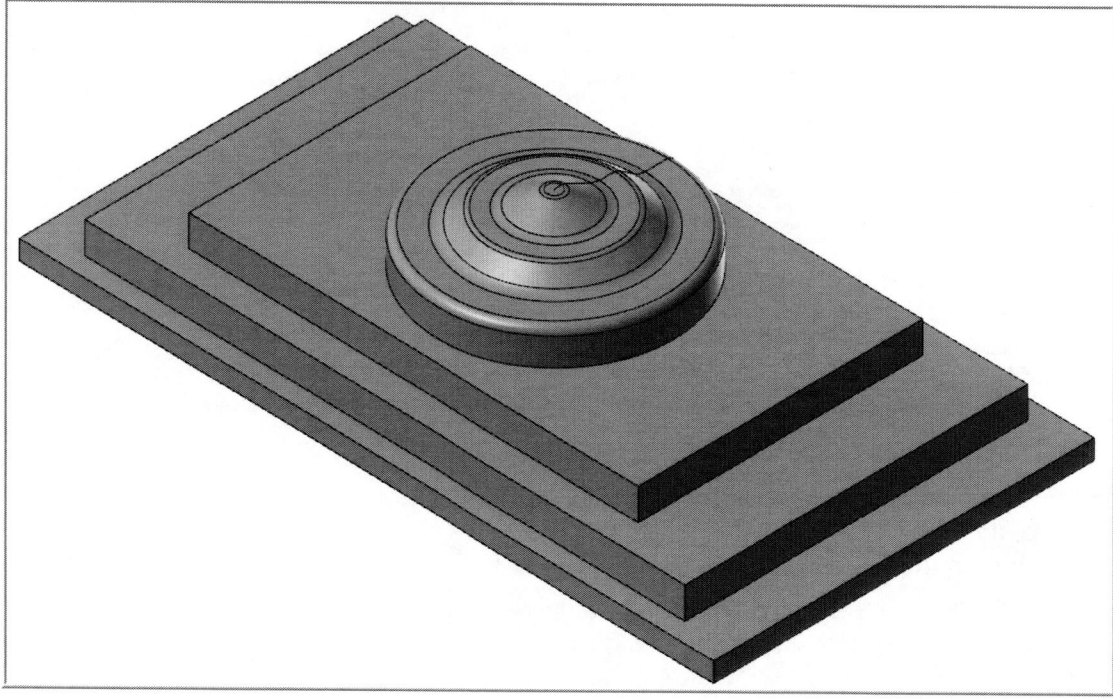

⊃ The Solids tree up to this point.

⊃ The Levels Manager.

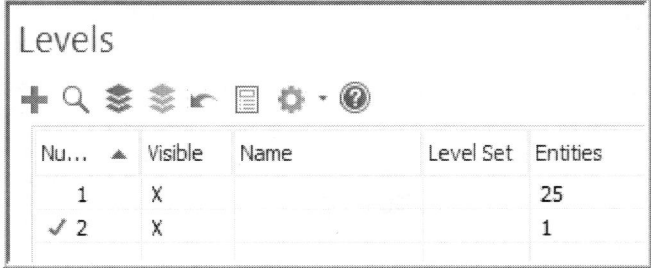

TASK 7:
CREATE THE FILLETS ON THE SOLID BODY

➪ **Create the .250 Fillets on the Base**

1. Click on the **Solids** tab and in the **Modify** section select **Constant Fillet**.
2. Make sure the **Select Edge** button is depressed (activated) and **all other buttons are off** as shown below in the **Solid Selection** dialog box:

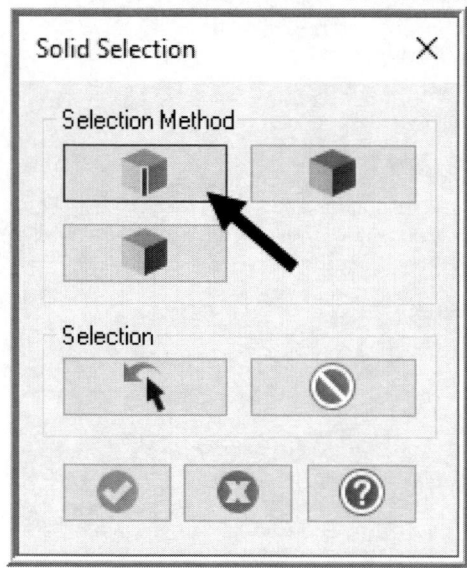

3. Switch to a Wireframe view.
4. On the graphics screen you are now prompted: **Select one or more entities to fillet.** Pick the 4 edges of the solid body as shown below: **Note:** the edge changes when selected.

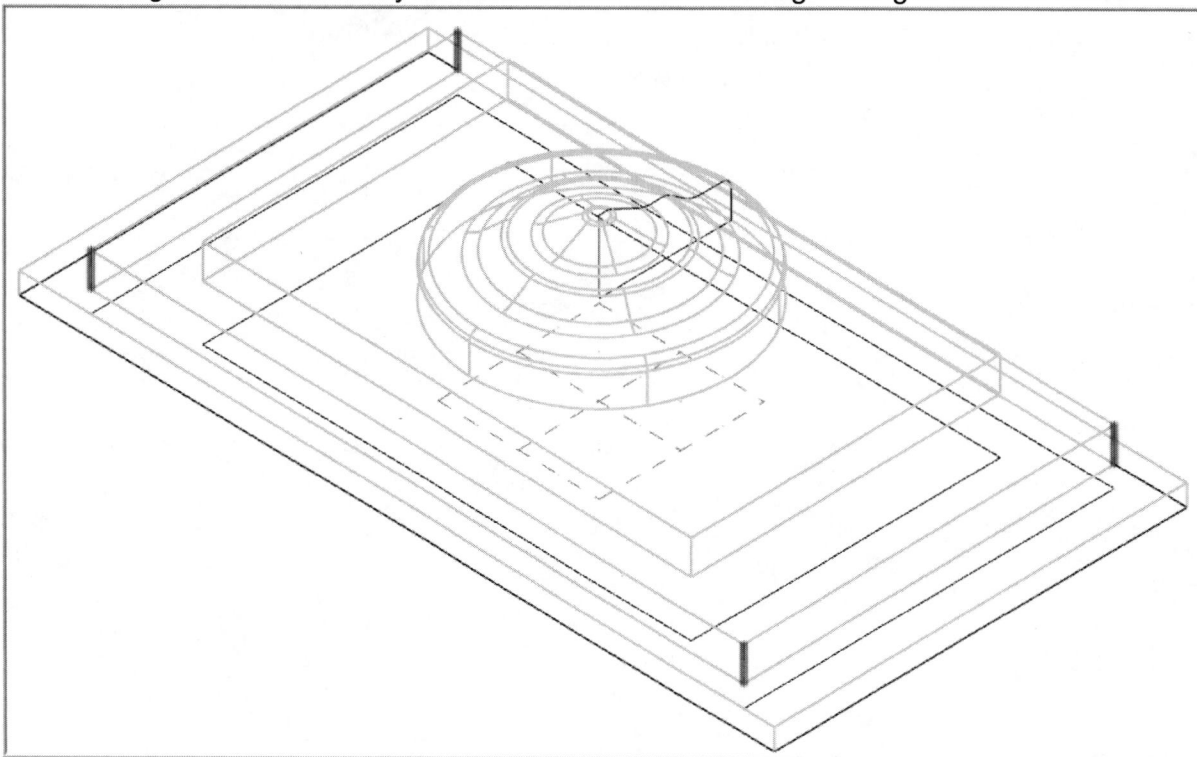

5. After picking the edge click on the OK icon  in the **Solid Selection** window.
6. Make the necessary changes as shown below in the **Constant Radius Fillet** panel

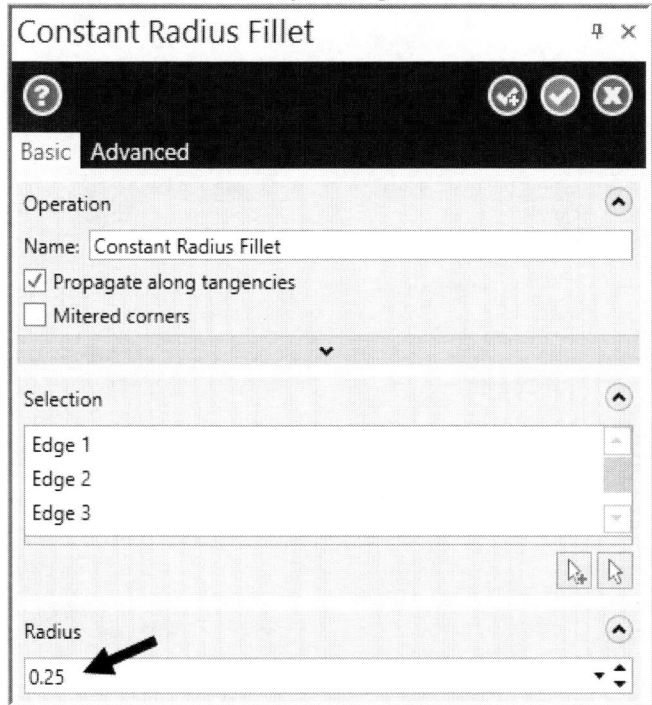

7. Click on the **OK** and **Create New Operation** icon.
8. Switch back to the **Outline Shaded** view.
9. On the graphics screen you are now prompted: **Select one or more entities to fillet.** Pick the edge of the solid body as shown below: **Note:** the edge changes when selected.

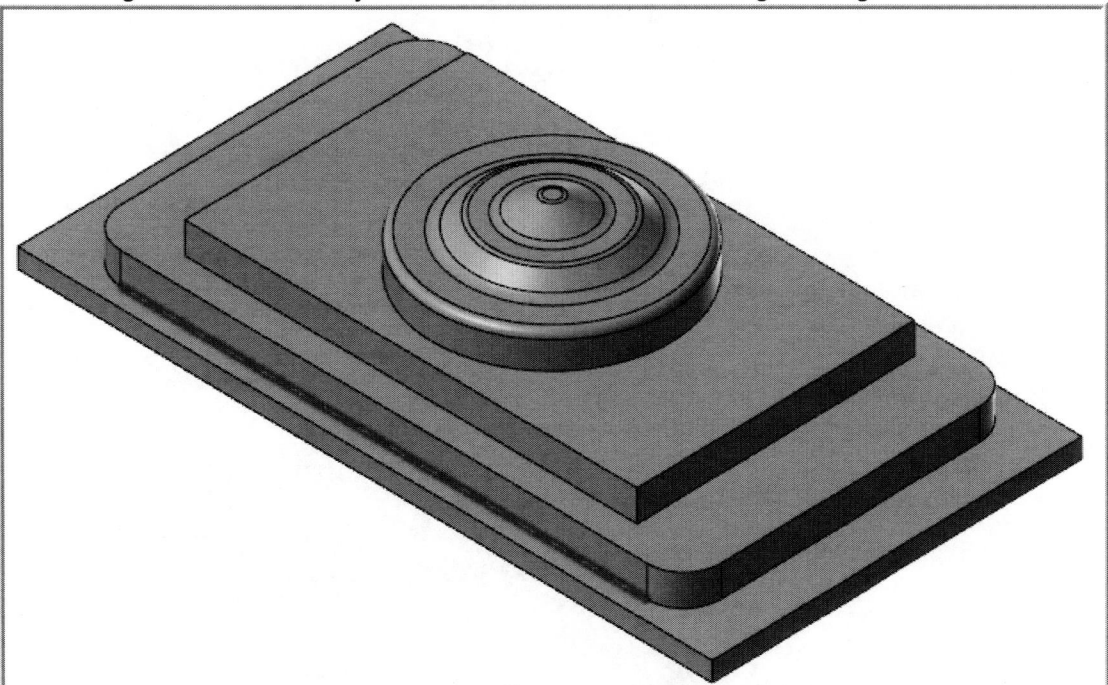

10. After picking the edge click on the OK icon  in the **Solid Selection** window.

11. Make the necessary changes as shown below in the **Constant Radius Fillet** panel.

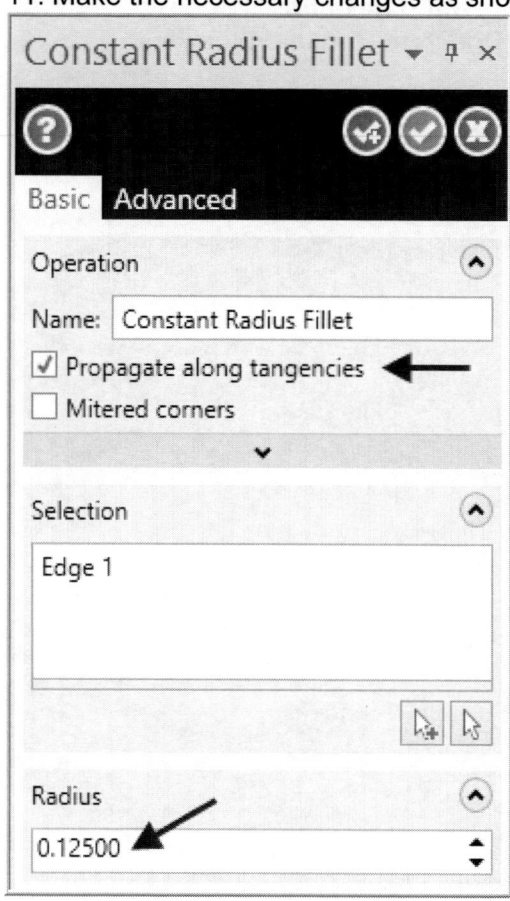

12. Click on the **OK** and **Create New Operation** icon .

⊃ Your screen should look like the image below:

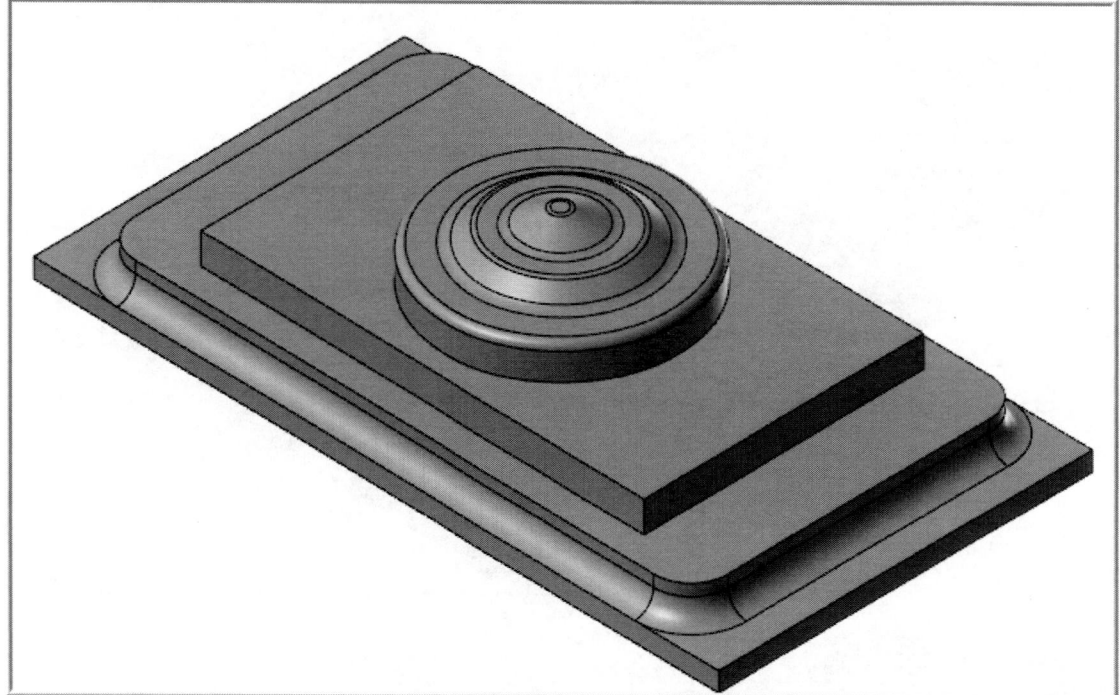

Ↄ Create the .125 Fillet on the mid-section

13. Make sure the **Select Edge** button is depressed (activated) and **all other buttons are off** as shown below in the **Solid Selection** dialog box:

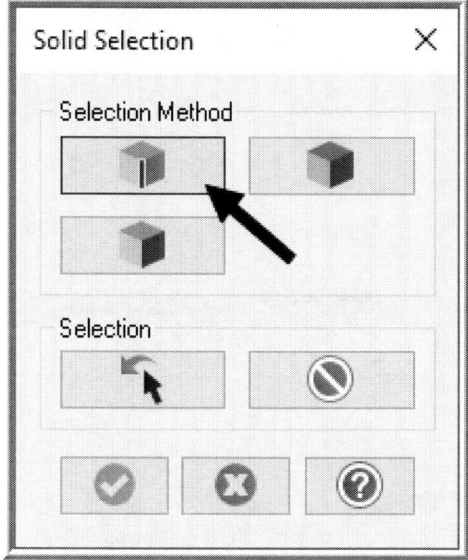

14. On the graphics screen you are now prompted: **Select Entities to fillet.** Pick all 4 edges of the solid body as shown below: **Note:** the edge changes when selected.

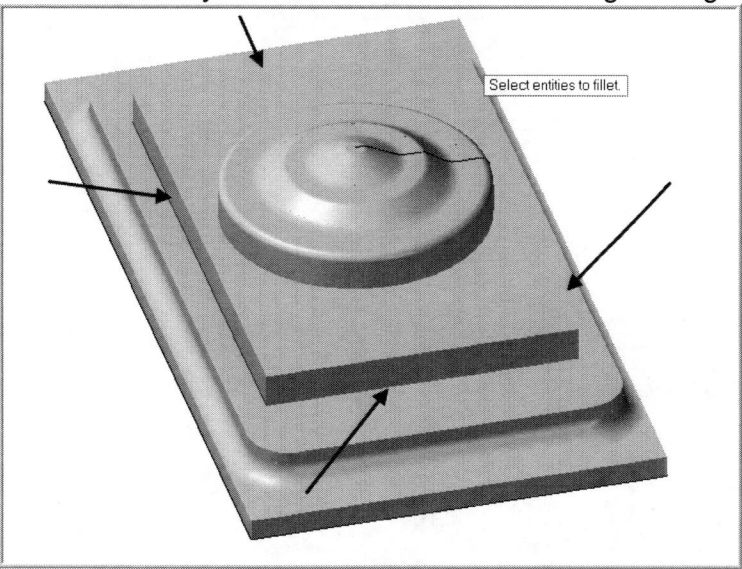

15. After picking the edge click on the OK icon [✓] in the **Solid Selection** window.

16. Make the necessary changes as shown below in the **Constant Radius Fillet** panel.

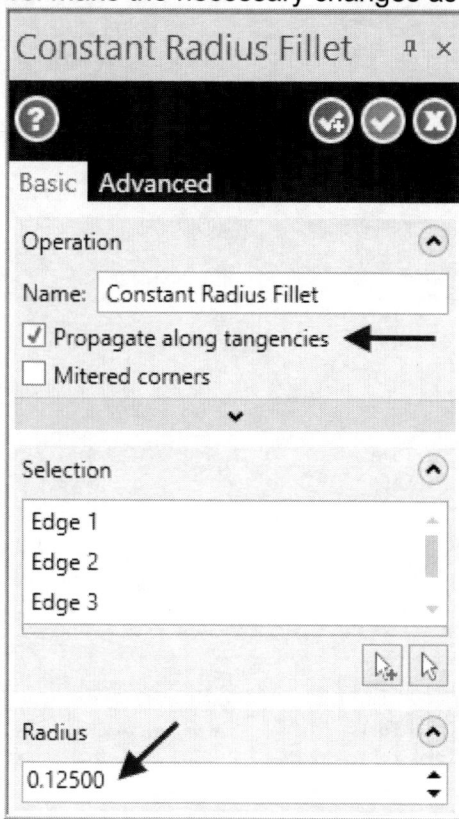

17. Click on the **OK** and **Create New Operation** icon 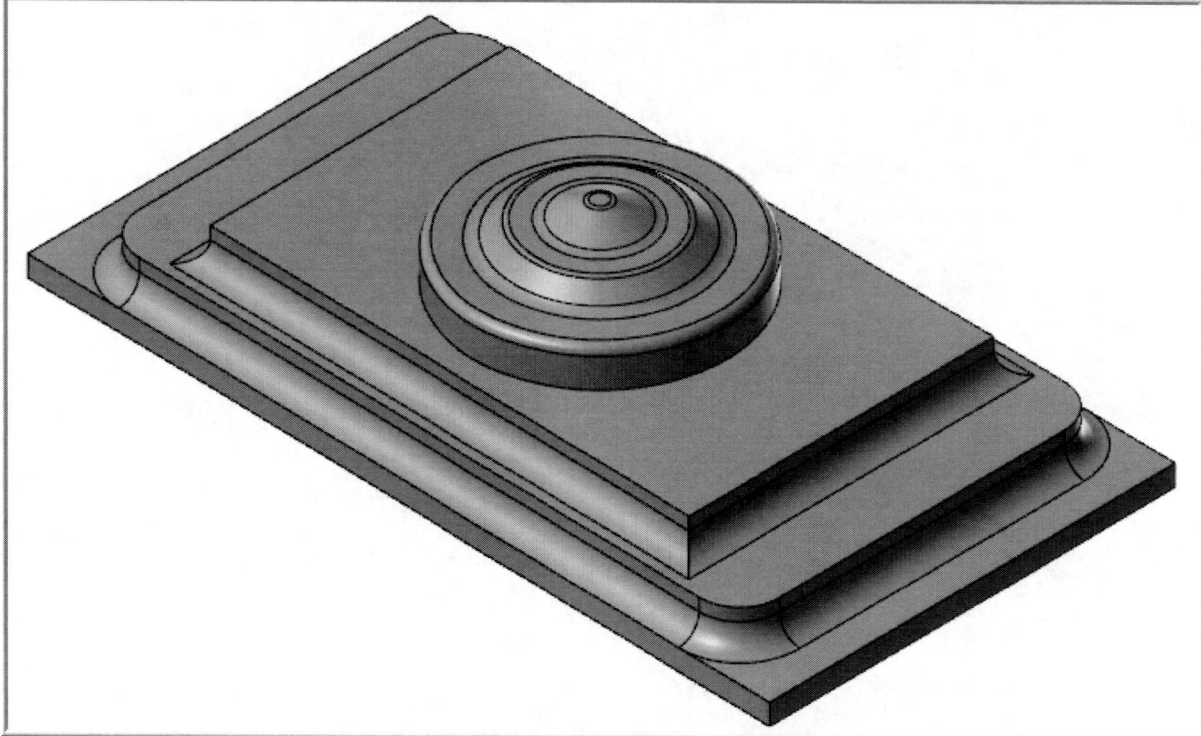.

➲ Your screen should look like the image below:

⊃ **Create the .125 Fillet on the revolved solid**

18. Make sure the **Select Edge** button is depressed (activated) and **all other buttons are off** as shown below in the **Solid Selection** dialog box:

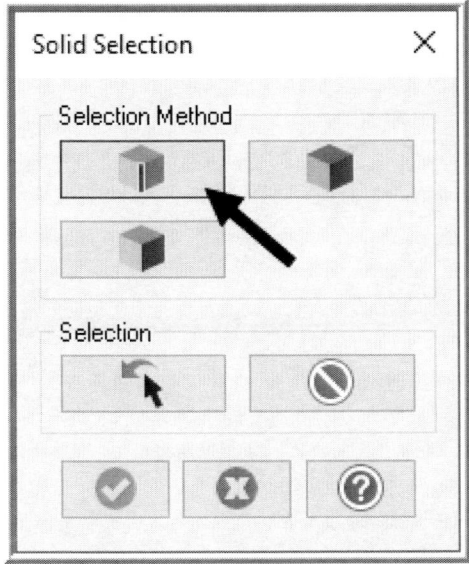

19. On the graphics screen you are now prompted: **Select Entities to fillet.** Pick the edge of the solid body as shown below: **Note:** the edge changes when selected.

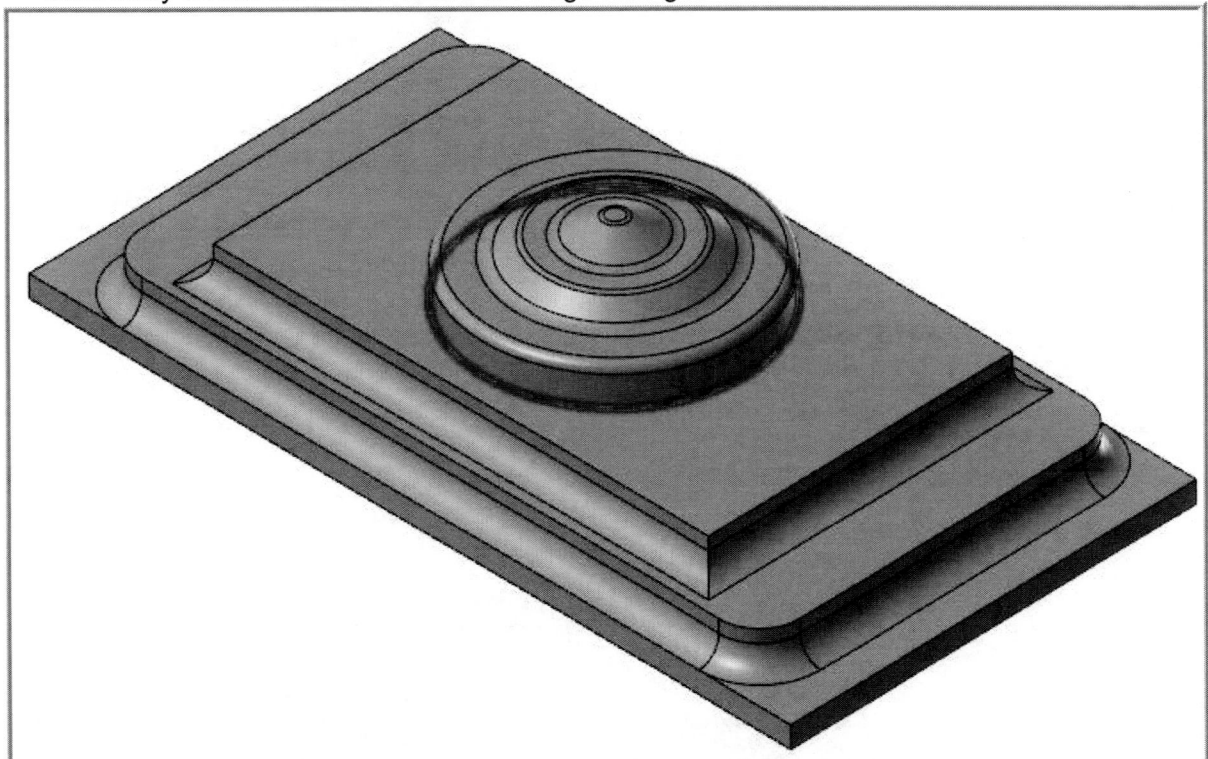

20. After picking the edge click on the OK icon [✓] in the **Solid Selection** window.

21. Make the necessary changes as shown below in the **Constant Radius Fillet** panel and then click on the **OK** icon 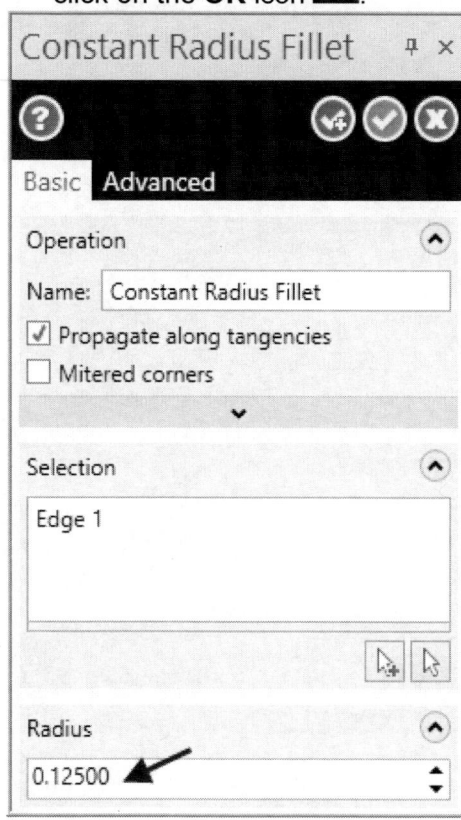.

22. **Close** the **Solids Manager**.

➲ Your screen should look like the image below:

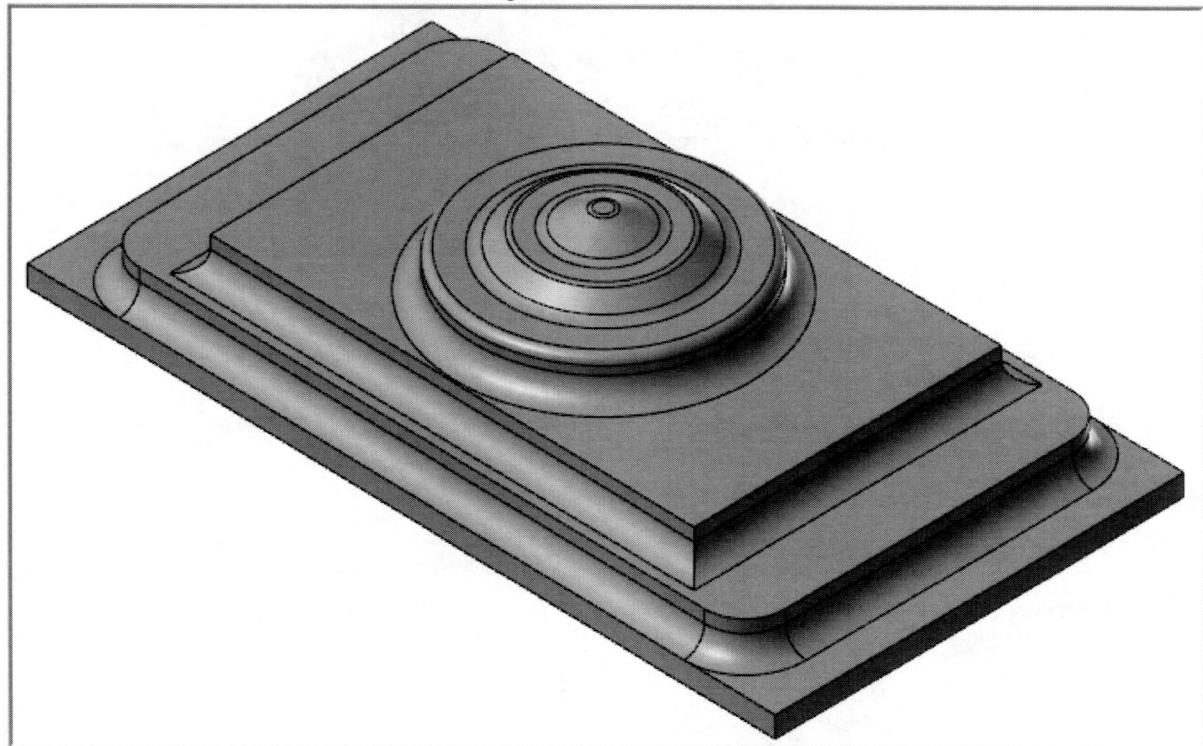

TASK 8:
HIDE THE 2D CONSTRUCTION ENTITIES

➲ All the construction entities were created on level 1 and the Solid Body on level 2. You will now turn off level 1 so all that all that will be visible is the Solid Body.
➲

> **Levels** are a primary organizational tool in Mastercam. A Mastercam file can contain separate levels for wireframe, surfaces, drafting entities, and toolpaths.
>
> By organizing your files into levels, you can more easily control which areas of the drawing are visible at any time and which parts are selectable so that you do not inadvertently make changes to areas of the drawing you do not want to change.
>
> You are always drawing on the main level. You can create and name up to *2 billion* levels and set any one to be the main level. You use the Level Manager dialog box to create and edit levels and to set the main level. You can configure Mastercam to always display the name of the level
>
> You can copy or move geometry from level to level, hide levels from view, name levels, and organize several levels into sets.

➲
1. Select the **View tab** and click on **Levels** to display the **Levels Manager**. The keyboard short cut is **ALT+Z**.
2. At the top of the **Level Manager** window click on the **X checkmark** as shown below: This will **turn off level 1** and make it invisible.

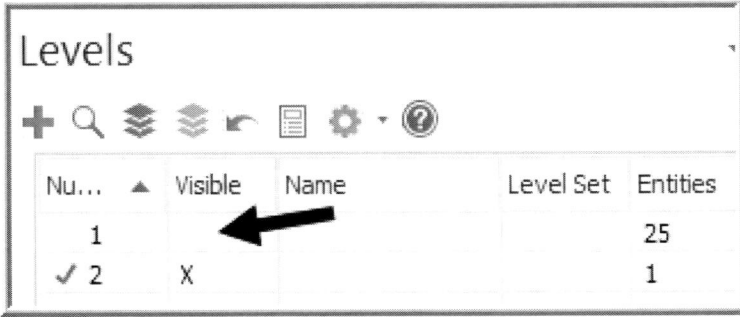

3. Select the ⊠ in the top right corner of the **Levels** manager to close the **Levels** manager.

TASK 9:
CREATE A BOX TO REPRESENT THE BOUNDARY OF THE PART

1. Right mouse click in the graphics area and toggle to **3D construction**.
2. On the **Wireframe** tab in the **Shapes** section click on **Bounding Box**.
3. You are prompted to **"Select entities, use Ctrl-A to select all"**. On your keyboard select **Ctrl-A** to select all the entities.
4. Click on **End Selection** ✅ to move onto the next step. The Bounding box window appears.

➲ Take note of the X, Y and Z values Mastercam has calculated for the stock size and the preview on the graphics screen.

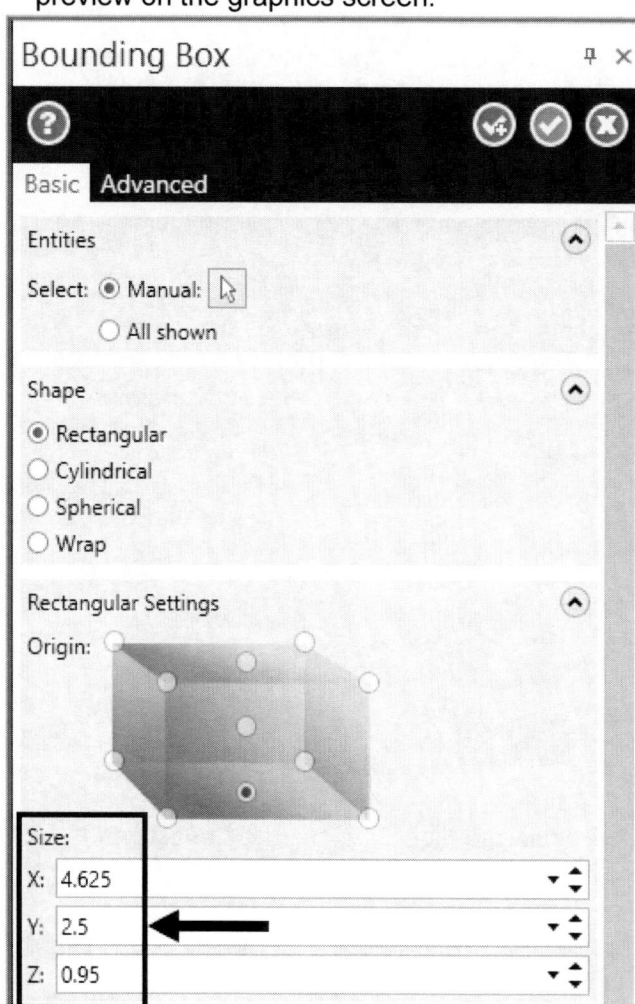

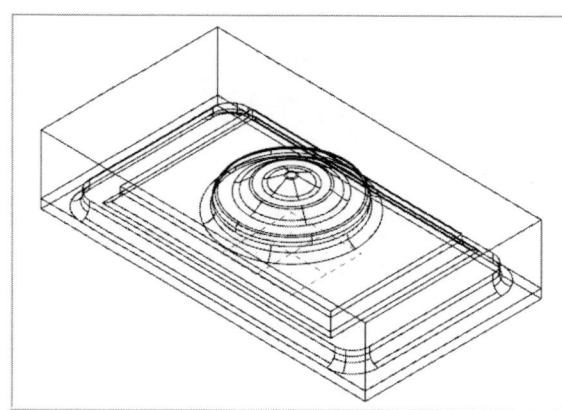

5. Scroll down to the bottom of the Bounding box window and ensure **Lines and arcs** are activated.

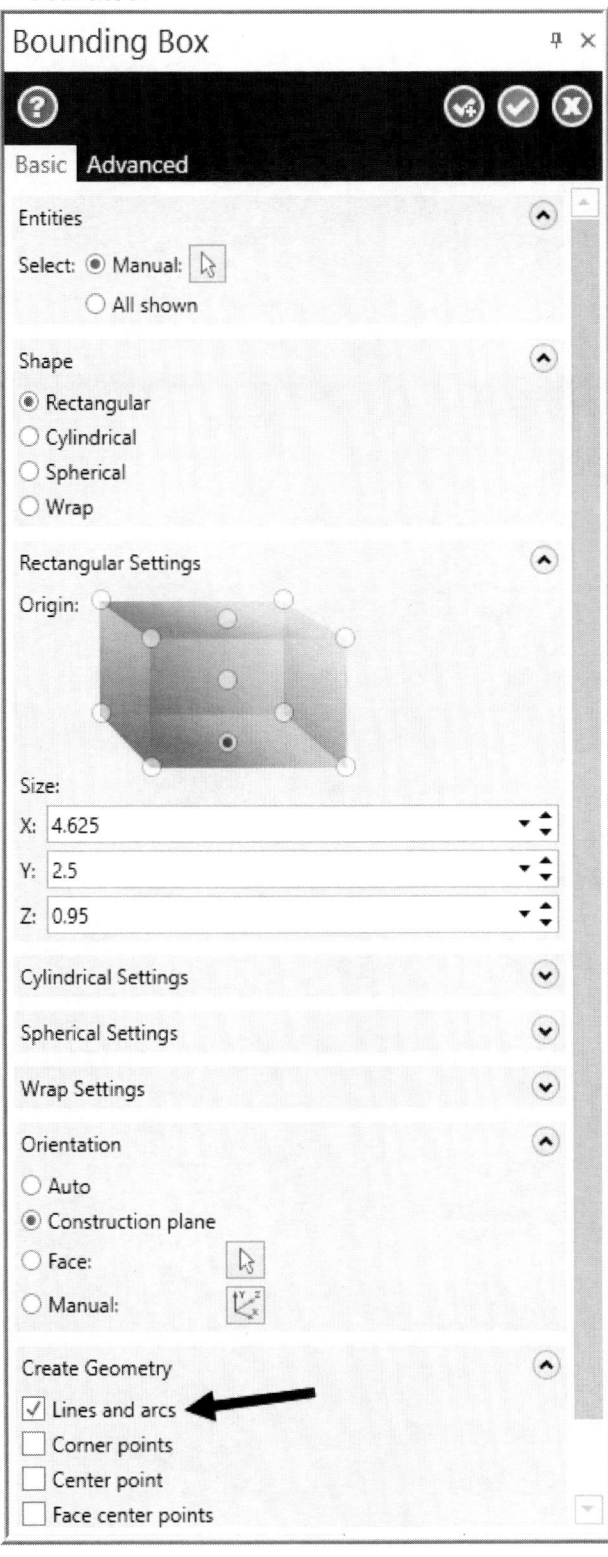

Use this panel to create a rectangular or cylindrical boundary around selected entities in the graphics window. Bounding box creates wireframe geometry, a solid model, or a stock model. You can also use Bounding box to check the overall dimensions of a part.

Note: To enable the Solids option in the Create Geometry area when the current geometry is 2D, enter a value for Z (for a rectangular shape) or Radius (for a cylindrical shape). For 3D geometry, the Solids option is already enabled.

Create lines, arcs, points
Select the entity types for the bounding box:
- Lines Arcs creates a closed boundary of lines if the shape is rectangular, and lines and arcs if the shape is cylindrical.

- Points create points at the corners or extents of the bounding box.

- Center point creates a point at the center.

6. Now click on the **OK** icon in the Bounding box window.

➲ Your screen should look like the image below:

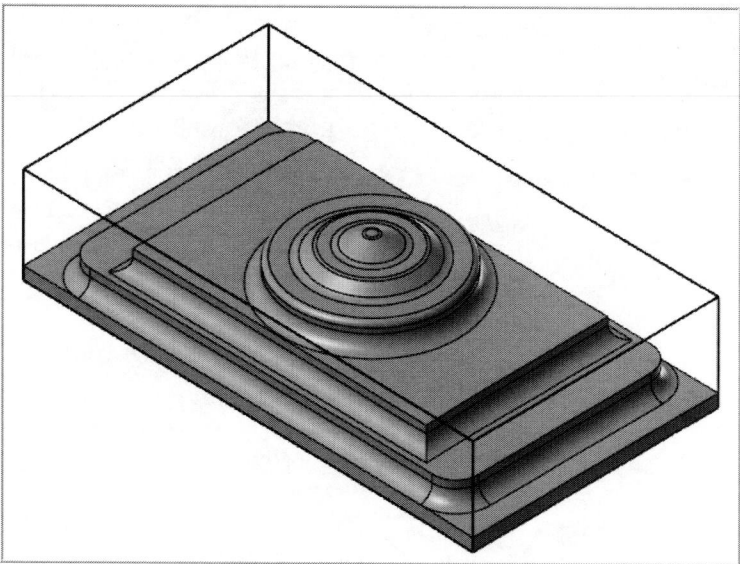

TASK 10:
SAVE THE DRAWING

1. Select **File**.
2. Select **Save As...**
3. Click on the **Browse** icon.
4. In the File name box, type **Mill-Lesson-14**
5. Save to an appropriate location.
6. Select the Save button to save the file and complete this function.

Toolpath Creation

TASK 11:
DEFINE THE ROUGH STOCK USING STOCK SETUP

1. Select the **View tab** and click on **Toolpaths** in the **Managers** section to display the Toolpaths Manager. **Alt-O** will **Show/Hide** Toolpaths Manager pane.
2. Select the **plus** in front of **Properties** to expand the Toolpaths Group Properties.
3. Select **Stock setup** in the Toolpaths Manager window.
4. On the **Stock Setup** page select **Bounding box**.

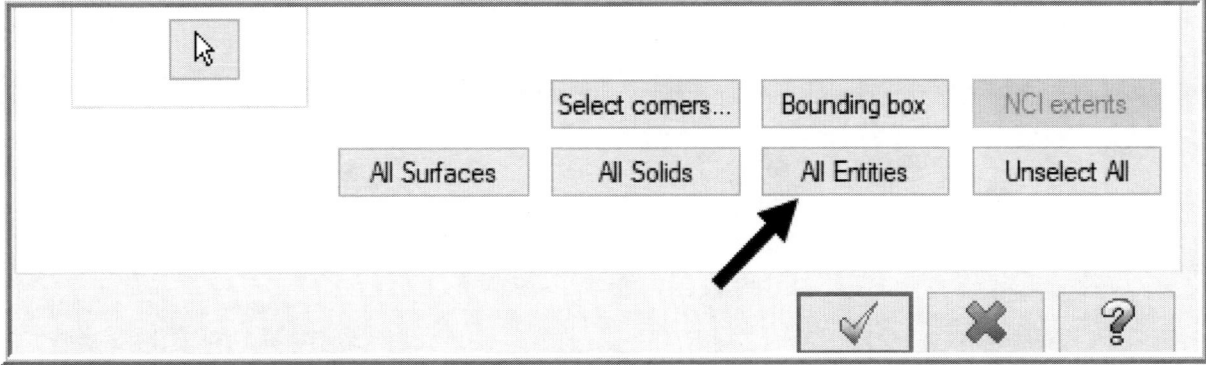

➲ An additional 0.05" of stock will be added to this setup.
➲ Take note of the **Stock Origin** values in the lower left of the Stock Setup dialog box. Z is set to 1.0 and the **arrow is pointing to the top of the stock**. This is because the **bottom of the part is at Z zero** and the arrow is pointing to the top of the part which is a **Z1.0**.

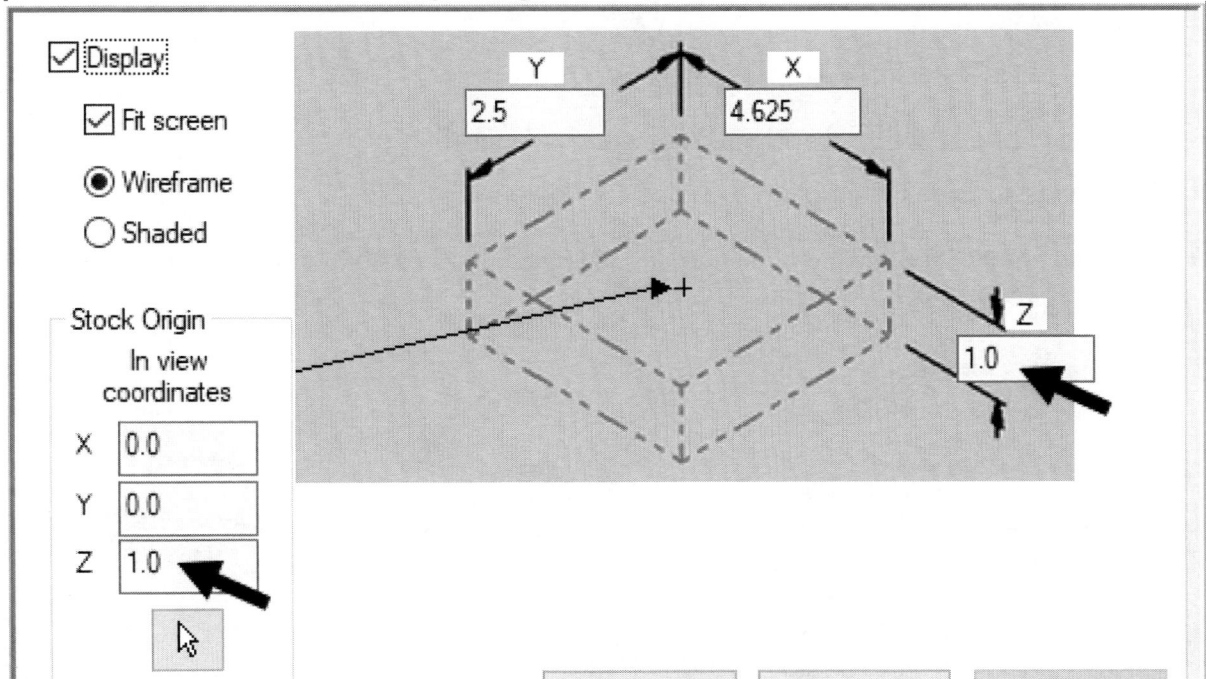

5. Select the **Tool Settings** tab and change the parameters to match the Tool Settings screenshot below: To change the Material type follow the instructions below:

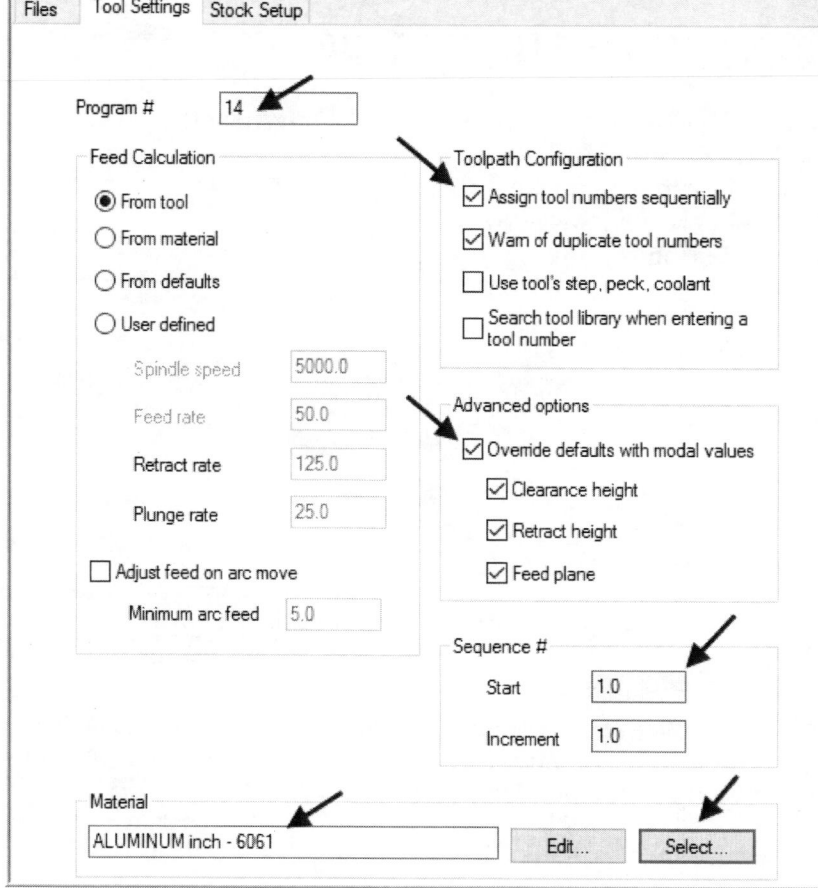

6. To change the Material type to Aluminum 6061 pick the Select button at the bottom of the Tool Settings page.

7. At the **Material List** dialog box open the **Source** drop down list and select **Mill – library**.

8. From the Default Materials list select **ALUMINUM inch - 6061** and then select ✓.

9. Select the OK button ✓ again to complete this function.

10. Right mouse click in the graphics area and click on the **Fit** icon ⊞.

➲ Your part should look similar to the screen shot below: With X0 Y0 at the center and Z zero on the bottom of the stock.

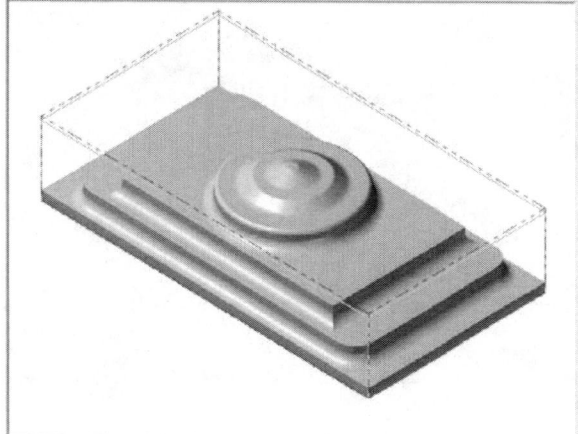
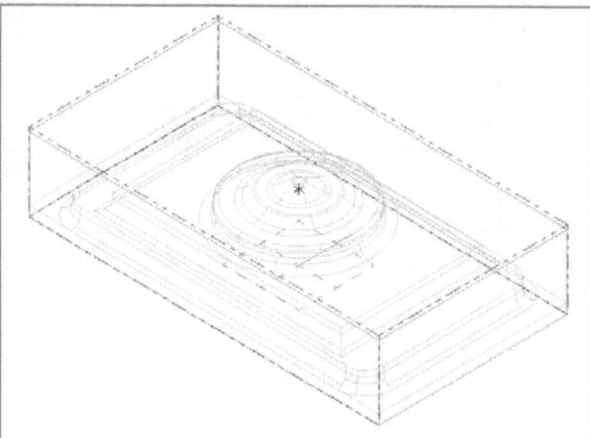

TASK 12:
ROUGH USING SURFACE ROUGH POCKET TOOLPATH

➲ In this task you will use a 0.500 diameter end mill with a 0.125 corner radius to rough the part.

1. Select the **Toolpaths** tab at the top right side of the screen.
2. Select **Pocket** in the **3D** toolpath section.

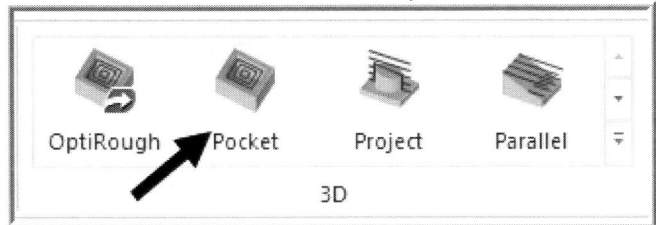

3. To satisfy the prompt **Triple Click** on the **Solid Model** and note how it changes color.
4. Click the **End Selection** icon 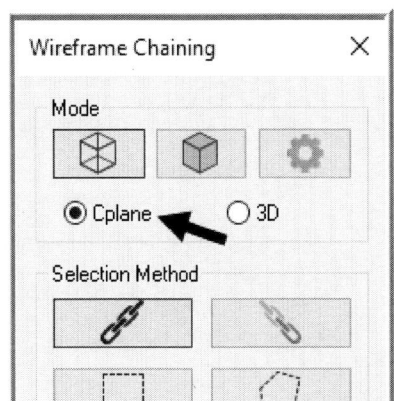.
5. Click on the **Containment Select** button. When the Chaining dialog menu appears, enable Cplane chaining.

6. Click on the rectangle as shown below:

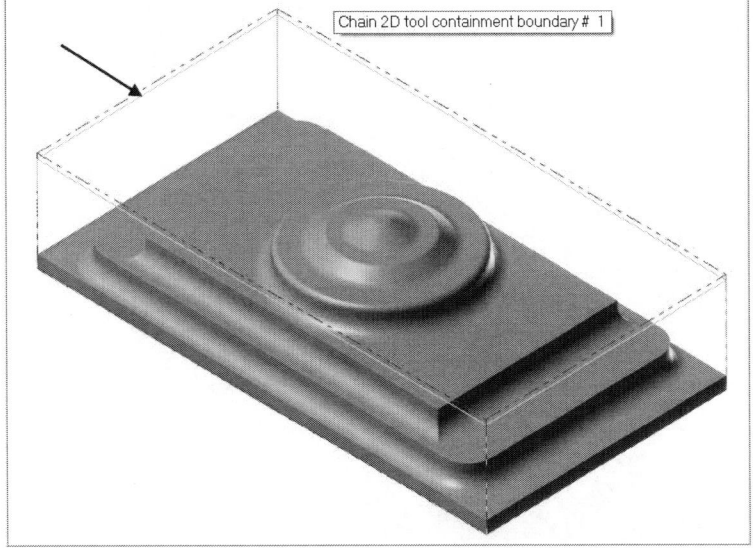

7. Select the **OK** button [✓] in the **Chaining** window.

8. Select **OK** [✓] in the **Toolpath/surface selection** window.
9. In the lower left corner of the **Toolpath parameters** page select the **Select library tool...** button.
10. Use the slider bar on the right of this dialog box to scroll down and locate a **0.5 diameter bull end mill with a 0.125 corner radius**. Select the end mill by picking anywhere along its row.
11. Select the OK button [✓] to complete the selection of this tool.
12. Make changes to the **Toolpath parameters** page as shown below: Set **coolant on**.

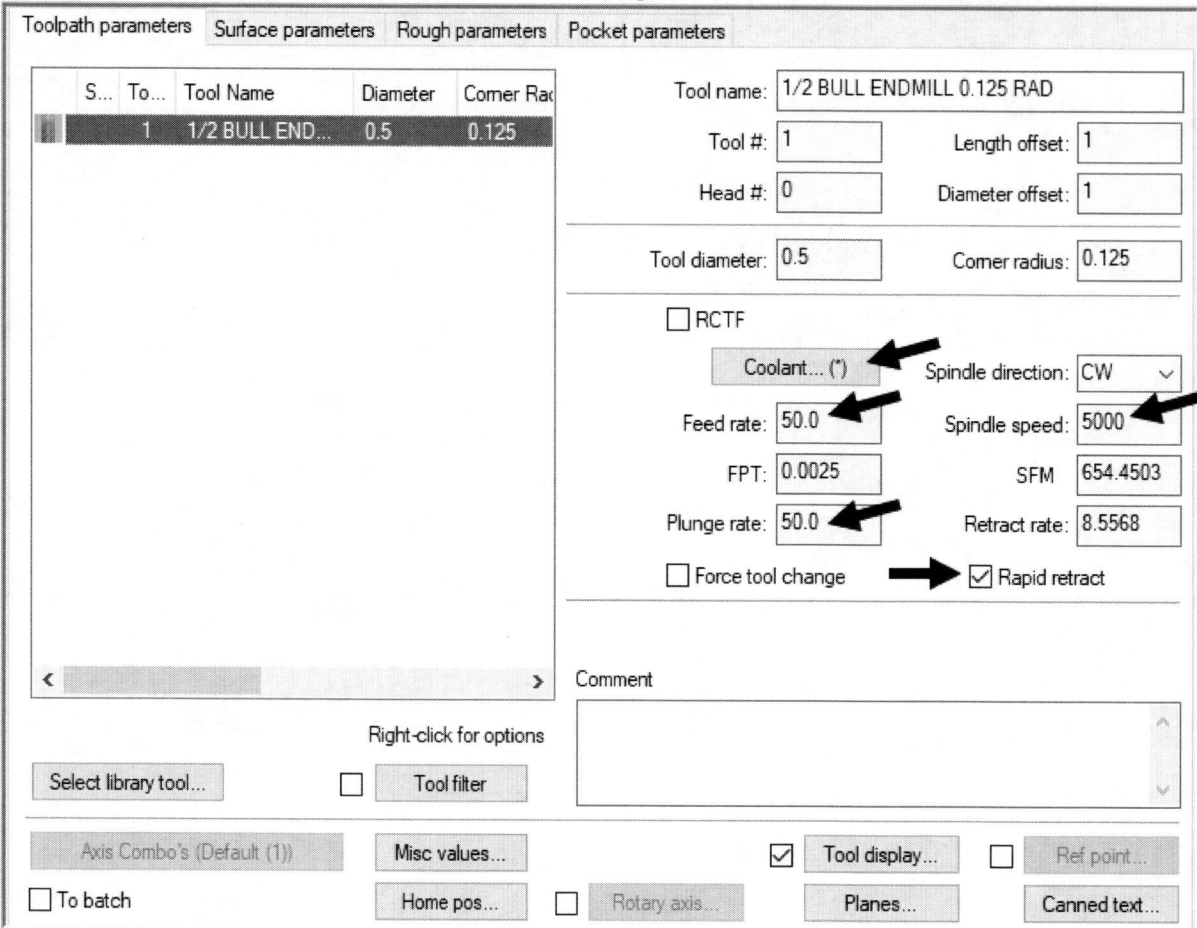

13. Select the **Surface parameters** page and make changes to this page as shown below:
Stock to leave on drive is set to **0.015**. **Tool containment** is set to **Outside and -0.2**.

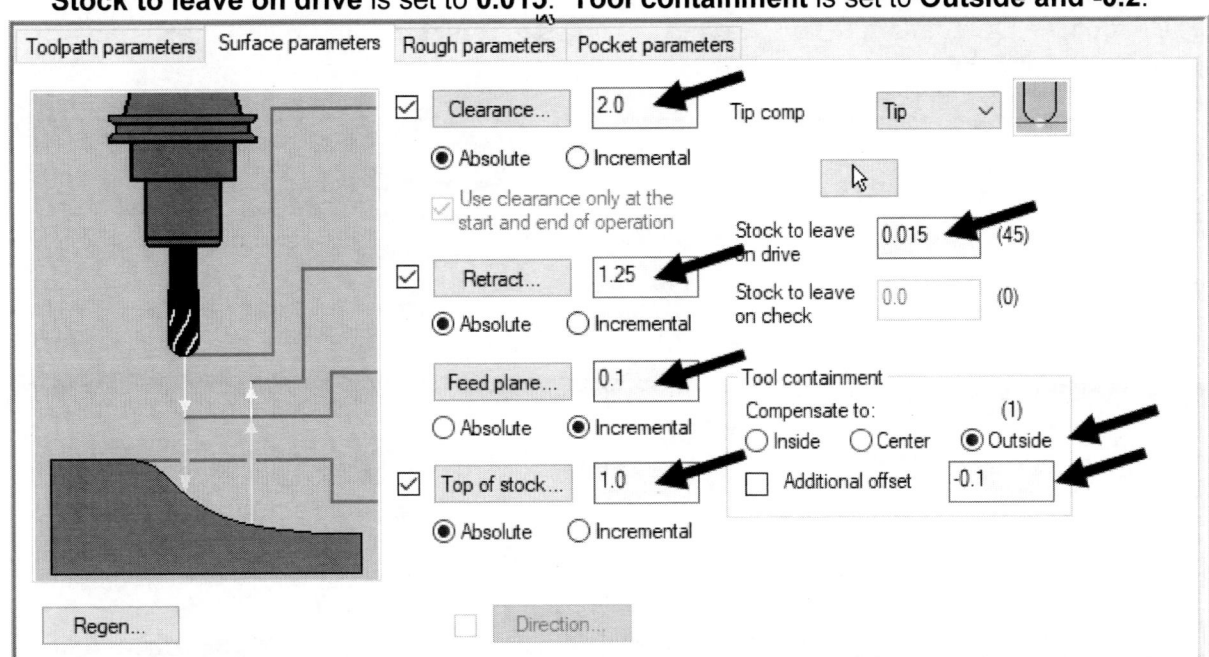

Compensation set to Outside with a negative value of -0.1 will leave 0.4 of our selected 0.5 diameter endmill outside of the selected boundary. If this was left at 0 for this part, our tools first pass would follow the boundary but not cut it. This could be reduced further to make the first cut heavier, but some material will be missed on the lowest level.

14. Select the **Rough parameters** page and make changes to this page as shown below:

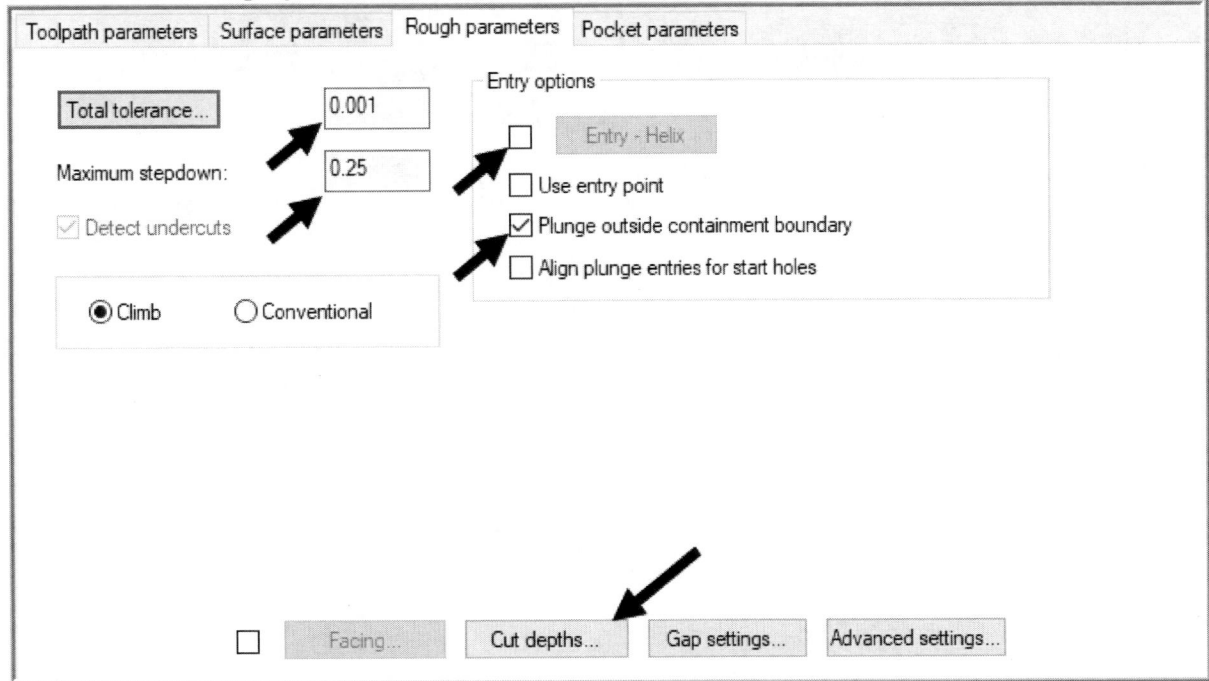

15. Select the **Cuts depths** button.
16. Activate **Absolute** on the **Cuts depths** page.
17. Click on the **Detect flats** button. **Note**: If prompted to **Reset minimum and maximum depths**, select **Yes.**
18. Your values should now be as shown below:

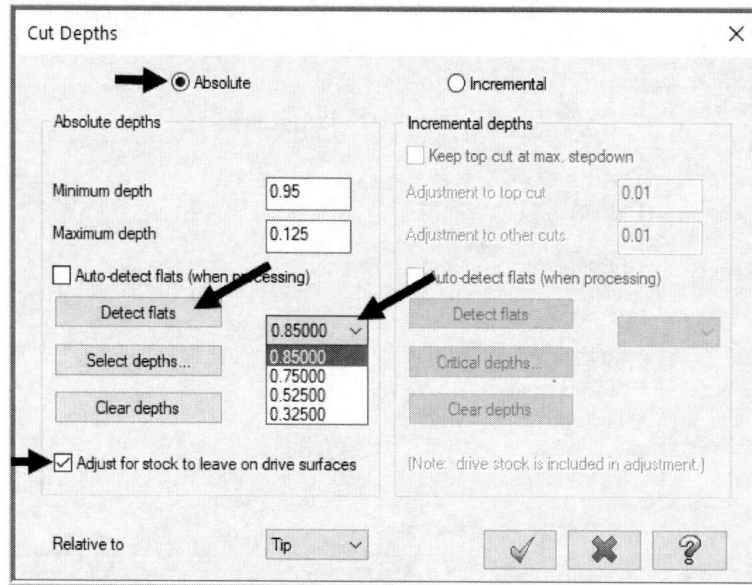

Cut depths specify the placement of Z-axis cuts for all rough surface toolpaths and for finish contour toolpaths.

Absolute cut depths
Absolute cut depths allow you to select a fixed location for the minimum and maximum depths.
Cuts are spaced at the **Maximum stepdown** except when flats are detected. Cut spacing will be changed to cut on the flats or above them if **Adjust for stock to leave of drive surfaces** is selected.

19. Select the OK button [✓] to complete this feature.
20. Select the **Pocket parameters** page and make changes to this page as shown below:

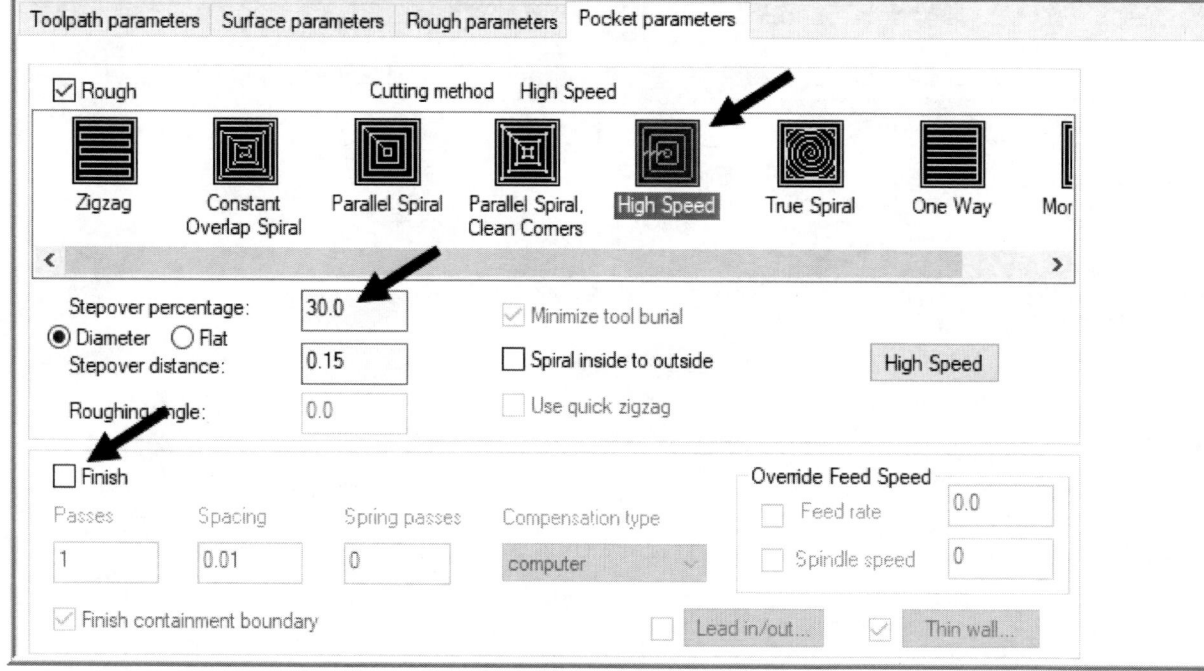

21. Select the OK button [✓] to exit Surface Rough pocket parameters.

22. When prompted about finish passes, click **OK**.

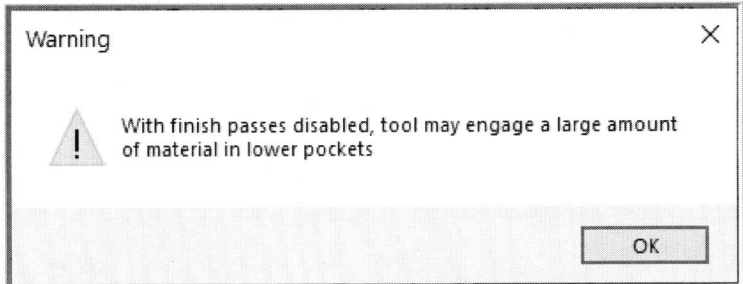

Warning   ✕

!   With finish passes disabled, tool may engage a large amount of material in lower pockets

     OK

➲ The toolpath is displayed as shown as below:

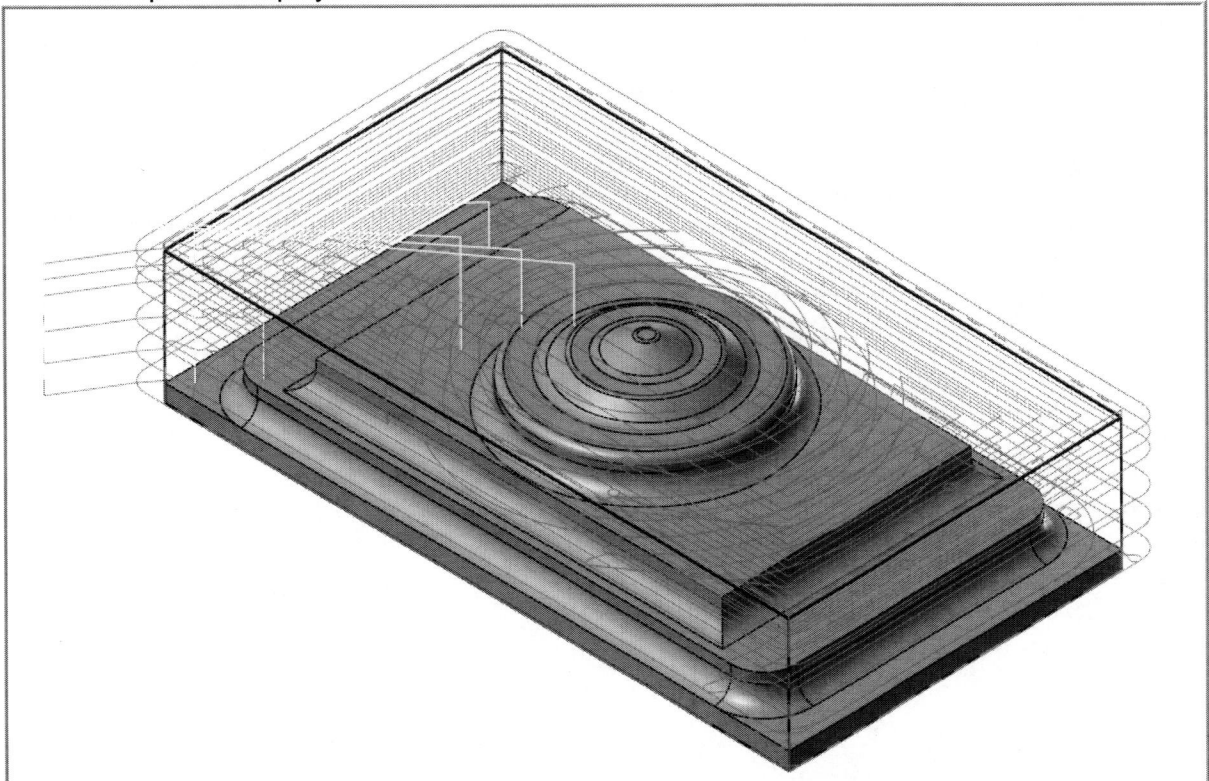

TASK 13:
VERIFY THE ROUGH TOOLPATH AND CREATE MODELS

STL is an acronym for **StereoLithography**, a 3D model file type developed by 3D Systems, Inc. An STL file is composed of triangular facets of data that represent surface and solid models. STL files are, in fact, large collections of oriented triangles. The triangles consist of three points and one vector. The three points are intended to define a plane; the vector is intended to be perpendicular—or normal—to the plane defined by the three points.

STL comparison allows you to check the accuracy of the part model created by Verify against an STL file (a 3D model file). STL comparison is available in Mill and Router, and only when using box-shaped stock.

Stock Model operations are associative to the source toolpath operations and parameters on which they are based. If you change the source operation parameters, Mastercam marks the operation and the stock model operation as "dirty", requiring regeneration.
Once created, you can use stock model operations to:
-Verify stock
-Define stock for rest machining
-Visualize stock
-Generate stock model compares

1. In the Toolpaths Manager pick all the operations by picking the **Select all operations** icon.
2. If required set to **Isometric** and **Fit** the part to the screen.
3. Select the **Verify selected** operations button shown below.
4. **Maximize** the Backplot/Verify window if required.
5. Activate the options shown below in the **Visibility** section of the **Home** tab. **Initial Stock not** activated.

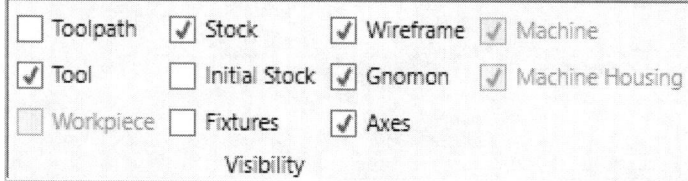

6. Open up the **Stop Conditions** dropdown menu and activate the **Collision** option.

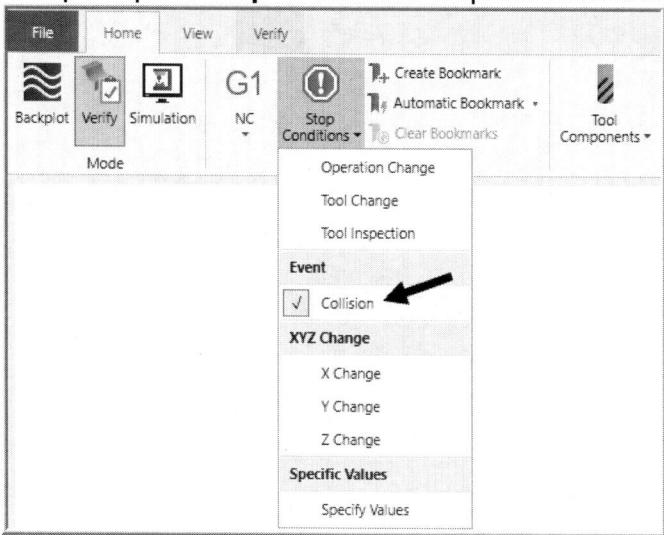

7. In the lower part of the screen now set the run Speed to slow by moving the slider bar pointer over to the left as shown below, and then press **Play.**

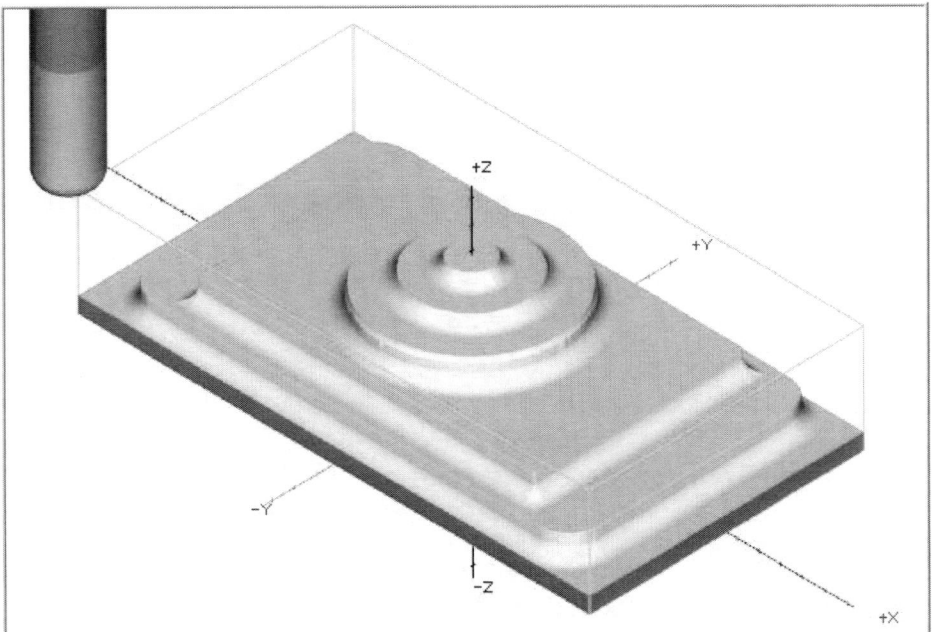

8. When Verify finished, click on the **Verify** Tab click on **Save Stock as STL.**

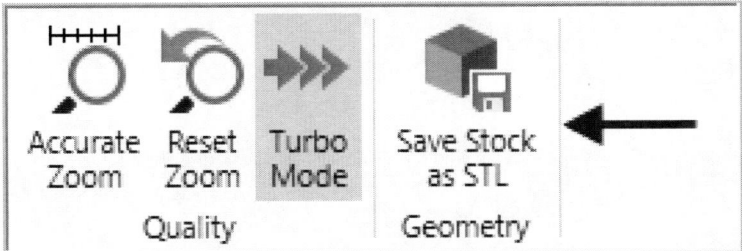

9. Save the **STL** file name as the same name as the Mastercam file name: **Mill-Lesson-14**. **Make note of where you save this STL file**, you will be using it shortly.

10. Select the Save button to save the STL file.

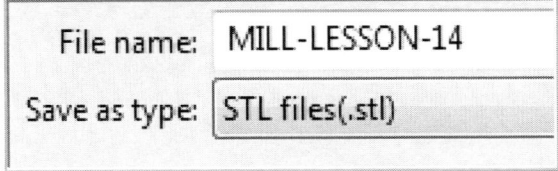

11. Select the **Close** button ⊠ in the top right-hand corner to exit Verify.

⊃ Another method for creating in process models is using the Stock Model function.

12. On the Toolpaths page, click Stock Model.

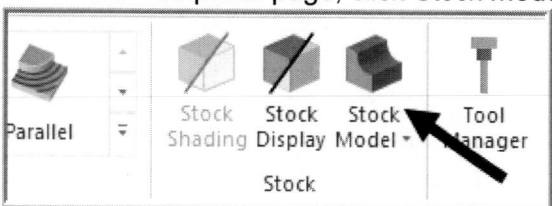

13. On the Stock Definition page, **name the Stock Model, Roughing Done**. Set the initial stock shape to **Rectangle** and then click **Stock Setup**. This will define our stock the same as defined in the Machine Properties Stock Setup we did earlier.

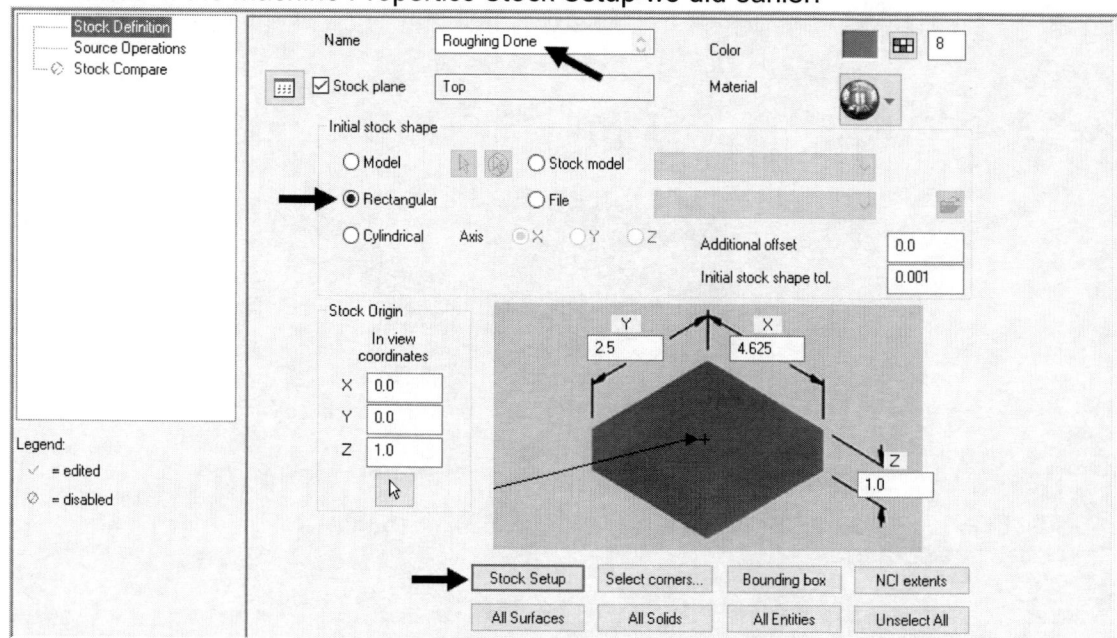

14. On the Source Operations page, select the **Surface Rough Pocket** toolpath. Click **Ok**.

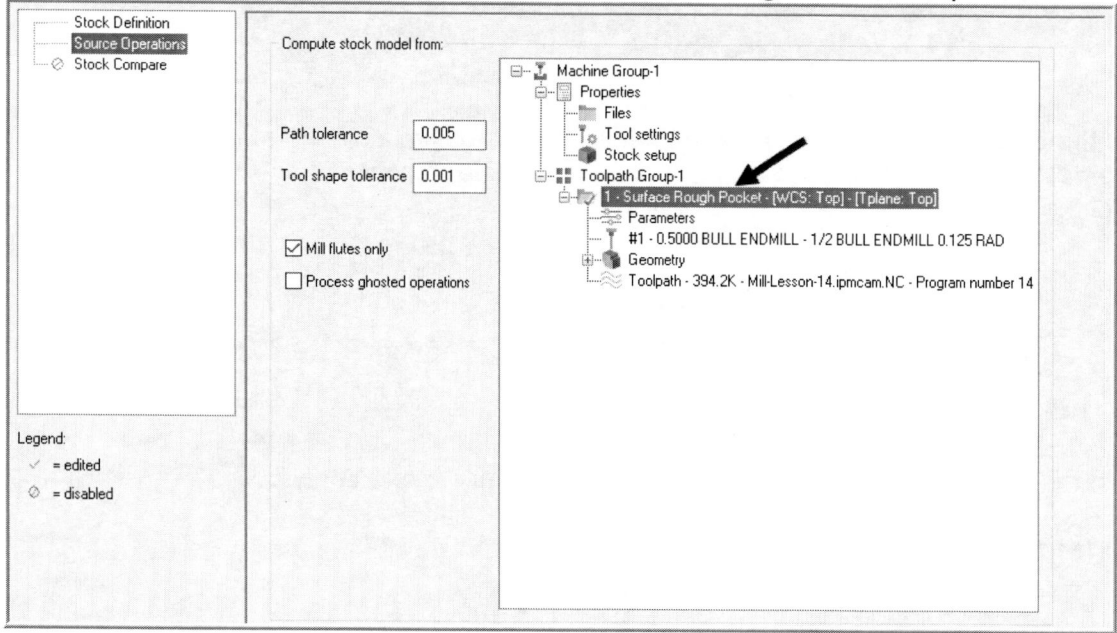

15. This will create a Stock Model in the Toolpaths Manager, you will also see this model in the graphics area.

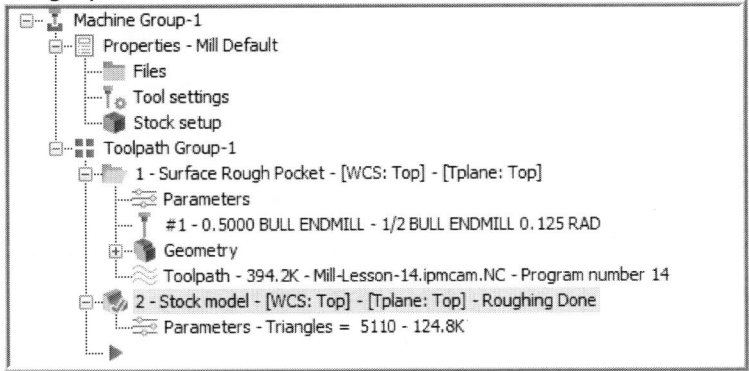

16. Toggle the display of the Stock Model the same as you would a toolpath, using Alt-T or clicking the Toggle Display Toolpaths button.

TASK 14:
FINISH USING SURFACE FINISH CONTOUR

➲ In this task you will use a 0.500 diameter end mill with a 0.125 corner radius to finish the walls of the part.

1. In the Toolpaths Manager pick all the operations by picking the **Select all operations** icon  and then select the Toggle toolpath display on selected operations to hide the toolpaths.

2. On the **Toolpaths** tab open the drop-down menu in the **3D** toolpath section and select **Contour** in the **Finishing** section.
3. To satisfy the prompt **Triple Click** on the **Solid Model** and note how it changes color.
4. the **End Selection** icon ⊙.
5. Click on the **Containment Select** button.

6. Click on **C-plane** and then click on the rectangle as shown below:

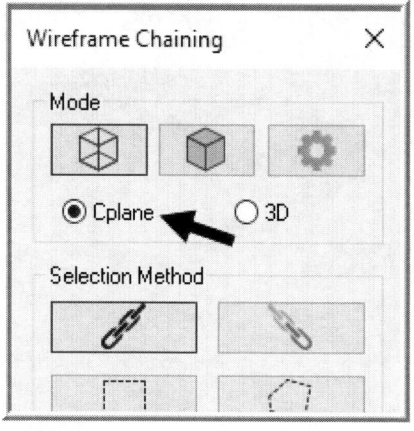
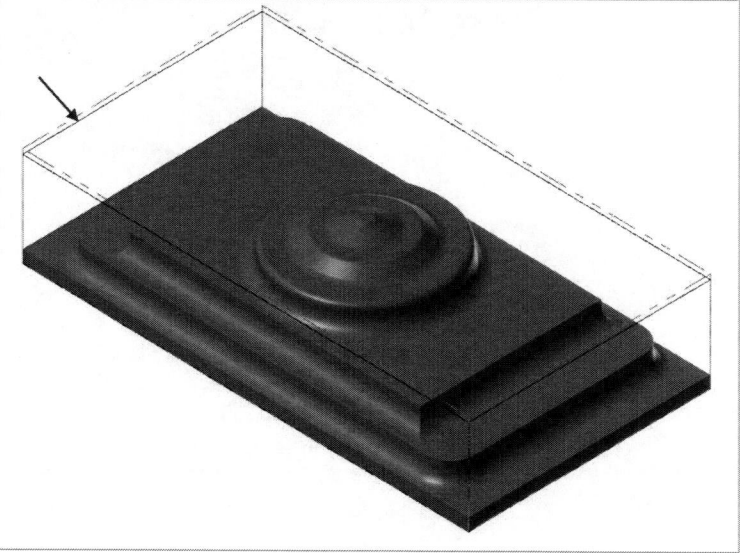

7. Select the OK button ✓ in the Chaining window.
8. Select OK ✓ in the Toolpath/surface selection window.

9. Select the 0.500 diameter end mill with a 0.125 corner radius and make changes to the **Toolpath parameters** page as shown below: Set **Coolant on**.

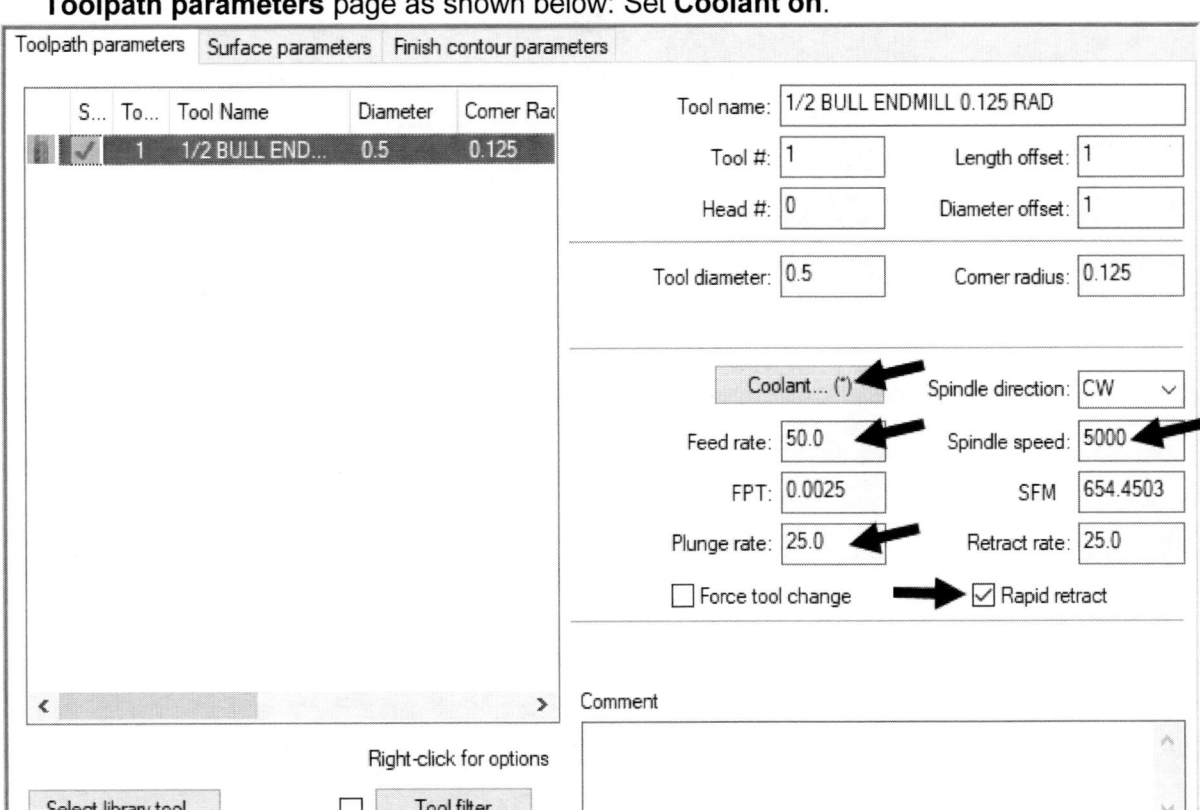

10. Click on the **Surface parameters** tab and make changes as shown below. **Tool containment** is set to **Outside**.

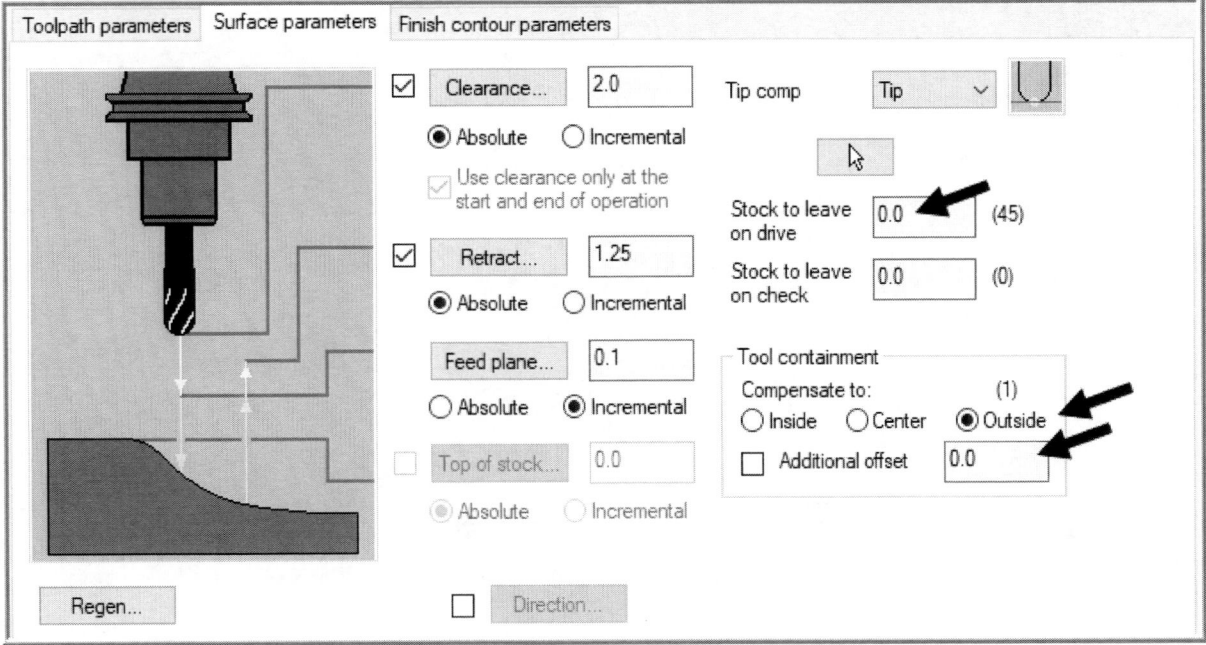

11. Click on the **Finish contour parameters** tab and make as shown below:

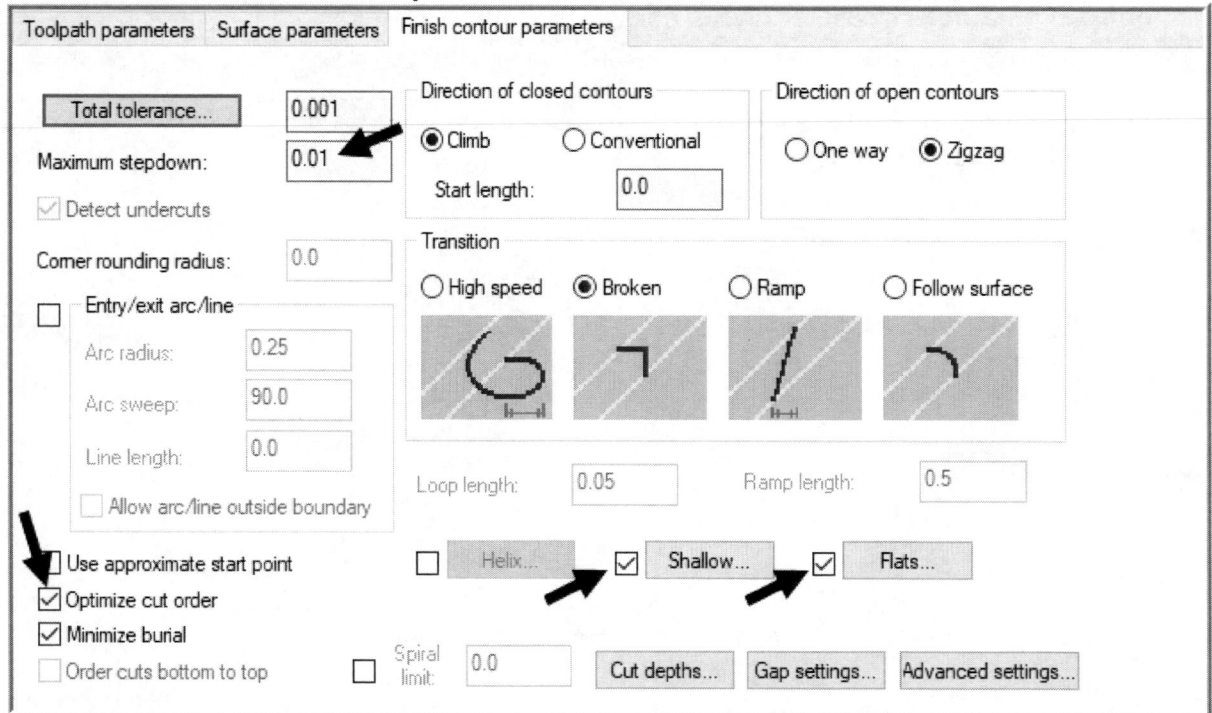

12. Activate **Shallow** click on the **Shallow** button and set values as shown below:

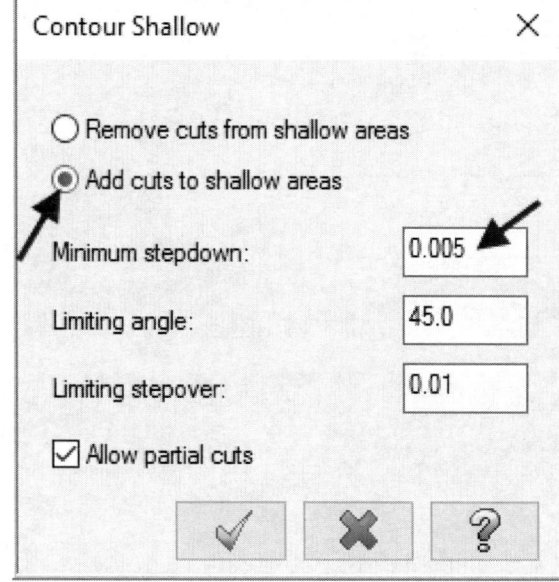

13. Select the OK button ✓ to exit Shallow.

Contour shallow dialog box
Shallow parameters add or remove cuts from shallow areas in a surface rough or finish contour (constant Z) toolpath.
You can add or remove full cuts or partial cuts from the shallow areas.

---

14. Activate **Flats** click on the Flats button and set values as shown below:

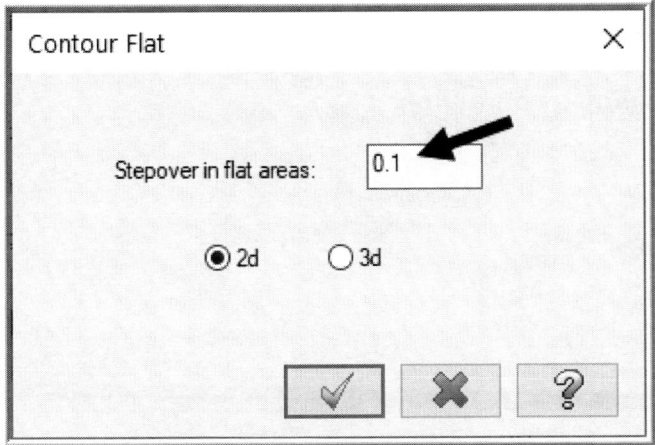

> **Contour flat dialog box**
> Use this dialog box to add additional cuts to flat or very shallow areas of a surface rough or
> finish contour toolpath. Mastercam already includes the Shallow option, which adds additional
> cuts in shallow areas of the part, but these additional passes are at different Z depths.
> In contrast, the extra cuts added with the Flats option are at the same Z depth, making them
> appropriate for perfectly flat areas.

15. Select the OK button to exit Flats.

16. Select the **Cuts depths** button and activate **Absolute** and set the values as shown below:

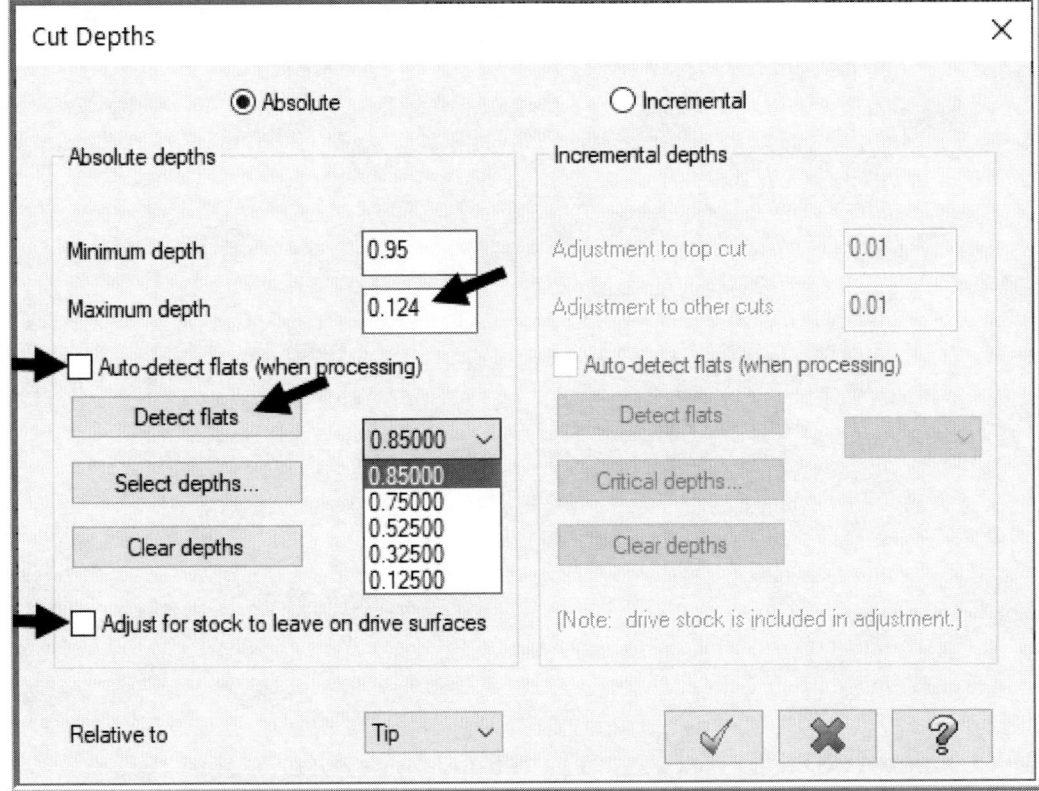

17. Select the OK button to complete this feature.

18. Select the OK button to exit the Surface Finish Contour parameter screen.

TASK 15:
VERIFY THE TOOLPATH

1. In the Toolpaths Manager select **only the Finish contour** operation.
2. In the Toolpaths Manager pick the **Simulator Options** icon.

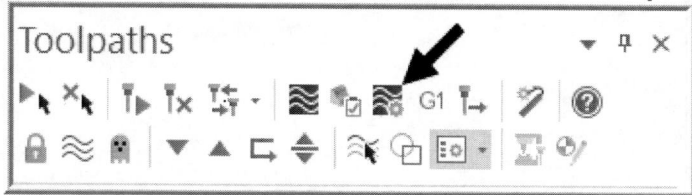

3. In the **Simulator Options** window activate the radio button for **File** and then select the **Browse** icon.

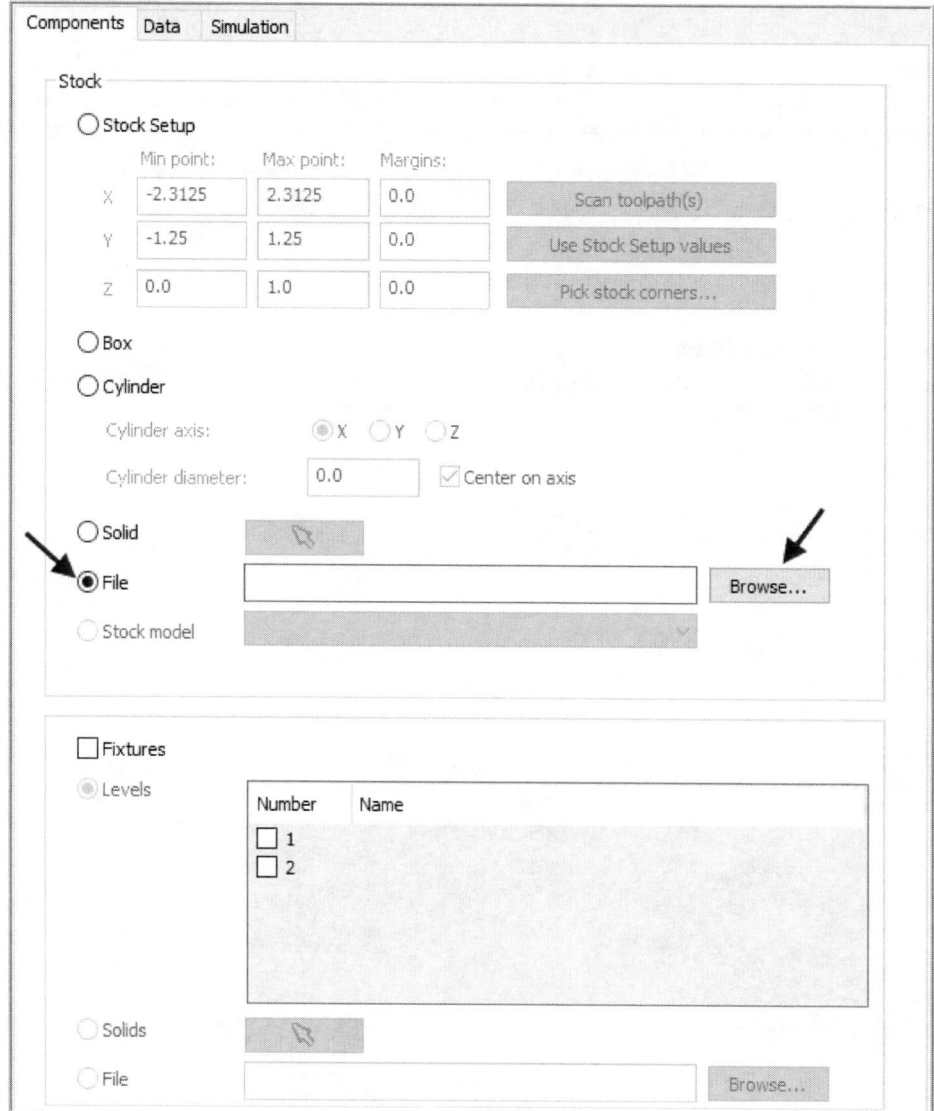

4. Select the **Mill-Lesson-14.STL** file you created earlier and then click on **Open**.
5. Select the **OK** button [✓] to exit **Simulator Options**.

6. Select the **Verify selected operations** icon.
➲ The stock appears as below:

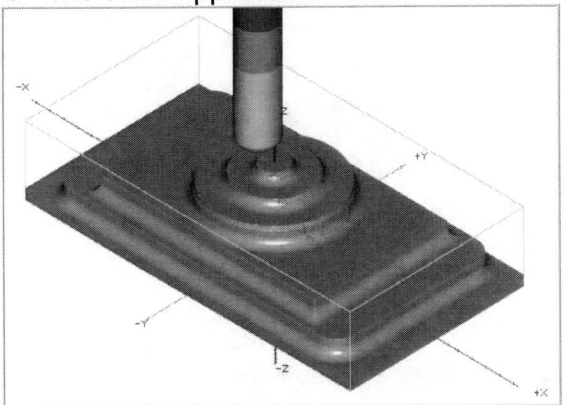

7. Activate the options shown below in the Visibility section of the Home tab. Initial Stock not activated.

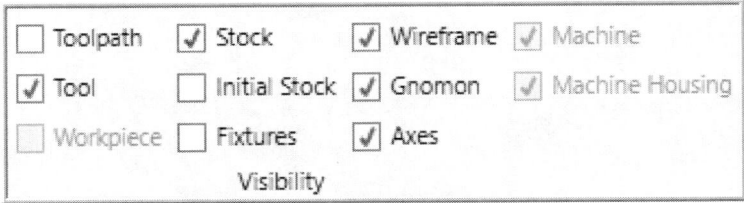

8. At the top of the screen select the **Verify** tab and activate the **Color Loop**.
9. At the top of the screen select the **View** tab, the **Isometric** icon and then select **Fit**.
10. In the lower part of the screen now set the run Speed to slow by moving the slider bar pointer over to the left as shown below.

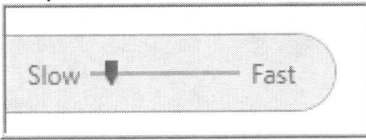

11. Now select the **Play** Simulation button to review the toolpaths.
➲ The verified toolpaths are shown below:

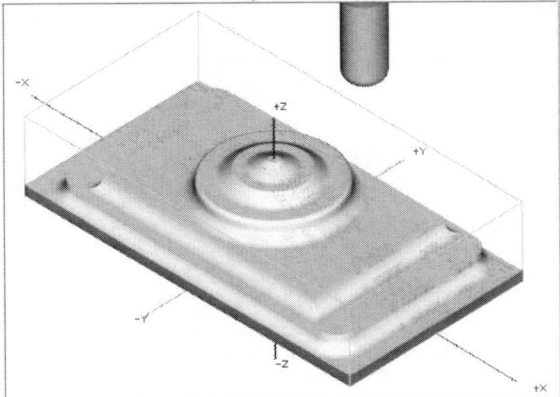

12. Select the Close button [×] in the top right-hand corner to exit Verify.

TASK 16:
SAVE THE UPDATED MASTERCAM FILE

1. Select the **Save** icon from the **Quick Access** toolbar at the top left of the screen.

TASK 17:
POST AND CREATE THE CNC CODE FILE

1. Ensure all the operations are selected by picking the **Select all operations** icon 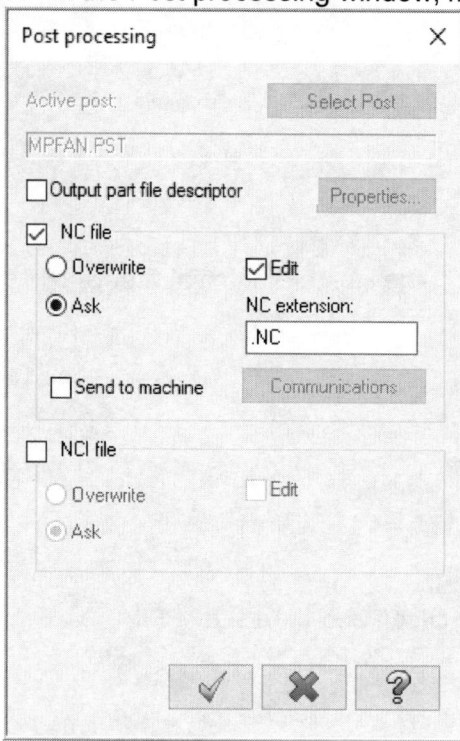 from the Toolpaths Manager.
2. Select the **Post selected operations** button from the Toolpaths Manager.
3. In the Post processing window, make the necessary changes as shown below:

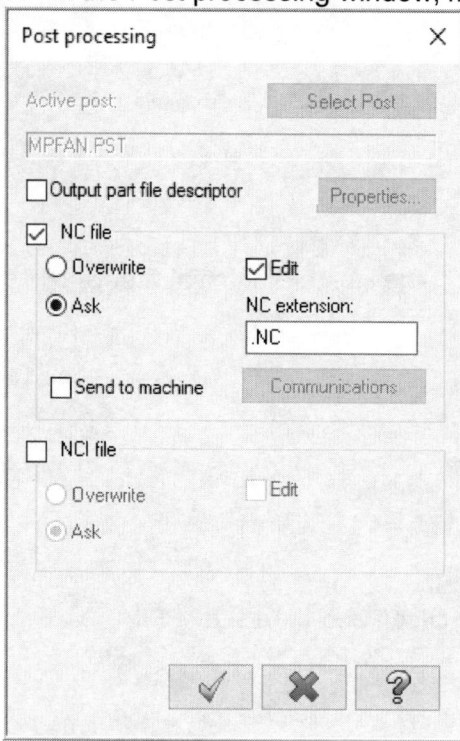

4. Select the OK button ✓ to continue.
5. Enter the same name as your Mastercam part file name in the NC File name field **Mill-Lesson-14**.
6. Select the Save button.
7. The CNC code file opens up in the default editor:

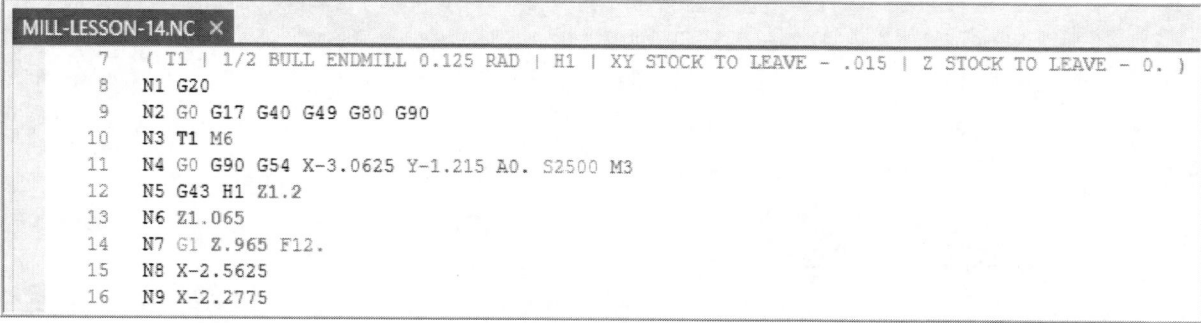

```
MILL-LESSON-14.NC  ×
     7    ( T1 | 1/2 BULL ENDMILL 0.125 RAD | H1 | XY STOCK TO LEAVE - .015 | Z STOCK TO LEAVE - 0. )
     8    N1 G20
     9    N2 G0 G17 G40 G49 G80 G90
    10    N3 T1 M6
    11    N4 G0 G90 G54 X-3.0625 Y-1.215 A0. S2500 M3
    12    N5 G43 H1 Z1.2
    13    N6 Z1.065
    14    N7 G1 Z.965 F12.
    15    N8 X-2.5625
    16    N9 X-2.2775
```

8. Select the ⊠ in the top right corner to exit the CNC editor

9. This completes Mill-Lesson-14.

MILL-LESSON-14-EXERCISE-A

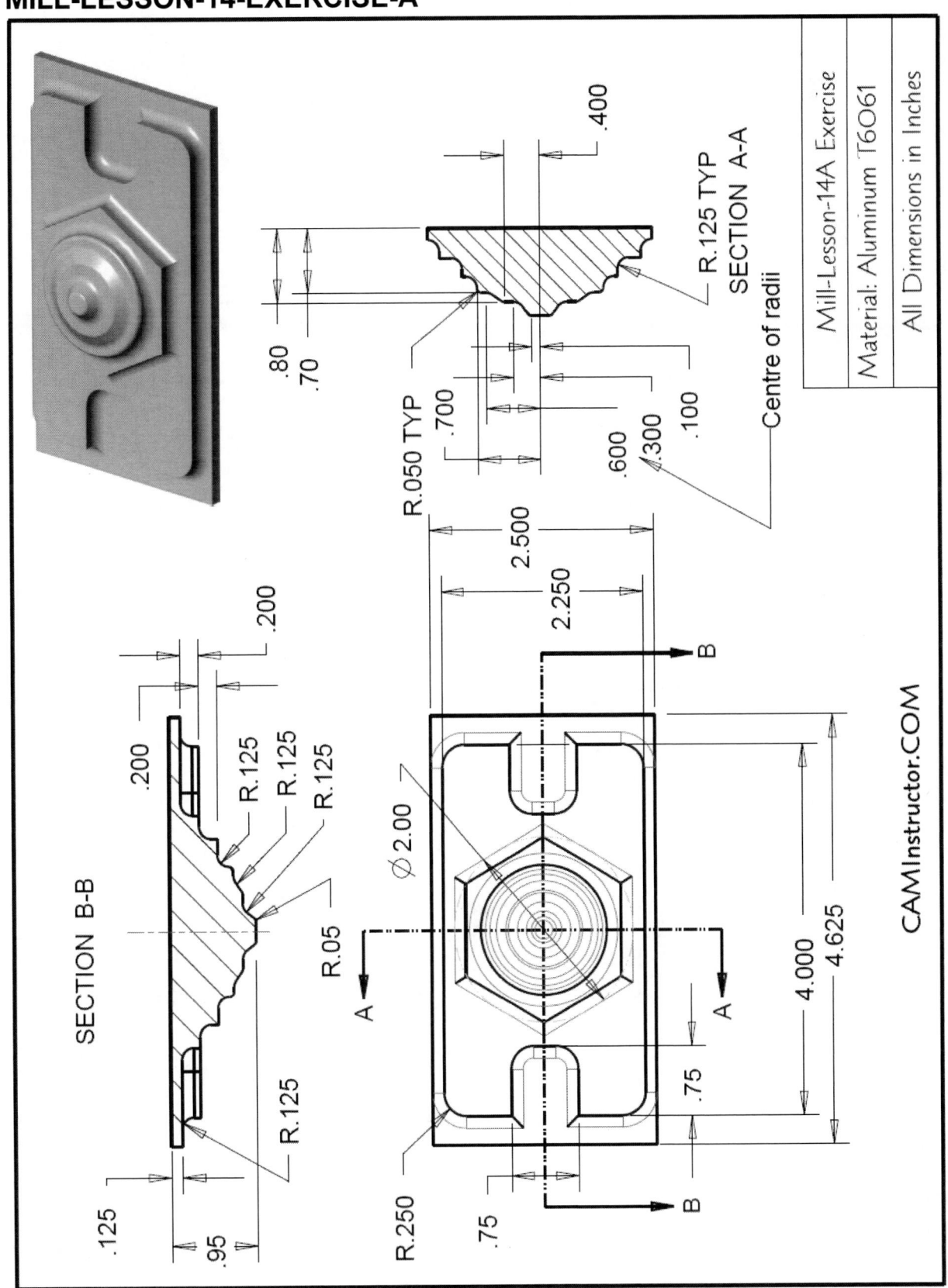

R.125 TYP
SECTION A-A

Centre of radii

.400

.80
.70

R.050 TYP
.700

.600
.300
.100

2.500

2.250

SECTION B-B

.200
.200

R.125
R.125
R.125

R.05

R.125

.125
.95

Ø 2.00

4.625
4.000

.75

R.250

.75

A   A

B   B

Mill-Lesson-14A Exercise

Material: Aluminum T6O61

All Dimensions in Inches

CAMInstructor.COM

MILL-LESSON-14-EXERCISE-B

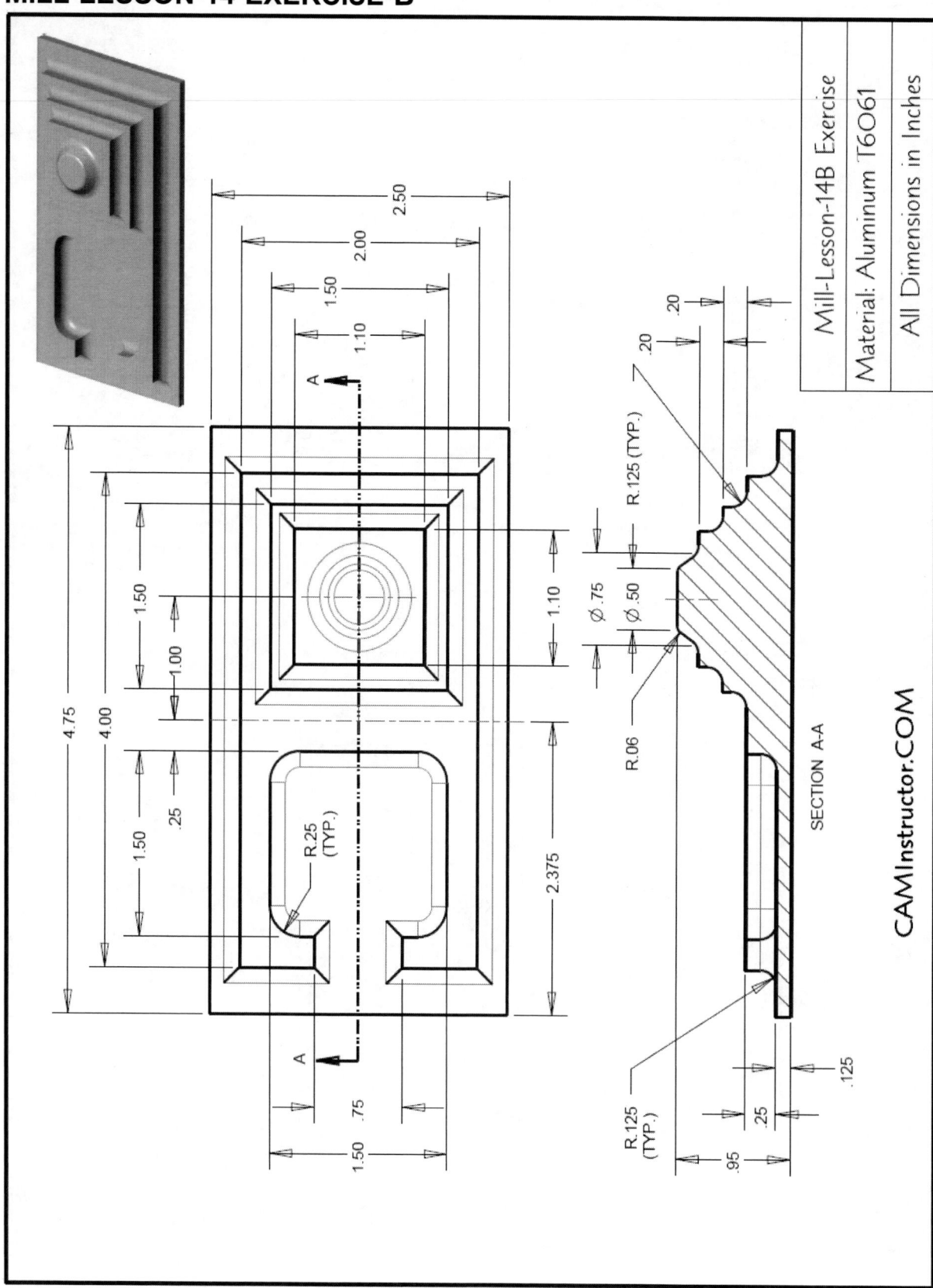

Mill-Lesson-14B Exercise

Material: Aluminum T6061

All Dimensions in Inches

SECTION A-A

CAMInstructor.COM

Mastercam 2022

TRAINING
GUIDE

MILL-LESSON-15
DYNAMIC OPTIROUGH,
WATERLINE, AND
SURFACE HIGH SPEED PENCIL

camInstructor

Objectives

You will use a provided model for Mill-Lesson-15, then generate the toolpaths to machine the part on a CNC vertical milling machine. This Lesson covers the following topics:

Establish Stock Setup settings:
Stock size using Bounding Box.
Material for the part.
Feed calculation.

Generate 2 and 3-dimensional milling toolpaths consisting of:
Dynamic OptiRough
Waterline
Contour
Surface High Speed Pencil

Inspect the toolpath using Mastercam's Verify by:
Launching the Verify function to machine the part on the screen.
Comparing a verified part to the original stock stl file.
Generating the NC- code.

TOOL LIST

1.000 diameter bull end mill 0.03125 corner radius to rough and finish machine.
.500 diameter ball end mill to finish machine.
.250 diameter flat end mill to finish machine.
.250 diameter ball end mill to finish machine.

MILL-LESSON-15 - THE PROCESS

Toolpath Creation

TASK 1:   Setting the environment
TASK 2:   Open an existing Mastercam file
TASK 3:   Define the rough stock using stock setup
TASK 4:   Roughing with OptiRough
TASK 5:   Finish surfaces with Waterline
TASK 6:   Finish profile using 2D Contour
TASK 7:   Finish radii using Pencil
TASK 8:   Verify the toolpaths and Compare to solid model
TASK 9:   Save the updated Mastercam file
TASK 10: Post and create the CNC code file
TASK 11: Create an ActiveReport

TASK 1:
SETTING THE ENVIRONMENT
➲ Before starting the geometry creation, you should set up the grid and machine type as outlined in the Setting the environment section at the beginning of this text:
1. Set up the Grid. This will help identify the location of the origin.

Please Note:
Review the videos **before** working through each task.

There are some intricate geometry selection techniques used in this lesson and reviewing the procedures in the **Videos** will make it easier for you to complete this lesson.

TASK 2:
OPEN AN EXISTING MASTERCAM FILE

➲ The required file for this Lesson is available in one of the Steps in **Lesson 15** on the **caminstructor Course Site**.
➲ **The part is already setup for: Default Mill.**

1. Select **File>Open>Mill-Lesson-15.**
2. If confronted with the System Configuration dialog box activate the radio button for **All settings**.

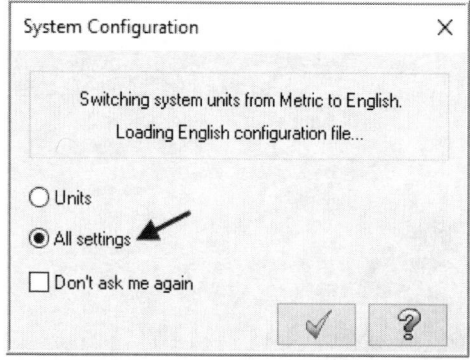

System Configuration (switch units) dialog box
When you open a part file that uses different units (English or metric) from those currently in use, Mastercam automatically displays this dialog box, which informs you that Mastercam is switching units and loading an alternate default configuration file. In order to complete the operation, select one of the following options:
Units: Tells Mastercam to use only the units from the new configuration file. (default)
All settings: Tells Mastercam to load all settings from the new configuration file.

---

3. Select the OK button [✓] to exit the **System Configuration** dialog box.
4. In the **View** tab click on **Outline Shaded** in the **Appearance** section to display the part in shaded mode.

TASK 3:
DEFINE THE ROUGH STOCK USING STOCK SETUP

1. Select the **View tab** and click on **Toolpaths** in the **Managers** section to display the Toolpaths Manager.
2. Select the **plus** in front of **Properties** to expand the Toolpaths Group Properties.
3. Select **Stock setup** in the Toolpaths Manager window.
4. On the **Stock Setup** page select **Bounding box**.

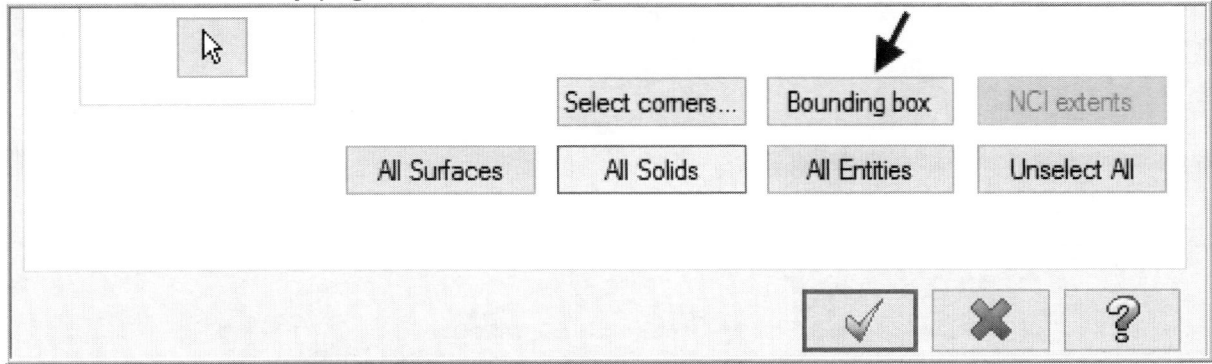

5. You are prompted to **"Select one or more entities. Use Ctrl-A to select all"**. On your keyboard select **Ctrl-A** to select all the entities.

6. Click on **End Selection** to move onto the next step. The Bounding box window appears.

➲ Take note of the X, Y and Z values Mastercam has calculated for the stock size and the preview on the graphics screen.

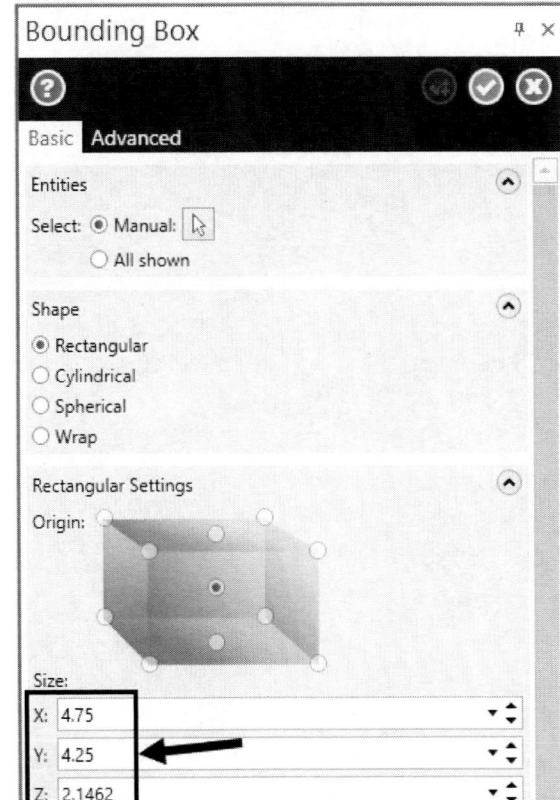

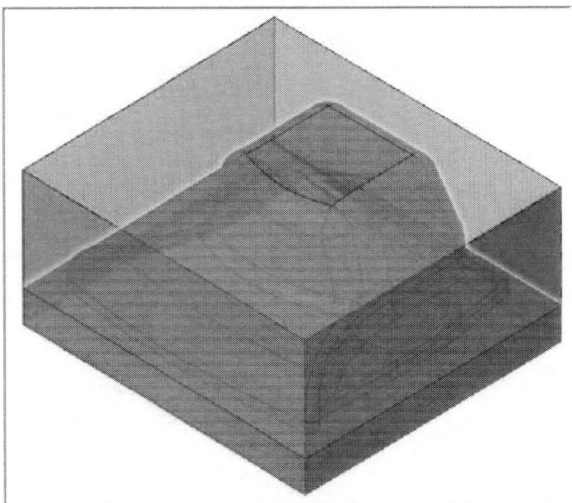

7. Move the stock origin to the bottom and then in the **Size** section **click in the Z value** after the last digit and input **+0.1** as shown below. This will add all the extra stock to the top of the part.

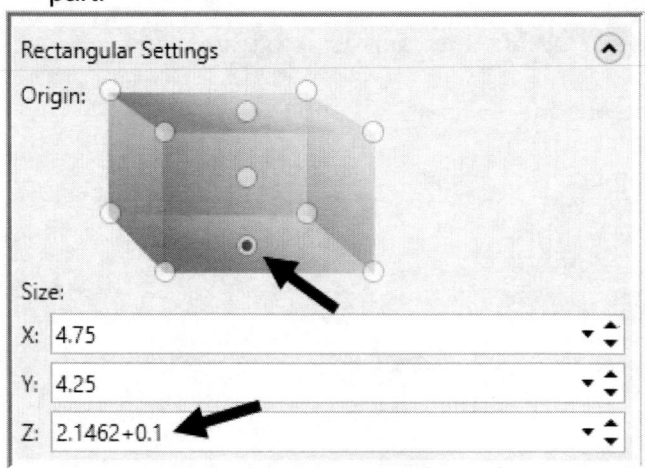

8. Now click on the **OK** icon in the Bounding box window.
9. Set the parameters to match the **Stock Setup** screenshot shown below.

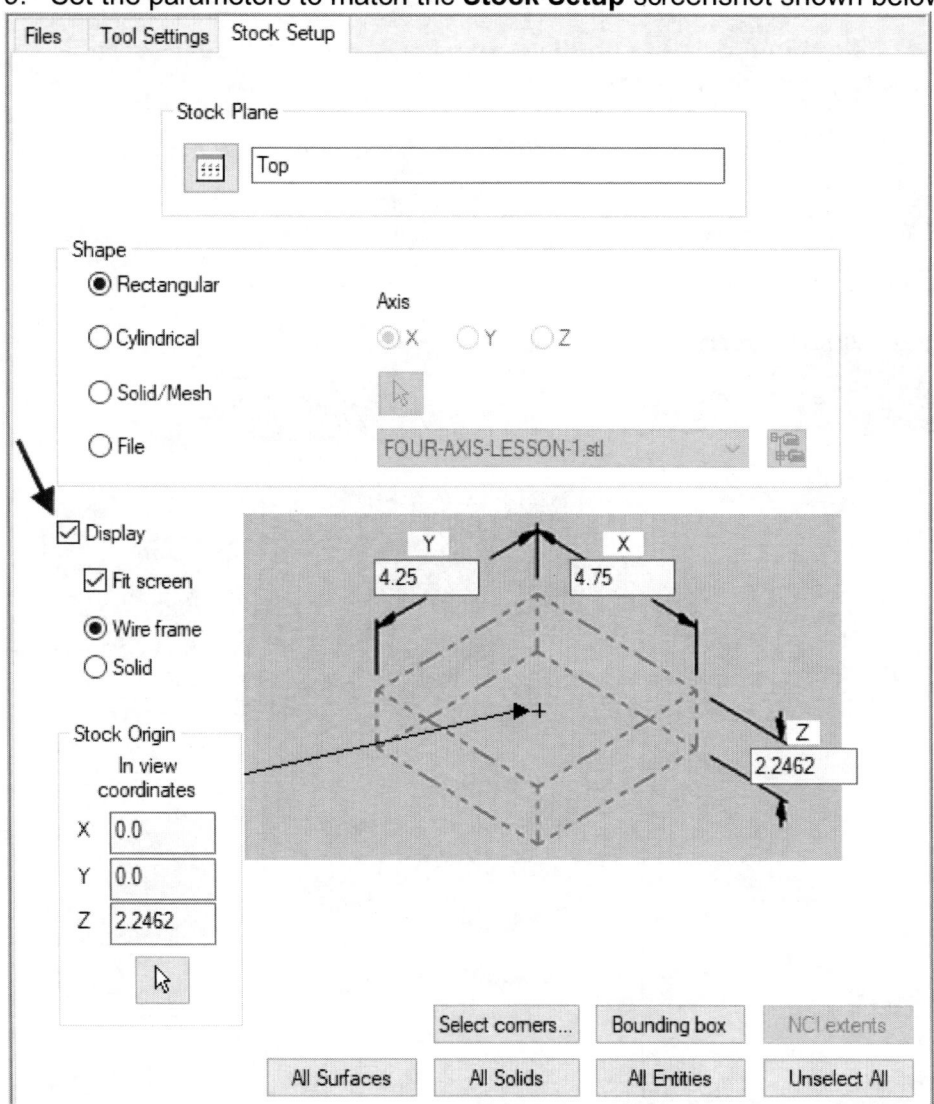

10. Select the **Tool Settings** tab and change the parameters to match the Tool Settings screenshot below. **Note**: The **Feed Calculation** is set to **From material**. To change the Material type follow the instructions below:

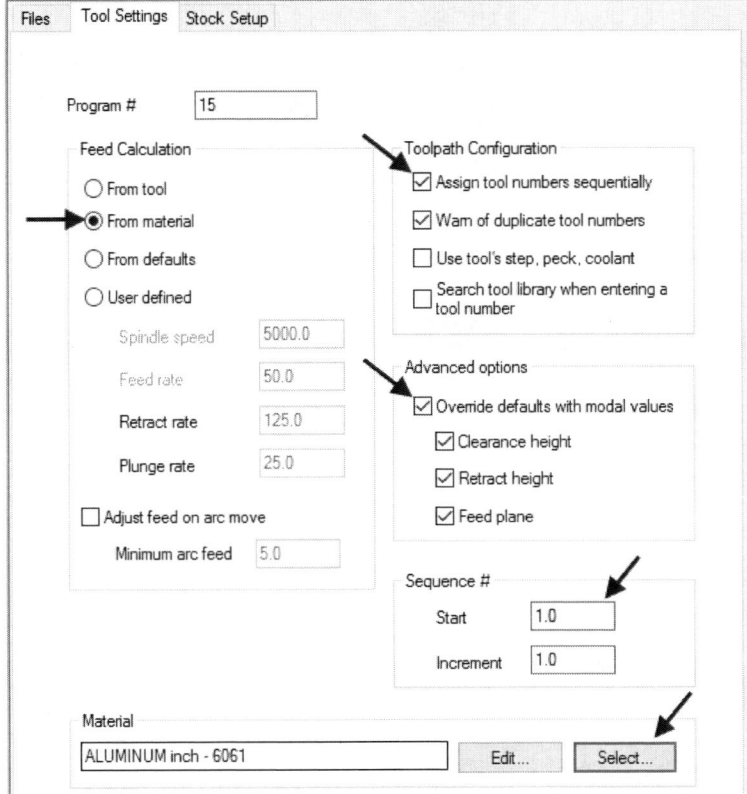

11. To change the **Material** type to **Aluminum 6061** pick the **Select** button at the bottom of the **Tool Settings** page.

12. At the **Material List** dialog box open the **Source** drop down list and select **Mill – library**.

13. From the Default Materials list select **ALUMINUM inch - 6061** and then select the **OK button**.

14. Select the **Edit** button to enter the material definition. Set the SFM% for carbide to **400**. This will set the SFM (Surface Feet per Minute) at 4x the Base cutting speed, 400. 400x4=1600 SFM for carbide tools. The Operation Type can also adjust the SFM. If we were Drilling, it would run at 60% of the base SFM, 400x0.6=240 SFM and if it was a carbide drill, 240x4=960 SFM. These same settings can be applied to the FPT (feed per tooth) as well.

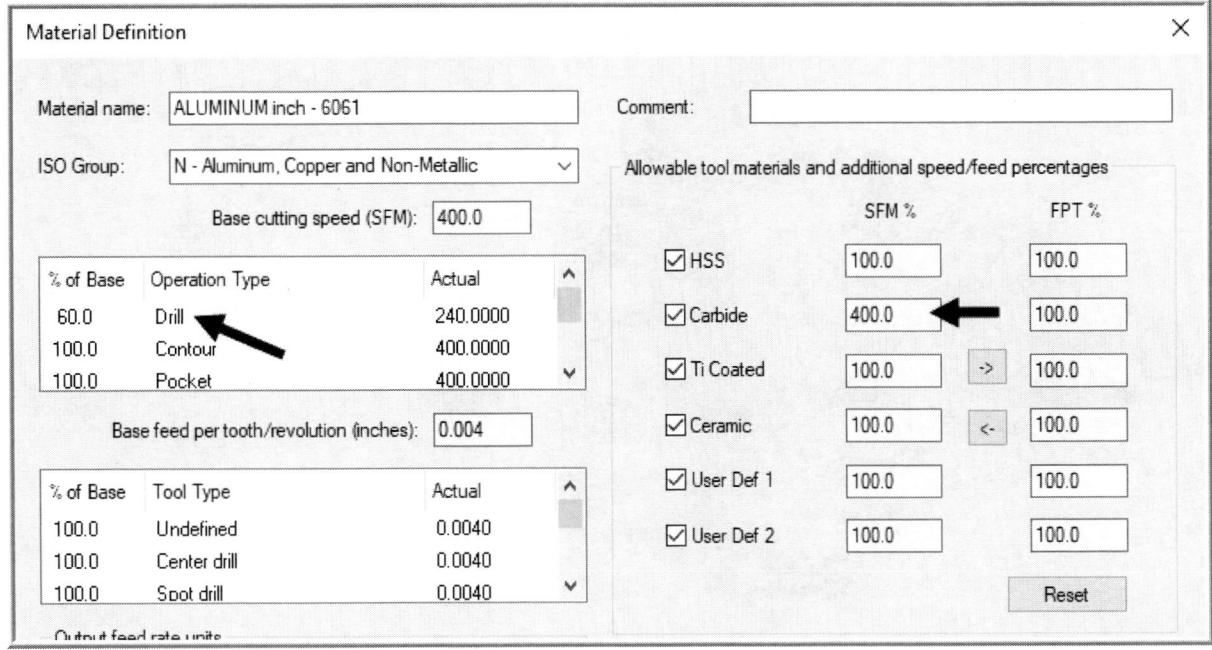

Material Definition allows the user to enter the **Base cutting speed** (Surface Feet per Minute) and **Base feed per tooth/revolution** (Chip Load). These base values can be arrived at based on the material used. Mastercam's default values are very conservative so we will use them for safety purposes during this lesson.

% of Base by Operation Type allows the user to specify a variation in SFM based on the operation type. Eg, contour milling will have a much higher SFM than profile milling.

% of Base by Tool Type allows the user to vary feed per tooth by the tool. Eg. endmills will typically have a much higher feed per tooth (FPT) than a ballnose tool will.

Allowable tool materials and additional speed/feed percentages allows the user to further customize based on the tool type.

The user can further adjust SFM and chip load percentages in each tool definition. This is demonstrated during the first toolpath operation.

When cutting on a machine it is extremely important that you research recommended SFM and FPT for your tools and material and make the appropriate settings in Mastercam.

15. Select the **OK button** ✓ again to complete this function.
16. Select the **OK button** ✓ again to exit the **Machine Group Properties**.
17. Right mouse click in the graphics area and click on **Isometric**.

18. Right mouse click in the graphics area and click on the **Fit** icon ⊞.

➲ Your part should look like the screen shot below: With X0 Y0 at the center and Z zero on the bottom of the part.

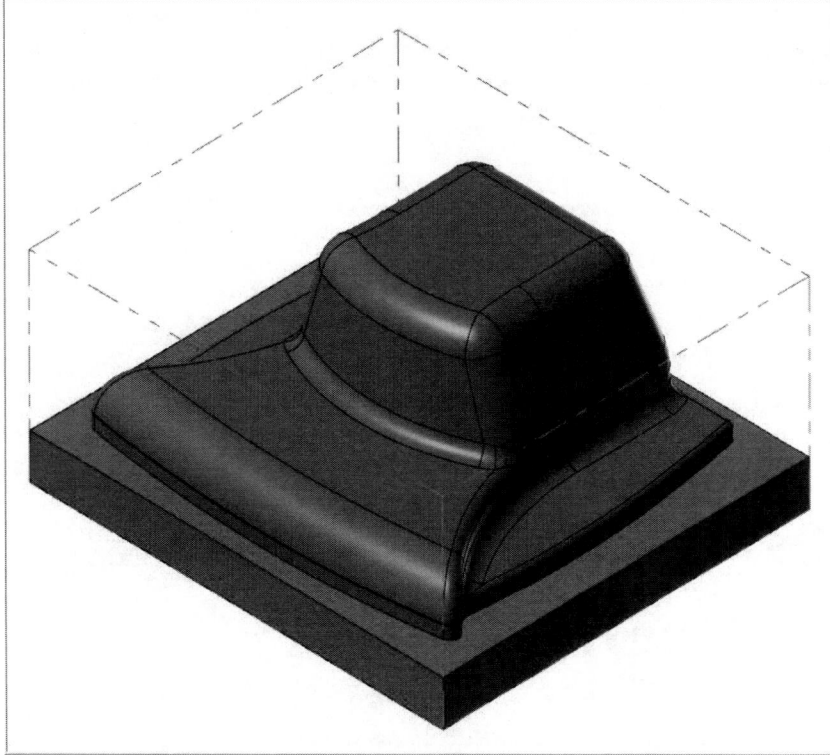

TASK 4:
ROUGHING WITH OPTIROUGH

➲ In this task you will use a 1.000 diameter bull end mill with a 0.03125 corner radius to rough the part.

1. There is only one Level in this part, Level 1 contains the solid geometry of this part.

2. Switch to the Toolpaths Manager, activate the display if needed.
3. Select the **Toolpaths** tab at the top right side of the screen.
4. Select **OptiRough** in the **3D** toolpath section.
5. On the **Model Geometry** page set the **Wall Stock to 0.01** and **Floor stock** to **Zero.**

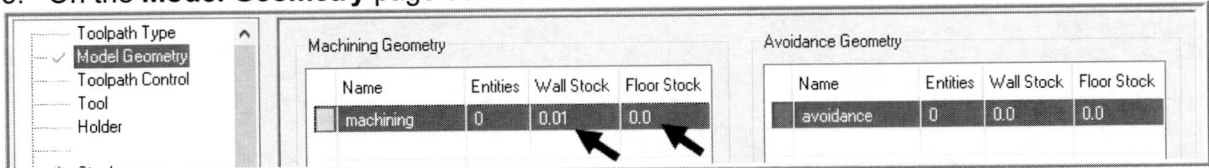

6. At the bottom of the **Model Geometry** page click on the **Select entities** button.

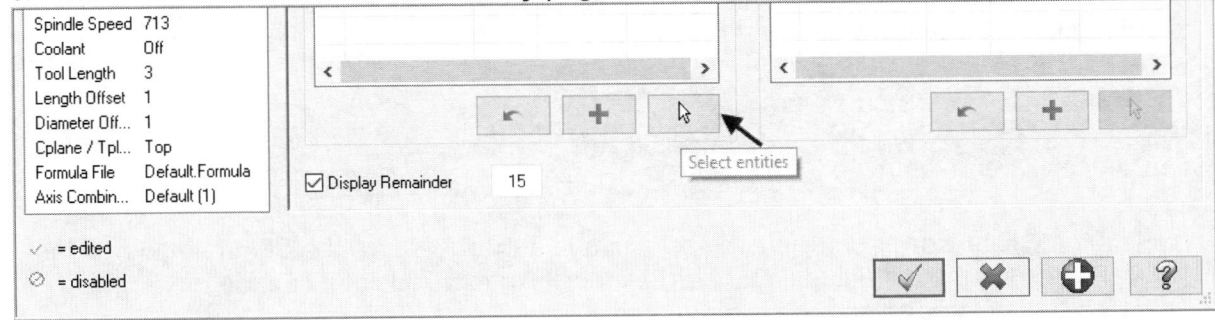

7. Now you will be returned to the graphics screen. To satisfy the prompt on the screen use **Ctrl-A on your keyboard** select to select all the entities.

8. To move onto the next step, you now need to pick the **End Selection** icon ⊘.

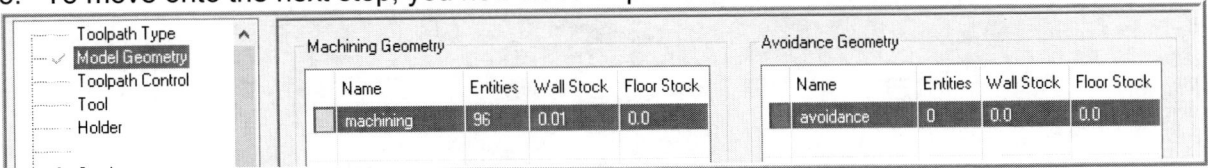

9. Select the **Toolpath Control** page, make changes as shown below.

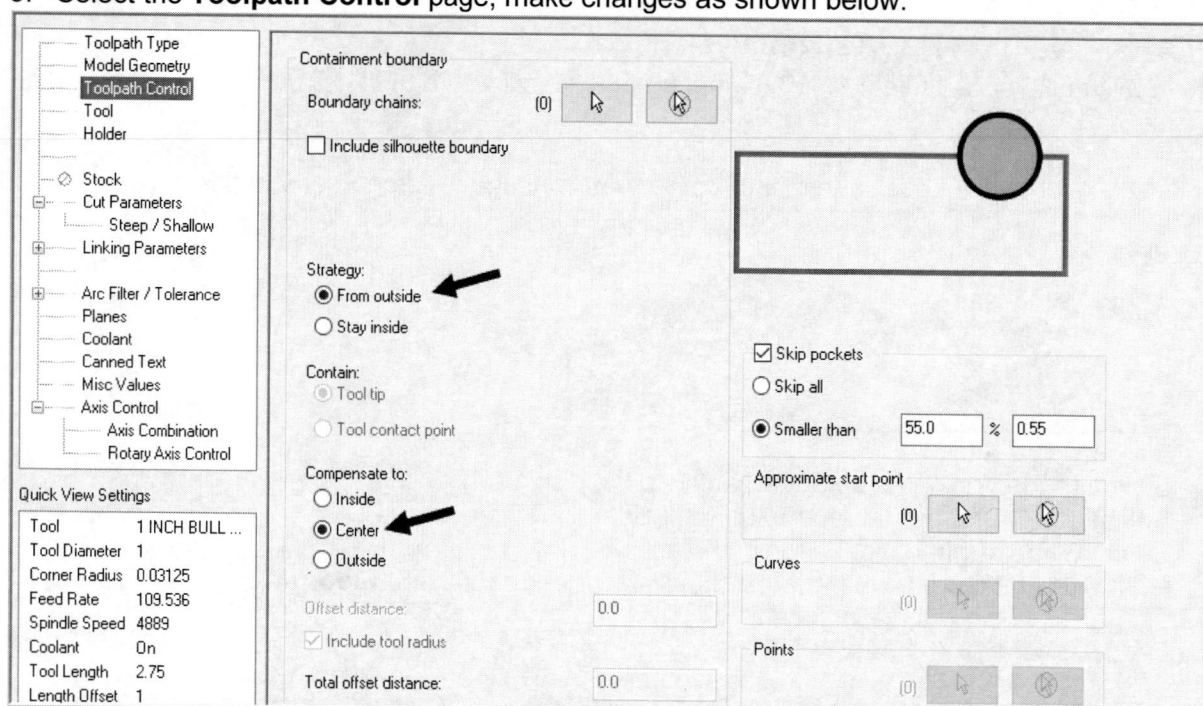

10. Next, select the **Tool** page. In the lower left corner of the page select the **Select library tool...** button. **Deactivate Filter Active**.

11. Use the scroll bar on the right of this dialog box to locate and select the **1.0" Bull Endmill with a 0.0312 corner radius**.

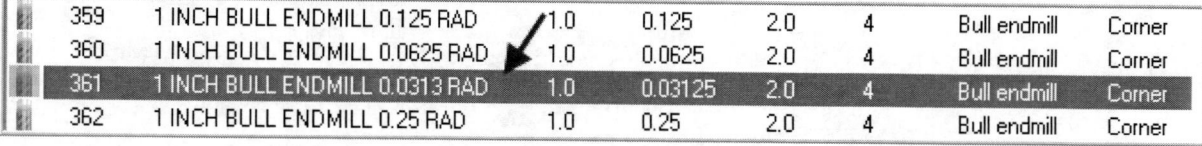

359	1 INCH BULL ENDMILL 0.125 RAD	1.0	0.125	2.0	4	Bull endmill	Corner
360	1 INCH BULL ENDMILL 0.0625 RAD	1.0	0.0625	2.0	4	Bull endmill	Corner
361	1 INCH BULL ENDMILL 0.0313 RAD	1.0	0.03125	2.0	4	Bull endmill	Corner
362	1 INCH BULL ENDMILL 0.25 RAD	1.0	0.25	2.0	4	Bull endmill	Corner

12. Select the **OK button** to complete the selection of this tool. Notice the SFM of the imported tool. This is due the current tool material defined. To update this to a carbide tool, **right click** on the tool and select **Edit tool.**

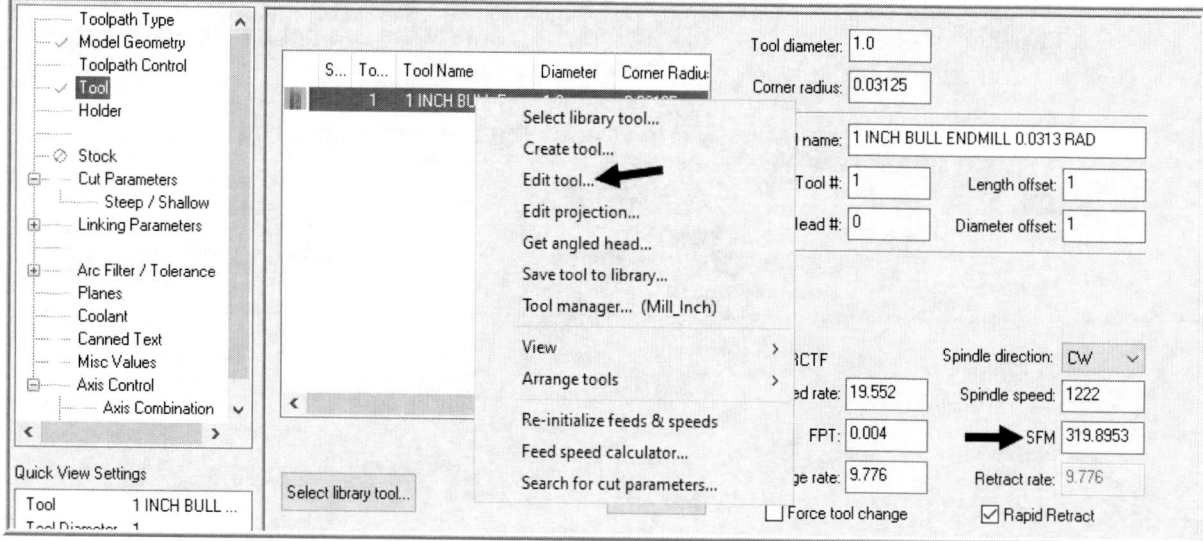

13. Switch to the **Finalize Properties** tab (1), change the Material **to Carbide** (2), click
Recalculate the feeds and speeds (3). You should see **1600 in the SFM** field. Click Finish.

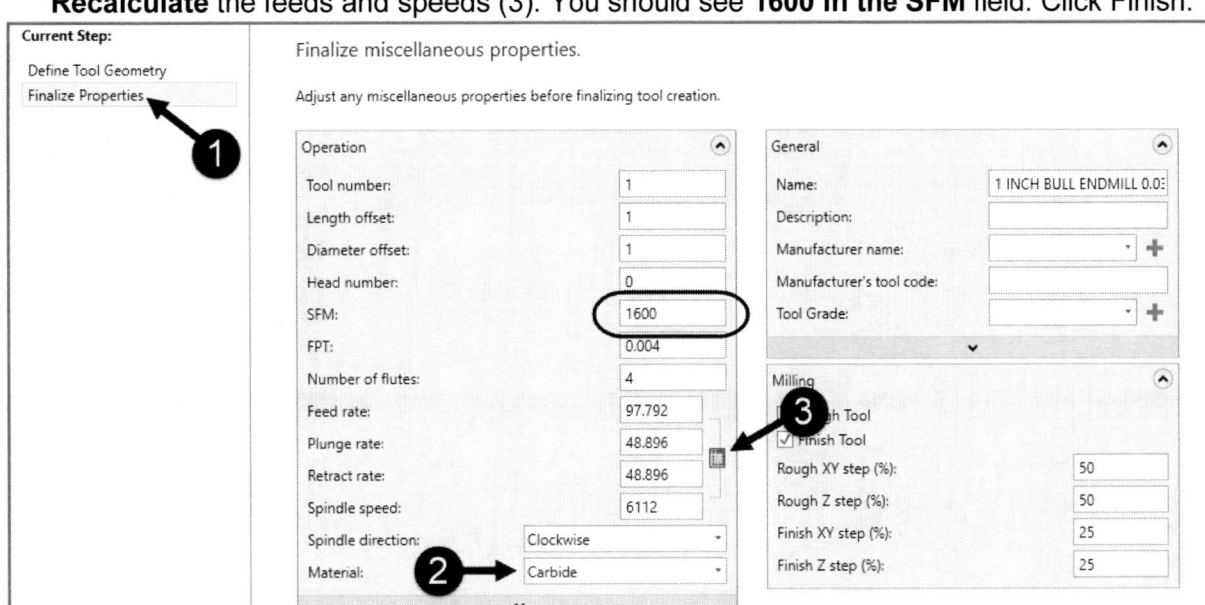

14. The tool should now show the updated SFM. Enable **RCTF** (Radial Chip Thinning).

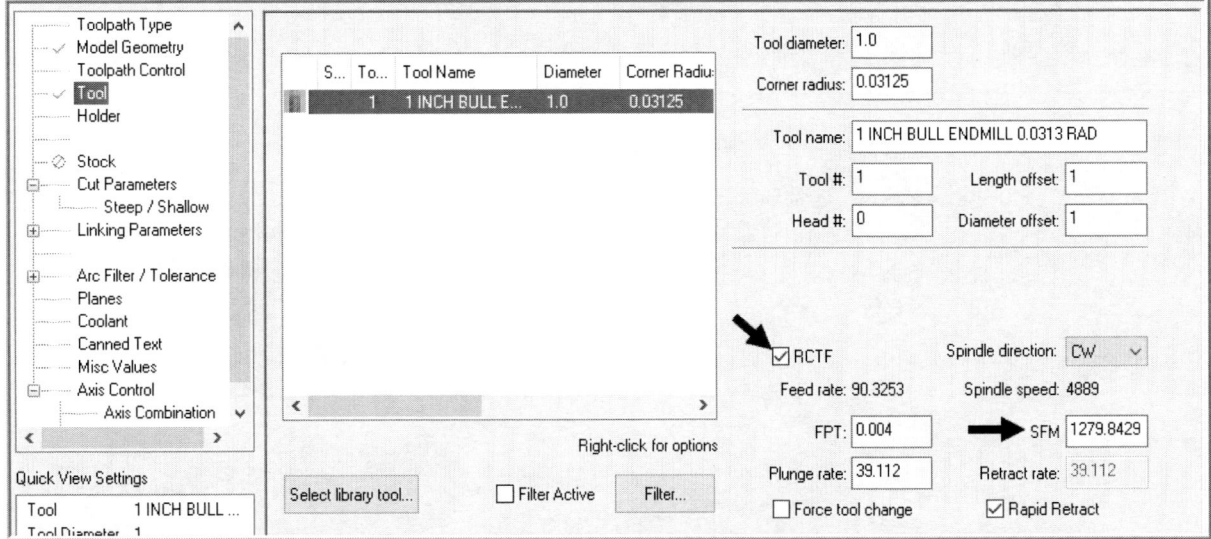

➔ Notice the SFM is now approx. 1280. This is reduced from the 1600 set in the tool due to the operation type, Surfacing, which was set to 80%. 1600x0.8 = 1280.

RCTF = Radial Chip Thinning Factor
For more information on RCTF review the Mastercam Blog:
Radial Chip Thinning Revisited at:
https://www.mastercam.com/en-us/Communities/Blog/postid/73/Mastercam-Radial-Chip-Thinning-Revisited

---

15. Select the **Holder** page and make changes to this page as shown below. Holder to be selected is a **B3E4-1000**. **Tool Projection** is set to **0.25 more** than the shoulder length at **2.75**.

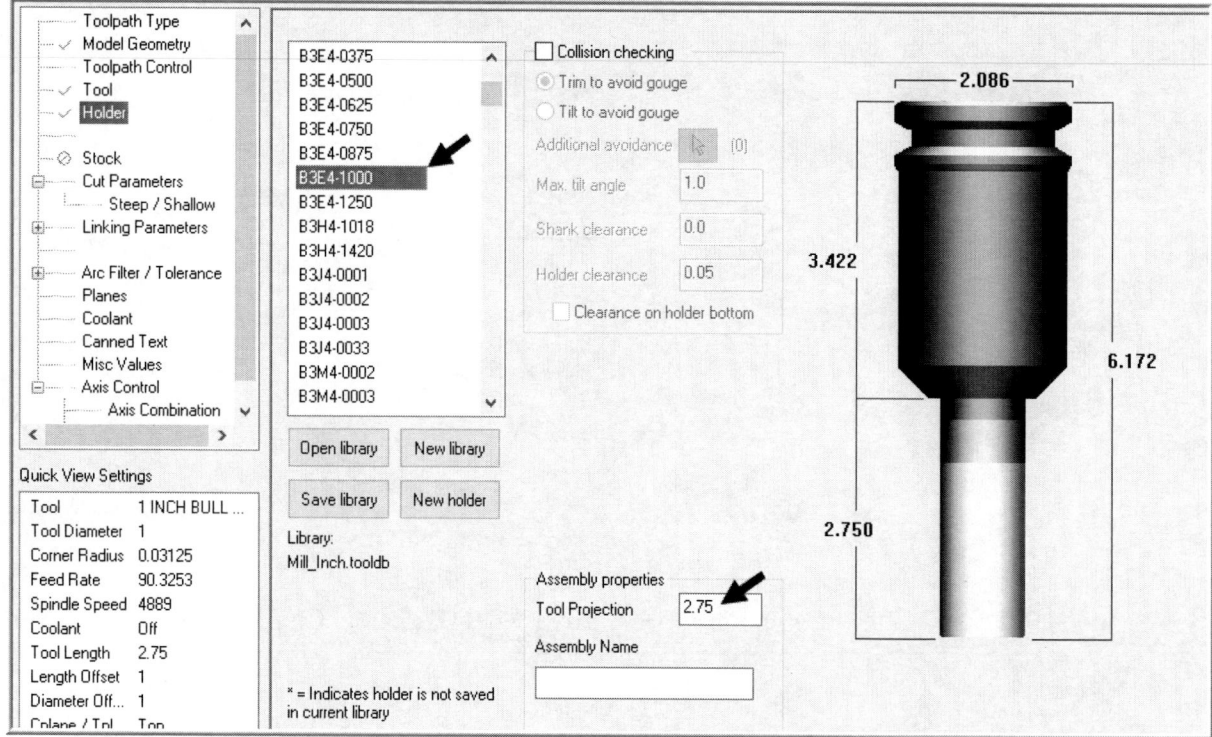

16. Select the **Cut Parameters** page and make changes to this page as shown below:

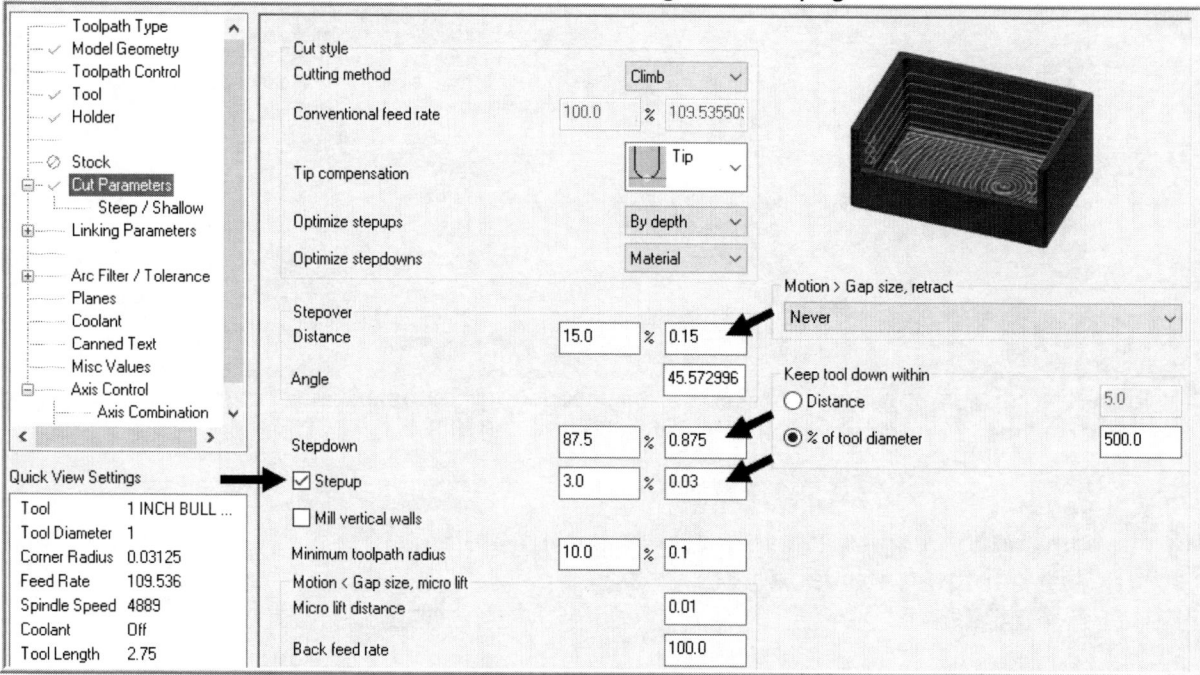

17. On the **Steep/Shallow** page, enable **Maximum depth** and then right click in the Maximum depth field then select **Z = Z coordinate of a point**.

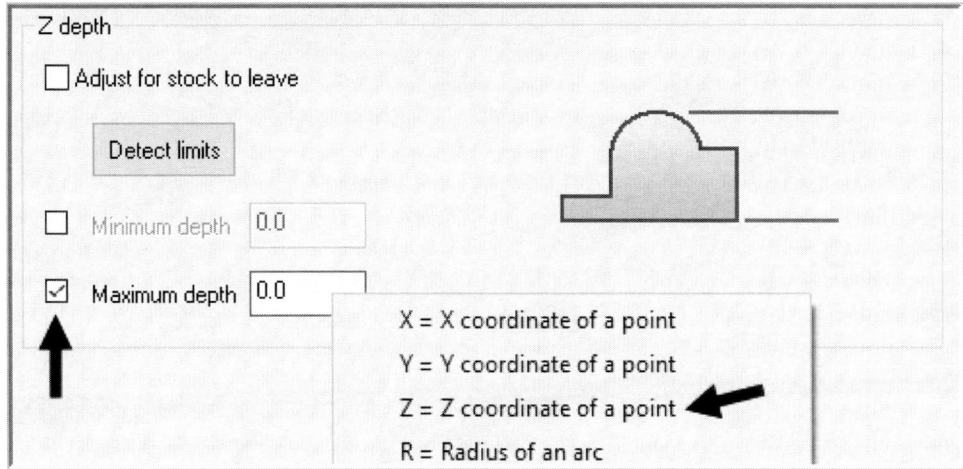

18. When prompted to "**Select a point**" select the point shown below as the Z at the top of the mold base as shown below:

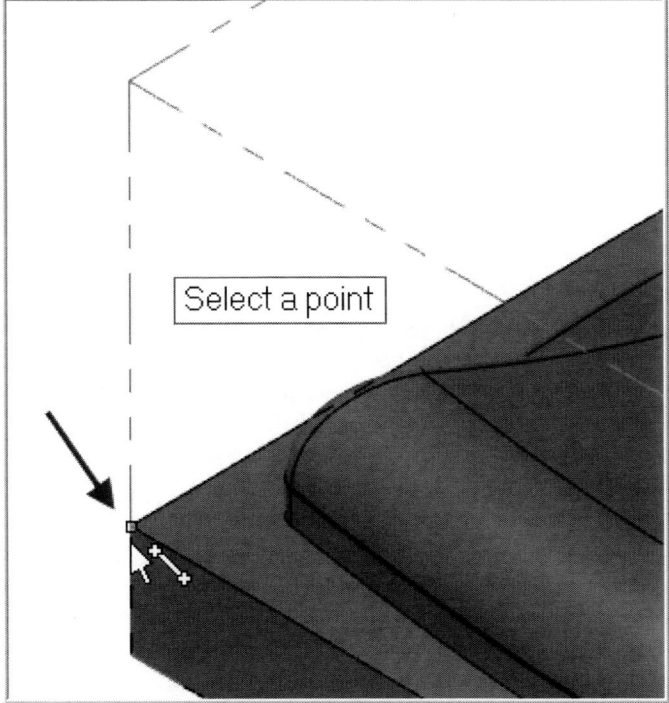

19. The resulting **Steep/Shallow** page values should match the following image:

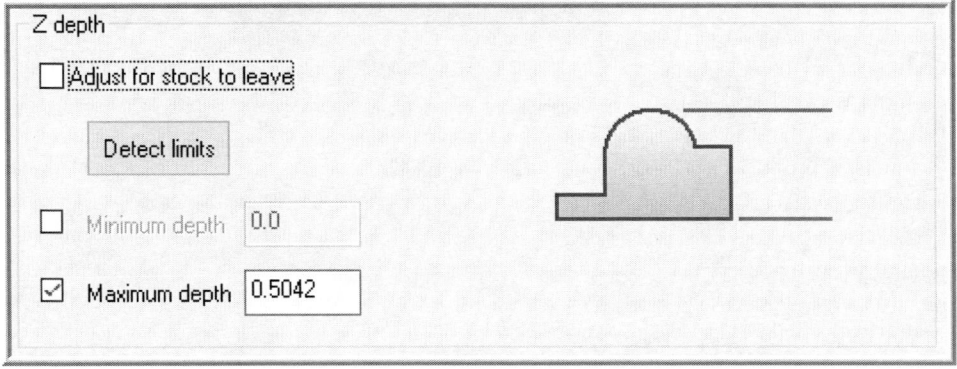

20. Make the following selections on the **Linking Parameters** page: Open up the top drop-down menu first and select **Minimum Distance**.

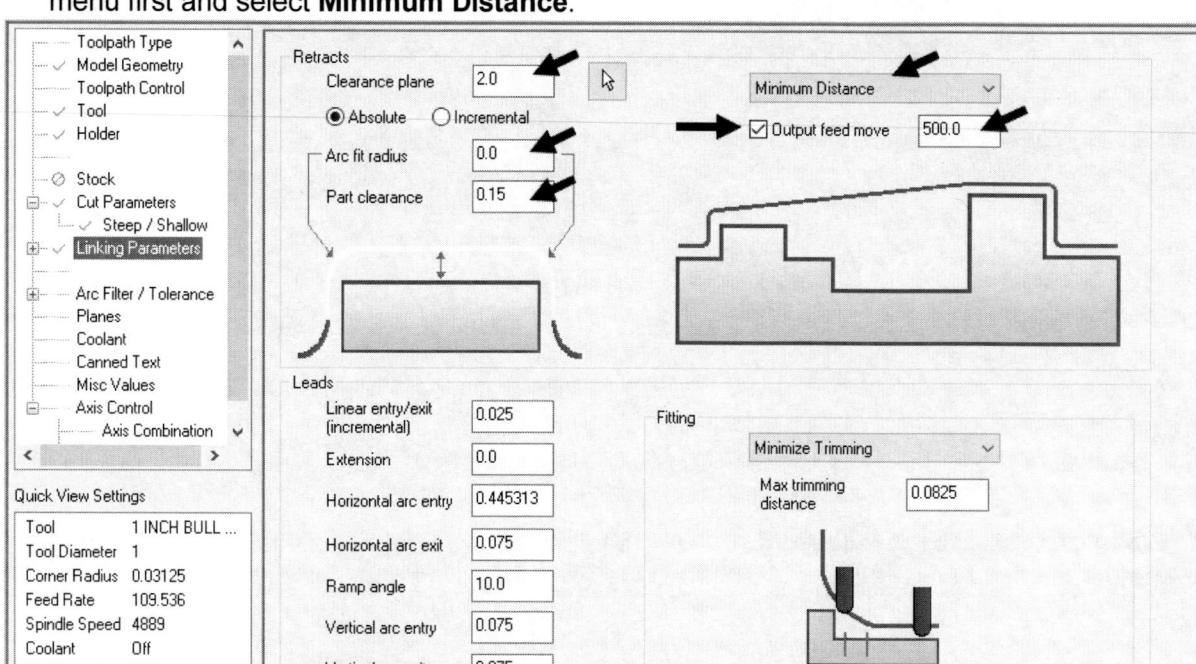

Use this page to create the links between the cutting passes. In general, you can think of linking moves as air moves when the tool is not in contact with the part, compared cutting moves which are configured on the toolpath's Cut parameters page.

First, select a **retract method**. This determines how the tool will move between the end of one pass and the beginning of another. Then, use the **Leads** fields to control how the tool moves onto and off of the part at the start and end of each cutting pass. These moves are applied to each pass no matter which cutting pass is selected. Finally, select a **Fitting** option to control how the entry and exit arcs will be fit into each pass.

Note: Mastercam creates linking moves only when the spacing between cutting passes is greater than the Keep tool down within distance on the

21. Go to the **Arc Filter/Tolerance** page set the **Total tolerance to 0.005**.

Tolerance Distribution		**Total tolerance**
	Total tolerance: 0.005	For the purposes of this Lesson we will do all roughing at .005 overall tolerance to speed calculation times.

22. Still on the **Arc Filter/Tolerance** page and make the following changes:

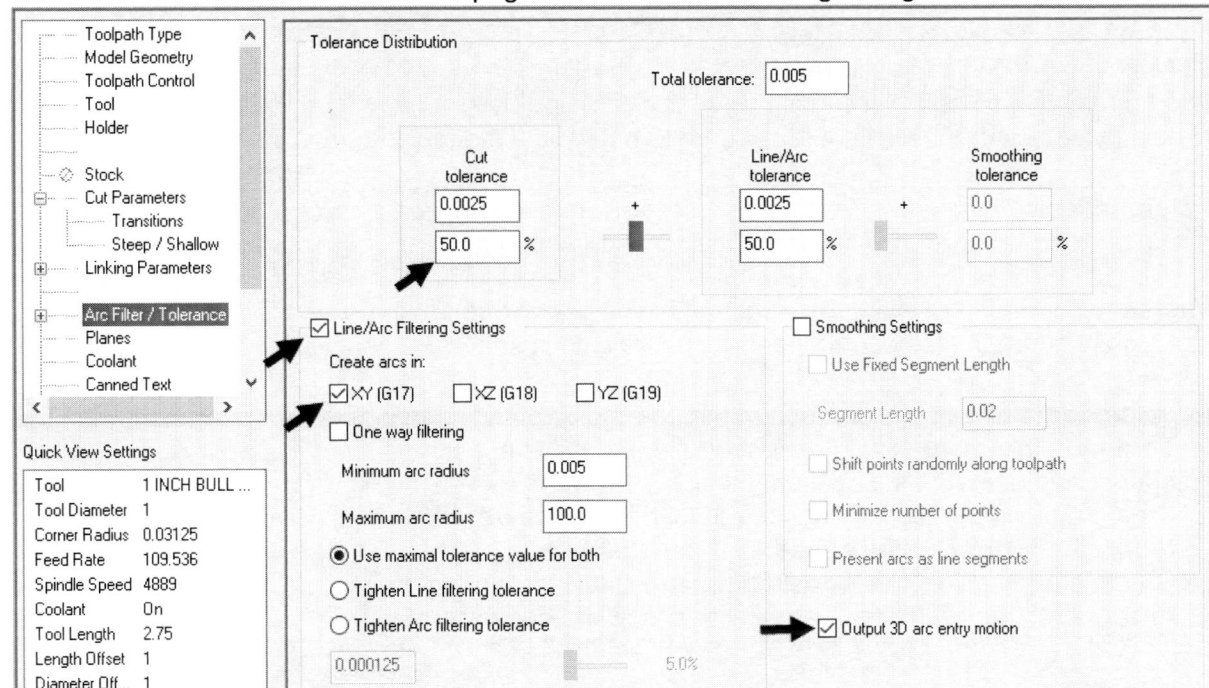

23. Finally, move to the **Coolant** tab and turn **Flood** coolant on.
24. Select the **OK button** [✓] to complete the toolpath.
25. **Verify** the new toolpath.

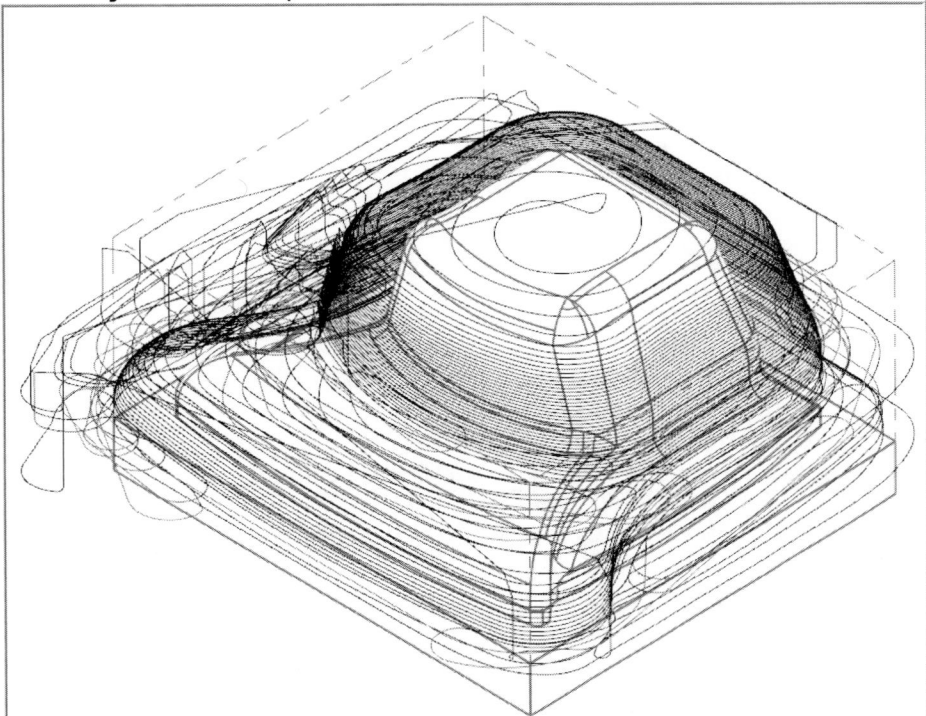

TASK 5:
FINISH SURFACES USING WATERLINE

➲ Next you will finish the part using the Surface High Speed Waterline toolpath.
➲ You may find it useful to toggle the display of toolpaths on and off during this lesson. Do this by selecting Alt-T on your keyboard to hide/show the toolpath display.

Waterline toolpaths are best suited for surfaces whose angles are between 30 and 90 degrees. This is because the distance between passes is measured along the tool axis.

Where the surfaces are shallower, material typically won't be removed as efficiently. However, you can configure the toolpath to generate extra cuts in shallow or flat areas.

---

1. In the **Toolpaths Manager** confirm that the red arrow used to locate new operations is in the **Toolpath Group,** just after the first operation. If it is not, simply grab it with the left mouse button, and drag it to the desired location.
2. Create a new operation, by right clicking in the **Toolpaths Manager** window, select **Mill toolpaths>Surface high speed toolpaths>Waterline...**.
3. On the screen select the **Model Geometry** page, if required.
4. Ensure both the **Wall Stock** and **Floor stock** are set to **Zero.**

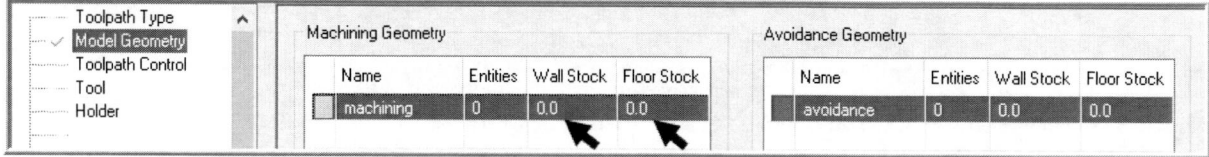

5. At the bottom of the **Model Geometry** page click on the **Select entities** button.

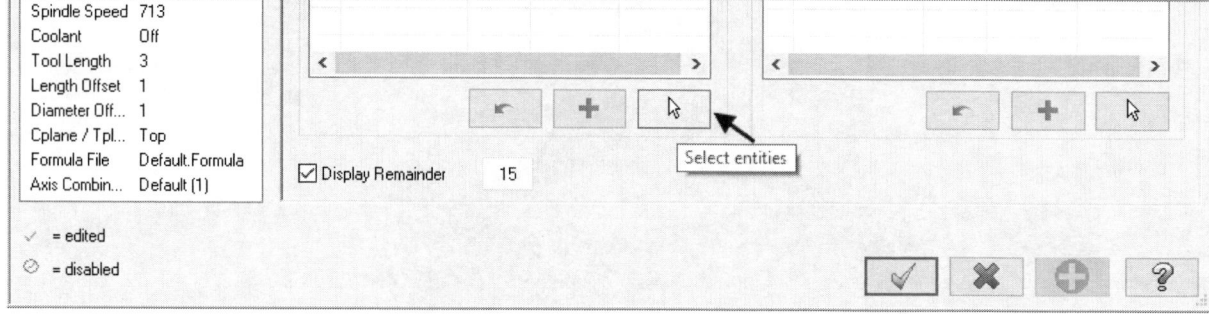

6. Now you will be returned to the graphics screen. To satisfy the prompt on the screen use **Ctrl-A on your keyboard** select to select all the entities.

7. To move onto the next step you now need to pick the **End Selection** icon .

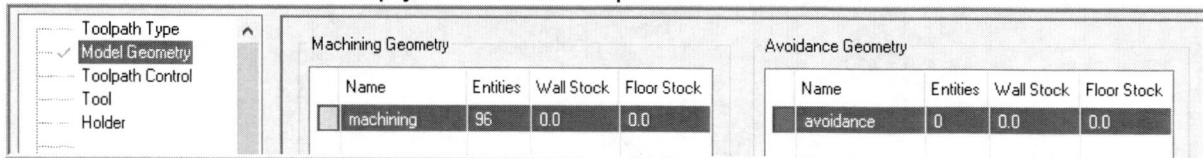

---

8. Select the **Toolpath Control** page, make changes as shown below, if required.

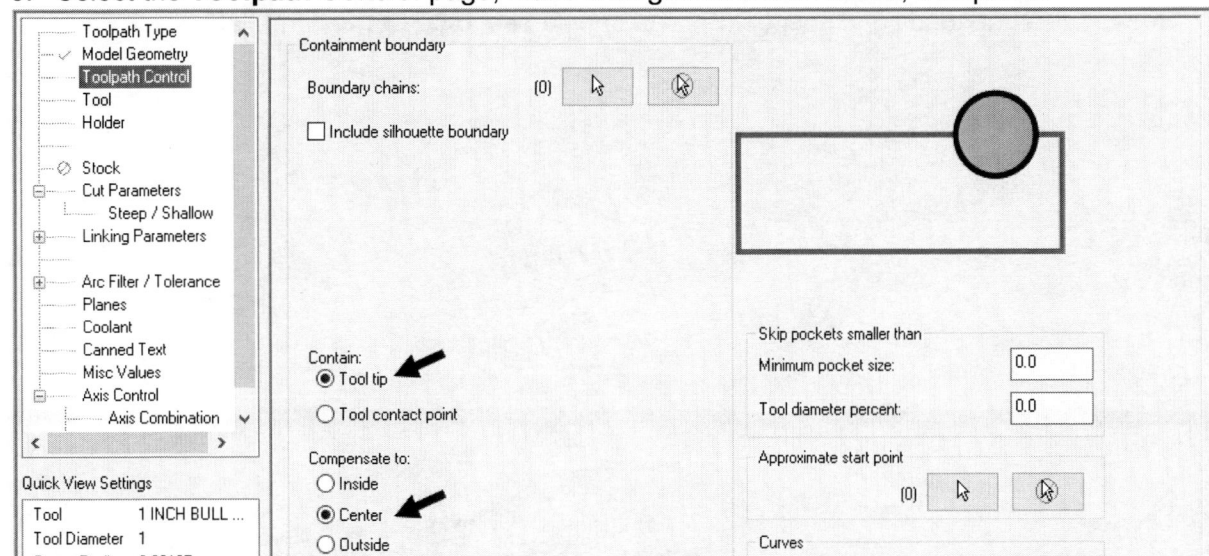

Skip pockets smaller than
Use this value to specify a minimum pocket size that Mastercam will consider creating a cutting pass for. This solves the problem where Mastercam thinks that a pocket is large enough to accommodate the tool, but the entry move is so compressed that the tool is effectively plunging into the part. A common value is 110% of the tool diameter.
If you want to ensure that the entire surface is machined, you can set this to 0. However, if the cutting area is too small for the programmed entry moves, the tool will plunge straight down into the pocket.

9. Navigate to the **Tool** page select the **Select Library tool...** icon. **Deactivate Filter Active**. Select a **0.500 Ball Endmill**. This tool will need to be changed to carbide. **Right click** on the 1/2 Ballmill in the Toolpaths tool list and select **Edit Tool**.

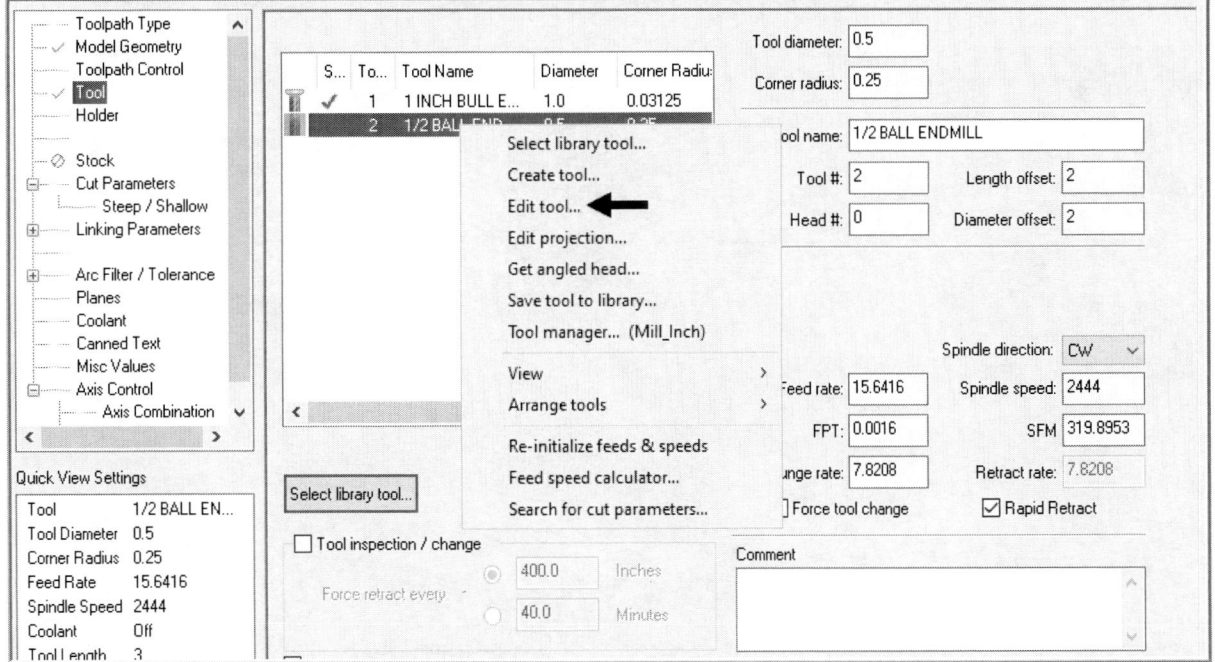

10. Switch to the **Finalize Properties** tab (1), change the Material **to Carbide** (2), click **Recalculate** the feeds and speeds (3). You should see **1600 in the SFM** field. Click Finish.

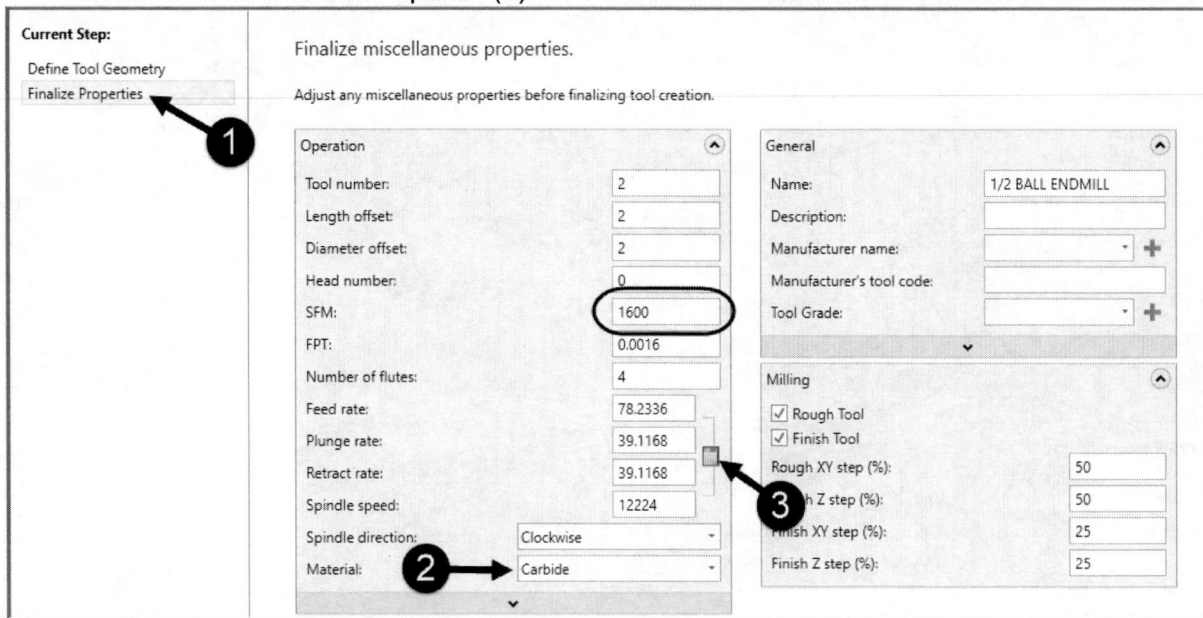

11. Speeds and feeds should now be set as shown below...

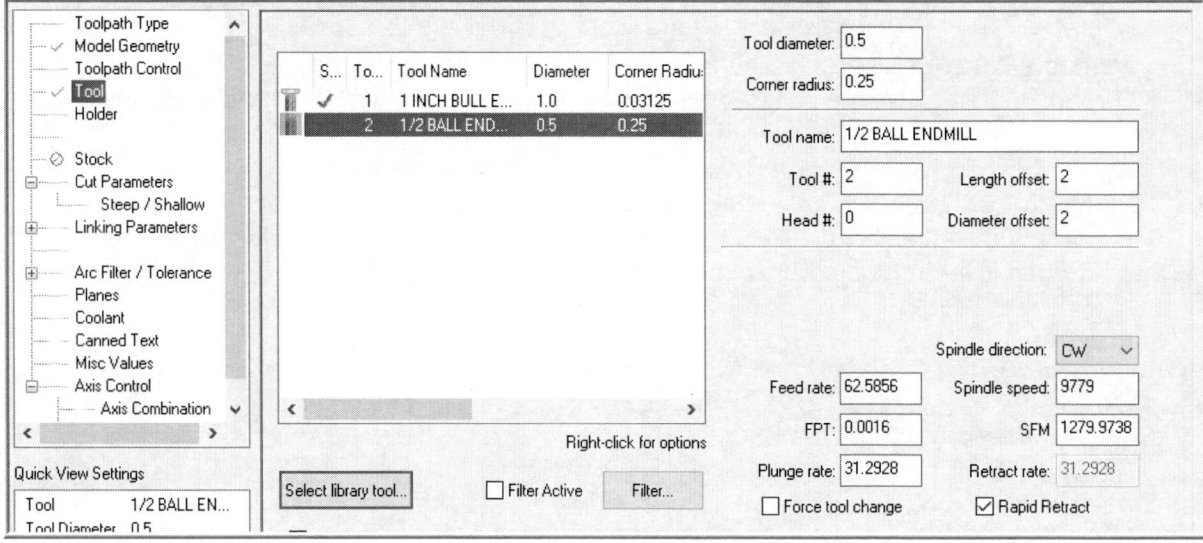

12. Select the **Holder** page and make changes to this page as shown below. Holder to be selected is a **B3E4-0500**. **Tool Projection** is set to **1.75**.

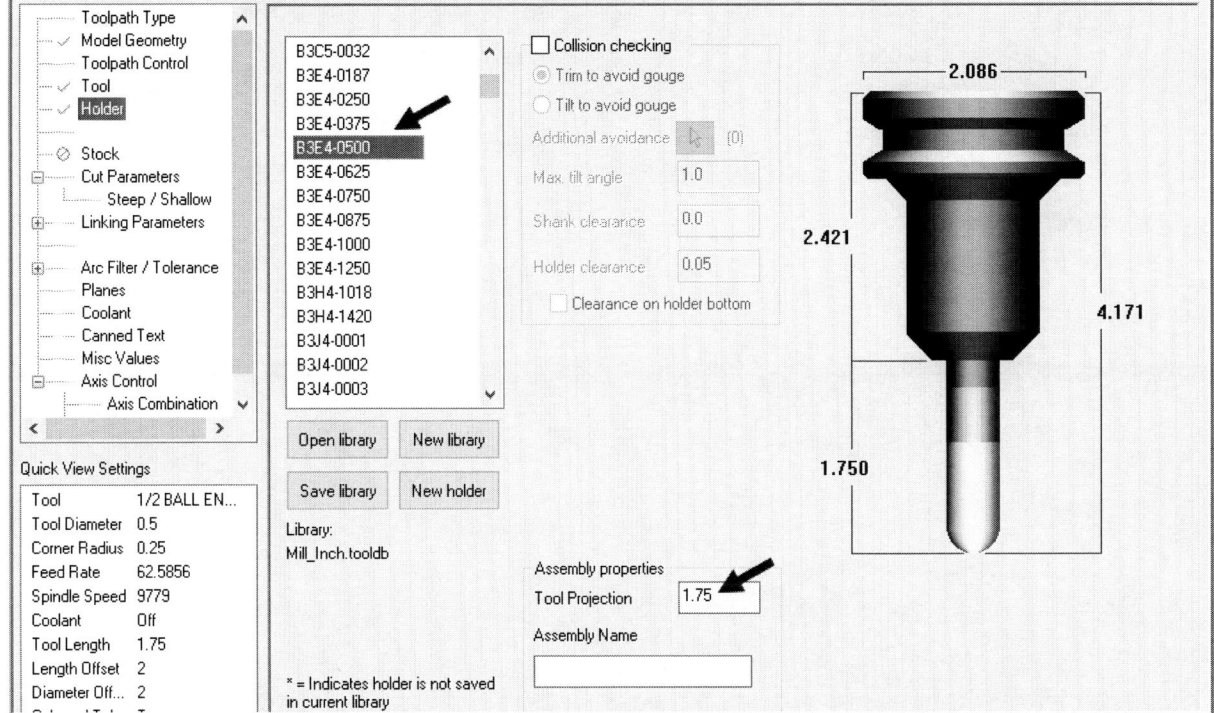

13. Make the appropriate selections on the **Cut Parameters** page shown below.

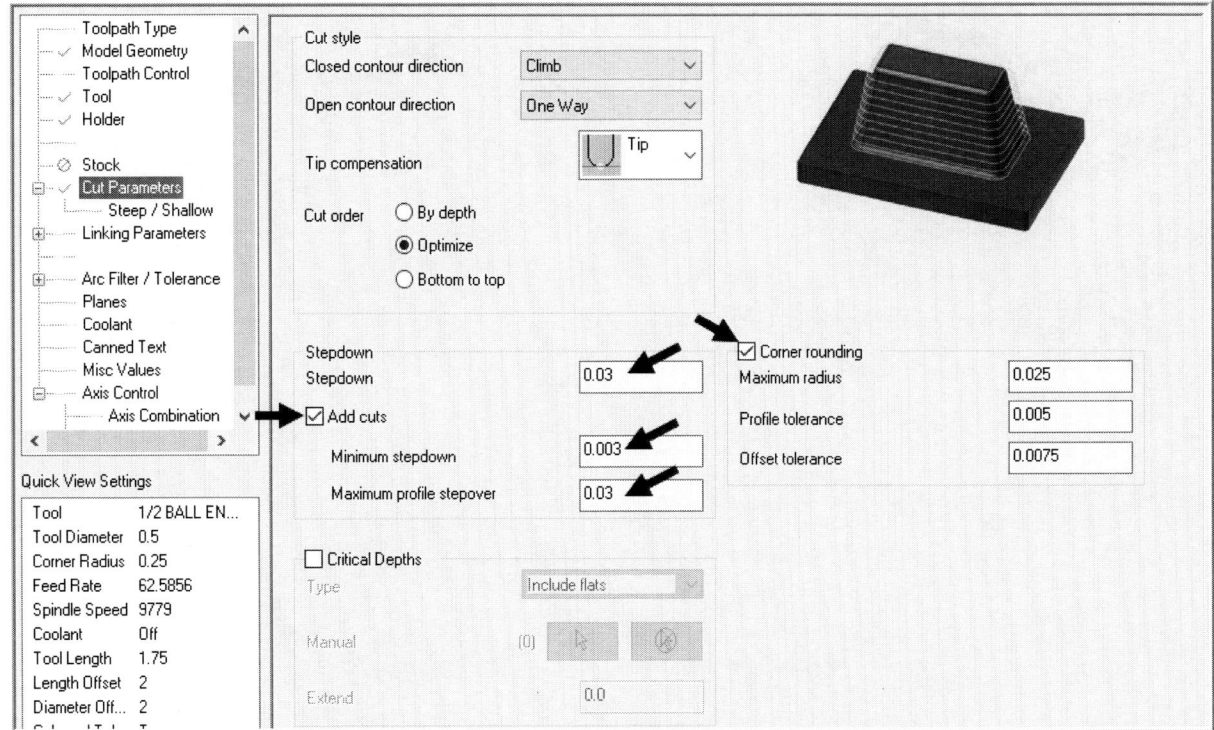

14. Set the **Transitions** parameters as shown below, no changes should be required.

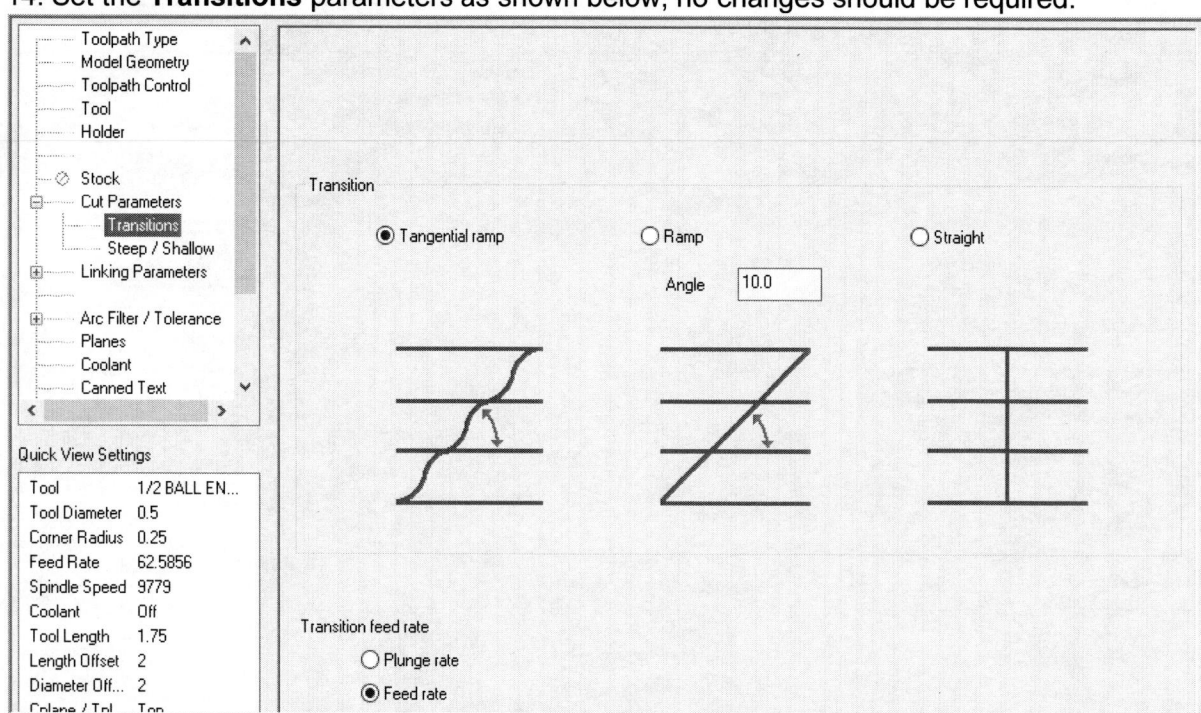

Transitions

Use this page to configure the entry moves that the tool will make as it transitions to new Z levels. These moves control the transition to a new set of cuts on a different Z level.

Select **Tangential ramp** to create a true high speed transition between the cutting passes. Mastercam inserts arcs at the beginning and end of the ramp for the smoothest tool motion into and out of the move.

Ramp/Angle

The moves between passes with a straight line at the specified angle.

Note: The Angle field applies only to Ramp moves. It is not used for Tangential ramp transitions.

15. On the **Steep/Shallow** page, enable **Maximum depth** and then right click in the Maximum depth field then select **Z = Z coordinate of a point**.

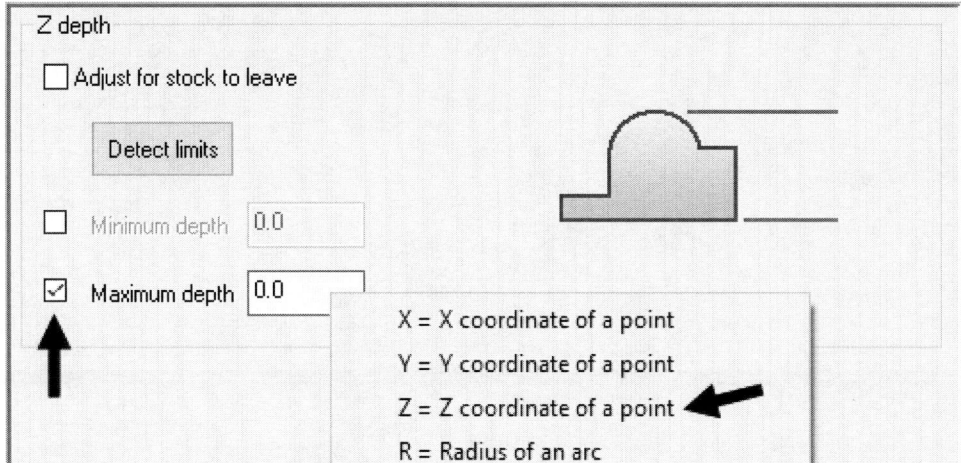

16. When prompted to "**Select a point**" select the point shown below as the Z at the top of the mold base as shown below:

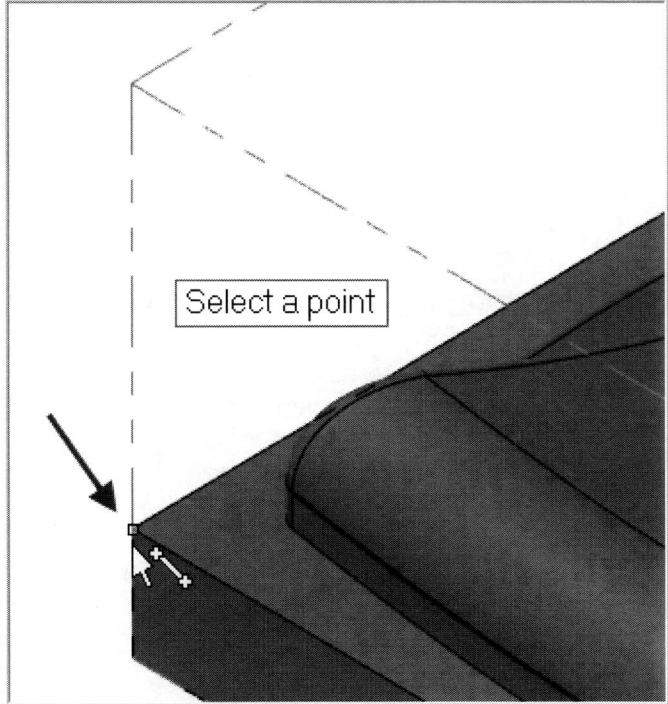

17. The resulting **Steep/Shallow** page values should match the following image:

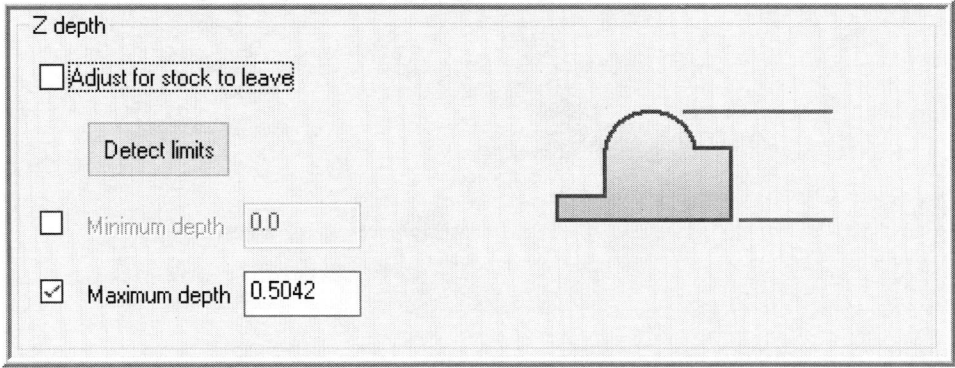

18. Set the **Linking Parameters** as shown below:

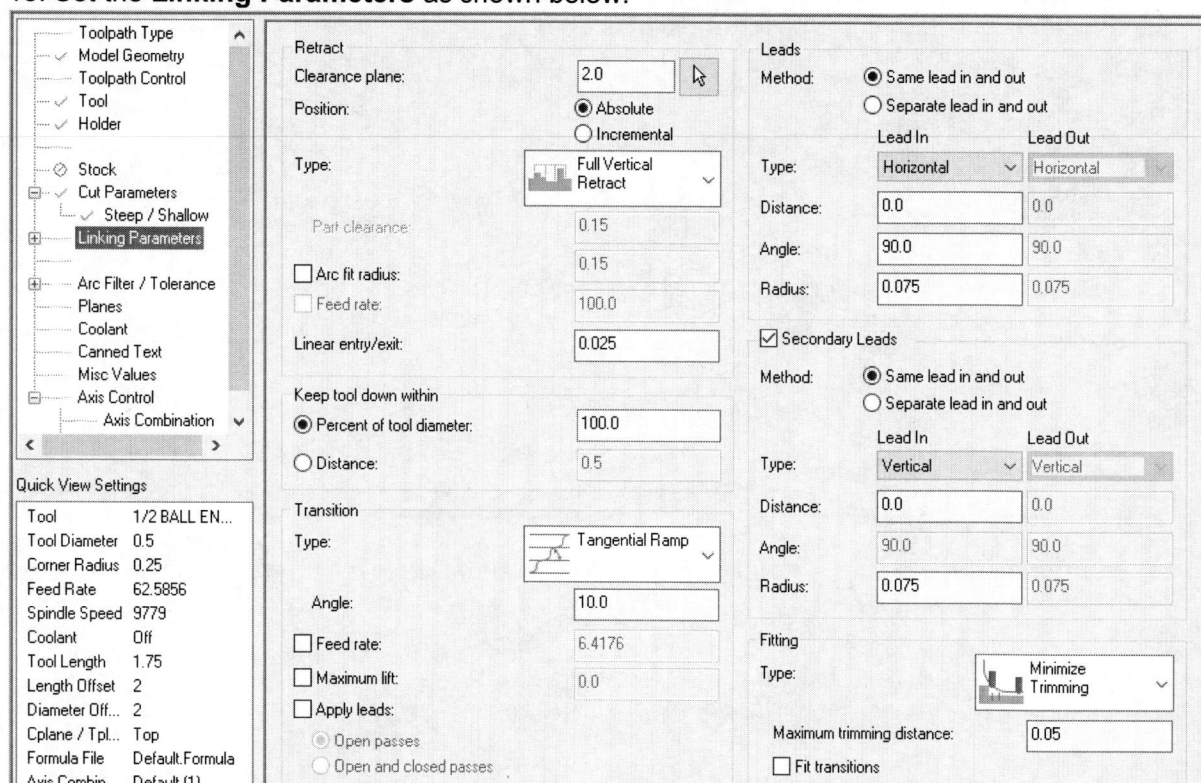

Retracts and Leads

These moves control the transition to a new set of cuts on a different Z level.

Mastercam divides the moves which link cutting passes into a number of discrete components so that you can have the maximum degree of control over them.

The picture below shows the relationship between the different parameters when you select the Minimum distance retract method. Mastercam divides the move into two zones: to/from the retract plane, and to/from the part. Each move is a separate arc.

Curl down is the radius of the arc as the tool moves away from the retract height.

Vertical arc entry is the radius of the arc as the tool moves toward the part.

Vertical arc exit is the radius of the arc as the tool comes off the part.

Linear entry/exit distance extends the entry and exit vectors.

Curl up is the radius of the arc as the tool moves to the retract height.

Use the **Fitting parameters** to modify how the entry and exit arcs are actually applied to the cutting pass.

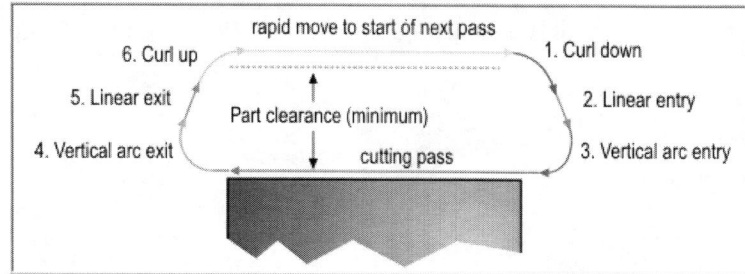

19. Set the **Arc Filter/Tolerance** values as shown below:

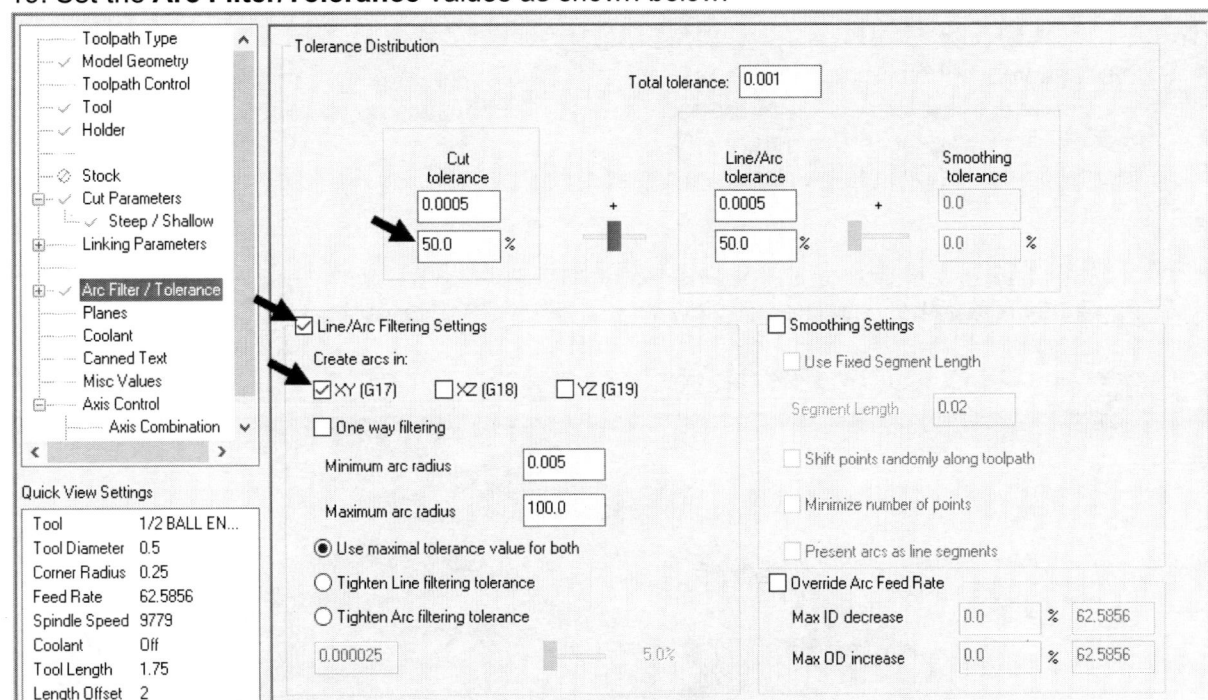

20. Navigate to the **Coolant** tab and turn the **Flood** coolant on.
21. Select the **OK button** ✓ to complete the toolpath.
22. Review Operation 2 using **Backplot**.

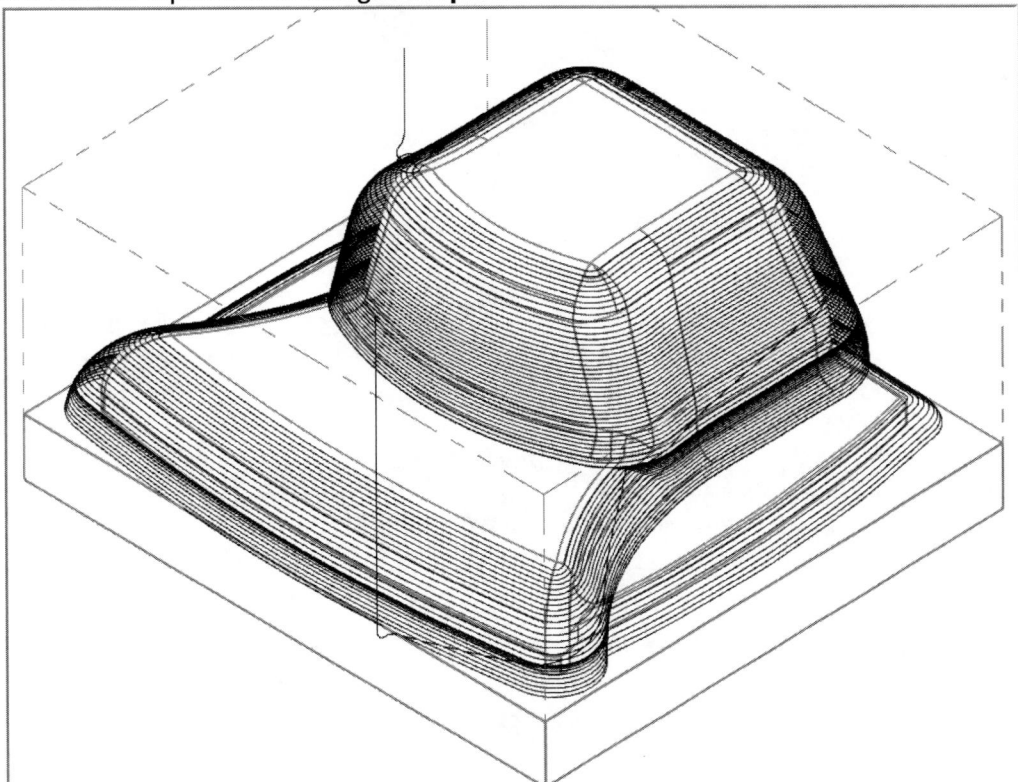

TASK 6:
FINISH PROFILE USING 2D CONTOUR

- ➲ In this task you will machine the contour with a 0.25 diameter flat end mill.
- ➲ You will also edit the projection of the tool in this task. This will be used to identify that the holder will not collide with the part.
- ➲ At the beginning of this task a Point will be created that will be used to edit the projection of the tool.

1. In the **Wireframe** tab click on **Point Position** in the **Points** section.
2. Dynamically rotate the view like the view shown below. Now select the **Midpoint** of the edge shown below.
3. Click on the **OK** icon to complete this point.

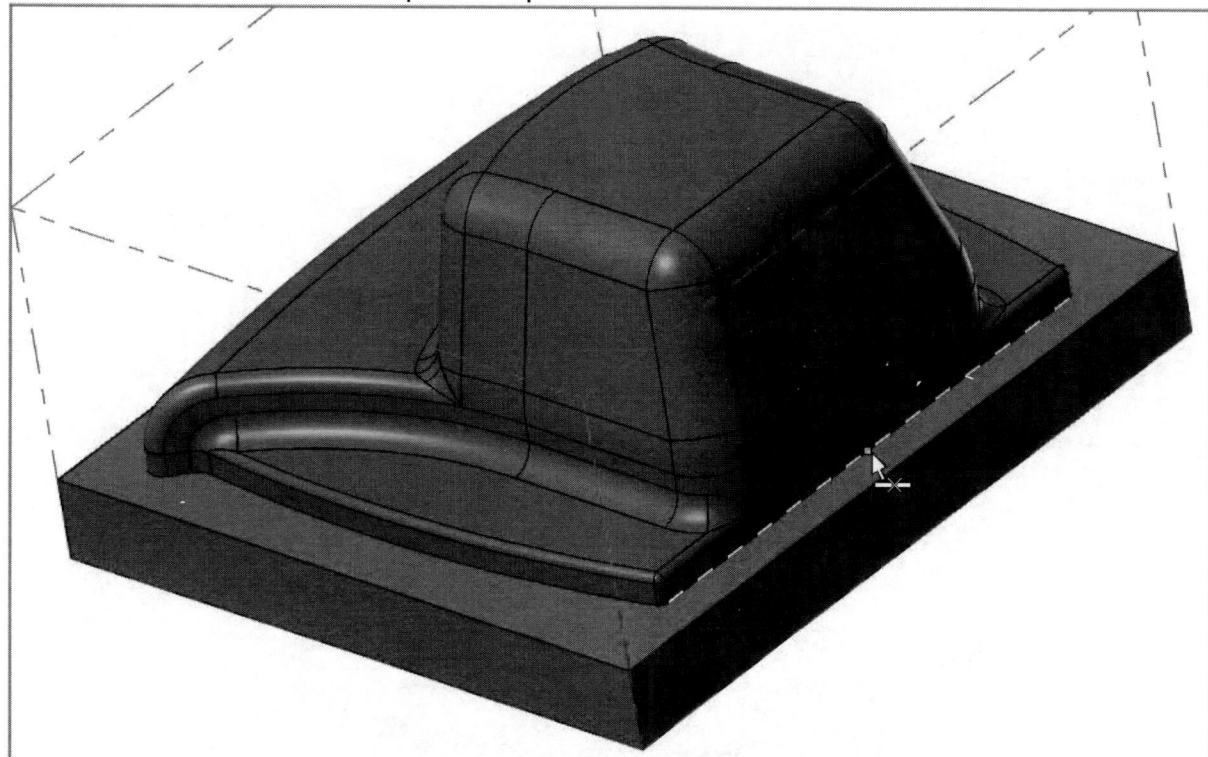

- ➲ In these next steps you will move the point just created 0.125 in the positive Y direction. This .125 value is the radius of the 0.250 diameter end mill. This point will be used later when you edit the projection of the tool.

4. In the **Home** tab click on **Analyze Entity** in the **Analyze** section.
5. **Zoom in** and select the Point just created.
6. In the Point Properties dialog box you will now add 0.125 to the Y value. Click at the end of the Y value and input **+0.125** and then hit **Enter**. The Y value has now been updated and is shown below right.

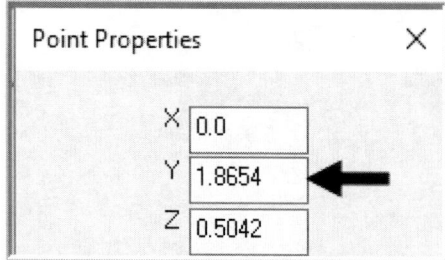

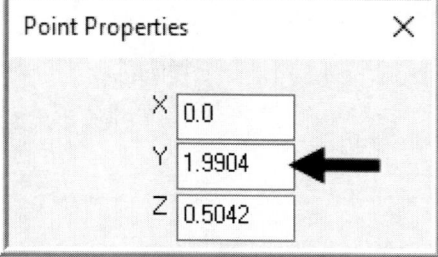

7. Select the **OK** button to complete this function.
8. Right mouse click and select a **Top** view.
9. Activate an **Outline Shaded** view.
➲ The new position of the Point is shown below.

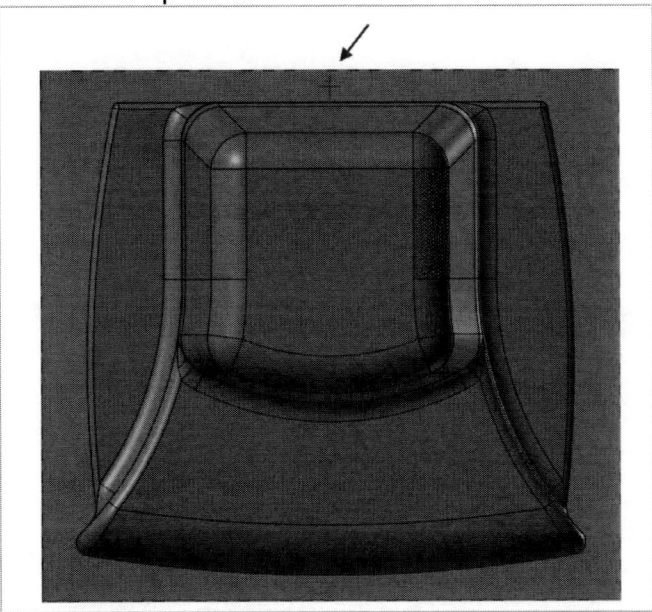

10. Right mouse click and select an **Isometric** view.
11. Select the **Toolpaths** tab at the top right side of the screen if required.
12. Select **Contour** in the **2D Milling** section.
13. On the screen you will now see the **Chaining dialog box** activate **Solids mode.** Only **Loop** should be activated. To satisfy the prompt select the edge shown below. Direction arrow is pointing to the left. Wireframe view showed for clarity.
14. When the edge has been selected click on **OK** in the **Pick Reference Face** dialog box.
15. Select the **OK** button at the bottom of the Chaining dialog box.

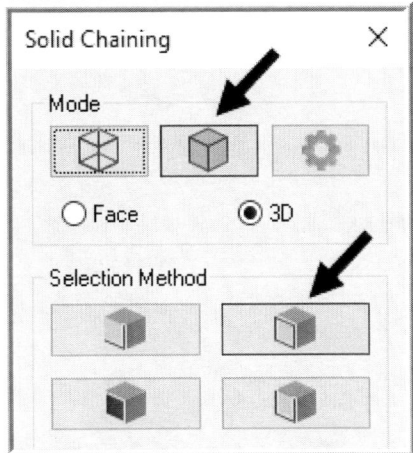

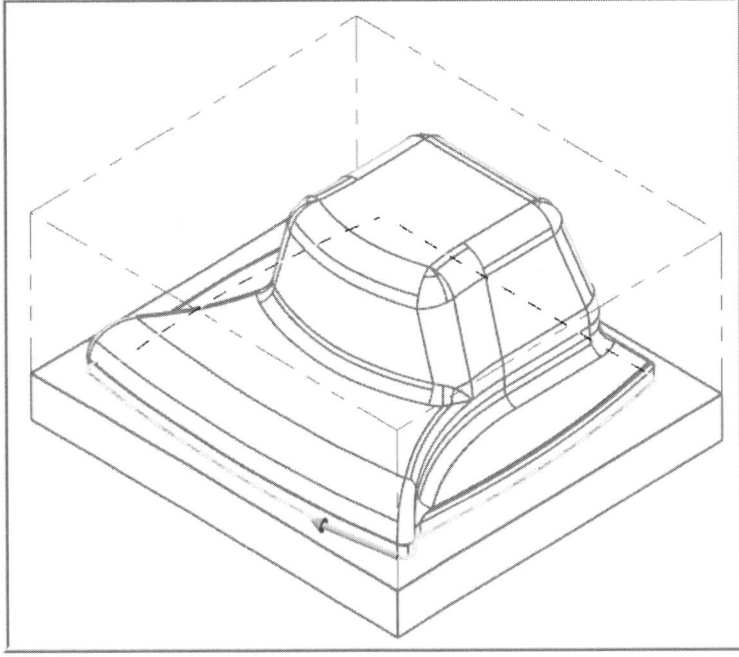

16. Select the **Tool** page. In the lower left corner of the page select the **Select library tool...** button. **Deactivate Filter Active**.
17. Scroll down and select a **0.25" diameter Flat end mill**.

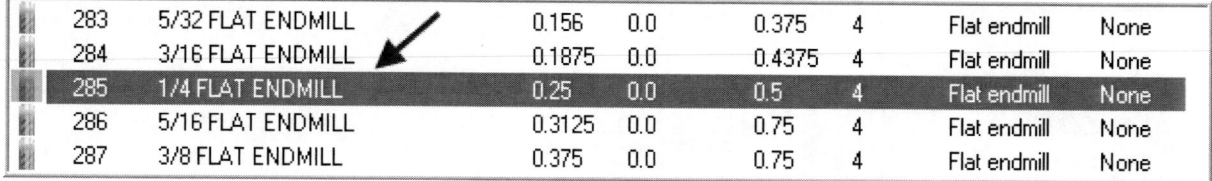

	283	5/32 FLAT ENDMILL	0.156	0.0	0.375	4	Flat endmill	None
	284	3/16 FLAT ENDMILL	0.1875	0.0	0.4375	4	Flat endmill	None
	285	1/4 FLAT ENDMILL	0.25	0.0	0.5	4	Flat endmill	None
	286	5/16 FLAT ENDMILL	0.3125	0.0	0.75	4	Flat endmill	None
	287	3/8 FLAT ENDMILL	0.375	0.0	0.75	4	Flat endmill	None

18. Select the **OK button** to complete the selection of this tool.
19. Right click on the **1/4 FLAT ENDMILL** and select **Edit tool**.
20. Switch to the **Finalize Properties** tab and set the tool material to **Carbide**.
21. Click the **Recalculate** speeds and feeds icon. Select **Finish** to complete the tool edit.
➲ The resulting RPM will be too high for the machine to achieve (24448rpm) and the tool holding/stickout would not be optimal to run even at machine max RPM (10000).
22. Reduce the SFM of the operation to a safer value of **500**. The FPT will remain at **0.001**.

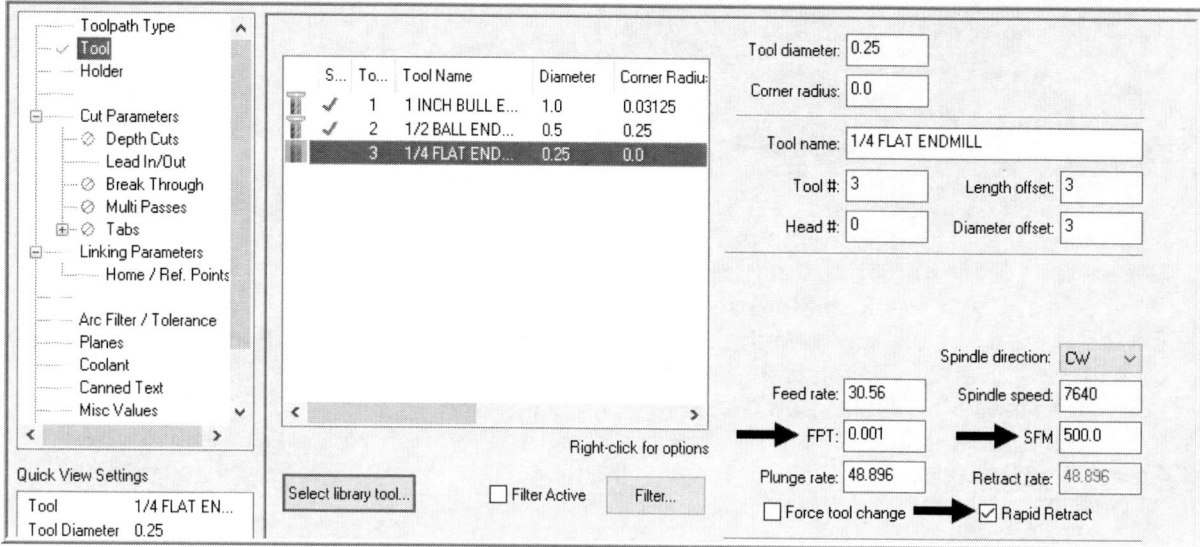

23. Select the **Holder** page and make changes to this page as shown below. Holder to be selected is a **B3C4-0020**. Note the **Tool Projection** value. In the next series of steps, the Tool Projection length is going to be changed.

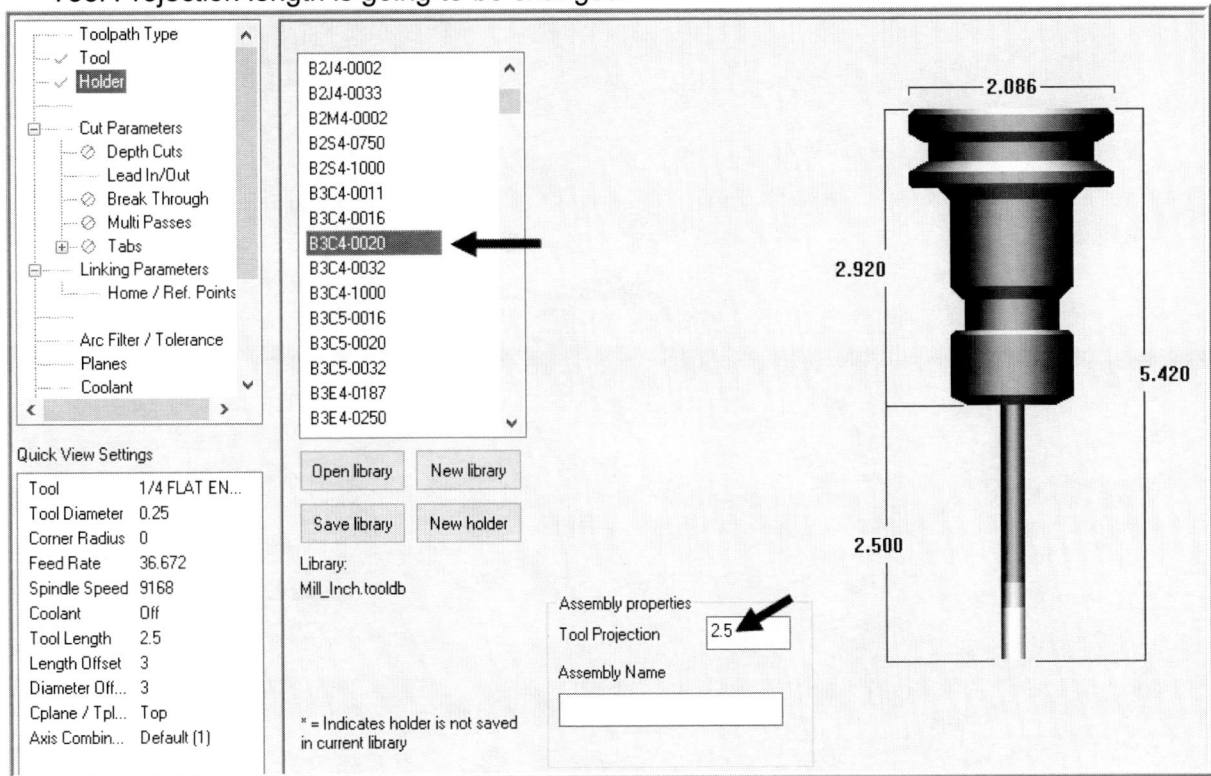

24. Select the **Tool** page.
25. Right mouse click over the 0.20 FLAT END MILL and select **Edit projection**.

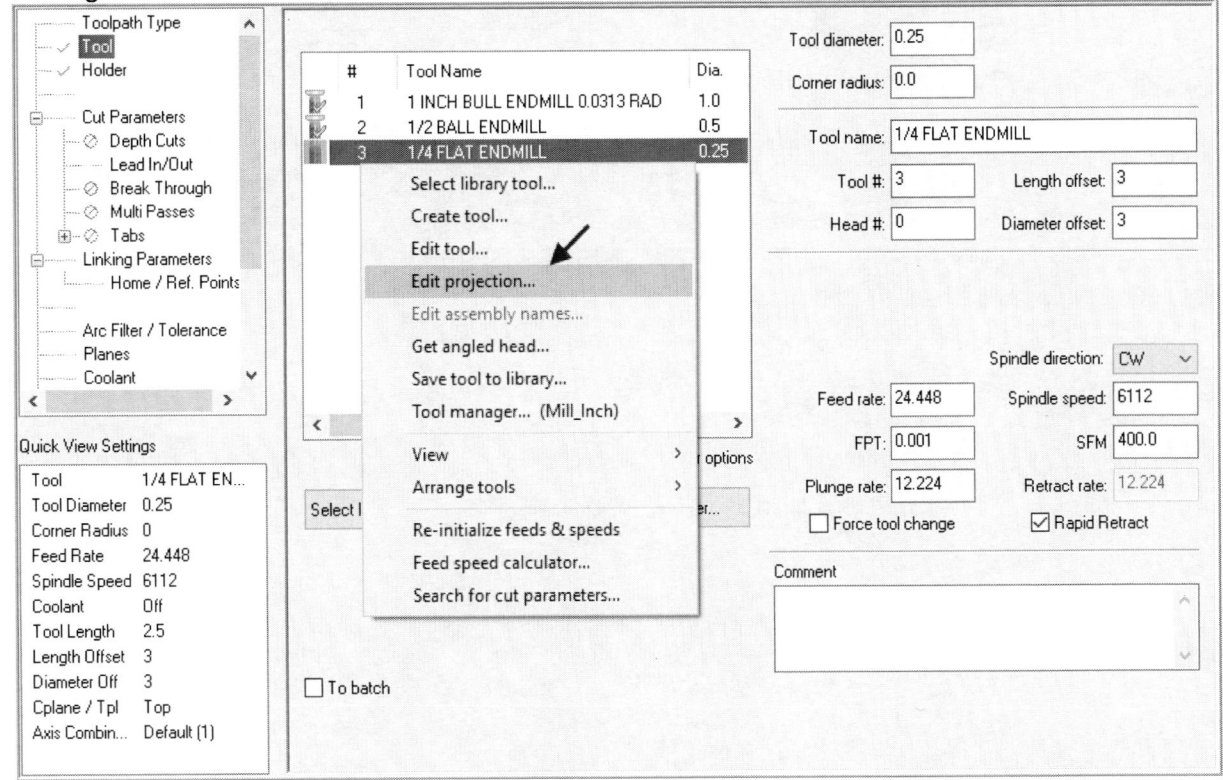

26. To satisfy the prompt on the screen **"Click a location on the drawing screen to place the assemble"** select the **point created earlier**. Dynamically rotate the view similar to the view shown below. Wireframe view shown for clarity.

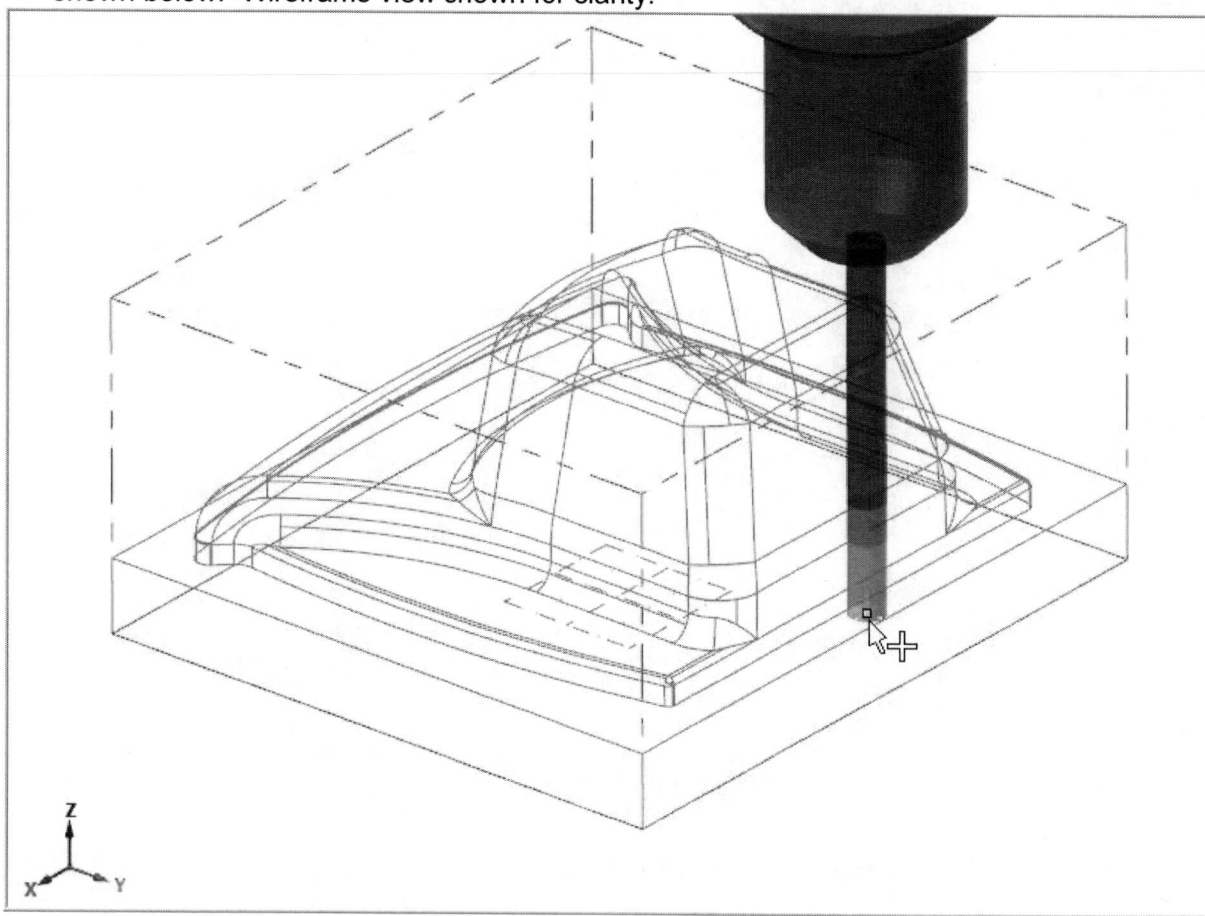

27. Return to an **Outline Shaded** view if required.

Edit projection
Let's you edit the projection value of tools and multiple holder assemblies (sometimes referred to as composite holders) using a graphical representation of the tool assembly in the graphics window.

---

28. Dynamically rotate the view similar to the view shown below.
29. The new prompt is now **"Select the tool to place the assembly, or select the holder to adjust the projection. Press Enter to accept changes or Escape to cancel."** Now **click on the Holder**.

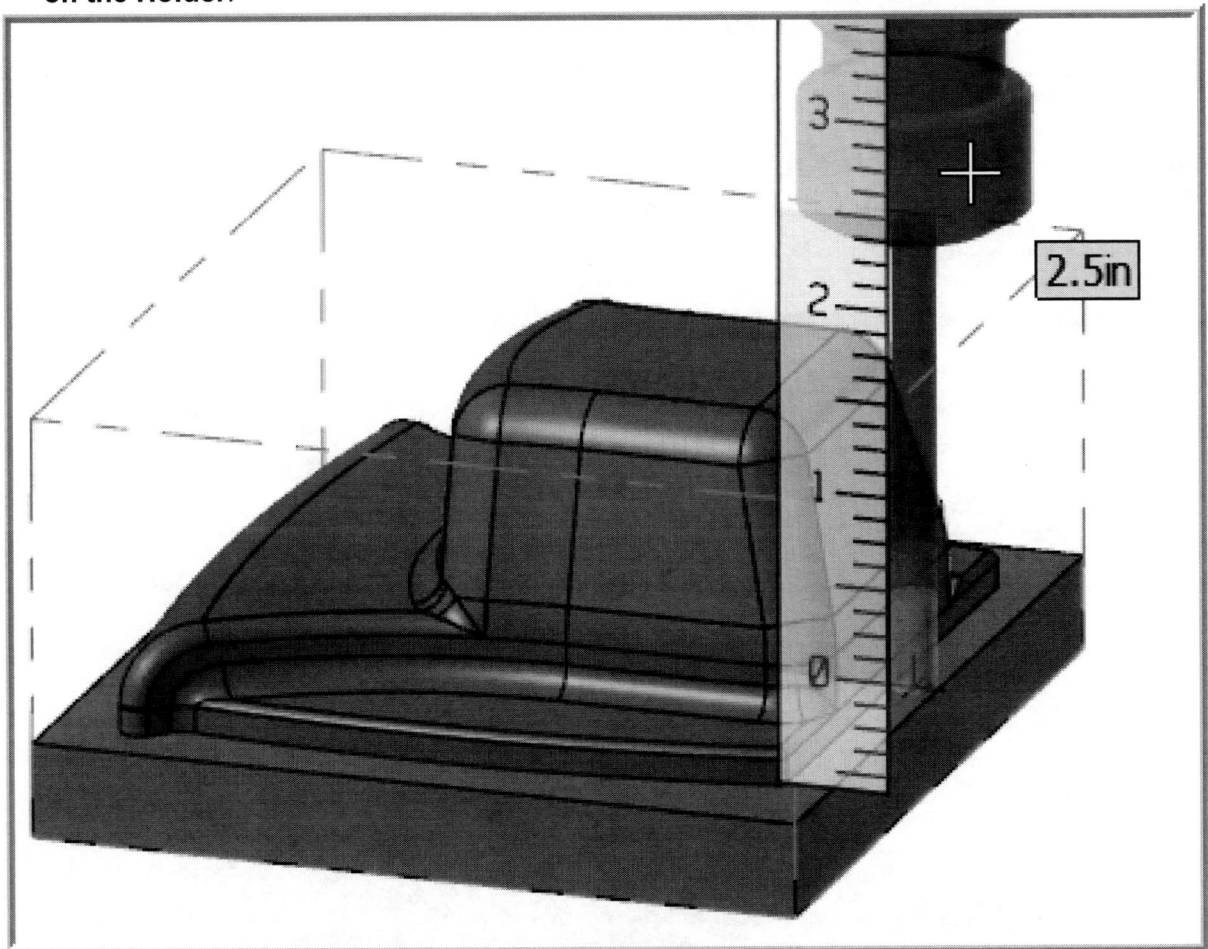

This displays the part and tool assembly in a **Temporary Viewsheet**.
Notice that the tool tip follows your mouse movements.
If you are in top view when you enter this function, you will be looking down the axis of the tool.
You may need to switch to a different GView (choose isometric or dynamically rotate to a view).

If you find that the current projection values cause collisions, edit the value by clicking the holder to display a ruler.
Click the ruler and slide the holder up or down to reset the project value of the tool. Alternatively, you can type a value that displays in the text box next to the ruler

30. Right mouse click and select a **Right view**.
31. To satisfy the new prompt on the screen **"Click along the ruler to set the projection, or type in a value and press enter."** Type in **1.625 and hit Enter**.

➲ Note the clearance between the holder and the part.

> If you find that the current projection values cause collisions, edit the value by clicking the holder to display a ruler.
> Click the ruler and slide the holder up or down to reset the project value of the tool.
> Alternatively, you can type a value that displays in the text box next to the ruler.

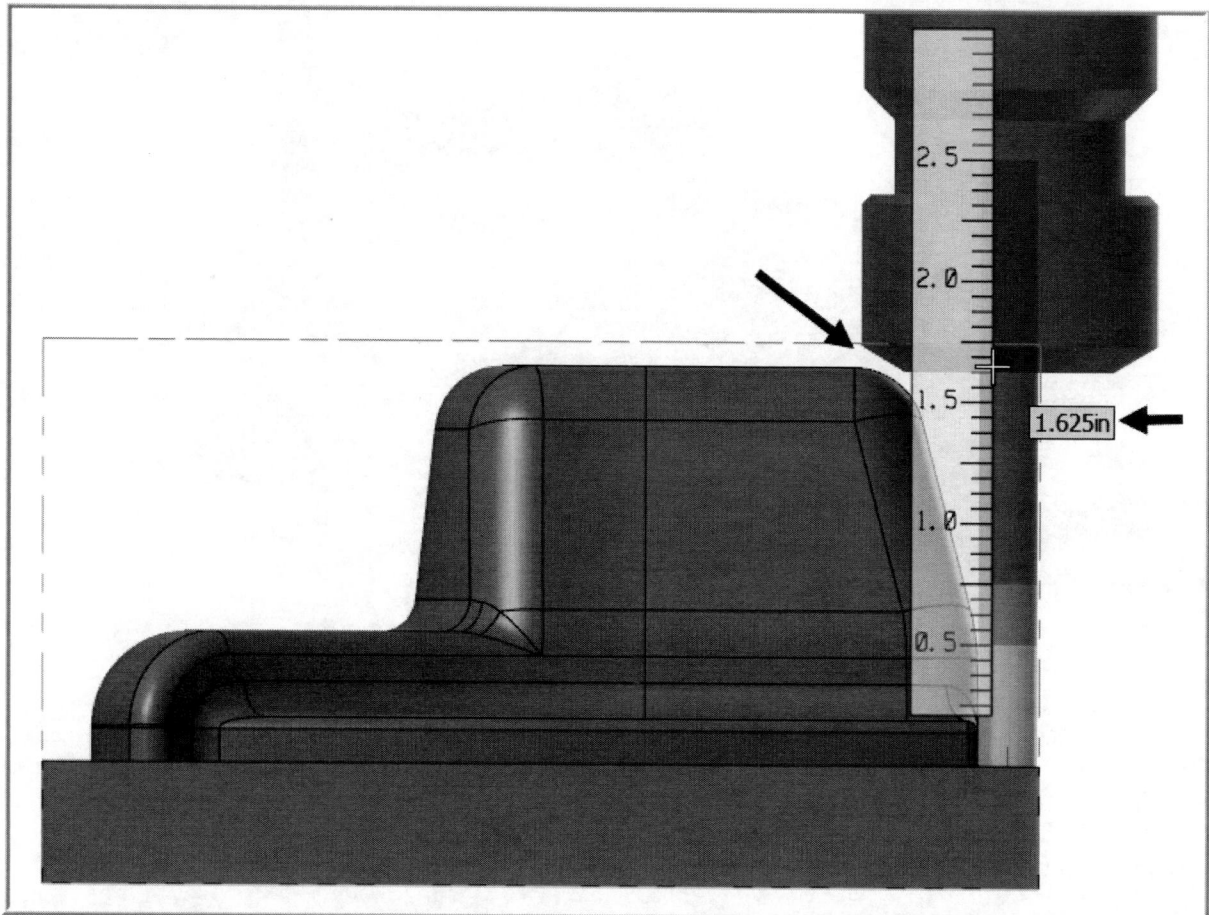

32. After hitting the prompt changes to **"Select the tool to place the assembly, or select the holder to adjust the projection. Press Enter to accept changes or Escape to cancel."** Hit **Enter**. You are now returned to the Tool page.

33. Select the **Cut Parameters** page and make changes to this page as shown below, if required.

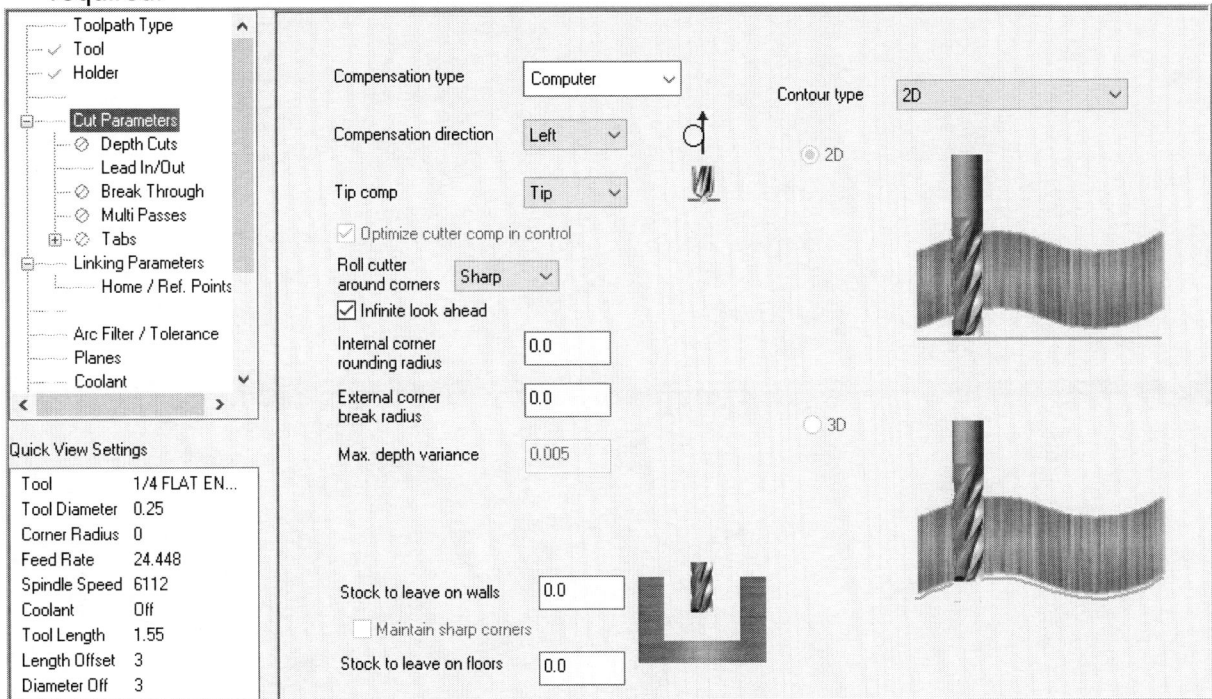

34. Set the **Linking Parameters** as shown below. Top of stock is set to 0 incremental to reduce the amount of Z feed motion to get to the cutting depth.

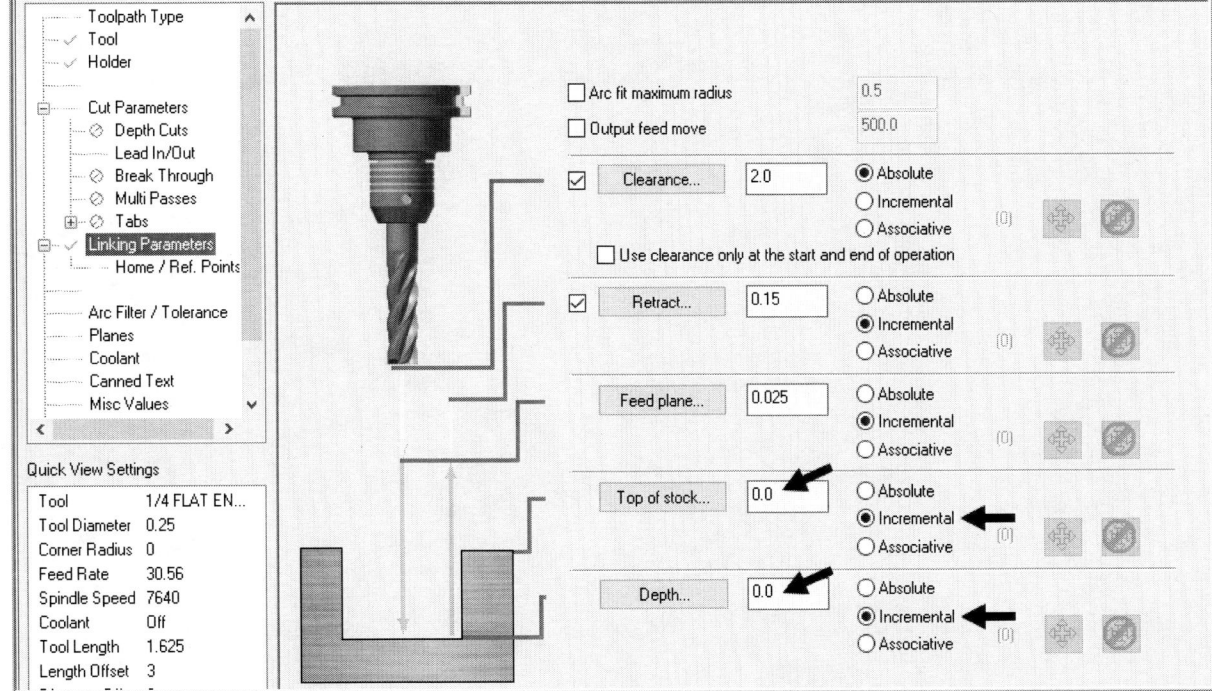

35. Finally, move to the **Coolant** tab and turn **Flood** coolant on.

36. Select **OK** ✓ to create the toolpath then **Backplot** after generation is complete.

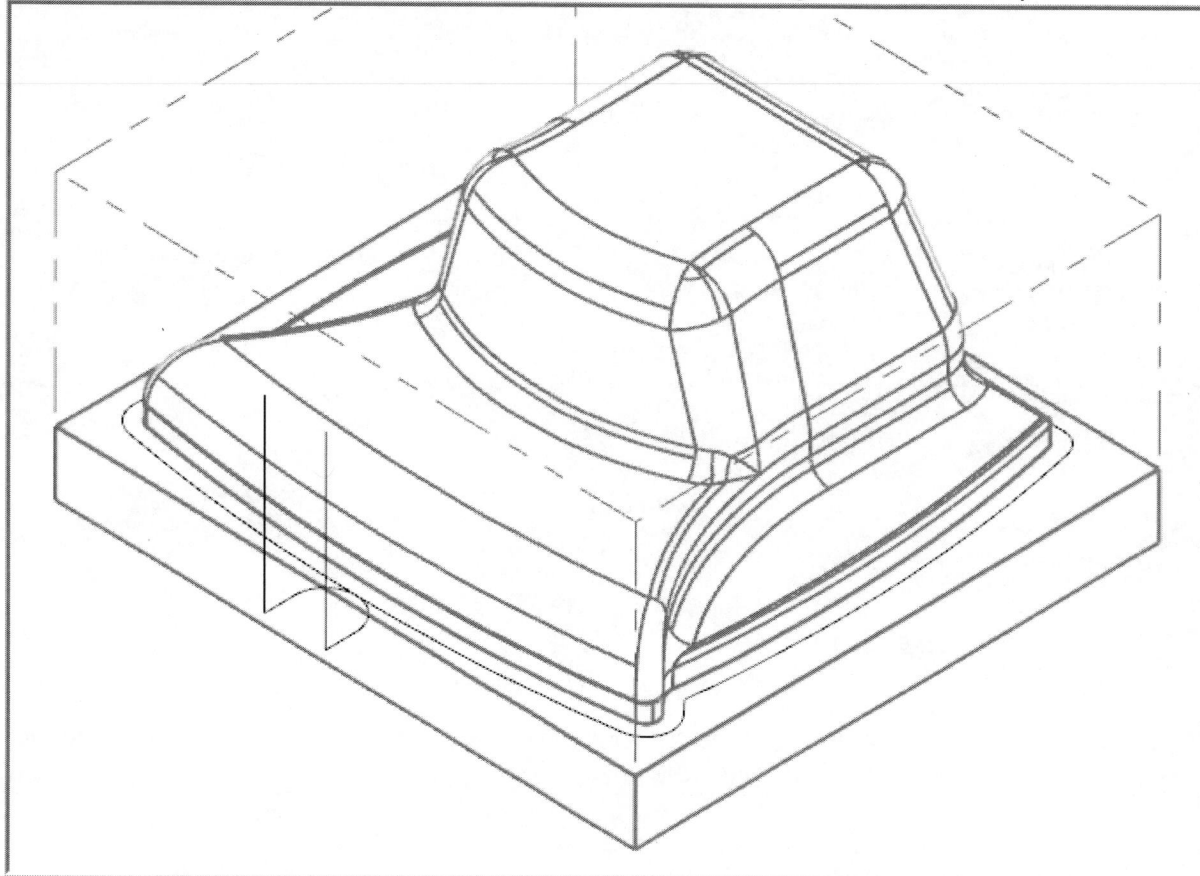

TASK 7:
FINISH RADII USING PENCIL
➲ Next you will finish the part using the Surface High Speed Pencil toolpath.

3D high speed pencil toolpaths
Are used to clean out the corners of a part. The tool follows a contour defined by the
intersection of two or more surfaces.
You can create pencil toolpaths with either single or multiple passes.
High speed pencil toolpaths are similar to Mastercam's standard pencil toolpaths, but are
enhanced to produce the smoother, free-flowing tool motion and transitions necessary for high
speed machining.
You can define the size of the cutting zone by creating multiple offset profiles from the surface
boundary.

---

1. Select the **Toolpaths** tab at the top right side of the screen if required.
2. Click on the **Expand gallery** down arrow in the **3D** section and select **Pencil** from the
    Finishing selections.

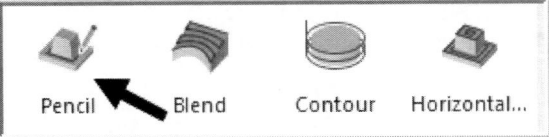

3. On the screen select the **Model Geometry** page, if required.
4. Ensure both the **Wall Stock** and **Floor stock** are set to **Zero.**

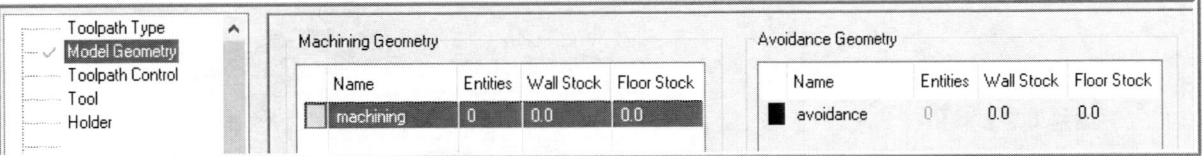

5. At the bottom of the **Model Geometry** page click on the **Select entities** button.

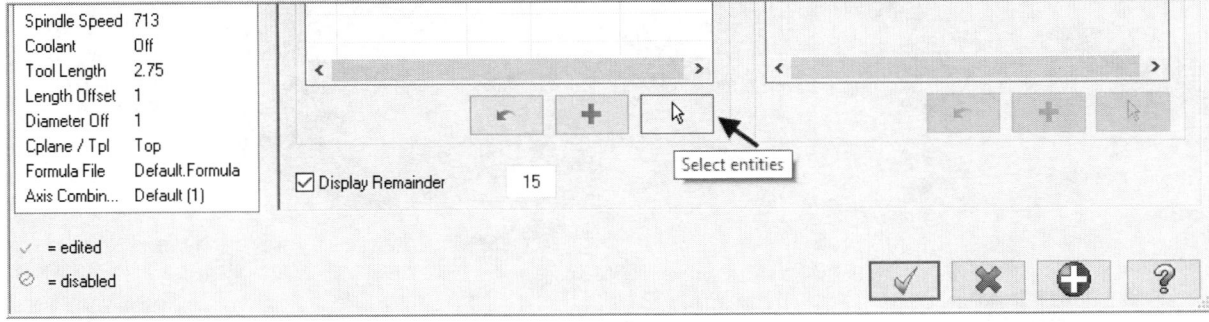

6. Now you will be returned to the graphics screen. To satisfy the prompt on the screen use
    Ctrl-A on your keyboard select to select all the entities.
7. To move onto the next step, you now need to pick the **End Selection** icon.

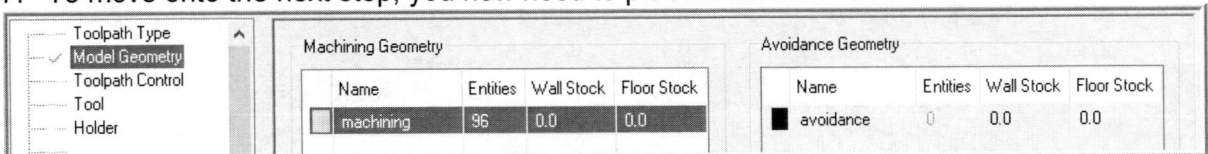

8. Select the **Toolpath Control** page, make changes as shown below, and then click the Boundary Chains selection button.

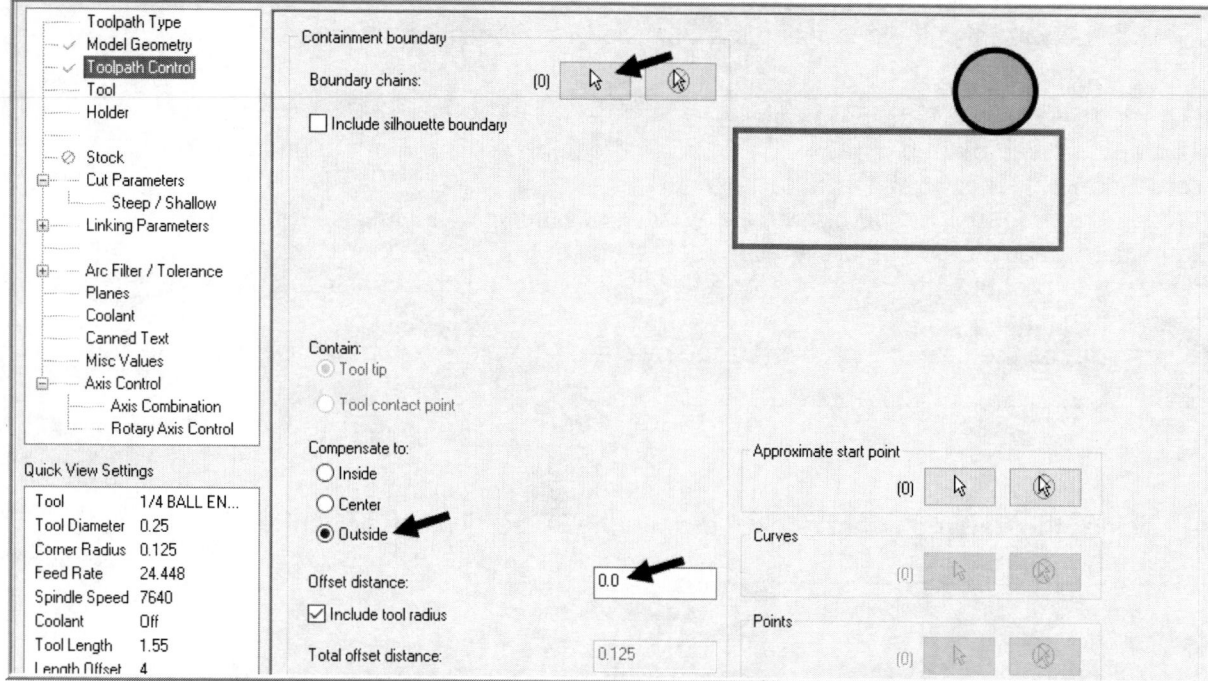

9. While in the **Solid Chaining** mode, enable **Loop** and select the boundary of the upper section of the model as shown below right. Click **OK** to complete.

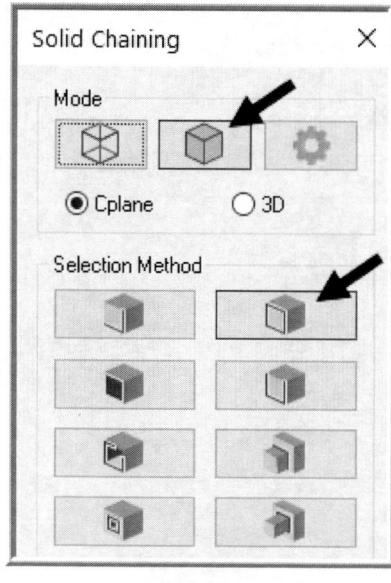

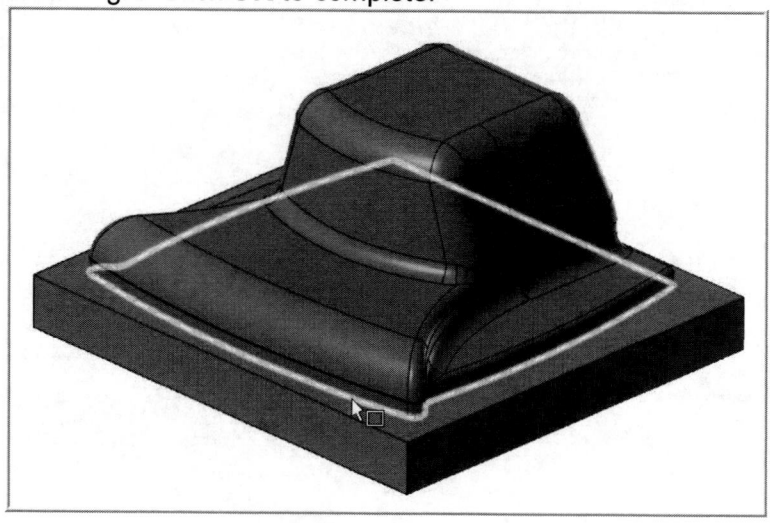

10. Next, select the **Tool** page. In the lower left corner of the page select the **Select library tool...** button. **Deactivate Filter Active**.
11. Use the scroll bar on the right of this dialog box to locate and select the **0.25 Ball endmill**.

	305	5/32 BALL ENDMILL	0.156	0.07813	0.375	4	Ball endmill	Full
	306	3/16 BALL ENDMILL	0.1875	0.09375	0.4375	4	Ball endmill	Full
	307	1/4 BALL ENDMILL	0.25	0.125	0.5	4	Ball endmill	Full
	308	5/16 BALL ENDMILL	0.3125	0.15625	0.75	4	Ball endmill	Full

12. Select the **OK button** to complete the selection of this tool.

13. Set the SFM for this tool to **500**. FPT will remain at 0.0008.

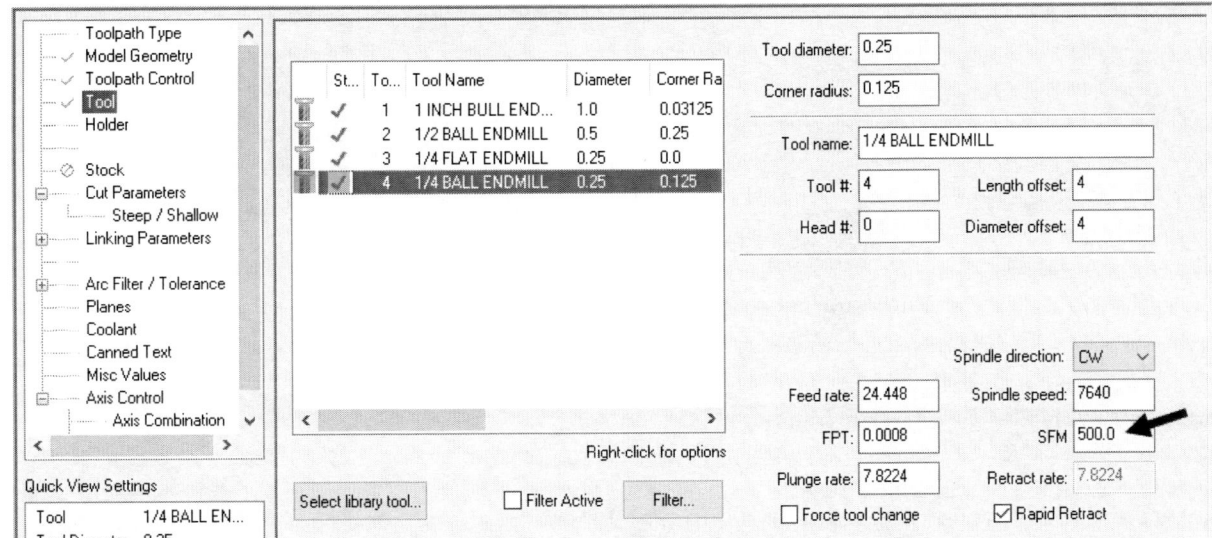

14. Select the **Holder** page and make changes to this page as shown below. Holder to be selected is a **B3E4-0250**. **Tool Projection** is set to **1.55**.

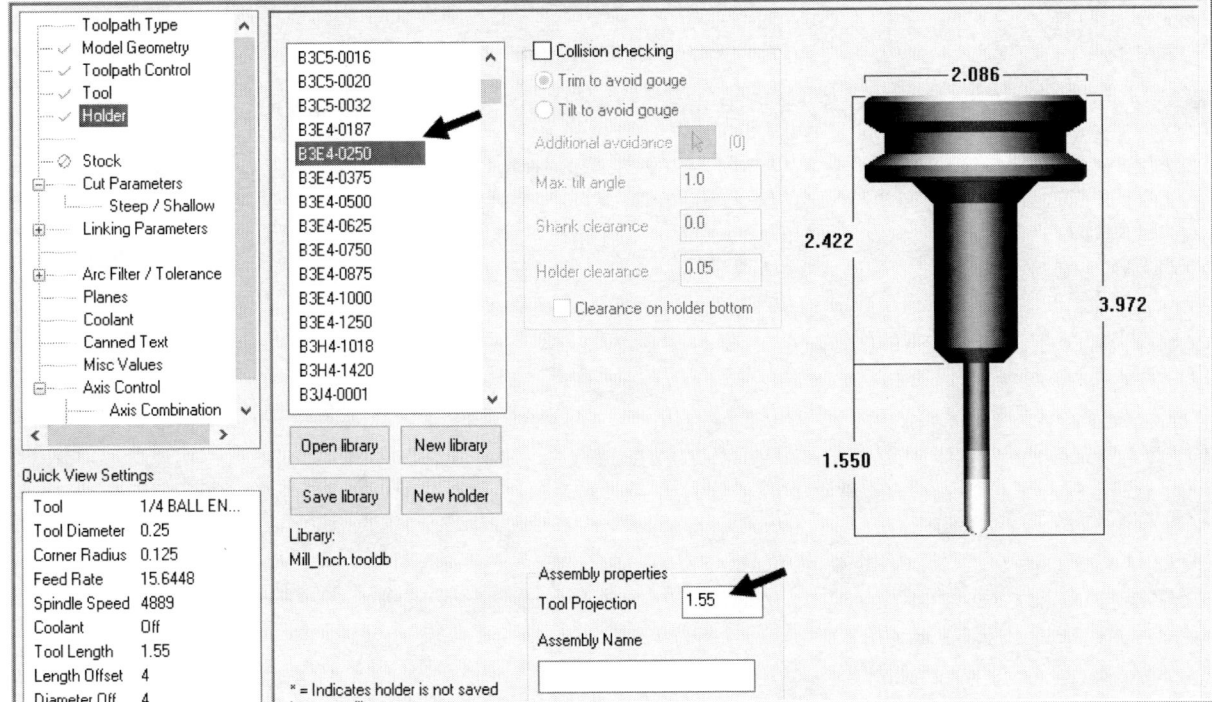

15. Select the **Cut Parameters** page and make changes to this page as shown below:

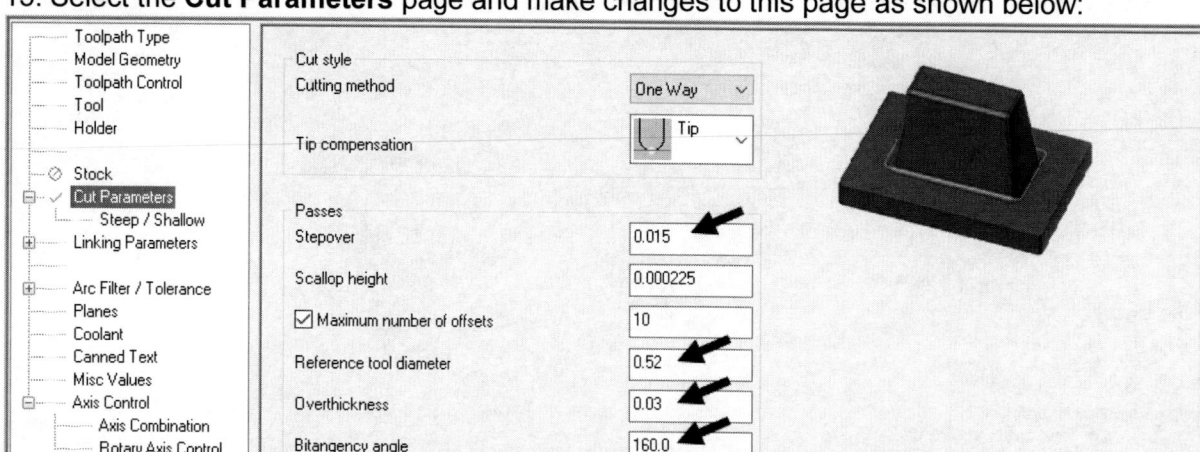

Reference tool diameter: This setting is available when you use multiple offsets. It represents the size of the theoretical roughing tool that would have machined the cutting zone defined for your pencil toolpath. Use it as a guide to make sure that you are in fact machining all of the areas that were missed by your roughing tool. In other words, if the value is greater than the actual tool you used for your roughing operation, you can be confident that the pencil toolpath will reach all of the areas that could not be roughed.

16. On the **Steep/Shallow** page, enable **Maximum depth** and set it to **0.510**. You could right click and use Z coordinate of a point again. The step will return a value of 0.5042, the value of 0.510 is used to keep the toolpath off of this shoulder. Any value above would work.

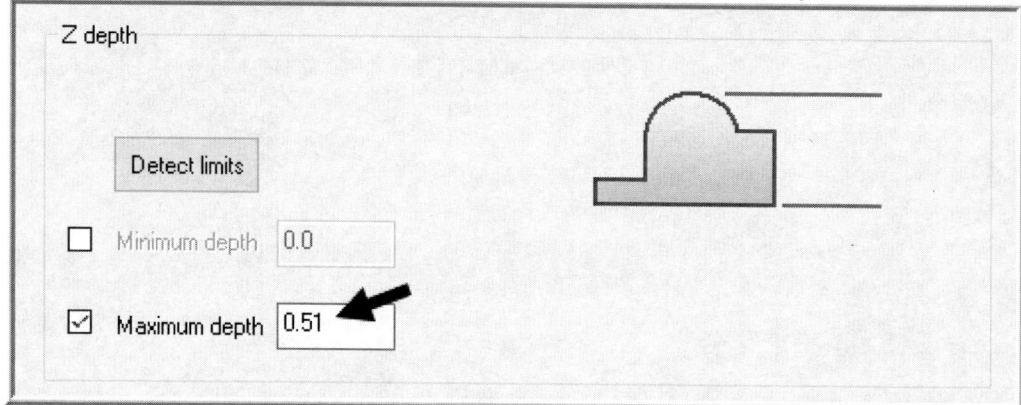

17. Make the following selections on the **Linking Parameters** page:

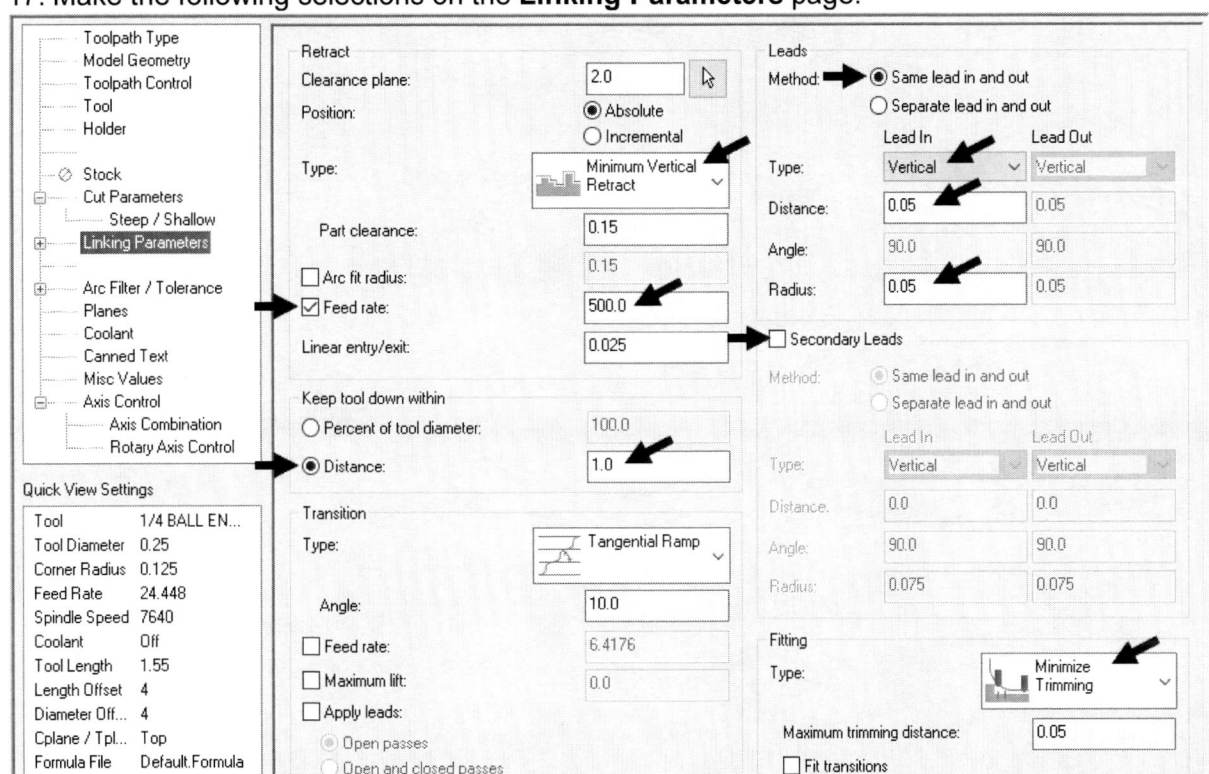

Use this page to create the links between the cutting passes. In general, you can think of linking moves as air moves when the tool is not in contact with the part, compared cutting moves which are configured on the toolpath's Cut parameters page.

First, select a **retract method**. This determines how the tool will move between the end of one pass and the beginning of another. Then, use the **Leads** fields to control how the tool moves onto and off of the part at the start and end of each cutting pass. These moves are applied to each pass no matter which cutting pass is selected. Finally, select a **Fitting** option to control how the entry and exit arcs will be fit into each pass.

Note: Mastercam creates linking moves only when the spacing between cutting passes is greater than the Keep tool down within distance on the

18. Go to the **Arc Filter/Tolerance** page and make the following changes.

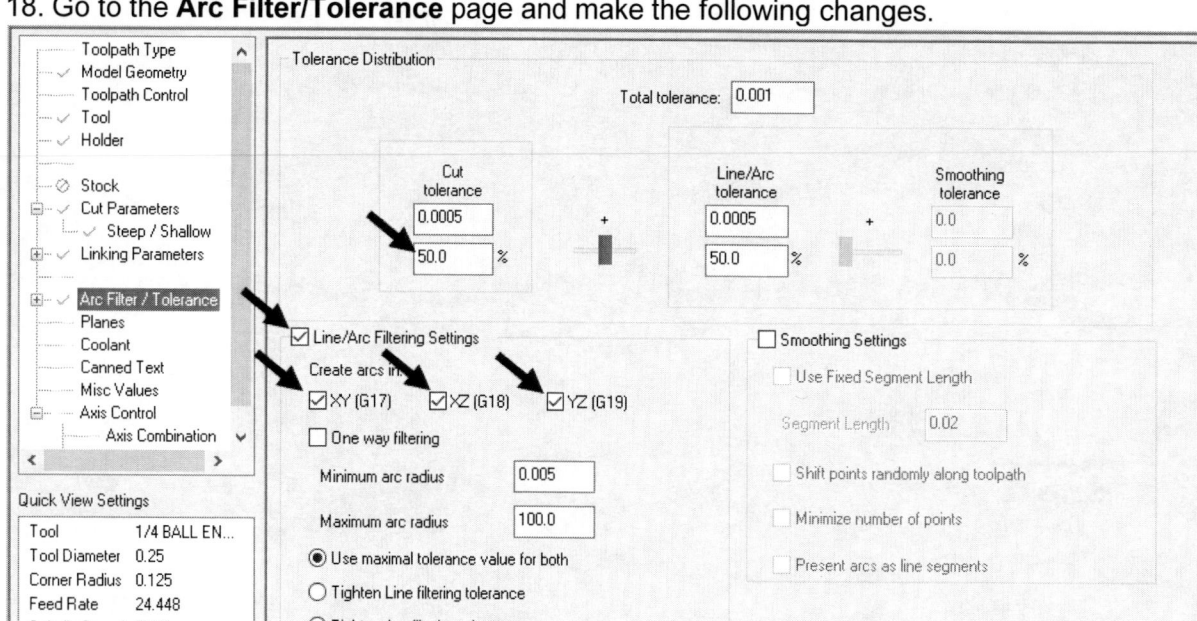

19. Finally, move to the **Coolant** tab and turn **Flood** coolant on.

20. Select the **OK button** to complete the toolpath.

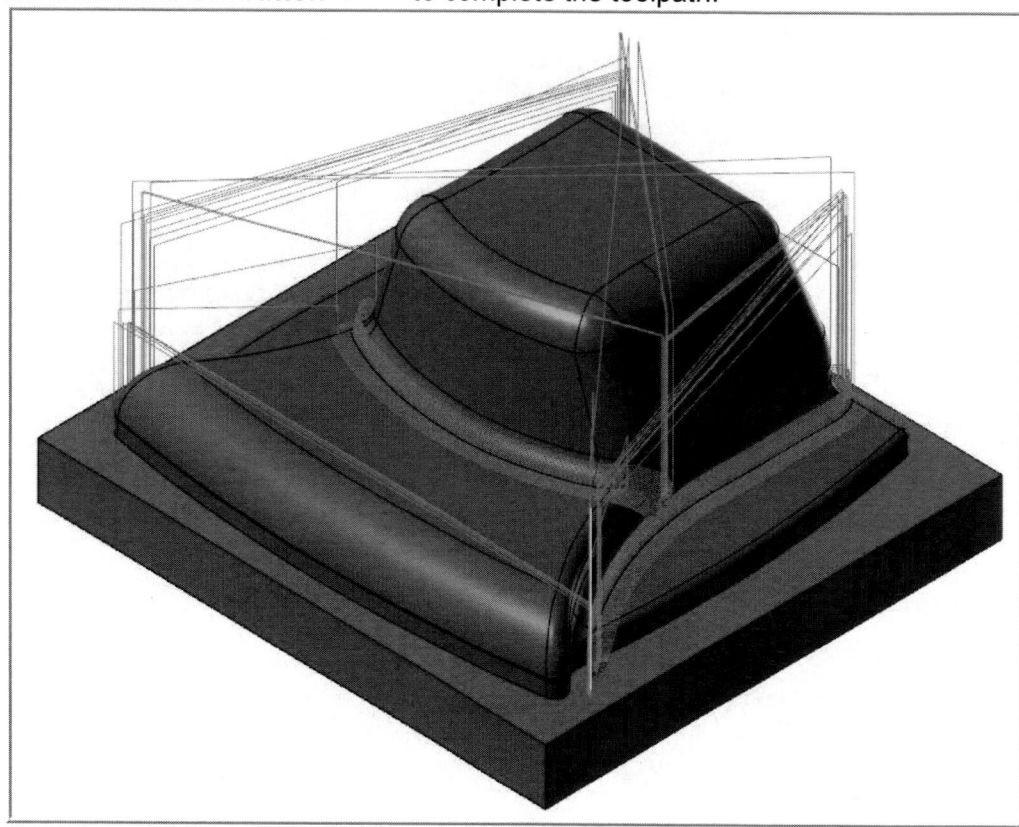

TASK 8:
VERIFY THE TOOLPATHS AND COMPARE TO SOLID MODEL

> **Comparing Verification/Simulation Results**
> You can compare your verification or simulation results to the workpiece or a selected STL file (a 3D model file) to check accuracy. Mastercam Simulator colors the part model according to the amount of stock, if any, left on the model above or below tolerances you specify in the Compare dialog box.

1. Select all of the operations you have completed so far by picking the **Select all operations** icon ⬚.

2. Select the **Verify selected** operations icon.

3. **Maximize** the Backplot/Verify window if required.

4. On the **Home** page open the **Stop Conditions** drop down menu and activate stop on **Collision**.

5. Activate the options shown below in the **Visibility** section of the **Home** tab. **Initial Stock and Toolpath not** activated.

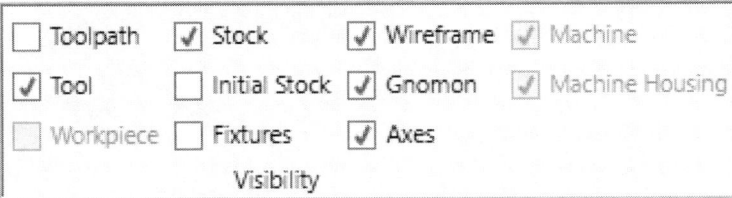

6. Select the **Verify** tab and activate the **Color Loop** to change the color of the tools for the verified part.

7. On the **Verify** tab and in the **Quality** section activate **Turbo Mode**.

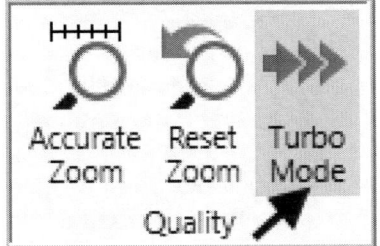

8. Now select the **Play Simulation** button to review the toolpaths.

9. After reviewing the toolpaths select the **Compare** icon in the **Analyze** section of the **Verify** page.

10. The **Compare** dialog box opens up on the right of the screen. Now click on **the Compare Options** icon.

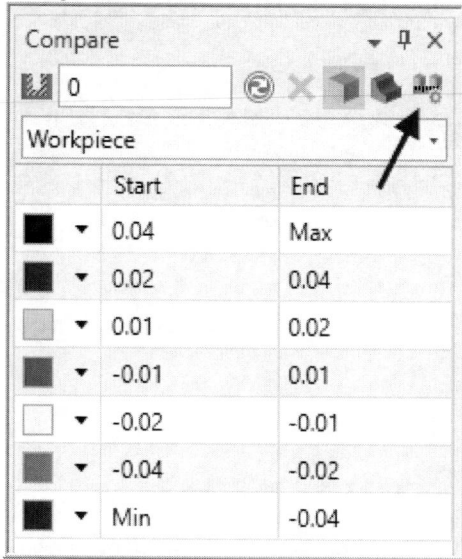

> **Click Options** to adjust the increment between the colors.
> Enter a Tolerance in the Compare Options dialog box and click OK to update the comparison results.

11. For the **Tolerance input 0.002** and click on **OK**.

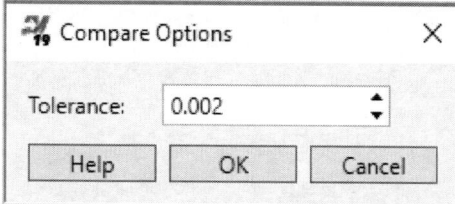

12. Hit the green **Refresh** icon. The computed results are shown below:

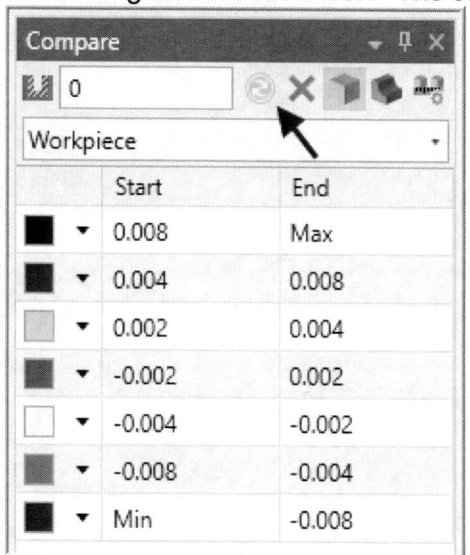

> Compare the colors on the model with those on the chart at the right.
>
> The light blue shaded areas indicate additional stock to remove.
>
> Purple to red shaded areas would indicate part gouges and areas in previous toolpaths that need to be addressed!

13. Select the **Close** button [×] in the top right-hand corner to exit Verify

TASK 9:
SAVE THE UPDATED MASTERCAM FILE

1. Select the **Save** icon from the **Quick Access** toolbar at the top left of the screen.

TASK 10:
POST AND CREATE THE CNC CODE FILE

1. Ensure all the operations are selected by picking the **Select all operations** icon 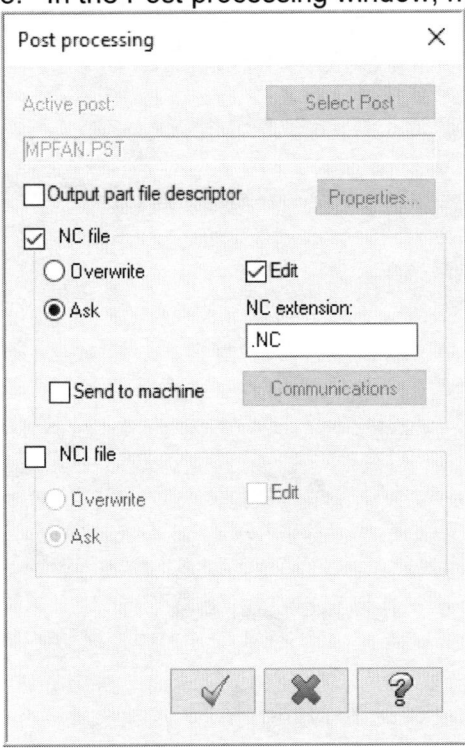 from the Toolpaths Manager.
2. Select the **Post selected operations** button from the Toolpaths Manager.
3. In the Post processing window, make the necessary changes as shown below:

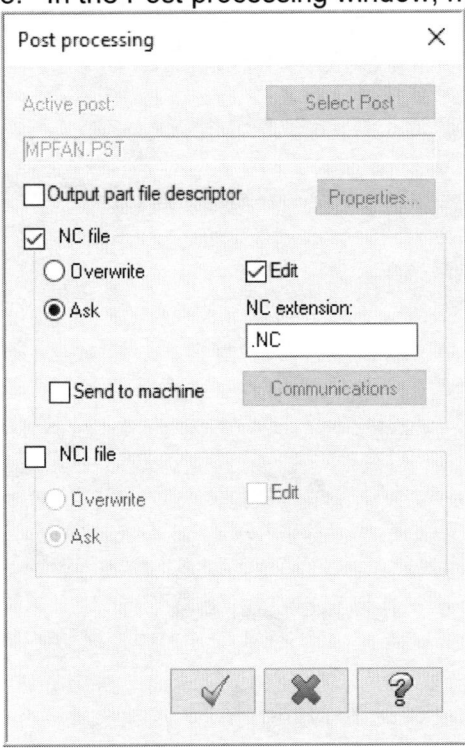

4. Select the **OK button** ✓ to continue.
5. Enter the same name as your Mastercam part file name in the NC File name field **Mill-Lesson-15**.
6. Select the **Save** button.
7. The CNC code file opens up in the default editor.
8. Select the ✕ in the top right corner to exit the CNC editor

TASK 11:
CREATE AN ACTIVEREPORT

➲ Finally, you will create a report to help with part setup at the machine.

1. Select **File>Configuration>Reports** and ensure the **Setup Sheet program** is set to **ActiveReport**.

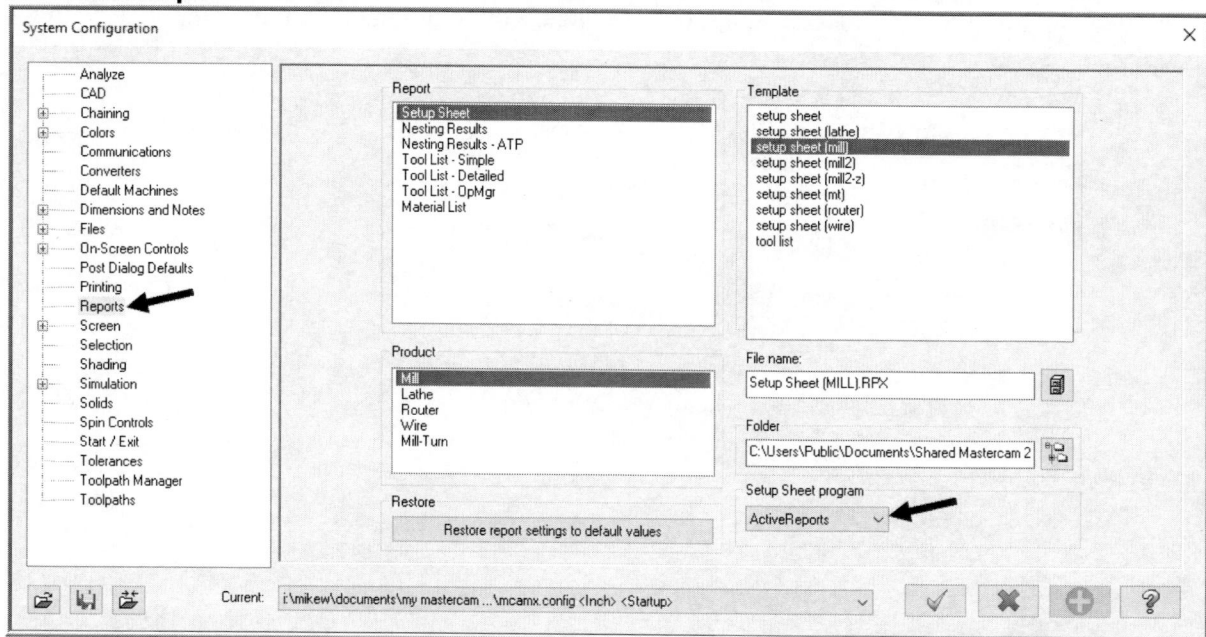

2. Select the **OK button** to exit. Select **Yes** to save changes if required.
3. Right click inside the **Toolpaths Manager** window and select **Setup sheet....**
4. Select the **OK button** to generate the report.
5. The **ActiveReports Viewer** will load automatically. Note it may take a while to load.
6. Print the report and go through the various pages comparing the report information to the toolpaths in the **Toolpaths Manager**.
7. You have the option of saving the report as any of the following file formats.

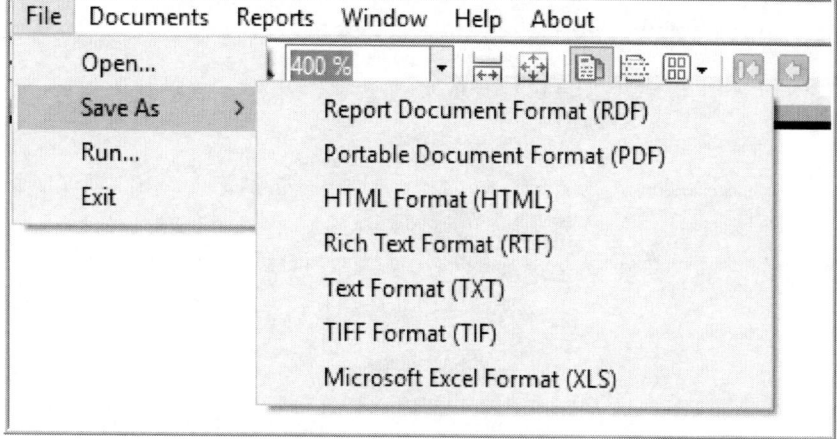

This completes Mill-Lesson-15.

MILL-LESSON-15 EXERCISE-A

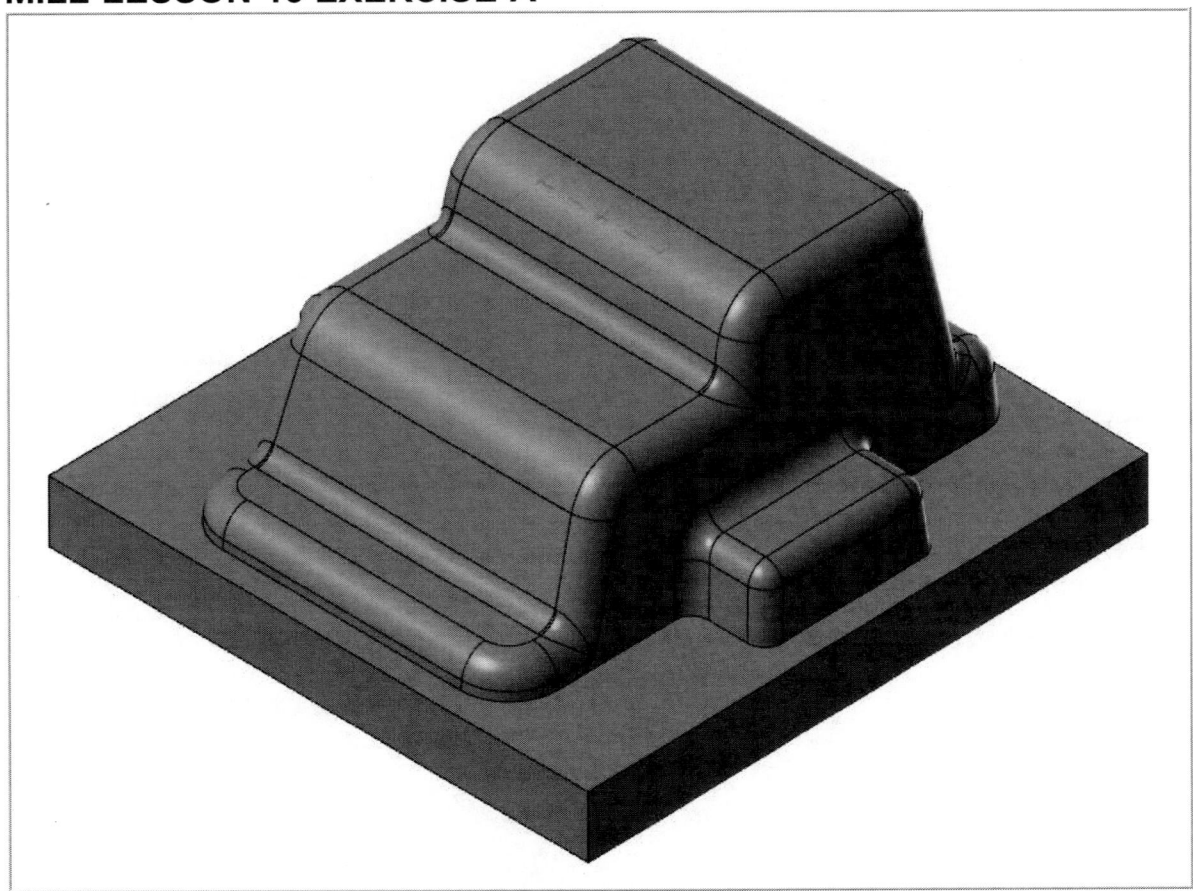

MILL-LESSON-15 EXERCISE-B

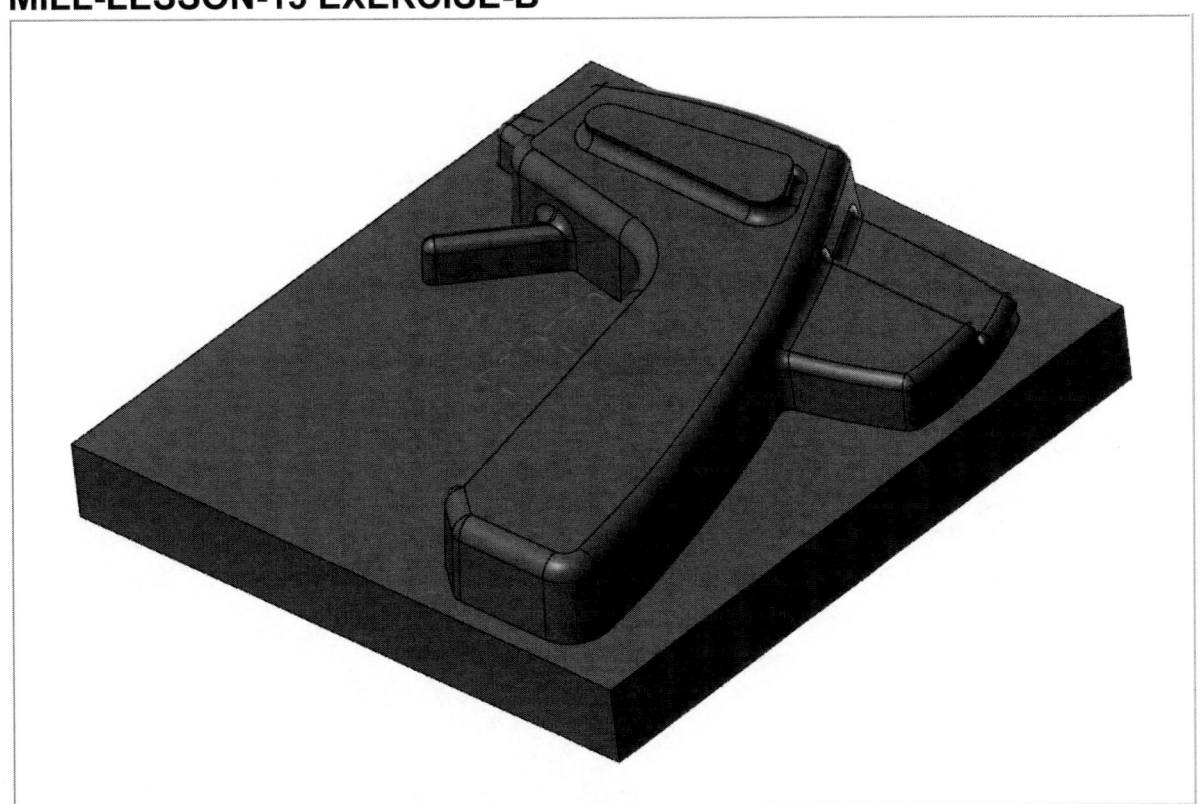

Mastercam 2022

TRAINING
GUIDE

MILL-LESSON-16

IMPORTING TOOLPATHS, DYNAMIC OPTIROUGH & OPTIREST, STOCK MODELS, 2D HIGH SPEED AREA MILL, SURFACE HIGH SPEED EQUAL SCALLOP, SPIRAL AND PENCIL REST TOOLPATHS

camInstructor

Objectives

You will use a provided model for Mill-Lesson-16, and then generate the toolpaths to machine the part on a CNC vertical milling machine. This Lesson covers the following topics:

➲ **Prepare model for cutting by:**
Creating Edge Curves
Creating surfaces from solid faces.
Creating flat boundary surfaces.

➲ **Generate 3-dimensional milling toolpaths consisting of:**
Importing toolpaths
Dynamic OptiRough & OptiRest
Stock Models
2D High Speed Area Mill
Surface High Speed Equal Scallop, Spiral and Pencil Rest

➲ **Inspect the toolpath using Mastercam's Verify by:**
Launching the Verify function to machine the part on the screen.
Verify the part using a stock model.
Generating the NC- code.

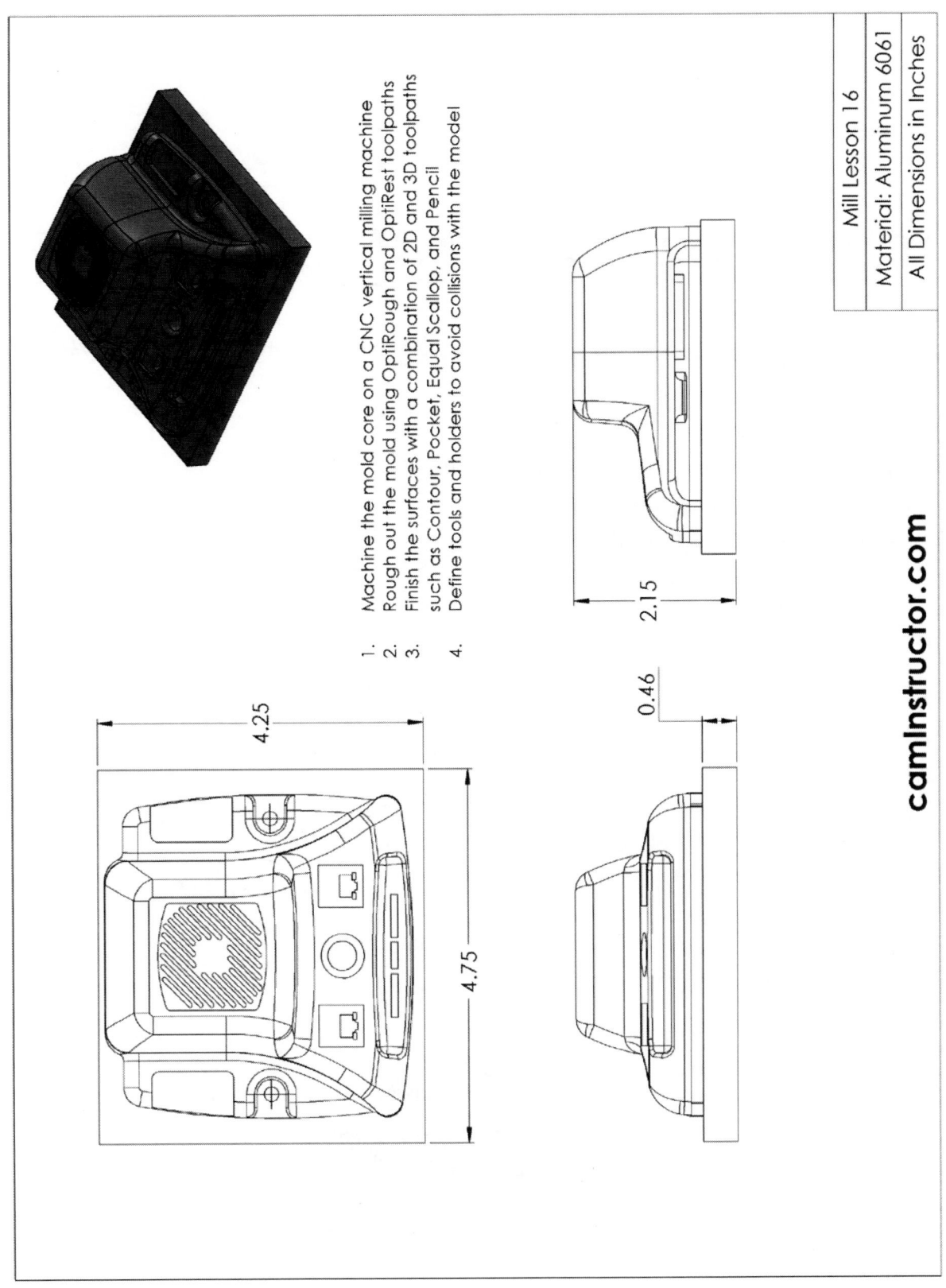

Mill Lesson 16

Material: Aluminum 6061

All Dimensions in Inches

1. Machine the mold core on a CNC vertical milling machine
2. Rough out the mold using OptiRough and OptiRest toolpaths
3. Finish the surfaces with a combination of 2D and 3D toolpaths such as Contour, Pocket, Equal Scallop, and Pencil
4. Define tools and holders to avoid collisions with the model

4.25

4.75

2.15

0.46

caminstructor.com

TOOL LIST

➲ 1.000 diameter bull end mill 0.0313 corner radius.
➲ 0.250 diameter bull end mill 0.0313 corner radius.
➲ 0.500 diameter flat end mill.
➲ 0.1875 diameter flat end mill.
➲ 0.375 diameter ball end mill.
➲ 0.1875 diameter ball end mill

MILL-LESSON-16 - THE PROCESS

Toolpath Creation

TASK 1: Open an existing Mastercam file
TASK 2: Prepare geometry for toolpath creation
TASK 3: Import the Roughing toolpath
TASK 4: Create a Stock Model from the Roughing toolpath
TASK 5: Rest Roughing using Dynamic OptiRough
TASK 6: Create Stock Model from the First Two Toolpaths
TASK 7: Finish flat surfaces using 2D High Speed 2D Area Mill
TASK 8: Use Analyze Dynamic to Identify Part Dimensions
TASK 9: Finish Machine Open Pockets – 2 places
TASK 10: Finish Machine Open radiused Pockets – 2 places
TASK 11: Finish Machine contour of mold base
TASK 12: Create Stock Model from the 2D Toolpaths
TASK 13: Semi Finish using Surface High Speed Equal Scallops
TASK 14: Finish Circular Feature using Surface High Speed Spiral
TASK 15: Create Stock Model ready for Pencil Toolpath
TASK 16: Finish using Surface High Speed Pencil rest passes
TASK 17: Verify the toolpaths
TASK 18: Save the updated Mastercam file
TASK 19: Post and create the CNC code file

Please Note:
Review the videos **before** working through each task.

There are some intricate geometry selection techniques used in this lesson, reviewing the videos will make it easier for you to complete this lesson.

TASK 1:
OPEN AN EXISTING MASTERCAM FILE

➲ The required file for this Lesson is is available in a step in **Lesson 16** on the **camInstructor Course Site.**

1. Select **File>Open> Mill-Lesson-16.**
2. If confronted with the System Configuration dialog box activate the radio button for **All settings**.

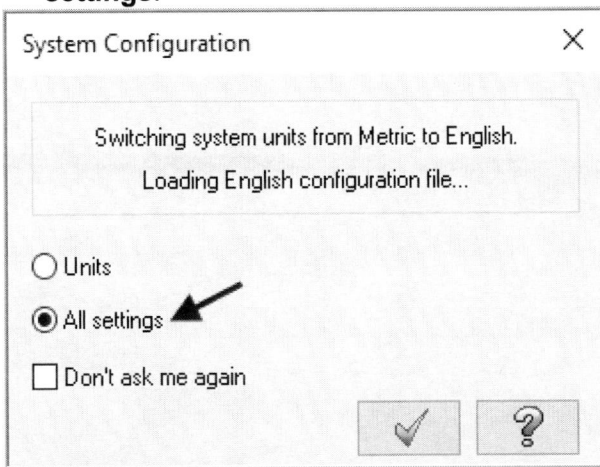

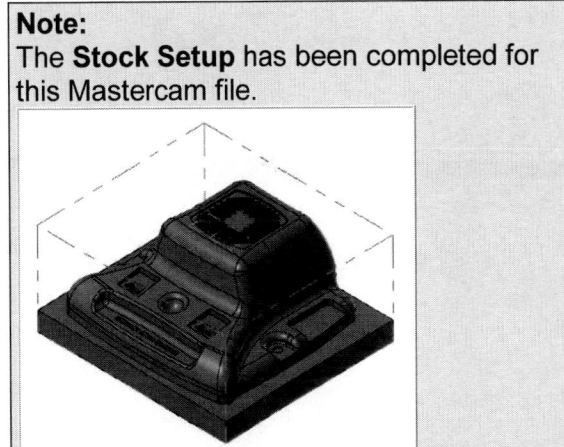

Note:
The **Stock Setup** has been completed for this Mastercam file.

System Configuration (switch units) dialog box
When you open a part file that uses different units (English or metric) from those currently in use, Mastercam automatically displays this dialog box, which informs you that Mastercam is switching units and loading an alternate default configuration file. In order to complete the operation, select one of the following options:
Units: Tells Mastercam to use only the units from the new configuration file. (default)
All settings: Tells Mastercam to load all settings from the new configuration file.

---

3. Select the OK button ☑ to exit the **System Configuration** dialog box.
4. In the View tab click on Outline Shaded in the Appearance section to display the part in shaded mode.

The existing Mastercam file for Lesson 16 has had some settings made already. The model has been located correctly in the Top plane relative to the required datum (origin). The stock setup has been defined. The Tool settings have been set as has the material type. The material type has been edited as was done in Lesson 15, for carbide tools. The machine has also had a new limit applied to the spindle. The steps to add this limit will be explained in the next few steps.

5. Select the **plus** in front of **Properties** to expand the Toolpaths Group Properties.
6. Select the **Tool Settings** tab.

The program number, Feed Calculation type, Toolpath Configuration options and Advanced options have all been set as shown.

The material has also been set to Aluminum 6061. Click Edit to view the material changes that have already been made.

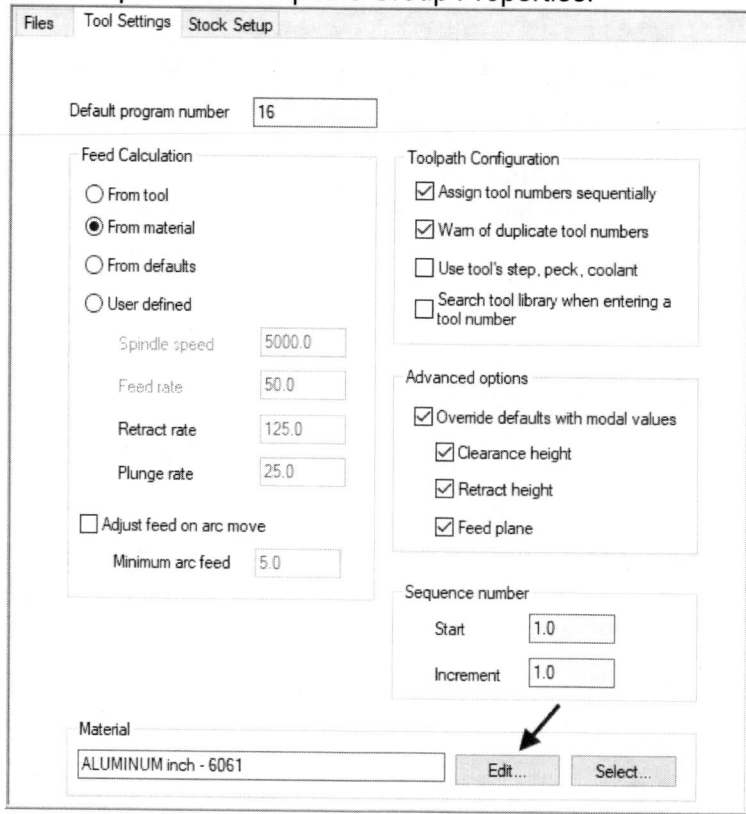

7. Notice the value for Carbide SFM has been increased to 400%. For more explanation on this setting refer to Lesson 15.

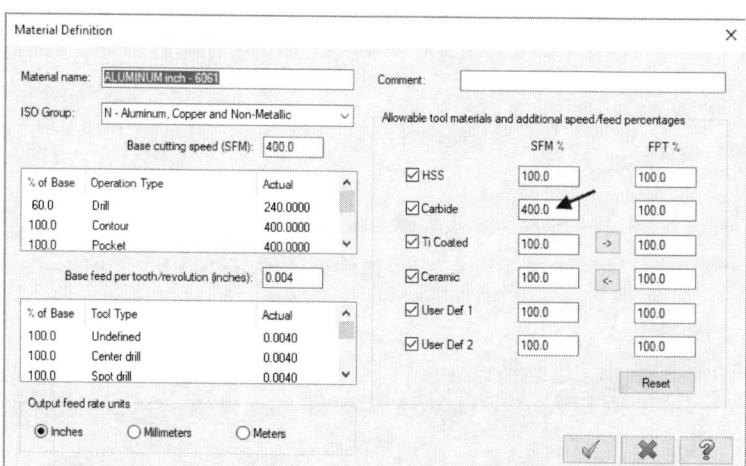

The user can further adjust SFM and chip load percentages in each tool definition. This is demonstrated during the first operation in **TASK 4**.

When cutting on a machine it is extremely important that you research recommended SFM and FPT for your tools and material and make the appropriate settings in Mastercam.

8. Select the **OK button** [✓] on the **Material Definition** dialog box to complete this function.

9. Select the **Files** tab, and click on the **Edit Machine** button.

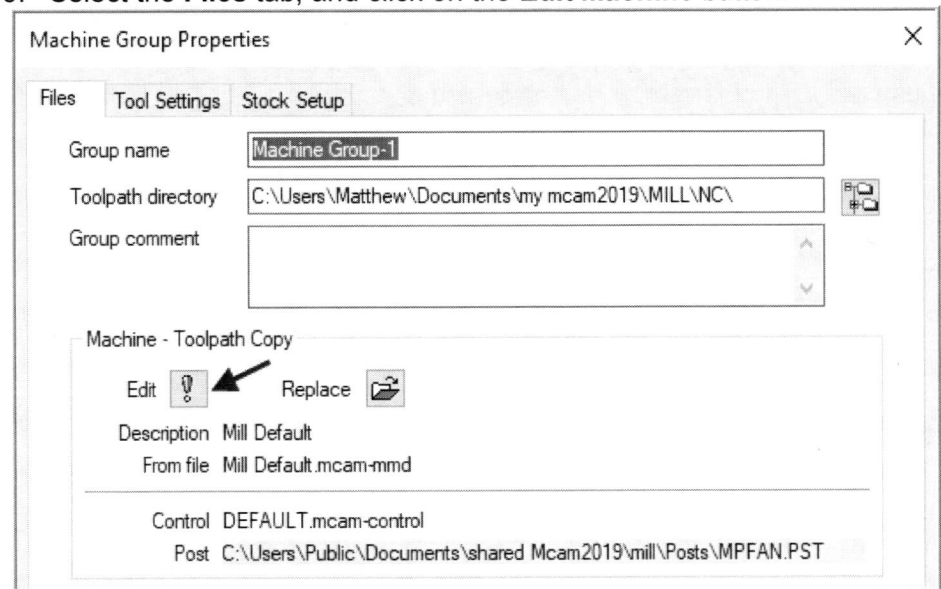

Edit machine (button)
Click to open and edit the machine definition.

Changes you make are only be saved to the local copy stored in your part file, **not the master copy stored on your workstation**.

Not all Machine Definition Manager and Control Definition Manager functions are available.

10. In the **Machine Configuration** section expand all the options for **Mill Spindle Group** and double click on **Tool Spindle**.

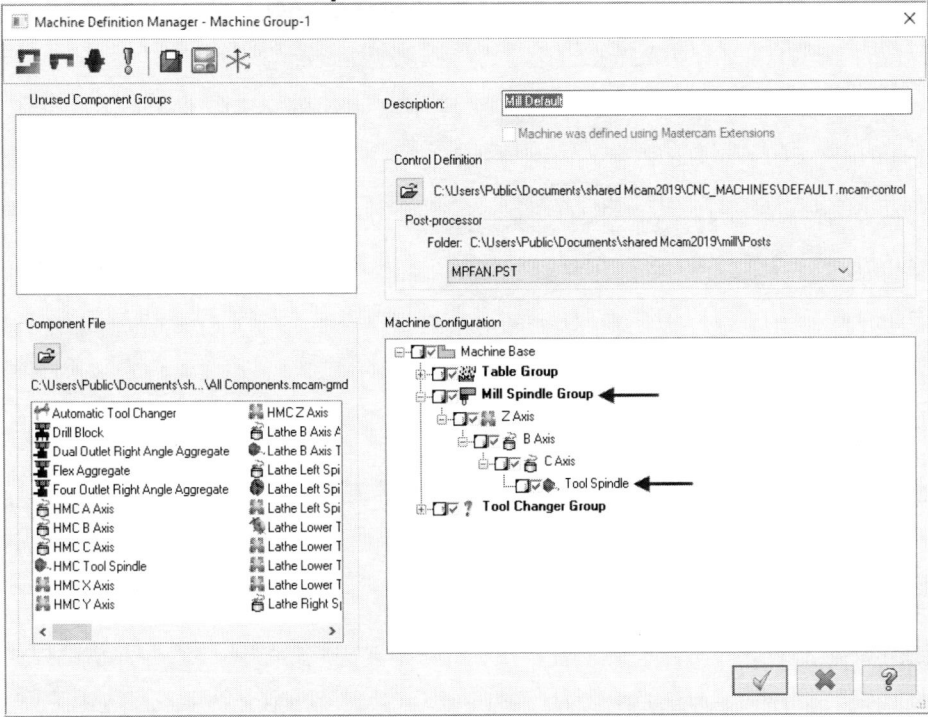

Machine Definition Manager

Use the Machine Definition Manager to assemble machine components, set machine and component properties, select a control definition, and select a post processor.

Once a machine definition has been created and selected, you can begin creating toolpath operations for the machine.

The **Machine Configuration window** displays a schematic model of your machine tool. Individual components and groups of components are organized in a tree structure. Right-click in the tree to add new components or to set properties for individual components. Add components and groups by dragging them from the other windows. Use the checkbox in front of each component to select it for simulation.

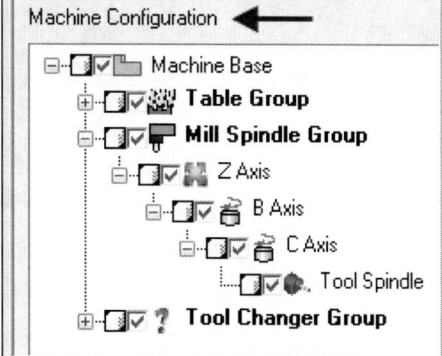

11. On the **Parameters** page, the default **Maximum spindle speed** has been changed from 50000 to **10000 rpm**.

The objective for setting the **Maximum spindle speed** to **10,000 RPM** is to prohibit excessive spindle speeds.

The default **Maximum spindle speed** was **50,000 RPM**, spindle speeds generated for carbide in aluminum will exceed typical RPM ranges on a Vertical Machining Center.

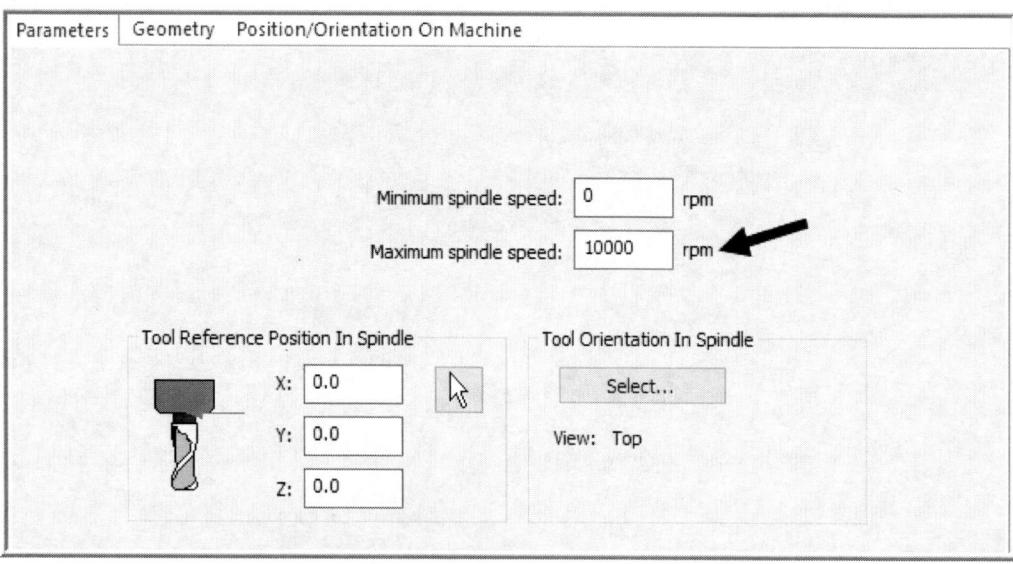

Minimum/maximum spindle speed

The spindle speeds are used to limit the spindle speed set in the Toolpath parameters for an operation.

12. Select the **OK button** ✓ again to exit the **Machine Component Manager**.
13. Select the **OK button** ✓ again to exit the **Machine Definition Manager**.
14. Select the **OK button** ✓ again to exit the **Machine Group Properties**.
15. Right mouse click in the graphics area and click on **Isometric**.

16. Right mouse click in the graphics area and click on the **Fit** icon ⊞.

➲ Your part should look similar to the screen shot below: With X0 Y0 at the center and Z zero on the top of the part.

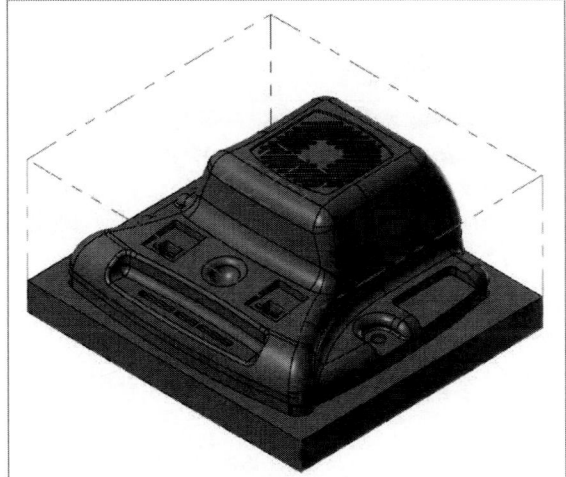 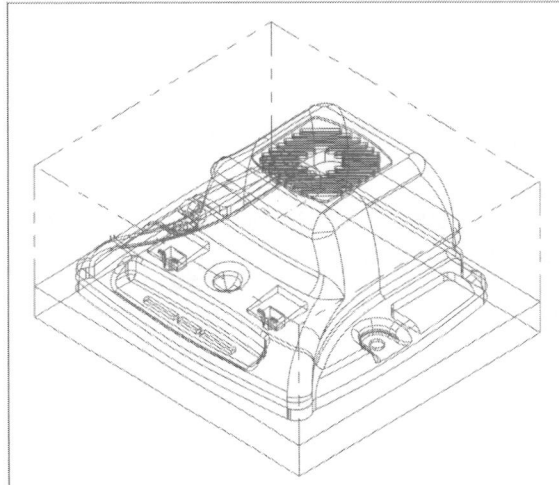

TASK 2:
PREPARE GEOMETRY FOR TOOLPATH CREATION
➲ In this task you will create surfaces and containment boundaries for machining.
➲ The first step will be to use **Curve On One Edge** to create curves on the part.
➲ The second step will use **Flat Boundary** to cover areas of the part that will later be machined by electrode.

Please Note:
Review the videos **before** working through each task.

There are some intricate geometry selection techniques used in this lesson and reviewing the videos will make it easier for you to complete this lesson.

---

1. Select the **View tab** and click on **Levels** to display the **Levels Manager**. The keyboard short cut is **ALT+Z**.
2. In the **Number** field click on **10 in the Number column**. Level 10 is now the main level, the **active level**.

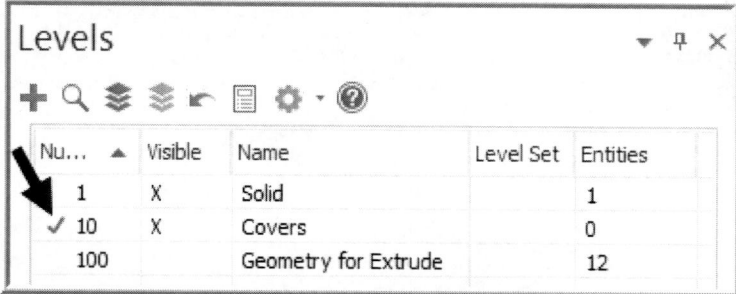

The **Levels Manager** is a good way to organize your geometry for easy reference.

The highlighted level is the main level. Any geometry created always goes onto the current main level. To select a level as main simply click on the number of the level in the level list.

The X under the column called **Visible** indicates whether or not the geometry on a certain level is showing. The main level is always visible.

It is possible to leave the **Levels Manager** open at all times.

---

3. Right mouse click in the graphics area and set the **Wireframe and Surface Color** to color **137**.

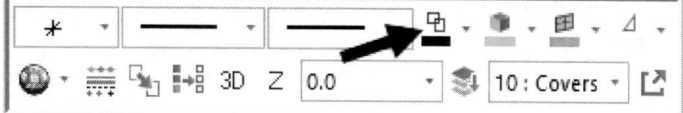

4. Click on the **Wireframe** tab and in the **Curves** section select **Curve One Edge**.

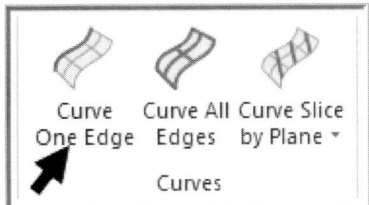

5. To satisfy the prompt, zoom in as required and select the edges shown in any order – **the three areas are shown below** as shown below. There is a total of 9 entities.

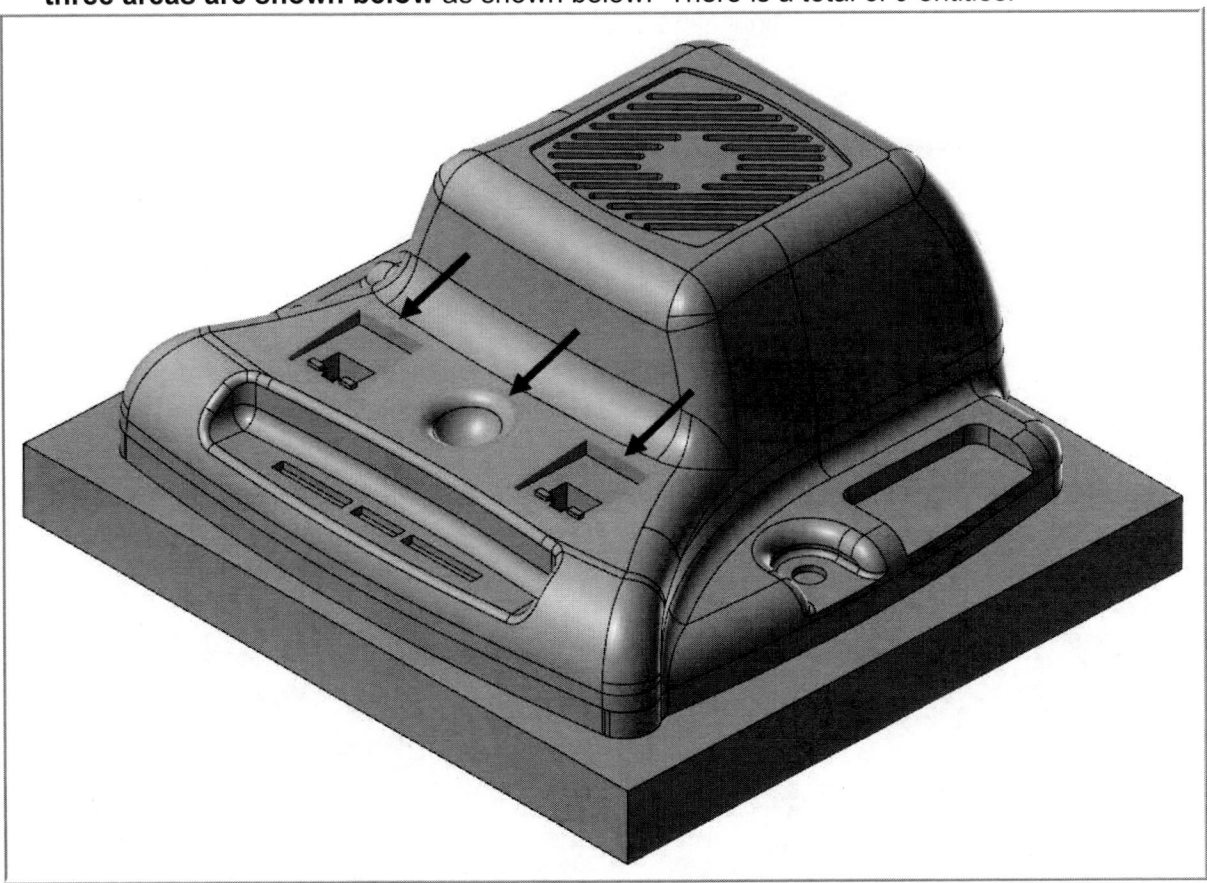

6. Select the **OK button**  to create the curves and exit.
7. Level 10 should now have **9 entities**.

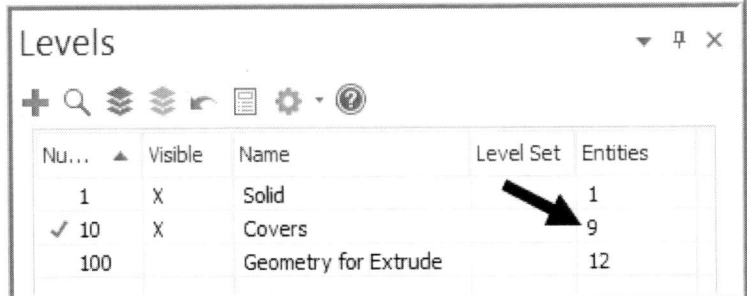

Nu... ▲	Visible	Name	Level Set	Entities
1	X	Solid		1
✓ 10	X	Covers		9
100		Geometry for Extrude		12

⊃ Next we will create eight surfaces shown below that will be used later for machining.

8. Click on the **Surfaces** tab and in the **Create** section select **Flat Boundary**.

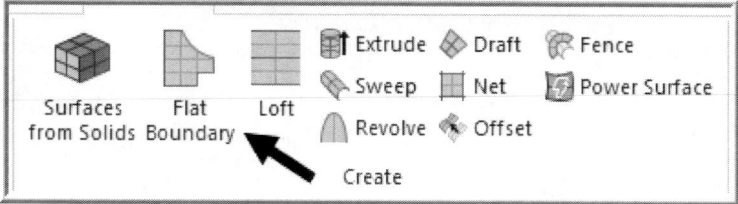

9. The chaining dialog appears with chain set. **C-Plane is not activated**.

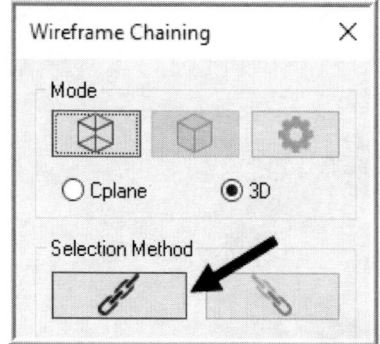

10. Select the **three chains** in any order as shown below.

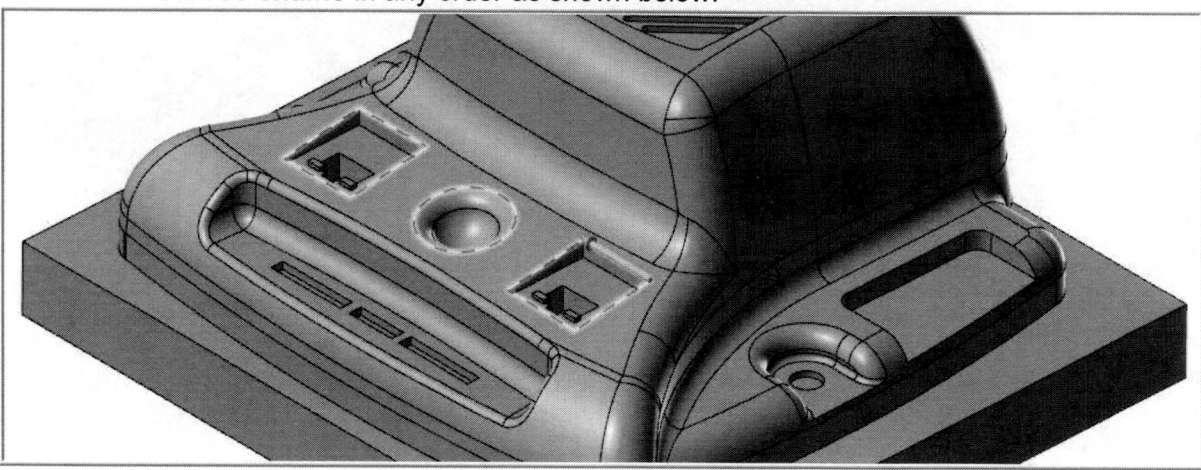

11. Select the **OK button** to create the Flat Boundary surfaces and exit.

12. Level 10 should now have **53 entities**.

Nu... ▲	Visible	Name	Level Set	Entities
1	X	Solid		1
✓ 10	X	Covers		15
100		Geometry for Extrude		12

⮎ The Flat Boundary surfaces are shown below.

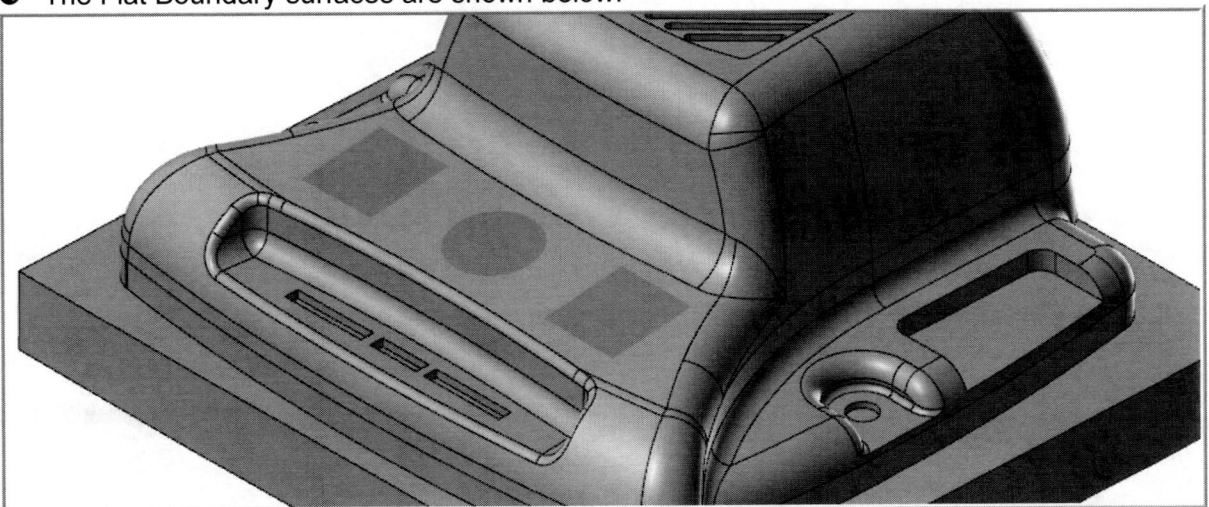

⮎ Alternatively, Fill Holes can be used to cover features. This function allows you to skip the step of creating the curves first. You can fill internal (completely contained in the surface) and external holes (lie on the boundary of the surface).

13. On the Surface tab in the Modify section, select **Fill Holes**.

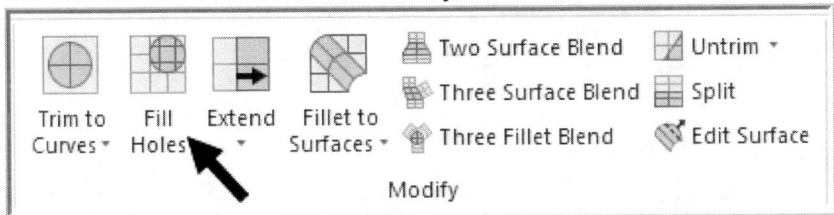

14. Fill Holes requires you to select a face, a solid face or surface will work, and then select the edge of the hole. Select the top face and then move the arrow to the inner edge.

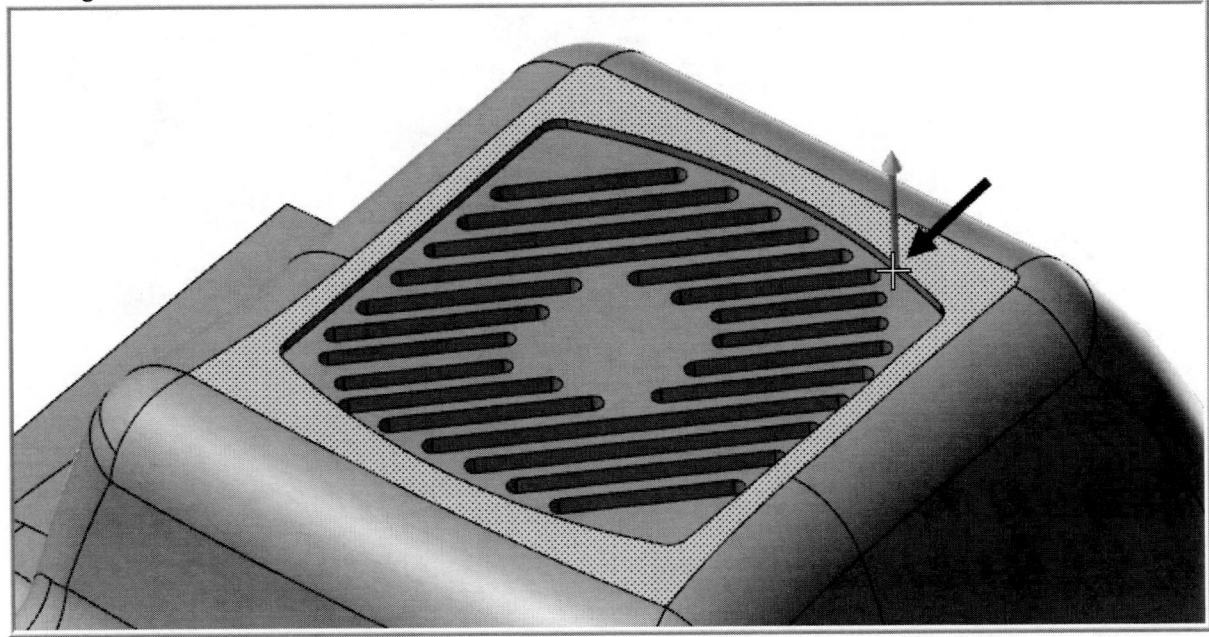

15. Left click on this inner edge and the surface cover will be created.

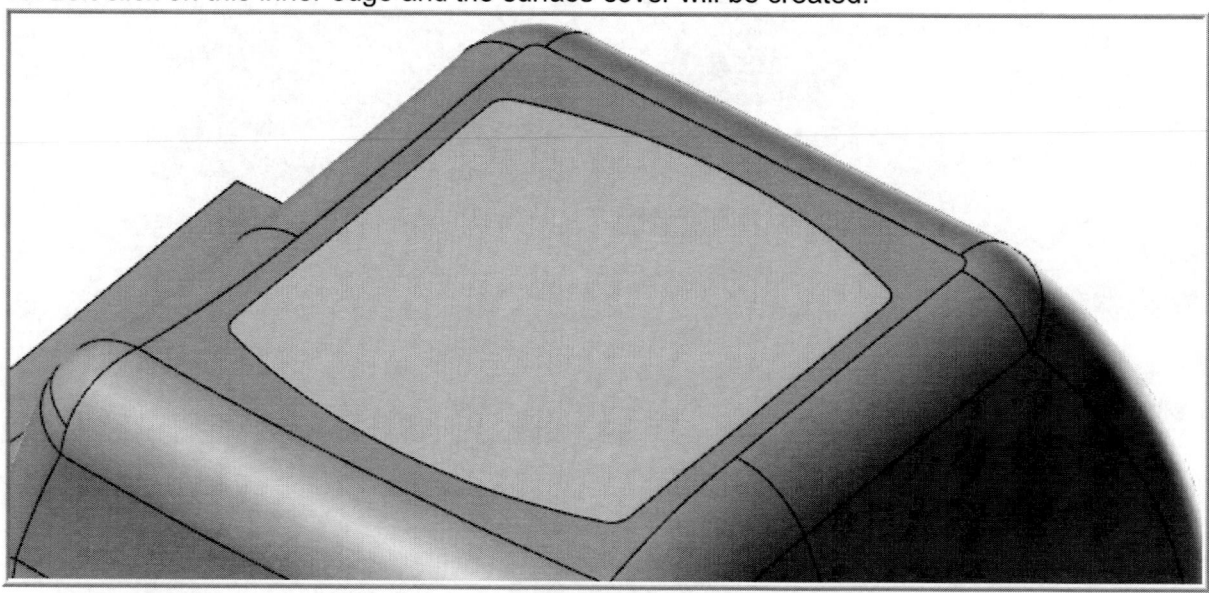

16. Repeat these steps for the **5** remaining features.

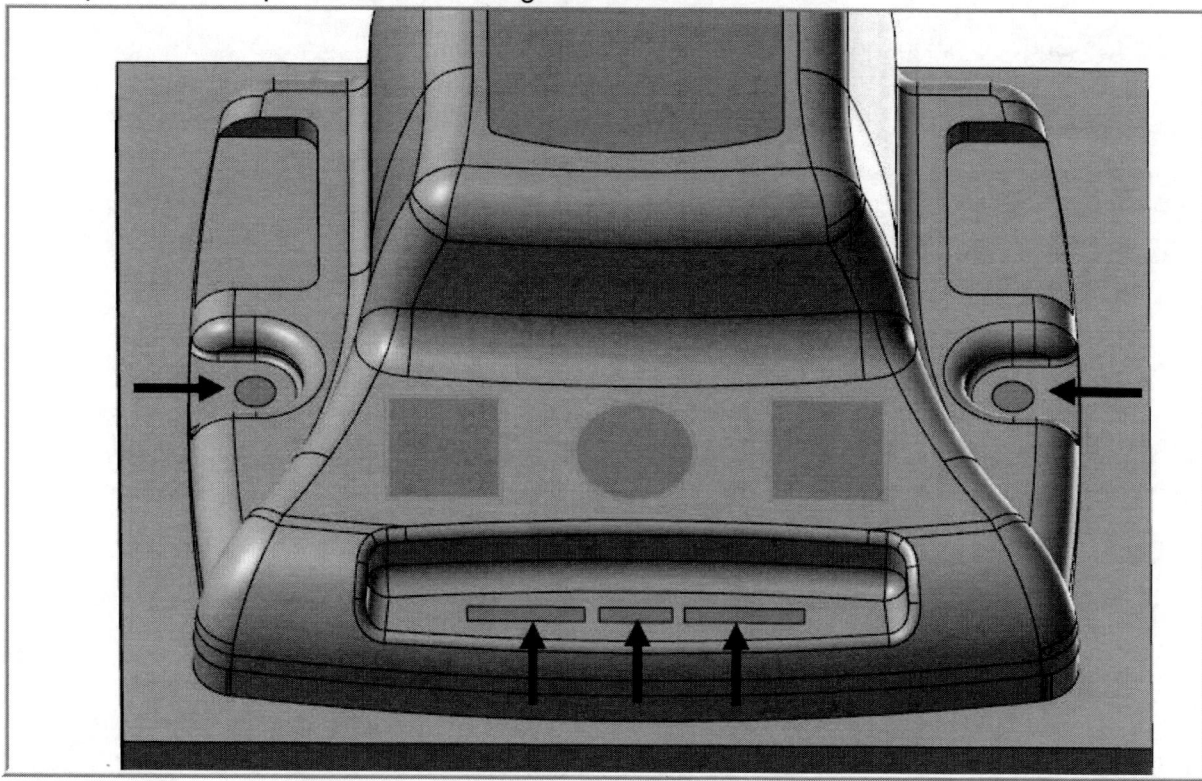

17. You should now have 29 entities on level 10.

Nu... ▲	Visible	Name	Level Set	Entities
1	X	Solid		1
✓ 10	X	Covers	➤	29
100		Geometry for Extrude		12

TASK 3:
IMPORT THE ROUGHING TOOLPATH

⊃ In this task you will import the roughing toolpath used in Lesson 15 and alter it to rough this part. The tool being used is a 1.000 diameter bull end mill with a 0.03125 corner radius.

1. Display the Toolpaths Manager, if required.
2. Right click in the **Toolpaths Manager** and select **Import** from the list as shown below:

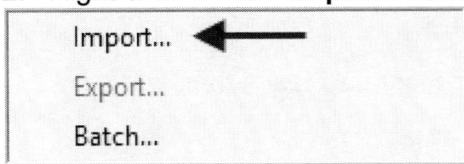

3. The **Import Toolpath Operations** window will now appear. Using the **Select Operations File** button [icon] browse to the source folder and select and open the **Mill-Lesson-15 Mastercam** file stored within it - **Change the types of files** to **Mastercam Files** as shown below right. *If your Lesson 15 file was done in the HLE version you will need to select the **Mastercam Education Files** option.

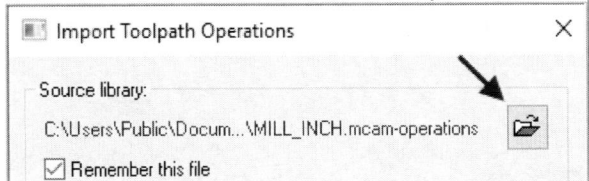 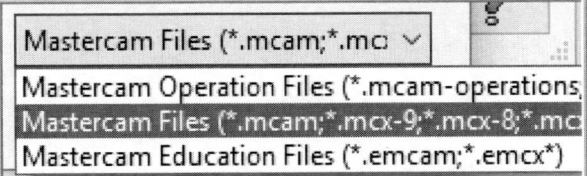

4. **Select the first operation only**, **Surface High Speed (Dynamic OptiRough)**.

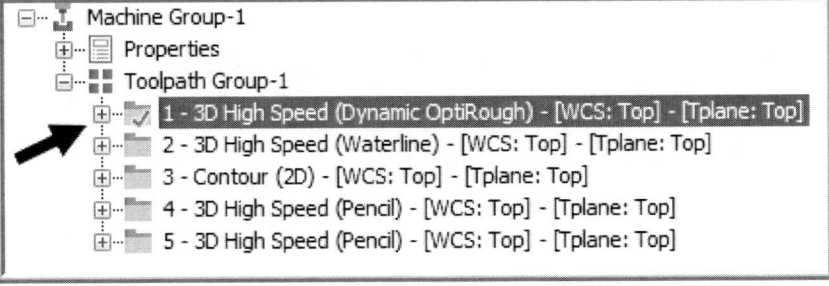

5. Select the **Import Operations button** [icon] to import the operation.
6. A message will appear indicating 1 operation has successfully been imported. Hit the **OK** button and then the **Cancel button** [icon] to return to the Toolpaths Manager.

7. Your Toolpaths manager should now have one dirty operation as shown below:

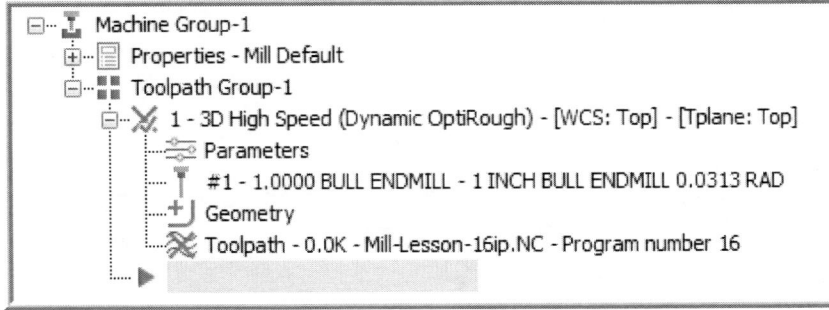

8. Select the **Geometry** icon from the first operation.
9. On the **Model Geometry** page select the machining row in the **Machine Geometry** section.
10. In the **Machine Geometry** section set the **Floor stock to 0.010**. Wall Stock should already be set to 0.010.

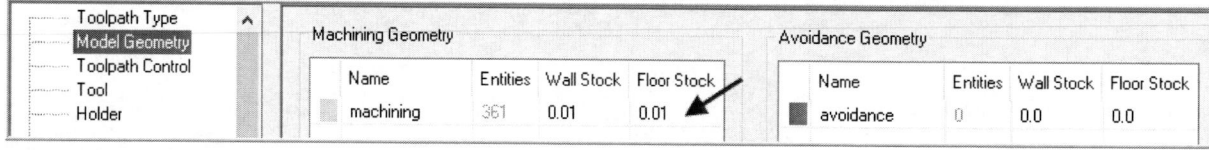

11. At the bottom of the **Model Geometry** page click on the **Select entities** button.

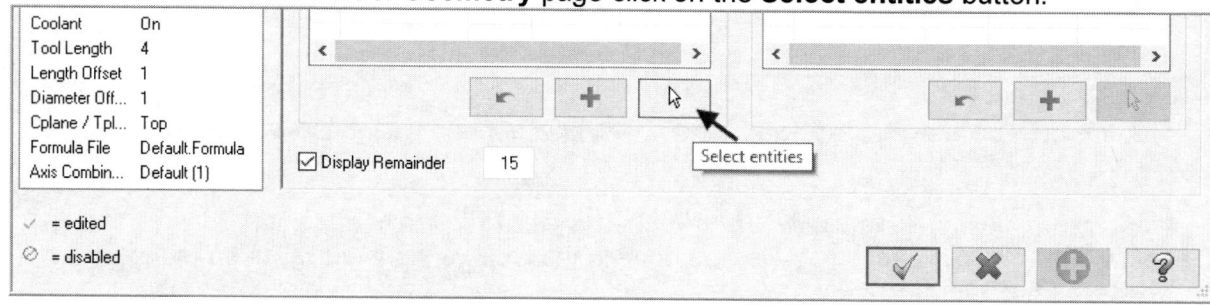

12. To satisfy the prompt **window select all of the entities** on the screen.

13. Click the **End Selection** icon 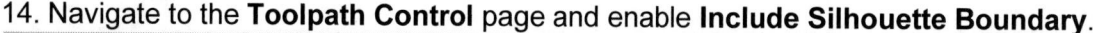.

14. Navigate to the **Toolpath Control** page and enable **Include Silhouette Boundary**.

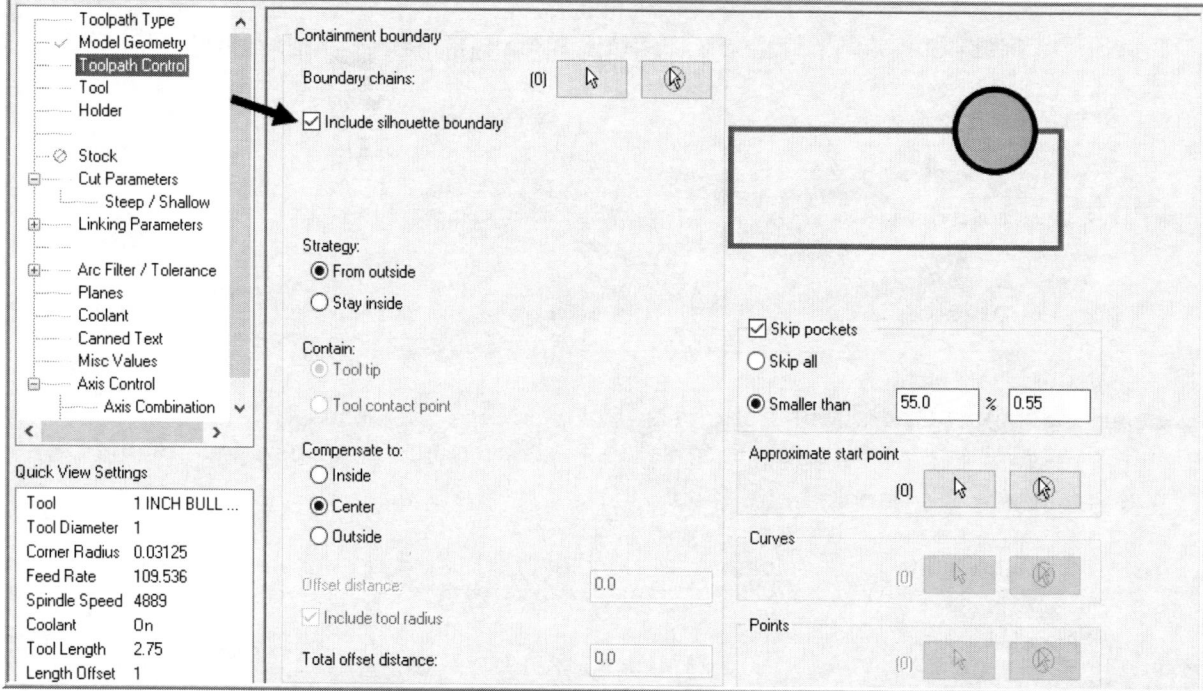

Include Silhouette Boundary
Mastercam will create a silhouette boundary around the selected Machining geometry and use it as a containment boundary. You can use this in conjunction with Boundary Chains.

15. Navigate to the **Tool** page. The tool being used is a **1 INCH BULL END MILL** with **a 0.313 corner radius**, this is a Carbide tool. If your tool did not import with a Spindle Speed of 4889 RPM you will need to edit the tool again. **Right mouse click** over the tool and select **Edit tool**.

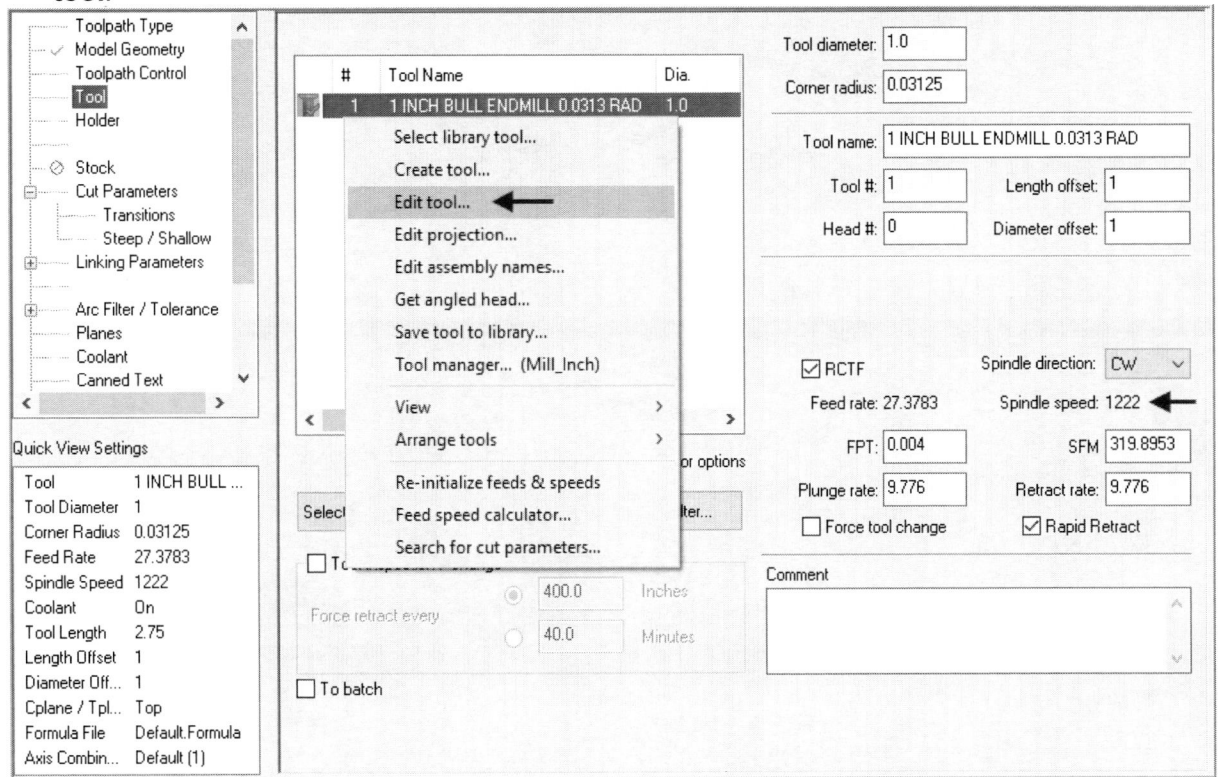

16. On the **Define Tool Geometry** page click on **Next** in the lower right-hand corner.
17. Open the drop-down menu for **Material** and notice it is set to **Carbide**. If not, adjust it now.

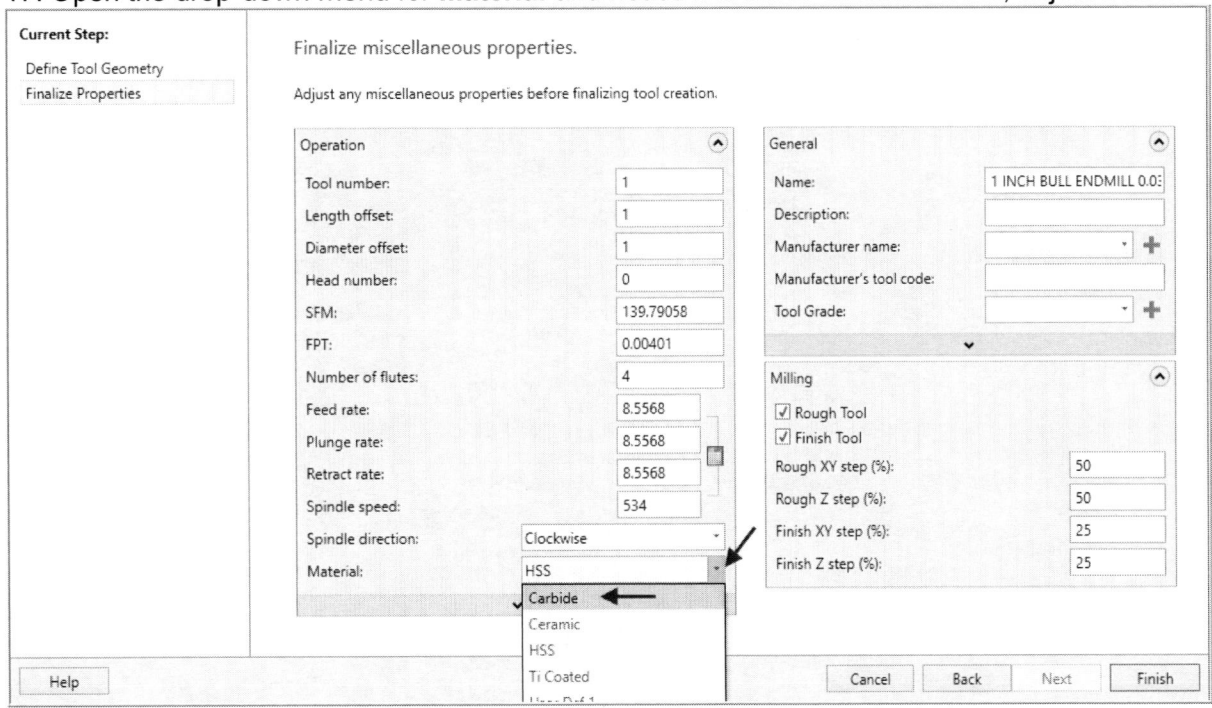

18. Click on **Finish** in the lower right-hand corner.

19. If you changed the tool material type you will have to **right mouse click** over the tool and select **Re-initialize feeds & speeds**.

➲ Take note of the feeds and speeds for the **carbide** cutter.

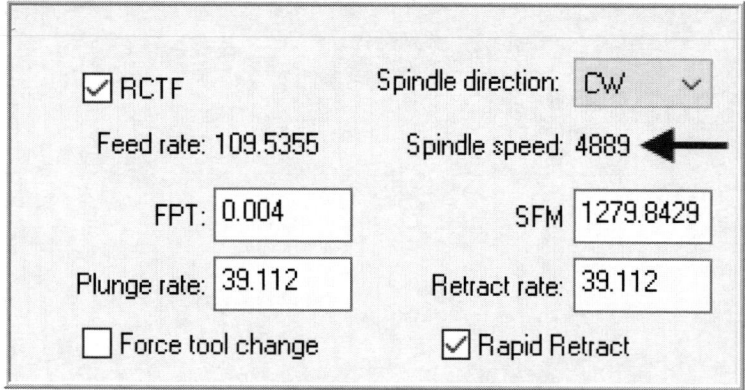

20. No changes are needed on the **Holder**, **Cut Parameters, or Transitions** pages as the imported settings are good.

➲ As the imported operation from Mill-Lesson-15 has **Z Zero at the bottom of the part** we will now need to adjust the parameters as Mill Lesson-16 has **Z Zero at the top of the part**.

21. On the **Steep/Shallow** page set the **Minimum depth** of the cut to **0.1** (this is the top of stock). Right click in the **Maximum depth** then select **Z = Z coordinate of a point**.

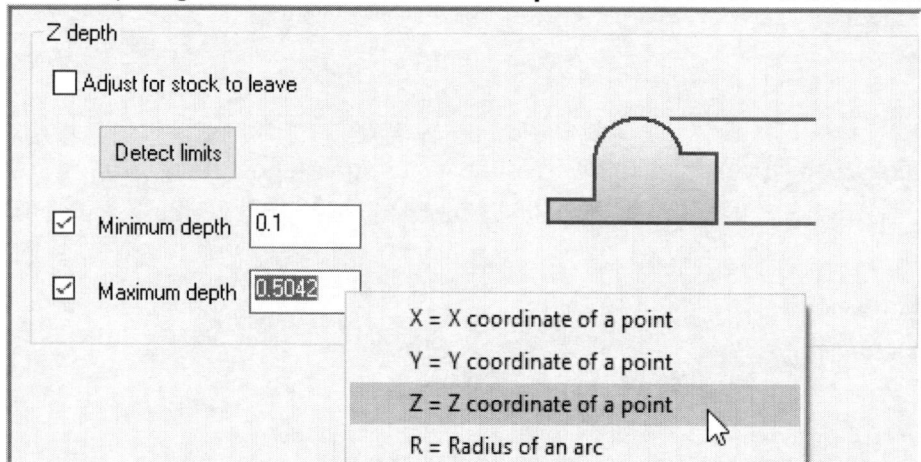

22. When prompted to "**Select a point**" select the end point shown below as the Z at the top of the mold base as shown below:

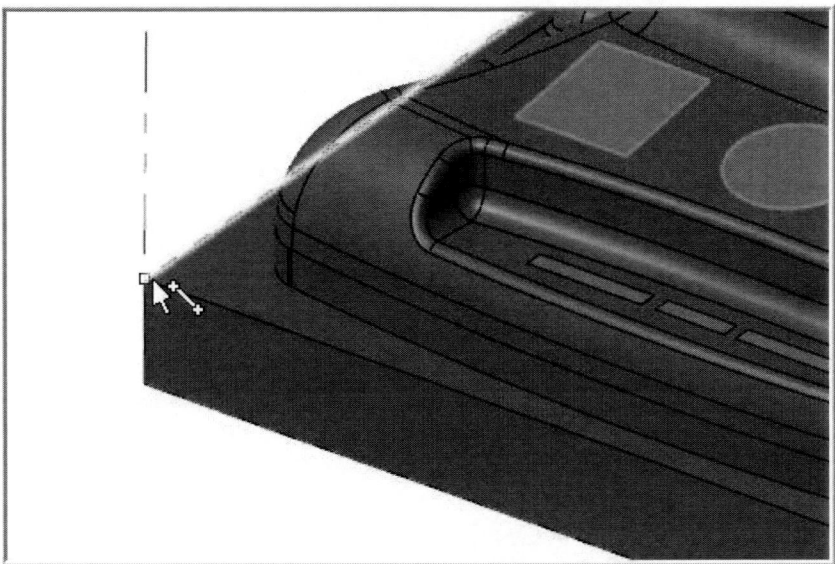

23. The resulting **Steep/Shallow** page values should match the following image:

☑ Minimum depth `0.1`

☑ Maximum depth `-1.6875`

24. Select the **Linking Parameters** page and set the **Clearance plane to 1.0** as shown below:

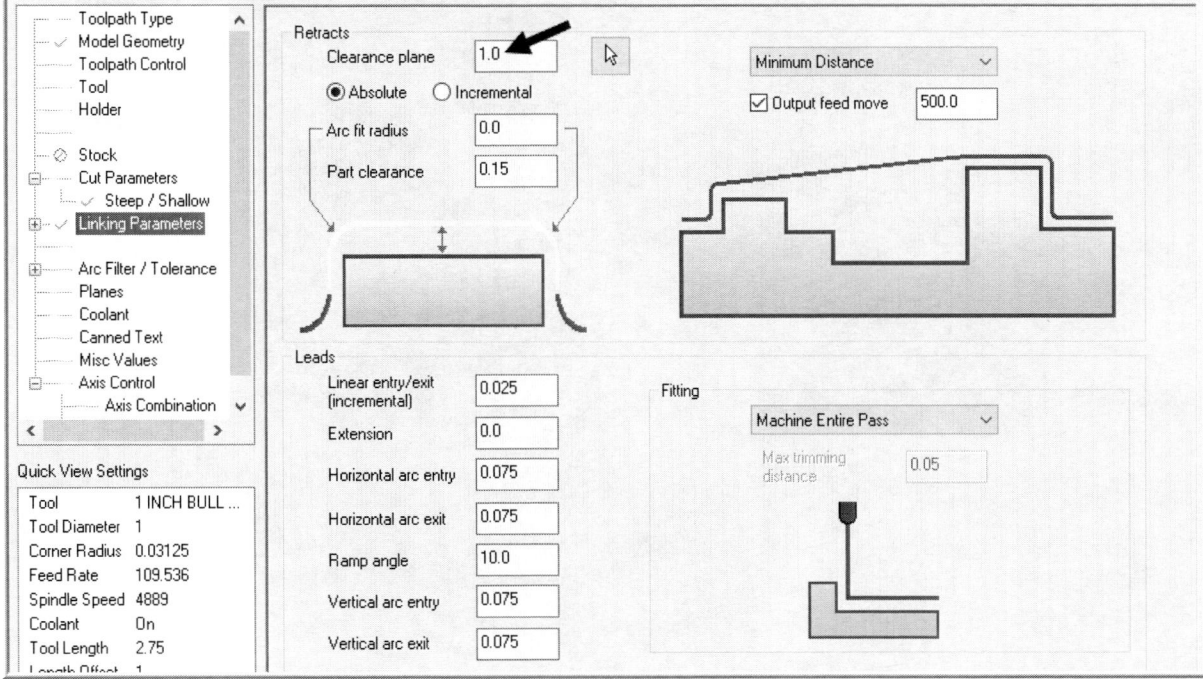

25. Ensure the Generate Toolpath is checked. This will automatically rebuild the operation once the Green Check is clicked.

26. Click the **Green Check button** to exit this toolpath.
27. The toolpath should rebuild.

➲ Now you will inspect the toolpath using Mastercam's **Backplot** function.
28. In the Toolpaths Manager, click on the **+** sign to the left of the toolpath to expand it if required. Now click on the **+** sign to the left of Geometry to expand it.
29. Then, left click on the bottom line with the toolpath information to review the toolpath using Backplot.

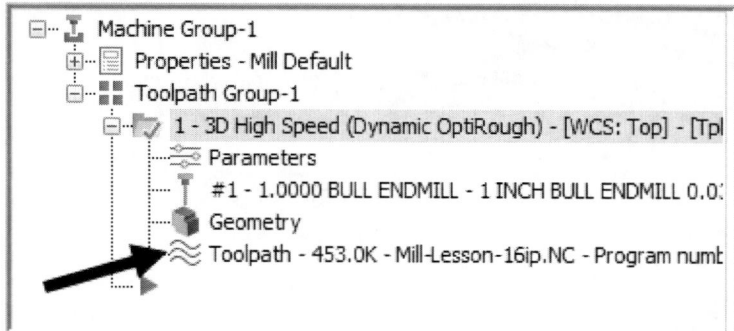

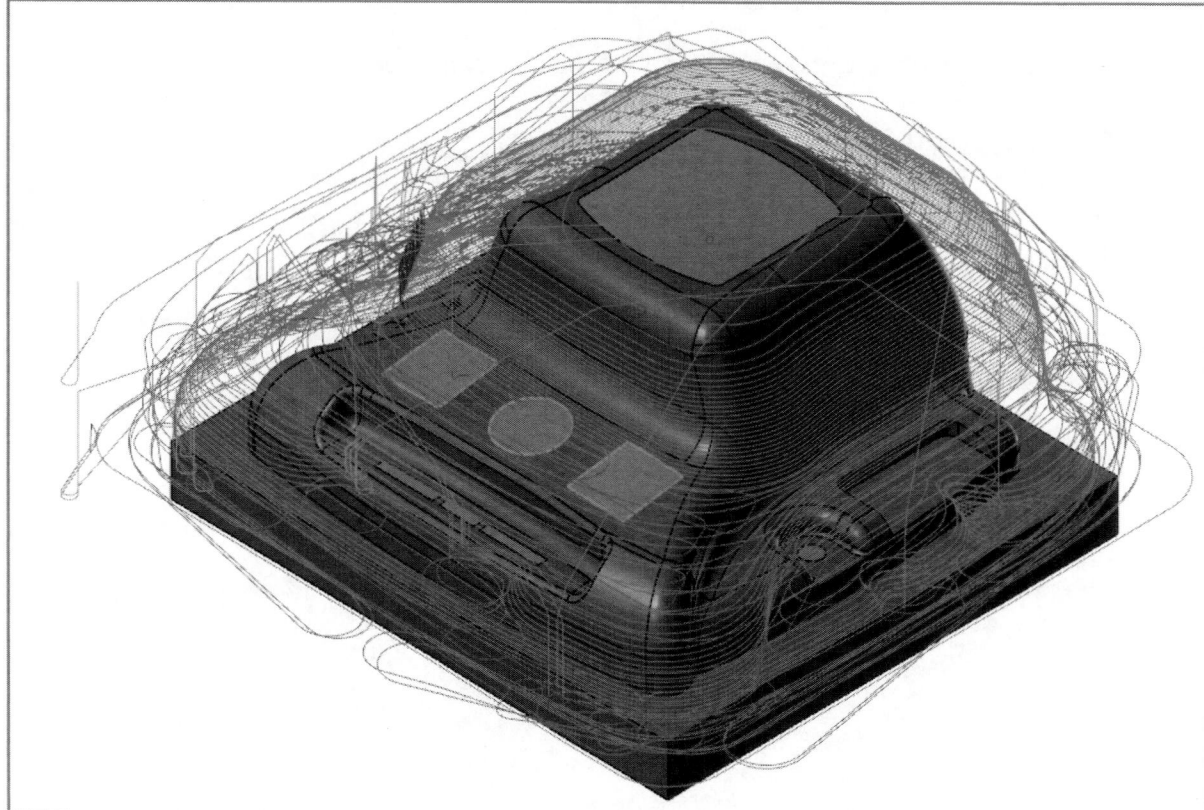

30. Click on the **OK** icon to exit Backplot.

TASK 4:
CREATE A STOCK MODEL FROM THE ROUGHING TOOLPATH
- ➲ In this task you will create a Stock Model.
- ➲ In this lesson we will create a **series of Stock Models** that will be used to verify the toolpaths as we create the various roughing and finishing toolpaths.
- ➲ For example, after creating a Stock Model we are then able to verify a finishing toolpath based on the previous roughing toolpaths as opposed to verifying all the toolpaths.
- ➲ Mastercam computes the stock model by processing toolpath operations selected in the Source Operations page against the stock you define.

Working with Stock Model Operations

You create and manage stock models in the Toolpaths Manager in the same manner as other types of toolpath operations. This includes using the toolpath display option to turn the display on and off.

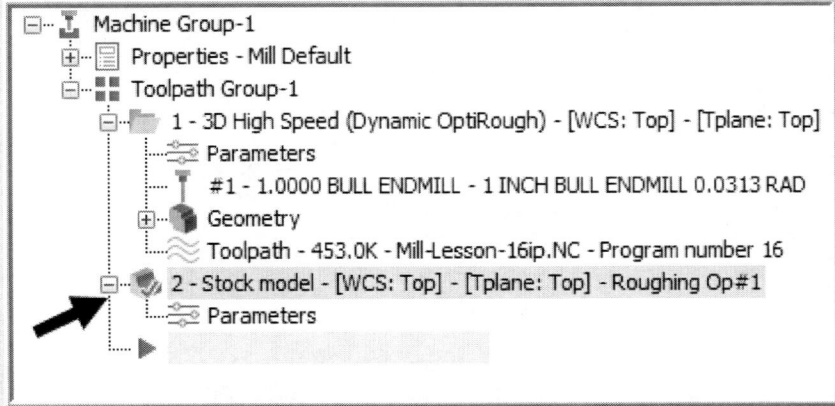

After choosing Stock model from the selected machine's Toolpaths tab, use property pages in the Stock Model dialog box to define it.

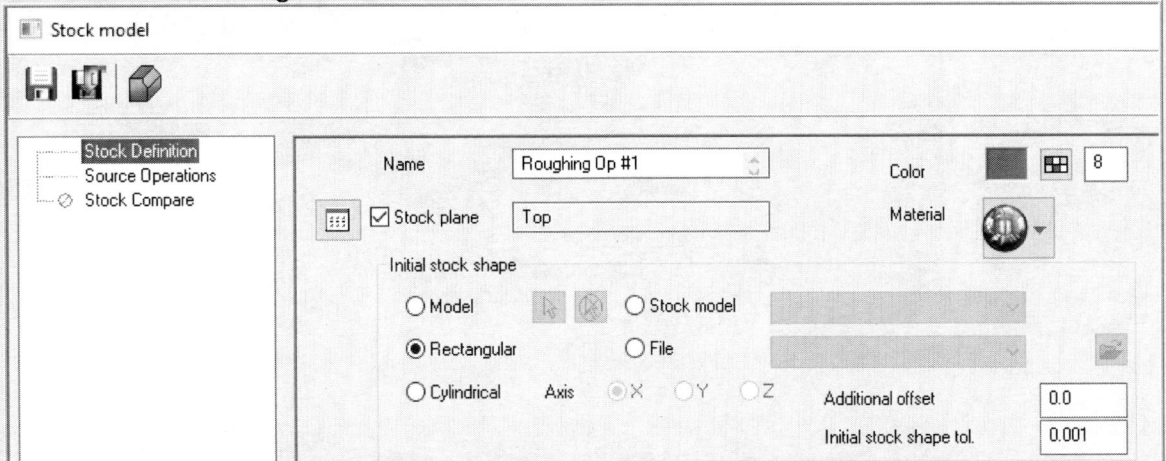

Creating a stock model operation consists of the following basic steps:
- Defining the stock to use for the operation.
- Choosing source operations in the existing part to process on the defined stock.
- Activating the stock compare (optional), which includes selecting the part model to use in the comparison and configuring its display.

Once created, you can use stock model operations to:
Verify stock, Define stock for rest machining, Visualize stock, Generate stock model compares.

1. On the **Toolpaths** tab select **Stock Model** in the **Stock** section.

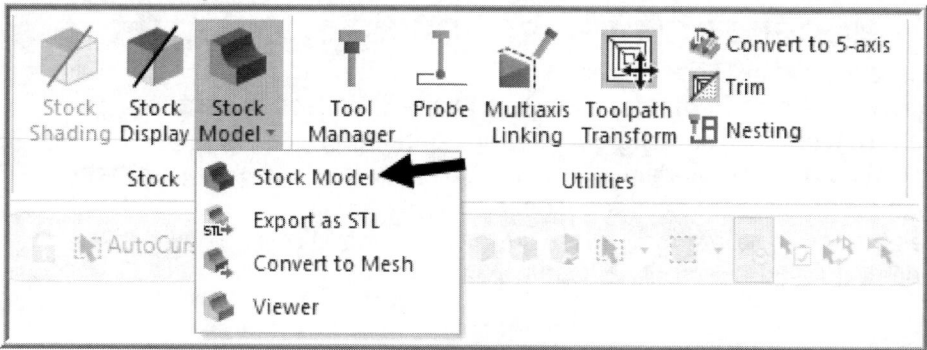

2. On the **Stock Definition** page enter **Roughing Op #1** for the name of this Stock Model.
3. Click on the **Stock Setup** button to automatically fill in the Stock dimensions and Stock Origin from the Stock Definition page.

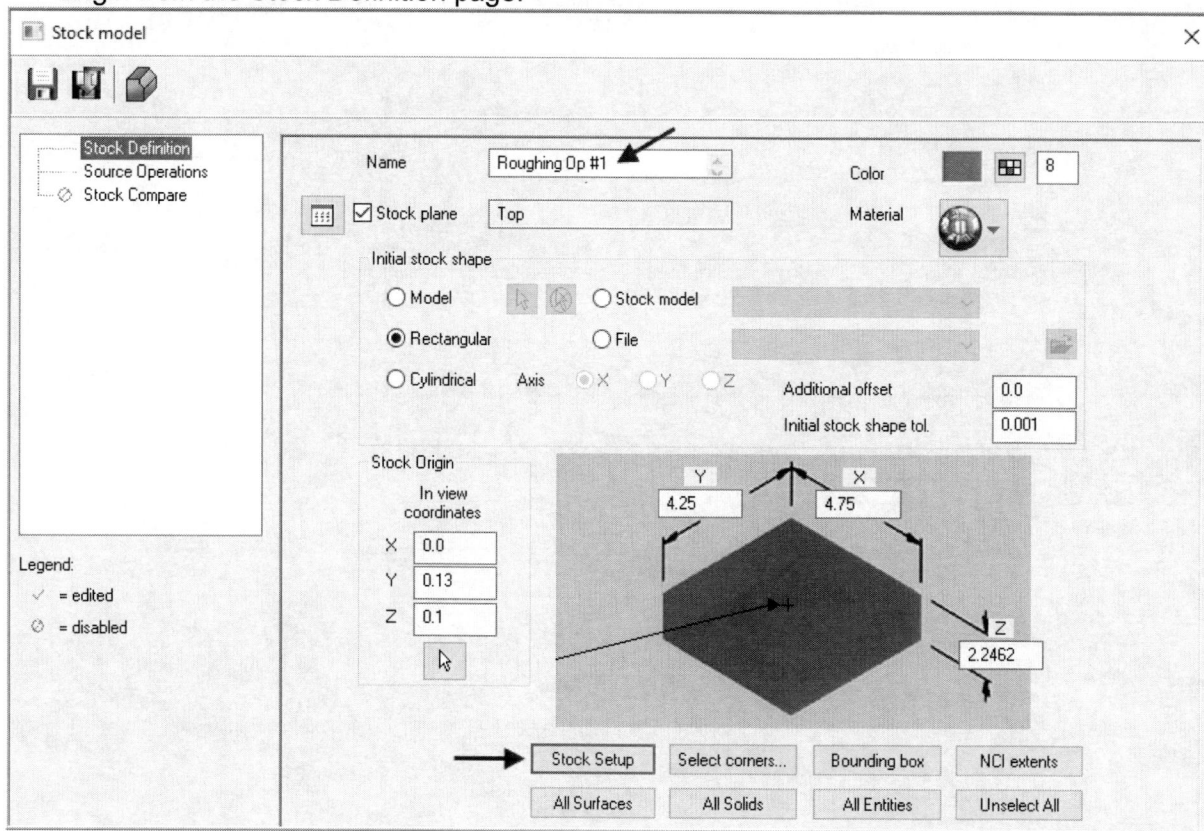

4. Click on **Source Operations** at the left of the Stock model dialog box.
5. Ensure there is a **check mark** on this first toolpath.

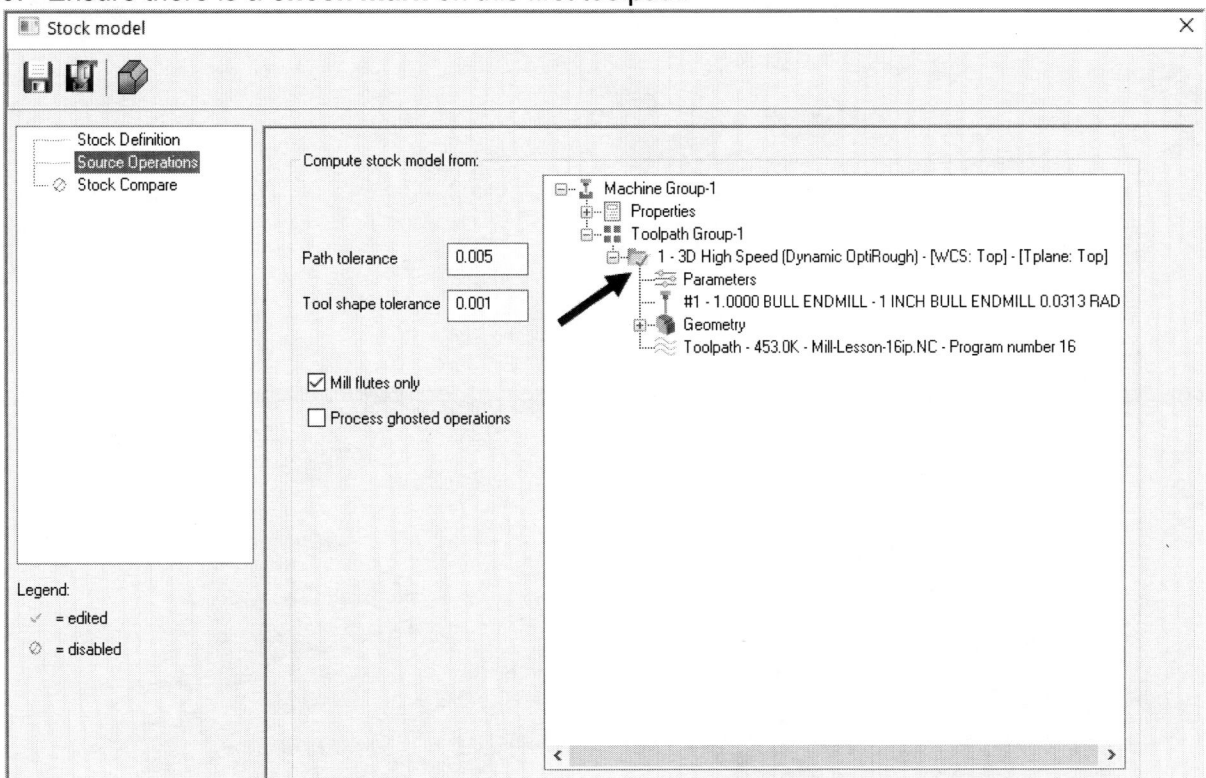

6. Click on the **OK** icon to complete this Stock model operation.
➲ The image below shows the **Stock model** in the Toolpaths Manager.
➲ We will be using this **Stock Model** later when verifying the next toolpath we create. It will also be used to drive the Rest-milling operation.

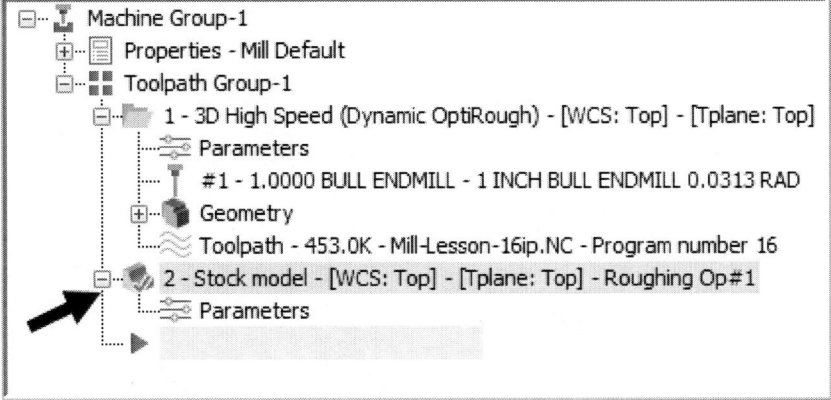

7. The image below left shows the Stock Model displayed. With a check mark on the Stock model **click** on the **Toggle display on selected operations** icon to hide the display of the Stock Model.

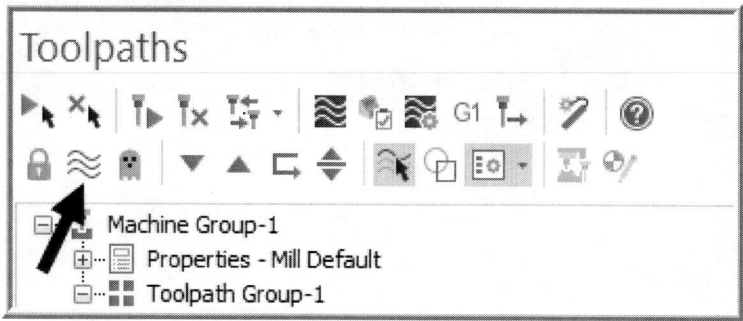

Stock Model Displayed	Stock Model Display - Toggled Off

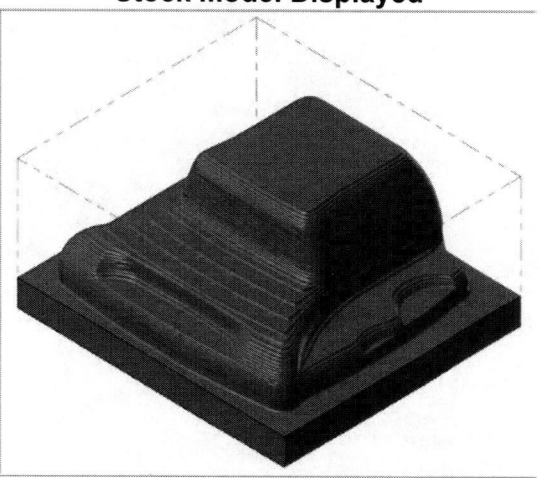 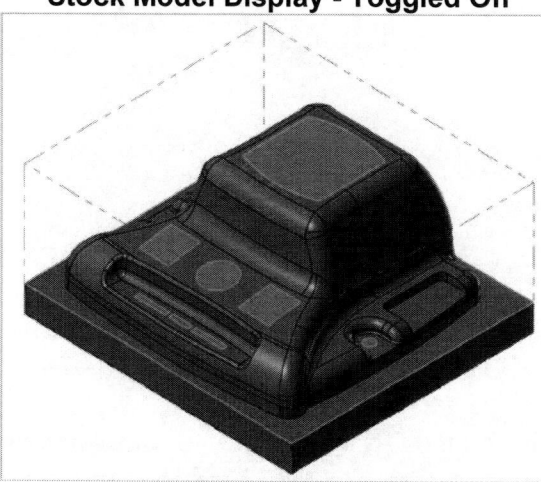

➲ After toggling the display of the Stock Model take note of the **shading of the folder** that denotes the Stock Model display is **toggled off**.

Visibility On

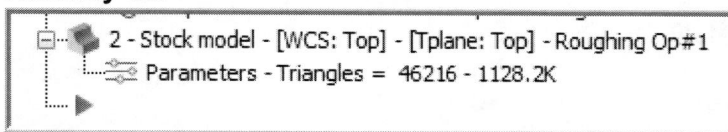

Visibility Off

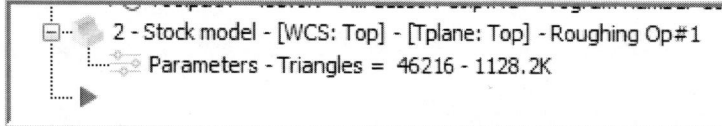

TASK 5:
REST ROUGHING USING DYNAMIC OPTIROUGH

➲ In this task you will use a .250 diameter Bull End Mill with a 0.0313 corner radius to continue roughing the part.

➲ You will copy the first toolpath and change the parameters to suit this Bull End Mill.

1. Turn off the display of toolpaths by using the keyboard short cut **ALT+T**.
2. Click on the **minus sign** beside each operation in the **Toolpath manager** to **collapse** them.
3. In the **Toolpaths Manager**, **copy operation 1** by selecting it with your mouse then pressing **Ctrl+C**. To paste the operation, select the red arrow with your mouse then press **Ctrl+V**.

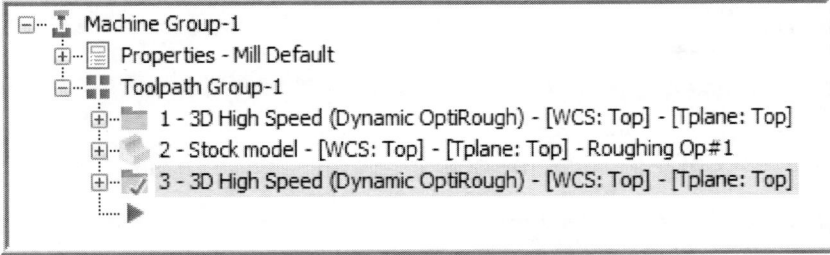

4. Move to the **Tool** page, press the **Select library tool...**, and select a **.250 diameter Bull End Mill with a 0.0313 corner radius** and return to the **Tool** page.

➲ We now need to change this **High Speed Steel tool to Carbide**.
5. **Right mouse click** over the **.250 diameter Bull End Mill** and select **Edit tool**.
6. On the **Define Tool Geometry** page click on **Next** in the lower right-hand corner.

7. Open up the drop-down menu for **Material** and change it to **Carbide**.

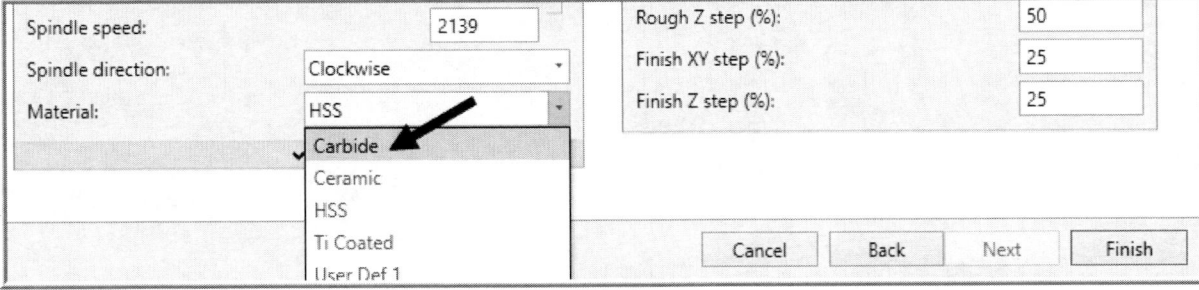

8. Click the **calculator icon** to recalculate the speeds and feeds for the material type. Note the updated values below.

9. Click on **Finish** in the lower right-hand corner.

⮥ Take note of the updated feeds and speeds using the **carbide** cutter. The spindle speed in *italics* relates to the maximum spindle speed setup earlier at 10,000 RPM. Note, you may need to reinitialize the speeds and feeds by right clicking on the tool and selecting reinitialize.

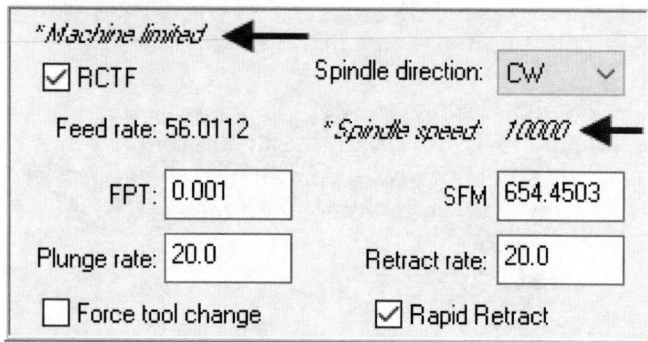

10. Select the **Holder** page and select **B3E4-0250** as the holder. **Tool Projection** is set to **1.625**.

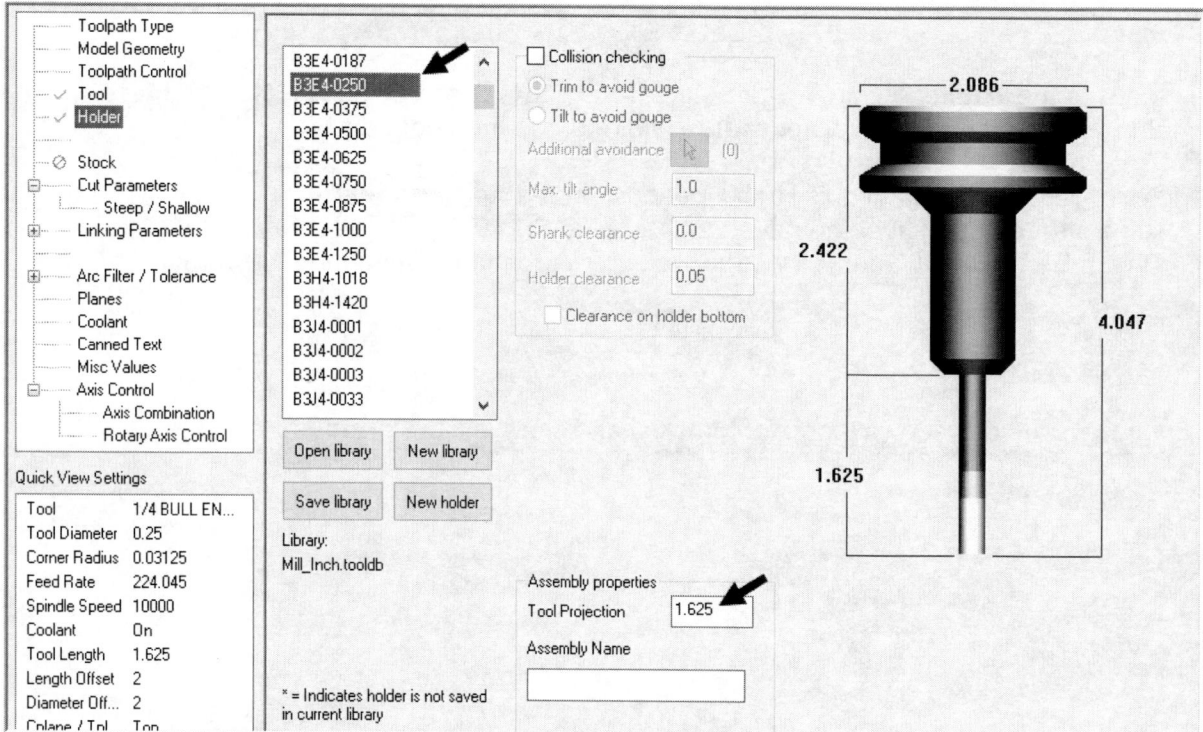

11. Select the **Stock** page and **activate Rest material** and make the appropriate changes as shown in the **Stock** page below:

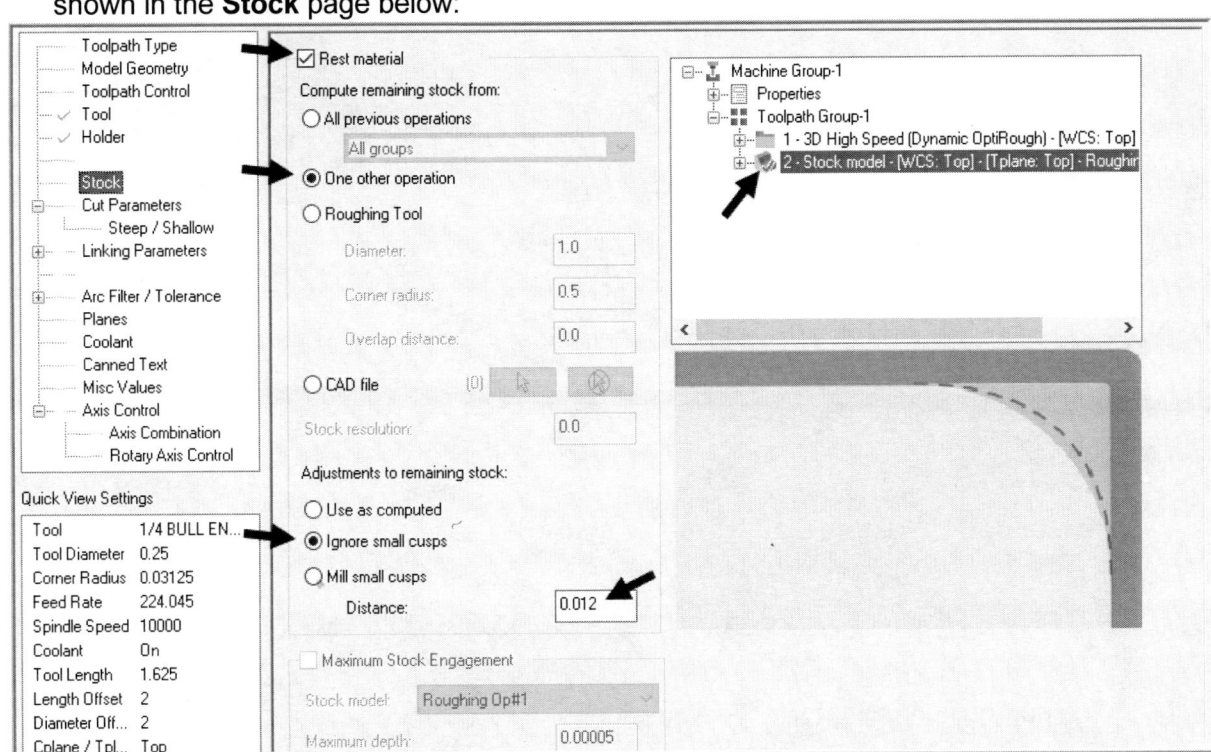

Rest Material

Compute remaining stock from:

All previous operations
This option calculates the remaining stock using all operations in the Toolpath Manager. This method determines the areas of stock where the tool did not go. Use the drop-down list (shown below) to choose the operations by group type to which the remaining stock parameters are applied.

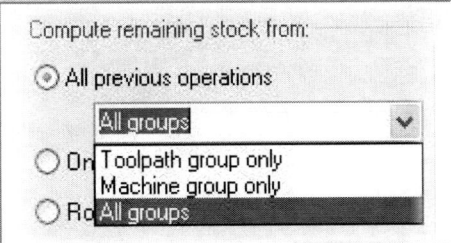

One other operation
This calculates the remaining stock from a single operation. Select the operation from the operations list on the right.

Roughing Tool
Use the dimensions of the roughing tool to create the stock to be machined by the toolpath.

12. Select **Cut Parameters** from the list on the left and make changes to this page.

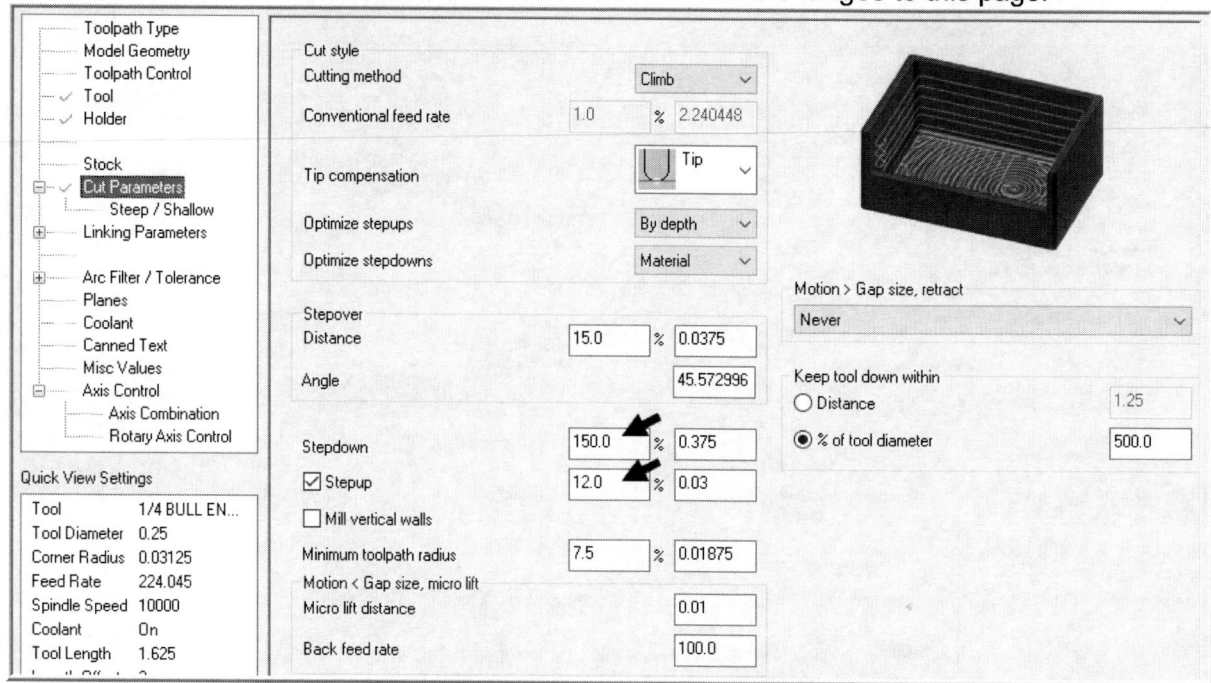

13. Make the appropriate changes to the **Transitions** page as shown below:

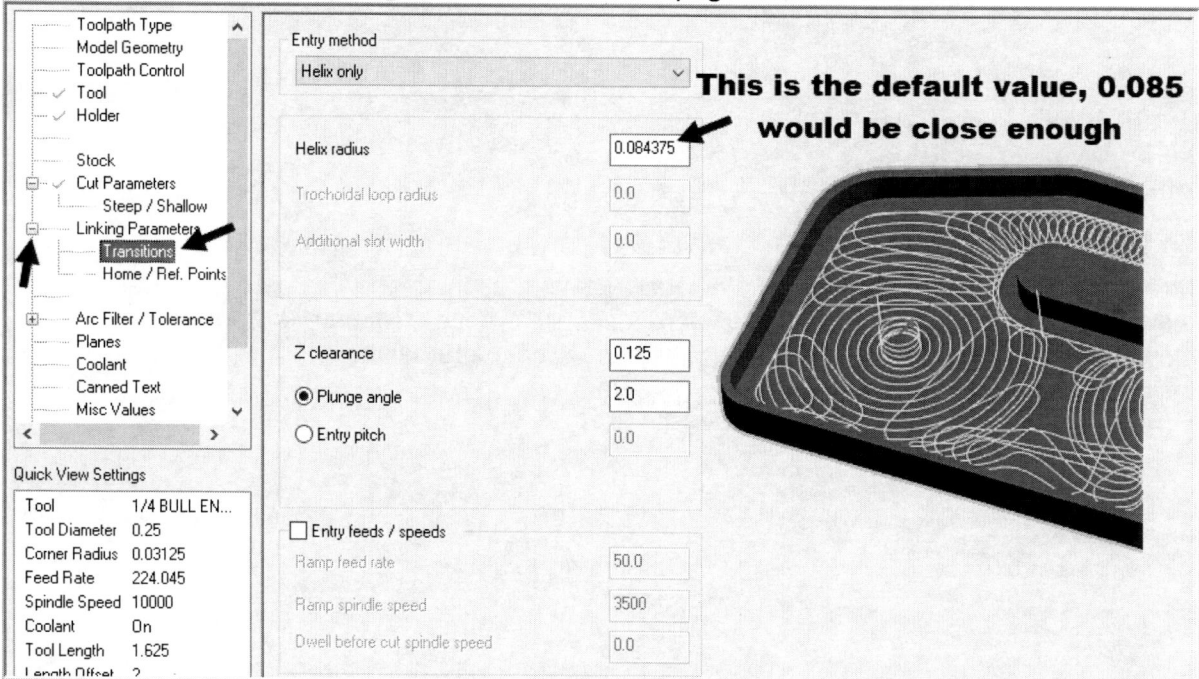

14. Now move to the **Model Geometry** page select the machining row in the **Machine Geometry** section.

15. At the bottom of the **Model Geometry** page click on the **Select entities** button.

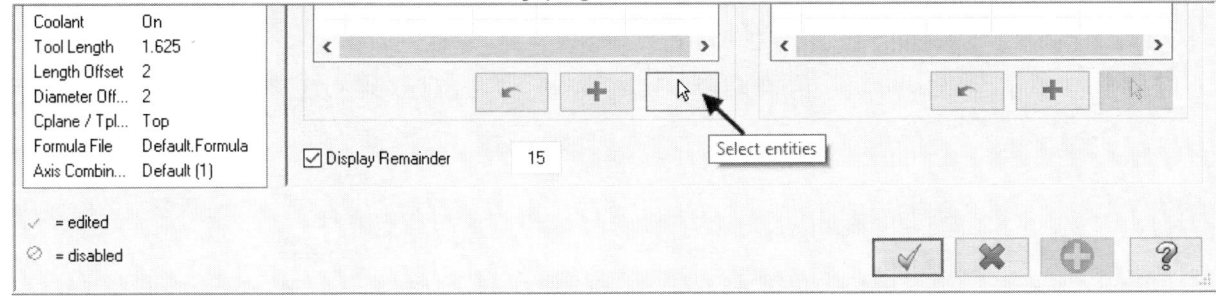

➔ At present all the entities on the part are selected. What we will do now is remove the circular surface shown below to allow the cutter to sink into and machine the circular shaped feature.

16. To satisfy the prompt **select the circular surface shown below left**. The image below right shows the part after selection of the circular surface.

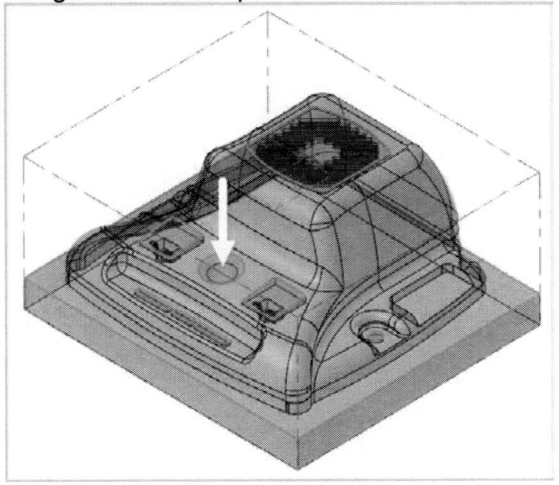 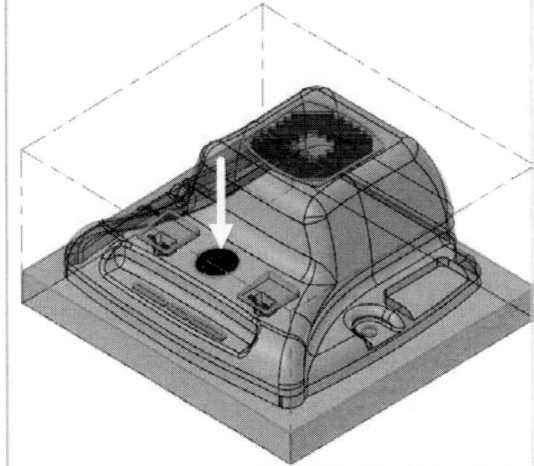

17. Click on **End Selection** to move onto the next step.

➔ Note that there are now **361 Entities** in the **Machining Geometry** section.

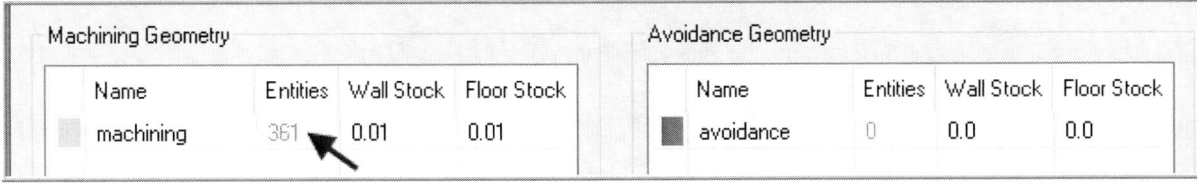

18. To allow the tool into the circle pocket area of the part, the Skip Pockets setting must be adjusted. On the **Toolpath Control** page, set the **Smaller Than** value to **0.1**.

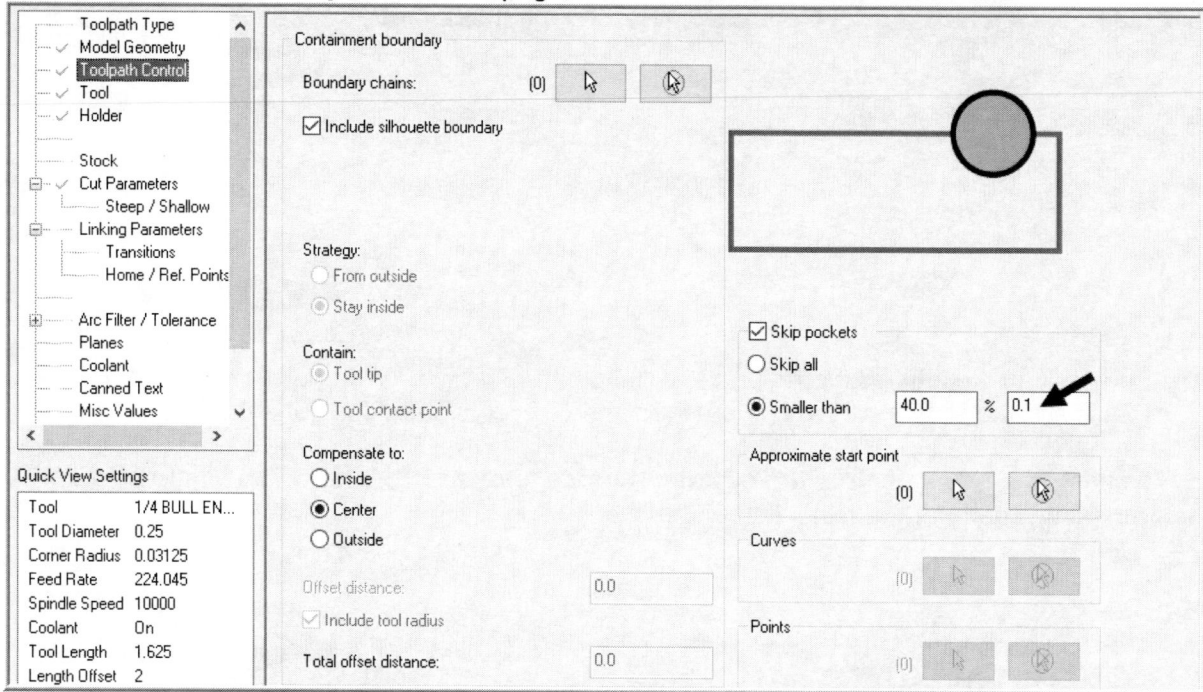

19. Press the **OK button** to complete the toolpath.
20. Regenerate the operation by selecting the **Regenerate all dirty operations** icon in the **Toolpaths Manager** if needed.

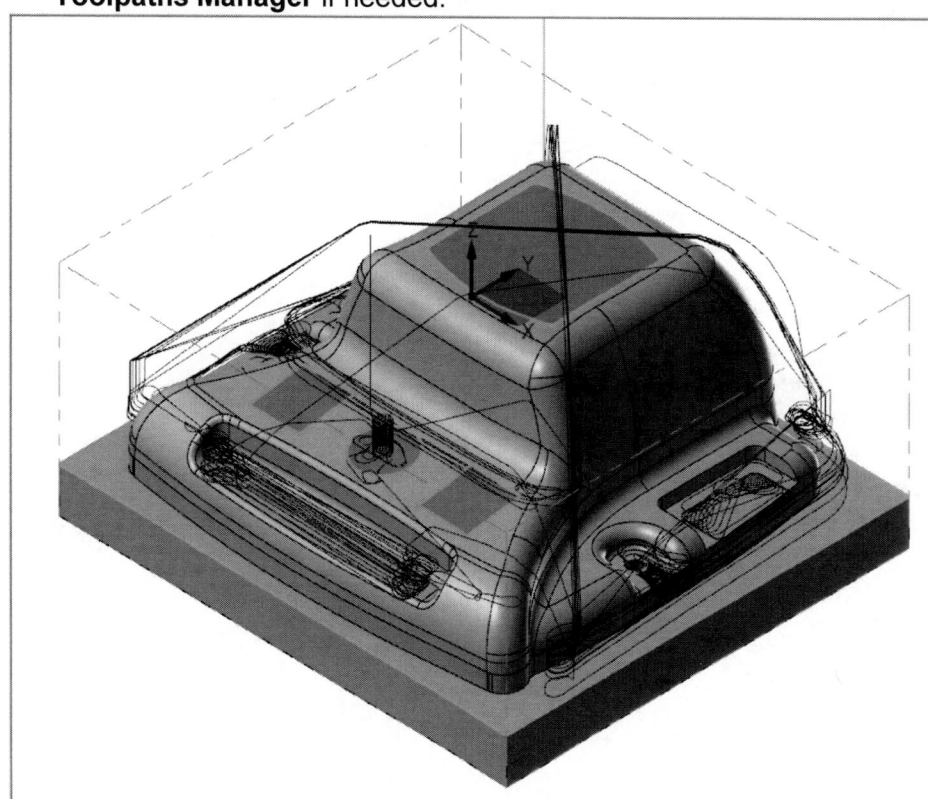

⮕ Now we will Verify this toolpath using the Stock model created earlier.

21. Click on the **Simulator Options** icon in the Toolpaths Manager.

22. Activate **Stock model** where the stock model being used is **Roughing Op #1**.

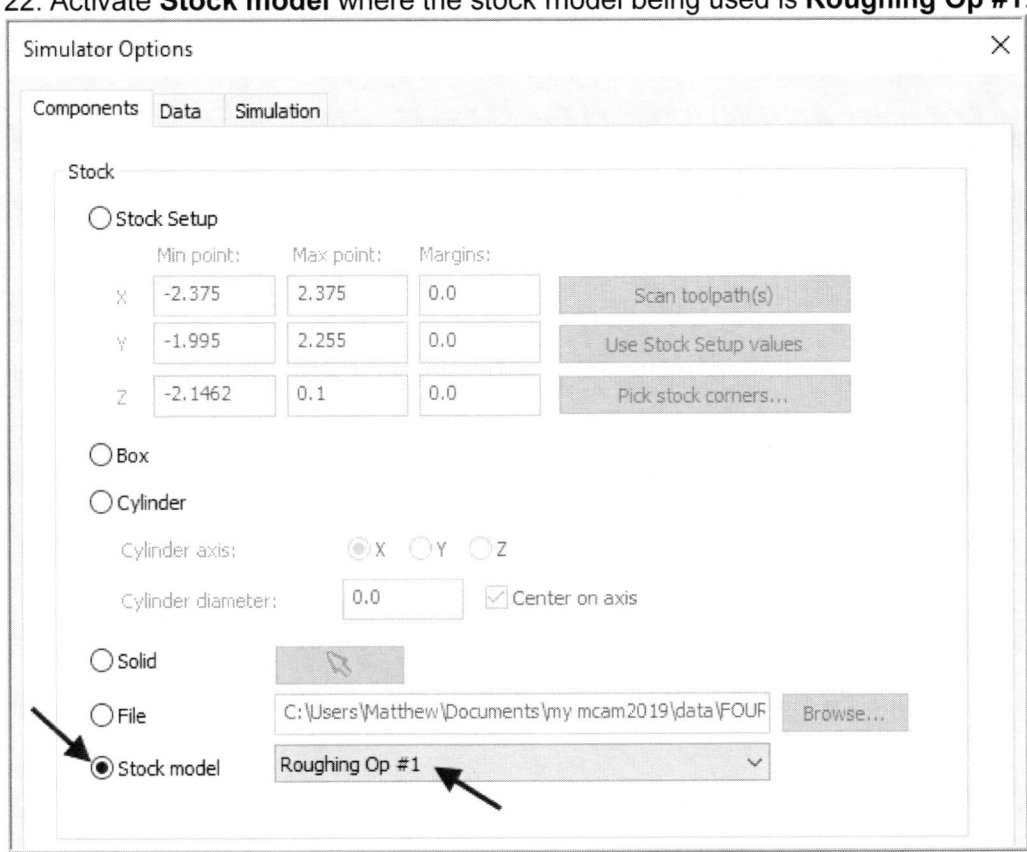

23. Verify the third operation only.

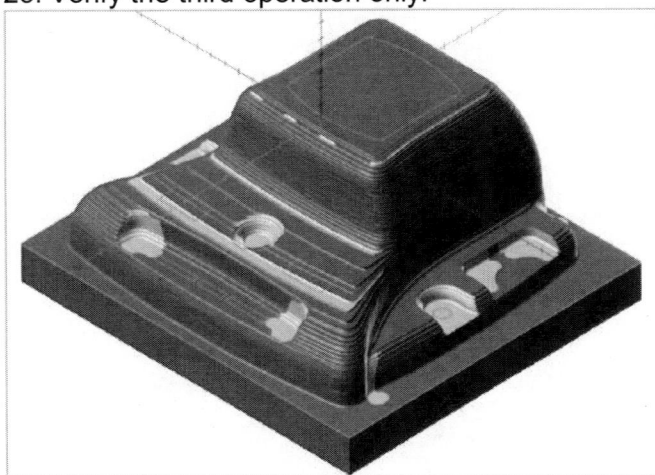

TASK 6:
CREATE A STOCK MODEL FROM THE FIRST TWO TOOLPATHS
➲ The previous stock model and the toolpath just created will be used to create the next Stock model.

Using an Existing Stock model
Uses an existing stock model operation defined in the current part file as stock.
After choosing this option, select the stock model operation to use from the corresponding drop-down list.

---

24. On the **Toolpaths** tab select **Stock Model** in the **Stock** section.

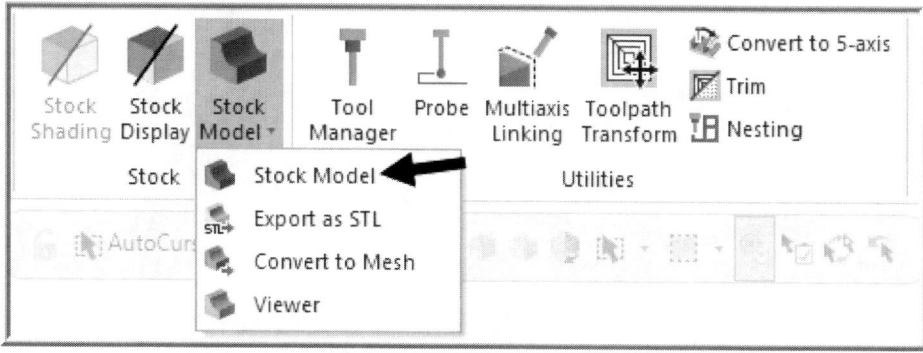

25. On the **Stock Definition** page enter **Roughing Done** for the **Name** of this Stock Model.
26. Activate **Stock model**. **Note** that the Stock model is **Roughing Op #1**. Select a new color. This will allow some contrast between the starting stock and the cuts made to this new Stock Model.

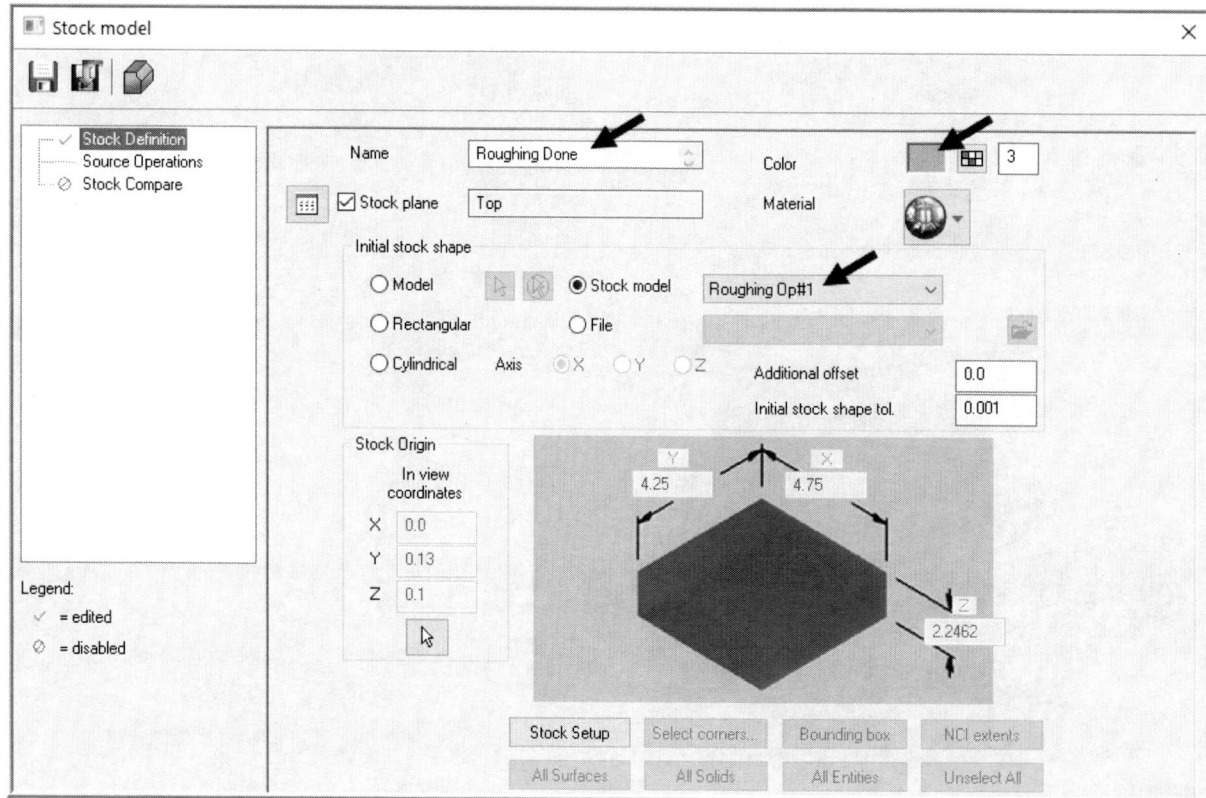

27. Click on **Source Operations** at the left of the Stock model dialog box.
28. Ensure there is a **check mark** on the **Dynamic OptiRest toolpath** as shown below.

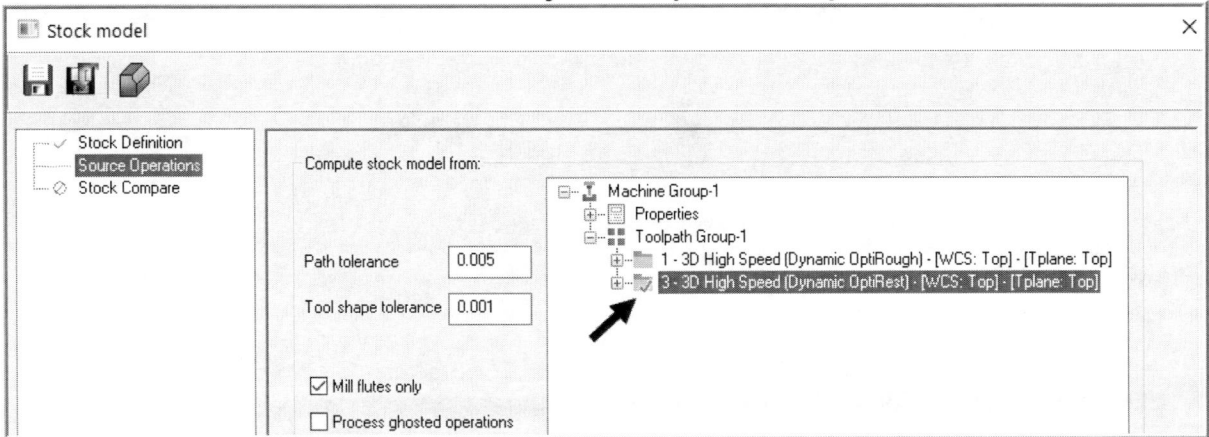

29. Click on the **OK** icon to complete this Stock model operation. The model is shown below
    with Level 10s visibility turned off.

➲ The image below shows the **Stock model** in the Toolpaths Manager.
➲ We will be using this **Stock Model** later when verifying the next toolpath we create.

30. With a check mark on the Stock model **click** on the **Toggle display on selected operations** icon to hide the display of the Stock Model.

➲ After toggling the display of the Stock Model take note of the **shading of the folder** that denotes the Stock Model display is **toggled off**.

TASK 7:
FINISH FLAT SURFACES USING 2D HIGH SPEED (2D AREA MILL)

➲ Next you will finish the flat portions of the part using the 2D High Speed (2D Area Mill) toolpath.

➲ The tool being used is a 0.5" diameter flat end mill.

> Using the bottom of a flat endmill will give a better surface finish on floor surfaces than a ballnose endmill will because there will be no scallops.
> Alternatively, a ballnose tool will provide a much better surfaces finish for shape profiling.

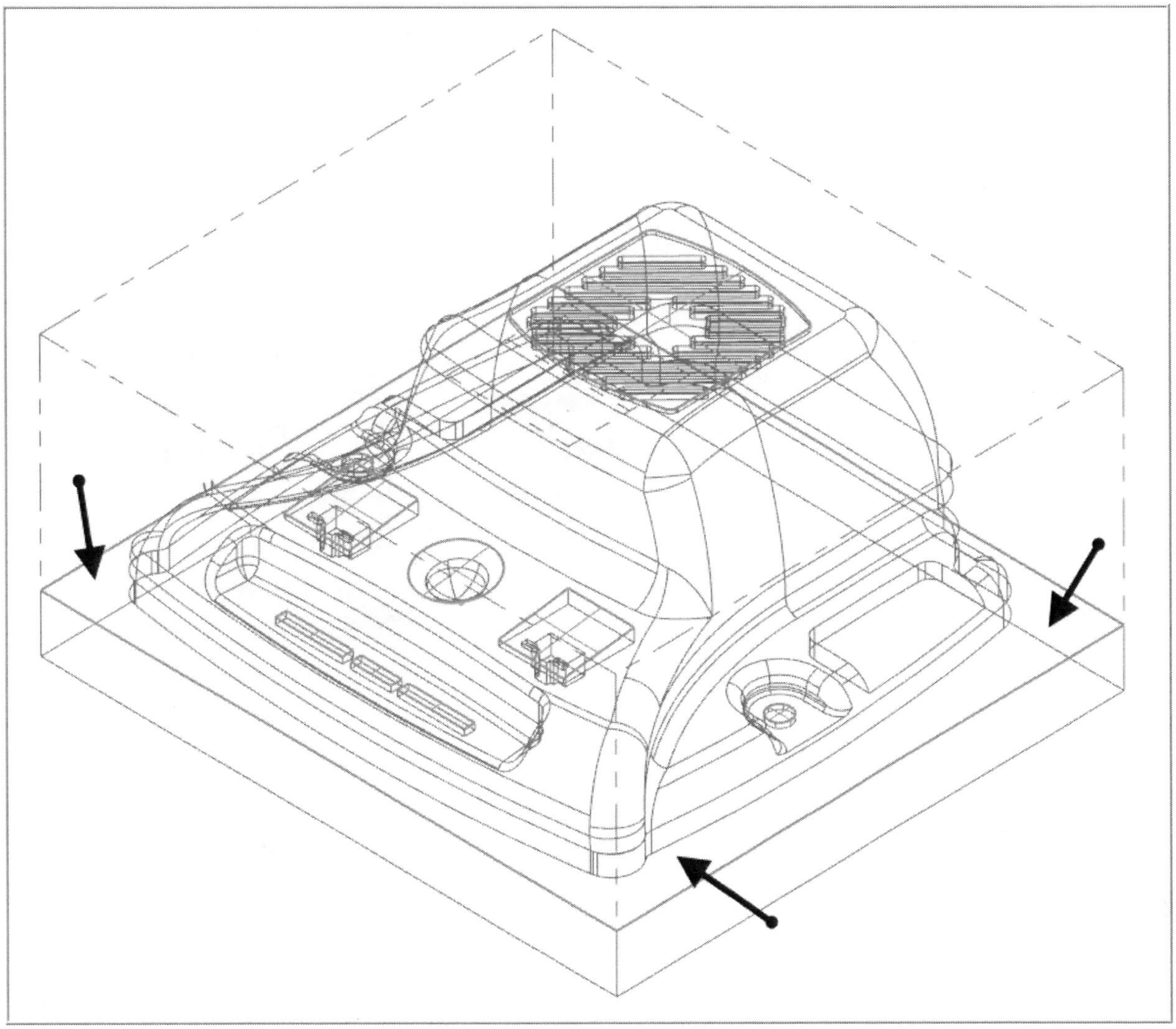

1. Create a new operation, by right mouse clicking in the **Toolpaths Manager** window, select **Mill toolpaths>2D high speed>Area Mill** or select **Area Mill** from the 2D toolpath gallery.

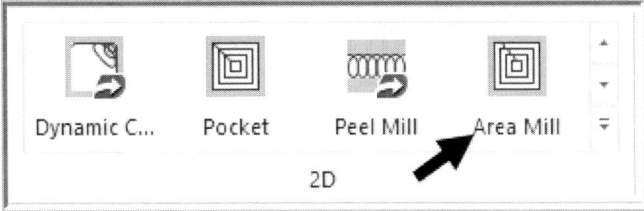

2. In the Chain Options dialog box activate From Outside in the Machining region strategy section. Select None (ignore stock) in the Open chain extension to stock section.
3. Now click on the selection arrow in the **Avoidance regions** section. Switch to the **Solids** chaining mode, ensure **loop** is enabled. Chain the loop around the base of the boss.

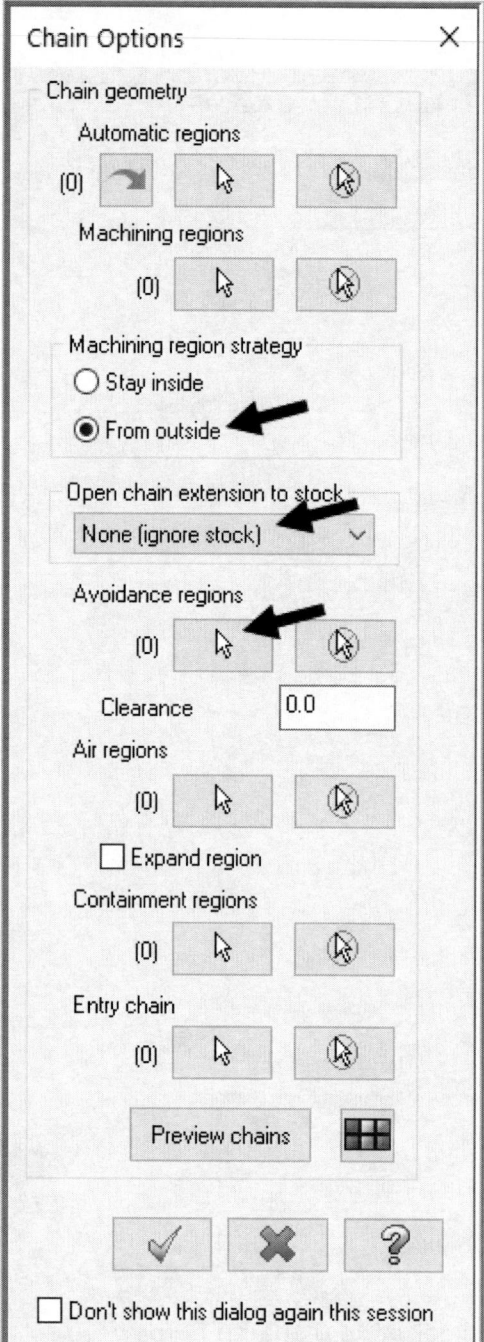

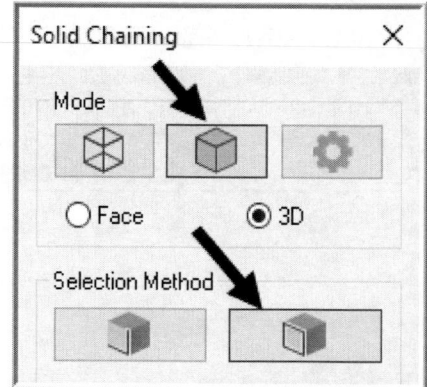

4. Click on **OK**  to exit Chaining.
5. Click on **OK** to exit Chain Options.

6. Next, select the **Tool** page. In the lower left corner of the page select the **Select library tool…** button and select a **0.5" diameter Flat End Mill**.

➲ We now need to change this **High Speed Steel tool to Carbide**.

7. **Right mouse click** over the **0.5" diameter Flat End Mill** and select **Edit tool**.
8. On the **Define Tool Geometry** page click on **Next** in the lower right-hand corner.
9. Open the drop-down menu for **Material** and change it to **Carbide**.
10. Click the **calculator icon** to recalculate the speeds and feeds based on the new material.
11. Click on **Finish** in the lower right-hand corner.
12. Right **mouse click** over the **0.5" diameter Flat End Mill** and select **Re-initialize feeds & speeds**.
13. Select the **Holder** page and select **B3E4-0500** as the holder.

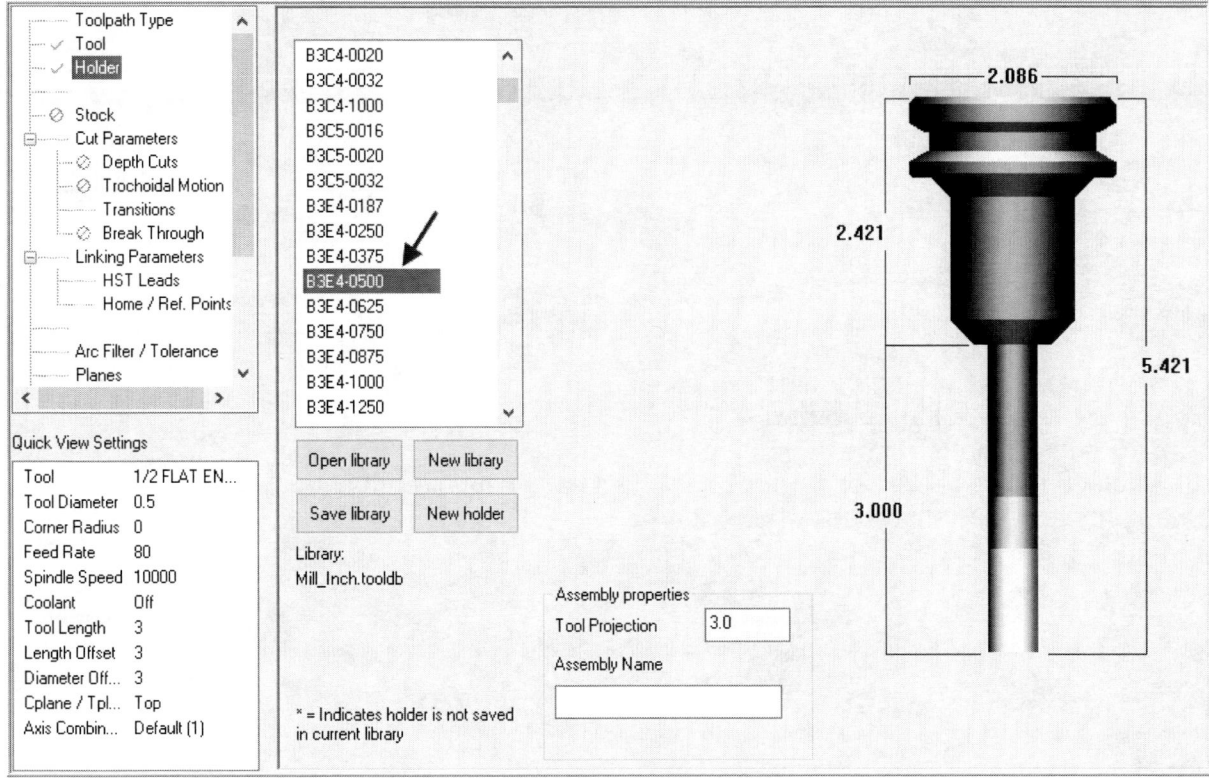

14. Make the appropriate selections on the **Cut Parameters** page shown below.

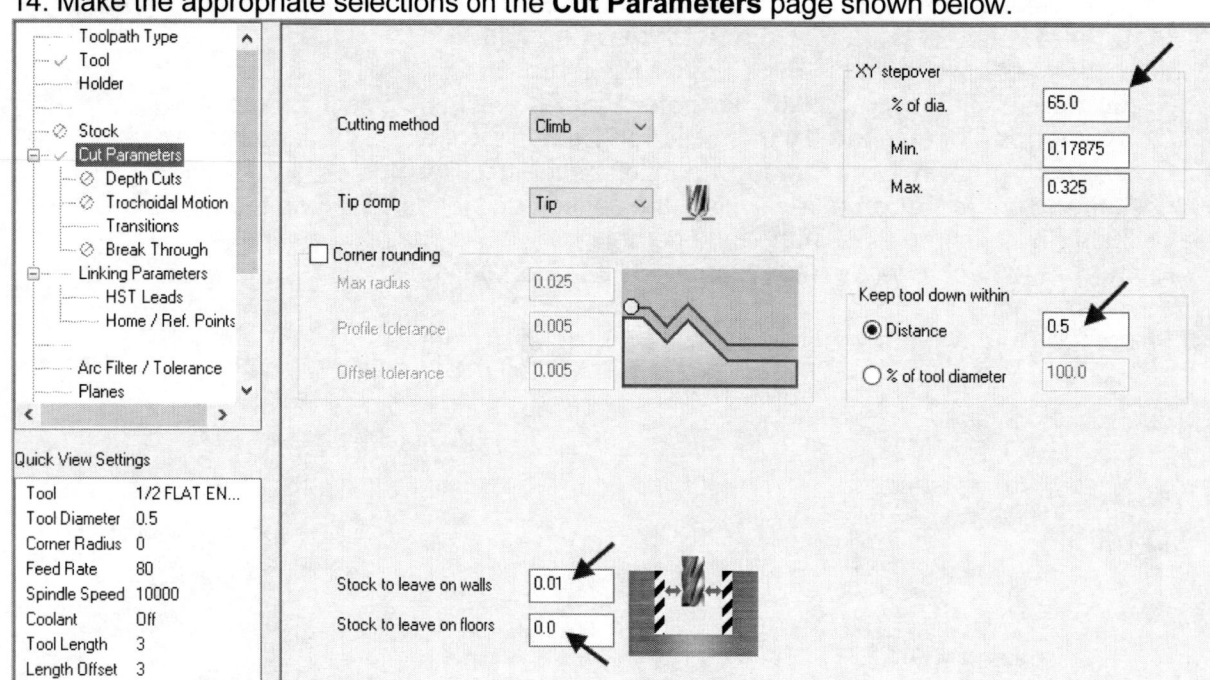

15. Navigate to the **Linking Parameters** page.
16. Activate the **Depth** to **Absolute**.
17. Click on the **Depth button**.
18. When prompted to "**Select a point**" select the end point shown below as the Z at the top of the mold base as shown below:

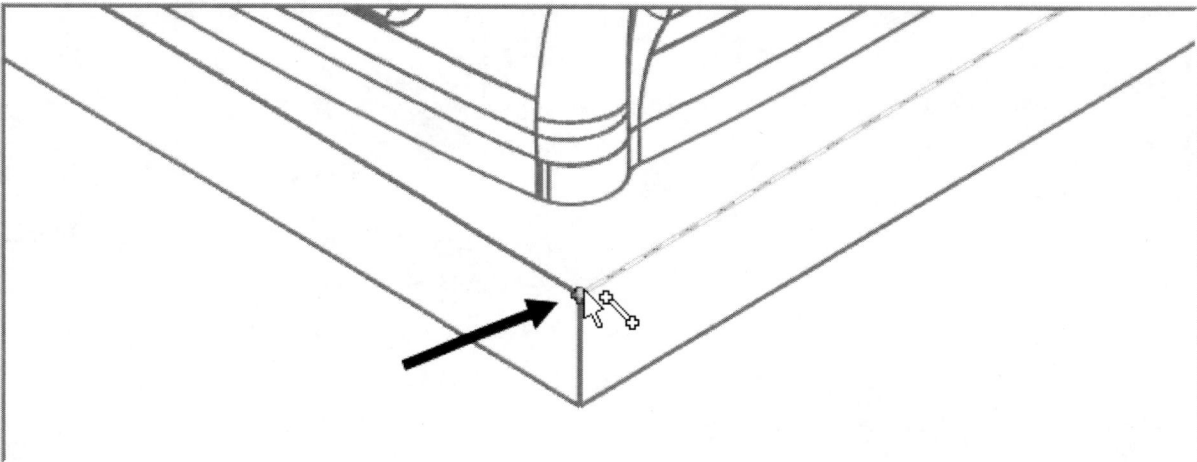

19. Set the remaining **Linking Parameters** as shown below:

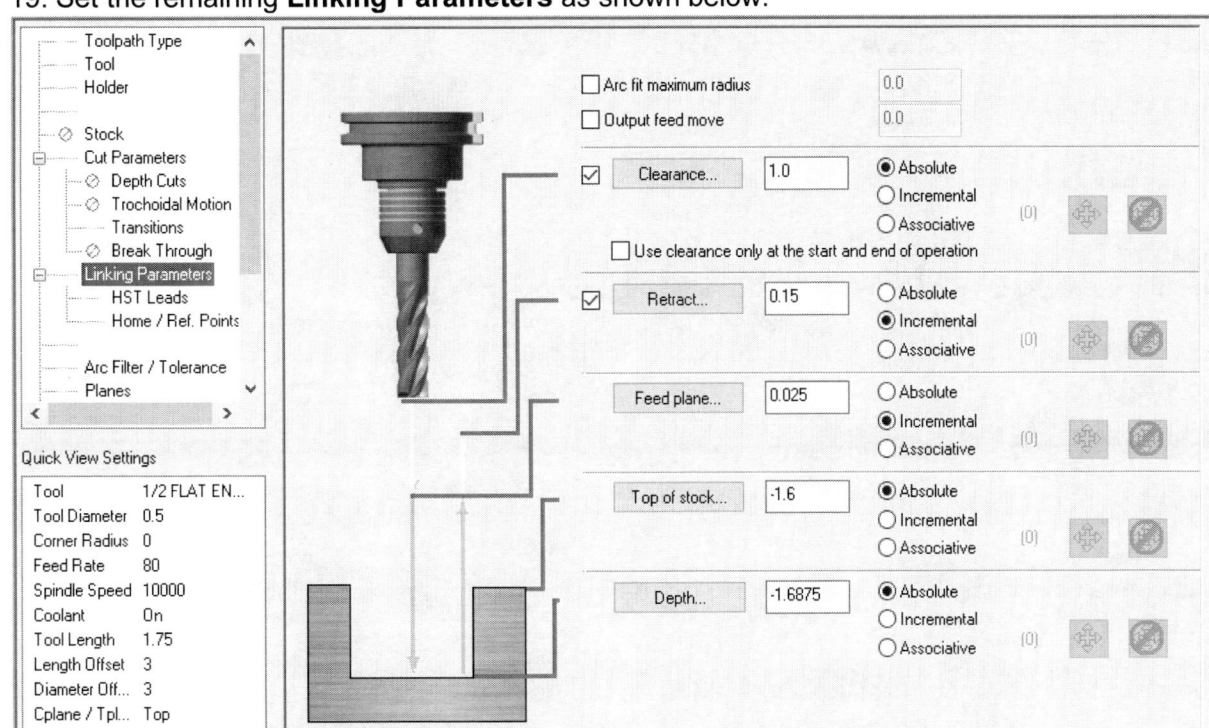

20. Turn the flood coolant on.
21. Select the **OK button** to complete the toolpath.

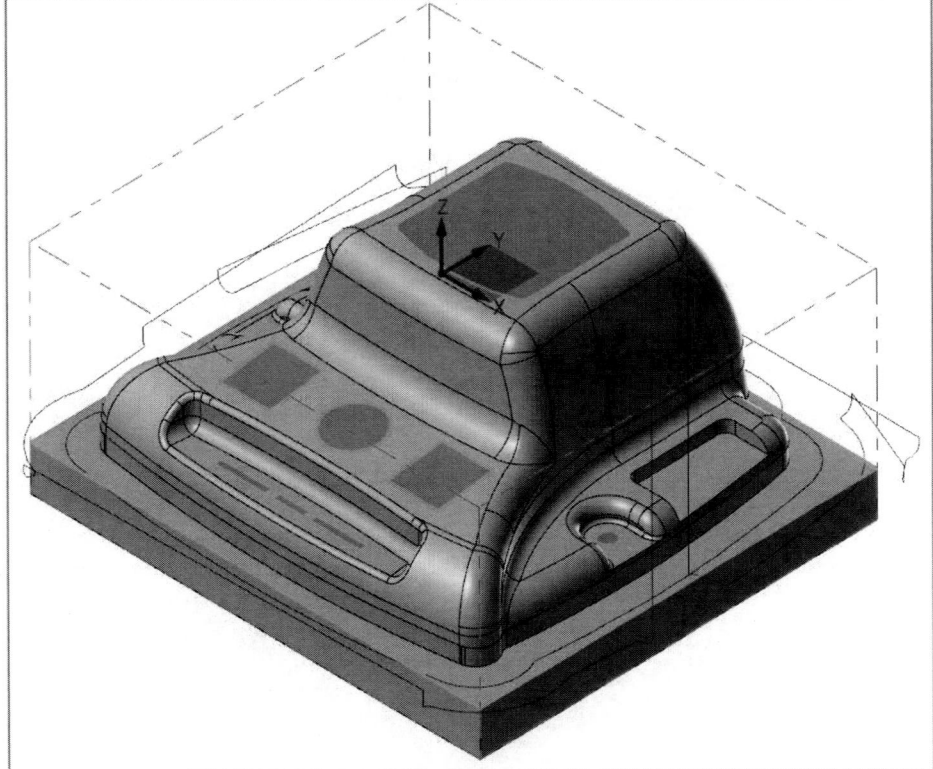

TASK 8:
USE ANALYZE DYNAMIC TO IDENTIFY PART DIMENSION

⮕ Before we move onto the next toolpath, we will use Analyze Dynamic to identify some of the dimensions on the part.

⮕ Utilizing Analyze Dynamic will aid in the selection of the appropriate cutter diameters and corner radii to machine this part.

Analyze Dynamic

Use the Analyze Dynamic dialog box to view information on any position you choose along an entity. When you select the entity, use the cursor to move the arrow endpoint to the position you want to analyze. The information that appears in the dialog box fields for the selected entity type includes:

Lines and solid edges: Point and tangent XYZ coordinates.

Arcs and splines: Point and tangent XYZ coordinates and the radius of curvature.

Surfaces and solid faces: Point XYZ coordinates, the normal XYZ coordinates, and the minimum radius of curvature.

Additionally, Analyze Dynamic displays information about the color (including RGB values) of the selected entity.

Type a value in the Arrow scale factor field to resize the arrow representing the vector direction. Use Reverse vector at the top of the dialog to change the direction of the vector by 180 degrees.

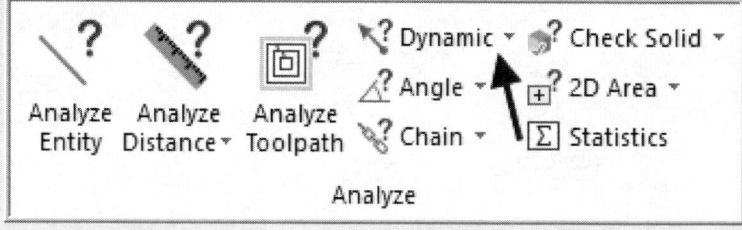

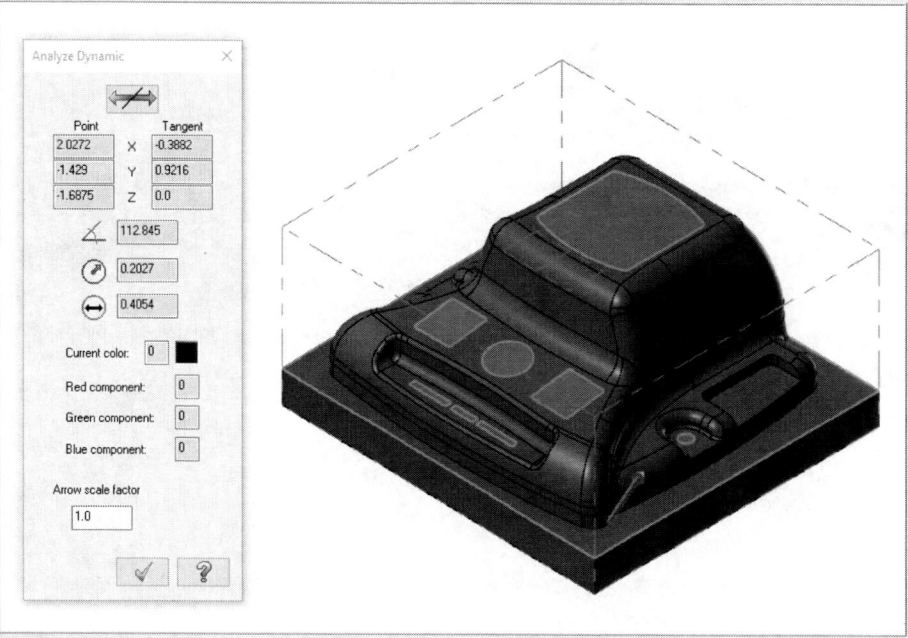

⮕ To start with we will zoom in on the right-hand open pocket and identify the radius of the fillets in the corner of this pocket.

◌ This pocket will be finished machined with a flat end mill.
◌ By identifying the size of the fillets on this part we will be able to select suitable end mills to machine the part.

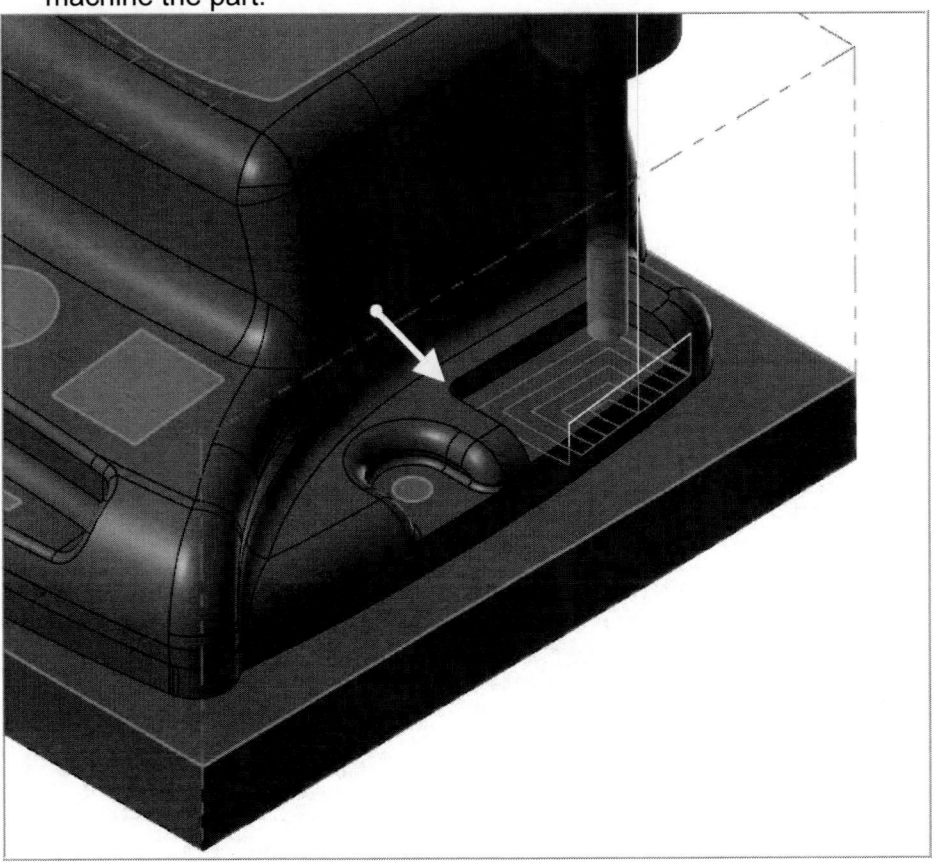

1. Select the **Home** page tab and in the **Analyze** section select **Dynamic**.

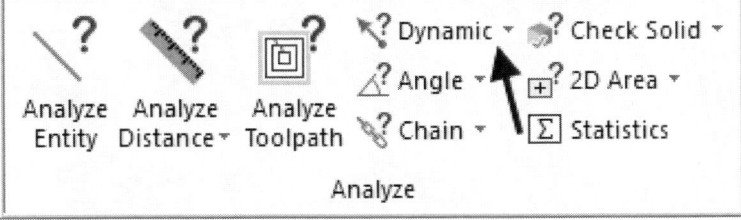

2. On the **Selection Bar, Edge** and **Face** are activated.

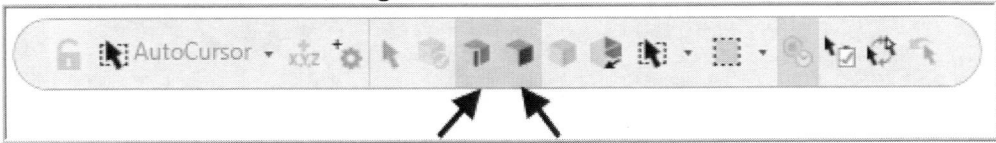

3. Zoom and rotate the display as shown below.
4. To satisfy the prompt **"Select the entities to analyze"** pick the face of the fillet shown below.

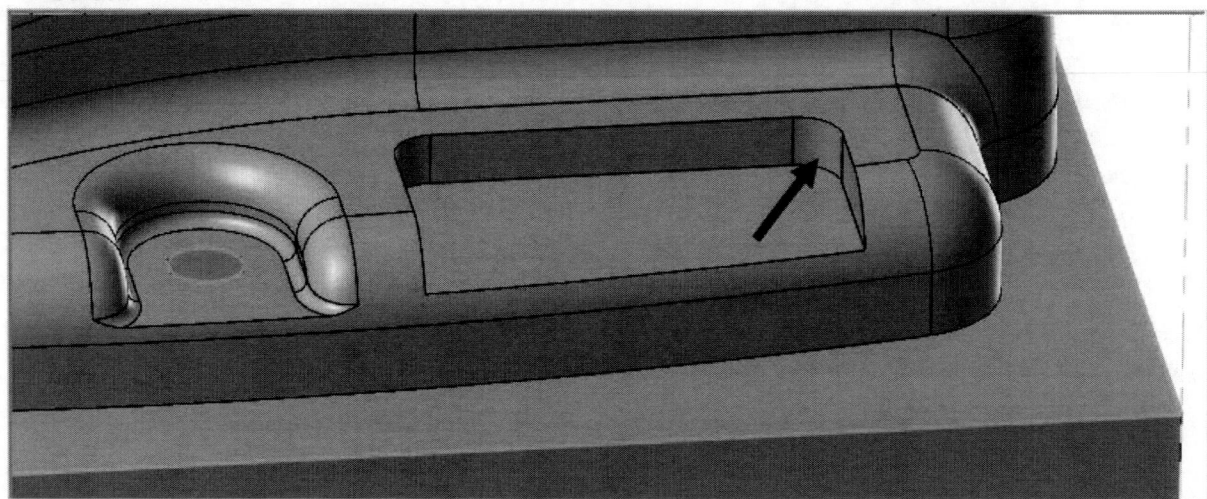

5. After selecting the fillet face the Analyze Dynamic dialog box displays. Using the mouse move around this face and you will see the **Point** and **Normal X, Y and Z** change.

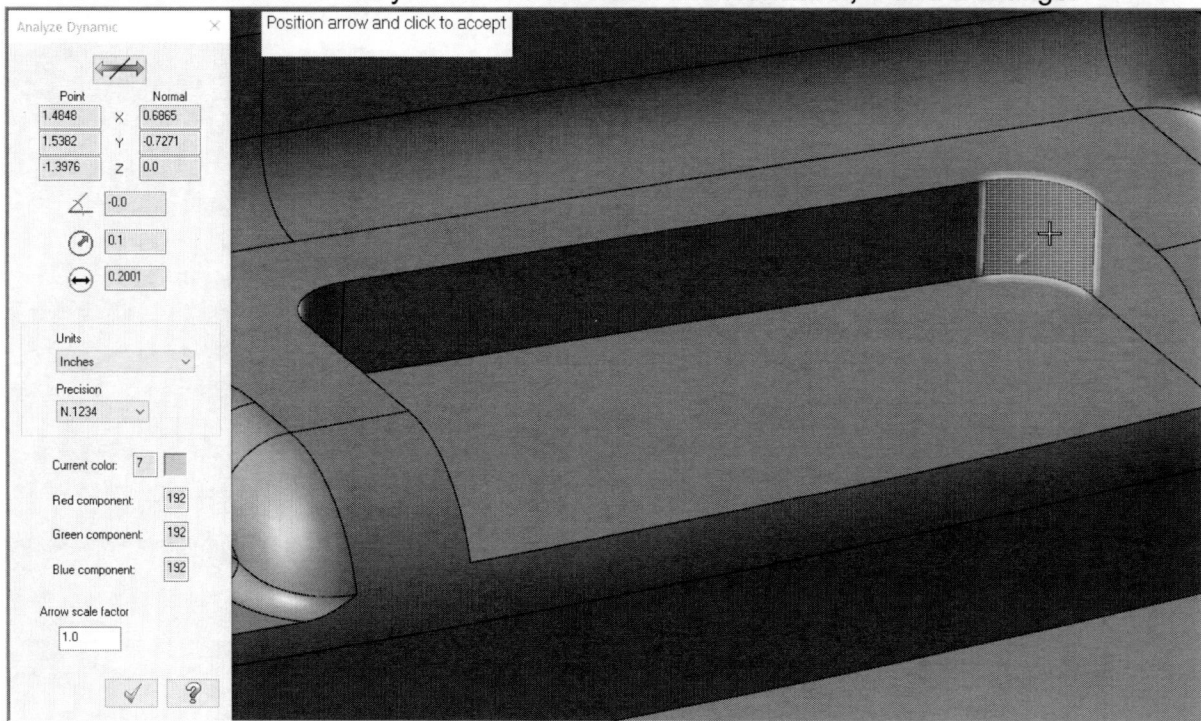

➲ In the Analyze Dynamic dialog box the radius and diameter are identified. **The diameter is 0.2001**.

➲ To finish machine this open pocket a **0.1875" diameter flat end** can be used.

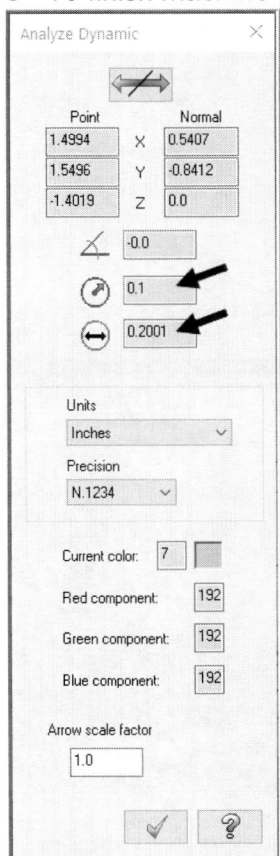

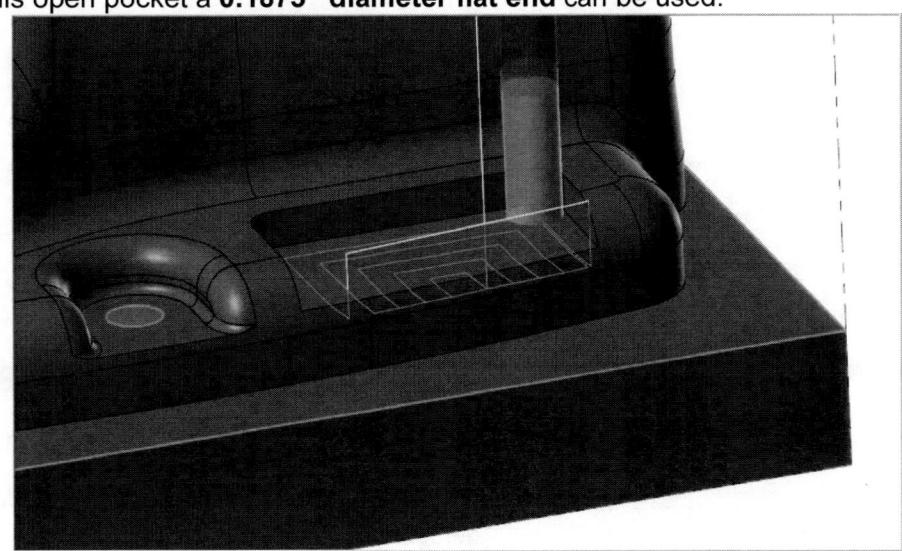

6. Now let's check the other radius in this pocket. Select the face of the fillet shown below. The diameter of this fillet is 0.2001.

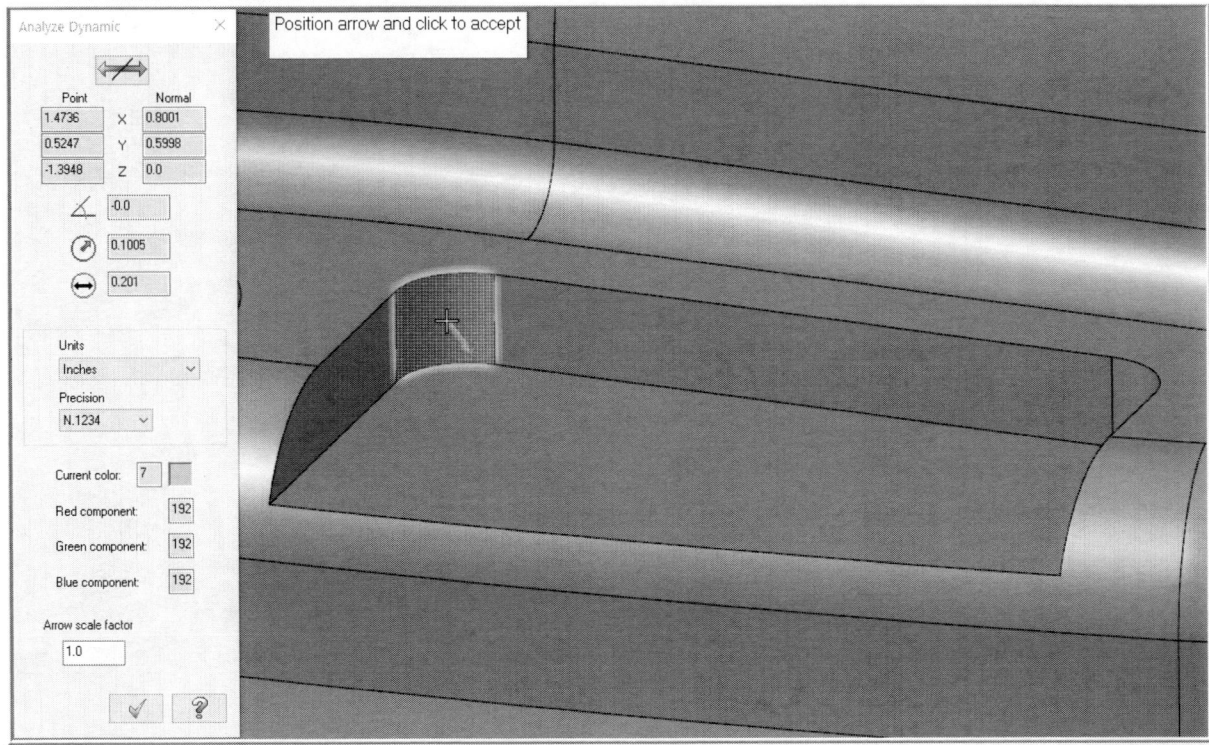

7. Pan the part and zoom the display as shown below. Select the face of the fillet shown below. **The radius of this fillet is 0.0310**. The 0.250 bull end mill with the 0.031 corner radius can be used here to finish machine.

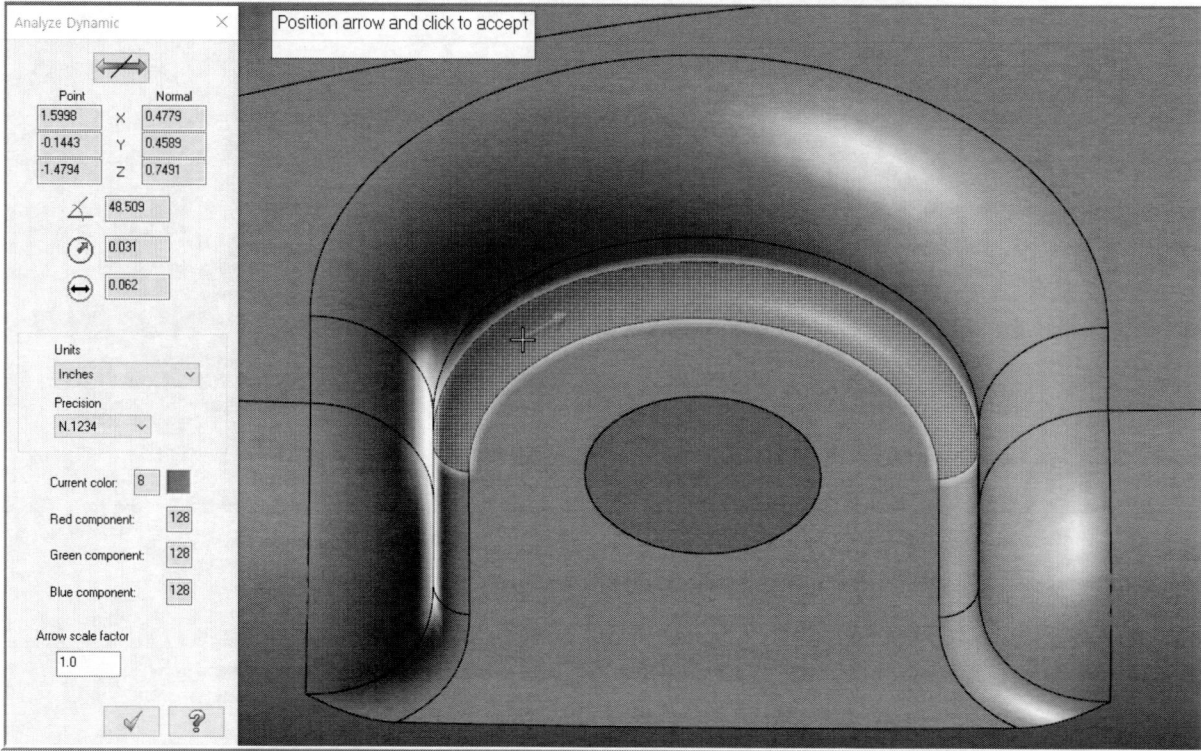

8. Pan the part and zoom the display as shown below.
9. Select the face of the fillet shown below. **The radius of this fillet is 0.1**. The 0.1875 diameter ball end mill can be used here to finish machine.

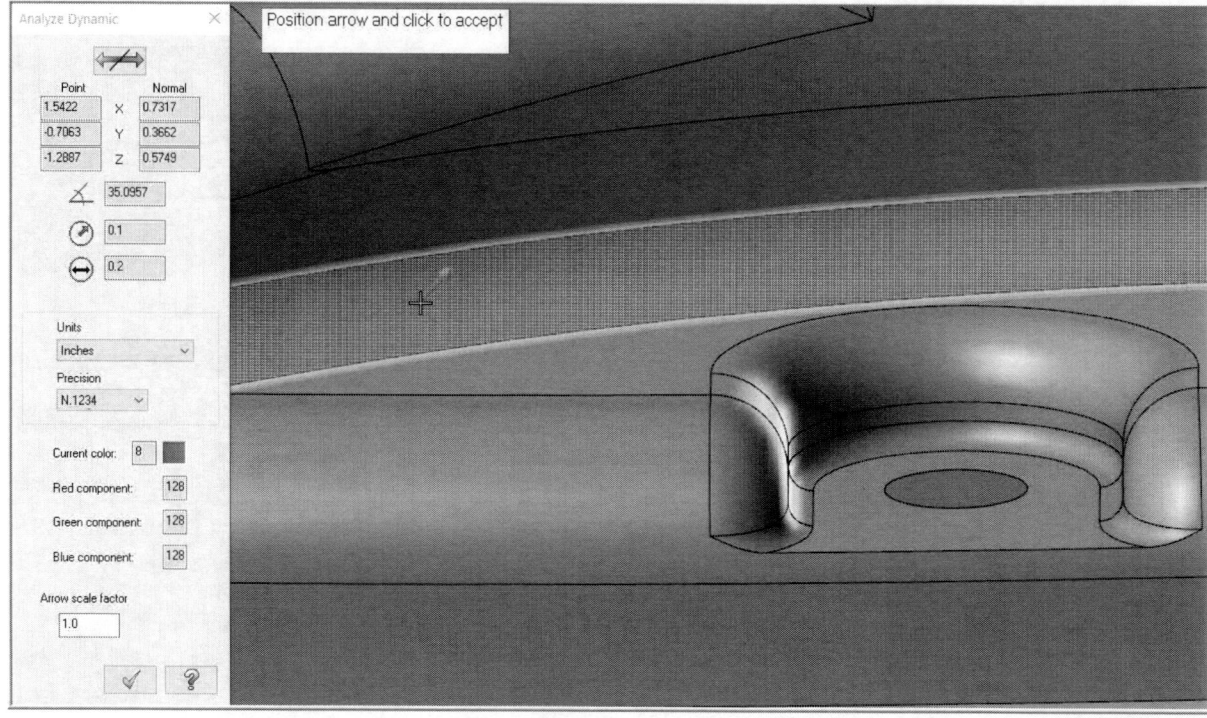

10. Pan the part and zoom the display as shown below.
11. Select the face of the fillet shown below. Using the mouse move around this face and you will see the **curvature change**. **The radius of this fillet ranges approximately from 0.1009 to 0.0992.** The 0.1875 diameter flat end mill can be used here to finish machine this contour.

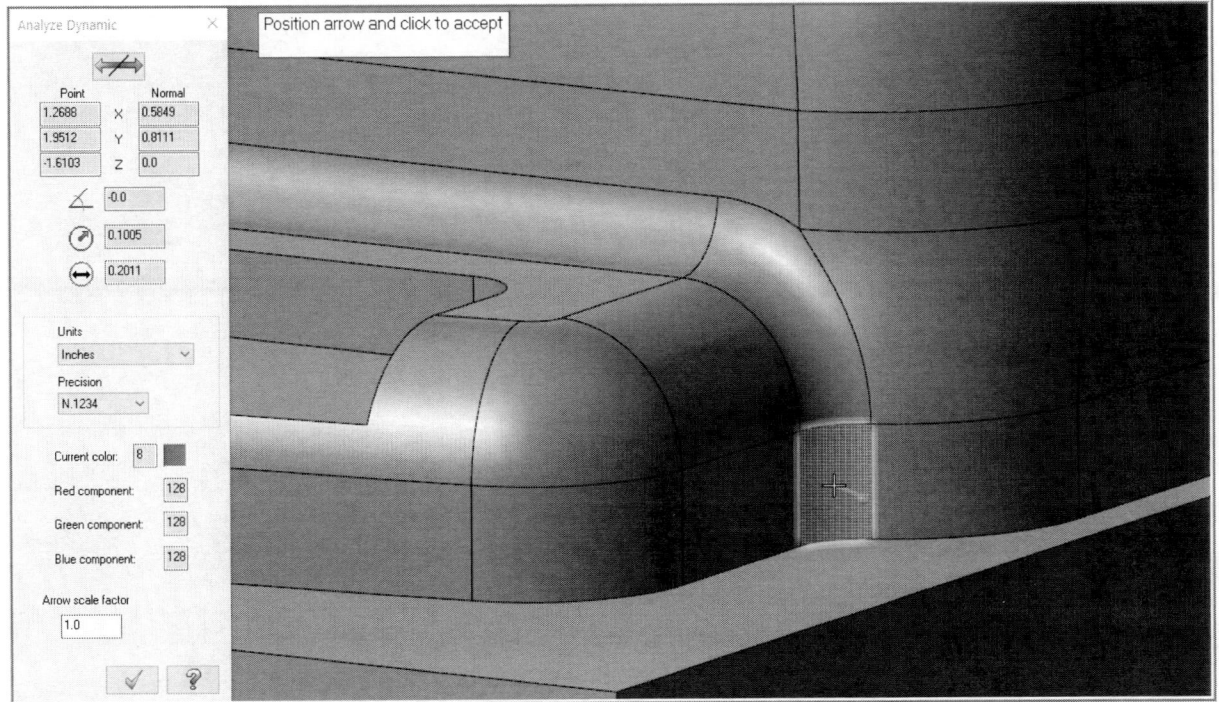

12. Select the OK button 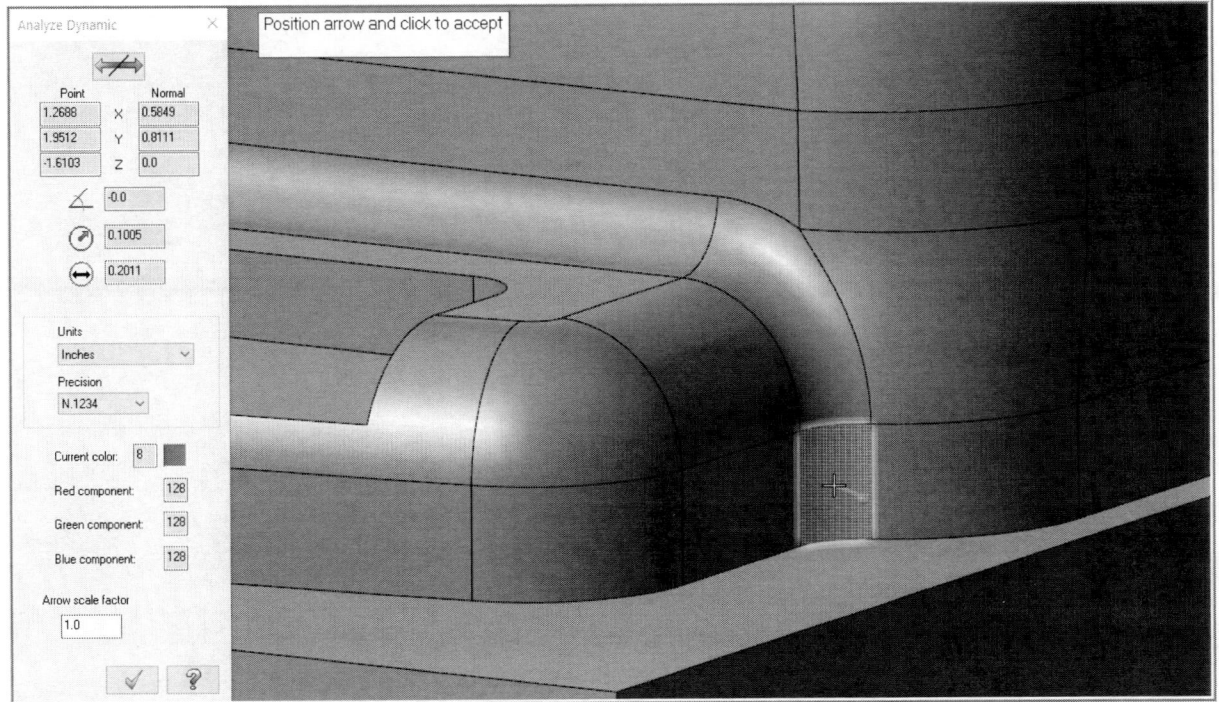 to exit the Analyze Dynamic dialog box.

TASK 9:
FINISH MACHINE OPEN POCKETS – 2 PLACES

➲ In this task we will finish the two open pockets on the sides of the part using a 0.1875"
  diameter flat end mill.

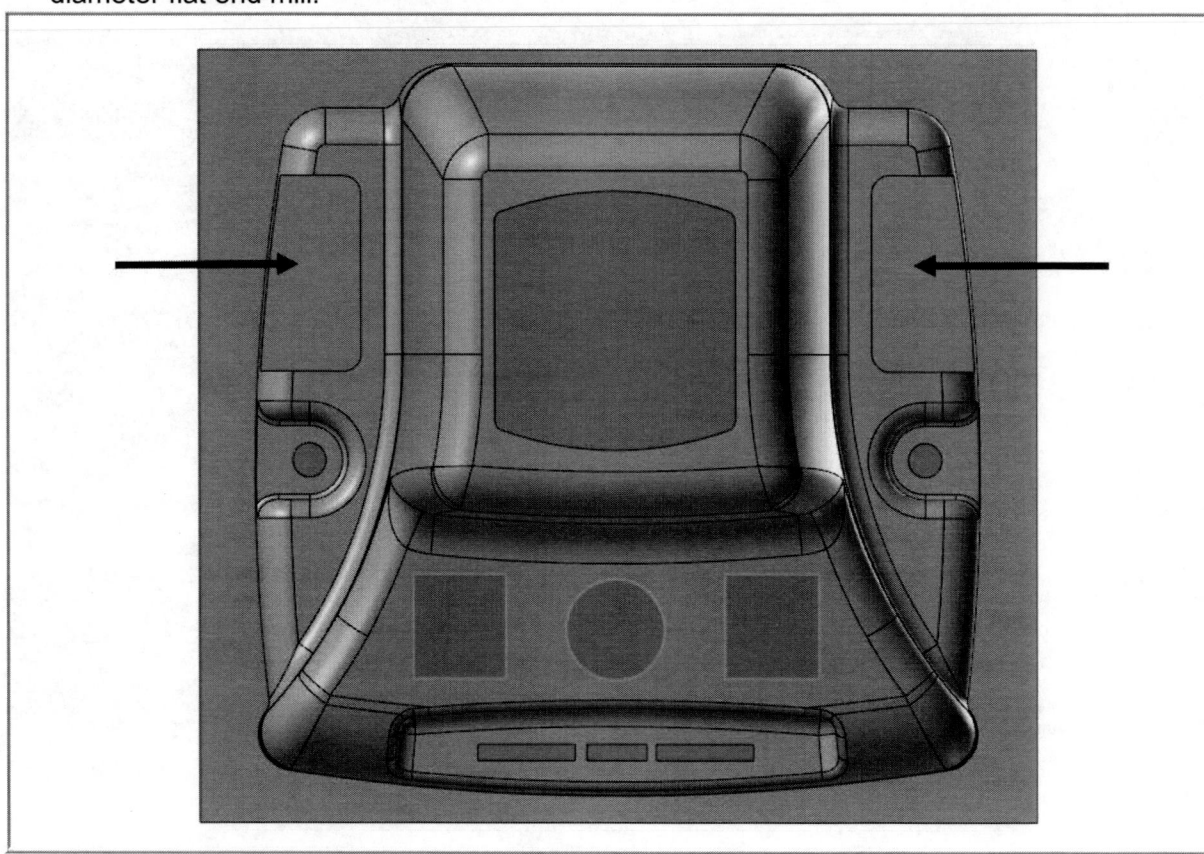

1. Select **Pocket** in the **2D Milling** section.
2. Click on the **Solids Mode** icon in the Chaining dialog box if required.
3. Activate only **Outer Shared** in the Chaining dialog box as shown below.

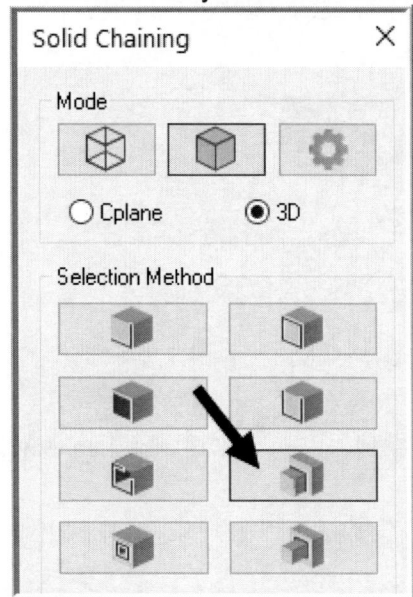

4. Rotate and Zoom the part similar to the view below. (Right Pocket)
5. To satisfy the prompt on the screen select the **face** of the pocket shown below. The partial chain will be created automatically with the correct direction. If your direction is opposite that shown, reverse it using the Reverse button on the Chaining Dialog Menu.

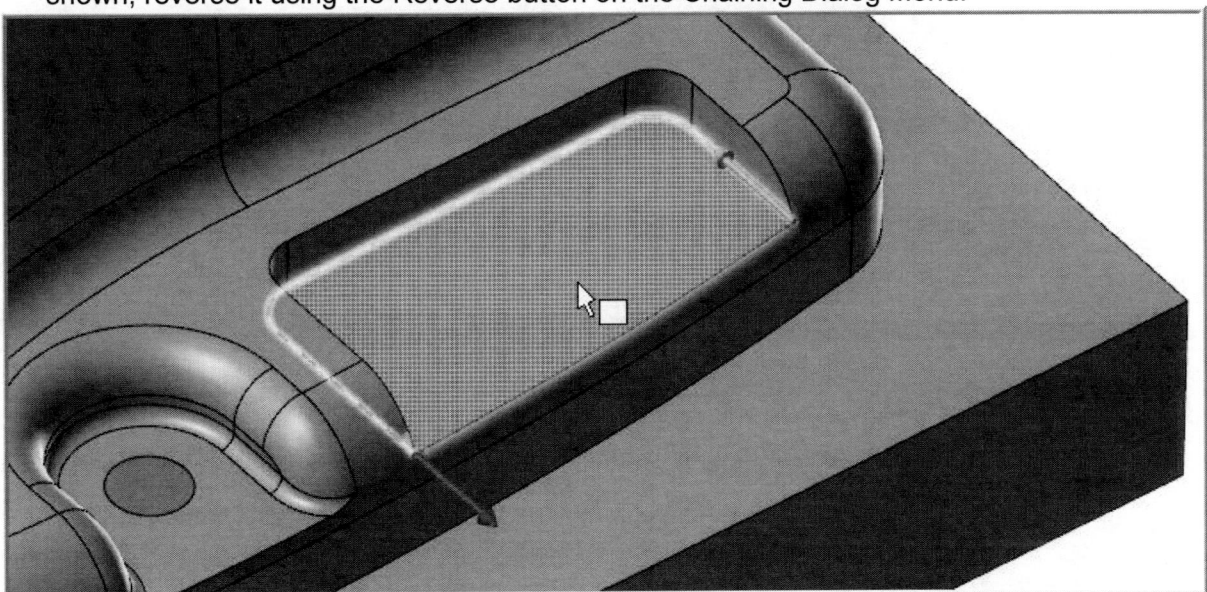

➲ Now we will select the geometry for the other open pocket.
6. Rotate and Zoom the part like the view below. (Left Pocket)
7. To satisfy the prompt on the screen select the **face** of the pocket shown below.

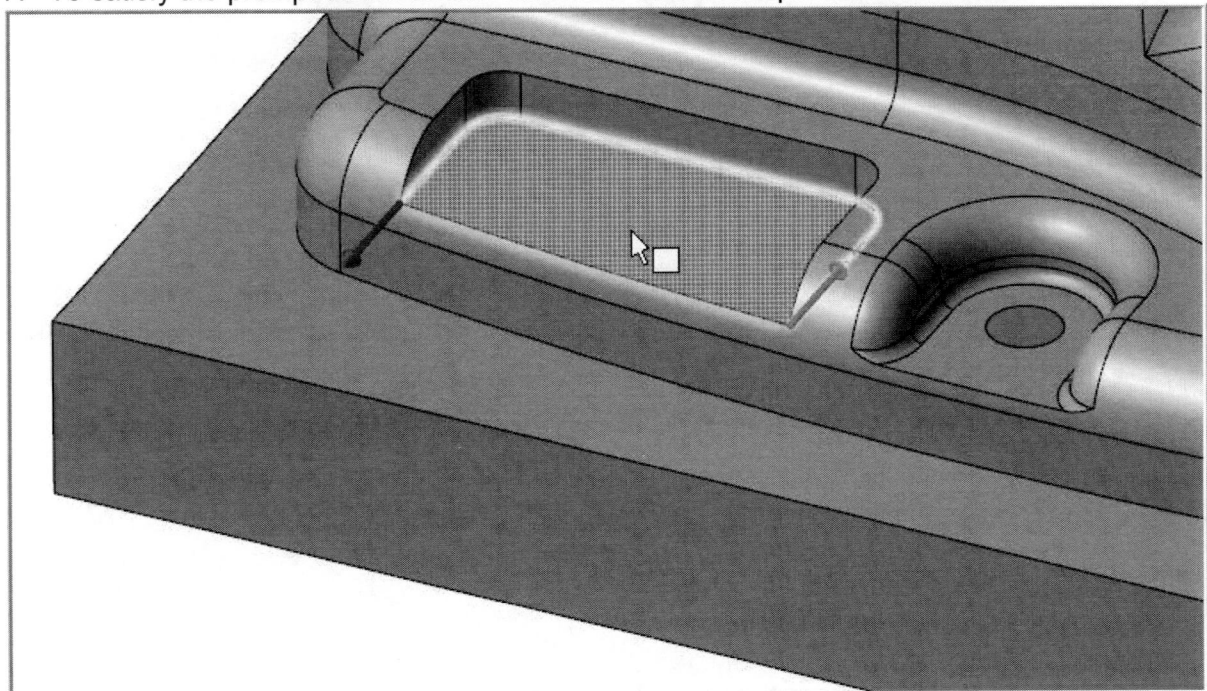

8. After the pocket has been successfully chained, select the **OK** button at the bottom of the Chaining dialog box.
9. Select **Tool** from the list on the left and click on the **Select library tool** button in the lower left corner.
10. Use the slider bar on the right of this dialog box to scroll down and locate a **0.1875 diameter flat end mill**.
⊃ We now need to change this **High Speed Steel tool to Carbide**.
11. **Right mouse click** over the **0.1875" diameter Flat End Mill** and select **Edit tool**.
12. **On** the **Define Tool Geometry** page click on **Next** in the lower right-hand corner.
13. Open the drop-down menu for **Material** and change it to **Carbide**.
14. Click the **calculator icon** to recalculate the speeds and feeds based on the new material.
15. Click on **Finish** in the lower right-hand corner.
16. Right **mouse click** over the **0.1875" diameter Flat End Mill** and select **Re-initialize feeds & speeds**.
17. Select the **Holder** page and select **B3E4-0187** as the holder.

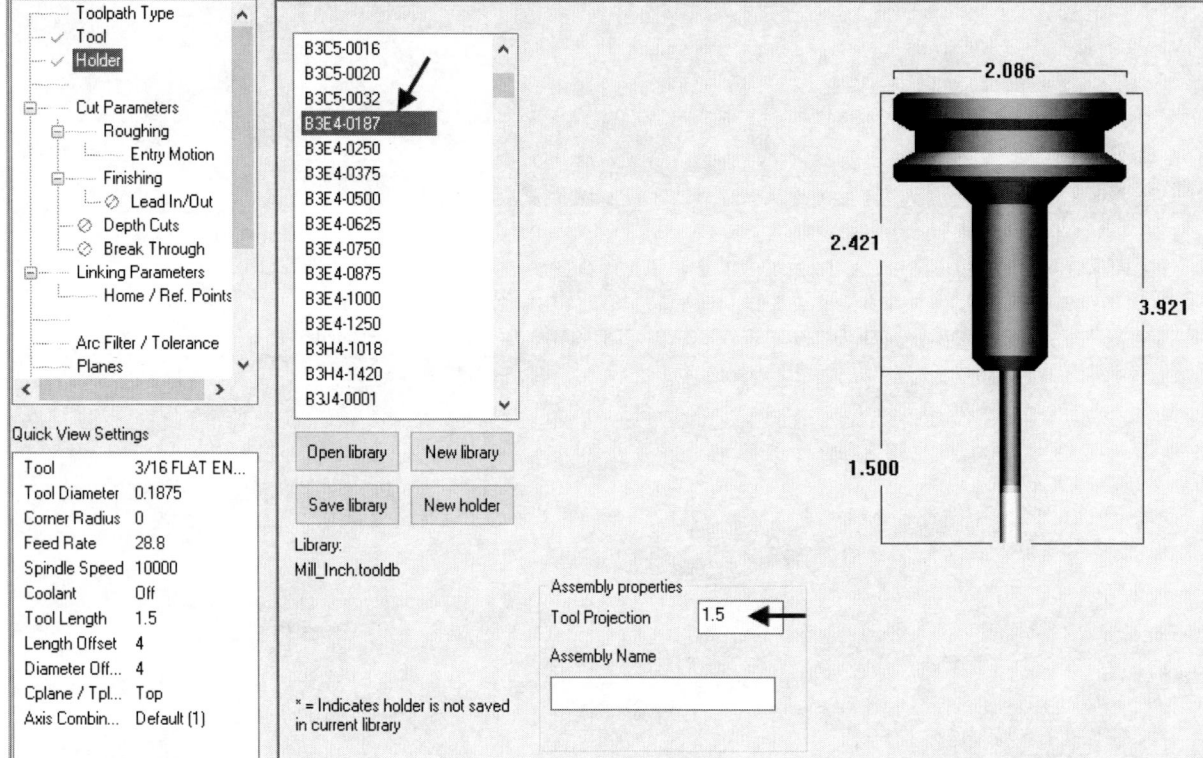

18. Select **Cut Parameters** from the list on the left and make changes to this page. The Pocket type should be set to **Open**.

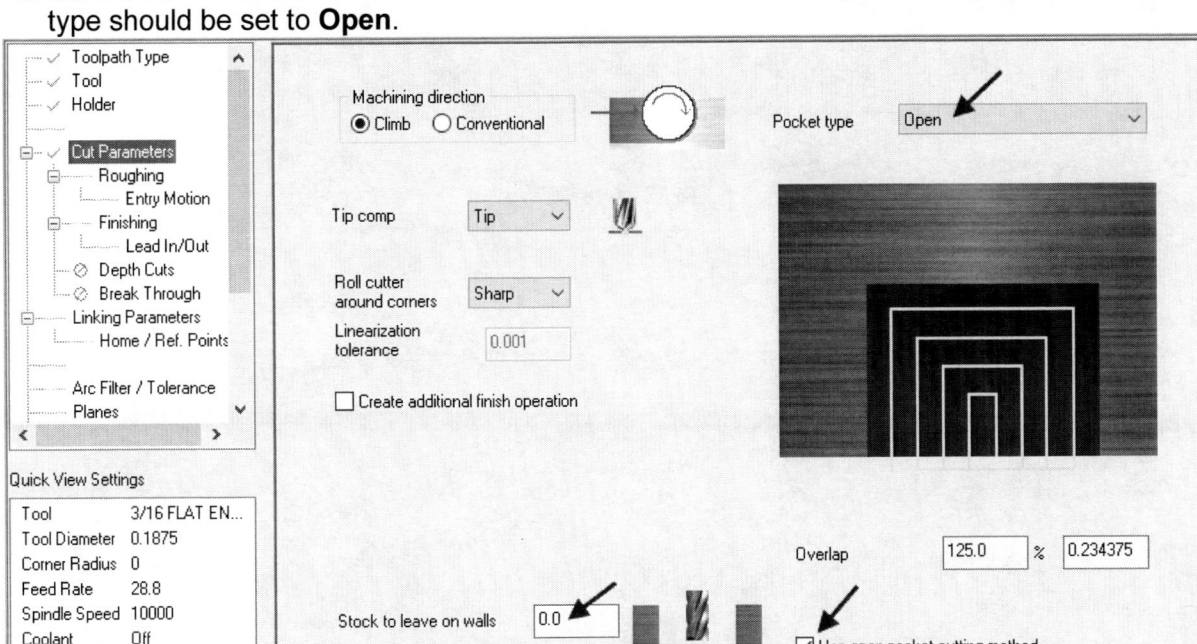

19. Select **Roughing** from the list on the left and make changes to this page, if required.

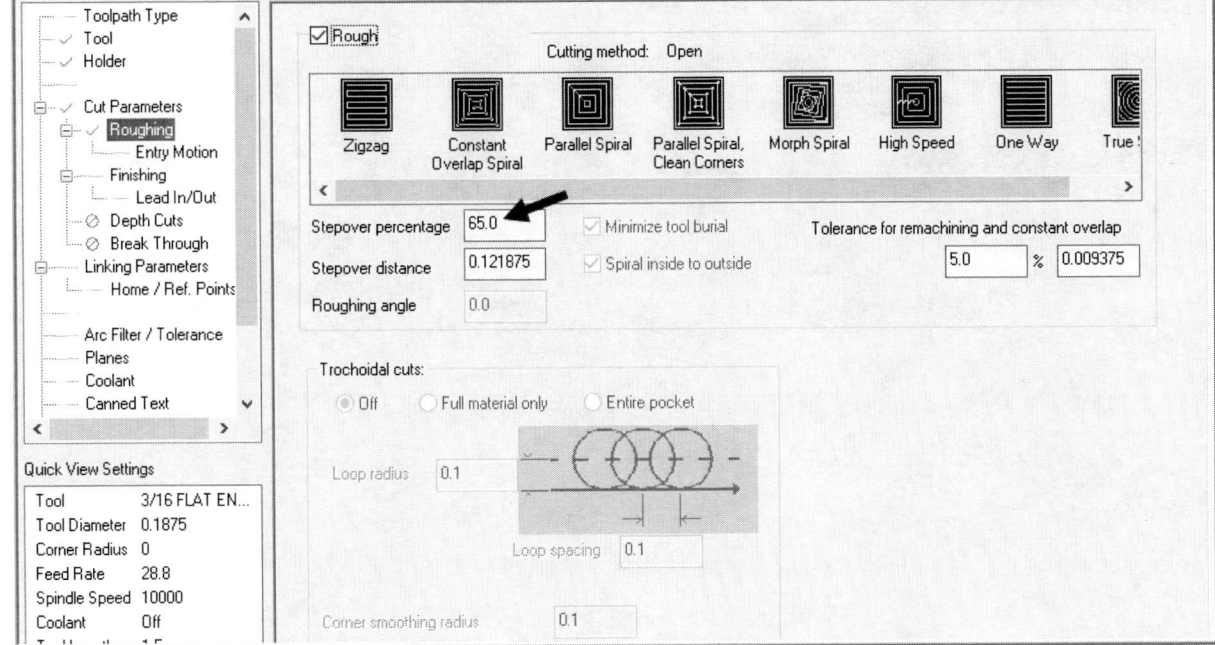

20. Select **Finishing** from the list on the left and make changes to this page

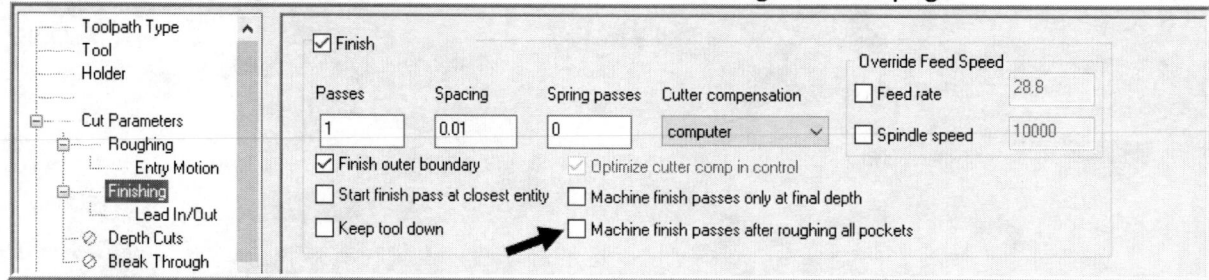

21. Select **Lead In/Out** from the list on the left and **deactivate**.

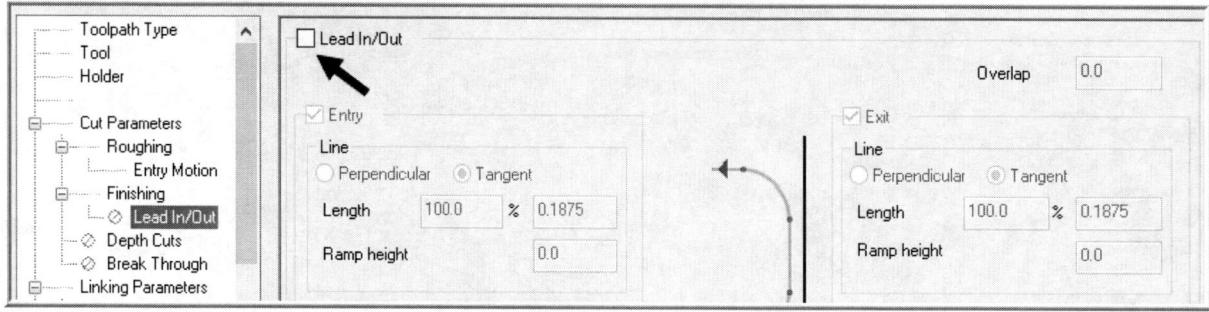

22. Navigate to the **Linking Parameters** page.
23. Activate the **Top of stock** to **Absolute**.
24. Click in the **Top of stock** button.
25. When prompted to "**Select a point**" select the end point shown below as the Z at the **top edge of this open pocket** as shown below:

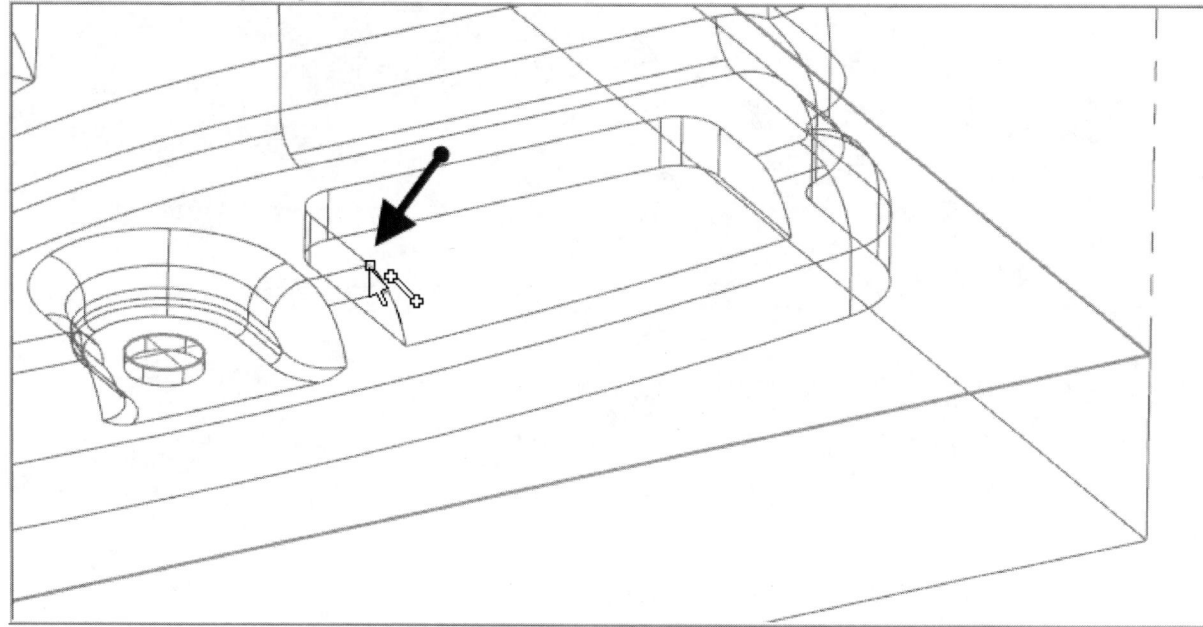

26. Set the remaining **Linking Parameters** as shown below:

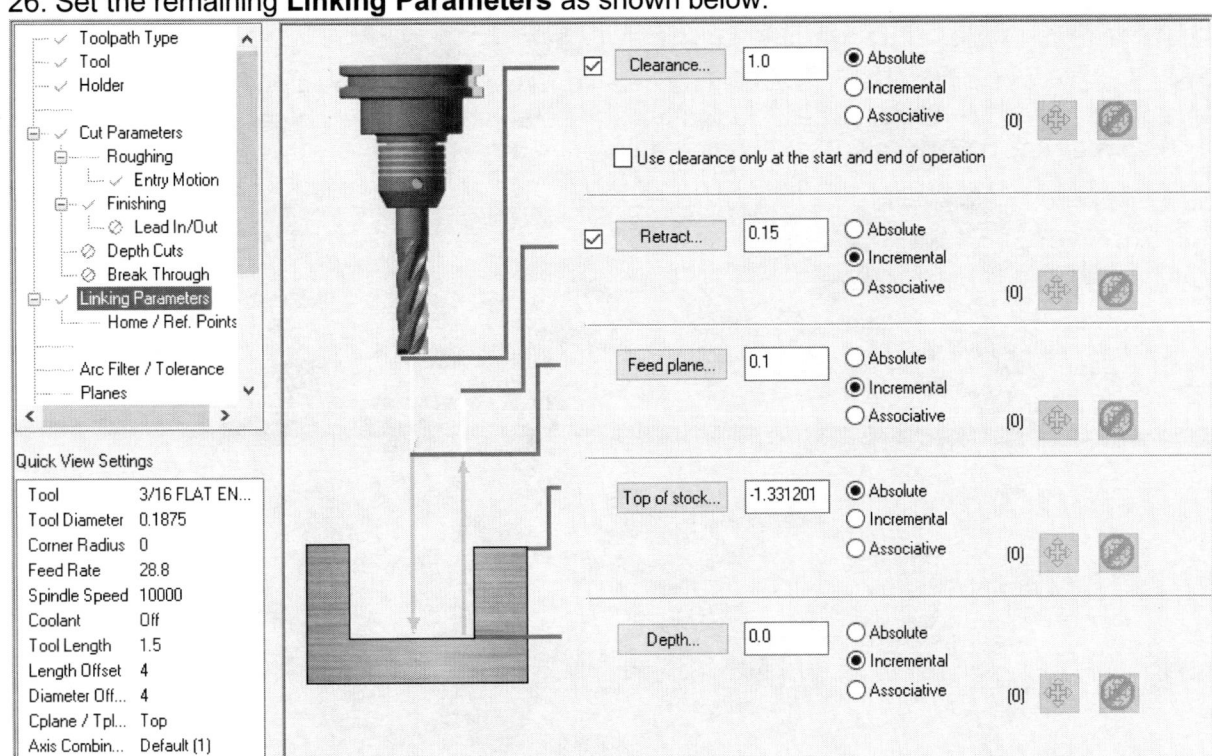

27. Select the OK button [✓] to exit Pocket operation.
28. Verify this toolpath only using the **Stock model: Roughing done**.

TASK 10:
FINISH MACHINE OPEN RADIUSED POCKETS – 2 PLACES

➲ In this task we will finish the two open radiused pockets on the sides of the part.
➲ You will copy the Pocket (Open)) toolpath just created and change the parameters to suit a 0.25" bull end mill with a 0.0313" corner radius.

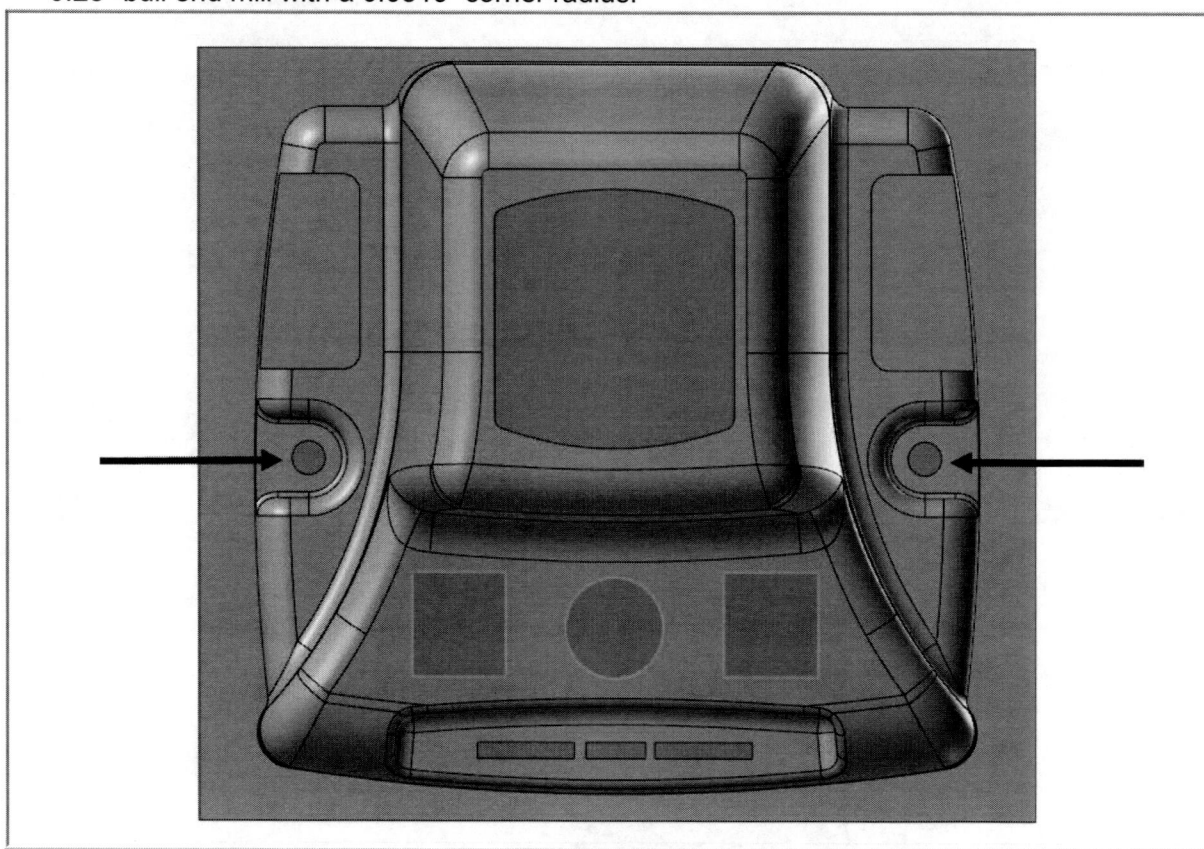

➲ In the **Toolpaths Manager**, copy **Operation 6**, which was just created, and paste the operation directly after, to create **Operation 7**.
➲ Select the **Parameters** option under **Operation 7**.

➲ Navigate to the **Toolpath Type** page and click on the **Remove selected chains** icon.
➲ Now click on the **Select chains** icon to select the new geometry for this toolpath.

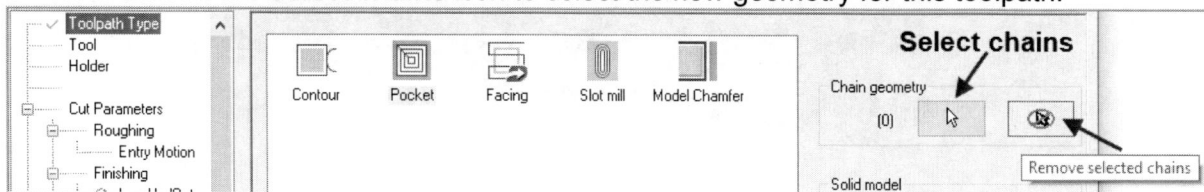

⮕ Click on the **Solids Mode** icon in the Chaining dialog box if required.
⮕ Activate only **Outer Shared Edges** in the Chaining dialog box as shown below.

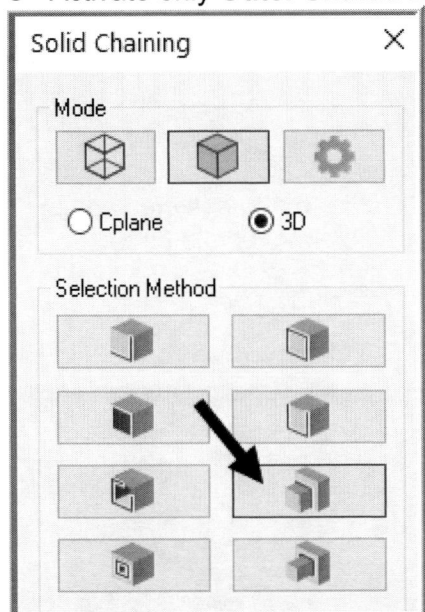

⮕ Rotate and Zoom in on the right side of the part similar to the view below.
⮕ To satisfy the prompt on the screen select the **face** of the pocket shown below. The partial chain will automatically be created.

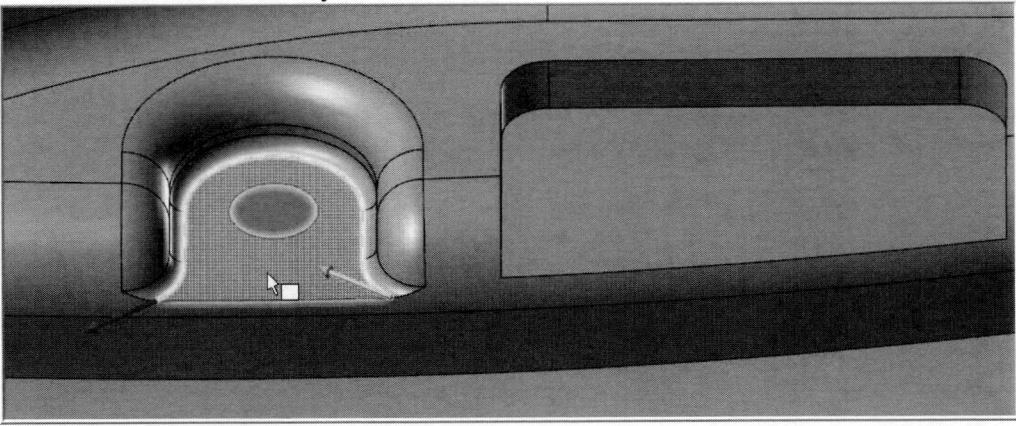

⮕ Repeat the chaining for the opposite side of the part.

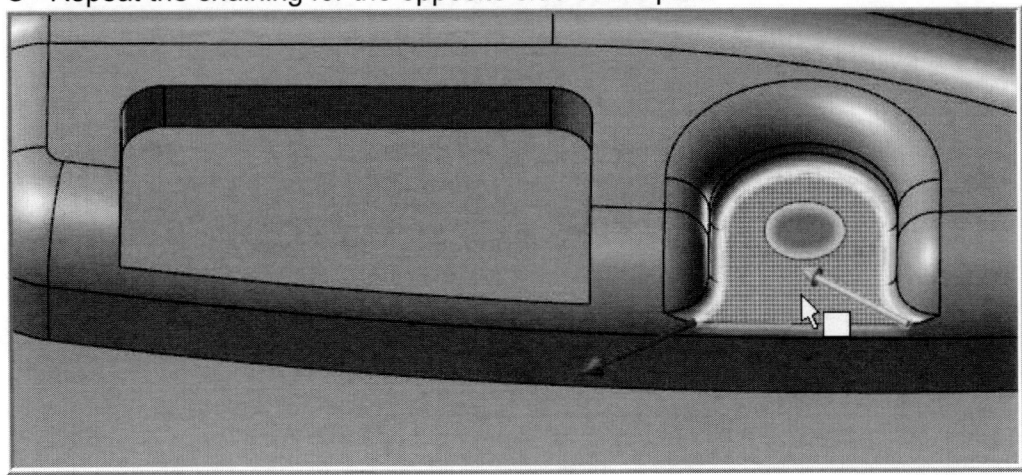

➲ After the pocket has been successfully chained, select the OK button 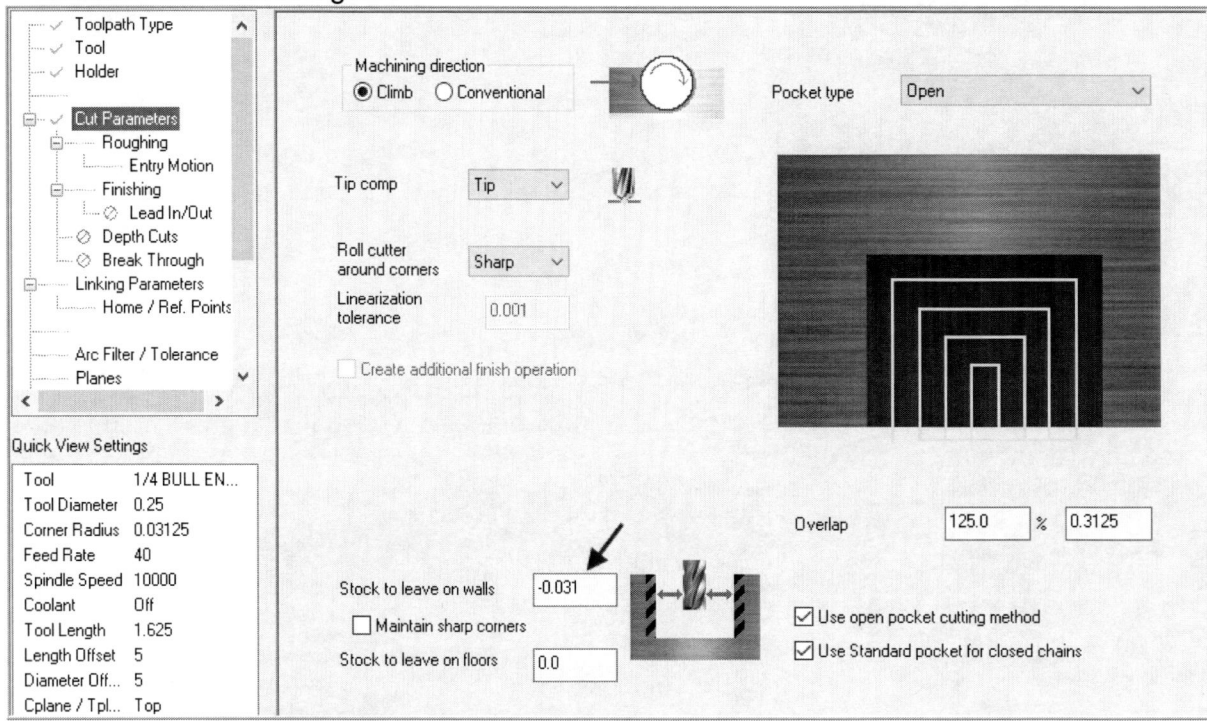 at the bottom of the Chaining dialog box.

➲ Select **Tool** from the list on the left.

➲ Now select the **0.25" bull end mill with a 0.0313" corner radius.**

➲ Right **mouse click** over the **0.25" bull end mill with a 0.0313" corner radius** and select **Re-initialize feeds & speeds**.

➲ Select **Cut Parameters** from the list on the left and make changes to this page. The Stock to leave on walls is set to **NEGATIVE 0.031**. This is because the geometry selected earlier was offset from the walls by 0.031. Subsequently the negative value moves the cutter towards the walls being cut.

➲ Select the **OK** button to exit Pocket operation.

➲ Verify this toolpath only using the **Stock model: Roughing done**.

TASK 11:
FINISH MACHINE CONTOUR OF MOLD BASE

➪ In this task we will finish the contour of the mold base using a 0.1875" diameter flat end mill.

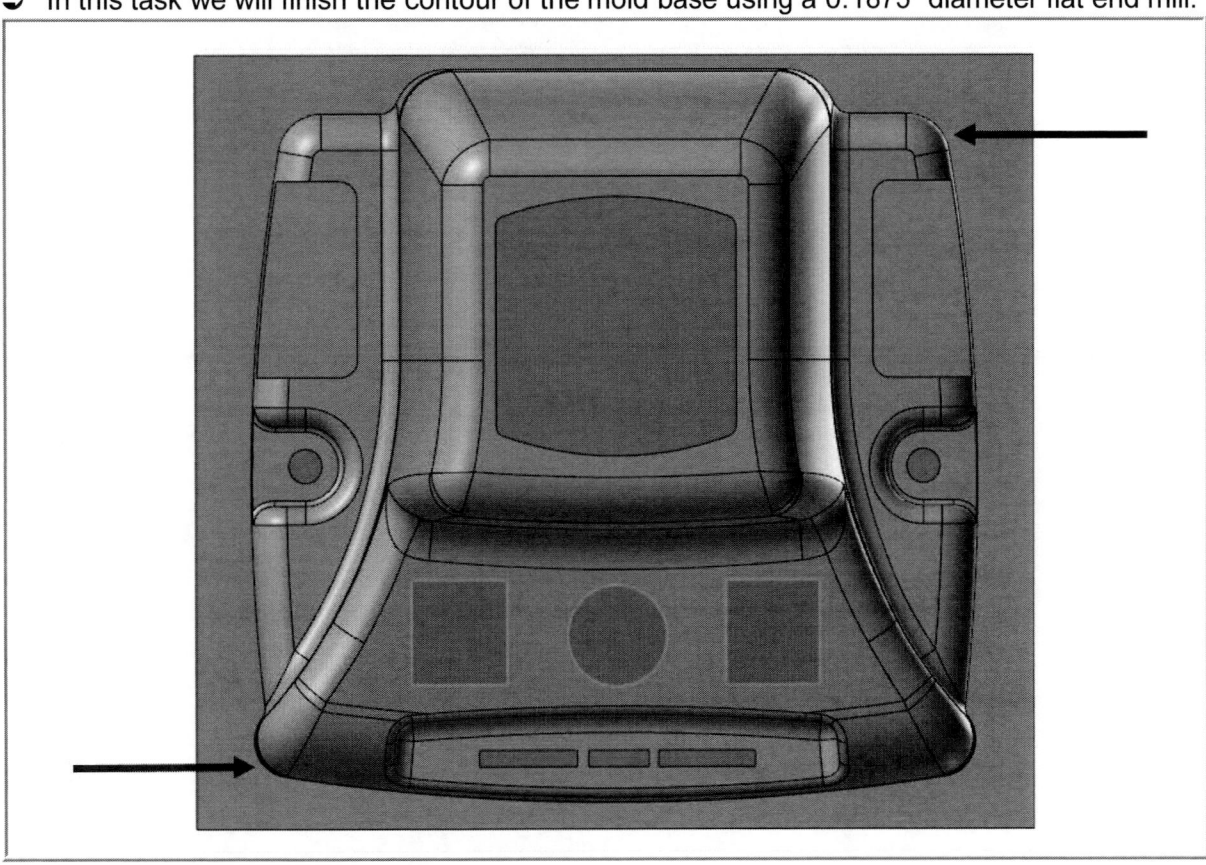

1. Select **Contour** in the **2D Milling** section.
2. Click on the **Solids Mode** icon in the Chaining dialog box if required.
3. Activate only **Loop** in the Chaining dialog box as shown below. Position the part in an **isometric** view for loop selection.

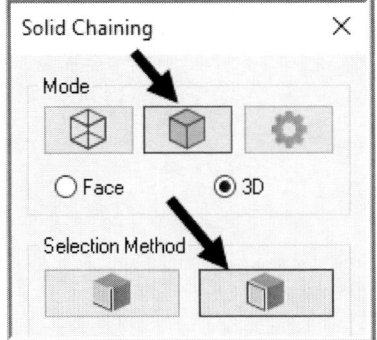

4. Select the loop in the general direction of the arrow below. Notice the resulting Green Arrow **direction** and its **position**. The direction is important.

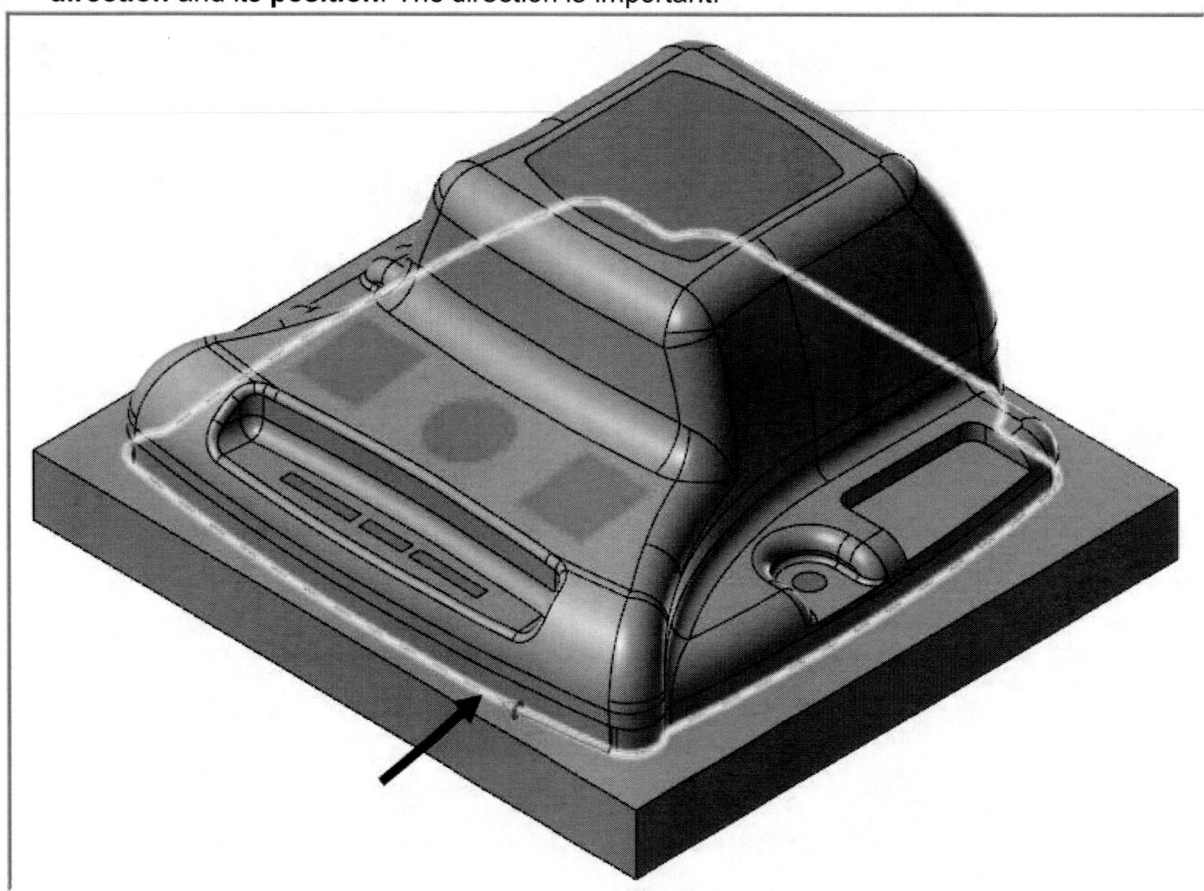

5. If your chain differs, use the controls at the bottom of the chaining manager.

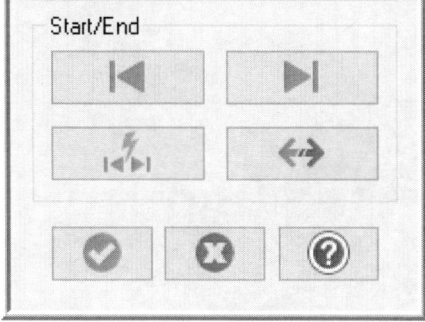

6. After the contour has been successfully chained, select the OK button ☑ at the bottom of the Chaining dialog box.

7. Select **Tool** from the list on the left and select the **0.1875 diameter flat end mill**.
8. Select **Cut Parameters** from the list on the left and make changes to this page, if required.

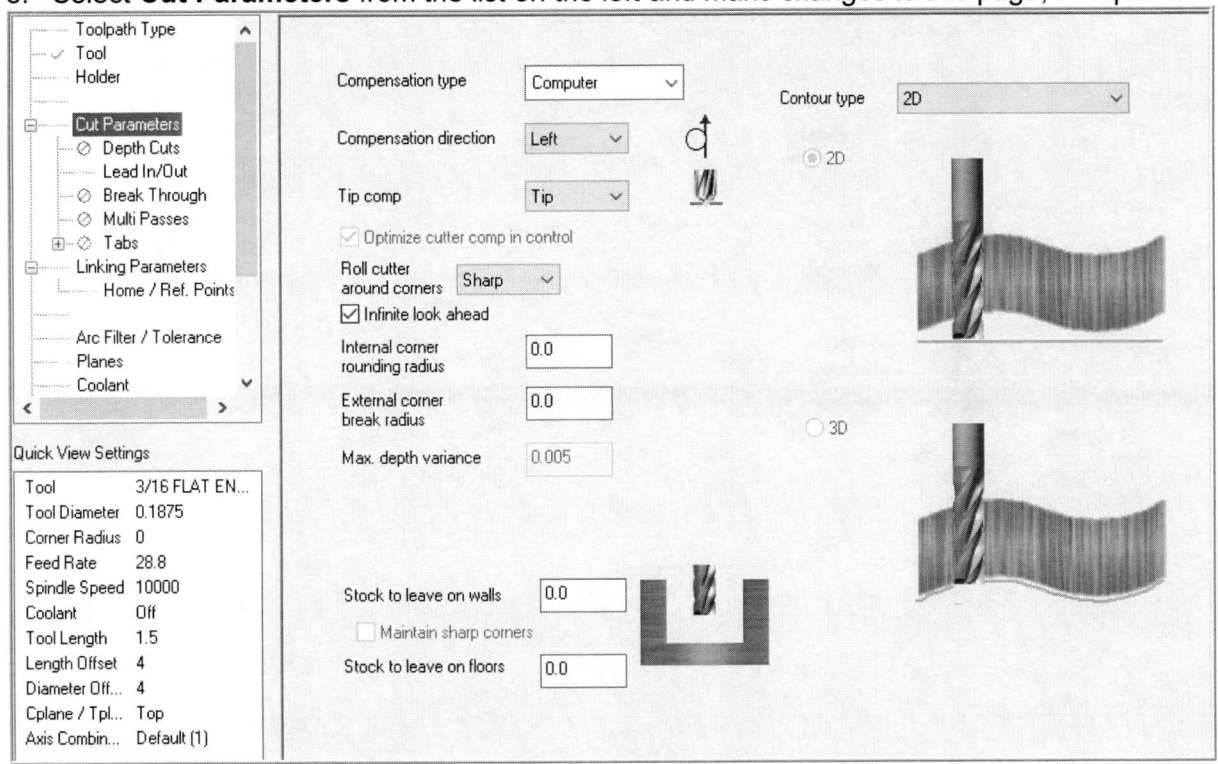

9. Select **Lead In/Out** from the list on the left and make changes to this page.

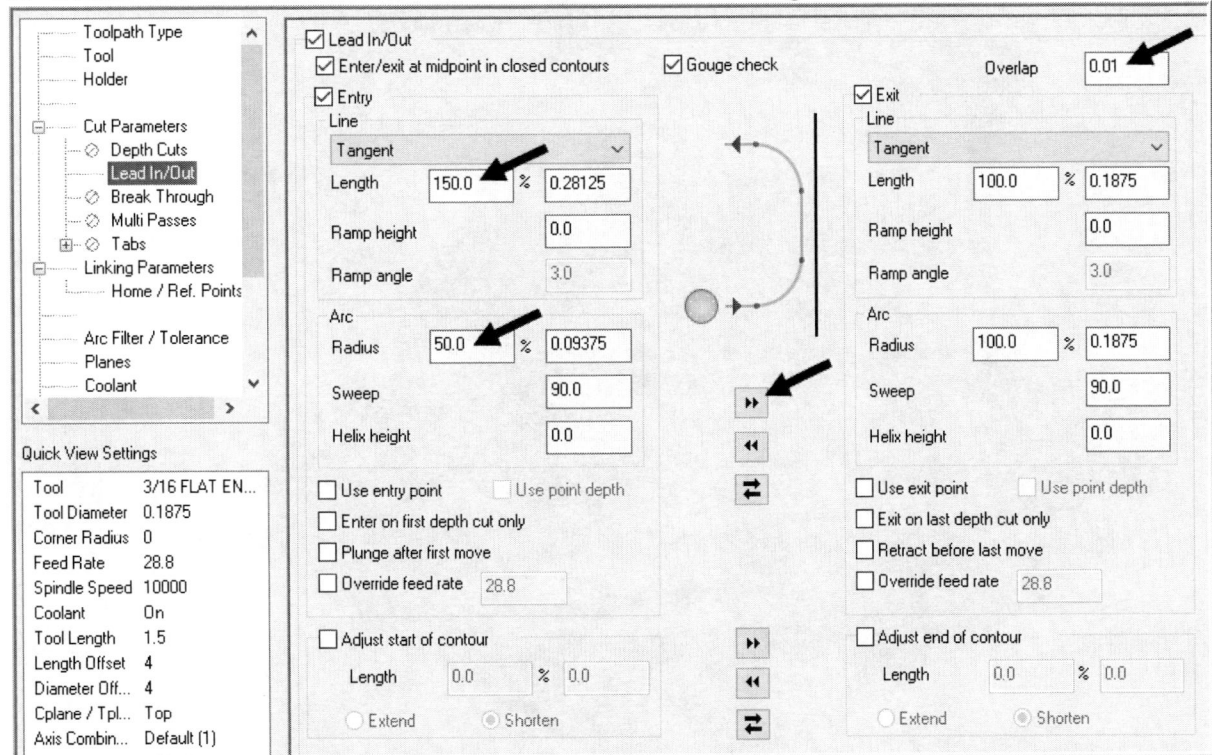

Overlap
Sets how far the tool goes past the end of the toolpath before exiting for a cleaner finish.

10. Navigate to the **Linking Parameters** page and make changes to this page.

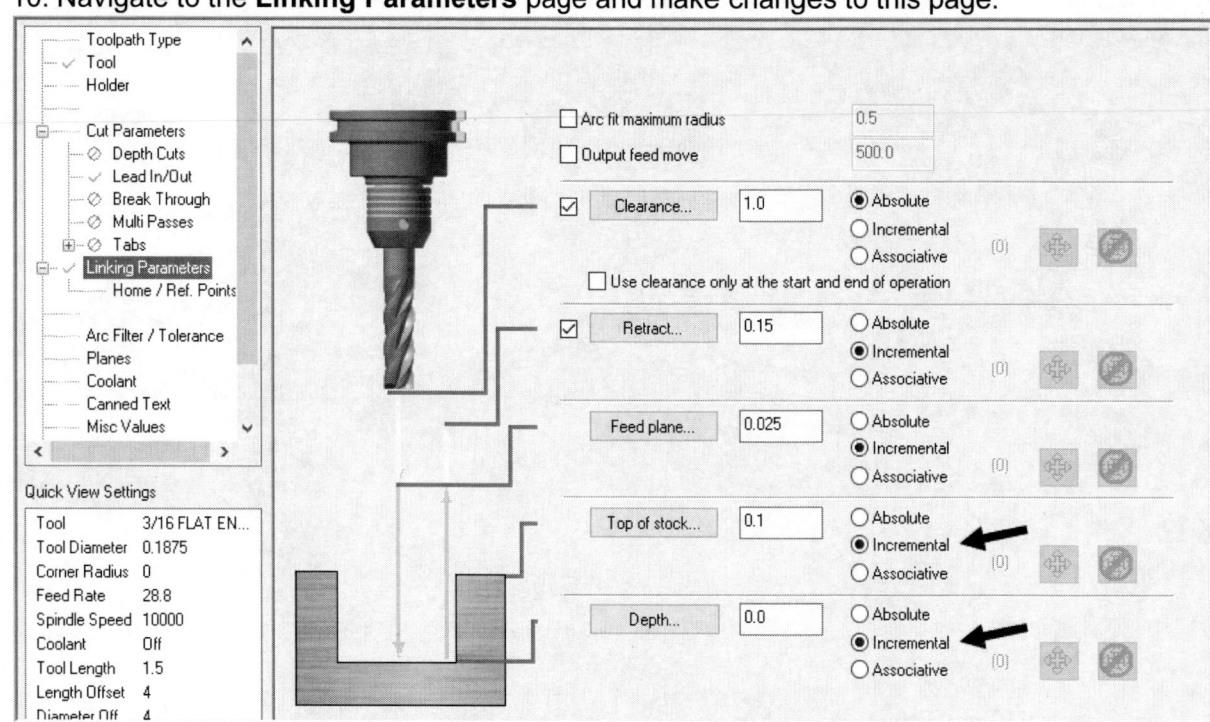

11. Select the OK button [✓] to exit Contour operation.

12. Backplot this toolpath. **Note** that the toolpath rapids down to depth in air.

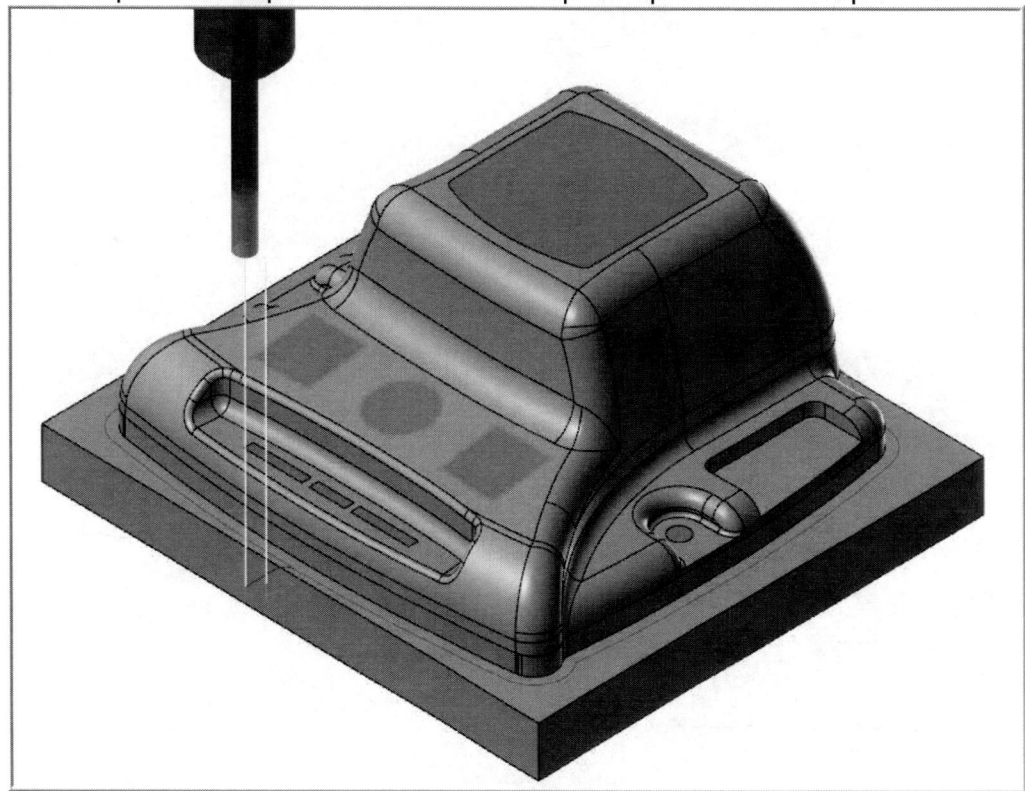

TASK 12:
CREATE A STOCK MODEL FROM THE 2D TOOLPATHS
⊃ In this task we will create a Stock Model from the four 2D toolpaths.

1. On the **Toolpaths** tab select **Stock Model** in the **Stock** section.

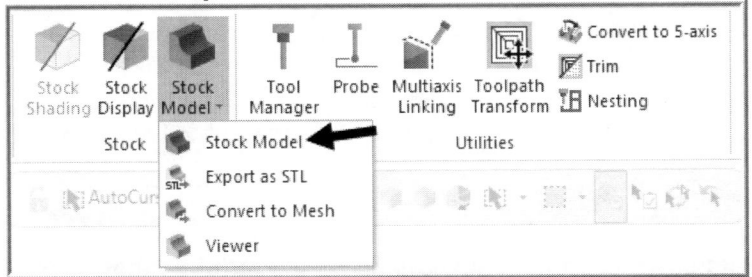

2. On the **Stock Definition** page enter **2D Finishing Done** for the **Name** of this Stock Model.
3. Activate **Stock model**. **Note** that the Stock model is **Roughing Done**. Give this Stock Model a new color as well.

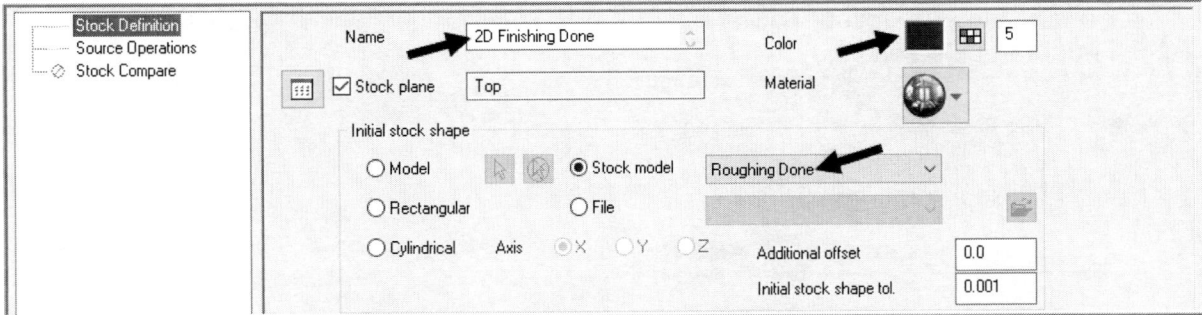

4. Click on **Source Operations** at the left of the Stock model dialog box.
5. Ensure there are **check marks** on the **four 2D toolpaths** as shown below.

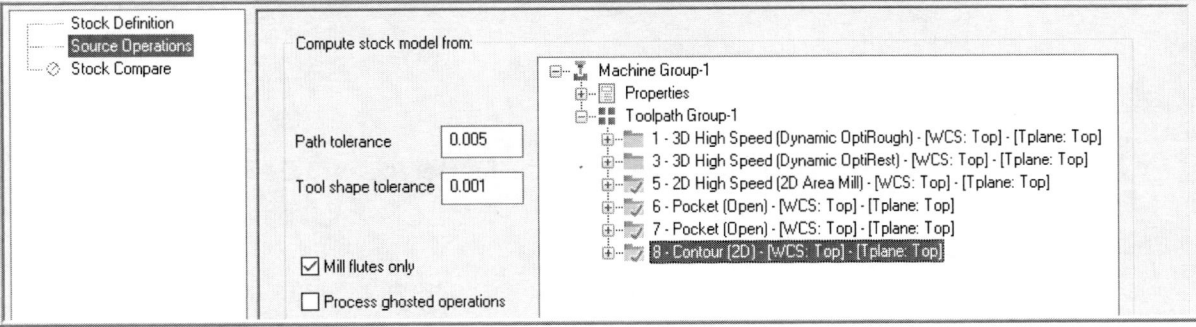

6. Click on the **OK** icon to complete this Stock model operation.

TASK 13:
FINISH USING SURFACE HIGH SPEED EQUAL SCALLOPS
➲ Next you will finish the part using the Surface High Speed Equal Scallops toolpath.

> **3D high speed Equal Scallops toolpaths**
> The stepover distance for high speed scallop toolpaths is measured along the surface, instead of parallel to the tool plane. This ensures a consistent scallop height across the surface, regardless of the surface direction. This is an ideal strategy to use on the boundaries generated by rest machining, or in any circumstances where you want to ensure a constant 3D distance between passes.
>
> Scallop toolpaths are also known as constant stepover toolpaths. Since the stepover is measured along the surface, the spacing between cuts is maintained as the surface angle varies, producing a consistent scallop height across the surface.

1. Select the **Toolpaths** tab at the top right side of the screen if required.
2. Click on the **Expand gallery** down arrow in the **3D** section and select **Equal Scallops** from the **Finishing** selections.

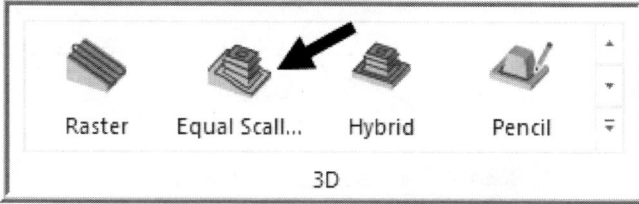

3. On the screen select the **Model Geometry** page, if required.
4. Ensure both the **Wall Stock** and **Floor stock** are set to **Zero.**

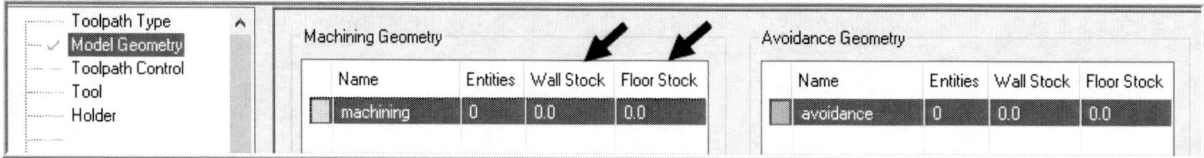

5. At the bottom of the **Model Geometry** page click on the **Select entities** button.

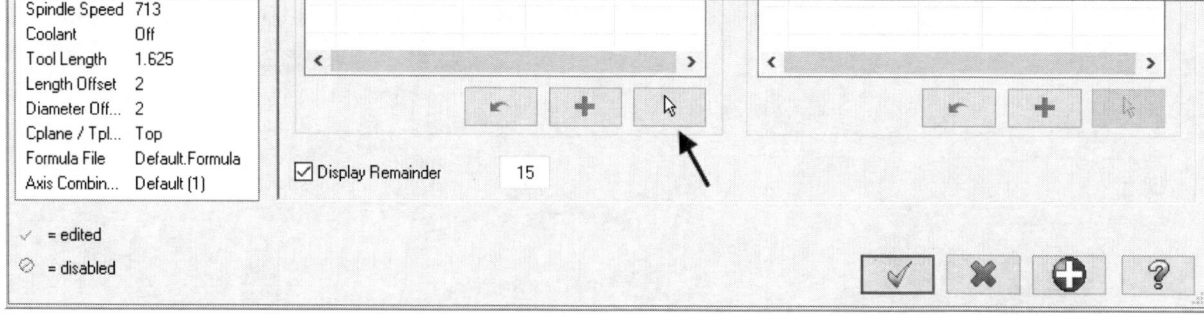

6. Now you will be returned to the graphics screen. To satisfy the prompt on the screen use **Ctrl-A on your keyboard** select to **select all the entities**.

7. To move onto the next step you now need to pick the **End Selection** icon ![icon].

---

8. Back at the Model Geometry page **select the avoidance row** in the **Avoidance Geometry** section.

9. At the bottom of the **Model Geometry** page click on the **Select entities** button for **Avoidance Geometry**.

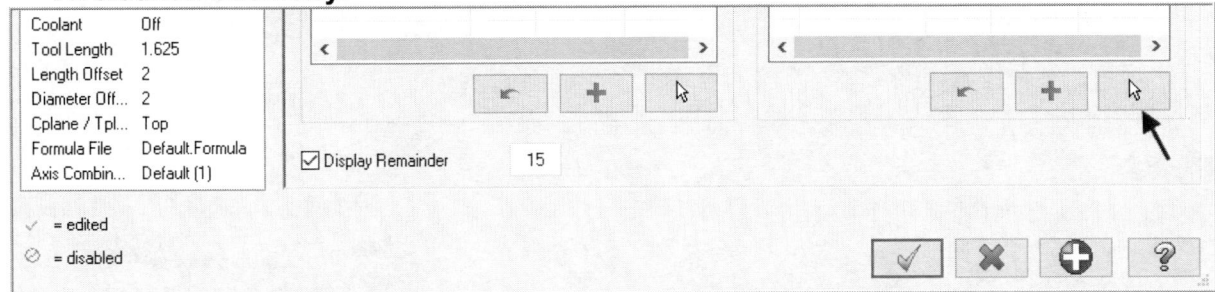

10. Now you will be returned to the graphics screen. To satisfy the prompt on the screen select the **five faces** of the **rectangular** shaped feature. Top and the four side faces. Selecting the bottom is not necessary.

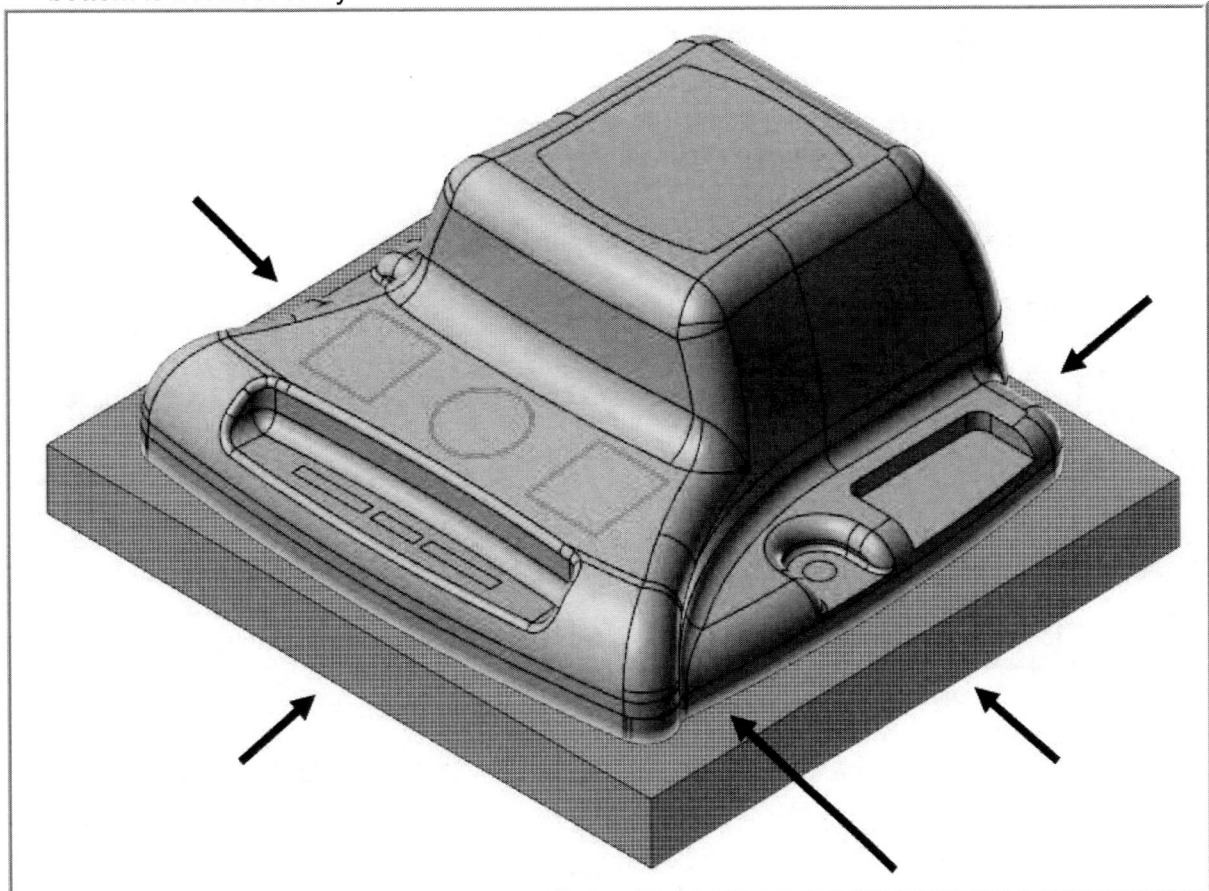

11. To move onto the next step you now need to pick the **End Selection** icon.

12. Select the **Toolpath Control** page, make changes as shown below, if required.

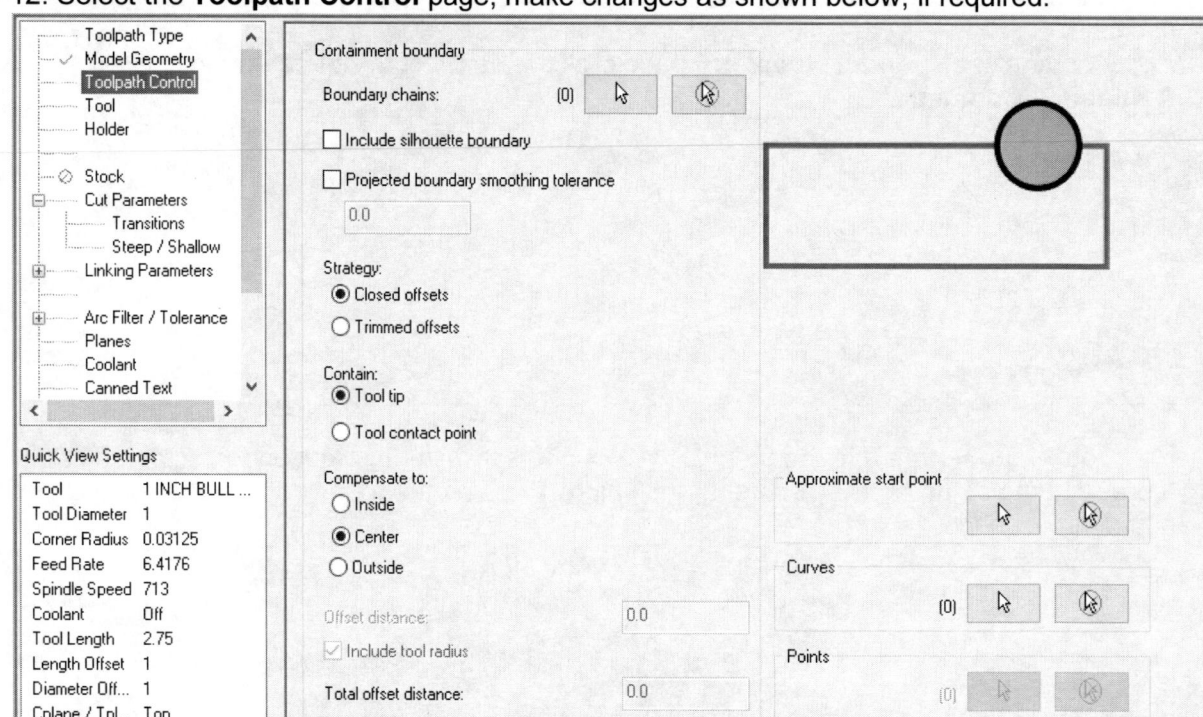

13. Next, select the **Tool** page. In the lower left corner of the page select the **Select library tool...** button. **Deactivate Filter Active**.
14. Use the scroll bar on the right of this dialog box to locate and select the **0.375 Ball endmill**.

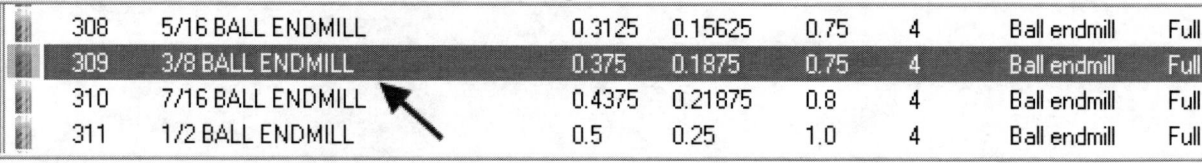

	308	5/16 BALL ENDMILL	0.3125	0.15625	0.75	4	Ball endmill	Full
	309	3/8 BALL ENDMILL	0.375	0.1875	0.75	4	Ball endmill	Full
	310	7/16 BALL ENDMILL	0.4375	0.21875	0.8	4	Ball endmill	Full
	311	1/2 BALL ENDMILL	0.5	0.25	1.0	4	Ball endmill	Full

15. Select the **OK button** to complete the selection of this tool.
➲ We now need to change this **High Speed Steel tool to Carbide**.
16. Right **mouse click** over the **0.375 Ball endmill** and select **Edit tool**.
17. On the **Define Tool Geometry** page click on **Next** in the lower right-hand corner.
18. Open the drop-down menu for **Material** and change it to **Carbide**.
19. Click the **calculator icon** to recalculate the speeds and feeds based on the new material.
20. Click on **Finish** in the lower right-hand corner.
21. Right **mouse click** over the **0.375 Ball endmill** and select **Re-initialize feeds & speeds**.

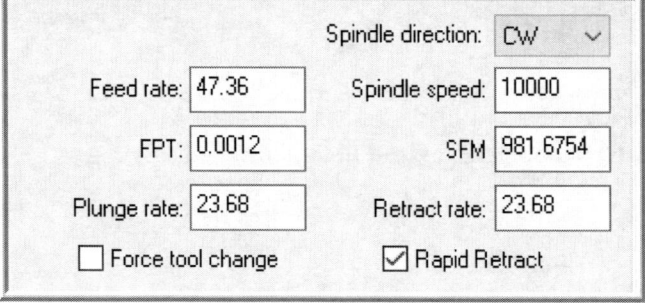

22. Select the **Holder** page and select **B3E4-0375** as the holder.

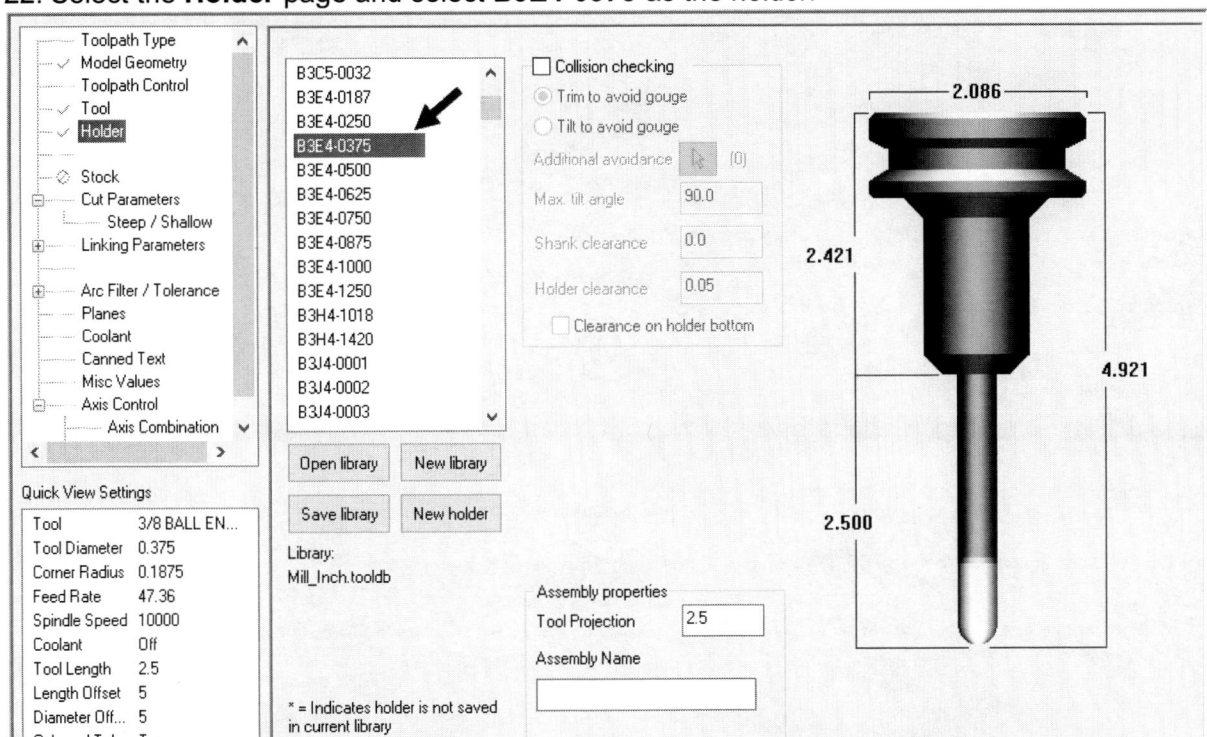

23. Select the **Cut Parameters** page and make changes to this page as shown below:

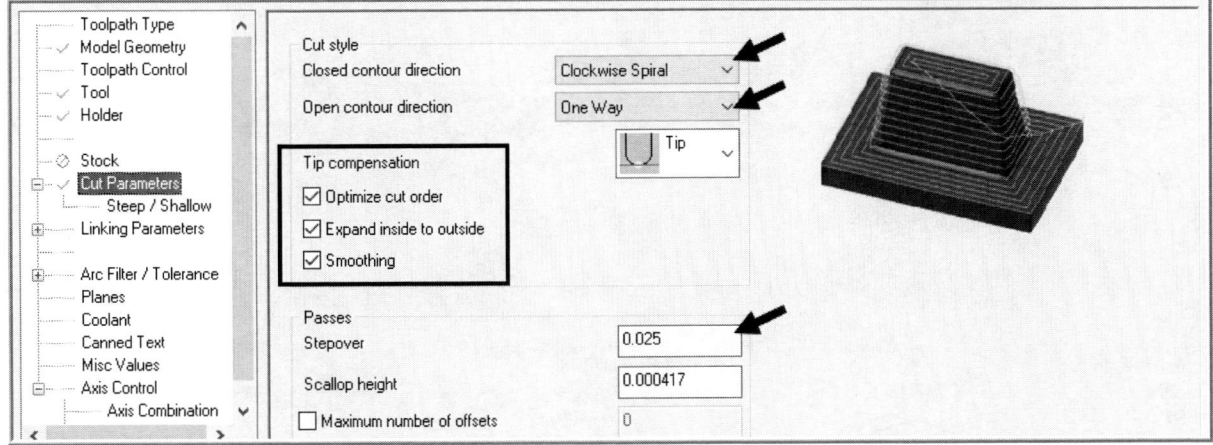

Spiral: Select to eliminate stepovers when machining.

Smoothing: Equal Scallop only. Use this option to smooth sharp corners and replace them with curves. Eliminating sharp changes of direction results in a more even load on the tool and lets you consistently maintain a higher feed rate.

Stepover: Defines the spacing between cutting passes. This is a 3D value measured along the surface profile. It is linked to Scallop height, so that you can specify the spacing between the passes in terms of the stepover distance or the scallop height. When you make an entry in one field, it automatically updates the other.

24. Select the **Steep/Shallow** page and make changes as shown below, if required.

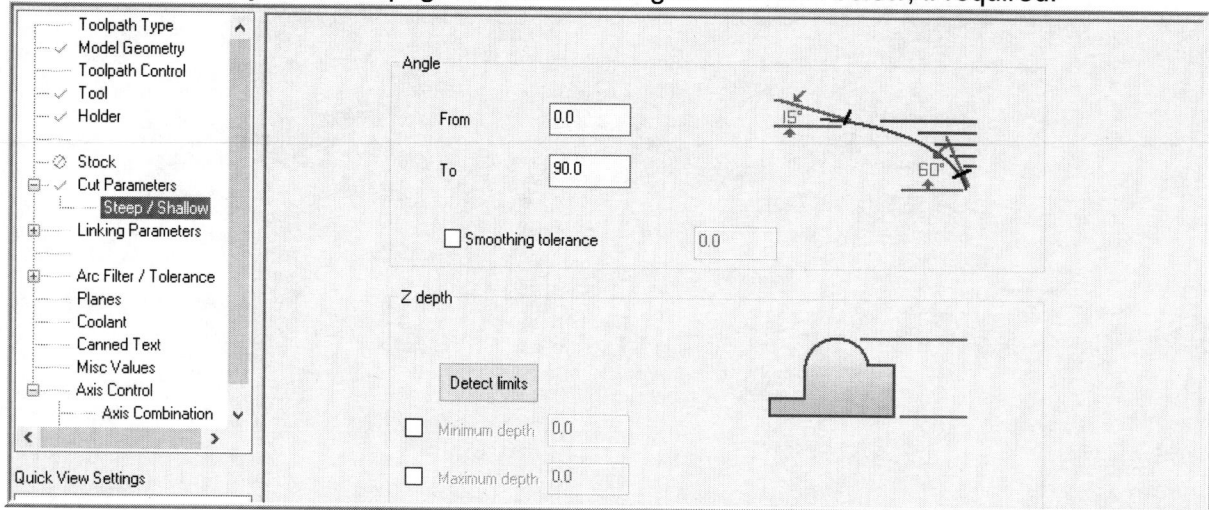

25. Make the following selections on the **Linking Parameters** page:

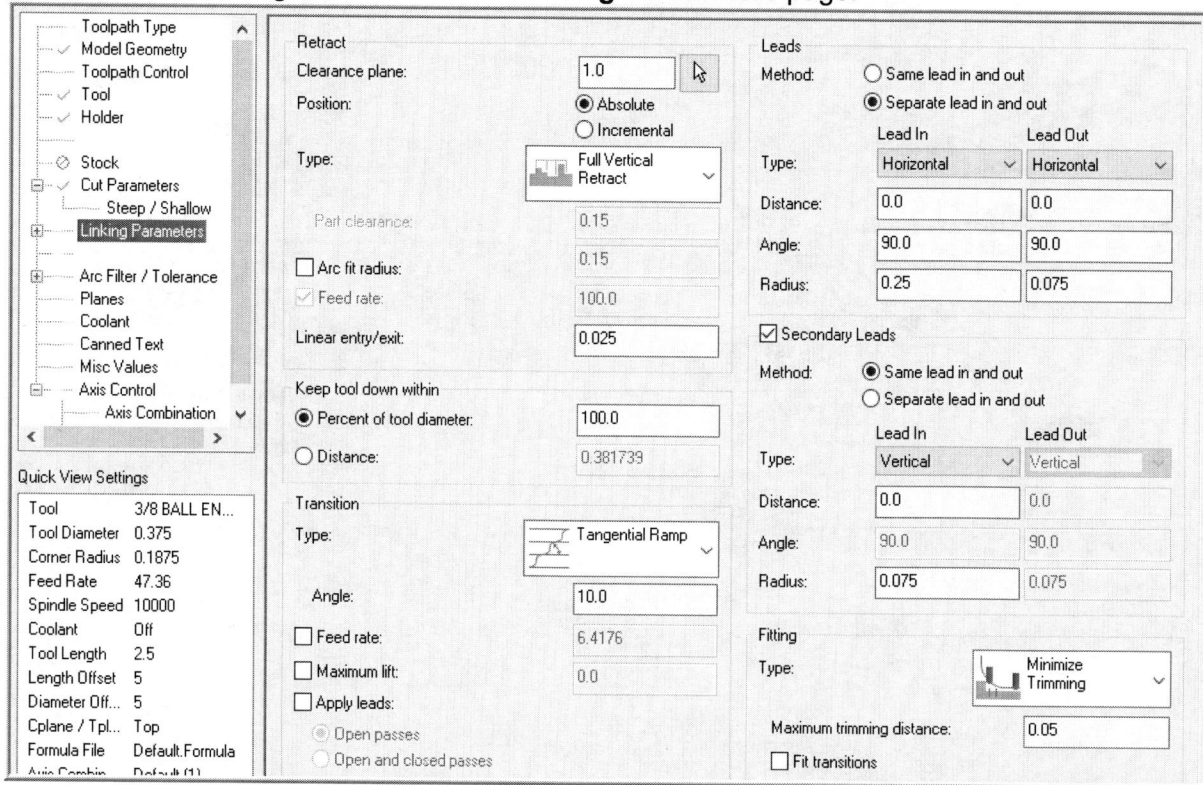

Retract Type. This determines how the tool will move between the end of one pass and the beginning of another. Then, use the **Leads** fields to control how the tool moves onto and off of the part at the start and end of each cutting pass. These moves are applied to each pass no matter which cutting pass is selected. Finally, select a **Fitting** option to control how the entry and exit arcs will be fit into each pass.

Note: Mastercam creates linking moves only when the spacing between cutting passes is greater than the Keep tool down within distance on the

26. Go to the **Arc Filter/Tolerance** page and make the following changes.

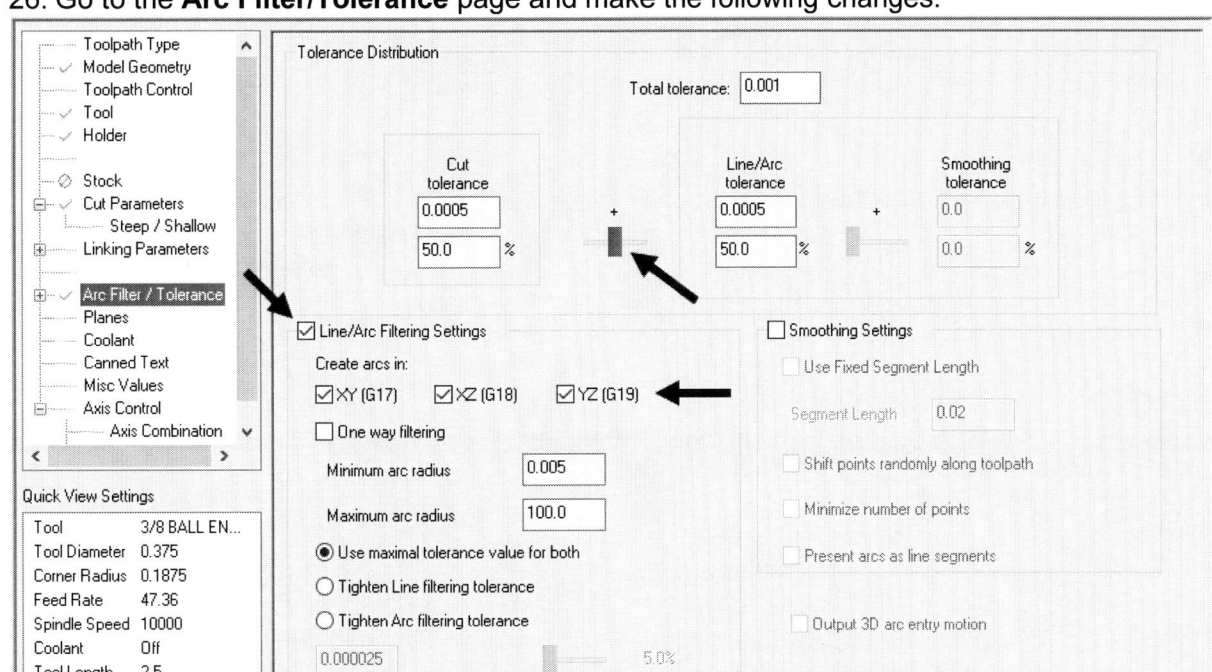

27. Select the **OK button** ☑ to complete the toolpath.
28. Verify this toolpath only using the **Stock model: 2D Finishing done**.

TASK 14:
FINISH THE CIRCULAR FEATURE USING SPIRAL

➲ Next you will finish the circular feature part using the **Surface High Speed Spiral** toolpath.

Spiral Toolpaths
Use a Spiral toolpath to create cutting passes where the tool feeds into the part in a continuous spiral instead of several discrete passes at a constant Z height. The spacing between each pass is a 2D distance measured in the XY plane, so this toolpath type works best on shallow parts whose features can be effectively machined with a circular motion. The following picture shows an example of a Spiral toolpath.

To define the machining zone, you need to enter the outer radius of the spiral, and the coordinates of its center point. Mastercam will project this circle onto your selected drive surfaces and calculate the toolpath within this area.

This is different from a waterline toolpath, in which each cutting pass represents the actual profile of the drive surface at a particular Z depth. Use the Cutting method together with the Spiral clockwise option to orient the cutting passes. For most applications, the One-way cutting method will cut from the center point outwards, while the Other way cutting method will cut from outside in.

If the center point and radius of the spiral do not match your drive surfaces, Mastercam will simply cut that portion of each spiral pass that lies on the drive surface.
To select the radius or center point coordinate based on geometry in your part file, right-click in the desired field and choose from the short-cut menu.

---

1. Open the **Levels Manager** and make only **Level 1 visible.** Set Level 1 as the main level.
2. Select the **Toolpaths** tab at the top right side of the screen.
3. Click on the **Expand gallery** down arrow in the **3D** section and select **Spiral** from the **Finishing** selections.

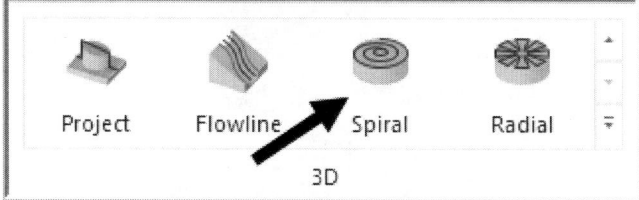

4. On the screen select the **Model Geometry** page, if required.
5. At the bottom of the **Model Geometry** page click **Reset Stock Values**, this will set Wall and Floor Stock to 0, and then click on the **Select entities** button.

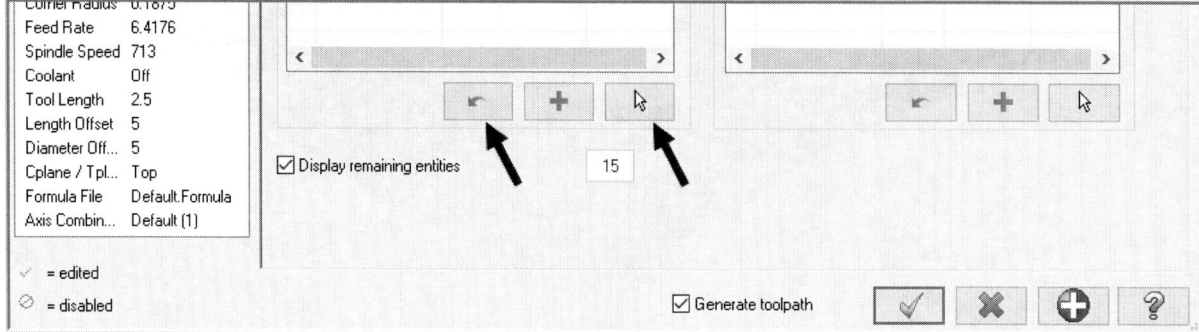

---

6. To satisfy the prompt on the screen select the **two faces** shown below. You may need to turn off the visibility of Level 10.

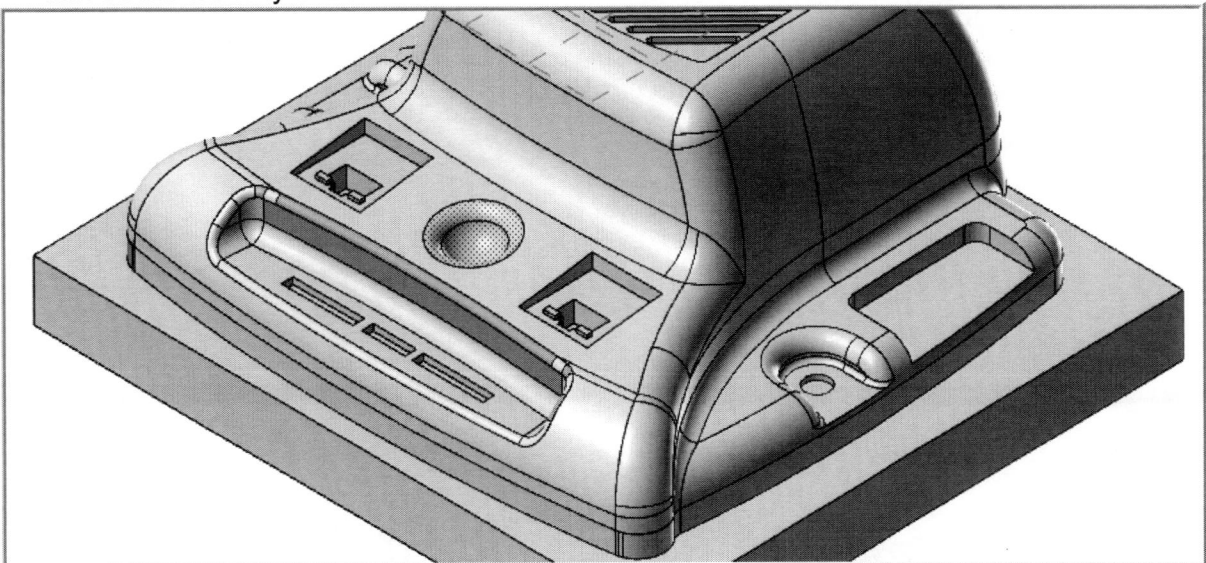

7. To move onto the next step, you now need to pick the **End Selection** icon.
8. Back at the Model Geometry page **select the avoidance row** in the **Avoidance Geometry** section.
9. At the bottom of the **Model Geometry** page click on the **Select entities** button for **Avoidance Geometry**.

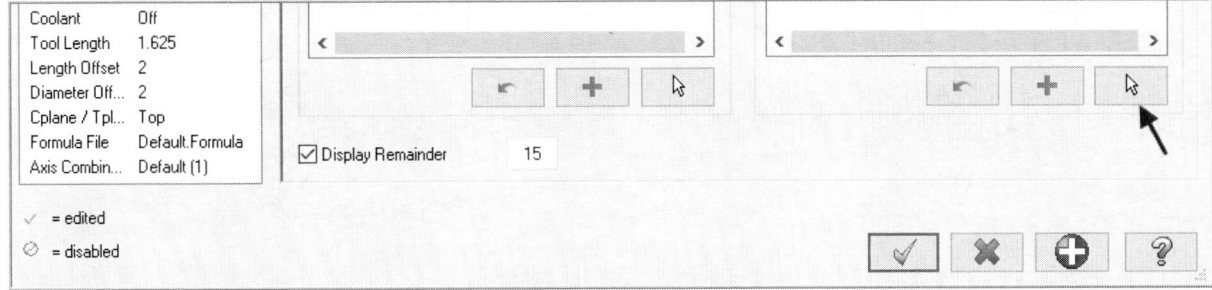

10. Now you will be returned to the graphics screen. To satisfy the prompt on the screen select the **flat** feature shown below.

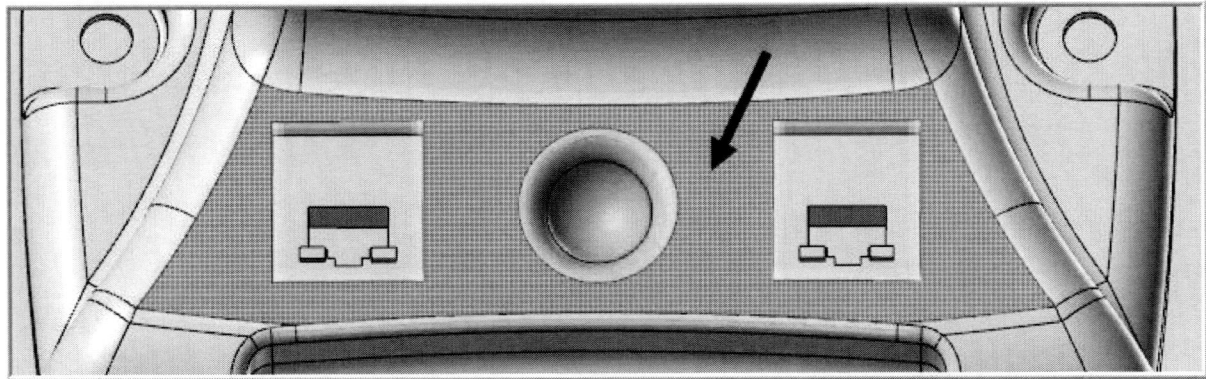

11. To move onto the next step, you now need to pick the **End Selection** icon.
12. Next, select the **Tool** page
13. Select a **3/16 diameter ball endmill**.
14. Edit the tools material to **carbide** and recalculate the speeds and feeds.
15. The tool page should be the same as the picture below.

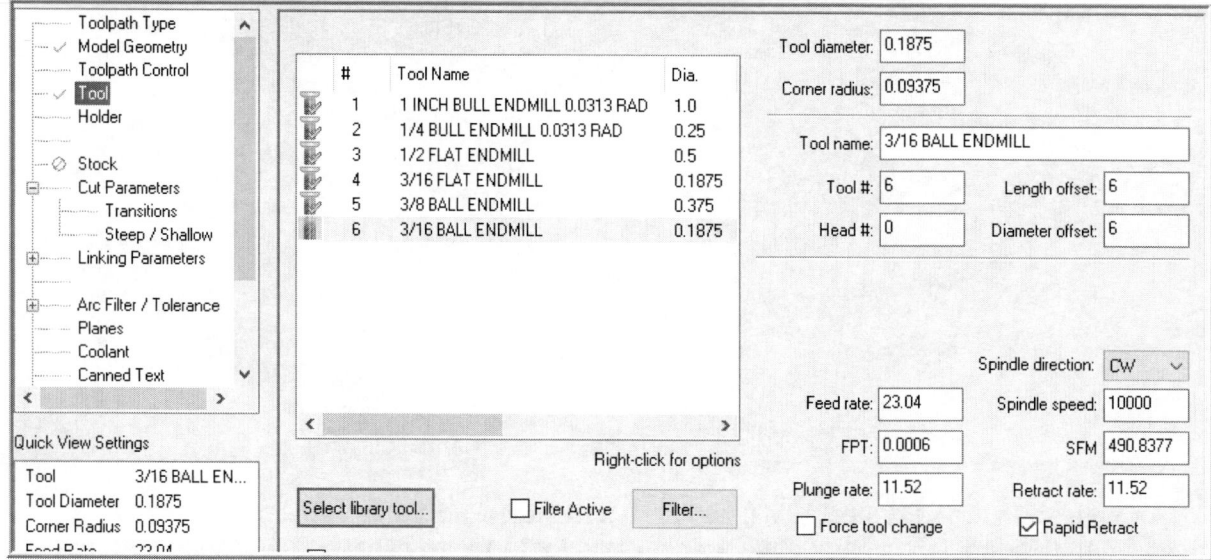

16. Select the **Holder** page and select **B3E4-0187** as the holder and edit the projection to 1.5.

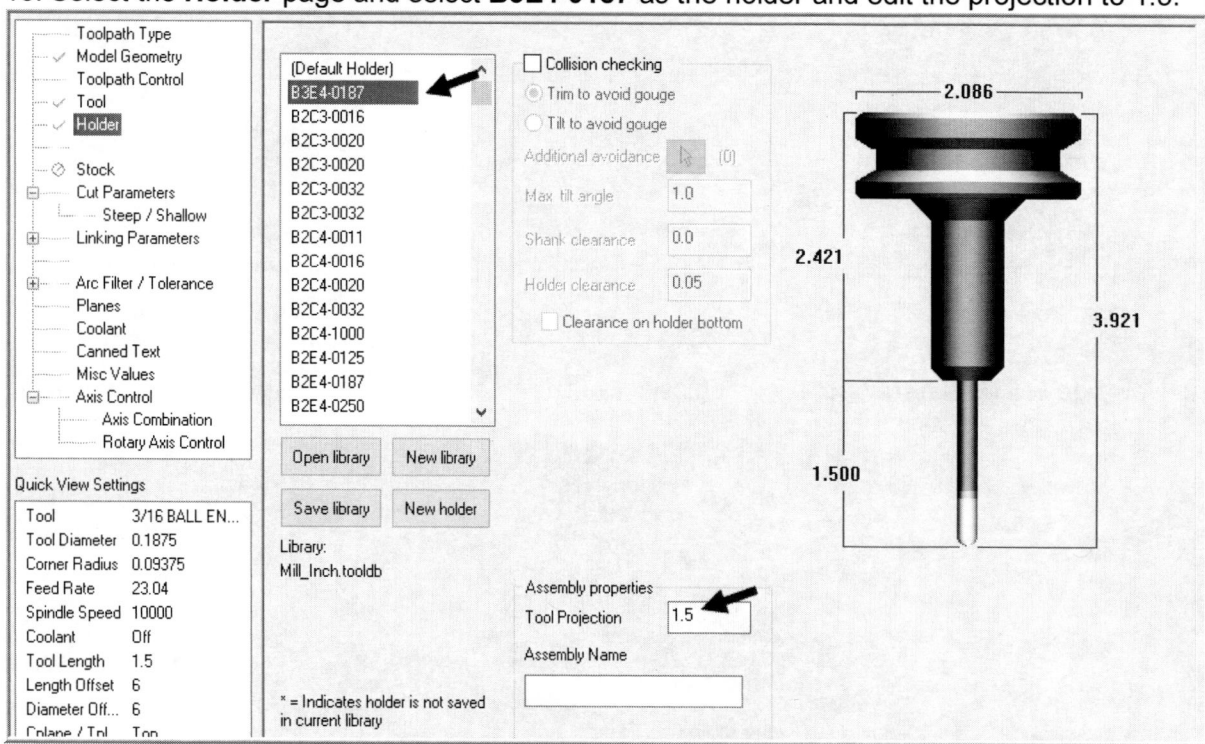

17. Select the **Cut Parameters** page and make changes shown below. The **Y-0.915** is the approximate location of the center of this feature which was taken from the cad drawing.

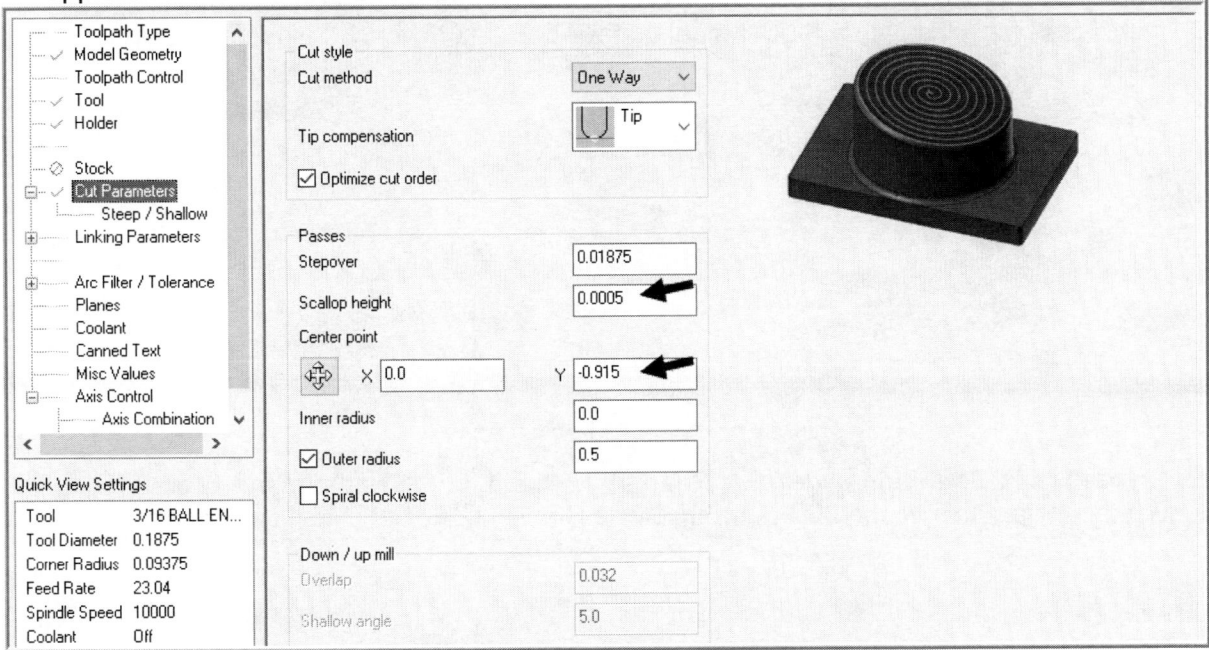

18. Make the following selections on the **Linking Parameters** page:

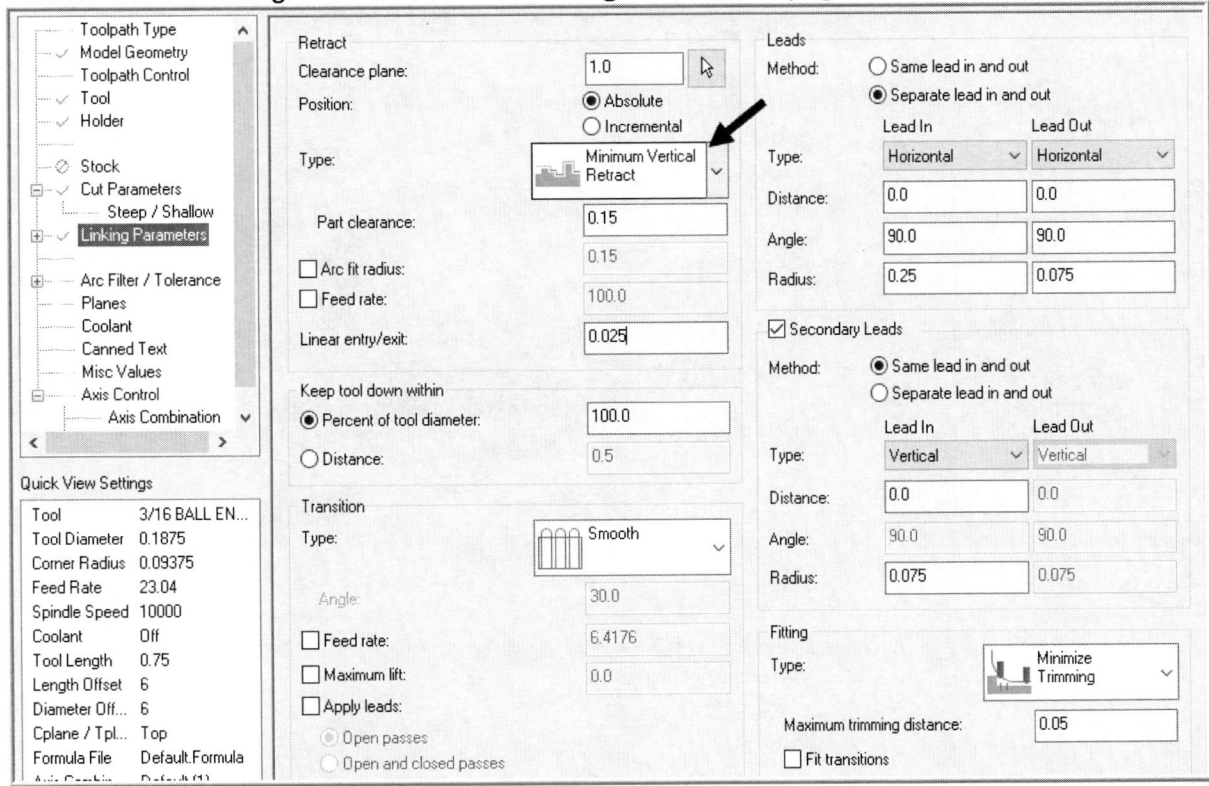

19. Select the **OK button** [✓] to complete the toolpath.

TASK 15:
CREATE STOCK MODEL FOR THE PENCIL TOOLPATH
➲ In this task we will create a Stock Model that will be used to verify the upcoming Pencil Toolpath.

1. On the **Toolpaths** tab select **Stock Model** in the **Stock** section.

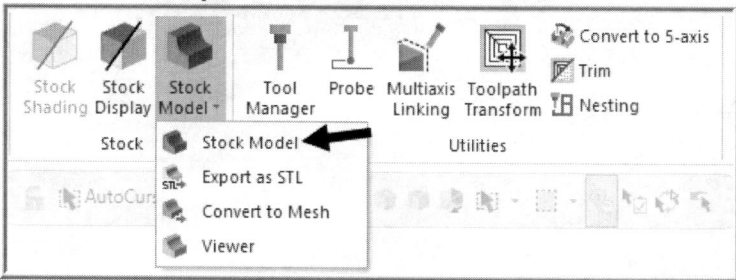

2. On the **Stock Definition** page enter **Ready for Pencil** for the **Name** of this Stock Model.
3. Set the Initial Stock to the **2D Finishing Done** Stock Model and select a new color.

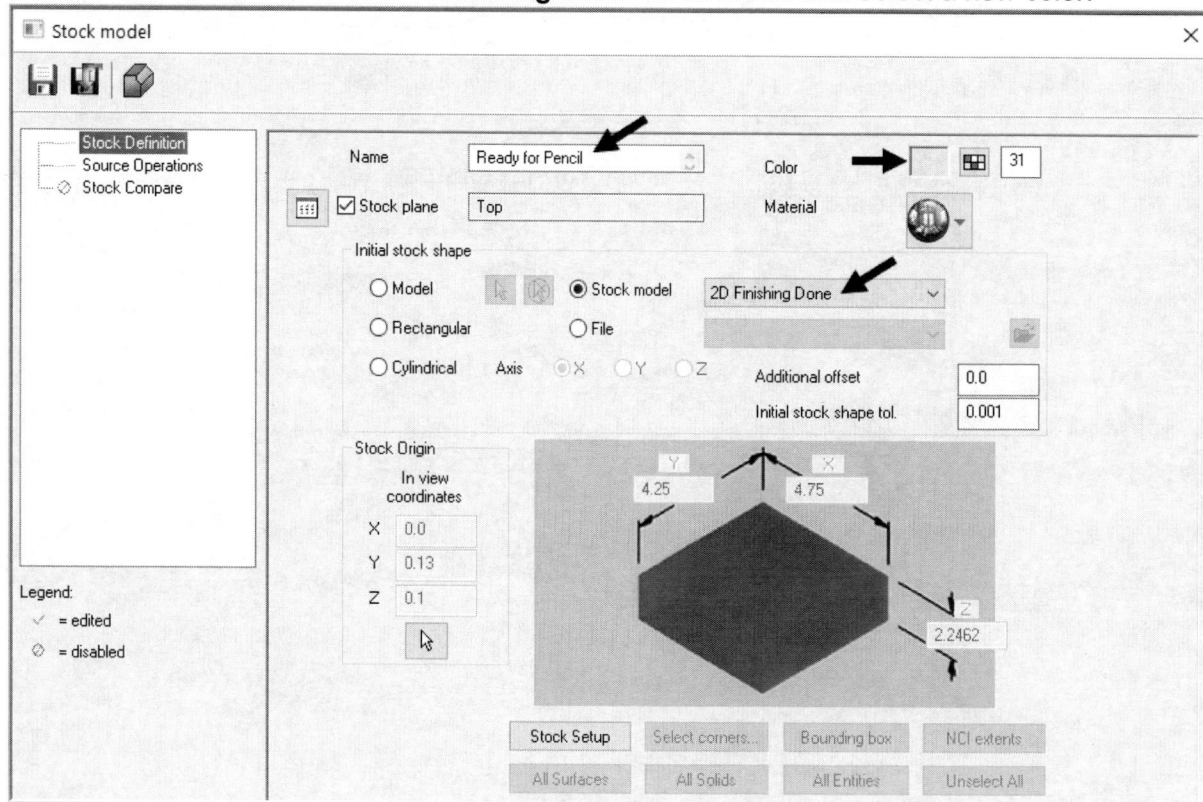

4. Click on **Source Operations** at the left of the Stock model dialog box.
5. Ensure there are **check marks on the final 2 toolpaths** as shown below.

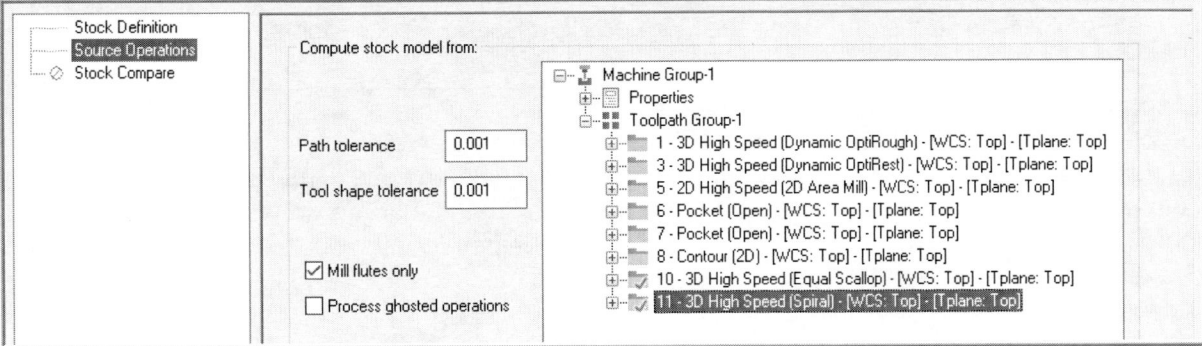

6. Click on the **OK** icon to complete this Stock model operation.
➲ The image below shows the **Stock model** in the Toolpaths Manager and it is the only visible toolpath.

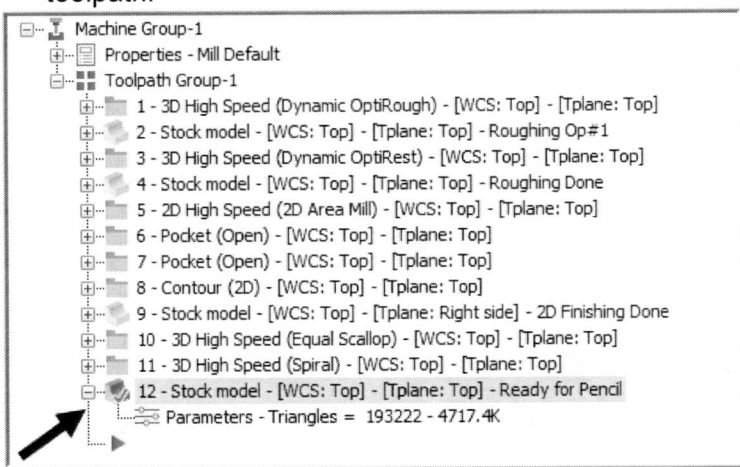

➲ Stock Model shown, all other levels are hidden.

7. With a check mark on the Stock model **click** on the **Toggle display on selected operations** icon to hide the display of the Stock Model.

TASK 16:
FINISH USING SURFACE HIGH SPEED PENCIL

➲ Next you will finish the part using the Surface High Speed Pencil toolpath.

> **3D high speed pencil toolpaths** are used to clean out the corners of a job. The tool follows a contour defined by the intersection of two or more surfaces.
> You can create pencil toolpaths with either single or multiple passes. High speed pencil toolpaths are similar to Mastercam's standard pencil toolpaths, but are enhanced to produce the smoother, free-flowing tool motion and transitions necessary for high speed machining.
> You can define the size of the cutting zone by creating multiple offset profiles from the surface boundary.

1. Open the **Levels Manager** and make only **Level 1 an 10 visible.** Set Level 1 as the main level.
2. Select the **Toolpaths** tab at the top right side of the screen.
3. Click on the **Expand gallery** down arrow in the **3D** section and select **Pencil** from the **Finishing** selections.

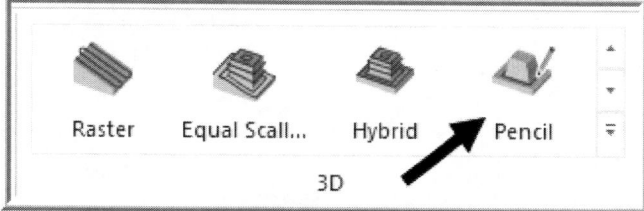

4. On the screen select the **Model Geometry** page, if required.
5. Ensure both the **Wall Stock** and **Floor stock** are set to **Zero.**

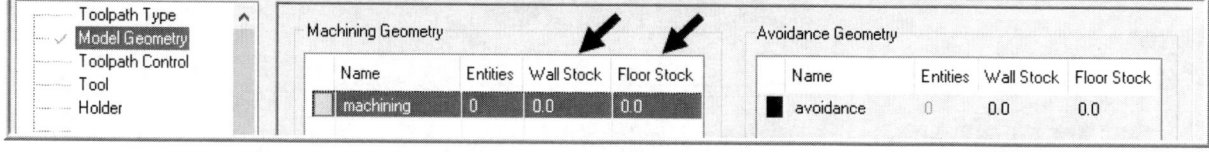

6. At the bottom of the **Model Geometry** page click on the **Select entities** button.

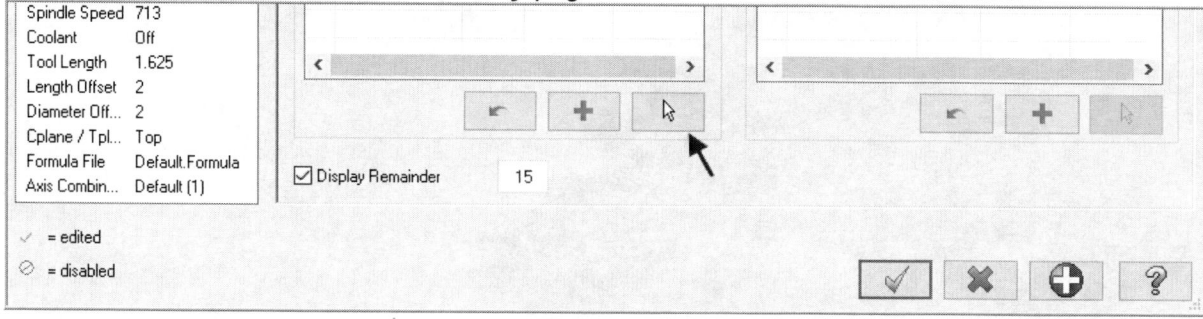

7. Now you will be returned to the graphics screen. To satisfy the prompt on the screen use **Ctrl-A on your keyboard** select to **select all the entities**.

8. To move onto the next step you now need to pick the **End Selection** icon ⊚.

9. Next, select the **Tool** page and select the **0.1875 Ball endmill**.
10. Select the **Stock** page and make changes to this page as shown below. Only the last Stock model is selected.

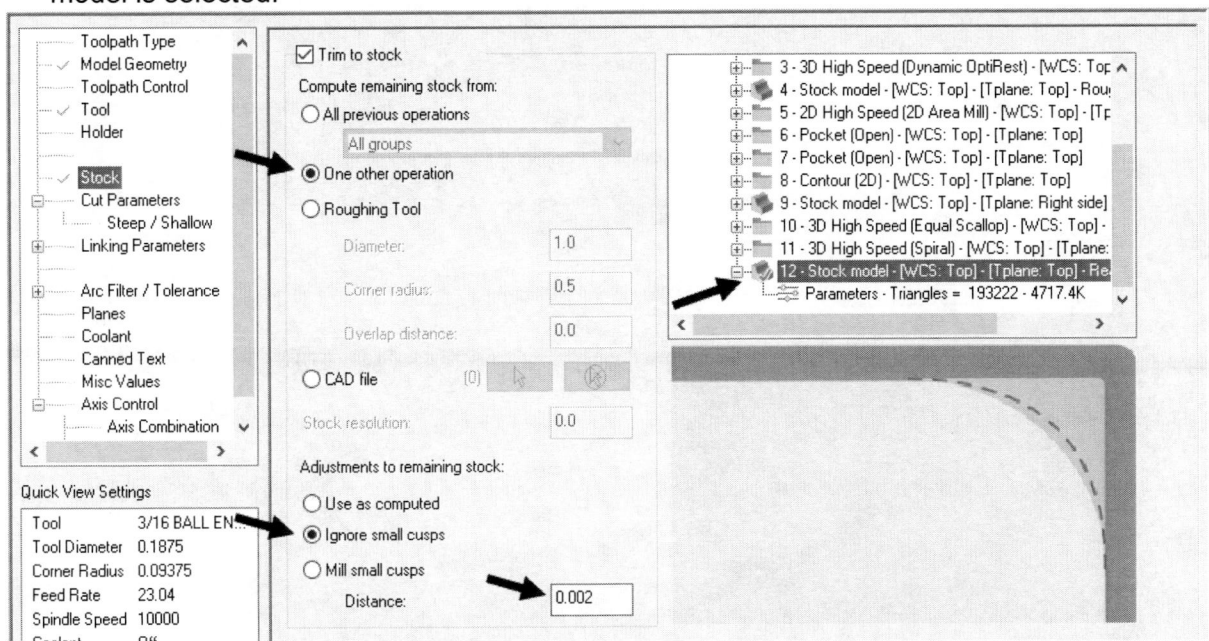

11. Select the **Cut Parameters** page and make changes to this page as shown below.

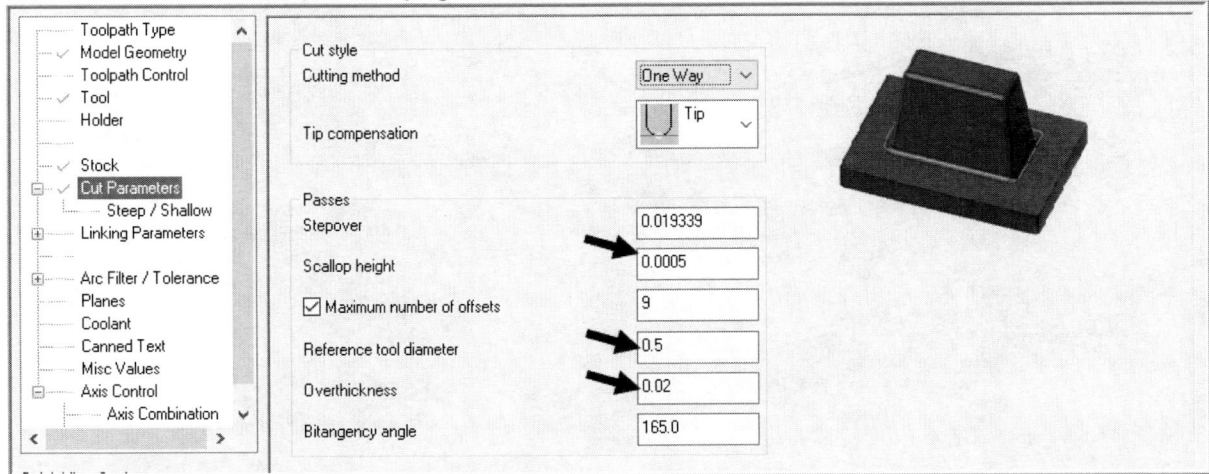

12. Make the following selections on the **Linking Parameters** page:

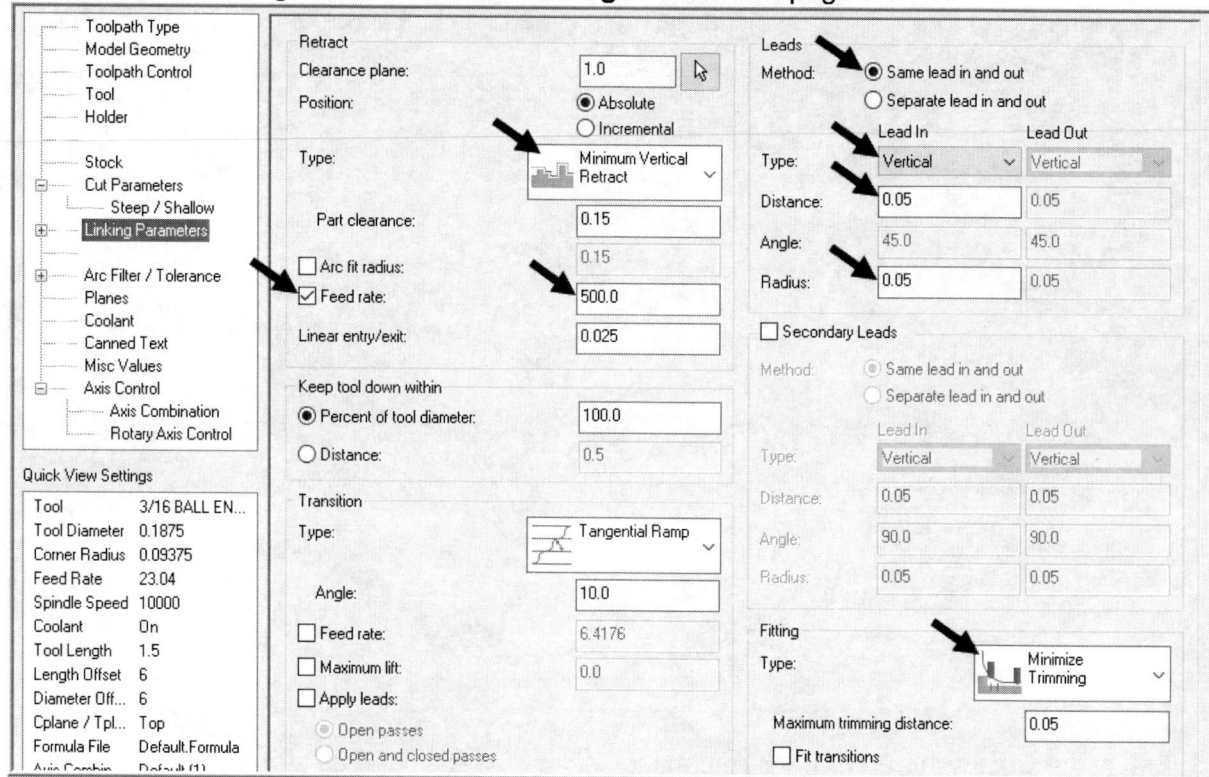

13. Turn Arc Filtering on for this toolpath with the following settings.

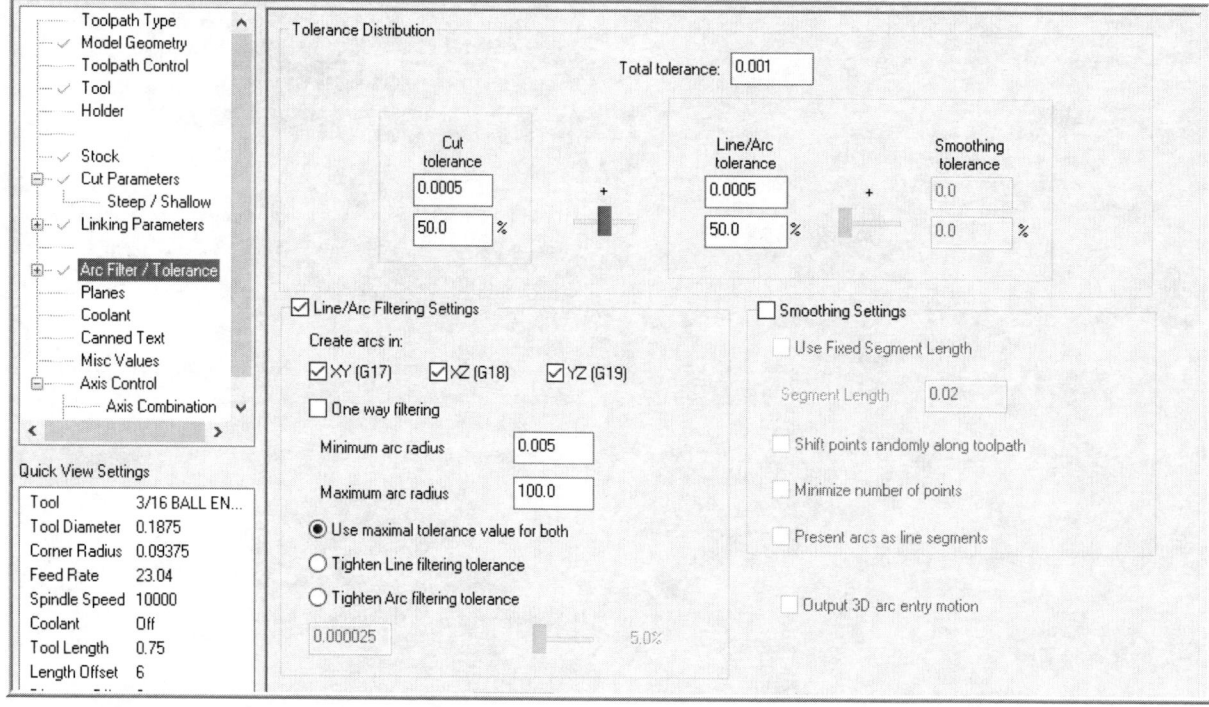

14. Activate the flood coolant.

15. Select the **OK button** ✓ to complete the toolpath.

16. Verify this toolpath only using the **Stock model: Ready for Pencil**.

TASK 17:
VERIFY ALL THE TOOLPATHS

1. In the Toolpaths Manager pick the **Simulator Options** icon.

2. In the **Simulator Options** window activate the radio button for **Stock Setup**.

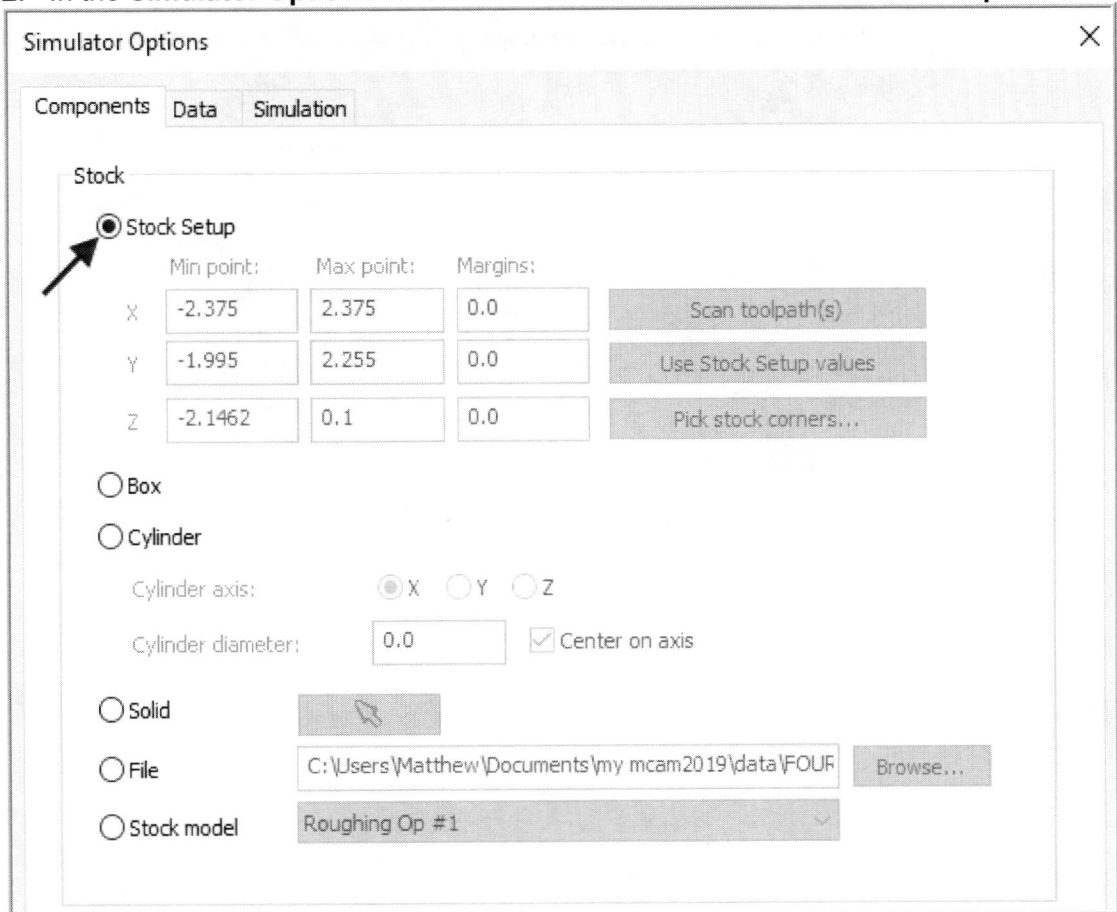

3. Select the **OK** button [✓] to exit **Simulator Options**.
4. Right mouse click in the graphics area and click on **Isometric**.
5. In the **Toolpaths Manager** pick all the operations to verify by picking the **Select all operations** icon.

6. Select the **Verify selected operations** icon.
7. At the top of the screen select the **Verify** tab and activate the **Color Loop**.
8. Now select the **Play Simulation** button to review the toolpaths.

➲ The verified toolpaths are shown below:

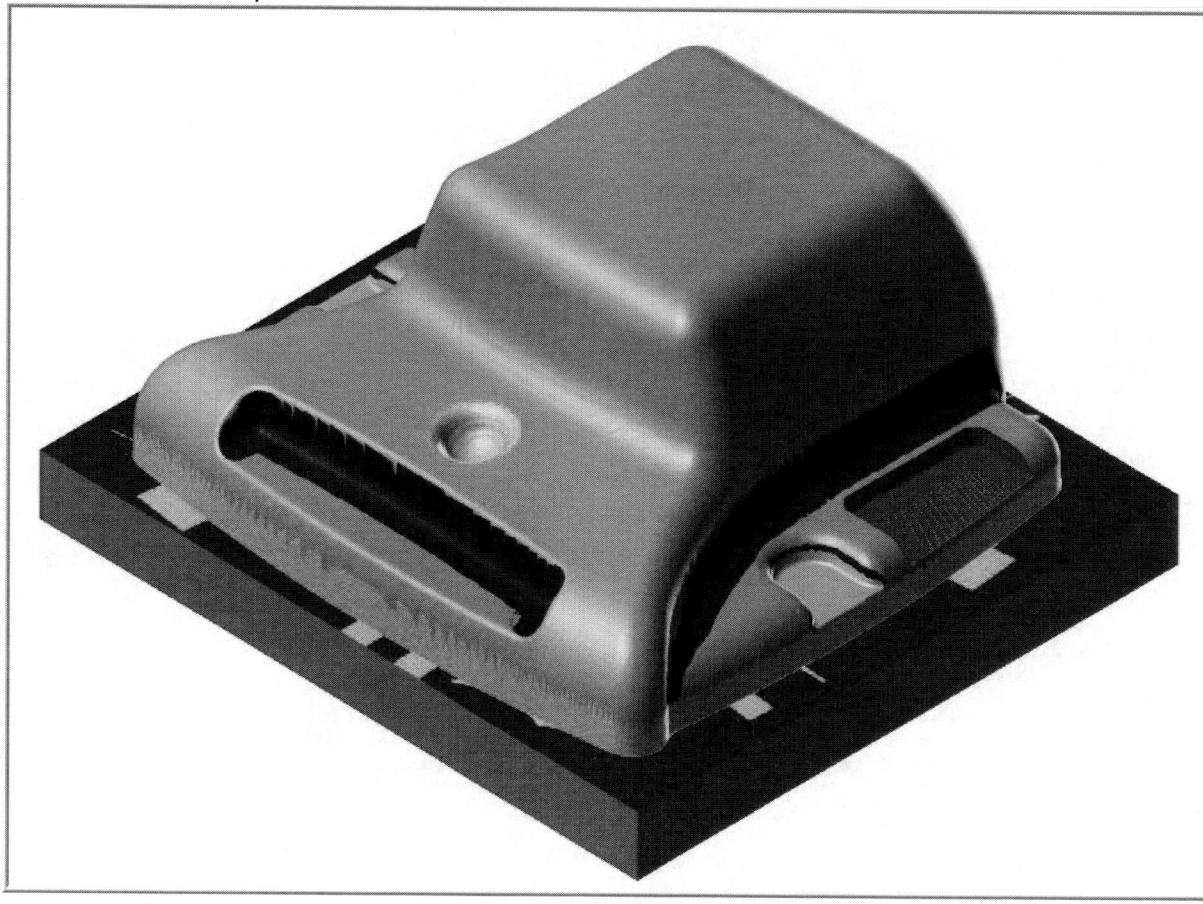

9. Select the Close button [×] in the top right hand corner to exit Verify.

TASK 18:
SAVE THE UPDATED MASTERCAM FILE

1. Select the **Save** icon from the **Quick Access** toolbar at the top left of the screen.

TASK 19:
POST AND CREATE THE CNC CODE FILE

1. Ensure all the operations are selected by picking the **Select all operations** icon 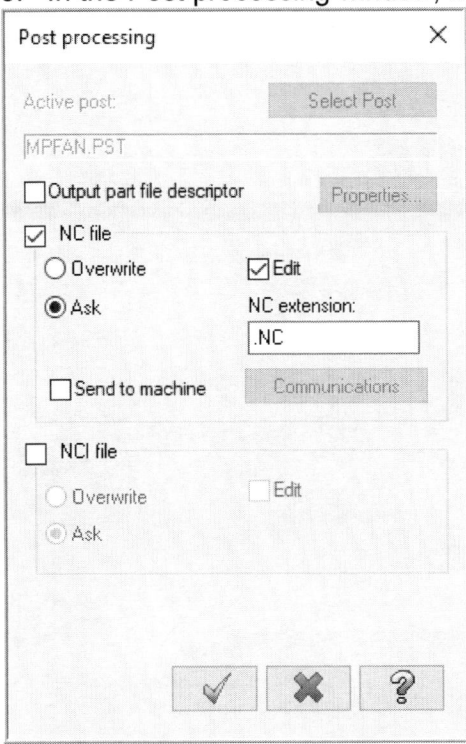 from the Toolpath manager.
2. Select the **Post selected operations** button from the Toolpaths Manager.
3. In the Post processing window, make the necessary changes as shown below:

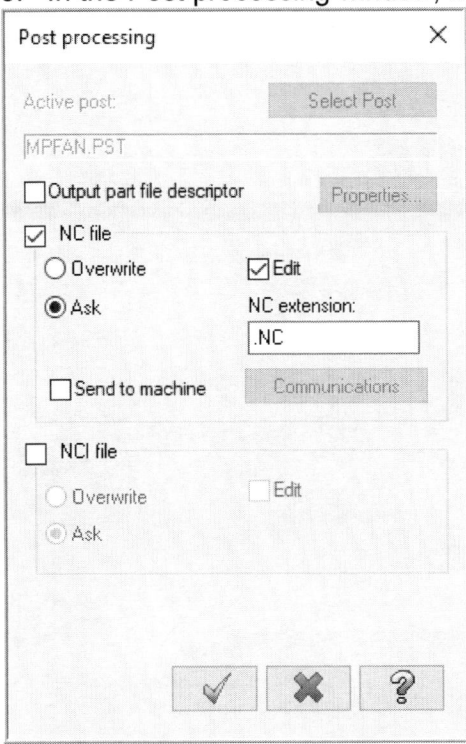

4. Select the **OK button** to continue.
5. Enter the same name as your Mastercam part file name in the NC File name field **Mill-Lesson-16**.
6. Select the **Save** button.
7. The CNC code file opens up in the default editor.

8. Select the in the top right corner to exit the CNC editor

➲ This completes Mill-Lesson-16.

MILL-LESSON-16 EXERCISE-A

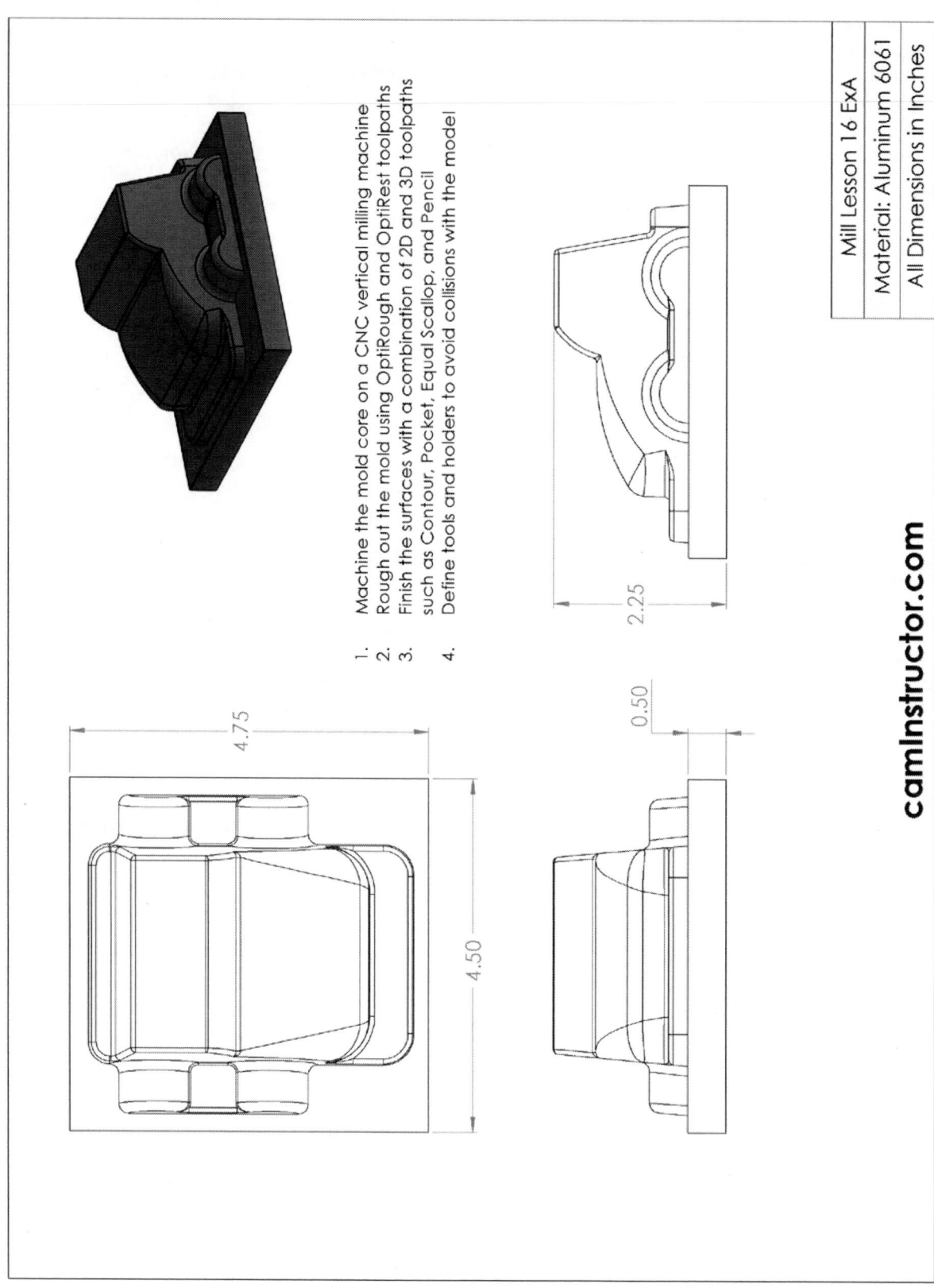

1. Machine the mold core on a CNC vertical milling machine
2. Rough out the mold using OptiRough and OptiRest toolpaths
3. Finish the surfaces with a combination of 2D and 3D toolpaths such as Contour, Pocket, Equal Scallop, and Pencil
4. Define tools and holders to avoid collisions with the model

2.25

0.50

4.75

4.50

Mill Lesson 16 ExA

Material: Aluminum 6061

All Dimensions in Inches

caminstructor.com

MILL-LESSON-16 EXERCISE-B

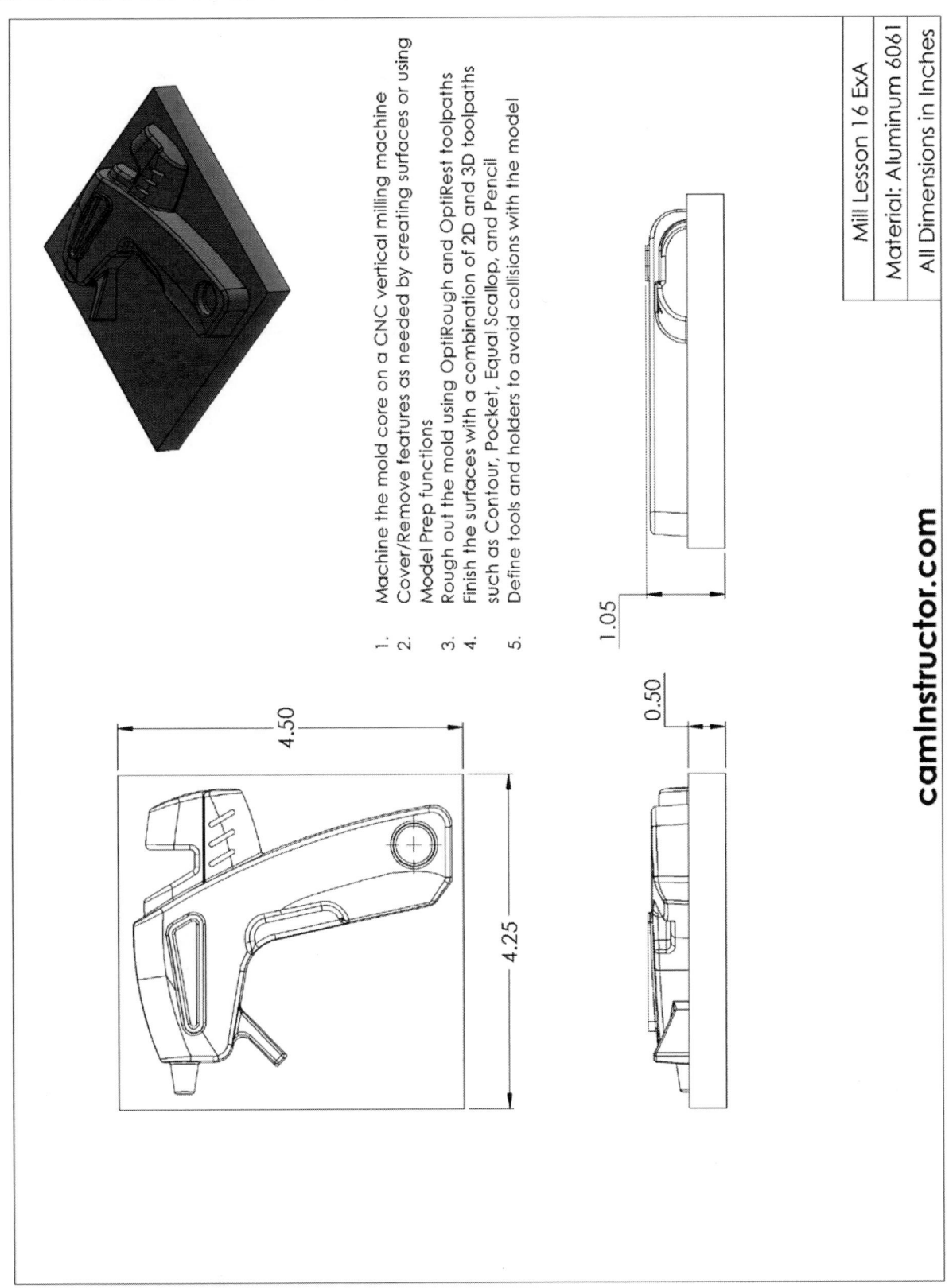

1. Machine the mold core on a CNC vertical milling machine
2. Cover/Remove features as needed by creating surfaces or using Model Prep functions
3. Rough out the mold using OptiRough and OptiRest toolpaths
4. Finish the surfaces with a combination of 2D and 3D toolpaths such as Contour, Pocket, Equal Scallop, and Pencil
5. Define tools and holders to avoid collisions with the model

Mill Lesson 16 ExA
Material: Aluminum 6061
All Dimensions in Inches

4.50

4.25

1.05

0.50

caminstructor.com